RON SHANDLER'S **2017**

BASEBALL FORECASTER

AND ENCYCLOPEDIA OF FANALYTICS

TRIUMPH
BOOKS

This book is available in quantity at special discounts for your group or organization. For further information, contact:

Triumph Books LLC
814 North Franklin Street
Chicago, Illinois 60610
(312) 337-0747
www.triumphbooks.com

Printed in U.S.A.
ISBN: 978-1-62937-309-6

Rotisserie League Baseball is a registered trademark of the Rotisserie League Baseball Association, Inc.

Statistics provided by Baseball Info Solutions

Cover design by Brent Hershey
Front cover photograph by John Hefti/USA TODAY Sports Images
Author photograph by Kevin Hurley

Ron Shandler's
BASEBALL FORECASTER

Editors
Ray Murphy
Brent Hershey

Associate Editor
Brandon Kruse

• • • • • •

Technical Wizard
Rob Rosenfeld

Design
Brent Hershey

Data and Charts
Matt Cederholm

Player Commentaries
Ryan Bloomfield
Rob Carroll
Matt Cederholm
Matt Dodge
Alec Dopp
Brent Hershey
Brandon Kruse
Ray Murphy
Stephen Nickrand
Kristopher Olson
Greg Pyron
Brian Rudd
Paul Sporer
Jock Thompson
Rod Truesdell

Research and Articles
Patrick Davitt
Ed DeCaria
Matt Dodge
Arik Florimonte
Brad Kullman
Brian Slack

Prospects
Rob Gordon
Jeremy Deloney
Tom Mulhall

Injury Chart
Rick Wilton

Acknowledgments

Producing the *Baseball Forecaster* has been a team effort for a number of years now; the list of credits to the left is where the heavy lifting gets done. On behalf of Ron, Brent, and Ray, our most sincere thanks to each of those key contributors.

We are just as grateful to the rest of the BaseballHQ.com staff, who do the yeoman's work in populating the website with 12 months of incredible content: Dave Adler, Andy Andres, Matt Beagle, Dan Becker, Alex Beckey, Bob Berger, Chris Blessing, Derrick Boyd, Brian Brickley, Brant Chesser, Doug Dennis, Greg Fishwick, Neil FitzGerald, Brandon Gavett, Sam Grant, Rick Green, Phil Hertz, Joe Hoffer, Scott Holmes, Ed Hubbard, Tom Kephart, Chris Lee, Glenn Lowy, Troy Martell, David Martin, Harold Nichols, Frank Noto, Josh Paley, Joseph Pytleski, Nick Richards, Mike Shears, Peter Sheridan, Skip Snow, Matthew St-Germain, Jeffrey Tomich, Nick Trojanowski, Michael Weddell and Mike Werner.

Thank you to our behind-the-scenes troopers: our technical dynamic duo of Mike Krebs and Rob Rosenfeld.

Thank you to all our industry colleagues, a truly impressive group. They are competitors, but they are also colleagues working to grow this industry, which is never a more evident than at our annual First Pitch Arizona gathering each November.

Thank you to Dave Morgan, Chris Pirrone, Ryan Bonini, and the team at USA Today Sports Media Group.

Thank you for all the support from the folks at Triumph Books and Action Printing.

And of course, thank *you*, readers, for your interest in what we all have to say. Your kind words, support and (respectful) criticism move us forward on the fanalytic continuum more than you know. We are grateful for your readership.

From Ray Murphy The annual process of constructing this book should be a fire drill, but the great people involved transform it into a symphony. Rob Rosenfeld's work on the construction of the player pages sets a tone, much like a double bass. The writers add so much pith in the player commentaries, with the varied yet complementary sounds of a woodwind section. The prospect coverage, the year-long work of our research team, the charts and data slices, all add the oomph of a brass section. Brent and I share the conductor's role year-round, which is a testament to Brent's boundless patience. Ron may not actually wield the day-to-day baton anymore, but he will always be our original virtuoso. In my other band, the home one, my wife Jennifer is the perfect blend of tag-team partner and co-conspirator, while Grace and Bridget keep bringing the fun.

From Brent Hershey This project always makes me appreciate of the rewards of hard work. To each contributor, thanks for your individual insights, digging and uncovering the raw materials. To Ray, thanks for your willing collaboration as we divide up the assembly process—fitting these pieces together into a cohesive unit. It's always a balancing act, and each year we get closer to that mythical centerline. You are a joy to work with. Thanks to Ron, for entrusting us as foremen on this job, and providing additional finishing work when necessary. And to Lorie, Dillon, and Eden: thank you for the "after hours" delight you each supply, your graciousness, and your strength of support. Our family, too, is building something special.

From Ron Shandler I owe a huge debt of gratitude to Ray, Brent and the entire BaseballHQ family for their continued fine work on this annual project. While we have the process down to a near science—milestone-scheduled weekly from July through November—it is still a thrill to put all the pieces together and sort out those first projections. Mookie Betts, No. 1? Well, that's exciting!

Thank you to 31 years' worth of dedicated readers, who wait for those numbers as anxiously as we do. And thank you to my family who continues to provide unending support. Darielle, Justina, Michele and Sue are changing the world through theatre, music and empathy. They are all doing important work.

Despite some buzz to the contrary, I am not retired even though I've moved to Florida. I just get to share my office these days with a family of sandhill cranes. A writer has to write; that will never change.

TABLE OF CONTENTS

Devaluation

by Ron Shandler

I once spent several years marveling at a certain player whose underlying power metrics *screamed* 40 home run potential. Forty is a big number, a feat, a milestone reserved for the very best, and this player seemed poised to take that leap.

Yet, for a variety of reasons, he kept falling short. Maybe it was his 60 percent contact rate and periodic sub-.200 batting average. Maybe it was his streakiness—.164 one month, .289 the next; .171 another month, .344 the next. Whatever the reason, the magical 40 remained elusive.

He came closest in 2014:

AB	R	HR	RBI	SB	BA
507	68	37	88	5	.227

The *2015 Forecaster* said, "He could be a monster. UP: 45 HRs."

But, the forecasting gods were unkind and 2015 turned out to be a bust. Naturally, our recency bias depressed his 2016 expectations to near nothing. His average draft position ranking (ADP) coming into last season was No. 305, which in real terms meant, "Undraftable even in a 13-team mixed league."

In the 13-team FSTA/SiriusXM experts league, he was selected in the fourth reserve round, or No. 339. That meant I did not deem him worthy enough to be among my first 26 picks even though I had seen 45-HR upside just one year earlier.

You can probably guess where this is going. The stubborn few who kept the faith last March—all six of you—were duly rewarded:

AB	R	HR	RBI	SB	BA
549	84	41	94	3	.222

I suppose this is the long-awaited validation for my pre-2016 Chris Carter projections. I don't know; he only managed the feat by going on an 11-HR tear from September 3 on. Regardless, we evaluate players on a full season's performance; 40 HRs is 40 HRs, right?

Maybe not. There is one nagging little piece of data that takes something away from the accomplishment:

Year	AB	R	HR	RBI	SB	BA	R$
2014	507	68	37	88	5	.227	**$20**
2016	549	84	41	94	3	.222	**$15**

Despite hitting four more HRs, scoring 16 more runs and driving in six more runners—discounting the minor dips in steals and BA—Carter's 15-team mixed league Rotisserie earnings were $5 less than in 2014 (and pretty crappy for a 40-HR hitter, all in all).

How could that be? The problem: *everyone* hit in 2016. When it came to home runs, *everyone* punched a power ticket:

- Every Upton.
- Every Seager.
- Every Davis.
- Two long-term singles hitters who had career power years at age 35. [1]
- Three declining sluggers with sudden power spikes at ages 37 and older. [2]
- Seven rookies who hit more HRs in their first partial MLB season than in any full minor league season. [3]
- My brother-in-law's neighbor's nephew. [4]
- Brad Miller.

Everyone. So in a year when balls were flying over the Green Monster, onto Waveland Avenue and into San Francisco Bay with wanton abandon, *the value of any individual homer took a dive.*

Rotisserie earnings are benched to the level of offense in any given season, thereby reflecting the context of the day. So, a bigger leaguewide offense will mean a lower value per homer… and every other offensive event. That's how Carter earned $5 less in a season when he put up bigger numbers.

This phenomenon tends to skew our perspective. I suppose we can't help but talk about a player's individual power growth as if it occurred in a vacuum. But everything has to be evaluated within its own context.

So no, this was not a career power year for Evan Longoria (he showed better skill in every season prior to 2014). Brad Miller's huge breakout was not as big as we think (his expected power index of 116 was just a tick above 2014's 105). And get this: Todd Frazier's career power year came along with the lowest xPX of his career. By a lot.

So we can debate whether Chris Carter's first 40-HR season is an accurate reflection of the skills befitting of that milestone. His xPX has been essentially flat for four straight years. This has been the same player since 2013.

It's possible that hitting 40 home runs is not as elite of a feat as it used to be.

Power and the balls

Take a look at how the power environment has evolved since around the turn of the century:

Year	Tot HR	20+ home run hitters		
		No.	Avg. HR	% of total
1998	5064	85	30.0	50%
1999	5528	103	29.7	55%
2000	5693	102	29.7	53%
2001	5458	90	30.8	51%
2002	5059	81	29.3	47%
2003	5207	86	28.8	48%
2004	5451	93	28.9	49%
2005	5017	78	28.3	44%
2006	5386	91	29.1	49%
2007	4957	86	26.9	47%
2008	4878	92	26.8	51%
2009	5042	87	27.8	48%
2010	4613	77	26.5	44%
2011	4552	68	27.4	41%
2012	4934	79	27.3	44%
2013	4661	70	25.6	38%
2014	4186	57	25.6	35%
2015	4909	64	28.4	37%
2016	5610	111	27.6	55%

The last three columns represent the number of players who hit at least 20 HR each year, the average number of HRs those players produced, and the percentage that their homers represented of baseball's entire HR output.

---

[1] Rajai Davis, Angel Pagan
[2] Carlos Beltran, Adrian Beltre, Chase Utley
[3] Tim Anderson, Willson Contreras, Aledmys Diaz, Max Kepler, Gary Sanchez, Trevor Story, Trea Turner
[4] Daniel Murphy (though admittedly, it might not be the same Daniel Murphy)

In 2014, only 57 players hit 20 or more HRs; their output represented 35% of all the homers hit that year. Just two years later, there were nearly twice as many 20-HR hitters making up more than half of all the HRs hit.

That meant, every owner in a 15-team mixed league could have rostered *seven* 20-HR hitters (and six teams could have owned eight). Essentially, you would have been hard-pressed not to trip over a 20-HR hitter in your drafts last March.

I actually projected this, right here, one year ago:

…barring a revelation that some external variable changed in 2015, one would expect power to regress off of this year's spike. But wait… this 2015 "correction" was the largest single season spike since 1993. Back then it set off a whole new era in power performance. Could we be entering a new cycle?

It's possible. As you scan all the player boxes in this book, you'll see many new players being projected for 20 HRs or more, driven by nothing more than normal trends… In all, I count 78 players projected for 20 or more HRs. Last year, only 64 players hit at least 20 HRs. This "correction" may have legs.

Right idea, wrong magnitude.

There has been a lot written to analyze this sudden phenomenon. Here is an excerpt of what I wrote back on May 19:

Everyone has their opinions about why baseballs are flying out of ballparks at the most frequent rate in the history of the sport. (Most explanations) can be discounted. There's only one other popularly-held explanation left. But MLB's Powers That Be will never reveal the truth about the baseballs that are being produced.

Yes, I wrote this on May 19.

May 19, 2000. Seventeen years ago. The more things change, the more they stay the same.

But it's interesting to compare the phenomenon from the Steroids Era to the current Post-PED-Power-and-Punchout Era. Something extraordinary happened in 1999 and carried over into the following season on an even bigger scale.

From 1998 to 1999, the major league home run rate jumped from 2.08 bombs per game, to 2.28. By the end of May 2000, hitters were slamming an amazing 2.62 home runs per game. At the time, the talk was about how someone had "flipped a switch." This discounted any explanation that would lend itself to a more gradual change—warmer weather, smaller ballparks, the impact of expansion or suddenly stronger hitters (steroids had not yet become a part of the popular vernacular). Thus, the conclusion was that the baseballs had to be juiced.

Seventeen years later, we're once again using a switch-flipping metaphor for the recent power spike. Prior to the 2015 All Star Break, the home run rate was 1.76 per game; after the Break, 2.20. Our surge continued into 2016, the home run rate climbed to 2.32.

The consensus opinion? It's the balls. (Some attribute the record-breaking summer heat, but it's tough to switch climate on and off at will.)

But that's not the end of the story…

The sudden power surge in early 2000 forced us to start reassessing our benchmarks. The juiced ball theory took on greater life after Rawlings refused to allow photographs of the machines that wound the yarn around balls.

But then the surge abated as suddenly as it had begun. By September, the homer rate had faded to 2.06 and finished the year at 2.34. It was as if someone had flipped the switch OFF. Any talk of juiced balls vanished as "steroids" became a more attractive headline magnet. We never found out the truth about the balls.

The point is, these tectonic shifts can occur at any time, in any direction. They are not necessarily gradual and they don't have to follow any expected trend. Look at the chart; we can no sooner explain the 2015-2016 spike than we can the 2000-2002 drop during the height of the Steroids Era. And so, neither can we draw any conclusions about the direction this trend will take in 2017.

Balls.

There were 111 players who hit at least 20 HRs last year. A quick scan of the projections here—admittedly, a rough number at this time of year—and I count 101 potential 20-HR sluggers. That level remains pretty significant though it does reflect some minimal regression. Still, I'm not betting the rent that this home run barrage will continue into 2017.

Deceleration

While home runs were a dime a dozen, stolen bases have become scarcer commodities. The number of elite speedsters dropped to its lowest level in over a decade.

Year	Tot SB	20+ base stealers		
		No.	Avg. SB	% of total
2000	2924	42	29.3	42%
2001	3103	44	29.9	42%
2002	2750	33	29.8	36%
2003	2573	26	30.8	31%
2004	2589	27	31.3	33%
2005	2565	27	33.1	35%
2006	2767	35	34.1	43%
2007	2918	42	32.1	46%
2008	2799	37	31.4	42%
2009	2970	46	29.0	45%
2010	2959	35	32.7	39%
2011	3279	50	28.8	44%
2012	3229	48	28.8	43%
2013	2693	40	28.7	43%
2014	2764	39	28.8	41%
2015	2505	30	27.8	33%
2016	2537	28	30.6	34%

These days, in a 15-team league, teams will average about two players with 20-SB potential. Compare that to five years ago when every team could have rostered three players with 20+ stolen bases.

The *2016 Baseball Forecaster* spoke to this phenomenon:

Given that steals have always been centralized in a smaller group of elite players, it has made sense to assign a somewhat inflated value to their contribution. But these days it's even more prevalent. It makes a strong argument for drafting a Jose Altuve or Dee Gordon in the first round, or for $30-plus. I think that approach has become more reasonable to consider these days; just plan the rest of the roster around it.

Will this phenomenon continue?

Year	S+BB/PA	BIP/PA	SBO	SB%
1998	24.6%	80.4%	10.4%	68.6%
1999	25.3%	80.7%	10.3%	69.3%
2000	25.2%	80.5%	8.9%	68.8%
2001	23.8%	79.8%	10.1%	68.8%
2002	24.0%	80.5%	9.0%	68.2%
2003	24.0%	80.8%	8.2%	69.4%
2004	24.1%	80.2%	8.1%	70.2%
2005	23.8%	80.9%	8.2%	70.6%
2006	24.2%	80.3%	8.5%	71.4%
2007	24.4%	80.3%	8.5%	74.4%
2008	24.3%	79.9%	8.4%	73.0%
2009	24.3%	79.3%	9.0%	72.4%
2010	23.9%	79.0%	9.2%	72.4%
2011	23.4%	78.9%	10.5%	72.2%
2012	23.2%	77.5%	10.2%	74.0%
2013	23.3%	77.6%	8.6%	72.8%
2014	23.1%	77.4%	9.0%	72.8%
2015	22.9%	76.9%	8.5%	70.2%
2016	23.1%	75.8%	8.3%	71.7%

The first column is the percentage of all plate appearances that have been singles and walks. While this is not a perfect measure of events that create stolen base opportunities, it does provide a rough gauge to track the trend. You can see that this has been declining over time. The 2% decline since 1999 seems small, but that equates to around 4,000 fewer baserunners per year who could potentially put up SBs.

The second column is a bit tangential but interesting nonetheless. It shows the larger Power-and-Punchouts environment in which those potential stolen base opportunities exist. This is the percentage of plate appearances that result in a ball in play—essentially reflecting the global rise in baseball's three true outcomes (homers, walks and strikeouts). The decline here is even steeper, 5% over the past decade alone.

The third column is Stolen Base Opportunity Pct., which measures how often a stolen base is attempted when a batter reaches first by either a single or walk. This trend has fluctuated within a 2% range over time, but as been in decline from its recent 2011 peak. The last two years' decline compares with the corresponding spike in power. No point stealing second when odds are a homer is right around the corner, right?

The final column is the Stolen Base Success Rate, or how often a base-stealer is successful in his attempts. While the last two years have seen a bit of decline, steals success is still better than it was 15 years ago. It would be tough to draw a conclusion that the decline in steals has any connection to runner skill.

So, the decline in bags is a decline in the events that potentially create stolen base opportunities. Writer Joe Sheehan also attributes the phenomenon to the decline in singles, not only to create baserunners but also for driving in those runners who've stolen second base. The risk of a failed steal outweighs the benefit of putting a runner into scoring position if there are fewer run-scoring singles. Again, odds are a homer is right around the corner.

This environment seems like more of a core trend. It might continue. It might stabilize. Or not. If you look at 2002-2007, you might conclude that we're just going through a similar trough now.

So I'm not taking bets for 2017. It's an easy speculation to see how things could turn around. Dee Gordon doesn't get suspended. Roman Quinn potentially sits at the top of the Phillies batting order. Full seasons for Mallex Smith, Keon Broxton, Jose Peraza, and on and on. There were 28 players who stole at least 20 bases last year. A quick scan of the projections here—admittedly, a rough number at this time of year—and I count 40 potential 20-SB speedsters. And we're back out of the trough.

Trickle-down trends

The more that we can't project the environment in which our stats live, the tougher it is to get a read on individual player projections. They are moving targets as well. This book provides a better understanding of skill so you can take aim at those targets with as much precision as is possible. But as Fanalytic Fundamental No. 1 notes: *"This is not a game of accuracy or precision; it is a game of human beings and tendencies."*

Still, no matter how much we might intuitively know this is true, we are going to obsess over who to rank where and how much to pay for Player A, Player B and Player Z. We can't help it.

QUESTION: If you have the No. 1 seed in your 2017 draft, will you draft Mike Trout, Mookie Betts or Jose Altuve?

ANSWER: It almost doesn't matter.

For starters, owning the No. 1 seed hasn't exactly been a stone cold lock anyway.

Year	No. 1 Pick	Finish
2007	Albert Pujols	24
2008	Alex Rodriguez	11
2009	Hanley Ramirez	2
2010	Albert Pujols	2
2011	Albert Pujols	14
2012	Matt Kemp	96
2013	Ryan Braun	314
2014	Mike Trout	4
2015	Mike Trout	10
2016	Mike Trout	3

For 2017, Trout seems like the safest pick, given what appears to be a high floor. But we could have said the same thing about Albert Pujols not too long ago. One day, the Trout Era will end too.

As far as the best player, well, he can come from anywhere:

Year	No. 1 Earner	Pre-season ADP
2007	Alex Rodriguez	4
2008	Albert Pujols	10
2009	Albert Pujols	2
2010	Carlos Gonzalez	119
2011	Matt Kemp	23
2012	Mike Trout	228
2013	Miguel Cabrera	2
2014	Jose Altuve	92
2015	Jake Arrieta	97
2016	Mookie Betts	16

In fact, our ability to nail *anyone* in the first round of a 15-team draft is just as imprecise. For years I've been parading around the research stating that our success rate in identifying each season's top 15 players is—using the scientific term—"awful."

As in 35.5% awful since 2004.

Several of my industry colleagues have dismissed this research. Their contention is that a player drafted in the first round doesn't need to return first round value, only some reasonably close level. For instance, in 2016, Miguel Cabrera was drafted No. 13 as a $30 player. He finished ranked No. 19, earning $27. That's clearly an acceptable result, even though he didn't finish in the top 15.

However, some might also make a case that the owners of Josh Donaldson (No. 5, $38) should not have been disappointed with his finish at No. 23, earning $26. But in real terms, any player whose end-of-season value is lower than projection means that you are taking a loss on your investment. As much as Donaldson owners may have been satisfied, they still took a $12 loss. I suppose it comes down to your own tolerance level, but I wouldn't be happy with a $12 loss.

Part of the problem is that the slope of player value at the high end of our rankings is incredibly steep. If the 90th ranked player finishes No. 125, your real loss is only about $4. If your No. 1 pick finishes 36th—the same span of picks—your loss is more than $20. The early round misses have far more impact.

But the bottom line is, those failed first-round picks are not finishing just outside the top 15 anyway. They are barely in the top 30. Look:

	Percentage of top 15 picks who	
Year	Earn top 15 value	Earn top 30 value
2004	40%	47%
2005	47%	53%
2006	27%	67%
2007	33%	60%
2008	47%	60%
2009	33%	53%
2010	33%	47%
2011	40%	60%
2012	27%	40%
2013	33%	40%
2014	27%	47%
2015	27%	53%
2016	47%	60%
Mean	35.5%	52.8%

In fact, most of the players in the ADP top 15 finish nowhere near their draft spot. Look at the past three seasons:

2014 ADP		Earned
1	Mike Trout	4
2	Miguel Cabrera	11
3	Paul Goldschmidt	54
4	Andrew McCutchen	10
5	Carlos Gonzalez	434
6	Clayton Kershaw	2
7	Chris Davis	271
8	Ryan Braun	108
9	Adam Jones	26
10	Bryce Harper	319
11	Robinson Cano	32
12	Hanley Ramirez	76
13	Jacoby Ellsbury	31
14	Prince Fielder	637
15	Troy Tulowitzki	63

2015 ADP		Earned
1	Mike Trout	10
2	Andrew McCutchen	32
3	Clayton Kershaw	3
4	Giancarlo Stanton	156
5	Paul Goldschmidt	4
6	Miguel Cabrera	53
7	Jose Abreu	33
8	Carlos Gomez	148
9	Jose Bautista	27
10	Edwin Encarnacion	26
11	Felix Hernandez	104
12	Jose Altuve	9
13	Anthony Rizzo	19
14	Adam Jones	80
15	Troy Tulowitzki	115

2016 ADP		Earned
1	Mike Trout	3
2	Paul Goldschmidt	7
3	Bryce Harper	98
4	Clayton Kershaw	9
5	Josh Donaldson	23
6	Carlos Correa	71
7	Nolan Arenado	10
8	Manny Machado	30
9	Anthony Rizzo	34
10	Giancarlo Stanton	260
11	Jose Altuve	2
12	Kris Bryant	12
13	Miguel Cabrera	19
14	Andrew McCutchen	141
15	Max Scherzer	6

Admittedly, 2016 was one of our better years. But, for all the pre-season obsessing we do over getting the best seed and trying to decide who to draft where, these lists look like a whole bunch of blind dart-throws.

The point of all this

When you combine…

- the volatility of the statistical environment
- the imprecision of player projections, and
- the uncertainty of the drafting process

…you get one hot mess.

Each year, we respond to these variables in pretty much the same way, looking for a silver bullet that doesn't exist. But we don't need to resign ourselves to another year of wanton randomness either.

When it comes to the *environment volatility*, analysts will do their best job at forecasting, but will ultimately fall back on Merkin's Maxim: "When in doubt, predict that the current trend will continue." There are worse approaches, but frankly, there is not much more we can do. Observe, and react.

When it comes to *projective imprecision*, forecasters will build ever more elaborate models, scratching and clawing for each thousandth of a decimal point in mean squared error. That's a lot of unnecessary effort.

Your energy will be better spent learning the tools in this book. They'll help you get a better handle on each player's potential. Focus on the peripheral metrics and commentaries, not the projections; that's where the treasures are hidden.

When it comes to *drafting uncertainty,* tacticians will devise increasingly brilliant strategies to game our opponents, always hoping they respond as lab rats might.

But the year that you try to deplete pitching resources by over-drafting your staff is the year that Chris Archer, Matt Harvey, Dallas Keuchel and Zack Greinke go belly up. The year that you try to corner the market on speed is the year that Dee Gordon gets suspended and Manny Machado stops running. Besides, your league's winner is still going to be the guy who drafts Jonathan Villar and Rick Porcello anyway.

The best we can do here is look for small tactical advantages. It's the little stuff that can give us an unexpected edge. I've found two such tactics that have helped my process over the past few years.

Categorizing foundation players

History has shown that four types of players generally populate the early rounds in most drafts, or get auctioned for $25 or more:

1. Veteran early round earners are players who've been consistently atop the end-of-season leaderboards. These are players like Trout, Altuve, Goldschmidt and Kershaw. These are the lowest risk players to own.

2. New early-round earners are players who earned elite value for the first time last season. These are players like Bryant, Marte, Villar and Blackmon. Recency bias will push many of them in to the early ADPs and $30 bids in 2017, but not all deserve to be there.

3. Possible rebounds are players who were previous top talents and still have the skills to potentially return to the top. In 2017, these will be players like Harper, McCutchen and Stanton. Here again, there is greater risk for a rebound, but some of these types could well bounce back.

4. New season risers are players who have the potential to develop into elite level earners but have never previously achieved that level over a full season. These Draft Day speculations included players like Carlos Correa and Kyle Schwarber in 2016. Expect Trea Turner and Gary Sanchez to be part of this group in 2017.

Consider these four groups as a high-level hierarchy of the types of players to target, the vets at the top and risers at the bottom. Using this logic, I might be more inclined to look at a Kris Bryant or Charlie Blackmon before a Bryce Harper. Heresy? Perhaps. But preconceptions are what often get us into trouble.

Let's take a look at last year's top 30 players to see what group each fell into coming into 2016, and how they each fared.

In the chart below, "Grp" is the Group the player would have been in on Draft Day 2016. "ADP$" are the equivalent auction dollars converted from each average draft position. "Earnings" are the actual dollar earnings at the end of the season. "Net" is each pick's net profit or loss.

Seed	Player	Grp	ADP$	Earnings	Net
1	Mike Trout	1	$45	$42	-$3
2	Paul Goldschmidt	1	$43	$34	-$9
3	Bryce Harper	2	$41	$15	-$26
4	Clayton Kershaw	1	$39	$32	-$7
5	Josh Donaldson	2	$38	$26	-$12
6	Carlos Correa	4	$37	$17	-$20
7	Nolan Arenado	2	$36	$32	-$4
8	Manny Machado	2	$35	$25	-$10
9	Anthony Rizzo	1	$34	$23	-$11
10	Giancarlo Stanton	3	$33	$5	-$28
11	Jose Altuve	1	$32	$45	+$13
12	Kris Bryant	2	$31	$33	+$2
13	Miguel Cabrera	3	$30	$28	-$2
14	Andrew McCutchen	3	$29	$10	-$19
15	Max Scherzer	3	$29	$37	+$8
16	Mookie Betts	2	$28	$47	+$19
17	Dee Gordon	2	$28	$5	-$23
18	Buster Posey	1	$27	$21	-$6
19	Jose Abreu	3	$27	$16	-$11
20	Jake Arrieta	2	$27	$22	-$5
21	Starling Marte	2	$26	$29	+$3
22	George Springer	4	$26	$19	-$7
23	Chris Sale	3	$26	$26	$0
24	Chris Davis	3	$25	$8	-$17
25	Edwin Encarnacion	1	$25	$23	-$2
26	Madison Bumgarner	2	$24	$30	+$6
27	Jose Bautista	1	$24	$4	-$20
28	Charlie Blackmon	1	$23	$34	+$11
29	Matt Harvey	4	$23	-$8	-$31
30	Jose Fernandez	4	$23	$24	+$1

Only eight of the 30 players turned a profit, but that's okay. We are not looking for profit in this part of the player pool. Here, the goal is par, and to minimize the risk of big losses. In addition to the eight, another six came within $5 of their acquisition cost. That makes 14 of the 30 (47%) accomplishing about what we needed them to do. Still, a hit rate of less than 50% is nothing to write home about.

But we can do better. Let's summarize the above picks based on where they fell in our four groups.

			|——Average——|	
Group		No.	ADP$	Earnings	Net
1	Veterans	9	$32	$29	-$3
2	New earners	10	$31	$27	-$5
3	Rebounds	7	$28	$19	-$9
4	New risers	4	$27	$13	-$14

Yes, it's only one season and the sample sizes are small, but the risk of loss did increase the further down the hierarchy you drafted. These results reinforce the need to play it conservative in these early rounds.

Matt Harvey's ill-fated season drags down Group 4 (without him, the average net loss would have been $9), but I still stand by the oft-advised adage: "Never pay for a level of performance a player has not previously achieved."

Once the 2017 ADPs start taking shape, it will be a helpful exercise to slot the top players into these groups and adjust your draft strategy accordingly. This goes for auctions as well as snake drafts. A Group 4 player priced at $35 is just as much of a risk.

As an aside, if you were wondering where the big profit went last year, take a look:

Speedster	SB	ADP	ADP$	Earned	Net
Jonathan Villar	62	325	Res	$35	$35
Billy Hamilton	58	86	$14	$19	$5
Starling Marte	47	21	$26	$29	$3
Rajai Davis	43	347	Res	$17	$17
Eduardo Nunez	40	761	Res	$25	$25
Hernan Perez	34	955	Res	$16	$16
Jean Segura	33	185	$7	$33	$26
Trea Turner	33	299	$1	$20	$19

These were your top eight SB sources in 2016. Every one returned a profit. Read all you want into that.

Maximizing draft odds

When given the opportunity to choose your own seeding in a snake draft, my standard advice had always been, "earlier is better." That's because a snake draft is not the most equitable method for distributing talent. As noted earlier, the slope of player value at the high end of our rankings is incredibly steep, leaving the lower seeds to play catch-up in every round after Round 1.

For years, I have suggested that drafting from a higher seed is always better than a lower seed. But this assertion contains a flaw.

The ranked values are based on perfect forecasts. They assume that the No. 1 seeded owner selects the player who will earn the most value, and each successive owner makes their selections with perfect knowledge of how the players will be ranked at the end of the season. Obviously, that assumption is faulty.

I was talking with *Forecaster* co-editor Ray Murphy about this topic. Ray won the FSTA/SiriusXM league last year (I finished 3rd) and he finished 4th overall in the National Fantasy Baseball Championship (NFBC). He said: "Screw the ADP, screw the way that value decays after the first few picks. Just start your draft with two good picks and you're way ahead of the game."

Never discount the words of a winner.

But how do you give yourself the best chance to get two good picks? As I've shown, landing the No. 1 seed guarantees you little. In fact, in a vacuum, there is little correlation between any draft seed and winning. The NFBC concurs; each year's results show league winners coming from all of the 15 seeds.

If we have little control over how much the top players will earn, you want as many chances as possible to try to find the best players. If you have the No. 1 seed, you may get first dibs but then you have to wait until pick No. 30 for your second player. There is a better seed to draft from. I'd rather have two shots within the top 16 picks than two shots within the top 30 picks.

So I want the No. 15 seed—the wheel. That gives me picks No. 15 and 16.

Some have responded, "Well, the No. 1 seed gives me *three* shots at the top 31 picks. I'd rather have that than three shots at the top 45." Maybe. But by the third round, the difference in potential earnings between the first pick in that round (No. 31) and last pick (No. 45) may be only about $4. That's statistical noise, assuming we do even a marginal job of identifying the best players. The biggest variances are in rounds 1 and 2.

The point is control, not value, because we don't know where the value is going to land.

Nearly every player has warts and baggage, which is why it's more important to have as many pokes at the upper end of the pool as possible. And the best way to get multiple pokes is when the talent pool is deepest and the downward slope of player value is potentially the steepest.

2017

Here are a few random truths and opinions for this coming season:

1. There will be more Group 1 players to choose from. In addition to the regulars, we can add Betts, Donaldson, Arenado, Bryant and maybe Scherzer and Machado. Falling out of Group 1 into Group 3 are Bautista, Abreu and Posey.

2. A player dropping from Group 2 to Group 3 is a steeper plummet because there is less of a track record to fall back on. Players like Harper, Gordon and Arrieta might continue to be high-end considerations but have yet to prove that they are more than one-year wonders. Yes, heresy. I know.

3. The above lists are not all-inclusive. I have no idea where to slot guys like Starling Marte and even Miguel Cabrera.

4. As noted earlier, Trea Turner and Gary Sanchez are likely to be the top drafted Group 4 players. That means their owners will be pretty much giving up a chance for profit. I prefer to wait for lower-cost players who might have upside. If I am going to speculate and be wrong, I'd rather spend $25 for Wil Myers than spend $35 for Turner.

5. There were eight players who were members of the 40-HR Club in 2016.

40-HR hitters	HR	R$	Rank
Mark Trumbo	47	$21	59
Nelson Cruz	43	$25	36
Brian Dozier	42	$29	22
Edwin Encarnacion	42	$23	41
Khris Davis	42	$17	106
Nolan Arenado	41	$32	8
Chris Carter	41	$15	148
Todd Frazier	40	$19	99
Mean	42	$23	65

Frankly, it's astounding how little roto value this elite power group earned.

How sustainable are these levels? Only one player—Arenado—was among the top 10 hitters in hard contact rate (minimum 400 AB). The rest were barely on the HctX radar. Encarnacion was next at No. 33, then Trumbo (No. 44), Davis (No. 67), Dozier (No. 79), Cruz (No. 83), Carter (No. 107) and Frazier (No. 147). Frazier actually pulled off his feat with a HctX level below league average.

The marketplace devalued these players in 2016. Questionable skills may filter many of them out of the club completely in 2017.

And I will be left wondering whether Chris Carter will ever be a legitimate 40-home run hitter.

Welcome to the 31st Edition

If you are new to the *Baseball Forecaster*, the sheer volume of information in this book may seem a bit daunting. We don't recommend you assessing its contents over a single commute to work, particularly if you drive. But do set aside some time this winter—instead of staring out the window, waiting for baseball to begin again, try immersing yourself in all the wisdom contained in this tome. There's a ton of it, and the payoff—Yoo-Hoo or otherwise—is worth it.

But where to begin?

The best place to start is with the Encyclopedia of Fanalytics, which provides the foundation concepts for everything else that appears in these pages. It's our research archive and collective memory, just as valuable for veterans as it is for rookies. Take a cursory read-through, lingering at any section that looks interesting. You'll keep coming back here frequently.

Then just jump in. Close your eyes, flip to a random page, and put your finger down anywhere. Oh, look—Trevor Story *wasn't* just a one-month wonder. He showed legit power skills, and a willingness to run, right up until his thumb shut him down. There's more upside than you might think.

See, you've learned something already!

What's New in 2017?

Updated PQS: Though our Pure Quality Start metric has been a staple for over a decade, pitching performances have only gotten better—to the point where a PQS-DOM start happened just as often as not in 2015. So we set out to re-calibrate the PQS scale to better distinguish the top starting pitching performances from the rest—all while maintaining the inherent simplicity of the PQS model. So newPQS appears throughout these pages:

- The rationale and detailed update on newPQS heads our research abstracts.
- A second essay tackles the predictive value of newPQS.
- The pitcher boxes include PQS-DOM/DIS scores that reflect the updated system.
- The charts also incorporate the new version of PQS.

Look for additional research in BaseballHQ.com and in future editions Baseball Forecaster as we continue to explore ways in which newPQS gives you an edge.

Answers to questions, such as: Does pitch framing have a fantasy application? Can pitchers control home runs that clear the fence by "Just Enough"? Is the newest "strategy" enough to take into your fantasy draft? Can playing both DFS and season-long leagues be mutually beneficial? And much more.

Updates

The Baseball Forecaster page at BaseballHQ.com is at www.baseballhq.com/bf2017. This is your headquarters for all information and updates regarding this book. Here you will find links to the following:

Content Updates: In a project of this magnitude, there are occasionally items that need clarification or correction. You can find them here.

Free Projections Update: As a buyer of this book, you get one free 2017 projections update. This is a set of Excel spreadsheet files that will be posted on or about March 1, 2017. Remember to keep the book handy when you visit as the access codes are hidden within these pages.

Electronic book: The complete PDF version of the *Forecaster*—plus Excel versions of most key charts—is available free to those who bought the book directly through the BaseballHQ.com website. These files will be available in January 2017 for most of you; those who have an annual standing order should have received the PDF just before Thanksgiving. Contact us if you do not receive information via e-mail about access. Information about the e-book version can be found at the above website.

If you purchased the book through an online vendor or bookstore, or would like these files earlier, you can purchase them from us for $9.95. Contact us at support@baseballhq.com for more information.

Beyond the Forecaster

The *Baseball Forecaster* is just the beginning. The following companion products and services are described in more detail in the back of the book.

BaseballHQ.com is our home website. It provides regular updates to everything in this book, including daily updated statistics and projections. A subscription to BHQ gets you more than 1,000 articles over the course of a year updated daily from spring training through the end of the regular season, customized tools, access to data going back over a decade, plus much more. Sign up for our free BaseballHQFriday newsletter at www.baseballhq.com/friday.

First Pitch Forums are a series of conferences we run all over the country, where you can meet top industry analysts and network with fellow fantasy leaguers in your area. We'll be in cities from coast to coast in February and March. Our big annual symposium at the Arizona Fall League is the first weekend in November.

The 12th edition of the *Minor League Baseball Analyst*, by Rob Gordon and Jeremy Deloney, is the minor league companion to this book, with stat boxes for 1,000-plus prospects, essays on prospects, lists upon lists, and more. It is available in January.

RotoLab is the best draft software on the market and comes pre-loaded with our projections. Learn more at www.rotolab.com.

Even further beyond the Forecaster

Visit us on *Facebook* at www.facebook.com/baseballhq. "Like" the BaseballHQ page for updates, photos from events and links to other important stuff.

Follow us on *Twitter*. Site updates are tweeted from @BaseballHQ and many of our writers share their insights from their own personal accounts. We even have a list to follow: www.twitter.com/BaseballHQ/lists/hq-staff.

But back to baseball. Your winter comfort awaits.

—Brent Hershey and Ray Murphy

CONSUMER ADVISORY

AN IMPORTANT MESSAGE FOR FANTASY LEAGUERS
REGARDING PROPER USAGE OF THE *BASEBALL FORECASTER*

This document is provided in compliance with authorities to outline the prospective risks and hazards possible in the event that the Baseball Forecaster is used incorrectly. Please be aware of these potentially dangerous situations and avoid them. The publisher assumes no risk related to any financial loss or stress-induced illnesses caused by ignoring the items as described below.

1. The statistical projections in this book are intended as general guidelines, not as gospel. It is highly dangerous to use the projected statistics alone, and then live and die by them. That's like going to a ballgame, being given a choice of any seat in the park, and deliberately choosing the last row in the right field corner with an obstructed view. The projections are there, you can look at them, but there are so many better places to sit.

We have to publish those numbers, but they are stagnant, inert pieces of data. This book focuses on a live forecasting process that provides the tools so that you can understand the leading indicators and draw your own conclusions. If you at least attempt your own analyses of the data, and enhance them with the player commentaries, you can paint more robust, colorful pictures of the future.

In other words...

If you bought this book purely for the projected statistics and do not intend to spend at least some time learning about the process, then you might as well just buy an $8 magazine.

2. The player commentaries in this book are written by humans, just like you. These commentaries provide an overall evaluation of performance and likely future direction, but 60-word capsules cannot capture everything. Your greatest value will be to use these as a springboard to your own analysis of the data. Odds are, if you take the time, you'll find hidden indicators that we might have missed. Forecaster veterans say that this self-guided excursion is the best part of owning the book.

3. This book does not attempt to tackle playing time. Rather than making arbitrary decisions about how roles will shake out, the focus is on performance. The playing time projections presented here are merely to help you better evaluate each player's talent. Our online preseason projections update provides more current AB and IP expectations based on how roles are being assigned.

4. The dollar values in this book are intended solely for player-to-player comparisons. They are not driven by a finite pool of playing time—which is required for valuation systems to work properly—so they cannot be used for bid values to be used in your own draft.

There are two reasons for this:

a. The finite pool of players that will generate the finite pool of playing time will not be determined until much closer to Opening Day. And, if we are to be brutally honest, there is really no such thing as a finite pool of players.

b. Your particular league's construction will drive the values; a $10 player in a 10-team mixed league will not be the same as a $10 player in a 12-team NL-only league.

Note that book dollar values also cannot be compared to those published at BaseballHQ.com as the online values are generated by a more finite player pool.

5. Do not pass judgment on the effectiveness of this book based on the performance of a few individual players. The test, rather, is on the collective predictive value of the book's methods. Are players with better base skills more likely to produce good results than bad ones? Years of research suggest that the answer is "yes." Does that mean that every high skilled player will do well? No. But many more of them will perform well than will the average low-skilled player. You should always side with the better percentage plays, but recognize that there are factors we cannot predict. Good decisions that beget bad outcomes do not invalidate the methods.

6. If your copy of this book is not marked up and dog-eared by Draft Day, you probably did not get as much value out of it as you might have.

7. This edition of the Forecaster is not intended to provide absorbency for spills of more than 7.5 ounces.

8. This edition is not intended to provide stabilizing weight for more than 18 sheets of 20 lb. paper in winds of more than 45 mph.

9. The pages of this book are not recommended for avian waste collection. In independent laboratory studies, 87% of migratory water fowl refused to excrete on interior pages, even when coaxed.

10. This book, when rolled into a cylindrical shape, is not intended to be used as a weapon for any purpose, including but not limited to insect extermination, canine training or to influence bidding behavior at a fantasy draft.

ENCYCLOPEDIA OF FANALYTICS

For new readers...

Everything begins here. The information in the following pages represents the foundation that powers everything we do.

You'll learn about the underlying concepts for our unique mode of analysis. You'll find answers to long-asked questions, interesting insights into what makes players tick, and innovative applications for all this newfound knowledge.

This Encyclopedia is organized into several logical sections:

1. Fundamentals
2. Batters
3. Pitchers
4. Prospects
5. Gaming

Enough talking. Jump in.
Remember to breathe.

For veteran readers...

As we do in each edition, this year's ever-expanding Encyclopedia includes relevant research results we've published over the past year. We've added some of the essays from the Research Abstracts and Gaming Abstracts sections in the 2016 *Forecaster* as well as some other essays from BaseballHQ.com.

And we continue to mold the content to best fit how fantasy leaguers use their information. Many readers consider this their fantasy information bible.

Okay, time to jump-start the analytical process for 2017. Remember to breathe—it's always good advice.

Abbreviations

Fundamentals

What is Fanalytics?

Fanalytics is the scientific approach to fantasy baseball analysis. A contraction of "fantasy" and "analytics," fanalytic gaming might be considered a mode of play that requires a more strategic and quantitative approach to player analysis and game decisions.

The three key elements of fanalytics are:

1. Performance analysis
2. Performance forecasting
3. Gaming analysis

For performance analysis, we tap into the vast knowledge of the sabermetric community. Founded by Bill James, this area of study provides objective and progressive new ways to assess skill. What we do in this book is called "component skills analysis." We break down performance into its component parts, then reverse-engineer it back into the traditional measures with which we are more familiar.

Our forecasting methodology is one part science and one part art. We start with a computer-generated baseline for each player. We then make subjective adjustments based on a variety of factors, such as discrepancies in skills indicators and historical guidelines gleaned from more than 20 years of research. We don't rely on a rigid model; our method forces us to get our hands dirty.

You might say that our brand of forecasting is more about finding logical journeys than blind destinations.

Gaming analysis is an integrated approach designed to help us win our fantasy leagues. It takes the knowledge gleaned from the first two elements and adds the strategic and tactical aspect of each specific fantasy game format.

Component Skills Analysis

Familiar gauges like HR and ERA have long been used to measure skill. In fact, these gauges only measure the outcome of an individual event, or series of events. They represent statistical output. They are "surface stats."

Raw skill is the talent beneath the stats. Players use these skills to create the individual events, or components, that are the building blocks of measures like HR and ERA. Our approach:

1. It's not about batting average; it's about seeing the ball and making contact. We target hitters based on elements such as their batting eye (walks to strikeouts ratio), how often they make contact and the type of contact they make. We then combine these components into an "expected batting average." By comparing each hitter's actual BA to how he should be performing, we can draw conclusions about the future.

2. It's not about home runs; it's about power. From the perspective of a round bat meeting a round ball, it may be only a fraction of an inch at the point of contact that makes the difference between a HR or a long foul ball. When a ball is hit safely, often it is only a few inches that separate a HR from a double. We tend to neglect these facts in our analyses, although the outcomes—the doubles, triples, long fly balls—may be no less a measure of that batter's raw power skill. We must incorporate all these components to paint a complete picture.

3. It's not about ERA; it's about getting the ball over the plate and keeping it in the park. Forget ERA. You want to draft pitchers who walk few batters (Control), strike out many (Dominance) and succeed at both in tandem (Command). You generally want pitchers who keep the ball on the ground (because home runs are bad), though some fly ball pitchers can succeed under the right conditions. All of this translates into an "expected ERA" that you can use to validate a pitcher's actual performance.

4. It's never about wins. For pitchers, winning ballgames is less about skill than it is about offensive support. As such, projecting wins is a very high-risk exercise and valuing hurlers based on their win history is dangerous. Target skill; wins will come.

5. It's not about saves; it's about opportunity first and skills second. While the highest-skilled pitchers have the best potential to succeed as closers, they still have to be given the ball with the game on the line in the 9th inning, and that is a decision left to others. Over the past 15 years, about 40% of relievers drafted for saves failed to hold the role for the entire season. The lesson: Don't take chances on draft day. There will always be saves in the free agent pool.

Accounting for "luck"

Luck has been used as a catch-all term to describe random chance. When we use the term here, we're talking about unexplained variances that shape the statistics. While these variances may be random, they are also often measurable and projectable. To get a better read on "luck," we use formulas that capture the external variability of the data.

Through our research and the work of others, we have learned that when raw skill is separated from statistical output, what's remaining is often unexplained variance. The aggregate totals of many of these variances, for all players, is often a constant. For instance, while a pitcher's ERA might fluctuate, the rate at which his opposition's batted balls fall for hits will tend towards 30%. Large variances can be expected to regress towards 30%.

Why is all this important? Analysts complain about the lack of predictability of many traditional statistical gauges. The reason they find it difficult is that they are trying to project performance using gauges that are loaded with external noise. Raw skills gauges follow better defined trends during a player's career. Then, as we get a better handle on the variances—explained and unexplained—we can construct a complete picture of what a player's statistics really mean.

Baseball Forecasting

Forecasting in perspective

The crystal ball aura of this process conceals the fact it is a process. We might define it as "the systematic process of determining likely end results." At its core, it's scientific.

However, the *outcomes* of forecasted events are what is most closely scrutinized, and are used to judge the success or failure of the forecast. That said, as long as the process is sound, the forecast has done the best job it can do. *In the end, forecasting is about analysis, not prophecy.*

Baseball performance forecasting is inherently a high-risk exercise with a very modest accuracy rate. This is because the process involves not only statistics, but also unscientific elements, from random chance to human volatility. And even from within the statistical aspect there are multiple elements that need to be evaluated, from skill to playing time to a host of external variables.

Every system is comprised of the same core elements:

- Players will tend to perform within the framework of past history and/or trends.
- Skills will develop and decline according to age.
- Statistics will be shaped by a player's health, expected role and venue.

While all systems are built from these same elements, they also are constrained by the same limitations. We are all still trying to project a bunch of human beings, each one...

- with his own individual skill set
- with his own rate of growth and decline
- with his own ability to resist and recover from injury
- limited to opportunities determined by other people
- generating a group of statistics largely affected by external noise.

Research has shown that the best accuracy rate that can be attained by any system is about 70%. In fact, a simple system that uses three-year averages adjusted for age ("Marcel") can attain a success rate of 65%. This means all the advanced systems are fighting for occupation of the remaining 5%.

But there is a bigger question... *what exactly are we measuring?* When we search for accuracy, what does that mean? In fact, any quest for accuracy is going to run into a brick wall of paradoxes:

- If a slugging average projection is dead on, but the player hits 10 fewer HRs than expected (and likely, 20 more doubles), is that a success or a failure?
- If a projection of hits and walks allowed by a pitcher is on the mark, but the bullpen and defense implodes, and inflates his ERA by a run, is that a success or a failure?
- If the projection of a speedster's rate of stolen base success is perfect, but his team replaces the manager with one that doesn't run, and the player ends up with half as many SBs as expected, is that a success or a failure?
- If a batter is traded to a hitters' ballpark and all the touts project an increase in production, but he posts a statistical line exactly what would have been projected had he not been traded to that park, is that a success or a failure?
- If the projection for a bullpen closer's ERA, WHIP and peripheral numbers is perfect, but he saves 20 games instead of 40 because the GM decided to bring in a high-priced free agent at the trading deadline, is that a success or a failure?
- If a player is projected to hit .272 in 550 AB and only hits .249, is that a success or failure? Most will say "failure." But wait a minute! The real difference is only two hits per month. That shortfall of 23 points in batting average is because a fielder might have made a spectacular play, or a screaming liner might have been hit right at someone, or a long shot to the outfield might have been held up by the wind... once every 14 games. Does that constitute "failure"?

Even if we were to isolate a single statistic that measures "overall performance" and run our accuracy tests on it, the results will still be inconclusive.

According to OPS, these players are virtually identical:

BATTER	HR	RBI	SB	BA	OBA	SLG	OPS
Gattis,E	32	72	0	.251	.319	.508	.826
Villar,J	19	63	62	.285	.369	.457	.826
Pedroia,D	15	74	7	.318	.376	.449	.825

If I projected Villar-caliber stats and ended up with Evan Gattis's numbers, I'd hardly call that an accurate projection, especially if my fantasy team was in dire need of steals.

According to Roto dollars, these players are also dead-on:

BATTER	HR	RBI	Runs	SB	BA	R$
Marte,S	9	46	71	47	.311	$26
Donaldson,J	37	99	122	7	.284	$26
LeMahieu,DJ	11	66	104	11	.348	$26

It's not so simple for someone to claim they have accurate projections. And so, it is best to focus on the bigger picture, especially when it comes to winning at fantasy baseball.

More on this: "The Great Myths of Projective Accuracy"

http://www.baseballhq.com/great-myths-projective-accuracy

Baseball Forecaster's forecasting process

We are all about component skills. Our approach is to assemble these evaluators in such a way that they can be used to validate our observations, analyze their relevance and project a likely future direction.

In a perfect world, if a player's raw skills improve, then so should his surface stats. If his skills decline, then his stats should follow as well. But, sometimes a player's skill indicators increase while his surface stats decline. These variances may be due to a variety of factors.

Our forecasting process is based on the expectation that events tend to move towards universal order. Surface stats will eventually approach their skill levels. Unexplained variances will regress to a mean. And from this, we can identify players whose performance may potentially change.

For most of us, this process begins with the previous year's numbers. Last season provides us with a point of reference, so it's a natural way to begin the process of looking at the future. Component skills analysis allows us to validate those numbers. A batter with few HRs but a high linear weighted power level has a good probability of improving his future HR output. A pitcher whose ERA was poor while his command ratio was solid might be a good bet for ERA improvement.

Of course, these leading indicators do not always follow the rules. There are more shades of grey than blacks and whites. When indicators are in conflict—for instance, a pitcher who is displaying both a rising strikeout rate and a rising walk rate—then we have to find ways to sort out what these indicators might be saying.

It is often helpful to look at leading indicators in a hierarchy. A rank of the most important pitching indicators might be: Command (k/bb), Dominance (k/9), Control (bb/9) and GB/FB rate. For batters, contact rate tops the list, followed by power, walk rate and speed.

Assimilating additional research

Once we've painted the statistical picture of a player's potential, we then use additional criteria and research results to help us add some color to the analysis. These other criteria include the player's health, age, changes in role, ballpark and a variety of other factors. We also use the research results described in the following pages. This research looks at things like traditional periods of peak performance and breakout profiles.

The final element of the process is assimilating the news into the forecast. This is the element that many fantasy leaguers tend to rely on most since it is the most accessible. However, it is also the element that provides the most noise. Players, management and the media have absolute control over what we are allowed to know. Factors such as hidden injuries, messy divorces and clubhouse unrest are routinely kept from us, while we are fed red herrings and media spam. *We will never know the entire truth.*

Quite often, all you are reading is just other people's opinions... a manager who believes that a player has what it takes to be a regular or a team physician whose diagnosis is that a player is healthy enough to play. These words from experts have some element of truth, but cannot be wholly relied upon to provide an accurate expectation of future events. As such, it is often helpful to develop an appropriate cynicism for what you read.

For instance, if a player is struggling for no apparent reason and there are denials about health issues, don't dismiss the possibility that an injury does exist. There are often motives for such news to be withheld from the public.

And so, as long as we do not know all the facts, we cannot dismiss the possibility that any one fact is true, no matter how often the media assures it, deplores it, or ignores it. Don't believe everything you read; use your own judgment. If your observations conflict with what is being reported, that's powerful insight that should not be ignored.

Also remember that nothing lasts forever in major league baseball. *Reality is fluid.* One decision begets a series of events that lead to other decisions. Any reported action can easily be reversed based on subsequent events. My favorite examples are announcements of a team's new bullpen closer. Those are about the shortest realities known to man.

We need the media to provide us with context for our analyses, and the real news they provide is valuable intelligence. But separating the news from the noise is difficult. In most cases, the only thing you can trust is how that player actually performs.

Embracing imprecision

Precision in baseball prognosticating is a fool's quest. There are far too many unexpected variables and noise that can render our projections useless. The truth is, the best we can ever hope for is to accurately forecast general tendencies and percentage plays.

However, even when you follow an 80% percentage play, for instance, you will still lose 20% of the time. That 20% is what skeptics use as justification to dismiss prognosticators; they conveniently ignore the more prevalent 80%. The paradox, of course, is that fantasy league titles are often won or lost by those exceptions. Still, long-term success dictates that you always chase the 80% and accept the fact that you will be wrong 20% of the time. Or, whatever that percentage play happens to be.

For fantasy purposes, playing the percentages can take on an even less precise spin. The best projections are often the ones that are just far enough away from the field of expectation to alter decision-making. In other words, it doesn't matter if I project Player X to bat .320 and he only bats .295; it matters that I project .320 and everyone else projects .280. Those who follow my less-accurate projection will go the extra dollar to acquire him in their draft.

Or, perhaps we should evaluate the projections based upon their intrinsic value. For instance, coming into 2016, would it have been more important for me to tell you that Anthony Rizzo was going to hit 30 HRs or that Brad Miller would hit 15 HRs (when all other touts predicted 10)? By season's end, the Rizzo projection would have been more accurate, but the Miller projection—even though it was off by more than 10 HRs—would have been far more *valuable*. The Miller projection might have persuaded you to go an extra buck on Draft Day, yielding far more profit.

And that has to be enough. Any tout who projects a player's statistics dead-on will have just been lucky with his dart throws that day.

Perpetuity

Forecasting is not an exercise that produces a single set of numbers. It is dynamic, cyclical and ongoing. Conditions are constantly changing and we must react to those changes by adjusting our expectations. A pre-season projection is just a snapshot in time. Once the first batter steps to the plate on Opening Day, that projection has become obsolete. Its value is merely to provide a starting point, a baseline for what is about to occur.

During the season, if a projection appears to have been invalidated by current performance, the process continues. It is then that we need to ask... What went wrong? What conditions have changed? In fact, has *anything* changed? We need to analyze the situation and revise our expectation, if necessary. This process must be ongoing.

When good projections go bad

Although we'd like to think otherwise, we cannot predict the future. All we can do is provide a sound process for constructing a "most likely expectation for future performance." If we've captured as much information as is available, used the best methodology and analyzed the results correctly, that's the best we can do.

All we can control is the process. We simply can't control outcomes.

However, one thing we *can* do is analyze the misses to see *why* they occurred. This is always a valuable exercise each year. It puts a proper focus on the variables that were out of our control as well as providing perspective on those players with whom we might have done a better job.

In general, we can organize these forecasting misses into several categories. To demonstrate, here are all the players whose 2016 Rotisserie earnings varied from projections by at least $10.

The performances that exceeded expectation

Development beyond the growth trend: These are young players for whom we knew there was skill. Some of them were prized prospects in the past who have taken their time ascending the growth curve. Others were a surprise only because their performance spike arrived sooner than anyone anticipated... Jackie Bradley, Xander Bogaerts, Kris Byrant, Adam Duvall, Jacob Lamb, Jose Ramirez, Wilson Ramos, Trevor Story, Trea Turner, Jonathan Villar, Danny Duffy, Michael Fulmer, Aaron Sanchez.

Skilled players who just had big years: We knew these guys were good too; we just didn't anticipate they'd be this good... Brian Dozier, D.J. Lemahieu, Daniel Murphy, Brad Brach, JA Happ, Kyle Hendricks, Jon Lester, Kenta Maeda, Seung-Hwan Oh, Rick Porcello, Max Scherzer.

Unexpected health: We knew these players had the goods; we just didn't know whether they'd be healthy or would stay healthy all year... Carlos Beltran, Freddie Freeman, Wil Myers, Dustin Pedroia.

Unexpected playing time: These players had the skills—and may have even displayed them at some time in the past—but had ques-tionable playing time potential coming into this season. Some benefited from another player's injury, a rookie who didn't pan out or leveraged a short streak into a regular gig... Aledmys Diaz.

Unexpected return to form: These players had the skills, having displayed them at some point in the past. But those skills had been M.I.A. long enough that we began to doubt that they'd ever return; our projections model got tired of waiting. Or those previous skills displays were so inconsistent that projecting an "up year" would have been a shot in the dark. Yes, "once you display a skill, you own it" but still... Chris Carter, Ian Desmond, Rajai Davis, Cameron Maybin, Jean Segura, Melvin Upton, Tanner Roark, Dan Straily.

Unexpected role: This category is reserved for 2016's surprise closers: Alex Colome, Edwin Diaz, Sam Dyson, Jeanmar Gomez, Jeremy Jeffress, Brandon Kintzler, Ryan Madson, Tyler Thornburg.

Unexpected discovery of the Fountain of Youth: These players should have been done, or nearly done, or at least headed down the far side of the bell curve. That's what the trends were pointing to. The trends were wrong... Mike Napoli, David Ortiz, Bartolo Colon, Rich Hill, John Lackey, Justin Verlander.

Celebrate and claim we're geniuses: How these players put up the numbers they did is a mystery, but fantasy owners will likely chalk it up to their own superior scouting skills as they count their winnings. The truth is, who knows? However, the odds of a comparable follow-up for these players—particularly those with soft peripherals—will be small: Eduardo Nunez!

The performances that fell short of expectation

The DL denizens: These are players who got hurt, may not have returned fully healthy, or may have never been fully healthy (whether they'd admit it or not)... Jose Bautista, Michael Brantley, Lorenzo Cain, Shin-Soo Choo, Lucas Duda, Prince Fielder, Alex Gordon, Austin Jackson, Hunter Pence, David Peralta, Ben Revere, Giancarlo Stanton, Mark Teixeira, Carlos Carrasco, Gerrit Cole, Wade Davis, Jacob deGrom, Jaime Garcia, Sonny Gray, Matt Harvey, Clayton Kershaw, Garrett Richards, Tyson Ross, Luis Severino, Jordan Zimmermann.

Accelerated skills erosion: These are players who we knew were on the downside of their careers or had soft peripherals but who we did not think would plummet so quickly. In some cases, there were injuries involved, but all in all, 2016 might be the beginning of the end for some of these guys... Carlos Gomez, Felix Hernandez, Jonathan Papelbon, James Shields, Adam Wainwright.

Inflated expectations: Here are players who we really should not have expected much more than what they produced. Some had short or spotty track records, others had soft peripherals coming into 2016, and still others were inflated by media hype. Yes, for some of these, it was "What the heck was I thinking?" For others, we've almost come to expect players to ascend the growth curve faster these days. (You're 23 and you haven't broken out yet? What's the problem??) The bottom line is that player performance trends simply don't progress or regress in a straight line; still, the trends were intriguing enough to take a leap of faith. We were wrong... Billy Burns, Byron Buxton, Joe Panik, Gerardo Parra, Yasiel Puig, Miguel Sano, Zack Greinke, Drew Smyly, Marcus Stroman, Michael Wacha.

Misplaced regression: Sometimes, we're so bullish on a player that we ignore the potential for regression within the bounds of normal random variance. Gravity is a powerful force, for... Jose Abreu, Chris Davis, Adrian Gonzalez, Collin McHugh, David Price.

Unexpected loss of role: This category is usually composed of closers who lost their job, sometimes through no fault of their own... Ken Giles, Jonathan Papelbon, Trevor Rosenthal, Huston Street, Glen Perkins, Brad Ziegler. Oh, and we'll throw Dee Gordon in this category as well.

Throw our hands up and yell at the TV: These are the players for whom there is little explanation for what happened. We can speculate that they hid an injury, went off of PEDs, or just didn't have their head on right in 2016. For some, it was just the turn of an unlucky card this year: Bryce Harper, Buster Posey, Jason Heyward, Andrew McCutchen, Justin Upton, Dallas Keuchel.

About fantasy baseball touts

As a group, there is a strong tendency for all pundits to provide numbers that are publicly palatable, often at the expense of poten-tial accuracy. That's because committing to either end of the range of expectation poses a high risk. Few touts will put their credibility on the line like that, even though we all know that those outliers are inevitable. Among our projections, you will find no .350 hitters or 70-steal speedsters (well, OK, maybe one). *Someone* is going to post a sub-2.50 ERA next year, but damned if any of us will commit to that. So we take an easier road. We'll hedge our numbers or split the difference between two equally possible outcomes.

In the world of prognosticating, this is called the *comfort zone*. This represents the outer tolerances for the public acceptability of a set of numbers. In most circumstances, even if the evidence is outstanding, prognosticators will not stray from within the comfort zone.

As for this book, occasionally we do commit to outlying numbers when we feel the data support it. But on the whole, most of the numbers here can be nearly as cowardly as everyone else's.

We get around this by providing "color" to the projections in the capsule commentaries, often listing UPside or DOWNside projections. That is where you will find the players whose projection has the best potential to stray beyond the limits of the comfort zone.

As analyst John Burnson once wrote: "The issue is not the success rate for one player, but the success rate for all players. No system is 100% reliable, and in trying to capture the outliers, you weaken the middle and thereby lose more predictive pull than you gain. At some level, everyone is an exception!"

Formula for consistent success

Anyone can win a league in any given season. Winning once proves very little, especially in redraft leagues. True success has to be defined as the ability to win consistently. It is a feat in itself to reach the mountaintop, but the battle isn't truly won unless you can stay atop that peak while others keep trying to knock you off.

What does it take to win that battle? We surveyed 12 of the most prolific fantasy champions in national experts league play. Here is how they rated six variables:

	Percent ranked			
	1-2	3-4	5-6	Score
Better in-draft strategy/tactics	77%	15%	7%	5.00
Better sense of player value	46%	46%	7%	4.15
Better luck	46%	23%	31%	3.85
Better grasp of contextual elements that affect players	31%	38%	31%	3.62
Better in-season roster management	31%	38%	31%	3.54
Better player projections	12%	31%	54%	2.62

Validating Performance

Performance validation criteria

The following is a set of support variables that helps determine whether a player's statistical output is an accurate reflection of his skills. From this we can validate or refute stats that vary from expectation, essentially asking, is this performance "fact or fluke?"

1. Age: Is the player at the stage of development when we might expect a change in performance?

2. Health: Is he coming off an injury, reconditioned and healthy for the first time in years, or a habitual resident of the disabled list?

3. Minor league performance: Has he shown the potential for greater things at some level of the minors? Or does his minor league history show a poor skill set that might indicate a lower ceiling?

4. Historical trends: Have his skill levels over time been on an upswing or downswing?

5. Component skills indicators: Looking beyond batting averages and ERAs, what do his support ratios look like?

6. Ballpark, team, league: Pitchers going to Colorado will see their ERA spike. Pitchers going to Oakland will see their ERA improve.

7. Team performance: Has a player's performance been affected by overall team chemistry or the environment fostered by a winning or losing club?

8. Batting stance, pitching style/mastery: Has a change in performance been due to a mechanical adjustment?

9. Usage pattern, lineup position, role: Has a change in RBI opportunities been a result of moving further up or down in the batting order? Has pitching effectiveness been impacted by moving from the bullpen to the rotation?

10. Coaching effects: Has the coaching staff changed the way a player approaches his conditioning, or how he approaches the game itself?

11. Off-season activity: Has the player spent the winter frequenting workout rooms or banquet tables?

12. Personal factors: Has the player undergone a family crisis? Experienced spiritual rebirth? Given up red meat? Taken up testosterone?

Skills ownership

Once a player displays a skill, he owns it. That display could occur at any time—earlier in his career, back in the minors, or even in winter ball play. And while that skill may lie dormant after its initial display, the potential is always there for him to tap back into that skill at some point, barring injury or age. That dormant skill can reappear at any time given the right set of circumstances.

Caveats:

1. The initial display of skill must have occurred over an extended period of time. An isolated 1-hit shut-out in Single-A ball amidst a 5.00 ERA season is not enough. The shorter the display of skill in the past, the more likely it can be attributed to random chance. The longer the display, the more likely that any reemergence is for real.

2. If a player has been suspected of using performance enhancing drugs at any time, all bets are off.

Corollaries:

1. Once a player displays a vulnerability or skills deficiency, he owns that as well. That vulnerability could be an old injury problem, an inability to hit breaking pitches, or just a tendency to go into prolonged slumps.

2. The probability of a player correcting a skills deficiency declines with each year that deficiency exists.

Contract year performance *(Tom Mullooly)*

There is a contention that players step up their game when they are playing for a contract. Research looked at contract year players and their performance during that year as compared to career levels. Of the batters and pitchers studied, 53% of the batters performed as if they were on a salary drive, while only 15% of the pitchers exhibited some level of contract year behavior.

How do players fare *after* signing a large contract (minimum $4M per year)? Research from 2005-2008 revealed that only 30% of pitchers and 22% of hitters exhibited an increase of more than 15% in BPV after signing a large deal either with their new team, or re-signing with the previous team. But nearly half of the pitchers (49%) and nearly half of the hitters (47%) saw a drop in BPV of more than 15% in the year after signing.

Risk Analysis

Risk management and reliability grades

Forecasts are constructed with the best data available, but there are factors that can impact the variability. One way we manage this risk is to assign each player Reliability Grades. The more certainty we see in a data set, the higher the reliability grades assigned to that player. The following variables are evaluated:

Health: Players with a history of staying healthy and off the DL are valuable to own. Unfortunately, while the ability to stay healthy can be considered skill, it is not very projectable. We can track the number of days spent on the disabled list and draw rough conclusions. The grades in the player boxes also include an adjustment for older players, who have a higher likelihood of getting hurt. That is the only forward-looking element of the grade.

"A" level players would have accumulated fewer than 30 days on the major league DL over the past five years. "F" grades go to those who've spent more than 120 days on the DL. Recent DL stays are given a heavier weight in the calculation.

Playing Time and Experience (PT/Exp): The greater the pool of MLB history to draw from, the greater our ability to construct a viable forecast. Length of service—and consistent service—is important. So players who bounce up and down from the majors to the minors are higher risk players. And rookies are all high risk.

For batters, we simply track plate appearances. Major league PAs have greater weight than minor league PAs. "A" level players would have averaged at least 550 major league PAs per year over the past three years. "F" graded players averaged fewer than 250 major league PA per year.

For pitchers, workload can be a double-edged sword. On one hand, small IP samples are deceptive in providing a read on a pitcher's true potential. Even a consistent 65-inning reliever can be considered higher risk since it would take just one bad outing to skew an entire season's work.

On the flipside, high workload levels also need to be monitored, especially in the formative years of a pitcher's career. Exceeding those levels elevates the risk of injury, burnout, or breakdown. So, tracking workload must be done within a range of innings. The grades capture this.

Consistency: Consistent performers are easier to project and garner higher reliability grades. Players that mix mediocrity with occasional flashes of brilliance or badness generate higher risk projections. Even those who exhibit a consistent upward or downward trend cannot be considered truly consistent as we do not know whether those trends will continue. Typically, they don't. *(See below: Using 3-year trends as leading indicators)*

"A" level players are those whose runs created per game level (xERA for pitchers) has fluctuated by less than half a run during each of the past three years. "F" grades go to those whose RC/G or xERA has fluctuated by two runs or more.

Remember that these grades have nothing to do with quality of performance; they strictly refer to confidence in our expectations. So a grade of **AAA** for Tom Koehler for instance, only means that there is a high probability he will perform as poorly as we've projected.

Using 3-year trends as leading indicators *(Ed DeCaria)*

It is almost irresistibly tempting to look at three numbers moving in one direction and expect that the fourth will continue that progression. However, for both hitters and pitchers riding positive trends over any consecutive three-year period, not only do most players not continue their positive trend into a fourth year, their Year 4 performance usually regresses significantly. This is true for every metric tested (whether related to playing time, batting skills, pitching skills, running skills, luck indicators, or valuation). Negative trends show similar reversals, but tend to be more "sticky," meaning that rebounds are neither as frequent nor as strong as positive trend regressions.

Reliability and age

Peak batting reliability occurs at ages 29 and 30, followed by a minor decline for four years. So, to draft the most reliable batters, and maximize the odds of returning at least par value on your investments, you should target the age range of 28-34.

The most reliable age range for pitchers is 29-34. While we are forever looking for "sleepers" and hot prospects, it is very risky to draft any pitcher under 27 or over 35.

Evaluating Reliability *(Bill Macey)*

Fantasy baseball owners are like investors who are always looking for a good return. Calculating our expected return includes assessing the risk of our draft-day investment.

Managing risk leads to two kinds of valuation adjustments. We downgrade talented players we believe to be higher injury risks, who have a history of inconsistent performance, or whose playing time (PT) is less certain. But we upgrade players we deem more reliable with respect to health, consistency, PT, or all three.

When you head into an upcoming auction or draft, consider the following with regard to reliability:

- Reliability grades do help identify more stable investments: players with "B" grades in both Health and PT/Experience are more likely to return a higher percentage of their projected value.
- While top-end starting pitching may be more reliable than ever, the overall pool of pitchers is fraught with uncertainty and they represent a less reliable investment than batters.
- There does not appear to be a significant market premium for reliability, at least according to the criteria measured by BaseballHQ.com.
- There are only two types of players: risky and riskier. So while it may be worth going the extra buck for a more reliable player, be warned that even the most reliable player can falter—don't go overboard bidding up a AAA-rated player simply due to his Reliability grades.

Normal production variance *(Patrick Davitt)*

Even if we have a perfectly accurate understanding of a player's "normal" performance level, his actual performance can and does vary widely over any particular 150-game span—including the 150-game span we call "a season." A .300 career hitter can perform in a range of .250-.350, a 40-HR hitter from 30-50, and a 3.70/1.15 pitcher from 2.60/0.95 to 6.00/1.55. And all of these results must be considered "normal."

Health Analysis

Disabled list statistics

Year	#Players	3yr Avg	DL Days	3yr Avg
2010	393	408	22,911	25,783
2011	422	408	25,610	24,924
2012	409	408	30,408	27,038
2013	442	419	29,551	28,523
2014	422	424	25,839	28,599
2015	454	439	28,982	28,124
2016	478	451	31,329	28,717

D.L. days as a leading indicator *(Bill Macey)*

Players who are injured in one year are likely to be injured in a subsequent year:

% DL batters in Year 1 who are also DL in year 2	38%
Under age 30	36%
Age 30 and older	41%
% DL batters in Year 1 and 2 who are also DL in year 3	54%
% DL pitchers in Year 1 who are also DL in year 2	43%
Under age 30	45%
Age 30 and older	41%
% DL pitchers in Yr 1 and 2 who are also DL in year 3	41%

Previously injured players also tend to spend a longer time on the DL. The average number of days on the DL was 51 days for batters and 73 days for pitchers. For the subset of these players who get hurt again the following year, the average number of days on the DL was 58 days for batters and 88 days for pitchers.

Spring training spin *(Dave Adler)*

Spring training sound bites raise expectations among fantasy leaguers, but how much of that "news" is really "noise"? Thanks to a summary listed at RotoAuthority.com, we were able to compile the stats for 2009. Verdict: Noise.

BATTERS	No.	IMPROVED	DECLINED
Weight change	30	33%	30%
Fitness program	3	0%	67%
Eye surgery	6	50%	33%
Plans more SB	6	17%	33%

PITCHERS	No.	IMPROVED	DECLINED
Weight change	18	44%	44%
Fitness program	4	50%	50%
Eye surgery	2	0%	50%
New pitch	5	60%	40%

In-Season Analysis

April performance as a leading indicator

We isolated all players who earned at least $10 more or $10 less than we had projected in March. Then we looked at the April stats of these players to see if we could have picked out the $10 outliers after just one month.

	Identifiable in April
Earned $10+ more than projected	
BATTERS	39%
PITCHERS	44%
Earned -$10 less than projected	
BATTERS	56%
PITCHERS	74%

Nearly three out of every four pitchers who earned at least $10 less than projected also struggled in April. For all the other surprises—batters or pitchers—April was not a strong leading indicator. Another look:

	Pct.
Batters who finished +$25	45%
Pitchers who finished +$20	44%
Batters who finished under $0	60%
Pitchers who finished under -$5	78%

April surgers are less than a 50/50 proposition to maintain that level all season. Those who finished April at the bottom of the roto rankings were more likely to continue struggling, especially pitchers. In fact, of those pitchers who finished April with a value *under -$10*, 91% finished the season in the red. Holes are tough to dig out of.

The weight of early season numbers

Early season strugglers who surge later in the year often get little respect because they have to live with the weight of their early num-bers all season long. Conversely, quick starters who fade late get far more accolades than they deserve.

For instance, take Joey Votto's month-by-month batting average. The perception is that his .326 BA was just a typical Votto season. Well, it was more than just typical. His awful .213 start after two months masked what was an incredible 4-month run. From June 1 on, he batted an amazing .378. From July 1 on, he batted .397!

Month	BA	Cum BA
April	.229	.229
May	.200	.213
June	.319	.249
July	.413	.285
August	.394	.309
Sept-Oct	.389	.326

Courtship period

Any time a player is put into a new situation, he enters into a courtship period. This period might occur when a player switches leagues, or switches teams. It could be the first few games when a minor leaguer is called up. It could occur when a reliever moves into the rotation, or when a lead-off hitter is moved to another spot in the lineup. There is a team-wide courtship period when a manager is replaced. Any external situation that could affect a player's performance sets off a new decision point in evaluating that performance.

During this period, it is difficult to get a true read on how a player is going to ultimately perform. He is adjusting to the new situation. Things could be volatile during this time. For instance, a role change that doesn't work could spur other moves. A rookie hurler might buy himself a few extra starts with a solid debut, even if he has questionable skills.

It is best not to make a decision on a player who is going through a courtship period. Wait until his stats stabilize. Don't cut a struggling pitcher in his first few starts after a managerial change. Don't pick up a hitter who smacks a pair of HRs in his first game after having been traded. Unless, of course, talent and track record say otherwise.

Half-season fallacies

A popular exercise at the midpoint of each season is to analyze those players who are consistent first half to second half surgers or faders. There are several fallacies with this analytical approach.

1. Half-season consistency is rare. There are very few players who show consistent changes in performance from one half of the season to the other.

Research results from a three-year study conducted in the late-1990s: The test groups... batters with min. 300 AB full season, 150 AB first half, and pitchers with min. 100 IP full season, 50 IP first half. Of those groups (size noted):

3-year consistency in	BATTERS (98)	PITCHERS (42)
1 stat category	40%	57%
2 stat categories	18%	21%
3 stat categories	3%	5%

When the analysis was stretched to a fourth year, only 1% of all players showed consistency in even one category.

2. Analysts often use false indicators. Situational statistics provide us with tools that can be misused. Several sources offer up 3- and 5-year stats intended to paint a picture of a long-term performance. Some analysts look at a player's half-season swing over that multi-year period and conclude that he is demonstrating consistent performance.

The fallacy is that those multi-year scans may not show any consistency at all. They are not individual season performances but *aggregate* performances. A player whose 5-year batting average shows a 15-point rise in the 2nd half, for instance, may actually have experienced a BA decline in several of those years, a fact that might have been offset by a huge BA rise in one of the years.

3. It's arbitrary. The season's midpoint is an arbitrary delineator of performance swings. Some players are slow starters and might be more appropriately evaluated as pre-May 1 and post-May 1. Others bring their game up a notch with a pennant chase and might see a performance swing with August 15 as the cut-off. Each player has his own individual tendency, if, in fact, one exists at all. There's nothing magical about mid-season as the break point, and certainly not over a multi-year period.

Half-season tendencies

Despite the above, it stands to reason logically that there might be some underlying tendencies on a more global scale, first half to second half. In fact, one would think that the player population as a whole might decline in performance as the season drones on. There are many variables that might contribute to a player wearing down—workload, weather, boredom—and the longer a player is on the field, the higher the likelihood that he is going to get hurt. A recent 5-year study uncovered the following tendencies:

Batting

Overall, batting skills held up pretty well, half to half. There was a 5% erosion of playing time, likely due, in part, to September roster expansion.

Power: First half power studs (20 HRs in 1H) saw a 10% drop-off in the second half. 34% of first half 20+ HR hitters hit 15 or fewer in the second half and only 27% were able to improve on their first half output.

Speed: Second half speed waned as well. About 26% of the 20+ SB speedsters stole *at least 10 fewer bases* in the second half. Only 26% increased their second half SB output at all.

Batting average: 60% of first half .300 hitters failed to hit .300 in the second half. Only 20% showed any second half improvement at all. As for 1H strugglers, managers tended to stick with their full-timers despite poor starts. Nearly one in five of the sub-.250 1H hitters managed to hit *more than* .300 in the second half.

Pitching

Overall, there was some slight erosion in innings and ERA despite marginal improvement in some peripherals.

ERA: For those who pitched at least 100 innings in the first half, ERAs rose an average of 0.40 runs in the 2H. Of those with first half ERAs less than 4.00, only 49% were able to maintain a sub-4.00 ERA in the second half.

Wins: Pitchers who won 18 or more games in a season tended to pitch *more* innings in the 2H and had slightly better peripherals.

Saves: Of those closers who saved 20 or more games in the first half, only 39% were able to post 20 or more saves in the 2H, and 26% posted fewer than 15 saves. Aggregate ERAs of these pitchers rose from 2.45 to 3.17, half to half.

In-season trends in hitting and pitching *(Bob Berger)*

A study of monthly trends in traditional statistical categories found:

- Batting average, HR/game and RBI/game rise from April through August, then fall in September/October.
- Stolen bases decline in July and August before rebounding in September.
- ERA worsens in July/August and improves in September.
- WHIP gets worse in July/August.
- K/9 rate improves all season.

The bold statement that hitters perform better in warmer weather seems to be true broadly.

Teams

Johnson Effect *(Bryan Johnson)*: Teams whose actual won/loss record exceeds or falls short of their statistically projected record in one season will tend to revert to the level of their projection in the following season.

Law of Competitive Balance *(Bill James)*: The level at which a team (or player) will address its problems is inversely related to its current level of success. Low performers will tend to make changes to improve; high performers will not. This law explains the existence of the Plexiglass and Whirlpool Principles.

Plexiglass Principle *(Bill James)*: If a player or team improves markedly in one season, it will likely decline in the next. The opposite is true but not as often (because a poor performer gets fewer opportunities to rebound).

Whirlpool Principle *(Bill James)*: All team and player performances are forcefully drawn to the center. For teams, that center is a .500 record. For players, it represents their career average level of performance.

Other Diamonds

The Fanalytic Fundamentals

1. This is not a game of accuracy or precision. It is a game of human beings and tendencies.
2. This is not a game of projections. It is a game of market value versus real value.
3. Draft skills, not stats. Draft skills, not roles.
4. A player's ability to post acceptable stats despite lousy support metrics will eventually run out.
5. Once you display a skill, you own it.
6. Virtually every player is vulnerable to a month of aberrant performance. Or a year.
7. Exercise excruciating patience.

Aging Axioms

1. Age is the only variable for which we can project a rising trend with 100% accuracy. (Or, age never regresses.)
2. The aging process slows down for those who maintain a firm grasp on the strike zone. Plate patience and pitching command can preserve any waning skill they have left.
3. Negatives tend to snowball as you age.

Steve Avery List

Players who hang onto MLB rosters for six years searching for a skill level they only had for three.

Bylaws of Badness

1. Some players are better than an open roster spot, but not by much.
2. Some players have bad years because they are unlucky. Others have *many* bad years because they are bad... and lucky.

George Brett Path to Retirement

Get out while you're still putting up good numbers and the public perception of you is favorable. Like Chipper Jones, Mariano Rivera, and David Ortiz.

Steve Carlton Path to Retirement

Hang around the majors long enough for your numbers to become so wretched that people begin to forget your past successes. Recent players who have taken this path include Miguel Tejada, Jason Giambi, Dan Uggla and Brian Roberts. Current players who could be on a similar course include Ichiro Suzuki, Josh Hamilton, and Carl Crawford.

Christie Brinkley Law of Statistical Analysis

Never get married to the model.

Employment Standards

1. If you are right-brain dominant, own a catcher's mitt and are under 40, you will always be gainfully employed.
2. Some teams believe that it is better to employ a player with any experience because it has to be better than the devil they don't know.
3. It's not so good to go *pffft* in a contract year.

Laws of Prognosticating Perspective

- *Berkeley's 17th Law:* A great many problems do not have accurate answers, but do have approximate answers, from which sensible decisions can be made.
- *Ashley-Perry Statistical Axiom #4:* A complex system that works is invariably found to have evolved from a simple system that works.
- *Baseball Variation of Harvard Law:* Under the most rigorously observed conditions of skill, age, environment, statistical rules and other variables, a ballplayer will perform as he damn well pleases.

Brad Fullmer List

Players whose leading indicators indicate upside potential, year after year, but consistently fail to reach that full potential. Players like Michael Pineda, Taijuan Walker, Dexter Fowler and Justin Smoak are on the list right now.

Good Luck Truism

Good luck is rare and everyone has more of it than you do. That's the law.

The Gravity Principles

1. It is easier to be crappy than it is to be good.
2. All performance starts at zero, ends at zero and can drop to zero at any time.
3. The odds of a good performer slumping are far greater than the odds of a poor performer surging.
4. Once a player is in a slump, it takes several 3-for-5 days to get out of it. Once he is on a streak, it takes a single 0-for-4 day to begin the downward spiral. *Corollary:* Once a player is in a slump, not only does it take several 3-for-5 days to get out of it, but he also has to get his name back on the lineup card.
5. Eventually all performance comes down to earth. It may take a week, or a month, or may not happen until he's 45, but eventually it's going to happen.

Health Homilies

1. Staying healthy is a skill (and "DL Days" should be a Rotisserie category).
2. A $40 player can get hurt just as easily as a $5 player but is eight times tougher to replace.
3. Chronically injured players never suddenly get healthy.
4. There are two kinds of pitchers: those that are hurt and those that are not hurt... yet.
5. Players with back problems are always worth $10 less.
6. "Opting out of surgery" usually means it's coming anyway, just later.

The Health Hush

Players get hurt and potentially have a lot to lose, so there is an incentive for them to hide injuries. HIPAA laws restrict the disclosure of health information. Team doctors and trainers have been instructed not to talk with the media. So, when it comes to information on a player's health status, we're all pretty much in the dark.

The Livan Level

The point when a player's career Runs Above Replacement level has dropped so far below zero that he has effectively cancelled out any possible remaining future value. (Similarly, the Dontrelle Demarcation.)

The Momentum Maxims

1. A player will post a pattern of positive results until the day you add him to your roster.
2. Patterns of negative results are more likely to snowball than correct.
3. When an unstoppable force meets an immovable object, the wall always wins.

Noise

Irrelevant or meaningless pieces of information that can distort the results of an analysis. In news, this is opinion or rumor. In forecasting, this is random variance or irrelevant data. In ballparks, this is a screaming crowd cheering for a team down 12-3 with two outs and bases empty in the bottom of the ninth.

Paradoxes and Conundrums

1. Is a player's improvement in performance from one year to the next a point in a growth trend, an isolated outlier or a complete anomaly?
2. A player can play through an injury, post rotten numbers and put his job at risk… or… he can admit that he can't play through an injury, allow himself to be taken out of the lineup/rotation, and put his job at risk.
3. Did irregular playing time take its toll on the player's performance or did poor performance force a reduction in his playing time?
4. Is a player only in the game versus right-handers because he has a true skills deficiency versus left-handers? Or is his poor performance versus left-handers because he's never given a chance to face them?
5. The problem with stockpiling bench players in the hope that one pans out is that you end up evaluating performance using data sets that are too small to be reliable.
6. There are players who could give you 20 stolen bases if they got 400 AB. But if they got 400 AB, they would likely be on a bad team that wouldn't let them steal.

Process-Outcome Matrix *(Russo and Schoemaker)*

	Good Outcome	Bad Outcome
Good Process	Deserved Success	Bad Break
Bad Process	Dumb Luck	Poetic Justice

Quack!

An exclamation in response to the educated speculation that a player has used performance enhancing drugs. While it is rare to have absolute proof, there is often enough information to suggest that, "if it looks like a duck and quacks like a duck, then odds are it's a duck."

Situation Dependent

An event that is affected by the context of team, ballpark, or other outside variables.

RBI: You can't drive in runs if there is nobody on base.

Runs: You can't score a run if no one drives you in.

Wins: You can't win a game unless your offense scores runs, no matter how well you pitch.

Surface Stats

All those wonderful statistics we grew up with that those mean bean counters are telling us don't matter anymore. Home runs, RBIs, batting average, won-loss record. Let's go back to the 1960s and make baseball great again! [EDITOR: No.]

Tenets of Optimal Timing

1. If a second half fader had put up his second half stats in the first half and his first half stats in the second half, then he probably wouldn't even have had a second half.
2. Fast starters can often buy six months of playing time out of one month of productivity.
3. Poor 2nd halves don't get recognized until it's too late.
4. "Baseball is like this. Have one good year and you can fool them for five more, because for five more years they expect you to have another good one." — Frankie Frisch

The Three True Outcomes

1. Strikeouts
2. Walks
3. Home runs

The Three True Handicaps

1. Has power but can't make contact.
2. Has speed but can't hit safely.
3. Has potential but is too old.

Zombie

A player who is indestructible, continuing to get work, year-after-year, no matter how dead his skills metrics are. Like Brett Wallace, Gordon Beckham, Mike Pelfrey, Brett Oberholtzer and Ryan Vogelsong.

Batters

Batting Eye, Contact and Batting Average

Batting average (BA, or Avg)

This is where it starts. BA is a grand old nugget that has long outgrown its usefulness. We revere .300 hitting superstars and scoff at .250 hitters, yet the difference between the two is one hit every five games. BA is a poor evaluator of performance in that it neglects the offensive value of the base on balls and assumes that all hits are created equal.

Walk rate (bb%)

(BB / (AB + BB))

A measure of a batter's plate patience. **BENCHMARKS:** The best batters will have levels more than 10%. Those with poor plate patience will have levels of 5% or less.

Walk rate and batting average *(Patrick Davitt)*

Analysts have long told us that a hitter's walk rate (bb%) is a reliable leading indicator of batting average (BA), and that changes in bb% are clues about expected improvements or declines in BA. This was probably because analysts used bb% as a proxy for a hitter's ability to "be selective" by laying off pitches outside the zone and swinging at pitches in the zone.

While the idea makes intuitive sense, a BaseballHQ.com review of several seasons' bb% and BA data showed that bb% and BA are as unconnected as they could be. In any single season, and for all seasons in the study combined, the overall correlation between the two variables was +0.01 (a score of 0.00 means two variables are completely uncorrelated).

On base average (OB)

(H + BB + HBP) / (AB + BB + HBP + Sac Flies)

Addressing a key deficiency with BA, OB gives value to events that get batters on base, but are not hits. An OB of .350 can be read as "this batter gets on base 35% of the time." When a run is scored, there is no distinction made as to how that runner reached base. So, two-thirds of the time—about how often a batter comes to the plate with the bases empty—a walk really is as good as a hit. **BENCHMARKS:** We know what a .300 hitter is, but what represents "good" for OB? That comparable level would likely be .400, with .275 representing the comparable level of futility.

Ground ball, line drive, fly ball percentages (G/L/F)

The percentage of all balls in play that are hit on the ground, as line drives and in the air. For batters, increased fly ball tendency may foretell a rise in power skills; increased line drive tendency may foretell an improvement in batting average. For a pitcher, the ability to keep the ball on the ground can contribute to his statistical output exceeding his demonstrated skill level.

*BIP Type	Total%	Out%
Ground ball	45%	72%
Line drive	20%	28%
Fly ball	35%	85%
TOTAL	*100%*	*69%*

*Data only includes fieldable balls and is net of HRs.

Line drives and luck *(Patrick Davitt)*

Given that each individual batter's hit rate sets its own baseline, and that line drives (LD) are the most productive type of batted ball, a study looked at the relationship between the two. Among the findings were that hit rates on LDs are much higher than on FBs or GBs, with individual batters consistently falling into the 72-73% range. Ninety-five percent of all batters fall between the range of 60%-86%; batters outside this range regress very quickly, often within the season.

Note that batters' BAs did not always follow their LD% up or down, because some of them enjoyed higher hit rates on other batted balls, improved their contact rates, or both. Still, it's justifiable to bet that players hitting the ball with authority but getting fewer hits than they should will correct over time.

Batting eye (Eye)

(Walks / Strikeouts)

A measure of a player's strike zone judgment. **BENCHMARKS:** The best hitters have Eye ratios more than 1.00 (indicating more walks than strikeouts) and are the most likely to be among a league's .300 hitters. Ratios less than 0.50 represent batters who likely also have lower BAs.

Batting eye as a leading indicator

There is a correlation between strike zone judgment and batting average. However, research shows that this is more descriptive than predictive:

	Batting Average				
Batting Eye	2012	2013	2014	2015	2016
0.00 - 0.25	.243	.242	.238	.243	.248
0.26 - 0.50	.255	.253	.253	.257	.255
0.51 - 0.75	.268	.265	.268	.267	.271
0.76 - 1.00	.276	.277	.270	.280	.286
1.01 and over	.292	.284	.304	.293	.255

We have been running the above chart for years and have always had large enough samples to make each group statistically significant. But not the past three years. The last group—1.01 and over—contained only six players in 2014, eight players in 2015 and seven players in 2016. This past year, for the first time, the small sample broke the correlation. In fact, all the other cohorts demonstrated higher batting averages than in the past, which has been an ongoing trend as well.

We can create percentage plays for the different levels:

For Eye	Pct who bat	
Levels of	.300+	.250-
0.00 - 0.25	7%	39%
0.26 - 0.50	14%	26%
0.51 - 0.75	18%	17%
0.76 - 1.00	32%	14%
1.01 - 1.50	51%	9%
1.51 +	59%	4%

Any batter with an eye ratio more than 1.50 has about a 4% chance of hitting less than .250 over 500 at bats.

Of all .300 hitters, those with ratios of at least 1.00 have a 65% chance of repeating as .300 hitters. Those with ratios less than 1.00 have less than a 50% chance of repeating.

Only 4% of sub-.250 hitters with ratios less than 0.50 will mature into .300 hitters the following year.

In this study, only 37 batters hit .300-plus with a sub-0.50 eye ratio over at least 300 AB in a season. Of this group, 30% were able to accomplish this feat on a consistent basis. For the other 70%, this was a short-term aberration.

Contact rate (ct%)

((AB - K) / AB)

Measures a batter's ability to get wood on the ball and hit it into the field of play. **BENCHMARKS:** Those batters with the best contact skill will have levels of 90% or better. The hackers will have levels of 75% or less.

Contact rate as a leading indicator

The more often a batter makes contact with the ball, the higher the likelihood that he will hit safely.

	Batting Average				
Contact Rate	2012	2013	2014	2015	2016
0% - 60%	.197	.203	.176	.194	.207
61% - 65%	.226	.211	.217	.217	.223
66% - 70%	.231	.232	.230	.236	.232
71% - 75%	.252	.246	.243	.254	.253
76% - 80%	.255	.261	.257	.257	.262
81% - 85%	.268	.268	.266	.268	.271
86% - 90%	.278	.272	.276	.277	.285
Over 90%	.282	.270	.324	.284	.254

Once again, the size of the highest-skilled group has dwindled, here to only 17 players in 2014, 25 players in 2015 and just 12 in 2016, effectively breaking the correlation.

Contact rate and walk rate as leading indicators

A matrix of contact rates and walk rates can provide expectation benchmarks for a player's batting average:

	Walk rate (bb%)			
	0-5	6-10	11-15	16+
65-	.179	.195	.229	.237
66-75	.190	.248	.254	.272
76-85	.265	.267	.276	.283
86+	.269	.279	.301	.309

(*Contact rate (ct%)* labels the left axis)

A contact rate of 65% or lower offers virtually no chance for a player to hit even .250, no matter how high a walk rate he has. The .300 hitters most often come from the group with a minimum 86% contact and 11% walk rate.

HCt and HctX *(Patrick Davitt)*

HCt= hard hit ball rate x contact rate
HctX= Player HCt divided by league average Hct, normalized to 100

The combination of making contact and hitting the ball hard might be the most important skills for a batter. HctX correlates very strongly with BA, and at higher BA levels often does so with high accuracy. Its success with HR was somewhat limited, probably due to GB/FB differences. **BENCHMARKS:** The average major-leaguer in a given year has a HctX of 100. Elite batters have an HctX of 135 or above; weakest batters have HctX of 55 or below.

Balls in play (BIP)

(AB – K)

The total number of batted balls that are hit fair, both hits and outs. An analysis of how these balls are hit—on the ground, in the air, hits, outs, etc.—can provide analytical insight, from player skill levels to the impact of luck on statistical output.

Batting average on balls in play *(Voros McCracken)*

(H – HR) / (AB – HR – K)

Or, BABIP. Also called hit rate (h%). The percent of balls hit into the field of play that fall for hits. **BENCHMARK:** Every hitter establishes his own individual hit rate that stabilizes over time. A batter whose seasonal hit rate varies significantly from the h% he has established over the preceding three seasons (variance of at least +/- 3%) is likely to improve or regress to his individual h% mean (with over-performer declines more likely and sharper than under-performer recoveries). Three-year h% levels strongly predict a player's h% the following year.

Pitches/Plate Appearance as a leading indicator for BA *(Paul Petera)*

The art of working the count has long been considered one of the more crucial aspects of good hitting. It is common knowledge that the more pitches a hitter sees, the greater opportunity he has to reach base safely.

P/PA	OBA	BA
4.00+	.360	.264
3.75-3.99	.347	.271
3.50-3.74	.334	.274
Under 3.50	.321	.276

Generally speaking, the more pitches seen, the lower the BA, but the higher the OBA. But what about the outliers, those players that bucked the trend in year #1?

	YEAR TWO	
	BA Improved	BA Declined
Low P/PA and Low BA	77%	23%
High P/PA and High BA	21%	79%

In these scenarios, there was a strong tendency for performance to normalize in year #2.

Expected batting average *(John Burnson)*

$xCT\% * [xH1\% + xH2\%]$
where
$xH1\% = GB\% \times [0.0004\ PX + 0.062\ ln(SX)]$
$+ LD\% \times [0.93 - 0.086\ ln(SX)]$
$+ FB\% \times 0.12$
and
$xH2\% = FB\% \times [0.0013\ PX - 0.0002\ SX - 0.057]$
$+ GB\% \times [0.0006\ PX]$

A hitter's expected batting average as calculated by multiplying the percentage of balls put in play (contact rate) by the chance that a ball in play falls for a hit. The likelihood that a ball in play falls for a hit is a product of the speed of the ball and distance it is hit (PX), the speed of the batter (SX), and distribution of ground balls, fly balls, and line drives. We further split it out by non-homerun hit rate (xH1%) and homerun hit rate (xH2%). **BENCHMARKS:** In general, xBA should approximate batting average fairly closely. Those hitters who have large variances between the two gauges are candidates for further analysis. LIMITATION: xBA tends to understate a batter's true value if he is an extreme ground ball hitter (G/F ratio over 3.0) with a low PX. These players are not inherently weak, but choose to take safe singles rather than swing for the fences.

Expected batting average variance
xBA – BA

The variance between a batter's BA and his xBA is a measure of over- or under-achievement. A positive variance indicates the potential for a batter's BA to rise. A negative variance indicates the potential for BA to decline. BENCHMARK: Discount variances that are less than 20 points. Any variance more than 30 points is regarded as a strong indicator of future change.

Power

Slugging average (Slg)
(Singles + (2 x Doubles) + (3 x Triples) + (4 x HR)) / AB

A measure of the total number of bases accumulated (or the minimum number of runners' bases advanced) per at bat. It is a misnomer; it is not a true measure of a batter's slugging ability because it includes singles. Slg also assumes that each type of hit has proportionately increasing value (i.e. a double is twice as valuable as a single, etc.) which is not true. For instance, with the bases loaded, a HR always scores four runs, a triple always scores three, but a double could score two or three and a single could score one, or two, or even three. BENCHMARKS: Top batters will have levels over .500. The bottom batters will have levels less than .300.

Fly ball tendency and power *(Mat Olkin)*

There is a proven connection between a hitter's ground ball/fly ball tendencies and his power production.

1. *Extreme ground ball hitters generally do not hit for much power.* It's almost impossible for a hitter with a ground/fly ratio over 1.80 to hit enough fly balls to produce even 25 HRs in a season. However, this does not mean that a low G/F ratio necessarily guarantees power production. Some players have no problem getting the ball into the air, but lack the strength to reach the fences consistently.

2. *Most batters' ground/fly ratios stay pretty steady over time.* Most year-to-year changes are small and random, as they are in any other statistical category. A large, sudden change in G/F, on the other hand, can signal a conscious change in plate approach. And so...

3. *If a player posts high G/F ratios in his first few years, he probably isn't ever going to hit for all that much power.*

4. *When a batter's power suddenly jumps, his G/F ratio often drops at the same time.*

5. *Every so often, a hitter's ratio will drop significantly even as his power production remains level. In these rare cases, impending power development is likely, since the two factors almost always follow each other.*

Home runs to fly ball rate (hr/f)
The percent of fly balls that are hit for HRs.

hr/f rate as a leading indicator *(Joshua Randall)*
Each batter establishes an individual home run to fly ball rate that stabilizes over rolling three-year periods; those levels strongly predict the hr/f in the subsequent year. A batter who varies significantly from his hr/f is likely to regress toward his individual hr/f mean, with over-performance decline more likely and more severe than under-performance recovery.

Estimating HR Rate for Young Hitters *(Matt Cederholm)*
Over time, hitters establish a baseline hr/f, but how do we measure the HR output of young hitters with little track record? Since power is a key indicator of HR output, we can look at typical hr/f for various levels of power, as measures by xPX:

	hr/f percentiles				
xPX	10	25	50	75	90
<=70	0.9%	2.0%	3.8%	5.5%	7.4%
71-80	3.3%	5.1%	6.4%	8.1%	10.0%
81-90	3.8%	5.4%	7.4%	9.0%	11.0%
91-100	4.7%	6.6%	8.9%	11.3%	13.0%
101-110	6.6%	8.3%	10.9%	13.0%	16.2%
111-120	7.4%	9.8%	11.9%	14.7%	17.1%
121-130	8.5%	10.9%	12.8%	15.5%	17.4%
131-140	9.7%	11.9%	14.6%	17.1%	20.4%
141-160	11.3%	13.1%	16.5%	19.2%	21.5%
161+	14.4%	16.5%	19.4%	22.0%	25.8%

To predict changes in HR output, just look at a player and project his HR as if his hr/f was at the median for his xPX level. For example, if a player with a 125 xPX exceeds a 12.8% hr/f, we would expect a decline in the following season. The greater the deviation from the mean, the greater the probability of an increase or decline.

Hard-hit flies as a sustainable skill *(Patrick Davitt)*
A study of data from 2009-2011 found that we should seek batters with a high Hard-Hit Fly Ball percentage (HHFB%). Among the findings:

- Avoiding pop-ups and hitting HHFBs are sustainable core power skills.
- Consistent HHFB% performance marks batters with power potential.
- When looking for candidates to regress, we should look at individual past levels of HR/HHFB, perhaps using a three-year rolling average.

Linear weighted power (LWPwr)
((Doubles x .8) + (Triples x .8) + (HR x 1.4)) / (At bats- K) x 100

A variation of the linear weights formula that considers only events that are measures of a batter's pure power. BENCHMARKS: Top sluggers typically top the 17 mark. Weak hitters will have a LWPwr level of less than 10.

Linear weighted power index (PX)
(Batter's LWPwr / League LWPwr) x 100

LWPwr is presented in this book in its normalized form to get a better read on a batter's accomplishment in each year. For instance, a 30-HR season today is much less of an accomplishment than 30 HRs hit in a lower offense year like 2014. BENCHMARKS: A level of 100 equals league average power skills. Any player with a value more than 100 has above average power skills, and those more than 150 are the Slugging Elite.

Expected LW power index (xPX) *(Bill Macey)*

2.6 + 269*HHLD% + 724*HHFB%

Previous research has shown that hard-hit balls are more likely to result in hits and hard-hit fly balls are more likely to end up as HRs. As such, we can use hard-hit ball data to calculate an expected skills-based power index. This metric starts with hard-hit ball data, which measures a player's fundamental skill of making solid contact, and then places it on the same scale as PX (xPX). In the above formula, HHLD% is calculated as the number of hard hit line-drives divided by the total number of balls put in play. HHFB% is similarly calculated for fly balls.

Pitches/Plate Appearance as a leading indicator for PX *(Paul Petera)*

Working the count has a positive effect on power.

P/PA	PX
4.00+	123
3.75-3.99	108
3.50-3.74	96
Under 3.50	84

As for the year #1 outliers:

	YEAR TWO	
	PX Improved	PX Declined
Low P/PA and High PX	11%	89%
High P/PA and Low PX	70%	30%

In these scenarios, there was a strong tendency for performance to normalize in year #2.

Doubles as a leading indicator for home runs *(Bill Macey)*

There is little support for the theory that hitting many doubles in year x leads to an increase in HR in year x+1. However, it was shown that batters with high doubles rates (2B/AB) also tend to hit more HR/AB than the league average; oddly, they are unable to sustain the high 2B/AB rate but do sustain their higher HR/AB rates. Batters with high 2B/AB rates and low HR/AB rates are more likely to see HR gains in the following year, but those rates will still typically trail the league average. And, batters who experience a surge in 2B/AB typically give back most of those gains in the following year without any corresponding gain in HR.

Opposite field home runs *(Ed DeCaria)*

From 2001-2008, nearly 75% of all HRs were hit to the batter's pull field, with the remaining 25% distributed roughly evenly between straight away and opposite field. Left-handers accomplished the feat slightly more often than right-handers (including switch-hitters hitting each way), and younger hitters did it significantly more often than older hitters. The trend toward pulled home runs was especially strong after age 36.

Power Quartile	AB/HR	Opp. Field	Straight Away	Pull Field
Top 25%	17.2	16%	16%	68%
2nd 25%	28.0	11%	12%	77%
3rd 25%	44.1	9%	10%	8%
Bot 25%	94.7	5%	6%	89%

Opposite field HRs serve as a strong indicator of overall home run power (AB/HR). Power hitters (smaller AB/HR rates) hit a far higher percentage of their HR to the opposite field or straight away (over 30%). Conversely, non-power hitters hit almost 90% of their home runs to their pull field.

	Performance in Y2-Y4 (% of Group)		
Y1 Trigger	<=30 AB/HR	5.5+ RC/G	$16+ R$
2+ OppHR	69%	46%	33%
<2 OppHR	29%	13%	12%

Players who hit just two or more OppHR in one season were 2-3 times as likely as those who hit zero or one OppHR to sustain strong AB/HR rates, RC/G levels, or R$ values over the following three seasons.

	Y2-Y4 Breakout Performance (% Breakout by Group, Age <=26 Only)		
	AB/HR	RC/G	R$
Y1 Trigger	>35 to <=30	<4.5 to 5.5+	<$8 to $16+
2+ OppHR	32%	21%	30%
<2 OppHR	23%	12%	10%

Roughly one of every 3-4 batters age 26 or younger experiences a *sustained three-year breakout* in AB/HR, RC/G or R$ after a season in which they hit 2+ OppHR, far better odds than the one in 8-10 batters who experience a breakout without the 2+ OppHR trigger.

Home runs in bunches *(Patrick Davitt)*

A study from HR data from 2010-2012 showed that batters hit HRs in a random manner, with game-gaps between HRs that correspond roughly to their average days per HR. Thus, the theory that batters hit HRs in "bunches" is a fallacy. It appears pointless to try to "time the market" by predicting the beginning or end of a drought or a bunch, or by assuming the end of one presages the beginning of the other, despite what the ex-player in the broadcast booth tells you.

Power breakout profile

It is not easy to predict which batters will experience a power spike. We can categorize power breakouts to determine the likelihood of a player taking a step up or of a surprise performer repeating his feat. Possibilities:

- Increase in playing time
- History of power skills at some time in the past
- Redistribution of already demonstrated extra base hit power
- Normal skills growth
- Situational breakouts, particularly in hitter-friendly venues
- Increased fly ball tendency
- Use of illegal performance-enhancing substances
- Miscellaneous unexplained variables

Speed

Wasted talent on the base paths

We refer to some players as having "wasted talent," a high level skill that is negated by a deficiency in another skill. Among these types are players who have blazing speed that is negated by a sub-.300 on base average.

These players can have short-term value. However, their stolen base totals are tied so tightly to their "green light" that any change in managerial strategy could completely erase that value. A higher OB mitigates that downside; the good news is that plate patience can be taught.

In the past, there were always a handful of players who had at least 20 SBs with an OBP less than .300, putting their future SBs at risk. In 2016, there was only one: Melvin Upton (27 SB, .291 OBP). There were two players who had managed to succeed in spite of this handicap multiple times, but Billy Hamilton (.321) and Jean Segura (.368) both pushed their respective OBPs well out of the danger zone.

Speed score *(Bill James)*

A measure of the various elements that comprise a runner's speed skills. Although this formula (a variation of James' original version) may be used as a leading indicator for stolen base output, SB attempts are controlled by managerial strategy which makes speed score somewhat less valuable.

Speed score is calculated as the mean value of the following four elements:

1. Stolen base efficiency = $(((SB + 3)/(SB + CS + 7)) - .4) \times 20$

2. Stolen base freq. = *Square root of $((SB + CS)/(Singles + BB))$ / .07*

3. Triples rating = $(3B / (AB - HR - K))$ and the result assigned a value based on the following chart:

< 0.001	0	0.0105	6
0.001	1	0.013	7
0.0023	2	0.0158	8
0.0039	3	0.0189	9
0.0058	4	0.0223+	10
0.008	5		

4. Runs scored as a percentage of times on base = $(((R - HR) / (H + BB - HR)) - .1) / .04$

Speed score index (SX)

(Batter's speed score / League speed score) x 100

Normalized speed scores get a better read on a runner's accomplishment in context. A level of 100 equals league average speed skill. Values more than 100 indicate above average skill, more than 200 represent the Fleet of Feet Elite.

Statistically scouted speed (Spd) *(Ed DeCaria)*

$(104 + \{[(Runs–HR+10*age\_wt)/(RBI–HR+10)]/lg\_av*100\} / 5$
$+ \{[(3B+5*age\_wt)/(2B+3B+5)]/lg\_av*100\} / 5$
$+ \{[(SoftMedGBhits+25*age\_wt)/(SoftMedGB+25)]/lg\_av*100\} / 2$
$- \{[Weight (Lbs)/Height (In)^2 * 703]/lg\_av*100\}$

A skills-based gauge that measures speed without relying on stolen bases. Its components are:

- *(Runs – HR) / (RBI – HR)*: This metric aims to minimize the influence of extra base hit power and team run-scoring rates on perceived speed.

- *3B / (2B + 3B)*: No one can deny that triples are a fast runner's stat; dividing them by 2B+3B instead of all balls in play dampens the power aspect of extra base hits.

- *(Soft + Medium Ground Ball Hits) / (Soft + Medium Ground Balls)*: Faster runners are more likely than slower runners to beat out routine grounders. Hard hit balls are excluded from numerator and denominator.

- *Body Mass Index (BMI)*: Calculated as *Weight (lbs) / Height (in)2 * 703*. All other factors considered, leaner players run faster than heavier ones.

In this book, the formula is scaled as an index with a midpoint of 100.

Stolen base opportunity percent (SBO)

(SB + CS) / (BB + Singles)

A rough approximation of how often a baserunner attempts a stolen base. Provides a comparative measure for players on a given team and, as a team measure, the propensity of a manager to give a "green light" to his runners.

Stolen base success rate (SB%)

SB / (SB + CS)

The rate at which baserunners are successful in their stolen base attempts. **BENCHMARK:** It is generally accepted that an 80% rate is the minimum required for a runner to be providing value to his team.

Roto Speed (RSpd)

(Spd x (SBO + SB%))

An adjustment to the measure for raw speed that takes into account a runner's opportunities to steal and his success rate. This stat is intended to provide a more accurate predictive measure of stolen bases for the Mayberry Method.

Stolen base breakout profile *(Bob Berger)*

To find stolen base breakouts (first 30+ steal season in the majors), look for players that:

- are between 22-27 years old
- have 3-7 years of professional (minors and MLB) experience
- have previous steals at the MLB level
- have averaged 20+ SB in previous three seasons (majors and minors combined)
- have at least one professional season of 30+ SB

Overall Performance Analysis

On base plus slugging average (OPS)

A simple sum of the two gauges, it is considered one of the better evaluators of overall performance. OPS combines the two basic elements of offensive production—the ability to get on base (OB) and the ability to advance baserunners (Slg). **BENCHMARKS:** The game's top batters will have OPS levels more than .900. The worst batters will have levels less than .600.

Base Performance Value (BPV)

(Walk rate - 5) x 2)
+ ((Contact rate - 75) x 4)
+ ((Power Index - 80) x 0.8)
+ ((Spd - 80) x 0.3)

A single value that describes a player's overall raw skill level. This is more useful than traditional statistical gauges to track player performance trends and project future statistical output. This formula combines the individual raw skills of batting eye, contact rate, power and speed. **BENCHMARKS:** The best hitters will have a BPV of 50 or greater.

Base Performance Index (BPX)
BPV scaled to league average to account for year-to-year fluctuations in league-wide statistical performance. It's a snapshot of a player's overall skills compared to an average player. **BENCHMARK:** A level of 100 means a player had a league-average BPV in that given season.

Linear weights *(Pete Palmer)*
((Singles x .46) + (Doubles x .8) + (Triples x 1.02)
+ (Home runs x 1.4) + (Walks x .33) + (Stolen Bases x .3)
- (Caught Stealing x .6) - ((At bats - Hits) x Normalizing Factor)
(Also referred to as Batting Runs.) Formula whose premise is that all events in baseball are linear; that is, the output (runs) is directly proportional to the input (offensive events). Each of these events is then weighted according to its relative value in producing runs. Positive events—hits, walks, stolen bases—have positive values. Negative events—outs, caught stealing—have negative values.

The normalizing factor, representing the value of an out, is an offset to the level of offense in a given year. It changes every season, growing larger in high offense years and smaller in low offense years. The value is about .26 and varies by league.

LW is not included in the player forecast boxes, but the LW concept is used with the linear weighted power gauge.

Runs above replacement (RAR)
An estimate of the number of runs a player contributes above a "replacement level" player. "Replacement" is defined as the level of performance at which another player can easily be found at little or no cost to a team. What constitutes replacement level is a topic that is hotly debated. There are a variety of formulas and rules of thumb used to determine this level for each position (replacement level for a catcher will be very different from replacement level for an outfielder). Our estimates appear below.

One of the major values of RAR for fantasy applications is that it can be used to assemble an integrated ranking of batters and pitchers for drafting purposes.

To calculate RAR for batters:
- Start with a batter's runs created per game (RC/G).
- Subtract his position's replacement level RC/G.
- Multiply by number of games played: (AB - H + CS) / 25.5.

Replacement levels used in this book:

POS	NL	AL
CA	4.41	3.87
1B	5.34	4.86
2B	4.87	4.73
3B	4.98	4.80
SS	4.62	4.31
LF	4.63	4.28
CF	4.65	4.37
RF	4.68	4.71
DH		5.50

RAR can also be used to calculate rough projected team won-loss records. *(Roger Miller)* Total the RAR levels for all the players on a team, divide by 10 and add to 53 wins.

Runs created *(Bill James)*
(H + BB – CS) x (Total bases + (.55 x SB)) / (AB + BB)
A formula that converts all offensive events into a total of runs scored. As calculated for individual teams, the result approximates a club's actual run total with great accuracy.

Runs created per game (RC/G)
Runs Created / ((AB - H + CS) / 25.5)
RC expressed on a per-game basis might be considered the hypothetical ERA compiled against a particular batter. Another way to look at it: A batter with a RC/G of 7.00 would be expected to score 7 runs per game if he were cloned nine times and faced an average pitcher in every at bat. Cloning batters is not a practice we recommend. **BENCHMARKS:** Few players surpass the level of a 10.00 RC/G, but any level more than 7.50 can still be considered very good. At the bottom are levels less than 3.00.

Plate Appearances as a leading indicator *(Patrick Davitt)*
While targeting players "age 26 with experience" as potential breakout candidates has become a commonly accepted concept, a study has found that cumulative plate appearances, especially during the first two years of a young player's career, can also have predictive value in assessing a coming spike in production. Three main conclusions:

- When projecting players, MLB experience is more important than age.
- Players who amass 800+ PAs in their first two seasons are highly likely to have double-digit Rotisserie dollar value in Year 3.
- Also target young players in the season where they attain 400 PAs, as they are twice as likely as other players to grow significantly in value.

Handedness
1. While pure southpaws account for about 27% of total ABs (RHers about 55% and switch-hitters about 18%), they hit 31% of the triples and take 30% of the walks.
2. The average lefty posts a batting average about 10 points higher than the average RHer. The on base averages of pure LHers are nearly 20 points higher than RHers, but only 10 points higher than switch-hitters.
3. LHers tend to have a better batting eye ratio than RHers, but about the same as switch-hitters.
4. Pure righties and lefties have virtually identical power skills. Switch-hitters tend to have less power, on average.
5. Switch-hitters tend to have the best speed, followed by LHers, and then RHers.
6. On an overall production basis, LHers have an 8% advantage over RHers and a 14% edge over switch-hitters.

Skill-specific aging patterns for batters *(Ed DeCaria)*
Baseball forecasters obsess over "peak age" of player performance because we must understand player ascent toward and decline

from that peak to predict future value. Most published aging analyses are done using composite estimates of value such as OPS or linear weights. By contrast, fantasy GMs are typically more concerned with category-specific player value (HR, SB, AVG, etc.). We can better forecast what matters most by analyzing peak age of individual baseball skills rather than overall player value.

For batters, recognized peak age for overall batting value is a player's late 20s. But individual skills do not peak uniformly at the same time:

Contact rate (ct%): Ascends modestly by about a half point of contact per year from age 22 to 26, then holds steady within a half point of peak until age 35, after which players lose a half point of contact per year.

Walk rate (bb%): Trends the opposite way with age compared to contact rate, as batters tend to peak at age 30 and largely remain there until they turn 38.

Stolen Base Opportunity (SBO): Typically, players maintain their SBO through age 27, but then reduce their attempts steadily in each remaining year of their careers.

Stolen base success rate (SB%): Aggressive runners (>14% SBO) tend to lose about 2 points per year as they age. However, less aggressive runners (<=14% SBO) actually improve their SB% by about 2 points per year until age 28, after which they reverse course and give back 1-2 pts every year as they age.

GB%/LD%/FB%: Both GB% and LD% peak at the start of a player's career and then decline as many hitters seemingly learn to elevate the ball more. But at about age 30, hitter GB% ascends toward a second late-career peak while LD% continues to plummet and FB% continues to rise through age 38.

Hit rate (h%): Declines linearly with age. This is a natural result of a loss of speed and change in batted ball trajectory.

Isolated Power (ISO): Typically peaks from age 24-26. Similarly, home runs per fly ball, opposite field HR %, and Hard Hit % all peak by age 25 and decline somewhat linearly from that point on.

Catchers and late-career performance spikes *(Ed Spaulding)*
Many catchers—particularly second line catchers—have their best seasons late in their careers. Some possible reasons why:

1. Catchers, like shortstops, often get to the big leagues for defensive reasons and not their offensive skills. These skills take longer to develop.
2. The heavy emphasis on learning the catching/ defense/ pitching side of the game detracts from their time to learn about, and practice, hitting.
3. Injuries often curtail their ability to show offensive skills, though these injuries (typically jammed fingers, bruises on the arms, rib injuries from collisions) often don't lead to time on the disabled list.
4. The time spent behind the plate has to impact the ability to recognize, and eventually hit, all kinds of pitches.

Spring training Slg as leading indicator *(John Dewan)*
A hitter's spring training Slg .200 or more above his lifetime Slg is a leading indicator for a better than normal season.

Overall batting breakout profile *(Brandon Kruse)*
We define a breakout performance as one where a player posts a Roto value of $20+ after having never posted a value of $10. These criteria are used to validate an apparent breakout in the current season but may also be used carefully to project a potential upcoming breakout:

- Age 27 or younger
- An increase in at least two of: h%, PX or Spd
- Minimum league average PX or Spd (100)
- Minimum contact rate of 75%
- Minimum xBA of .270

In-Season Analysis

Batting order facts *(Ed DeCaria)*
Eighty-eight percent of today's leadoff hitters bat leadoff again in their next game, 78% still bat leadoff 10 games later, and 68% still bat leadoff 50 games later. Despite this level of turnover after 50 games, leadoff hitters have the best chance of retaining their role over time. After leadoff, #3 and #4 hitters are the next most likely to retain their lineup slots.

On a season-to-season basis, leadoff hitters are again the most stable, with 69% of last year's primary leadoff hitters retaining the #1 slot next year.

Plate appearances decline linearly by lineup slot. Leadoff batters receive 10-12% more PAs than when batting lower in the lineup. AL #9 batters and NL #8 batters get 9-10% fewer PAs. These results mirror play-by-play data showing a 15-20 PA drop by lineup slot over a full season.

Walk rate is largely unaffected by lineup slot in the AL. Beware strong walk rates by NL #8 hitters, as much of this "skill" will disappear if ever moved from the #8 slot.

Batting order has no discernable effect on contact rate.

Hit rate slopes gently upward as hitters are slotted deeper in the lineup.

As expected, the #3-4-5 slots are ideal for non-HR RBIs, at the expense of #6 hitters. RBIs are worst for players in the #1-2 slots. Batting atop the order sharply increases the probability of scoring runs, especially in the NL.

The leadoff slot easily has the highest stolen base attempt rate. #4-5-6 hitters attempt steals more often when batting out of those slots than they do batting elsewhere. The NL #8 hitter is a SB attempt sink hole. A change in batting order from #8 to #1 in the NL could nearly double a player's SB output due to lineup slot alone.

DOMination and DISaster rates
Week-to-week consistency is measured using a batter's BPV compiled in each week. A player earns a DOMinant week if his BPV was greater or equal to 50 for that week. A player registers a DISaster if his BPV was less than 0 for that week. The percentage of Dominant weeks, DOM%, is simply calculated as the number of DOM weeks divided by the total number of weeks played.

Is week-to-week consistency a repeatable skill? *(Bill Macey)*
To test whether consistent performance is a repeatable skill for batters, we examined how closely related a player's DOM% was from year to year.

YR1 DOM%	AVG YR2 DOM%
< 35%	37%
35%–45%	40%
46%–55%	45%
56%+	56%

Quality/consistency score (QC)
(DOM% – (2 x DIS%)) x 2
Using the DOM/DIS percentages, this score measures both the quality of performance as well as week–to–week consistency.

Sample size reliability *(Russell Carleton)*
At what point during the season do stats become reliable indicators of skill? Measured in PA *(unlisted=did not stablize over full season)*:
- 60: Contact rate
- 120: Walk rate
- 160: ISO (Isolated power)
- 170: HR rate
- 320: Slg
- 460: OBP

Measured via balls in play:
- 80: GB%; FB%
- 50: hr/f
- 600: LD%
- 820: hit rate (BABIP)

Projecting RBIs *(Patrick Davitt)*
Evaluating players in-season for RBI potential is a function of the interplay among four factors:
- Teammates' ability to reach base ahead of him and to run the bases efficiently
- His own ability to drive them in by hitting, especially XBH
- Number of Games Played
- Place in the batting order

3-4-5 Hitters:
(0.69 x GP x TOB) + (0.30 x ITB) + (0.275 x HR) – (.191 x GP)

6-7-8 Hitters:
(0.63 x GP x TOB) + (0.27 x ITB) + (0.250 x HR) – (.191 x GP)

9-1-2 Hitters:
(0.57 x GP x TOB) + (0.24 x ITB) + (0.225 x HR) – (.191 x GP)

...where *GP = games played, TOB = team on-base pct.* and *ITB = individual total bases (ITB)*.

Apply this pRBI formula after 70 games played or so (to reduce the variation from small sample size) to find players more than 9 RBIs over or under their projected RBI. There could be a correction coming.

You should also consider other factors, like injury or trade (involving the player or a top-of-the-order speedster) or team SB philosophy and success rate.

Remember: the player himself has an impact on his TOB. When we first did this study, we excluded the player from his TOB and got better results. The formula overestimates projected RBI for players with high OBP who skew his teams' OBP but can't benefit in RBI from that effect.

Ten-Game hitting streaks as a leading indicator *(Bob Berger)*
Research of hitting streaks from 2011 and 2012 showed that a 10-game streak can reliably predict improved longer-term BA performance during the season. A player who has put together a hitting streak of at least 10 games will improve his BA for the remainder of the season about 60% of the time. This improvement can be significant, on average as much as .020 of BA.

Other Diamonds

It's a Busy World Shortcut
For marginal utility-type players, scan their PX and Spd history to see if there's anything to mine for. If you see triple digits anywhere, stop and look further. If not, move on.

Chronology of the Classic Free-Swinger with Pop
1. Gets off to a good start.
2. Thinks he's in a groove.
3. Gets lax, careless.
4. Pitchers begin to catch on.
5. Fades down the stretch.

Errant Gust of Wind
A unit of measure used to describe the difference between your home run projection and mine.

Hannahan Concession
Players with a .218 BA rarely get 500 plate appearances, but when they do, it's usually once.

Mendoza Line
Named for Mario Mendoza, it represents the benchmark for batting futility. Usually refers to a .200 batting average, but can also be used for low levels of other statistical categories. Note that Mendoza's lifetime batting average was actually a much more robust .215.

Old Player Skills
Power, low batting average, no speed and usually good plate patience. Young players, often those with a larger frame, who possess these "old player skills" tend to decline faster than normal, often in their early 30s.

Small Sample Certitude
If players' careers were judged based what they did in a single game performance, then Tuffy Rhodes and Mark Whiten would be in the Hall of Fame.

Esix Snead List
Players with excellent speed and sub-.300 on base averages who get a lot of practice running down the line to first base, and then back to the dugout. Also used as an adjective, as in "Esix-Sneadian."

Pitchers

Strikeouts and Walks

Fundamental skills

The contention that pitching performance is unreliable is a fallacy driven by the practice of attempting to project pitching stats using gauges that are poor evaluators of skill.

How can we better evaluate pitching skill? We can start with the statistical categories that are generally unaffected by external factors. These stats capture the outcome of an individual pitcher versus batter match-up without regard to supporting offense, defense or bullpen:

Walks Allowed, Strikeouts and Ground/Fly Balls

Even with only these stats to observe, there is a wealth of insight that these measures can provide.

Control rate (Ctl, bb/9), or opposition walks per game
BB allowed x 9 / IP

Measures how many walks a pitcher allows per game equivalent. BENCHMARK: The best pitchers will have bb/9 of 2.8 or less.

Dominance rate (Dom, k/9), or opposition strikeouts/game
Strikeouts recorded x 9 / IP

Measures how many strikeouts a pitcher allows per game equivalent. BENCHMARK: The best pitchers will have k/9 levels of 7.0 or higher.

Command ratio (Cmd)
(Strikeouts / Walks)

A measure of a pitcher's ability to get the ball over the plate. There is no more fundamental a skill than this, and so it is used as a leading indicator to project future rises and falls in other gauges, such as ERA. BENCHMARKS: Baseball's best pitchers will have ratios in excess of 3.0. Pitchers with ratios less than 1.0—indicating that they walk more batters than they strike out—have virtually no potential for long-term success. If you make no other changes in your approach to drafting pitchers, limiting your focus to only pitchers with a command ratio of 2.5 or better will substantially improve your odds of success.

Command ratio as a leading indicator

The ability to get the ball over the plate—command of the strike zone—is one of the best leading indicators for future performance. Command ratio (K/BB) can be used to project potential in ERA as well as other skills gauges.

1. Research indicates that there is a high correlation between a pitcher's Cmd ratio and his ERA.

	Earned Run Average				
Command	2012	2013	2014	2015	2016
0.0 - 1.0	6.22	5.98	6.81	6.31	7.71
1.1 - 1.5	5.03	4.91	4.97	5.23	5.51
1.6 - 2.0	4.48	4.42	4.37	4.54	4.66
2.1 - 2.5	4.09	3.96	3.80	4.19	4.30
2.6 - 3.0	3.88	3.81	3.78	3.87	4.02
3.1 - 3.5	3.67	3.46	3.43	3.51	3.95
3.6 - 4.0	3.34	3.32	3.16	3.56	3.51
4.1+	3.12	2.86	2.92	3.07	3.30

On the pitching flipside, the number of arms comprising the 4.1+ group has nearly doubled since 2012. That year, 58 pitchers made up this group; in 2014 there were 93, 90 in 2015 and 88 this year.

We can create percentage plays for the different levels:

For Cmd	% with ERA of	
Levels of	3.50-	4.50+
0.0 - 1.0	0%	100%
1.1 - 1.5	9%	70%
1.6 - 2.0	19%	54%
2.1 - 2.5	33%	41%
2.6 - 3.0	35%	31%
3.1 – 3.5	37%	18%
3.6 – 4.0	56%	15%
4.1 +	61%	11%

Pitchers who maintain a Cmd over 2.5 have a high probability of long-term success. For fantasy drafting purposes, it is best to avoid pitchers with sub-2.0 ratios. Avoid bullpen closers if they have a ratio less than 2.5.

2. A pitcher's Command in tandem with Dominance (strikeout rate) provides even greater predictive abilities.

	Earned Run Average	
Command	-5.6 Dom	5.6+ Dom
0.0-0.9	6.71	n/a
1.0-1.4	5.56	n/a
1.5-1.9	4.78	4.26
2.0-2.4	4.33	4.10
2.5-2.9	4.31	3.74
3.0-3.9	4.10	3.66
4.0+	3.79	3.09

This helps to highlight the limited upside potential of soft-tossers with pinpoint control. The extra dominance makes a huge difference.

Swinging strike rate as leading indicator *(Stephen Nickrand)*
An emerging indicator for predicting starting pitching performance is swinging strike rate (SwK%), which measures the percentage of total pitches against which a batter swings and misses. SwK% can help us validate and forecast a SP's Dominance (K/9) rate, which in turn allows us to identify surgers and faders with greater accuracy.

Follow these rules of thumb when targeting starting pitchers based on SwK%: SwK% baselines for SP are 8.0% in AL, 8.4% in NL; Expected Dom (xDom) can be estimated from SwK%; and a pitcher's individual SwK% does not regress to league norms.

The few starters per year who have a 12.0% or higher SwK% are near-locks to have a 9.0 Dom or greater. In contrast, starters with a 7.0% or lower SwK% have nearly no chance at posting even an average Dom. Finally, use an 8.5% SwK% as an acceptable threshold when searching for SP based on this metric; raise it to 9.5% to begin to find SwK% difference-makers.

Fastball velocity and Dominance rate *(Stephen Nickrand)*
It is intuitive that an increase in fastball velocity for starting pitchers leads to more strikeouts. But how much? We analyzed the historical link between fastball velocity and Dominance (K/9) rate. Among the findings:

The vast majority of SP with significant fastball velocity gains

- experience a significant Dom gain during the same season.
- are likely to give back those gains during the following season.
- are likely to increase their Dom the following season, but the magnitude of the Dom increase usually is small.

The vast majority of SP with significant fastball velocity losses

- are likely to experience a significant Dom decrease during the same season.

Those SP with significant fastball velocity losses from one season to the next are just as likely to experience a fastball velocity or Dom increase as they are to experience a fastball or Dom decrease, and the amounts of the increase/decrease are nearly identical.

First-pitch strike rate as leading indicator *(Stephen Nickrand)*

The measurement of a pitcher's rate of first-pitch strikes (FpK%) can help us validate and forecast a pitcher's Control (BB/9) rate. As first-pitch strike rate increases, walks are very likely to go down, and WHIP will follow. As it goes up, walks are likely to increase, as will WHIP. So if you're wondering if a pitcher's newfound good control is likely to hold, check out his FpK%.

The FpK% baseline is 60% for starting pitchers and does not vary significantly by league. Expected Ctl (xCtl) can be estimated from FpK%, and a starting pitcher's individual FpK% does not regress to league norms. BENCHMARKS: Elite pitchers will have a FpK% above 68% and most of them will have a Ctl below 2.0. Avoid pitchers with a FpK% below 55%, as they are likely to have a Ctl at or above 4.0.

First pitch strikes increase with age *(Ed DeCaria)*

On average, pitchers lose about 0.2 mph per season off their fastballs. Over time, this coincides with decreases in swinging strike rate (SwK%) and overall strikeout rate (K/PA)—the inevitable effects of aging. But one thing that pitchers can do to delay these effects is to throw more first pitch strikes.

Individual pitcher first pitch strike rates (FpK%) increase at a rate of 0.5% per year from age 22 to 26. Pitchers then typically add another 0.5-1.0% as they settle into their respective peak levels. Once pitchers reach their peaks, first pitch strike rate tends not to decline with age—it is a skill that pitchers own until retirement, even as their other physical skills deteriorate.

Younger pitchers (under age 26) with above average SwK% but below average FpK% make for great breakout targets.

Power/contact rating

(BB + K) / IP

Measures the level by which a pitcher allows balls to be put into play. In general, extreme power pitchers can be successful even with poor defensive teams. Power pitchers tend to have greater longevity in the game. Contact pitchers with poor defenses behind them are high risks to have poor W-L records and ERA. BENCHMARKS: A level of 1.13+ describes pure throwers. A level of .93 or less describes high contact pitchers.

Balls in Play

Balls in play (BIP)

(Batters faced – (BB + HBP + SAC)) + H – K

The total number of batted balls that are hit fair, both hits and outs. An analysis of how these balls are hit—on the ground, in the air, hits, outs, etc.—can provide analytical insight, from player skill levels to the impact of luck on statistical output.

Batting average on balls in play *(Voros McCracken)*

(H – HR) / (Batters faced – (BB + HBP + SAC)) + H – K – HR

Abbreviated as BABIP; also called hit rate (H%), this is the percent of balls hit into the field of play that fall for hits. In 2000, Voros McCracken published a study that concluded "there is little if any difference among major league pitchers in their ability to prevent hits on balls hit in the field of play." His assertion was that, while a Johan Santana would have a better ability to prevent a batter from getting wood on a ball, or perhaps keeping the ball in the park, once that ball was hit in the field of play, the probability of it falling for a hit was virtually no different than for any other pitcher.

Among the findings in his study were:

- There is little correlation between what a pitcher does one year in the stat and what he will do the next. This is not true with other significant stats (BB, K, HR).
- You can better predict a pitcher's hits per balls in play from the rate of the rest of the pitcher's team than from the pitcher's own rate.

This last point brings a team's defense into the picture. It begs the question, when a batter gets a hit, is it because the pitcher made a bad pitch, the batter took a good swing, or the defense was not positioned correctly?

BABIP as a leading indicator *(Voros McCracken)*

The league average is 30%, which is also the level that individual performances will regress to on a year to year basis. Any +/- variance of 3% or more can affect a pitcher's ERA.

Pitchers will often post hit rates per balls-in-play that are far off from the league average, but then revert to the mean the following year. As such, we can use that mean to project the direction of a pitcher's ERA.

Subsequent research has shown that ground ball or fly ball propensity has some impact on this rate.

Hit rate *(See Batting average on balls in play)*

Opposition batting average (OBA)

Hits allowed / (Batters faced – (BB + HBP + SAC))

The batting average achieved by opposing batters against a pitcher. BENCHMARKS: The best pitchers will have levels less than .250; the worst pitchers levels more than .300.

Opposition on base average (OOB)

(Hits allowed + BB) / ((Batters faced – (BB + HBP + SAC)) + Hits allowed + BB)

The on base average achieved by opposing batters against a pitcher. BENCHMARK: The best pitchers will have levels less than .300; the worst pitchers levels more than .375.

Walks plus hits divided by innings pitched (WHIP)

Essentially the same measure as opposition on base average, but used for Rotisserie purposes. BENCHMARKS: A WHIP of less than 1.20 is considered top level; more than 1.50 indicative of poor performance. Levels less than 1.00—allowing fewer runners than IP—represent extraordinary performance and are rarely maintained over time.

Ground ball, line drive, fly ball percentage (G/L/F)

The percentage of all balls-in-play that are hit on the ground, in the air and as line drives. For a pitcher, the ability to pitch to a ground ball or fly ball extreme can contribute to his statistical output exceeding his demonstrated skill level.

Ground ball tendency as a leading indicator *(John Burnson)*

Ground ball pitchers tend to give up fewer HRs than do fly ball pitchers. There is also evidence that GB pitchers have higher hit rates. In other words, a ground ball has a higher chance of being a hit than does a fly ball that is not out of the park.

GB pitchers have lower strikeout rates. We should be more forgiving of a low strikeout rate (under 5.5 K/9) if it belongs to an extreme ground ball pitcher.

GB pitchers have a lower ERA but a higher WHIP than do fly ball pitchers. On balance, GB pitchers come out ahead, even when considering strikeouts, because a lower ERA also leads to more wins.

Groundball and strikeout tendencies as indicators

(Mike Dranchak)

Pitchers were assembled into 9 groups based on the following profiles (minimum 23 starts in 2005):

Profile	Ground Ball Rate
Ground Ball	higher than 47%
Neutral	42% to 47%
Fly Ball	less than 42%

Profile	Strikeout Rate (k/9)
Strikeout	higher than 6.6 k/9
Average	5.4 to 6.6 k/9
Soft-Tosser	less than 5.4 k/9

Findings: Pitchers with higher strikeout rates had better ERAs and WHIPs than pitchers with lower strikeout rates, regardless of ground ball profile. However, for pitchers with similar strikeout rates, those with higher ground ball rates had better ERAs and WHIPs than those with lower ground ball rates.

Pitchers with higher strikeout rates tended to strand more baserunners than those with lower K rates. Fly ball pitchers tended to strand fewer runners than their GB or neutral counterparts within their strikeout profile.

Ground ball pitchers (especially those who lacked high-dominance) yielded more home runs per fly ball than did fly ball pitchers. However, the ERA risk was mitigated by the fact that ground ball pitchers (by definition) gave up fewer fly balls to begin with.

Extreme GB/FB pitchers *(Patrick Davitt)*

Among pitchers with normal strikeout levels, extreme GB pitchers (>3–7% of all batters faced) have ERAs about 0.4 runs lower than normal-GB% pitchers but only slight WHIP advantages. Extreme FB% pitchers (32% FB) show no ERA benefits.

Among High-K (>=24% of BF), however, extreme GBers have ERAs about 0.5 runs lower than normal-GB pitchers, and WHIPs about five points lower. Extreme FB% pitchers have ERAs about 0.2 runs lower than normal-FB pitchers, and WHIPs about 10 points lower.

Revisting flyballs *(Jason Collette)*

The increased emphasis on defensive positioning is often associated with infield shifting, but the same data also influences how outfielders are positioned. Some managers are positioning OFs more aggressively than just the customary few steps per a right- or left-handed swinging batter. BaseballHQ.com found that five of the top 10 defensive efficiency teams in 2013 —OAK, STL, MIA, LAA and KC—also had parks among the top 10 in HR suppression.

Before dismissing flyball pitchers as toxic assets, pay more attention to park factors and OF defensive talent. In particular, be a little more willing to roster fly ball pitchers who pitch both in front of good defensive OFs and in good pitchers' parks.

Line drive percentage as a leading indicator *(Seth Samuels)*

The percentage of ball-in-play that are line drives is beyond a pitcher's control. Line drives do the most damage; from 1994-2003, here were the expected hit rates and number of total bases per type of BIP.

	┣------ Type of BIP ------┫		
	GB	FB	LD
H%	26%	23%	56%
Total bases	0.29	0.57	0.80

Despite the damage done by LDs, pitchers do not have any innate skill to avoid them. There is little relationship between a pitcher's LD% one year and his rate the next year. All rates tend to regress towards a mean of 22.6%.

However, GB pitchers do have a slight ability to prevent LDs (21.7%) and extreme GB hurlers even moreso (18.5%). Extreme FB pitchers have a slight ability to prevent LDs (21.1%) as well.

Home run to fly ball rate (hr/f)

HR / FB

The percent of fly balls that are hit for home runs.

hr/f as a leading indicator *(John Burnson)*

McCracken's work focused on "balls in play," omitting home runs from the study. However, pitchers also do not have much control over the percentage of fly balls that turn into HR. Research shows that there is an underlying rate of HR as a percentage of fly balls of about 10%. A pitcher's HR/FB rate will vary each year but always tends to regress to that 10%. The element that pitchers do have control over is the number of fly balls they allow. That is the underlying skill or deficiency that controls their HR rate.

Pitchers who keep the ball out of the air more often correlate well with Roto value.

Opposition home runs per game (hr/9)

(HR Allowed x 9 / IP)

Also, expected opposition HR rate = (FB x 0.10) x 9 / IP

Measures how many HR a pitcher allows per game equivalent. Since FB tend to go yard at about a 10% rate, we can also estimate this rate off of fly balls. BENCHMARK: The best pitchers will have hr/9 levels of less than 1.0.

Runs

Expected earned run average (xERA)

Gill and Reeve version: *(.575 x H [per 9 IP]) + (.94 x HR [per 9 IP]) + (.28 x BB [per 9 IP]) – (.01 x K [per 9 IP]) – Normalizing Factor*

John Burnson version (used in this book):
(xER x 9)/IP, where xER is defined as
xER% x (FB/10) + (1-xS%) x [0.3 x (BIP – FB/10) + BB]
where xER% = 0.96 – (0.0284 x (GB/FB))
and
xS% = (64.5 + (K/9 x 1.2) – (BB/9 x (BB/9 + 1)) / 20)
+ ((0.0012 x (GB%^2)) – (0.001 x GB%) - 2.4)

xERA represents the an equivalent of what a pitcher's real ERA might be, calculated solely with skills-based measures. It is not influenced by situation-dependent factors.

Expected ERA variance

xERA – ERA

The variance between a pitcher's ERA and his xERA is a measure of over or underachievement. A positive variance indicates the potential for a pitcher's ERA to rise. A negative variance indicates the potential for ERA improvement. BENCHMARK: Discount variances that are less than 0.50. Any variance more than 1.00 (one run per game) is regarded as a strong indicator of future change.

Projected xERA or projected ERA?

Which should we be using to forecast a pitcher's ERA? Projected xERA is more accurate for looking ahead on a purely skills basis. Projected ERA includes *situation-dependent* events—bullpen support, park factors, etc.—which are reflected better by ERA. The optimal approach is to use both gauges as *a range of expectation* for forecasting purposes.

Strand rate (S%)

(H + BB – ER) / (H + BB – HR)

Measures the percentage of allowed runners a pitcher strands (earned runs only), which incorporates both individual pitcher skill and bullpen effectiveness. BENCHMARKS: The most adept at stranding runners will have S% levels over 75%. Those with rates over 80% will have artificially low ERAs which will be prone to relapse. Levels below 65% will inflate ERA but have a high probability of regression.

Expected strand rate *(Michael Weddell)*

*73.935 + K/9 - 0.116 * (BB/9*(BB/9+1))*
*+ (0.0047 * GB%^2 - 0.3385 * GB%)*
+ (MAX(2,MIN(4,IP/G))/2-1)
+ (0.82 if left-handed)

This formula is based on three core skills: strikeouts per nine innings, walks per nine innings, and groundballs per balls in play, with adjustments for whether the pitcher is a starter or reliever (measured by IP/G), and his handedness.

Strand rate as a leading indicator *(Ed DeCaria)*

Strand rate often regresses/rebounds toward past rates (usually 69-74%), resulting in Year 2 ERA changes:

% of Pitchers with Year 2 Regression/Rebound

Y1 S%	RP	SP	LR
<60%	100%	94%	94%
65	81%	74%	88%
70	53%	48%	65%
75	55%	85%	100%
80	80%	100%	100%
85	100%	100%	100%

Typical ERA Regression/Rebound in Year 2

Y1 S%	RP	SP	LR
<60%	-2.54	-2.03	-2.79
65	-1.00	-0.64	-0.93
70	-0.10	-0.05	-0.44
75	0.24	0.54	0.75
80	1.15	1.36	2.29
85	1.71	2.21	n/a

Starting pitchers (SP) have a narrower range of strand rate outcomes than do relievers (RP) or swingmen/long relievers (LR). **Relief pitchers** with Y1 strand rates of <=67% or >=78% are likely to experience a +/- ERA regression in Y2. **Starters and swingmen/long relievers** with Y1 strand rates of <=65% or >=75% are likely to experience a +/- ERA regression in Y2. Pitchers with strand rates that deviate more than a few points off of their individual expected strand rates are likely to experience some degree of ERA regression in Y2. Over-performing (or "lucky") pitchers are more likely than underperforming (or "unlucky") pitchers to see such a correction.

Wins

Expected Wins (xW) *(Matt Cederholm)*

[(Team runs per game)^1.8]/[(Pitcher ERA)^1.8 + (Team runs per game)^1.8] x 0.72 x GS

Starting pitchers' win totals are often at odds with their ERA. Attempts to find a strictly skill-based analysis of this phenomenon haven't worked, but there is a powerful tool in the toolbox: Bill James' Pythagorean Theorem. While usually applied to team outcomes, recent research has shown that its validity holds up when applied to individual starting pitchers.

One key to applying the Pythagorean Theorem is factoring in no-decisions. Research shows that the average no-decision rate is 28% of starts, regardless of the type or quality of the pitcher or his team, with no correlation in ND% from one season to the next.

Overall, 70% of pitchers whose expected wins varied from actual wins showed regression in wins per start in the following year, making variation from Expected Wins a good leading indicator.

Projecting/chasing wins

There are five events that need to occur in order for a pitcher to post a single win...

1. He must pitch well, allowing few runs.
2. The offense must score enough runs.
3. The defense must successfully field all batted balls.
4. The bullpen must hold the lead.
5. The manager must leave the pitcher in for 5 innings, and not remove him if the team is still behind.

Of these five events, only one is within the control of the pitcher. As such, projecting or chasing wins based on skills alone can be an exercise in futility.

Home field advantage *(John Burnson)*

A 2006 study found that home starting pitchers get credited with a win in 38% of their outings. Visiting team starters are credited with a win in 33% of their outings.

Usage

Batters faced per game *(Craig Wright)*

((Batters faced – (BB + HBP + SAC)) + H + BB) / G

A measure of pitcher usage and one of the leading indicators for potential pitcher burnout.

Workload

Research suggests that there is a finite number of innings in a pitcher's arm. This number varies by pitcher, by development cycle, and by pitching style and repertoire. We can measure a pitcher's potential for future arm problems and/or reduced effectiveness (burnout):

Sharp increases in usage from one year to the next. Common wisdom has suggested that pitchers who significantly increase their workload from one year to the next are candidates for burnout symptoms. This has often been called the Verducci Effect, after writer Tom Verducci. BaseballHQ.com analyst Michael Weddell tested pitchers with sharp workload increases during the period 1988-2008 and found that no such effect exists.

Starters' overuse. Consistent "batters faced per game" (BF/G) levels of 28.0 or higher, combined with consistent seasonal IP totals of 200 or more may indicate burnout potential, especially with pitchers younger than 25. Within a season, a BF/G of more than 30.0 with a projected IP total of 200 may indicate a late season fade.

Relievers' overuse. Warning flags should be up for relievers who post in excess of 100 IP in a season, while averaging fewer than 2 IP per outing.

When focusing solely on minor league pitchers, research results are striking:

Stamina: Virtually every minor league pitcher who had a BF/G of 28.5 or more in one season experienced a drop-off in BF/G the following year. Many were unable to ever duplicate that previous level of durability.

Performance: Most pitchers experienced an associated drop-off in their BPVs in the years following the 28.5 BF/G season.

Some were able to salvage their effectiveness later on by moving to the bullpen.

Protecting young pitchers *(Craig Wright)*

There is a link between some degree of eventual arm trouble and a history of heavy workloads in a pitcher's formative years. Some recommendations from this research:

Teenagers (A-ball): No 200 IP seasons and no BF/G over 28.5 in any 150 IP span. No starts on three days rest.

Ages 20-22: Average no more than 105 pitches per start with a single game ceiling of 130 pitches.

Ages 23-24: Average no more than 110 pitches per start with a single game ceiling of 140 pitches.

When possible, a young starter should be introduced to the majors in long relief before he goes into the rotation.

Overall Performance Analysis

Base Performance Value (BPV)

((Dominance Rate - 5.0) x 18)
+ ((4.0 - Walk Rate) x 27))
+ (Ground ball rate as a whole number - 40%)

A single value that describes a player's overall raw skill level. This is more useful than traditional statistical gauges to track player performance trends and project future statistical output. The formula combines the individual raw skills of power, control and the ability to keep the ball down in the zone, all characteristics that are unaffected by most external factors. In tandem with a pitcher's strand rate, it provides a more complete picture of the elements that contribute to ERA, and therefore serves as an accurate tool to project likely changes in ERA. **BENCHMARKS:** A BPV of 50 is the minimum level required for long-term success. The elite of the bullpen aces will have BPVs in excess of 100 and it is rare for these stoppers to enjoy long term success with consistent levels under 75.

Base Performance Index (BPX)

BPV scaled to league average to account for year-to-year fluctuations in league-wide statistical performance. It's a snapshot of a player's overall skills compared to an average player. **BENCHMARK:** A level of 100 means a player had a league-average BPV in that given season.

Runs above replacement (RAR)

An estimate of the number of runs a player contributes above a "replacement level" player.

Batters create runs; pitchers save runs. But are batters and pitchers who have comparable RAR levels truly equal in value? Pitchers might be considered to have higher value. Saving an additional run is more important than producing an additional run. A pitcher who throws a shutout is guaranteed to win that game, whereas no matter how many runs a batter produces, his team can still lose given poor pitching support.

To calculate RAR for pitchers:

1. Start with the replacement level league ERA.
2. Subtract the pitcher's ERA. (To calculate projected RAR, use the pitcher's xERA.)
3. Multiply by number of games played, calculated as plate appearances (IP x 4.34) divided by 38.
4. Multiply the resulting RAR level by 1.08 to account for the variance between earned runs and total runs.

Handedness

1. LHers tend to peak about a year after RHers.
2. LHers post only 15% of the total saves. Typically, LHers are reserved for specialist roles so few are frontline closers.
3. RHers have slightly better command and HR rate.
4. There is no significant variance in ERA.
5. On an overall skills basis, RHers have ~6% advantage.

Skill-specific aging patterns for pitchers *(Ed DeCaria)*

Baseball forecasters obsess over "peak age" of player performance because we must understand player ascent toward and decline from that peak to predict future value. Most published aging analyses are done using composite estimates of value such as OPS or linear weights. By contrast, fantasy GMs are typically more concerned with category-specific player value (K, ERA, WHIP, etc.). We can better forecast what matters most by analyzing peak age of individual baseball skills rather than overall player value.

For pitchers, prior research has shown that pitcher value peaks somewhere in the late 20s to early 30s. But how does aging affect each demonstrable pitching skill?

Strikeout rate (k/9): Declines fairly linearly beginning at age 25.

Walk rate (bb/9): Improves until age 25 and holds somewhat steady until age 29, at which point it begins to steadily worsen. Deteriorating k/9 and bb/9 rates result in inefficiency, as it requires far more pitches to get an out. For starting pitchers, this affects the ability to pitch deep into games.

Innings Pitched per game (IP/G): Among starters, it improves slightly until age 27, then tails off considerably with age, costing pitchers nearly one full IP/G by age 33 and one more by age 39.

Hit rate (H%): Among pitchers, H% appears to increase slowly but steadily as pitchers age, to the tune of .002-.003 points per year.

Strand rate (S%): Very similar to hit rate, except strand rate decreases with age rather than increasing. GB%/LD%/FB%: Line drives increase steadily from age 24 onward, and outfield flies increase beginning at age 31. Because 70%+ of line drives fall for hits, and 10%+ of fly balls become home runs, this spells trouble for aging pitchers.

Home runs per fly ball (hr/f): As each year passes, a higher percentage of a pitcher's fly balls become home runs allowed increases with age.

Catchers' effect on pitching *(Thomas Hanrahan)*

A typical catcher handles a pitching staff better after having been with a club for a few years. Research has shown that there is an improvement in team ERA of approximately 0.37 runs from a catcher's rookie season to his prime years with a club. Expect a pitcher's ERA to be higher than expected if he is throwing to a rookie backstop.

First productive season *(Michael Weddell)*

To find those starting pitchers who are about to post their first productive season in the majors (10 wins, 150 IP, ERA of 4.00 or less), look for:

- Pitchers entering their age 23-26 seasons, especially those about to pitch their age 25 season.
- Pitchers who already have good skills, shown by an xERA in the prior year of 4.25 or less.
- Pitchers coming off of at least a partial season in the majors without a major health problem.
- To the extent that one speculates on pitchers who are one skill away, look for pitchers who only need to improve their control (bb/9).

Overall pitching breakout profile *(Brandon Kruse)*

A breakout performance is defined here as one where a player posts a Rotisserie value of $20 or higher after having never achieved $10 previously. These criteria are primarily used to validate an apparent breakout in the current season but may also be used carefully to project a potential breakout for an upcoming season.

- Age 27 or younger
- Minimum 5.6 Dom, 2.0 Cmd, 1.1 hr/9 and 50 BPV
- Maximum 30% hit rate
- Minimum 71% strand rate
- Starters should have a H% no greater than the previous year; relievers should show improved command
- Maximum xERA of 4.00

Career year drop-off *(Rick Wilton)*

Research shows that a pitcher's post-career year drop-off, on average, looks like this:

- ERA increases by 1.00
- WHIP increases by 0.14.
- Nearly 6 fewer wins

Bounceback fallacy *(Patrick Davitt)*

It is conventional wisdom that a pitcher often or even usually follows a bad year (value decline of more than 50%) with a significant "bounceback" that offers profit opportunity for the canny owner. But BaseballHQ.com research showed the owner is extremely unlikely to get a full bounceback, and in fact, is more likely to suffer a further decline or uselessly small recovery than even a partial bounceback. The safest bet is a $30+ pitcher who has a collapse—but even then, bid to only about half of the previous premium value.

Pitchers crossing leagues *(Bob Berger)*

The AL has higher league-wide ERA and lower K/9 when compared to the NL. Fantasy owners should consider adjusting their ERA, WHIP, and K/9 expectations for pitchers moving to the "other" league. Pitchers moving to the NL may perform better than expected based on their recent career trends; pitchers moving to the AL may perform worse than expected.

Closers

Saves

There are six events that need to occur in order for a relief pitcher to post a single save:

1. The starting pitcher and middle relievers must pitch well.
2. The offense must score enough runs.
3. It must be a reasonably close game.
4. The manager must put the pitcher in for a save opportunity.
5. The pitcher must pitch well and hold the lead.
6. The manager must let him finish the game.

Of these six events, only one is within the control of the relief pitcher. As such, projecting saves for a reliever has less to do with skills than opportunity. However, pitchers with excellent skills may create opportunity for themselves.

Saves conversion rate (Sv%)

Saves / Save Opportunities

The percentage of save opportunities that are successfully converted. **BENCHMARK:** We look for a minimum 80% for long-term success.

Leverage index (LI) *(Tom Tango)*

Leverage index measures the amount of swing in the possible change in win probability indexed against an average value of 1.00. Thus, relievers who come into games in various situations create a composite score and if that average score is higher than 1.00, then their manager is showing enough confidence in them to try to win games with them. If the average score is below 1.00, then the manager is using them, but not showing nearly as much confidence that they can win games.

Saves chances and wins *(Patrick Davitt)*

Some fantasy owners think that good teams get more saves because they generate more wins. Other owners think that poor teams get more saves because more of their wins are by narrow margins. The "good-team" side is probably on firmer ground, though there are enough exceptions that we should be cautious about drawing broad inferences.

The 2014 study confirmed what Craig Neuman found years earlier: The argument "more wins leads to more saves" is generally correct. Over five studied seasons, the percentage of wins that were saved (Sv%W) was about 50%, and half of all team-seasons fell in the Sv%W range of 48%-56%. As a result, high-saves seasons were more common for high-win teams.

That wins-saves connection for individual team-seasons was much less solid, however, and we observed many outliers. Data for individual team-seasons showed wide ranges of both Sv%W and actual saves.

Finally, higher-win teams do indeed get more blowout wins, but while poorer teams had a higher percentage (73%) of close wins (three runs or fewer) than better teams (56%), good teams' higher number of wins meant they still had more close wins, more save opportunities and more saves, again with many outliers among individual team-seasons.

Origin of closers

History has long maintained that ace closers are not easily recognizable early on in their careers, so that every season does see its share of the unexpected. Jeanmar Gomez, Sam Dyson, Ryan Madson, Seung-Hwan Oh, Tony Cingrani, Edwin Diaz, Brandon Kintzler … who would have thought it a year ago?

Accepted facts, all of which have some element of truth:

- You cannot find major league closers from pitchers who were closers in the minors.
- Closers begin their careers as starters.
- Closers are converted set-up men.
- Closers are pitchers who were unable to develop a third effective pitch.

More simply, closers are a product of circumstance.

Are the minor leagues a place to look at all?

From 1990-2004, there were 280 twenty-save seasons in Double-A and Triple-A. Over that period, there were only 13 pitchers ever saved 20 games in the majors and only five who ever posted more than one 20-save season: John Wetteland, Mark Wohlers, Ricky Bottalico, Braden Looper and Francisco Cordero.

More recent data is even more pessimistic:

Year	# with 20 Svs	MLB closers
2006	25	none
2007	22	none
2008	19	none
2009	17	none
2010	14	Craig Kimbrel
2011	16	none
2012	16	A.J. Ramos
2013	16	none
2014	12	none
2015	17	none

That's 177 twenty-save seasons and only two major league closers.

One of the reasons that minor league closers rarely become major league closers is because, in general, they do not get enough innings in the minors to sufficiently develop their arms into big-league caliber.

In fact, organizations do not look at minor league closing performance seriously, assigning that role to pitchers who they do not see as legitimate prospects. The average age of minor league closers over the past decade has been 27.5.

Elements of saves success

The task of finding future closing potential comes down to looking at two elements:

Talent: The raw skills to mow down hitters for short periods of time. Optimal BPVs over 100, but not under 75.

Opportunity: The more important element, yet the one that pitchers have no control over.

There are pitchers that have Talent, but not Opportunity. These pitchers are not given a chance to close for a variety of reasons (e.g. being blocked by a solid front-liner in the pen, being left-handed, etc.), but are good to own because they will not likely hurt your pitching staff. You just can't count on them for saves, at least not in the near term.

There are pitchers that have Opportunity, but not Talent. MLB managers decide who to give the ball to in the 9th inning based on their own perceptions about what skills are required to succeed, even if those perceived "skills" don't translate into acceptable metrics.

Those pitchers without the metrics may have some initial short-term success, but their long-term prognosis is poor and they are high risks to your roster. Classic examples of the short life span of these types of pitchers include Matt Karchner, Heath Slocumb, Ryan Kohlmeier, Dan Miceli, Joe Borowski and Danny Kolb. More recent examples include Tom Wilhelmsen, Kevin Gregg and Tony Cingrani.

Closers' job retention *(Michael Weddell)*

Of pitchers with 20 or more saves in one year, only 67.5% of these closers earned 20 or more saves the following year. The variables that best predicted whether a closer would avoid this attrition:

- *Saves history:* Career saves was the most important factor.
- *Age:* Closers are most likely to keep their jobs at age 27. For long-time closers, their growing career saves totals more than offset the negative impact of their advanced ages. Older closers without a long history of racking up saves tend to be bad candidates for retaining their roles.
- *Performance:* Actual performance, measured by ERA+, was of only minor importance.
- *Being right-handed:* Increased the odds of retaining the closer's role by 9% over left-handers.

How well can we predict which closers will keep their jobs? Of the 10 best closers during 1989-2007, 90% saved at least 20 games during the following season. Of the 10 worst bets, only 20% saved at least 20 games the next year.

Closer volatility history

Year	Closers Drafted	Avg R$	Closers Failed	Failure %	New Sources
2008	32	$17.78	10	31%	11
2009	28	$17.56	9	32%	13
2010	28	$16.96	7	25%	13
2011	30	$15.47	11	37%	8
2012	29	$15.28	19	66%	18
2013	29	$15.55	9	31%	13
2014	28	$15.54	11	39%	15
2015	29	$14.79	13	45%	16
2016	33	$13.30	19	58%	17

Drafted refers to the number of saves sources purchased in both LABR and Tout Wars experts leagues each year. These only include relievers drafted for at least $10*, specifically for saves speculation. *Avg R$* refers to the average purchase price of these pitchers in the AL-only and NL-only leagues. *Failed* is the number (and percentage) of saves sources drafted that did not return at least 50% of their value that year. The failures include those that lost their value due to ineffectiveness, injury or managerial decision. *New Sources* are arms that were drafted for less than $10 (if drafted at all) but finished with at least double-digit saves.

The failed saves investments in 2016 were Brad Boxberger, Wade Davis, Sean Doolittle, Ken Giles, Jason Grilli, J.J. Hoover, Jake McGee, Jonathan Papelbon, Glen Perkins, Fernando Rodney, Hector Rondon, Trevor Rosenthal, Will Smith, Drew Storen, Huston Street, Shawn Tolleson and Arodys Vizcaino. In addition, Craig Kimbrel and David Robertson both returned less than 50% of their owners' investments despite each saving at least 30 games. The new sources in 2016 were Tony Cingrani, Alex Colome, Sam Dyson, Edwin Diaz, Carlos Esteves, Jeanmar Gomez, Luke Gregerson, Kelvin Herrera, Jeremy Jeffress, Jim Johnson, Brandon Kintzler, Ryan Madson, Brandon Maurer, Seung-Hwan Oh, Tyler Thornburg, Tony Watson, and Will Harris. Note that only four of these new sources fared well enough to earn double-digit roto value, and another four earned zero dollars or less.

The fantasy bullpen environment continued to erode in 2016. Owners spread their bullpen dollars more than ever before, further depressing the record low closer prices. In 2015, there were five potential closers drafted for less than $10; in 2016, there were 10. As MLB managers continue to micro-manage their bullpens, investments in closers will likely continue to be depressed.

Closers and multi-year performance *(Patrick Davitt)*

A team having an "established closer"—even a successful one—in a given year does not affect how many of that team's wins are saved in the next year. However, a top closer (40-plus saves) in a given year has a significantly greater chance to retain his role in the subsequent season.

Research of saves and wins data over several seasons found that the percentage of wins that are saved is consistently 50%-54%, irrespective of whether the saves were concentrated in the hands of a "top closer" or passed around to the dreaded "committee" of lesser closers. But it also found that about two-thirds of high-save closers reprised their roles the next season, while three-quarters of low-save closers did not. Moreover, closers who held the role for two or three straight seasons averaged 34 saves per season while closers new to the role averaged 27.

BPV as a leading indicator *(Doug Dennis)*

Research has shown that base performance value (BPV) is an excellent indicator of long-term success as a closer. Here are 20-plus saves seasons, by year:

Year	No.	BPV 100+	75+	<75
1999	26	27%	54%	46%
2000	24	25%	54%	46%
2001	25	56%	80%	20%
2002	25	60%	72%	28%
2003	25	36%	64%	36%
2004	23	61%	61%	39%
2005	25	36%	64%	36%
2006	25	52%	72%	28%
2007	23	52%	74%	26%
MEAN	*25*	*45%*	*66%*	*34%*

Though 20-saves success with a 75+ BPV is only a 66% percentage play in any given year, the below-75 group is composed of closers who are rarely able to repeat the feat in the following season:

Year	No. with BPV < 75	No. who followed up 20+ saves <75 BPV
1999	12	2
2000	11	2
2001	5	2
2002	7	3
2003	9	3
2004	9	2
2005	9	1
2006	7	3
2007	6	0

Other Relievers

Projecting holds *(Doug Dennis)*

Here are some general rules of thumb for identifying pitchers who might be in line to accumulate holds. The percentages represent the portion of 2003's top holds leaders who fell into the category noted.

1. Left-handed set-up men with excellent BPIs. (43%)
2. A "go-to" right-handed set-up man with excellent BPIs. This is the one set-up RHer that a manager turns to with a small lead in the 7th or 8th innings. These pitchers also tend to vulture wins. (43%, but 6 of the top 9)
3. Excellent BPIs, but not a firm role as the main LHed or RHed set-up man. Roles change during the season; cream rises to the top. Relievers projected to post great BPIs often overtake lesser set-up men in-season. (14%)

Reliever efficiency percent (REff%)

(Wins + Saves + Holds) / (Wins + Losses + SaveOpps + Holds)

This is a measure of how often a reliever contributes positively to the outcome of a game. A record of consistent, positive impact on game outcomes breeds managerial confidence, and that confidence could pave the way to save opportunities. For those pitchers suddenly thrust into a closer's role, this formula helps gauge their potential to succeed based on past successes in similar roles. BENCHMARK: Minimum of 80%.

Vulture

A pitcher, typically a middle reliever, who accumulates an unusually high number of wins by preying on other pitchers' misfortunes. More accurately, this is a pitcher typically brought into a game after a starting pitcher has put his team behind, and then pitches well enough and long enough to allow his offense to take the lead, thereby "vulturing" a win from the starter.

In-Season Analysis

Pure Quality Starts

(This section is updated to reflect the new PQS scoring system we unveiled in 2016, as detailed on page 57. Note that the PQS figures in the pitcher boxes also reflect the new system.)

We've always approached performance measures on an aggregate basis. Each individual event that our statistics chronicle gets dumped into a huge pool of data. We then use our formulas to try to sort and slice and manipulate the data into more usable information.

Pure Quality Starts (PQS) take a different approach. It says that the smallest unit of measure should not be the "event" but instead be the "game." Within that game, we can accumulate all the strikeouts, hits and walks, and evaluate that outing as a whole. After all, when a pitcher takes the mound, he is either "on" or "off" his game; he is either dominant or struggling, or somewhere in between.

In PQS, we give a starting pitcher credit for exhibiting certain skills in each of his starts. Then by tracking his "PQS Score" over time, we can follow his progress. A starter earns one point for each of the following criteria:

1. *The pitcher must go more than 6 innings (record at least one out in the 7th). This measures stamina.*
2. *He must allow fewer hits than innings pitched. This measures hit prevention.*
3. *His number of strikeouts must equal to or more than 5. This measures dominance.*
4. *He must strike out at least three times as many batters as he walks (or have a minumum of three strikeouts if he hasn't walked a batter). This measures command.*
5. *He must not allow a home run. This measures his ability to keep the ball in the park.*

A perfect PQS score is 5. Any pitcher who averages 3 or more over the course of the season is probably performing admirably. The nice thing about PQS is it allows you to approach each start as more than an all-or-nothing event.

Note the absence of earned runs. No matter how many runs a pitcher allows, if he scores high on the PQS scale, he has hurled a good game in terms of his base skills. The number of runs allowed—a function of not only the pitcher's ability but that of his bullpen and defense—will tend to even out over time.

It doesn't matter if a few extra balls got through the infield, or the pitcher was given the hook in the fourth or sixth inning, or the bullpen was able to strand their inherited baserunners. When we look at performance in the aggregate, those events do matter, and will affect a pitcher's peripherals and ERA. But with PQS, the minutia is less relevant than the overall performance.

In the end, a dominating performance is a dominating performance, whether Clayton Kershaw is hurling a 4-hit shutout or giving up three runs while striking out 10 in 6 IP. And a disaster is still a disaster, whether Kyle Lohse gets a 5th inning hook after giving up 5 runs on 10 hits, or "takes one for the team" and gets shelled for 8 runs in 3.1 innings.

Skill versus consistency

Two pitchers have identical 4.50 ERAs and identical 3.0 PQS averages. Their PQS logs look like this:

```
PITCHER A:   3   3   3   3   3
PITCHER B:   5   0   5   0   5
```

Which pitcher would you rather have on your team? The risk-averse manager would choose Pitcher A as he represents the perfectly known commodity. Many fantasy leaguers might opt for Pitcher B because his occasional dominating starts show that there is an upside. His Achilles Heel is inconsistency—he is unable to sustain that high level. Is there any hope for Pitcher B?

- If a pitcher's inconsistency is characterized by more poor starts than good starts, his upside is limited.

- Pitchers with extreme inconsistency rarely get a full season of starts.
- However, inconsistency is neither chronic nor fatal.

The outlook for Pitcher A is actually worse. Disaster avoidance might buy these pitchers more starts, but history shows that the lack of dominating outings is more telling of future potential. In short, consistent mediocrity is bad.

PQS DOMination and DISaster rates *(Gene McCaffrey)*
DOM% is the percentage of a starting pitcher's outings that rate as a PQS-4 or PQS-5. DIS% is the percentage that rate as a PQS-0 or PQS-1.

DOM/DIS percentages open up a new perspective, providing us with two separate scales of performance. In tandem, they measure consistency.

Quality/consistency score (QC)
(DOM% – (2 x DIS%)) x 2
Using PQS and DOM/DIS percentages, this score measures both the quality of performance as well as start-to-start consistency.

PQS correlation with Quality Starts *(Paul Petera)*

PQS	QS%
0	8%
1	18%
2	38%
3	63%
4	87%
5	99%

In-season ERA/xERA variance as a leading indicator
(Matt Cederholm)
Pitchers with large first-half ERA/xERA variances will see regression towards their xERA in the second half, if they are allowed (and are able) to finish out the season. Starters have a stronger regression tendency than relievers, which we would expect to see given the larger sample size. In addition, there is substantial attrition among all types of pitchers, but those who are "unlucky" have a much higher rate.

An important corollary: While a pitcher underperforming his xERA is very likely to rebound in the second half, such regression hinges on his ability to hold onto his job long enough to see that regression come to fruition. Healthy veteran pitchers with an established role are more likely to experience the second half boost than a rookie starter trying to make his mark.

Pure Quality Relief *(Patrick Davitt)*
A system for evaluating reliever outings. The scoring :

1. Two points for the first out, and one point for each subsequent out, to a maximum of four points.
2. One point for having at least one strikeout for every four full outs (one K for 1-4 outs, two Ks for 5-8 outs, etc.).
3. One point for zero baserunners, minus one point for each baserunner, though allowing the pitcher one unpenalized runner for each three full outs (one baserunner for 3-5 outs, two for 6-8 outs, three for nine outs)

4. Minus one point for each earned run, though allowing one ER for 8– or 9-out appearances.
5. An automatic PQR-0 for allowing a home run.

Avoiding relief disasters *(Ed DeCaria)*
Relief disasters (defined as ER>=3 and IP<=3), occur in 5%+ of all appearances. The chance of a disaster exceeds 13% in any 7-day period. To minimize the odds of a disaster, we created a model that produced the following list of factors, in order of influence:

1. Strength of opposing offense
2. Park factor of home stadium
3. BB/9 over latest 31 days (more walks is bad)
4. Pitch count over previous 7 days (more pitches is bad)
5. Latest 31 Days ERA>xERA (recent bad luck continues)

Daily league owners who can slot relievers by individual game should also pay attention to days of rest: pitching on less rest than one is accustomed to increases disaster risk.

Sample size reliability *(Russell Carleton)*
At what point during the season do statistics become reliable indicators of skill? Measured in batters faced:

60: K/PA
120: BB/PA

Measured in balls in play:

50: hr/f
80: GB%, FB%
600: LD%
820: h% (or BABIP)

Unlisted stats did not stabilize over a full season of play. *(Note that 150 BF is roughly equivalent to six outings for a starting pitcher; 550 BF would be 22 starts, etc.)*

April ERA as a leading indicator *(Stephen Nickrand)*
A starting pitcher's April ERA can act as a leading indicator for how his ERA is likely to fare during the balance of the season. A study looked at extreme April ERA results to see what kind of in-season forecasting power they may have. From 2010-2012, 42 SP posted an ERA in April that was at least 2.00 ER better than their career ERA. The findings:

- Pitchers who come out of the gates quickly have an excellent chance at finishing the season with an ERA much better than their career ERA.
- While April ERA gems see their in-season ERA regresses towards their career ERA, their May-Sept ERA is still significantly better than their career ERA.
- Those who stumble out of the gates have a strong chance at posting an ERA worse than their career average, but their in-season ERA improves towards their career ERA.
- April ERA disasters tend to have a May-Sept ERA that closely resembles their career ERA.

Second-half ERA reduction drivers *(Stephen Nickrand)*
It's easy to dismiss first-half-to-second-half improvement among starting pitchers as an unpredictable event. After all, the midpoint

of the season is an arbitrary cutoff. Performance swings occur throughout the season.

A study of SP who experienced significant 1H-2H ERA improvement from 2010-2012 examined what indicators drove second-half ERA improvement. Among the findings for those 79 SP with a > 1.00 ERA 1H-2H reduction:

- 97% saw their WHIP decrease, with an average decrease of 0.26
- 97% saw their strand (S%) rate improve, with an average increase of 9%
- 87% saw their BABIP (H%) improve, with an average reduction of 5%
- 75% saw their control (bb/9) rate improve, with an average reduction of 0.8
- 70% saw their HR/9 rate improve, with an average decrease of 0.5
- 68% saw their swinging strike (SwK%) rate improve, with an average increase of 1.4%
- 68% saw their BPV improve, with an average increase of 37
- 67% saw their HR per fly ball rate (hr/f) improve, with an average decrease of 4%
- 53% saw their ground ball (GB%) rate improve, with an average increase of 5%
- 52% saw their dominance (k/9) rate improve, with an average increase of 1.3

These findings highlight the power of H% and S% regression as it relates to ERA and WHIP improvement. In fact, H% and S% are more often correlated with ERA improvement than are improved skills. They also suggest that improved control has a bigger impact on ERA reduction than does increased strikeouts.

Pitcher home/road splits *(Stephen Nickrand)*

One overlooked strategy in leagues that allow frequent transactions is to bench pitchers when they are on the road. Research reveals that several pitching stats and indicators are significantly and consistently worse on the road than at home.

Some home/road rules of thumb for SP:

- If you want to gain significant ground in ERA and WHIP, keep all your average or worse SP benched on the road.
- A pitcher's win percentage drops by 15% when on the road, so don't bank on road starts as a means to catch up in wins.
- Control erodes by 10% on the road, so be especially careful with keeping wild SP in your active lineups when they are away from home.
- NL pitchers at home produce significantly more strikeouts than their AL counterparts and vs. all pitchers on the road.
- hr/9, groundball rate, hit rate, strand rate, and hr/f do not show significant home vs. road variances.

Other Diamonds

The Pitching Postulates

1. Never sign a soft-tosser to a long-term contract.
2. Right-brain dominance has a very long shelf life.

3. A fly ball pitcher who gives up many HRs is expected. A GB pitcher who gives up many HRs is making mistakes.
4. Never draft a contact fly ball pitcher who plays in a hitter's park.
5. Only bad teams ever have a need for an inning-eater.
6. Never chase wins.

Dontrelle Willis List

Pitchers with peripherals so incredibly horrible that you have to wonder how they can possibly draw a major league paycheck year after year.

Chaconian

Having the ability to post many saves despite sub-Mendoza peripherals and an ERA in the stratosphere.

ERA Benchmark

A half run of ERA over 200 innings comes out to just one earned run every four starts.

Gopheritis (also, Acute Gopheritis and Chronic Gopheritis)

The dreaded malady in which a pitcher is unable to keep the ball in the park. Pitchers with gopheritis have a FB rate of at least 40%. More severe cases have a FB% over 45%.

The Knuckleballers Rule

Knuckleballers don't follow no stinkin' rules.

Brad Lidge Lament

When a closer posts a 62% strand rate, he has nobody to blame but himself.

LOOGY (Lefty One Out GuY)

A left-handed reliever whose job it is to get one out in important situations.

Vin Mazzaro Vindication

Occasional nightmares (2.1 innings, 14 ER) are just a part of the game.

Meltdown

Any game in which a starting pitcher allows more runs than innings pitched.

The Five Saves Certainties

1. On every team, there will be save opportunities and someone will get them. At a bare minimum, there will be at least 30 saves to go around, and not unlikely more than 45.
2. Any pitcher could end up being the chief beneficiary. Bullpen management is a fickle endeavor.
3. Relief pitchers are often the ones that require the most time at the start of the season to find a groove. The weather is cold, the schedule is sparse and their usage is erratic.
4. Despite the talk about "bullpens by committee," managers prefer a go-to guy. It makes their job easier.
5. As many as 50% of the saves in any year will come from pitchers who are unselected at the end of Draft Day.

Soft-tosser

A pitcher with a strikeout rate of 5.5 or less.

Soft-tosser land

The place where feebler arms leave their fortunes in the hands of the defense, variable hit and strand rates, and park dimensions. It's a place where many live, but few survive.

Prospects

General

Minor league prospecting in perspective

In our perpetual quest to be the genius who uncovers the next Mike Trout when he's still in high school, there is an obsessive fascination with minor league prospects. That's not to say that prospecting is not important. The issue is perspective:

1. During the 10 year period of 1996 to 2005, only 8% of players selected in the first round of the Major League Baseball First Year Player Draft went on to become stars.

2. Some prospects are going to hit the ground running (Carlos Correa) and some are going to immediately struggle (Daniel Norris), no matter what level of hype follows them.

3. Some prospects are going to start fast (since the league is unfamiliar with them) and then fade (as the league figures them out). Others will start slow (since they are unfamiliar with the opposition) and then improve (as they adjust to the competition). So if you make your free agent and roster decisions based on small early samples sizes, you are just as likely to be an idiot as a genius.

4. How any individual player will perform relative to his talent is largely unknown because there is a psychological element that is vastly unexplored. Some make the transition to the majors seamlessly, some not, completely regardless of how talented they are.

5. Still, talent is the best predictor of future success, so major league equivalent base performance indicators still have a valuable role in the process. As do scouting reports, carefully filtered.

6. Follow the player's path to the majors. Did he have to repeat certain levels? Was he allowed to stay at a level long enough to learn how to adjust to the level of competition? A player with only two great months at Double-A is a good bet to struggle if promoted directly to the majors because he was never fully tested at Double-A, let alone Triple-A.

7. Younger players holding their own against older competition is a good thing. Older players reaching their physical peak, regardless of their current address, can be a good thing too. The Adam Duvalls and Seung-Hwan Ohs can have some very profitable years.

8. Remember team context. A prospect with superior potential often will not unseat a steady but unspectacular incumbent, especially one with a large contract.

9. Don't try to anticipate how a team is going to manage their talent, both at the major and minor league level. You might think it's time to promote Manuel Margot and give him an everyday role. You are not running the Padres.

10. Those who play in shallow, one-year leagues should have little cause to be looking at the minors at all. The risk versus reward is so skewed against you, and there is so much talent available with a track record, that taking a chance on an unproven commodity makes little sense.

11. Decide where your priorities really are. If your goal is to win, prospect analysis is just a *part* of the process, not the entire process.

Factors affecting minor league stats *(Terry Linhart)*

1. Often, there is an exaggerated emphasis on short-term performance in an environment that is supposed to focus on the long-term. Two poor outings don't mean a 21-year-old pitcher is washed up.

2. Ballpark dimensions and altitude create hitters parks and pitchers parks, but a factor rarely mentioned is that many parks in the lower minors are inconsistent in their field quality. Minor league clubs have limited resources to maintain field conditions, and this can artificially depress defensive statistics while inflating stats like batting average.

3. Some players' skills are so superior to the competition at their level that you can't get a true picture of what they're going to do from their stats alone.

4. Many pitchers are told to work on secondary pitches in unorthodox situations just to gain confidence in the pitch. The result is an artificially increased number of walks.

5. The #3, #4, and #5 pitchers in the lower minors are truly longshots to make the majors. They often possess only two pitches and are unable to disguise the off-speed offerings. Hitters can see inflated statistics in these leagues.

Minor league level versus age

When evaluating minor leaguers, look at the age of the prospect in relation to the median age of the league he is in:

Low level A	Between 19-20
Upper level A	Around 20
Double-A	21
Triple-A	22

These are the ideal ages for prospects at the particular level. If a prospect is younger than most and holds his own against older and more experienced players, elevate his status. If he is older than the median, reduce his status.

Triple-A experience as a leading indicator

The probability that a minor leaguer will immediately succeed in the majors can vary depending upon the level of Triple-A experience he has amassed at the time of call-up.

	BATTERS		PITCHERS	
	< 1 Yr	Full	<1 Yr	Full
Performed well	57%	56%	16%	56%
Performed poorly	21%	38%	77%	33%
2nd half drop-off	21%	7%	6%	10%

The odds of a batter achieving immediate MLB success was slightly more than 50-50. More than 80% of all pitchers promoted with less than a full year at Triple-A struggled in their first year in the majors. Those pitchers with a year in Triple-A succeeded at a level equal to that of batters.

Major League Equivalency (MLE) *(Bill James)*

A formula that converts a player's minor or foreign league statistics into a comparable performance in the major leagues. These are not projections, but conversions of current performance. MLEs contain adjustments for the level of play in individual leagues and teams. They work best with Triple-A stats, not quite as well with Double-A stats, and hardly at all with the lower levels. Foreign conversions are still a work in process. James' original formula only addressed batting. Our research has devised conversion formulas for pitchers, however, their best use comes when looking at peripherals, not traditional stats.

Adjusting to the competition

All players must "adjust to the competition" at every level of professional play. Players often get off to fast or slow starts. During their second tour at that level is when we get to see whether the slow starters have caught up or whether the league has figured out the fast starters. That second half "adjustment" period is a good baseline for projecting the subsequent season, in the majors or minors.

Premature major league call-ups often negate the ability for us to accurately evaluate a player due to the lack of this adjustment period. For instance, a hotshot Double-A player might open the season in Triple-A. After putting up solid numbers for a month, he gets a call to the bigs, and struggles. The fact is, we do not have enough evidence that the player has mastered the Triple-A level. We don't know whether the rest of the league would have caught up to him during his second tour of the league. But now he's labeled as an underperformer in the bigs when in fact he has never truly proven his skills at the lower levels.

Bull Durham prospects

There is some potential talent in older players—age 26, 27 or higher—who, for many reasons (untimely injury, circumstance, bad luck, etc.), don't reach the majors until they have already been downgraded from prospect to suspect. Equating potential with age is an economic reality for major league clubs, but not necessarily a skills reality.

Skills growth and decline is universal, whether it occurs at the major league level or in the minors. So a high-skills journeyman in Triple-A is just as likely to peak at age 27 as a major leaguer of the same age. The question becomes one of opportunity—will the parent club see fit to reap the benefits of that peak performance?

Prospecting these players for your fantasy team is, admittedly, a high risk endeavor, though there are some criteria you can use. Look for a player who is/has:

- Optimally, age 27-28 for overall peak skills, age 30-31 for power skills, or age 28-31 for pitchers.
- At least two seasons of experience at Triple-A. Career Double-A players are generally not good picks.
- Solid base skills levels.
- Shallow organizational depth at their position.
- Notable winter league or spring training performance.

Players who meet these conditions are not typically draftable players, but worthwhile reserve or FAAB picks.

Batters

MLE PX as a leading indicator *(Bill Macey)*

Looking at minor league performance (as MLE) in one year and the corresponding MLB performance the subsequent year:

	Year 1 MLE	Year 2 MLB
Observations	496	496
Median PX	95	96
Percent PX > 100	43%	46%

In addition, 53% of the players had a MLB PX in year 2 that exceeded their MLE PX in year 1. A slight bias towards improved performance in year 2 is consistent with general career trajectories.

Year 1 MLE PX	Year 2 MLB PX	Pct. Incr	Pct. MLB PX > 100
<= 50	61	70.3%	5.4%
51-75	85	69.6%	29.4%
76-100	93	55.2%	39.9%
101-125	111	47.4%	62.0%
126-150	119	32.1%	66.1%
> 150	142	28.6%	76.2%

Slicing the numbers by performance level, there is a good amount of regression to the mean.

Players rarely suddenly develop power at the MLB level if they didn't previously display that skill at the minor league level. However, the relatively large gap between the median MLE PX and MLB PX for these players, 125 to 110, confirms the notion that the best players continue to improve once they reach the major leagues.

MLE contact rate as a leading indicator *(Bill Macey)*

There is a strong positive correlation (0.63) between a player's MLE ct% in Year 1 and his actual ct% at the MLB level in Year 2.

MLE ct%	Year 1 MLE ct%	Year 2 MLB ct%
< 70%	69%	68%
70% - 74%	73%	72%
75% - 79%	77%	75%
80% - 84%	82%	77%
85% - 89%	87%	82%
90% +	91%	86%
TOTAL	**84%**	**79%**

There is very little difference between the median MLE BA in Year 1 and the median MLB BA in Year 2:

MLE ct%	Year 1 MLE BA	Year 2 MLB BA
< 70%	.230	.270
70% - 74%	.257	.248
75% - 79%	.248	.255
80% - 84%	.257	.255
85% - 89%	.266	.270
90% +	.282	.273
TOTAL	.261	.262

Excluding the <70% cohort (which was a tiny sample size), there is a positive relationship between MLE ct% and MLB BA.

Pitchers

Skills metrics as a leading indicator for pitching success

The percentage of hurlers that were good investments in the year that they were called up varied by the level of their historical minor league peripherals prior to that year.

Pitchers who had:	Fared well	Fared poorly
Good indicators	79%	21%
Marginal or poor indicators	18%	82%

The data used here were MLE levels from the previous two years, not the season in which they were called up. The significance? Solid current performance is what merits a call-up, but this is not a good indicator of short-term MLB success, because a) the performance data set is too small, typically just a few month's worth of statistics, and b) for those putting up good numbers at a new minor league level, there has typically not been enough time for the scouting reports to make their rounds.

Japanese Baseball *(Tom Mulhall)*

Comparing MLB and Japanese Baseball

The Japanese major leagues are generally considered to be equivalent to Triple-A ball and the pitching is thought to be even better. However, statistics are difficult to convert due to differences in the way the game is played in Japan.

1. While strong on fundamentals, Japanese baseball's guiding philosophy is risk avoidance. Mistakes are not tolerated. Runners rarely take extra bases, batters focus on making contact rather than driving the ball, and managers play for one run at a time. Bunts are more common. As a result, offenses score fewer runs per number of hits, and pitching stats tend to look better than the talent behind them.

2. Stadiums in Japan usually have much shorter fences. This should mean more HRs, but given #1 above, it is the American players who make up the majority of Japan's power elite. No power hitters have made an equivalent transition to the MLB.

3. There are more artificial turf fields, which increases the number of ground ball singles. Only a small number of stadiums have infield grass and a few still use all dirt infields.

4. The quality of umpiring is questionable and even inept. Fewer errors are called, reflecting the cultural philosophy of low tolerance for mistakes and the desire to avoid publicly embarrassing a player. Moreover, umpires are routinely intimidated, even physically.

5. Teams have smaller pitching staffs and use a six-man rotation. Starters usually pitch once a week, typically on the same day since Monday is an off-day for the entire league. Many starters will also occasionally pitch in relief between starts. Moreover, managers push for complete games, no matter what the score or situation. Because of the style of offense, higher pitch counts are common. Despite superior conditioning, Japanese pitchers tend to burn out early due to overuse.

6. The ball is smaller and lighter, and the strike zone is closer to the batter. A new ball was introduced in 2011 with lower-elasticity rubber surrounding the cork, which limited offense and inflated pitching stats. A more hitter-friendly ball was used in 2013 and home runs increased. But continue to exercise some skepticism when analyzing pitching stats and look for possible signs of optimism in hitting stats other than the power categories.

7. Tie games are allowed. If the score remains even after 12 innings, the game goes into the books as a tie.

8. There are 18 fewer games in the Japanese schedule.

Japanese players as fantasy farm selections

When evaluating the potential of Japanese League prospects, the key is not to just identify the best Japanese players—the key is to identify impact players who have the desire and opportunity to sign with a MLB team. With the success of Yu Darvish and Masahiro Tanaka, it is easy to overestimate the value of drafting these players. But since 1995, less than four dozen Japanese players have made a big league roster, and about half of them were middle relievers. Still, for owners who are allowed to carry a large reserve or farm team at reduced salaries, these players could be a real windfall, especially if your competitors do not do their homework.

A list of Japanese League players who could jump to the majors appears in the Prospects section.

Other Diamonds

A-Rod 10-Step Path to Stardom

Not all well-hyped prospects hit the ground running. More often they follow an alternative path:

1. Prospect puts up phenomenal minor league numbers.
2. The media machine gets oiled up.
3. Prospect gets called up, but struggles, Year 1.
4. Prospect gets demoted.
5. Prospect tears it up in the minors, Year 2.
6. Prospect gets called up, but struggles, Year 2.
7. Prospect gets demoted.
8. The media turns their backs. Fantasy leaguers reduce their expectations.
9. Prospect tears it up in the minors, Year 3. The public shrugs its collective shoulders.
10. Prospect is promoted in Year 3 and explodes. Some lucky fantasy leaguer lands a franchise player for under $5.

Some players that are currently stuck at one of the interim steps, and may or may not ever reach Step 10, include Jesus Montero, Jonathan Singleton and Dalton Pompey.

Rule 5 Reminder

Don't ignore the Rule 5 draft lest you ignore the possibility of players like Jose Bautista, Josh Hamilton, Johan Santana, Joakim Soria, Dan Uggla, Shane Victorino and Jayson Werth. All were Rule 5 draftees.

Trout Inflation

The tendency for rookies to go for exorbitant draft prices following a year when there was a very good rookie crop.

Gaming

Standard Rules and Variations

Rotisserie Baseball was invented as an elegant confluence of baseball and economics. Whether by design or accident, the result has lasted for more than three decades. But what would Rotisserie and fantasy have been like if the Founding Fathers knew then what we know now about statistical analysis and game design? You can be sure things would be different.

The world has changed since the original game was introduced yet many leagues use the same rules today. New technologies have opened up opportunities to improve elements of the game that might have been limited by the capabilities of the 1980s. New analytical approaches have revealed areas where the original game falls short.

As such, there are good reasons to tinker and experiment; to find ways to enhance the experience.

Following are the basic elements of fantasy competition, those that provide opportunities for alternative rules and experimentation. This is by no means an exhaustive list, but at minimum provides some interesting food-for-thought.

Player pool

Standard: American League-only, National League-only or Mixed League.

AL/NL-only typically drafts 8-12 teams (pool penetration of 49% to 74%). Mixed leagues draft 10-18 teams (31% to 55% penetration), though 15 teams (46%) is a common number.

Drafting of reserve players will increase the penetration percentages. A 12-team AL/NL-only league adding six reserves onto 23-man rosters would draft 93% of the available pool of players on all teams' 25-man rosters.

The draft penetration level determines which fantasy management skills are most important to your league. The higher the penetration, the more important it is to draft a good team. The lower the penetration, the greater the availability of free agents and the more important in-season roster management becomes.

There is no generally-accepted optimal penetration level, but we have often suggested that 75% (including reserves) provides a good balance between the skills required for both draft prep and in-season management.

Alternative pools: There is a wide variety of options here. Certain leagues draft from within a small group of major league divisions or teams. Some competitions, like home run leagues, only draft batters.

Bottom-tier pool: Drafting from the entire major league population, the only players available are those who posted a Rotisserie dollar value of $5 or less in the previous season. Intended as a test of an owner's ability to identify talent with upside. Best used as a pick-a-player contest with any number of teams participating.

Positional structure

Standard: 23 players. One at each defensive position (though three outfielders may be from any of LF, CF or RF), plus one additional catcher, one middle infielder (2B or SS), one corner infielder (1B or 3B), two additional outfielders and a utility player/designated hitter (which often can be a batter who qualifies anywhere). Nine pitchers, typically holding any starting or relief role.

Open: 25 players. One at each defensive position (plus DH), 5-man starting rotation and two relief pitchers. Nine additional players at any position, which may be a part of the active roster or constitute a reserve list.

40-man: Standard 23 plus 17 reserves. Used in many keeper and dynasty leagues.

Reapportioned: In recent years, new obstacles are being faced by 12-team AL/NL-only leagues thanks to changes in the real game. The 14/9 split between batters and pitchers no longer reflects how MLB teams structure their rosters. Of the 30 teams, each with 25-man rosters, not one contains 14 batters for any length of time. In fact, many spend a good part of the season with only 12 batters, which means teams often have more pitchers than hitters.

For fantasy purposes in AL/NL-only leagues, that leaves a disproportionate draft penetration into the batter and pitcher pools:

	BATTERS	PITCHERS
On all MLB rosters	195	180
Players drafted	168	108
Pct.	86%	60%

These drafts are depleting 26% more batters out of the pool than pitchers. Add in those leagues with reserve lists—perhaps an additional six players per team removing another 72 players—and post-draft free agent pools are very thin, especially on the batting side.

The impact is less in 15-team mixed leagues, though the FA pitching pool is still disproportionately deep.

	BATTERS	PITCHERS
On all rosters	381	369
Drafted	210	135
Pct.	55%	37%

One solution is to reapportion the number of batters and pitchers that are rostered. Adding one pitcher slot and eliminating one batter slot may be enough to provide better balance. The batting slot most often removed is the second catcher, since it is the position with the least depth.

Beginning in the 2012 season, the Tout Wars AL/NL-only experts leagues opted to eliminate one of the outfield slots and replace it with a "swingman" position. This position could be any batter or pitcher, depending upon the owner's needs at any given time during the season.

Selecting players

Standard: The three most prevalent methods for stocking fantasy rosters are:

Snake/Straight/Serpentine draft: Players are selected in order with seeds reversed in alternating rounds. This method has become the most popular due to its speed, ease of implementation and ease of automation.

In these drafts, the underlying assumption is that value can be ranked relative to a linear baseline. Pick #1 is better than pick #2, which is better than pick #3, and the difference between each pick is assumed to be somewhat equivalent. While a faulty assumption, we must believe in it to assume a level playing field.

Auction: Players are sold to the highest bidder from a fixed budget, typically $260. Auctions provide the team owner with more control over which players will be on his team, but can take twice as long as snake drafts.

The baseline is $0 at the beginning of each player put up for bid. The final purchase price for each player is shaped by many wildly variable factors, from roster need to geographic location of the draft. A $30 player can mean different things to different drafters.

One option that can help reduce the time commitment of auctions is to force minimum bids at each hour mark. You could mandate $15 openers in hour #1; $10 openers in hour #2, etc.

Pick-a-player / Salary cap: Players are assigned fixed dollar values and owners assemble their roster within a fixed cap. This type of roster-stocking is an individual exercise which results in teams typically having some of the same players.

In these leagues, the "value" decision is taken out of the hands of the owners. Each player has a fixed value, pre-assigned based on past season performance and/or future expectation.

Hybrid snake-auction: Each draft begins as an auction. Each team has to fill its first seven roster slots from a budget of $154. Opening bid for any player is $15. After each team has filled seven slots, it becomes a snake draft.

This method is intended to reduce draft time while still providing an economic component for selecting players.

Stat categories

Standard: The standard statistical categories for Rotisserie leagues are:

4x4: HR, RBI, SB, BA, W, Sv, ERA, WHIP

5x5: HR, R, RBI, SB, BA, W, Sv, K, ERA, WHIP

6x6: Categories typically added are Holds and OPS.

7x7, etc.: Any number of categories may be added.

In general, the more categories you add, the more complicated it is to isolate individual performance and manage the categorical impact on your roster. There is also the danger of redundancy; with multiple categories measuring like stats, certain skills can get over-valued. For instance, home runs are double-counted when using the categories of both HR and slugging average. (Though note that HRs are actually already triple-counted in standard 5x5—HRs, runs, and RBIs)

If the goal is to have categories that create a more encompassing picture of player performance, it is actually possible to accomplish more with less:

Modified 4x4: HR, (R+RBI-HR), SB, OBA, (W+QS), (Sv+Hld), K, ERA

This provides a better balance between batting and pitching in that each has three counting categories and one ratio category. In fact, the balance is shown to be even more notable here:

	BATTING	PITCHING
Pure skill counting stat	HR	K
Ratio category	OBA	ERA
Dependent upon managerial decision	SB	(Sv+Hold)
Dependent upon team support	(R+RBI-HR)	(W+QS)

Replacing saves: The problem with the Saves statistic is that we have a scarce commodity that is centered on a small group of players, thereby creating inflated demand for those players. With the rising failure rate for closers these days, the incentive to pay full value for the commodity decreases. The higher the risk, the lower the prices.

We can increase the value of the commodity by reducing the risk. We might do this by increasing the number of players that contribute to that category, thereby spreading the risk around. One way we can accomplish this is by changing the category to Saves + Holds.

Holds are not perfect, but the typical argument about them being random and arbitrary can apply to saves these days as well. In fact, many of the pitchers who record holds are far more skilled and valuable than closers; they are often called to the mound in much higher leverage situations (a fact backed up by a scan of each pitcher's Leverage Index).

Neither stat is perfect, but together they form a reasonable proxy for overall bullpen performance.

In tandem, they effectively double the player pool of draftable relievers while also flattening the values allotted to those pitchers. The more players around which we spread the risk, the more control we have in managing our pitching staffs.

Replacing wins: Using reasons similar to replacing Saves with Saves + Holds, some have argued for replacing the Wins statistic with W + QS (quality starts). This method of scoring gives value to a starting pitcher who pitches well, but fails to receive the win due to his team's poor offense or poor luck.

Keeping score

Standard: These are the most common scoring methods:

Rotisserie: Players are evaluated in several statistical categories. Totals of these statistics are ranked by team. The winner is the team with the highest cumulative ranking.

Points: Players receive points for events that they contribute to in each game. Points are totaled for each team and teams are then ranked.

Head-to-Head (H2H): Using Rotisserie or points scoring, teams are scheduled in daily or weekly matchups. The winner of each matchup is the team that finishes higher in more categories (Rotisserie) or scores the most points.

Hybrid H2H-Rotisserie: Rotisserie's category ranking system can be converted into a weekly won-loss record. Depending upon where your team finishes for that week's statistics determines how many games you win for that week. Each week, your team will play seven games.

*Place	Record	*Place	Record
1st	7-0	7th	3-4
2nd	6-1	8th	2-5
3rd	6-1	9th	2-5
4th	5-2	10th	1-6
5th	5-2	11th	1-6
6th	4-3	12th	0-7

* Based on overall Rotisserie category ranking for the week.

At the end of each week, all the statistics revert to zero and you start over. You never dig a hole in any category that you can't climb out of, because all categories themselves are incidental to the standings.

The regular season lasts for 23 weeks, which equals 161 games. Weeks 24, 25 and 26 are for play-offs.

Free agent acquisition

Standard: Three methods are the most common for acquiring free agent players during the season.

First come first served: Free agents are awarded to the first owner who claims them.

Reverse order of standings: Access to the free agent pool is typically in a snake draft fashion with the last place team getting the first pick, and each successive team higher in the standings picking afterwards.

Free agent acquisition budget (FAAB): Teams are given a set budget at the beginning of the season (typically $100 or $1000) from which they bid on free agents in a closed auction process.

Vickrey FAAB: Research has shown that more than 50% of FAAB dollars are lost via overbid on an annual basis. Given that this is a scarce commodity, one would think that a system to better manage these dollars might be desirable. The Vickrey system conducts a closed auction in the same way as standard FAAB, but the price of the winning bid is set at the amount of the second highest bid, plus $1. In some cases, gross overbids (at least $10 over) are reduced to the second highest bid plus $5.

This method was designed by William Vickrey, a Professor of Economics at Columbia University. His theory was that this process reveals the true value of the commodity. For his work, Vickrey was awarded the Nobel Prize for Economics (and $1.2 million) in 1996.

Double-Bid FAAB: One of the inherent difficulties in the current FAAB system is that we have so many options for setting a bid amount. You can bid $47, or $51, or $23. You might agonize over whether to go $38 or $39. With a $100 budget, there are 100 decision points. And while you may come up with a rough guesstimate of the range in which your opponents might bid, the results for any individual player bidding are typically random within that range.

The first part of this process reduces the number of decision points. Owners must categorize their interest by bidding a fixed number of pre-set dollar amounts for each player. In a $100 FAAB league, for instance, those levels might be $1, $5, $10, $15, $20, $30, $40 or $50. All owners would set the general market value for free agents in these eight levels of interest. (This system sets a $50 maximum, but that is not absolutely necessary.)

The initial stage of the bidding process serves to screen out those who are not interested in a player at the appropriate market level. That leaves a high potential for tied owners, those who share the same level of interest.

The tied owners must then submit a second bid of equal or greater value than their first bid. These bids can be in $1 increments. The winning owner gets the player; if there is still a tie, then the player would go to the owner lower in the standings.

An advantage of this second bid is that it gives owners an opportunity to see who they are going up against, and adjust. If you are bidding against an owner close to you in the standings,

you may need to be more aggressive in that second bid. If you see that the tied owner(s) wouldn't hurt you by acquiring that player, then maybe you resubmit the original bid and be content to potentially lose out on the player. If you're ahead in the standings, it's actually a way to potentially opt out on that player completely by resubmitting your original bid and forcing another owner to spend his FAAB.

Some leagues will balk at adding another layer to the weekly deadline process; it's a trade-off to having more control over managing your FAAB.

The season

Standard: Leagues are played out during the course of the entire Major League Baseball season.

Split-season: Leagues are conducted from Opening Day through the All-Star break, then re-drafted to play from the All-Star break through the end of the season.

50-game split-season: Leagues are divided into three 50-game seasons with one-week break in between.

Monthly: Leagues are divided into six seasons or rolling four-week seasons.

The advantages of these shorter time frames:

- Shorter time frames can help to maintain interest. There would be fewer abandoned teams.
- There would be more shots at a title each year.
- Given that drafting is considered the most fun aspect of the game, these splits multiply the opportunities to participate in some type of draft. Leagues may choose to do complete re-drafts and treat the year as distinct mini-seasons. Or, leagues might allow teams to drop their five worst players and conduct a restocking draft at each break.

Daily games: Participants select a roster of players from one day's MLB schedule. Scoring is based on an aggregate points-based system rather than categories, with cash prizes awarded based on the day's results. The structure and distribution of that prize pool varies across different types of events, and those differences can affect roster construction strategies. Although scoring and prizes are based on one day's play, the season-long element of bankroll management provides a proxy for overall standings.

In terms of projecting outcomes, daily games are drastically different than full-season leagues. Playing time is one key element of any projection, and daily games offer near-100% accuracy in projecting playing time: you can check pre-game lineups to see exactly which players are in the lineup that night. The other key component of any projection is performance, but that is plagued by variance in daily competitions. Even if you roster a team full of the most advantageous matchups (for instance, Mike Trout facing Franklin Morales at Coors Field), Trout will sometimes go 0-for-4 on that one night.

Single game (Quint-Inning): A game that drafts from the active rosters of two major league teams in a single game. The rules:

1. Start with five owners.

2. Prior to first pitch, conduct a simple snake draft where each owner selects five players. If you're ambitious, auction off the 25 players giving each owner a budget of $50 of real or fake money.

3. Scoring is simple. For batters, singles, walks, hit-by-pitches and stolen bases are one point each. Doubles are 2 points. Triples are 3 points. Home runs are 4 points. Pitchers get one point for each complete inning pitched but lose one point for every run they allow.

4. At the beginning of the 5th inning, each owner has the option of doubling any future points for one player on his roster. We call that player the Quint. Points for all batters are doubled beginning in the 9th inning. That means the Quint's points would be quadrupled.

5. At the end of each inning, you can cut players, claim players from the free agent pool or trade players. You must maintain five players at all times, so all adds, drops and trades must keep your roster square. Free agent claims are done in reverse order of the standings. If two teams are tied and both want the same player, it can be helpful to have a deck of cards handy - the owner who draws high card would get the player.

6. Quint-Inning is a betting game (which makes it technically illegal). Owners need to ante up to play, typically $5, though if you're using a $50 auction budget, that works fine. It then costs $1 per inning to stay in the game for the second through fourth innings. Beginning in the 5th inning, the stakes increase to $2 per inning to stay in the game. You can use higher or lower stakes if you prefer.

7. Owners can fold at any time, forfeiting any monies they contributed to the pot. Their players are released into the free agent pool and are available to the remaining owners in reverse order of the standings.

8. The owner with the most points at the end of the game wins the pot.

Post-season league: Some leagues re-draft teams from among the MLB post-season contenders and play out a separate competition. It is possible, however, to make a post-season competition that is an extension of the regular season.

Start by designating a set number of regular season finishers as qualifying for the post-season. The top four teams in a league is a good number.

These four teams would designate a fixed 23-man roster for all post-season games. First, they would freeze all of their currently-owned players who are on MLB post-season teams.

In order to fill the roster holes that will likely exist, these four teams would then pick players from their league's non-playoff teams (for the sake of the post-season only). This would be in the form of a snake draft done on the day following the end of the regular season. Draft order would be regular season finish, so the play-off team with the most regular season points would get first pick. Picks would continue until all four rosters are filled with 23 men.

Regular scoring would be used for all games during October. The team with the best play-off stats at the end of the World Series is the overall champ.

Snake Drafting

Snake draft first round history

The following tables record the comparison between pre-season projected player rankings (using Average Draft Position data from Mock Draft Central and National Fantasy Baseball

Championship) and actual end-of-season results. The 13-year success rate of identifying each season's top talent is only 35%. This had been a declining trend over the past few years until 2016, when the ADPs posted their best success rate since 2008.

2009	ADP		ACTUAL = 5
1	Hanley Ramirez	1	Albert Pujols (2)
2	Albert Pujols	2	Hanley Ramirez (1)
3	Jose Reyes	3	Tim Lincecum
4	David Wright	4	Dan Haren
5	Grady Sizemore	5	Carl Crawford
6	Miguel Cabrera	6	Matt Kemp
7	Ryan Braun	7	Joe Mauer
8	Jimmy Rollins	8	Derek Jeter
9	Ian Kinsler	9	Zach Greinke
10	Josh Hamilton	10	Ryan Braun (7)
11	Ryan Howard	11	Jacoby Ellsbury
12	Mark Teixeira	12	Mark Reynolds
13	Alex Rodriguez	13	Prince Fielder
14	Matt Holliday	14	Chase Utley (15)
15	Chase Utley	15	Miguel Cabrera (6)

2010	ADP		ACTUAL = 5
1	Albert Pujols	1	Carlos Gonzalez
2	Hanley Ramirez	2	Albert Pujols (1)
3	Alex Rodriguez	3	Joey Votto
4	Chase Utley	4	Roy Halladay
5	Ryan Braun	5	Carl Crawford (15)
6	Mark Teixeira	6	Miguel Cabrera (9)
7	Matt Kemp	7	Josh Hamilton
8	Prince Fielder	8	Adam Wainwright
9	Miguel Cabrera	9	Felix Hernandez
10	Ryan Howard	10	Robinson Cano
11	Evan Longoria	11	Jose Bautista
12	Tom Lincecum	12	Paul Konerko
13	Joe Mauer	13	Matt Holliday
14	David Wright	14	Ryan Braun (5)
15	Carl Crawford	15	Hanley Ramirez (2)

2011	ADP		ACTUAL = 6
1	Albert Pujols	1	Matt Kemp
2	Hanley Ramirez	2	Jacoby Ellsbury
3	Miguel Cabrera	3	Ryan Braun (10)
4	Troy Tulowitzki	4	Justin Verlander
5	Evan Longoria	5	Clayton Kershaw
6	Carlos Gonzalez	6	Curtis Granderson
7	Joey Votto	7	Adrian Gonzalez (8)
8	Adrian Gonzalez	8	Miguel Cabrera (3)
9	Robinson Cano	9	Roy Halladay (15)
10	Ryan Braun	10	Cliff Lee
11	David Wright	11	Jose Bautista
12	Mark Teixeira	12	Dustin Pedroia
13	Carl Crawford	13	Jered Weaver
14	Josh Hamilton	14	Albert Pujols (1)
15	Roy Halladay	15	Robinson Cano (9)

2012	ADP		ACTUAL = 4
1	Matt Kemp	1	Mike Trout
2	Ryan Braun	2	Ryan Braun (2)
3	Albert Pujols	3	Miguel Cabrera (4)
4	Miguel Cabrera	4	Andrew McCutchen
5	Troy Tulowitzki	5	R.A. Dickey
6	Jose Bautista	6	Clayton Kershaw
7	Jacoby Ellsbury	7	Justin Verlander (8)
8	Justin Verlander	8	Josh Hamilton
9	Adrian Gonzalez	9	Fernando Rodney
10	Justin Upton	10	Adrian Beltre
11	Robinson Cano	11	Alex Rios
12	Joey Votto	12	David Price
13	Evan Longoria	13	Chase Headley
14	Carlos Gonzalez	14	Robinson Cano (11)
15	Prince Fielder	15	Edwin Encarnacion

2013	ADP		ACTUAL = 5
1	Ryan Braun	1	Miguel Cabrera (2)
2	Miguel Cabrera	2	Mike Trout (3)
3	Mike Trout	3	Clayton Kershaw (15)
4	Matt Kemp	4	Chris Davis
5	Andrew McCutchen	5	Paul Goldschmidt
6	Albert Pujols	6	Andrew McCutchen (5)
7	Robinson Cano	7	Adam Jones
8	Jose Bautista	8	Jacoby Ellsbury
9	Joey Votto	9	Max Scherzer
10	Carlos Gonzalez	10	Carlos Gomez
11	Buster Posey	11	Hunter Pence
12	Justin Upton	12	Robinson Cano (7)
13	Giancarlo Stanton	13	Alex Rios
14	Prince Fielder	14	Adrian Beltre
15	Clayton Kershaw	15	Matt Harvey

2014	ADP		ACTUAL = 4
1	Mike Trout	1	Jose Altuve
2	Miguel Cabrera	2	Clayton Kershaw (6)
3	Paul Goldschmidt	3	Michael Brantley
4	Andrew McCutchen	4	Mike Trout (1)
5	Carlos Gonzalez	5	Johnny Cueto
6	Clayton Kershaw	6	Felix Hernandez
7	Chris Davis	7	Victor Martinez
8	Ryan Braun	8	Jose Abreu
9	Adam Jones	9	Giancarlo Stanton
10	Bryce Harper	10	Andrew McCutchen (4)
11	Robinson Cano	11	Miguel Cabrera (2)
12	Hanley Ramirez	12	Carlos Gomez
13	Jacoby Ellsbury	13	Jose Bautista
14	Prince Fielder	14	Dee Gordon
15	Troy Tulowitzki	15	Anthony Rendon

2015	ADP		ACTUAL = 4
1	Mike Trout	1	Jake Arrieta
2	Andrew McCutchen	2	Zack Greinke
3	Clayton Kershaw	3	Clayton Kershaw (3)
4	Giancarlo Stanton	4	Paul Goldschmidt (5)
5	Paul Goldschmidt	5	A.J. Pollock
6	Miguel Cabrera	6	Dee Gordon
7	Jose Abreu	7	Bryce Harper
8	Carlos Gomez	8	Josh Donaldson
9	Jose Bautista	9	Jose Altuve (12)
10	Edwin Encarnacion	10	Mike Trout (1)
11	Felix Hernandez	11	Nolan Arenado
12	Jose Altuve	12	Manny Machado
13	Anthony Rizzo	13	Dallas Keuchel
14	Adam Jones	14	Max Scherzer
15	Troy Tulowitzki	15	Nelson Cruz

2016	ADP		ACTUAL = 7
1	Mike Trout	1	Mookie Betts
2	Paul Goldschmidt	2	Jose Altuve (11)
3	Bryce Harper	3	Mike Trout (1)
4	Clayton Kershaw	4	Jonathan Villar
5	Josh Donaldson	5	Jean Segura
6	Carlos Correa	6	Max Scherzer (15)
7	Nolan Arenado	7	Paul Goldschmidt (2)
8	Manny Machado	8	Charlie Blackmon
9	Anthony Rizzo	9	Clayton Kershaw (4)
10	Giancarlo Stanton	10	Nolan Arenado (7)
11	Jose Altuve	11	Daniel Murphy
12	Kris Bryant	12	Kris Bryant (12)
13	Miguel Cabrera	13	Joey Votto
14	Andrew McCutchen	14	Jon Lester
15	Max Scherzer	15	Madison Bumgarner

The 2016 success rate is even better than it appears, as Miguel Cabrera (13) and Josh Donaldson (5) finished just outside the Top 15.

ADP attrition

Why is our success rate so low in identifying what should be the most easy-to-project players each year? We rank and draft players based on the expectation that those ranked higher will return greater value in terms of productivity and playing time, as well as being the safest investments. However, there are many variables affecting where players finish.

Earlier, it was shown that players spend an inordinate number of days on the disabled list. In fact, of the players projected to finish in the top 300, the number who lost playing time due to injuries, demotions and suspensions has been extreme:

Year	Pct. of top-ranked 300 players who lost PT
2009	51%
2010	44%
2011	49%
2012	45%
2013	51%
2014	53%
2015	47%
2016	47%

When you consider that about half of each season's very best players had fewer at-bats or innings pitched than we projected, it shows how tough it is to rank players each year.

The fallout? Consider: It is nearly a foregone conclusion that a player like Jonathan Villar—someone who finished in the top 15 for the first time last year—will be a consideration for a first round pick in 2017. The above data provide a strong argument against him returning first-round value.

Yes, he is an excellent player, in 2016 anyway. But the issue is not his skills profile. The issue is the profile of what makes a worthy first rounder.

Since 2004:

- Two-thirds of players finishing in the Top 15 were not in the Top 15 the previous year. There is a great deal of turnover in the first round, year-to-year.
- Of those who were first-timers, only 14% repeated in the first round the following year.
- Established superstars who finished in the Top 15 were no guarantee to repeat.

As such, the odds are against Villar repeating in the first round. In past years, sudden stars like Carlos Gonzalez, Curtis Granderson and Dustin Pedroia have failed to repeat. As talented as these players are, it's not just about skill; it's also about skill relative to the rest of a volatile player pool.

Importance of the early rounds *(Bill Macey)*

It's long been said that you can't win your league in the first round, but you can lose it there. An analysis of data from actual drafts reveals that this holds true—those who spend an early round pick on a player that severely under-performs expectations rarely win their league and seldom even finish in the top 3.

At the same time, drafting a player in the first round that actually returns first-round value is no guarantee of success. In fact, those that draft some of the best values still only win their league about a quarter of the time and finish in the top 3 less than half the time. Research also shows that drafting pitchers in the first round is a risky proposition. Even if the pitchers deliver first-round value, the opportunity cost of passing up on an elite batter makes you less likely to win your league.

What is the best seed to draft from?

Most drafters like mid-round so they never have to wait too long for their next player. Some like the swing pick, suggesting that getting two players at 15 and 16 is better than a 1 and a 30. Many drafters assume that the swing pick means you'd be getting something like two $30 players instead of a $40 and $20.

Equivalent auction dollar values reveal the following facts about the first two snake draft rounds:

In an AL/NL-only league, the top seed would get a $44 player (at #1) and a $24 player (at #24) for a total of $68; the 12th seed would get two $29s (at #12 and #13) for $58.

In a mixed league, the top seed would get a $47 and a $24 ($71); the 15th seed would get two $28s ($56).

Since the talent level flattens out after the 2nd round, low seeds never get a chance to catch up:

Dollar value difference between
first player selected and last player selected

Round	12-team	15-team
1	$15	$19
2	$7	$8
3	$5	$4
4	$3	$3
5	$2	$2
6	$2	$1
7-17	$1	$1
18-23	$0	$0

The total value each seed accumulates at the end of the draft is hardly equitable:

Seed	Mixed	AL/NL-only
1	$266	$273
2	$264	$269
3	$263	$261
4	$262	$262
5	$259	$260
6	$261	$260
7	$260	$260
8	$261	$260
9	$261	$258
10	$257	$260
11	$257	$257
12	$258	$257
13	$254	
14	$255	
15	$256	

Of course, the draft is just the starting point for managing your roster and player values are variable. Still, assuming reasonably accurate projections, it's tough to imagine a scenario where the top seed wouldn't have an advantage over the bottom seed.

Using ADPs to determine when to select players *(Bill Macey)*

Although average draft position (ADP) data provides a good idea of where in the draft each player is selected, it can be misleading when trying to determine how early to target a player. This chart summarizes the percentage of players drafted within 15 picks of his ADP as well as the average standard deviation by grouping of players.

ADP Rank 1-25	% within 15 picks 100%	Standard Deviation 2.5
26-50	97%	6.1
51-100	87%	9.6
100-150	72%	14.0
150-200	61%	17.4
200-250	53%	20.9

As the draft progresses, the picks for each player become more widely dispersed and less clustered around the average. Most top 100 players will go within one round of their ADP-converted round. However, as you reach the mid-to-late rounds, there is much more uncertainty as to when a player will be selected. Pitchers have slightly smaller standard deviations than do batters (i.e. they tend to be drafted in a narrower range). This suggests that drafters may be more likely to reach for a batter than for a pitcher.

Using the ADP and corresponding standard deviation, we can to estimate the likelihood that a given player will be available at a certain draft pick. We estimate the predicted standard deviation for each player as follows:

Stdev = -0.42 + 0.42*(ADP - Earliest Pick)

(That the figure 0.42 appears twice is pure coincidence; the numbers are not equal past two decimal points.)

If we assume that the picks are normally distributed, we can use a player's ADP and estimated standard deviation to estimate the likelihood that the player is available with a certain pick (MS Excel formula):

=1-normdist(x,ADP,Standard Deviation,True)
where «x» represents the pick number to be evaluated.

We can use this information to prepare for a snake draft by determining how early we may need to reach in order to roster a player. Suppose you had the 8th pick in a 15-team league draft and your target was 2009 sleeper candidate Nelson Cruz. His ADP was 128.9 and his earliest selection was with the 94th pick. This yielded an estimated standard deviation of 14.2. You could have then entered these values into the formula above to estimate the likelihood that he was still available at each of the following picks:

Pick	Likelihood Available
83	100%
98	99%
113	87%
128	53%
143	16%
158	2%

ADPs and scarcity *(Bill Macey)*

Most players are selected within a round or two of their ADP with tight clustering around the average. But every draft is unique and every pick in the draft seemingly affects the ordering of subsequent picks. In fact, deviations from "expected" sequences can sometimes start a chain reaction at that position. This is most often seen in runs at scarce positions such as the closer; once the first one goes, the next seems sure to closely follow.

Research also suggests that within each position, there is a correlation within tiers of players. The sooner players within a generally accepted tier are selected, the sooner other players within the same tier will be taken. However, once that tier is exhausted, draft order reverts to normal.

How can we use this information? If you notice a reach pick, you can expect that other drafters may follow suit. If your draft plan is to get a similar player within that tier, you'll need to adjust your picks accordingly.

Mapping ADPs to auction value *(Bill Macey)*

Reliable average auction values (AAV) are often tougher to come by than ADP data for snake drafts. However, we can estimate predicted auction prices as a function of ADP, arriving at the following equation:

$$y = -9.8ln(x) + 57.8$$

where ln(x) is the natural log function, x represents the actual ADP, and y represents the predicted AAV.

This equation does an excellent job estimating auction prices ($r^2 = 0.93$), though deviations are unavoidable. The asymptotic nature of the logarithmic function, however, causes the model to predict overly high prices for the top players. So be aware of that, and adjust.

The value of mock drafts *(Todd Zola)*

Most assume the purpose of a mock draft is to get to know the market value of the player pool. But even more important, mock drafting is general preparation for the environment and process, thereby allowing the drafter to completely focus on the draft when it counts. Mock drafting is more about fine-tuning your strategy than player value. Here are some tips to maximize your mock drafting experience.

1. Make sure you can seamlessly use an on-line drafting room, draft software or your own lists to track your draft or auction. The less time you spend looking, adding and adjusting names, the more time you can spend on thinking about what player is best for your team. This also gives you the opportunity to make sure your draft lists are complete, and assures all the players are listed at the correct position(s).

2. Alter the positions from which you mock. The flow of each mock will be different, but if you do a few mocks with an early initial pick, a few in the middle and a few with a late first pick, you may learn you prefer one of the spots more than the others. If you're in a league where you can choose your draft spot, this helps you decide where to select. Once you know your spot, a few mocks from that spot will help you decide how to deal with positional runs.

3. Use non-typical strategies and consider players you rarely target. We all have our favorite players. Intentionally passing on those players not only gives you an idea when others may draft them but it also forces you to research players you normally don't consider. The more players you have researched, the more prepared you'll be for any series of events that occurs during your real draft.

How a strong draft contributes to a winning season *(Todd Zola)*

You can't win a league at the draft but you can lose it. We've all read this cliché, it's classic writer-speak. But have you ever wondered about how much a strong draft or auction contributes to winning?

Standings correlation based on draft to final ranges from 0.42 to 0.94 with mean around 0.73. The top hitting counting stat drafted is home runs, stolen bases fewest. The top pitching counting stat drafted is saves, wins fewest. More hitting is acquired at the draft or auction than pitching. Influx of stats is greatest in Mixed Leagues suggesting practicing patience in AL/NL-only formats while being cautiously aggressive in Mixed formats.

Top teams almost always improve ratios from drafted, despite available free agents sporting poorer aggregate ratios. This is most apropos if favoring improving pitching staff as the year progresses; it's easier said than done.

Being top-three in saves is far more important in Mixed leagues than AL/NL only. Most Mixed champions draft the majority of saves while AL/NL only winners often acquire in season.

Auction Value Analysis

Auction values (R$) in perspective

R$ is the dollar value placed on a player's statistical performance in a Rotisserie league, and designed to measure the impact that player has on the standings.

There are several methods to calculate a player's value from his projected (or actual) statistics.

One method is Standings Gain Points, described in the book, *How to Value Players for Rotisserie Baseball*, by Art McGee (2nd edition available at BaseballHQ.com). SGP converts a player's statistics in each Rotisserie category into the number of points those stats will allow you to gain in the standings. These are then converted back into dollars.

Another popular method is the Percentage Valuation Method. In PVM, a least valuable, or replacement performance level is set for each category (in a given league size) and then values are calculated representing the incremental improvement from that base. A player is then awarded value in direct proportion to the level he contributes to each category.

As much as these methods serve to attach a firm number to projected performance, the winning bid for any player is still highly variable depending upon many factors:

- the salary cap limit
- the number of teams in the league
- each team's roster size
- the impact of any protected players
- each team's positional demands at the time of bidding
- the statistical category demands at the time of bidding
- external factors, e.g. media inflation or deflation of value

In other words, a $30 player is only a $30 player if someone in your draft pays $30 for him.

Roster slot valuation *(John Burnson)*

When you draft a player, what have you bought?

"You have bought the stats generated by this player."

No. You have bought the stats generated by his slot. Initially, the drafted player fills the slot, but he need not fill the slot for the season, and he need not contribute from Day One. If you trade the player during the season, then your bid on Draft Day paid for the stats of the original player plus the stats of the new player. If the player misses time due to injury or demotion, then you bought the stats of whoever fills the time while the drafted player is missing. At season's end, there will be more players providing positive value than there are roster slots.

Before the season, the number of players projected for positive value has to equal the total number of roster slots. However, the projected productivity should be adjusted by the potential to capture extra value in the slot. This is especially important for injury-rehab cases and late-season call-ups. For example, if we think that a player will miss half the season, then we would augment his projected stats with a half-year of stats from a replacement-level player at his position. Only then would we calculate prices. Essentially, we want to apportion $260 per team among the slots, not the players.

Average player value by draft round

Rd	AL/NL	Mxd
1	$34	$34
2	$26	$26
3	$23	$23
4	$20	$20
5	$18	$18
6	$17	$16
7	$16	$15
8	$15	$13
9	$13	$12
10	$12	$11
11	$11	$10
12	$10	$9
13	$9	$8
14	$8	$8
15	$7	$7
16	$6	$6
17	$5	$5
18	$4	$4
19	$3	$3
20	$2	$2
21	$1	$2
22	$1	$1
23	$1	$1

Benchmarks for auction players:

- All $30 players will go in the first round.
- All $20-plus players will go in the first four rounds.
- Double-digit value ends pretty much after Round 11.
- The $1 end game starts at about Round 21.

Dollar values: expected projective accuracy

There is a 65% chance that a player projected for a certain dollar value will finish the season with a value within plus-or-minus $5 of that projection. Therefore, if you value a player at $25, you only have about a 2-in-3 shot of him finishing between $20 and $30.

If you want to raise your odds to 80%, the range becomes +/- $9, so your $25 player has to finish somewhere between $16 and $34.

Dollar values by lineup position *(Michael Roy)*

How much value is derived from batting order position?

Pos	PA	R	RBI	R$
#1	747	107	72	$18.75
#2	728	102	84	$19.00
#3	715	95	100	$19.45
#4	698	93	104	$19.36
#5	682	86	94	$18.18
#6	665	85	82	$17.19
#7	645	81	80	$16.60
#8	623	78	80	$16.19
#9	600	78	73	$15.50

So, a batter moving from the bottom of the order to the clean-up spot, with no change in performance, would gain nearly $4 in value from runs and RBIs alone.

How likely is it that a $30 player will repeat? *(Matt Cederholm)*

From 2003-2008, there were 205 players who earned $30 or more (using single-league 5x5 values). Only 70 of them (34%) earned $30 or more in the next season.

In fact, the odds of repeating a $30 season aren't good. As seen below, the best odds during that period were 42%. And as we would expect, pitchers fare far worse than hitters.

	Total>$30	# Repeat	% Repeat
Hitters	167	64	38%
Pitchers	38	6	16%
Total	205	70	34%
*High-Reliability**			
Hitters	42	16	38%
Pitchers	7	0	0%
Total	49	16	33%
100+ BPV			
Hitters	60	25	42%
Pitchers	31	6	19%
Total	91	31	19%
*High-Reliability and 100+ BPV**			
Hitters	12	5	42%
Pitchers	6	0	0%
Total	18	5	28%

Reliability figures are from 2006-2008

For players with multiple seasons of $30 or more, the numbers get better. Players with consecutive $30 seasons, 2003-2008:

	Total>$30	# Repeat	% Repeat
Two Years	62	29	55%
Three+ Years	29	19	66%

Still, a player with two consecutive seasons at $30 in value is barely a 50/50 proposition. And three consecutive seasons is only a 2/3 shot. Small sample sizes aside, this does illustrate the nature of the beast. Even the most consistent, reliable players fail 1/3 of the time. Of course, this is true whether they are kept or drafted anew, so this alone shouldn't prevent you from keeping a player.

Predicting player value from year 1 performance *(Patrick Davitt)*

Year-1 (Y1, first season >=100AB) batter results predict some—but not all—subsequent-year performance. About half of all Y1 players have positive value. Players with higher Y1 value were likelier to get PT in subsequent seasons. Players with −$6 to −$10 in Y1 got more chances than players +$5 to −$5 and performed better. Batters with Y1 value of $16 or more are excellent bets to at least provide positive value in subsequent seasons, and those above $21 in Y1 value play in all subsequent seasons and return an average of $26. But even a $21 batter is only a 50-50 bet to do better in Y2.

How well do elite pitchers retain their value? *(Michael Weddell)*

An elite pitcher (one who earns at least $24 in a season) on average keeps 80% of his R$ value from year 1 to year 2. This compares to the baseline case of only 52%.

Historically, 36% of elite pitchers improve, returning a greater R$ in the second year than they did the first year. That is an impressive performance considering they already were at an elite level. 17% collapse, returning less than a third of their R$ in the second year. The remaining 47% experience a middling outcome, keeping more than a third but less than all of their R$ from one year to the next.

Valuing closers

Given the high risk associated with the closer's role, it is difficult to determine a fair draft value. Typically, those who have successfully held the role for several seasons will earn the highest draft price, but valuing less stable commodities is troublesome.

A rough rule of thumb is to start by paying $10 for the role alone. Any pitcher tagged the closer on draft day should merit at least $10. Then add anywhere from $0 to $15 for support skills.

In this way, the top level talents will draw upwards of $20-$25. Those with moderate skill will draw $15-$20, and those with more questionable skill in the $10-$15 range.

Profiling the end game

What types of players are typically the most profitable in the end-game? First, our overall track record on $1 picks:

Avg Return	%Profitable	Avg Prof	Avg. Loss
$1.89	51%	$10.37	($7.17)

On aggregate, the hundreds of players drafted in the end-game earned $1.89 on our $1 investments. While they were profitable overall, only 51% of them actually turned a profit. Those that did cleared more than $10 on average. Those that didn't—the other 49%—lost about $7 apiece.

Pos	Pct.of tot	Avg Val	%Profit	Avg Prof	Avg Loss
CA	12%	($1.68)	41%	$7.11	($7.77)
CO	9%	$6.12	71%	$10.97	($3.80)
MI	9%	$3.59	53%	$10.33	($4.84)
OF	22%	$2.61	46%	$12.06	($5.90)
SP	29%	$1.96	52%	$8.19	($7.06)
RP	19%	$0.35	50%	$11.33	($10.10)

These results bear out the danger of leaving catchers to the end; only catchers returned negative value. Corner infielder returns say leaving a 1B or 3B open until late.

Age	Pct.of tot	Avg Val	%Profit	Avg Prof	Avg Loss
< 25	15%	($0.88)	33%	$8.25	($8.71)
25-29	48%	$2.59	56%	$11.10	($8.38)
30-35	28%	$2.06	44%	$10.39	($5.04)
35+	9%	$2.15	41%	$8.86	($5.67)

The practice of speculating on younger players—mostly rookies—in the end game was a washout. Part of the reason was that those that even made it to the end game were often the long-term or fringe type. Better prospects were typically drafted earlier.

	Pct.of tot	Avg Val	%Profit	Avg Prof	Avg Loss
Injury rehabs	20%	$3.63	36%	$15.07	($5.65)

One in five end-gamers were players coming back from injury. While only 36% of them were profitable, the healthy ones returned a healthy profit. The group's losses were small, likely because they weren't healthy enough to play.

Realistic expectations of $1 endgamers *(Patrick Davitt)*

Many fantasy articles insist leagues are won or lost with $1 batters, because "that's where the profits are." But are they?

A 2011 analysis showed that when considering $1 players in deep leagues, managing $1 endgamers should be more about minimizing losses than fishing for profit. In the cohort of batters projected $0 to -$5, 82% returned losses, based on a $1 bid. Two-thirds of the projected $1 cohort returned losses. In addition, when considering $1 players, speculate on speed.

Advanced Draft Strategies

Stars & Scrubs v. Spread the Risk

Stars & Scrubs (S&S): A Rotisserie auction strategy in which a roster is anchored by a core of high priced stars and the remaining positions filled with low-cost players.

Spread the Risk (STR): An auction strategy in which available dollars are spread evenly among all roster slots.

Both approaches have benefits and risks. An experiment was conducted in 2004 whereby a league was stocked with four teams assembled as S&S, four as STR and four as a control group. Rosters were then frozen for the season.

The Stars & Scrubs teams won all three ratio categories. Those deep investments ensured stability in the categories that are typically most difficult to manage. On the batting side, however, S&S teams amassed the least amount of playing time, which in turn led to bottom-rung finishes in HRs, RBIs and Runs.

One of the arguments for the S&S approach is that it is easier to replace end-game losers (which, in turn, may help resolve the playing time issues). Not only is this true, but the results of this experiment show that replacing those bottom players is critical to success.

The Spread the Risk teams stockpiled playing time, which led to strong finishes in many counting stats, including clear victories in RBIs, wins and strikeouts. This is a key tenet in drafting philosophy; we often say that the team that compiles the most ABs will be among the top teams in RBI and Runs.

The danger is on the pitching side. More innings did yield more wins and Ks, but also destroyed ERA/WHIP.

So, what approach makes the most sense? **The optimal strategy might be to STR on offense and go S&S with your pitching staff.** STR buys more ABs, so you immediately position yourself well in four of the five batting categories. On pitching, it might be more advisable to roster a few core arms, though that immediately elevates your risk exposure. Admittedly, it's a balancing act, which is why we need to pay more attention to risk analysis and look closer at strategies like the Portfolio3 Plan.

The LIMA Plan

The LIMA Plan is a strategy for Rotisserie leagues (though the underlying concept can be used in other formats) that allows you to target high skills pitchers at very low cost, thereby freeing up dollars for offense. LIMA is an acronym for Low Investment Mound Aces, and also pays tribute to Jose Lima, a $1 pitcher in 1998 who exemplified the power of the strategy. In a $260 league:

1. Budget a maximum of $60 for your pitching staff.
2. Allot no more than $30 of that budget for acquiring saves. In 5x5 leagues, it is reasonable to forego saves at the draft (and acquire them during the season) and re-allocate this $30 to starters ($20) and offense ($10).
3. Ignore ERA. Draft only pitchers with:
   • Command ratio (K/BB) of 2.5 or better.
   • Strikeout rate of 7.0 or better.
   • Expected home run rate of 1.0 or less.
4. Draft as few innings as your league rules will allow. This is intended to manage risk. For some game formats, this should be a secondary consideration.
5. Maximize your batting slots. Target batters with:
   • Contact rate of at least 80%
   • Walk rate of at least 10%
   • PX or Spd level of at least 100

Spend no more than $29 for any player and try to keep the $1 picks to a minimum.

The goal is to ace the batting categories and carefully pick your pitching staff so that it will finish in the upper third in ERA, WHIP and saves (and Ks in 5x5), and an upside of perhaps 9th in wins. In a competitive league, that should be enough to win, and definitely enough to finish in the money. Worst case, you should have an excess of offense available that you can deal for pitching.

The strategy works because it better allocates resources. Fantasy leaguers who spend a lot for pitching are not only paying for expected performance, they are also paying for better defined roles—#1 and #2 rotation starters, ace closers, etc.—which are expected to translate into more IP, wins and saves. But roles are highly variable. A pitcher's role will usually come down to his skill and performance; if he doesn't perform, he'll lose the role.

The LIMA Plan says, let's invest in skill and let the roles fall where they may. In the long run, better skills should translate into more innings, wins and saves. And as it turns out, pitching skill costs less than pitching roles do.

In *snake draft leagues,* don't start drafting starting pitchers until Round 10. In *shallow mixed leagues,* the LIMA Plan may not be necessary; just focus on the peripheral metrics. In *simulation leagues,* build your staff around those metrics.

Variations on the LIMA Plan

LIMA Extrema: Limit your total pitching budget to only $30, or less. This can be particularly effective in shallow leagues where LIMA-caliber starting pitcher free agents are plentiful during the season.

SANTANA Plan: Instead of spending $30 on saves, you spend it on a starting pitcher anchor. In 5x5 leagues where you can reasonably punt saves at the draft table, allocating those dollars to a high-end LIMA-caliber starting pitcher can work well as long as you pick the right anchor.

Total Control Drafting (TCD)

On Draft Day, we make every effort to control as many elements as possible. In reality, the players that end up on our teams are largely controlled by the other owners. Their bidding affects your ability to roster the players you want. In a snake draft, the other owners control your roster even more. We are really only able to get the players we want within the limitations set by others.

However, an optimal roster can be constructed from a fanalytic assessment of skill and risk combined with more assertive draft day demeanor.

Why this makes sense

1. Our obsession with projected player values is holding us back. If a player on your draft list is valued at $20 and you agonize when the bidding hits $23, odds are about two chances in three that he could really earn anywhere from $15 to $25. What this means is, in some cases, and within reason, you should just pay what it takes to get the players you want.

2. There is no such thing as a bargain. Most of us *don't* just pay what it takes because we are always on the lookout for players who go under value. But we really don't know which players will cost less than they will earn because prices are still driven by the draft table. The concept of "bargain" assumes that we even know what a player's true value is.

3. "Control" is there for the taking. Most owners are so focused on their own team that they really don't pay much attention to what you're doing. There are some exceptions, and bidding wars do happen, but in general, other owners will not provide that much resistance.

How it's done

1. Create your optimal draft pool.
2. Get those players.

Start by identifying which players will be draftable based on the LIMA or Portfolio3 criteria. Then, at the draft, focus solely on your roster. When it's your bid opener, toss a player you need at about 50%-75% of your projected value. Bid aggressively and just pay what you need to pay. Of course, don't spend $40 for a player with $25 market value, but it's okay to exceed your projected value within reason.

From a tactical perspective, mix up the caliber of openers. Drop out early on some bids to prevent other owners from catching on to you.

In the end, it's okay to pay a slight premium to make sure you get the players with the highest potential to provide a good return on your investment. It's no different than the premium you might pay for a player with position flexibility or to get the last valuable shortstop. With TCD, you're just spending those extra dollars up front to ensure you are rostering your targets. As a side benefit, TCD almost asssures that you don't leave money on the table.

Mayberry Method

The foundation of the Mayberry Method (MM) is the assertion that we really can't project player performance with the level of precision that advanced metrics and modeling systems would like us to believe.

MM is named after the fictional TV village where life was simpler. MM evaluates skill by embracing the imprecision of the forecasting process and projecting performance in broad strokes rather than with hard statistics.

MM reduces every player to a 7-character code. The format of the code is 5555 AAA, where the first four characters describe elements of a player's skill on a scale of 0 to 5. These skills are indexed to the league average so that players are evaluated within the context of the level of offense or pitching in a given year.

The three alpha characters are our reliability grades (Health, Experience and Consistency) on the standard A-to-F scale. The skills numerics are forward-looking; the alpha characters grade reliability based on past history.

Batting

The first character in the MM code measures a batter's power skills. It is assigned using the following table:

Power Index	MM
0 - 49	0
50 - 79	1
80 - 99	2
100 - 119	3
120 - 159	4
160+	5

The second character measures a batter's speed skills. RSpd takes our Statistically Scouted Speed metric (Spd) and adds the elements of opportunity and success rate, to construct the formula of RSpd = Spd x (SBO + SB%).

RSpd	MM
0 - 39	0
40 - 59	1
60 - 79	2
80 - 99	3
100 - 119	4
120+	5

The third character measures expected batting average.

xBA Index	MM
0-87	0
88-92	1
93-97	2
98-102	3
103-107	4
108+	5

The fourth character measures playing time.

Role	PA	MM
Potential full-timers	450+	5
Mid-timers	250-449	3
Fringe/bench	100-249	1
Non-factors	0-99	0

Pitching

The first character in the pitching MM code measures xERA, which captures a pitcher's overall ability and is a proxy for ERA, and even WHIP.

xERA Index	MM
0-80	0
81-90	1
91-100	2
101-110	3
111-120	4
121+	5

The second character measures strikeout ability.

K/9 Index	MM
0-76	0
77-88	1
89-100	2
101-112	3
113-124	4
125+	5

The third character measures saves potential.

Description	Saves est.	MM
No hope for saves; starting pitchers	0	0
Speculative closer	1-9	1
Closer in a pen with alternatives	10-24	2
Frontline closer with firm bullpen role	25+	3

The fourth character measures **playing time**.

Role	IP	MM
Potential #1-2 starters	180+	5
Potential #3-4 starters	130-179	3
#5 starters/swingmen	70-129	1
Relievers	0-69	0

Overall Mayberry Scores

The real value of Mayberry is to provide a skills profile on a player-by-player basis. I want to be able to see this…

Player A	4455 AAB
Player B	5245 BBD
Player C	5255 BAB
Player D	5155 BAF

…and make an objective, unbiased determination about these four players without being swayed by preconceived notions and baggage. But there is a calculation that provides a single, overall value for each player.

This is the calculation for the overall MM batting score:

MM Score =
(PX score + Spd score + xBA score + PA score)
x PA score

An overall MM pitching score is calculated as:

MM Score =
((xERA score x 2) + K/9 score + Saves score + IP score)
x (IP score + Saves score)

The highest score you can get for either is 100. That makes the result of the formula easy to assess.

BaseballHQ.com analyst Patrick Davitt did some great research about using Reliability Grades to adjust the Mayberry scores. His research showed that "higher-reliability players met their Mayberry targets more often than their lower-reliability counterparts, and players with all "D" or "F" reliability scores underperform Mayberry projections far more often. Those results can be reflected by multiplying a player's MM Score by each of three reliability bonuses or penalties:"

I've taken his work a minor step further and applied slightly different multipliers to each Reliability element.

	Health	Experience	Consistency
A	x 1.10	x 1.10	x 1.10
B	x 1.05	x 1.05	x 1.05
C	x 1.00	x 1.00	x 1.00
D	x 0.90	x 0.95	x 0.95
F	x 0.80	x 0.90	x 0.90

So, let's perform the overall calculations for Player A above, using these Reliability adjustments.

Player A: 4455 AAB
= (4+4+5+5) x 5
= 90 x 1.10 x 1.10 x 1.05
= 114.3

The Portfolio3 Plan (P3)

When it comes to profitability, all players are not created equal. Every player has a different role on your team by virtue of his skill set, dollar value/draft round, position and risk profile. When it comes to a strategy for how to approach a specific player, one size does not fit all.

We need some players to return fair value more than others. A $40/first round player going belly-up is going to hurt you far more than a $1/23rd round bust. End-gamers are easily replaceable.

We rely on some players for profit more than others. First-rounders do not provide the most profit potential; that comes from players further down the value rankings.

We can afford to weather more risk with some players than with others. Since high-priced early-rounders need to return at least fair value, we cannot afford to take on excessive risk. Our risk tolerance opens up with later-round/lower cost picks.

Players have different risk profiles based solely on what roster spot they are going to fill. Catchers are more injury prone. A closer's value is highly dependent on managerial decision. These types of players are high risk even if they have great skills. That needs to affect their draft price or draft round.

For some players, the promise of providing a scarce skill, or productivity at a scarce position, may trump risk. Not always, but sometimes. The determining factor is usually price.

In the end, we need a way to integrate all these different types of players, roles and needs. We need to put some structure to the concept of a diversified draft approach. Thus:

The Portfolio3 Plan provides a three-tiered structure to the draft. Just like most folks prefer to diversify their stock portfolio, P3 advises to diversify your roster with three different types of players. Depending upon the stage of the draft (and budget constraints in auction leagues), P3 uses a different set of rules for each tier that you'll draft from. The three tiers are:

1. Core Players
2. Mid-Game Players
3. End-Game Players

Mayberry scores can be used as proxies for the skills filters. When planning your draft, pretty much all you need to remember is the number "3". That essentially represents "just over league average" and makes it easy to set your targets.

TIER 1: CORE PLAYERS
General Roster Goals

Auction target: Budget a maximum of $160. Any player purchased for $20 or more should meet the Tier 1 skills criteria

Snake draft target: 5-8 players, with an emphasis on those drafted in the earlier rounds

Reliability grades: No worse than "B" for each variable (Health, Experience and Consistency)

Playing time: No restrictions, however, pricier early round players should have more guaranteed playing time

Batter skills: Minimum MM scores of 3 in xBA *plus* either PX or RSpd

Pitcher skills: Minimum MM scores of 3 in xERA *and* K/9

Tier 1 players provide the foundation to your roster. These are your prime contributors and where you will invest the largest percentage of your budget or early round picks. There is no room for risk here, so the majority of these players should be batters.

TIER 2: MID-GAME PLAYERS
General Roster Goals

Auction target: Budget between $50 and $100; players should be under $20

Snake draft target: 7-13 players

Reliability grades: No worse than "B" for Health, no worse than "C" for Experience and Consistency

Playing time: Must have a MM score of 5 for batters (meaning full-time batters) and minimum 3 for pitchers (meaning at least mid-rotation starting pitchers)

Batter skills: Minimum MM scores of 3 in xBA or PX or RSpd

Pitcher skills: Minimum MM score of 3 in xERA or K/9

Tier 1 players are all about skill. Tier 2 is all about accumulating playing time, particularly on the batting side, with lesser regard to skill. This is where you can beef up on runs and RBI. If a player is getting 500 AB, he is likely going to provide positive value in those categories just from opportunity alone. And given that his team is seeing fit to give him those AB, he is probably also contributing somewhere else.

For pitchers, we use Tier 2 to accumulate arms whose innings provide some level of positive support, either by stockpiling strikeouts or by building your ERA foundation.

TIER 3: END-GAME PLAYERS
General Roster Goals

Auction target: Budget up to $50; players should be under $10

Snake draft target: 5-10 players

Reliability grades: No restrictions, except no "F" Health grades.

Playing time: No restrictions

Batter skills: Minimum MM scores of 3 in xBA plus either PX or RSpd (same as Tier 1)

Pitcher skills: Minimum MM score of 3 in xERA

Tier 3 players are your gambling chips, but every end-gamer must provide the promise of upside. For that reason, the focus must remain on skill and conditional opportunity. MP3 drafters should fill the majority of their pitching slots from this group.

By definition, end-gamers are typically high risk players, but risk is something you'll want to embrace here. If a Tier 3 player does not pan out, he can be easily replaced.

As such, the best Tier 3 options should possess the MM skill levels noted above, and at least one of the following:

- playing time upside as a back-up to a risky front-liner
- an injury history that has depressed his value (but not chronically injured players)
- solid skills demonstrated at some point in the past
- minor league potential even if he has been more recently a major league bust

A complete list of players in each tier appears in the back of the book starting on page 251. One of the major benefits of the MP3 process is that any player failing to find a home in one of the tiers can be safely ignored. Either his skills are not draft-worthy or his risk-profile too dangerous, regardless of skill. By shrinking the draftable player pool, it makes the roster planning and construction process easier.

Category Targets

The final task is to set MM targets for each category.

If you are in a league with good trading activity, this may not be important—you can always deal away excesses to beef up weak categories. But for those in leagues with little or no trading, drafting a balanced team is critical.

For skills budgeting purposes, here are targets for several standard leagues:

BATTING	PX	RSpd	xBA	PA
12-team mixed	41	28	40	66
15-team mixed	41	26	39	64
12-team AL/NL	37	23	32	54
PITCHING	**xERA***	**K/9***	**Sv**	**IP**
12-team mixed	23	33	7	29
15-team mixed	20	30	6	30
12-team AL/NL	17	27	5	25

* Make sure the majority of these points come from starting pitchers.

As you draft, track each MM score and keep a running total of all the categories. With the above goals will allow you to shift your in-draft targets if you see you are falling behind in any area.

Consistency in Head-to-Head leagues *(Dylan Hedges)*

Few things are as valuable to H2H league success as filling your roster with players who can produce a solid baseline of stats, week in and week out. In traditional leagues, while consistency is not as important—all we care about are aggregate numbers—filling your team with consistent players can make roster management easier.

Consistent batters have good plate discipline, walk rates and on base percentages. These are foundation skills. Those who add power to the mix are obviously more valuable, however, the ability to hit home runs consistently is rare.

Consistent pitchers demonstrate similar skills in each outing; if they also produce similar results, they are even more valuable.

We can track consistency but predicting it is difficult. Many fantasy leaguers try to predict a batter's hot or cold streaks, or individual pitcher starts, but that is typically a fool's errand. The best we can do is find players who demonstrate seasonal consistency; in-season, we must manage players and consistency tactically.

Building a consistent Head-to-Head team *(David Martin)*

Teams in head-to-head leagues need batters who are consistent. Focusing on certain metrics helps build consistency, which is the roster holy grail for H2H players. Our filters for such success are:

- Contact rate = minimum 80%
- xBA = minimum .280
- PX (or Spd) = minimum 120
- RC/G = minimum 5.00

Ratio insulation in Head-to-Head leagues *(David Martin)*

On a week-to-week basis, inequities are inherent in the head-to-head game. One way to eliminate your competitor's advantage in the pure numbers game is to build your team's pitching foundation around the ratio categories.

One should normally insulate at the end of a draft, once your hitters are in place. To obtain several ratio insulators, target pitchers that have:

- Cmd greater than 3.0
- Dom greater than 7.5
- xERA less than 3.30

While adopting this strategy may compromise wins, research has shown that wins come at a cost to ERA and WHIP. Roster space permitting, adding two to four insulators to your team will improve your team's weekly ERA and WHIP.

Consistency in points leagues *(Bill Macey)*

Previous research has demonstrated that week-to-week statistical consistency is important for Rotisserie-based head-to-head play. But one can use the same foundation in points-based games. A study showed that not only do players with better skills post more overall points in this format, but that the format caters to consistent performances on a week-to-week basis, even after accounting for differences in total points scored and playing-time.

Therefore, when drafting your batters in points-based head-to-head leagues, ct% and bb% make excellent tiebreakers if you are having trouble deciding between two players with similarly projected point totals. Likewise, when rostering pitchers, favor those who tend not to give up home runs.

In-Season Analyses

The efficacy of streaming *(John Burnson)*

In leagues that allow weekly or daily transactions, many owners flit from hot player to hot player. But published dollar values don't capture this traffic—they assume that players are owned from April to October. For many leagues, this may be unrealistic.

We decided to calculate these "investor returns." For each week, we identified the top players by one statistic—BA for hitters, ERA for pitchers—and took the top 100 hitters *[cont. on page 56]*

Daily Fantasy Baseball

Daily Fantasy Sports (DFS) is an offshoot of traditional fantasy sports. Many of the same analytic methods that are integral to seasonal fantasy baseball are just as relevant for DFS.

General Format

1. The overwhelming majority of DFS contests are pay-for-play where the winners are compensated a percentage of their entry fee, in accordance with the rules of that game.

2. DFS baseball contests are generally based on a single day's slate of games, or a subset of the day's games (i.e., all afternoon games or all evening games)

3. Most DFS formats are points-based salary cap games.

Most Popular Contests

1. Cash Games: Three variants (50/50, Multipliers, and Head-to-Head) all pay out a flat prize to a portion of the entries.

2. GPP (Guaranteed prize pool) Tournaments: The overall winner earns the largest prize and prizes scale downward.

3. Survivor: A survivor contest is a multiple-slate format where a portion of the entries survives to play the following day.

4. Qualifiers/Satellites: Tournaments where the prize(s) consist of entry tickets to a larger tournament.

DFS Analysis

1. Predicting single-day performance entails adjusting a baseline projection based on that day's match-up. This adjusted expectation is considered in context with his salary to determine his potential contributions relative to the other players.

2. Weighted on base average (wOBA) is a souped-up version of OBP, and is a favorite metric to help evaluate both hitters and pitchers. (For more useful DFS metrics, see next section)

3. Pitching: In DFS, innings and strikeouts are the two chief means of accruing points, so they need to be weighed heavily in pitching evaluation.

Tips for Players New to DFS

1. Start slow and be prepared to lose: While cogent analysis can increase your chances of winning, the variance associated with a single day's worth of outcomes doesn't assure success. Short-term losing streaks are inevitable, so start with low cost cash games before embarking on tournament play.

2. Minimize the number of sites you play: The DFS space is dominated by two sites but there are other options. At the beginning, stick to one or two then once you're comfortable, consider expanding to others.

3. Bankroll management: The recommended means to manage your bankroll is to risk no more than 10% on a given day. Within that portion, the suggested ratio is 80% cash games to 20% GPP tournament action.

4. General Strategies

A. Cash Games: Conventional wisdom preaches to be conservative in cash games. Upper level starting pitchers make excellent cash game options. For hitters, it's best to spread your choices among several teams. In general, you're looking for players with a high floor rather than a high ceiling.

B: GPP Tournaments: In tournaments (with a larger number of entrants), a common ploy is to select a lesser priced, though risky, pitcher with a favorable match-up. It's also very common to overload—or stack—several batters from the same team, hoping that squad scores a bunch of runs.

5. Miscellaneous Tips

A. Pay extra attention to games threatened by weather, as well as players who are not a lock to be in the lineup.

B. Avoid playing head-to-head against strangers until you're comfortable and have enjoyed some success.

C. Stay disciplined. The worst thing you can do is eat up your bankroll quickly by entering into tournaments.

D. Most importantly, have fun. Obviously, you want to win, but hopefully you're also in it for the challenge of mastering the unique skills intrinsic to DFS.

Using BaseballHQ Tools in DFS

Here are some of the additional skill metrics to consider:

Cash Game BPIs

bb%: this simple indicator may receive only a quick glance when building lineups, but it is imperative in providing insight on a batter's underlying approach and plate discipline. Walks also equal points in all DFS scoring structures.

ct%: Another byproduct of good plate discipline, reflecting the percentage of balls put in play. Players with strong contact rates tend to provide a higher floor, and less chance of a negative score from a free swinger with a high strikeout rate.

xBA: Measures a hitter's BA by multiplying his contact rate by the chance that a ball in play falls for a hit. Hitters whose BA is far below their xBA may be "due" for some hits.

Tournament / GPP BPIs

PX / xPX: Home runs are the single greatest multi-point event. Using PX (power index) and xPX (expected power index) together can help identify underperformers who are due in the power category.

Choosing Pitchers in DFS

The criteria for choosing a pitcher(s) may be more narrow than for full-season league, but the skills focus should remain.

Major Considerations

• Overall skills. Look for the following minimums: 2.9 Ctl (bb/9), 7.7 Dom (k/9), 2.6 Cmd (k/bb), and 1.0 HR/9.

• Home/Away. In 2016, MLB pitchers logged a 4.02 ERA, 8.2 Dom, 2.8 Cmd at home; 4.37 ERA, 8.0 Dom, 2.4 Cmd on the road.

• Is he pitching at Coors Field? (Even the best pitchers are a risky start there.)

Moderate Considerations

• Recent performance. Examine Ks and BBs over last 4-5 starts.

• Strength of opponent. Refer to opposing team's OPS for the season, as well as more recent performance.

Minor Considerations

• L/R issues. Does the pitcher/opponent have wide platoon splits?

• Park. Is the game at a hitter's/pitcher's/neutral park?

• Previous outings. Has he faced this team already this season? If so, how did he fare? (Skills; not just his ERA.)

You will hopefully be left with a tiered list of pitching options, ripe for comparing individual risk/reward level against their price point.

and top 50 pitchers. We then said that, at the end of the week, the #1 player was picked up (or already owned) by 100% of teams, the #2 player was picked up or owned by 99% of teams, and so on, down to the 100th player, who was on 1% of teams. (For pitchers, we stepped by 2%.) Last, we tracked each player's performance in the next week, when ownership matters.

We ran this process anew for every week of the season, tabulating each player's "investor returns" along the way. If a player was owned by 100% of teams, then we awarded him 100% of his performance. If the player was owned by half the teams, we gave him half his performance. If he was owned by no one (that is, he was not among the top players in the prior week), his performance was ignored. A player's cumulative stats over the season was his investor return.

The results...

- 60% of pitchers had poorer investor returns, with an aggregate ERA 0.40 higher than their true ERA.
- 55% of batters had poorer investor returns, but with an aggregate batting average virtually identical to the true BA.

Sitting stars and starting scrubs *(Ed DeCaria)*

In setting your pitching rotation, conventional wisdom suggests sticking with trusted stars despite difficult matchups. But does this hold up? And can you carefully start inferior pitchers against weaker opponents? Here are the ERAs posted by varying skilled pitchers facing a range of different strength offenses:

	OPPOSING OFFENSE (RC/G)				
Pitcher (ERA)	5.25+	5.00	4.25	4.00	<4.00
3.00-	3.46	3.04	3.04	2.50	2.20
3.50	3.98	3.94	3.44	3.17	2.87
4.00	4.72	4.57	3.96	3.66	3.24
4.50	5.37	4.92	4.47	4.07	3.66
5.00+	6.02	5.41	5.15	4.94	4.42

Recommendations:

1. Never start below replacement-level pitchers.
2. Always start elite pitchers.
3. Other than that, never say never or always.

Playing matchups can pay off when the difference in opposing offense is severe.

Two-start pitcher weeks *(Ed DeCaria)*

A two-start pitcher is a prized possession. But those starts can mean two DOMinant outings, two DISasters, or anything else in between, as shown by these results:

PQS Pair	% Weeks	ERA	WHIP	Win/Wk	K/Wk
DOM-DOM	20%	2.53	1.02	1.1	12.0
DOM-AVG	28%	3.60	1.25	0.8	9.2
AVG-AVG	14%	4.44	1.45	0.7	6.8
DOM-DIS	15%	5.24	1.48	0.6	7.9
AVG-DIS	17%	6.58	1.74	0.5	5.7
DIS-DIS	6%	8.85	2.07	0.3	5.0

Weeks that include even one DISaster start produce terrible results. Unfortunately, avoiding such disasters is much easier in hindsight. But what is the actual impact of this decision on the stat categories?

ERA and WHIP: When the difference between opponents is extreme, inferior pitchers can be a better percentage play. This is

true both for 1-start pitchers and 2-start pitchers, and for choosing inferior one-start pitchers over superior two-start pitchers.

Strikeouts per Week: Unlike the two rate stats, there is a massive shift in the balance of power between one-start and two-start pitchers in the strikeout category. Even stars with easy one-start matchups can only barely keep pace with two-start replacement-level arms in strikeouts per week.

Wins per week are also dominated by the two-start pitchers. Even the very worst two-start pitchers will earn a half of a win on average, which is the same rate as the very best one-start pitchers.

The bottom line: If strikeouts and wins are the strategic priority, use as many two-start weeks as the rules allow, even if it means using a replacement-level pitcher with two tough starts instead of a mid-level arm with a single easy start. But if ERA and/or WHIP management are the priority, two-start pitchers can be very powerful, as a single week might impact the standings by over 1.5 points in ERA/WHIP, positively or negatively.

Six tips on category management *(Todd Zola)*

1. Disregard whether you are near the top or the bottom of a category; focus instead on the gaps directly above and below your squad.
2. Prorate the difference in stats between teams.
3. ERA tends to move towards WHIP.
4. As the season progresses, the number of AB/IF do not preclude a gain/loss in the ratio categories.
5. An opponent's point lost is your point gained.
6. *Most important!* Come crunch time, forget value, forget names, and forget reputation. It's all about stats and where you are situated within each category.

Other Diamonds

Cellar value

The dollar value at which a player cannot help but earn more than he costs. Always profit here.

Crickets

The sound heard when someone's opening draft bid on a player is also the only bid.

FAAB Forewarnings

1. Spend early and often.
2. Emptying your budget for one prime league-crosser is a tactic that should be reserved for the desperate.
3. If you chase two rabbits, you will lose them both.

Hope

A commodity that routinely goes for $5 over value at the draft table.

Seasonal Assessment Standard

If you still have reason to be reading the boxscores during the last weekend of the season, then your year has to be considered a success.

The Three Cardinal Rules for Winners

If you cherish this hobby, you will live by them or die by them...

1. Revel in your success; fame is fleeting.
2. Exercise excruciating humility.
3. 100% of winnings must be spent on significant others.

Extreme Makeovers: PQS Edition

by Ed DeCaria

Pure Quality Starts (PQS) has been BaseballHQ.com's go-to metric for assessing starting pitcher game-level performance for over a decade. To "calculate" a PQS score, we need only look at a starting pitcher's box score, cross our eyes, and count up to five:

- Did pitcher pitch deep into game? 1 if Yes, 0 if No.
- Did pitcher limit hits? 1 if Yes, 0 if No.
- Did pitcher strike out batters? 1 if Yes, 0 if No.
- Did pitcher limit walks? 1 if Yes, 0 if No.
- Did pitcher limit home runs? 1 if Yes, 0 if No.

For a given start, this works well: a score of 4 or 5 is relatively "dominant" (or "PQS-DOM"), a score of 0 or 1 is a relative "disaster" ("PQS-DIS"), and a score of 2 or 3 is somewhere in between. However, in recent seasons, when we aggregate PQS data for all pitchers, we see that the distribution of PQS scores has become rather imbalanced:

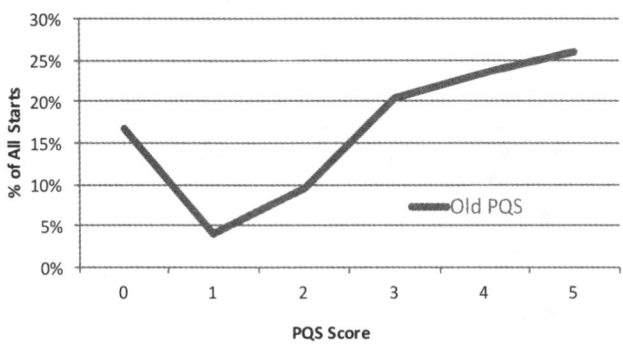

oldPQS Distribution 2012-2014

From 2012-2014, the "average" PQS score was *way* above average, such that the league-wide DOM:DIS ratio was 50%:21%. So what's the problem? Hasn't PQS always tilted more toward DOM than DIS? Yes, but as the balance of power has shifted from hitters to pitchers in recent years, PQS has started to lose its ability to distinguish great pitchers from good ones, good ones from average ones, and average ones from bad ones.

So last offseason we set out to re-define PQS to better reflect today's statistical era (without losing what we love about it), and maybe fix a few other problems along the way. Here is the challenge we gave ourselves:

1. Must still be able to calculate PQS in our heads.
2. All PQS variables must be available in the starting pitcher's simple box score.
3. Must maintain our familiar 0-5 scale.
4. Must account for recent league-wide uptick in strikeouts.
5. Should fix abnormal distribution of current PQS methodology.
6. Must still pass "the smell test" at the individual game level.

We considered all sorts of new methodologies, but they all violated at least one of the above constraints. Then the skies cleared and rainbows appeared and a very simple solution presented itself: set the threshold for each PQS category so that, on a given day, an average major league starting pitcher has a roughly 50% chance of earning that PQS point. This should result in an average PQS score of about 2.5/5.0, and yield a more "normal" distribution of PQS scores across pitchers (in both the intuitive and statistical sense).

NewPQS

We used 2002-2014 data, with a particular focus on 2012-2014, to determine what game-level thresholds yield a 50/50 yes/no split for each PQS category. Pitchers must now reach the following thresholds to earn a newPQS point:

Innings Pitched: >6 IP. 21.4% of all 2002-2014 starts were exactly 6 IP. NewPQS now requires SPs to successfully "pitch into the seventh inning" (vs. "finish the sixth inning") to earn a PQS point for IP. We also removed the auto PQS-0 caveat for starts that lasted less than 5 IP.

Hits allowed: H<IP. This subtle change (vs. H<=IP) gets us closer to a 50% success rate.

Strikeouts: K>=5. Using this absolute count (a) is a tougher threshold than oldPQS's K>=(IP-2) threshold for starts that end before the third out of the seventh inning, (b) doesn't raise the strikeout bar too high for starts that last into the eighth inning and beyond, and (c) holds up well in early exits that are no longer automatic PQS-0s.

Command: (K/BB)>=3 (or if BB=0, K>=3). League average K/BB is now closer to 3.0 than 2.0. Though 2.5 may have worked as well, it's harder on the brain and 3.0 gets us closer to a 50% success rate in recent years.

Home runs: HR=0. This was an easy call, as yielding zero vs. 1+HR in a given start is a 50/50 proposition. The oldPQS threshold of HR<=1 was met in over 85% of starts.

With these changes, starting pitchers under newPQS now have close to a 50/50 achievement rate in all five components, and far closer than oldPQS:

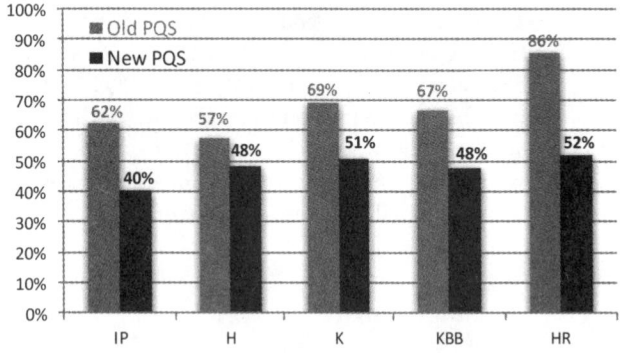

% of Starts where PQS Criteria Met, 2012-2014

And as we had expected, newPQS is distributed more normally:

oldPQS vs. newPQS Distribution 2012-2014

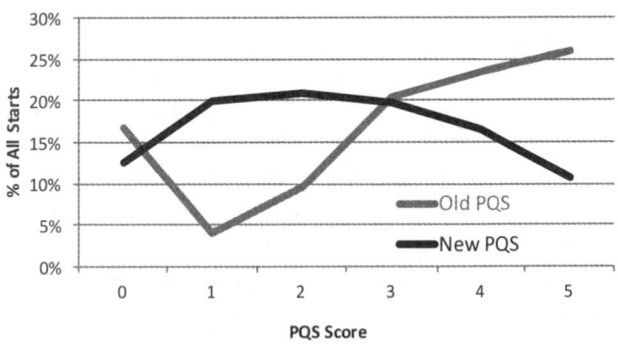

From 2012-2014, the average newPQS DOM:DIS ratio is closer to 1:1 (vs. 2.5:1 using oldPQS), and the average newPQS score is 2.40 (vs. 3.08 using oldPQS).

With a more central midpoint and wider distribution of scores around it, newPQS now gives us an up-to-date framework for evaluating game-level starting pitcher performance, while creating more distinction between starts at each tier.

Here is how performance shakes out in aggregate for each PQS score:

newPQS	Freq	IP	H	ER	HR	BB	K	ERA	WHIP
0	13%	4.3	7.3	4.8	1.5	2.3	2.3	10.01	2.23
1	20%	4.8	6.8	3.6	0.8	2.2	3.1	6.75	1.86
2	21%	5.5	6.1	2.8	0.7	1.9	4.5	4.56	1.45
3	20%	6.2	5.4	2.0	0.5	1.8	5.3	2.89	1.16
4	16%	6.9	4.8	1.5	0.5	1.4	6.5	2.00	0.91
5	11%	7.4	4.2	0.8	0.0	1.0	7.5	0.95	0.71

oldPQS	Freq	IP	H	ER	HR	BB	K	ERA	WHIP
0	17%	3.4	6.6	4.6	0.9	2.2	2.8	12.08	2.59
1	4%	5.2	7.7	4.2	1.2	2.5	2.2	7.21	1.95
2	10%	5.5	7.2	3.6	1.0	2.2	3.3	5.84	1.72
3	20%	5.9	6.3	2.7	0.7	2.0	4.0	4.07	1.41
4	24%	6.5	5.6	2.0	0.5	1.6	5.2	2.84	1.10
5	26%	6.9	4.5	1.3	0.3	1.4	7.1	1.74	0.86

At every step up the PQS ladder, results get demonstrably better. And now we see some real separation between the absolute disaster and absolute dominant starts (PQS-0s and PQS-5s) from the simply very bad and very good starts (PQS-1s and PQS-4s) both skills-wise and results-wise.

When we roll these up one more level, we also see a much more distinct and useful distribution of PQS scores:

newPQS	Freq	IP	H	ER	HR	BB	K	ERA	WHIP
DIS (0-1)	32%	4.6	7.0	4.1	1.0	2.2	2.8	7.92	1.99
DEC (2-3)	40%	5.9	5.8	2.4	0.6	1.9	4.9	3.70	1.30
DOM (4-5)	27%	7.1	4.6	1.2	0.3	1.3	6.9	1.56	0.83

oldPQS	Freq	IP	H	ER	HR	BB	K	ERA	WHIP
DIS (0-1)	21%	3.7	6.9	4.7	1.0	2.3	2.3	11.20	2.46
DEC (2-3)	30%	5.9	6.6	3.0	0.8	2.3	3.5	4.54	1.49
DOM (4-5)	50%	6.8	5.2	1.7	0.5	1.5	6.0	2.32	0.99

The best place to start here might be in the middle with our newly termed PQS-DECent starts (PQS-2s and PQS-3s). From oldPQS to newPQS, these have shifted toward more average results. That's because newPQS pulls more statistically average starts down from the DOMinant level, pushes very poor starts from DECent down to the DISaster level, and even brings up some not-so-bad-just-really-short starts up from DISaster to DECent.

At the DISaster level, the results are still awful whether you're looking at old or new PQS, but notice that newPQS DISasters now incorporate a much larger group of outings, 32% vs. 21%. The average innings pitched are also way up with new PQS, because it is no longer automatically weighed down by every start that lasted less than 5 innings.

Lastly, we see the DOMinant level, which is where newPQS really shines. The PQS-DOM group is now just over half of its previous size under oldPQS. Because of this, the term DOMinant is now reserved for only genuinely valuable fantasy starts. On average, a DOMinant outing means that the starter pitched into the eighth inning, gave up only 4-5 hits, 1-2 walks, 0 home runs, and struck out close to 7 batters. And a just barely DOMinant start might be something like 6.1 innings pitched, 6 hits, 3 walks, 0 home runs, and 6 strikeouts. Still pretty dominant.

And while PQS-DOM starts are definitely now more rare, earning a PQS-DOM is not now "too hard." Rather, under oldPQS, earning a PQS-DOM was just way too easy. With 50% of starts classified as DOMinant, anything league average or better was considered DOMinant, and any start that wasn't tagged as DOMinant was statistically very bad. NewPQS restores the middle class (in the form of PQS-DECent starts: PQS-2s and PQS-3s).

Just as importantly, it brings the extremes (PQS-0s and PQS-5s) into sharper focus. It should be news-worthy when a pitcher throws a PQS-5 or a PQS-0. With 20-30 pitchers throwing most nights, newPQS helps highlight the 2-4 that that were outright DOMinant and the 2-4 that were truly DISastrous.

All references to PQS in this book and on BaseballHQ.com now use our newPQS framework, and additional research using the newPQS system is underway. It's a big change that may take long-time readers time to get used to, but we believe it's a big improvement that will pay dividends for years to come.

The Predictive Value of newPQS

by Arik Florimonte

In April 2016, BaseballHQ.com released an updated version of PQS (summarized in the preceeding article). Thus we now revisit the question of whether PQS-DOM starts have any predictive value, using the new PQS definitions and approaching the problem slightly differently than in the past, in the hopes that we can tease out some additional signal in all the noise.

Background

Using data from 2010-2015, we test whether a streak of PQS-DOM starts leads to a better results in the start immediately following. We examine streaks of between one and four DOM starts. But, since better pitchers tend to have more DOM streaks, and those pitchers are likely to throw more DOMinant starts any time they pitch, we need to remove that effect. As done previously, we divide pitchers into cohorts based on their YTD PQS mean, or their last-five start PQS mean.

The following terms are used in this article:

- PQS: refers to the newPQS. When old PQS is intended, it will be called oldPQS
- SEQ5: The PQS average of 5 starts
- SEQ5 Cohort: tier of pitchers with a SEQ5 in a given range
- YTD Cohort: the tier of pitchers with a year-to-date PQS average in a given range.

We will be using PQS means to evaluate the predictive value of different scenarios. But how big a change in mean should we care about? What does a fractional difference in PQS mean… mean? We plotted YTD PQS average against YTD ERA, YTD WHIP, K/GS, and Wins/GS, and found the following relationships:

ERA	-1.25 / PQS
K/GS	+1.8 / PQS
W/GS	+0.1 / PQS
WHIP	-0.24 / PQS

Clearly, shifting by a tenth of a point for a start here and there isn't going to help you much. But if we can find a process for consistently gaining an advantage over the whole season, it can add up. Consider: if you can manage your staff in a way that improves your rotation's mean PQS by just 0.1, you could move up 0.11 ERA and 0.02 in WHIP, and gain around 40 Ks.

Single Start

Is a single PQS start predictive? Since good starters earn higher PQS scores, we expect high PQS starts would tend to be followed by high PQS starts, resulting in a higher mean score. But what we are really interested in knowing is whether a single PQS-DOM is an indicator that a pitcher is now more likely than he previously was to pitch a good game. To find this, we separate our pitchers into SEQ5 cohorts, and examine six-start sequences: the first five starts are averaged to determine the SEQ5 bin, and the sixth start results are evaluated. Then, we repeat the same analysis, using the YTD Cohort—the PQS mean of all of the pitchers prior starts—and evaluate the next start following.

We find that even after only one PQS-DOM start, there is a slight uptick in both mean PQS and rate of throwing another DOM.

Streaks

If one DOM start is good, we would guess a streak is even better. We look again at the SEQ5 and YTD cohorts, this time finding cases when the SP is coming off a streak of DOMinant starts. We find that a streak does portend better results to come, and the longer the streak, the better the results. We summarize the findings in the table below, where the columns (Str2, Str3, & Str4) are the length of the DOM streak.

	Mean 6th Start PQS and DOM% by DOM Streak									
SEQ5	—6th Start Mean PQS—					——6th Start DOM%——				
Cohort	All	Str1	Str2	Str3	Str4	All	Str1	Str2	Str3	Str4
0.0-0.9	1.69					12%				
1.0-1.9	2.06	2.35	2.38			20%	25%	25%		
2.0-2.9	2.40	2.44	2.59	2.90		27%	28%	32%	35%	
3.0-3.9	2.75	2.75	2.79	2.79	2.67	36%	37%	39%	38%	33%
4.0-5.0	3.19	3.19	3.23	3.25	3.26	48%	48%	49%	51%	52%
Overall	2.42	2.66	2.87	3.02	3.12	27%	28%	40%	45%	48%

	Mean Next Start PQS and DOM% by DOM Streak									
YTD PQS	—Next Start Mean PQS—					——Next Start DOM%——				
Cohort	All	Str1	Str2	Str3	Str4	All	Str1	Str2	Str3	Str4
0.0-0.9	1.59					10%				
1.0-1.9	1.94	2.07	2.48			17%	18%	24%		
2.0-2.9	2.42	2.51	2.63	2.76	2.81	27%	30%	33%	37%	35%
3.0-3.9	2.95	2.97	3.04	3.11	3.16	42%	43%	45%	47%	49%
4.0-5.0	3.27	3.28	3.22	3.21	3.30	53%	53%	50%	52%	59%
Overall	2.42	2.66	2.87	3.02	3.12	27%	28%	40%	45%	48%

Conclusions

- The lowest tier is useless and should be avoided.
- In the next two tiers we see improvement following even a single DOM starts, and the longer the streak, the greater the improvement. (Note: these two tiers cover 68% of pitchers using SEQ5, and 79% of all pitchers using YTD)
- The SEQ5 Cohort 3.0-3.9 sees only slight improvement from streaks. This is probably because 1) it's not possible to have long DOM streaks and stay in this tier without having some other disasters as well; 2) pitchers in this tier are probably good enough to start regardless; and 3) the YTD Cohort 3.0-3.9 sees steady improvement as the streak lengthens.
- The upper tier are elite. Just plug 'em in and go.
- And finally, a tier's best-case outcomes are not quite as good as the baseline of the tier above (which makes sense: if a pitcher has a long enough string of DOM starts, they are probably going to end up in the tier above).

The fantasy owners who would be best positioned to take advantage of this are those who frequently can choose from multiple similar SP options, such as in a DFS league, or in traditional leagues if you have structured your SP strategy around streaming. In either case, make your evaluations as you normally would (e.g. talent first, then matchups or ballpark or by simply using the HQ Pitcher Matchups Tool)—and then give a value bump to the pitcher with the hot streak.

Pitchers, "Just Enough" Home Runs, and HR/FB%

by Brian Slack

For anyone who's ever seen a baseball barely clear the outfield fence, the natural inclination is to think that a fraction of an inch at the point of contact or an "errant gust of wind" would have turned that not-exactly-clobbered home run into a long fly-ball out. By extension, it might be easy to conclude that the hitter got lucky or the pitcher unlucky in that particular instance. Well, thanks to a closer inspection of home run types—with a focus on the "Just Enough" variety—we can see interesting correlations and test whether our natural assumptions are in fact correct, or if perhaps our eyes are playing tricks on us.

Methodology

Using ESPN's Home Run Tracker data, we analyzed year-to-year consistency across the league, focusing on the 528 starting pitchers who logged enough innings to qualify for the ERA title in consecutive years—from 2006 through the end of the 2016 season. From there, we took a more granular look at 10 individual 2015 performances to see how those results carried over to 2016.

League-wide consistency

Home runs, for this study, fall into one of three classifications: (1) Just Enough, meaning the ball cleared the fence by less than 10 vertical feet or landed less than one fence height past the fence, (2) No Doubt, which encompasses those that cleared the fence by at least 20 vertical feet and landed at least 50 feet past the fence, and (3) Plenty, accounting for all other HRs not captured by either of the above classifications.

Across the 11-year period at issue, the portion of MLB yearly totals that each makes up has remained remarkably consistent. For instance, the number of Plenty home runs has generally comprised about half of the yearly totals, with a single-year high of 52% and low of 48%. The No Doubters have tended to hover between 16-18%, with this past year seeing a spike to 19.9%, the highest since 2009's 20.5%. Meanwhile the Just Enough (JE) set, the focus of this analysis, has stayed more or less confined to the 31-33% range, with an 11-year average of 32.4%.

Pitcher variance

Zooming in on ten pitchers—those with the five highest/lowest 2015 percentages of JE home runs (JE%)—we can stack their total HR numbers against those that barely left the yard, comparing the percentages to determine the delta. We wondered if the larger the delta, the more likely an impact on that pitcher's HR/FB.

	2015 HR (JE)	2016 HR (JE)	2015 JE%	2016 JE%	JE% +/-
G.Gonzalez	8 (4)	19 (6)	50%	32%	18%
F.Liriano	15 (7)	26 (10)	47%	39%	8%
CC.Sabathia	28 (13)	22 (4)	46%	18%	28%
C.Martinez	13 (6)	15 (3)	46%	20%	26%
C.Kluber	22 (10)	22 (7)	45%	32%	17%
J.Cueto	21 (4)	15 (6)	19%	40%	-21%
J.A.Happ	16 (3)	22 (9)	19%	41%	-22%
C.Hamels	22 (4)	24 (6)	18%	25%	-7%
R.A.Dickey	25 (4)	28 (4)	16%	14%	2%
Y.Ventura	14 (1)	23 (9)	7%	39%	-32%

Heading into 2016 we might have expected Gio Gonzalez's (50%) and Francisco Liriano's (47%) percentage of JE home runs to fall, perhaps even dramatically. And sure enough, those rates did drop to 32% and 39%, respectively. Conversely, four of the five pitchers with the lowest JE% in 2015—Ventura (7%), Hamels (18%), Happ (19%) and Cueto (19%)—saw their rates balloon in 2016.

While the amount of rise/fall varied depending on the pitcher, most did gravitate back toward the league average (32%) during the second year, with 29 of the 40 qualifying pitchers (i.e., 72.5%) moving back in that direction in 2016, a number consistent with the eleven-year average of 73%.

But does it affect home runs per fly ball?

The question still remains: what impact, if any, does this have on the pitcher's HR/FB rate? First, we look to the correlation between a given pitcher's HR/FB and JE% within a single year.

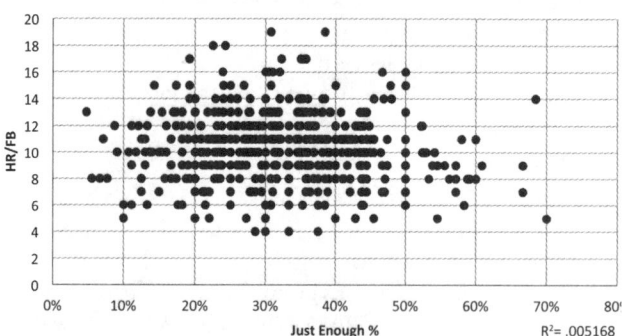

JE% in relation to HR/FB

R^2= .005168

Rather than a tight clustering around a sloping line, we see instead the spread of data points, highlighting the weak correlation between JE% and HR/FB rates. In other words, just because a pitcher gives up a higher percentage of JE home runs does not mean he'll have a (relatively) higher HR/FB rate, or vice versa.

Given the lack of correlation within a single year, it would logically follow that we are unlikely to see a change in JE% impacting the pitcher's HR/FB from one year to the next. Again, the results hold true. Of the 260 pitchers whose JE% went down in Year2, something conventional wisdom might interpret as a positive sign, only 99 (38%) saw their HR/FB improve, while the remainder either held steady (15%) or got worse (47%).

Conclusion

- The percentage of Just Enough home runs that a pitcher gives up gravitates towards league average (32%) the following year.
- There only a tenuous connection between a pitcher's ability to limit the percentage of Just Enough home runs and a pitcher's HR/FB rate. So we should avoid the assumption that a pitcher with a high percentage of Just Enough home runs will necessarily improve his HR/FB rate (and presumably ERA) the following year, or vice versa.
- For 2017, this means being careful not to over-draft Dallas Keuchel (50%), Jose Quintana (45%) or Jake Odorizzi (45%) based solely on the idea of HR/FB improvement, or avoid such pitchers as Julio Teheran (9%), Hector Santiago (12%) or Rick Porcello (13%) due to perceived HR/FB downside.

Using K–BB% to Find SP Buying Opportunties

by Arik Florimonte

Looking for SP Help

It's the middle of summer, and you really need an extra arm or two until your ace returns. But the names on the waiver wire elicit a feeling best described as "meh." Desperate, you filter to look at the last month's stats and *voila!* There are some good performances—surely too small a sample to learn anything from—but you can't help but hope. Can we trust those last 30 days? We turn to strikeout rate minus walk rate (k–bb%) to answer this question.

Methodology

We will filter for pitchers likely to be available in different league types, and then find those who have recently seen an uptick in k–bb%. We estimate the likelihood that they remain rosterable, or even become elite, in the following month.

Background

Using 2014-2016 player-seasons and filtering for SP with ≥ 100 IP, the k–bb% mean is about 13%. The overall MLB mean is approximately 12%, and the top 50 SP tend to be 14% or higher.

We begin with SP game logs from 2010-2015. Since the stabilization points for strikeout and walk rate are 60 and 120 total batters faced (TBF), respectively, we include only pitchers with >120 TBF in both the last 30 days and the next 30 days. We are left with 13587 player-months (a month is a rolling 30-day period).

To see how well k–bb% correlates with the next-30-days results, we plot last-30 k–bb% versus next-30 ERA, WHIP, and K, and calculate the R^2 value of the relationship. Here are those R^2 values summarized:

Next 30 Parameter	Last30 Parameter	R^2
ERA	k–bb%	.038
ERA	BPV	.032
ERA	ERA	.010
WHIP	k–bb%	.067
WHIP	BPV	.058
WHIP	WHIP	.029
K	k–bb%	.225
K	BPV	.157
K	Dom	.258

We find last-30 k–bb% correlates better with next-30 performance than BPV, and in the case of ERA and WHIP, exhibits a much better R^2 than the core statistic itself. Next we will determine if those pitchers showing improvement are likely to be better than the general population of available pitchers.

Setting the Thresholds

We are interested in SP who are likely to be available, so we need to exclude pitchers with YTD numbers higher than a certain threshold. We should also exclude SP with a certain "reputation," as these pitchers will likely be held even if they are struggling, so we will exclude players with a prior year k–bb% above a certain threshold. We also define thresholds for what level performance we would find valuable going forward.

To make this relevant for different league depths, we will define three different sets of thresholds as follows:

- The Study Threshold: players with k–bb% above this in YTD or prior year are expected to be owned everywhere, so they are excluded.
- The Roster Threshold: how well a pitcher has to perform to remain rosterable
- The Elite Threshold: chosen such that players above it would be performing like a top-two SP

League Depth	Study Threshold (YTD or Prior year)		Roster threshold (next 30 days)		Elite Threshold (next 30 days)	
	Tier	k–bb%	Tier	k–bb%	Tier	k–bb%
Shallow (10-tm mxd)	Top 35	16%	Top 80	12%	Top 20	18%
Medium (16-tm mxd)	Top 50	14%	Top 100	10%	Top 35	16%
Deep (12-tm "only")	Top 80	12%	Top 120	8%	Top 50	14%

Shallow Leagues

We exclude all SP that meet any of the following conditions:

- Prior Year: k–bb % ≥ 16% AND TBF ≥ 300; OR no data
- YTD: TBF < 240 [OR] k–bb% > 16%
- Last 30 < 120 TBF
- Next 30 < 120 TBF

The k–bb% Rosterable Threshold is 12%, and Elite Threshold is 18%. We are left with 3209 30-day samples, 222 unique starting pitchers. For a given improvement in k–bb%, how often did those SP stay rosterable, i.e. greater than 12% k–bb% for our shallow league case?

k–bb% improvement	N	Results Next30		"Rosterable" Next30 > 12%		"Elite" Next30 > 18%	
		WHIP	k–bb%	Count	Rate	Count	Rate
All Gainers	1701	1.30	11.3%	757	45%	196	11.5%
≥ 5%	671	1.30	11.4%	301	45%	78	11.6%
≥ 8%	279	1.29	11.7%	133	48%	37	13.3%
≥ 10%	153	1.30	11.4%	72	47%	21	13.7%
All avail SP	3209	1.31	10.9%	1245	42%	325	10.1%

(Note: WHIP is included here has a sanity check, since high k% reduces balls in play, which reduces hits, while low bb% obviously reduces bb)

On average, there is improvement for k–bb% gainers relative to the overall population. Moreover, with a k–bb% improvement of 8% or more, a pitcher has greatly improved odds not only of remaining rosterable, but also of continuing to have an elite month following.

Medium-depth leagues

We tweak our thresholds slightly for medium-depth leagues as outlined above and build our table again:

k–bb% improvement	N	Results Next30		"Rosterable" Next30 > 10%		"Elite" Next30 > 16%	
		WHIP	k–bb%	Count	Rate	Count	Rate
All Gainers	1331	1.30	10.7%	731	55%	236	17.7%
≥ 5%	528	1.31	10.8%	290	55%	97	18.4%
≥ 8%	223	1.30	10.9%	121	54%	38	17.0%
≥ 10%	125	1.31	10.5%	66	53%	14	11.2%
All avail SP	2466	1.32	10.3%	1283	52%	372	15.1%

For this group, pitchers coming off any uptick in k–bb% are more likely to go on to claim an elite month than similar pitchers who have not seen such an uptick.

Deep Leagues

We apply the filters for deep leagues and rebuild the table:

k–bb% improvement	N	Results WHIP	Next30 k–bb%	"Rosterable" Next30 > 8% Count	Rate	"Elite" Next30 > 14% Count	Rate
All Gainers	856	1.33	9.4%	513	60%	162	18.9%
≥ 5%	351	1.33	9.7%	217	62%	76	21.7%
≥ 8%	151	1.31	10.1%	99	66%	36	23.8%
≥ 10%	84	1.32	9.7%	57	68%	16	19.0%
All avail SP	1618	1.34	9.2%	953	59%	271	16.7%

As in shallow and medium leagues, pitchers with an improving k–bb% are more likely to be rosterable or elite than the general population.

Conclusions

- Last 30 days k–bb% is useful as a gauge of next 30 days performance.
- Pitchers on the upswing are more likely to climb into the elite ranks than other pitchers of similar YTD numbers; pitchers with a larger uptick show a greater likelihood.
- Last-30 k–bb% surgers could be good mid-season pickups if they are being overlooked by the other owners in your league.

Seeking Impact Hitters? Look the Other Way

by Brad Kullman

Insightful research by Ed DeCaria a few years back in regard to opposite field home runs has become part of our Encyclopedia. Specifically, the study revealed that opposite field home runs serve as a strong indicator of overall home run power. Could the ability to hit the ball *hard* to the opposite field provide similar insight as to a hitter's all-around hitting ability?

Method

Ignoring trajectory and hit result, we examined hard hit balls of all types (flies, liners, and grounders) from the 2015 season by hitters with 100 or more plate appearances. We broke down opposite-field hard-hit rates into tiers, and then did the same with pull-rates.

The Results

The average opposite field hard contact percentage among 445 qualifiers (100 overall plate appearances) was 22.1%, with 212 players coming in above that average line and 233 coming in below. Moving to round number thresholds from there, 154 players had opposite field hard contact rates above 25%, while 182 players were below 20%. Moving farther away from the average, 80 players topped the 30% mark, while 93 players fell short of 15%.

Opposite Field Hard Hit Rates with Corresponding Overall Averages

Opp-HH Rate	Players	AVG	SLG	ISO	OBP
>30%	80	.273	.462	.189	.346
>25%	154	.269	.446	.176	.338
Above Avg (22.1%)	212	.267	.441	.174	.335
Below Avg (22.1%)	233	.253	.390	.137	.312
<20%	182	.251	.387	.135	.309
<15%	93	.251	.374	.123	.303

Not only do we find players with the best opposite field hard contact percentage having the best batting average, which might

be expected, but we also find that they have the most overall power! Both slugging percentage and isolated power appear to correspond with the ability to drive the ball to all fields.

But power hitters *pull* the ball, right? In order to get a perspective on our top opposite field hard contact hitters, we also looked at the players who consistently pull the ball the most.

Pull Rates with Corresponding Overall Averages

Pull Rate	Players	AVG	SLG	ISO	OBP
50% +	25	.239	.456	.216	.326
45% +	85	.248	.443	.195	.321
Above Avg (39.4%)	220	.253	.428	.175	.319
Below Avg (39.44%)	225	.267	.403	.136	.328

The average player in this study pulled the ball just under 40% of the time, with 85 players topping 45% and 25 players pulling over half the balls they put into play. While the 50% plus group produces significant power, it comes at the expense of batting average. In addition, when the 85 players that pull the ball over 45% of the time are matched against the 80 who top a 30% opposite field hard contact rate, the power numbers are almost identical, while the opposite field group comes in with a batting average some 25 points higher.

Summary

Hitters who can effectively use the whole field are more productive in virtually every facet of hitting than those with an exclusively pull-oriented approach. Especially as MLB teams continue to use batted ball data in order to aggressively defend the turf with exaggerated shifts, single-field hitters are going to have little green to work with, causing this phenomena to become increasingly magnified.

How Pitch Framing Affects Staring Pitcher Value

By Arik Florimonte

Introduction

Pitch framing ability has long been valued in catchers, but only recently have analysts begun to quantify it. Good framers are coveted by savvy teams, and some have been rewarded with lucrative long-term contracts. However, projection systems for pitchers do not appear to have kept pace. While park factors and team defense are routinely incorporated into projections for pitchers, framing ability of the catcher is not. We can estimate the effects of catcher pitch framing on a starting pitcher's statistics—particularly strikeouts, WHIP, ERA, and wins—and determine by how much the framing skill of a catcher impacts a pitcher's projection.

Orientation

This analysis uses several framing statistics that may not be familiar:

- Called Strike Above Average (CSAA, from Baseball Prospectus' Catcher stats database) is the total number of called strikes a catcher gains (or loses) through his pitch framing ability.
- Framing Opportunity (FO) is a pitch taken by the batter, but was near enough to the strike zone to have a nonzero chance of being called a strike.

- CSAA% is CSAA/FO. The distribution of a catcher's CSAA% rates in a season generally spans +/- 3%, with 0% being league average (by definition).

To calculate the effect of an extra strike, we used the 2015 MLB splits by count at baseball-reference.com. Using the first pitch as an example, here are the average rates of key outcomes, depending on whether the first pitch is a strike or not:

	BB/PA	H/PA	K/PA	Outs/PA*
After 1-0	.140	.225	.162	.647
After 0-1	.043	.207	.282	.758
Difference	-.097	-.018	+.080	+.111

Outs are calculated as AB+SH+SF+DP-H-ROE

On average, the first-pitch strike reduces the pitcher's total walks and hits, and increases strikeouts. It also theoretically increases the pitcher's IP total, because that PA is now more likely to result in an out, and the pitcher can go further in his start.

Performing a similar exercise for all possible counts, and weighting by how often historically a pitch is taken on a particular count, we calculate the weighted average value of an extra strike across all counts:

Change per extra strike

BB/PA	-.141
H/PA	-.028
K/PA	.260
IP/PA	.085

We can now estimate the impact of catcher pitch framing on a starting pitcher's fantasy value. To do so, we created a fictional starting pitcher, Joe Average, whose stat line is the per-game average of all 2015 SP with >120 IP, multiplied by 32 starts:

	IP	W	ER	ERA	WHIP	K
Joe Average	193.8	12.7	81.9	3.803	1.245	166.7

There are, on average league-wide, 7.13 FO per IP. So while Joe Average is on the mound, his catchers will have 1,382 opportunities to steal or give away a strike. If we put Joe with a +1.0% framer, his catcher will steal 13.8 strikes over a season.

Impact on Fantasy Statistics

The framer's impact on Strikeouts and WHIP are simple to calculate using the values above. A +1.0% framer will steal Joe an extra 1.2 IP and 3.6 K, and reduce his walks issued by 1.9, and his hits allowed by 0.4. His new strikeout total for the year is 168.3, and his new WHIP is reduced by 0.020 to 1.225.

The impact on ERA is also direct to estimate. In 2015 Dan Meyer of the Hardball Times estimated the run value of an extra strike to be .143. We use that value and assume that any run saved is an earned run saved. The +1.0% framer will reduce ER by 2.0 and increase Joe's IP by 1.2, dropping his ERA from 3.803 to 3.688

Those extra runs saved will lead to a small tick up in Expected Wins. Using Matthew Cederholm's formula for Expected Wins, and inputting the 2014-2016 average RS/G of 4.26 and Joe's unadjusted 3.803 ERA, we calculate 12.69 Expected Wins. Using Joe's framing-adjusted ERA of 3.688 gives 13.01 projected wins. The impact of +1.0% framing is 0.32 wins.

SP value changes due to pitch framing

Given these estimates, what does the quality of a framer do to Joe's overall fantasy value?

with +/- Framer	IP	W	K	ERA	WHIP	Rank	15$
Joe Average +3%	197.4	13.6	177.5	3.46	1.19	25	13
Joe Average +2%	196.2	13.3	173.9	3.57	1.21	29	11
Joe Average +1%	195.0	13.0	170.3	3.69	1.23	34	10
Joe Average	193.8	12.7	166.7	3.80	1.25	44	9
Joe Average -1%	192.6	12.4	163.1	3.92	1.26	54	8
Joe Average -2%	191.4	12.0	159.5	4.04	1.28	66	6
Joe Average -3%	190.2	11.7	155.9	4.16	1.30	69	5

A small change in framing ability has a small but significant effect on a pitcher's fantasy value—enough to bump him a round or two in your draft. Bigger changes would have even more dramatic effects.

CSAA% from year to year

To properly take advantage of this, the last piece of the puzzle is identifying catchers who are good and bad framers. Fortunately, CSAA% is fairly sticky from year to year: using data from 2008-2015 and filtering for catchers with minimum 1500 FO in both the current and prior year, CSAA%=0.79 * PY-CSAA%, with an R^2 of 0.57.

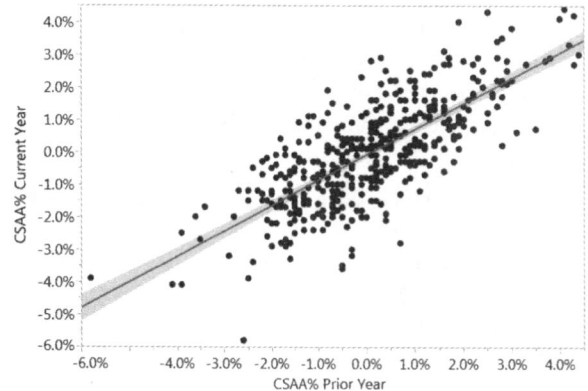

Conclusion

The projections say that a move to a different catcher should have a small effect on each of the fantasy stats that we care about for starting pitchers. The change in any one category by itself could be dismissed as part of the noise, but since framing affects all four simultaneously, the cumulative effect can be significant.

Based on 2016's pitch framing results, there are 11 framers with expected CSAA for 2017 above 1%:

Player	pCSAA	Player	pCSAA
Miguel Montero	+2.2%	Roberto Perez	+1.3%
Yasmani Grandal	+2.1%	Tyler Flowers	+1.3%
Buster Posey	+2.0%	Rene Rivera	+1.3%
Tony Wolters	+1.3%	Russell Martin	+1.0%
Jason Castro	+1.3%	Francisco Cervelli	+1.0%

As your 2017 draft approaches, it is worthwhile to identify pitchers with expected impact due to the framing skill of their new receiver(s)—pitchers who changed teams or pitchers on teams that changed catchers. Look for not only the quality of the framer, but the delta between their old and new receiver(s). The projections will likely be based on the past receiver(s) and not reflect the change in catcher. You may then confidently go a round earlier or a dollar extra for starting pitchers with favorable catcher changes, and let someone else overdraft or overspend on those whose new catchers represent a downgrade in framing ability.

GAMING RESEARCH ABSTRACTS

2016 Trends, 2017 Responses

by Patrick Davitt

The 2016 season featured several actionable trends: increased overall HR production and a change in HR distribution; a decline in SBs and a change in their distribution; and a continued trend toward even more strikeouts.

This article looks at how these trends from 2016 might affect fantasy play in 2017, along with some players who might gain or lose value as a result of how the trends might affect them individually. In this article, "elite" individual players are the top 15% in the category being discussed, and all individual players mentioned or included in stat-gathering are "qualified" (except where noted) by having met PT minimums:

- Batters: 100 PA. Reference to a stat like "SB/650" means per 650 PA
- Starters: 100 IP, 10 starts, 90% of appearances as starts
- Relievers 20 IP, 90% of appearances in relief, 2 starts or fewer

The season saw five important trends and some minor ones. Among the lesser trends were a small but ongoing increase in the number of pitchers used and a parallel decrease in the number of innings starting pitchers were reaching in their starts.

Home Runs

The biggest change in 2016 was the HR increase. Qualifying batters in 2016 hit about 23.0 HR/650, up a full 5.0 HR/650 from last season. It's the highest mark ever, surpassing even the Steroid Era. Notwithstanding the Commissioner's denials, the most convincing explanation is the baseballs, whose manufacturing changed just as the HR spike began in the second half of 2015:

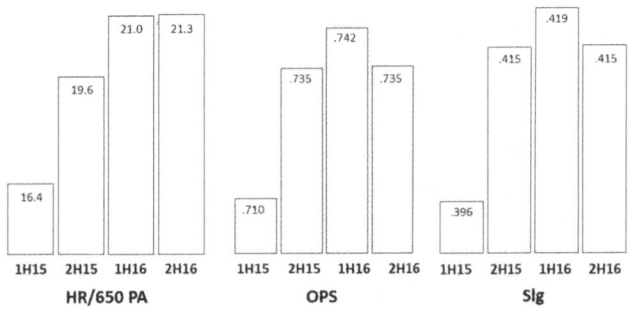

In these power stats, we see power numbers jump noticeably in the 2H2015, with HR/650 up about 20%, OPS up about 3.5% and Slg up about 5%. Those gains jumped again in 2016.

More important than the number of big flies was distribution of HRs:

	HR Season Cohort				
	40+	30-39	20-29	10-19	<10
2014	1	10	46	106	280
2015	9	11	44	135	246
2016	8	30	73	103	220

The nine hitters who mashed 40+ big flies in 2015 were as many as in 2012-14 combined. But the real jump to be aware of is in the next tiers down. The 30 batters in the 30-39 HR cohort were almost triple 2015's total, and the 20-29 group jumped by about two-thirds, to 73. Combine the two tiers, and 2016 had more than 100 hitters who chipped in with 20-39 taters, more than any other season in history—including the Steroid Era. This stands to reason—if we assume the juiceball adds a few extra feet to flyballs, the greatest jumps should occur with the hitters who are having balls die on the warning track, not those who are whacking 'em into the tenth row of the bleachers.

How to Play It: De-emphasize your valuations of the top handful of HR-only sluggers—guys like Jedd Gyorko, Brandon Moss, Miguel Sano and Corey Dickerson, who provide mid-20s HR or more but low BAs, surprisingly few runs and RBI, and few to no SBs. Choose instead from the abundant 20-30 HR guys who give runs and RBIs as well as BA (Nelson Cruz, Nolan Arenado, Robinson Cano, Manny Machado), SB (Jason Kipnis, Adam Eaton), or both (Charlie Blackmon, Francisco Lindor, Xander Bogaerts). And that's not even considering the top-tier elite all-rounders like Mookie Betts, Mike Trout and Paul Goldschmidt.

For 2017, it should be possible to get competitive HRs by focusing on those abundant mid-tier, multi-contributing sluggers. It usually takes about 300 HR to get a top-three in HR in a typical 15-mixed league, about 21 HR per offensive roster slot. With more than 100 hitters in the 20-39 HR tier, there's no need to spend on the high-HR guys who come without other benefits. Oh, and don't go for a leak when Nick Franklin is nominated.

The emphasis on HR also affects how to consider pitchers. We always knew low-HR pitchers enjoy higher Strand Rates and therefore reduced ERAs. BaseballHQ.com includes HR/9 as a core pitcher evaluation metric, but you might want to give a little more value weight to potentially underappreciated low-HR/9 starters like James Paxton (SEA), Joe Ross (WAS), Tanner Roark (WAS) and Junior Guerra (MIL), and ultra-low-HR relievers like Matt Strahm (KC), Dan Otero (CLE), Cam Bedrosian (LAA) and Seung Hwan Oh (STL).

Stolen Bases

A moment ago we mentioned Nick Franklin because of his HR potential; he is also interesting because he pro-rated to more than 20 SB in 2016 had he enjoyed 650 PA. The value of 20+ SB producers is amplified by the other important big offensive trends: a continuing rapid decline in SB attempts and a decline in the number of teams ready to run:

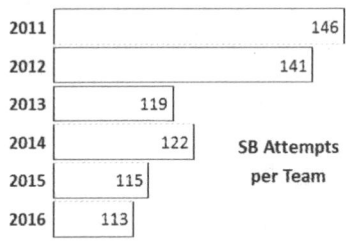

SB Attempts Team Count By Season					
	40+	30-39	20-29	10-19	<10
2011	8	10	9	3	0
2012	3	12	13	2	0
2013	3	9	10	7	1
2014	2	6	15	7	0
2015	0	5	18	7	0
2016	2	8	8	10	2

Average SB attempts (SBA) sagged to 113 SBA/team, 12 SBA/650 overall, the lowest mark since free agency began in 1976. There is a team split to consider: 12 teams had fewer than 100 SBA in 2016, compared with seven teams in 2014 and only three in 2011. Meanwhile, teams with 100+ SBA declined to 10 in 2016 from 18 in 2011. In fact, of the 30 lowest team SBA totals in the free-agent era, six are 2016 teams, and with just 32 SBA, the 2016 Orioles had half the SBA of the lowest previous teams.

At the same time, SBA distribution didn't spread the wealth like HRs. In fact, the opposite appears to be true:

SB Player Cohorts By Season						
	40+	30-39	20-29	10-19	5-9	1-4	0
2011	15	23	33	79	92	162	48
2012	13	21	39	72	85	174	55
2013	13	10	35	55	93	181	66
2014	11	9	36	61	97	176	53
2015	6	12	33	66	89	167	72
2016	9	14	27	64	88	169	67

In 2011, 71 different players attempted 20+ SBs. That number eased downward over the next few years, then dropped to 56 in 2014. Since then, it has slid still further, to 50 this season. We also see an increase in the number of hitters whose feet are nailed to the bases.

As a result, elite players accounted for almost 60% of SBA (and SB) in 2016, and the ultra-elite, the top five percent, amassed more than 25% of all SBA and SB. The top 1%—Jonathan Villar, Billy Hamilton, Starling Marte, Eduardo Nunez, Rajai Davis and Travis Jankowski—compiled more than 10% of the SBA. On the other end, 67 batters, 15% of qualifiers, had no attempts at all.

How to Play It: The change in SB distribution has changed how the category plays in roto-style fantasy, with a couple of owners typically running away from the field, a few more jockeying for top-half points, and the rest competing in the lower points levels.

It appears the play could be to target one or two of the elite SB guys, but to concentrate on the ones who also provide some additional benefit. Hamilton and Davis, for instance, will provide SBs that will position an owner well in SB, but not much else. By contrast, Villar and Segura will add useful stats across-the-board, and Nunez, if he's healthy, will be in that conversation.

Also keep in mind the team issue. We should already discount speed sources on SB-averse teams like BAL, NYM, STL, LA, OAK, TOR and SEA. If the juiceball continues, more teams will play "station-to-station," eschewing the risk of a CS in favor of waiting for the three-run bomb. Manny Machado seems highly unlikely

to justify first-round or high-dollar bidding if he repeats the zero SB he had this year, and given BAL's all-way stop philosophy, Machado's SB value looks fixed at or very near zero.

If HRs continue to look prevalent, you'll have to re-revalue top SB sources upwards, and add an extra buck to runners on SB-heavy teams like MIL, CIN, SD, CLE, ARI, PIT and WAS. Watch for changes in front offices and/or managers. MIL was the most larcenous big-league team, with three players in the top 25. Villar was 2016's big story, and is well positioned to earn the big-bucks he'll cost in 2017. Put 3B-OF Hernan Perez on your radar— he swiped 30+ with near-20 HR/650 pop. A lot of whiffing in his game, and he doesn't walk enough, but coaching and experience might help. OF Keon Broxton made very poor contact—bottom 10 of the game—but walked 15% of his PA, helping his SB opportunities and making him more viable in OBP leagues.

Strikeouts

The overall K% of 21.5% in 2016 pushed to a new frontier beyond 2015's previous alltime high of 20%, and the 21.2% K% among our qualified hitters was a 12.1% jump over 2015. Since 2011, the K% among qualified hitters has risen 2.4 percentage points, about a 13% increase. The 2016 season also saw a new mark in sustained whiffing, as 16 different qualified hitters struck out in more than one-third of their PA. The highest BA among these human wind machines: just .247, by TAM OF Steven Souza. The 2016 elite contact hitters whiffed at a 12.1% clip, substantially better than their peers but likewise still a new high (or low) strikeout rate. Only nine hitters notched K rates under 10%. Add a buck or three to HOU 2B Jose Altuve, if you need another reason to target him. Also remember HOU IF Yuliesky Gourriel (8.8% in a short PA sample), and CLE 3B Jose Ramirez (10.0%), a breakout favorite next year.

Strikeouts moved slightly higher for pitchers as well as for hitters, nosing over 8.0 K/9 for the first time. Relievers crept over 9.0, about 1 whiff more than starters.

How to Play It: Tweak your strikeout targets before 2017 drafts to reflect the higher rates. Remember that elite K-makers among starters SPs are now over 9.5 K/9, elite RPs top 11.0. NYY starter Michael Pineda's 10.6 K/9 was ninth-best among starters, but again had disappointing results in 2016 that might depress his 2017 price. Aaron Nola flirted with 10 K/9 but a strand rate barely 60% killed his ERA. Among relievers, Hector Neris played second fiddle in the PHI bullpen to Jeanmar Gomez, but Neris' K/9 almost doubled Gomez's. And the Angels' Cam Bedrosian had his 2016 cut short by a blood-clotting issue in his pitching arm, but he had taken over as closer, and his 11.9 K/9 was elite. He also reined in the walks.

SP Game Depth

The fourth 2016 trend with fantasy implications was a sharp decline in the number of innings and pitches starting pitchers provided. Back in 2011, starters went at least 5 IP (and therefore qualified for a Win) in 86% of starts, threw seven innings 34% of starts, and threw 100 pitches in 49% of starts. Over the last three seasons, all those numbers have dropped, and 2016 set new lows (chart includes all starters without season-innings qualifications):

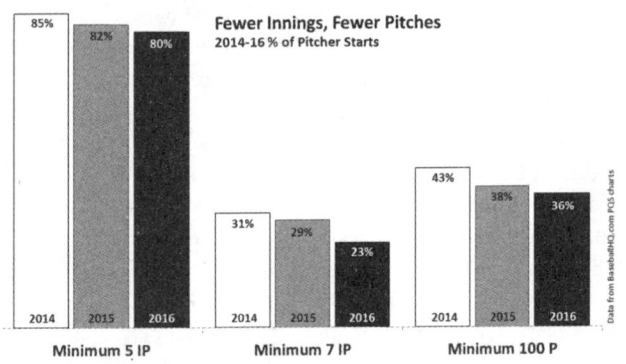

Fewer Innings, Fewer Pitches
2014-16 % of Pitcher Starts

This change has a couple of important effects on wins and strikeouts. With wins, it's as basic as it gets: Pitch more innings, win more games. For 2014-16:

Innings	Win%
5.0-5.2	26%
6.0-6.2	39%
7.0-7.2	54%
8+	74%

Pitchers who go 7+ IP win about twice as often as pitchers who don't reach 6 IP, and pitchers getting through 8 IP win at triple the rate of those pulled before six. And as the chart shows, fewer pitchers are reaching that 7-IP threshold (and fewer still are getting to 8 IP). At the same time, increasing unwillingness to extend starters even to 100 pitches—now barely more than one-third of starts—obviously limits a pitcher's chances of getting deeper into the game, and therefore less likely to get the win.

The capacity to get deep into games also affects strikeout totals, again for obvious reasons: A pitcher not in the game can't get strikeouts. Over the last three seasons (2014-16, qualified 100-IP starters only), about 33% of starts went 7+ IP. But the distribution of those starts is not even; only about a third of starters reached that 33% threshold. The elite level performers over the period reached 7+ IP 46% of all games—but again that number was part of an ongoing decline, from 52% in 2014 to 47% in 2015 and just 41% in 2016.

How To Play It: If you don't already, give a little extra credit to starters who have a demonstrated ability to pitch deep into their starts. As noted, they're getting tougher to find and what it means to be "elite" is declining as well. Most of the elite names are well-recognized as top performers (Kershaw, Sale, Price, etc.), but some names might be worth stashing:

Aaron Sanchez (TOR) wasn't on any list in 2014-15 because he wasn't starting, but in 2016 reached 7 IP in half his starts. And he won the ERA title. There will be some pre-season anxiety over workload as the Jays made their playoff run after running Sanchez out there more than they planned. But he'll be 25 next July, so it's not like he's a teenager.

Sanchez' teammate Marcus Stroman missed 2015 but quietly posted 40% 7+ marks both in 2014 and this year, when he averaged 6.1 IP per start. Some bad luck on HR/F killed his ERA but he pitched like a 3.50 ERA guy. Not a ton of Ks, but a 60% GB rate on balls in play in front of a solid infield defense should keep that ERA down, especially if the HR/F regresses to more normal levels.

Rick Porcello (BOS) has reached the 7-IP level in 48% of his starts in 2014. And 2015. And 2016. This year, it was good enough to make the elite. Porcello is an example of how just staying out there pays dividends. His 7.6 Dom was just average, but he stayed in games long enough to amass 223 IP. And when you multiply a 66th-best Dom by a sixth-best IP total, you get a 16th-best, and very useful, 189 strikeouts. Porcello's Cy Young caliber 2016 was already being dissed as "lucky," with references to his run support. But Porcello is a seasoned veteran (just 27 next Opening Day despite eight MLB seasons and almost 1,470 IP), and his Cmd, just under 6.0, was second-best among starters (to some guy named Kershaw) and contributed to a WHIP under 1.0. Take advantage of any discount.

And while it was easy to ignore pretty much anyone playing in Atlanta, Julio Teheran deserves notice. For the second time in three years he was elite at getting deep, with just under half his starts going 7+ innings and 60% of his starts going 100+ pitches. He's not an elite Dom pitcher but he's right around 8.0 K/9, and if he can get back to the 220 IP level he attained in 2014, he could recover to 200+ K as well.

Conclusion

Rating SPs for draft and auction prep doesn't take place in a contextual vacuum. The game is changing all the time. It wasn't so long ago that a 7.5 Dom was pretty darn good, but these days it's barely acceptable. Other situations and usage patterns change as well, and the smart fantasy owner knows to spot the trends and take advantage. So during this year's prep, keep your eyes open for mid-tier HR guys with other production values, for higher-contact guys, and for pitchers who have shown the knack for getting deep into games.

Draft Preparation with a Full-Season Mindset

by Matt Dodge

The astute fantasy participant will look at the six-month major league (and fantasy) baseball season, and develop a draft day plan in concert with a season-long strategy for success.

League Variations

The original rules of the Rotisserie Baseball Founding Fathers have evolved along several different dimensions in the past 30+ years, each having in-season management implications that can drive draft day tactics. Your league variations could include one or more of the following:

- Player pool: AL only, NL only, mixed AL/NL, or something else.
- Reserve list: Larger reserve lists result in a smaller Free Agent pool, which is a significant consideration for AL- or NL- only leagues.
- Transactional type and frequency (daily, weekly, monthly).
- Scoring categories: 4x4, 5x5, others. Note the balance between counting stats and "average" stats. In traditional 4x4, one of the four categories (batting average) can have a negative impact on team scoring, but two of the

four pitching categories (ERA, WHIP), can drag your team down. In 5x5, those impacts are reduced from 25% to 20% for hitting, and 50% to 40% for pitching, but still twice as impactful on the pitching side of the ledger.

Each of these individual dimensions should impact your draft day plan, but it may also be helpful to look at them in combination. Using a matrix format, the groupings raise some interesting considerations.

Sources of Additional Stats after Draft Day

League Player Pool

Reserve List	Mixed 15 team	AL- or NL-only 12 team
Short	free agents	trades, free agents
Long	free agents, trades	trades

Whether the "new guy" or a long-time league member, look at the prior season's transactional summary for your league, to analyze the proportional category contributions from trade acquisitions and free agent pickups for the successful teams. Trades are often necessary to add specific stats in AL/NL-only leagues as the player pool penetration is generally much deeper, and the size of a reserve roster further reduces the help possible from the free agent pool.

Draft Strategies Related to In-season Player Acquisition

Trade Activity

FA Pool	Low	High
Shallow	solid foundation (STR)	tradable commodoties surplus counting stats
Deep	gamble on upside (S&S)	ultimate flexibility

Trading activity is a function of multiple factors. Keeper leagues tend to keep owners engaged longer during the season by providing trading opportunities to "play for next year" when current season success appears unlikely. However, those increased opportunities are often controlled by special rules to prevent undesirable "dump trading." Also, stratification of the standings, especially in a redraft league, can cause owners at the bottom of the standings to lose interest, reducing the number of effective trading partners as the season goes on.

When deep rosters create a shallow free agent pool in a league with little trading, the onus is squarely on the draft day acquisition of solid contributors. In this case, a Spread the Risk strategy designed to accumulate at bats, innings, and saves would be the recommended approach. If the free agent pool is deep, the drafter can take more risks with the Stars and Scrubs approach, acquiring "lottery ticket" players with upside, knowing that replacements are readily available if the upside plays don't hit in a reasonable amount of time.

In leagues where trading is prevalent, a shallow free agent pool means you should acquire players on draft day with the intent of trading them. This could mean a traditional strategy of acquiring a category surplus (frequently saves and/or steals), and then trading them in mid-season to shore up other categories. In a keeper league, this includes grabbing a few bargains (to interest those who are rebuilding) or grabbing top performers to flip in trade (if you are already on "the two year plan").

Draft Day Considerations for In-season Roster Management

Reserve List Txn Freq	4 x 4 League Format	5 x 5 League Format
Daily	careful SP management batting platoons positional flexibility	RP (K, ERA, WHIP) batting platoons positional flexibility
Weekly	SP (2 start weeks) cover risky starters	SP (2 start weeks) cover risky starters

Expanding on the considerations noted above, owners must be careful with pitching, due to the negative impact potential of ERA and WHIP. Blindly streaming pitchers on a daily basis can be counter-productive, particularly in 4x4 leagues. In 5x5, the Strikeouts category can make a foundation of high Dom relievers a useful source of mitigation for the invariable starting pitching disappointments.

The degree that these recommendations can be implemented is also dependent on the depth of the reserve list itself. Obviously those with longer reserve lists can do more than those with a shorter list, but the key is deciding up front how you plan to use that reserve list, however long it is, and then tailor your draft strategy toward that usage.

Of course, it is frequently more complicated than just two dimensions. A 15-team, mixed, 5x5 league with a seven player reserve list will roster about 180 pitchers on draft day, or the six best pitchers on each of the 30 MLB teams. If this is a keeper league, it is likely that many of the starting pitchers with positive ERA and WHIP contributions are already rostered. If this league has daily transactions, the owner could consider loading up on high Dom starting pitchers at the draft, planning to churn them daily to build up strikeouts and hope for wins, while relying on skilled middle relievers to mitigate ERA and WHIP damage.

Conversely, a drafter in an AL/NL-only league, with deep reserve lists and weekly transactions, may want to target a wide range of starting pitchers during the draft. That will provide a greater choice of options when selecting starting pitchers for weekly roster decisions, and leave the relievers in the free agent pool.

These are only some of the possible combinations as Rotisserie baseball has evolved. The key is to actively consider the specifics of your league, and how those nuances of in-season management provide insights into your draft day preparation, through analyses similar to the above.

It's Still LIMA Time: Drafting Hitters During the New Pitching Era

by Brad Kullman

As scoring has decreased in this "post-steroid era," we have seen a corresponding improvement in pitching, leading many pundits to advise increasing the draft focus on pitchers. The stance seems to be rooted in the "fact" that you may be left behind if you don't load up on arms in this "new era of the pitcher." Not so fast!

Looking back to when the very first Rotisserie League rules were laid out in 1980, the 14-hitter/9-pitcher structure that remains an industry standard resulted in roughly three-quarters of both hitters and pitchers of the 12-team National League being rostered by the ten original Rotisserie League teams. Over the next three-and-a-half decades, however, the nature of how pitchers are managed at the MLB level changed drastically. Starters pitching deep into a game became a rare occurrence, due to the evolution of one-inning closers and single-batter matchup relief specialists.

In 1980, MLB pitchers registered 856 complete games, as 27 pitchers topped 230 innings and 17 reached the 250 mark, led by Steve Carlton's ridiculous 304! A designated "ninth-inning guy" was unheard of, as multi-inning saves were quite common and top starters would scowl at the sight of action in the bullpen. Goose Gossage and Dan Quisenberry each posted an MLB-high 33 saves. Of those 66 combined saves, well over half (42) were more than one inning. Gossage recorded 14 two-plus inning saves, while Quisenberry picked up 18 of his own two-plus variety, including one four-inning save (changing times, indeed!). Just six pitchers reached the 25-save plateau, while 18 managed to top 15 saves. Though the "hold" had yet to be coined, in retrospect, we can see there were only 344 such accomplishments. In such an environment, the only thing a deep bullpen would bring about is pitchers who need more work. Accordingly, MLB teams routinely carried a roster of ten pitchers and 15 hitters, sometimes even dropping down to a 9/16 mix, depending on off-days and perceived starter workloads.

Fast-forward to 2016 where, even in the midst of a perceived pitching "renaissance," we see a different game, played in a different way. A grand total of 83 complete games were thrown in 2016 (a 90% decrease), while only David Price managed to reach the 230-inning threshold. The 25-save tier was reached by 20 closers, while 32 pitchers tallied 15 or more, and "holds" were up more than seven-fold to 2,421. The result is that MLB teams have taken to routinely carrying 12 pitchers and only 13 hitters, sometimes even adding a 13th arm for a stretch.

In fantasy leagues maintaining the original 14-hitter/9-pitcher roster structure, the culture change within MLB has unwittingly resulted in a saturation of the hitter market while leaving a multitude of arms to sift through in the free agent pool.

1980 Single League

(10-man MLB pitching staffs)	Hitters	Pitchers
Available (12 NL teams)	15h x 12tm = 180	10p x 12tm = 120
10-Team Single-League	14h x 10 tm = 140	9p x 10tm = 90
Roster Usage Rate	78%	75%

2016 Single League

(12-man MLB pitching staffs)	Hitters	Pitchers
Available (15 NL teams)	13h x 15tm = 195	12p x 15tm = 180
12-Team Single-League	14h x 12 tm = 168	9p x 12tm = 108
Roster Usage Rate	86%	60%

2016 Mixed League

(12-man MLB pitching staffs)	Hitters	Pitchers
Available (30 MLB teams)	13h x 30tm = 390	12p x 30tm = 360
15-Team Mixed League	14h x 15 tm = 210	9p x 15tm = 135
Roster Usage Rate	54%	37.5%

In both single-league and mixed-league play, the apparent plan of the original Rotisserie League founders to roster a comparable percentage of the available player pool has fallen out of balance. The result is that the in-season opportunity to find useful offense has become far more difficult than adding productive pitching. But there is one more factor that may convince you to move some of your pitching funds over to the hitting budget.

Next, Add Risk

Change in MLB roster construction has coincided with increasingly conservative management of pitchers in general. Not only do they get extra rest whenever possible, but disabled list stints come at seemingly the slightest twinge.

According to Spotrac.com, there were 475 players who spent a combined total of 33,057 days on the disabled list in 2016. Of those, 274 (58%) were pitchers. Even more disconcerting, those 274 pitchers accounted for a staggering 20,440 (62%) of the DL days. A baseball team fields nine players at a time on the diamond and one of those positions accounts for almost two-thirds of all missed time due to injury! This does make some sense, as many pitching (arm-related) injuries require lengthy recovery times, whereas position players tend to suffer more of the muscular sprain/strain variety that heal nicely in a matter of days.

But back to the 62% DL days number. If 39% of your fantasy team (9 pitchers on a standard 23-man roster) is in danger of being hit with almost two-thirds of the injury-related missed time, investing significant capital in this position represents extreme risk, relatively speaking. And this is before factoring in what is oftentimes decreased performance leading up to the diagnosis of an underlying injury.

Load Up the Lumber

So, how does the smart fantasy baseball competitor profit from this information? If you are competing in a typical fantasy league where traditional roster structure provides such an exploitable inefficiency, then get ready to load up the bats on draft day. Championships are rarely won on draft day, but as the season gets underway, and you begin trawling for assets to supplement your title drive, where would you rather be fishing? Angling in the fertile free agent pitching pool is a lot more fun (and productive) than spending the summer trying to catch something useful in the relatively shallow power and speed waters.

What Strategy? Take What the Table Gives You

by Patrick Davitt

As we start looking ahead to our drafts each year, we see a lot of website articles, podcast discussions and bar fights about the best strategies for drafts and auctions. Some web articles had headlines like, "When to Start the Closer Run" (a tactic, not a strategy) and "The Over-30 All-Stars Strategy."

We can add those newcomers to a tall pile. If you've been around fantasy baseball for any kind of while, you'll have seen lots of strategies. "Stars and Scrubs" is a strategy. So are "Spread the Risk," "All Lefthanders," "Punting a Category," "No Player over $29," and "No Player under $10." "Labadini" (the $9 pitching staff) is a strategy. Fantasy baseball has more strategies than the Kardashians have scandals.

And all the strategies have something in common: They don't work. To be more accurate, they work, but only work if all your opponents at the table cooperate to benefit you, which is kind of like having an Asian military strategy that works only if Kim-Jong Un is on board.

The Tyson Philosophy

There's a famous Mike Tyson quote about boxing, usually cited as, "Everybody has a plan until they get punched in the face." This neatly summarizes the problem with fantasy baseball strategies: Your opponents will punch you in the face. If they see your strategic goals, they'll try to mess you up by drafting the players you need. More often, they'll mess you up just because they happen to want the same players you do, for their own reasons.

Think about "Stars and Scrubs." It's a great strategy, unless other teams are also Stars and Scrubsing. At that point, economists say the laws of supply and demand will force up prices on the stars and the scrubs. Thus, the bargains will then fall to the middle-tier players for owners playing Spread the Risk. But if there's also a bunch of them, they will bid up the middle-tier players! As a result, all players end up going way over their value. Which is impossible, of course, and another reason to mistrust economists.

Or take that "Over-30 All-Stars Strategy." The article implied that owners could dominate 2015 fantasy auctions by targeting:

- C Brian McCann
- 1B Miguel Cabrera
- 2B Robinson Cano
- 3B Josh Donaldson
- SS Troy Tulowitzki
- OFs Jose Bautista, Chris Davis and Nelson Cruz
- SP Max Scherzer
- and CL Frankie Rodriguez

Ignore for now the issue that Cano and Cruz just broke even, and McCann, Cabrera, Donaldson, Tulo, Bautista and Davis combined to produce about $90 less than projected value.

Even if all of these players had been profitable, following this "strategy" meant the owner had to roster 10 players, whose 2015 BHQ projections added up to $207. That left $53 to get 13 additional players, including five or six more starting pitchers and another closer. This wasn't a new strategy; it was Stars and Scrubs,

with the stars wearing pants well above their navels and driving with their turn signals on. (And the whole thing needed opponents who agreed to eschew face-punching by never bidding past projected values on any of these players. Did Josh Donaldson go for $29 in your league? Didn't think so.)

In fact, even though the "Over-30 players" article has the word "strategy" in the title, it likely wasn't intended as an actual strategy. More like, "these older players might be undervalued in some leagues."

There has been one genuine strategic breakthrough in fantasy baseball. Many years ago, Ron Shandler noticed and exploited a market-valuation inefficiency in 4x4 involving high-skilled pitchers with less prominent roles. His "LIMA Plan" budgeted $60 for arms who would create a ERA/WHIP/Saves foundation, then budgeted the resulting savings towards outspending everyone in hitting.

It actually worked, for a while. But when it did, word got out. And pretty soon other owners started using it, and ended up punching each other in the face over those low-cost LIMA relievers, just as the economists predicted, raising their team average to .012. We've never seen another LIMA. And we never will.

Conclusion

So, there is not strategy for fantasy drafting. But there is a set of tenets (and remember that to win a set of tenets, you have to win by two games).

Here they are:

1. Know what players are available, right to the bottom of the pool.
2. Know what every player is worth in your league format.*
3. Know why you think each player is worth what you think he's worth.
4. Identify players you believe you value differently from the other owners.
5. Know each player's risks.
6. Know your opponents' patterns.
7. For sure, know the league rules and its history, and what it takes to win.

When many fantasy owners say they're looking for "a strategy," they mean something more like "a shortcut" or "a gimmick." But there are no shortcuts, and gimmicks only work by fluke.

That earlier Mike Tyson quote is actually not quite complete. A few years ago, Tyson gave a fuller telling to the fine columnist Mike Berardino, then of the *South Florida Sun-Sentinel.* Iron Mike said, "Everybody has a plan until they get hit. Then, like a rat, they stop in fear and freeze. ... If you're good, and your plan is working, somewhere during ... the event you're involved in, you're going to get ... the bad end of the stick. Let's see how you deal with it. Normally, people don't deal with it that well."

There's your winning strategy. Know your stuff, take what the table gives you. But be ready to get punched in the face, and when it happens, deal with it well.

---

* You'll see disagreements about the precision of player valuations—very successful fantasy champions Larry Schechter and Tristan Cockcroft advocate valuing players to the penny, while others like Ron Shandler and Todd Zola say such precision is impossible given the variabilities of the game and player performance.

The Daily Season-Long Fantasy Grind

by Brad Kullman

Season-long fantasy players understand the competition is a grind. As the excitement of Opening Day gradually fades, staying focused can often be a challenge. What if there was a fun way to help you maintain your daily focus that might even put a few bucks in your pocket? While it has been something of a hot button topic in the industry, it is slowly gaining acceptance as a viable fantasy format to consider, overzealous politicians notwithstanding.

That's right, we're talking daily fantasy sports (DFS). Consider how the two formats—season-long and DFS—may actually complement each other. Playing both simultaneously could actually provide a competitive advantage—playing DFS could actually help your season-long efforts, and vice-versa.

Winter/Spring Training

This is the time when season-long players engage in exhaustive research, preparing for the critical pre-season draft. Devouring the *Baseball Forecaster*, along with various other sources of information, is part of the fun and anticipation of preparing for the upcoming season. The knowledge base obtained during this period will be advantageous, not only for your season-long efforts, but for DFS as well.

Opening Day

As the regular season gets underway, the season-long owner sits back to see where he may need to shore up weaknesses as they become apparent. In DFS, however, this early period is a sweet spot for the season-long player. Much early season DFS pricing is inefficient, as players are valued on the basis of the prior year's performance. Now-healthy players returning from an injury-plagued season may be underpriced, while many players are not priced appropriately for job battles won in spring training. Season-long competitors who have been closely monitoring these developments throughout the spring may well have a significant advantage in the early going.

One of the joys of season-long that quickly evaporates in the daily game, however, is the pleasure that comes with accurately identifying the breakout sleeper. When your late-round sleeper busts out of the gates, you can look forward to reading the box scores with a smile all summer long, knowing that you have him for the entire season, and possibly longer. If you were smart enough to target him in DFS during the first week of the season, that smile will be short-lived as you find your great scouting (and good fortune) quickly evaporates when the DFS sites quickly jack up his salary to reflect his strong play.

The Daily Grind

Opening Day turns into opening week, which grows into opening month, and the excitement of a new season gradually wears off. Monitoring your season-long team becomes something of a grind, especially if your team is not off to the best of starts. You fight the urge to shake things up, cognizant of the inherent danger in tinkering too much on the basis of small sample sizes

with your well-thought-out roster. Putting some DFS lineups together on a regular basis can be a conduit for expending your "nervous energy" while at the same time helping you to accumulate information that might be helpful from a season-long perspective.

As you scour the daily lineups building your DFS team, you might notice an overlooked player on draft day is beginning to get starts for his respective MLB team. Because he is a cheap play, you stick him in your DFS lineup, carefully monitoring his production in that night's game. If he has success, you might quickly conclude it makes sense to take a low-risk, season-long flyer on a player who might otherwise have flown under your radar.

The research and attention that inherently goes into "drafting" a fantasy team on a daily basis helps to maintain the focus on important developments in MLB. In addition, when your $50/first round stud goes down with an injury, effectively torpedoing your season-long aspirations, constructing a new team each day—one without the scourge of your season-long efforts—can be a cathartic exercise.

Dog Days of Summer

As spring turns to summer, the grind of the marathon heightens. From vacation time to the distractions of general outdoor activity, our fantasy baseball focus can naturally waver. Especially in a lost fantasy season, it may be tempting to tune out and "wait 'til next year." Playing DFS can help to maintain the joy of watching baseball all summer long. It can also help to keep you engaged, regardless of how your season-long entries may be faring. This engagement, in turn, will help you stay abreast of mid-season call-ups. Pouncing on an unheralded rookie who runs with an opportunity might just be enough to jump-start your season-long efforts and help you climb into contention.

Expanded Rosters and the Pennant Race

For the season-long player, the month of September generally has two separate feels, both of which can be aided by playing DFS. Even if your season-long team is in the title chase, it is basically running on auto-pilot, leaving little to do, short of managing injuries. Playing DFS, however, will keep you engaged with developments across the MLB landscape, providing valuable knowledge that may help in your preparation for next year, even if you don't need it now. At the opposite end of the spectrum, if a confluence of misfortune has your season-long team out of contention, playing DFS can be especially helpful in keeping you abreast of MLB developments during this time of year.

Summary

Developing a regular habit of putting together a DFS lineup can be beneficial for your season-long efforts. Having skin in the game, even if it is only a buck or two in a 50/50, will help maintain a discipline to stay in tune with what is transpiring during the course of the marathon that is the MLB season. Best of all, you can choose to play DFS only on days where you have sufficient time to research and prepare a lineup. Making it a priority to find that daily time might just help to make you a season-long champion.

The following section contains player boxes for every batter who had significant playing time in 2016 and/or is expected to get fantasy roster-worthy plate appearances in 2017. In most cases, high-end prospects who have yet to make their major league debuts will not appear here; you can find scouting reports for them in the Prospects section.

Snapshot Section

The top band of each player box contains the following information:

Age as of Opening Day 2017.

Bats shows which side of the plate he bats from—(L)eft, (R)ight or (B)oth.

Positions: Up to three defensive positions are listed and represent those for which he appeared a minimum of 20 games in 2016.

Ht/Wt: Each batter's height and weight.

Reliability Grades analyze each batter's forecast risk, on an A-F scale. High grades go to those who have accumulated few disabled list days (Health), have a history of substantial and regular major league playing time (PT/Exp) and have displayed consistent performance over the past three years, using RC/G (Consist).

LIMA Plan Grade evaluates how well a batter would fit into a team using the LIMA Plan draft strategy. Best grades go to batters who have excellent base skills, are expected to see regular playing time, and are in the $10-$30 Rotisserie dollar range. Lowest grades will go to poor skills, few AB and values less than $5 or more than $30.

Random Variance Score (Rand Var) measures the impact random variance had on the batter's 2016 stats and the probability that his 2017 performance will exceed or fall short of 2016. The variables tracked are those prone to regression—h%, hr/f and xBA to BA variance. Players are rated on a scale of −5 to +5 with positive scores indicating rebounds and negative scores indicating corrections. Note that this score is computer-generated and the projections will override it on occasion.

Mayberry Method (MM) acknowledges the imprecision of the forecasting process by projecting player performance in broad strokes. The four digits of MM each represent a fantasy-relevant skill—power, speed, batting average and playing time (PA)—and are all on a scale of 0 to 5.

Commentaries for each batter provide a brief analysis of his skills and the potential impact on performance in 2017. MLB statistics are listed first for those who played only a portion of 2016 at the major league level. Note that these commentaries generally look at performance related issues only. Role and playing time expectations may impact these analyses, so you will have to adjust accordingly. Upside (UP) and downside (DN) statistical potential appears for some players; these are less grounded in hard data and more speculative of skills potential.

Player Stat Section

The past five years' statistics represent the total accumulated in the majors as well as in Triple-A, Double-A ball and various foreign leagues during each year. All non-major league stats have been converted to a major league equivalent (MLE) performance level. Minor league levels below Double-A are not included.

Nearly all baseball publications separate a player's statistical experiences in the major leagues from the minor leagues and outside leagues. While this may be appropriate for official record-keeping purposes, it is not an easy-to-analyze snapshot of a player's complete performance for a given year.

Bill James has proven that minor league statistics (converted to MLEs), at Double-A level or above, provide as accurate a record of a player's performance as major league statistics. Other researchers have also devised conversion factors for foreign leagues. Since these are adequate barometers, we include them in the pool of historical data for each year.

Team designations: An asterisk (*) appearing with a team name means that Triple-A and/or Double-A numbers are included in that year's stat line. Any stints of less than 20 AB are not included (to screen out most rehab appearances). A designation of "a/a" means the stats were accumulated at both AA and AAA levels that year. "for" represents a foreign or independent league. The designation "2TM" appears whenever a player was on more than one major league team, crossing leagues, in a season. "2AL" and "2NL" represent more than one team in the same league. Players who were cut during the season and finished 2016 as a free agent are designated as FAA (Free agent, AL) and FAN (Free agent, NL).

Stats: Descriptions of all the categories appear in the Encyclopedia.

- The leading decimal point has been suppressed on some categories to conserve space.
- Data for platoons (vL, vR), balls-in-play (G/L/F) and consistency (Wk#, DOM, DIS) are for major league performance only.
- Formulas that use BIP data, like xBA and xPX, only appear for years in which G/L/F data is available.

Batting average is presented alongside xBA. On base average and slugging average appear next, and the combined On Base Plus Slugging (OPS). OPS splits vs. left-handed and right-handed pitchers appear after the overall OPS column.

Batting eye and contact skill are measured with walk rate (bb%), contact rate (ct%). Eye is the ratio of walks to strikeouts.

Once the ball leaves the bat, it will either be a (G)round ball, (L)ine drive or (F)ly ball. Hit rate (h%), the also referred to as batting average on balls-in-play (BABIP), measures how often a ball put into play results in a base hit. Hard contact index (HctX) measures the frequency of hard contact, compared to overall league levels. Looking at the ratio of fly balls is a good springboard to the Power gauges. Linear weighted power index (PX) measures a batter's skill at hitting extra base hits as compared to overall league levels. xPX measures power by assessing how hard the ball is being hit (rather than the outcomes of those hits). And the ratio of home runs to fly balls shows the results of those hits.

To assess speed, first look at on base average (does he get on base?), then Spd (is he fast enough to steal bases?), then SBO (how often is he attempting to steal bases?) and finally, SB% (when he attempts, what is his rate of success?).

In looking at consistency, we use weekly Base Performance Value (BPV) levels. Starting with the total number of weeks the batter accumulated stats (#Wk), the percentage of DOMinating weeks (BPV over 50) and DISaster weeks (BPV under 0) is shown. The larger the variance between DOM and DIS, the greater the consistency.

The final section includes several overall performance measures: runs created per game (RC/G), runs above replacement (RAR), Base performance value (BPV), Base performance index (BPX, which is BPV indexed to each year's league average) and the Rotisserie value (R$).

2017 Projections

Forecasts are computed from a player's trends over the past five years. Adjustments were made for leading indicators and variances between skill and statistical output. After reviewing the leading indicators, you might opt to make further adjustments.

Although each year's numbers include all playing time at the Double-A level or above, the 2017 forecast only represents potential playing time at the major league level, and again is highly preliminary.

Note that the projected Rotisserie values in this book will not necessarily align with each player's historical actuals. Since we currently have no idea who is going to play first base for the Rangers, or whether Josh Bell is going to break camp with the Pirates, it is impossible to create a finite pool of playing time, something which is required for valuation. So the projections are roughly based on a 12-team AL/NL league, and include an inflated number of plate appearances, league-wide. This serves to flatten the spread of values and depress individual player dollar

projections. In truth, a $25 player in this book might actually be worth $21, or $28. This level of precision is irrelevant in a process that is driven by market forces anyway. So, don't obsess over it.

Be aware of other sources that publish perfectly calibrated Rotisserie values over the winter. They are likely making arbitrary decisions as to where free agents are going to sign and who is going to land jobs in the spring. We do not make those leaps of faith here.

Bottom line… It is far too early to be making definitive projections for 2017, especially on playing time. Focus on the skill levels and trends, then consult BaseballHQ.com for playing time revisions as players change teams and roles become more defined. A free projections update will be available online in March.

Do-it-yourself analysis

Here are some data points you can look at in doing your own player analysis:

- Variance between vLH and vRH OPS
- Growth or decline in walk rate (bb%)
- Growth or decline in contact rate (ct%)
- Growth or decline in G/L/F individually, or concurrent shifts
- Variance in 2016 hit rate (h%) to 2013-2015 three-year average
- Variance between Avg and xBA each year
- Growth or decline in HctX level
- Growth or decline in power index (PX) rate
- Variance between PX and xPX each year
- Variance in 2016 hr/f rate to 2013-2015 three-year average
- Growth or decline in statistically scouted speed (Spd) score
- Concurrent growth/decline of gauges like ct%, FB, PX, xPX, hr/f
- Concurrent growth/decline of gauges like OB, Spd, SBO, SB%
- Trends in DOM/DIS splits

Abreu,Jose

Age: 30	Bats: R	Pos: 1B	Health A	LIMA Plan B
Ht: 6' 3"	Wt: 255		PT/Exp A	Rand Var 0
			Consist C	MM 3045

Plate skills surge, healthy LD, h% bumps fueled 2H turnaround. But PX, xPX suddenly look very average, and remained depressed even during the rebound. Age, health, solid HctX say performance shouldn't fall off a cliff, and could even uptick. But xBA, secondary skill trends suggest his very best years are in the rear-view.

Yr	Tm	AB	R	HR	RBI	SB	BA	xBA	OBP	SLG	OPS	vL	vR	bb%	ct%	Eye	G	L	F	h%	HctX	PX	xPX	hr/f	Spd	SBO	SB%	#Wk	DOM	DIS	RC/G	RAR	BPV	BPX	R$
12	for	297	72	18	91	1	339		447	582	1029			16	85	1.28				35		138			90	1%	100%				10.06	36.2	111	278	$22
13	for	285	59	10	54	2	320		406	480	886			13	84	0.90				35		103			86	8%	21%				6.76	17.0	72	180	$16
14	CHW	556	80	36	107	3	317	307	383	581	964	1098	919	8	76	0.39	45	23	31	36	120	185	132	27%	67	3%	75%	24	71%	21%	8.09	59.0	93	251	$35
15	CHW	613	88	30	101	0	290	276	347	502	850	658	908	6	77	0.28	47	21	32	33	116	136	116	20%	76	0%	0%	26	54%	31%	6.01	18.2	54	146	$26
16	CHW	624	67	25	100	0	293	263	353	468	820	840	816	7	80	0.38	45	21	33	33	106	103	93	15%	66	1%	0%	27	44%	33%	5.71	14.8	38	109	$22
1st Half		318	30	11	49	0	267	253	325	437	762	728	769	6	78	0.31	48	18	34	31	102	106	92	13%	76	3%	0%	14	36%	50%	4.66	-4.1	33	94	$16
2nd Half		306	37	14	51	0	320	278	381	500	881	927	867	8	82	0.46	43	24	33	35	110	99	94	17%	56	0%	0%	13	54%	15%	6.97	15.3	43	123	$28
17	**Proj**	**613**	**80**	**28**	**102**	**1**	**288**	**275**	**355**	**482**	**837**	**809**	**845**	**8**	**79**	**0.41**	**46**	**22**	**32**	**32**	**112**	**114**	**107**	**18%**	**71**	**2%**	**33%**				**5.88**	**13.3**	**38**	**109**	**$24**

Ackley,Dustin

Age: 29	Bats: L	Pos: 1B	Health F	LIMA Plan D
Ht: 6' 1"	Wt: 195		PT/Exp D	Rand Var +5
			Consist C	MM 1211

Another injury (torn labrum) mercy-killed his season in May. Contact has always been decent, and he's shown flashes of power and patience. But the sum of the parts is consistently unimpressive. Handedness, age keep the window open. Now a durability-challenged flyer in search of opportunity; speculate only if he has it.

Yr	Tm	AB	R	HR	RBI	SB	BA	xBA	OBP	SLG	OPS	vL	vR	bb%	ct%	Eye	G	L	F	h%	HctX	PX	xPX	hr/f	Spd	SBO	SB%	#Wk	DOM	DIS	RC/G	RAR	BPV	BPX	R$
12	SEA	607	84	12	50	13	226	234	294	328	622	675	593	9	80	0.48	45	19	35	27	97	67	74	7%	119	10%	81%	28	29%	36%	3.22	-24.9	27	68	$8
13	SEA *	488	54	5	41	2	262	253	330	354	685	664	659	9	82	0.55	51	22	27	31	105	68	62	5%	105	3%	40%	24	33%	42%	3.97	0.0	33	83	$8
14	SEA	502	64	14	65	8	245	265	293	398	692	553	749	6	82	0.36	45	18	36	27	108	106	105	9%	100	11%	67%	27	44%	33%	3.85	2.3	57	154	$13
15	2 AL	238	28	10	30	2	231	263	284	429	712	422	742	7	81	0.40	44	16	40	25	119	118	143	13%	98	8%	50%	23	48%	26%	3.94	-3.2	64	173	$3
16	NYY	61	6	0	4	0	148	177	243	148	390	421	382	12	85	0.89	43	15	42	17	72	0	56	0%	110	0%	0%	8	25%	38%	1.09	-6.4	0	0	-$3
1st Half		61	6	0	4	0	148	177	243	148	390	421	382	12	85	0.89	43	15	42	17	72	0	56	0%	110	0%	0%	8	25%	38%	1.09	-6.9	-1	-3	-$3
2nd Half																																			
17	**Proj**	**211**	**24**	**4**	**21**	**2**	**214**	**235**	**282**	**316**	**598**	**550**	**613**	**9**	**83**	**0.55**	**45**	**17**	**37**	**24**	**98**	**59**	**88**	**6%**	**106**	**5%**	**62%**				**2.88**	**-14.5**	**20**	**56**	**$2**

Adames,Cristhian

Age: 25	Bats: B	Pos: SS	Health A	LIMA Plan D
Ht: 6' 0"	Wt: 180		PT/Exp D	Rand Var +3
			Consist B	MM 0221

PRO: Seemingly learned to take a walk. CON: The good news ends there. Zero power and anemic contact were glaring in .452 OPS away from Coors. BA should rise from here, but inability to leverage good speed into a running game seals his fate as fringe player. He'll need more injury help to accumulate another 200+ AB.

Yr	Tm	AB	R	HR	RBI	SB	BA	xBA	OBP	SLG	OPS	vL	vR	bb%	ct%	Eye	G	L	F	h%	HctX	PX	xPX	hr/f	Spd	SBO	SB%	#Wk	DOM	DIS	RC/G	RAR	BPV	BPX	R$
12																																			
13	aa	389	36	3	29	10	257		305	337	642			7	80	0.35				31		62			103	17%	58%				3.38		16	40	$7
14	COL *	490	43	2	36	8	254	267	295	322	617	1000	0	6	81	0.31	70	20	10	31	35	53	-15	0%	108	15%	43%	3	0%	67%	3.01	-4.2	12	32	$7
15	COL *	516	45	8	37	7	269	261	304	365	669	729	515	5	87	0.38	58	18	25	30	113	58	71	0%	116	12%	45%	6	17%	50%	3.65	-1.7	39	105	$10
16	COL	225	25	2	17	2	218	254	304	302	607	611	604	10	79	0.51	64	18	18	27	66	51	23	6%	131	8%	40%	27	30%	59%	2.77	-12.9	18	51	-$1
1st Half		90	8	1	7	0	211	277	311	311	622	684	602	11	81	0.65	64	22	14	25	57	62	14	10%	101	4%	0%	14	36%	50%	2.85	-4.6	28	80	-$2
2nd Half		135	17	1	10	2	222	238	300	296	596	578	607	9	78	0.43	63	15	21	28	72	43	29	5%	148	11%	50%	13	23%	69%	2.71	-7.3	9	26	$0
17	**Proj**	**116**	**12**	**1**	**9**	**1**	**240**	**252**	**309**	**316**	**626**	**668**	**603**	**8**	**81**	**0.44**	**61**	**18**	**21**	**29**	**85**	**47**	**42**	**4%**	**119**	**11%**	**44%**				**3.00**	**-5.2**	**5**	**15**	**$1**

Adams,Matt

Age: 28	Bats: L	Pos: 1B	Health F	LIMA Plan D+
Ht: 6' 3"	Wt: 230		PT/Exp C	Rand Var +1
			Consist C	MM 4023

Song remains the same: Left-handed power still teases 25 HR upside; high BAs aren't likely to return; injuries and platoon profile cap AB. Improved patience and career-best small-sample performance vL (46 AB) are encouraging, not definitive. Age suggests time for more productive years ahead, but health needs to cooperate.

Yr	Tm	AB	R	HR	RBI	SB	BA	xBA	OBP	SLG	OPS	vL	vR	bb%	ct%	Eye	G	L	F	h%	HctX	PX	xPX	hr/f	Spd	SBO	SB%	#Wk	DOM	DIS	RC/G	RAR	BPV	BPX	R$
12	STL *	344	38	14	50	2	267	255	300	465	765	440	739	5	74	0.18	44	18	39	32	99	142	126	8%	70	5%	66%	5	20%	60%	4.81	-6.0	41	103	$9
13	STL	296	46	17	51	0	284	262	335	503	839	654	876	7	73	0.29	44	19	36	34	123	153	145	22%	80	1%	0%	26	54%	42%	5.93	11.2	55	138	$12
14	STL	527	55	15	68	3	288	265	321	457	779	528	854	5	78	0.23	35	24	41	34	109	124	130	9%	89	4%	60%	26	54%	19%	5.22	15.3	51	138	$19
15	STL	175	14	5	24	1	240	237	280	377	657	499	683	5	77	0.24	41	20	39	29	125	95	120	10%	60	3%	100%	13	38%	31%	3.59	-9.2	13	35	$1
16	STL	297	37	16	54	0	249	252	309	471	780	822	773	8	73	0.31	32	20	48	29	108	142	159	15%	73	2%	0%	25	40%	36%	4.85	-4.2	44	126	$7
1st Half		178	22	9	34	0	281	248	330	489	819	808	821	7	72	0.27	38	19	43	34	94	133	129	16%	81	2%	0%	14	36%	43%	5.58	2.4	36	103	$10
2nd Half		119	15	7	20	0	202	258	278	445	724	865	707	9	73	0.38	23	20	57	21	128	156	203	14%	66	0%	0%	11	45%	27%	3.91	-4.4	57	163	$2
17	**Proj**	**326**	**36**	**15**	**52**	**1**	**248**	**253**	**299**	**449**	**748**	**667**	**763**	**7**	**75**	**0.29**	**34**	**21**	**45**	**29**	**116**	**127**	**150**	**14%**	**68**	**2%**	**56%**				**4.51**	**-5.7**	**28**	**79**	**$9**

Aguilar,Jesus

Age: 27	Bats: R	Pos: 1B	Health A	LIMA Plan D
Ht: 6' 3"	Wt: 241		PT/Exp C	Rand Var +1
			Consist A	MM 3011

0-0-.000 in 9 AB at CLE. Third consecutive AAA season, led Int'l League in HR with acceptable patience / contact, held his own vR. But BA history isn't promising; lacks both speed and defensive versatility. Needs opportunity that his profile makes difficult to come by. An end-gamer at best, and time is running out.

Yr	Tm	AB	R	HR	RBI	SB	BA	xBA	OBP	SLG	OPS	vL	vR	bb%	ct%	Eye	G	L	F	h%	HctX	PX	xPX	hr/f	Spd	SBO	SB%	#Wk	DOM	DIS	RC/G	RAR	BPV	BPX	R$
12	aa	72	11	3	12	0	277		380	474	854			14	64	0.46				40		169			87	0%	0%				6.35		47	118	$1
13	aa	499	49	11	78	0	233		291	352	643			8	75	0.33				29		90			75	1%	0%				3.37		13	33	$6
14	CLE *	460	55	15	62	0	251	242	327	407	733	471	133	10	73	0.41	48	19	33	31	90	125	92	0%	67	0%	0%	8	0%	88%	4.52	6.4	33	89	$11
15	CLE *	529	48	16	81	0	244	281	296	394	690	583	818	7	75	0.29	42	33	25	30	215	107	171	0%	58	0%	0%	4	0%	50%	3.93	-23.7	17	46	$9
16	CLE *	521	51	25	75	0	215	199	274	407	681	0	0	8	76	0.34	80	0	20	23	62	115	125	0%	53	0%	0%	3	0%	33%	3.62	-30.0	29	83	$5
1st Half		302	29	14	41	0	195	248	262	374	636			8	77	0.39				20		104			65	0%	0%				3.10		29	83	$2
2nd Half		219	21	11	34	0	242	204	292	452	744	0	0	7	75	0.28	80	0	20	28	61	132	125	0%	56	0%	0%	3	0%	33%	4.44	-6.9	37	106	$7
17	**Proj**	**162**	**16**	**6**	**24**	**0**	**240**	**240**	**298**	**407**	**705**	**705**	**705**	**8**	**75**	**0.33**	**38**	**20**	**42**	**28**		**107**		**12%**	**68**	**0%**	**0%**				**4.06**	**-5.0**	**8**	**23**	**$3**

Ahmed,Nick

Age: 27	Bats: R	Pos: SS	Health C	LIMA Plan D
Ht: 6' 3"	Wt: 205		PT/Exp C	Rand Var +2
			Consist A	MM 1311

World-class defender saw near-everyday playing time until hip impingement shelved him in July and surgery ended his season. Maintained good ct%, even nudged his LD% and HctX forward. But h% didn't cooperate as speed and anemic power headed in the wrong direction. A poor speculative profile regardless of venue.

Yr	Tm	AB	R	HR	RBI	SB	BA	xBA	OBP	SLG	OPS	vL	vR	bb%	ct%	Eye	G	L	F	h%	HctX	PX	xPX	hr/f	Spd	SBO	SB%	#Wk	DOM	DIS	RC/G	RAR	BPV	BPX	R$
12																																			
13	aa	487	49	4	39	22	223		265	309	574			5	84	0.36				26		59			122	28%	74%				2.69		33	83	$9
14	ARI *	477	45	4	34	9	247	236	286	334	620	428	577	5	84	0.35	42	18	40	29	88	66	85	4%	123	15%	53%	9	22%	56%	3.08	-3.1	40	108	$7
15	ARI	421	49	9	34	4	226	242	275	359	634	803	575	6	81	0.36	46	17	37	26	77	82	78	7%	139	10%	44%	25	24%	52%	3.12	-8.3	45	122	$3
16	ARI	284	26	4	20	5	218	239	265	299	564	633	536	5	80	0.26	48	21	30	26	88	50	92	6%	107	11%	71%	16	19%	50%	2.51	-18.5	2	6	$0
1st Half		244	25	4	19	4	230	246	275	324	599	682	561	5	79	0.23	48	23	30	28	90	59	95	7%	107	9%	80%	14	21%	50%	2.87	-11.8	5	14	$1
2nd Half		40	1	0	1	1	150	186	205	150	355	0	413	7	85	0.50	51	14	34	18	79	0	76	0%	104	22%	50%	2	0%	50%	0.89	-4.9	-13	-37	-$7
17	**Proj**	**205**	**21**	**3**	**16**	**4**	**234**	**239**	**275**	**333**	**608**	**639**	**597**	**5**	**82**	**0.32**	**47**	**17**	**35**	**27**	**82**	**60**	**82**	**5%**	**120**	**14%**	**63%**				**2.98**	**-9.3**	**17**	**48**	**$3**

Albies,Ozhaino

Age: 20	Bats: B	Pos: 2B/SS	Health A	LIMA Plan C+
Ht: 5' 9"	Wt: 160		PT/Exp F	Rand Var 0
			Consist F	MM 2533

Elite ATL prospect with fine athleticism, bat-to-ball skills and speed took big step toward MLB debut by hitting .321 in AA at ridiculously young age. Subsequent AAA scuffles (.248 BA) aren't alarming over the long haul, but may need more time before he's ready. Or not; outstanding glove could force the issue even if bat lags behind.

Yr	Tm	AB	R	HR	RBI	SB	BA	xBA	OBP	SLG	OPS	vL	vR	bb%	ct%	Eye	G	L	F	h%	HctX	PX	xPX	hr/f	Spd	SBO	SB%	#Wk	DOM	DIS	RC/G	RAR	BPV	BPX	R$
12																																			
13																																			
14																																			
15																																			
16	a/a	552	81	6	52	29	287		349	410	758			9	81	0.50				35		77			123	26%	69%				4.96		43	123	$25
1st Half		324	43	3	26	12	286		344	394	739			8	83	0.51				34		68			131	20%	62%				4.65		43	123	$24
2nd Half		228	38	3	25	18	290		355	431	786			9	79	0.48				36		90			133	36%	74%				5.41		49	140	$27
17	**Proj**	**288**	**42**	**3**	**26**	**15**	**278**	**260**	**340**	**410**	**751**	**751**	**751**	**9**	**81**	**0.49**	**47**	**20**	**33**	**34**		**83**		**4%**	**136**	**27%**	**68%**				**4.77**	**-0.3**	**52**	**148**	**$13**

JOCK THOMPSON

Alfaro,Jorge

Age: 24 Bats: R Pos: CA | Ht: 6' 2" Wt: 225
Health A | PT/Exp F | Consist B
LIMA Plan F | Rand Var -2 | MM 2201

0-0-.125 in 16 AB at PHI. Key piece of Hamels trade was good-not-great in third AA stint before mid-Sept sip of coffee in MLB. Big bat and cannon behind the dish are the carrying tools, but all aspects of his game still need refinement. Improvement at CA has quelled talk of a new position; excelling in AAA could expedite arrival.

Yr	Tm	AB	R	HR	RBI	SB	BA	xBA	OBP	SLG	OPS	vL	vR	bb%	ct%	Eye	G	L	F	h%	HctX	PX	xPX	hr/f	Spd	SBO	SB%	#Wk	DOM	DIS	RC/G	RAR	BPV	BPX	R$
12																																			
13																																			
14	aa	88	10	3	11	0	239		280	393	673			5	72	0.20				29		116			91	0%	0%				3.68		21	57	$0
15	aa	190	17	4	16	2	222		251	369	621			4	66	0.11				32		124			100	9%	59%				2.99		1	3	$0
16	PHI *	420	55	14	54	2	248	234	281	400	681	333	286	4	69	0.15	63	13	25	33	0	103	-24	0%	88	5%	52%	3	0%	100%	3.74	-8.2	-3	-9	$8
1st Half		234	35	9	36	0	259	249	280	438	718			3	73	0.10				32		114			97	5%	0%				4.03		19	54	$11
2nd Half		186	20	5	19	2	235	207	283	351	634	333	286	6	65	0.19	63	13	25	34	0	89	-24	0%	81	6%	100%	3	0%	100%	3.38	-4.3	-32	-91	$4
17	**Proj**	**134**	**15**	**3**	**14**	**1**	**236**	**225**	**269**	**367**	**636**	**636**	**636**	**4**	**67**	**0.14**	**48**	**20**	**32**	**33**		**98**		**10%**	**92**	**6%**	**65%**				**3.27**	**-3.5**	**-19**	**-53**	**$0**

Almonte,Abraham

Age: 28 Bats: B Pos: RF LF | Ht: 5' 9" Wt: 205
Health A | PT/Exp D | Consist C
LIMA Plan D+ | Rand Var 0 | MM 2223

1-22-.264 with 8 SB in 194 AB at CLE. Generated some intrigue after 2015 2nd half before promptly erasing it with an 80-game PED suspension. PX returned to pre-CLE levels upon his return—huge surprise. We said last year a breakout at his age was unlikely despite flurry w/CLE, if anything it's less likely a year later.

Yr	Tm	AB	R	HR	RBI	SB	BA	xBA	OBP	SLG	OPS	vL	vR	bb%	ct%	Eye	G	L	F	h%	HctX	PX	xPX	hr/f	Spd	SBO	SB%	#Wk	DOM	DIS	RC/G	RAR	BPV	BPX	R$
12	aa	319	38	4	20	24	245		310	344	654			9	80	0.46				30		69			114	34%	81%				3.74		27	68	$9
13	SEA *	512	73	13	62	21	259	248	332	398	731	475	872	10	74	0.43	50	20	30	33	68	102	29	14%	90	21%	70%	6	50%	50%	4.48	2.9	27	68	$20
14	2 TM *	481	47	7	35	9	218	223	263	309	572	670	573	6	71	0.21	50	21	28	29	85	75	107	8%	87	15%	53%	13	31%	62%	2.52	-20.6	-16	-43	$4
15	2 TM *	484	73	8	53	16	248	261	317	389	705	548	779	9	78	0.46	49	21	31	30	93	97	74	10%	91	18%	74%	18	50%	39%	4.16	-8.8	37	100	$14
16	CLE *	209	29	2	25	10	280	274	319	426	745	771	649	5	78	0.26	48	21	31	35	97	110	85	2%	67	21%	100%	13	38%	38%	5.09	2.3	32	91	$7
1st Half		30	5	1	3	2	347	310	424	537	961	0	0	12	78	0.60	100	0	0	43	0	114	-24	0%	93	15%	100%	1	0%	100%	9.39	3.6	56	160	$0
2nd Half		179	24	1	22	8	268	273	298	408	706	805	649	4	78	0.20	47	22	31	34	98	109	85	2%	64	24%	100%	12	42%	33%	4.51	-0.9	28	80	$9
17	**Proj**	**261**	**33**	**4**	**26**	**9**	**248**	**256**	**298**	**382**	**680**	**660**	**691**	**7**	**76**	**0.30**	**49**	**21**	**30**	**31**	**88**	**92**	**82**	**7%**	**78**	**20%**	**76%**				**3.87**	**-6.4**	**28**	**81**	**$8**

Almora,Albert

Age: 23 Bats: R Pos: CF | Ht: 6' 2" Wt: 190
Health A | PT/Exp D | Consist B
LIMA Plan D+ | Rand Var -1 | MM 2353

3-14-.277 in 117 AB at CHC. Better real life player than fantasy asset with defense as his top skill and mostly 50-grade (MLB average) tools on offense. Drop in system was due more to influx of talent than fall-off in skills. Best case scenario: hit tool improves and yields .300+ BA w/double-double HR/SB; likely a 4th OF for now.

Yr	Tm	AB	R	HR	RBI	SB	BA	xBA	OBP	SLG	OPS	vL	vR	bb%	ct%	Eye	G	L	F	h%	HctX	PX	xPX	hr/f	Spd	SBO	SB%	#Wk	DOM	DIS	RC/G	RAR	BPV	BPX	R$
12																																			
13																																			
14	aa	142	16	2	8	0	212		220	312	532			1	83	0.07				24		72			117	5%	0%				2.13		30	81	-$2
15	aa	405	56	5	37	7	248		294	361	655			6	87	0.51				27		74			107	12%	63%				3.52		55	149	$7
16	CHC *	432	50	6	48	8	273	281	293	391	684	827	724	3	84	0.18	43	28	29	31	96	73	92	12%	109	12%	70%	12	42%	17%	3.98	-8.3	34	97	$11
1st Half		272	32	3	29	8	291	272	313	409	722	933	745	3	84	0.19	44	24	31	34	96	74	81	7%	116	15%	78%	5	40%	40%	4.61	0.8	37	106	$16
2nd Half		160	18	3	18	0	243	292	259	361	620	727	700	2	85	0.14	42	31	27	27	97	71	103	17%	104	4%	0%	7	43%	0%	3.04	-7.1	32	91	$2
17	**Proj**	**270**	**33**	**8**	**26**	**4**	**249**	**299**	**276**	**414**	**690**	**738**	**659**	**4**	**85**	**0.24**	**43**	**28**	**28**	**27**	**97**	**93**	**94**	**13%**	**114**	**12%**	**67%**				**3.81**	**-5.6**	**53**	**150**	**$7**

Alonso,Yonder

Age: 30 Bats: L Pos: 1B | Ht: 6' 2" Wt: 230
Health C | PT/Exp C | Consist B
LIMA Plan D+ | Rand Var +1 | MM 1133

This era's Doug Mientkiewicz isn't even putting up the skills of an average middle infielder given the power surge at those positions in 2016. PX was 2nd-worst among 1B (min. 400 AB) as he gave back all of his 2015 gains vR. Bat slowing? Career-worst performance on fastballs says yes, especially vL. Hard pass.

Yr	Tm	AB	R	HR	RBI	SB	BA	xBA	OBP	SLG	OPS	vL	vR	bb%	ct%	Eye	G	L	F	h%	HctX	PX	xPX	hr/f	Spd	SBO	SB%	#Wk	DOM	DIS	RC/G	RAR	BPV	BPX	R$
12	SD	549	47	9	62	3	273	264	348	393	741	693	760	10	82	0.61	45	24	31	32	107	88	106	6%	57	2%	100%	27	44%	22%	4.83	-7.2	36	90	$11
13	SD	334	34	6	45	6	281	247	341	368	710	637	736	9	86	0.68	46	21	33	31	110	57	84	6%	62	6%	100%	19	26%	32%	4.62	0.1	28	70	$10
14	SD	267	27	7	27	6	240	279	285	397	682	607	699	6	87	0.47	43	19	38	25	120	110	121	8%	68	13%	86%	16	44%	13%	3.85	-2.3	68	184	$5
15	SD	354	50	5	31	2	282	269	361	381	742	669	762	11	86	0.88	49	23	28	32	108	65	73	6%	84	6%	29%	19	37%	11%	4.64	-3.0	46	124	$9
16	OAK	482	52	7	56	3	253	268	316	367	683	617	694	9	85	0.61	44	23	33	29	111	76	94	5%	59	3%	75%	27	41%	30%	3.97	-12.4	36	103	$7
1st Half		248	28	3	22	2	250	261	309	339	648	592	657	8	85	0.61	47	22	31	28	114	58	92	5%	66	4%	67%	14	36%	36%	3.57	-11.2	26	74	$6
2nd Half		234	24	4	34	1	256	275	323	397	721	645	731	9	84	0.61	41	23	36	29	108	95	96	6%	60	2%	100%	13	46%	23%	4.43	-4.6	49	140	$8
17	**Proj**	**351**	**40**	**6**	**39**	**3**	**261**	**269**	**326**	**379**	**705**	**640**	**719**	**9**	**85**	**0.65**	**45**	**22**	**33**	**29**	**111**	**75**	**93**	**6%**	**65**	**5%**	**64%**				**4.24**	**-8.8**	**38**	**107**	**$9**

Altherr,Aaron

Age: 26 Bats: R Pos: RF LF | Ht: 6' 5" Wt: 190
Health D | PT/Exp D | Consist F
LIMA Plan C+ | Rand Var 0 | MM 2425

2015 audition yielded alluring HR/SB potential paired with clear path to playing time, but March wrist surgery lopped off 2/3rds of season before it started. Once back, an already-flimsy ct% fell further, and HctX, xPX nosedived—signs that the wrist wasn't 100%. He'll get another shot, but the time is now.

Yr	Tm	AB	R	HR	RBI	SB	BA	xBA	OBP	SLG	OPS	vL	vR	bb%	ct%	Eye	G	L	F	h%	HctX	PX	xPX	hr/f	Spd	SBO	SB%	#Wk	DOM	DIS	RC/G	RAR	BPV	BPX	R$
12																																			
13																																			
14	PHI *	454	41	12	43	9	201	172	235	337	572	0	0	4	71	0.16	33	0	67	25	103	110	235	0%	105	21%	58%	2	0%	50%	2.40	-24.5	16	43	$3
15	PHI *	570	75	17	74	18	250	260	315	434	750	636	936	9	75	0.39	40	22	38	30	95	128	96	14%	138	19%	74%	8	50%	0%	4.61	-4.1	64	173	$19
16	PHI	198	23	4	22	7	197	222	300	288	587	723	553	10	65	0.33	51	26	22	28	78	67	76	14%	109	17%	78%	11	27%	55%	2.62	-12.9	-29	-83	$1
1st Half																																			
2nd Half		198	23	4	22	7	197	222	300	288	587	723	553	10	65	0.33	51	26	22	28	78	67	76	14%	109	17%	78%	11	27%	55%	2.62	-13.1	-30	-86	$1
17	**Proj**	**421**	**46**	**12**	**46**	**12**	**235**	**245**	**311**	**374**	**685**	**660**	**694**	**7**	**70**	**0.27**	**47**	**25**	**29**	**31**	**85**	**96**	**84**	**14%**	**121**	**17%**	**69%**				**3.58**	**-14.4**	**3**	**8**	**$11**

Altuve,Jose

Age: 27 Bats: R Pos: 2B | Ht: 5' 7" Wt: 170
Health A | PT/Exp A | Consist D
LIMA Plan C | Rand Var -4 | MM 2455

After nearly doubling hr/f in 2015, it was hard to see a repeat... instead, he nearly doubled it again. However, his evolution into heart-of-the-order stud may be coming at the expense of speed. After 21 SBs w/an 88% success rate in the 1st half, he nabbed just 9 at a 56% clip, exclusively batting 3rd. A top-5 star.

Yr	Tm	AB	R	HR	RBI	SB	BA	xBA	OBP	SLG	OPS	vL	vR	bb%	ct%	Eye	G	L	F	h%	HctX	PX	xPX	hr/f	Spd	SBO	SB%	#Wk	DOM	DIS	RC/G	RAR	BPV	BPX	R$
12	HOU	576	80	7	37	33	290	277	340	399	740	911	676	6	87	0.54	53	20	27	32	86	72	73	5%	143	27%	75%	27	44%	7%	4.79	10.3	64	160	$24
13	HOU	626	64	5	52	35	283	264	316	363	678	733	656	5	86	0.38	49	23	28	32	94	58	78	3%	105	28%	73%	27	37%	15%	4.05	5.8	35	88	$27
14	HOU	660	85	7	59	56	341	296	377	453	830	1013	775	5	92	0.68	48	23	30	36	95	81	77	4%	127	32%	86%	27	78%	7%	6.86	60.3	83	224	$50
15	HOU	638	86	15	66	38	313	281	353	459	812	973	743	5	89	0.49	47	18	35	33	104	89	92	7%	131	29%	75%	27	67%	19%	5.82	27.2	80	216	$40
16	HOU	640	108	24	96	30	338	311	396	531	928	885	942	9	89	0.86	42	26	32	35	122	104	120	13%	116	20%	75%	27	70%	15%	7.96	55.0	94	269	$46
1st Half		322	62	14	49	21	351	322	424	568	992	1011	986	11	90	1.18	40	27	33	36	127	117	122	14%	112	21%	88%	14	71%	7%	9.66	40.4	110	314	$54
2nd Half		318	46	10	47	9	324	301	367	494	860	774	893	6	88	0.57	43	25	31	34	117	92	117	11%	119	17%	56%	13	69%	23%	6.42	14.1	77	220	$37
17	**Proj**	**634**	**93**	**20**	**92**	**25**	**325**	**304**	**373**	**499**	**872**	**924**	**853**	**7**	**90**	**0.69**	**45**	**23**	**32**	**34**	**110**	**94**	**102**	**11%**	**121**	**19%**	**69%**				**6.78**	**34.1**	**81**	**232**	**$42**

Alvarez,Pedro

Age: 30 Bats: L Pos: DH | Ht: 6' 2" Wt: 225
Health A | PT/Exp C | Consist B
LIMA Plan B | Rand Var +1 | MM 4135

Quietly had a strong vR platoon season, but Mark Trumbo's surge vR curbed the AB. Leaguewide HR binge also diminished the value of his output. Save a 2015 spike in groundballs, this is a firm base of skills that will continue to yield high power, low BA results with AB count ultimately deciding overall value.

Yr	Tm	AB	R	HR	RBI	SB	BA	xBA	OBP	SLG	OPS	vL	vR	bb%	ct%	Eye	G	L	F	h%	HctX	PX	xPX	hr/f	Spd	SBO	SB%	#Wk	DOM	DIS	RC/G	RAR	BPV	BPX	R$
12	PIT	525	64	30	85	1	244	244	317	467	784	648	833	10	66	0.32	47	19	34	31	97	164	144	25%	71	1%	100%	27	44%	37%	5.01	1.9	37	93	$14
13	PIT	558	70	36	100	2	233	256	296	473	770	537	842	8	67	0.26	43	20	36	28	115	176	168	26%	74	2%	100%	27	48%	30%	4.64	2.3	48	120	$17
14	PIT	398	46	18	56	8	231	235	312	405	717	504	770	10	72	0.40	45	16	39	28	117	125	138	16%	73	10%	73%	23	39%	39%	4.13	0.9	31	84	$11
15	PIT	437	60	27	77	2	243	265	318	469	787	712	799	10	70	0.37	53	20	27	28	113	154	114	33%	53	2%	100%	27	52%	30%	5.04	-5.2	41	111	$13
16	BAL	337	43	22	49	1	249	264	322	504	826	654	848	10	71	0.38	47	17	36	28	112	163	120	25%	68	1%	100%	26	50%	15%	5.56	0.6	57	163	$8
1st Half		165	18	9	26	1	242	247	317	461	778	332	839	10	70	0.38	50	16	34	29	104	144	108	23%	72	2%	100%	14	50%	29%	5.01	-2.4	38	109	$7
2nd Half		172	25	13	23	0	256	276	326	547	873	1011	857	9	73	0.38	45	17	38	28	120	180	131	27%	72	0%	0%	12	50%	0%	6.11	3.1	77	220	$10
17	**Proj**	**411**	**53**	**26**	**63**	**2**	**244**	**261**	**317**	**483**	**800**	**651**	**825**	**10**	**71**	**0.36**	**48**	**18**	**34**	**28**	**113**	**151**	**126**	**26%**	**64**	**3%**	**83%**				**5.17**	**-4.0**	**39**	**112**	**$14**

PAUL SPORER

Amarista,Alexi

Age: 28 Bats: L Pos: 2B	Health B	LIMA Plan D	
Ht: 5' 8" Wt: 150	PT/Exp D	Rand Var -3	
	Consist B	MM 0411	

0-11-.257 in 140 AB at SD. Missed a month with hamstring injury late in the year. While BA marked a career high and he continues to hit tons of line drives, lack of punch in his bat and high h% (for him) give little hope for BA repeat. Sure, he can run a little, but can you afford to roster 10 SB alone?

Yr	Tm	AB	R	HR	RBI	SB	BA	xBA	OBP	SLG	OPS	vL	vR	bb%	ct%	Eye	G	L	F	h%	HctX	PX	xPX	hr/f	Spd	SBO	SB%	#Wk	DOM	DIS	RC/G	RAR	BPV	BPX	R$
12	2 TM *	401	48	6	44	11	235	271	271	362	633	705	657	5	86	0.35	50	19	30	26	87	78	78	7%	137	18%	73%	22	55%	23%	3.25	-10.4	59	148	$6
13	SD	368	35	5	32	4	236	252	282	337	619	557	627	6	85	0.39	43	23	34	27	84	65	72	5%	122	7%	67%	27	52%	22%	3.12	-4.2	40	100	$3
14	SD	423	39	5	40	12	239	252	286	314	600	446	651	6	84	0.42	49	23	28	28	76	53	55	5%	112	12%	92%	27	30%	48%	3.15	-1.8	26	70	$7
15	SD	324	28	3	30	5	204	244	257	287	544	507	549	7	83	0.44	48	21	31	24	71	52	49	4%	127	8%	83%	26	19%	54%	2.41	-13.7	28	76	-$1
16	SD *	193	15	1	15	10	261	238	301	296	597	293	612	5	81	0.30	47	25	28	32	80	25	34	0%	96	21%	83%	18	6%	56%	3.21	-7.9	-13	-37	$4
1st Half		93	9	0	7	6	270	236	337	300	637	382	629	9	81	0.54	37	29	34	33	62	25	49	0%	96	22%	86%	9	11%	56%	3.78	-1.8	-6	-17	$6
2nd Half		100	6	1	8	4	254	237	264	292	557	200	583	1	81	0.08	62	19	19	31	105	24	13	0%	107	19%	79%	9	0%	56%	2.69	-5.3	-18	-51	$3
17	Proj	199	17	1	17	7	239	244	278	294	572	398	605	5	82	0.32	50	22	28	29	82	35	42	2%	109	16%	83%				2.84	-11.8	-1	-3	$2

Anderson,Tim

Age: 24 Bats: R Pos: SS	Health A	LIMA Plan C+	
Ht: 6' 1" Wt: 185	PT/Exp C	Rand Var -1	
	Consist A	MM 2525	

9-30-.283 with 10 SB in 410 AB at CHW. Speed skills and high SB% track record foretell of legit SB upside, though lack of walks and fringy contact will ultimately limit OBP. xBA, ct% issues in minors paint doubtful picture for BA repeat. Building blocks for power showed in 2nd half, but don't get too optimistic just yet.

Yr	Tm	AB	R	HR	RBI	SB	BA	xBA	OBP	SLG	OPS	vL	vR	bb%	ct%	Eye	G	L	F	h%	HctX	PX	xPX	hr/f	Spd	SBO	SB%	#Wk	DOM	DIS	RC/G	RAR	BPV	BPX	R$
12																																			
13																																			
14	aa	44	5	1	5	0	326		326	445	771			0	77	0.00				41		97			94	10%	0%				4.88		15	41	$0
15	aa	513	70	5	41	43	287		318	389	707			4	75	0.18				38		69			145	42%	75%				4.37		8	22	$29
16	CHW *	657	89	12	46	19	277	248	298	403	701	797	721	3	72	0.11	54	21	25	37	94	85	86	12%	171	17%	75%	18	28%	50%	4.21	-1.9	15	43	$21
1st Half		347	47	6	22	11	276	252	293	394	687	690	814	2	71	0.08	51	27	22	37	81	82	61	20%	156	20%	71%	5	20%	0%	3.99	-4.8	3	9	$22
2nd Half		310	42	6	24	8	277	250	306	413	718	816	686	4	73	0.14	55	19	26	36	100	87	93	10%	173	14%	80%	13	31%	69%	4.45	-0.1	22	63	$20
17	Proj	607	83	12	45	31	264	254	292	395	687	719	679	4	73	0.14	53	22	24	34	92	84	80	11%	179	30%	76%				3.95	-9.1	16	45	$25

Andrus,Elvis

Age: 28 Bats: R Pos: SS	Health A	LIMA Plan B+	
Ht: 6' 0" Wt: 185	PT/Exp A	Rand Var -3	
	Consist C	MM 1545	

Eighth straight season of 20+ SB, so you can ink that in. Continues to make quality contact, but that .300+ BA was driven by an elevated 2nd half h% which will likely decline. Still, his xBA floor remains high and sets himself up well for a solid follow-up.

Yr	Tm	AB	R	HR	RBI	SB	BA	xBA	OBP	SLG	OPS	vL	vR	bb%	ct%	Eye	G	L	F	h%	HctX	PX	xPX	hr/f	Spd	SBO	SB%	#Wk	DOM	DIS	RC/G	RAR	BPV	BPX	R$
12	TEX	629	85	3	62	21	286	275	349	378	727	687	742	8	85	0.59	57	22	21	33	101	61	76	3%	145	16%	68%	27	48%	22%	4.59	12.2	50	125	$21
13	TEX	620	91	4	67	42	271	257	328	331	659	698	644	8	84	0.54	56	21	22	32	91	40	54	3%	143	26%	84%	27	33%	37%	3.99	10.1	30	75	$30
14	TEX	619	72	2	41	27	263	268	314	333	647	760	607	7	84	0.48	59	20	21	31	75	59	36	2%	110	25%	64%	27	37%	19%	3.49	5.7	34	92	$19
15	TEX	596	69	7	62	25	258	266	309	357	667	757	618	7	87	0.59	47	21	32	29	104	67	70	4%	110	22%	74%	27	59%	15%	3.81	-10.3	51	138	$19
16	TEX	506	75	8	69	24	302	289	362	439	800	899	771	8	86	0.67	48	24	29	34	95	80	68	6%	143	21%	75%	27	48%	7%	5.77	20.6	71	203	$26
1st Half		274	37	3	36	11	281	278	336	391	726	929	661	8	87	0.64	45	25	29	31	86	62	54	4%	151	21%	65%	14	50%	0%	4.49	0.2	60	171	$23
2nd Half		232	38	5	33	13	328	301	392	496	887	850	896	9	85	0.71	51	22	27	37	105	100	84	9%	130	20%	87%	13	46%	15%	7.55	19.1	81	231	$30
17	Proj	548	75	7	63	26	286	281	343	400	743	805	721	8	86	0.61	50	22	27	32	96	70	65	5%	130	21%	75%				4.90	6.7	55	156	$27

Aoki,Norichika

Age: 35 Bats: L Pos: LF	Health B	LIMA Plan B	
Ht: 5' 9" Wt: 180	PT/Exp C	Rand Var 0	
	Consist A	MM 1453	

4-28-.283 in 417 AB at SEA. Aging vet progressively lost AB as season wore on. Sharp SB% decline removes utility of still-strong Spd, which is one of only few select skills at this point. Ct% remains in fine shape, and xBA floor is still high. A source of cheap BA/SB in deeper formats at the very least.

Yr	Tm	AB	R	HR	RBI	SB	BA	xBA	OBP	SLG	OPS	vL	vR	bb%	ct%	Eye	G	L	F	h%	HctX	PX	xPX	hr/f	Spd	SBO	SB%	#Wk	DOM	DIS	RC/G	RAR	BPV	BPX	R$
12	MIL	520	81	10	50	30	288	294	355	433	787	711	828	8	89	0.78	55	17	28	31	98	91	81	8%	126	27%	79%	27	59%	19%	5.35	11.6	86	215	$24
13	MIL	597	80	8	37	20	286	282	356	370	726	781	703	8	93	1.38	60	18	22	30	100	50	69	7%	137	16%	63%	27	56%	4%	4.43	7.8	73	183	$22
14	KC	491	63	1	43	17	285	292	349	360	710	863	658	8	90	0.88	62	21	17	32	73	53	40	1%	131	16%	68%	25	48%	4%	4.34	9.1	60	162	$17
15	SF	355	42	5	26	14	287	294	353	380	733	774	717	8	93	1.20	61	19	20	30	64	52	36	8%	126	17%	74%	17	53%	6%	4.65	2.6	69	186	$13
16	SEA *	513	75	5	33	10	275	280	327	372	700	557	793	7	88	0.63	61	17	22	31	71	59	32	5%	139	13%	52%	22	45%	23%	4.09	-2.7	56	160	$13
1st Half		272	39	1	13	5	246	270	309	315	624	434	728	8	86	0.63	67	17	16	28	58	41	10	3%	142	15%	40%	12	17%	33%	3.03	-11.9	36	103	$9
2nd Half		241	36	4	20	5	308	288	348	438	786	1079	866	6	90	0.62	52	18	30	33	90	79	62	7%	131	11%	72%	10	80%	10%	5.57	7.4	77	220	$18
17	Proj	357	49	4	26	11	285	288	347	384	731	711	737	7	90	0.81	59	18	22	31	75	57	43	5%	128	15%	66%				4.51	0.6	55	156	$13

Arcia,Orlando

Age: 22 Bats: R Pos: SS	Health A	LIMA Plan B+	
Ht: 6' 0" Wt: 165	PT/Exp D	Rand Var +1	
	Consist F	MM 1535	

4-17-.219 with 8 SB in 201 AB at MIL. Didn't "wow" in MLB debut, but showed some skills. Plus speed, SB% track record point to solid SB totals, though you'd like to see a few more walks. Good contact and line-drive swing path suggest future BA impact. Needs time to tap into power, but enjoy his thefts in the meantime.

Yr	Tm	AB	R	HR	RBI	SB	BA	xBA	OBP	SLG	OPS	vL	vR	bb%	ct%	Eye	G	L	F	h%	HctX	PX	xPX	hr/f	Spd	SBO	SB%	#Wk	DOM	DIS	RC/G	RAR	BPV	BPX	R$
12																																			
13																																			
14																																			
15	aa	512	67	7	63	23	296		332	432	764			5	85	0.36				34		90			104	24%	73%				5.11		55	149	$25
16	MIL *	605	65	10	57	19	230	250	275	348	623	845	564	6	78	0.28	54	17	29	28	80	73	59	9%	148	21%	69%	10	40%	40%	3.10	-28.1	29	83	$10
1st Half		310	37	5	28	9	237	235	277	332	609			5	81	0.30				28		54			159	21%	58%				2.91		29	83	$11
2nd Half		295	28	6	29	10	223	254	272	365	637	845	564	6	75	0.27	54	17	29	28	77	94	59	9%	134	21%	82%	10	40%	40%	3.31	-10.4	30	86	$9
17	Proj	596	69	9	56	20	255	270	295	384	679	900	611	5	81	0.29	53	20	27	30	69	80	53	7%	143	21%	72%				3.83	-11.3	38	108	$18

Arcia,Oswaldo

Age: 26 Bats: L Pos: RF	Health C	LIMA Plan D	
Ht: 6' 0" Wt: 220	PT/Exp D	Rand Var 0	
	Consist C	MM 3001	

Lived out of his suitcase, and issues persisted each destination. Ct% woes continue to hamper his consistency, and while the liners are there, still struggles to keep BA above Mendoza line via poor HctX trend. Past HR/xPX output is tempting to dream on, especially given his age, but don't let those stats obscure your judgment.

Yr	Tm	AB	R	HR	RBI	SB	BA	xBA	OBP	SLG	OPS	vL	vR	bb%	ct%	Eye	G	L	F	h%	HctX	PX	xPX	hr/f	Spd	SBO	SB%	#Wk	DOM	DIS	RC/G	RAR	BPV	BPX	R$
12	aa	262	45	8	56	2	305		362	500	862			8	75	0.36				38		136			105	6%	53%				6.49		57	143	$12
13	MIN *	479	54	21	67	3	257	231	315	446	761	659	769	8	67	0.25	42	17	41	34	94	145	131	15%	91	5%	45%	19	42%	37%	4.72	9.3	29	73	$14
14	MIN *	449	59	24	72	2	240	254	295	464	759	574	848	7	68	0.24	37	22	42	30	94	175	144	19%	83	4%	48%	20	45%	50%	4.52	9.9	52	141	$14
15	MIN *	340	32	12	43	0	195	223	238	335	573	624	779	5	70	0.18	36	23	41	24	69	100	64	11%	77	2%	0%	5	20%	40%	2.48	-24.0	-4	-11	-$1
16	4 TM	202	17	8	23	1	203	216	270	366	637	539	659	8	60	0.23	42	25	34	29	76	120	101	20%	65	5%	50%	22	36%	59%	3.09	-9.7	-24	-69	-$1
1st Half		128	12	5	16	1	242	226	310	414	724	795	709	9	59	0.23	38	30	32	37	75	130	101	21%	75	3%	100%	14	43%	57%	4.32	-0.5	-17	-49	$2
2nd Half		74	5	3	7	0	135	192	200	284	484	125	569	8	62	0.21	48	15	37	16	77	105	101	18%	67	9%	0%	8	25%	63%	1.54	-7.4	-30	-86	-$5
17	Proj	194	19	8	25	1	227	223	292	397	689	568	735	7	65	0.23	41	21	38	30	79	117	101	17%	69	4%	32%				3.64	-6.3	-14	-40	$3

Arenado,Nolan

Age: 26 Bats: R Pos: 3B	Health A	LIMA Plan C	
Ht: 6' 1" Wt: 205	PT/Exp A	Rand Var -1	
	Consist B	MM 4155	

How much better can this guy get? Second straight year with 40 HR/130 RBI, and this time around, he added OBP skills to his arsenal. Expect BA to hold steady with solid contact and walks surge, while heavy fly-ball lean and elite HctX and xPX suggest his HR floor is exceptionally high. A proven asset worth investing in early.

Yr	Tm	AB	R	HR	RBI	SB	BA	xBA	OBP	SLG	OPS	vL	vR	bb%	ct%	Eye	G	L	F	h%	HctX	PX	xPX	hr/f	Spd	SBO	SB%	#Wk	DOM	DIS	RC/G	RAR	BPV	BPX	R$
12	aa	516	48	13	49	0	289		333	440	773			6	89	0.59				31		95			82	2%	0%				5.16		71	178	$13
13	COL *	552	58	12	65	2	273	284	306	424	730	846	652	5	85	0.32	43	24	34	30	103	103	103	7%	99	3%	47%	23	43%	17%	4.50	7.9	64	160	$14
14	COL	432	58	18	61	2	287	300	328	500	828	973	776	5	87	0.43	38	21	42	30	127	142	134	11%	91	3%	67%	20	80%	10%	5.80	25.3	100	270	$18
15	COL	616	97	42	130	2	287	307	323	575	898	778	931	5	82	0.31	34	22	44	29	133	172	151	19%	90	6%	29%	27	70%	15%	6.46	31.1	106	286	$32
16	COL	618	116	41	133	2	294	290	362	570	932	875	951	10	83	0.66	35	18	47	30	128	146	148	17%	111	3%	40%	27	78%	11%	7.38	41.4	105	300	$32
1st Half		313	58	22	66	1	288	293	363	569	931	986	911	10	85	0.75	36	15	48	28	131	150	151	17%	94	5%	25%	14	86%	7%	7.10	19.6	110	314	$30
2nd Half		305	58	19	67	1	302	287	362	570	932	765	993	9	82	0.58	34	21	45	32	125	142	144	16%	127	1%	100%	13	69%	15%	7.69	23.4	100	286	$33
17	Proj	616	101	39	119	2	291	299	342	563	905	870	916	7	84	0.49	36	20	44	29	126	147	142	17%	103	3%	41%				6.84	33.7	92	262	$33

ALEC DOPP

Asche,Cody

Age: 27	Bats: L	Pos: LF	Health	C	LIMA Plan	D
Ht: 6' 1"	Wt: 205		PT/Exp	C	Rand Var	+4
			Consist	A	MM	2211

4-18-.213 in 197 AB at PHI. Lost April and May to oblique injury, then posted his only good month in June when h%, HctX, and LD% sparked a 142 xPX. Subsequent 2nd half collapse rendered 2016 indicators nearly indistiguishable from 2013-15. At this point, just a AAAA player / end-game filler.

Yr Tm	AB	R	HR	RBI	SB	BA	xBA	OBP	SLG	OPS	vL	vR	bb%	ct%	Eye	G	L	F	h%	HctX	PX	xPX	hr/f	Spd	SBO	SB%	#Wk	DOM	DIS	RC/G	RAR	BPV	BPX	R$
12 aa	263	33	8	37	1	269		315	450	765			6	76	0.28				32		127			93	3%	42%				4.87		49	123	$6
13 PHI *	566	58	17	75	10	252	246	304	411	715	608	710	7	73	0.28	44	21	35	32	92	116	111	12%	104	10%	74%	10	40%	40%	4.24	3.1	33	83	$16
14 PHI	397	43	10	46	0	252	249	309	390	699	733	690	8	74	0.32	41	24	35	32	95	113	102	10%	86	1%	0%	24	50%	29%	4.07	3.3	31	84	$7
15 PHI *	486	46	13	41	1	245	241	290	388	678	585	713	6	75	0.25	38	23	39	30	96	99	112	10%	95	3%	33%	26	27%	35%	3.74	-14.0	21	57	$6
16 PHI *	324	40	10	32	4	218	243	282	383	665	734	621	8	71	0.31	39	22	39	27	97	116	108	7%	65	7%	79%	16	38%	38%	3.53	-10.9	16	46	$3
1st Half	132	18	6	17	3	244	294	294	470	765	896	829	7	75	0.28	42	27	31	29	115	154	134	13%	70	17%	75%	6	67%	17%	4.63	0.7	58	166	$6
2nd Half	192	22	5	15	1	201	198	274	322	596	496	453	9	69	0.33	36	16	48	26	80	88	81	3%	75	2%	100%	10	20%	50%	2.84	-9.7	-10	-29	$0
17 Proj	**162**	**18**	**4**	**16**	**1**	**235**	**237**	**296**	**375**	**671**	**684**	**668**	**7**	**73**	**0.30**	**39**	**22**	**39**	**30**	**94**	**98**	**106**	**9%**	**82**	**5%**	**70%**				**3.62**	**-4.1**	**6**	**16**	**$1**

Asuaje,Carlos

Age: 25	Bats: L	Pos: 2B	Health	A	LIMA Plan	D
Ht: 5' 9"	Wt: 160		PT/Exp	D	Rand Var	0
			Consist	B	MM	1211

0-2-.208 in 24 AB at SD. Led PCL in hits and runs—but also led in plate appearances and AB. Checks the utility infielder boxes (LH bat, decent plate approach, plus speed) but lack of power and poor SB success rate will prevent similar AB totals in the majors.

Yr Tm	AB	R	HR	RBI	SB	BA	xBA	OBP	SLG	OPS	vL	vR	bb%	ct%	Eye	G	L	F	h%	HctX	PX	xPX	hr/f	Spd	SBO	SB%	#Wk	DOM	DIS	RC/G	RAR	BPV	BPX	R$
12																																		
13																																		
14																																		
15 aa	495	47	6	48	7	226		289	331	620			8	80	0.45				27		71			110	11%	51%				3.04		29	78	$4
16 SD *	559	68	6	48	7	255	244	298	363	661	556	517	6	81	0.32	35	25	40	31	99	67	88	0%	125	9%	53%	2	50%	50%	3.59	-21.1	29	83	$9
1st Half	312	40	3	27	5	254	240	302	349	651			6	82	0.39				30		58			133	10%	57%				3.51		30	86	$11
2nd Half	247	27	4	21	2	257	250	293	380	673	556	517	5	80	0.25	35	25	40	31	97	80	88	0%	115	8%	46%	2	50%	50%	3.70	-8.0	29	83	$8
17 Proj	**196**	**21**	**2**	**18**	**2**	**244**	**240**	**294**	**353**	**647**	**647**	**647**	**7**	**81**	**0.36**	**42**	**20**	**38**	**29**		**69**		**4%**	**119**	**10%**	**52%**				**3.38**	**-8.4**	**20**	**56**	**$3**

Austin,Tyler

Age: 25	Bats: R	Pos: 1B	Health	A	LIMA Plan	D+
Ht: 6' 1"	Wt: 220		PT/Exp	C	Rand Var	-3
			Consist	D	MM	4213

5-12-.241 in 83 AB at NYY. Removed from the 40-man roster at end of 2015, and underwent an epiphany in second AAA tour (1.051 OPS in 201 AB). Rewarded with call-up and slugged all five HR in friendly home stadium. Weak, infrequent contact with few LD will keep BA low, but 2016 power surge has our attention.

Yr Tm	AB	R	HR	RBI	SB	BA	xBA	OBP	SLG	OPS	vL	vR	bb%	ct%	Eye	G	L	F	h%	HctX	PX	xPX	hr/f	Spd	SBO	SB%	#Wk	DOM	DIS	RC/G	RAR	BPV	BPX	R$
12																																		
13 aa	319	36	6	34	3	236		312	342	655			10	73	0.41				31		84			92	4%	100%				3.63		10	25	$3
14 aa	396	45	8	37	2	243		295	363	659			7	77	0.32				30		89			107	5%	52%				3.56		27	73	$6
15 a/a	341	35	6	30	10	218		280	312	592			8	68	0.27				30		72			101	15%	74%				2.86		-23	-62	$3
16 NYY *	461	62	23	83	6	265	246	355	488	842	1097	621	12	66	0.41	43	17	40	35	91	162	135	26%	69	6%	85%	9	33%	67%	6.04	15.7	40	114	$16
1st Half	278	39	11	50	4	251	253	346	453	800			13	69	0.46				33		145			75	6%	76%				5.35		40	114	$17
2nd Half	183	23	11	33	3	286	246	367	540	907	1097	621	11	62	0.34	43	17	40	40	86	191	135	26%	68	5%	100%	9	33%	67%	7.19	10.7	46	131	$15
17 Proj	**284**	**34**	**12**	**39**	**4**	**250**	**235**	**324**	**441**	**765**	**1104**	**626**	**10**	**68**	**0.35**	**43**	**17**	**40**	**32**	**77**	**132**	**122**	**16%**	**79**	**7%**	**78%**				**4.86**	**-2.0**	**21**	**59**	**$9**

Avila,Alex

Age: 30	Bats: L	Pos: CA	Health	F	LIMA Plan	F
Ht: 5' 11"	Wt: 210		PT/Exp	D	Rand Var	-5
			Consist	C	MM	2001

7-11-.213 in 169 AB at CHW. Walk rate has benefited from 687 career games behind the plate, and he still can provide a small handful of HRs. But 2016's plummeting ct% and HctX, two right hamstring strains and F Health Grade indicate that the rest of the body is not as healthy as his eyes.

Yr Tm	AB	R	HR	RBI	SB	BA	xBA	OBP	SLG	OPS	vL	vR	bb%	ct%	Eye	G	L	F	h%	HctX	PX	xPX	hr/f	Spd	SBO	SB%	#Wk	DOM	DIS	RC/G	RAR	BPV	BPX	R$
12 DET	367	42	9	48	2	243	245	352	384	736	539	796	14	72	0.59	46	24	30	31	105	106	130	11%	76	2%	100%	26	35%	38%	4.57	4.7	25	63	$5
13 DET *	374	43	12	51	0	225	238	316	369	685	455	767	12	66	0.39	42	28	30	31	100	116	138	17%	67	0%	0%	24	25%	42%	3.84	1.4	4	10	$4
14 DET	390	44	11	47	0	218	222	327	359	686	589	720	14	61	0.40	45	25	30	32	105	136	147	15%	59	3%	0%	27	37%	44%	3.68	4.2	1	3	$3
15 DET	178	21	4	13	0	191	207	339	287	626	424	666	18	63	0.61	41	28	32	28	84	77	123	11%	79	2%	0%	19	26%	53%	3.00	-4.1	-23	-62	-$3
16 CHW *	193	22	8	13	0	219	203	360	374	734	844	715	18	55	0.49	52	25	23	35	72	129	111	33%	78	0%	0%	19	37%	53%	4.40	3.1	-15	-43	$0
1st Half	129	13	3	6	0	217	211	349	326	675	730	706	17	59	0.50	49	29	22	34	76	90	89	19%	78	0%	0%	12	33%	58%	3.70	-1.7	-32	-91	-$1
2nd Half	64	9	5	7	0	224	184	382	476	859	906	747	20	46	0.47	63	11	26	39	69	230	199	80%	82	0%	0%	7	43%	43%	5.99	3.6	36	103	$1
17 Proj	**174**	**21**	**4**	**16**	**0**	**213**	**193**	**350**	**325**	**675**	**662**	**678**	**17**	**58**	**0.49**	**47**	**23**	**30**	**34**	**83**	**94**	**144**	**14%**	**73**	**1%**	**10%**				**3.64**	**-2.7**	**-50**	**-143**	**$1**

Aybar,Erick

Age: 33	Bats: B	Pos: SS	Health	B	LIMA Plan	B
Ht: 5' 10"	Wt: 195		PT/Exp	B	Rand Var	+2
			Consist	B	MM	1245

3-34-.243 with 3 SB in 415 AB at ATL/DET. Lost AB due to multiple aches/pains (abdomen, ribs, hamstring, foot) which likely impacted ct% in 1st half and SB success all year. Health and SB% must both rebound to win back SB opps (and value). At this age, odds are low for a full rebound.

Yr Tm	AB	R	HR	RBI	SB	BA	xBA	OBP	SLG	OPS	vL	vR	bb%	ct%	Eye	G	L	F	h%	HctX	PX	xPX	hr/f	Spd	SBO	SB%	#Wk	DOM	DIS	RC/G	RAR	BPV	BPX	R$
12 LAA	517	67	8	45	20	290	279	324	416	740	879	690	4	88	0.36	52	19	29	32	91	79	63	6%	105	19%	83%	25	52%	24%	4.84	13.6	58	145	$19
13 LAA	550	68	6	54	12	271	287	301	382	683	723	666	4	89	0.39	50	23	27	29	91	75	63	5%	97	15%	63%	25	52%	20%	3.90	7.5	56	140	$16
14 LAA	589	77	7	68	16	278	282	321	379	700	622	727	6	89	0.58	49	23	28	30	88	69	54	5%	91	16%	64%	27	41%	15%	4.16	16.7	54	146	$21
15 LAA	597	74	3	44	15	270	265	301	338	639	597	657	4	88	0.34	53	21	26	30	88	50	58	2%	93	14%	71%	27	33%	33%	3.51	-15.3	29	78	$15
16 2 TM *	444	36	3	35	4	236	255	288	310	598	532	655	7	84	0.45	57	20	23	28	71	49	39	4%	97	8%	47%	24	29%	38%	2.88	-23.4	18	51	$2
1st Half	242	18	0	14	3	214	237	256	259	514	501	580	5	81	0.30	56	20	24	26	64	37	29	0%	84	14%	46%	12	8%	67%	2.03	-18.5	-8	-23	-$1
2nd Half	202	18	3	21	1	262	274	324	371	696	590	720	9	87	0.70	58	19	23	29	80	62	49	8%	107	3%	50%	12	50%	8%	4.13	-2.0	47	134	$5
17 Proj	**428**	**45**	**4**	**38**	**9**	**259**	**271**	**307**	**345**	**652**	**592**	**673**	**6**	**86**	**0.47**	**54**	**20**	**25**	**29**	**81**	**54**	**49**	**4%**	**97**	**13%**	**67%**				**3.56**	**-11.5**	**30**	**87**	**$11**

Baez,Javier

Age: 24	Bats: R	Pos: 3B 2B SS	Health	A	LIMA Plan	C+
Ht: 6' 1"	Wt: 195		PT/Exp	C	Rand Var	-2
			Consist	C	MM	2415

Now a modest five-category contributor as ct% approaches tolerable level. 2nd half fade in HctX, xPX, FB% likely just noise, though favorable speed metrics indicate SB could eclipse HR in 2017. Age and three-position eligibility ensure he will be high on everyone's list at the draft table (and probably overbid).

Yr Tm	AB	R	HR	RBI	SB	BA	xBA	OBP	SLG	OPS	vL	vR	bb%	ct%	Eye	G	L	F	h%	HctX	PX	xPX	hr/f	Spd	SBO	SB%	#Wk	DOM	DIS	RC/G	RAR	BPV	BPX	R$
12																																		
13 aa	218	31	16	43	6	268		317	557	874			7	66	0.21				33		224			79	20%	75%				6.07		81	203	$11
14 CHC *	601	74	26	81	17	209	213	260	393	654	569	546	6	60	0.17	41	14	45	30	82	166	120	17%	93	24%	64%	9	33%	67%	3.17	-4.2	16	43	$15
15 CHC *	357	41	11	51	14	287	249	325	443	768	1082	617	5	69	0.18	37	31	31	39	103	117	121	6%	112	21%	72%	6	33%	67%	5.06	9.1	15	41	$16
16 CHC	421	50	14	59	12	273	241	314	423	737	850	689	3	74	0.14	44	20	36	34	88	95	89	13%	112	16%	80%	26	27%	38%	4.44	-5.1	16	46	$15
1st Half	193	25	8	27	5	275	251	314	456	770	1009	674	4	76	0.15	42	18	40	33	93	114	97	15%	101	15%	83%	13	46%	15%	4.84	0.2	33	94	$14
2nd Half	228	25	6	32	7	272	232	314	395	709	724	702	3	73	0.13	46	21	34	35	84	78	82	11%	124	16%	78%	13	8%	62%	4.10	-4.6	1	3	$16
17 Proj	**500**	**60**	**15**	**73**	**16**	**266**	**239**	**309**	**412**	**721**	**900**	**654**	**5**	**72**	**0.18**	**41**	**23**	**36**	**34**	**92**	**97**	**104**	**12%**	**112**	**18%**	**75%**				**4.27**	**-9.1**	**7**	**19**	**$21**

Bandy,Jett

Age: 27	Bats: R	Pos: CA	Health	A	LIMA Plan	D+
Ht: 6' 4"	Wt: 210		PT/Exp	D	Rand Var	0
			Consist	A	MM	2113

8-25-.234 in 209 AB at LAA. Started strong after May callup but faded down the stretch (.198/.234/.342 after August 1). Average power with a FB tilt plus above average speed (for a catcher) make for an interesting late-round target. But buyer beware of the BA hit.

Yr Tm	AB	R	HR	RBI	SB	BA	xBA	OBP	SLG	OPS	vL	vR	bb%	ct%	Eye	G	L	F	h%	HctX	PX	xPX	hr/f	Spd	SBO	SB%	#Wk	DOM	DIS	RC/G	RAR	BPV	BPX	R$
12																																		
13 aa	245	22	3	24	0	213		248	325	573			4	82	0.26				25		83			97	3%	0%				2.55		35	88	-$2
14 aa	312	32	10	34	2	220		281	352	633			8	77	0.37				25		94			83	8%	27%				3.05		25	68	$3
15 LAA *	311	32	8	40	0	229	127	254	358	612	2500	0	3	75	0.13	0	0	100	28	162	93	358	50%	81	0%	0%	2	50%	0%	3.01	-6.8	7	19	$2
16 LAA *	304	32	9	39	2	228	230	258	367	625	696	664	4	80	0.20	27	21	52	26	89	85	101	9%	86	6%	66%	21	52%	29%	3.10	-7.1	23	66	$2
1st Half	146	15	3	24	1	228	208	250	346	596	1352	493	3	79	0.14	20	20	61	27	47	77	63	7%	95	10%	53%	8	63%	25%	2.77	-6.1	14	40	$2
2nd Half	158	17	6	15	1	228	243	275	386	661	513	723	5	80	0.26	30	21	49	25	105	92	115	10%	90	3%	100%	13	46%	31%	3.41	-3.5	34	97	$3
17 Proj	**301**	**31**	**10**	**36**	**1**	**225**	**235**	**268**	**378**	**646**	**777**	**595**	**5**	**78**	**0.22**	**27**	**21**	**52**	**25**	**82**	**93**	**94**	**9%**	**87**	**4%**	**50%**				**3.19**	**-8.7**	**12**	**35**	**$5**

MATT DODGE

Barnes,Austin

Age: 27	Bats: R	Pos: CA	Health A	LIMA Plan D+
Ht: 5' 9"	Wt: 190		PT/Exp D	Rand Var -2
			Consist B	MM 1311

0-1-.207 with 1 SB in 29 AB at LA. Not your garden-variety backup catcher, this one totes a full cadre of gloves, also playing 2B, 3B, and OF in minors. Solid plate skills, a career .299 minors BA, AND swiped 18 bags at Triple-A. A multi-positional #2 CA who doesn't kill your BA and might get some SB? That's worth a buck.

Yr	Tm	AB	R	HR	RBI	SB	BA	xBA	OBP	SLG	OPS	vL	vR	bb%	ct%	Eye	G	L	F	h%	HctX	PX	xPX	hr/f	Spd	SBO	SB%	#Wk	DOM	DIS	RC/G	RAR	BPV	BPX	R$
12																																			
13	aa	62	8	1	6	0	307		404	431	835			14	82	0.90				37		73			142	0%	0%				6.40		59	148	$0
14	aa	284	41	7	32	6	245		332	399	730			11	85	0.89				26		105			100	7%	100%				4.60		81	219	$7
15	LA *	321	33	7	32	10	251	269	315	374	689	625	644	8	84	0.59	48	22	30	28	76	79	71	0%	72	14%	80%	9	56%	33%	4.06	2.2	42	114	$8
16	LA *	368	48	5	32	14	231	187	298	339	637	795	297	9	80	0.47	32	9	59	28	70	70	89	0%	114	19%	79%	9	11%	56%	3.40	-11.2	29	83	$7
1st Half		216	28	2	18	11	223	138	299	309	607	500	250	10	78	0.49	27	0	73	28	79	59	112	0%	98	22%	81%	3	0%	100%	3.13	-6.7	10	29	$9
2nd Half		152	20	2	13	3	243	242	298	382	680	929	393	7	82	0.44	36	18	45	28	61	85	67	0%	121	12%	71%	6	17%	33%	3.81	-1.5	51	146	$4
17	Proj	**204**	**25**	**3**	**19**	**6**	**243**	**239**	**309**	**353**	**662**	**662**	**662**	**9**	**83**	**0.55**	**41**	**18**	**41**	**28**		**70**		**4%**	**102**	**14%**	**83%**				**3.75**	**-2.4**	**38**	**107**	**$3**

Barney,Darwin

Age: 31	Bats: R	Pos: 2B 3B SS	Health A	LIMA Plan D
Ht: 5' 10"	Wt: 185		PT/Exp D	Rand Var -2
			Consist C	MM 1221

Known more for his former CHC prospect status. He has carved out a role as a UT who can hit lefties, posting a .306/.361/.418 slash vs. LHP in 2016. But he doesn't do any one thing particularly well, and now at age 31, there's little room for skills growth. However, he knows full well about survival of the fittest.

Yr	Tm	AB	R	HR	RBI	SB	BA	xBA	OBP	SLG	OPS	vL	vR	bb%	ct%	Eye	G	L	F	h%	HctX	PX	xPX	hr/f	Spd	SBO	SB%	#Wk	DOM	DIS	RC/G	RAR	BPV	BPX	R$
12	CHC	548	73	7	44	6	254	273	299	354	653	636	659	6	89	0.57	48	22	30	27	81	62	58	5%	120	5%	86%	27	41%	22%	3.61	-8.9	57	143	$9
13	CHC	501	49	7	41	4	208	252	266	303	569	725	515	7	87	0.56	45	19	36	23	74	66	74	4%	88	6%	67%	24	38%	21%	2.53	-18.6	43	108	$0
14	2 NL *	272	27	3	24	1	232	243	281	323	604	707	614	6	85	0.46	43	20	37	26	94	64	79	4%	127	2%	100%	24	38%	21%	3.03	-2.9	44	119	$1
15	2 TM *	374	39	5	25	5	210	219	239	282	522	1111	652	4	84	0.25	44	16	40	24	54	49	74	20%	89	13%	48%	6	33%	0%	2.07	-24.7	12	32	-$1
16	TOR	279	35	4	19	2	269	260	322	373	695	779	649	7	83	0.46	47	22	30	31	93	64	68	6%	120	5%	50%	26	31%	42%	4.11	-4.9	35	100	$4
1st Half		168	19	3	10	2	292	260	346	387	733	746	723	7	85	0.50	47	23	30	33	89	53	61	7%	123	8%	50%	14	43%	36%	4.62	-0.9	34	97	$7
2nd Half		111	16	1	9	0	234	260	287	351	638	849	557	8	80	0.41	48	21	31	28	98	81	80	4%	106	0%	0%	12	17%	50%	3.41	-4.6	34	97	$0
17	Proj	**230**	**27**	**3**	**17**	**2**	**239**	**253**	**289**	**335**	**625**	**727**	**580**	**6**	**84**	**0.41**	**46**	**21**	**33**	**27**	**90**	**60**	**73**	**5%**	**111**	**6%**	**55%**				**3.17**	**-11.3**	**20**	**57**	**$3**

Barnhart,Tucker

Age: 26	Bats: B	Pos: CA	Health A	LIMA Plan D+
Ht: 5' 10"	Wt: 185		PT/Exp D	Rand Var 0
			Consist C	MM 1025

Has gradually raised offensive game from "awful" to "palatable" (precise analytic verbiage). Drove the ball with a bit more authority without sacrificing solid plate skills; xBA growth a better indicator of progress. Solving LHers is his next step, but can he? Skills batting RH show few signs of life, so this isn't the time to speculate.

Yr	Tm	AB	R	HR	RBI	SB	BA	xBA	OBP	SLG	OPS	vL	vR	bb%	ct%	Eye	G	L	F	h%	HctX	PX	xPX	hr/f	Spd	SBO	SB%	#Wk	DOM	DIS	RC/G	RAR	BPV	BPX	R$
12	aa	130	9	2	11	1	190		247	280	527			7	82	0.41				22		56			103	7%	46%				2.12		19	48	-$3
13	aa	339	28	3	40	1	245		326	331	656			11	81	0.64				29		66			86	1%	100%				3.65		28	70	$2
14	CIN *	310	16	2	21	0	202	189	259	258	517	167	568	7	84	0.48	60	7	33	24	79	39	38	7%	103	1%	0%	9	22%	44%	2.10	-13.2	14	38	-$4
15	CIN	242	23	3	18	0	252	245	324	326	650	433	700	9	81	0.56	47	25	28	30	66	52	45	5%	82	1%	0%	24	42%	33%	3.52	-2.0	13	35	$1
16	CIN	377	34	7	51	1	257	270	323	379	702	546	744	9	81	0.50	48	25	28	30	92	79	93	8%	81	1%	100%	27	37%	26%	4.21	-2.1	30	86	$5
1st Half		194	16	2	15	1	268	266	336	376	713	776	693	8	76	0.39	51	27	22	34	91	79	89	6%	98	2%	100%	14	36%	43%	4.36	1.2	17	49	$4
2nd Half		183	18	5	36	0	246	273	309	383	691	261	797	9	86	0.69	44	23	33	26	93	80	97	10%	72	0%	0%	13	38%	8%	4.05	-0.5	49	140	$7
17	Proj	**416**	**37**	**7**	**50**	**1**	**255**	**254**	**319**	**357**	**676**	**434**	**738**	**9**	**82**	**0.53**	**49**	**22**	**29**	**30**	**81**	**64**	**68**	**7%**	**80**	**1%**	**45%**				**3.87**	**-3.2**	**10**	**28**	**$8**

Barreto,Franklin

Age: 21	Bats: R	Pos: SS	Health A	LIMA Plan D
Ht: 5' 9"	Wt: 175		PT/Exp F	Rand Var 0
			Consist F	MM 2331

Top OAK prospect held his own as a 20-year-old in the high minors. And as splits indicate, really stepped it up in the 2H, a strong sign. Lots of rough edges to file down (see Eye, SB%), but power/speed upside is enticing. May have to move off SS, but expect him to arrive sometime during 2017. Keeper league must-own.

Yr	Tm	AB	R	HR	RBI	SB	BA	xBA	OBP	SLG	OPS	vL	vR	bb%	ct%	Eye	G	L	F	h%	HctX	PX	xPX	hr/f	Spd	SBO	SB%	#Wk	DOM	DIS	RC/G	RAR	BPV	BPX	R$
12																																			
13																																			
14																																			
15																																			
16	a/a	479	58	9	47	27	271		317	396	712			6	80	0.33				32		78			106	36%	60%				3.99		28	80	$20
1st Half		292	27	5	24	15	224		272	331	603			6	76	0.28				28		68			115	37%	61%				2.73		9	26	$17
2nd Half		187	29	3	21	11	334		373	478	851			6	85	0.40				38		88			117	34%	56%				6.05		58	166	$25
17	Proj	**165**	**21**	**3**	**16**	**7**	**291**	**263**	**334**	**424**	**758**	**758**	**758**	**6**	**81**	**0.34**	**45**	**22**	**33**	**34**		**82**		**7%**	**117**	**29%**	**57%**				**4.66**	**0.9**	**38**	**109**	**$8**

Bautista,Jose

Age: 36	Bats: R	Pos: RF DH	Health D	LIMA Plan A
Ht: 6' 1"	Wt: 190		PT/Exp A	Rand Var +2
			Consist C	MM 4135

This is a smaller decline than it appears. Sure, there are signs: leg/toe injuries, a ct% dip that accelerated in the 2H. But HctX is right there with five-year average, so he's hitting the ball as hard as ever; AB dip, FB rate regression did in the HR totals, not any loss of raw power. Despite age, he's a solid bounce-back candidate.

Yr	Tm	AB	R	HR	RBI	SB	BA	xBA	OBP	SLG	OPS	vL	vR	bb%	ct%	Eye	G	L	F	h%	HctX	PX	xPX	hr/f	Spd	SBO	SB%	#Wk	DOM	DIS	RC/G	RAR	BPV	BPX	R$
12	TOR	332	64	27	65	5	241	280	358	527	886	718	942	15	81	0.94	37	14	49	22	130	165	145	20%	84	7%	71%	17	76%	12%	6.25	13.9	113	283	$14
13	TOR	452	82	28	73	7	259	282	358	498	856	910	842	13	81	0.82	41	16	43	26	129	150	138	18%	90	7%	78%	21	71%	5%	6.12	24.2	101	253	$20
14	TOR	553	101	35	103	6	286	290	403	524	928	1079	888	16	83	1.08	40	18	42	29	124	152	121	18%	96	4%	75%	27	81%	7%	7.46	55.4	115	311	$32
15	TOR	543	108	40	114	8	250	285	377	536	913	834	932	17	80	1.04	37	14	49	24	123	168	151	18%	102	6%	80%	27	81%	7%	6.88	33.9	123	332	$26
16	TOR	423	68	22	69	2	234	261	366	452	817	752	834	17	76	0.84	40	19	42	26	126	133	131	16%	76	3%	50%	21	67%	14%	5.42	9.1	68	194	$10
1st Half		235	41	12	41	1	230	272	360	455	815	797	821	17	79	0.98	39	18	43	24	123	133	122	15%	80	3%	50%	11	73%	9%	5.38	4.9	83	237	$11
2nd Half		188	27	10	28	1	239	247	372	447	819	661	848	17	71	0.72	40	20	40	28	130	132	143	18%	79	3%	50%	10	60%	20%	5.47	4.4	51	146	$8
17	Proj	**503**	**85**	**30**	**89**	**3**	**248**	**267**	**374**	**486**	**859**	**816**	**870**	**17**	**78**	**0.89**	**39**	**17**	**44**	**26**	**126**	**137**	**137**	**18%**	**88**	**3%**	**54%**				**6.07**	**20.5**	**72**	**207**	**$19**

Beckham,Gordon

Age: 30	Bats: R	Pos: 2B	Health D	LIMA Plan D
Ht: 6' 0"	Wt: 190		PT/Exp D	Rand Var +2
			Consist A	MM 2211

"Another season of futility. Not even worthy of short half of platoon, as he's overmatched by both LHP and RHP. It's been years since he hit ball with authority or got on base at acceptable level, and time is running out." Alas, this is from LAST season's Forecaster entry. 2H collapse confirms it's as apt now as a year ago. Pass.

Yr	Tm	AB	R	HR	RBI	SB	BA	xBA	OBP	SLG	OPS	vL	vR	bb%	ct%	Eye	G	L	F	h%	HctX	PX	xPX	hr/f	Spd	SBO	SB%	#Wk	DOM	DIS	RC/G	RAR	BPV	BPX	R$
12	CHW	525	62	16	60	5	234	245	296	371	668	689	659	7	83	0.45	38	20	42	25	92	86	90	9%	89	7%	56%	27	37%	33%	3.50	-17.6	44	110	$8
13	CHW *	407	51	5	28	5	267	247	317	367	684	510	745	7	84	0.47	35	23	41	31	95	73	105	4%	111	6%	83%	20	40%	35%	4.08	1.0	45	113	$8
14	2 AL *	489	56	10	48	4	217	242	255	335	590	780	560	5	82	0.28	45	16	39	25	98	89	85	6%	73	4%	100%	24	42%	33%	2.82	-13.3	32	86	$4
15	CHW	211	24	6	20	0	209	237	275	332	607	626	593	8	80	0.44	45	19	35	23	74	79	55	10%	80	2%	0%	26	31%	46%	2.86	-11.9	24	65	-$1
16	2 NL	245	25	5	31	1	212	234	294	347	641	667	629	10	79	0.50	45	14	40	25	99	89	123	6%	82	2%	100%	19	32%	37%	3.25	-13.0	32	91	$0
1st Half		95	12	2	16	1	284	268	382	442	824	865	806	11	88	1.09	48	13	39	30	103	91	105	6%	110	3%	100%	7	57%	14%	5.82	2.5	84	240	$5
2nd Half		150	13	3	15	0	167	208	237	287	523	546	512	9	73	0.34	43	15	42	21	97	87	137	6%	63	0%	0%	12	17%	50%	2.09	-13.7	-2	-6	-$4
17	Proj	**192**	**21**	**4**	**21**	**1**	**217**	**238**	**288**	**345**	**632**	**662**	**618**	**8**	**80**	**0.46**	**44**	**16**	**39**	**25**	**92**	**82**	**98**	**7%**	**83**	**3%**	**72%**				**3.17**	**-9.7**	**21**	**59**	**$2**

Beckham,Tim

Age: 27	Bats: R	Pos: SS	Health D	LIMA Plan D+
Ht: 6' 0"	Wt: 190		PT/Exp F	Rand Var -2
			Consist C	MM 4421

After abysmal 1H, was turning it around, especially vs. LH—then got demoted to the minors for lack of hustle in late Aug and never returned. Just now hitting peak age, still owns tantalizing power and speed skills; xBA, 2H ct% offer glimmers of hope. If head matches tools, former #1 pick could take a step up. UP: 15 HR, 15 SB

Yr	Tm	AB	R	HR	RBI	SB	BA	xBA	OBP	SLG	OPS	vL	vR	bb%	ct%	Eye	G	L	F	h%	HctX	PX	xPX	hr/f	Spd	SBO	SB%	#Wk	DOM	DIS	RC/G	RAR	BPV	BPX	R$
12	aaa	285	33	5	23	5	225		284	311	595			8	72	0.30				30		62			101	7%	100%				3.00		-13	-33	$2
13	TAM *	467	59	3	43	14	247	231	300	341	641	900	667	7	74	0.29	63	13	25	33	39	74	-15	0%	143	18%	64%	2	0%	0%	3.37	-0.7	13	33	$10
14	aaa	62	7	0	3	0	225		245	252	498			3	74	0.10				30		30			101	16%	0%				1.66		-42	-114	-$2
15	TAM *	242	28	9	40	5	228	246	279	422	701	725	676	7	66	0.21	50	19	31	30	81	142	87	21%	103	14%	68%	21	48%	38%	3.81	-4.2	26	70	$5
16	TAM	198	25	5	16	2	247	235	300	434	735	792	688	7	66	0.21	46	18	36	35	97	131	97	11%	159	7%	67%	21	38%	43%	4.33	0.1	32	91	$2
1st Half		96	10	3	7	1	177	197	248	365	612	673	545	8	59	0.21	37	12	51	26	87	144	133	10%	133	13%	50%	14	36%	50%	2.61	-5.8	10	29	-$2
2nd Half		102	15	2	9	1	314	272	352	500	852	951	793	6	73	0.21	53	22	25	42	106	122	68	11%	159	4%	100%	7	43%	29%	6.61	5.9	49	140	$5
17	Proj	**228**	**28**	**8**	**24**	**4**	**246**	**247**	**301**	**443**	**744**	**785**	**707**	**7**	**69**	**0.23**	**48**	**18**	**34**	**32**	**91**	**131**	**92**	**15%**	**140**	**11%**	**71%**				**4.41**	**-0.4**	**29**	**84**	**$6**

ROD TRUESDELL

Bell,Josh

Age: 24 Bats: B Pos: 1B
Ht: 6' 2" Wt: 235

Health	A	LIMA Plan	D+
PT/Exp	C	Rand Var	0
Consist	C	MM	1143

3-19-.273 in 128 AB at PIT. Former 1st-rd talent showing small signs of tapping into that upside: 2H plate skills, extra-base pop vs. RH, makes hard contact, still young. Missing piece is lack of uppercut in swing. As a 1B/OF type, he needs it to be an asset to you. History of GB lean suggests caution. A long-term investment.

Yr Tm	AB	R	HR	RBI	SB	BA	xBA	OBP	SLG	OPS	vL	vR	bb%	ct%	Eye	G	L	F	h%	HctX	PX	xPX	hr/f	Spd	SBO	SB%	#Wk	DOM	DIS	RC/G	RAR	BPV	BPX	R$
12																																		
13																																		
14 aa	94	10	0	5	3	249		292	268	559			6	86	0.44				29		17			102	15%	73%				2.67		3	8	$0
15 a/a	489	57	5	66	8	285		356	390	747			10	86	0.77				32		65			115	8%	63%				4.89		52	141	$15
16 PIT *	549	70	15	74	3	269	271	354	414	767	515	820	12	82	0.73	50	21	29	31	110	86	96	9%	70	7%	24%	9	56%	22%	4.83	-8.2	43	123	$14
1st Half	296	41	10	46	1	295	270	371	478	849			11	81	0.64				34		106			88	8%	12%	1	100%	0%	5.90		59	169	$20
2nd Half	253	29	5	27	2	239	257	334	340	673	515	820	12	83	0.85	50	21	29	27	112	63	96	9%	62	5%	46%	8	50%	25%	3.72	-10.6	29	83	$7
17 Proj	**346**	**43**	**9**	**47**	**5**	**269**	**273**	**337**	**403**	**740**	**528**	**777**	**10**	**84**	**0.71**	**50**	**21**	**29**	**30**	**101**	**76**	**86**	**10%**	**75**	**8%**	**54%**				**4.69**	**-4.2**	**43**	**122**	**$10**

Belt,Brandon

Age: 29 Bats: L Pos: 1B
Ht: 6' 5" Wt: 195

Health	B	LIMA Plan	B
PT/Exp	B	Rand Var	-1
Consist	B	MM	4225

Long-awaited power breakout still in mothballs. Blame loss of 20 ft in FB distance for hr/f dip, so don't assume correction there. But another year of LDs, fewer GBs and surging xPX keep a potential HR breakout on our radar. Upticks in ct%, bb% reflect growing maturity. Each year the odds increase for UP: 30 HR, 100 RBI

Yr Tm	AB	R	HR	RBI	SB	BA	xBA	OBP	SLG	OPS	vL	vR	bb%	ct%	Eye	G	L	F	h%	HctX	PX	xPX	hr/f	Spd	SBO	SB%	#Wk	DOM	DIS	RC/G	RAR	BPV	BPX	R$
12 SF	411	47	7	56	12	275	247	360	421	781	768	786	12	74	0.51	38	26	37	36	95	107	112	6%	118	11%	86%	27	41%	37%	5.42	-0.1	43	108	$13
13 SF	509	76	17	67	5	289	266	360	481	841	755	867	9	75	0.42	34	24	41	35	116	143	132	11%	111	5%	71%	27	59%	22%	6.09	21.5	70	175	$21
14 SF	214	30	12	27	3	243	244	306	449	755	715	772	8	70	0.28	38	18	44	29	90	152	119	18%	115	8%	75%	14	71%	21%	4.54	2.3	54	146	$6
15 SF	492	73	18	68	9	280	257	356	478	834	802	845	10	70	0.38	33	29	38	37	123	145	156	14%	105	9%	75%	24	50%	25%	5.97	8.5	51	138	$20
16 SF	542	77	17	82	0	275	259	394	474	868	883	861	16	73	0.70	26	28	46	35	108	134	163	9%	113	2%	0%	27	59%	30%	6.36	15.9	66	189	$15
1st Half	284	42	10	44	0	299	284	402	518	920	940	910	15	79	0.80	28	27	45	35	111	139	145	10%	99	4%	0%	14	71%	21%	7.21	16.8	86	246	$20
2nd Half	258	35	7	38	0	248	230	385	426	811	818	808	18	66	0.63	24	28	47	35	103	126	188	9%	132	0%	0%	13	46%	38%	5.50	3.0	43	123	$11
17 Proj	**547**	**79**	**22**	**82**	**5**	**271**	**252**	**370**	**477**	**847**	**837**	**851**	**13**	**71**	**0.52**	**30**	**26**	**44**	**34**	**108**	**137**	**154**	**13%**	**115**	**5%**	**61%**				**6.06**	**15.1**	**50**	**142**	**$21**

Beltran,Carlos

Age: 40 Bats: B Pos: DH RF
Ht: 6' 1" Wt: 200

Health	B	LIMA Plan	B
PT/Exp	B	Rand Var	-3
Consist	C	MM	3135

Continues to stave off Father Time, but 2016 likely was his last hurrah. League-average xPX in two of last three seasons hidden in 2016 by unbankable h% and hr/f rates. 19 of 29 HR came in NYY and TEX hitter parks; watch where he ends up before bidding. The risk-averse should use 2014/2015 as baseline.

Yr Tm	AB	R	HR	RBI	SB	BA	xBA	OBP	SLG	OPS	vL	vR	bb%	ct%	Eye	G	L	F	h%	HctX	PX	xPX	hr/f	Spd	SBO	SB%	#Wk	DOM	DIS	RC/G	RAR	BPV	BPX	R$
12 STL	547	83	32	97	13	269	274	346	495	842	867	832	11	77	0.52	42	20	38	29	116	142	124	20%	77	12%	68%	27	56%	22%	5.88	15.8	69	173	$25
13 STL	554	79	24	84	2	296	282	339	491	830	729	871	6	84	0.42	35	24	41	32	131	122	128	13%	96	2%	67%	27	63%	11%	6.05	23.7	76	190	$25
14 NYY	403	46	15	49	3	233	258	301	402	703	564	777	8	80	0.46	44	16	39	26	105	120	101	12%	78	4%	75%	23	43%	35%	3.98	-0.8	59	159	$8
15 NYY	478	57	19	67	0	276	276	337	471	808	752	831	9	82	0.53	35	22	43	30	122	125	133	11%	81	0%	0%	25	60%	16%	5.61	2.2	72	195	$15
16 2AL	552	73	29	93	1	295	284	337	513	850	970	805	6	82	0.35	42	21	37	32	119	124	103	17%	78	1%	100%	27	56%	22%	6.27	11.7	63	180	$23
1st Half	265	42	19	53	0	298	288	339	574	913	985	879	6	80	0.30	42	18	40	31	113	156	117	22%	81	0%	0%	14	64%	21%	7.05	11.3	81	231	$25
2nd Half	287	31	10	40	1	293	280	336	456	792	953	743	6	84	0.40	42	24	34	32	124	96	91	12%	77	1%	100%	13	46%	23%	5.56	0.5	49	140	$20
17 Proj	**487**	**59**	**19**	**72**	**1**	**280**	**269**	**332**	**459**	**791**	**802**	**786**	**7**	**82**	**0.43**	**40**	**21**	**39**	**31**	**118**	**106**	**112**	**12%**	**79**	**1%**	**59%**				**5.38**	**-1.6**	**40**	**113**	**$18**

Beltre,Adrian

Age: 38 Bats: R Pos: 3B
Ht: 5' 11" Wt: 225

Health	B	LIMA Plan	B+
PT/Exp	A	Rand Var	0
Consist	C	MM	3155

Model of dependability now with $25+ in 6 of last 7 years after big finishes to last two. With elite contact and steady pop, you can put a near-.300 BA and 20 HR in stone. Hoping for another 30 HR a risky proposition, as dwindling pre-2016 xPX tempers optimism there. Still, his consistency is golden.

Yr Tm	AB	R	HR	RBI	SB	BA	xBA	OBP	SLG	OPS	vL	vR	bb%	ct%	Eye	G	L	F	h%	HctX	PX	xPX	hr/f	Spd	SBO	SB%	#Wk	DOM	DIS	RC/G	RAR	BPV	BPX	R$
12 TEX	604	95	36	102	1	321	299	359	561	921	737	985	6	86	0.44	39	21	40	33	135	136	139	17%	74	1%	100%	27	74%	11%	7.59	48.9	90	225	$33
13 TEX	631	88	30	92	1	315	287	371	509	880	948	857	7	88	0.64	38	22	40	32	130	115	127	14%	60	1%	100%	27	63%	7%	6.94	50.6	77	193	$32
14 TEX	549	79	19	77	1	324	286	388	492	879	984	845	9	87	0.77	42	22	36	35	125	111	122	11%	79	1%	50%	26	73%	12%	7.16	50.9	79	214	$28
15 TEX	567	83	18	83	1	287	288	334	453	788	929	715	7	89	0.63	42	23	36	30	130	97	109	10%	89	1%	100%	25	60%	16%	5.45	14.0	74	200	$21
16 TEX	583	89	32	104	1	300	287	358	521	879	1004	842	8	89	0.73	40	18	42	29	128	114	125	15%	64	1%	50%	27	67%	15%	6.68	30.2	82	234	$26
1st Half	293	42	12	52	0	280	271	329	451	780	955	719	6	88	0.54	45	18	37	28	119	91	109	12%	63	0%	0%	14	50%	21%	5.16	2.3	58	166	$20
2nd Half	290	47	20	52	1	321	302	386	593	979	1070	957	9	89	0.94	36	17	47	31	137	137	140	16%	65	2%	50%	13	85%	8%	8.43	27.5	106	303	$33
17 Proj	**550**	**83**	**25**	**90**	**1**	**295**	**287**	**351**	**495**	**846**	**942**	**813**	**8**	**88**	**0.70**	**40**	**20**	**40**	**30**	**129**	**105**	**123**	**13%**	**75**	**1%**	**59%**				**6.24**	**20.5**	**70**	**199**	**$26**

Benintendi,Andrew

Age: 22 Bats: L Pos: LF
Ht: 5' 10" Wt: 170

Health	A	LIMA Plan	B+
PT/Exp	F	Rand Var	0
Consist	F	MM	4355

2-14-.295 in 105 AB at BOS. Top prospect surged through minors on back of elite plate coverage and toolsy skills. Gaudy September with BOS figures to rev up the hype machine, but it's still just 100 AB. May not be a cornerstone quite yet, but... UP: 20 HR, .300 BA

Yr Tm	AB	R	HR	RBI	SB	BA	xBA	OBP	SLG	OPS	vL	vR	bb%	ct%	Eye	G	L	F	h%	HctX	PX	xPX	hr/f	Spd	SBO	SB%	#Wk	DOM	DIS	RC/G	RAR	BPV	BPX	R$
12																																		
13																																		
14																																		
15																																		
16 BOS *	342	50	8	51	8	288	287	346	480	825	429	984	8	83	0.53	36	25	39	33	111	117	116	6%	113	18%	51%	8	50%	25%	5.56	12.6	79	226	$13
1st Half	161	22	4	22	5	275	285	331	459	790			8	84	0.52				31		110			114	27%	49%				4.82		76	217	$11
2nd Half	181	28	4	29	3	299	291	358	497	856	429	984	8	83	0.53	36	25	39	34	110	124	116	6%	111	10%	56%	8	50%	25%	6.29	9.3	82	234	$14
17 Proj	**451**	**66**	**13**	**68**	**10**	**288**	**293**	**348**	**497**	**845**	**415**	**900**	**8**	**83**	**0.52**	**36**	**25**	**39**	**32**	**99**	**125**	**104**	**9%**	**116**	**17%**	**54%**				**5.82**	**17.7**	**86**	**247**	**$21**

Bethancourt,Christian

Age: 25 Bats: R Pos: CA
Ht: 6' 2" Wt: 190

Health	B	LIMA Plan	D
PT/Exp	D	Rand Var	-2
Consist	B	MM	1201

Reputation as excellent defensive catcher supported by superb pop times. But stagnant hit tool makes him a liability at dish, even as your 2nd catcher. And now they're talking about turning him into a super-utility type who could pitch too. That's nice and all, but doesn't change immediate marginal fanalytic outlook.

Yr Tm	AB	R	HR	RBI	SB	BA	xBA	OBP	SLG	OPS	vL	vR	bb%	ct%	Eye	G	L	F	h%	HctX	PX	xPX	hr/f	Spd	SBO	SB%	#Wk	DOM	DIS	RC/G	RAR	BPV	BPX	R$
12 aa	268	26	2	23	7	227		254	270	524			3	82	0.19				27		28			103	21%	52%				2.10		-11	-28	$1
13 ATL *	359	37	10	40	10	256	260	284	397	681	0	0	4	82	0.22	44	20	36	29	0	97	-15	0%	89	23%	56%	1	0%	100%	3.62	-0.8	42	105	$10
14 ATL *	456	31	6	44	6	243	222	263	323	586	889	465	3	78	0.13	54	15	31	30	86	63	54	0%	92	8%	74%	8	0%	75%	2.86	-8.0	0	0	$6
15 ATL *	357	38	5	39	5	251	254	282	366	648	433	551	4	80	0.22	50	19	31	30	83	86	62	5%	96	8%	84%	17	29%	53%	3.55	-2.8	30	81	$6
16 SD	193	20	6	25	1	228	219	265	368	633	677	620	5	71	0.18	47	16	37	29	80	95	109	12%	101	8%	33%	22	36%	50%	3.10	-7.7	2	6	$1
1st Half	90	10	4	13	1	267	242	316	433	750	1087	662	7	76	0.32	49	18	34	31	77	98	86	17%	110	13%	33%	14	43%	50%	4.43	0.8	30	86	$4
2nd Half	103	10	2	12	0	194	198	217	311	528	341	582	3	67	0.09	45	14	41	27	83	92	131	7%	99	0%	0%	8	25%	50%	2.13	-6.5	-21	-60	-$2
17 Proj	**201**	**20**	**4**	**23**	**2**	**235**	**226**	**267**	**346**	**613**	**618**	**611**	**4**	**75**	**0.17**	**49**	**17**	**34**	**29**	**82**	**76**	**86**	**7%**	**100**	**9%**	**56%**				**3.01**	**-6.9**	**-11**	**-32**	**$3**

Betts,Mookie

Age: 24 Bats: R Pos: RF
Ht: 5' 9" Wt: 156

Health	A	LIMA Plan	C
PT/Exp	A	Rand Var	-2
Consist	C	MM	3555

Cover boy's surge to superstardom is backed by peripherals. Room for more? Merely-solid xPX foretells power regression, as does its two-year decline. SB efficiency, improving OBP give him a higher SB ceiling, but move to middle of lineup threatens green light. Firmly elite now, and 2nd half points to... UP: batting title.

Yr Tm	AB	R	HR	RBI	SB	BA	xBA	OBP	SLG	OPS	vL	vR	bb%	ct%	Eye	G	L	F	h%	HctX	PX	xPX	hr/f	Spd	SBO	SB%	#Wk	DOM	DIS	RC/G	RAR	BPV	BPX	R$
12																																		
13																																		
14 BOS *	588	106	14	72	34	318	281	392	479	871	843	798	11	86	0.85	41	21	39	35	133	114	117	8%	132	23%	76%	12	67%	8%	7.00	50.0	97	262	$40
15 BOS	597	92	18	77	21	291	277	341	479	820	843	813	7	86	0.56	38	19	42	31	119	114	114	8%	146	18%	78%	26	69%	12%	5.89	18.8	96	259	$30
16 BOS	672	122	31	113	26	318	295	363	534	897	814	917	7	88	0.61	41	19	39	33	119	114	107	13%	138	16%	87%	27	59%	7%	7.40	48.8	100	286	$44
1st Half	360	70	17	55	13	294	295	332	517	849	672	885	6	86	0.40	44	19	37	31	122	119	112	15%	145	16%	93%	14	50%	7%	6.39	16.9	94	269	$42
2nd Half	312	52	14	58	13	346	296	397	554	952	940	955	8	91	1.00	39	19	42	35	117	109	101	12%	127	16%	81%	13	69%	8%	8.68	32.4	108	309	$47
17 Proj	**646**	**107**	**24**	**102**	**26**	**316**	**286**	**368**	**514**	**882**	**862**	**888**	**8**	**87**	**0.67**	**40**	**20**	**41**	**33**	**121**	**109**	**110**	**11%**	**141**	**18%**	**81%**				**7.08**	**42.0**	**93**	**265**	**$43**

STEPHEN NICKRAND

Bird,Gregory

Age: 24	Bats: L	Pos: DH	Health	F	LIMA Plan	B+
Ht: 6' 4"	Wt: 215		PT/Exp	F	Rand Var	0
			Consist	A	MM	5135

Shoulder surgery on torn labrum ended season before it began. Played through it in 2015 with tantalizing xPX in 157 MLB AB, while PX history and fly-ball swing further hint at significant power ceiling. Plate patience can't hide ct% warts, however, so BA risk, limited track record suggest we give him time to take flight.

Yr	Tm	AB	R	HR	RBI	SB	BA	xBA	OBP	SLG	OPS	vL	vR	bb%	ct%	Eye	G	L	F	h%	HctX	PX	xPX	hr/f	Spd	SBO	SB%	#Wk	DOM	DIS	RC/G	RAR	BPV	BPX	R$
12																																			
13																																			
14	aa	95	13	6	9	0	230		334	504	838			13	69	0.50				26		218			95	0%	0%				5.58		106	286	$1
15	NYY *	475	65	23	77	1	259	256	329	470	799	752	915	10	75	0.43	27	22	51	30	146	142	203	20%	97	2%	45%	9	78%	22%	5.29	4.8	65	176	$15
16																																			
1st Half																																			
2nd Half																																			
17	Proj	**404**	**55**	**25**	**55**	**1**	**248**	**264**	**333**	**505**	**838**	**726**	**879**	**11**	**70**	**0.42**	**30**	**22**	**48**	**29**	**131**	**169**	**183**	**18%**	**98**	**1%**	**50%**				**5.65**	**1.8**	**50**	**144**	**$11**

Blackmon,Charlie

Age: 31	Bats: L	Pos: CF	Health	B	LIMA Plan	D+
Ht: 6' 2"	Wt: 185		PT/Exp	A	Rand Var	-4
			Consist	C	MM	3455

Third straight $30 season—with a twist. Maintained 2015's xPX gains, which hinted at HR spike, and hr/f complied. April DL stint (toe) might explain SBO dip, though can't expect full SB recovery at this age. Rock-solid xBA/LD%, narrowing splits (.313 BA, 17 HR on road), steady BPV growth equals an early-round anchor.

Yr	Tm	AB	R	HR	RBI	SB	BA	xBA	OBP	SLG	OPS	vL	vR	bb%	ct%	Eye	G	L	F	h%	HctX	PX	xPX	hr/f	Spd	SBO	SB%	#Wk	DOM	DIS	RC/G	RAR	BPV	BPX	R$
12	COL *	341	47	6	29	7	260	266	302	392	694	853	701	6	81	0.32	49	21	30	31	88	93	86	7%	116	11%	77%	8	63%	25%	4.09	-5.9	47	118	$7
13	COL *	503	66	8	44	11	266	268	302	395	697	752	824	5	81	0.27	42	27	31	32	90	90	66	10%	141	15%	64%	16	38%	25%	4.04	-0.8	50	125	$14
14	COL	593	82	19	72	28	288	269	335	440	775	697	801	5	84	0.32	41	22	37	32	103	100	94	10%	108	25%	74%	27	52%	19%	5.02	20.1	60	162	$32
15	COL	614	93	17	58	43	287	266	347	450	797	709	828	7	82	0.41	38	25	37	33	117	100	119	9%	142	34%	77%	27	59%	22%	5.37	18.7	66	178	$36
16	COL	578	111	29	82	17	324	295	381	552	933	843	972	7	82	0.42	34	28	38	35	115	127	129	16%	114	16%	65%	26	62%	19%	7.45	43.9	81	231	$36
1st Half		269	48	12	42	8	309	282	377	509	887	812	916	9	83	0.56	34	26	40	33	123	110	148	14%	107	15%	67%	13	54%	23%	6.71	16.4	72	206	$30
2nd Half		309	63	17	40	9	337	306	384	589	973	867	1024	6	82	0.32	35	29	36	37	108	143	113	19%	119	17%	64%	13	69%	15%	8.12	29.7	89	254	$42
17	Proj	**588**	**99**	**25**	**71**	**24**	**304**	**286**	**361**	**507**	**868**	**791**	**898**	**7**	**82**	**0.40**	**37**	**26**	**37**	**34**	**111**	**114**	**115**	**14%**	**121**	**22%**	**71%**				**6.34**	**30.1**	**74**	**210**	**$37**

Blanco,Gregor

Age: 33	Bats: L	Pos: RF LF	Health	B	LIMA Plan	D+
Ht: 5' 11"	Wt: 170		PT/Exp	C	Rand Var	+3
			Consist	D	MM	1513

Career-lows across the board, but were 2H knee, shoulder issues to blame? First half xBA was in line with previous norms, so BA should improve with h%. Declining xPX, HctX leave him with no pop, but pre-injury Spd, plate skills looked fine. Previous R$ stability, offseason recovery should yield mild rebound.

Yr	Tm	AB	R	HR	RBI	SB	BA	xBA	OBP	SLG	OPS	vL	vR	bb%	ct%	Eye	G	L	F	h%	HctX	PX	xPX	hr/f	Spd	SBO	SB%	#Wk	DOM	DIS	RC/G	RAR	BPV	BPX	R$
12	SF	393	56	5	34	26	244	227	333	344	676	694	667	11	74	0.49	44	24	32	32	73	69	73	6%	144	26%	81%	27	19%	59%	3.99	-8.7	18	45	$12
13	SF	452	50	3	41	14	265	250	341	350	690	650	696	10	79	0.55	44	28	28	33	87	60	69	3%	157	16%	61%	27	22%	30%	4.01	-0.6	34	85	$12
14	SF	393	51	5	38	16	260	241	333	374	707	730	697	9	80	0.53	40	21	39	31	93	81	93	4%	139	18%	76%	27	37%	37%	4.27	5.6	49	132	$13
15	SF	327	59	5	26	13	291	268	368	413	781	741	792	11	82	0.68	45	24	30	34	85	83	76	6%	136	17%	72%	23	39%	30%	5.42	6.5	59	159	$14
16	SF	241	28	1	18	6	224	236	309	311	620	686	597	11	79	0.57	46	21	33	28	63	55	42	2%	142	13%	67%	24	21%	54%	3.11	-11.2	26	74	$1
1st Half		181	25	0	15	3	249	253	328	337	665	707	648	10	82	0.66	46	23	31	30	64	54	42	0%	151	11%	50%	14	29%	43%	3.58	-4.7	41	117	$3
2nd Half		60	3	1	3	3	150	182	250	233	483	573	466	12	68	0.42	48	13	40	20	61	61	38	6%	94	21%	100%	10	10%	70%	1.96	-5.0	-24	-69	-$4
17	Proj	**300**	**36**	**4**	**22**	**12**	**255**	**238**	**337**	**357**	**694**	**738**	**680**	**11**	**79**	**0.57**	**45**	**20**	**35**	**31**	**74**	**64**	**60**	**5%**	**128**	**16%**	**78%**				**4.16**	**-4.7**	**25**	**72**	**$9**

Bogaerts,Xander

Age: 24	Bats: R	Pos: SS	Health	A	LIMA Plan	B
Ht: 6' 3"	Wt: 175		PT/Exp	A	Rand Var	-3
			Consist	C	MM	2435

Sure looks like he's arrived, as R$ excellence at this age is seldom seen. But before a hefty investment, consider: paltry xPX questions hr/f spike and puts HR repeat in doubt; xBA hints at serious BA risk, particularly if 2H FB% sticks. Elite keeper play with bright future, but skills don't support a 2017 repeat.

Yr	Tm	AB	R	HR	RBI	SB	BA	xBA	OBP	SLG	OPS	vL	vR	bb%	ct%	Eye	G	L	F	h%	HctX	PX	xPX	hr/f	Spd	SBO	SB%	#Wk	DOM	DIS	RC/G	RAR	BPV	BPX	R$
12	aa	92	10	4	15	1	326		332	581	913			1	77	0.04				39		187			80	12%	46%				7.00		84	210	$3
13	BOS *	488	64	12	58	7	277	291	349	427	777	1089	463	10	77	0.48	47	34	19	34	120	107	87	17%	137	7%	67%	7	43%	57%	5.22	25.0	55	138	$16
14	BOS	538	60	12	46	2	240	230	297	362	660	755	621	7	74	0.28	38	21	41	30	110	98	111	7%	116	4%	40%	26	42%	42%	3.47	4.7	26	70	$7
15	BOS	613	84	7	81	10	320	269	355	421	776	892	735	5	84	0.32	53	21	26	37	100	71	60	5%	134	7%	83%	27	44%	11%	5.62	20.0	43	116	$28
16	BOS	652	115	21	89	13	294	262	356	446	802	873	785	8	81	0.47	45	20	35	34	101	91	73	11%	122	9%	76%	27	56%	19%	5.68	24.9	52	149	$29
1st Half		333	60	9	51	10	333	274	391	480	871	936	859	9	83	0.56	50	19	31	38	106	91	68	10%	120	11%	83%	14	64%	7%	7.25	24.4	62	177	$38
2nd Half		319	55	12	38	3	254	250	320	411	731	827	702	8	79	0.40	41	21	39	29	96	91	79	12%	128	6%	60%	13	46%	31%	4.32	-1.4	43	123	$20
17	Proj	**628**	**95**	**16**	**78**	**10**	**286**	**258**	**343**	**422**	**765**	**858**	**737**	**7**	**80**	**0.40**	**46**	**20**	**33**	**34**	**102**	**84**	**75**	**10%**	**131**	**8%**	**76%**				**5.12**	**11.6**	**32**	**92**	**$26**

Bour,Justin

Age: 29	Bats: L	Pos: 1B	Health	C	LIMA Plan	B
Ht: 6' 3"	Wt: 265		PT/Exp	C	Rand Var	0
			Consist	C	MM	3045

On path to 30-HR season until July ankle sprain. Power dragged upon return, and while 1H PX/xPX were on right track, low FB% caps HR upside. Won't (and shouldn't) play against lefties, so even though underlying Eye, xBA gains hint at some BA growth, this is a vanilla skill set in today's HR-friendly environment.

Yr	Tm	AB	R	HR	RBI	SB	BA	xBA	OBP	SLG	OPS	vL	vR	bb%	ct%	Eye	G	L	F	h%	HctX	PX	xPX	hr/f	Spd	SBO	SB%	#Wk	DOM	DIS	RC/G	RAR	BPV	BPX	R$
12	aa	506	50	13	86	3	245		313	387	700			9	74	0.38				31		106			70	3%	73%				4.09		21	53	$10
13	aa	317	36	14	47	0	200		263	374	638			8	77	0.38				22		119			79	4%	0%				3.03		45	113	$2
14	MIA *	459	48	11	58	2	246	249	298	372	670	600	734	7	81	0.39	53	16	31	28	127	93	126	6%	56	3%	61%	12	33%	58%	3.73	-6.1	31	84	$9
15	MIA *	460	48	24	77	1	258	254	321	458	779	573	845	9	77	0.40	48	17	35	29	113	128	110	21%	41	1%	100%	25	48%	32%	5.06	-4.1	40	108	$14
16	MIA	280	35	15	51	0	264	276	349	475	824	533	857	12	80	0.68	44	22	35	28	114	117	107	19%	50	0%	0%	18	61%	28%	5.80	3.7	54	154	$8
1st Half		213	30	15	46	0	268	280	347	526	873	500	914	11	78	0.59	44	20	37	28	121	145	123	24%	44	0%	0%	13	69%	15%	6.41	8.0	67	191	$11
2nd Half		67	5	0	5	0	254	262	354	313	668	625	671	14	85	1.10	44	28	28	30	95	35	59	0%	75	0%	0%	5	40%	60%	3.84	-2.5	21	60	-$4
17	Proj	**408**	**45**	**20**	**63**	**1**	**261**	**276**	**337**	**463**	**800**	**577**	**831**	**10**	**80**	**0.58**	**47**	**21**	**33**	**28**	**111**	**113**	**100**	**19%**	**51**	**1%**	**67%**				**5.39**	**3.5**	**46**	**133**	**$13**

Bourjos,Peter

Age: 30	Bats: R	Pos: RF	Health	B	LIMA Plan	D
Ht: 6' 1"	Wt: 180		PT/Exp	D	Rand Var	0
			Consist	C	MM	2511

PHI gave him a chance, but he failed to take advantage. Eye/HctX combo was among the worst you'll see, and it's reflected in mediocre xBA. Ineffective on basepaths (SB%) despite elite wheels; failure to sustain 2015's bb% gains says he won't get a chance to use them anyway. His chances are fading fast.

Yr	Tm	AB	R	HR	RBI	SB	BA	xBA	OBP	SLG	OPS	vL	vR	bb%	ct%	Eye	G	L	F	h%	HctX	PX	xPX	hr/f	Spd	SBO	SB%	#Wk	DOM	DIS	RC/G	RAR	BPV	BPX	R$
12	LAA *	197	30	3	21	3	223	214	285	325	610	606	607	8	74	0.33	52	13	35	29	58	73	64	7%	135	8%	75%	25	8%	72%	3.04	-9.8	12	30	$1
13	LAA *	223	34	4	16	6	247	222	287	356	643	608	740	5	70	0.19	59	14	27	33	71	77	65	9%	178	11%	100%	12	17%	58%	3.60	-3.2	9	23	$4
14	STL	264	32	4	24	9	231	234	294	348	643	582	680	7	70	0.26	53	20	27	31	89	89	80	9%	183	19%	75%	27	30%	59%	3.30	-4.2	24	65	$5
15	STL	195	32	4	13	5	200	222	290	333	623	651	609	9	70	0.32	49	16	35	27	71	95	56	9%	150	30%	38%	27	41%	56%	2.46	-11.8	20	54	$0
16	PHI	355	40	5	23	6	251	243	292	389	681	695	676	5	74	0.19	51	17	32	32	69	90	66	6%	178	14%	60%	25	32%	44%	3.66	-10.4	34	97	$5
1st Half		213	25	3	17	4	268	245	307	399	706	788	674	5	74	0.20	53	18	29	35	68	86	65	7%	175	16%	50%	14	36%	43%	3.97	-3.4	30	86	$8
2nd Half		142	15	2	6	2	225	242	270	373	643	457	679	4	75	0.17	48	16	36	29	70	98	68	5%	156	8%	100%	11	27%	45%	3.22	-5.6	34	97	$0
17	Proj	**230**	**30**	**4**	**16**	**5**	**229**	**235**	**288**	**364**	**652**	**625**	**663**	**6**	**72**	**0.24**	**51**	**17**	**33**	**30**	**72**	**88**	**66**	**7%**	**169**	**18%**	**58%**				**3.18**	**-10.7**	**14**	**39**	**$4**

Bourn,Michael

Age: 34	Bats: L	Pos: CF LF RF	Health	B	LIMA Plan	D
Ht: 5' 11"	Wt: 190		PT/Exp	C	Rand Var	-2
			Consist	B	MM	1413

5-38-.264 with 15 SB in 375 AB at ARI/BAL. Clung to relevance despite being released twice, but grip is slipping. GB stroke pairs well with (still) above-average Spd to form solid h%, but subpar ct%, HctX, xBA lag behind. Still useful steals source per SB%/SBO, but when he loses a step, his value will quickly fade.

Yr	Tm	AB	R	HR	RBI	SB	BA	xBA	OBP	SLG	OPS	vL	vR	bb%	ct%	Eye	G	L	F	h%	HctX	PX	xPX	hr/f	Spd	SBO	SB%	#Wk	DOM	DIS	RC/G	RAR	BPV	BPX	R$
12	ATL	624	96	9	57	42	274	251	348	391	739	728	745	10	75	0.45	54	22	25	35	100	80	86	8%	140	28%	76%	26	38%	42%	4.80	-1.0	29	73	$28
13	CLE	525	75	6	50	23	263	243	316	360	676	655	685	7	75	0.30	57	20	24	34	68	72	60	7%	149	24%	66%	25	28%	56%	3.79	-7.0	18	45	$19
14	CLE *	487	58	3	29	11	242	239	294	338	632	569	724	7	73	0.28	50	24	25	32	69	73	71	4%	152	14%	64%	19	26%	63%	3.27	-9.0	13	35	$7
15	2 TM	425	39	0	30	17	238	223	310	282	592	599	590	10	75	0.43	47	25	28	32	72	39	62	0%	106	18%	71%	27	15%	67%	2.96	-20.0	-15	-41	$7
16	2 TM *	397	49	5	39	16	262	245	310	365	675	844	648	7	75	0.28	51	22	26	34	78	64	74	7%	125	19%	76%	21	24%	52%	3.92	-8.4	5	14	$12
1st Half		163	19	2	17	7	257	244	308	361	669	691	695	7	72	0.27	45	27	28	34	95	76	112	7%	86	23%	69%	8	38%	50%	3.74	-3.8	-9	-26	$9
2nd Half		234	30	3	22	9	265	246	311	368	678	1055	624	6	77	0.30	55	20	25	33	68	56	53	7%	149	17%	82%	13	15%	54%	4.05	-3.1	14	40	$14
17	Proj	**259**	**30**	**2**	**22**	**10**	**246**	**241**	**302**	**337**	**639**	**678**	**627**	**8**	**75**	**0.32**	**50**	**23**	**26**	**32**	**76**	**59**	**72**	**5%**	**122**	**20%**	**73%**				**3.44**	**-8.3**	**1**	**4**	**$7**

RYAN BLOOMFIELD

Bradley,Jackie

Age: 27 Bats: L Pos: CF
Ht: 5' 10" Wt: 195

Health	A	LIMA Plan	A
PT/Exp	B	Rand Var	-1
Consist	D	MM	4235

Impressive 1H: carried over late 2015 power gains, crushed RHP, seemed to be fixing previous MLB contact woes (68%). But power faded in 2H, and from July 28 to end of year, ct% was back down to 68%. High GB%, modest xPX warn of HR regression, which could negatively impact BA. Odds are, he'll fall short of repeat.

Yr Tm	AB	R	HR	RBI	SB	BA	xBA	OBP	SLG	OPS	vL	vR	bb%	ct%	Eye	G	L	F	h%	HctX	PX	xPX	hr/f	Spd	SBO	SB%	#Wk	DOM	DIS	RC/G	RAR	BPV	BPX	R$
12 aa	229	31	5	24	7	262		346	414	760			11	77	0.56				32		110			97	15%	68%				4.86		52	130	$5
13 BOS *	415	62	10	37	7	239	268	307	401	708	327	722	9	73	0.36	63	16	22	30	91	130	79	21%	104	16%	49%	11	36%	45%	3.90	-4.2	47	118	$8
14 BOS *	450	50	2	34	8	197	197	252	262	514	640	473	7	69	0.24	46	18	36	28	104	64	119	1%	86	9%	88%	25	16%	68%	2.15	-24.7	-31	-84	-$1
15 BOS *	503	75	17	68	6	267	264	337	460	796	918	791	9	76	0.44	48	16	36	32	106	132	133	18%	97	8%	59%	15	53%	47%	5.27	11.2	61	165	$17
16 BOS	558	94	26	87	9	267	269	349	486	835	673	902	10	74	0.44	47	18	34	32	109	133	109	18%	99	7%	82%	27	56%	22%	5.79	22.9	56	160	$21
1st Half	278	46	13	51	7	295	287	381	547	927	697	1004	11	76	0.49	48	18	34	35	118	151	124	18%	103	10%	88%	14	71%	21%	7.39	22.3	79	226	$27
2nd Half	280	48	13	36	2	239	249	318	425	743	651	787	10	73	0.39	47	19	35	28	100	114	95	18%	90	4%	67%	13	38%	23%	4.43	-0.7	31	89	$15
17 Proj	538	82	23	70	8	256	263	334	458	792	728	821	10	74	0.41	49	17	34	31	105	127	112	17%	94	8%	71%				5.10	9.3	51	145	$17

Brantley,Michael

Age: 30 Bats: L Pos: LF
Ht: 6' 2" Wt: 200

Health	F	LIMA Plan	B+
PT/Exp	C	Rand Var	+5
Consist	F	MM	2355

0-7-.231 in 39 AB at CLE. Season-opening DL stint was supposed to be brief, but after multiple setbacks with shoulder, year was pretty much wiped out. Additional surgery in Aug, so questions remain about future health and power outlook. Monitor status in spring, but take any "100 percent healthy" statements with grain of salt.

Yr Tm	AB	R	HR	RBI	SB	BA	xBA	OBP	SLG	OPS	vL	vR	bb%	ct%	Eye	G	L	F	h%	HctX	PX	xPX	hr/f	Spd	SBO	SB%	#Wk	DOM	DIS	RC/G	RAR	BPV	BPX	R$
12 CLE	552	63	6	60	12	288	286	348	402	750	680	785	9	90	0.95	49	23	29	31	100	75	76	4%	105	13%	57%	27	59%	0%	4.87	4.7	70	175	$17
13 CLE	556	66	10	73	17	284	277	332	396	728	664	757	7	88	0.60	47	23	30	31	89	72	76	7%	105	13%	81%	27	56%	19%	4.74	11.9	56	140	$23
14 CLE	611	94	20	97	23	327	324	385	506	890	826	923	8	91	0.93	46	26	28	34	133	116	105	13%	91	13%	96%	26	85%	4%	7.54	62.1	101	273	$42
15 CLE	529	68	15	84	15	310	308	379	480	859	785	908	10	90	1.18	46	23	32	32	121	107	88	10%	74	10%	94%	26	77%	0%	6.92	36.1	92	249	$28
16 CLE *	67	7	0	9	1	196	257	254	252	506	821	504	7	87	0.62	44	24	32	22	115	43	108	0%	101	7%	100%	3	33%	67%	2.09	-4.5	31	89	-$2
1st Half	60	7	0	9	1	219	256	282	281	563	821	504	8	86	0.62	44	24	32	25	113	48	108	0%	100	7%	100%	3	33%	67%	2.67	-3.3	30	86	-$2
2nd Half	7	1	0	0	0	0	0	0	0	0			0	100	0.00				0		0			101	0%	0%				0.00		32	91	-$4
17 Proj	417	54	12	61	11	280	302	338	440	779	800	770	8	89	0.82	46	24	30	29	115	91	95	11%	93	11%	88%				5.40	11.2	75	214	$19

Braun,Ryan

Age: 33 Bats: R Pos: LF
Ht: 6' 1" Wt: 200

Health	A	LIMA Plan	B+
PT/Exp	A	Rand Var	-2
Consist	C	MM	3345

Another outstanding year, capped by late-season power explosion (16 HR from Aug 2 on). But unsustainable hr/f played large role, and PX, xPX, FB% all reached career lows. Also at an age where speed is typically declining, so while he should be a five-category contributor once again, may be a little overpriced.

Yr Tm	AB	R	HR	RBI	SB	BA	xBA	OBP	SLG	OPS	vL	vR	bb%	ct%	Eye	G	L	F	h%	HctX	PX	xPX	hr/f	Spd	SBO	SB%	#Wk	DOM	DIS	RC/G	RAR	BPV	BPX	R$
12 MIL	598	108	41	112	30	319	296	391	595	987	1209	915	10	79	0.49	44	18	38	35	127	170	153	23%	107	21%	81%	27	74%	15%	8.57	62.4	104	260	$45
13 MIL	225	30	9	38	4	298	268	372	498	869	1053	777	11	75	0.48	52	16	32	36	120	142	150	16%	118	13%	44%	14	43%	21%	6.31	14.4	73	183	$10
14 MIL	530	68	19	81	11	266	277	324	453	777	823	760	7	79	0.36	47	20	33	31	115	130	125	14%	114	13%	69%	25	56%	24%	4.94	17.7	69	186	$21
15 MIL	506	87	25	84	24	285	282	356	498	854	957	821	10	77	0.47	50	19	31	33	121	136	139	20%	105	20%	86%	25	52%	28%	6.40	24.1	71	192	$31
16 MIL	511	80	30	91	16	305	303	365	538	903	1010	869	8	81	0.47	56	19	25	33	113	127	97	29%	104	14%	76%	26	58%	23%	7.11	35.0	75	214	$30
1st Half	262	35	13	44	6	328	305	383	546	929	1020	897	7	83	0.48	55	20	25	36	111	122	95	24%	97	12%	67%	14	57%	14%	7.66	22.5	76	217	$30
2nd Half	249	45	17	47	10	281	299	347	530	877	997	842	9	78	0.46	56	19	25	30	115	133	99	35%	112	17%	83%	12	58%	33%	6.58	15.0	73	209	$31
17 Proj	505	77	23	84	14	292	282	356	493	848	954	814	9	79	0.45	52	19	29	33	117	115	117	20%	109	12%	78%				6.25	25.5	59	169	$28

Bregman,Alex

Age: 23 Bats: R Pos: 3B
Ht: 6' 0" Wt: 180

Health	A	LIMA Plan	B+
PT/Exp	F	Rand Var	+1
Consist	F	MM	3335

8-34-.264 with 2 SB in 201 AB at HOU. Dug an early hole with 1-for-34 start in majors, but made necessary adjustments and hit .311 afterward. A lot to like here, as he's already providing plus power, while minor league track record suggests ct% will rise and BA surge will continue. It's a high-floor package, with ... UP: 30 HR

Yr Tm	AB	R	HR	RBI	SB	BA	xBA	OBP	SLG	OPS	vL	vR	bb%	ct%	Eye	G	L	F	h%	HctX	PX	xPX	hr/f	Spd	SBO	SB%	#Wk	DOM	DIS	RC/G	RAR	BPV	BPX	R$
12																																		
13																																		
14																																		
15																																		
16 HOU *	515	86	25	81	7	270	286	336	497	833	735	813	9	82	0.54	29	28	43	29	106	129	118	13%	121	9%	63%	9	56%	44%	5.73	13.8	86	246	$19
1st Half	253	47	13	42	4	277	304	363	514	877			12	86	0.94				28		128			115	10%	54%				6.36		105	300	$21
2nd Half	262	39	11	39	4	264	272	309	480	789	735	813	6	78	0.29	29	28	43	30	101	130	118	13%	123	8%	76%	9	56%	44%	5.12	1.8	66	189	$18
17 Proj	545	89	22	85	8	269	270	329	473	802	757	819	8	81	0.48	33	23	44	30	102	119	106	11%	122	9%	69%				5.38	7.7	71	204	$23

Brinson,Lewis

Age: 23 Bats: R Pos: OF
Ht: 6' 3" Wt: 195

Health	A	LIMA Plan	C+
PT/Exp	F	Rand Var	0
Consist	F	MM	3423

Was scuffling at AA before trade to MIL, though lingering shoulder injury may deserve part of the blame. Hit .382 at AAA post-trade, thanks to 47% h%. Outstanding pedigree, with already-intriguing power/speed combo, but plate approach still needs refining. Valuable commodity in dynasty leagues, but don't count on breakout just yet.

Yr Tm	AB	R	HR	RBI	SB	BA	xBA	OBP	SLG	OPS	vL	vR	bb%	ct%	Eye	G	L	F	h%	HctX	PX	xPX	hr/f	Spd	SBO	SB%	#Wk	DOM	DIS	RC/G	RAR	BPV	BPX	R$
12																																		
13																																		
14																																		
15 a/a	140	19	6	22	4	291		343	482	825			7	74	0.30				36		131			96	14%	79%				5.95		46	124	$6
16 a/a	393	50	13	50	12	249		278	423	701			4	77	0.17				30		106			108	25%	66%				3.84		33	94	$11
1st Half	192	28	7	28	7	212		260	397	657			6	79	0.31				24		105			146	31%	70%				3.24		58	166	$8
2nd Half	201	25	7	25	6	295		312	476	788			2	75	0.10				37		118			114	21%	64%				5.15		34	97	$14
17 Proj	332	43	9	43	9	255	250	293	419	713	713	713	5	76	0.22	44	19	37	31		104		10%	125	19%	70%				4.13	#N/A	36	102	$12

Brito,Socrates

Age: 24 Bats: L Pos: CF
Ht: 6' 2" Wt: 205

Health	B	LIMA Plan	D+
PT/Exp	F	Rand Var	0
Consist	D	MM	3431

4-12-.179 with 2 SB in 95 AB at ARI. Struggled in semi-regular role early on, spent two months in AAA, then fractured toe immediately after recall. Wasn't done any favors with MLB 19% h%, but didn't help himself with steps back in bb%, ct%. Poor OBP renders speed moot, so for now, both PT and value will likely be minimal.

Yr Tm	AB	R	HR	RBI	SB	BA	xBA	OBP	SLG	OPS	vL	vR	bb%	ct%	Eye	G	L	F	h%	HctX	PX	xPX	hr/f	Spd	SBO	SB%	#Wk	DOM	DIS	RC/G	RAR	BPV	BPX	R$
12																																		
13																																		
14																																		
15 ARI *	523	63	8	48	18	285	286	318	432	750	200	862	5	81	0.25	58	23	19	34	95	84	42	0%	177	18%	73%	5	20%	60%	4.83	7.8	56	151	$20
16 ARI *	398	42	8	39	7	236	243	256	370	626	167	609	3	77	0.12	38	25	37	29	82	76	67	15%	130	18%	50%	12	42%	25%	2.96	-20.5	15	43	$5
1st Half	256	25	5	25	3	244	249	258	388	646	0	649	2	76	0.08	41	26	33	30	103	80	96	22%	141	16%	40%	4	25%	25%	3.12	-10.8	16	46	$6
2nd Half	142	16	3	14	4	221	238	253	338	591	182	578	4	79	0.20	36	25	39	26	71	68	50	12%	109	22%	62%	8	50%	25%	2.69	-8.1	12	34	$3
17 Proj	202	23	7	19	4	251	265	279	440	718	520	747	4	78	0.18	42	23	34	29	84	102	68	13%	131	19%	59%				3.98	-3.2	39	112	$6

Brown,Trevor

Age: 25 Bats: R Pos: CA
Ht: 6' 2" Wt: 195

Health	A	LIMA Plan	D
PT/Exp	F	Rand Var	+1
Consist	B	MM	1011

Known for his glove, but came out swinging, with 3 HR in first 8 AB. Predictably, he was pretty useless the rest of the season. Doesn't look capable of providing much in the way of power, average, or OBP, so even if that Posey guy wasn't around, he's nothing more than a defense-first backup catcher.

Yr Tm	AB	R	HR	RBI	SB	BA	xBA	OBP	SLG	OPS	vL	vR	bb%	ct%	Eye	G	L	F	h%	HctX	PX	xPX	hr/f	Spd	SBO	SB%	#Wk	DOM	DIS	RC/G	RAR	BPV	BPX	R$
12																																		
13																																		
14 aaa	72	4	0	9	0	262		309	308	617			6	79	0.33				33		46			88	0%	0%				3.29		-5	-14	-$1
15 SF *	322	27	1	25	2	218	213	261	283	544	160	774	6	78	0.27	59	13	28	28	74	55	70	0%	80	4%	63%	3	33%	33%	2.40	-14.0	-5	-14	-$2
16 SF	173	17	5	19	0	237	238	283	364	647	679	628	5	77	0.26	43	21	37	28	68	79	74	10%	108	3%	0%	25	28%	44%	3.30	-5.7	18	51	$0
1st Half	106	12	4	13	0	245	247	286	396	682	650	697	5	77	0.21	41	22	37	28	54	90	61	13%	113	0%	0%	14	36%	50%	3.74	-1.3	26	74	$2
2nd Half	67	5	1	6	0	224	221	278	313	591	714	499	7	78	0.33	44	19	37	27	91	61	96	5%	105	6%	0%	11	18%	36%	2.67	-3.1	7	20	-$2
17 Proj	165	14	4	15	0	227	236	275	345	620	683	581	6	78	0.28	43	20	37	27	76	76	82	8%	106	4%	28%				3.02	-5.6	-4	-12	$2

BRIAN RUDD

Broxton,Keon

Age: 27 Bats: R Pos: CF
Ht: 6' 3" Wt: 187

Health	A	LIMA Plan	C
PT/Exp	C	Rand Var	-2
Consist	B	MM	4505

9-19-.242 with 23 SB in 207 AB at MIL. After two demotions, third time was charm: Post-July 26, hit .294/.399/.538 in 169 PA with strong HctX. Low ct% ensures BA drag, while too few FB, unsustainable hr/f will cap HR. But strong bb% should keep running opps coming, meaning SB will be top note in power-speed blend.

Yr	Tm	AB	R	HR	RBI	SB	BA	xBA	OBP	SLG	OPS	vL	vR	bb%	ct%	Eye	G	L	F	h%	HctX	PX	xPX	hr/f	Spd	SBO	SB%	#Wk	DOM	DIS	RC/G	RAR	BPV	BPX	R$
12																																			
13	aa	334	34	7	35	5	217		272	338	610			7	63	0.20				32		102			116	8%	82%				3.03		-16	-40	$2
14	aa	407	48	9	37	18	226		295	367	663			9	67	0.30				32		117			120	25%	72%				3.53		16	43	$10
15	PIT *	493	72	7	55	32	233	256	306	360	666	0	0	10	65	0.30	100	0	0	35	0	101	-16	0%	142	40%	64%	2	0%	50%	3.43	-13.6	3	8	$18
16	MIL *	385	49	15	37	35	238	227	326	430	756	916	694	12	59	0.31	45	25	30	37	103	148	139	26%	139	48%	72%	17	29%	53%	4.53	-1.4	19	54	$19
1st Half		183	22	6	14	18	185	210	276	325	601	486	382	11	57	0.29	60	17	23	28	52	113	67	14%	108	57%	72%	9	11%	78%	2.75	-10.8	-24	-69	$13
2nd Half		202	26	9	23	17	286	244	370	525	895	1217	791	12	60	0.33	40	28	33	44	123	179	164	29%	153	41%	72%	8	50%	25%	6.67	12.8	54	154	$24
17	**Proj**	**471**	**60**	**14**	**50**	**36**	**237**	**230**	**315**	**408**	**724**	**807**	**663**	**10**	**62**	**0.30**	**48**	**23**	**29**	**35**	**95**	**126**	**125**	**17%**	**142**	**42%**	**70%**				**4.14**	**-5.5**	**16**	**46**	**$20**

Bruce,Jay

Age: 30 Bats: L Pos: RF
Ht: 6' 2" Wt: 210

Health	A	LIMA Plan	B+
PT/Exp	A	Rand Var	+2
Consist	B	MM	4235

Rep is low BA and plentiful power, but xBA, upward trajectory of ct% suggest FA suitors may be pleasantly surprised. Second-highest HctX, xPX of career say plenty left in tank. Where he lands matters a bit (16.4 AB/HR in Great American, 22.9 AB/HR elsewhere), but may only make or break run at 30 HR.

Yr	Tm	AB	R	HR	RBI	SB	BA	xBA	OBP	SLG	OPS	vL	vR	bb%	ct%	Eye	G	L	F	h%	HctX	PX	xPX	hr/f	Spd	SBO	SB%	#Wk	DOM	DIS	RC/G	RAR	BPV	BPX	R$
12	CIN	560	89	34	99	9	252	270	327	514	841	754	879	10	72	0.40	35	20	44	29	118	178	162	19%	91	9%	75%	27	59%	26%	5.69	9.0	81	203	$22
13	CIN	626	89	30	109	7	262	264	329	478	807	734	841	9	70	0.34	37	24	39	33	102	165	133	17%	82	7%	70%	27	52%	33%	5.40	14.3	59	148	$25
14	CIN	493	71	18	66	12	217	240	281	373	654	556	685	8	70	0.30	45	21	34	27	99	122	109	15%	89	14%	80%	26	35%	46%	3.44	-9.9	22	59	$12
15	CIN	580	72	26	87	9	226	256	294	434	729	666	754	9	75	0.40	37	19	44	26	116	140	144	13%	77	11%	64%	27	48%	22%	4.16	-12.3	55	149	$14
16	2 NL	539	74	33	99	4	250	279	309	506	815	678	872	8	77	0.35	37	22	41	27	119	147	153	19%	95	5%	67%	27	56%	19%	5.25	9.0	70	200	$17
1st Half		298	45	17	60	3	268	290	315	544	858	790	885	6	77	0.28	37	23	40	30	123	159	158	18%	104	5%	100%	14	64%	0%	5.98	11.0	81	231	$22
2nd Half		241	29	16	39	1	228	264	302	461	763	547	855	9	76	0.43	37	21	42	23	114	131	145	21%	75	5%	33%	13	46%	38%	4.44	-1.9	52	149	$11
17	**Proj**	**513**	**72**	**27**	**88**	**6**	**256**	**262**	**319**	**479**	**797**	**679**	**845**	**8**	**75**	**0.36**	**38**	**21**	**41**	**29**	**114**	**134**	**142**	**17%**	**86**	**8%**	**67%**				**5.17**	**7.1**	**50**	**144**	**$20**

Bryant,Kris

Age: 25 Bats: R Pos: 3B LF
Ht: 6' 5" Wt: 230

Health	A	LIMA Plan	D+
PT/Exp	A	Rand Var	0
Consist	C	MM	5335

Bad news, pitchers: ct% on rise with no harm to PX/xPX. Consistent hard contact suggests outperforming xBA may continue, and LHP, in particular, had little chance in 2nd half. Ran a bit less as SB% faltered, but really, who's complaining? Given high FB rate, next stop... UP: 45 HR

Yr	Tm	AB	R	HR	RBI	SB	BA	xBA	OBP	SLG	OPS	vL	vR	bb%	ct%	Eye	G	L	F	h%	HctX	PX	xPX	hr/f	Spd	SBO	SB%	#Wk	DOM	DIS	RC/G	RAR	BPV	BPX	R$
12																																			
13																																			
14	a/a	492	91	33	85	12	290		377	559	935			12	63	0.37				40		229			85	11%	72%				7.48		86	232	$32
15	CHC *	587	92	28	107	15	276	233	361	492	854	797	875	12	64	0.38	34	21	45	38	105	165	148	16%	124	11%	78%	26	54%	35%	6.28	26.8	52	141	$29
16	CHC	603	121	39	102	8	292	273	385	554	939	1060	896	11	74	0.49	31	24	46	33	122	158	159	19%	109	7%	62%	27	59%	19%	7.25	38.4	81	231	$31
1st Half		307	64	23	61	3	277	281	367	564	931	953	921	11	73	0.45	33	22	45	31	123	176	177	22%	87	6%	60%	14	79%	0%	6.94	18.0	84	240	$31
2nd Half		296	57	16	41	5	307	266	403	544	947	1214	872	11	76	0.53	28	26	46	36	120	140	141	15%	129	9%	63%	13	38%	38%	7.57	21.9	78	223	$32
17	**Proj**	**595**	**108**	**37**	**107**	**10**	**288**	**264**	**381**	**546**	**927**	**1005**	**902**	**11**	**72**	**0.45**	**32**	**23**	**46**	**34**	**118**	**162**	**153**	**19%**	**117**	**8%**	**67%**				**7.12**	**37.6**	**70**	**199**	**$34**

Burns,Billy

Age: 27 Bats: B Pos: CF
Ht: 5' 9" Wt: 170

Health	A	LIMA Plan	D
PT/Exp	C	Rand Var	+2
Consist	F	MM	0511

0-13-.235 with 17 SB in 112 AB at OAK/KC. Just when we thought he'd be the next great SB burner, the flame went out. Lack of HctX, bb%, bad turn of h% led the regression. Given Spd, h% should recover, but lack of patience is more problematic for SB opps. Might be best to forget 2015 "breakout," lest you get... burned.

Yr	Tm	AB	R	HR	RBI	SB	BA	xBA	OBP	SLG	OPS	vL	vR	bb%	ct%	Eye	G	L	F	h%	HctX	PX	xPX	hr/f	Spd	SBO	SB%	#Wk	DOM	DIS	RC/G	RAR	BPV	BPX	R$
12																																			
13	aa	114	21	0	6	16	288		373	320	692			12	84	0.82				34		29			110	41%	88%				4.91		16	40	$7
14	OAK *	479	55	1	19	40	189	323	248	240	488	333	0	7	80	0.39	50	50	0	23	0	44	-15	0%	122	45%	83%	6	0%	67%	2.05	-28.6	8	22	$8
15	OAK *	611	84	5	44	30	290	257	326	385	711	768	707	5	84	0.33	50	22	28	34	52	57	29	4%	179	23%	74%	23	30%	35%	4.48	-0.4	46	124	$27
16	2 AL *	357	44	0	16	20	234	247	257	289	547	685	526	3	84	0.20	53	19	28	28	42	35	-2	0%	142	31%	80%	24	21%	33%	2.55	-19.8	16	46	$7
1st Half		265	32	0	12	14	242	269	276	313	589	674	563	3	89	0.31	53	20	27	27	44	42	-6	0%	142	29%	82%	14	36%	7%	2.90	-12.9	41	117	$10
2nd Half		92	12	0	4	6	211	178	231	221	452	721	265	3	71	0.09	53	16	32	30	37	9	22	0%	111	37%	74%	10	0%	70%	1.69	-8.3	-70	-200	-$1
17	**Proj**	**233**	**31**	**1**	**12**	**16**	**240**	**234**	**291**	**297**	**589**	**726**	**525**	**5**	**80**	**0.27**	**52**	**19**	**29**	**30**	**45**	**37**	**18**	**2%**	**139**	**34%**	**80%**				**2.88**	**-11.5**	**7**	**19**	**$8**

Butler,Billy

Age: 31 Bats: R Pos: DH 1B
Ht: 6' 0" Wt: 260

Health	A	LIMA Plan	D+
PT/Exp	B	Rand Var	0
Consist	A	MM	2043

Bit of a disruptive force (ask Danny Valencia), which might work with Bondsian production, but not best employment strategy for power-challenged DH/1B. HctX/Eye combo says he could be useful, particularly vL, though lack of FB% makes double-digit HR a stretch. Now on wrong side of 30, opportunities may dwindle.

Yr	Tm	AB	R	HR	RBI	SB	BA	xBA	OBP	SLG	OPS	vL	vR	bb%	ct%	Eye	G	L	F	h%	HctX	PX	xPX	hr/f	Spd	SBO	SB%	#Wk	DOM	DIS	RC/G	RAR	BPV	BPX	R$
12	KC	614	72	29	107	2	313	288	373	510	882	1042	827	8	82	0.49	47	24	29	34	132	120	118	20%	40	2%	67%	27	52%	26%	6.94	34.1	54	135	$29
13	KC	582	62	15	82	0	289	251	374	412	787	797	783	12	82	0.77	53	20	26	33	111	84	92	12%	30	0%	0%	27	33%	37%	5.52	16.6	32	80	$19
14	KC	549	57	9	66	0	271	258	323	379	702	847	653	7	83	0.43	49	22	28	32	132	83	111	7%	37	0%	0%	27	33%	37%	4.27	3.4	23	62	$13
15	OAK	538	63	15	65	0	251	251	323	390	713	687	722	9	81	0.51	51	18	32	28	108	91	103	11%	49	0%	0%	27	44%	41%	4.21	-19.5	32	86	$10
16	2 AL	250	27	5	35	0	284	291	336	416	752	739	765	8	83	0.50	42	29	29	33	110	86	95	8%	36	0%	0%	26	31%	38%	5.03	-3.2	30	86	$5
1st Half		133	13	2	21	0	248	285	294	376	670	880	494	6	82	0.38	45	27	27	29	121	89	96	7%	30	0%	0%	14	43%	29%	3.77	-6.8	23	66	$3
2nd Half		117	14	3	14	0	325	298	382	462	843	611	1136	9	85	0.67	39	31	31	36	99	83	94	10%	53	0%	0%	12	17%	50%	6.76	3.9	41	117	$8
17	**Proj**	**289**	**32**	**7**	**38**	**0**	**270**	**274**	**330**	**402**	**732**	**709**	**900**	**8**	**83**	**0.51**	**46**	**25**	**30**	**31**	**113**	**83**	**100**	**10%**	**42**	**0%**	**67%**				**4.64**	**-7.2**	**23**	**66**	**$8**

Buxton,Byron

Age: 23 Bats: R Pos: CF
Ht: 6' 2" Wt: 189

Health	B	LIMA Plan	B
PT/Exp	F	Rand Var	-1
Consist	A	MM	3505

10-38-.225 with 10 SB in 298 AB at MIN. Promising flourish as Sept callup—.287/.357/.653 with 9 HR in 113 PA—but don't overlook how much h% helped. Contact still a struggle; xPX doesn't buy power. With elite prospects, compelling case to be ahead of curve, but be careful. Path to stardom may yet have some detours.

Yr	Tm	AB	R	HR	RBI	SB	BA	xBA	OBP	SLG	OPS	vL	vR	bb%	ct%	Eye	G	L	F	h%	HctX	PX	xPX	hr/f	Spd	SBO	SB%	#Wk	DOM	DIS	RC/G	RAR	BPV	BPX	R$
12																																			
13																																			
14																																			
15	MIN *	421	61	8	43	20	261	221	310	411	721	318	704	7	74	0.27	43	14	43	34	88	96	104	6%	186	24%	79%	10	20%	70%	4.43	-0.9	44	119	$16
16	MIN *	488	81	20	60	16	249	231	300	466	766	735	704	7	63	0.20	35	22	43	35	70	157	85	14%	171	18%	89%	20	30%	50%	4.84	6.8	46	131	$17
1st Half		260	39	6	23	10	253	230	296	442	737	483	630	6	66	0.18	33	23	43	36	74	138	74	3%	163	19%	100%	10	20%	40%	4.66	1.2	37	106	$16
2nd Half		228	41	13	37	7	245	232	305	493	798	969	771	8	60	0.22	37	20	43	34	66	180	95	23%	158	18%	77%	10	40%	60%	5.04	3.6	50	143	$18
17	**Proj**	**554**	**85**	**15**	**66**	**24**	**247**	**221**	**304**	**420**	**724**	**646**	**761**	**7**	**67**	**0.23**	**38**	**18**	**43**	**34**	**77**	**118**	**93**	**9%**	**187**	**23%**	**85%**				**4.34**	**-2.8**	**28**	**81**	**$22**

Cabrera,Asdrubal

Age: 31 Bats: B Pos: SS
Ht: 6' 0" Wt: 170

Health	B	LIMA Plan	B+
PT/Exp	A	Rand Var	-2
Consist	B	MM	3335

Big 2nd half, just like 2015, which led to best HR total since 2011. xPX says, "Don't assume HR will recede to mid-teens." That might be enough to forecast strong follow-up but periodic knee woes warn us off from being too optimistic. Otherwise, most skills remarkably consistent. Given high floor, a solid investment.

Yr	Tm	AB	R	HR	RBI	SB	BA	xBA	OBP	SLG	OPS	vL	vR	bb%	ct%	Eye	G	L	F	h%	HctX	PX	xPX	hr/f	Spd	SBO	SB%	#Wk	DOM	DIS	RC/G	RAR	BPV	BPX	R$
12	CLE	555	70	16	68	9	270	269	338	423	762	796	745	9	82	0.53	41	23	36	30	117	101	105	10%	82	9%	69%	27	56%	30%	4.88	12.3	53	133	$17
13	CLE	508	66	14	64	9	242	256	299	402	700	639	730	6	78	0.31	36	23	41	29	107	118	138	9%	106	11%	75%	25	36%	16%	3.92	6.3	51	128	$13
14	2 TM	553	74	14	61	10	241	250	307	387	694	689	696	8	80	0.45	38	19	42	28	118	105	126	8%	122	9%	83%	27	52%	30%	3.97	11.1	61	165	$13
15	TAM	505	66	15	58	6	265	248	315	430	744	725	752	7	79	0.34	36	21	44	31	92	107	107	9%	114	7%	67%	25	48%	20%	4.64	12.7	50	135	$14
16	NYM	521	65	23	62	5	280	273	336	474	810	835	803	7	80	0.37	37	23	40	31	119	114	142	14%	93	5%	83%	26	38%	15%	5.54	13.6	56	160	$17
1st Half		294	33	10	27	0	262	256	320	418	738	827	709	6	79	0.30	41	22	37	30	116	97	120	12%	86	1%	0%	14	36%	14%	4.37	-0.8	32	91	$12
2nd Half		227	32	13	35	5	304	290	357	546	904	848	916	8	82	0.48	33	24	43	32	124	135	169	16%	109	8%	100%	12	42%	17%	7.32	17.7	88	251	$24
17	**Proj**	**519**	**68**	**18**	**64**	**7**	**266**	**261**	**323**	**438**	**761**	**746**	**767**	**7**	**80**	**0.39**	**37**	**22**	**41**	**30**	**112**	**103**	**133**	**10%**	**104**	**7%**	**81%**				**4.87**	**6.1**	**47**	**135**	**$18**

KRISTOPHER OLSON

Cabrera,Melky

Age: 32 Bats: B Pos: LF	Health B	LIMA Plan A	
Ht: 6' 0" Wt: 200	PT/Exp A	Rand Var 0	
	Consist C	MM 2255	

BA has more historical skill support (in particular, ct%, LD%, HctX) than power, which makes recent run of double-digit HR and above-average RBI totals the dicier side of his value equation. Probably best to view him as sub-$20 player who can deliver fluky upside, rather than $20+ guy who sometimes has an off year.

Yr	Tm	AB	R	HR	RBI	SB	BA	xBA	OBP	SLG	OPS	vL	vR	bb%	ct%	Eye	G	L	F	h%	HctX	PX	xPX	hr/f	Spd	SBO	SB%	#Wk	DOM	DIS	RC/G	RAR	BPV	BPX	R$
12	SF	459	84	11	60	13	346	298	390	516	906	1111	826	7	86	0.57	52	22	26	38	105	99	80	11%	151	12%	72%	20	65%	10%	7.84	39.1	86	215	$28
13	TOR	344	39	3	30	2	279	255	322	360	682	595	717	6	86	0.49	46	22	31	32	120	57	85	3%	106	4%	50%	15	27%	20%	4.07	0.9	37	93	$7
14	TOR	568	81	16	73	6	301	297	351	458	808	785	817	7	88	0.64	49	21	30	32	117	104	90	11%	101	5%	75%	23	61%	9%	5.84	33.6	82	222	$25
15	CHW	629	70	12	77	3	273	278	314	394	709	600	748	6	86	0.45	46	24	30	30	101	79	66	7%	77	2%	100%	26	42%	19%	4.41	0.3	44	119	$16
16	CHW	591	70	14	86	2	296	289	345	455	800	847	788	7	88	0.68	43	22	35	32	103	92	79	8%	89	1%	100%	27	67%	19%	5.76	24.2	70	200	$20
1st Half		279	35	8	39	0	294	290	344	462	807	911	782	8	88	0.68	46	21	32	31	102	93	82	10%	89	0%	0%	14	57%	21%	5.81	10.4	70	200	$17
2nd Half		312	35	6	47	2	298	286	346	449	795	798	794	7	89	0.69	41	22	37	32	103	90	77	6%	91	2%	100%	13	77%	15%	5.72	10.9	71	203	$21
17	Proj	**573**	**70**	**13**	**77**	**3**	**293**	**286**	**340**	**439**	**778**	**765**	**783**	**7**	**88**	**0.60**	**45**	**22**	**32**	**32**	**105**	**85**	**78**	**8%**	**92**	**2%**	**77%**				**5.41**	**15.3**	**56**	**160**	**$19**

Cabrera,Miguel

Age: 34 Bats: R Pos: 1B	Health B	LIMA Plan D+	
Ht: 6' 2" Wt: 210	PT/Exp A	Rand Var -1	
	Consist C	MM 4055	

Skills indicate power rebound was legit—especially in 2H—despite playing through nagging injuries most of year. BA has run higher than xBA in 11 of 14 seasons thanks to consistently elite h%, but as ct% creeps downward, .300+ BA becomes a riskier proposition. Post-2013 R$ highlights shift to different Miggy era.

Yr	Tm	AB	R	HR	RBI	SB	BA	xBA	OBP	SLG	OPS	vL	vR	bb%	ct%	Eye	G	L	F	h%	HctX	PX	xPX	hr/f	Spd	SBO	SB%	#Wk	DOM	DIS	RC/G	RAR	BPV	BPX	R$
12	DET	622	109	44	139	4	330	315	393	606	999	913	1027	10	84	0.67	42	22	36	34	159	161	161	23%	80	3%	80%	27	81%	7%	9.08	62.1	111	278	$42
13	DET	555	103	44	137	3	348	317	442	636	1078	1210	1038	14	83	0.96	39	24	37	36	157	170	165	25%	79	1%	100%	26	69%	19%	10.96	90.2	122	305	$46
14	DET	611	101	25	109	1	313	302	371	524	895	900	894	9	81	0.51	40	25	35	35	157	154	163	14%	85	1%	50%	27	70%	15%	7.23	51.0	92	249	$33
15	DET	429	64	18	76	1	338	290	440	534	974	1016	964	15	81	0.94	42	25	33	39	142	126	124	16%	87	1%	50%	21	62%	14%	8.97	45.0	83	224	$25
16	DET	595	92	38	108	0	316	293	393	563	956	926	966	11	81	0.65	42	23	36	34	134	137	144	22%	81	0%	0%	27	52%	22%	8.24	53.9	80	229	$31
1st Half		309	47	18	51	0	298	290	379	531	909	616	1008	11	81	0.68	45	21	34	32	118	130	128	21%	87	0%	0%	14	36%	29%	7.29	18.6	79	226	$27
2nd Half		286	45	20	57	0	336	299	409	598	1007	1264	921	11	80	0.61	38	24	38	36	152	146	163	23%	75	0%	0%	13	69%	15%	9.37	31.8	84	240	$35
17	Proj	**586**	**88**	**33**	**105**	**0**	**308**	**294**	**391**	**540**	**930**	**960**	**921**	**12**	**81**	**0.70**	**41**	**24**	**35**	**34**	**144**	**132**	**146**	**20%**	**83**	**0%**	**38%**				**7.74**	**42.1**	**64**	**183**	**$32**

Cain,Lorenzo

Age: 31 Bats: R Pos: CF RF	Health C	LIMA Plan B	
Ht: 6' 2" Wt: 185	PT/Exp B	Rand Var -3	
	Consist C	MM 2535	

Several concerns here: injuries have cut into AB in 4 of last 5 seasons, L/R splits have grown into a chasm, and even during supposedly healthy 1st half, xBA, HctX, and xPX all fell short of 2015's career highs. If we give 2016 Spd a pass for hammy strain, running game seems like only part to invest in with confidence.

Yr	Tm	AB	R	HR	RBI	SB	BA	xBA	OBP	SLG	OPS	vL	vR	bb%	ct%	Eye	G	L	F	h%	HctX	PX	xPX	hr/f	Spd	SBO	SB%	#Wk	DOM	DIS	RC/G	RAR	BPV	BPX	R$
12	KC *	274	33	8	36	10	256	252	298	407	705	844	681	6	75	0.24	47	22	31	31	85	101	92	13%	125	16%	100%	12	42%	33%	4.37	-3.8	33	83	$8
13	KC	399	54	4	46	14	251	247	310	348	658	617	676	8	77	0.37	49	22	29	31	78	76	69	4%	131	19%	70%	24	38%	42%	3.61	-7.5	27	68	$11
14	KC	471	55	5	53	28	301	260	339	412	751	827	720	5	77	0.22	51	23	26	38	72	90	68	5%	136	26%	85%	25	28%	28%	5.20	17.1	33	89	$25
15	KC	551	101	16	72	28	307	283	361	477	838	959	777	6	82	0.38	46	23	31	35	114	108	109	11%	144	23%	82%	26	54%	27%	6.22	26.1	73	197	$35
16	KC	397	56	9	56	14	287	257	339	408	747	1016	668	7	79	0.37	47	23	30	35	96	76	79	9%	102	16%	74%	20	40%	30%	4.91	6.2	23	66	$17
1st Half		286	39	8	39	6	290	258	336	416	752	1099	661	6	78	0.30	48	24	28	35	93	78	74	13%	91	12%	60%	13	31%	38%	4.84	2.7	15	43	$20
2nd Half		111	17	1	17	8	279	254	346	387	734	859	685	10	82	0.60	47	19	34	33	103	72	90	3%	120	26%	89%	7	57%	14%	5.10	1.9	43	123	$9
17	Proj	**500**	**75**	**10**	**64**	**26**	**281**	**263**	**335**	**411**	**746**	**886**	**691**	**7**	**80**	**0.38**	**47**	**22**	**31**	**34**	**97**	**82**	**87**	**8%**	**130**	**22%**	**83%**				**4.95**	**6.3**	**41**	**117**	**$26**

Calhoun,Kole

Age: 29 Bats: L Pos: RF	Health A	LIMA Plan B	
Ht: 5' 10" Wt: 205	PT/Exp A	Rand Var 0	
	Consist B	MM 3135	

No, he didn't hit 25+ HR again. But if you fixate on that, you miss: 1) restoration of ct%; 2) improved Eye, HctX; 3) highest FB% of career; 4) xPX holding steady; 5) better results vL. And if your opponents fixate on HR drop, they might miss: repeat of 2015, with better BA.

Yr	Tm	AB	R	HR	RBI	SB	BA	xBA	OBP	SLG	OPS	vL	vR	bb%	ct%	Eye	G	L	F	h%	HctX	PX	xPX	hr/f	Spd	SBO	SB%	#Wk	DOM	DIS	RC/G	RAR	BPV	BPX	R$
12	LAA *	433	53	8	48	9	224	253	274	354	628	0	578	6	74	0.26	41	29	29	29	95	95	150	0%	87	14%	71%	9	0%	33%	3.16	-22.6	11	28	$5
13	LAA *	435	58	15	62	8	274	267	335	443	777	889	782	8	81	0.49	41	23	36	31	133	106	131	14%	91	10%	64%	10	70%	20%	5.10	10.2	56	140	$16
14	LAA *	515	94	18	61	5	276	281	326	456	782	710	793	7	79	0.35	44	24	32	32	99	129	94	13%	93	7%	53%	23	39%	17%	5.11	17.9	63	170	$20
15	LAA	630	78	26	83	4	256	248	308	422	731	663	763	7	74	0.27	42	23	35	31	90	109	117	16%	75	3%	80%	27	26%	37%	4.42	-6.4	21	57	$17
16	LAA	594	91	18	75	2	271	261	348	438	786	830	770	10	80	0.57	38	22	40	31	115	100	113	9%	78	3%	40%	27	41%	26%	5.20	8.3	46	131	$16
1st Half		314	48	10	44	2	283	258	352	443	795	873	768	9	80	0.50	35	25	41	33	110	91	114	10%	85	4%	50%	14	36%	21%	5.38	6.1	39	111	$20
2nd Half		280	43	8	31	0	257	264	344	432	776	784	773	11	80	0.64	42	19	39	30	121	110	112	9%	76	1%	0%	13	46%	31%	5.00	2.5	55	157	$12
17	Proj	**608**	**90**	**22**	**76**	**4**	**272**	**262**	**336**	**449**	**785**	**779**	**787**	**9**	**78**	**0.43**	**40**	**22**	**38**	**32**	**109**	**107**	**113**	**12%**	**80**	**4%**	**56%**				**5.19**	**8.6**	**41**	**117**	**$21**

Canha,Mark

Age: 28 Bats: R Pos: 1B	Health F	LIMA Plan D+	
Ht: 6' 2" Wt: 195	PT/Exp D	Rand Var +5	
	Consist F	MM 3223	

Hip surgery ended season in May, leaving us with data sample too small to be meaningful. At 28, there are still some peak years left, and don't forget that he posted 121 HctX, 132 xPX after Aug 1 in 2015. Could have nice late-round value, especially if injury makes others dismiss him as one-hit wonder.

Yr	Tm	AB	R	HR	RBI	SB	BA	xBA	OBP	SLG	OPS	vL	vR	bb%	ct%	Eye	G	L	F	h%	HctX	PX	xPX	hr/f	Spd	SBO	SB%	#Wk	DOM	DIS	RC/G	RAR	BPV	BPX	R$
12																																			
13	aa	425	52	9	48	5	241		314	382	696			10	73	0.40				31		114			93	6%	81%				4.05		33	83	$7
14	aaa	465	55	11	54	2	240		297	373	671			7	72	0.29				31		107			94	3%	62%				3.71		18	49	$8
15	OAK	441	61	16	70	7	254	252	315	426	742	587	821	7	78	0.34	42	18	40	29	107	111	114	11%	110	9%	78%	27	56%	33%	4.46	-6.1	51	138	$14
16	OAK	41	4	3	6	0	122	190	140	341	481	632	352	0	51	0.00	36	18	45	11	81	167	157	30%	94	50%	0%	6	17%	67%	0.94	-5.6	-30	-86	-$2
1st Half		41	4	3	6	0	122	190	140	341	481	632	352	0	51	0.00	36	18	45	11	81	167	157	30%	94	50%	0%	6	17%	67%	0.94	-6.0	-31	-89	-$2
2nd Half																																			
17	Proj	**321**	**39**	**12**	**38**	**4**	**245**	**246**	**315**	**421**	**737**	**715**	**752**	**8**	**76**	**0.36**	**40**	**18**	**41**	**29**	**91**	**111**	**140**	**12%**	**86**	**6%**	**79%**				**4.37**	**-6.9**	**33**	**95**	**$8**

Cano,Robinson

Age: 34 Bats: L Pos: 2B	Health A	LIMA Plan B+	
Ht: 6' 0" Wt: 190	PT/Exp A	Rand Var 0	
	Consist C	MM 3055	

Terrific comeback season, but biggest HR total of career came with noteworthy PX/xPX imbalance, and required highest FB% and second-highest hr/f of career. Add in age and home park, and regression seems very likely. And if he keeps fly ball approach with fewer HR, some BA slippage could come into play, too.

Yr	Tm	AB	R	HR	RBI	SB	BA	xBA	OBP	SLG	OPS	vL	vR	bb%	ct%	Eye	G	L	F	h%	HctX	PX	xPX	hr/f	Spd	SBO	SB%	#Wk	DOM	DIS	RC/G	RAR	BPV	BPX	R$
12	NYY	627	105	33	94	3	313	324	379	550	929	646	1108	9	85	0.64	49	26	26	33	141	145	115	24%	87	3%	60%	27	70%	7%	7.57	57.7	101	253	$32
13	NYY	605	81	27	107	7	314	312	383	516	899	788	969	10	86	0.76	44	26	30	33	139	128	115	17%	83	4%	88%	26	65%	19%	7.34	58.9	92	230	$34
14	SEA	595	77	14	82	10	314	301	382	454	836	746	891	9	89	0.90	53	23	25	34	109	95	82	11%	87	7%	77%	27	59%	11%	6.38	48.2	77	208	$29
15	SEA	624	82	21	79	2	287	285	334	446	779	715	815	6	83	0.40	50	24	25	32	118	100	107	16%	80	5%	25%	27	52%	11%	5.11	14.7	50	135	$22
16	SEA	655	107	39	103	0	298	290	350	533	882	770	955	7	85	0.47	46	18	36	30	122	124	96	19%	81	1%	0%	27	59%	7%	6.63	34.3	78	223	$29
1st Half		336	59	19	54	0	304	299	360	539	898	709	1017	7	85	0.50	44	21	35	31	122	128	90	19%	85	1%	0%	14	64%	0%	6.89	19.3	82	234	$30
2nd Half		319	48	20	49	0	292	281	339	527	866	831	888	6	85	0.44	48	15	37	29	123	121	102	20%	79	0%	0%	13	54%	15%	6.36	13.8	75	214	$28
17	Proj	**631**	**93**	**29**	**93**	**1**	**298**	**290**	**352**	**494**	**846**	**752**	**905**	**7**	**85**	**0.51**	**48**	**21**	**31**	**31**	**121**	**108**	**99**	**17%**	**81**	**2%**	**19%**				**6.17**	**23.8**	**55**	**156**	**$29**

Carpenter,Matt

Age: 31 Bats: L Pos: 3B 1B 2B	Health B	LIMA Plan B+	
Ht: 6' 3" Wt: 205	PT/Exp A	Rand Var +1	
	Consist B	MM 4055	

Oblique strain thwarted what could have been career-best season, as he combined elite bb%, HctX, LD%, and power in 1st half. PX/xPX differential even suggests there's further untapped HR potential, as does 190 xPX, 22% hr/f in 2nd half of 2015. With return to health... UP: .300 BA, 35 HR.

Yr	Tm	AB	R	HR	RBI	SB	BA	xBA	OBP	SLG	OPS	vL	vR	bb%	ct%	Eye	G	L	F	h%	HctX	PX	xPX	hr/f	Spd	SBO	SB%	#Wk	DOM	DIS	RC/G	RAR	BPV	BPX	R$
12	STL	296	44	6	46	1	294	268	365	463	828	784	846	10	79	0.54	40	24	36	36	118	116	114	7%	105	2%	50%	24	58%	21%	6.07	12.1	62	155	$9
13	STL	626	126	11	78	3	318	293	392	481	873	820	897	10	84	0.73	39	27	34	36	117	116	103	6%	125	3%	50%	27	63%	11%	6.89	48.8	90	225	$30
14	STL	595	99	8	59	5	272	253	375	375	750	722	762	14	81	0.86	41	24	35	32	117	80	97	5%	111	4%	63%	26	50%	27%	4.86	19.6	52	141	$17
15	STL	574	101	28	84	4	272	278	365	505	871	752	926	12	74	0.54	30	29	42	32	119	164	167	16%	95	4%	57%	27	59%	26%	6.32	27.1	81	219	$23
16	STL	473	81	21	68	0	271	282	380	505	885	809	920	15	77	0.75	31	26	43	31	131	144	174	13%	84	3%	0%	24	63%	21%	6.46	20.3	80	229	$15
1st Half		275	56	14	51	0	298	301	421	575	996	883	1048	17	79	0.98	30	27	43	33	144	165	190	15%	92	1%	0%	14	71%	14%	8.63	28.5	112	320	$22
2nd Half		198	25	7	17	0	232	255	319	409	728	701	740	11	75	0.48	32	26	43	28	113	114	152	11%	81	6%	0%	10	50%	30%	4.02	-5.3	38	109	$4
17	Proj	**549**	**95**	**28**	**81**	**2**	**278**	**284**	**374**	**520**	**893**	**819**	**927**	**13**	**77**	**0.64**	**31**	**26**	**43**	**32**	**122**	**147**	**151**	**16%**	**90**	**4%**	**31%**				**6.63**	**27.4**	**74**	**212**	**$24**

BRANDON KRUSE

Carrera,Ezequiel

Age: 30 Bats: L Pos: RF LF	Health A	LIMA Plan D
Ht: 5' 11" Wt: 175	PT/Exp D	Rand Var -2
	Consist A	MM 1411

Contact, walk rates tanked in 2nd half, exacerbated by Achilles' issue that brought running game to a near halt. Three-year xBA, GB, and PX outline a fourth OF ceiling, and 65% career SB rate hasn't been commensurate with Spd. Unless SBO bounces back, there's little reason for even short-term rostering.

Yr Tm	AB	R	HR	RBI	SB	BA	xBA	OBP	SLG	OPS	vL	vR	bb%	ct%	Eye	G	L	F	h%	HctX	PX	xPX	hr/f	Spd	SBO	SB%	#Wk	DOM	DIS	RC/G	RAR	BPV	BPX	R$
12 CLE *	541	69	6	42	27	251	258	290	353	643	810	660	5	80	0.28	47	26	28	30	86	67	89	7%	119	28%	75%	9	33%	44%	3.47	-22.4	23	58	$15
13 2 TM *	433	49	4	26	35	207	198	260	282	542	0	533	7	75	0.28	42	17	42	27	72	56	131	0%	141	49%	71%	5	0%	100%	2.31	-27.5	2	5	$11
14 DET *	443	62	4	32	38	257	239	316	350	666	866	590	8	80	0.44	60	12	29	31	101	66	77	0%	158	44%	70%	10	20%	50%	3.66	-3.2	38	103	$20
15 TOR *	288	42	4	34	7	258	241	309	343	652	782	675	7	77	0.32	61	17	23	32	80	63	76	11%	100	13%	67%	22	23%	59%	3.59	-10.0	6	16	$7
16 TOR	270	47	6	23	7	248	236	323	356	679	824	626	9	74	0.39	58	17	26	31	76	68	53	13%	131	14%	64%	26	27%	58%	3.73	-7.9	10	29	$6
1st Half	139	30	3	9	5	288	256	385	396	781	1003	678	11	81	0.69	56	17	27	34	82	67	74	11%	127	16%	63%	14	36%	36%	5.06	1.5	42	120	$10
2nd Half	131	17	3	14	2	206	215	254	313	566	528	576	6	66	0.20	60	16	24	29	70	71	27	15%	128	10%	67%	12	17%	83%	2.56	-8.8	-24	-69	$2
17 Proj	**194**	**29**	**4**	**18**	**7**	**245**	**241**	**307**	**349**	**656**	**768**	**623**	**7**	**75**	**0.33**	**58**	**17**	**25**	**31**	**81**	**66**	**62**	**10%**	**123**	**21%**	**68%**				**3.49**	**-7.1**	**5**	**15**	**$4**

Carter,Chris

Age: 30 Bats: R Pos: 1B	Health A	LIMA Plan B+
Ht: 6' 5" Wt: 245	PT/Exp B	Rand Var +1
	Consist C	MM 5115

Another season of loud extremes, leading the NL in both HR and whiffs. While BA continues to suffer, the power hasn't paid a price for all the Ks (witness ridiculous PX/xPX, hr/f), and Eye is remarkably steady. Safe to count on more of the same, but he's someone around whom you have to plan complementary pieces.

Yr Tm	AB	R	HR	RBI	SB	BA	xBA	OBP	SLG	OPS	vL	vR	bb%	ct%	Eye	G	L	F	h%	HctX	PX	xPX	hr/f	Spd	SBO	SB%	#Wk	DOM	DIS	RC/G	RAR	BPV	BPX	R$
12 OAK *	494	70	23	75	3	225	228	316	423	739	898	837	12	65	0.38	34	20	46	30	97	154	126	25%	67	4%	73%	15	47%	27%	4.39	-15.5	29	73	$10
13 HOU	506	64	29	82	2	223	226	320	451	770	782	765	12	58	0.33	31	22	47	32	95	197	171	21%	79	2%	100%	27	44%	33%	4.72	2.0	40	100	$12
14 HOU	507	68	37	88	5	227	252	308	491	799	869	772	10	64	0.31	27	22	51	27	106	210	171	22%	74	6%	71%	26	50%	31%	4.89	10.8	69	186	$18
15 HOU	391	50	24	64	1	199	223	307	427	734	736	733	13	61	0.38	30	18	52	25	99	177	176	19%	64	3%	33%	27	44%	30%	4.03	-16.5	34	92	$5
16 MIL	549	84	41	94	3	222	245	321	499	821	875	803	12	62	0.37	32	20	49	27	103	194	174	24%	70	3%	75%	27	52%	37%	5.18	-2.6	52	149	$14
1st Half	279	39	20	49	0	229	247	315	498	813	889	790	11	63	0.33	34	20	46	28	105	190	168	24%	70	0%	0%	14	50%	43%	5.16	0.5	49	140	$13
2nd Half	270	45	21	45	3	215	242	328	500	828	863	816	13	62	0.41	29	19	52	25	100	199	181	24%	73	6%	75%	13	54%	31%	5.19	0.8	58	166	$15
17 Proj	**524**	**75**	**36**	**88**	**2**	**220**	**237**	**318**	**478**	**796**	**822**	**785**	**12**	**62**	**0.36**	**30**	**20**	**50**	**27**	**101**	**181**	**172**	**22%**	**70**	**3%**	**57%**				**4.86**	**-3.8**	**35**	**101**	**$15**

Casali,Curtis

Age: 28 Bats: R Pos: CA	Health B	LIMA Plan D
Ht: 6' 2" Wt: 220	PT/Exp F	Rand Var +3
	Consist B	MM 4201

8-25-.186 in 226 AB at TAM. Few expected a repeat of 2015 power output (see hr/f), and after April 15, his BA was never north of the Mendoza Line. History shows that crushing one occasionally is his only avenue to positive value; he's otherwise torpedoed by poor ct% and cement feet. Will do more harm than good.

Yr Tm	AB	R	HR	RBI	SB	BA	xBA	OBP	SLG	OPS	vL	vR	bb%	ct%	Eye	G	L	F	h%	HctX	PX	xPX	hr/f	Spd	SBO	SB%	#Wk	DOM	DIS	RC/G	RAR	BPV	BPX	R$
12																																		
13 aa	120	20	4	25	0	324		406	497	903			12	82	0.75				37		123			84	0%	0%				7.61		77	193	$5
14 TAM *	298	24	3	25	0	202	201	303	282	585	521	460	13	65	0.42	44	23	33	30	50	82	69	0%	71	0%	0%	11	9%	73%	2.73	-5.5	-23	-62	-$3
15 TAM *	213	24	13	28	1	199	228	271	425	696	864	911	9	67	0.30	43	12	46	23	93	161	116	32%	73	2%	100%	12	75%	25%	3.69	-0.2	39	105	$1
16 TAM *	289	27	10	37	0	190	203	281	326	608	747	543	11	66	0.38	37	19	44	25	88	96	104	13%	74	0%	0%	23	26%	61%	2.89	-8.9	-10	-29	-$2
1st Half	157	17	6	18	0	172	193	257	331	588	702	528	9	61	0.26	35	17	48	24	89	123	107	13%	86	0%	0%	14	29%	71%	2.54	-8.2	-13	-37	-$3
2nd Half	132	10	4	19	0	211	227	319	320	639	881	575	14	73	0.59	41	24	35	26	77	69	98	12%	74	0%	0%	9	22%	44%	3.30	-3.4	0	0	-$1
17 Proj	**155**	**16**	**8**	**21**	**0**	**210**	**229**	**307**	**402**	**709**	**799**	**673**	**11**	**69**	**0.41**	**41**	**18**	**41**	**25**	**81**	**126**	**102**	**17%**	**75**	**0%**	**100%**				**3.89**	**-1.2**	**7**	**20**	**$2**

Castellanos,Nick

Age: 25 Bats: R Pos: 3B	Health B	LIMA Plan B+
Ht: 6' 4" Wt: 210	PT/Exp B	Rand Var -4
	Consist B	MM 4125

Breakout, Interrupted (by Aug hand injury)? NO: BA dropped every healthy month after .363 April, while plate skills, xBA were consistent with prior years. YES: GB/FB reversal paired with PX, xPX, and hr/f say he's growing into his power. VERDICT: Further skills consolidation in 2017 could yield... UP: 2016 1st half x 2.

Yr Tm	AB	R	HR	RBI	SB	BA	xBA	OBP	SLG	OPS	vL	vR	bb%	ct%	Eye	G	L	F	h%	HctX	PX	xPX	hr/f	Spd	SBO	SB%	#Wk	DOM	DIS	RC/G	RAR	BPV	BPX	R$
12 aa	322	29	6	21	4	245		270	345	616			3	76	0.15				30		71			98	12%	50%				3.02		0	0	$3
13 DET *	551	70	15	65	3	258	242	315	408	723	545	571	8	81	0.44	59	6	35	29	60	106	-15	0%	97	3%	76%	5	0%	20%	4.41	7.4	56	140	$13
14 DET	533	50	11	66	2	259	252	306	394	700	693	702	6	74	0.26	35	29	37	33	109	108	135	8%	101	3%	50%	27	33%	41%	4.10	6.6	26	70	$11
15 DET	549	42	15	73	0	255	243	303	419	721	970	656	7	72	0.26	36	23	40	33	103	118	118	9%	95	2%	0%	27	30%	37%	4.26	-4.9	27	73	$9
16 DET	411	54	18	58	1	285	260	331	496	827	656	894	7	73	0.25	31	26	43	35	106	135	166	14%	125	2%	50%	20	50%	35%	5.80	11.6	52	149	$13
1st Half	304	40	14	43	1	299	262	340	513	854	763	888	6	74	0.24	30	26	44	36	109	132	173	14%	125	3%	50%	14	64%	29%	6.30	11.8	53	151	$18
2nd Half	107	14	4	15	0	243	255	305	449	754	370	911	8	70	0.28	36	24	41	31	97	143	146	13%	115	0%	0%	6	17%	50%	4.56	-1.1	47	134	$0
17 Proj	**555**	**63**	**22**	**77**	**1**	**266**	**255**	**316**	**467**	**783**	**702**	**811**	**7**	**73**	**0.27**	**35**	**23**	**43**	**33**	**103**	**130**	**140**	**13%**	**111**	**2%**	**39%**				**5.06**	**2.8**	**30**	**85**	**$17**

Castillo,Welington

Age: 30 Bats: R Pos: CA	Health A	LIMA Plan C+
Ht: 6' 0" Wt: 200	PT/Exp C	Rand Var -2
	Consist A	MM 3225

Where's the beef, Welington? Career-low FB% and HR dip fed sense of disappointment in 2016 results. Admitted he was distracted by family health concerns in 2nd half, but HctX, LD% rate confirm solid contact while xPX suggests plus power is still there. Maybe he's not prime cut, but he's not hamburger, either.

Yr Tm	AB	R	HR	RBI	SB	BA	xBA	OBP	SLG	OPS	vL	vR	bb%	ct%	Eye	G	L	F	h%	HctX	PX	xPX	hr/f	Spd	SBO	SB%	#Wk	DOM	DIS	RC/G	RAR	BPV	BPX	R$
12 CHC *	327	34	11	43	0	245	225	324	394	717	1199	604	10	70	0.39	46	20	34	32	92	111	99	12%	76	0%	0%	16	38%	38%	4.30	0.1	15	38	$5
13 CHC	380	41	8	32	2	274	240	349	397	746	707	758	8	74	0.35	44	22	34	35	112	99	110	8%	78	2%	100%	25	36%	40%	4.68	10.7	19	48	$8
14 CHC	380	28	13	46	0	237	228	296	389	686	855	631	6	73	0.25	41	19	40	29	103	118	121	12%	69	0%	0%	24	42%	29%	3.72	2.9	23	62	$5
15 3 TM	342	42	19	57	0	237	253	296	453	750	778	739	7	73	0.27	42	18	40	27	122	142	152	19%	72	0%	0%	27	37%	37%	4.37	5.7	43	116	$8
16 ARI	416	41	14	68	2	264	250	322	423	745	868	698	7	71	0.27	42	25	33	34	115	110	128	14%	77	2%	100%	25	32%	44%	4.70	3.5	11	31	$10
1st Half	226	24	10	30	2	283	255	328	469	797	1122	637	6	72	0.23	43	23	34	36	110	122	129	18%	88	4%	100%	14	36%	36%	5.53	8.8	25	71	$13
2nd Half	190	17	4	38	0	242	245	315	368	683	413	757	9	70	0.32	40	28	32	33	120	95	126	9%	69	0%	0%	11	27%	55%	3.81	-1.8	-4	-11	$6
17 Proj	**440**	**44**	**18**	**69**	**1**	**250**	**247**	**313**	**430**	**743**	**822**	**715**	**7**	**72**	**0.29**	**42**	**22**	**37**	**31**	**114**	**119**	**130**	**16%**	**73**	**1%**	**100%**				**4.49**	**4.5**	**9**	**27**	**$12**

Castro,Jason

Age: 30 Bats: L Pos: CA	Health A	LIMA Plan D+
Ht: 6' 3" Wt: 210	PT/Exp C	Rand Var +1
	Consist A	MM 3103

Heed the Momentum Maxim: Patterns of negative results are more likely to snowball than correct. Contact has dropped annually since 2010, creating too many null AB around the occasional dinger. As xPX slides into league average, nothing here suggests a reversal, portending a full immersion into the world of #2 backstops.

Yr Tm	AB	R	HR	RBI	SB	BA	xBA	OBP	SLG	OPS	vL	vR	bb%	ct%	Eye	G	L	F	h%	HctX	PX	xPX	hr/f	Spd	SBO	SB%	#Wk	DOM	DIS	RC/G	RAR	BPV	BPX	R$
12 HOU	257	29	6	29	0	257	264	334	401	735	361	831	11	76	0.51	43	28	30	32	93	101	107	10%	89	0%	0%	22	55%	32%	4.63	3.7	36	90	$3
13 HOU	435	63	18	56	2	276	270	350	485	835	738	864	10	70	0.38	39	25	35	36	109	167	140	17%	83	3%	67%	23	61%	22%	5.96	27.8	62	155	$15
14 HOU	465	43	14	56	1	222	225	286	366	651	619	662	7	68	0.23	45	20	36	30	87	119	110	12%	97	1%	100%	26	38%	46%	3.30	-0.3	10	27	$5
15 HOU	337	38	11	31	0	211	229	283	365	648	512	707	9	66	0.29	37	24	38	28	90	124	122	13%	76	0%	0%	25	32%	44%	3.31	-4.3	5	14	$0
16 HOU	329	41	11	32	2	210	222	307	377	684	478	757	12	63	0.37	46	20	34	30	90	124	102	16%	102	4%	67%	26	31%	46%	3.69	-1.7	6	17	$1
1st Half	179	28	6	21	2	212	222	338	391	729	395	853	16	59	0.47	46	21	33	32	98	142	120	18%	105	4%	100%	14	36%	43%	4.35	1.1	16	46	$3
2nd Half	150	13	5	11	0	207	221	265	360	625	586	639	7	67	0.22	45	19	35	27	80	105	84	14%	97	3%	0%	12	25%	50%	2.92	-5.7	-5	-14	-$2
17 Proj	**316**	**36**	**10**	**31**	**1**	**217**	**228**	**295**	**378**	**673**	**528**	**725**	**10**	**66**	**0.31**	**43**	**22**	**35**	**29**	**89**	**116**	**109**	**14%**	**92**	**2%**	**57%**				**3.58**	**-5.5**	**-4**	**-12**	**$3**

Castro,Starlin

Age: 27 Bats: R Pos: 2B	Health A	LIMA Plan B+
Ht: 6' 1" Wt: 160	PT/Exp A	Rand Var -1
	Consist C	MM 2335

Engimatic IF's odd career arc continues. Spike in hr/f saved him, but middling PX/xPX, FB% casts doubt on HR output, while vanishing SBO suggests running game won't return. Still valuable, but must reverse unwelcome trend in overall plate skills to avoid "what could have been" talk that seemed so unlikely five years ago.

Yr Tm	AB	R	HR	RBI	SB	BA	xBA	OBP	SLG	OPS	vL	vR	bb%	ct%	Eye	G	L	F	h%	HctX	PX	xPX	hr/f	Spd	SBO	SB%	#Wk	DOM	DIS	RC/G	RAR	BPV	BPX	R$
12 CHC	646	78	14	78	25	283	271	323	430	753	775	746	5	85	0.36	47	21	32	32	99	87	100	8%	173	23%	66%	27	63%	19%	4.72	10.3	72	180	$26
13 CHC	666	59	10	44	9	245	249	284	347	631	619	635	4	81	0.23	51	20	29	29	106	75	99	6%	130	10%	60%	27	37%	41%	3.18	-11.0	32	80	$9
14 CHC	528	58	14	65	4	292	272	339	438	777	788	773	6	81	0.35	45	23	32	34	102	107	105	10%	109	6%	50%	23	52%	17%	5.17	26.3	57	154	$19
15 CHC	547	52	11	69	5	265	251	296	375	671	643	679	4	83	0.23	54	17	29	30	86	70	75	8%	125	8%	50%	27	37%	33%	3.69	-9.3	36	97	$13
16 NYY	577	63	21	70	4	270	268	300	433	734	740	731	4	80	0.20	49	21	30	31	101	97	91	15%	117	3%	100%	25	52%	28%	4.58	-2.5	41	117	$15
1st Half	301	28	10	31	2	246	268	283	389	672	724	649	4	82	0.26	53	20	27	27	96	80	80	15%	125	3%	100%	14	43%	36%	3.71	-9.7	41	117	$10
2nd Half	276	35	11	39	2	297	268	320	482	801	762	815	3	77	0.16	45	21	34	35	105	117	103	15%	115	3%	100%	11	64%	18%	5.67	6.5	44	126	$21
17 Proj	**591**	**63**	**17**	**72**	**5**	**275**	**264**	**306**	**420**	**726**	**721**	**728**	**4**	**81**	**0.22**	**49**	**20**	**31**	**32**	**98**	**87**	**91**	**12%**	**122**	**5%**	**71%**				**4.47**	**-5.6**	**22**	**63**	**$19**

ROB CARROLL

Centeno,Juan	Health	A	LIMA Plan	D
Age: 27 Bats: L Pos: CA	PT/Exp	F	Rand Var	0
Ht: 5' 10" Wt: 172	Consist	B	MM	1141

3-25-.261 in 176 AB at MIN. PRO: Lifetime 87% ct% in minors. CON: Not much good happens after contact, small-sample 2016 xPX and 2nd-half LD% notwithstanding. Right-brain dominant catchers have long shelf lives, so he'll likely get a bunch more chances. For now, we're not interested.

Yr	Tm	AB	R	HR	RBI	SB	BA	xBA	OBP	SLG	OPS	vL	vR	bb%	ct%	Eye	G	L	F	h%	HctX	PX	xPX	hr/f	Spd	SBO	SB%	#Wk	DOM	DIS	RC/G	RAR	BPV	BPX	R$
12	aa	281	23	0	28	1	242		288	286	575			6	82	0.36				29		35			95	3%	41%				2.74		0	0	$0
13	NYM *	246	20	0	22	1	239	226	263	287	550	0	600	3	85	0.22	63	13	25	28	40	37	-15	0%	110	3%	37%	3	0%	33%	2.48	-8.9	11	28	-$1
14	NYM *	286	18	1	18	1	217	219	259	251	510	0	522	5	82	0.32	79	13	8	26	57	29	17	0%	87	4%	51%	6	17%	67%	2.09	-12.0	-8	-22	-$2
15	MIL *	197	7	0	16	1	217	283	238	266	504	1500	95	3	85	0.18	43	36	21	26	131	33	109	0%	109	9%	36%	6	17%	67%	1.96	-11.3	6	16	-$3
16	MIN *	225	20	4	29	1	250	275	298	367	665	562	751	6	81	0.36	51	25	24	29	91	75	104	9%	80	2%	100%	22	45%	50%	3.74	-0.8	23	66	$2
1st Half		121	10	3	14	1	226	240	258	327	585	513	669	4	81	0.23	52	19	30	26	104	60	119	13%	80	3%	100%	10	30%	60%	2.81	-4.9	8	23	$1
2nd Half		104	10	1	15	0	279	300	342	413	756	600	803	9	81	0.50	50	30	20	34	83	93	94	6%	91	0%	0%	12	58%	42%	5.00	2.5	44	126	$3
17	**Proj**	**165**	**12**	**3**	**17**	**1**	**246**	**274**	**290**	**357**	**647**	**518**	**690**	**5**	**82**	**0.32**	**51**	**25**	**24**	**28**	**91**	**68**	**104**	**9%**	**88**	**3%**	**53%**				**3.42**	**-3.5**	**11**	**32**	**$0**

Cervelli,Francisco	Health	F	LIMA Plan	C+
Age: 31 Bats: R Pos: CA	PT/Exp	D	Rand Var	-1
Ht: 6' 1" Wt: 210	Consist	B	MM	1215

Injuries (broken hand, concussion) played a role in xPX nosedive. Even in more representative 2nd half, lofty GB% puts a hard cap on HR potential. Long-shaky xBA and health grade point to the downside, as his value hinges on h% and racking up AB. 2015 output is now his ceiling, but we may not see that again.

Yr	Tm	AB	R	HR	RBI	SB	BA	xBA	OBP	SLG	OPS	vL	vR	bb%	ct%	Eye	G	L	F	h%	HctX	PX	xPX	hr/f	Spd	SBO	SB%	#Wk	DOM	DIS	RC/G	RAR	BPV	BPX	R$
12	NYY *	355	34	2	30	5	205	75	268	262	531	1000	0	8	73	0.32	0	0	100	28	320	47	737	0%	93	5%	100%	2	50%	50%	2.32	-21.7	-23	-58	-$1
13	NYY	52	12	3	8	0	269	300	377	500	877	684	1017	13	83	0.89	30	28	42	28	145	145	148	17%	84	0%	0%	4	100%	0%	6.40	4.0	101	253	$0
14	NYY *	172	19	2	13	1	274	247	328	384	712	735	830	7	73	0.30	44	26	30	36	112	97	126	6%	93	2%	100%	17	47%	35%	4.46	4.9	15	41	$2
15	PIT	451	56	7	43	1	295	249	370	401	771	856	747	9	79	0.49	52	21	27	36	106	69	100	7%	125	1%	50%	27	22%	41%	5.20	17.2	30	81	$13
16	PIT	326	42	1	33	6	264	236	377	322	699	888	663	15	78	0.78	56	20	24	34	85	44	59	2%	95	6%	75%	21	24%	43%	4.18	-2.1	7	20	$6
1st Half		167	19	0	21	3	257	241	373	293	667	751	642	15	79	0.86	56	24	20	33	84	25	37	0%	108	7%	60%	10	10%	60%	3.69	-2.2	1	3	$6
2nd Half		159	23	1	12	3	270	230	380	352	732	1268	682	14	77	0.70	56	15	28	35	87	64	83	3%	89	5%	100%	11	36%	27%	4.73	2.7	15	43	$7
17	**Proj**	**434**	**54**	**5**	**40**	**3**	**268**	**241**	**361**	**359**	**720**	**790**	**700**	**11**	**77**	**0.56**	**51**	**21**	**28**	**34**	**101**	**62**	**91**	**5%**	**103**	**3%**	**72%**				**4.39**	**3.1**	**4**	**10**	**$10**

Cespedes,Yoenis	Health	B	LIMA Plan	B+
Age: 31 Bats: R Pos: LF CF	PT/Exp	A	Rand Var	0
Ht: 5' 10" Wt: 220	Consist	B	MM	4245

Strained quad cost him about a month; SB impact likely felt all year. At peak age with a stable and consistent skill set, party line should be "expect more of same". But growth in bb% plus 2H upticks in FB% and ct% say there may yet be another level. With 600 AB... UP: 40 HR, especially in the right non-CitiField venue.

Yr	Tm	AB	R	HR	RBI	SB	BA	xBA	OBP	SLG	OPS	vL	vR	bb%	ct%	Eye	G	L	F	h%	HctX	PX	xPX	hr/f	Spd	SBO	SB%	#Wk	DOM	DIS	RC/G	RAR	BPV	BPX	R$
12	OAK	487	70	23	82	16	292	269	356	505	861	853	864	8	79	0.42	40	20	40	33	114	132	114	15%	104	15%	80%	26	50%	27%	6.36	22.8	71	178	$25
13	OAK	529	74	26	80	7	240	244	294	442	737	880	672	7	74	0.27	38	17	46	28	98	136	127	14%	110	12%	50%	24	46%	33%	4.11	0.2	53	133	$17
14	2 AL	600	89	22	100	7	260	255	301	450	751	666	777	6	79	0.27	34	18	48	30	106	134	127	10%	104	7%	78%	27	56%	11%	4.66	14.5	66	178	$23
15	2 TM	633	101	35	105	7	291	289	328	542	870	736	909	5	78	0.23	42	20	38	33	124	160	132	19%	92	9%	58%	27	56%	22%	6.20	33.7	78	211	$32
16	NYM	479	72	31	86	3	280	280	354	530	884	1081	839	10	77	0.47	37	21	41	30	123	145	137	20%	69	3%	75%	24	58%	17%	6.54	25.7	68	194	$20
1st Half		272	44	20	48	1	294	285	362	570	932	1188	869	9	73	0.38	37	26	38	34	124	165	144	27%	76	3%	50%	14	64%	21%	7.33	21.3	67	191	$24
2nd Half		207	28	11	38	2	261	271	343	478	821	924	800	10	84	0.68	37	17	46	27	123	121	129	14%	63	4%	100%	10	50%	10%	5.59	6.5	72	206	$15
17	**Proj**	**582**	**87**	**35**	**101**	**6**	**284**	**279**	**342**	**531**	**873**	**903**	**865**	**8**	**79**	**0.38**	**38**	**20**	**42**	**31**	**119**	**142**	**132**	**18%**	**85**	**6%**	**71%**				**6.35**	**31.1**	**69**	**197**	**$29**

Chirinos,Robinson	Health	F	LIMA Plan	D
Age: 33 Bats: R Pos: CA	PT/Exp	F	Rand Var	+2
Ht: 6' 1" Wt: 185	Consist	B	MM	4021

9-20-.224 in 147 AB at TEX. Missed two months with a broken right forearm, on top of 2015's shoulder strain and biceps tendon soreness. The xPX/FB% combination is intriguing from a catcher, even though it comes with a low BA. It's getting late for this, but if he ever stumbled into 400 AB... UP: 20 HR

Yr	Tm	AB	R	HR	RBI	SB	BA	xBA	OBP	SLG	OPS	vL	vR	bb%	ct%	Eye	G	L	F	h%	HctX	PX	xPX	hr/f	Spd	SBO	SB%	#Wk	DOM	DIS	RC/G	RAR	BPV	BPX	R$
12																																			
13	TEX *	293	26	6	27	1	199	194	269	305	574	445	583	9	75	0.37	24	19	57	25	100	77	175	0%	103	2%	100%	8	38%	38%	2.63	-9.9	11	28	-$2
14	TEX	306	36	13	40	0	239	259	290	415	705	759	682	5	77	0.24	42	21	37	27	100	126	129	15%	80	2%	0%	26	35%	35%	3.81	4.5	45	122	$6
15	TEX	233	33	10	34	0	232	253	325	438	762	845	717	11	73	0.45	35	19	45	27	89	145	133	19%	94	0%	0%	19	53%	26%	4.57	5.8	61	165	$3
16	TEX *	168	21	9	20	0	205	240	271	432	702	823	791	8	69	0.29	40	14	45	24	111	155	156	19%	77	3%	0%	19	42%	42%	3.65	-1.1	40	114	$0
1st Half		79	7	5	9	0	184	217	241	412	653	1306	766	7	63	0.20	42	17	42	21	117	159	184	33%	83	0%	0%	6	50%	33%	3.11	-2.6	18	51	-$1
2nd Half		89	14	4	11	0	225	256	311	449	760	508	807	9	74	0.39	40	13	47	26	109	152	141	13%	83	6%	0%	13	38%	46%	4.16	0.1	63	180	$1
17	**Proj**	**192**	**24**	**10**	**29**	**0**	**229**	**252**	**309**	**458**	**766**	**819**	**749**	**8**	**72**	**0.33**	**39**	**17**	**44**	**26**	**102**	**148**	**145**	**17%**	**81**	**2%**	**8%**				**4.38**	**1.4**	**36**	**103**	**$5**

Chisenhall,Lonnie	Health	B	LIMA Plan	B
Age: 28 Bats: L Pos: RF	PT/Exp	C	Rand Var	-1
Ht: 6' 1" Wt: 200	Consist	C	MM	2325

8-57-.286 in 385 AB at CLE. Former top prospect showing some signs of late development? Upticks in ct%, HctX and LD% signal some refinement of plate approach. 2nd half FB% spike is one component of potential power emergence: PX and hr/f didn't come along, but he has flashed those skills before. Worth one more look.

Yr	Tm	AB	R	HR	RBI	SB	BA	xBA	OBP	SLG	OPS	vL	vR	bb%	ct%	Eye	G	L	F	h%	HctX	PX	xPX	hr/f	Spd	SBO	SB%	#Wk	DOM	DIS	RC/G	RAR	BPV	BPX	R$
12	CLE *	260	28	8	29	2	267	275	297	431	729	442	848	4	80	0.21	43	25	32	31	82	110	67	14%	84	5%	67%	9	44%	22%	4.43	-3.2	42	105	$5
13	CLE *	394	48	16	58	3	256	262	302	445	747	408	705	6	79	0.31	38	20	42	29	83	130	92	11%	96	3%	100%	22	64%	23%	4.64	4.1	61	153	$11
14	CLE	478	62	13	59	3	280	261	343	427	770	729	782	8	79	0.39	38	24	38	33	83	109	93	9%	89	3%	75%	27	52%	22%	5.06	15.7	48	130	$16
15	CLE *	490	53	9	61	5	245	239	291	371	662	624	676	6	78	0.29	41	20	40	30	80	92	74	7%	82	5%	83%	21	38%	43%	3.67	-15.9	23	62	$8
16	CLE *	408	45	8	60	6	274	257	317	421	738	642	784	6	81	0.34	35	24	41	32	87	90	77	6%	110	6%	100%	25	44%	24%	4.77	0.8	45	129	$11
1st Half		213	26	5	25	4	276	265	332	430	762	743	836	8	80	0.43	37	27	35	32	88	88	85	9%	129	7%	100%	12	50%	17%	5.14	2.7	48	137	$12
2nd Half		195	19	3	35	2	272	251	303	410	713	435	737	4	83	0.24	33	21	47	32	87	92	69	4%	92	5%	100%	13	38%	31%	4.38	-1.8	41	117	$10
17	**Proj**	**428**	**48**	**11**	**60**	**5**	**266**	**252**	**313**	**418**	**731**	**617**	**752**	**6**	**80**	**0.32**	**36**	**21**	**43**	**31**	**84**	**96**	**78**	**7%**	**96**	**5%**	**92%**				**4.56**	**-1.7**	**38**	**107**	**$13**

Choi,Ji-Man	Health	A	LIMA Plan	D
Age: 26 Bats: L Pos: 1B LF	PT/Exp	F	Rand Var	0
Ht: 6' 1" Wt: 225	Consist	A	MM	3131

5-12-.170 in 112 AB at LAA. Rule 5 pick struggled in first MLB action. There are plenty of warts here, from lofty GB% (also an issue in minors) to injury history to prior PED suspension. But there are also raw materials of a patience-and-power profile, that are just enough to hold our attention... barely.

Yr	Tm	AB	R	HR	RBI	SB	BA	xBA	OBP	SLG	OPS	vL	vR	bb%	ct%	Eye	G	L	F	h%	HctX	PX	xPX	hr/f	Spd	SBO	SB%	#Wk	DOM	DIS	RC/G	RAR	BPV	BPX	R$
12																																			
13	a/a	243	24	8	36	2	234		314	400	713			10	84	0.71				25		103			101	6%	42%				4.06		71	178	$3
14	a/a	248	32	4	25	1	236		314	324	638			10	79	0.55				28		62			106	5%	39%				3.29		21	57	$2
15	aaa	57	5	1	11	0	239		318	330	649			10	70	0.39				33		79			87	7%	0%				3.23		-7	-19	-$1
16	LAA *	300	31	8	34	5	238	246	323	388	710	250	621	11	77	0.54	49	16	34	28	91	98	117	17%	71	15%	39%	18	33%	50%	3.86	-9.2	32	91	$4
1st Half		168	18	3	17	3	246	206	328	355	683	0	347	11	72	0.44	58	8	33	33	24	83	-3	0%	71	13%	45%	7	29%	71%	3.71	-7.1	0	0	$5
2nd Half		132	13	6	16	2	229	281	317	429	746	250	674	11	83	0.76	48	18	34	24	109	114	136	20%	78	19%	32%	11	36%	36%	4.01	-4.5	72	206	$4
17	**Proj**	**156**	**17**	**7**	**18**	**2**	**234**	**266**	**313**	**423**	**736**	**425**	**747**	**11**	**80**	**0.58**	**48**	**18**	**34**	**25**	**98**	**109**	**122**	**16%**	**83**	**11%**	**39%**				**4.20**	**-4.3**	**47**	**135**	**$4**

Choo,Shin-Soo	Health	C	LIMA Plan	C+
Age: 34 Bats: L Pos: RF	PT/Exp	C	Rand Var	0
Ht: 5' 11" Wt: 205	Consist	D	MM	2125

7-17-.242 with 6 SB in 178 AB at TEX. Injuries (calf, hamstring, back, fractured forearm) wrecked his season. Rediscovered SB game was a consolation prize, but age/health don't support a return to 20 SB. Stable plate skills, LD% and xPX say he should remain productive when healthy enough to make the lineup card.

Yr	Tm	AB	R	HR	RBI	SB	BA	xBA	OBP	SLG	OPS	vL	vR	bb%	ct%	Eye	G	L	F	h%	HctX	PX	xPX	hr/f	Spd	SBO	SB%	#Wk	DOM	DIS	RC/G	RAR	BPV	BPX	R$
12	CLE	598	88	16	67	21	283	268	373	441	815	605	926	11	75	0.49	50	23	27	35	99	118	107	13%	78	15%	75%	27	48%	33%	5.64	13.4	41	103	$24
13	CIN	569	107	21	54	20	285	273	423	462	885	612	1011	16	77	0.84	49	21	29	34	98	126	101	16%	111	14%	65%	27	59%	15%	6.46	35.6	76	190	$29
14	TEX	455	58	13	40	3	242	236	340	374	714	673	732	11	71	0.44	50	20	30	31	113	104	109	13%	88	5%	43%	21	33%	43%	4.01	1.5	19	51	$8
15	TEX	555	94	22	82	4	276	267	375	463	838	708	917	12	74	0.52	51	21	28	34	104	130	123	19%	83	3%	67%	27	48%	33%	5.89	17.7	49	132	$21
16	TEX *	209	28	8	21	7	251	250	339	403	742	1016	665	12	74	0.51	47	22	31	31	129	96	127	18%	71	19%	55%	13	23%	62%	4.36	-2.1	19	54	$5
1st Half		126	19	7	19	5	273	263	360	477	837	1223	775	12	75	0.53	46	20	34	32	139	123	154	25%	74	24%	51%	6	50%	33%	5.45	2.8	45	129	$10
2nd Half		83	9	1	2	2	217	229	330	289	619	840	523	12	72	0.48	48	25	27	29	117	53	96	6%	79	12%	67%	7	0%	86%	2.89	-4.7	-19	-54	-$1
17	**Proj**	**431**	**61**	**14**	**42**	**9**	**262**	**251**	**368**	**410**	**779**	**820**	**760**	**12**	**73**	**0.51**	**49**	**22**	**29**	**33**	**116**	**97**	**117**	**15%**	**79**	**12%**	**58%**				**4.82**	**1.6**	**19**	**53**	**$15**

GREG PYRON

Coghlan,Chris

Age: 32 Bats: L Pos: LF 2B | Ht: 6' 1" Wt: 190
Health C | PT/Exp C | Consist C
LIMA Plan D+ | Rand Var +4 | MM 3243

6-30-.188 in 261 AB at OAK/CHC. Why he'll be undervalued: Wretched 1st half obscures return to form (see 2nd half OPS, xBA, bb%). Why you should be cautious: 2nd half magic came in only 69 AB due to two DL trips; must re-earn "super utility" tag. If he can indeed find the at-bats, 2014-15 value represents the upside.

Yr	Tm	AB	R	HR	RBI	SB	BA	xBA	OBP	SLG	OPS	vL	vR	bb%	ct%	Eye	G	L	F	h%	HctX	PX	xPX	hr/f	Spd	SBO	SB%	#Wk	DOM	DIS	RC/G	RAR	BPV	BPX	R$
12	MIA *	410	40	6	32	7	209	250	287	307	594	186	451	10	83	0.64	63	13	23	24	52	65	28	5%	95	11%	62%	9	11%	33%	2.79	-25.0	34	85	$0
13	MIA	195	10	1	10	2	256	242	318	354	672	861	641	8	78	0.40	50	21	29	32	85	73	65	2%	119	4%	100%	15	33%	53%	3.90	-0.8	24	60	$0
14	CHC *	455	56	9	45	11	268	271	338	420	757	709	832	10	77	0.46	43	26	31	33	99	118	80	9%	113	13%	67%	22	45%	41%	4.86	14.2	58	157	$14
15	CHC	440	64	16	41	11	250	273	341	443	784	348	831	12	79	0.62	46	20	34	28	114	123	126	14%	131	11%	85%	27	48%	19%	5.15	5.6	77	208	$13
16	2 TM *	294	39	6	35	2	209	246	301	344	645	427	627	12	74	0.50	48	21	31	26	87	93	94	10%	77	4%	67%	23	39%	43%	3.33	-11.8	18	51	$1
1st Half		194	23	5	14	1	155	221	244	278	523	332	544	10	68	0.34	46	21	33	20	84	85	100	12%	81	5%	50%	13	15%	54%	1.96	-16.1	-14	-40	-$3
2nd Half		100	16	1	21	1	315	295	418	471	889	700	852	15	85	1.16	53	19	28	36	91	105	81	6%	90	3%	100%	10	70%	30%	7.42	7.9	82	234	$8
17	**Proj**	**247**	**35**	**8**	**32**	**5**	**261**	**276**	**351**	**444**	**795**	**578**	**825**	**12**	**78**	**0.61**	**48**	**21**	**32**	**31**	**94**	**114**	**92**	**12%**	**95**	**10%**	**70%**				**5.28**	**6.0**	**61**	**173**	**$7**

Collins,Tyler

Age: 27 Bats: L Pos: CF | Ht: 5' 11" Wt: 205
Health A | PT/Exp D | Consist A
LIMA Plan D | Rand Var 0 | MM 2211

4-15-.235 in 136 AB at DET. Profile stagnant as he reaches peak age—dwindling ct% means a low BA ceiling, and has yet to bring low-minors 20/20 profile to higher levels. Some success vR provides slim hope of platoon-OF upside, but only as your 5th OF.

Yr	Tm	AB	R	HR	RBI	SB	BA	xBA	OBP	SLG	OPS	vL	vR	bb%	ct%	Eye	G	L	F	h%	HctX	PX	xPX	hr/f	Spd	SBO	SB%	#Wk	DOM	DIS	RC/G	RAR	BPV	BPX	R$
12																																			
13	aa	466	53	17	62	3	212		274	374	649			8	72	0.31				26		123			78	9%	36%				3.18		28	70	$6
14	DET *	492	52	15	52	9	231	233	289	363	651	400	721	7	74	0.31	35	25	40	28	96	94	148	13%	91	11%	67%	7	14%	57%	3.42	-3.9	15	41	$10
15	DET *	382	34	5	40	9	237	235	292	346	638	643	739	7	77	0.34	40	22	38	29	85	78	107	7%	95	13%	72%	16	38%	44%	3.36	-11.9	16	43	$5
16	DET *	393	38	10	40	4	203	207	260	313	573	311	780	7	71	0.26	41	19	39	26	84	67	82	10%	111	7%	67%	15	40%	47%	2.58	-20.9	-12	-34	$0
1st Half		244	20	3	16	3	179	144	228	241	470	0	294	6	69	0.20	57	0	43	24	80	44	29	0%	84	7%	68%	3	33%	67%	1.71	-21.7	-49	-140	-$4
2nd Half		149	18	6	24	2	242	245	310	431	740	347	865	9	74	0.38	39	22	39	28	88	103	90	12%	127	7%	65%	12	42%	42%	4.43	-0.1	37	106	$6
17	**Proj**	**129**	**13**	**4**	**15**	**2**	**223**	**231**	**286**	**359**	**645**	**352**	**698**	**8**	**74**	**0.31**	**39**	**22**	**38**	**28**	**87**	**83**	**97**	**10%**	**100**	**10%**	**67%**				**3.30**	**-4.8**	**3**	**9**	**$2**

Conforto,Michael

Age: 24 Bats: L Pos: LF | Ht: 6' 1" Wt: 211
Health A | PT/Exp F | Consist B
LIMA Plan B | Rand Var 0 | MM 4035

12-42-.220 in 304 AB at NYM. Had us thinking stardom after sparkling 2015, explosive April, then... wow. Wheels completely fell off as the whiffs mounted. Then raked in minors and ended the season well, and is only 24 come March. Will have to earn his way back, but still owns exciting skills. UP: 25 HR.

Yr	Tm	AB	R	HR	RBI	SB	BA	xBA	OBP	SLG	OPS	vL	vR	bb%	ct%	Eye	G	L	F	h%	HctX	PX	xPX	hr/f	Spd	SBO	SB%	#Wk	DOM	DIS	RC/G	RAR	BPV	BPX	R$
12																																			
13																																			
14																																			
15	NYM *	347	48	13	48	1	277	274	346	479	825	481	872	10	77	0.47	39	23	39	32	137	137	157	17%	92	2%	46%	12	83%	17%	5.80	10.6	68	184	$11
16	NYM *	432	59	18	62	3	260	251	330	463	793	295	804	9	74	0.41	36	19	45	31	120	130	153	12%	70	6%	50%	22	36%	41%	5.14	6.5	43	123	$11
1st Half		245	32	11	33	2	222	242	292	414	706	219	854	9	73	0.36	38	19	44	26	123	122	152	15%	79	6%	67%	12	42%	42%	3.93	-3.9	33	94	$9
2nd Half		187	27	8	28	1	310	261	380	529	909	1000	702	10	76	0.48	32	19	48	37	110	140	157	7%	69	7%	37%	10	30%	40%	7.13	13.8	60	171	$15
17	**Proj**	**462**	**64**	**19**	**65**	**2**	**274**	**262**	**351**	**481**	**832**	**476**	**871**	**10**	**76**	**0.44**	**36**	**20**	**43**	**32**	**124**	**131**	**156**	**13%**	**74**	**4%**	**46%**				**5.71**	**16.7**	**49**	**139**	**$17**

Contreras,Willson

Age: 25 Bats: R Pos: CA LF | Ht: 6' 1" Wt: 210
Health A | PT/Exp D | Consist B
LIMA Plan B+ | Rand Var -1 | MM 4155

12-35-.282 in 252 AB at CHC. Followed up 2015 breakout with this gem, and let's just say we hope you heeded our advice and grabbed him LAST year. GB%, xPX say to tap brakes on any huge power explosion, but ct% was better in minors, so a regression there actually means BA upside. In short, a catching star is born.

Yr	Tm	AB	R	HR	RBI	SB	BA	xBA	OBP	SLG	OPS	vL	vR	bb%	ct%	Eye	G	L	F	h%	HctX	PX	xPX	hr/f	Spd	SBO	SB%	#Wk	DOM	DIS	RC/G	RAR	BPV	BPX	R$
12																																			
13																																			
14																																			
15	aa	454	56	7	59	3	297		361	422	784			9	84	0.65				34		85			94	5%	41%				5.37		54	146	$15
16	CHC *	456	63	19	67	5	293	277	360	495	855	854	841	9	77	0.45	54	18	28	34	101	123	105	24%	105	9%	43%	17	41%	29%	6.14	22.3	59	169	$18
1st Half		255	38	11	43	3	305	291	372	520	893	775	1062	10	79	0.51	51	20	29	35	119	129	133	40%	100	12%	35%	4	50%	50%	6.60	17.6	71	203	$22
2nd Half		201	25	8	24	2	279	263	348	463	811	875	784	9	75	0.39	55	17	28	34	94	116	98	20%	104	5%	67%	13	38%	23%	5.58	8.2	43	123	$13
17	**Proj**	**444**	**58**	**21**	**60**	**4**	**282**	**291**	**360**	**502**	**862**	**831**	**876**	**9**	**80**	**0.50**	**54**	**18**	**28**	**31**	**104**	**129**	**112**	**22%**	**103**	**8%**	**45%**				**6.00**	**23.7**	**63**	**179**	**$19**

Correa,Carlos

Age: 22 Bats: R Pos: SS | Ht: 6' 4" Wt: 215
Health A | PT/Exp C | Consist B
LIMA Plan B+ | Rand Var 0 | MM 4355

Not exactly a sophomore slump, really just a correction in power/speed as foretold in last year's Forecaster. And yes, this is still a skill set to own: HctX remained solid, fine bb% growth, and remember, this was his age-21 season. Don't be surprised to see a tick back up in 2017, and the long-term upside remains huge.

Yr	Tm	AB	R	HR	RBI	SB	BA	xBA	OBP	SLG	OPS	vL	vR	bb%	ct%	Eye	G	L	F	h%	HctX	PX	xPX	hr/f	Spd	SBO	SB%	#Wk	DOM	DIS	RC/G	RAR	BPV	BPX	R$
12																																			
13																																			
14																																			
15	HOU *	602	85	30	101	28	287	302	352	517	869	899	836	9	80	0.50	49	22	29	32	115	146	103	24%	87	21%	84%	18	67%	6%	6.59	37.4	82	222	$36
16	HOU	577	76	20	96	13	274	275	361	451	811	730	839	12	76	0.54	50	22	27	33	115	113	100	17%	105	9%	81%	26	46%	38%	5.69	22.9	50	143	$22
1st Half		298	40	13	51	8	265	271	362	466	829	597	900	12	73	0.53	49	23	28	32	117	125	102	21%	118	12%	73%	14	43%	36%	5.72	10.9	55	157	$23
2nd Half		279	36	7	45	5	283	276	359	434	792	850	770	11	79	0.56	51	22	27	34	112	101	97	12%	94	6%	100%	12	50%	42%	5.66	9.4	48	137	$20
17	**Proj**	**564**	**76**	**22**	**94**	**18**	**280**	**286**	**357**	**475**	**832**	**820**	**836**	**11**	**78**	**0.53**	**50**	**22**	**28**	**33**	**114**	**120**	**101**	**18%**	**100**	**13%**	**84%**				**6.07**	**25.7**	**61**	**175**	**$29**

Cozart,Zack

Age: 31 Bats: R Pos: SS | Ht: 6' 1" Wt: 185
Health D | PT/Exp C | Consist C
LIMA Plan B | Rand Var 0 | MM 2325

After 2015's season-ending knee injury cost him a career year, he just went out and did it again. Once again, season ended early—in Sept this time—with continuing soreness in the same knee. Solid health grade before the knee injury, so if that heals for good this time, there's no reason he can't re-repeat this output.

Yr	Tm	AB	R	HR	RBI	SB	BA	xBA	OBP	SLG	OPS	vL	vR	bb%	ct%	Eye	G	L	F	h%	HctX	PX	xPX	hr/f	Spd	SBO	SB%	#Wk	DOM	DIS	RC/G	RAR	BPV	BPX	R$
12	CIN	561	72	15	35	4	246	254	288	399	687	699	683	5	80	0.27	42	20	38	28	83	102	86	9%	139	3%	100%	26	35%	19%	3.89	-3.5	55	138	$8
13	CIN	567	74	12	63	0	254	255	284	381	665	686	658	4	82	0.25	50	18	32	29	80	88	63	8%	118	0%	0%	27	41%	19%	3.73	3.8	45	113	$11
14	CIN	506	48	4	38	7	221	231	268	300	568	702	532	5	84	0.32	45	18	38	26	84	55	77	3%	143	6%	100%	27	33%	33%	2.60	-10.6	36	97	$2
15	CIN	194	28	9	28	3	258	276	310	459	769	931	718	7	85	0.48	39	19	42	26	98	117	118	13%	104	14%	50%	10	70%	10%	4.61	4.9	81	219	$5
16	CIN	464	67	16	50	4	252	266	308	425	732	737	731	7	82	0.44	39	21	40	28	104	102	106	10%	99	5%	80%	23	43%	26%	4.46	-2.1	56	160	$10
1st Half		280	45	11	33	1	264	290	318	461	779	820	765	7	85	0.52	40	22	38	28	107	113	101	12%	88	3%	50%	14	64%	7%	5.02	4.5	73	209	$14
2nd Half		184	22	5	17	3	234	228	291	370	661	565	683	8	77	0.36	39	18	44	28	99	84	115	8%	118	7%	100%	9	11%	56%	3.67	-4.4	28	80	$5
17	**Proj**	**490**	**64**	**15**	**53**	**6**	**246**	**255**	**298**	**400**	**698**	**754**	**682**	**7**	**82**	**0.40**	**41**	**19**	**40**	**27**	**96**	**90**	**103**	**9%**	**114**	**7%**	**72%**				**3.99**	**-7.0**	**43**	**123**	**$12**

Crawford,Brandon

Age: 30 Bats: L Pos: SS | Ht: 6' 2" Wt: 200
Health A | PT/Exp A | Consist B
LIMA Plan B+ | Rand Var -2 | MM 2325

Despite power regression, HctX shows he was hitting ball as hard (or harder) than ever. That's what a 50% drop in HR/F will do. Made up for lost power with BA spike though, so it all came out in the wash. HR may inch back up, BA down a bit, but with stable skills overall and just now reaching age 30, he's a low-risk investment.

Yr	Tm	AB	R	HR	RBI	SB	BA	xBA	OBP	SLG	OPS	vL	vR	bb%	ct%	Eye	G	L	F	h%	HctX	PX	xPX	hr/f	Spd	SBO	SB%	#Wk	DOM	DIS	RC/G	RAR	BPV	BPX	R$
12	SF	435	44	4	45	1	248	246	304	349	653	631	661	7	78	0.35	47	23	30	31	98	77	85	4%	91	5%	20%	27	26%	37%	3.44	-8.6	18	45	$4
13	SF	499	52	9	43	1	248	246	311	363	674	546	727	8	81	0.44	49	19	32	29	83	80	78	7%	109	2%	33%	27	41%	41%	3.72	3.2	37	93	$6
14	SF	491	54	10	69	5	246	229	324	389	713	879	637	11	74	0.46	38	20	42	32	91	103	125	6%	131	6%	63%	27	48%	37%	4.26	14.1	40	108	$11
15	SF	507	65	21	84	6	256	274	321	462	782	716	808	7	77	0.33	48	19	34	30	111	137	136	16%	89	9%	60%	27	48%	15%	4.80	15.4	59	159	$16
16	SF	553	67	12	84	7	275	257	342	430	772	713	801	9	79	0.50	43	21	36	33	113	92	114	8%	126	4%	100%	27	41%	30%	5.27	10.2	49	140	$16
1st Half		283	34	8	53	3	272	255	347	431	778	715	811	10	79	0.53	39	23	38	32	118	93	122	9%	112	4%	100%	14	36%	29%	5.30	6.7	46	131	$18
2nd Half		270	33	4	31	4	278	260	337	430	766	710	791	8	80	0.45	47	20	34	34	108	90	107	5%	134	5%	100%	13	46%	31%	5.24	5.9	50	143	$15
17	**Proj**	**544**	**65**	**14**	**78**	**6**	**264**	**256**	**329**	**425**	**754**	**727**	**765**	**9**	**78**	**0.42**	**44**	**20**	**36**	**32**	**106**	**98**	**117**	**9%**	**115**	**6%**	**76%**				**4.80**	**5.4**	**41**	**116**	**$17**

ROD TRUESDELL

Crawford,J.P.

Age: 22 Bats: L Pos: SS
Ht: 6' 2" Wt: 180
Health A | PT/Exp D | Consist A
LIMA Plan D+ | Rand Var 0 | MM 1313

Top PHI shortstop prospect should arrive sometime soon, but is he ready? Overall, these skills say no. Fine plate control suggests he won't be completely overmatched, but there's little else to grab onto. Decent speed can't offset lack of power, so BA will suffer. Potential bright future for this 22-year-old, but don't bet on it arriving now.

Yr	Tm	AB	R	HR	RBI	SB	BA	xBA	OBP	SLG	OPS	vL	vR	bb%	ct%	Eye	G	L	F	h%	HctX	PX	xPX	hr/f	Spd	SBO	SB%	#Wk	DOM	DIS	RC/G	RAR	BPV	BPX	R$
12																																			
13																																			
14																																			
15	aa	351	43	5	27	6	240		318	363	681			10	86	0.80				27		77			122	8%	73%				3.87		64	173	$4
16	a/a	472	57	7	39	11	235		329	322	650			12	81	0.74				28		55			97	12%	59%				3.44		24	69	$7
1st Half		292	38	3	23	9	238		339	317	656			13	82	0.84				28		52			115	15%	63%				3.53		32	91	$10
2nd Half		180	19	4	16	2	230		311	330	640			10	80	0.59				27		59			105	7%	46%				3.28		23	66	$2
17	**Proj**	**375**	**44**	**6**	**41**	**7**	**248**	**243**	**329**	**352**	**681**	**681**	**681**	**11**	**83**	**0.71**	**42**	**20**	**38**	**29**		**63**		**5%**	**115**	**10%**	**64%**				**3.87**	**-6.6**	**32**	**91**	**$7**

Crisp,Coco

Age: 37 Bats: B Pos: LF CF
Ht: 6' 0" Wt: 180
Health D | PT/Exp C | Consist F
LIMA Plan D+ | Rand Var +2 | MM 1323

A decent little bounce-back, with skills better than stats overall even with a double/double. But keep in mind that was only a return to so-so 2014 skills, not to his heyday. And now 37, with a neck that seems ready to go at any time, there's major risk. And what's the upside? Most likely, 2016 again. Honestly, why bother?

Yr	Tm	AB	R	HR	RBI	SB	BA	xBA	OBP	SLG	OPS	vL	vR	bb%	ct%	Eye	G	L	F	h%	HctX	PX	xPX	hr/f	Spd	SBO	SB%	#Wk	DOM	DIS	RC/G	RAR	BPV	BPX	R$
12	OAK	455	68	11	46	39	259	274	325	418	742	682	774	9	86	0.70	44	20	36	28	88	95	76	8%	130	36%	91%	26	38%	23%	5.03	6.1	79	198	$22
13	OAK	513	93	22	66	21	261	278	335	444	779	645	857	11	87	0.94	41	20	40	26	89	107	85	12%	113	18%	81%	25	56%	16%	5.27	19.4	92	230	$25
14	OAK	463	68	9	47	19	246	252	336	363	699	640	726	12	86	1.00	39	20	40	27	88	79	76	6%	109	16%	79%	26	54%	23%	4.25	7.8	66	178	$15
15	OAK	126	11	0	6	2	175	209	252	222	474	531	448	9	80	0.52	44	18	39	22	55	43	48	0%	96	7%	100%	13	8%	46%	1.80	-10.5	5	14	-$4
16	2 AL	446	54	13	55	10	231	270	302	397	698	625	719	9	83	0.59	40	22	38	25	82	98	69	9%	106	14%	67%	27	48%	22%	3.91	-4.9	61	174	$8
1st Half		255	38	7	35	5	247	286	310	427	737	692	751	9	85	0.62	40	23	37	27	88	106	66	9%	112	16%	56%	14	57%	21%	4.33	-1.0	76	217	$12
2nd Half		191	16	6	20	5	209	247	291	356	647	514	679	10	80	0.56	39	21	40	23	75	86	74	10%	94	13%	83%	13	38%	23%	3.40	-6.3	38	109	$3
17	**Proj**	**315**	**36**	**7**	**31**	**8**	**228**	**250**	**304**	**355**	**659**	**610**	**677**	**10**	**82**	**0.63**	**41**	**20**	**39**	**26**	**76**	**76**	**67**	**7%**	**103**	**12%**	**78%**				**3.61**	**-8.1**	**41**	**117**	**$6**

Cron,C.J.

Age: 27 Bats: R Pos: 1B
Ht: 6' 4" Wt: 235
Health B | PT/Exp C | Consist B
LIMA Plan B+ | Rand Var 0 | MM 3135

Continued to make steady skills gains despite missing time with a broken hand. Note the ct% trend, earned without sacrificing power, which bodes well for BA gains. Odd reverse splits continued; with the sort of correction we'd expect from a RH batter, and if PT cooperates, he's not far from this... UP: 30 HR

Yr	Tm	AB	R	HR	RBI	SB	BA	xBA	OBP	SLG	OPS	vL	vR	bb%	ct%	Eye	G	L	F	h%	HctX	PX	xPX	hr/f	Spd	SBO	SB%	#Wk	DOM	DIS	RC/G	RAR	BPV	BPX	R$
12																																			
13	aa	519	48	11	71	7	242		269	372	641			4	82	0.20				28		93			79	11%	60%				3.29		35	88	$10
14	LAA *	432	46	15	57	1	250	255	283	413	697	751	731	4	75	0.18	35	25	40	30	109	123	122	15%	80	3%	50%	20	45%	45%	3.94	-2.5	31	84	$10
15	LAA *	471	47	20	66	3	260	263	290	448	738	672	774	4	79	0.20	45	18	37	29	96	120	108	14%	75	4%	75%	25	44%	32%	4.47	-6.4	44	119	$13
16	LAA	407	51	16	69	2	278	271	325	467	792	674	827	6	82	0.32	41	20	39	31	107	111	106	12%	81	5%	40%	22	41%	32%	5.10	2.8	53	151	$13
1st Half		241	31	9	42	1	282	271	335	465	799	701	827	6	84	0.42	41	19	40	30	112	105	112	11%	80	5%	33%	14	50%	14%	5.23	0.9	59	169	$15
2nd Half		166	20	7	27	1	271	269	311	470	781	634	827	5	78	0.22	42	21	37	31	100	120	97	14%	87	6%	50%	8	25%	63%	4.91	-0.9	44	126	$10
17	**Proj**	**520**	**58**	**22**	**79**	**3**	**265**	**268**	**306**	**457**	**763**	**683**	**796**	**5**	**79**	**0.24**	**42**	**20**	**38**	**30**	**102**	**114**	**108**	**14%**	**80**	**5%**	**54%**				**4.67**	**-6.4**	**39**	**113**	**$17**

Cruz,Nelson

Age: 37 Bats: R Pos: DH RF
Ht: 6' 3" Wt: 225
Health A | PT/Exp A | Consist B
LIMA Plan B+ | Rand Var -2 | MM 4245

PRO: Elite PX and another healthy year netted 40-HR season, most skills holding steady. CON: Gradual HctX slide could erode HR totals, ct% still sitting on the precipice, turning 37 can't help. Will decline at some point, as they all (well, those not called Big Papi) do. But power base still looks solid—and good for another run at 40.

Yr	Tm	AB	R	HR	RBI	SB	BA	xBA	OBP	SLG	OPS	vL	vR	bb%	ct%	Eye	G	L	F	h%	HctX	PX	xPX	hr/f	Spd	SBO	SB%	#Wk	DOM	DIS	RC/G	RAR	BPV	BPX	R$
12	TEX	585	86	24	90	8	260	262	319	460	779	944	727	8	76	0.34	41	18	41	30	129	141	151	13%	86	9%	67%	27	48%	19%	4.94	0.9	60	150	$20
13	TEX	413	49	27	76	5	266	264	327	506	833	821	837	8	74	0.32	42	17	41	30	120	162	154	21%	65	6%	83%	20	70%	25%	5.71	14.4	61	153	$18
14	BAL	613	87	40	108	4	271	285	333	525	859	977	823	8	77	0.39	42	17	41	29	119	173	131	20%	91	6%	44%	27	63%	15%	5.91	33.0	93	251	$30
15	SEA	590	90	44	93	3	302	277	369	566	936	1107	866	9	72	0.36	46	20	34	35	113	169	137	30%	88	3%	60%	26	50%	31%	7.49	33.1	70	189	$33
16	SEA	589	96	43	105	2	287	274	360	555	915	1020	864	10	73	0.39	44	18	38	33	108	160	134	26%	88	1%	100%	26	62%	23%	7.07	25.8	67	191	$27
1st Half		304	50	21	56	0	283	265	365	543	908	1102	816	10	73	0.41	44	17	39	32	101	159	128	24%	85	0%	0%	14	57%	21%	6.85	11.6	67	191	$26
2nd Half		285	46	22	49	2	291	279	354	568	923	934	917	9	73	0.36	45	19	36	33	115	162	141	29%	91	3%	100%	12	67%	25%	7.30	14.3	69	197	$29
17	**Proj**	**567**	**87**	**39**	**97**	**3**	**286**	**271**	**354**	**540**	**894**	**1005**	**848**	**9**	**74**	**0.37**	**44**	**19**	**37**	**33**	**113**	**151**	**137**	**25%**	**88**	**3%**	**69%**				**6.73**	**19.6**	**53**	**151**	**$29**

Cuthbert,Cheslor

Age: 24 Bats: R Pos: 3B
Ht: 6' 1" Wt: 190
Health A | PT/Exp C | Consist B
LIMA Plan D+ | Rand Var -4 | MM 2321

12-46-.274 in 475 AB at KC. Held his own after May call-up, and overall posted a nice growth season. But skills don't support these stats (e.g., xBA). Late tailspin, not to mention assumed return to a reserve (or even minor league) role, clouds outlook now. Some nice building blocks, but likely not even close to $15 for 2017.

Yr	Tm	AB	R	HR	RBI	SB	BA	xBA	OBP	SLG	OPS	vL	vR	bb%	ct%	Eye	G	L	F	h%	HctX	PX	xPX	hr/f	Spd	SBO	SB%	#Wk	DOM	DIS	RC/G	RAR	BPV	BPX	R$
12																																			
13	aa	237	20	4	23	4	196		247	315	563			6	78	0.31				23		93			83	14%	65%				2.43		26	65	-$2
14	a/a	446	36	9	49	8	243		297	355	652			7	81	0.41				28		83			82	11%	64%				3.49		33	89	$8
15	KC *	443	51	9	50	4	247	263	300	371	671	636	660	7	83	0.46	46	22	32	28	49	81	38	8%	104	6%	65%	8	25%	25%	3.74	-10.8	46	124	$7
16	KC *	568	60	17	67	2	276	252	324	427	751	819	701	7	80	0.36	48	17	35	32	101	92	74	9%	112	2%	63%	23	39%	30%	4.85	0.8	44	126	$14
1st Half		275	31	12	42	1	279	251	321	450	771	808	712	6	80	0.31	51	15	33	31	84	95	67	15%	120	3%	46%	10	40%	40%	5.04	1.1	45	129	$17
2nd Half		293	29	5	25	1	273	252	324	406	730	822	694	7	81	0.41	45	18	37	32	111	90	78	6%	109	1%	100%	13	38%	23%	4.67	-1.9	45	129	$12
17	**Proj**	**202**	**21**	**5**	**22**	**2**	**255**	**252**	**304**	**399**	**703**	**781**	**677**	**7**	**81**	**0.38**	**48**	**17**	**35**	**29**	**100**	**88**	**74**	**9%**	**111**	**5%**	**67%**				**4.14**	**-4.4**	**28**	**81**	**$5**

D Arnaud,Travis

Age: 28 Bats: R Pos: CA
Ht: 6' 2" Wt: 195
Health F | PT/Exp D | Consist C
LIMA Plan D+ | Rand Var -2 | MM 1213

Another injury-marred year, and this one came with major power outage. These may not be independent events—rotator cuff (or another, hidden) injury could be culprit for PX crash. In any case, he'd lost his starting job by season's end. If healthy, 2014-2015 power skills are still there... but he hasn't stayed healthy yet.

Yr	Tm	AB	R	HR	RBI	SB	BA	xBA	OBP	SLG	OPS	vL	vR	bb%	ct%	Eye	G	L	F	h%	HctX	PX	xPX	hr/f	Spd	SBO	SB%	#Wk	DOM	DIS	RC/G	RAR	BPV	BPX	R$
12	aaa	279	31	12	36	1	287		318	492	810			4	76	0.19				34		139			89	3%	38%				5.51		52	130	$8
13	NYM *	182	18	3	15	0	208	225	315	325	639	298	630	13	74	0.61	47	18	35	26	71	93	74	4%	94	0%	0%	7	29%	43%	3.29	-2.2	29	73	-$2
14	NYM *	448	58	18	53	1	252	286	305	447	752	707	722	7	84	0.49	42	20	39	26	122	130	135	10%	89	1%	100%	23	57%	17%	4.66	15.8	84	227	$12
15	NYM *	267	33	12	42	0	260	270	319	461	780	1112	758	8	80	0.43	37	21	42	29	101	127	108	15%	84	0%	0%	16	56%	19%	5.07	9.7	64	173	$7
16	NYM	251	27	4	15	0	247	217	307	323	629	455	682	7	80	0.38	52	17	31	29	105	47	85	6%	95	0%	0%	19	11%	42%	3.28	-8.3	2	6	$1
1st Half		78	5	0	6	0	244	217	306	282	588	583	588	7	82	0.43	50	20	30	30	94	31	69	0%	87	0%	0%	7	14%	29%	2.83	-3.0	-5	-14	-$2
2nd Half		173	22	4	9	0	249	217	307	341	648	435	735	7	79	0.36	53	15	31	29	110	54	92	9%	108	0%	0%	12	8%	50%	3.48	-3.3	8	23	$2
17	**Proj**	**356**	**40**	**9**	**35**	**0**	**251**	**241**	**313**	**373**	**686**	**631**	**701**	**7**	**80**	**0.41**	**46**	**19**	**35**	**29**	**102**	**75**	**96**	**8%**	**89**	**0%**	**74%**				**3.91**	**-2.4**	**10**	**29**	**$7**

Dahl,David

Age: 23 Bats: L Pos: LF
Ht: 6' 2" Wt: 185
Health A | PT/Exp D | Consist F
LIMA Plan B | Rand Var -3 | MM 3535

7-24-.315 with 5 SB in 222 AB at COL. PRO: Strong debut at 22 with solid PX/Spd combo; SB upside with a greener light. CON: Unsustainable h% means BA will regress; shaky plate skills suggest it could REALLY tank, impacting SB. A volatile investment: $30-plus potential, but also the chance of... DN: .275, 10 HR/15 SB

Yr	Tm	AB	R	HR	RBI	SB	BA	xBA	OBP	SLG	OPS	vL	vR	bb%	ct%	Eye	G	L	F	h%	HctX	PX	xPX	hr/f	Spd	SBO	SB%	#Wk	DOM	DIS	RC/G	RAR	BPV	BPX	R$
12																																			
13																																			
14																																			
15	aa	288	38	5	20	18	274		296	408	704			3	76	0.13				34		93			123	40%	71%				4.07		24	65	$12
16	COL *	572	99	23	74	19	310	273	367	527	894	728	895	8	73	0.34	45	21	33	39	97	138	100	13%	140	17%	72%	11	27%	27%	7.03	37.8	65	186	$32
1st Half		288	46	12	39	14	277	265	352	493	845			10	72	0.41				35		144			111	25%	72%				5.99		58	166	$29
2nd Half		284	56	11	37	6	351	280	393	579	972	728	895	7	75	0.28	45	21	33	43	100	137	100	13%	153	9%	73%	11	27%	27%	8.85	32.1	72	206	$35
17	**Proj**	**526**	**85**	**16**	**56**	**18**	**287**	**264**	**331**	**470**	**801**	**665**	**839**	**6**	**75**	**0.26**	**45**	**21**	**33**	**36**	**90**	**117**	**90**	**13%**	**144**	**20%**	**71%**				**5.45**	**14.9**	**48**	**136**	**$26**

ROD TRUESDELL

Davis,Chris

Age: 31	Bats: L	Pos: 1B	Health	A	LIMA Plan	B+
Ht: 6' 4"	Wt: 235		PT/Exp	A	Rand Var	+2
			Consist	F	MM	5115

Lowest ct%, LD% of career, combined with HR regression, pulled rug out from under BA, and all skills got worse in nightmarish 2nd half. Battled sore left palm all year, so perhaps, as with oblique injury in 2014, that's the explanation, but this is scary start to his 30s. Career BA, xBA both now sit at .250; that might be 2017 ceiling.

Yr Tm	AB	R	HR	RBI	SB	BA	xBA	OBP	SLG	OPS	vL	vR	bb%	ct%	Eye	G	L	F	h%	HctX	PX	xPX	hr/f	Spd	SBO	SB%	#Wk	DOM	DIS	RC/G	RAR	BPV	BPX	R$
12 BAL	515	75	33	85	2	270	252	326	501	827	792	836	7	67	0.22	39	23	38	34	102	162	150	25%	71	4%	40%	27	41%	37%	5.46	2.6	35	88	$20
13 BAL	584	103	53	138	4	286	297	370	634	1004	763	1142	11	66	0.36	32	22	46	34	114	266	199	30%	63	3%	80%	27	78%	11%	8.24	59.5	119	298	$38
14 BAL	450	65	26	72	2	196	235	300	404	704	677	716	12	62	0.35	35	25	41	25	96	174	154	23%	62	3%	67%	22	36%	36%	3.71	-6.1	30	81	$8
15 BAL	573	100	47	117	2	262	271	361	562	923	799	984	13	64	0.40	32	25	43	32	115	224	196	29%	58	3%	40%	27	56%	22%	6.80	31.1	79	214	$28
16 BAL	566	99	38	84	1	221	231	332	459	792	711	828	13	61	0.40	36	20	44	28	100	168	179	25%	76	1%	100%	27	41%	41%	4.91	0.8	31	89	$12
1st Half	293	60	21	56	0	242	246	350	512	862	832	875	13	62	0.41	32	21	48	31	105	194	191	24%	77	0%	0%	14	43%	29%	5.91	7.1	55	157	$18
2nd Half	273	39	17	28	1	198	215	313	403	716	576	778	14	60	0.40	42	19	39	25	95	141	164	27%	84	1%	100%	13	38%	54%	3.95	-9.9	9	26	$6
17 Proj	**538**	**89**	**37**	**88**	**2**	**230**	**241**	**334**	**480**	**814**	**719**	**857**	**13**	**62**	**0.38**	**36**	**22**	**42**	**29**	**103**	**174**	**177**	**26%**	**67**	**2%**	**61%**				**5.18**	**1.4**	**30**	**85**	**$16**

Davis,Khristopher

Age: 29	Bats: R	Pos: LF DH	Health	A	LIMA Plan	B+
Ht: 6' 0"	Wt: 190		PT/Exp	B	Rand Var	+1
			Consist	B	MM	5135

Basically doubled 2H numbers from 2015 (.246 BA, 22 HR, 50 RBI). Elbow pain took a bite out of power skills in June (92 xPX, 29% FB), but didn't stop him from letting it rip after that. Good vL/vR splits, peak age, xBA indicates some BA upside... no reason he can't ride this wave for at least another year.

Yr Tm	AB	R	HR	RBI	SB	BA	xBA	OBP	SLG	OPS	vL	vR	bb%	ct%	Eye	G	L	F	h%	HctX	PX	xPX	hr/f	Spd	SBO	SB%	#Wk	DOM	DIS	RC/G	RAR	BPV	BPX	R$
12 a/a	241	36	11	37	2	305		387	516	903			12	70	0.45				40		160			80	6%	50%				7.13		58	145	$10
13 MIL *	379	51	21	52	7	233	265	294	455	749	1009	918	8	72	0.31	43	20	37	27	135	158	162	29%	92	15%	60%	16	63%	25%	4.30	-2.2	60	150	$11
14 MIL	501	70	22	69	4	244	278	299	457	756	777	749	6	76	0.26	39	21	40	28	132	161	157	14%	89	5%	80%	26	54%	23%	4.45	6.0	72	195	$15
15 MIL	392	54	27	66	6	247	260	323	505	828	729	864	10	69	0.36	42	17	40	29	105	174	170	25%	92	8%	75%	22	64%	18%	5.51	0.7	64	173	$15
16 OAK	555	85	42	102	1	247	266	307	524	831	881	815	7	70	0.25	43	17	40	27	111	171	145	27%	89	3%	33%	26	54%	35%	5.25	-4.0	60	171	$18
1st Half	278	37	19	53	1	259	263	295	507	802	859	787	3	72	0.13	43	19	38	29	115	148	126	25%	99	4%	50%	14	43%	43%	4.90	-4.8	45	129	$18
2nd Half	277	48	23	49	0	235	270	317	542	859	897	845	10	68	0.36	43	15	43	25	108	195	166	28%	84	2%	0%	12	67%	25%	5.58	0.7	77	220	$18
17 Proj	**547**	**81**	**38**	**92**	**3**	**249**	**267**	**316**	**516**	**832**	**843**	**828**	**8**	**71**	**0.30**	**42**	**18**	**40**	**28**	**115**	**167**	**157**	**25%**	**88**	**5%**	**54%**				**5.35**	**14.5**	**54**	**154**	**$21**

Davis,Rajai

Age: 36	Bats: R	Pos: CF LF	Health	A	LIMA Plan	C
Ht: 5' 10"	Wt: 195		PT/Exp	C	Rand Var	0
			Consist	A	MM	2523

PRO: Career-high HR built on steady gains in FB%, hr/f; SB rebound driven by SBO, SB% levels he's owned before. CON: 2nd-lowest Spd of career (and remember that 2015's Spd was spiked by 11 triples), tied for lowest ct%; ugly 2nd half validated by poor skills. Given age, consider 2nd half line as potential 2017 downside.

Yr Tm	AB	R	HR	RBI	SB	BA	xBA	OBP	SLG	OPS	vL	vR	bb%	ct%	Eye	G	L	F	h%	HctX	PX	xPX	hr/f	Spd	SBO	SB%	#Wk	DOM	DIS	RC/G	RAR	BPV	BPX	R$
12 TOR	447	64	8	43	46	257	248	309	378	687	783	638	6	77	0.28	45	23	32	32	80	86	75	7%	119	54%	78%	27	26%	44%	3.95	-12.2	27	68	$22
13 TOR	331	49	6	24	45	260	241	312	375	687	857	594	6	80	0.31	39	23	38	31	90	81	84	6%	128	61%	88%	23	26%	30%	4.34	1.0	36	90	$23
14 DET	461	64	8	51	36	282	269	320	401	721	939	617	5	84	0.29	50	19	31	32	74	88	58	7%	104	41%	77%	26	46%	23%	4.46	7.6	48	130	$26
15 DET	341	55	8	30	18	258	265	306	440	746	758	738	6	78	0.29	44	22	33	31	95	111	77	9%	178	35%	69%	26	50%	38%	4.39	-1.1	67	181	$13
16 CLE	454	74	12	48	43	249	244	306	388	693	670	708	7	77	0.31	45	19	36	30	82	88	75	10%	105	45%	88%	27	26%	48%	4.22	-2.0	24	69	$25
1st Half	255	42	9	31	22	271	258	330	447	777	772	779	7	76	0.33	47	18	35	32	84	109	76	13%	106	39%	88%	14	29%	43%	5.32	6.0	40	114	$30
2nd Half	199	32	3	17	21	221	228	274	312	586	577	595	6	77	0.29	42	20	37	27	81	62	74	5%	94	53%	88%	13	23%	54%	3.02	-9.2	2	6	$18
17 Proj	**362**	**57**	**8**	**35**	**31**	**253**	**251**	**303**	**392**	**695**	**724**	**676**	**6**	**78**	**0.29**	**45**	**20**	**35**	**30**	**84**	**85**	**73**	**8%**	**133**	**45%**	**82%**				**4.10**	**-4.5**	**45**	**129**	**$20**

Descalso,Daniel

Age: 30	Bats: L	Pos: SS	Health	B	LIMA Plan	D
Ht: 5' 10"	Wt: 190		PT/Exp	F	Rand Var	-2
			Consist	C	MM	1221

More of a Coors Nudge than a Coors Bump; other than hr/f, there's nothing here we haven't seen glimpses of in less favorable environments. Positional flexibility could make him intriguing bench bat if he retains Denver address, but without the mile high air, he reverts to being mostly dead weight.

Yr Tm	AB	R	HR	RBI	SB	BA	xBA	OBP	SLG	OPS	vL	vR	bb%	ct%	Eye	G	L	F	h%	HctX	PX	xPX	hr/f	Spd	SBO	SB%	#Wk	DOM	DIS	RC/G	RAR	BPV	BPX	R$
12 STL	374	41	4	26	6	227	235	303	324	627	812	564	9	78	0.45	45	23	32	28	103	60	100	4%	140	9%	67%	27	19%	48%	3.14	-11.0	21	53	$2
13 STL	328	43	5	43	6	238	262	290	366	656	529	684	6	83	0.39	48	18	34	27	102	96	85	5%	86	13%	67%	27	41%	30%	3.44	-0.5	49	123	$6
14 STL	161	20	0	10	1	242	220	333	311	644	899	575	11	80	0.61	43	17	39	30	72	68	50	0%	94	8%	25%	26	27%	42%	3.19	-0.4	25	68	$0
15 COL	185	22	5	22	1	205	223	283	324	607	468	628	10	76	0.44	44	19	36	24	68	71	75	10%	119	6%	33%	27	30%	48%	2.83	-5.4	17	46	-$1
16 COL	250	38	8	38	3	264	264	349	424	773	732	782	12	78	0.61	44	24	32	31	92	96	99	13%	86	4%	100%	22	27%	36%	5.25	4.6	39	111	$7
1st Half	60	13	2	17	0	367	279	465	533	998	671	1071	15	78	0.85	43	30	28	44	108	92	82	15%	113	0%	0%	9	33%	33%	9.98	8.2	54	154	$6
2nd Half	190	25	6	21	3	232	260	312	389	701	753	691	11	77	0.53	44	22	34	27	87	98	105	12%	77	6%	100%	13	23%	38%	4.16	-1.8	35	100	$7
17 Proj	**174**	**25**	**4**	**24**	**2**	**254**	**247**	**338**	**381**	**719**	**699**	**723**	**11**	**78**	**0.56**	**44**	**22**	**34**	**31**	**86**	**78**	**83**	**9%**	**97**	**5%**	**58%**				**4.33**	**-0.7**	**23**	**64**	**$5**

Deshields Jr.,Delino

Age: 24	Bats: R	Pos: CF LF	Health	A	LIMA Plan	C
Ht: 5' 9"	Wt: 200		PT/Exp	C	Rand Var	0
			Consist	D	MM	1513

4-13-.209 with 8 SB in 182 AB at TEX. Oof. 2015 xBA suggested regression was coming, but declines in ct%, HctX made it so much worse. Despite sudden hr/f outburst, hard to see much power upside when more than half his batted balls hit dirt. Good bb% may spare him an Esix Sneadian fate, but these are still costly SB.

Yr Tm	AB	R	HR	RBI	SB	BA	xBA	OBP	SLG	OPS	vL	vR	bb%	ct%	Eye	G	L	F	h%	HctX	PX	xPX	hr/f	Spd	SBO	SB%	#Wk	DOM	DIS	RC/G	RAR	BPV	BPX	R$
12																																		
13																																		
14 aa	411	58	9	44	41	206		288	309	598			10	69	0.38				28		81			105	51%	73%				2.85		-3	-8	$17
15 TEX *	451	85	2	39	25	262	237	340	374	714	765	693	11	76	0.50	47	19	34	34	72	80	56	2%	162	24%	76%	25	32%	48%	4.43	0.4	41	111	$18
16 TEX *	389	65	6	26	25	217	217	296	306	603	541	614	10	69	0.36	55	17	28	30	57	66	51	12%	101	33%	69%	18	22%	50%	2.91	-16.9	-18	-51	$10
1st Half	272	40	4	20	17	214	215	290	301	591	395	661	10	66	0.32	56	19	25	31	45	68	55	11%	93	33%	69%	6	0%	67%	2.78	-14.6	-32	-91	$13
2nd Half	117	25	2	7	8	225	226	312	318	630	634	507	11	75	0.51	55	14	31	28	78	63	44	13%	108	33%	70%	12	33%	42%	3.22	-4.6	9	26	$5
17 Proj	**250**	**45**	**4**	**20**	**17**	**232**	**234**	**317**	**347**	**664**	**668**	**661**	**11**	**73**	**0.44**	**52**	**17**	**31**	**30**	**67**	**77**	**52**	**8%**	**134**	**33%**	**73%**				**3.58**	**-7.2**	**21**	**59**	**$10**

Desmond,Ian

Age: 31	Bats: R	Pos: CF LF	Health	A	LIMA Plan	C+
Ht: 6' 2"	Wt: 210		PT/Exp	A	Rand Var	-3
			Consist	C	MM	2425

Best R$ of his career, BUT... that 2nd half. Collapse didn't actually start until after Aug 1, when already-low FB% dropped to 22%, and xPX (37), hr/f (5%) disappeared. Without a reported injury, we're left speculating. That, plus BA/xBA gap, steady declines in xPX, create situation ripe for overpayment. Play it cool.

Yr Tm	AB	R	HR	RBI	SB	BA	xBA	OBP	SLG	OPS	vL	vR	bb%	ct%	Eye	G	L	F	h%	HctX	PX	xPX	hr/f	Spd	SBO	SB%	#Wk	DOM	DIS	RC/G	RAR	BPV	BPX	R$
12 WAS	513	72	25	73	21	292	279	335	511	845	902	828	6	78	0.27	48	18	35	33	112	142	115	18%	113	23%	78%	24	46%	33%	6.06	17.3	72	180	$27
13 WAS	600	77	20	80	21	280	265	331	453	784	766	789	7	76	0.30	43	22	34	34	101	126	100	13%	95	18%	78%	26	46%	31%	5.26	17.6	48	120	$28
14 WAS	593	73	24	91	24	255	247	313	430	743	771	734	7	69	0.25	50	18	32	33	97	136	107	18%	103	20%	83%	27	41%	33%	4.60	12.4	33	89	$26
15 WAS	583	69	19	62	13	233	229	290	384	674	757	653	7	68	0.24	53	16	31	31	83	113	92	15%	109	14%	72%	27	26%	48%	3.65	-15.1	11	30	$13
16 TEX	625	107	22	86	21	285	264	335	446	782	880	753	7	74	0.28	53	21	26	35	92	101	81	18%	115	16%	78%	26	46%	38%	5.28	16.2	28	80	$30
1st Half	322	60	15	52	14	317	281	371	525	896	1069	834	7	74	0.31	49	23	28	39	98	132	103	22%	102	18%	82%	14	50%	21%	7.26	24.0	50	143	$40
2nd Half	303	47	7	34	7	251	244	296	363	659	596	674	6	75	0.23	58	18	24	32	85	69	59	13%	129	13%	70%	12	42%	58%	3.58	-8.4	5	14	$18
17 Proj	**621**	**88**	**20**	**77**	**19**	**264**	**248**	**316**	**416**	**732**	**793**	**714**	**7**	**72**	**0.26**	**53**	**19**	**29**	**34**	**91**	**99**	**88**	**16%**	**114**	**16%**	**77%**				**4.50**	**-0.1**	**17**	**49**	**$25**

Diaz,Aledmys

Age: 26	Bats: R	Pos: SS	Health	B	LIMA Plan	A
Ht: 6' 1"	Wt: 195		PT/Exp	D	Rand Var	-2
			Consist	F	MM	3335

Surprise rookie breakout featured crazy highs (.423 BA, 94% ct, 160 PX in April), disappointing lows (fractured thumb in Aug, 2H BA/xBA slump), but overall, we get a good picture. FB%, HctX, xPX all support plus power, while bb%, Spd, past SBO hint at SB upside. But .265 xBA after May 1, so just don't expect .300 encore.

Yr Tm	AB	R	HR	RBI	SB	BA	xBA	OBP	SLG	OPS	vL	vR	bb%	ct%	Eye	G	L	F	h%	HctX	PX	xPX	hr/f	Spd	SBO	SB%	#Wk	DOM	DIS	RC/G	RAR	BPV	BPX	R$
12																																		
13																																		
14 aa	117	11	2	14	5	251		260	381	642			1	77	0.06				31		103			95	33%	67%				3.22		23	62	$2
15 a/a	425	43	9	37	4	225		269	349	618			6	80	0.31				26		85			91	13%	38%				2.89		31	84	$3
16 STL	404	71	17	65	4	300	284	369	510	879	725	941	9	85	0.68	46	16	39	32	109	118	108	13%	135	7%	50%	22	59%	14%	6.57	21.9	96	274	$18
1st Half	268	52	11	42	2	317	295	377	530	907	766	969	8	86	0.63	45	18	37	34	114	123	110	13%	127	5%	50%	14	64%	7%	7.23	20.0	98	280	$23
2nd Half	136	19	6	23	2	265	261	354	471	825	620	892	11	84	0.77	46	11	42	28	99	108	105	13%	144	10%	50%	8	50%	25%	5.43	3.8	89	254	$8
17 Proj	**502**	**65**	**19**	**65**	**8**	**274**	**261**	**348**	**461**	**809**	**653**	**868**	**9**	**82**	**0.57**	**46**	**14**	**40**	**30**	**105**	**108**	**107**	**12%**	**135**	**11%**	**52%**				**5.32**	**12.4**	**59**	**169**	**$20**

BRANDON KRUSE

Dickerson,Alex

Age: 27	Bats: L	Pos: LF	Health	A	LIMA Plan	B+
Ht: 6' 3"	Wt: 230		PT/Exp	D	Rand Var	0
			Consist	C	MM	4245

10-37-.257 with 5 SB in 253 AB at SD. 1st half included .382 BA, 41% hit rate at AAA, then bb%, HctX improvements in 2H (all in majors) provide foundation for BA growth. Age limits upside, but with those plate skills, a solid SLG and that LD/FB profile he's not far away from ... UP 20 HR, .280 BA

Yr	Tm	AB	R	HR	RBI	SB	BA	xBA	OBP	SLG	OPS	vL	vR	bb%	ct%	Eye	G	L	F	h%	HctX	PX	xPX	hr/f	Spd	SBO	SB%	#Wk	DOM	DIS	RC/G	RAR	BPV	BPX	R$
12																																			
13	aa	451	48	12	54	8	251		284	413	697			4	79	0.22				29		118			90	18%	50%				3.76		48	120	$11
14	aa	137	16	2	19	0	274		311	416	727			5	76	0.22				35		113			101	4%	0%				4.38		36	97	$2
15	SD *	467	53	8	46	3	243	254	288	380	667	0	667	6	74	0.24	20	40	40	31	128	101	84	0%	97	3%	100%	4	0%	75%	3.71	-13.9	19	51	$6
16	SD *	470	72	17	71	5	279	275	329	465	794	717	810	7	83	0.45	37	22	40	30	115	107	105	12%	92	5%	83%	17	53%	35%	5.43	10.6	62	177	$16
1st Half		240	36	9	40	1	296	275	325	476	801	0	797	4	84	0.27	39	22	39	32	90	101	101	29%	86	2%	100%	4	50%	25%	5.63	7.8	52	149	$18
2nd Half		230	36	8	31	4	261	277	341	452	793	740	811	10	83	0.63	37	22	41	29	117	113	106	10%	96	8%	80%	13	54%	38%	5.22	5.1	71	203	$15
17	Proj	**425**	**54**	**17**	**53**	**4**	**262**	**271**	**318**	**464**	**781**	**733**	**798**	**6**	**79**	**0.33**	**37**	**22**	**41**	**30**	**105**	**120**	**95**	**12%**	**96**	**6%**	**69%**				**4.93**	**5.9**	**55**	**156**	**$12**

Dickerson,Corey

Age: 28	Bats: L	Pos: LF DH	Health	C	LIMA Plan	B
Ht: 6' 2"	Wt: 210		PT/Exp	C	Rand Var	+3
			Consist	C	MM	4145

Is he still as valuable in TAM as in COL? PRO: Return to 500 AB says 2015 injuries no longer a factor. CON: Nearly everything else. Year-long HctX dive; struggles vL persist; ct% and power trends. In a year when everyone hit HRs, his 24 is pedestrian at best. At 28, there may stil be some life left, but don't chase it.

Yr	Tm	AB	R	HR	RBI	SB	BA	xBA	OBP	SLG	OPS	vL	vR	bb%	ct%	Eye	G	L	F	h%	HctX	PX	xPX	hr/f	Spd	SBO	SB%	#Wk	DOM	DIS	RC/G	RAR	BPV	BPX	R$
12	aa	266	34	13	32	6	274		313	508	821			5	81	0.29				30		143			104	16%	65%				5.42		82	205	$9
13	COL *	509	68	12	47	6	296	287	337	492	829	581	819	6	81	0.33	40	26	34	34	109	124	107	10%	153	16%	29%	14	64%	21%	5.42	13.3	85	213	$19
14	COL	436	74	24	76	8	312	298	364	567	931	724	985	8	77	0.37	37	27	36	36	123	176	135	20%	116	13%	53%	25	60%	28%	7.33	39.4	101	273	$28
15	COL *	252	32	11	33	0	296	293	325	514	839	662	938	4	76	0.18	38	30	32	35	123	149	136	19%	112	2%	0%	16	44%	25%	5.94	3.4	67	181	$9
16	TAM	510	57	24	70	0	245	256	293	469	761	589	807	6	74	0.25	38	17	45	29	95	144	119	14%	84	2%	0%	27	52%	33%	4.52	-14.7	49	140	$10
1st Half		233	22	13	34	0	215	242	264	446	710	485	749	6	72	0.24	38	15	47	24	99	143	120	16%	88	0%	0%	14	57%	29%	3.84	-11.9	42	120	$5
2nd Half		277	35	11	36	0	271	268	316	487	804	637	864	6	75	0.25	37	20	43	32	92	145	118	12%	86	4%	0%	13	46%	38%	5.17	-2.7	57	163	$14
17	Proj	**495**	**61**	**21**	**65**	**2**	**262**	**272**	**305**	**479**	**784**	**606**	**834**	**6**	**76**	**0.25**	**38**	**23**	**39**	**31**	**108**	**137**	**124**	**14%**	**100**	**6%**	**37%**				**4.89**	**6.3**	**47**	**135**	**$16**

Dietrich,Derek

Age: 27	Bats: L	Pos: 2B	Health	B	LIMA Plan	D+
Ht: 5' 11"	Wt: 200		PT/Exp	D	Rand Var	-4
			Consist	B	MM	3213

Gifted twice with playing time opportunities, but could not convert. 1st half hit rate spike boosted BA, then falling ct%, HctX in 2nd half made it easy to bench him when Dee Gordon returned. A multi-position past may offer him more playing time chances, but must solve LHP to earn his keep.

Yr	Tm	AB	R	HR	RBI	SB	BA	xBA	OBP	SLG	OPS	vL	vR	bb%	ct%	Eye	G	L	F	h%	HctX	PX	xPX	hr/f	Spd	SBO	SB%	#Wk	DOM	DIS	RC/G	RAR	BPV	BPX	R$
12	aa	133	18	3	14	0	233		263	358	622			4	69	0.13				31		95			103	4%	0%				3.01		-6	-15	$0
13	MIA *	433	61	17	54	3	226	256	285	414	699	786	644	8	72	0.29	40	25	35	28	90	136	114	16%	111	4%	100%	12	42%	33%	3.93	-1.6	45	113	$8
14	MIA *	240	41	9	28	2	235	246	281	399	680	372	762	6	75	0.26	43	19	38	28	99	114	100	11%	101	3%	100%	12	42%	42%	3.78	0.0	37	100	$5
15	MIA *	442	58	15	46	0	241	243	297	422	719	519	864	7	74	0.30	37	20	43	30	112	125	159	12%	106	5%	0%	18	44%	39%	4.03	-9.1	43	116	$7
16	MIA	351	39	7	42	1	279	245	374	425	798	556	852	8	76	0.38	40	22	38	35	86	93	99	7%	104	1%	100%	26	46%	31%	5.12	4.8	29	83	$8
1st Half		217	25	4	28	0	300	254	395	447	842	664	894	8	79	0.43	42	21	37	37	99	94	108	6%	99	0%	0%	14	50%	21%	5.84	8.2	39	111	$11
2nd Half		134	14	3	14	1	246	231	338	388	726	192	791	8	72	0.32	37	24	39	32	66	92	81	8%	110	3%	100%	12	42%	42%	4.09	-1.4	12	34	$3
17	Proj	**292**	**37**	**8**	**33**	**1**	**252**	**243**	**339**	**415**	**754**	**513**	**802**	**7**	**74**	**0.30**	**39**	**21**	**39**	**31**	**91**	**103**	**112**	**10%**	**104**	**3%**	**59%**				**4.32**	**-4.1**	**21**	**61**	**$7**

Donaldson,Josh

Age: 31	Bats: R	Pos: 3B	Health	A	LIMA Plan	C
Ht: 6' 1"	Wt: 215		PT/Exp	A	Rand Var	0
			Consist	C	MM	4345

BPV says he displayed even better skill in 2016 despite R$ drop. Walk rate, Eye entered elite territory, top-shelf HctX generated even more LD and FB. Plus, OPS growth vR (78% of his AB) continued. It's hard to imagine that he somehow had three bad weeks (11% DIS). Go the extra dollar.

Yr	Tm	AB	R	HR	RBI	SB	BA	xBA	OBP	SLG	OPS	vL	vR	bb%	ct%	Eye	G	L	F	h%	HctX	PX	xPX	hr/f	Spd	SBO	SB%	#Wk	DOM	DIS	RC/G	RAR	BPV	BPX	R$
12	OAK *	483	59	17	62	7	247	257	291	410	701	703	680	6	79	0.29	40	23	38	28	90	107	107	11%	70	10%	68%	17	35%	47%	3.98	-8.1	34	85	$11
13	OAK	579	89	24	93	5	301	282	384	499	883	1042	813	12	81	0.69	44	21	36	34	107	132	99	14%	103	4%	71%	27	48%	19%	6.92	47.4	86	215	$29
14	OAK	608	93	29	98	8	255	264	342	456	798	1007	727	11	79	0.58	45	13	41	28	118	138	126	15%	92	5%	100%	27	56%	30%	5.35	29.8	77	208	$24
15	TOR	620	122	41	123	6	297	297	371	568	939	1024	919	11	79	0.55	45	17	38	32	129	170	140	22%	85	3%	100%	27	74%	19%	7.71	53.6	99	268	$37
16	TOR	577	122	37	99	7	284	290	404	549	953	932	960	16	79	0.92	38	21	41	30	130	148	135	20%	104	4%	88%	27	74%	11%	7.84	49.3	101	289	$29
1st Half		312	73	20	56	6	298	295	410	583	994	1066	968	15	79	0.88	35	23	42	32	136	159	144	19%	119	6%	100%	14	71%	7%	8.74	33.0	113	323	$35
2nd Half		265	49	17	43	1	268	278	397	509	906	725	950	17	79	0.96	42	19	39	28	124	136	124	21%	75	2%	50%	13	77%	15%	6.86	15.0	84	240	$22
17	Proj	**583**	**112**	**34**	**103**	**6**	**280**	**282**	**380**	**523**	**903**	**932**	**895**	**13**	**79**	**0.73**	**42**	**19**	**39**	**30**	**124**	**139**	**130**	**19%**	**93**	**4%**	**86%**				**6.98**	**34.6**	**84**	**240**	**$30**

Dozier,Brian

Age: 30	Bats: R	Pos: 2B	Health	A	LIMA Plan	A
Ht: 6' 0"	Wt: 190		PT/Exp	A	Rand Var	0
			Consist	C	MM	4435

Just like ringing the carnival bell: harder contact with greater loft wins prize, but luck (like the 2H hr/f spike) cannot always be counted on. Ct% gains also pushed BA to positive side of ledger, while career best SB% delivered extra value. Should regress a bit because 29-HR half-seasons are not repeatable feats.

Yr	Tm	AB	R	HR	RBI	SB	BA	xBA	OBP	SLG	OPS	vL	vR	bb%	ct%	Eye	G	L	F	h%	HctX	PX	xPX	hr/f	Spd	SBO	SB%	#Wk	DOM	DIS	RC/G	RAR	BPV	BPX	R$
12	MIN *	497	45	7	47	11	223	232	264	318	581	775	547	5	81	0.29	42	21	38	26	77	65	80	6%	107	15%	73%	15	20%	40%	2.74	-21.8	19	48	$4
13	MIN	558	72	18	66	14	244	256	312	414	726	978	649	8	78	0.43	38	21	41	28	89	118	99	10%	125	16%	67%	27	48%	33%	4.19	7.8	65	163	$16
14	MIN	598	112	23	71	21	242	257	345	416	762	804	743	13	78	0.69	37	20	43	27	95	124	97	11%	105	16%	75%	27	44%	19%	4.77	24.9	72	195	$24
15	MIN	628	101	28	77	12	236	261	307	444	751	762	746	9	76	0.41	33	23	44	27	100	138	129	13%	105	12%	75%	26	58%	19%	4.48	3.7	67	181	$18
16	MIN	615	104	42	99	18	268	276	340	546	886	965	862	9	78	0.44	36	16	48	28	109	159	137	18%	127	14%	90%	26	65%	15%	6.47	30.8	96	274	$30
1st Half		286	45	13	41	6	262	266	345	476	820	1156	725	10	81	0.58	36	18	45	28	95	120	104	12%	124	8%	100%	14	57%	14%	5.63	6.9	81	231	$20
2nd Half		329	59	29	58	12	274	287	335	608	943	808	985	8	74	0.35	36	14	50	28	121	196	168	24%	124	20%	86%	12	75%	17%	7.19	22.5	109	311	$39
17	Proj	**604**	**99**	**35**	**85**	**17**	**253**	**268**	**326**	**496**	**822**	**868**	**806**	**9**	**77**	**0.45**	**36**	**18**	**45**	**27**	**103**	**142**	**127**	**16%**	**119**	**14%**	**82%**				**5.48**	**12.0**	**79**	**225**	**$27**

Dozier,Hunter

Age: 25	Bats: R	Pos: RF	Health	A	LIMA Plan	D
Ht: 6' 4"	Wt: 220		PT/Exp	C	Rand Var	-3
			Consist	C	MM	3211

0-1-.211 in 19 AB at KC. In his third tour of the upper minors, he cut the strikeouts, kept the walks and resuscitated his prospect status with an .899 OPS. Not yet a finished product, and the final step is the toughest, but his first round pedigree is his friend for now. One to tuck away.

Yr	Tm	AB	R	HR	RBI	SB	BA	xBA	OBP	SLG	OPS	vL	vR	bb%	ct%	Eye	G	L	F	h%	HctX	PX	xPX	hr/f	Spd	SBO	SB%	#Wk	DOM	DIS	RC/G	RAR	BPV	BPX	R$
12																																			
13																																			
14	aa	234	26	3	17	2	185		262	271	533			9	68	0.33				26		80			93	9%	52%				2.17		-13	-35	-$3
15	aa	475	50	9	41	5	183		238	294	532			7	65	0.21				26		95			90	8%	67%				2.17		-19	-51	-$3
16	KC *	505	65	17	59	5	255	252	313	439	752	550	545	8	71	0.30	45	18	36	33	52	133	44	0%	87	6%	82%	3	0%	100%	4.72	-1.1	35	100	$12
1st Half		293	33	11	36	4	265	250	319	452	770			7	70	0.26				35		135			79	7%	77%				4.99		27	77	$15
2nd Half		212	33	6	23	2	240	258	306	421	727	550	545	9	73	0.35	45	18	36	30	54	131	44	0%	99	3%	100%	3	0%	100%	4.37	-3.3	46	131	$7
17	Proj	**129**	**16**	**3**	**13**	**1**	**233**	**232**	**293**	**379**	**672**	**672**	**672**	**8**	**69**	**0.27**	**44**	**20**	**36**	**31**		**109**		**10%**	**93**	**6%**	**75%**				**3.69**	**-3.9**	**1**	**4**	**$2**

Drury,Brandon

Age: 24	Bats: R	Pos: LF RF 3B	Health	A	LIMA Plan	B+
Ht: 6' 2"	Wt: 190		PT/Exp	C	Rand Var	-1
			Consist	D	MM	3045

Made the team out of spring training (.389/ 4 HR), faced the common "success-struggle-growth" cycle, then finished with a flourish (.357/.417/.632 Sept). Still some work to do (bb%, G/F split, weekly DOM/DIS), but dual 3B/OF eligibility should provide ample opportunities.

Yr	Tm	AB	R	HR	RBI	SB	BA	xBA	OBP	SLG	OPS	vL	vR	bb%	ct%	Eye	G	L	F	h%	HctX	PX	xPX	hr/f	Spd	SBO	SB%	#Wk	DOM	DIS	RC/G	RAR	BPV	BPX	R$
12																																			
13																																			
14	aa	105	10	3	11	0	272		309	435	744			5	80	0.27				31		119			87	0%	0%				4.71		55	149	$1
15	ARI *	580	51	6	53	3	260	267	291	362	653	913	434	4	84	0.27	56	21	23	30	106	75	109	18%	77	9%	25%	5	20%	40%	3.40	-22.6	29	78	$8
16	ARI	461	59	16	53	1	282	271	329	458	786	804	779	6	78	0.31	50	20	30	33	105	111	97	15%	105	2%	50%	27	48%	37%	5.28	8.5	48	137	$13
1st Half		224	25	8	19	0	268	272	310	438	747	651	791	5	79	0.25	51	21	28	31	112	103	103	16%	108	2%	0%	14	43%	50%	4.56	0.7	41	117	$9
2nd Half		237	34	8	34	1	295	272	346	477	823	980	769	7	78	0.37	49	19	31	35	98	119	91	14%	107	2%	100%	13	54%	23%	6.03	10.3	56	160	$17
17	Proj	**504**	**56**	**18**	**54**	**2**	**271**	**277**	**315**	**449**	**764**	**912**	**690**	**5**	**81**	**0.29**	**51**	**20**	**29**	**31**	**105**	**110**	**101**	**15%**	**99**	**4%**	**33%**				**4.74**	**4.1**	**34**	**98**	**$15**

MATT DODGE

Duda,Lucas

Age: 31	Bats: L	Pos: 1B	Health F	LIMA Plan C	
Ht: 6' 5"	Wt: 225		PT/Exp C	Rand Var +4	
			Consist B	MM 4025	

Second consecutive season dealing with back issues; this year's (stress fracture) limited him to 47 games. Impact of injury on HctX, PX, and FB%—the main components of his game—shouldn't be minimized. Still needs to state his case vL (lifetime .224 BA, 65% ct%) to avoid pigeonholing himself as full-on platoon player.

Yr	Tm	AB	R	HR	RBI	SB	BA	xBA	OBP	SLG	OPS	vL	vR	bb%	ct%	Eye	G	L	F	h%	HctX	PX	xPX	hr/f	Spd	SBO	SB%	#Wk	DOM	DIS	RC/G	RAR	BPV	BPX	R$
12	NYM *	497	52	17	63	1	233	222	313	374	687	662	745	10	71	0.40	35	23	42	30	118	99	134	13%	62	1%	100%	23	22%	57%	3.90	-22.7	3	8	$7
13	NYM *	380	50	15	38	1	222	221	333	388	721	610	831	14	68	0.52	32	20	48	29	119	130	181	14%	79	3%	16%	18	39%	33%	4.12	-5.4	30	75	$4
14	NYM	514	74	30	92	3	253	263	349	481	830	516	915	12	74	0.51	31	20	49	29	132	165	181	16%	59	4%	60%	27	56%	15%	5.55	20.6	70	189	$20
15	NYM	471	67	27	73	0	244	263	352	486	838	878	823	12	71	0.48	27	22	51	29	120	174	168	16%	70	2%	0%	25	52%	32%	5.44	0.9	70	189	$13
16	NYM	153	20	7	23	0	229	259	302	412	714	454	776	9	76	0.42	37	24	39	25	102	110	110	15%	74	0%	0%	10	40%	40%	4.05	-5.9	36	103	$1
1st Half		130	16	7	19	0	231	261	297	431	727	271	834	8	78	0.38	36	22	42	24	104	114	114	16%	71	0%	0%	7	43%	43%	4.15	-3.7	41	117	$2
2nd Half		23	4	0	4	0	217	250	333	304	638	1400	439	15	70	0.57	44	31	25	31	88	84	85	0%	94	0%	0%	3	33%	33%	3.31	-1.3	5	14	-$3
17	**Proj**	**405**	**53**	**21**	**60**	**1**	**240**	**247**	**333**	**445**	**778**	**573**	**842**	**11**	**72**	**0.45**	**32**	**21**	**46**	**28**	**118**	**129**	**154**	**15%**	**64**	**2%**	**41%**				**4.79**	**-3.7**	**27**	**76**	**$9**

Duffy,Matt

Age: 26	Bats: R	Pos: 3B	Health C	LIMA Plan B	
Ht: 6' 2"	Wt: 170		PT/Exp C	Rand Var +2	
			Consist C	MM 1435	

ROY runner-up lost half-season to Achilles injury while dealing with league and position switches. Power regression continued (had 65 PX, 5% hr/f in 2H of 2015), low OBP undercut speed, while plate skills were flat across the board. Still a relative unknown, he'd benefit from healthier, less disruptive 2017 to define his value.

Yr	Tm	AB	R	HR	RBI	SB	BA	xBA	OBP	SLG	OPS	vL	vR	bb%	ct%	Eye	G	L	F	h%	HctX	PX	xPX	hr/f	Spd	SBO	SB%	#Wk	DOM	DIS	RC/G	RAR	BPV	BPX	R$
12																																			
13																																			
14	SF *	427	48	2	59	16	291	267	347	379	726	888	300	8	79	0.41	41	33	26	36	80	72	56	0%	120	17%	75%	11	18%	55%	4.74	17.5	28	76	$17
15	SF	573	77	12	77	12	295	276	334	428	762	642	803	5	83	0.31	53	21	27	34	103	83	90	9%	134	8%	100%	27	44%	26%	5.24	13.3	52	141	$24
16	2 TM	333	41	5	28	8	258	263	310	357	668	702	654	6	84	0.43	50	21	29	29	90	59	67	6%	133	15%	62%	17	35%	24%	3.65	-6.4	38	109	$7
1st Half		257	32	4	21	8	253	270	313	358	671	778	632	7	84	0.50	48	24	28	29	97	62	76	6%	137	18%	67%	12	42%	17%	3.67	-6.1	45	129	$9
2nd Half		76	9	1	7	0	276	227	300	355	655	477	736	4	83	0.23	56	14	30	32	63	50	38	5%	118	5%	0%	5	20%	40%	3.58	-1.9	17	49	-$1
17	**Proj**	**496**	**62**	**7**	**55**	**10**	**274**	**262**	**319**	**376**	**695**	**684**	**699**	**6**	**83**	**0.34**	**51**	**21**	**28**	**32**	**86**	**62**	**67**	**6%**	**133**	**11%**	**69%**				**4.10**	**-11.2**	**24**	**69**	**$16**

Duvall,Adam

Age: 28	Bats: R	Pos: LF	Health A	LIMA Plan B+	
Ht: 6' 1"	Wt: 220		PT/Exp B	Rand Var 0	
			Consist B	MM 4225	

The perfect union of FB% and PX, but will marriage last? NO: ct% spells trouble; FB% likely unrepeatable; PX, hr/f were earthbound in 2nd half. YES: Eye, bb% nearly doubled from 1st to 2nd half; FB% actually rose after June; HctX, xPX stable all year. VERDICT: Enjoy HR honeymoon, but expect some BA-related spats.

Yr	Tm	AB	R	HR	RBI	SB	BA	xBA	OBP	SLG	OPS	vL	vR	bb%	ct%	Eye	G	L	F	h%	HctX	PX	xPX	hr/f	Spd	SBO	SB%	#Wk	DOM	DIS	RC/G	RAR	BPV	BPX	R$
12																																			
13	aa	385	43	11	41	1	203		251	350	601			6	78	0.29				23		102			105	4%	55%				2.78		39	98	$0
14	SF *	432	51	18	63	1	219	243	258	395	653	525	629	5	72	0.19	38	21	42	26	105	132	155	14%	75	2%	100%	11	27%	45%	3.34	-5.8	27	73	$7
15	CIN *	561	62	31	77	4	224	248	265	444	709	498	895	5	70	0.18	29	24	47	26	111	153	129	28%	69	5%	77%	6	50%	50%	3.86	-14.6	34	92	$11
16	CIN	552	85	33	103	6	241	256	297	498	795	795	795	7	70	0.25	34	19	47	28	111	163	155	18%	104	11%	55%	27	44%	33%	4.77	2.3	59	169	$17
1st Half		279	45	22	58	2	254	288	292	570	862	783	885	5	71	0.17	33	22	45	28	112	201	158	24%	75	17%	29%	14	57%	36%	5.23	6.5	79	226	$21
2nd Half		273	40	11	45	4	227	224	301	425	726	808	704	9	70	0.33	35	17	48	28	110	124	152	12%	136	6%	100%	13	31%	31%	4.24	-1.8	38	109	$13
17	**Proj**	**557**	**76**	**33**	**90**	**5**	**232**	**252**	**291**	**475**	**766**	**635**	**816**	**6**	**70**	**0.23**	**33**	**21**	**46**	**27**	**110**	**154**	**146**	**18%**	**97**	**7%**	**66%**				**4.37**	**-1.4**	**46**	**131**	**$17**

Dyson,Jarrod

Age: 32	Bats: L	Pos: CF RF	Health B	LIMA Plan C+	
Ht: 5' 9"	Wt: 165		PT/Exp D	Rand Var 0	
			Consist A	MM 1543	

1-25-.278 with 30 SB in 299 AB at KC. Showed again how part-timer with single elite skill can deliver value. In this case, it was coupling baserunning proficiencies with pronounced Eye/ct% improvements and finding LD stroke in 2nd half. Even with regression, GB profile, Spd, and green light are givens. Pay for a repeat.

Yr	Tm	AB	R	HR	RBI	SB	BA	xBA	OBP	SLG	OPS	vL	vR	bb%	ct%	Eye	G	L	F	h%	HctX	PX	xPX	hr/f	Spd	SBO	SB%	#Wk	DOM	DIS	RC/G	RAR	BPV	BPX	R$
12	KC *	355	60	0	12	34	261	250	323	332	655	510	689	8	83	0.52	57	19	24	32	89	44	56	0%	194	38%	85%	25	20%	48%	3.99	-9.1	42	105	$14
13	KC *	265	36	2	18	37	231	248	293	324	617	531	741	8	78	0.39	58	17	25	29	70	66	68	5%	144	64%	86%	21	33%	33%	3.52	-6.2	24	60	$14
14	KC	260	33	1	24	36	269	233	324	327	651	604	663	8	80	0.42	63	14	23	33	56	37	39	2%	163	52%	84%	27	19%	48%	4.09	1.5	16	43	$17
15	KC	200	31	2	18	26	250	278	311	380	691	578	715	7	82	0.38	54	23	23	30	68	77	28	6%	162	60%	90%	26	42%	38%	4.29	-2.8	51	138	$12
16	KC *	321	51	1	26	33	275	280	334	378	712	1006	698	8	86	0.65	56	20	24	32	60	57	32	2%	155	42%	82%	25	52%	24%	4.66	-0.4	56	160	$18
1st Half		160	22	0	10	15	252	266	326	315	641	830	642	10	86	0.80	61	16	22	29	44	44	19	0%	118	36%	83%	12	42%	33%	3.75	-4.5	37	106	$15
2nd Half		161	29	1	16	18	298	289	347	441	788	1111	748	6	86	0.50	51	23	26	34	74	71	43	3%	167	49%	82%	13	62%	15%	5.64	4.3	67	191	$22
17	**Proj**	**259**	**40**	**1**	**22**	**30**	**267**	**273**	**326**	**373**	**699**	**716**	**696**	**7**	**84**	**0.49**	**56**	**20**	**24**	**31**	**64**	**58**	**36**	**3%**	**159**	**50%**	**85%**				**4.47**	**-0.3**	**52**	**150**	**$17**

Eaton,Adam

Age: 28	Bats: L	Pos: RF CF	Health B	LIMA Plan B+	
Ht: 5' 9"	Wt: 180		PT/Exp A	Rand Var -1	
			Consist A	MM 2445	

Line by line, a carbon copy of 2015, with best full-season HctX, xPX driving 2nd half power gain. Notable that season PX/FB% aren't truly aligned with modest power stroke, nor is middling SB total reflective of Spd (thanks, SBO). Solid peripheral history gives him projectability, and peak age could still provide HR/SB surprise.

Yr	Tm	AB	R	HR	RBI	SB	BA	xBA	OBP	SLG	OPS	vL	vR	bb%	ct%	Eye	G	L	F	h%	HctX	PX	xPX	hr/f	Spd	SBO	SB%	#Wk	DOM	DIS	RC/G	RAR	BPV	BPX	R$
12	ARI *	613	108	7	38	32	312	274	367	440	807	890	737	8	83	0.51	64	12	24	37	108	90	91	13%	142	26%	67%	4	50%	25%	5.76	18.3	65	163	$31
13	ARI *	285	43	4	25	5	235	261	282	341	623	708	665	6	81	0.35	57	19	25	28	84	71	63	6%	131	11%	71%	13	31%	23%	3.19	-7.8	36	90	$4
14	CHW	486	76	1	35	15	300	278	362	401	763	724	778	8	83	0.52	60	20	20	36	87	74	44	1%	158	16%	63%	23	43%	30%	5.05	15.9	57	154	$19
15	CHW	610	98	14	56	18	287	267	361	431	792	648	847	9	79	0.44	51	22	27	35	91	93	69	11%	144	14%	69%	26	38%	38%	5.29	13.6	51	138	$26
16	CHW	619	91	14	59	14	284	276	362	428	790	726	812	9	81	0.55	54	21	26	33	104	83	90	11%	130	10%	74%	27	48%	15%	5.33	16.8	52	149	$22
1st Half		320	40	4	27	9	272	275	356	391	747	835	719	9	83	0.57	60	19	21	32	87	66	67	7%	143	13%	75%	14	43%	14%	4.63	1.1	46	131	$19
2nd Half		299	51	10	32	5	298	278	368	468	836	622	915	9	80	0.53	47	23	31	34	123	102	116	14%	109	8%	71%	13	54%	15%	6.14	13.5	56	160	$25
17	**Proj**	**608**	**95**	**16**	**55**	**16**	**288**	**280**	**360**	**444**	**804**	**711**	**838**	**9**	**81**	**0.49**	**54**	**21**	**26**	**33**	**100**	**91**	**80**	**12%**	**136**	**13%**	**69%**				**5.47**	**13.3**	**52**	**149**	**$27**

Eibner,Brett

Age: 28	Bats: R	Pos: RF	Health A	LIMA Plan D	
Ht: 6' 4"	Wt: 225		PT/Exp D	Rand Var +2	
			Consist C	MM 2201	

6-22-.193 in 187 AB at KC/OAK. Former 2nd-round pick took six years to get to bigs. Overall hit tool lags (.244 BA in 2,037 MiLB AB) so sub-Mendoza MLB BA was no surprise, but HctX, xPX were in conflict with big power reputation. Expect a few bombs, a batting average hit, and perhaps a few more rides on AAA shuttle.

Yr	Tm	AB	R	HR	RBI	SB	BA	xBA	OBP	SLG	OPS	vL	vR	bb%	ct%	Eye	G	L	F	h%	HctX	PX	xPX	hr/f	Spd	SBO	SB%	#Wk	DOM	DIS	RC/G	RAR	BPV	BPX	R$
12																																			
13	aa	441	56	13	31	5	210		276	372	647			8	63	0.24				30		126			162	9%	60%				3.25		19	48	$3
14	aaa	274	28	4	18	3	192		246	290	536			7	67	0.22				27		85			108	10%	58%				2.20		-14	-38	-$2
15	aaa	389	49	13	61	8	252		302	411	713			7	76	0.30				30		108			81	8%	100%				4.34		31	84	$12
16	2 AL *	384	55	15	50	4	217	234	304	391	694	715	544	11	70	0.42	42	18	39	27	70	114	72	11%	90	8%	56%	19	42%	37%	3.78	-5.8	24	69	$5
1st Half		224	36	9	33	4	246	248	328	427	756	1082	657	11	69	0.39	33	30	37	32	100	123	133	10%	99	9%	77%	6	67%	17%	4.75	2.0	27	77	$10
2nd Half		160	18	6	17	0	177	227	269	340	609	644	506	11	72	0.46	45	15	40	21	64	103	57	11%	93	6%	0%	13	31%	46%	2.67	-9.3	24	69	-$3
17	**Proj**	**191**	**24**	**6**	**22**	**2**	**215**	**230**	**284**	**361**	**646**	**755**	**568**	**9**	**71**	**0.34**	**40**	**21**	**39**	**27**	**78**	**97**	**87**	**11%**	**93**	**8%**	**64%**				**3.31**	**-8.2**	**7**	**21**	**$3**

Ellsbury,Jacoby

Age: 33	Bats: L	Pos: CF	Health C	LIMA Plan B+	
Ht: 6' 1"	Wt: 185		PT/Exp A	Rand Var +1	
			Consist C	MM 1435	

He's always vexed me: high-profile, oft-injured, overvalued (him, not me). Lifetime .286/.342/.419 isn't that remarkable. Sure, there are the SBs. But Spd is waning and SBO is in free-fall. Ditto for PX. R$ says he's been a different hitter last two years, but no matter. The vexing will continue. When all else fails, nudge the trend.

Yr	Tm	AB	R	HR	RBI	SB	BA	xBA	OBP	SLG	OPS	vL	vR	bb%	ct%	Eye	G	L	F	h%	HctX	PX	xPX	hr/f	Spd	SBO	SB%	#Wk	DOM	DIS	RC/G	RAR	BPV	BPX	R$
12	BOS	303	43	4	26	14	271	259	313	370	682	648	701	6	86	0.44	47	20	33	30	85	70	91	5%	104	22%	82%	15	53%	20%	4.15	-6.2	44	110	$9
13	BOS	577	92	9	53	52	298	276	355	426	781	641	863	8	84	0.51	51	21	28	34	107	85	78	7%	138	33%	93%	25	56%	20%	5.90	26.6	63	158	$39
14	NYY	575	71	16	70	39	271	276	328	419	747	828	711	8	84	0.53	42	25	34	30	103	98	87	10%	110	28%	89%	25	60%	16%	5.06	19.4	64	173	$31
15	NYY	452	66	7	33	21	257	248	318	345	663	652	669	7	81	0.41	45	24	31	30	79	58	56	6%	132	24%	70%	21	24%	43%	3.61	-12.1	26	70	$15
16	NYY	551	71	9	56	20	263	267	330	374	703	618	744	9	85	0.64	46	23	31	30	91	64	67	6%	115	17%	71%	27	30%	22%	4.22	-2.3	44	126	$17
1st Half		267	35	3	25	16	277	272	347	397	744	655	787	9	86	0.71	50	20	30	31	96	68	77	4%	135	28%	73%	14	29%	21%	4.75	1.9	58	166	$23
2nd Half		284	36	6	31	4	250	263	313	352	665	579	704	9	84	0.59	43	25	32	28	87	60	57	8%	84	7%	67%	13	31%	23%	3.74	-6.5	28	80	$12
17	**Proj**	**514**	**69**	**9**	**50**	**18**	**260**	**263**	**322**	**369**	**692**	**649**	**712**	**8**	**84**	**0.54**	**45**	**23**	**31**	**30**	**90**	**64**	**68**	**7%**	**115**	**17%**	**72%**				**4.04**	**-7.1**	**38**	**109**	**$18**

ROB CARROLL

Encarnacion,Edwin

Age: 34 Bats: R Pos: DH 1B | Ht: 6' 2" Wt: 215
Health B | PT/Exp A | Consist B | LIMA Plan A | Rand Var 0 | MM 4155

Bottom line consistency speaks volumes: Five years of averaging almost 39 HR, 110 RBI and a .360+ OBP. Yes, there are signs of aging: some ct% and HctX slippage, a FB% decline, even the fraying xPX are warnings. But he remains a gold standard among run-producers, and money-in-the-bank that won't kill your BA.

Yr	Tm	AB	R	HR	RBI	SB	BA	xBA	OBP	SLG	OPS	vL	vR	bb%	ct%	Eye	G	L	F	h%	HctX	PX	xPX	hr/f	Spd	SBO	SB%	#Wk	DOM	DIS	RC/G	RAR	BPV	BPX	R$
12	TOR	542	93	42	110	13	280	285	384	557	941	1086	892	13	83	0.89	33	18	49	27	131	157	153	19%	83	9%	81%	27	81%	7%	7.47	39.7	110	275	$31
13	TOR	530	90	36	104	7	272	311	370	534	904	859	916	13	88	1.32	35	22	43	25	135	150	152	18%	73	5%	88%	25	84%	8%	6.95	37.1	124	310	$28
14	TOR	477	75	34	98	2	268	300	354	547	901	870	909	12	83	0.76	36	16	47	26	137	176	153	18%	81	2%	100%	22	68%	14%	6.75	36.9	121	327	$24
15	TOR	528	94	39	111	3	277	297	372	557	929	836	950	13	81	0.79	36	19	45	27	129	166	142	20%	59	3%	60%	27	81%	4%	7.17	25.9	104	281	$28
16	TOR	601	99	42	127	2	263	284	357	529	886	902	881	13	77	0.63	38	20	41	28	118	155	137	22%	60	1%	100%	27	78%	7%	6.54	18.1	77	220	$24
1st Half		310	54	22	76	2	265	294	357	545	903	1035	860	12	77	0.61	36	22	42	28	116	166	141	21%	57	2%	100%	14	71%	14%	6.74	11.1	86	246	$27
2nd Half		291	45	20	51	0	261	269	356	512	868	688	902	13	77	0.65	41	19	41	28	119	144	132	22%	70	0%	0%	13	85%	0%	6.33	7.0	71	203	$21
17	**Proj**	**551**	**92**	**38**	**110**	**3**	**265**	**286**	**358**	**528**	**886**	**858**	**893**	**13**	**80**	**0.71**	**38**	**19**	**42**	**27**	**125**	**148**	**142**	**20%**	**67**	**2%**	**80%**				**6.53**	**16.4**	**79**	**227**	**$24**

Escobar,Alcides

Age: 30 Bats: R Pos: SS | Ht: 6' 1" Wt: 175
Health A | PT/Exp A | Consist B | LIMA Plan B+ | Rand Var 0 | MM 1535

Apart from a vL/R splits reversal and a few more HR, a carbon copy of 2015. SBs drove value; speed and ct% kept BA barely above water. Sub-par power, HctX and track record suggest that anything more requires h% luck and a return of his green light on the basepaths. With these... UP: 2014. But don't pay for it.

Yr	Tm	AB	R	HR	RBI	SB	BA	xBA	OBP	SLG	OPS	vL	vR	bb%	ct%	Eye	G	L	F	h%	HctX	PX	xPX	hr/f	Spd	SBO	SB%	#Wk	DOM	DIS	RC/G	RAR	BPV	BPX	R$
12	KC	605	68	5	52	35	293	271	331	390	721	676	739	4	83	0.27	53	23	24	34	76	65	51	4%	144	25%	88%	27	33%	26%	4.73	14.0	40	100	$25
13	KC	607	57	4	52	22	234	250	259	300	559	620	532	3	86	0.23	46	23	31	27	75	45	60	3%	141	17%	100%	26	23%	27%	2.74	-12.5	31	78	$11
14	KC	579	74	3	50	31	285	265	317	377	694	784	663	4	86	0.28	44	24	32	33	82	70	62	2%	140	25%	84%	27	41%	22%	4.31	18.7	50	135	$25
15	KC	612	76	3	47	17	257	255	293	320	614	653	598	4	88	0.35	48	22	30	29	80	41	53	2%	138	14%	77%	27	37%	22%	3.18	-22.0	35	95	$14
16	KC	637	57	7	55	17	261	256	292	350	642	584	660	4	85	0.28	50	20	30	30	77	52	49	4%	137	13%	81%	27	44%	48%	3.55	-14.0	32	91	$14
1st Half		349	29	1	21	11	264	250	284	324	608	471	640	3	85	0.20	53	19	28	31	71	40	50	1%	121	18%	73%	14	36%	57%	3.18	-13.2	17	49	$15
2nd Half		288	28	6	34	6	257	263	301	382	683	670	688	6	84	0.38	46	21	32	29	84	67	48	8%	149	8%	100%	13	54%	38%	4.03	-3.7	49	140	$14
17	**Proj**	**603**	**64**	**6**	**53**	**19**	**263**	**260**	**299**	**350**	**649**	**652**	**647**	**4**	**86**	**0.32**	**48**	**22**	**30**	**30**	**79**	**51**	**53**	**4%**	**142**	**15%**	**84%**				**3.65**	**-14.4**	**31**	**88**	**$18**

Escobar,Eduardo

Age: 28 Bats: B Pos: SS 3B | Ht: 5' 10" Wt: 175
Health A | PT/Exp C | Consist B | LIMA Plan D+ | Rand Var +2 | MM 1123

Recent PX/xPX gains were M.I.A. all year. 1st half contact dive accompanied big LD spike; both turned around in 2nd half. Only plate skills remained consistent, exceeding career norms in 2nd half—when depressed h% took over. Age, health say he can rebound, but ceiling, role uncertainty look more like "end-gamer."

Yr	Tm	AB	R	HR	RBI	SB	BA	xBA	OBP	SLG	OPS	vL	vR	bb%	ct%	Eye	G	L	F	h%	HctX	PX	xPX	hr/f	Spd	SBO	SB%	#Wk	DOM	DIS	RC/G	RAR	BPV	BPX	R$
12	2 AL *	269	34	1	17	6	207	227	257	270	526	844	419	6	78	0.30	51	21	28	26	80	41	42	0%	145	11%	84%	19	26%	68%	2.28	-13.6	3	8	-$1
13	MIN *	331	39	6	30	4	251	244	300	383	683	655	619	7	77	0.31	42	21	37	31	77	97	94	6%	130	11%	51%	18	33%	39%	3.76	3.3	41	103	$5
14	MIN	433	52	6	37	1	275	264	315	406	721	877	654	5	79	0.26	41	24	35	34	99	110	93	5%	110	2%	50%	27	41%	26%	4.44	15.6	48	130	$10
15	MIN	409	48	12	58	2	262	267	309	445	754	789	737	6	79	0.33	42	19	39	31	102	125	118	10%	106	6%	40%	27	44%	30%	4.62	2.7	63	170	$10
16	MIN	352	32	6	37	1	236	240	280	338	618	552	648	6	80	0.29	39	23	37	28	84	63	73	6%	85	5%	25%	25	36%	44%	3.03	-13.5	7	20	$2
1st Half		182	17	2	20	1	258	237	284	357	641	757	603	4	77	0.17	35	27	39	32	75	64	64	4%	107	7%	33%	12	25%	50%	3.36	-6.0	2	6	$4
2nd Half		170	15	4	17	0	212	236	276	318	593	412	706	8	82	0.45	44	20	36	24	95	62	82	8%	69	3%	0%	13	46%	38%	2.72	-9.3	15	43	$0
17	**Proj**	**328**	**34**	**5**	**33**	**1**	**245**	**246**	**293**	**361**	**654**	**644**	**659**	**6**	**79**	**0.32**	**41**	**22**	**37**	**29**	**92**	**76**	**88**	**6%**	**96**	**5%**	**39%**				**3.47**	**-9.7**	**13**	**36**	**$5**

Escobar,Yunel

Age: 34 Bats: R Pos: 3B | Ht: 6' 2" Wt: 200
Health B | PT/Exp A | Consist C | LIMA Plan B+ | Rand Var -3 | MM 1035

So the question now is who owns his soul and for how much? Average remained largely intact, fueled by shift-neutralizing all-fields approach and more h% luck. Rock-solid plate skills and soaring GB% prevailed even as HctX and anemic power waned. Do you feel lucky? It's the ultimate BA-only profile with... DN: .260 BA.

Yr	Tm	AB	R	HR	RBI	SB	BA	xBA	OBP	SLG	OPS	vL	vR	bb%	ct%	Eye	G	L	F	h%	HctX	PX	xPX	hr/f	Spd	SBO	SB%	#Wk	DOM	DIS	RC/G	RAR	BPV	BPX	R$
12	TOR	558	58	9	51	5	253	261	300	344	644	644	643	6	87	0.50	56	19	25	28	88	57	69	7%	95	4%	83%	27	44%	22%	3.51	-17.0	38	95	$8
13	TAM	508	61	9	56	4	256	266	332	366	698	750	674	10	86	0.78	53	19	27	28	117	76	98	8%	93	5%	50%	27	59%	19%	4.07	1.8	53	133	$10
14	TAM	476	33	7	39	1	258	244	324	340	664	689	656	8	87	0.72	49	20	31	28	105	57	75	6%	76	1%	50%	25	56%	20%	3.72	0.7	37	100	$6
15	WAS	535	75	9	56	2	314	275	375	415	790	760	800	8	87	0.64	55	22	23	35	105	65	72	8%	105	2%	50%	26	46%	19%	5.61	15.0	49	132	$20
16	LAA	517	68	5	39	0	304	271	355	391	745	852	714	7	87	0.60	58	21	21	34	96	56	64	5%	106	2%	0%	26	42%	23%	4.94	2.0	41	117	$14
1st Half		283	34	3	22	0	318	276	367	417	784	986	726	7	87	0.58	57	22	22	36	97	66	68	6%	89	2%	0%	14	50%	21%	5.53	4.9	44	126	$16
2nd Half		234	34	2	17	0	286	268	340	359	699	695	700	8	87	0.61	60	21	20	32	95	44	60	5%	124	1%	0%	12	33%	25%	4.28	-4.0	36	103	$11
17	**Proj**	**516**	**64**	**7**	**44**	**1**	**288**	**268**	**347**	**377**	**724**	**759**	**713**	**8**	**87**	**0.65**	**56**	**21**	**23**	**32**	**100**	**55**	**69**	**6%**	**105**	**2%**	**32%**				**4.57**	**-4.6**	**22**	**62**	**$15**

Espinosa,Danny

Age: 30 Bats: B Pos: SS | Ht: 6' 0" Wt: 190
Health A | PT/Exp C | Consist B | LIMA Plan D+ | Rand Var 0 | MM 3303

2015 ct% hike held up in 1H, complementing FB-fueled HR binge before everything fell apart. A closer look shows that June—9 HR; his only month with a BA above .228—made his season. Power, decent glove at skill position have kept him in AB thus far. Contact woes and streakiness keep him risky and a scourge for H2Hers.

Yr	Tm	AB	R	HR	RBI	SB	BA	xBA	OBP	SLG	OPS	vL	vR	bb%	ct%	Eye	G	L	F	h%	HctX	PX	xPX	hr/f	Spd	SBO	SB%	#Wk	DOM	DIS	RC/G	RAR	BPV	BPX	R$
12	WAS	594	82	17	56	20	247	234	315	402	717	775	694	7	68	0.24	47	19	34	34	93	123	109	13%	110	19%	77%	27	33%	44%	4.11	0.0	21	53	$16
13	WAS *	441	33	4	27	6	169	173	199	245	444	529	448	4	63	0.10	51	10	39	26	70	74	95	7%	80	11%	83%	10	40%	50%	1.52	-28.6	-54	-135	-$7
14	WAS	333	31	8	27	8	219	215	283	351	634	859	532	5	63	0.15	44	22	34	32	100	115	134	12%	111	14%	89%	26	27%	54%	3.04	-2.5	-8	-22	$4
15	WAS	367	59	13	37	5	240	242	311	409	719	753	709	8	71	0.31	45	18	37	30	86	124	113	14%	104	8%	71%	24	33%	42%	4.12	3.9	33	89	$8
16	WAS	516	66	24	72	9	209	214	306	378	684	712	675	9	66	0.31	39	18	43	26	90	111	130	17%	79	9%	82%	27	30%	44%	3.49	-18.1	0	0	$8
1st Half		261	40	18	49	4	241	249	341	479	820	956	774	10	72	0.39	34	19	47	26	107	140	156	21%	73	6%	100%	14	36%	21%	5.16	5.4	45	129	$17
2nd Half		255	26	6	23	5	176	179	270	275	544	416	577	9	60	0.25	45	17	38	27	72	76	98	11%	93	12%	71%	13	23%	69%	2.15	-19.3	-51	-146	-$1
17	**Proj**	**354**	**45**	**13**	**39**	**6**	**215**	**217**	**296**	**367**	**662**	**721**	**644**	**8**	**66**	**0.26**	**43**	**18**	**39**	**29**	**88**	**106**	**119**	**14%**	**94**	**10%**	**79%**				**3.33**	**-12.4**	**-6**	**-17**	**$7**

Ethier,Andre

Age: 35 Bats: L Pos: LF | Ht: 6' 1" Wt: 205
Health F | PT/Exp D | Consist F | LIMA Plan C+ | Rand Var +2 | MM 3143

Spent all season recovering from a fractured tibia incurred in March. His 5-for-24 Sept tells us nothing. GB-driven 2014 outlier, age and lost 2016 may depress value. But consistent plate skills and left-handed production should generate another 400 AB if healthy. More-than-worthy speculation at the right price.

Yr	Tm	AB	R	HR	RBI	SB	BA	xBA	OBP	SLG	OPS	vL	vR	bb%	ct%	Eye	G	L	F	h%	HctX	PX	xPX	hr/f	Spd	SBO	SB%	#Wk	DOM	DIS	RC/G	RAR	BPV	BPX	R$
12	LA	556	79	20	89	2	284	271	351	460	812	606	945	8	78	0.40	43	24	33	33	109	120	106	14%	85	3%	50%	26	54%	27%	5.57	13.2	51	128	$20
13	LA	482	54	12	52	4	272	268	360	423	783	613	854	11	80	0.64	39	24	37	32	121	109	124	8%	98	5%	57%	25	60%	16%	5.17	15.4	62	155	$13
14	LA	341	29	4	42	2	249	259	322	370	691	567	710	8	78	0.42	52	22	26	31	84	88	63	6%	113	4%	50%	27	37%	30%	3.85	0.6	36	97	$5
15	LA	395	54	14	53	2	294	281	366	486	852	474	900	10	81	0.57	38	26	35	33	117	116	122	12%	115	4%	40%	27	63%	19%	6.22	16.6	73	197	$15
16	LA	24	2	1	2	0	208	201	269	375	644	0	671	8	75	0.33	39	11	50	24	68	102	114	11%	81	0%	0%	5	20%	40%	3.25	-0.9	23	66	-$2
1st Half																																			
2nd Half		24	2	1	2	0	208	201	269	375	644	0	671	8	75	0.33	39	11	50	24	68	102	114	11%	81	0%	0%	5	20%	40%	3.25	-0.9	23	66	-$2
17	**Proj**	**347**	**44**	**10**	**47**	**2**	**276**	**273**	**353**	**443**	**796**	**588**	**855**	**10**	**80**	**0.53**	**42**	**24**	**34**	**32**	**111**	**101**	**109**	**11%**	**102**	**4%**	**50%**				**5.31**	**8.5**	**45**	**128**	**$12**

Fielder,Prince

Age: 33 Bats: L Pos: DH | Ht: 6' 0" Wt: 270
Health F | PT/Exp C | Consist F | LIMA Plan F | Rand Var +5 | MM 0000

A herniated neck disk ended his season early in 2014, and despite a big 2015 rebound, the issue reocurred. Struggled until July '16, when he was told he needed more neck surgery and he'd never get medical clearance to return. He finishes a 12-year career with 319 HR - the same total as dad Cecil! - and an .887 OPS.

Yr	Tm	AB	R	HR	RBI	SB	BA	xBA	OBP	SLG	OPS	vL	vR	bb%	ct%	Eye	G	L	F	h%	HctX	PX	xPX	hr/f	Spd	SBO	SB%	#Wk	DOM	DIS	RC/G	RAR	BPV	BPX	R$
12	DET	581	83	30	108	1	313	304	412	528	940	808	1017	13	86	1.01	41	25	33	33	132	126	128	18%	47	0%	100%	27	70%	11%	7.88	46.8	85	213	$30
13	DET	624	82	25	106	1	279	275	362	457	819	819	819	11	81	0.64	41	23	36	31	117	119	127	14%	38	1%	50%	27	56%	11%	5.73	21.6	55	138	$24
14	TEX	150	19	3	16	0	247	251	360	360	720	688	733	14	84	1.04	50	19	31	28	94	83	68	8%	46	0%	0%	7	29%	14%	4.32	1.2	47	127	$1
15	TEX	613	78	23	98	0	305	259	378	463	841	724	923	9	86	0.73	46	18	35	33	120	94	107	12%	28	0%	0%	27	52%	22%	6.30	14.2	47	127	$26
16	TEX	326	29	8	44	0	212	237	292	334	626	524	667	9	81	0.51	44	19	37	24	93	76	92	8%	17	0%	0%	16	25%	31%	3.05	-24.6	9	26	$0
1st Half		290	26	7	41	0	217	244	293	345	638	590	657	9	82	0.56	43	19	38	24	91	79	90	8%	18	0%	0%	14	29%	21%	3.24	-20.1	17	49	$0
2nd Half		36	3	1	3	0	167	182	286	250	536	0	747	8	69	0.27	52	16	32	21	113	47	106	13%	47	0%	0%	2	0%	100%	1.77	-4.4	-53	-151	-$6
17	Proj																																		

JOCK THOMPSON

Flaherty,Ryan

Age: 30	Bats: L	Pos: 3B	Health A	LIMA Plan D
Ht: 6' 3"	Wt: 210		PT/Exp D	Rand Var 0
			Consist A	MM 2401

His moderate power, which has been the lone offset for ct% and BA issues, disappeared in this year's (small sample) body of work. xPX cratered in lockstep with PX, and mounting GB% is a further drag on any potential HR output. R$ column tells a bleak tale. Moving into his 30s won't help.

Yr Tm	AB	R	HR	RBI	SB	BA	xBA	OBP	SLG	OPS	vL	vR	bb%	ct%	Eye	G	L	F	h%	HctX	PX	xPX	hr/f	Spd	SBO	SB%	#Wk	DOM	DIS	RC/G	RAR	BPV	BPX	R$
12 BAL *	191	19	8	21	1	224	208	254	380	634	667	613	4	72	0.14	43	13	44	27	80	96	107	13%	118	3%	100%	24	25%	63%	3.20	-4.0	10	25	$1
13 BAL *	280	31	12	31	2	223	240	274	390	665	641	687	7	74	0.28	49	16	36	26	96	116	115	15%	83	3%	100%	24	38%	42%	3.55	1.1	31	78	$3
14 BAL	281	33	7	32	1	221	244	288	356	644	616	649	7	76	0.32	47	19	34	27	94	104	101	10%	77	2%	100%	26	42%	46%	3.25	0.6	26	70	$2
15 BAL	267	34	9	31	0	202	219	281	356	637	546	661	9	70	0.32	50	14	36	25	87	104	96	13%	114	0%	0%	24	29%	50%	3.11	-10.7	16	43	$0
16 BAL	157	16	3	15	2	217	218	291	318	610	717	593	10	69	0.35	56	17	27	29	79	75	54	10%	99	5%	100%	23	13%	61%	3.11	-5.7	-10	-29	-$1
1st Half	116	15	3	12	1	233	227	313	353	666	897	637	11	70	0.40	56	18	26	31	76	85	43	14%	103	3%	100%	13	15%	62%	3.75	-2.5	2	6	$1
2nd Half	41	1	0	3	1	171	184	227	220	447	444	447	7	68	0.23	56	15	30	25	86	48	87	0%	94	13%	100%	10	10%	60%	1.63	-3.8	-45	-129	-$4
17 Proj	**193**	**23**	**5**	**21**	**1**	**222**	**225**	**290**	**348**	**638**	**618**	**642**	**8**	**72**	**0.32**	**52**	**16**	**32**	**28**	**86**	**83**	**85**	**11%**	**99**	**2%**	**100%**				**3.28**	**-9.4**	**-5**	**-15**	**$0**

Flores,Wilmer

Age: 25	Bats: R	Pos: 3B 1B	Health A	LIMA Plan C+
Ht: 6' 3"	Wt: 190		PT/Exp C	Rand Var 0
			Consist B	MM 3043

Still-developing skills: lost some ct%, but improved bb% helped extend multi-year Eye growth. What looks like power gain was mostly 10-HR-in-59-AB binge vL in 2nd half. Lack of improvement vR dampens excitement, for now. Underwent minor Oct wrist surgery, but is expected to be ready for spring. Still in sight... UP: 20 HR

Yr Tm	AB	R	HR	RBI	SB	BA	xBA	OBP	SLG	OPS	vL	vR	bb%	ct%	Eye	G	L	F	h%	HctX	PX	xPX	hr/f	Spd	SBO	SB%	#Wk	DOM	DIS	RC/G	RAR	BPV	BPX	R$
12 aa	251	30	7	27	0	274		318	428	746			6	86	0.48				29		95			94	0%	0%				4.78		64	160	$5
13 NYM *	519	53	11	69	1	246	269	276	384	660	447	591	4	81	0.22	51	22	27	28	70	98	47	5%	84	4%	16%	8	50%	50%	3.48	-0.4	37	93	$9
14 NYM *	479	54	14	64	1	250	256	283	393	676	382	749	4	84	0.28	40	20	40	27	101	95	103	7%	113	3%	30%	20	40%	35%	3.71	5.8	55	149	$11
15 NYM	483	55	16	59	0	263	267	295	408	703	955	637	4	87	0.30	42	21	37	27	109	86	95	10%	95	1%	0%	26	46%	19%	4.06	4.1	55	149	$11
16 NYM	307	38	16	49	1	267	274	319	469	788	1093	642	7	84	0.48	33	22	45	27	93	108	107	14%	100	3%	50%	21	48%	29%	5.14	4.6	70	200	$9
1st Half	149	16	5	18	1	255	259	317	403	720	770	701	8	83	0.52	38	22	40	28	78	85	86	10%	109	3%	100%	12	42%	42%	4.38	-0.4	52	149	$5
2nd Half	158	22	11	31	0	278	291	322	532	853	1318	578	6	85	0.43	28	22	50	27	106	130	127	16%	96	3%	0%	9	56%	11%	5.88	6.4	88	251	$12
17 Proj	**397**	**48**	**18**	**58**	**1**	**264**	**273**	**306**	**451**	**757**	**977**	**668**	**5**	**85**	**0.39**	**37**	**21**	**42**	**27**	**97**	**101**	**99**	**13%**	**100**	**2%**	**34%**				**4.69**	**-2.3**	**45**	**128**	**$13**

Flowers,Tyler

Age: 31	Bats: R	Pos: CA	Health B	LIMA Plan D
Ht: 6' 4"	Wt: 260		PT/Exp C	Rand Var -5
			Consist C	MM 3003

Broken hand cost him a month in 2nd half. BA gains combined with established PX give him the sheen of a viable 2nd CA. Should we believe? PRO: HctX spike is extension of long-term trend; more FB% good for power output. CON: xBA and ct% are particularly dubious of so-called growth. Odds point to BA regression.

Yr Tm	AB	R	HR	RBI	SB	BA	xBA	OBP	SLG	OPS	vL	vR	bb%	ct%	Eye	G	L	F	h%	HctX	PX	xPX	hr/f	Spd	SBO	SB%	#Wk	DOM	DIS	RC/G	RAR	BPV	BPX	R$
12 CHW	136	19	7	13	2	213	225	296	412	708	905	586	8	59	0.21	53	18	29	30	64	165	87	30%	68	11%	67%	26	27%	62%	3.64	-2.6	6	15	$1
13 CHW	256	24	10	24	0	195	208	247	355	603	455	661	5	63	0.15	42	17	41	26	86	133	106	15%	60	2%	0%	22	32%	59%	2.62	-8.7	-9	-23	-$1
14 CHW	407	42	15	50	0	241	222	297	396	693	732	679	6	61	0.16	48	24	29	36	82	137	88	21%	63	1%	0%	26	31%	62%	3.74	3.4	-13	-35	$7
15 CHW	331	21	9	39	0	239	194	295	356	652	751	627	6	69	0.20	47	17	36	32	93	88	85	11%	62	1%	0%	26	27%	54%	3.34	-4.6	-22	-59	$2
16 ATL	281	27	8	41	0	270	217	357	420	777	767	781	9	68	0.32	42	19	39	37	120	113	153	11%	76	0%	0%	22	36%	45%	4.97	4.5	4	11	$5
1st Half	161	13	6	17	0	255	209	348	416	764	650	865	10	63	0.29	37	21	42	36	116	121	154	14%	71	0%	0%	14	43%	50%	4.64	2.3	-7	-20	$5
2nd Half	120	14	2	24	0	292	228	369	425	794	1244	712	9	73	0.38	48	16	36	38	126	103	152	6%	78	0%	0%	8	25%	38%	5.45	4.4	19	54	$7
17 Proj	**388**	**36**	**12**	**54**	**0**	**242**	**217**	**316**	**389**	**705**	**778**	**679**	**8**	**67**	**0.25**	**45**	**19**	**36**	**33**	**104**	**108**	**121**	**13%**	**68**	**1%**	**30%**				**3.91**	**-2.7**	**-21**	**-59**	**$7**

Forsythe,Logan

Age: 30	Bats: R	Pos: 2B	Health C	LIMA Plan B+
Ht: 6' 1"	Wt: 195		PT/Exp B	Rand Var -2
			Consist C	MM 3325

Hairline fracture in left shoulder blade sidelined him for a month in 1st half. Gave back the ct%/vL gains that drove last year's breakout, but offset them vR. HR/f should drop a couple of ticks; so 20 HR probably not repeatable. But overall skill set driven by HctX, LD% and moderate power is still playable.

Yr Tm	AB	R	HR	RBI	SB	BA	xBA	OBP	SLG	OPS	vL	vR	bb%	ct%	Eye	G	L	F	h%	HctX	PX	xPX	hr/f	Spd	SBO	SB%	#Wk	DOM	DIS	RC/G	RAR	BPV	BPX	R$
12 SD *	373	53	7	32	10	263	249	329	383	712	1010	603	9	79	0.46	36	29	35	32	112	77	107	7%	155	11%	83%	18	28%	28%	4.42	0.8	43	108	$9
13 SD *	245	26	7	22	6	221	254	291	360	651	651	593	9	74	0.38	42	28	29	27	100	94	105	13%	108	11%	86%	17	12%	35%	3.49	-1.2	25	63	$2
14 TAM	301	32	6	26	2	223	224	287	329	616	708	536	8	76	0.35	41	19	40	27	83	80	100	6%	104	3%	100%	27	30%	59%	3.08	-2.8	18	49	$2
15 TAM	540	69	17	68	9	281	255	359	444	804	972	728	9	79	0.50	40	20	41	33	108	109	105	10%	107	8%	69%	26	46%	23%	5.44	17.8	58	157	$20
16 TAM	511	76	20	52	6	264	259	333	444	778	775	778	8	75	0.36	42	23	35	32	110	110	115	15%	122	9%	50%	24	50%	25%	4.83	1.5	44	126	$14
1st Half	207	30	6	19	4	304	279	366	488	854	1186	752	8	76	0.35	43	26	31	38	110	121	107	12%	118	11%	67%	11	64%	27%	6.28	8.5	55	157	$15
2nd Half	304	46	14	33	2	237	244	312	414	726	475	796	9	74	0.37	41	21	38	27	110	102	120	16%	123	8%	33%	13	38%	23%	4.00	-7.4	35	100	$14
17 Proj	**512**	**69**	**18**	**53**	**7**	**262**	**255**	**334**	**430**	**764**	**834**	**735**	**9**	**77**	**0.40**	**41**	**22**	**37**	**31**	**105**	**102**	**109**	**13%**	**117**	**8%**	**62%**				**4.75**	**-0.7**	**33**	**96**	**$17**

Fowler,Dexter

Age: 31	Bats: B	Pos: CF	Health C	LIMA Plan B
Ht: 6' 4"	Wt: 175		PT/Exp A	Rand Var -3
			Consist B	MM 3525

Mid-June hamstring injury cost him a month. Overall picture stable, is there room for more? CON: Ct% remains shaky, xBA pessimistic, lukewarm SB% keeps his light on yellow. PRO: LD%/Spd have historically propped BA well above xBA, healthy bb% keeps OBP elite. VERDICT: Pay for the stability, anything more a bonus.

Yr Tm	AB	R	HR	RBI	SB	BA	xBA	OBP	SLG	OPS	vL	vR	bb%	ct%	Eye	G	L	F	h%	HctX	PX	xPX	hr/f	Spd	SBO	SB%	#Wk	DOM	DIS	RC/G	RAR	BPV	BPX	R$
12 COL	454	72	13	53	12	300	249	389	474	863	857	866	13	72	0.53	39	27	34	39	97	115	125	12%	179	10%	71%	27	33%	33%	6.67	25.1	61	153	$20
13 COL	415	71	12	42	19	263	246	369	407	776	860	741	14	75	0.62	42	23	34	33	81	102	102	11%	139	20%	68%	23	48%	35%	4.99	11.0	51	128	$18
14 HOU	434	61	8	35	11	276	240	375	399	774	887	737	13	75	0.61	44	21	35	35	95	94	107	7%	148	10%	73%	20	45%	30%	5.23	17.4	49	132	$15
15 CHC	596	102	17	46	20	250	245	346	411	757	865	726	12	74	0.55	43	20	36	31	90	109	98	11%	167	15%	74%	26	50%	27%	4.78	8.3	61	165	$19
16 CHC	456	84	13	48	13	276	250	393	447	840	876	827	15	73	0.64	41	24	36	35	90	110	100	11%	147	11%	76%	23	48%	35%	6.06	18.4	55	157	$18
1st Half	238	41	7	28	6	290	272	398	483	881	884	879	13	74	0.57	41	25	34	36	106	129	120	12%	122	12%	67%	11	55%	27%	6.49	13.3	65	186	$19
2nd Half	218	43	6	20	7	261	227	387	408	795	860	778	17	71	0.70	40	22	38	34	73	88	77	10%	172	9%	88%	12	42%	42%	5.58	6.8	42	120	$16
17 Proj	**511**	**89**	**15**	**48**	**16**	**269**	**247**	**377**	**434**	**811**	**881**	**788**	**14**	**73**	**0.62**	**42**	**23**	**36**	**34**	**89**	**104**	**99**	**11%**	**157**	**12%**	**76%**				**5.63**	**16.7**	**46**	**131**	**$21**

Franco,Maikel

Age: 24	Bats: R	Pos: 3B	Health B	LIMA Plan B+
Ht: 6' 1"	Wt: 180		PT/Exp B	Rand Var 0
			Consist F	MM 3235

First full MLB season was a bit of a mixed bag, but there are reasons for optimism. Consistent ct% combined with broad-based 2nd half gains (see ct%, LD%, HctX) set a nice floor while waiting for 2015's PX/xPX to return. If that happens sooner rather than later... UP: .275 BA, 30 HR.

Yr Tm	AB	R	HR	RBI	SB	BA	xBA	OBP	SLG	OPS	vL	vR	bb%	ct%	Eye	G	L	F	h%	HctX	PX	xPX	hr/f	Spd	SBO	SB%	#Wk	DOM	DIS	RC/G	RAR	BPV	BPX	R$
12																																		
13 aa	277	36	12	39	1	305		324	492	816			3	87	0.22				31		109			100	4%	26%				5.67		74	185	$11
14 PHI *	577	55	14	65	2	222	240	253	358	611	277	573	4	82	0.23	49	12	40	25	32	97	26	0%	118	3%	68%	5	0%	40%	2.96	-13.3	50	135	$6
15 PHI *	445	57	18	70	3	291	283	340	492	832	825	844	7	82	0.40	47	18	35	32	105	130	120	16%	104	2%	100%	16	69%	25%	6.06	17.1	78	211	$18
16 PHI	581	67	25	88	1	255	263	306	427	733	860	698	6	82	0.38	44	20	35	27	102	95	91	15%	90	1%	50%	27	48%	22%	4.40	-9.8	45	129	$14
1st Half	287	28	14	45	0	258	256	315	453	768	767	769	8	79	0.41	44	18	38	28	93	110	102	16%	99	1%	0%	14	57%	7%	4.83	-0.5	53	151	$13
2nd Half	294	39	11	43	1	252	270	297	401	698	964	631	5	84	0.34	45	22	33	27	110	82	81	13%	87	1%	100%	13	38%	38%	3.99	-7.8	40	114	$14
17 Proj	**594**	**70**	**24**	**86**	**2**	**264**	**268**	**310**	**442**	**751**	**778**	**741**	**6**	**83**	**0.35**	**46**	**18**	**36**	**28**	**93**	**101**	**91**	**14%**	**99**	**2%**	**68%**				**4.66**	**-3.9**	**40**	**115**	**$19**

Francoeur,Jeff

Age: 33	Bats: R	Pos: LF	Health A	LIMA Plan D
Ht: 6' 5"	Wt: 210		PT/Exp D	Rand Var -5
			Consist C	MM 2101

Long-underwhelming skill set deteriorated even further in 2016, making 2015 "resurgence" look like a dead cat bounce. Reverted to ineptitude vR; a problem since he doesn't hit lefties either. Only some h% fortune kept this from being a complete debacle. This combo of BPV and RandVar says one thing: stay FAR away.

Yr Tm	AB	R	HR	RBI	SB	BA	xBA	OBP	SLG	OPS	vL	vR	bb%	ct%	Eye	G	L	F	h%	HctX	PX	xPX	hr/f	Spd	SBO	SB%	#Wk	DOM	DIS	RC/G	RAR	BPV	BPX	R$
12 KC	561	58	16	49	4	235	252	287	378	665	695	652	6	79	0.29	45	21	34	27	100	93	106	11%	100	9%	36%	27	44%	37%	3.35	-30.7	33	83	$7
13 2 TM	245	20	3	17	3	204	219	238	298	536	539	534	4	75	0.15	47	17	36	26	79	71	86	5%	117	7%	100%	19	16%	58%	2.27	-17.8	1	3	-$2
14 SD *	480	31	8	38	6	187	223	211	272	483	393	83	3	71	0.10	39	28	33	25	51	68	82	0%	92	11%	69%	4	0%	75%	1.78	-35.6	-25	-68	-$3
15 PHI	326	34	13	45	0	258	260	286	433	718	645	769	4	76	0.17	40	24	37	30	83	115	81	14%	81	3%	0%	27	48%	33%	4.13	-6.9	32	86	$7
16 2 NL	307	33	7	34	2	254	225	297	378	675	726	636	6	71	0.22	49	19	33	34	84	87	89	10%	109	5%	50%	27	22%	63%	3.79	-7.9	0	0	$4
1st Half	173	19	3	18	0	254	233	292	364	656	787	501	5	75	0.23	47	20	33	32	97	78	89	7%	93	0%	0%	14	29%	64%	3.67	-5.2	4	11	$4
2nd Half	134	14	4	16	2	254	213	303	396	699	583	748	7	65	0.21	51	16	33	36	68	100	89	14%	124	12%	50%	13	15%	62%	3.94	-3.0	-7	-20	$5
17 Proj	**133**	**13**	**4**	**15**	**1**	**241**	**230**	**279**	**374**	**653**	**645**	**659**	**5**	**72**	**0.19**	**46**	**20**	**34**	**31**	**82**	**88**	**88**	**11%**	**103**	**7%**	**49%**				**3.42**	**-4.1**	**-10**	**-30**	**$2**

GREG PYRON

Franklin,Nick

Franklin,Nick		Health	B	LIMA Plan	D+
Age: 26	Bats: B Pos: LF	PT/Exp	D	Rand Var	-1
Ht: 6' 1"	Wt: 180	Consist	A	MM	3413

6-26-.270 with 6 SB in 174 AB at TAM. Baby steps. Cut down Ks in 2nd half MLB cameo (78% ct%). PX/xPX limit power upside, but FB% should yield modest HR total. Volatile SB% key to value; Spd hints at something closer to 2016 version. Can't hit lefties, BPV says breakout unlikely, but 15/15 is possible in part-time role.

Yr	Tm	AB	R	HR	RBI	SB	BA	xBA	OBP	SLG	OPS	vL	vR	bb%	ct%	Eye	G	L	F	h%	HctX	PX	xPX	hr/f	Spd	SBO	SB%	#Wk	DOM	DIS	RC/G	RAR	BPV	BPX	R$
12	a/a	472	53	8	45	10	239		300	373	673			8	74	0.33				31		98			109	13%	69%				3.71		25	63	$7
13	SEA *	511	58	15	59	11	240	239	323	385	709	599	727	11	73	0.46	35	24	41	30	102	111	140	11%	88	9%	92%	19	37%	37%	4.27	4.5	33	83	$12
14	2 AL *	460	52	10	54	11	227	208	310	337	647	369	492	11	70	0.40	41	18	41	30	71	90	103	5%	107	13%	67%	7	14%	71%	3.41	-4.0	7	19	$9
15	TAM *	293	32	12	32	4	205	226	277	381	658	592	490	9	68	0.31	32	23	45	26	68	126	109	11%	119	12%	56%	11	18%	55%	3.28	-10.3	29	78	$2
16	TAM *	414	40	10	49	14	240	226	297	379	676	554	828	8	74	0.31	38	18	44	30	92	94	101	11%	115	17%	87%	15	33%	40%	3.88	-4.9	22	63	$9
1st Half		245	21	5	31	8	213	227	284	339	623	1000	673	9	73	0.36	31	25	44	27	92	89	163	14%	98	16%	87%	4	50%	50%	3.21	-9.5	11	31	$7
2nd Half		169	19	5	19	7	278	236	318	436	754	452	854	5	75	0.23	39	17	43	34	93	102	93	10%	124	19%	87%	11	27%	36%	5.01	2.7	33	94	$12
17	**Proj**	**322**	**34**	**11**	**37**	**9**	**235**	**235**	**301**	**405**	**706**	**664**	**720**	**8**	**72**	**0.32**	**36**	**21**	**43**	**29**	**84**	**111**	**117**	**11%**	**115**	**16%**	**79%**				**4.02**	**-4.2**	**24**	**70**	**$7**

Frazier,Adam

Frazier,Adam		Health	A	LIMA Plan	D
Age: 25	Bats: L Pos: LF	PT/Exp	F	Rand Var	0
Ht: 5' 10"	Wt: 175	Consist	B	MM	1441

2-11-.301 with 4 SB in 146 AB at PIT. Held his own with support from xBA, though LD% is unsustainable. Three HR in 1,300+ minor league AB, awful PX squash any power upside, and will he keep running if thrown out half the time? Solid BA is likely given ct% history; Spd hints at end-game upside if he learns to steal.

Yr	Tm	AB	R	HR	RBI	SB	BA	xBA	OBP	SLG	OPS	vL	vR	bb%	ct%	Eye	G	L	F	h%	HctX	PX	xPX	hr/f	Spd	SBO	SB%	#Wk	DOM	DIS	RC/G	RAR	BPV	BPX	R$
12																																			
13																																			
14																																			
15	aa	377	47	1	24	9	281		328	356	684			7	88	0.57				32		51			115	15%	52%				3.92		41	111	$10
16	PIT *	407	51	2	31	19	300	297	359	390	749	840	753	8	86	0.67	44	33	23	34	110	57	93	7%	137	28%	51%	16	25%	56%	4.54	-11.4	51	146	$17
1st Half		275	32	0	22	18	310	376	368	396	764	2000	900	8	89	0.82	31	62	8	35	139	53	34	0%	128	39%	51%	3	33%	33%	4.55	-7.7	55	157	$24
2nd Half		132	19	2	9	1	280	277	342	379	721	618	740	8	81	0.48	45	30	25	33	101	66	101	7%	120	5%	50%	13	23%	62%	4.48	-3.9	32	91	$3
17	**Proj**	**194**	**25**	**3**	**13**	**7**	**288**	**273**	**343**	**406**	**749**	**676**	**762**	**7**	**86**	**0.56**	**46**	**23**	**31**	**32**	**91**	**70**	**91**	**7%**	**133**	**21%**	**56%**				**4.63**	**1.0**	**44**	**126**	**$8**

Frazier,Todd

Frazier,Todd		Health	A	LIMA Plan	B
Age: 31	Bats: R Pos: 3B	PT/Exp	A	Rand Var	+2
Ht: 6' 3"	Wt: 215	Consist	A	MM	4225

Counting stats piled up—as did the warning signs. BA plunge result of more Ks and low h%, which won't fully recover with FB% uptick; xPX suggests more of those might stay in yard despite career-high hr/f; ongoing Spd decline puts SB total at risk. We've likely seen his peak, and could see... DN: 25 HR, single-digit SB.

Yr	Tm	AB	R	HR	RBI	SB	BA	xBA	OBP	SLG	OPS	vL	vR	bb%	ct%	Eye	G	L	F	h%	HctX	PX	xPX	hr/f	Spd	SBO	SB%	#Wk	DOM	DIS	RC/G	RAR	BPV	BPX	R$
12	CIN *	461	58	20	72	5	265	258	321	480	801	858	817	8	75	0.32	33	22	45	32	99	143	127	13%	123	7%	72%	25	60%	24%	5.32	9.5	68	170	$15
13	CIN	531	63	19	73	6	234	251	314	407	721	782	696	9	76	0.40	42	18	40	27	103	121	121	12%	97	9%	55%	27	41%	22%	3.95	0.0	51	128	$12
14	CIN	597	88	29	80	20	273	263	336	459	795	750	807	8	77	0.37	41	22	37	31	114	127	123	17%	91	17%	71%	27	48%	19%	5.24	27.2	54	146	$30
15	CIN	619	82	35	89	13	255	273	309	498	806	908	773	7	78	0.32	33	19	48	28	125	157	156	15%	78	17%	62%	27	63%	30%	5.01	8.2	76	205	$24
16	CHW	590	89	40	98	15	225	245	302	464	767	803	758	10	72	0.39	36	16	49	24	92	142	111	19%	70	15%	75%	27	44%	26%	4.57	-4.0	46	131	$19
1st Half		299	47	23	51	6	204	245	299	455	754	912	727	11	73	0.46	37	15	48	20	92	142	109	22%	73	11%	75%	14	50%	14%	4.26	-5.9	50	143	$16
2nd Half		291	42	17	47	9	247	244	305	474	780	735	794	8	72	0.32	35	16	49	28	91	142	112	16%	76	18%	75%	13	38%	38%	4.92	0.3	43	123	$22
17	**Proj**	**591**	**84**	**32**	**91**	**13**	**245**	**250**	**310**	**459**	**769**	**802**	**759**	**8**	**75**	**0.36**	**36**	**18**	**46**	**27**	**104**	**130**	**125**	**16%**	**81**	**13%**	**71%**				**4.70**	**-3.4**	**45**	**130**	**$23**

Freeman,Freddie

Freeman,Freddie		Health	B	LIMA Plan	B+
Age: 27	Bats: L Pos: 1B	PT/Exp	A	Rand Var	-4
Ht: 6' 5"	Wt: 220	Consist	C	MM	4245

Powered up big, as hr/f, FB% reached new heights, fully backed by PX/xPX. Power gains came at expense of ct%, but it's a tradeoff we can live with given stable xBA, h% baseline. 15 HR, .348 surge in Aug/Sept. begs some regression, but gains vL (.513 SLG, 151 PX) bolster repeat odds. He's just entering peak years.

Yr	Tm	AB	R	HR	RBI	SB	BA	xBA	OBP	SLG	OPS	vL	vR	bb%	ct%	Eye	G	L	F	h%	HctX	PX	xPX	hr/f	Spd	SBO	SB%	#Wk	DOM	DIS	RC/G	RAR	BPV	BPX	R$
12	ATL	540	91	23	94	2	259	271	340	456	796	714	855	11	76	0.50	37	26	37	30	129	132	137	15%	87	1%	100%	27	52%	30%	5.32	-1.6	59	148	$18
13	ATL	551	89	23	109	1	319	274	396	501	897	764	958	11	78	0.55	38	27	35	38	123	121	152	15%	95	1%	100%	25	60%	16%	7.38	41.0	61	153	$31
14	ATL	607	93	18	78	3	288	283	386	461	847	756	885	13	76	0.62	37	31	32	35	131	134	159	12%	96	4%	43%	27	56%	22%	6.17	33.8	68	184	$24
15	ATL	416	62	18	66	3	276	279	370	471	841	656	912	12	76	0.57	37	28	36	32	129	133	152	16%	78	3%	75%	22	45%	23%	6.01	7.6	61	165	$16
16	ATL	589	102	34	91	6	302	279	400	569	968	902	1001	13	71	0.52	30	29	41	38	125	173	177	20%	107	4%	86%	27	59%	15%	8.21	46.4	82	234	$29
1st Half		308	39	14	31	3	292	267	375	516	891	912	879	10	71	0.40	30	31	39	37	119	145	166	16%	116	3%	100%	14	50%	14%	6.88	15.2	58	166	$23
2nd Half		281	63	20	60	3	313	295	425	626	1052	889	1112	16	71	0.65	31	27	42	38	132	205	189	24%	98	4%	75%	13	69%	15%	9.79	35.7	110	314	$37
17	**Proj**	**580**	**98**	**30**	**94**	**5**	**294**	**280**	**390**	**530**	**920**	**807**	**970**	**13**	**74**	**0.56**	**33**	**29**	**39**	**35**	**128**	**151**	**166**	**18%**	**95**	**3%**	**75%**				**7.34**	**36.1**	**68**	**194**	**$30**

Freese,David

Freese,David		Health	B	LIMA Plan	D+
Age: 34	Bats: R Pos: 3B 1B	PT/Exp	C	Rand Var	-5
Ht: 6' 3"	Wt: 220	Consist	A	MM	2013

Strong 1H unraveled down the stretch; peripherals cast doubt he can patch it back together. Hit rate explosion propped up BA despite ct% collapse; xBA confirms it. Double-digit HR in jeopardy given severe GB% swing, while subpar xPX questions hr/f spike. We'll bet R$ finally breaks though $10 floor; RandVar says it's not going up.

Yr	Tm	AB	R	HR	RBI	SB	BA	xBA	OBP	SLG	OPS	vL	vR	bb%	ct%	Eye	G	L	F	h%	HctX	PX	xPX	hr/f	Spd	SBO	SB%	#Wk	DOM	DIS	RC/G	RAR	BPV	BPX	R$
12	STL	501	70	20	79	3	293	265	372	467	839	886	824	10	76	0.47	52	22	26	35	119	116	119	20%	94	4%	50%	27	56%	26%	6.06	20.3	46	115	$20
13	STL	462	53	9	60	1	262	253	340	381	721	811	689	9	77	0.44	55	21	24	32	118	91	97	10%	77	2%	33%	25	24%	28%	4.28	3.8	25	63	$10
14	LAA	462	53	10	55	1	260	253	321	383	704	876	656	8	73	0.31	49	26	26	34	124	101	116	11%	77	3%	25%	25	28%	48%	4.07	4.8	14	38	$10
15	LAA *	445	54	15	60	1	254	250	306	413	719	719	752	7	75	0.29	54	18	28	31	109	114	108	16%	70	2%	50%	22	50%	32%	4.29	-5.0	27	73	$10
16	PIT	437	63	13	55	0	270	232	352	412	764	963	710	9	68	0.32	61	19	20	37	97	104	92	22%	97	0%	0%	26	27%	50%	4.87	-1.3	3	9	$10
1st Half		232	37	8	35	0	289	253	365	457	822	970	771	9	70	0.32	61	19	20	38	105	119	103	25%	86	0%	0%	14	43%	29%	5.74	5.5	21	60	$14
2nd Half		205	26	5	20	0	249	209	336	361	697	947	650	10	64	0.32	60	19	21	36	87	85	80	18%	106	0%	0%	12	8%	75%	3.98	-5.5	-20	-57	$6
17	**Proj**	**352**	**46**	**9**	**44**	**0**	**251**	**238**	**328**	**383**	**711**	**827**	**678**	**9**	**71**	**0.32**	**56**	**20**	**24**	**33**	**105**	**94**	**100**	**15%**	**89**	**1%**	**39%**				**4.09**	**-8.2**	**-11**	**-32**	**$8**

Johnson,Chris

Johnson,Chris		Health	B	LIMA Plan	F
Age: 32	Bats: R Pos: 1B	PT/Exp	C	Rand Var	+2
Ht: 6' 3"	Wt: 220	Consist	A	MM	1211

Remember when he nearly won a batting title? BA has consistently fallen from that 2013 peak; ct% trend tells us why. At least he recovered LD% stroke, but xBA says it's nowhere near enough to save him. Meager PX, lack of fly balls lock in single-digit HR, while effectiveness vL is fading fast as well. In a word: avoid.

Yr	Tm	AB	R	HR	RBI	SB	BA	xBA	OBP	SLG	OPS	vL	vR	bb%	ct%	Eye	G	L	F	h%	HctX	PX	xPX	hr/f	Spd	SBO	SB%	#Wk	DOM	DIS	RC/G	RAR	BPV	BPX	R$
12	2 NL	488	48	15	76	5	281	254	326	451	777	672	819	6	73	0.23	39	26	35	36	98	120	112	12%	105	5%	83%	27	33%	44%	5.19	8.0	33	83	$16
13	ATL	514	54	12	68	0	321	268	358	457	816	939	772	5	77	0.25	46	27	27	40	97	104	101	11%	68	0%	0%	26	42%	42%	6.13	29.3	26	65	$21
14	ATL	582	43	10	58	6	263	245	292	361	653	988	570	4	73	0.14	48	27	25	35	83	83	74	9%	70	4%	100%	27	19%	67%	3.69	-0.4	-11	-30	$12
15	2 TM	243	18	3	18	2	255	210	286	337	624	745	550	4	70	0.14	48	21	31	36	92	69	106	6%	69	5%	67%	21	10%	71%	3.27	-10.0	-35	-95	$2
16	MIA	243	20	5	24	0	222	230	281	329	611	618	606	7	68	0.24	45	27	28	31	93	80	92	11%	80	0%	0%	27	19%	44%	3.01	-14.5	-23	-66	-$1
1st Half		129	10	3	11	0	233	226	283	333	616	653	581	7	69	0.23	44	27	29	31	109	69	99	12%	93	0%	0%	14	21%	50%	3.13	-6.8	-26	-74	$0
2nd Half		114	10	2	13	0	211	235	280	325	605	559	627	8	67	0.26	46	28	26	30	75	92	84	10%	73	0%	0%	13	15%	38%	2.87	-7.1	-20	-57	-$1
17	**Proj**	**132**	**11**	**2**	**13**	**1**	**243**	**232**	**290**	**348**	**639**	**692**	**610**	**6**	**70**	**0.21**	**46**	**26**	**28**	**33**	**90**	**78**	**93**	**9%**	**77**	**2%**	**78%**				**3.38**	**-6.7**	**-35**	**-101**	**$2**

Gallo,Joey

Gallo,Joey		Health	A	LIMA Plan	D
Age: 23	Bats: L Pos: 3B	PT/Exp	D	Rand Var	0
Ht: 6' 5"	Wt: 235	Consist	A	MM	5303

1-1-.040 in 25 AB with TEX. Groin injury derailed hot start (7 HR, 1.008 OPS in April). Still waiting for him to shine, but piling up Ks at this rate means it'll be a while. Mammoth PX keeps us interested; small-sample xPX in MLB does nothing to change that. Still a pup who deserves a shot, but road to stardom looks bumpy.

Yr	Tm	AB	R	HR	RBI	SB	BA	xBA	OBP	SLG	OPS	vL	vR	bb%	ct%	Eye	G	L	F	h%	HctX	PX	xPX	hr/f	Spd	SBO	SB%	#Wk	DOM	DIS	RC/G	RAR	BPV	BPX	R$
12																																			
13																																			
14	aa	250	36	17	46	2	211		295	456	750			11	51	0.24				32		242			81	3%	100%				4.38		46	124	$6
15	TEX *	429	49	24	64	5	210	217	303	433	736	477	836	12	52	0.28	35	27	37	33	115	206	185	32%	76	5%	100%	10	40%	50%	4.29	-8.5	21	57	$7
16	TEX *	384	59	21	54	3	201	183	311	429	740	250	374	14	53	0.34	17	17	67	31	36	186	100	25%	113	3%	100%	7	0%	86%	4.30	-6.7	23	66	$4
1st Half		184	32	11	28	1	216	312	337	468	805	0	0	15	60	0.45	0	100	0	29	0	181	-24	0%	112	2%	100%	1	0%	0%	5.16	0.3	51	146	$6
2nd Half		200	27	10	26	2	186	148	287	393	680	250	390	12	46	0.26	20	0	80	33	37	192	125	25%	111	4%	100%	6	0%	100%	3.58	-9.7	-2	-6	$2
17	**Proj**	**276**	**38**	**15**	**41**	**3**	**204**	**212**	**302**	**428**	**730**	**475**	**856**	**12**	**52**	**0.29**	**35**	**27**	**37**	**32**	**104**	**189**	**167**	**28%**	**95**	**4%**	**100%**				**4.19**	**-6.0**	**15**	**42**	**$5**

RYAN BLOOMFIELD

Galvis,Freddy

Age: 27 Bats: B Pos: SS | Ht: 5' 10" Wt: 170

Health B | PT/Exp B | Consist A | LIMA Plan C | Rand Var 0 | MM 2313

Major spikes in both HR and SB; which to believe? 2H h% and hr/f were only changes in a static G/L/F, HctX profile, so lack of underlying skills growth says HR luck won't return. More green lights on bases were rewarded with improved SB%, but terrible plate discipline will limit future opportunities. 2016 likely career year.

Yr	Tm	AB	R	HR	RBI	SB	BA	xBA	OBP	SLG	OPS	vL	vR	bb%	ct%	Eye	G	L	F	h%	HctX	PX	xPX	hr/f	Spd	SBO	SB%	#Wk	DOM	DIS	RC/G	RAR	BPV	BPX	R$
12	PHI	190	14	3	24	0	226	265	254	363	617	735	562	4	85	0.24	41	21	38	25	106	95	116	5%	79	0%	0%	10	40%	30%	3.04	-6.1	48	120	-$1
13	PHI *	446	33	8	38	3	221	218	256	340	596	688	662	5	77	0.21	36	19	46	27	97	83	115	8%	130	5%	74%	18	39%	39%	2.85	-8.9	23	58	$1
14	PHI *	254	30	6	23	2	200	217	248	347	595	496	573	6	76	0.27	41	8	51	24	84	112	117	9%	111	7%	60%	12	25%	42%	2.70	-4.7	42	114	$0
15	PHI	559	63	7	50	10	263	229	302	343	645	602	662	5	82	0.29	41	22	37	31	88	49	90	4%	143	7%	91%	27	22%	41%	3.64	-1.9	21	57	$13
16	PHI	584	61	20	67	17	241	253	274	399	673	544	715	4	77	0.18	40	23	36	28	83	95	80	13%	103	20%	74%	27	37%	30%	3.62	-17.6	24	69	$14
1st Half		301	30	7	31	4	223	248	253	355	609	382	687	4	78	0.18	40	23	37	26	84	80	72	8%	120	11%	67%	14	36%	21%	2.90	-14.5	23	66	$7
2nd Half		283	31	13	36	13	261	260	297	445	742	734	744	4	75	0.18	40	24	36	31	83	113	90	17%	85	28%	76%	13	38%	38%	4.47	0.0	26	74	$23
17	Proj	**401**	**43**	**11**	**42**	**9**	**241**	**242**	**277**	**379**	**656**	**591**	**680**	**5**	**78**	**0.22**	**40**	**21**	**39**	**28**	**86**	**83**	**93**	**9%**	**109**	**14%**	**77%**				**3.51**	**-11.5**	**21**	**59**	**$8**

Gamel,Benjamin

Age: 25 Bats: L Pos: RF | Ht: 5' 10" Wt: 170

Health A | PT/Exp B | Consist C | LIMA Plan D | Rand Var -4 | MM 2321

1-5-.188 in 48 AB at NYY/SEA. After over 1000 PA in AAA, Spd looks to be worthy of minor interest here, but will need to improve SB% to continue to get the chances. He also posted a .304 BA at AAA, but MLEs show ct% must improve to attain similar results in the majors. Lack of power saddles him with ceiling of 4th OF.

Yr	Tm	AB	R	HR	RBI	SB	BA	xBA	OBP	SLG	OPS	vL	vR	bb%	ct%	Eye	G	L	F	h%	HctX	PX	xPX	hr/f	Spd	SBO	SB%	#Wk	DOM	DIS	RC/G	RAR	BPV	BPX	R$
12																																			
13	aa	67	4	1	4	1	221		259	318	578			5	71	0.18				30		84			95	6%	100%				2.76		-6	-15	-$2
14	aa	544	47	2	41	11	234		273	301	574			5	82	0.30				28		57			92	13%	66%				2.70		14	38	$5
15	aaa	500	68	10	56	11	276		331	427	757			8	76	0.34				35		100			129	13%	67%				4.89		39	105	$17
16	2 AL *	531	82	7	52	17	277	238	335	381	715	1162	404	8	77	0.37	44	22	34	35	80	69	69	9%	117	17%	66%	9	22%	56%	4.39	1.7	16	46	$19
1st Half		297	44	3	28	11	266	268	332	354	686	0	393	9	78	0.46	100	0	0	33	45	56	-24	0%	133	19%	62%	2	0%	50%	3.94	-4.6	18	51	$19
2nd Half		234	38	4	23	6	292	235	338	415	753	1278	406	6	75	0.28	28	28	44	37	87	86	96	9%	99	13%	74%	7	29%	57%	5.03	3.8	14	40	$17
17	Proj	**195**	**27**	**5**	**19**	**5**	**272**	**247**	**323**	**428**	**752**	**1531**	**515**	**7**	**77**	**0.33**	**28**	**28**	**44**	**33**	**78**	**96**	**86**	**8%**	**113**	**15%**	**67%**				**4.74**	**0.3**	**34**	**98**	**$7**

Garcia,Adonis

Age: 32 Bats: R Pos: 3B | Ht: 5' 9" Wt: 205

Health A | PT/Exp C | Consist B | LIMA Plan B | Rand Var -2 | MM 2135

14-65-.273 with 3 SB in 532 AB at ATL. BA fit the xBA model perfectly despite large 1H/2H variance vL, but that's where the perfection ends. 2nd half ct% boost a plus, but accompanying spike in h% looks flukish. Too few FB and low xPX will cap HR ceiling, and platoon split suggests best used as bad-side platoon option.

Yr	Tm	AB	R	HR	RBI	SB	BA	xBA	OBP	SLG	OPS	vL	vR	bb%	ct%	Eye	G	L	F	h%	HctX	PX	xPX	hr/f	Spd	SBO	SB%	#Wk	DOM	DIS	RC/G	RAR	BPV	BPX	R$
12	aa	118	13	3	10	1	237		260	406	666			3	82	0.17				26		118			85	15%	55%				3.40		55	138	$0
13	aaa	199	13	3	8	3	211		244	294	538			4	87	0.34				23		54			103	20%	39%				2.09		33	83	-$2
14	aaa	342	38	7	30	7	243		268	354	622			4	80	0.17				28		81			98	16%	65%				3.12		24	65	$6
15	ATL *	522	53	12	62	4	243	264	266	364	631	982	706	3	83	0.19	49	22	29	27	113	79	107	22%	49	5%	75%	13	54%	23%	3.26	-22.6	17	46	$8
16	ATL *	605	76	17	79	5	273	273	303	414	717	765	700	4	82	0.24	52	21	27	31	99	86	63	12%	60	6%	58%	25	40%	44%	4.34	-5.0	25	71	$17
1st Half		297	31	8	36	4	243	256	271	361	632	493	646	4	79	0.18	53	21	26	28	99	72	62	11%	56	7%	73%	12	33%	50%	3.29	-10.4	1	3	$11
2nd Half		308	45	9	43	1	302	289	340	464	805	1041	735	5	84	0.31	52	21	27	33	100	100	63	13%	67	4%	33%	13	46%	38%	5.54	9.2	49	140	$22
17	Proj	**471**	**49**	**13**	**50**	**5**	**254**	**269**	**287**	**392**	**679**	**784**	**638**	**4**	**81**	**0.22**	**51**	**21**	**28**	**29**	**105**	**84**	**80**	**12%**	**64**	**8%**	**60%**				**3.74**	**-16.0**	**20**	**58**	**$11**

Garcia,Avisail

Age: 26 Bats: R Pos: DH RF | Ht: 6' 3" Wt: 230

Health D | PT/Exp C | Consist A | LIMA Plan C+ | Rand Var +1 | MM 2225

Leg injuries (hamstring and knee) cost three weeks of AB, but he can't blame those for reversion to extreme GB ways. The few positives to build on (bb% improvement, 2nd half HctX) aren't enough to overcome stagnant xPX, ct%. He'll need something positive when 2nd half hr/f reverses but there is not enough here to build on.

Yr	Tm	AB	R	HR	RBI	SB	BA	xBA	OBP	SLG	OPS	vL	vR	bb%	ct%	Eye	G	L	F	h%	HctX	PX	xPX	hr/f	Spd	SBO	SB%	#Wk	DOM	DIS	RC/G	RAR	BPV	BPX	R$
12	DET *	262	33	5	21	7	296	292	318	407	725	745	588	3	81	0.17	62	27	11	35	135	67	63	0%	131	20%	54%	6	0%	100%	4.36	-3.6	27	68	$8
13	2 AL *	418	55	13	58	6	309	254	340	453	793	640	770	5	76	0.20	56	18	26	38	107	95	92	15%	138	10%	55%	17	29%	53%	5.49	13.9	33	83	$19
14	CHW *	222	25	8	31	4	253	242	300	405	705	992	620	6	72	0.23	56	15	28	32	81	119	89	19%	74	9%	80%	10	50%	30%	4.17	1.7	19	51	$6
15	CHW	553	66	13	59	7	257	243	309	365	675	759	650	6	75	0.26	49	25	27	32	96	73	90	12%	95	10%	50%	27	33%	48%	3.65	-18.3	0	0	$13
16	CHW	413	59	12	51	4	245	253	307	385	692	677	696	8	72	0.30	55	22	23	31	101	92	77	17%	90	8%	50%	25	36%	40%	3.81	-11.0	6	17	$8
1st Half		235	30	5	27	2	243	247	312	349	660	591	675	8	73	0.33	53	25	22	31	91	69	67	13%	84	6%	50%	14	21%	50%	3.49	-8.5	-10	-29	$7
2nd Half		178	29	7	24	2	247	262	301	433	733	739	730	7	71	0.25	58	17	25	31	113	122	91	22%	99	10%	50%	11	55%	27%	4.22	-2.6	28	80	$9
17	Proj	**425**	**57**	**12**	**52**	**6**	**255**	**249**	**308**	**392**	**700**	**749**	**683**	**7**	**73**	**0.26**	**54**	**20**	**25**	**32**	**99**	**88**	**86**	**15%**	**95**	**9%**	**55%**				**3.96**	**-19.4**	**4**	**11**	**$12**

Garcia,Greg

Age: 27 Bats: L Pos: 3B SS 2B | Ht: 6' 0" Wt: 175

Health A | PT/Exp D | Consist B | LIMA Plan D | Rand Var -2 | MM 1221

3-17-.276 in 214 AB at STL. To paraphrase Casey Stengel: In three years he has a chance to be 30 (with a matching BPX?). Walk rate improvement delivered plus OBP, but lack of speed and power skills doom this profile. Positional versatility makes him a valid short-term injury replacement. Emphasis on "short-term."

Yr	Tm	AB	R	HR	RBI	SB	BA	xBA	OBP	SLG	OPS	vL	vR	bb%	ct%	Eye	G	L	F	h%	HctX	PX	xPX	hr/f	Spd	SBO	SB%	#Wk	DOM	DIS	RC/G	RAR	BPV	BPX	R$
12	aa	412	62	7	39	8	243		342	347	690			13	78	0.67				30		72			105	10%	57%				3.91		27	68	$7
13	aaa	354	37	2	26	10	228		301	315	616			9	78	0.47				29		71			109	14%	82%				3.20		20	50	$3
14	STL *	411	46	6	30	6	222	229	276	304	580	1167	377	7	71	0.25	100	0	0	30	115	67	-15	0%	114	11%	49%	8	0%	50%	2.63	-9.6	-12	-32	$3
15	STL *	405	41	2	30	11	236	243	312	307	620	1171	688	10	80	0.55	57	18	25	29	103	56	71	13%	98	13%	76%	12	58%	17%	3.24	-11.3	16	43	$5
16	STL *	318	42	3	23	2	254	246	348	331	679	577	806	13	76	0.60	50	25	24	33	73	55	67	8%	111	5%	41%	23	22%	39%	3.83	-9.8	9	26	$3
1st Half		159	25	2	16	1	263	231	348	341	690	875	1027	12	76	0.55	48	23	30	33	72	51	88	17%	121	9%	29%	10	20%	40%	3.83	-4.6	7	20	$6
2nd Half		159	17	1	7	1	245	251	353	321	674	511	718	14	76	0.66	51	26	22	32	73	59	60	4%	107	2%	100%	13	23%	38%	3.81	-4.7	13	37	$1
17	Proj	**155**	**18**	**3**	**11**	**2**	**242**	**253**	**338**	**357**	**695**	**671**	**900**	**11**	**76**	**0.54**	**52**	**22**	**25**	**30**	**85**	**74**	**71**	**11%**	**110**	**8%**	**61%**				**3.87**	**-4.8**	**10**	**28**	**$3**

Gardner,Brett

Age: 33 Bats: L Pos: LF | Ht: 5' 11" Wt: 195

Health B | PT/Exp A | Consist A | LIMA Plan B+ | Rand Var 0 | MM 1425

Went 43 games between steals in the 2nd half due to sore foot (but no DL time). Sagging power indicators (FB, HctX, hr/f, PX) ensured HR drop, but OBP remained strong. A return to 20 SB is just a matter of health and SBO%, as Spd/SB% seem intact. But xPX never bought double-digit HR pop; that's likely gone for good.

Yr	Tm	AB	R	HR	RBI	SB	BA	xBA	OBP	SLG	OPS	vL	vR	bb%	ct%	Eye	G	L	F	h%	HctX	PX	xPX	hr/f	Spd	SBO	SB%	#Wk	DOM	DIS	RC/G	RAR	BPV	BPX	R$
12	NYY	31	7	0	3	2	323	266	417	387	804	2032	426	14	77	0.71	38	38	25	42	122	60	51	0%	90	31%	50%	5	20%	60%	5.24	0.6	14	35	$0
13	NYY	539	81	8	52	24	273	251	344	416	759	744	767	9	76	0.41	41	23	35	34	80	104	70	6%	136	22%	75%	24	38%	38%	4.89	14.3	49	123	$22
14	NYY	555	87	17	58	21	256	254	327	422	749	687	775	9	76	0.42	42	22	37	31	95	117	91	11%	136	18%	81%	27	48%	30%	4.73	17.0	58	157	$22
15	NYY	571	94	16	66	20	259	247	343	399	742	761	734	11	76	0.50	45	21	34	31	88	94	87	11%	111	15%	80%	27	37%	48%	4.70	5.1	37	100	$22
16	NYY	547	80	7	41	16	261	256	351	362	713	645	745	11	81	0.66	52	21	27	31	84	61	42	6%	124	11%	80%	27	30%	37%	4.38	1.6	33	94	$15
1st Half		264	46	5	16	12	254	258	357	348	706	528	779	13	80	0.73	55	21	24	30	85	59	49	10%	108	16%	86%	14	36%	43%	4.31	-1.1	28	80	$18
2nd Half		283	34	2	25	4	269	253	345	375	719	737	709	10	81	0.59	50	21	30	33	84	63	36	3%	125	7%	67%	13	23%	31%	4.44	-0.1	34	97	$12
17	Proj	**532**	**80**	**9**	**49**	**19**	**262**	**250**	**344**	**380**	**724**	**692**	**739**	**11**	**78**	**0.55**	**48**	**21**	**31**	**32**	**86**	**73**	**63**	**7%**	**123**	**15%**	**81%**				**4.53**	**1.1**	**34**	**97**	**$20**

Gattis,Evan

Age: 30 Bats: R Pos: DH CA | Ht: 6' 4" Wt: 230

Health B | PT/Exp B | Consist B | LIMA Plan B+ | Rand Var 0 | MM 4135

32-72-.251 in 447 AB at HOU. Remembered how to bash vL, and rode 2H hr/f spike and some newfound plate patience to a career high in HR. But the most important aspect of 2016? Try July 10—his 20th MLB game behind the dish, securing CA eligiblity for 2017. Stable skill set—ct% warts and all—points towards a repeat.

Yr	Tm	AB	R	HR	RBI	SB	BA	xBA	OBP	SLG	OPS	vL	vR	bb%	ct%	Eye	G	L	F	h%	HctX	PX	xPX	hr/f	Spd	SBO	SB%	#Wk	DOM	DIS	RC/G	RAR	BPV	BPX	R$
12	aa	182	19	7	29	1	221		283	430	714			8	81	0.45				24		130			102	6%	40%				3.90		76	190	$1
13	ATL *	375	45	22	66	0	244	264	285	483	768	808	757	5	77	0.24	41	14	45	26	117	163	136	17%	56	0%	0%	24	54%	21%	4.64	1.5	68	170	$11
14	ATL	369	41	22	52	0	263	259	317	493	810	970	773	6	74	0.23	39	17	45	30	123	163	165	18%	81	0%	0%	24	50%	21%	5.19	12.2	63	170	$13
15	HOU	566	66	27	88	0	246	267	285	463	748	698	775	5	79	0.25	46	17	37	27	110	126	117	16%	128	1%	0%	27	52%	30%	4.40	-17.5	67	181	$14
16	HOU *	487	63	36	79	2	254	264	315	516	832	886	795	8	73	0.33	41	18	41	28	96	156	119	24%	75	3%	67%	24	63%	17%	5.54	0.6	57	163	$16
1st Half		249	30	16	40	0	232	246	288	456	744	806	660	7	75	0.32	45	15	39	24	101	128	108	20%	68	0%	0%	12	50%	25%	4.36	-8.6	41	117	$11
2nd Half		238	33	20	39	2	277	278	346	580	926	964	907	9	70	0.34	37	20	43	31	91	188	129	28%	86	5%	67%	12	75%	8%	6.96	9.9	77	220	$21
17	Proj	**509**	**64**	**32**	**83**	**1**	**256**	**265**	**311**	**503**	**814**	**850**	**797**	**7**	**75**	**0.29**	**42**	**17**	**41**	**28**	**105**	**144**	**128**	**21%**	**97**	**2%**	**59%**				**5.26**	**-3.5**	**49**	**139**	**$19**

MATT DODGE

Gennett,Scooter

Age: 27 Bats: L Pos: 2B | Ht: 5' 9" Wt: 170
Health A | PT/Exp C | Consist C | LIMA Plan C | Rand Var -1 | MM 2235

Bottom line was an improvement, but skill gains not very apparent. Power metrics remain below average, while mediocre speed, past ineptitude on bases indicate he's not a viable SB source. Also, 1st half strides in bb%, vL appear to be small sample aberrations. Don't pay for full repeat, regression is likely on the way.

Yr Tm	AB	R	HR	RBI	SB	BA	xBA	OBP	SLG	OPS	vL	vR	bb%	ct%	Eye	G	L	F	h%	HctX	PX	xPX	hr/f	Spd	SBO	SB%	#Wk	DOM	DIS	RC/G	RAR	BPV	BPX	R$
12 aa	533	54	5	36	9	267		299	353	652			4	85	0.30				31		61			96	11%	62%				3.59		28	70	$10
13 MIL *	534	61	8	37	9	275	240	308	381	689	329	946	5	79	0.23	39	24	37	33	116	72	115	10%	146	11%	58%	14	43%	29%	3.99	5.1	30	75	$14
14 MIL	440	55	9	54	6	289	285	320	434	754	253	802	5	85	0.33	41	25	34	32	105	105	92	7%	95	8%	67%	27	52%	19%	4.95	19.3	63	170	$16
15 MIL *	450	50	7	37	1	262	262	285	384	670	310	713	3	82	0.19	49	22	30	30	78	80	77	7%	124	5%	19%	24	38%	21%	3.64	-6.9	39	105	$7
16 MIL	498	58	14	56	8	263	255	317	412	728	708	733	7	77	0.33	45	21	35	32	91	97	90	11%	91	7%	89%	26	42%	38%	4.55	-4.5	30	86	$13
1st Half	223	31	7	21	3	265	254	332	417	749	863	723	9	76	0.43	45	22	33	32	85	96	75	13%	97	6%	75%	13	38%	38%	4.82	0.1	30	86	$11
2nd Half	275	27	7	35	5	262	255	304	407	711	591	741	5	78	0.25	44	20	36	31	95	97	102	9%	92	8%	100%	13	46%	38%	4.32	-3.8	30	86	$14
17 Proj	**431**	**49**	**10**	**44**	**5**	**258**	**263**	**300**	**400**	**700**	**534**	**730**	**5**	**80**	**0.28**	**45**	**22**	**34**	**30**	**92**	**89**	**90**	**9%**	**102**	**8%**	**70%**				**4.06**	**-9.3**	**29**	**84**	**$9**

Giavotella,Johnny

Age: 29 Bats: R Pos: 2B | Ht: 5' 8" Wt: 180
Health B | PT/Exp C | Consist B | LIMA Plan D | Rand Var +2 | MM 1241

6-31-.260 with 4 SB in 346 AB at LAA. After fluky week in June (4 HR from 6/13 to 6/20), posted .568 OPS over next two months, resulting in demotion to AAA. Consistently puts ball in play, which provides respectable BA floor, but that's not enough to make up for lack of... everything else, really.

Yr Tm	AB	R	HR	RBI	SB	BA	xBA	OBP	SLG	OPS	vL	vR	bb%	ct%	Eye	G	L	F	h%	HctX	PX	xPX	hr/f	Spd	SBO	SB%	#Wk	DOM	DIS	RC/G	RAR	BPV	BPX	R$
12 KC *	543	67	7	64	8	256	260	306	351	657	547	591	7	85	0.49	47	23	30	29	89	62	50	2%	101	6%	87%	14	14%	36%	3.73	-7.0	36	90	$11
13 KC *	411	40	5	39	6	240	238	313	334	647	498	713	10	83	0.62	57	14	30	28	122	72	127	0%	82	9%	56%	6	50%	17%	3.42	-3.7	34	85	$5
14 KC *	478	51	5	45	13	241	278	288	339	627	347	661	6	90	0.66	55	18	27	26	94	70	76	11%	83	17%	69%	6	33%	33%	3.23	-2.3	55	149	$9
15 LAA	453	51	4	49	2	272	272	318	375	694	674	700	7	87	0.54	46	24	30	31	71	68	48	3%	109	2%	67%	23	39%	22%	4.19	-1.1	50	135	$9
16 LAA *	373	45	6	32	5	257	285	285	370	656	558	703	4	88	0.35	50	22	28	28	92	68	58	7%	81	9%	61%	20	40%	20%	3.55	-12.8	42	120	$6
1st Half	263	33	6	26	3	274	297	295	411	705	567	755	3	89	0.31	47	24	29	29	96	79	68	9%	80	10%	50%	14	50%	14%	4.13	-5.1	52	149	$10
2nd Half	110	12	0	6	2	217	252	257	273	530	535	522	5	87	0.42	58	16	26	25	77	43	27	0%	90	7%	100%	6	17%	33%	2.35	-8.3	22	63	-$3
17 Proj	**198**	**22**	**3**	**17**	**3**	**264**	**276**	**306**	**369**	**675**	**621**	**697**	**5**	**88**	**0.47**	**50**	**21**	**29**	**29**	**81**	**64**	**46**	**5%**	**93**	**8%**	**73%**				**3.88**	**-5.3**	**38**	**108**	**$5**

Gillaspie,Conor

Age: 29 Bats: L Pos: 3B | Ht: 6' 1" Wt: 200
Health A | PT/Exp D | Consist C | LIMA Plan D+ | Rand Var +1 | MM 2033

6-25-.262 in 191 AB at SF. Rebounded from down year with career-best ct% and moderate power. But post-season heroics aside, lack of patience suppresses OBP, which, combined with inability to hit LHP, leaves him locked into part-time role with little to no chance of making fantasy impact.

Yr Tm	AB	R	HR	RBI	SB	BA	xBA	OBP	SLG	OPS	vL	vR	bb%	ct%	Eye	G	L	F	h%	HctX	PX	xPX	hr/f	Spd	SBO	SB%	#Wk	DOM	DIS	RC/G	RAR	BPV	BPX	R$
12 SF *	433	42	8	35	0	216	284	262	315	577	0	467	6	84	0.40	39	33	28	24	62	62	17	0%	90	0%	0%	2	50%	50%	2.69	-25.5	28	70	$0
13 CHW	408	46	13	40	0	245	243	305	390	695	451	738	8	81	0.47	37	20	42	28	108	91	110	9%	115	1%	0%	27	48%	26%	4.01	0.2	49	123	$6
14 CHW	464	50	7	57	0	282	262	336	416	752	565	805	7	83	0.46	39	22	39	33	105	98	95	5%	110	3%	0%	25	40%	32%	4.76	13.8	61	165	$12
15 2 AL	237	14	4	24	0	228	254	269	359	627	583	630	5	80	0.28	45	21	35	27	76	91	87	6%	74	2%	0%	20	35%	40%	3.11	-11.2	28	76	-$1
16 SF *	242	28	7	28	2	257	269	295	415	710	591	767	5	85	0.36	38	23	38	28	110	84	102	10%	115	7%	46%	25	40%	32%	4.08	-6.3	55	157	$4
1st Half	133	16	3	13	2	265	249	301	387	688	500	808	5	86	0.36	38	20	42	29	123	70	120	7%	113	5%	100%	12	33%	33%	4.11	-3.0	45	129	$5
2nd Half	109	12	4	15	0	248	288	284	450	734	700	737	5	84	0.35	39	26	35	26	99	102	88	12%	114	9%	0%	13	46%	31%	4.01	-2.9	66	189	$3
17 Proj	**264**	**26**	**8**	**30**	**1**	**261**	**268**	**303**	**424**	**727**	**576**	**748**	**6**	**83**	**0.35**	**40**	**22**	**38**	**29**	**100**	**91**	**97**	**9%**	**101**	**5%**	**27%**				**4.28**	**-4.7**	**41**	**117**	**$6**

Goeddel,Tyler

Age: 24 Bats: R Pos: LF | Ht: 6' 4" Wt: 180
Health A | PT/Exp F | Consist C | LIMA Plan D | Rand Var +2 | MM 1501

Jump from AA to majors proved to be a bit much. Low h%, including 21% vs L, partly to blame for ugly line, but xBA and lack of power don't provide much reason for optimism, either. Excellent speed reveals path to fantasy relevance, but first needs to prove that he can actually reach first base.

Yr Tm	AB	R	HR	RBI	SB	BA	xBA	OBP	SLG	OPS	vL	vR	bb%	ct%	Eye	G	L	F	h%	HctX	PX	xPX	hr/f	Spd	SBO	SB%	#Wk	DOM	DIS	RC/G	RAR	BPV	BPX	R$
12																																		
13																																		
14																																		
15 aa	473	54	9	57	22	242		299	364	663			7	76	0.34				30		77			133	27%	69%				3.56		23	62	$15
16 PHI	213	17	4	16	3	192	225	258	291	549	448	632	7	76	0.33	54	17	29	24	77	54	79	9%	178	6%	100%	25	28%	52%	2.38	-15.1	16	46	-$2
1st Half	146	13	3	13	1	226	239	269	349	619	458	705	5	76	0.23	52	19	29	28	66	68	79	9%	183	3%	100%	14	29%	57%	3.10	-6.0	26	74	-$1
2nd Half	67	4	1	3	2	119	182	234	164	398	435	322	12	75	0.53	57	12	31	14	103	23	78	7%	113	13%	100%	11	27%	45%	1.17	-7.6	-23	-66	-$6
17 Proj	**160**	**14**	**3**	**14**	**5**	**227**	**222**	**299**	**331**	**629**	**569**	**701**	**8**	**76**	**0.38**	**53**	**15**	**32**	**28**	**88**	**58**	**78**	**9%**	**153**	**15%**	**78%**				**3.22**	**-6.1**	**-1**	**-3**	**$3**

Goldschmidt,Paul

Age: 29 Bats: R Pos: 1B | Ht: 6' 4" Wt: 245
Health B | PT/Exp A | Consist D | LIMA Plan D+ | Rand Var -1 | MM 4345

Career low FB%, huge jump in pop-up rate brought down power numbers, but made up for it by running wild on bases, particularly in 2nd half. So-so speed suggests betting against SB repeat, but even if he doesn't reach 30 HR or SB, overall package ensures he'll continue to be five-category anchor.

Yr Tm	AB	R	HR	RBI	SB	BA	xBA	OBP	SLG	OPS	vL	vR	bb%	ct%	Eye	G	L	F	h%	HctX	PX	xPX	hr/f	Spd	SBO	SB%	#Wk	DOM	DIS	RC/G	RAR	BPV	BPX	R$
12 ARI	514	82	20	82	18	286	274	359	490	850	1068	739	10	75	0.46	40	24	36	35	127	149	160	14%	77	15%	86%	27	56%	22%	6.41	14.3	64	160	$25
13 ARI	602	103	36	125	15	302	290	401	551	952	986	941	14	76	0.68	44	21	35	35	132	168	164	23%	91	11%	68%	27	67%	19%	7.94	56.1	96	240	$40
14 ARI	406	75	19	69	9	300	297	396	542	938	1115	894	14	73	0.58	45	22	33	37	139	194	173	19%	95	9%	75%	19	58%	16%	7.78	40.4	104	281	$24
15 ARI	567	103	33	110	21	321	284	435	570	1005	1081	984	17	73	0.78	42	23	35	39	132	169	152	22%	85	11%	81%	27	70%	7%	9.42	61.9	91	246	$42
16 ARI	579	106	24	95	32	297	273	411	489	899	1070	850	16	74	0.73	46	25	29	37	113	121	106	19%	86	17%	86%	27	48%	22%	7.48	34.6	53	151	$37
1st Half	298	47	15	55	11	292	276	418	510	929	1102	873	17	73	0.78	44	25	30	36	113	136	118	22%	84	12%	79%	14	57%	7%	7.67	21.6	62	177	$34
2nd Half	281	59	9	40	21	302	271	402	466	868	1028	827	14	75	0.68	49	24	27	37	113	106	94	15%	90	22%	91%	13	38%	38%	7.28	16.9	44	126	$40
17 Proj	**564**	**104**	**25**	**100**	**24**	**304**	**277**	**409**	**514**	**923**	**1065**	**900**	**15**	**74**	**0.69**	**45**	**24**	**31**	**37**	**123**	**136**	**132**	**19%**	**86**	**14%**	**83%**				**7.83**	**42.5**	**68**	**195**	**$39**

Gomes,Yan

Age: 29 Bats: R Pos: CA | Ht: 6' 2" Wt: 215
Health D | PT/Exp C | Consist D | LIMA Plan D+ | Rand Var +5 | MM 3213

Skills took another step back, and luck wasn't on his side, either. Had 12% h% vR, and just as he was about to return from separated shoulder, suffered wrist fracture. Some sort of rebound is likely, but between poor plate approach, declining power, and injury risk, not nearly as intriguing as he was a couple years ago.

Yr Tm	AB	R	HR	RBI	SB	BA	xBA	OBP	SLG	OPS	vL	vR	bb%	ct%	Eye	G	L	F	h%	HctX	PX	xPX	hr/f	Spd	SBO	SB%	#Wk	DOM	DIS	RC/G	RAR	BPV	BPX	R$
12 TOR *	403	38	13	51	3	254	237	292	427	719	701	567	5	71	0.19	48	15	37	33	93	133	127	16%	69	3%	100%	15	27%	53%	4.30	1.9	23	58	$8
13 CLE	293	45	11	38	2	294	261	345	481	826	934	766	6	77	0.27	43	18	39	35	104	131	126	12%	112	3%	100%	26	54%	38%	5.85	17.3	61	153	$11
14 CLE	485	61	21	74	0	278	266	313	472	785	879	745	5	75	0.20	37	24	39	33	101	139	128	14%	98	0%	0%	26	54%	23%	5.21	25.9	53	143	$18
15 CLE	363	38	12	45	0	231	248	267	391	659	545	702	3	71	0.13	34	26	40	29	86	120	102	11%	59	0%	0%	20	35%	40%	3.35	-4.2	8	22	$4
16 CLE	251	22	9	34	0	167	221	201	327	527	740	445	3	73	0.13	39	16	45	19	80	102	99	11%	77	0%	0%	18	33%	33%	1.96	-15.5	4	11	-$4
1st Half	220	21	8	31	0	182	224	216	345	561	847	451	4	73	0.14	39	16	45	21	82	104	100	11%	79	0%	0%	14	29%	36%	2.27	-13.2	9	26	-$3
2nd Half	31	1	1	3	0	65	189	94	194	287	0	403	3	68	0.10	38	19	43	5	65	87	95	11%	85	0%	0%	4	50%	25%	0.49	-4.1	-26	-74	-$7
17 Proj	**368**	**42**	**13**	**51**	**1**	**240**	**243**	**278**	**412**	**691**	**680**	**695**	**4**	**74**	**0.18**	**38**	**21**	**42**	**29**	**82**	**111**	**106**	**12%**	**79**	**1%**	**100%**				**3.79**	**-3.8**	**13**	**38**	**$8**

Gomez,Carlos

Age: 31 Bats: R Pos: CF LF | Ht: 6' 2" Wt: 215
Health B | PT/Exp B | Consist C | LIMA Plan C+ | Rand Var 0 | MM 3425

13-53-.231 with 18 SB in 411 AB at HOU/TEX. Was a mess in HOU, as ct% and power were way down. Still a lot of whiffs after move to TEX, but FB%, exit velocity skyrocketed, resulting in 8 HR, .905 OPS in 130 PA. All told, he clearly carries risk, particularly when it comes to BA. But also still offers... UP: 25 HR, 25 SB

Yr Tm	AB	R	HR	RBI	SB	BA	xBA	OBP	SLG	OPS	vL	vR	bb%	ct%	Eye	G	L	F	h%	HctX	PX	xPX	hr/f	Spd	SBO	SB%	#Wk	DOM	DIS	RC/G	RAR	BPV	BPX	R$
12 MIL	415	72	19	51	37	260	250	305	463	768	778	762	5	76	0.20	40	17	43	30	108	128	124	14%	123	50%	86%	25	40%	40%	4.85	3.5	56	140	$24
13 MIL	536	80	24	73	40	284	263	338	506	843	993	797	6	73	0.25	40	21	38	35	113	153	137	16%	147	37%	85%	27	48%	30%	6.07	32.1	73	183	$36
14 MIL	574	95	23	73	34	284	262	356	477	833	828	835	8	75	0.33	38	22	41	34	117	142	132	13%	118	31%	74%	26	54%	35%	5.63	32.1	68	184	$36
15 2 TM	435	61	12	56	17	255	251	314	409	724	646	745	7	77	0.31	43	19	38	31	101	110	99	10%	86	26%	65%	23	22%	35%	4.09	-3.9	36	97	$16
16 2 AL *	444	48	14	55	18	230	227	285	382	666	636	699	7	66	0.23	44	21	35	31	81	110	87	14%	104	25%	74%	25	20%	52%	3.57	-9.6	1	3	$11
1st Half	239	22	5	21	8	217	218	275	331	606	706	589	7	64	0.22	46	24	30	32	82	93	85	10%	94	21%	71%	13	15%	54%	2.93	-11.4	-25	-71	$7
2nd Half	205	26	9	34	10	245	240	296	441	738	547	820	7	69	0.24	43	18	40	31	81	129	90	18%	112	29%	77%	12	25%	50%	4.39	-0.4	29	83	$16
17 Proj	**489**	**65**	**17**	**64**	**24**	**250**	**244**	**312**	**425**	**737**	**684**	**754**	**7**	**72**	**0.26**	**42**	**20**	**38**	**32**	**95**	**116**	**102**	**13%**	**108**	**29%**	**74%**				**4.30**	**-3.1**	**32**	**90**	**$21**

BRIAN RUDD

Gonzalez,Adrian

Age: 35 Bats: L Pos: 1B | Ht: 6' 2" Wt: 225
Health A | PT/Exp A | Consist A | LIMA Plan B+ | Rand Var -1 | MM 3045

Ripples in the force. Typical hr/f was negated by career-low FB%, and torrid Aug kept lifetime-worst HctX, PX (with a feeble 41 PX vL) from being, well, worse. LD% magic remained intact, and box at left vouches for his consistency. Still, BPV took quite a tumble, and he's never been 35 before. Sliding into middle tier of 1B.

Yr Tm	AB	R	HR	RBI	SB	BA	xBA	OBP	SLG	OPS	vL	vR	bb%	ct%	Eye	G	L	F	h%	HctX	PX	xPX	hr/f	Spd	SBO	SB%	#Wk	DOM	DIS	RC/G	RAR	BPV	BPX	R$
12 2 TM	629	75	18	108	2	299	279	344	463	806	846	783	6	83	0.38	40	24	36	34	121	111	134	10%	58	1%	100%	27	56%	30%	5.79	6.2	51	128	$24
13 LA	583	69	22	100	1	293	272	342	461	803	747	829	7	83	0.48	38	23	39	32	125	110	140	11%	67	1%	100%	27	59%	15%	5.77	19.1	58	145	$24
14 LA	590	83	27	116	1	276	292	335	483	818	588	903	9	81	0.50	38	24	38	30	136	145	145	15%	47	1%	50%	28	64%	11%	5.74	26.0	74	200	$26
15 LA	571	76	28	90	0	275	290	350	480	830	782	850	10	81	0.58	37	26	37	30	128	127	154	16%	49	1%	0%	27	48%	26%	5.80	7.0	63	170	$20
16 LA	568	69	18	90	0	285	275	349	435	784	602	859	9	79	0.47	46	26	27	33	106	93	94	14%	61	1%	0%	27	33%	33%	5.33	-0.1	30	86	$18
1st Half	288	29	6	39	0	278	249	352	385	737	626	768	10	78	0.52	51	24	25	34	97	70	85	11%	68	0%	0%	14	36%	43%	4.79	-2.5	10	29	$13
2nd Half	280	40	12	51	0	293	299	346	486	832	587	976	7	81	0.42	42	29	30	33	115	115	104	18%	57	3%	0%	13	31%	23%	5.86	5.9	50	143	$22
17 Proj	**576**	**74**	**22**	**87**	**0**	**283**	**282**	**345**	**459**	**804**	**662**	**866**	**9**	**81**	**0.48**	**42**	**26**	**33**	**32**	**119**	**106**	**122**	**15%**	**57**	**1%**	**15%**				**5.56**	**7.5**	**34**	**97**	**$20**

Gonzalez,Carlos

Age: 31 Bats: L Pos: RF | Ht: 6' 1" Wt: 180
Health B | PT/Exp B | Consist C | LIMA Plan B+ | Rand Var -2 | MM 4245

Was chasing 2015 HR pace in 1st half until HR/f fell off a cliff (4% after ankle injury in early Aug). Nobody likes swapping taters for gappers, but 2nd half HctX, xPX bode well for power rebound. SB gone since injury-plagued 2014, but batting skills remain steadfast. Rumblings of move to 1B add a bit of intrigue.

Yr Tm	AB	R	HR	RBI	SB	BA	xBA	OBP	SLG	OPS	vL	vR	bb%	ct%	Eye	G	L	F	h%	HctX	PX	xPX	hr/f	Spd	SBO	SB%	#Wk	DOM	DIS	RC/G	RAR	BPV	BPX	R$
12 COL	518	89	22	85	20	303	285	371	510	881	742	961	10	78	0.49	49	22	29	35	116	134	116	19%	109	16%	80%	26	50%	23%	6.94	25.7	73	183	$30
13 COL	391	72	26	70	21	302	281	367	591	958	875	1004	9	70	0.35	38	22	41	37	112	206	170	24%	139	23%	88%	22	50%	45%	8.09	37.7	107	268	$30
14 COL	260	35	11	38	3	238	256	292	431	723	635	766	7	73	0.27	47	15	38	28	109	146	119	15%	96	6%	100%	15	40%	27%	4.25	1.2	53	143	$6
15 COL	554	87	40	97	2	271	284	325	540	864	530	997	8	76	0.35	47	16	36	29	114	166	126	26%	96	2%	100%	27	63%	19%	6.19	21.0	83	224	$25
16 COL	584	87	25	100	2	298	282	350	505	855	786	883	7	78	0.36	46	21	33	35	117	129	127	17%	98	3%	50%	27	52%	22%	6.34	26.8	61	174	$24
1st Half	308	54	18	51	2	321	288	370	568	939	815	989	7	75	0.32	47	22	31	38	107	148	125	25%	120	4%	67%	14	50%	29%	7.86	26.0	72	206	$32
2nd Half	276	33	7	49	0	272	272	327	435	761	754	764	7	81	0.42	45	21	34	31	129	109	129	9%	78	2%	0%	13	54%	15%	4.88	1.5	51	146	$16
17 Proj	**551**	**82**	**30**	**93**	**2**	**280**	**277**	**333**	**513**	**845**	**712**	**904**	**7**	**77**	**0.34**	**46**	**18**	**36**	**32**	**116**	**141**	**127**	**20%**	**96**	**2%**	**80%**				**6.04**	**20.9**	**55**	**157**	**$24**

Gonzalez,Marwin

Age: 28 Bats: B Pos: 3B SS | Ht: 6' 1" Wt: 195
Health A | PT/Exp C | Consist B | LIMA Plan C | Rand Var 0 | MM 2233

A year after trading ct% for power without hurting already mediocre xBA, became jack of more trades by adding running game. Although Spd/SB% doesn't guarantee it will stick, the prime number to heed is 35746, the positions for which he may be eligible in 2017. You could do worse at the end of your draft.

Yr Tm	AB	R	HR	RBI	SB	BA	xBA	OBP	SLG	OPS	vL	vR	bb%	ct%	Eye	G	L	F	h%	HctX	PX	xPX	hr/f	Spd	SBO	SB%	#Wk	DOM	DIS	RC/G	RAR	BPV	BPX	R$
12 HOU *	244	22	3	19	3	241	262	286	342	628	296	713	6	85	0.41	54	20	27	28	90	74	67	4%	84	11%	50%	20	35%	30%	3.17	-10.1	37	93	$1
13 HOU *	376	34	5	25	9	221	240	251	307	559	575	570	4	83	0.24	54	15	30	26	93	62	84	8%	100	16%	74%	20	25%	35%	2.53	-16.4	21	53	$2
14 HOU	285	33	6	23	2	277	253	327	400	727	776	719	6	80	0.29	52	18	30	33	93	92	68	9%	92	8%	33%	26	46%	38%	4.26	4.8	33	89	$7
15 HOU	344	44	12	34	4	279	265	317	442	759	843	701	4	78	0.22	44	23	33	33	109	107	100	14%	95	11%	44%	27	48%	44%	4.62	0.5	39	105	$11
16 HOU	484	55	13	51	12	254	253	293	401	694	724	678	4	76	0.19	47	21	32	31	102	94	99	12%	99	17%	67%	27	30%	37%	3.83	-13.9	18	51	$12
1st Half	233	30	6	22	8	253	256	301	403	705	773	664	5	76	0.23	42	25	33	31	105	97	122	11%	109	24%	67%	14	29%	36%	3.90	-6.9	25	71	$13
2nd Half	251	25	7	29	4	255	246	285	398	684	672	689	3	76	0.15	53	17	31	31	100	92	78	13%	91	12%	67%	13	31%	38%	3.77	-8.3	12	34	$11
17 Proj	**368**	**42**	**10**	**36**	**6**	**262**	**257**	**299**	**407**	**706**	**742**	**689**	**4**	**78**	**0.20**	**48**	**20**	**31**	**31**	**101**	**91**	**91**	**11%**	**95**	**14%**	**58%**				**3.98**	**-9.9**	**19**	**54**	**$11**

Gordon,Alex

Age: 33 Bats: L Pos: LF | Ht: 6' 2" Wt: 220
Health C | PT/Exp C | Consist B | LIMA Plan B | Rand Var 0 | MM 3225

17-40-.220 in 445 AB at KC. A lost season. Peripherals suggest wrist fractured in May never healed. Overcome by toxic ct% and mundane HctX, his BA/xBA and SLG were full-season worsts. Plate patience, xPX state best case for rebound, although contact and health may prove to be persistent adversaries going forward.

Yr Tm	AB	R	HR	RBI	SB	BA	xBA	OBP	SLG	OPS	vL	vR	bb%	ct%	Eye	G	L	F	h%	HctX	PX	xPX	hr/f	Spd	SBO	SB%	#Wk	DOM	DIS	RC/G	RAR	BPV	BPX	R$
12 KC	642	93	14	72	10	294	272	368	455	822	668	908	10	78	0.52	42	25	33	36	96	116	103	8%	85	8%	67%	27	56%	15%	5.95	24.9	54	135	$24
13 KC	633	90	20	81	11	265	247	327	422	749	877	683	8	78	0.37	40	20	39	31	112	104	125	10%	120	8%	79%	26	42%	38%	4.71	13.5	47	118	$22
14 KC	563	87	19	74	12	266	260	351	432	783	787	782	10	78	0.52	43	19	38	31	108	123	118	11%	69	9%	80%	27	48%	26%	5.16	24.0	52	141	$22
15 KC *	382	44	14	52	2	276	250	367	435	802	817	805	13	74	0.55	38	25	38	34	108	111	125	13%	75	6%	29%	20	45%	35%	5.39	10.9	34	92	$12
16 KC *	467	64	18	44	8	223	226	306	381	687	665	704	11	67	0.36	38	24	38	29	100	107	147	15%	90	7%	89%	24	17%	46%	3.89	-5.5	3	9	$7
1st Half	199	25	7	17	3	222	216	301	357	659	532	710	10	66	0.33	34	25	41	30	84	94	139	13%	74	6%	100%	11	18%	45%	3.61	-5.1	-16	-46	$4
2nd Half	268	39	11	27	5	224	234	311	399	711	730	700	11	67	0.38	41	23	36	29	111	116	152	17%	100	9%	83%	13	15%	46%	4.09	-3.0	15	43	$9
17 Proj	**499**	**67**	**18**	**56**	**7**	**251**	**244**	**344**	**414**	**758**	**747**	**763**	**11**	**72**	**0.44**	**39**	**23**	**38**	**31**	**104**	**105**	**134**	**13%**	**82**	**7%**	**72%**				**4.66**	**3.1**	**21**	**61**	**$15**

Gordon,Dee

Age: 29 Bats: L Pos: 2B | Ht: 5' 11" Wt: 150
Health A | PT/Exp B | Consist D | LIMA Plan D+ | Rand Var +1 | MM 0535

1-14-.268 with 30 SB in 325 AB at MIA. 80-game PED suspension torpedoed season early, batted ball fortunes got him later. Assured h% backslide with more FB, fewer LD—an awful trend when HctX + PX < 100. But never mind, that Spd is absurd. Even a slight reversal of bad habits will put him back in $30+ territory.

Yr Tm	AB	R	HR	RBI	SB	BA	xBA	OBP	SLG	OPS	vL	vR	bb%	ct%	Eye	G	L	F	h%	HctX	PX	xPX	hr/f	Spd	SBO	SB%	#Wk	DOM	DIS	RC/G	RAR	BPV	BPX	R$
12 LA *	333	40	1	18	33	226	246	272	276	548	415	632	6	80	0.32	59	21	21	28	52	36	20	2%	148	53%	75%	18	17%	56%	2.51	-19.3	8	20	$9
13 LA *	468	53	1	28	43	234	224	299	295	594	577	623	8	77	0.41	49	21	30	30	53	45	33	5%	170	44%	74%	12	33%	33%	2.98	-10.0	16	40	$18
14 LA	609	92	2	34	64	289	274	326	378	704	719	699	5	82	0.29	60	21	19	35	62	62	27	2%	197	49%	77%	27	37%	19%	4.39	17.7	50	135	$38
15 MIA	615	88	4	46	58	333	280	359	418	776	823	760	4	85	0.27	60	22	19	39	68	54	40	4%	176	40%	74%	25	44%	24%	5.62	24.5	47	127	$47
16 MIA *	360	52	1	16	32	263	257	300	332	631	579	656	5	83	0.31	59	19	23	31	57	37	29	2%	212	40%	82%	15	13%	40%	3.61	-13.3	38	109	$16
1st Half	94	13	0	5	6	266	249	289	340	629	682	613	3	82	0.18	53	20	27	32	65	43	33	0%	158	35%	75%	4	25%	75%	3.40	-3.9	18	51	$2
2nd Half	266	39	1	11	26	262	260	303	329	632	537	673	6	83	0.36	61	18	21	31	54	35	27	3%	214	42%	84%	11	9%	27%	3.69	-8.8	39	111	$21
17 Proj	**600**	**85**	**3**	**33**	**55**	**282**	**265**	**317**	**360**	**677**	**661**	**683**	**5**	**83**	**0.30**	**58**	**20**	**22**	**34**	**61**	**45**	**31**	**3%**	**196**	**42%**	**78%**				**4.10**	**-12.2**	**30**	**85**	**$35**

Gosselin,Phil

Age: 28 Bats: R Pos: 2B | Ht: 6' 1" Wt: 190
Health C | PT/Exp F | Consist F | LIMA Plan D+ | Rand Var -2 | MM 1431

There's nothing truly attractive or overtly repellent here. Plate skills are passable, and while power certainly falls short, Spd appears untapped. While lack of standout proficiencies has limited his PT and exacerbated reliability grades, still useful for plug-and-play without threatening irreparable damage. There IS a skill in that.

Yr Tm	AB	R	HR	RBI	SB	BA	xBA	OBP	SLG	OPS	vL	vR	bb%	ct%	Eye	G	L	F	h%	HctX	PX	xPX	hr/f	Spd	SBO	SB%	#Wk	DOM	DIS	RC/G	RAR	BPV	BPX	R$
12 aa	484	45	2	38	10	216		273	284	556			7	79	0.36				27		52			96	12%	69%				2.50		1	3	$1
13 ATL *	431	37	2	30	5	220	183	255	271	526	1100	0	4	81	0.24	67	0	33	27	84	39	-15	0%	112	6%	80%	2	0%	100%	2.28	-18.2	-1	-3	$0
14 ATL *	506	58	4	25	6	276	250	301	371	672	653	603	3	79	0.17	58	17	25	34	91	77	61	4%	144	8%	66%	11	9%	36%	3.88	7.1	30	81	$11
15 2 NL *	127	21	3	18	2	303	309	352	485	837	857	875	7	85	0.52	56	19	26	34	93	123	65	13%	109	9%	67%	13	54%	31%	6.15	7.0	89	241	$4
16 ARI	220	26	2	13	3	277	252	324	368	692	685	694	6	79	0.33	52	21	27	34	87	63	57	4%	134	5%	100%	27	33%	48%	4.29	-3.5	22	63	$4
1st Half	114	13	1	7	0	263	241	317	351	668	596	691	7	77	0.35	57	19	24	33	85	59	55	5%	134	0%	0%	14	29%	50%	3.85	-3.1	13	37	$2
2nd Half	106	13	1	6	3	292	260	330	387	717	785	697	5	81	0.30	47	24	29	35	88	68	58	4%	122	10%	100%	13	38%	46%	4.79	0.0	28	80	$6
17 Proj	**231**	**29**	**4**	**18**	**4**	**278**	**268**	**325**	**399**	**724**	**723**	**724**	**6**	**81**	**0.32**	**54**	**20**	**26**	**33**	**90**	**80**	**60**	**7%**	**126**	**8%**	**82%**				**4.55**	**-1.6**	**28**	**79**	**$7**

Grandal,Yasmani

Age: 28 Bats: B Pos: CA | Ht: 6' 2" Wt: 215
Health B | PT/Exp C | Consist A | LIMA Plan B | Rand Var 0 | MM 4025

Discordant 1st half was prelude to powerful crescendo in second as PX/xPX, FB% blew through the roof. But yearlong refrain was familiar: weak ct%, subpar BA/xBA, lots of grounders. Body of work and chasm between the two halves dissuade full buy-in, but appears poised to pepper his next ballad with more loud passages.

Yr Tm	AB	R	HR	RBI	SB	BA	xBA	OBP	SLG	OPS	vL	vR	bb%	ct%	Eye	G	L	F	h%	HctX	PX	xPX	hr/f	Spd	SBO	SB%	#Wk	DOM	DIS	RC/G	RAR	BPV	BPX	R$
12 SD *	386	55	12	60	0	281	248	374	432	806	971	821	13	79	0.69	53	17	30	33	116	102	87	17%	102	0%	0%	15	53%	33%	5.73	15.6	54	135	$12
13 SD *	124	15	1	10	0	221	255	326	327	653	752	635	13	77	0.69	48	24	28	28	114	94	112	5%	85	0%	0%	6	50%	0%	3.49	-0.7	39	98	-$2
14 SD	377	47	15	49	3	225	242	327	401	728	512	781	13	69	0.50	43	19	38	28	108	139	132	15%	75	3%	100%	27	44%	44%	4.38	10.6	40	108	$7
15 LA	355	43	16	47	0	234	229	353	403	756	794	749	15	74	0.71	46	17	37	27	97	110	117	16%	70	1%	0%	27	37%	48%	4.68	9.2	38	103	$6
16 LA	390	49	27	72	1	228	251	339	477	816	780	824	14	70	0.55	45	16	39	25	111	152	155	25%	69	4%	25%	26	50%	31%	5.17	9.1	54	154	$9
1st Half	178	16	8	30	0	185	235	298	365	663	670	662	14	73	0.60	52	18	31	20	102	113	96	20%	56	4%	0%	13	46%	31%	3.27	-5.0	29	83	-$1
2nd Half	212	33	19	42	1	264	259	373	571	944	830	978	14	68	0.51	38	15	47	30	119	187	209	28%	92	3%	50%	13	54%	31%	7.19	18.8	79	226	$17
17 Proj	**402**	**51**	**24**	**69**	**1**	**241**	**247**	**350**	**461**	**811**	**773**	**820**	**14**	**72**	**0.59**	**44**	**17**	**39**	**28**	**108**	**135**	**141**	**21%**	**70**	**2%**	**37%**				**5.33**	**14.3**	**36**	**102**	**$13**

ROB CARROLL

Granderson,Curtis

Age: 36 Bats: L Pos: RF CF | Health B | LIMA Plan A
Ht: 6' 1" Wt: 195 | PT/Exp A | Rand Var +2
Consist B | MM 4235

Historically low RBI total for 30-HR season dinged R$, but skills remained rock solid. Though hr/f spike may not hold, power metrics still firmly in place, and FB% allows them to flourish. Career-low h% hurt BA, but xBA is optimistic, especially if 2H ct% spike holds. Few signs of age-related decline, so think 2015 without the SB.

Yr Tm	AB	R	HR	RBI	SB	BA	xBA	OBP	SLG	OPS	vL	vR	bb%	ct%	Eye	G	L	F	h%	HctX	PX	xPX	hr/f	Spd	SBO	SB%	#Wk	DOM	DIS	RC/G	RAR	BPV	BPX	R$
12 NYY	596	102	43	106	10	232	251	319	492	811	762	839	11	67	0.38	33	23	44	27	91	175	132	24%	98	9%	77%	27	52%	19%	5.17	0.3	63	158	$22
13 NYY *	240	33	8	17	8	238	231	322	411	734	792	695	11	69	0.40	34	23	44	31	97	134	135	11%	142	16%	80%	12	42%	33%	4.48	-0.9	48	120	$5
14 NYM	564	73	20	66	8	227	236	326	388	714	742	703	12	75	0.56	34	19	47	27	105	119	132	10%	91	6%	80%	27	56%	26%	4.15	0.8	49	132	$12
15 NYM	580	98	26	70	11	259	260	364	457	821	558	892	14	74	0.60	31	27	42	31	118	135	154	14%	100	9%	65%	27	44%	15%	5.55	11.8	63	170	$21
16 NYM	545	88	30	59	4	237	265	335	464	799	723	826	12	76	0.57	36	22	42	26	114	131	127	17%	96	4%	67%	27	48%	22%	5.06	6.2	64	183	$12
1st Half	285	39	14	24	2	232	255	327	449	776	711	799	11	74	0.47	40	19	42	26	116	128	131	16%	101	6%	50%	14	36%	29%	4.58	-1.0	54	154	$9
2nd Half	260	49	16	35	2	242	277	343	481	824	735	855	13	78	0.70	33	24	43	25	112	135	124	18%	88	3%	100%	13	62%	15%	5.60	7.0	75	214	$16
17 Proj	**521**	**84**	**26**	**68**	**5**	**249**	**257**	**347**	**459**	**806**	**714**	**838**	**12**	**75**	**0.57**	**34**	**23**	**43**	**28**	**111**	**126**	**135**	**15%**	**93**	**5%**	**64%**				**5.29**	**9.1**	**53**	**150**	**$16**

Gregorius,Didi

Age: 27 Bats: L Pos: SS | Health A | LIMA Plan B+
Ht: 6' 3" Wt: 160 | PT/Exp B | Rand Var -1
Consist B | MM 2435

Joined league-wide HR surge via perfect storm of FB%, hr/f spikes; latter shouldn't stick given subpar xPX. Made notable gains vL, as ct% off them continued to rise (73%, 82%, 92% since 2014), while xBA bolstered solid BA. Spd, SB% hint at untapped SB upside, so while HR repeat unlikely, there's plenty of staying power.

Yr Tm	AB	R	HR	RBI	SB	BA	xBA	OBP	SLG	OPS	vL	vR	bb%	ct%	Eye	G	L	F	h%	HctX	PX	xPX	hr/f	Spd	SBO	SB%	#Wk	DOM	DIS	RC/G	RAR	BPV	BPX	R$
12 CIN *	521	60	7	47	3	247	256	293	357	650	1000	556	6	82	0.36	67	13	20	29	0	67	-11	0%	178	7%	28%	4	0%	50%	3.37	-11.4	49	123	$6
13 ARI *	388	51	8	29	1	258	245	324	384	708	512	789	9	83	0.58	37	21	42	29	80	83	87	6%	157	2%	24%	23	52%	22%	4.19	7.8	65	163	$6
14 ARI *	496	62	8	43	5	239	241	292	362	654	424	706	7	83	0.45	37	20	43	27	101	82	106	6%	152	4%	100%	19	42%	26%	3.59	4.4	61	165	$7
15 NYY	525	57	9	56	5	265	252	318	370	688	626	712	6	84	0.39	45	21	34	30	82	68	64	6%	120	6%	63%	27	37%	26%	3.91	-7.4	40	108	$11
16 NYY	562	68	20	70	7	276	271	304	447	751	834	721	3	85	0.23	40	20	40	29	85	96	78	10%	120	7%	88%	27	56%	15%	4.74	6.9	63	180	$18
1st Half	275	34	9	38	4	291	281	319	444	763	843	733	4	88	0.31	46	21	34	30	74	82	61	11%	124	7%	80%	14	57%	14%	5.05	4.5	65	186	$20
2nd Half	287	34	11	32	3	261	262	289	449	739	825	709	3	83	0.18	35	19	47	28	95	111	95	10%	118	6%	100%	13	54%	15%	4.46	0.0	63	180	$16
17 Proj	**585**	**69**	**16**	**64**	**6**	**264**	**259**	**307**	**410**	**717**	**697**	**725**	**5**	**84**	**0.33**	**40**	**20**	**40**	**29**	**87**	**84**	**81**	**8%**	**128**	**6%**	**78%**				**4.27**	**-3.3**	**42**	**119**	**$17**

Grichuk,Randal

Age: 25 Bats: R Pos: CF | Health B | LIMA Plan B+
Ht: 6' 1" Wt: 205 | PT/Exp C | Rand Var +1
Consist F | MM 4325

24-68-.240 in 446 AB with STL. Strong finish (.275 BA, 12 HR after 8/1) saved otherwise trying season. Stable power skills support HR total, but mediocre ct% and poor 2nd half Eye raise overall risk. Middling BA hampers odds of full breakout, though 2nd half PX/xPX with FB stroke hint at... UP: 35 HR.

Yr Tm	AB	R	HR	RBI	SB	BA	xBA	OBP	SLG	OPS	vL	vR	bb%	ct%	Eye	G	L	F	h%	HctX	PX	xPX	hr/f	Spd	SBO	SB%	#Wk	DOM	DIS	RC/G	RAR	BPV	BPX	R$
12																																		
13 aa	500	74	18	55	8	231		266	412	678			4	80	0.24				26		117			124	15%	59%				3.51		62	155	$12
14 STL *	546	63	20	59	6	224	231	257	392	649	689	662	4	72	0.16	39	15	46	27	141	127	162	8%	100	14%	43%	11	27%	45%	3.13	-11.8	32	86	$10
15 STL	323	49	17	47	4	276	265	329	548	877	819	907	6	66	0.20	38	21	42	37	107	202	139	19%	134	9%	67%	22	55%	14%	6.12	16.7	80	216	$13
16 STL *	527	75	28	81	5	237	251	277	472	750	806	754	5	70	0.19	41	16	44	28	113	154	142	18%	106	10%	56%	25	44%	32%	4.27	-6.0	48	137	$13
1st Half	252	36	11	38	3	208	237	263	407	670	547	727	7	73	0.27	44	12	44	24	104	123	116	12%	109	9%	75%	12	33%	25%	3.44	-8.4	38	109	$8
2nd Half	275	39	17	43	2	263	264	291	532	823	1131	773	4	67	0.12	37	19	44	33	122	186	167	24%	106	11%	40%	13	54%	38%	5.13	5.0	60	171	$18
17 Proj	**497**	**70**	**26**	**70**	**5**	**255**	**256**	**299**	**498**	**798**	**797**	**798**	**5**	**70**	**0.19**	**39**	**18**	**43**	**31**	**116**	**158**	**146**	**17%**	**124**	**11%**	**55%**				**4.89**	**5.6**	**51**	**146**	**$18**

Grossman,Robert

Age: 27 Bats: B Pos: LF | Health A | LIMA Plan D+
Ht: 6' 1" Wt: 215 | PT/Exp C | Rand Var -2
Consist F | MM 2113

11-37-.280 in 332 AB with MIN. Career year after CLE release in May, but further gains unlikely: power skills backed HR boost, but recent xPX doubts he can hold it; 2H BA inflated by fluky h%, which xBA confirms; stopped running after years of futile SB%. Skill growth vL could unlock more AB, but still just an end-game option.

Yr Tm	AB	R	HR	RBI	SB	BA	xBA	OBP	SLG	OPS	vL	vR	bb%	ct%	Eye	G	L	F	h%	HctX	PX	xPX	hr/f	Spd	SBO	SB%	#Wk	DOM	DIS	RC/G	RAR	BPV	BPX	R$
12 aa	485	60	8	35	10	228		311	346	657			11	71	0.42				31		89			115	17%	44%				3.29		14	35	$5
13 HOU *	510	61	6	36	17	254	223	332	339	671	785	669	10	71	0.40	47	23	30	35	85	72	90	7%	108	21%	52%	12	25%	58%	3.56	-10.5	-2	-5	$13
14 HOU *	535	63	9	47	16	247	231	334	355	689	566	703	12	72	0.46	41	24	35	33	63	92	76	7%	84	17%	56%	21	19%	43%	3.82	-1.0	10	27	$13
15 HOU *	396	42	5	29	9	191	176	267	266	534	345	567	9	69	0.34	55	6	39	26	47	61	57	8%	84	19%	49%	6	33%	50%	2.09	-31.2	-28	-76	-$1
16 MIN *	453	61	16	49	5	264	248	365	425	789	994	729	14	72	0.57	38	25	37	33	92	106	96	13%	81	6%	56%	21	38%	38%	5.26	11.8	28	80	$12
1st Half	261	35	11	30	3	251	254	365	430	795	1070	767	15	74	0.69	38	23	39	30	94	115	88	15%	75	7%	51%	8	50%	25%	5.20	5.4	43	123	$13
2nd Half	192	26	5	19	2	281	236	370	417	787	936	700	12	70	0.43	38	27	35	38	89	93	101	11%	94	5%	67%	13	31%	46%	5.35	4.6	7	20	$10
17 Proj	**309**	**38**	**7**	**28**	**6**	**244**	**233**	**336**	**370**	**705**	**797**	**664**	**12**	**71**	**0.46**	**40**	**25**	**35**	**32**	**80**	**87**	**88**	**10%**	**88**	**11%**	**52%**				**3.99**	**-4.4**	**0**	**-1**	**$7**

Gurriel,Yulieski

Age: 33 Bats: R Pos: 3B | Health A | LIMA Plan B+
Ht: 6' 0" Wt: 190 | PT/Exp D | Rand Var +3
Consist F | MM 3245

3-15-.262 in 130 AB with HOU. Modest debut despite rapid adjustment period—signed in July, in uniform by August. Contact ability carried over well, though HctX, xPX say contact was weak. Cuban MLEs point toward improvement, but wait for better stateside skills before investing. Most important number? Age 33.

Yr Tm	AB	R	HR	RBI	SB	BA	xBA	OBP	SLG	OPS	vL	vR	bb%	ct%	Eye	G	L	F	h%	HctX	PX	xPX	hr/f	Spd	SBO	SB%	#Wk	DOM	DIS	RC/G	RAR	BPV	BPX	R$
12 for	289	50	5	51	7	293		371	437	808			11	93	1.87				30		83			109	14%	56%				5.60	8.4	97	243	$12
13 for	297	61	10	67	9	292		382	491	873			13	90	1.48				30		119			113	19%	50%				6.24	19.5	117	293	$17
14 for	414	84	11	63	13	299		352	480	833			8	87	0.62				32		131			92	14%	85%				6.24	29.2	96	259	$23
15 for	175	39	4	34	10	320		395	511	906			11	90	1.28				34		121			96	22%	82%				7.64	14.4	111	300	$12
16 HOU *	165	15	4	18	1	233	250	261	347	608	537	739	4	85	0.25	42	20	38	26	98	68	74	7%	79	6%	50%	6	67%	0%	2.95	-9.1	27	77	$0
1st Half																																		
2nd Half	165	15	4	18	1	233	250	261	347	608	537	739	4	85	0.25	42	20	38	26	98	68	74	7%	79	6%	50%	6	67%	0%	2.95	-9.7	27	77	$0
17 Proj	**449**	**77**	**12**	**72**	**8**	**264**	**278**	**327**	**431**	**758**	**582**	**900**	**8**	**85**	**0.59**	**42**	**20**	**38**	**29**	**88**	**101**	**67**	**8%**	**100**	**10%**	**69%**				**4.80**	**-1.2**	**72**	**205**	**$17**

Gutierrez,Franklin

Age: 34 Bats: R Pos: RF | Health C | LIMA Plan D
Ht: 6' 2" Wt: 195 | PT/Exp F | Rand Var -1
Consist A | MM 4111

Lefty masher lived up to billing with 12 HR vL backed by 148 PX, though 2H hr/f a more realistic expectation. Contact issues persisted, while xBA confirms subpar BA. Inflammatory condition that cost him 2014 isn't going away, so health risk further limits use as power option against southpaws. It's an awful narrow niche.

Yr Tm	AB	R	HR	RBI	SB	BA	xBA	OBP	SLG	OPS	vL	vR	bb%	ct%	Eye	G	L	F	h%	HctX	PX	xPX	hr/f	Spd	SBO	SB%	#Wk	DOM	DIS	RC/G	RAR	BPV	BPX	R$
12 SEA *	212	25	5	22	3	236	250	284	382	666	1160	397	6	77	0.29	43	21	36	28	117	104	125	9%	98	12%	57%	9	44%	33%	3.52	-8.6	35	88	$2
13 SEA *	339	34	12	39	5	193	210	225	353	578	664	846	4	64	0.11	44	13	43	26	91	138	122	23%	93	19%	60%	11	45%	27%	2.42	-20.1	3	8	$1
14																																		
15 SEA *	351	48	19	54	1	258	257	312	478	790	973	978	7	68	0.24	41	24	36	33	119	161	162	36%	71	2%	100%	16	63%	25%	5.14	3.8	37	100	$11
16 SEA	248	33	14	39	1	246	235	329	452	780	884	456	10	66	0.34	50	18	32	32	125	137	144	26%	69	1%	100%	27	33%	52%	4.99	2.0	16	46	$5
1st Half	135	22	9	25	0	252	247	329	489	818	934	534	9	67	0.31	55	16	29	31	113	154	113	35%	79	0%	0%	14	43%	50%	5.37	2.7	34	97	$7
2nd Half	113	11	5	14	1	239	219	328	407	735	832	312	12	65	0.38	44	20	36	32	140	117	182	19%	70	3%	100%	13	23%	54%	4.53	-0.6	-1	-3	$3
17 Proj	**224**	**28**	**11**	**31**	**2**	**240**	**235**	**308**	**428**	**736**	**809**	**608**	**8**	**67**	**0.28**	**45**	**19**	**35**	**31**	**120**	**129**	**149**	**20%**	**77**	**4%**	**72%**				**4.35**	**-2.3**	**3**	**9**	**$6**

Guyer,Brandon

Age: 31 Bats: R Pos: LF | Health D | LIMA Plan D+
Ht: 6' 1" Wt: 210 | PT/Exp D | Rand Var 0
Consist A | MM 2331

Received career-high PA vR for some reason, which weighed down overall line. June hamstring strain didn't help Spd, but SB% decline at this age says legs are no longer a weapon. Skills vL were fine (86% ct%, 123 PX), and LD% stroke suggests he'll hold decent BA, but health, splits make him unusable in weekly formats.

Yr Tm	AB	R	HR	RBI	SB	BA	xBA	OBP	SLG	OPS	vL	vR	bb%	ct%	Eye	G	L	F	h%	HctX	PX	xPX	hr/f	Spd	SBO	SB%	#Wk	DOM	DIS	RC/G	RAR	BPV	BPX	R$
12 TAM *	92	9	3	11	2	233	243	274	379	654	714	0	5	79	0.27	83	0	17	26	115	87	114		104	8%	100%	1	100%	0%	3.54	-3.6	29	73	$0
13 aaa	356	55	5	31	17	244		288	368	656			6	78	0.28				30		88			130	25%	82%				3.65		36	90	$11
14 TAM	259	37	3	26	6	266	253	334	367	701	762	656	6	80	0.31	50	20	30	32	98	81	79	5%	111	11%	86%	25	48%	44%	4.01	0.8	31	84	$7
15 TAM	332	51	8	28	10	265	266	359	413	771	844	673	7	82	0.41	44	21	35	30	104	98	90	9%	102	17%	71%	27	48%	30%	4.47	-2.8	52	141	$10
16 2 AL	293	39	9	32	3	266	263	372	423	795	1021	628	6	81	0.35	41	22	38	30	93	95	80	10%	91	7%	60%	23	48%	26%	4.50	-1.7	42	120	$7
1st Half	163	24	7	17	1	264	271	356	466	823	1164	654	5	78	0.22	34	23	43	30	96	128	95	13%	88	6%	50%	11	55%	27%	4.72	0.1	52	149	$8
2nd Half	130	15	2	15	2	269	255	391	369	760	912	581	8	85	0.58	48	20	32	30	91	57	63	6%	100	8%	67%	12	42%	25%	4.16	-2.0	35	100	$5
17 Proj	**229**	**32**	**5**	**23**	**5**	**264**	**260**	**363**	**401**	**763**	**893**	**637**	**7**	**81**	**0.38**	**44**	**21**	**35**	**30**	**98**	**84**	**81**	**8%**	**102**	**12%**	**72%**				**4.31**	**-1.0**	**37**	**106**	**$8**

RYAN BLOOMFIELD

Gyorko,Jedd

Age: 28	Bats: R	Pos: 2B 3B SS	Health	B	LIMA Plan	B+
Ht: 5' 10"	Wt: 195		PT/Exp	C	Rand Var	+1
			Consist	C	MM	3025

Power of rookie season on display in monster 2H, though unsustainable hr/f helped. Newfound effectiveness vR a positive sign, raising hopes for BA improvement, despite stagnant underlying plate discipline. Big question: Are 25+ HR here to stay? FB%, xPX suggest, "Quite possibly." If not, positional flexibility still a plus.

Yr Tm	AB	R	HR	RBI	SB	BA	xBA	OBP	SLG	OPS	vL	vR	bb%	ct%	Eye	G	L	F	h%	HctX	PX	xPX	hr/f	Spd	SBO	SB%	#Wk	DOM	DIS	RC/G	RAR	BPV	BPX	R$
12 a/a	499	58	19	72	4	249		302	409	712			7	77	0.33				29		106			75	7%	43%				4.07		30	75	$12
13 SD	486	62	23	63	1	249	261	301	444	745	829	715	6	75	0.27	38	23	40	29	115	138	140	16%	90	2%	50%	24	54%	29%	4.45	13.5	51	128	$13
14 SD *	424	41	11	54	3	210	239	275	333	608	669	594	8	75	0.36	44	22	35	25	95	93	115	10%	71	5%	60%	20	30%	40%	2.93	-4.8	15	41	$3
15 SD *	482	39	19	63	0	242	231	289	391	679	803	654	6	75	0.26	42	21	37	29	113	96	129	14%	65	2%	0%	25	24%	56%	3.72	-0.7	10	27	$8
16 STL	400	58	30	59	0	243	265	306	495	801	735	836	8	76	0.39	41	19	40	24	107	137	135	24%	93	0%	0%	27	56%	19%	5.11	5.8	60	171	$10
1st Half	137	18	7	18	0	234	248	295	416	711	575	834	8	78	0.40	44	19	37	25	104	95	111	18%	119	0%	0%	14	43%	29%	4.09	-1.6	42	120	$1
2nd Half	263	40	23	41	0	247	274	311	536	848	875	836	9	75	0.38	39	19	42	24	109	160	148	28%	76	0%	0%	13	69%	8%	5.67	9.4	70	200	$15
17 Proj	517	61	27	72	1	248	251	308	441	748	754	746	8	76	0.35	41	20	38	28	108	111	130	18%	81	2%	40%				4.53	-4.1	20	58	$13

Hamilton,Billy

Age: 26	Bats: B	Pos: CF	Health	B	LIMA Plan	D+
Ht: 6' 1"	Wt: 160		PT/Exp	B	Rand Var	-3
			Consist	B	MM	0515

Best yet to come? Speedster took walk rate (13%), OBP (.376) to new heights from August on. More ground balls, too. Suddenly, batting him leadoff not the worst idea. Oblique injury ended season, also dealt with concussion, but neither should have long-term impact. With health and if gains hold... UP: 90 SB. Really.

Yr Tm	AB	R	HR	RBI	SB	BA	xBA	OBP	SLG	OPS	vL	vR	bb%	ct%	Eye	G	L	F	h%	HctX	PX	xPX	hr/f	Spd	SBO	SB%	#Wk	DOM	DIS	RC/G	RAR	BPV	BPX	R$
12 aa	175	29	1	13	45	271		383	360	744			15	73	0.67				37		56			157	89%	73%				4.66		17	43	$16
13 CIN *	523	72	6	36	76	238	276	285	319	604	0	950	6	77	0.29	50	36	14	30	40	59	-15	0%	163	71%	81%	5	20%	40%	3.25	-13.8	19	48	$34
14 CIN	563	72	6	48	56	250	237	292	355	648	669	641	6	79	0.29	42	21	37	31	70	77	55	4%	167	58%	71%	26	46%	35%	3.37	-8.0	42	114	$28
15 CIN	412	56	4	28	57	226	216	274	289	563	641	532	6	82	0.37	43	20	38	27	69	38	58	3%	164	61%	88%	22	23%	55%	3.01	-16.6	22	59	$23
16 CIN	411	69	3	17	58	260	239	321	343	664	576	696	8	77	0.39	48	22	30	33	60	57	32	3%	183	56%	88%	23	35%	57%	4.27	-4.6	28	80	$28
1st Half	214	34	3	12	19	243	252	291	364	656	675	648	6	77	0.28	47	21	31	30	56	83	32	6%	152	48%	83%	14	43%	50%	3.69	-5.3	33	94	$21
2nd Half	197	35	0	5	39	279	226	352	320	671	456	744	10	78	0.51	48	22	30	36	65	30	31	0%	188	61%	91%	9	22%	67%	4.92	2.3	15	43	$36
17 Proj	512	84	4	29	74	256	234	319	332	651	619	663	9	79	0.44	47	21	32	32	65	49	44	3%	178	56%	86%				4.08	-6.7	25	71	$38

Hamilton,Josh

Age: 36	Bats: L	Pos: DH	Health	F	LIMA Plan	D
Ht: 6' 4"	Wt: 205		PT/Exp	F	Rand Var	0
			Consist	A	MM	3221

Lost season due to knee woes. Early June surgery entailed repair of cartilage, ACL reconstruction. Released in late August as procedural move, but hopes to try to earn some of $28.4 million he's owed, despite battered body, declining HctX, and FB becoming GB. At this point, odds stacked against him. DN: Retirement

Yr Tm	AB	R	HR	RBI	SB	BA	xBA	OBP	SLG	OPS	vL	vR	bb%	ct%	Eye	G	L	F	h%	HctX	PX	xPX	hr/f	Spd	SBO	SB%	#Wk	DOM	DIS	RC/G	RAR	BPV	BPX	R$
12 TEX	562	103	43	128	7	285	282	354	577	930	853	965	10	71	0.37	38	21	41	33	115	196	166	26%	90	8%	64%	27	63%	30%	7.15	36.0	90	225	$33
13 LAA	576	73	21	79	4	250	251	307	432	739	596	802	8	73	0.30	39	22	39	31	99	133	128	13%	118	3%	100%	27	52%	30%	4.55	0.7	49	123	$15
14 LAA	338	43	10	44	3	263	238	331	414	745	884	695	9	68	0.30	37	25	39	36	97	132	136	11%	83	7%	50%	17	35%	35%	4.57	5.1	22	59	$10
15 TEX *	226	30	9	31	0	258	247	296	429	724	726	736	5	70	0.18	46	23	32	33	91	126	121	21%	79	0%	0%	14	36%	50%	4.35	-7.1	17	46	$4
16																																		
1st Half																																		
2nd Half																																		
17 Proj	162	22	6	24	1	248	246	303	420	723	683	741	7	71	0.27	40	23	37	31	99	117	133	14%	93	4%	68%				4.29	-5.8	14	40	$5

Haniger,Mitch

Age: 26	Bats: R	Pos: CF	Health	A	LIMA Plan	D
Ht: 6' 2"	Wt: 180		PT/Exp	D	Rand Var	-2
			Consist	C	MM	3221

5-17-.229 in 109 AB at ARI. Earned first MLB promotion in mid-Aug after huge July in PCL (.402, 11 HR in 102 AB). Generating pop proved more difficult at MLB level (96 PX), though xPX (135) sees hope. Did draw walks at 10% clip, but other plate skills lacking. Unless those improve, full-time work may prove elusive.

Yr Tm	AB	R	HR	RBI	SB	BA	xBA	OBP	SLG	OPS	vL	vR	bb%	ct%	Eye	G	L	F	h%	HctX	PX	xPX	hr/f	Spd	SBO	SB%	#Wk	DOM	DIS	RC/G	RAR	BPV	BPX	R$
12																																		
13																																		
14 aa	267	36	8	30	3	232		277	366	643			6	81	0.33				26		89			99	5%	100%				3.42		39	105	$4
15 aa	153	18	1	15	3	250		307	340	648			8	76	0.35				32		73			100	20%	41%				3.22		10	27	$1
16 ARI *	567	68	24	87	9	265	251	338	469	806	583	760	10	75	0.44	39	18	43	32	113	126	135	14%	125	9%	65%	7	57%	14%	5.40	12.8	59	169	$18
1st Half	287	33	11	36	5	264	259	336	447	783			10	76	0.44				32		115			114	11%	59%				5.06		51	146	$17
2nd Half	280	35	13	50	4	265	255	340	490	830	583	760	10	74	0.43	39	18	43	32	111	138	135	14%	132	7%	76%	7	57%	14%	5.77	10.7	67	191	$20
17 Proj	192	23	8	25	3	254	249	321	448	769	660	808	9	76	0.39	39	18	43	30	100	118	122	13%	122	13%	52%				4.65	0.8	42	121	$6

Hardy,J.J.

Age: 34	Bats: R	Pos: SS	Health	D	LIMA Plan	D+
Ht: 6' 2"	Wt: 190		PT/Exp	B	Rand Var	-1
			Consist	D	MM	1215

Lost six weeks to yet another injury after strong April. Recovered a bit after shoulder, oblique, groin injuries sapped power in 2015, but 2nd half surge also aided by favorable h%. HctX, xPX say he still owns skills to get back to double-digit HR, but at 34, ceiling is low.

Yr Tm	AB	R	HR	RBI	SB	BA	xBA	OBP	SLG	OPS	vL	vR	bb%	ct%	Eye	G	L	F	h%	HctX	PX	xPX	hr/f	Spd	SBO	SB%	#Wk	DOM	DIS	RC/G	RAR	BPV	BPX	R$
12 BAL	663	85	22	68	0	238	249	282	389	671	767	639	5	84	0.36	43	17	40	25	114	91	109	10%	103	0%	0%	27	52%	19%	3.64	-5.2	53	133	$10
13 BAL	601	66	25	76	2	263	267	306	433	738	783	720	6	88	0.52	45	17	38	26	104	101	99	12%	94	2%	67%	27	63%	19%	4.58	20.0	74	185	$17
14 BAL	529	56	9	52	0	268	234	309	372	682	621	702	5	80	0.28	43	19	38	32	104	81	96	6%	100	0%	0%	27	30%	37%	3.98	12.1	28	76	$11
15 BAL	411	45	8	37	0	219	221	253	311	564	494	593	5	79	0.23	49	17	33	26	82	62	69	7%	95	0%	0%	22	23%	50%	2.60	-22.6	4	11	$0
16 BAL	405	43	9	48	0	269	254	309	407	716	782	693	6	83	0.38	45	18	36	30	117	89	110	7%	85	0%	0%	22	55%	18%	4.45	1.7	44	126	$7
1st Half	137	14	2	14	0	241	253	274	358	632	610	642	5	86	0.37	44	18	38	27	143	76	130	4%	79	0%	0%	9	56%	0%	3.34	-4.6	41	117	$0
2nd Half	268	29	7	34	0	284	254	326	433	759	900	716	7	82	0.39	46	18	35	33	104	95	100	9%	91	0%	0%	13	54%	31%	5.10	4.8	46	131	$11
17 Proj	463	50	10	50	0	253	244	293	376	668	674	900	6	82	0.33	46	18	36	29	107	77	98	7%	91	0%	67%				3.79	-9.2	12	35	$9

Harper,Bryce

Age: 24	Bats: L	Pos: RF	Health	B	LIMA Plan	B+
Ht: 6' 2"	Wt: 230		PT/Exp	B	Rand Var	+4
			Consist	F	MM	4235

After huge April, power skills retreated to mortal. In 2nd half, ct%, FB%, hr/f tanked; neck, shoulder woes didn't help. Cold comfort for those who paid for 2015 repeat, but not all went south: elite bb% kept OBP up; SB spiked despite weak SB%; ct% nudged up. 2013 a good baseline, but if last year's issue was just health? Hmm...

Yr Tm	AB	R	HR	RBI	SB	BA	xBA	OBP	SLG	OPS	vL	vR	bb%	ct%	Eye	G	L	F	h%	HctX	PX	xPX	hr/f	Spd	SBO	SB%	#Wk	DOM	DIS	RC/G	RAR	BPV	BPX	R$
12 WAS *	607	105	23	61	19	265	272	334	459	793	715	869	9	78	0.47	45	23	33	31	103	122	107	16%	131	16%	73%	24	54%	8%	5.27	2.1	69	173	$23
13 WAS	424	71	20	58	11	274	281	368	486	854	648	947	13	78	0.65	47	20	33	31	116	142	118	18%	87	12%	73%	22	64%	27%	6.18	19.2	78	195	$20
14 WAS	352	41	13	32	2	273	234	344	423	768	765	769	10	70	0.37	44	22	35	35	92	110	115	15%	117	4%	50%	18	44%	39%	5.02	9.3	26	70	$10
15 WAS	521	118	42	99	6	330	309	460	649	1109	986	1160	19	75	0.95	39	22	39	37	134	208	161	27%	87	5%	60%	27	81%	7%	11.16	87.2	132	357	$40
16 WAS	506	84	24	86	21	243	252	373	441	814	764	833	18	77	0.92	40	17	42	27	106	117	111	14%	77	17%	68%	26	54%	31%	5.48	12.3	61	174	$21
1st Half	264	47	17	48	11	261	262	405	496	902	886	906	20	80	1.23	40	14	46	27	111	129	111	17%	62	16%	65%	14	71%	14%	6.76	16.3	83	237	$26
2nd Half	242	37	7	38	10	223	241	336	380	716	619	752	15	74	0.67	41	21	38	27	102	102	110	10%	94	19%	71%	12	33%	50%	4.23	-3.5	36	103	$14
17 Proj	518	89	30	91	10	273	269	388	510	898	817	930	16	75	0.76	40	20	40	31	111	141	124	19%	86	8%	67%				6.87	32.6	73	208	$27

Harrison,Josh

Age: 29	Bats: R	Pos: 2B	Health	B	LIMA Plan	B+
Ht: 5' 8"	Wt: 185		PT/Exp	B	Rand Var	-2
			Consist	C	MM	1535

As PX and xPX decline, 2014 HR output looks irretrievable. Spd is plus skill, and to his credit, he used it to set personal best in SB, though more opps via higher bb% seems not in cards. Stable ct%, but struggles vR creeping in, and HctX now subpar, too. Expecting more than some SB help may be unwise.

Yr Tm	AB	R	HR	RBI	SB	BA	xBA	OBP	SLG	OPS	vL	vR	bb%	ct%	Eye	G	L	F	h%	HctX	PX	xPX	hr/f	Spd	SBO	SB%	#Wk	DOM	DIS	RC/G	RAR	BPV	BPX	R$
12 PIT	249	34	3	16	7	233	241	279	345	624	580	647	4	85	0.27	37	22	41	26	101	66	111	3%	157	20%	70%	27	33%	41%	2.96	-10.4	50	125	$2
13 PIT *	356	48	6	40	16	261	276	294	412	705	981	466	4	85	0.31	47	19	35	29	120	103	122	12%	103	34%	66%	18	33%	28%	3.96	3.2	63	158	$13
14 PIT	520	77	13	52	18	315	284	347	490	837	856	832	4	84	0.27	37	24	39	35	116	121	117	8%	126	20%	72%	27	52%	15%	6.15	39.2	83	224	$29
15 PIT	418	57	4	28	10	287	263	327	390	717	761	702	4	83	0.27	41	25	34	34	104	77	97	3%	112	17%	56%	27	32%	27%	4.21	0.5	38	103	$13
16 PIT	487	57	4	59	19	283	250	311	388	699	810	674	4	84	0.24	44	19	36	33	95	63	99	3%	143	19%	83%	23	35%	35%	4.34	-7.3	40	114	$18
1st Half	284	33	3	38	13	282	257	307	387	694	776	669	3	85	0.24	45	21	34	32	97	61	91	4%	133	20%	93%	14	29%	29%	4.41	-3.1	38	109	$22
2nd Half	203	24	1	21	6	286	240	317	389	706	911	679	4	83	0.24	43	18	39	34	92	66	111	1%	142	18%	67%	9	44%	44%	4.23	-3.3	38	109	$12
17 Proj	504	65	6	50	17	278	259	312	398	710	799	686	4	84	0.25	42	21	37	32	101	74	105	4%	133	20%	71%				4.23	-8.3	43	124	$19

KRISTOPHER OLSON

Hazelbaker,Jeremy

Age: 29 Bats: L Pos: LF CF | Ht: 6' 3" Wt: 200
Health A | PT/Exp D | Consist C
LIMA Plan D | Rand Var 0 | MM 4411

12-28-.235 with 5 SB in 200 AB with STL. Hot start screamed for regression (65% ct, 240 PX, 45% hr/f in April), but that doesn't mean he's a flash in the pan. In small 2nd half sample, bb%, FB%, xPX stand out as skills he could build on. If you can stand the BA downside, makes for a solid power/speed end-game target.

Yr	Tm	AB	R	HR	RBI	SB	BA	xBA	OBP	SLG	OPS	vL	vR	bb%	ct%	Eye	G	L	F	h%	HctX	PX	xPX	hr/f	Spd	SBO	SB%	#Wk	DOM	DIS	RC/G	RAR	BPV	BPX	R$
12	a/a	466	63	15	53	29	247		289	413	702			6	71	0.20				32		119			106	41%	70%				3.85		23	58	$18
13	aaa	428	45	8	39	27	218		263	308	571			6	64	0.17				32		75			103	36%	77%				2.67		-37	-93	$11
14	a/a	361	26	5	26	13	177		217	269	486			5	66	0.15				25		73			123	37%	53%				1.61		-28	-76	-$1
15	a/a	403	49	8	46	16	242		295	389	684			7	66	0.22				35		113			124	20%	87%				3.97		6	16	$11
16	STL *	240	40	13	35	6	236	244	301	458	759	585	822	8	67	0.28	50	15	36	30	84	144	96	25%	120	18%	66%	22	50%	36%	4.47	-1.4	36	103	$7
1st Half		149	24	7	23	5	254	239	300	458	758	633	811	6	63	0.18	53	16	30	35	77	140	86	29%	127	26%	62%	11	36%	45%	4.42	-1.2	18	51	$10
2nd Half		91	17	6	12	1	208	254	303	457	760	455	837	12	72	0.48	45	13	43	22	94	150	109	21%	101	5%	100%	11	64%	27%	4.52	-0.5	63	180	$2
17	Proj	**161**	**23**	**7**	**19**	**5**	**224**	**241**	**283**	**425**	**708**	**522**	**748**	**8**	**67**	**0.26**	**49**	**16**	**35**	**29**	**87**	**132**	**100**	**19%**	**113**	**21%**	**71%**				**3.90**	**-2.7**	**31**	**88**	**$3**

Headley,Chase

Age: 33 Bats: B Pos: 3B | Ht: 6' 2" Wt: 230
Health A | PT/Exp A | Consist A
LIMA Plan C+ | Rand Var 0 | MM 2225

About as boring as skill sets get; not bad enough to cost him AB, not good enough for any foreseeable upside, just blandly consistent. Even BPV has given up, seemingly counting down to a future season where his game achieves zero sum monotony. We'll commemorate it with a bowl of rice and a side of dry toast.

Yr	Tm	AB	R	HR	RBI	SB	BA	xBA	OBP	SLG	OPS	vL	vR	bb%	ct%	Eye	G	L	F	h%	HctX	PX	xPX	hr/f	Spd	SBO	SB%	#Wk	DOM	DIS	RC/G	RAR	BPV	BPX	R$
12	SD	604	95	31	115	17	286	268	376	498	875	801	906	12	74	0.55	48	19	32	34	117	141	134	21%	75	12%	74%	27	52%	37%	6.64	35.8	58	145	$32
13	SD	520	59	13	50	8	250	253	347	400	747	764	740	11	73	0.47	46	23	31	32	106	119	107	11%	77	8%	67%	25	48%	28%	4.52	8.8	34	85	$11
14	2 TM	470	55	13	49	7	243	251	328	372	700	721	693	10	74	0.42	41	27	32	30	113	99	120	12%	63	8%	70%	26	35%	42%	3.95	3.9	16	43	$10
15	NYY	580	74	11	62	0	259	252	324	369	693	743	670	8	77	0.38	43	27	30	32	94	80	91	8%	79	1%	0%	27	26%	44%	3.98	-9.8	13	35	$11
16	NYY	467	58	14	51	8	253	246	331	385	716	697	726	10	75	0.43	44	24	32	31	95	83	108	12%	83	7%	80%	26	31%	42%	4.32	-6.5	12	34	$11
1st Half		241	25	5	21	4	245	232	320	349	668	610	700	10	76	0.44	44	22	34	31	93	65	114	8%	94	7%	80%	14	29%	43%	3.78	-8.0	4	11	$8
2nd Half		226	33	9	30	4	261	260	342	425	767	797	753	10	74	0.42	44	25	30	32	98	103	101	18%	72	8%	80%	12	33%	42%	4.93	0.3	22	63	$14
17	Proj	**474**	**60**	**14**	**54**	**6**	**255**	**250**	**333**	**390**	**723**	**731**	**720**	**10**	**74**	**0.42**	**44**	**25**	**31**	**32**	**100**	**87**	**106**	**12%**	**77**	**6%**	**73%**				**4.36**	**-7.4**	**10**	**28**	**$13**

Healy,Ryon

Age: 25 Bats: R Pos: 3B | Ht: 6' 5" Wt: 205
Health A | PT/Exp D | Consist F
LIMA Plan B | Rand Var -2 | MM 3035

13-37-.305 in 269 AB at OAK. We hate to be a wet blanket, but before you get carried away with stellar MLB results, please note discrepancies between BA/xBA, PX and xPX/HctX. Surface stats say "Future star!", skills say "Middling BA with poor Eye and only average power." We know, we know. We're not fun at parties.

Yr	Tm	AB	R	HR	RBI	SB	BA	xBA	OBP	SLG	OPS	vL	vR	bb%	ct%	Eye	G	L	F	h%	HctX	PX	xPX	hr/f	Spd	SBO	SB%	#Wk	DOM	DIS	RC/G	RAR	BPV	BPX	R$
12																																			
13																																			
14																																			
15	aa	507	47	7	46	0	258		290	357	646			4	82	0.25				30		70			85	1%	0%				3.52		21	57	$6
16	OAK *	606	86	24	90	1	298	269	339	503	842	886	853	6	76	0.27	42	20	39	36	93	132	102	16%	108	1%	42%	13	62%	15%	6.15	22.6	58	166	$23
1st Half		313	48	10	50	1	291	269	344	491	834			7	75	0.32				36		131			117	3%	42%				6.00		58	166	$22
2nd Half		293	38	14	40	0	304	269	333	516	850	886	853	4	78	0.20	42	20	39	35	95	132	102	16%	94	0%	0%	13	62%	15%	6.31	11.3	55	157	$24
17	Proj	**433**	**52**	**16**	**54**	**0**	**275**	**265**	**313**	**462**	**774**	**797**	**767**	**5**	**79**	**0.24**	**43**	**20**	**38**	**32**	**86**	**115**	**92**	**12%**	**105**	**1%**	**33%**				**5.01**	**1.5**	**34**	**97**	**$14**

Hechavarria,Adeiny

Age: 28 Bats: R Pos: SS | Ht: 5' 11" Wt: 185
Health A | PT/Exp B | Consist B
LIMA Plan C | Rand Var +3 | MM 1425

Previous xBA marks warned of BA drop, which in turn deflated OBP, which in turn killed already meager running game, like a Rube Goldberg contraption built to ruin R$. That said, HctX, xPX both say there's more pop here than he's shown, and ct%/LD% combo should support better BA (see 1st half xBA). Odds are he'll rebound a bit.

Yr	Tm	AB	R	HR	RBI	SB	BA	xBA	OBP	SLG	OPS	vL	vR	bb%	ct%	Eye	G	L	F	h%	HctX	PX	xPX	hr/f	Spd	SBO	SB%	#Wk	DOM	DIS	RC/G	RAR	BPV	BPX	R$
12	TOR *	569	64	6	58	5	264	236	300	360	660	590	677	5	77	0.23	48	21	31	33	81	68	98	7%	123	5%	71%	10	30%	50%	3.72	-6.3	12	30	$11
13	MIA	543	30	3	42	11	227	240	267	298	565	589	555	5	82	0.31	52	20	28	27	77	46	55	2%	155	16%	52%	26	31%	50%	2.49	-17.1	25	63	$3
14	MIA	536	53	1	34	7	276	262	308	356	664	742	645	5	84	0.30	54	22	24	33	100	55	73	1%	172	8%	58%	25	40%	44%	3.80	7.8	43	116	$11
15	MIA	470	54	5	48	7	281	253	315	374	689	912	637	5	83	0.29	51	20	29	33	92	58	84	5%	135	7%	78%	22	32%	32%	4.19	5.5	32	86	$13
16	MIA	508	52	3	38	1	236	254	283	311	594	570	600	6	86	0.45	48	22	30	27	112	43	86	2%	138	1%	100%	27	30%	26%	2.95	-25.4	32	91	$1
1st Half		273	29	3	25	0	245	272	282	348	630	577	644	5	88	0.44	47	24	29	27	115	54	91	4%	147	0%	0%	14	29%	14%	3.35	-9.0	50	143	$4
2nd Half		235	23	0	13	1	226	231	283	268	552	560	549	7	83	0.46	48	21	31	27	109	31	81	0%	112	2%	100%	13	31%	38%	2.50	-14.0	8	23	-$1
17	Proj	**529**	**54**	**5**	**42**	**5**	**253**	**255**	**294**	**339**	**633**	**686**	**619**	**5**	**84**	**0.36**	**48**	**22**	**30**	**29**	**102**	**50**	**82**	**4%**	**143**	**5%**	**74%**				**3.40**	**-16.6**	**18**	**52**	**$9**

Hedges,Austin

Age: 24 Bats: R Pos: CA | Ht: 6' 1" Wt: 210
Health A | PT/Exp D | Consist C
LIMA Plan D+ | Rand Var -4 | MM 1013

0-1-.125 in 24 BA at SD. Sept sip of coffee tells us nothing, but AAA stats offered first signs of offensive life for glove-first backstop, even if they did only last for 113 AB. 2nd half dip possibly caused by hamate bone fracture that made him miss all of May, though we can't rule out 1st half sample size fluke. Wait for more data.

Yr	Tm	AB	R	HR	RBI	SB	BA	xBA	OBP	SLG	OPS	vL	vR	bb%	ct%	Eye	G	L	F	h%	HctX	PX	xPX	hr/f	Spd	SBO	SB%	#Wk	DOM	DIS	RC/G	RAR	BPV	BPX	R$
12																																			
13	aa	67	3	0	7	3	198		255	235	490			7	85	0.51				23		34			94	23%	70%				1.92		11	28	-$2
14	aa	427	26	5	36	1	196		231	276	507			4	77	0.19				25		63			91	5%	20%				1.95		-4	-11	-$4
15	SD *	208	21	4	21	1	202	226	250	308	558	420	483	6	77	0.28	45	19	36	24	67	74	55	8%	71	2%	100%	23	17%	74%	2.47	-8.7	3	8	-$2
16	SD *	337	40	15	57	1	257	223	277	447	724	1000	148	3	79	0.13	44	6	50	28	108	111	59	0%	72	5%	24%	3	33%	67%	4.13	-2.7	35	100	$8
1st Half		113	19	10	28	0	341	313	376	664	1040			5	80	0.28				35		175			79	4%	0%				9.26		97	277	$15
2nd Half		224	21	5	29	1	216	198	226	340	566	1000	148	1	79	0.06	44	6	50	25	107	79	59	0%	79	5%	40%	3	33%	67%	2.45	-11.7	8	23	$5
17	Proj	**369**	**39**	**8**	**40**	**1**	**233**	**235**	**264**	**347**	**612**	**620**	**607**	**4**	**78**	**0.20**	**45**	**19**	**36**	**28**	**60**	**73**	**50**	**7%**	**75**	**4%**	**45%**				**3.01**	**-12.6**	**-1**	**-3**	**$5**

Heredia,Guillermo

Age: 26 Bats: R Pos: LF | Ht: 5' 10" Wt: 180
Health A | PT/Exp F | Consist F
LIMA Plan D+ | Rand Var -2 | MM 1333

1-12-.250 in 92 AB at SEA. Cuban defector not known for power, but 13 xPX is pitcher-batting territory. Takes walks, good ct%, Spd is nice, SB% is not... let's see what he does in larger sample, but you gotta wonder why opponents will do anything other than go aggressively after empty contact. DN: Stuck in AAA

Yr	Tm	AB	R	HR	RBI	SB	BA	xBA	OBP	SLG	OPS	vL	vR	bb%	ct%	Eye	G	L	F	h%	HctX	PX	xPX	hr/f	Spd	SBO	SB%	#Wk	DOM	DIS	RC/G	RAR	BPV	BPX	R$
12	for	245	42	4	23	9	247		323	341	663			10	92	1.38				26		54			113	20%	62%				3.59	-7.8	67	168	$6
13	for	192	38	1	9	4	238		315	336	652			10	89	1.00				27		66			150	15%	45%				3.32	-4.1	75	188	$2
14																																			
15																																			
16	SEA *	435	67	4	51	5	257	242	334	328	662	658	669	10	84	0.71	49	20	31	30	57	44	13	4%	128	8%	43%	10	30%	60%	3.60	-8.7	30	86	$9
1st Half		246	38	2	32	2	252	231	332	319	652			11	83	0.73				30		41			125	9%	22%				3.32		27	77	$9
2nd Half		189	29	3	19	3	263	245	337	339	676	658	669	10	84	0.68	49	20	31	30	57	47	13	4%	110	7%	78%	10	30%	60%	3.98	-2.6	27	77	$8
17	Proj	**283**	**49**	**3**	**24**	**5**	**251**	**259**	**339**	**341**	**680**	**674**	**687**	**10**	**87**	**0.85**	**49**	**20**	**31**	**28**	**57**	**53**	**12**	**4%**	**147**	**12%**	**52%**				**3.65**	**-6.8**	**42**	**120**	**$7**

Hernandez,Cesar

Age: 27 Bats: B Pos: 2B | Ht: 5' 10" Wt: 165
Health A | PT/Exp B | Consist C
LIMA Plan B | Rand Var -4 | MM 1535

Increased patience seemed to drive 2nd half breakout, as pitches per PA rose from 3.56 in 1st half to 4.22. Low FB% limits xPX, but HctX bump in 2H adds legitimacy to hr/f gain. SB% history is terrible; PHI claims he gets poor jumps, so could be fixable issue. Not a .300 hitter (see xBA), but he could deliver... UP: 30 SB

Yr	Tm	AB	R	HR	RBI	SB	BA	xBA	OBP	SLG	OPS	vL	vR	bb%	ct%	Eye	G	L	F	h%	HctX	PX	xPX	hr/f	Spd	SBO	SB%	#Wk	DOM	DIS	RC/G	RAR	BPV	BPX	R$
12	a/a	532	53	2	48	18	264		299	361	660			5	84	0.30				31		65			117	27%	53%				3.41		34	85	$12
13	PHI *	522	64	2	38	25	278	243	331	344	674	581	722	7	77	0.34	52	25	23	36	68	49	48	0%	160	23%	68%	7	14%	57%	3.92	3.9	12	30	$19
14	PHI *	373	40	4	22	7	242	246	299	314	613	626	551	8	76	0.34	53	26	21	31	63	54	50	6%	130	15%	44%	16	19%	56%	2.92	-5.3	4	11	$5
15	PHI	405	57	1	35	19	272	257	339	348	687	769	653	9	79	0.47	54	24	22	34	80	58	68	2%	143	19%	79%	24	38%	42%	4.19	0.3	24	65	$14
16	PHI	547	67	6	39	17	294	263	371	393	764	789	756	11	79	0.57	55	24	21	36	83	55	58	7%	180	15%	57%	27	19%	33%	5.01	2.1	37	106	$20
1st Half		262	25	2	19	4	279	253	319	366	685	576	723	6	79	0.29	53	24	23	35	68	50	48	4%	160	12%	44%	14	7%	29%	3.90	-6.8	16	46	$12
2nd Half		285	42	4	20	13	309	270	414	418	832	988	782	15	79	0.83	57	25	19	38	97	59	67	10%	181	17%	62%	13	31%	38%	6.09	10.4	49	140	$27
17	Proj	**529**	**67**	**6**	**39**	**20**	**280**	**259**	**360**	**378**	**738**	**759**	**730**	**11**	**79**	**0.58**	**53**	**24**	**23**	**35**	**82**	**58**	**59**	**6%**	**161**	**17%**	**63%**				**4.65**	**-2.3**	**21**	**60**	**$20**

BRANDON KRUSE

Hernandez,Enrique

Age: 25	Bats: R	Pos: LF CF	Health C	LIMA Plan D	
Ht: 5' 11"	Wt: 170		PT/Exp D	Rand Var +4	
			Consist B	MM 2311	

Showed willingness to take a walk, and before going down in late June with rib cage injury, flashed a little pop too. A punishing h% played role in struggles, but he's been overmatched by breaking balls, RHP for a while. Until he solves at least one of those issues, he'll have a hard time earning consistent AB or fantasy value.

Yr	Tm	AB	R	HR	RBI	SB	BA	xBA	OBP	SLG	OPS	vL	vR	bb%	ct%	Eye	G	L	F	h%	HctX	PX	xPX	hr/f	Spd	SBO	SB%	#Wk	DOM	DIS	RC/G	RAR	BPV	BPX	R$
12	aa	81	5	1	2	2	216		245	268	513			4	88	0.31				24		33			100	21%	41%				1.92		16	40	-$2
13	aa	437	42	11	36	4	210		256	328	584			6	82	0.35				23		77			102	8%	55%				2.65		34	85	$1
14	2 TM *	497	55	10	45	4	266	264	313	401	714	581	796	6	87	0.52	38	21	41	29	94	92	115	7%	124	9%	39%	9	56%	22%	4.16	5.4	72	195	$12
15	LA *	261	28	8	29	1	269	261	306	427	733	1215	592	5	76	0.22	46	23	30	33	110	106	98	15%	129	5%	27%	20	45%	40%	4.42	-2.2	41	111	$5
16	LA	216	25	7	18	2	190	211	283	324	607	668	524	11	70	0.44	41	17	42	23	79	89	91	11%	100	4%	100%	23	35%	48%	2.93	-11.6	8	23	-$2
1st Half		127	16	5	12	1	189	221	280	346	626	786	483	11	75	0.50	39	15	46	21	102	97	123	11%	90	3%	100%	13	38%	62%	3.09	-5.5	28	80	-$1
2nd Half		89	9	2	6	1	191	198	287	292	579	558	632	12	64	0.38	44	21	35	27	46	76	37	10%	119	4%	100%	10	30%	30%	2.70	-5.0	-22	-63	-$3
17	Proj	**224**	**24**	**7**	**20**	**2**	**241**	**239**	**308**	**386**	**694**	**778**	**615**	**9**	**74**	**0.37**	**43**	**21**	**37**	**29**	**87**	**92**	**87**	**11%**	**121**	**5%**	**63%**				**3.93**	**-3.5**	**8**	**23**	**$2**

Hernandez,Teoscar

Age: 24	Bats: R	Pos: LF	Health A	LIMA Plan D+	
Ht: 6' 2"	Wt: 180		PT/Exp D	Rand Var -1	
			Consist C	MM 3511	

4-11-.230 in 100 AB at HOU. Speedster dramatically improved plate approach, leading to more SB opps, though SB% suffered as he moved up (73% in AA, 45% in AAA/MLB). Showed more power in 2H, though small sample xPX not convinced. Still must prove gains are real, but legs alone make him an attractive end-gamer.

Yr	Tm	AB	R	HR	RBI	SB	BA	xBA	OBP	SLG	OPS	vL	vR	bb%	ct%	Eye	G	L	F	h%	HctX	PX	xPX	hr/f	Spd	SBO	SB%	#Wk	DOM	DIS	RC/G	RAR	BPV	BPX	R$
12																																			
13																																			
14	aa	95	9	3	8	2	252		264	409	673			2	57	0.04				41		146			109	27%	32%				3.12		-16	-43	$1
15	aa	470	70	14	36	25	191		231	310	541			5	69	0.17				24		81			124	37%	76%				2.26		-7	-19	$9
16	HOU *	523	70	12	51	25	256	232	315	395	710	881	632	8	77	0.36	48	12	40	31	102	91	75	14%	130	34%	57%	9	56%	22%	3.88	-7.8	36	103	$18
1st Half		296	43	6	25	22	259	242	316	386	702			8	76	0.35				32		84			118	44%	63%				3.84		26	74	$26
2nd Half		227	27	6	25	4	253	238	313	408	721	881	632	8	77	0.38	48	12	40	31	102	101	75	14%	131	19%	36%	9	56%	22%	3.92	-4.1	45	129	$9
17	Proj	**228**	**31**	**8**	**21**	**11**	**230**	**233**	**280**	**395**	**675**	**798**	**604**	**7**	**74**	**0.28**	**48**	**12**	**40**	**28**	**92**	**104**	**68**	**12%**	**138**	**35%**	**62%**				**3.43**	**-7.4**	**29**	**83**	**$8**

Herrera,Odubel

Age: 25	Bats: L	Pos: CF	Health A	LIMA Plan B	
Ht: 5' 11"	Wt: 205		PT/Exp B	Rand Var -3	
			Consist B	MM 1525	

Strong out of the gate, with 22% bb%, .462 OBP in April, but slipped to 7%, .342 rest of year. Figured out how to make most of speed, successfully converting last 13 SB attempts. Futility vL could cost him some AB, and subpar power hints at HR regression, but should continue to provide counting stats in bulk.

Yr	Tm	AB	R	HR	RBI	SB	BA	xBA	OBP	SLG	OPS	vL	vR	bb%	ct%	Eye	G	L	F	h%	HctX	PX	xPX	hr/f	Spd	SBO	SB%	#Wk	DOM	DIS	RC/G	RAR	BPV	BPX	R$
12																																			
13	aa	389	32	2	26	13	246		274	323	596			4	82	0.21				30		50			145	20%	71%				2.95		21	53	$6
14	aa	368	37	2	37	10	289		331	359	690			6	79	0.30				36		55			110	16%	55%				4.04		7	19	$12
15	PHI	495	64	8	41	16	297	248	344	418	762	720	776	5	74	0.22	47	23	29	39	85	93	83	8%	125	18%	67%	27	41%	30%	4.94	8.7	20	54	$20
16	PHI	583	87	15	49	25	286	249	361	420	781	599	841	10	77	0.47	46	22	32	35	85	79	88	11%	145	17%	78%	27	26%	26%	5.38	12.2	36	103	$26
1st Half		302	47	9	30	12	301	254	390	430	820	600	904	12	80	0.72	45	23	32	35	87	71	77	12%	133	16%	67%	14	29%	21%	5.96	12.3	44	126	$29
2nd Half		281	40	6	19	13	270	244	328	409	737	597	775	7	74	0.27	49	20	32	35	83	89	99	9%	144	19%	93%	13	23%	31%	4.77	2.1	24	69	$22
17	Proj	**553**	**75**	**12**	**50**	**22**	**284**	**251**	**342**	**412**	**753**	**633**	**792**	**7**	**77**	**0.33**	**47**	**22**	**31**	**35**	**85**	**79**	**87**	**9%**	**136**	**18%**	**77%**				**4.91**	**6.3**	**24**	**69**	**$25**

Herrmann,Chris

Age: 29	Bats: L	Pos: CA	Health B	LIMA Plan D	
Ht: 6' 0"	Wt: 195		PT/Exp F	Rand Var -5	
			Consist F	MM 2401	

6-28-.284 with 4 SB in 148 AB at ARI. Put on surprising power display in 1H before injuries struck. Hamstring strain knocked him out for two months, then broke hand in second game back. Probably earned another chance as backup CA, but contact woes, less than impressive power history suggest betting against repeat.

Yr	Tm	AB	R	HR	RBI	SB	BA	xBA	OBP	SLG	OPS	vL	vR	bb%	ct%	Eye	G	L	F	h%	HctX	PX	xPX	hr/f	Spd	SBO	SB%	#Wk	DOM	DIS	RC/G	RAR	BPV	BPX	R$
12	MIN *	508	70	7	48	2	229	245	293	317	610	0	237	8	79	0.43	69	15	15	28	27	63	46	0%	88	2%	57%				3.05	-19.0	11	28	$4
13	MIN *	404	38	5	34	2	193	202	257	280	537	545	624	8	70	0.29	43	19	38	26	106	69	156	10%	102	6%	39%	14	29%	43%	2.20	-19.2	-14	-35	-$3
14	MIN *	279	31	4	24	4	246	234	295	377	672	544	496	7	75	0.28	46	12	39	31	73	107	55	0%	118	8%	77%	13	8%	54%	3.76	2.5	37	100	$4
15	MIN *	176	20	3	15	2	175	211	241	277	518	224	550	8	70	0.29	48	17	35	23	86	78	69	9%	89	7%	100%	20	25%	65%	2.12	-9.6	-11	-30	-$3
16	ARI *	171	23	6	30	4	254	230	325	440	765	1071	804	9	68	0.33	44	17	38	34	123	116	206	15%	145	9%	100%	16	31%	50%	5.03	3.1	31	89	$4
1st Half		134	20	6	27	3	291	247	356	507	863	1100	819	9	71	0.36	44	17	39	37	122	130	199	16%	138	8%	100%	14	36%	43%	6.70	9.5	50	143	$7
2nd Half		37	3	0	3	1	121	179	203	196	398	500	670	9	60	0.25	44	22	33	20	161	54	281	0%	121	15%	100%	2	0%	100%	1.24	-3.7	-61	-174	-$7
17	Proj	**161**	**20**	**3**	**19**	**2**	**230**	**217**	**293**	**365**	**658**	**640**	**662**	**8**	**70**	**0.28**	**46**	**16**	**38**	**31**	**95**	**92**	**116**	**8%**	**114**	**7%**	**86%**				**3.56**	**-2.8**	**1**	**4**	**$3**

Heyward,Jason

Age: 27	Bats: L	Pos: RF CF	Health A	LIMA Plan B+	
Ht: 6' 4"	Wt: 235		PT/Exp A	Rand Var +4	
			Consist D	MM 2335	

Not much went right in first year of mega-deal. Hit the ball with less authority than ever, and xPX continued to slide. Was also less effective on bases, and posted career-worst numbers vR. Even when he bumped up ct%, FB% in 2H, couldn't find a hole or clear the wall. Should rebound some, but ceiling not as enticing anymore.

Yr	Tm	AB	R	HR	RBI	SB	BA	xBA	OBP	SLG	OPS	vL	vR	bb%	ct%	Eye	G	L	F	h%	HctX	PX	xPX	hr/f	Spd	SBO	SB%	#Wk	DOM	DIS	RC/G	RAR	BPV	BPX	R$
12	ATL	587	93	27	82	21	269	261	335	479	814	635	934	9	74	0.38	44	19	37	32	112	138	132	17%	108	19%	72%	27	56%	19%	5.51	6.1	59	148	$26
13	ATL	382	67	14	38	2	254	272	349	427	776	801	766	11	81	0.66	44	21	35	28	101	116	95	13%	101	6%	33%	20	65%	25%	4.75	1.5	71	178	$10
14	ATL	573	74	11	58	20	271	251	351	384	735	477	820	10	83	0.68	45	19	36	31	95	80	80	6%	111	13%	83%	26	50%	12%	4.75	10.8	52	141	$21
15	STL	547	79	13	60	23	293	288	359	439	797	709	835	9	84	0.62	57	19	23	33	105	94	74	12%	107	16%	88%	27	48%	19%	5.84	14.9	62	168	$27
16	CHC	530	61	7	49	11	230	249	306	325	631	586	647	9	82	0.58	46	21	33	27	88	62	72	5%	84	11%	73%	27	26%	37%	3.25	-23.1	25	71	$6
1st Half		281	38	4	26	7	231	248	321	320	641	659	633	11	78	0.54	49	23	28	28	73	61	56	6%	82	12%	70%	14	21%	43%	3.31	-11.9	9	26	$9
2nd Half		249	23	3	23	4	229	250	289	329	619	478	661	8	87	0.66	43	18	38	25	105	62	89	4%	90	8%	80%	13	31%	31%	3.17	-11.5	43	123	$4
17	Proj	**538**	**70**	**13**	**57**	**15**	**262**	**263**	**336**	**399**	**735**	**633**	**900**	**9**	**83**	**0.61**	**46**	**20**	**34**	**30**	**97**	**82**	**80**	**9%**	**96**	**12%**	**80%**				**4.62**	**-1.1**	**47**	**134**	**$19**

Hicks,Aaron

Age: 27	Bats: B	Pos: RF LF CF	Health C	LIMA Plan D+	
Ht: 6' 1"	Wt: 205		PT/Exp C	Rand Var +2	
			Consist D	MM 1213	

By May 1, injury paved way for regular PT, but couldn't take advantage. Power/speed combo showed signs of life in Aug (4 HR, 3 SB) before suffering hamstring injury. Low h% played role in down year, particularly with surprise struggles vL (19%), but stagnant power, inability to hit RHP suggest breakout not imminent.

Yr	Tm	AB	R	HR	RBI	SB	BA	xBA	OBP	SLG	OPS	vL	vR	bb%	ct%	Eye	G	L	F	h%	HctX	PX	xPX	hr/f	Spd	SBO	SB%	#Wk	DOM	DIS	RC/G	RAR	BPV	BPX	R$
12	aa	472	80	10	49	26	258		347	401	748			12	73	0.51				33		96			141	26%	68%				4.63		37	93	$18
13	MIN *	353	42	8	31	10	192	219	258	328	586	713	566	8	70	0.29	45	17	38	25	91	102	104	11%	133	18%	76%	16	38%	44%	2.68	-18.0	18	45	$2
14	MIN *	406	52	5	41	6	235	241	340	330	670	792	512	14	75	0.64	54	20	26	30	78	81	45	3%	98	11%	45%	16	25%	56%	3.57	-4.1	24	65	$6
15	MIN *	501	69	13	49	15	268	259	331	418	750	870	661	9	80	0.48	42	23	35	31	90	94	93	11%	119	13%	78%	18	33%	22%	4.84	1.0	51	138	$17
16	NYY	327	32	8	31	3	217	232	281	336	617	484	691	8	79	0.44	46	17	37	25	93	72	104	8%	87	9%	43%	25	28%	40%	2.98	-17.6	19	54	$1
1st Half		168	18	3	16	0	208	232	273	315	588	469	667	9	81	0.50	49	16	35	24	85	70	102	6%	77	5%	0%	14	21%	29%	2.67	-10.7	22	63	-$1
2nd Half		159	14	5	15	3	226	228	289	358	648	502	713	8	77	0.39	41	18	40	26	102	75	106	10%	109	13%	60%	11	36%	55%	3.32	-6.7	20	57	$3
17	Proj	**317**	**37**	**8**	**31**	**6**	**247**	**240**	**318**	**375**	**692**	**685**	**696**	**9**	**78**	**0.47**	**45**	**19**	**36**	**30**	**91**	**78**	**93**	**9%**	**103**	**12%**	**60%**				**3.93**	**-7.2**	**20**	**58**	**$8**

Hill,Aaron

Age: 35	Bats: R	Pos: 3B 2B	Health B	LIMA Plan D	
Ht: 5' 11"	Wt: 205		PT/Exp C	Rand Var -1	
			Consist A	MM 1121	

After brutal April (.454 OPS), bat came alive during 5 HR, 1.038 OPS May. After July trade to BOS, both PT and production took a hit. HctX, xPX both hint at a little something left in his tank, and versatility could help him stick a few more years. But futility vR says that even an expanded opportunity isn't good news.

Yr	Tm	AB	R	HR	RBI	SB	BA	xBA	OBP	SLG	OPS	vL	vR	bb%	ct%	Eye	G	L	F	h%	HctX	PX	xPX	hr/f	Spd	SBO	SB%	#Wk	DOM	DIS	RC/G	RAR	BPV	BPX	R$
12	ARI	609	93	26	85	14	302	286	360	522	882	839	901	8	86	0.60	34	21	45	32	129	132	145	11%	110	12%	74%	27	63%	7%	6.75	37.1	100	250	$30
13	ARI *	351	49	11	44	1	290	275	345	455	800	911	789	8	85	0.57	39	22	40	31	110	108	120	10%	92	5%	20%	18	61%	22%	5.39	13.9	72	180	$12
14	ARI	501	52	10	60	4	244	252	287	367	654	680	645	5	82	0.30	34	25	41	28	114	89	116	6%	83	6%	57%	27	37%	30%	3.45	-3.2	35	95	$9
15	ARI	313	32	6	39	7	230	248	295	345	640	595	663	9	83	0.57	42	20	38	26	114	79	121	6%	59	11%	78%	26	46%	31%	3.45	-10.6	32	86	$4
16	2 TM	378	48	10	38	4	262	247	336	378	714	745	696	10	84	0.69	37	22	41	29	112	66	102	8%	74	5%	67%	26	42%	31%	4.34	-5.0	34	97	$8
1st Half		242	33	7	26	4	277	253	354	405	759	671	797	11	83	0.71	37	23	40	31	107	74	100	8%	74	8%	67%	14	43%	29%	5.01	0.8	37	106	$12
2nd Half		136	15	3	12	0	235	234	302	331	633	830	449	8	87	0.67	38	19	42	25	122	52	107	6%	79	0%	0%	12	42%	33%	3.28	-6.6	31	89	$0
17	Proj	**192**	**22**	**5**	**21**	**2**	**250**	**249**	**314**	**370**	**684**	**732**	**657**	**8**	**84**	**0.58**	**38**	**21**	**41**	**28**	**116**	**71**	**113**	**7%**	**76**	**6%**	**69%**				**3.91**	**-5.6**	**29**	**84**	**$5**

BRIAN RUDD

Holliday,Matt

Age: 37 Bats: R Pos: LF | Ht: 6' 4" Wt: 235
Health F | PT/Exp C | Consist A | LIMA Plan D+ | Rand Var +3 | MM 3033

Lost 52 days to thumb surgery before end-of-season cameo. Prior to injury, plunges in Eye, batted-ball fortunes were bane for BA/OBP, and power was already receding in 2H. Toll of recent injuries, age-related erosion are significant obstacles to overcome. Expecting a repeat of 2016 production would be pushing it.

Yr	Tm	AB	R	HR	RBI	SB	BA	xBA	OBP	SLG	OPS	vL	vR	bb%	ct%	Eye	G	L	F	h%	HctX	PX	xPX	hr/f	Spd	SBO	SB%	#Wk	DOM	DIS	RC/G	RAR	BPV	BPX	R$
12	STL	599	95	27	102	4	295	270	379	497	877	1021	827	11	78	0.57	46	19	35	34	135	132	145	16%	94	4%	50%	27	52%	22%	6.61	31.4	70	175	$27
13	STL	520	103	22	94	6	300	288	389	490	879	799	903	12	83	0.80	46	21	34	33	134	123	126	15%	84	4%	86%	25	68%	0%	6.86	40.1	83	208	$29
14	STL	574	83	20	90	4	272	268	370	441	811	1004	751	11	83	0.74	46	17	38	30	140	119	142	11%	68	3%	80%	26	77%	12%	5.49	27.9	71	192	$22
15	STL	229	24	4	35	2	279	265	394	410	804	796	807	15	79	0.80	48	23	28	34	112	96	74	8%	78	4%	67%	17	53%	29%	5.56	5.5	46	124	$6
16	STL	382	48	20	62	0	246	264	322	461	782	797	776	8	81	0.49	50	14	36	25	127	120	126	18%	75	0%	0%	21	52%	19%	4.82	2.2	63	180	$8
1st Half		274	35	15	50	0	248	273	324	474	798	784	803	9	81	0.53	54	13	33	25	137	127	141	20%	72	0%	0%	14	50%	14%	5.08	5.0	69	197	$11
2nd Half		108	13	5	12	0	241	247	317	426	743	822	697	7	81	0.40	41	16	43	25	102	104	89	13%	84	0%	0%	7	57%	29%	4.19	-0.8	50	143	$0
17	Proj	376	48	16	56	1	260	268	350	453	803	860	780	10	81	0.61	46	18	36	28	120	113	108	15%	79	1%	45%				5.22	8.4	49	139	$10

Holt,Brock

Age: 29 Bats: L Pos: LF | Ht: 5' 10" Wt: 185
Health B | PT/Exp C | Consist A | LIMA Plan D+ | Rand Var 0 | MM 1343

7-34-.255 in 290 AB at BOS. Mid-season concussion didn't appear to forestall him to extent that LHP did (4 hits in 39 AB). Small sample size, sure, and hr/f (all vR, natch) rescued his season, but tepid power peripherals subdue LD% stroke. Lost some position eligiblity in 2016, PT reduction likely on deck for 2017.

Yr	Tm	AB	R	HR	RBI	SB	BA	xBA	OBP	SLG	OPS	vL	vR	bb%	ct%	Eye	G	L	F	h%	HctX	PX	xPX	hr/f	Spd	SBO	SB%	#Wk	DOM	DIS	RC/G	RAR	BPV	BPX	R$
12	PIT *	542	60	2	44	13	305	275	356	396	751	517	732	7	85	0.54	62	19	19	35	49	64	22	0%	136	17%	47%	6	17%	67%	4.77	0.6	50	125	$18
13	BOS *	350	35	2	29	7	220	221	279	261	540	384	536	8	81	0.44	57	17	26	26	84	31	33	0%	76	11%	67%	8	13%	50%	2.37	-17.3	-9	-23	$1
14	BOS *	557	84	5	34	17	280	272	327	384	711	763	682	7	80	0.35	50	26	23	34	97	80	66	5%	138	13%	84%	19	42%	26%	4.53	13.3	40	108	$19
15	BOS	454	56	2	45	8	280	263	349	379	727	807	701	9	79	0.47	53	24	24	35	89	74	62	2%	120	7%	89%	26	31%	38%	4.72	4.1	30	81	$12
16	BOS *	315	47	7	36	4	258	276	325	382	707	342	762	9	80	0.49	54	24	22	30	75	81	50	14%	92	8%	57%	22	41%	36%	4.17	-0.9	31	89	$7
1st Half		146	23	3	22	2	262	274	340	379	719	688	706	11	80	0.58	53	25	22	31	80	76	66	14%	96	4%	100%	9	44%	33%	4.54	0.4	31	89	$7
2nd Half		169	24	4	14	2	254	276	319	385	704	170	806	8	80	0.41	56	23	21	30	72	84	39	14%	93	12%	40%	13	38%	38%	3.86	-3.0	32	91	$6
17	Proj	288	40	4	28	5	267	272	331	378	709	610	734	9	80	0.47	54	24	22	32	81	73	53	8%	106	9%	67%				4.29	-1.4	24	69	$9

Holt,Tyler

Age: 28 Bats: R Pos: CF RF | Ht: 5' 10" Wt: 187
Health A | PT/Exp D | Consist A | LIMA Plan D | Rand Var 0 | MM 0501

Sports a zero in the hr/f column... for his career (280 AB). With hard-hit metrics like his, may as well have been a pitcher. Hit tool reduces the 30-SB seasons he had in minors to a pipe dream here. Will only have value if "organizational depth" becomes a fantasy category.

Yr	Tm	AB	R	HR	RBI	SB	BA	xBA	OBP	SLG	OPS	vL	vR	bb%	ct%	Eye	G	L	F	h%	HctX	PX	xPX	hr/f	Spd	SBO	SB%	#Wk	DOM	DIS	RC/G	RAR	BPV	BPX	R$
12	aa	216	27	0	11	12	230		300	267	567			9	79	0.48				29		27			124	25%	73%				2.70		-4	-10	$2
13	aa	521	61	1	31	20	221		276	290	566			7	80	0.37				28		52			131	22%	72%				2.61		16	40	$6
14	CLE *	422	60	2	25	26	258	206	339	315	654	659	507	11	74	0.47	50	16	34	35	41	55	42	0%	144	25%	74%	10	20%	70%	3.73	-1.2	7	19	$15
15	2 TM *	399	56	0	23	22	253	254	327	307	634	311	258	10	80	0.54	47	29	24	32	52	43	14	0%	110	22%	79%	5	0%	80%	3.54	-9.1	8	22	$12
16	CIN	179	21	0	13	4	235	226	327	296	623	615	625	11	73	0.48	52	23	25	32	64	41	33	0%	158	12%	57%	27	22%	56%	3.09	-8.5	-1	-3	$1
1st Half		107	13	0	7	4	224	219	294	262	556	575	547	9	73	0.34	50	25	25	31	62	26	35	0%	133	23%	57%	14	14%	57%	2.37	-7.2	-29	-83	$2
2nd Half		72	8	0	6	0	250	232	372	347	719	653	755	15	74	0.68	55	20	25	34	66	63	30	0%	150	0%	0%	13	31%	54%	4.31	-0.4	22	63	-$1
17	Proj	124	16	0	8	4	244	224	336	307	643	653	636	11	76	0.52	52	20	29	32	55	44	36	0%	140	15%	71%				3.42	-4.1	-4	-10	$3

Hosmer,Eric

Age: 27 Bats: L Pos: 1B | Ht: 6' 4" Wt: 230
Health A | PT/Exp A | Consist C | LIMA Plan B | Rand Var 0 | MM 2145

Sacrificing BA for pop wasn't necessarily in his best interest, and FB%, xPX suggest it might not even stick. GB%, paucity of LD% and Spd are forces pulling him in opposite directions. 1H/2H and seesaw xBA over course of career show him especially prone to vagaries of h%. 2017 could fall anywhere within a wide spectrum.

Yr	Tm	AB	R	HR	RBI	SB	BA	xBA	OBP	SLG	OPS	vL	vR	bb%	ct%	Eye	G	L	F	h%	HctX	PX	xPX	hr/f	Spd	SBO	SB%	#Wk	DOM	DIS	RC/G	RAR	BPV	BPX	R$
12	KC	535	65	14	60	16	232	262	304	359	663	591	700	9	82	0.59	54	18	28	26	121	80	95	11%	81	12%	94%	26	54%	27%	3.76	-24.6	38	95	$11
13	KC	623	86	17	79	11	302	287	353	448	801	797	803	8	84	0.51	53	22	25	34	129	96	105	13%	96	8%	73%	26	46%	8%	5.77	20.1	59	148	$28
14	KC	503	54	9	58	4	270	259	318	398	716	676	732	7	82	0.38	51	17	32	32	117	99	100	7%	76	5%	67%	23	35%	26%	4.39	3.6	43	116	$13
15	KC	599	98	18	93	7	297	290	363	459	822	730	885	9	82	0.56	52	24	24	34	116	102	94	15%	101	5%	70%	27	44%	22%	6.00	17.6	60	162	$27
16	KC	605	80	25	104	5	266	263	328	433	761	656	813	9	78	0.43	59	16	25	30	109	97	89	21%	71	5%	63%	26	46%	27%	4.91	0.8	31	89	$19
1st Half		310	43	12	48	4	303	276	363	484	846	800	864	9	78	0.43	59	17	24	36	112	110	82	20%	88	5%	80%	14	50%	29%	6.44	11.4	46	131	$25
2nd Half		295	37	13	56	1	227	246	292	380	672	544	751	9	78	0.44	59	16	25	25	106	83	97	22%	60	4%	33%	12	42%	25%	3.59	-13.6	17	49	$13
17	Proj	601	81	21	94	6	270	271	333	429	762	674	809	9	80	0.48	55	19	26	31	113	93	94	17%	79	5%	67%				4.96	-2.5	36	104	$22

Howard,Ryan

Age: 37 Bats: L Pos: 1B | Ht: 6' 4" Wt: 240
Health C | PT/Exp B | Consist A | LIMA Plan D | Rand Var +5 | MM 4021

Thirty-eight percent of his 65 hits left the yard, all but one vR, against whom he played almost exclusively. Owners who remained on board enjoyed 2H surge even while hr/f, OPS strained credibilty. He'll take that immense PX/xPX to retirement. Until then, he'll take the HR trot at the expense of everything else.

Yr	Tm	AB	R	HR	RBI	SB	BA	xBA	OBP	SLG	OPS	vL	vR	bb%	ct%	Eye	G	L	F	h%	HctX	PX	xPX	hr/f	Spd	SBO	SB%	#Wk	DOM	DIS	RC/G	RAR	BPV	BPX	R$
12	PHI	260	28	14	56	0	219	237	295	423	718	604	784	9	62	0.25	43	26	31	29	98	159	143	27%	50	0%	0%	13	38%	54%	3.98	-11.5	10	25	$4
13	PHI	286	34	11	43	0	266	251	319	465	784	539	878	7	67	0.24	39	24	38	36	122	163	160	15%	83	0%	0%	14	36%	43%	5.17	4.8	39	98	$7
14	PHI	569	65	23	95	0	223	225	310	380	690	770	658	11	67	0.35	41	22	37	29	97	123	154	16%	57	0%	0%	27	33%	44%	3.80	-6.6	5	14	$11
15	PHI	467	53	23	77	0	229	269	277	443	720	418	802	5	70	0.20	36	28	37	27	115	154	152	19%	39	0%	0%	24	54%	33%	3.98	-19.6	30	81	$9
16	PHI	331	35	25	59	0	196	250	257	453	710	355	749	8	66	0.24	35	23	43	21	122	165	192	27%	42	2%	0%	27	48%	26%	3.64	-17.7	24	69	$3
1st Half		192	16	11	25	0	151	223	213	344	557	345	581	8	65	0.24	32	23	45	16	118	125	188	19%	43	0%	0%	14	29%	36%	2.23	-18.3	-11	-31	-$3
2nd Half		139	19	14	34	0	259	287	318	604	922	368	979	7	67	0.24	38	23	40	28	129	219	198	38%	59	4%	0%	13	69%	15%	6.32	5.0	77	220	$11
17	Proj	227	26	15	42	0	223	255	284	461	745	516	900	7	67	0.24	37	24	39	26	117	156	173	24%	51	1%	0%				4.20	-6.2	18	51	$6

Hundley,Nick

Age: 33 Bats: R Pos: CA | Ht: 6' 1" Wt: 210
Health C | PT/Exp D | Consist C | LIMA Plan D+ | Rand Var 0 | MM 3123

Uneven follow-up to solid 2015. Odd, isolated 1H surges in bb%, ct%, GB% might have been related to concussion, oblique strain, but BA regression was foretold by 2015 xBA. Worth noting as he enters free agency: 36% hit rate at Coors last two seasons. Prone to inconsistency, but less risky when part of a job share.

Yr	Tm	AB	R	HR	RBI	SB	BA	xBA	OBP	SLG	OPS	vL	vR	bb%	ct%	Eye	G	L	F	h%	HctX	PX	xPX	hr/f	Spd	SBO	SB%	#Wk	DOM	DIS	RC/G	RAR	BPV	BPX	R$
12	SD *	246	16	3	26	0	153	193	209	235	444	306	568	7	72	0.26	39	18	43	20	98	59	100	5%	94	10%	0%	14	14%	79%	1.34	-24.5	-19	-48	-$7
13	SD	373	35	13	44	1	233	240	290	389	679	553	721	7	74	0.27	43	20	37	28	87	115	99	13%	81	1%	100%	27	37%	48%	3.68	-0.2	26	65	$5
14	2 TM	218	18	6	22	1	243	219	273	358	631	570	641	4	71	0.16	37	23	40	32	98	89	109	10%	70	2%	100%	27	22%	52%	3.35	-0.6	-12	-32	$2
15	COL	366	45	10	43	5	301	267	339	467	807	727	832	5	79	0.28	43	23	34	36	97	108	107	10%	121	12%	45%	23	57%	26%	5.46	16.9	52	141	$14
16	COL	289	30	10	48	0	260	256	320	439	759	923	674	8	78	0.38	46	18	36	30	118	115	109	12%	79	0%	0%	22	50%	32%	4.82	3.4	44	126	$6
1st Half		111	12	4	17	0	234	264	346	432	779	976	681	14	83	0.95	53	11	36	25	127	116	106	12%	87	0%	0%	10	60%	20%	4.91	2.6	80	229	$1
2nd Half		178	18	6	31	0	275	253	301	444	745	892	667	4	74	0.15	41	23	37	34	113	114	111	12%	75	0%	0%	12	42%	42%	4.73	3.0	20	57	$8
17	Proj	261	27	8	36	1	260	251	310	422	733	795	708	7	77	0.31	43	20	37	31	108	103	108	11%	91	4%	46%				4.44	2.3	21	59	$7

Iannetta,Chris

Age: 34 Bats: R Pos: CA | Ht: 5' 11" Wt: 225
Health A | PT/Exp D | Consist C | LIMA Plan D | Rand Var +1 | MM 1003

Difficult to mine for positives in a negative BPV. Did approximate his annual OBP trick (BA+.100) and hit some bombs in 1st half. But everything was crickets in the second half when bat, defense, and playing time plummeted to a level that will be tough to reverse. This is a number two catcher who really CAN hurt you.

Yr	Tm	AB	R	HR	RBI	SB	BA	xBA	OBP	SLG	OPS	vL	vR	bb%	ct%	Eye	G	L	F	h%	HctX	PX	xPX	hr/f	Spd	SBO	SB%	#Wk	DOM	DIS	RC/G	RAR	BPV	BPX	R$
12	LAA *	243	29	9	27	1	235	228	321	385	706	636	756	11	71	0.44	44	20	36	29	99	100	115	16%	79	6%	25%	16	25%	44%	3.94	-1.4	14	35	$3
13	LAA	325	40	11	39	0	225	218	358	372	731	835	663	17	69	0.68	37	19	43	29	97	115	125	11%	65	1%	0%	27	41%	56%	4.34	6.2	25	63	$3
14	LAA	306	41	7	43	3	252	233	373	392	765	880	697	15	70	0.59	38	20	41	34	93	125	100	8%	68	3%	100%	26	46%	35%	4.93	14.4	33	89	$7
15	LAA	272	28	10	34	0	188	196	293	335	628	764	575	13	69	0.49	39	13	48	23	80	105	105	11%	67	1%	0%	26	31%	54%	3.04	-6.0	10	27	-$2
16	SEA	295	23	7	24	0	210	224	303	329	631	740	557	11	72	0.46	41	22	36	27	102	83	94	9%	62	0%	0%	26	27%	58%	3.19	-6.1	-2	-6	-$2
1st Half		211	19	7	20	0	227	242	321	374	695	849	601	12	75	0.54	38	23	39	27	106	93	97	11%	67	0%	0%	14	36%	50%	3.93	-1.3	21	60	$0
2nd Half		84	4	0	4	0	167	176	255	214	470	515	426	11	63	0.32	51	21	28	26	92	50	84	0%	59	0%	0%	12	17%	67%	1.67	-6.8	-67	-191	-$7
17	Proj	245	22	5	24	0	203	205	306	310	616	695	569	13	69	0.47	42	19	39	27	93	80	98	7%	64	1%	50%				3.00	-8.7	-25	-72	$0

ROB CARROLL

Iglesias,Jose

Age: 27 Bats: R Pos: SS
Ht: 5' 11" Wt: 175
Health F | PT/Exp D | Consist C
LIMA Plan C | Rand Var +3 | MM 0335

August hamstring strain likely affected 2nd half Spd and SB%, but pre-injury SB profile was merely average anyway. Made plenty of contact despite h%-induced BA plunge; xBA tells us to split the difference. No pop (a 28 xPX!?), growing injury rap sheet, passive approach on basepaths suggest 2015 might have been peak.

Yr Tm	AB	R	HR	RBI	SB	BA	xBA	OBP	SLG	OPS	vL	vR	bb%	ct%	Eye	G	L	F	h%	HctX	PX	xPX	hr/f	Spd	SBO	SB%	#Wk	DOM	DIS	RC/G	RAR	BPV	BPX	R$
12 BOS *	421	44	2	22	11	235	233	281	279	560	536	284	6	85	0.42	59	16	25	27	55	32	23	8%	112	13%	78%	7	0%	43%	2.65	-15.9	12	30	$3
13 2AL *	469	52	6	41	9	272	250	304	357	661	769	716	4	83	0.27	56	18	26	32	68	59	37	4%	137	11%	63%	22	23%	32%	3.71	3.9	31	78	$12
14																																		
15 DET	416	44	2	23	11	300	273	347	370	717	889	663	6	89	0.57	56	21	23	33	65	46	30	2%	141	15%	58%	22	36%	14%	4.40	0.0	50	135	$13
16 DET	467	57	4	32	7	255	271	306	336	643	704	618	6	89	0.56	51	20	28	28	66	53	28	3%	115	9%	64%	26	46%	23%	3.37	-12.9	47	134	$7
1st Half	258	37	3	20	5	260	276	318	345	663	670	660	8	89	0.72	52	22	26	28	57	53	25	5%	121	8%	83%	14	50%	21%	3.80	-5.0	51	146	$10
2nd Half	209	20	1	12	2	249	262	292	325	617	744	565	3	90	0.33	51	19	30	27	78	52	32	2%	106	11%	40%	12	42%	25%	2.86	-10.1	42	120	$3
17 Proj	**451**	**50**	**4**	**29**	**9**	**266**	**268**	**317**	**344**	**661**	**753**	**621**	**5**	**89**	**0.49**	**54**	**20**	**27**	**29**	**67**	**49**	**30**	**4%**	**126**	**12%**	**61%**				**3.54**	**-12.3**	**31**	**87**	**$9**

Inciarte,Ender

Age: 26 Bats: L Pos: CF
Ht: 5' 11" Wt: 165
Health B | PT/Exp B | Consist B
LIMA Plan B | Rand Var -1 | MM 1545

April hammy led to slow start; safe to say he recovered in 2H. Stable xBA, superb ct% in this K-friendly age set high BA floor, while Spd fits GB/LD profile like a glove. Gains vL seem legit too (90% ct%), though feeble power skills limit any HR upside. Said this last year; bb% gains make it even more attainable... UP: 35 SB

Yr Tm	AB	R	HR	RBI	SB	BA	xBA	OBP	SLG	OPS	vL	vR	bb%	ct%	Eye	G	L	F	h%	HctX	PX	xPX	hr/f	Spd	SBO	SB%	#Wk	DOM	DIS	RC/G	RAR	BPV	BPX	R$
12																																		
13 aa	473	59	4	21	37	264		298	341	639			5	89	0.45				29		50			136	37%	81%				3.64		49	123	$20
14 ARI *	527	68	5	35	23	273	271	314	358	671	646	691	6	85	0.40	52	24	25	31	87	60	51	5%	135	20%	81%	23	43%	22%	4.02	2.9	43	116	$19
15 ARI	524	73	6	45	21	303	284	338	408	747	530	826	5	89	0.45	52	22	26	33	102	66	72	5%	139	21%	68%	23	57%	9%	4.88	8.4	62	168	$24
16 ATL	522	85	3	29	16	291	275	351	381	732	749	726	8	87	0.66	49	24	27	33	80	53	50	2%	167	14%	70%	24	50%	29%	4.71	0.9	58	166	$18
1st Half	203	24	0	10	8	236	259	307	305	612	597	620	9	88	0.76	47	22	31	27	61	41	30	0%	149	20%	73%	11	45%	27%	3.09	-8.8	47	134	$6
2nd Half	319	61	3	19	8	326	286	379	429	809	903	783	8	87	0.60	51	25	24	37	93	61	64	4%	166	11%	67%	13	54%	31%	6.01	12.9	62	177	$26
17 Proj	**555**	**82**	**5**	**35**	**22**	**288**	**279**	**338**	**382**	**720**	**646**	**748**	**7**	**87**	**0.57**	**51**	**23**	**26**	**32**	**89**	**55**	**58**	**4%**	**153**	**19%**	**73%**				**4.56**	**0.8**	**47**	**134**	**$24**

Jackson,Austin

Age: 30 Bats: R Pos: CF
Ht: 6' 1" Wt: 203
Health F | PT/Exp C | Consist A
LIMA Plan B | Rand Var +2 | MM 2435

Recovery from June knee surgery dragged all year, and could create buying opportunity, as xPX says not to worry about HR shutout, while SB drop a product of red light on basepaths. Health a concern, but still owns 2012-13 skills, and young enough to recover. Previously stable R$ makes him potentially lucrative dart throw.

Yr Tm	AB	R	HR	RBI	SB	BA	xBA	OBP	SLG	OPS	vL	vR	bb%	ct%	Eye	G	L	F	h%	HctX	PX	xPX	hr/f	Spd	SBO	SB%	#Wk	DOM	DIS	RC/G	RAR	BPV	BPX	R$
12 DET	543	103	16	66	12	300	260	377	479	856	856	856	11	75	0.50	42	24	34	37	112	118	117	11%	166	12%	57%	25	44%	24%	6.33	22.4	69	173	$25
13 DET	552	99	12	49	8	272	263	337	417	754	681	784	9	77	0.40	42	28	31	34	105	103	101	9%	145	8%	67%	22	41%	23%	4.83	9.3	52	130	$18
14 2AL	597	71	4	47	20	256	238	308	347	655	735	622	7	76	0.33	42	26	33	33	86	75	87	3%	131	16%	77%	27	26%	48%	3.72	-2.9	19	51	$16
15 2TM *	529	58	9	49	18	261	248	303	372	675	770	657	6	73	0.22	51	24	25	34	95	83	77	10%	98	21%	64%	25	32%	60%	3.75	-11.9	2	5	$16
16 CHW	181	24	0	18	2	254	256	318	343	661	411	741	9	78	0.44	37	30	32	32	109	66	97	0%	122	6%	67%	10	40%	40%	3.70	-3.4	23	66	$1
1st Half	181	24	0	18	2	254	256	318	343	661	411	741	9	78	0.44	37	30	32	32	109	66	97	0%	122	6%	67%	10	40%	40%	3.70	-4.3	23	66	$1
2nd Half																																		
17 Proj	**418**	**57**	**10**	**39**	**10**	**263**	**264**	**323**	**412**	**735**	**719**	**742**	**8**	**76**	**0.37**	**42**	**27**	**31**	**32**	**100**	**95**	**93**	**10%**	**131**	**13%**	**68%**				**4.53**	**0.3**	**33**	**93**	**$14**

Jankowski,Travis

Age: 26 Bats: L Pos: CF RF
Ht: 6' 2" Wt: 185
Health A | PT/Exp D | Consist B
LIMA Plan C | Rand Var -2 | MM 1523

Gained regular PT in July and literally took off running. PRO: Spd confirms the wheels are elite; bb% growth means passable OBP; made better contact in minors. CON: MLB ct%, xBA suggest poor BA here to stay; power of a flea; futility vL caps AB total. Useful SB source, but you'll be way behind in other categories.

Yr Tm	AB	R	HR	RBI	SB	BA	xBA	OBP	SLG	OPS	vL	vR	bb%	ct%	Eye	G	L	F	h%	HctX	PX	xPX	hr/f	Spd	SBO	SB%	#Wk	DOM	DIS	RC/G	RAR	BPV	BPX	R$
12																																		
13																																		
14 aa	100	11	0	8	8	207		256	257	513			6	84	0.41				25		39			111	45%	78%				2.22		15	41	$1
15 SD *	469	59	3	30	25	268	236	325	349	674	650	572	8	82	0.47	63	10	27	32	47	52	12	12%	171	28%	65%	8	38%	50%	3.78	-7.3	39	105	$17
16 SD	335	53	2	12	30	245	244	332	313	646	398	727	11	70	0.42	58	26	16	34	68	53	28	6%	150	39%	71%	27	15%	74%	3.47	-12.1	-7	-20	$13
1st Half	90	18	1	5	11	256	225	356	322	678	476	756	13	64	0.44	60	26	13	39	62	43	4	14%	144	41%	79%	14	7%	79%	4.17	-0.9	-36	-103	$9
2nd Half	245	35	1	7	19	241	251	324	310	634	363	716	10	72	0.41	58	26	16	33	70	56	36	4%	139	38%	68%	13	23%	69%	3.23	-9.8	-2	-6	$15
17 Proj	**318**	**46**	**3**	**17**	**25**	**249**	**248**	**320**	**329**	**649**	**513**	**691**	**9**	**76**	**0.42**	**61**	**19**	**20**	**32**	**59**	**52**	**18**	**6%**	**147**	**37%**	**72%**				**3.52**	**-9.7**	**9**	**24**	**$14**

Jaso,John

Age: 33 Bats: L Pos: 1B
Ht: 6' 2" Wt: 205
Health D | PT/Exp D | Consist C
LIMA Plan D+ | Rand Var 0 | MM 3043

A true head scratcher, as 1st-2nd half plate/power skills splits question if this was even the same person. Kicked his GB% tilt midseason (lingering effect of 2015 wrist injury?). Second half xPX, HctX surged, though he gave up ct% to do it. Issues vL, health grade suggest less AB overall—no matter which version shows up.

Yr Tm	AB	R	HR	RBI	SB	BA	xBA	OBP	SLG	OPS	vL	vR	bb%	ct%	Eye	G	L	F	h%	HctX	PX	xPX	hr/f	Spd	SBO	SB%	#Wk	DOM	DIS	RC/G	RAR	BPV	BPX	R$
12 SEA	294	41	10	50	5	276	294	394	456	850	393	927	16	83	1.10	46	25	28	30	108	115	86	14%	88	5%	100%	26	73%	15%	6.41	8.2	83	208	$10
13 OAK	207	31	3	21	2	271	247	387	372	759	442	802	16	78	0.84	40	25	35	33	76	80	58	5%	90	4%	67%	17	35%	35%	4.97	2.3	37	93	$4
14 OAK	307	42	9	40	2	264	273	337	430	767	468	793	8	80	0.47	37	26	38	30	105	117	120	10%	96	3%	100%	21	57%	14%	4.89	6.2	63	170	$8
15 TAM	185	23	5	22	1	286	282	380	459	839	911	831	13	79	0.72	53	22	26	34	129	127	116	13%	82	5%	33%	14	64%	29%	6.04	3.5	70	189	$4
16 PIT	380	45	8	42	0	268	270	353	413	766	258	795	11	81	0.61	52	21	27	32	100	92	77	10%	82	4%	0%	27	56%	30%	4.78	-6.1	43	123	$7
1st Half	239	27	4	22	0	272	265	352	393	745	259	776	10	84	0.67	59	17	23	31	81	73	45	9%	92	3%	0%	14	57%	29%	4.57	-3.6	42	120	$8
2nd Half	141	18	4	20	0	262	277	354	447	801	250	826	12	75	0.54	39	27	34	32	132	126	136	11%	69	5%	0%	13	54%	31%	5.12	0.1	48	137	$5
17 Proj	**278**	**35**	**7**	**34**	**1**	**272**	**276**	**362**	**434**	**796**	**508**	**900**	**12**	**79**	**0.64**	**46**	**23**	**30**	**32**	**113**	**105**	**104**	**11%**	**81**	**4%**	**29%**				**5.26**	**1.3**	**43**	**122**	**$8**

Jay,Jon

Age: 32 Bats: L Pos: CF
Ht: 5' 11" Wt: 200
Health F | PT/Exp D | Consist F
LIMA Plan D | Rand Var -3 | MM 0233

Reason #374 why spring stats don't matter: Hit 5 HR with .968 OPS in the Cactus League. Brutal xPX/FB% combo suggests it might take years to match that HR total, while SBO has vanished. Notable BA gains, but pin them on wild h% swing; underlying ct%, xBA suggest repeat is unlikely. Lots of reasons not to own.

Yr Tm	AB	R	HR	RBI	SB	BA	xBA	OBP	SLG	OPS	vL	vR	bb%	ct%	Eye	G	L	F	h%	HctX	PX	xPX	hr/f	Spd	SBO	SB%	#Wk	DOM	DIS	RC/G	RAR	BPV	BPX	R$
12 STL	443	70	4	40	19	305	278	373	400	773	697	804	7	84	0.48	59	22	19	36	95	64	53	6%	120	19%	73%	23	30%	22%	5.15	5.7	39	98	$19
13 STL	548	75	7	67	10	276	270	351	370	721	620	749	9	81	0.50	50	27	23	33	87	70	58	7%	91	9%	67%	27	37%	33%	4.36	4.1	27	68	$18
14 STL	413	52	3	46	6	303	269	372	378	750	859	721	6	81	0.36	52	28	20	37	94	57	63	4%	109	7%	67%	26	19%	50%	4.75	10.5	17	46	$15
15 STL	210	25	1	10	0	210	248	306	257	563	414	596	8	83	0.53	60	22	18	25	84	32	47	3%	104	4%	0%	18	17%	56%	2.18	-13.9	7	19	-$3
16 SD	347	49	2	26	2	291	267	339	389	728	752	713	5	78	0.24	55	24	21	37	93	76	65	4%	100	2%	100%	16	19%	44%	4.63	-0.1	13	37	$8
1st Half	270	35	2	23	2	296	272	345	407	752	840	708	6	77	0.26	54	25	21	38	99	88	78	5%	91	3%	100%	12	25%	33%	5.01	3.7	19	54	$11
2nd Half	77	14	0	3	0	273	246	317	325	642	459	730	4	79	0.19	58	22	20	34	73	33	18	0%	119	0%	0%	4	0%	75%	3.42	-2.4	-12	-34	-$1
17 Proj	**295**	**42**	**1**	**20**	**2**	**268**	**261**	**333**	**338**	**672**	**611**	**693**	**6**	**80**	**0.34**	**56**	**24**	**20**	**33**	**86**	**48**	**48**	**3%**	**109**	**4%**	**59%**				**3.66**	**-7.3**	**1**	**2**	**$6**

Jennings,Desmond

Age: 30 Bats: R Pos: LF CF
Ht: 6' 2" Wt: 180
Health F | PT/Exp D | Consist A
LIMA Plan D+ | Rand Var +3 | MM 2413

Anatomy of a rough year: Mendoza line BA in 1H; quad, hamstring issues in July; knee contusion, release in August. Piled up Ks, which torpedoed BA/xBA, while leg issues likely limited SB attempts. Health grade peppers him with risk, but still a former top prospect with 2012-14 skill ownership. You could do worse in end-game.

Yr Tm	AB	R	HR	RBI	SB	BA	xBA	OBP	SLG	OPS	vL	vR	bb%	ct%	Eye	G	L	F	h%	HctX	PX	xPX	hr/f	Spd	SBO	SB%	#Wk	DOM	DIS	RC/G	RAR	BPV	BPX	R$
12 TAM	505	85	13	47	31	246	236	314	388	702	735	691	8	76	0.38	42	20	38	30	102	92	99	9%	169	25%	94%	24	54%	33%	4.32	-4.8	48	120	$19
13 TAM	527	82	14	54	20	252	258	334	414	748	857	697	11	78	0.56	47	17	36	30	115	113	110	10%	139	19%	71%	25	72%	20%	4.65	9.9	68	170	$19
14 TAM	479	64	10	36	15	244	252	319	378	697	833	653	9	77	0.44	49	18	34	30	104	105	103	8%	132	17%	71%	22	45%	32%	3.94	2.9	53	143	$12
15 TAM *	118	10	1	7	5	239	240	304	311	615	717	646	8	80	0.47	57	18	24	29	80	48	69	5%	119	24%	63%	6	17%	50%	3.04	-4.8	14	38	$0
16 TAM	200	22	7	20	2	200	224	281	350	631	549	672	10	71	0.36	46	16	37	24	76	95	99	13%	120	4%	100%	14	29%	57%	3.13	-8.2	17	49	-$1
1st Half	193	22	7	19	2	202	224	286	352	638	536	687	10	72	0.38	47	16	37	24	79	93	102	14%	124	4%	100%	13	31%	54%	3.21	-7.5	19	54	$0
2nd Half	7	0	0	1	0	143	231	143	286	429	750	0	0	57	0.00	25	25	50	25	0	167	-24	0%	101	0%	0%	1	0%	100%	1.21	-0.8	-6	-17	-$5
17 Proj	**285**	**36**	**7**	**24**	**8**	**232**	**241**	**308**	**364**	**672**	**697**	**662**	**9**	**76**	**0.44**	**49**	**17**	**33**	**28**	**93**	**83**	**97**	**10%**	**133**	**15%**	**72%**				**3.65**	**-7.0**	**23**	**65**	**$7**

RYAN BLOOMFIELD

Johnson,Kelly

Age: 35	Bats: L	Pos: 2B 3B	Health	B	LIMA Plan	D
Ht: 6' 1"	Wt: 205		PT/Exp	D	Rand Var	+1
			Consist	B	MM	2221

Versatile veteran posted best ct% since 2009, but Father Time is catching up with power skills. Half of HR came in torrid Aug stretch; outside of that, it was once again tons of ground balls and an inability to sustain 2015's HctX. Might be able to cling to bench spot, but fantasy relevance continues to fade.

Yr	Tm	AB	R	HR	RBI	SB	BA	xBA	OBP	SLG	OPS	vL	vR	bb%	ct%	Eye	G	L	F	h%	HctX	PX	xPX	hr/f	Spd	SBO	SB%	#Wk	DOM	DIS	RC/G	RAR	BPV	BPX	R$
12	TOR	507	61	16	55	14	225	226	313	365	678	607	705	11	69	0.39	45	21	34	30	94	102	113	14%	87	12%	88%	27	33%	52%	3.80	-25.1	6	15	$9
13	TAM	366	41	16	52	7	235	227	305	410	715	686	723	9	73	0.35	39	15	46	28	86	119	116	13%	101	12%	64%	26	50%	35%	4.03	-6.1	37	93	$9
14	3 AL	265	29	7	27	2	215	252	296	362	659	708	653	10	73	0.41	49	21	30	27	81	114	77	12%	86	6%	50%	24	46%	29%	3.37	-6.7	32	86	$1
15	2 NL	310	38	14	47	2	265	253	314	435	750	678	758	7	74	0.28	44	23	33	32	110	112	122	19%	86	4%	67%	23	30%	48%	4.73	-5.6	27	73	$9
16	2 NL	304	25	10	34	4	247	255	306	391	698	707	695	8	79	0.38	48	21	32	28	94	88	90	13%	75	5%	100%	27	48%	44%	4.10	-11.0	25	71	$5
1st Half		167	14	4	15	2	246	245	314	371	685	845	643	9	78	0.44	48	19	33	29	104	82	100	9%	87	5%	100%	14	50%	43%	3.98	-5.5	25	71	$4
2nd Half		137	11	6	19	2	248	266	297	416	713	461	754	6	79	0.31	47	23	30	27	82	96	79	18%	68	6%	100%	13	46%	46%	4.24	-3.5	27	77	$5
17	Proj	**226**	**22**	**8**	**28**	**3**	**249**	**252**	**310**	**406**	**715**	**670**	**724**	**8**	**76**	**0.35**	**46**	**22**	**32**	**29**	**94**	**96**	**97**	**15%**	**80**	**6%**	**82%**				**4.26**	**-3.6**	**13**	**37**	**$4**

Jones,Adam

Age: 31	Bats: R	Pos: CF	Health	A	LIMA Plan	B
Ht: 6' 3"	Wt: 220		PT/Exp	A	Rand Var	0
			Consist	A	MM	3235

Slow start due in part to rib injury, but by season's end he was where we thought he'd be, albeit with career-high FB%. Odd struggles vL seem fluky, and xPX says not to sweat PX dip. AAA reliability comforting, and career arcs rarely as smooth as this one. Sit back, relax as we continue our gentle descent from 2012-13 peak.

Yr	Tm	AB	R	HR	RBI	SB	BA	xBA	OBP	SLG	OPS	vL	vR	bb%	ct%	Eye	G	L	F	h%	HctX	PX	xPX	hr/f	Spd	SBO	SB%	#Wk	DOM	DIS	RC/G	RAR	BPV	BPX	R$
12	BAL	648	103	32	82	16	287	290	334	505	839	800	852	5	81	0.27	46	21	33	31	125	136	108	19%	107	16%	70%	27	59%	19%	5.70	15.5	75	188	$30
13	BAL	653	100	33	108	14	285	284	318	493	811	732	846	4	79	0.18	48	20	32	32	124	137	126	20%	93	12%	82%	26	62%	19%	5.49	23.0	64	160	$34
14	BAL	644	88	29	96	7	281	270	311	469	780	1003	709	3	79	0.14	47	17	36	32	113	127	119	16%	101	6%	88%	27	52%	30%	5.05	21.0	57	154	$29
15	BAL	546	74	27	82	3	269	274	308	474	782	754	792	4	81	0.24	46	18	36	29	109	122	120	17%	94	3%	75%	25	44%	36%	4.96	7.0	61	165	$20
16	BAL	619	86	29	83	2	265	248	310	436	746	580	798	6	81	0.34	43	17	41	28	108	92	110	14%	83	1%	100%	27	44%	26%	4.69	5.7	38	109	$18
1st Half		310	53	16	51	1	261	256	310	455	764	617	816	7	80	0.35	46	15	39	28	117	108	127	16%	74	1%	100%	14	36%	21%	4.89	3.4	44	126	$20
2nd Half		309	33	13	32	1	269	240	310	417	728	537	780	5	83	0.32	40	18	42	29	98	78	94	12%	97	1%	100%	13	54%	31%	4.48	-0.2	35	100	$16
17	Proj	**600**	**82**	**28**	**85**	**1**	**263**	**260**	**303**	**448**	**751**	**690**	**771**	**5**	**81**	**0.27**	**44**	**18**	**38**	**28**	**109**	**102**	**113**	**15%**	**94**	**1%**	**75%**				**4.61**	**1.8**	**35**	**99**	**$20**

Jones,JaCoby

Age: 25	Bats: R	Pos: 3B	Health	A	LIMA Plan	D
Ht: 6' 2"	Wt: 205		PT/Exp	F	Rand Var	0
			Consist	B	MM	3501

0-2-.214 in 28 AB at DET. Coming off 50-game drug suspension to start season, 20-game tear at AA gained him promotion to AAA, where things got considerably tougher (.665 OPS in 324 PA, 67% ct%, 0.26 Eye). Natural SS, DET played him at 3B, OF. Has 20/20 upside but will need to refine plate approach to reach it.

Yr	Tm	AB	R	HR	RBI	SB	BA	xBA	OBP	SLG	OPS	vL	vR	bb%	ct%	Eye	G	L	F	h%	HctX	PX	xPX	hr/f	Spd	SBO	SB%	#Wk	DOM	DIS	RC/G	RAR	BPV	BPX	R$
12																																			
13																																			
14																																			
15	aa	146	22	5	18	9	241		311	408	719			9	63	0.27				35		130			120	33%	73%				4.18		11	30	$5
16	DET *	397	39	6	37	11	233	225	286	365	651	294	909	7	65	0.21	44	25	31	34	99	99	147	0%	139	18%	66%	5	20%	40%	3.39	-17.1	-3	-9	$5
1st Half		175	17	5	23	7	229	233	288	412	700			8	66	0.24				32		125			142	27%	66%				3.77		24	69	$8
2nd Half		222	22	1	14	4	235	210	285	329	613	294	909	6	64	0.19	44	25	31	36	97	78	147	0%	130	12%	65%	5	20%	40%	3.07	-12.3	-28	-80	$3
17	Proj	**194**	**23**	**4**	**20**	**8**	**235**	**219**	**295**	**377**	**671**	**418**	**1057**	**8**	**64**	**0.23**	**48**	**20**	**32**	**35**	**87**	**105**	**132**	**10%**	**131**	**24%**	**72%**				**3.66**	**-7.3**	**-2**	**-6**	**$6**

Joseph,Caleb

Age: 31	Bats: R	Pos: CA	Health	B	LIMA Plan	F
Ht: 6' 3"	Wt: 180		PT/Exp	D	Rand Var	+3
			Consist	D	MM	1001

0-0-.174 in 132 AB at BAL. That he didn't bump into a single RBI in majors was quite a shock after he looked in 2015 like prototypical catcher with late-blooming power. Made just as much contact, but now it was exceedingly weak. In theory, still owns power skills, but prospects of grabbing many AB look dim.

Yr	Tm	AB	R	HR	RBI	SB	BA	xBA	OBP	SLG	OPS	vL	vR	bb%	ct%	Eye	G	L	F	h%	HctX	PX	xPX	hr/f	Spd	SBO	SB%	#Wk	DOM	DIS	RC/G	RAR	BPV	BPX	R$
12	a/a	347	34	10	43	2	224		283	373	657			8	77	0.36				26		102			86	2%	100%				3.50		31	78	$3
13	aa	518	52	17	68	3	243		281	395	676			5	79	0.24				28		104			83	5%	53%				3.68		34	85	$10
14	BAL *	338	27	10	35	0	205	224	247	340	588	643	603	5	72	0.20	33	22	46	25	93	106	138	11%	84	2%	0%	21	24%	57%	2.66	-6.9	9	24	$0
15	BAL	320	38	11	49	0	234	249	299	394	693	712	683	8	78	0.38	33	23	43	27	104	105	121	10%	97	0%	0%	26	42%	42%	3.85	1.1	41	111	$4
16	BAL *	193	10	1	4	0	185	191	223	218	440	191	494	5	78	0.21	41	19	39	23	69	23	89	0%	120	3%	0%	20	15%	55%	1.46	-14.9	-22	-63	-$5
1st Half		90	6	1	1	0	185	216	242	242	483	180	521	7	75	0.29	44	24	33	24	83	41	89	0%	119	6%	0%	10	20%	60%	1.70	-7.1	-17	-49	-$5
2nd Half		103	3	0	3	0	184	155	203	194	397	200	460	2	80	0.12	39	14	47	23	51	8	88	0%	116	0%	0%	10	10%	50%	1.23	-9.6	-31	-89	-$6
17	Proj	**199**	**17**	**5**	**21**	**0**	**216**	**220**	**261**	**323**	**583**	**516**	**613**	**5**	**77**	**0.25**	**37**	**20**	**43**	**26**	**82**	**66**	**107**	**7%**	**103**	**2%**	**17%**				**2.67**	**-9.0**	**-17**	**-48**	**$1**

Joseph,Tommy

Age: 25	Bats: R	Pos: 1B	Health	A	LIMA Plan	B
Ht: 6' 1"	Wt: 220		PT/Exp	F	Rand Var	-2
			Consist	F	MM	4035

21-47-.257 in 315 AB at PHI. Plenty to get excited about from big 2nd half, including prodigious power both vL and vR, and improved bb% and Eye. FB% dipped a bit, but was still healthy. It all speaks to a hitter settling in nicely and ready for full-time duty. Time to jump on the bandwagon.

Yr	Tm	AB	R	HR	RBI	SB	BA	xBA	OBP	SLG	OPS	vL	vR	bb%	ct%	Eye	G	L	F	h%	HctX	PX	xPX	hr/f	Spd	SBO	SB%	#Wk	DOM	DIS	RC/G	RAR	BPV	BPX	R$
12	aa	404	35	9	38	0	230		279	354	633			6	74	0.26				29		93			79	5%	0%				3.11		9	23	$2
13	a/a	78	5	2	12	0	192		230	309	539			5	77	0.22				22		76			93	7%	0%				2.08		9	23	-$3
14	aa	78	6	4	14	0	247		282	473	755			5	81	0.26				26		145			97	0%	0%				4.52		79	214	$0
15	aaa	166	7	3	14	0	165		177	260	437			1	77	0.06				20		70			80	0%	0%				1.41		-7	-19	-$5
16	PHI *	410	57	27	63	1	272	272	315	523	838	912	774	6	78	0.29	37	18	45	29	116	144	144	19%	65	4%	32%	22	41%	32%	5.65	3.7	62	177	$14
1st Half		230	25	14	31	1	259	261	280	494	773	841	582	3	78	0.13	32	19	50	27	119	135	141	16%	62	8%	32%	9	22%	33%	4.56	-3.7	46	131	$12
2nd Half		180	32	13	32	0	289	282	364	561	925	964	910	10	79	0.50	41	17	42	30	115	154	146	21%	76	0%	0%	13	54%	31%	7.18	10.4	83	237	$16
17	Proj	**465**	**53**	**27**	**70**	**0**	**255**	**258**	**296**	**478**	**774**	**856**	**900**	**5**	**77**	**0.23**	**39**	**18**	**43**	**28**	**117**	**131**	**144**	**17%**	**63**	**2%**	**21%**				**4.72**	**-5.1**	**33**	**93**	**$15**

Joyce,Matt

Age: 32	Bats: L	Pos: RF LF	Health	B	LIMA Plan	D
Ht: 6' 2"	Wt: 185		PT/Exp	D	Rand Var	-1
			Consist	F	MM	3011

Rejuvenated—at least somewhat—career that had been on life support by rediscovering power skills. Still, in second half, threatened to flatline once more. Walk rate is impressive, though, and it helped propel career-best OBP. Whether that's enough to keep him gainfully employed remains to be seen.

Yr	Tm	AB	R	HR	RBI	SB	BA	xBA	OBP	SLG	OPS	vL	vR	bb%	ct%	Eye	G	L	F	h%	HctX	PX	xPX	hr/f	Spd	SBO	SB%	#Wk	DOM	DIS	RC/G	RAR	BPV	BPX	R$
12	TAM	399	55	17	59	4	241	244	341	429	769	631	810	12	74	0.54	38	19	43	28	106	124	117	13%	103	6%	57%	24	50%	29%	4.71	-0.2	54	135	$9
13	TAM	413	61	18	47	7	235	259	328	419	747	499	783	13	79	0.68	37	20	43	26	89	124	90	13%	88	9%	70%	27	44%	41%	4.58	6.5	68	170	$11
14	TAM	418	51	9	52	2	254	232	349	383	732	408	758	13	73	0.56	43	19	38	33	99	104	105	8%	111	5%	29%	26	35%	42%	4.40	7.6	38	103	$9
15	LAA *	283	19	6	25	0	182	209	268	299	567	262	592	10	72	0.42	41	18	42	23	78	87	92	7%	95	5%	0%	20	30%	50%	2.38	-21.4	9	24	-$5
16	PIT	231	45	13	42	1	242	255	403	463	866	763	884	20	71	0.88	46	18	36	28	104	138	126	22%	100	2%	50%	27	56%	37%	6.13	10.3	67	191	$6
1st Half		120	23	8	27	1	300	275	425	575	1000	970	1006	17	68	0.66	45	21	34	38	102	179	140	29%	105	4%	50%	14	64%	29%	8.63	13.9	85	243	$11
2nd Half		111	22	5	15	0	180	227	381	342	723	322	766	23	74	1.17	47	16	37	19	106	96	111	17%	96	0%	0%	13	46%	46%	3.97	-1.7	50	143	$1
17	Proj	**147**	**22**	**6**	**20**	**1**	**222**	**239**	**352**	**397**	**750**	**575**	**773**	**16**	**73**	**0.70**	**43**	**18**	**38**	**26**	**96**	**111**	**110**	**15%**	**100**	**3%**	**35%**				**4.42**	**-1.2**	**29**	**82**	**$3**

Judge,Aaron

Age: 25	Bats: R	Pos: RF	Health	A	LIMA Plan	D+
Ht: 6' 7"	Wt: 255		PT/Exp	D	Rand Var	-1
			Consist	B	MM	4203

4-10-.179 in 84 AB at NYY. Those 84 AB also included 42 Ks. Prior to mid-Aug promotion, second tour of AAA had gone a bit better (.855 OPS, 72% ct%), raising hopes that next shot at MLB will bring similar improvement. No one doubts 30+ HR upside, but you can't launch what you don't hit.

Yr	Tm	AB	R	HR	RBI	SB	BA	xBA	OBP	SLG	OPS	vL	vR	bb%	ct%	Eye	G	L	F	h%	HctX	PX	xPX	hr/f	Spd	SBO	SB%	#Wk	DOM	DIS	RC/G	RAR	BPV	BPX	R$
12																																			
13																																			
14																																			
15	a/a	478	55	20	63	6	238		306	422	728			9	66	0.29				31		138			91	7%	74%				4.31		23	62	$11
16	NYY *	436	67	24	69	5	239	216	321	448	769	289	679	11	65	0.34	35	14	51	31	129	143	196	18%	81	5%	82%	6	33%	50%	4.83	1.6	22	63	$12
1st Half		300	46	17	46	5	251	252	329	467	796			10	69	0.38				31		140			85	6%	100%				5.33		37	106	$16
2nd Half		136	21	7	24	0	214	189	303	406	709	289	679	11	56	0.29	35	14	51	32	111	151	196	18%	80	3%	0%	6	33%	50%	3.86	-3.5	-7	-20	$1
17	Proj	**347**	**48**	**17**	**53**	**3**	**230**	**217**	**310**	**425**	**735**	**342**	**822**	**10**	**64**	**0.30**	**35**	**18**	**47**	**31**	**100**	**139**	**176**	**16%**	**83**	**5%**	**68%**				**4.29**	**-4.3**	**9**	**24**	**$9**

KRISTOPHER OLSON

Kang,Jung-ho

Age: 30	Bats: R	Pos: 3B		Health	C	LIMA Plan	B+
Ht: 6' 0"	Wt: 205			PT/Exp	C	Rand Var	+5
				Consist	F	MM	4145

21-62-.255 in 318 AB at PIT. Positive signs abound: growth in FB%, xPX support increased HR output; 2H gains in bb%, Eye very encouraging; xBA says BA will bounce back. Only reasons to hesitate are health grade and age, and even those are fairly minor concerns. If you feel like speculating... UP: 35 HR, 100 RBI

Yr	Tm	AB	R	HR	RBI	SB	BA	xBA	OBP	SLG	OPS	vL	vR	bb%	ct%	Eye	G	L	F	h%	HctX	PX	xPX	hr/f	Spd	SBO	SB%	#Wk	DOM	DIS	RC/G	RAR	BPV	BPX	R$
12	for	436	75	15	80	19	293		375	469	843			12	83	0.77				32		115			78	18%	77%				6.34	21.7	73	183	$24
13	for	450	65	13	94	14	271		350	413	763			11	77	0.53				33		99			88	16%	60%				4.87	11.8	38	95	$21
14	for	418	100	24	114	3	332		410	605	1015			12	76	0.55				39		200			90	5%	45%				9.24	61.5	116	314	$33
15	PIT	421	60	15	58	5	287	272	355	461	816	721	840	6	76	0.28	50	22	28	35	116	117	104	17%	85	8%	56%	24	33%	33%	5.33	7.7	39	105	$16
16	PIT *	366	49	22	68	3	237	271	314	473	787	757	896	10	75	0.45	42	20	37	25	120	142	146	23%	62	6%	57%	21	57%	29%	4.88	-1.0	54	154	$9
1st Half		192	21	12	32	2	223	264	273	448	721	808	862	6	75	0.27	46	19	35	24	131	133	171	27%	70	9%	62%	10	60%	30%	3.94	-5.6	41	117	$8
2nd Half		174	28	11	36	1	251	278	356	500	856	624	921	14	75	0.65	39	22	39	28	110	152	122	20%	63	4%	50%	11	55%	27%	5.98	5.6	71	203	$11
17	**Proj**	**473**	**75**	**26**	**80**	**5**	**271**	**279**	**365**	**498**	**863**	**753**	**890**	**10**	**76**	**0.45**	**44**	**21**	**35**	**31**	**118**	**138**	**127**	**21%**	**76**	**7%**	**59%**				**5.85**	**13.1**	**57**	**164**	**$19**

Kemp,Anthony

Age: 25	Bats: L	Pos: LF		Health	A	LIMA Plan	D
Ht: 5' 6"	Wt: 165			PT/Exp	C	Rand Var	+1
				Consist	A	MM	0321

1-7-.217 with 2 SB in 120 AB at HOU. Scouts say he's a utility guy, skills suggest maybe something more... PRO: Solid HctX, LD%, and 10% bb% in first taste of bigs; history of plus ct%, Spd. CON: Lack of power may cap BA around .260; SB% raises serious doubts about running game. Wait for skills to make stronger case.

Yr	Tm	AB	R	HR	RBI	SB	BA	xBA	OBP	SLG	OPS	vL	vR	bb%	ct%	Eye	G	L	F	h%	HctX	PX	xPX	hr/f	Spd	SBO	SB%	#Wk	DOM	DIS	RC/G	RAR	BPV	BPX	R$
12																																			
13																																			
14	aa	233	32	3	16	10	253		316	364	680			8	84	0.58				29		74			130	26%	59%				3.69		54	146	$6
15	a/a	464	56	2	35	25	259		319	324	642			8	83	0.52				31		44			117	30%	61%				3.33		22	59	$15
16	HOU *	375	41	3	24	9	242	249	312	327	639	440	660	9	82	0.56	45	24	31	29	108	49	77	4%	128	18%	47%	15	40%	47%	3.17	-12.8	25	71	$5
1st Half		181	20	1	11	6	254	240	339	346	686	286	754	11	80	0.65	48	21	30	31	121	47	97	0%	147	21%	46%	6	33%	33%	3.63	-4.6	28	80	$7
2nd Half		194	20	2	13	3	230	257	285	309	594	485	602	7	83	0.45	43	26	31	27	101	50	66	6%	101	14%	47%	9	44%	56%	2.75	-10.2	19	54	$3
17	**Proj**	**192**	**22**	**2**	**13**	**7**	**249**	**252**	**309**	**333**	**642**	**445**	**682**	**8**	**83**	**0.53**	**45**	**24**	**31**	**29**	**109**	**49**	**78**	**3%**	**115**	**23%**	**55%**				**3.27**	**-7.0**	**22**	**63**	**$5**

Kemp,Matt

Age: 32	Bats: R	Pos: RF LF		Health	C	LIMA Plan	B
Ht: 6' 2"	Wt: 215			PT/Exp	A	Rand Var	0
				Consist	B	MM	4135

2nd highest HR total of his career (39 in 2011) and both times required massive numbers of plate appearances - 2016 output required most AB of career. Injury history doesn't bode well for repeat on all counts. That said, a full season out of PETCO (.684 OPS last year) will help (pending SunTrust Park tendencies).

Yr	Tm	AB	R	HR	RBI	SB	BA	xBA	OBP	SLG	OPS	vL	vR	bb%	ct%	Eye	G	L	F	h%	HctX	PX	xPX	hr/f	Spd	SBO	SB%	#Wk	DOM	DIS	RC/G	RAR	BPV	BPX	R$
12	LA	403	74	23	69	9	303	277	367	538	906	1105	818	9	74	0.39	43	22	35	36	122	155	158	22%	94	11%	69%	21	48%	19%	7.08	26.3	70	175	$23
13	LA	263	35	6	33	9	270	237	328	395	723	853	671	8	71	0.29	40	25	35	36	107	103	142	9%	70	13%	100%	14	29%	57%	4.72	5.0	5	13	$9
14	LA	541	77	25	89	8	287	287	346	506	852	781	879	9	73	0.36	43	26	31	35	128	168	139	20%	80	9%	62%	27	59%	15%	6.18	36.7	71	192	$27
15	SD	596	80	23	100	12	265	258	312	443	755	824	736	6	75	0.27	44	21	35	32	136	119	149	14%	83	10%	86%	26	38%	35%	4.82	1.7	36	97	$23
16	2 NL	623	89	35	108	1	268	270	304	499	803	954	761	5	75	0.23	40	20	40	31	109	143	136	18%	59	1%	100%	27	37%	15%	5.37	13.2	45	129	$21
1st Half		325	38	16	54	0	255	259	273	458	731	1021	638	3	76	0.13	42	20	38	29	104	125	119	17%	51	0%	0%	14	29%	14%	4.36	-0.9	26	74	$17
2nd Half		298	51	19	54	1	282	280	335	544	879	858	884	8	74	0.34	38	21	41	32	115	164	155	20%	75	1%	100%	13	46%	15%	6.58	17.8	68	194	$26
17	**Proj**	**555**	**81**	**27**	**94**	**4**	**274**	**267**	**320**	**484**	**804**	**883**	**781**	**7**	**74**	**0.28**	**41**	**22**	**37**	**32**	**120**	**133**	**143**	**18%**	**73**	**4%**	**73%**				**5.46**	**12.1**	**41**	**117**	**$24**

Kendrick,Howie

Age: 33	Bats: R	Pos: LF 2B		Health	C	LIMA Plan	B
Ht: 5' 10"	Wt: 200			PT/Exp	A	Rand Var	+3
				Consist	A	MM	1345

Lowest BA, OPS of career, and while some of that can be blamed on 1st half calf, shoulder injuries, there's also not a single elite skill to be found here. Even xBA questions return to the .290s. BPV/BPX illustrates that age is subtly chipping away at value, which means you can't dismiss possibility of him plateauing at 2016 level.

Yr	Tm	AB	R	HR	RBI	SB	BA	xBA	OBP	SLG	OPS	vL	vR	bb%	ct%	Eye	G	L	F	h%	HctX	PX	xPX	hr/f	Spd	SBO	SB%	#Wk	DOM	DIS	RC/G	RAR	BPV	BPX	R$
12	LAA	550	57	8	67	14	287	265	325	400	725	797	694	5	79	0.25	59	21	21	35	110	81	87	9%	98	14%	70%	27	33%	37%	4.56	-2.5	23	58	$18
13	LAA	478	55	13	54	6	297	289	335	439	775	862	745	5	81	0.26	51	27	21	34	115	93	88	16%	110	7%	67%	23	48%	26%	5.19	15.0	44	110	$18
14	LAA	617	85	7	75	14	293	272	347	397	744	834	714	7	82	0.44	60	19	21	35	133	78	88	7%	104	10%	74%	27	26%	22%	4.92	19.6	39	105	$25
15	LA	464	64	9	54	6	295	286	336	409	746	721	753	5	82	0.33	59	24	17	34	108	75	71	14%	95	6%	75%	22	27%	36%	4.94	2.9	31	84	$17
16	LA	487	65	8	40	10	255	272	326	366	691	626	722	9	80	0.52	61	19	20	30	110	72	63	10%	98	9%	83%	26	31%	38%	4.11	-7.4	29	83	$10
1st Half		230	32	3	15	7	239	275	298	326	624	751	581	8	81	0.44	67	19	14	28	103	54	41	11%	104	11%	100%	13	23%	38%	3.41	-7.1	17	49	$9
2nd Half		257	33	5	25	3	268	268	351	401	751	551	872	11	79	0.58	56	20	25	32	116	88	84	10%	89	6%	60%	13	38%	38%	4.78	2.4	38	109	$12
17	**Proj**	**484**	**60**	**8**	**47**	**8**	**265**	**275**	**325**	**380**	**705**	**667**	**720**	**8**	**80**	**0.43**	**59**	**21**	**20**	**32**	**114**	**73**	**73**	**11%**	**98**	**8%**	**75%**				**4.25**	**-2.9**	**25**	**71**	**$14**

Kepler,Max

Age: 24	Bats: L	Pos: RF		Health	A	LIMA Plan	A
Ht: 6' 4"	Wt: 180			PT/Exp	D	Rand Var	+1
				Consist	C	MM	4345

17-63-.235 with 6 SB in 396 AB at MIN. Not quite a breakout, but perhaps the heralding of a breakout to come. You can see makings of something good in glimpses of plus ct%, HctX, xPX, and Spd; just needs to put them all together. Skills vL (71% ct%, 0.29 Eye) may hold him back slightly, so invest with patience.

Yr	Tm	AB	R	HR	RBI	SB	BA	xBA	OBP	SLG	OPS	vL	vR	bb%	ct%	Eye	G	L	F	h%	HctX	PX	xPX	hr/f	Spd	SBO	SB%	#Wk	DOM	DIS	RC/G	RAR	BPV	BPX	R$
12																																			
13																																			
14																																			
15	MIN *	414	58	7	54	14	288	280	365	457	822	0	333	11	83	0.72	75	0	25	33	90	107	-16	0%	137	15%	76%	2	0%	100%	5.96	12.0	83	224	$17
16	MIN *	506	66	18	80	7	243	259	318	425	743	595	792	10	79	0.52	47	16	36	28	106	105	103	15%	119	8%	69%	22	55%	36%	4.51	-5.2	57	163	$12
1st Half		227	30	6	40	3	263	271	339	454	793	663	895	10	79	0.55	44	20	36	31	122	113	117	16%	139	7%	73%	9	56%	33%	5.30	1.3	73	209	$12
2nd Half		279	36	12	40	4	226	248	302	401	703	553	756	10	78	0.49	49	15	36	25	99	98	97	15%	105	9%	67%	13	54%	38%	3.93	-10.0	44	126	$12
17	**Proj**	**534**	**72**	**22**	**78**	**10**	**260**	**280**	**337**	**474**	**811**	**644**	**886**	**10**	**80**	**0.59**	**47**	**18**	**35**	**29**	**108**	**121**	**105**	**14%**	**120**	**10%**	**71%**				**5.44**	**11.7**	**76**	**217**	**$20**

Kiermaier,Kevin

Age: 27	Bats: L	Pos: CF		Health	B	LIMA Plan	B+
Ht: 6' 1"	Wt: 195			PT/Exp	C	Rand Var	+1
				Consist	A	MM	2535

Was establishing new FB%, power baselines when fractured left hand knocked him out for nearly two months. Now we're left wondering what to believe, though solid bb% growth gives reason to keep the faith. We know he can steal 20+, xBA history says he can hit .270, and with health, might be able to add... UP: 20 HR

Yr	Tm	AB	R	HR	RBI	SB	BA	xBA	OBP	SLG	OPS	vL	vR	bb%	ct%	Eye	G	L	F	h%	HctX	PX	xPX	hr/f	Spd	SBO	SB%	#Wk	DOM	DIS	RC/G	RAR	BPV	BPX	R$
12																																			
13	TAM *	508	72	5	33	17	263	240	312	381	693	0	0	7	81	0.37	44	20	36	32	0	74	-15	0%	181	23%	56%	1	0%	100%	3.83	-6.1	51	128	$15
14	TAM *	459	58	12	46	14	264	270	314	436	750	507	837	7	79	0.34	53	17	31	31	92	116	82	13%	145	18%	73%	22	45%	32%	4.69	10.7	67	181	$16
15	TAM	505	62	10	40	18	263	275	298	420	718	625	754	5	81	0.25	48	23	29	31	88	96	59	8%	154	21%	78%	26	50%	31%	4.31	-2.8	59	159	$16
16	TAM	366	55	12	37	21	246	260	331	410	741	816	718	10	80	0.54	42	21	38	28	102	98	78	11%	102	25%	88%	19	42%	16%	4.62	2.7	50	143	$14
1st Half		123	18	5	16	6	236	276	307	447	754	747	754	8	82	0.50	43	16	41	25	111	124	110	12%	100	32%	75%	7	57%	14%	4.39	-0.4	76	217	$7
2nd Half		243	37	7	21	15	251	253	343	391	734	854	699	11	79	0.56	41	23	36	29	97	85	59	11%	105	23%	94%	12	33%	17%	4.71	1.4	37	106	$17
17	**Proj**	**517**	**72**	**15**	**48**	**23**	**258**	**267**	**322**	**424**	**746**	**706**	**759**	**8**	**80**	**0.42**	**46**	**21**	**34**	**30**	**96**	**97**	**73**	**10%**	**129**	**23%**	**80%**				**4.64**	**1.9**	**59**	**168**	**$21**

Kim,Hyun-Soo

Age: 29	Bats: L	Pos: LF		Health	A	LIMA Plan	B
Ht: 6' 2"	Wt: 210			PT/Exp	B	Rand Var	-4
				Consist	B	MM	1145

Did not make great first impression, with lousy spring, weight concerns, and refusal to go to minors, but bat quickly silenced critics. Yet skills suggest critics had a point, as xBA exposes fluky BA, and high GB% approach limits power potential. BA is really the only help here, but the floor is potentially soft.

Yr	Tm	AB	R	HR	RBI	SB	BA	xBA	OBP	SLG	OPS	vL	vR	bb%	ct%	Eye	G	L	F	h%	HctX	PX	xPX	hr/f	Spd	SBO	SB%	#Wk	DOM	DIS	RC/G	RAR	BPV	BPX	R$
12	for	437	46	4	63	5	271		328	345	673			8	89	0.78				30		48			88	7%	62%				3.91	-9.3	39	98	$10
13	for	434	61	10	88	2	281		355	407	763			10	85	0.74				31		84			88	5%	29%				4.96	11.7	54	135	$16
14	for	463	73	10	88	2	300		359	421	780			8	91	1.00				31		81			78	1%	100%				5.54	22.9	70	189	$21
15	for	512	100	17	118	10	304		399	453	852			14	88	1.36				32		88			77	8%	64%				6.52	27.8	76	205	$30
16	BAL	305	36	6	22	1	302	264	382	420	801	217	839	11	83	0.71	53	21	27	35	102	72	78	9%	115	4%	25%	25	40%	24%	5.56	10.9	48	137	$8
1st Half		130	17	3	11	1	338	279	423	477	900	273	943	11	86	0.89	56	19	25	38	116	85	76	11%	117	4%	50%	13	54%	15%	7.41	10.1	72	206	$10
2nd Half		175	19	3	11	0	274	252	350	377	727	167	762	10	81	0.61	50	22	28	32	92	62	80	8%	107	4%	0%	12	25%	33%	4.42	-0.2	29	83	$6
17	**Proj**	**406**	**58**	**7**	**42**	**3**	**291**	**271**	**374**	**401**	**774**	**218**	**811**	**11**	**86**	**0.86**	**52**	**21**	**27**	**32**	**98**	**66**	**78**	**8%**	**109**	**5%**	**47%**				**5.18**	**8.3**	**38**	**108**	**$15**

BRANDON KRUSE

Kinsler,Ian

Age: 35 Bats: R Pos: 2B
Ht: 6' 0" Wt: 200

Health	A	LIMA Plan	B+
PT/Exp	A	Rand Var	-3
Consist	B	MM	2335

Sold out for more power with career-low ct%. With FB% uptick, hit as many HR as past two years combined. Durablity, across-the-board production make him valuable commodity, but he's had power spikes before in his 11-year career and was never able to repeat them. Odds are he won't suddenly find a new skill at age 35.

Yr Tm	AB	R	HR	RBI	SB	BA	xBA	OBP	SLG	OPS	vL	vR	bb%	ct%	Eye	G	L	F	h%	HctX	PX	xPX	hr/f	Spd	SBO	SB%	#Wk	DOM	DIS	RC/G	RAR	BPV	BPX	R$
12 TEX	655	105	19	72	21	256	268	326	423	749	988	671	8	86	0.67	38	20	42	27	100	103	88	8%	104	19%	70%	27	48%	19%	4.54	7.3	77	193	$22
13 TEX	545	85	13	72	15	277	275	344	413	757	814	733	9	89	0.86	37	24	39	29	123	87	109	7%	97	17%	58%	24	75%	8%	4.71	15.5	75	188	$23
14 DET	684	100	17	92	15	275	267	307	420	727	740	722	4	88	0.37	38	20	43	29	92	96	84	7%	113	12%	79%	27	59%	4%	4.50	21.7	75	203	$28
15 DET	624	94	11	73	10	296	265	342	428	770	798	763	6	87	0.54	34	25	41	33	102	81	94	5%	125	9%	63%	26	38%	15%	5.20	16.0	66	178	$25
16 DET	618	117	28	83	14	288	264	348	484	831	893	809	7	81	0.39	32	24	45	32	112	109	122	13%	119	12%	70%	27	56%	15%	5.74	17.7	64	183	$29
1st Half	331	67	16	52	8	293	267	352	502	853	956	813	7	81	0.39	31	24	45	32	108	118	122	13%	118	13%	73%	14	50%	7%	6.13	12.3	69	197	$34
2nd Half	287	50	12	31	6	282	261	343	463	806	810	805	7	82	0.39	32	24	44	31	117	99	121	12%	112	12%	67%	13	62%	23%	5.31	4.2	57	163	$24
17 Proj	**608**	**102**	**18**	**76**	**13**	**285**	**261**	**339**	**440**	**779**	**830**	**763**	**7**	**85**	**0.46**	**34**	**23**	**43**	**31**	**107**	**87**	**107**	**8%**	**119**	**12%**	**68%**				**5.14**	**5.8**	**57**	**164**	**$26**

Kipnis,Jason

Age: 30 Bats: L Pos: 2B
Ht: 5' 10" Wt: 175

Health	A	LIMA Plan	B+
PT/Exp	A	Rand Var	-1
Consist	C	MM	3345

Altered his approach, taking different route to nearly identical year-end value. Drop in ct%, BA were offset by career high in FB% and HR, and he even mashed LH in 2nd half (5 HR, 171 PX). Power numbers will likely regress a bit, but durability and five category contributions leave him locked in as a top MI option.

Yr Tm	AB	R	HR	RBI	SB	BA	xBA	OBP	SLG	OPS	vL	vR	bb%	ct%	Eye	G	L	F	h%	HctX	PX	xPX	hr/f	Spd	SBO	SB%	#Wk	DOM	DIS	RC/G	RAR	BPV	BPX	R$
12 CLE	591	86	14	76	31	257	259	335	379	714	581	787	10	82	0.61	47	23	30	29	97	76	91	10%	108	21%	82%	27	48%	26%	4.44	4.7	42	105	$23
13 CLE	564	86	17	84	30	284	264	366	452	818	850	801	12	75	0.53	43	25	32	35	110	125	128	12%	101	21%	81%	27	48%	44%	6.03	37.0	55	138	$32
14 CLE	500	61	6	41	22	240	249	310	330	640	500	710	9	80	0.50	46	23	31	29	92	72	84	5%	98	18%	88%	23	30%	30%	3.58	2.8	27	73	$13
15 CLE	565	86	9	52	12	303	284	372	451	823	908	779	9	81	0.53	45	27	28	36	109	103	97	7%	122	12%	60%	24	50%	21%	5.87	25.1	64	173	$23
16 CLE	610	91	23	82	15	275	268	343	469	811	790	822	9	76	0.41	39	24	37	33	110	123	122	13%	95	11%	83%	27	52%	26%	5.66	16.3	51	146	$24
1st Half	314	40	11	46	5	264	262	324	439	763	650	816	8	77	0.38	39	25	36	31	107	103	113	13%	102	7%	83%	14	50%	29%	4.95	1.3	39	111	$20
2nd Half	296	51	12	36	10	287	274	362	500	862	921	828	10	75	0.45	39	22	39	35	114	144	132	14%	97	15%	83%	13	54%	23%	6.48	14.0	66	189	$28
17 Proj	**571**	**85**	**17**	**71**	**15**	**278**	**271**	**348**	**447**	**795**	**731**	**829**	**9**	**78**	**0.47**	**42**	**24**	**34**	**33**	**107**	**108**	**110**	**11%**	**101**	**13%**	**76%**				**5.45**	**10.6**	**52**	**148**	**$25**

La Stella,Tommy

Age: 28 Bats: L Pos: 3B
Ht: 5' 11" Wt: 185

Health	F	LIMA Plan	D+
PT/Exp	F	Rand Var	0
Consist	A	MM	1141

2-11-.270 in 148 AB at CHC. After solid start, had two interruptions—in June, a hamstring strain, and later, refusal to report to AAA. This is not a place to go for counting stats. High LD%, bb% set a nice foundation for BA, and that's all you get. In an age of role players, he's your 23rd pick to help temper Chris Carter's BA downside.

Yr Tm	AB	R	HR	RBI	SB	BA	xBA	OBP	SLG	OPS	vL	vR	bb%	ct%	Eye	G	L	F	h%	HctX	PX	xPX	hr/f	Spd	SBO	SB%	#Wk	DOM	DIS	RC/G	RAR	BPV	BPX	R$
12																																		
13 aa	283	27	3	35	6	308		378	423	800			10	86	0.80				35		82			92	7%	84%				5.95		59	148	$10
14 ATL *	486	35	2	47	3	247	257	322	308	630	818	603	10	88	0.94	48	23	29	28	104	47	79	1%	77	3%	55%	19	42%	16%	3.34	-0.7	35	95	$4
15 CHC *	136	13	2	18	2	254	302	306	379	685	0	771	7	91	0.86	38	30	33	27	91	81	74	5%	80	6%	100%	8	63%	25%	4.05	-0.4	70	189	$1
16 CHC *	196	22	3	13	0	262	267	333	384	717	856	748	10	81	0.55	36	28	36	31	105	82	100	5%	86	2%	0%	20	40%	30%	4.33	-3.0	35	100	$1
1st Half	97	12	3	9	0	270	287	337	458	794	650	896	9	79	0.49	36	28	36	32	111	119	128	9%	92	0%	0%	11	36%	36%	5.38	1.6	61	174	$3
2nd Half	99	10	0	4	0	254	248	330	311	641	1007	566	10	82	0.61	35	28	37	31	99	47	68	0%	86	3%	0%	9	44%	22%	3.36	-4.2	12	34	$0
17 Proj	**204**	**20**	**2**	**18**	**1**	**271**	**276**	**342**	**380**	**722**	**734**	**720**	**9**	**85**	**0.66**	**38**	**28**	**34**	**31**	**99**	**71**	**84**	**4%**	**80**	**4%**	**63%**				**4.45**	**-2.6**	**35**	**100**	**$5**

Lagares,Juan

Age: 28 Bats: R Pos: CF
Ht: 6' 1" Wt: 175

Health	C	LIMA Plan	D+
PT/Exp	D	Rand Var	+2
Consist	A	MM	1523

Cut down on Ks early on, albeit in small sample, before June thumb injury. Tried to play through it, with poor results, and eventually had surgery. Elite defense will continue to provide chances, so could get back to double-digit SB. But given weak xBA history, dwindling xPX, unlikely to make an impact with the bat.

Yr Tm	AB	R	HR	RBI	SB	BA	xBA	OBP	SLG	OPS	vL	vR	bb%	ct%	Eye	G	L	F	h%	HctX	PX	xPX	hr/f	Spd	SBO	SB%	#Wk	DOM	DIS	RC/G	RAR	BPV	BPX	R$
12 aa	499	55	3	38	17	240		282	323	605			6	78	0.27				30		62			107	24%	60%				2.90		8	20	$8
13 NYM *	470	43	6	40	7	246	228	281	360	641	657	620	5	76	0.20	49	16	36	31	81	84	81	4%	151	13%	52%	24	25%	42%	3.27	-11.6	27	68	$7
14 NYM	416	46	4	47	13	281	249	321	382	703	875	658	5	79	0.23	46	22	32	35	93	81	89	4%	128	16%	76%	22	45%	32%	4.27	5.2	31	84	$14
15 NYM	441	47	6	41	7	259	236	289	358	647	771	599	4	80	0.18	55	14	31	31	107	64	72	6%	143	10%	70%	27	26%	30%	3.48	-10.7	24	65	$9
16 NYM	142	15	3	9	4	239	259	301	380	682	650	715	7	81	0.41	42	22	35	28	71	83	68	7%	142	18%	67%	19	32%	37%	3.66	-4.2	49	140	$1
1st Half	97	10	2	6	1	289	283	324	433	757	744	771	5	86	0.36	39	27	35	32	74	85	66	7%	135	4%	100%	13	38%	23%	5.09	1.6	62	177	$2
2nd Half	45	5	1	3	3	133	214	259	267	526	423	616	12	71	0.46	52	12	36	16	64	78	74	8%	137	56%	60%	6	17%	67%	1.66	-4.6	13	37	-$2
17 Proj	**327**	**35**	**6**	**26**	**11**	**253**	**244**	**312**	**373**	**685**	**682**	**687**	**7**	**80**	**0.36**	**49**	**17**	**34**	**30**	**83**	**71**	**75**	**6%**	**148**	**20%**	**64%**				**3.73**	**-7.6**	**27**	**76**	**$9**

Lamb,Jacob

Age: 26 Bats: L Pos: 3B
Ht: 6' 2" Wt: 220

Health	B	LIMA Plan	B+
PT/Exp	B	Rand Var	+2
Consist	C	MM	4335

Appeared to be on way to full-fledged breakout, but hr/f proved unsustainable, and HctX, h% suddenly tanked. Bruised hand in July only cost him a couple games, but may have played role in 2nd half slide. Power looks legit, bb% on rise, and gains vL (117 PX) masked by 20% h%. So don't let 2nd half scare you off.

Yr Tm	AB	R	HR	RBI	SB	BA	xBA	OBP	SLG	OPS	vL	vR	bb%	ct%	Eye	G	L	F	h%	HctX	PX	xPX	hr/f	Spd	SBO	SB%	#Wk	DOM	DIS	RC/G	RAR	BPV	BPX	R$
12																																		
13																																		
14 ARI *	518	59	15	70	2	268	258	323	451	774	364	692	8	70	0.27	52	17	31	36	98	153	105	14%	92	3%	71%	9	33%	56%	5.07	20.2	47	127	$15
15 ARI	350	38	6	34	3	263	234	331	386	716	541	743	9	72	0.37	45	23	32	35	115	87	114	7%	115	5%	60%	21	29%	57%	4.37	-3.0	14	38	$6
16 ARI	523	81	29	91	6	249	271	332	509	840	625	898	11	71	0.42	46	17	37	30	113	164	149	21%	102	6%	86%	27	67%	22%	5.73	11.6	68	194	$17
1st Half	272	46	19	58	3	290	300	367	607	974	751	1027	10	72	0.40	46	20	34	34	123	196	166	28%	104	6%	75%	14	86%	0%	7.88	22.7	97	277	$26
2nd Half	251	35	10	33	3	203	238	294	402	696	507	753	12	69	0.43	45	15	40	25	102	129	130	14%	101	5%	100%	13	46%	46%	3.87	-8.0	36	103	$7
17 Proj	**504**	**78**	**25**	**89**	**5**	**267**	**264**	**340**	**501**	**840**	**762**	**858**	**10**	**71**	**0.38**	**45**	**19**	**36**	**33**	**114**	**147**	**128**	**20%**	**101**	**5%**	**76%**				**5.92**	**15.0**	**57**	**164**	**$21**

Lawrie,Brett

Age: 27 Bats: R Pos: 2B
Ht: 5' 11" Wt: 225

Health	F	LIMA Plan	C+
PT/Exp	C	Rand Var	-3
Consist	A	MM	3215

With jump in FB%, was on pace for career-high in HR before July hamstring injury ended season. However, was second straight year with sizable drops in both HctX and xPX, while ct% dipped to dangerous levels. MI power isn't as hard to find as it used to be, and Health grade and xBA highlight the sizeable risk here.

Yr Tm	AB	R	HR	RBI	SB	BA	xBA	OBP	SLG	OPS	vL	vR	bb%	ct%	Eye	G	L	F	h%	HctX	PX	xPX	hr/f	Spd	SBO	SB%	#Wk	DOM	DIS	RC/G	RAR	BPV	BPX	R$
12 TOR	494	73	11	48	13	273	265	324	405	729	813	697	6	83	0.38	50	20	30	31	94	85	78	9%	100	16%	62%	23	43%	39%	4.37	2.9	43	108	$16
13 TOR *	422	45	12	48	10	252	254	308	393	701	613	742	7	81	0.43	49	17	34	28	104	91	89	10%	107	14%	66%	20	60%	25%	4.04	3.9	48	120	$11
14 TOR	259	27	12	38	0	247	238	301	421	722	595	760	6	81	0.33	47	14	39	26	118	112	121	14%	63	0%	0%	14	43%	36%	4.15	5.8	46	124	$6
15 OAK	562	64	16	60	5	260	244	299	407	706	825	660	5	74	0.19	49	18	33	32	98	103	108	12%	94	6%	71%	27	26%	48%	4.12	-2.5	20	54	$13
16 CHW	351	35	12	36	7	248	229	310	413	723	802	704	8	69	0.28	38	19	42	33	81	119	92	12%	68	12%	70%	16	38%	44%	4.25	-4.9	9	26	$7
1st Half	307	33	11	32	6	254	237	320	433	754	833	737	8	69	0.29	38	20	42	34	81	131	100	12%	68	12%	67%	14	43%	36%	4.61	-1.8	19	54	$9
2nd Half	44	2	1	4	1	205	170	234	273	507	676	436	4	70	0.15	41	16	44	27	80	38	38	7%	83	10%	100%	2	0%	100%	2.19	-3.6	-52	-149	-$7
17 Proj	**425**	**48**	**14**	**49**	**6**	**243**	**238**	**295**	**402**	**697**	**776**	**670**	**7**	**74**	**0.27**	**44**	**17**	**39**	**30**	**92**	**102**	**85**	**12%**	**82**	**9%**	**66%**				**3.91**	**-11.4**	**16**	**45**	**$11**

Lee,Dae-ho

Age: 35 Bats: R Pos: 1B
Ht: 6' 4" Wt: 250

Health	A	LIMA Plan	D+
PT/Exp	B	Rand Var	0
Consist	A	MM	3033

14-49-.253 in 292 AB at SEA. A respectable debut, but not without some red flags. Rarely hit the ball in the air, but was saved by extremely high—and likely unsustainable—hr/f. Power metrics were rather unimpressive, and along with ct%, subsided in 2nd half. In all, a small window for value, even smaller for a 35-year-old.

Yr Tm	AB	R	HR	RBI	SB	BA	xBA	OBP	SLG	OPS	vL	vR	bb%	ct%	Eye	G	L	F	h%	HctX	PX	xPX	hr/f	Spd	SBO	SB%	#Wk	DOM	DIS	RC/G	RAR	BPV	BPX	R$
12 for	525	53	14	89	0	266		332	408	740			9	85	0.64				29		86			88	1%	0%				4.62	-11.1	54	135	$13
13 for	521	59	14	89	0	283		347	417	764			9	85	0.68				31		88			75	0%	0%				5.15	8.0	55	138	$17
14 for	566	59	11	66	0	280		324	393	717			6	84	0.40				32		82			78	2%	0%				4.40	3.7	38	103	$15
15 for	510	66	19	96	0	263		329	431	760			9	80	0.48				30		110			74	1%	0%				4.86	-4.3	49	132	$15
16 SEA *	319	35	15	53	0	266	260	312	449	761	775	699	6	76	0.28	53	22	25	31	82	108	72	25%	57	0%	0%	27	30%	41%	4.87	0.1	22	63	$8
1st Half	160	19	11	35	0	294	278	339	519	858	828	889	6	79	0.29	50	24	26	31	84	118	69	33%	63	0%	0%	14	43%	29%	6.28	5.2	42	120	$13
2nd Half	159	16	4	18	0	238	241	289	378	667	719	432	7	73	0.27	57	20	24	30	81	97	76	14%	61	0%	0%	13	15%	54%	3.66	-6.8	4	11	$3
17 Proj	**259**	**29**	**11**	**41**	**0**	**254**	**268**	**322**	**428**	**750**	**811**	**674**	**7**	**79**	**0.37**	**54**	**21**	**25**	**28**	**82**	**103**	**73**	**22%**	**58**	**1%**	**0%**				**4.49**	**-4.7**	**21**	**60**	**$7**

BRIAN RUDD

LeMahieu,DJ

Age: 28	Bats: R	Pos: 2B	Health	A	LIMA Plan	B+
Ht: 6' 4"	Wt: 185		PT/Exp	A	Rand Var	-5
			Consist	F	MM	1555

Batting title! Sure, won't repeat BA once h% falls back to earth, but there's a lot to like: ct%, xBA, LD% fully back another .300 season; harder contact (HctX, xPX) make HR gains repeatable; surged vL; top-notch Spd leaves SB rebound window open. Some counting stat risk, but this came with plenty of skill support.

Yr	Tm	AB	R	HR	RBI	SB	BA	xBA	OBP	SLG	OPS	vL	vR	bb%	ct%	Eye	G	L	F	h%	HctX	PX	xPX	hr/f	Spd	SBO	SB%	#Wk	DOM	DIS	RC/G	RAR	BPV	BPX	R$
12	COL *	484	46	3	41	9	281	261	318	370	689	681	764	5	85	0.37	56	19	25	33	93	61	72	4%	152	14%	50%	17	41%	35%	3.96	-5.4	46	115	$11
13	COL *	547	59	3	41	23	285	286	316	375	692	652	682	4	84	0.28	55	27	18	34	98	64	64	3%	148	22%	71%	20	30%	30%	4.16	7.8	42	105	$20
14	COL	494	59	5	42	10	267	250	315	348	663	669	660	6	80	0.34	56	21	23	32	98	57	84	5%	153	14%	50%	26	35%	38%	3.58	2.7	28	76	$13
15	COL	564	85	6	61	23	301	271	358	388	746	757	743	8	81	0.47	54	26	19	36	95	58	75	7%	146	14%	88%	26	42%	31%	5.26	16.9	33	89	$27
16	COL	552	104	11	66	11	348	303	416	495	911	931	903	11	86	0.83	51	27	23	39	122	84	95	10%	160	9%	61%	26	62%	19%	7.87	43.2	80	229	$32
1st Half		266	47	5	29	7	327	315	393	496	890	905	884	10	85	0.73	52	26	21	37	123	100	93	10%	152	14%	58%	14	64%	21%	7.08	16.5	87	249	$28
2nd Half		286	57	6	37	4	367	292	437	493	930	955	921	11	86	0.93	49	27	24	41	121	69	96	10%	158	5%	67%	12	58%	17%	8.65	27.6	72	206	$36
17	Proj	570	92	12	62	18	307	289	373	440	813	831	806	10	84	0.64	50	26	24	35	109	76	86	10%	158	13%	69%				5.95	18.2	52	148	$28

Leon,Sandy

Age: 28	Bats: B	Pos: CA	Health	A	LIMA Plan	D+
Ht: 5' 11"	Wt: 220		PT/Exp	F	Rand Var	-5
			Consist	D	MM	1013

7-35-.310 in 252 AB with BOS. Shot out of gate with .350 BA through Aug, but likely just a flash in the pan. BA was propped up by LD% and h%, both of which he's never held; ct%, xBA suggest BA is headed south. Power skills skeptical of HR spike—previous career-high was 6. Rand Var confirms: we've likely seen his best.

Yr	Tm	AB	R	HR	RBI	SB	BA	xBA	OBP	SLG	OPS	vL	vR	bb%	ct%	Eye	G	L	F	h%	HctX	PX	xPX	hr/f	Spd	SBO	SB%	#Wk	DOM	DIS	RC/G	RAR	BPV	BPX	R$
12	WAS *	217	21	2	21	1	286	229	346	401	748	1306	515	8	81	0.48	58	11	32	34	56	90	28	0%	94	1%	100%	6	0%	67%	4.99	4.3	43	108	$3
13	WAS *	311	28	2	20	0	154	216	241	216	457	0	0	10	80	0.57	44	20	36	19	0	47	-15	0%	83	0%	0%	2	0%	100%	1.57	-21.9	4	10	-$9
14	WAS *	234	26	4	21	1	182	225	254	275	528	511	413	9	74	0.37	53	19	28	23	67	74	38	8%	63	1%	100%	10	20%	70%	2.18	-9.5	-5	-14	-$3
15	BOS *	213	15	1	14	0	209	188	262	248	510	118	569	7	74	0.28	45	19	36	28	46	34	28	0%	71	4%	0%	19	16%	63%	1.99	-11.6	-37	-100	-$4
16	BOS *	367	47	9	47	0	283	253	341	424	765	1062	764	8	74	0.35	44	25	31	36	94	93	82	12%	117	0%	0%	18	39%	39%	5.15	13.2	26	74	$9
1st Half		150	18	3	21	0	278	268	343	397	740	1246	1176	9	77	0.43	46	29	25	35	100	79	92	14%	97	0%	0%	5	80%	0%	4.81	2.9	19	54	$6
2nd Half		217	29	6	26	0	286	252	343	442	785	1006	714	8	73	0.31	44	24	32	37	92	104	80	12%	117	0%	0%	13	23%	54%	5.38	7.5	27	77	$11
17	Proj	322	35	6	33	0	243	238	307	352	659	668	655	8	75	0.35	46	22	32	31	74	73	58	8%	95	1%	27%				3.58	-5.4	-7	-21	$5

Lind,Adam

Age: 33	Bats: L	Pos: 1B	Health	B	LIMA Plan	C+
Ht: 6' 1"	Wt: 220		PT/Exp	C	Rand Var	+4
			Consist	C	MM	3033

Age-related decline setting in? YES: Effectiveness vR, his niche, is waning; ct%, xBA hint he's no longer plus BA source; unlikely to hold hr/f spike. NO: career-low h% played role in BA drop; xPX, HctX suggest he can still mash. Expect more hits and a fewer dingers, but platoon role, BPV decline ultimately cap his upside.

Yr	Tm	AB	R	HR	RBI	SB	BA	xBA	OBP	SLG	OPS	vL	vR	bb%	ct%	Eye	G	L	F	h%	HctX	PX	xPX	hr/f	Spd	SBO	SB%	#Wk	DOM	DIS	RC/G	RAR	BPV	BPX	R$
12	TOR *	457	45	17	65	1	274	250	332	445	778	553	795	8	78	0.40	48	17	35	32	98	110	101	12%	82	1%	100%	18	56%	22%	5.21	-1.0	43	108	$12
13	TOR	465	67	23	67	1	288	279	357	497	854	573	924	10	78	0.50	46	21	33	33	131	140	141	19%	75	1%	100%	27	52%	22%	6.40	23.2	68	170	$19
14	TOR	290	38	6	40	0	321	283	381	479	860	223	942	9	83	0.58	47	21	33	37	134	119	123	8%	89	0%	0%	21	52%	19%	6.85	20.9	75	203	$12
15	MIL	502	72	20	87	0	277	264	360	460	820	575	883	12	80	0.66	46	19	35	31	130	120	138	14%	64	0%	0%	27	48%	19%	5.86	13.0	61	165	$18
16	SEA	401	48	20	58	0	239	258	286	431	717	638	729	6	78	0.29	44	20	36	26	114	111	128	18%	48	1%	0%	26	46%	35%	4.09	-9.2	28	80	$7
1st Half		211	26	12	36	0	246	248	278	455	733	715	735	5	77	0.20	43	16	41	27	124	120	151	18%	60	2%	0%	14	36%	36%	4.22	-5.5	32	91	$9
2nd Half		190	22	8	22	0	232	272	295	405	700	572	721	8	79	0.40	45	25	31	25	103	102	102	17%	48	0%	0%	12	58%	33%	3.92	-6.8	29	83	$5
17	Proj	384	49	16	57	0	264	265	327	445	772	555	813	9	79	0.45	45	20	34	30	120	108	126	15%	61	0%	19%				5.03	-0.8	33	94	$12

Lindor,Francisco

Age: 23	Bats: B	Pos: SS	Health	A	LIMA Plan	B
Ht: 5' 11"	Wt: 175		PT/Exp	A	Rand Var	-2
			Consist	C	MM	1445

Sophomore slump? Ha! Skills-wise, a similar version of rookie breakout. Continued Eye growth was a highlight, while elevated h% just might be his baseline. PX dipped towards xPX, but still enough pop for double-digit HR given mammoth AB totals. Should continue to flirt with .300, and green light could yield... UP: 30 SB.

Yr	Tm	AB	R	HR	RBI	SB	BA	xBA	OBP	SLG	OPS	vL	vR	bb%	ct%	Eye	G	L	F	h%	HctX	PX	xPX	hr/f	Spd	SBO	SB%	#Wk	DOM	DIS	RC/G	RAR	BPV	BPX	R$
12																																			
13	aa	76	11	1	6	4	259		351	342	693			12	90	1.40				28		52			118	23%	65%				4.00		64	160	$1
14	a/a	507	61	9	51	23	248		301	342	643			7	79	0.36				30		67			104	29%	57%				3.20		16	43	$16
15	CLE *	619	73	14	71	20	298	275	349	443	793	890	804	7	82	0.45	51	21	29	34	92	92	75	13%	139	17%	68%	17	71%	18%	5.49	19.1	62	168	$28
16	CLE	604	99	15	78	19	301	282	358	435	794	748	816	9	85	0.65	49	22	28	33	95	77	74	10%	121	13%	79%	27	44%	15%	5.78	24.6	59	169	$29
1st Half		313	52	10	39	13	300	287	356	450	807	790	815	8	85	0.58	52	21	26	33	88	84	72	14%	120	17%	81%	14	57%	14%	5.94	12.8	60	171	$33
2nd Half		291	47	5	39	6	302	276	360	419	780	705	817	9	86	0.73	46	23	31	34	103	69	77	6%	120	8%	75%	13	31%	15%	5.60	9.1	56	160	$25
17	Proj	612	86	15	74	20	292	275	344	427	772	765	775	8	84	0.52	49	22	29	33	95	78	75	10%	128	16%	70%				5.27	13.9	47	134	$30

Lobaton,Jose

Age: 32	Bats: B	Pos: CA	Health	B	LIMA Plan	D
Ht: 6' 0"	Wt: 170		PT/Exp	F	Rand Var	+2
			Consist	B	MM	1011

Skill set on life support showed a little blip in tiny sample. Improved BA with support from ct%, xBA, while xPX hints it came with some pop. Held similar skills over larger sample in 2013, but these skills are still barely rosterable as a #2 catcher in deep leagues.

Yr	Tm	AB	R	HR	RBI	SB	BA	xBA	OBP	SLG	OPS	vL	vR	bb%	ct%	Eye	G	L	F	h%	HctX	PX	xPX	hr/f	Spd	SBO	SB%	#Wk	DOM	DIS	RC/G	RAR	BPV	BPX	R$
12	TAM *	195	17	2	21	0	201	200	295	291	586	751	584	12	71	0.47	48	16	36	27	80	78	100	5%	86	2%	0%	21	29%	48%	2.68	-9.8	0	0	-$3
13	TAM	277	38	7	32	0	249	256	320	394	714	653	745	10	77	0.46	44	23	32	30	86	104	81	10%	119	1%	0%	27	56%	22%	4.25	4.5	47	118	$4
14	WAS	214	18	2	12	0	234	217	287	304	591	483	633	7	71	0.25	49	24	27	32	93	64	95	5%	105	0%	0%	24	21%	58%	2.87	-3.7	-15	-41	-$1
15	WAS	136	11	3	20	0	199	201	279	294	573	403	598	10	71	0.38	47	19	34	26	74	69	89	9%	92	0%	0%	24	33%	58%	2.60	-5.1	-12	-32	-$2
16	WAS	99	10	3	8	0	232	255	319	374	692	443	737	11	82	0.67	46	21	33	26	96	76	110	11%	115	0%	0%	19	42%	42%	3.91	-1.4	46	131	-$1
1st Half		65	5	1	4	0	185	223	284	277	561	83	656	11	78	0.57	55	16	29	22	87	49	88	7%	118	0%	0%	13	38%	46%	2.37	-3.7	12	34	-$2
2nd Half		34	5	2	4	0	324	326	385	559	943	1400	882	11	88	1.00	32	29	39	32	112	122	145	17%	108	0%	0%	6	50%	33%	8.32	3.8	106	303	$2
17	Proj	222	20	6	20	0	233	233	307	355	661	584	900	10	74	0.41	44	22	33	29	92	76	107	10%	111	0%	0%				3.60	-3.6	-10	-28	$2

Loney,James

Age: 33	Bats: L	Pos: 1B	Health	B	LIMA Plan	D+
Ht: 6' 2"	Wt: 220		PT/Exp	B	Rand Var	+2
			Consist	A	MM	1043

9-34-.265 in 343 AB with NYM. BA dip was the product of lower h%; excellent ct%, LD% remained intact. Good news ends there, as struggles vL limit him to platoon role, and though xPX bounced back, this was likely his HR ceiling. "A" consistency just means more of the same, which isn't really a good thing.

Yr	Tm	AB	R	HR	RBI	SB	BA	xBA	OBP	SLG	OPS	vL	vR	bb%	ct%	Eye	G	L	F	h%	HctX	PX	xPX	hr/f	Spd	SBO	SB%	#Wk	DOM	DIS	RC/G	RAR	BPV	BPX	R$
12	2 TM	434	37	6	41	0	249	266	293	336	630	508	662	6	88	0.55	46	25	29	27	93	58	65	5%	55	3%	0%	27	33%	26%	3.26	-27.9	30	75	$4
13	TAM	549	54	13	75	3	299	297	348	430	778	729	797	7	86	0.57	42	30	28	33	102	89	77	10%	60	2%	75%	27	44%	22%	5.48	13.5	50	125	$20
14	TAM	600	59	9	69	4	290	271	336	380	716	601	762	6	87	0.51	42	27	31	32	92	65	78	6%	60	2%	100%	27	48%	26%	4.62	7.2	32	86	$19
15	TAM	361	25	4	32	2	280	267	322	357	680	568	713	6	91	0.68	42	25	33	30	75	51	42	4%	69	6%	33%	22	41%	23%	3.93	-14.8	38	103	$6
16	NYM *	501	43	10	51	0	260	270	290	368	658	487	742	4	89	0.40	42	24	35	27	107	60	82	8%	61	0%	0%	19	53%	21%	3.68	-24.1	34	97	$7
1st Half		277	26	5	31	0	268	273	304	380	684	804	832	5	89	0.46	41	24	35	29	123	64	89	11%	67	0%	0%	6	67%	33%	4.02	-8.6	38	109	$8
2nd Half		224	17	5	20	0	250	267	284	353	637	334	693	3	90	0.32	42	24	34	26	99	55	79	7%	62	0%	0%	13	46%	15%	3.27	-12.1	31	89	$4
17	Proj	299	25	6	30	1	269	275	310	375	685	547	719	5	89	0.49	42	25	33	29	97	60	71	7%	64	2%	45%				3.96	-9.8	24	70	$7

Longoria,Evan

Age: 31	Bats: R	Pos: 3B	Health	A	LIMA Plan	B
Ht: 6' 2"	Wt: 180		PT/Exp	A	Rand Var	0
			Consist	B	MM	4135

The rebirth we'd been waiting for, as he rekindled 2012-13 power skills and paired them with career-high FB%. Didn't sell out for it either, as ct% held steady and xBA supported gains. Lots of positives tempered somewhat by the fact that EVERYONE hit in 2016. Note that 2013 still generated higher roto value.

Yr	Tm	AB	R	HR	RBI	SB	BA	xBA	OBP	SLG	OPS	vL	vR	bb%	ct%	Eye	G	L	F	h%	HctX	PX	xPX	hr/f	Spd	SBO	SB%	#Wk	DOM	DIS	RC/G	RAR	BPV	BPX	R$
12	TAM *	303	39	17	57	2	276	264	357	491	848	1064	842	11	76	0.53	38	22	40	31	126	137	147	20%	94	6%	40%	14	64%	21%	5.99	12.5	67	168	$11
13	TAM	614	91	32	88	1	269	264	343	498	842	950	799	10	74	0.43	37	19	45	32	127	164	173	16%	94	1%	100%	27	63%	33%	5.98	35.8	76	190	$23
14	TAM	624	83	22	91	5	253	249	320	404	724	824	691	8	79	0.43	39	20	41	29	109	105	118	11%	106	3%	100%	27	48%	19%	4.40	13.3	49	132	$19
15	TAM	604	74	21	73	3	270	254	328	435	764	960	695	8	78	0.39	39	21	40	31	105	111	121	11%	103	3%	75%	27	44%	33%	4.97	6.8	50	135	$18
16	TAM	633	81	36	98	0	273	276	318	521	840	753	864	6	77	0.29	32	21	47	30	114	148	146	16%	112	2%	0%	27	63%	15%	5.71	16.5	75	214	$21
1st Half		313	45	18	45	0	278	274	330	524	854	897	843	7	75	0.32	30	22	48	32	123	154	165	16%	98	3%	0%	14	64%	7%	5.97	9.7	71	203	$21
2nd Half		320	36	18	53	0	269	277	306	519	825	628	886	5	79	0.25	34	21	46	29	105	141	129	15%	127	2%	0%	13	62%	23%	5.45	5.2	79	226	$21
17	Proj	617	78	29	91	2	269	263	323	477	800	831	790	7	78	0.35	35	21	44	30	111	125	136	14%	110	3%	48%				5.29	7.2	44	125	$22

RYAN BLOOMFIELD

Lowrie,Jed

Age: 33 Bats: B Pos: 2B | Ht: 6' 0" Wt: 190

Health F | PT/Exp C | Consist A | LIMA Plan D+ | Rand Var -2 | MM 1313

Annual talk of upside is muted by essential career split: 799 games played/532 DL days. 2016 maladies (shin, toe) gutted his power before felling him completely in early Aug. Lauded for comebacks and LD stroke, but cumulative toll of injuries may now be too much to overcome. Best left to the "what-if" hangers-on.

Yr	Tm	AB	R	HR	RBI	SB	BA	xBA	OBP	SLG	OPS	vL	vR	bb%	ct%	Eye	G	L	F	h%	HctX	PX	xPX	hr/f	Spd	SBO	SB%	#Wk	DOM	DIS	RC/G	RAR	BPV	BPX	R$
12	HOU	340	43	16	42	2	244	253	331	438	769	623	819	11	81	0.66	29	19	51	26	125	121	162	11%	89	2%	100%	18	50%	22%	4.90	7.4	72	180	$7
13	OAK	603	80	15	75	1	290	272	344	446	791	772	800	8	85	0.55	33	23	43	32	96	108	99	7%	90	1%	100%	26	65%	12%	5.53	30.3	70	175	$21
14	OAK	502	59	6	50	0	249	250	321	355	676	598	707	9	84	0.65	31	24	44	29	107	79	112	3%	101	0%	0%	25	40%	16%	3.83	6.5	51	138	$7
15	HOU	230	35	9	30	1	222	263	312	400	712	908	641	11	81	0.65	35	21	44	24	128	115	153	11%	80	2%	100%	15	60%	27%	4.04	-1.6	65	176	$2
16	OAK	338	30	2	27	0	263	239	314	322	637	667	627	7	81	0.40	43	25	32	32	91	40	81	2%	103	0%	0%	17	24%	53%	3.53	-11.7	2	6	$3
1st Half		243	23	2	25	0	292	251	347	362	709	631	732	8	83	0.51	40	26	33	35	97	45	80	3%	113	0%	0%	13	31%	46%	4.55	-1.7	20	57	$6
2nd Half		95	7	0	2	0	189	209	228	221	449	734	323	5	75	0.21	49	23	28	25	76	28	85	0%	87	0%	0%	4	0%	75%	1.60	-9.7	-41	-117	-$7
17	**Proj**	**354**	**39**	**5**	**31**	**1**	**235**	**240**	**298**	**328**	**626**	**725**	**588**	**8**	**80**	**0.45**	**39**	**23**	**37**	**28**	**101**	**61**	**110**	**5%**	**89**	**1%**	**100%**				**3.25**	**-16.4**	**3**	**9**	**$2**

Lucroy,Jonathan

Age: 31 Bats: R Pos: CA | Ht: 6' 0" Wt: 185

Health B | PT/Exp B | Consist D | LIMA Plan B+ | Rand Var -3 | MM 3345

Injury-free, continued to fine-tune all-around game by muscling up: FB%, hr/f were career bests. Sacrificed a bit of ct% for launch, but even if hr/f ebbs, HctX and LD% will keep hits coming. He's not a plodder, and xBA is backslide insurance. Heed age and the rigors of the position, but bid aggressively.

Yr	Tm	AB	R	HR	RBI	SB	BA	xBA	OBP	SLG	OPS	vL	vR	bb%	ct%	Eye	G	L	F	h%	HctX	PX	xPX	hr/f	Spd	SBO	SB%	#Wk	DOM	DIS	RC/G	RAR	BPV	BPX	R$
12	MIL	316	46	12	58	4	320	284	368	513	881	1169	782	7	86	0.50	41	21	37	34	131	112	129	12%	124	6%	80%	20	60%	15%	7.00	24.2	86	215	$16
13	MIL	521	59	18	82	9	280	281	340	455	795	859	775	8	87	0.67	39	23	38	29	133	104	135	10%	112	7%	90%	27	48%	7%	5.53	26.6	82	205	$21
14	MIL	585	73	13	69	4	301	298	373	465	837	838	837	10	88	0.93	42	22	36	33	132	119	128	7%	100	5%	50%	27	78%	0%	6.19	46.4	99	268	$23
15	MIL	371	51	7	43	1	264	275	326	391	717	639	743	9	83	0.56	44	26	29	30	124	83	104	8%	99	1%	100%	21	38%	29%	4.48	7.9	47	127	$8
16	2 TM	490	67	24	81	5	292	276	355	500	855	796	874	9	80	0.47	37	24	39	33	114	118	131	16%	109	4%	100%	27	48%	22%	6.44	35.0	65	186	$21
1st Half		273	40	10	39	3	300	272	360	491	851	646	919	9	80	0.47	38	24	38	35	116	112	141	12%	133	4%	100%	14	50%	29%	6.54	18.0	68	194	$22
2nd Half		217	27	14	42	2	281	283	349	512	860	1001	819	9	79	0.47	36	25	39	30	112	126	119	21%	71	3%	100%	13	46%	15%	6.31	13.3	59	169	$19
17	**Proj**	**510**	**68**	**19**	**77**	**4**	**286**	**279**	**350**	**464**	**815**	**808**	**817**	**9**	**82**	**0.55**	**40**	**24**	**36**	**32**	**121**	**103**	**122**	**13%**	**101**	**3%**	**86%**				**5.82**	**24.1**	**54**	**154**	**$21**

Machado,Manny

Age: 24 Bats: R Pos: 3B SS | Ht: 6' 2" Wt: 180

Health B | PT/Exp A | Consist B | LIMA Plan D+ | Rand Var -1 | MM 4345

Let's get the SB issue out of the way: as a team, BAL had 19. Speed's still there; where's the green light? Dude is already a behemoth while consolidating his skills, namely making hard contact with elevation. This year brought inroads vL. And now with 3B/SS eligibility! A little Eye-tightening puts him in MVP conversation.

Yr	Tm	AB	R	HR	RBI	SB	BA	xBA	OBP	SLG	OPS	vL	vR	bb%	ct%	Eye	G	L	F	h%	HctX	PX	xPX	hr/f	Spd	SBO	SB%	#Wk	DOM	DIS	RC/G	RAR	BPV	BPX	R$
12	BAL *	593	73	17	74	13	254	251	310	417	727	801	716	8	81	0.44	46	14	40	29	115	103	100	12%	131	12%	75%	9	44%	44%	4.40	-2.4	64	160	$16
13	BAL	667	88	14	71	6	283	277	314	432	746	762	738	4	83	0.26	47	21	32	32	101	107	73	8%	119	9%	46%	26	62%	12%	4.64	13.2	64	160	$22
14	BAL	327	38	12	32	2	278	262	324	431	755	642	802	6	79	0.29	49	20	31	32	100	106	101	15%	109	2%	100%	16	56%	25%	4.91	11.5	48	130	$10
15	BAL	633	102	35	86	20	286	279	359	502	861	763	894	10	82	0.63	44	18	38	30	119	127	122	18%	110	15%	71%	27	67%	4%	6.30	31.3	86	232	$35
16	BAL	640	105	37	96	0	294	283	343	533	876	919	862	7	81	0.40	37	20	43	31	117	136	118	17%	108	2%	0%	27	63%	4%	6.47	29.8	82	234	$27
1st Half		316	58	18	50	0	329	297	384	592	976	1023	960	8	81	0.44	36	20	44	36	123	159	130	16%	107	4%	0%	14	79%	0%	8.28	28.6	100	286	$32
2nd Half		324	47	19	46	0	259	270	303	475	778	808	769	6	82	0.36	39	20	41	26	111	114	107	17%	117	0%	0%	13	46%	8%	4.98	0.8	68	194	$22
17	**Proj**	**642**	**99**	**36**	**100**	**7**	**287**	**280**	**340**	**510**	**850**	**822**	**860**	**7**	**81**	**0.43**	**40**	**20**	**40**	**31**	**116**	**125**	**112**	**17%**	**108**	**6%**	**70%**				**6.14**	**22.6**	**64**	**184**	**$32**

Mahtook,Mikie

Age: 27 Bats: R Pos: LF CF | Ht: 6' 1" Wt: 200

Health B | PT/Exp C | Consist B | LIMA Plan D | Rand Var -2 | MM 3301

3-11-.195 in 185 AB at TAM. Ugly follow-up to able debut was impacted by oblique and hand injuries. Weak plate skills were hyperexposed, how overall game translates to MLB is TBD. But in the rubble of the good (2015) and the bad (2016) are career 126 PX, 129 xPX, and 14% hr/f. Could really use a strong Act Three.

Yr	Tm	AB	R	HR	RBI	SB	BA	xBA	OBP	SLG	OPS	vL	vR	bb%	ct%	Eye	G	L	F	h%	HctX	PX	xPX	hr/f	Spd	SBO	SB%	#Wk	DOM	DIS	RC/G	RAR	BPV	BPX	R$
12	aa	153	14	3	20	3	212		255	338	592			5	77	0.25				26		90			90	23%	49%				2.57		19	48	$0
13	aa	511	56	5	54	20	218		266	327	593			6	77	0.28				27		80			120	27%	68%				2.77		22	55	$9
14	aaa	489	46	9	56	15	251		305	386	691			7	67	0.24				36		119			101	17%	72%				3.96		9	24	$13
15	TAM *	490	50	12	54	12	225	221	260	367	627	1030	856	5	69	0.15	33	23	44	30	120	109	193	28%	117	18%	74%	12	58%	17%	3.12	-19.2	11	30	$8
16	TAM *	290	29	4	17	4	216	183	259	317	576	678	438	5	66	0.17	38	14	47	31	86	77	94	5%	127	10%	65%	13	15%	85%	2.63	-14.7	-21	-60	$0
1st Half		143	15	1	7	3	223	172	279	303	582	667	254	7	68	0.24	40	12	48	32	73	56	41	0%	147	13%	73%	5	0%	100%	2.77	-7.4	-21	-60	$0
2nd Half		147	14	3	10	1	210	191	239	330	569	683	547	4	64	0.11	37	16	47	31	91	98	123	8%	98	7%	44%	8	25%	75%	2.48	-9.1	-26	-74	-$1
17	**Proj**	**199**	**20**	**6**	**17**	**3**	**223**	**216**	**277**	**382**	**658**	**819**	**515**	**5**	**68**	**0.18**	**37**	**18**	**45**	**30**	**98**	**111**	**131**	**10%**	**115**	**13%**	**62%**				**3.24**	**-7.4**	**0**	**0**	**$3**

Maile,Luke

Age: 26 Bats: R Pos: CA | Ht: 6' 3" Wt: 226

Health A | PT/Exp D | Consist B | LIMA Plan D | Rand Var -1 | MM 2003

3-15-.227 in 119 AB at TAM. Among the last to jump on team's catcher carousel in 2016, he showed a bit of pop but little else. Weak plate skills, hit tool consistent with undistinguished AAA seasons (.221 BA/.295 OBP). Has rep for strong defense, but woe is you if he racks up projected AB while on your team.

Yr	Tm	AB	R	HR	RBI	SB	BA	xBA	OBP	SLG	OPS	vL	vR	bb%	ct%	Eye	G	L	F	h%	HctX	PX	xPX	hr/f	Spd	SBO	SB%	#Wk	DOM	DIS	RC/G	RAR	BPV	BPX	R$
12																																			
13																																			
14	aa	351	34	4	29	2	232		289	324	613			7	75	0.32				30		75			104	3%	59%				3.09		9	24	$2
15	TAM *	329	33	4	26	1	177	212	243	251	494	571	214	8	80	0.43	41	19	41	21	103	50	86	0%	79	3%	42%	6	33%	50%	1.87	-19.9	1	3	-$6
16	TAM *	313	21	5	25	0	215	204	256	317	573	697	581	5	75	0.22	47	14	39	27	102	75	114	9%	74	2%	0%	13	23%	54%	2.58	-12.4	-5	-14	-$2
1st Half		175	8	2	9	0	200	217	247	277	524			6	78	0.28				25		56			79	3%	0%				2.11		-7	-20	-$5
2nd Half		138	13	3	16	0	233	214	268	367	635	697	581	5	71	0.17	47	14	39	31	98	101	114	9%	77	0%	0%	13	23%	54%	3.27	-3.6	0	0	$1
17	**Proj**	**294**	**26**	**7**	**25**	**1**	**206**	**222**	**258**	**334**	**593**	**652**	**900**	**7**	**76**	**0.30**	**47**	**14**	**39**	**25**	**88**	**84**	**103**	**8%**	**87**	**2%**	**42%**				**2.75**	**-12.8**	**-1**	**-2**	**$0**

Maldonado,Martin

Age: 30 Bats: R Pos: CA | Ht: 6' 1" Wt: 230

Health A | PT/Exp F | Consist C | LIMA Plan D+ | Rand Var +1 | MM 2003

Another caught up in a fluid CA situation, he actually (albeit modestly) stated a case. Patience became a virtue while flexing a bit of hr/f muscle, but xPX wasn't convinced. That's a monotonously low string of xBAs, but fact is, he's a lifetime backup. Best to treat him as such on draft day.

Yr	Tm	AB	R	HR	RBI	SB	BA	xBA	OBP	SLG	OPS	vL	vR	bb%	ct%	Eye	G	L	F	h%	HctX	PX	xPX	hr/f	Spd	SBO	SB%	#Wk	DOM	DIS	RC/G	RAR	BPV	BPX	R$
12	MIL *	354	30	11	40	1	233	230	281	370	651	612	766	6	72	0.24	43	23	34	29	78	97	78	14%	68	5%	23%	19	37%	53%	3.32	-10.3	0	0	$3
13	MIL	183	13	4	22	0	169	195	236	284	520	446	543	7	71	0.25	42	14	44	21	72	87	101	7%	80	0%	0%	26	27%	65%	1.96	-10.3	-6	-15	-$4
14	MIL	111	14	4	16	0	234	223	320	387	707	721	693	9	71	0.34	36	18	46	29	86	119	107	12%	82	0%	0%	26	31%	54%	3.91	1.5	25	68	$1
15	MIL	229	19	4	22	0	210	205	282	293	575	810	503	9	72	0.35	47	20	33	28	91	62	100	8%	51	2%	0%	25	12%	68%	2.61	-8.6	-27	-73	-$2
16	MIL	208	21	8	21	1	202	225	332	351	683	677	685	14	73	0.63	44	18	38	24	84	92	90	14%	50	2%	100%	25	44%	36%	3.58	-5.3	12	34	-$1
1st Half		59	5	2	4	0	153	169	306	271	577	508	606	17	76	0.86	44	9	47	16	81	67	81	10%	61	0%	0%	13	54%	38%	2.41	-3.4	13	37	-$5
2nd Half		149	16	6	17	1	221	240	343	383	725	752	716	13	72	0.55	44	22	34	27	85	103	93	17%	56	2%	100%	12	33%	33%	4.12	-0.1	15	43	$1
17	**Proj**	**371**	**36**	**12**	**39**	**1**	**205**	**216**	**308**	**336**	**644**	**685**	**628**	**12**	**73**	**0.48**	**44**	**18**	**38**	**25**	**85**	**84**	**94**	**12%**	**53**	**1%**	**59%**				**3.19**	**-11.0**	**-9**	**-27**	**$2**

Margot,Manuel

Age: 22 Bats: R Pos: CF | Ht: 5' 11" Wt: 180

Health A | PT/Exp F | Consist B | LIMA Plan C+ | Rand Var +3 | MM 1533

0-3-.243 with 2 SB in 37 AB at SD. First taste of bigs for top prospect who could excel as table-setter for next decade. Had 88% ct% at AAA using up-the-middle approach in order to maximize excellent speed. Power potential is still under question (HctX was small MLB sample), but he's a keeper—and he's close.

Yr	Tm	AB	R	HR	RBI	SB	BA	xBA	OBP	SLG	OPS	vL	vR	bb%	ct%	Eye	G	L	F	h%	HctX	PX	xPX	hr/f	Spd	SBO	SB%	#Wk	DOM	DIS	RC/G	RAR	BPV	BPX	R$
12																																			
13																																			
14																																			
15	aa	258	31	2	27	16	263		309	403	712			6	85	0.45				30		98			103	42%	65%				4.02		65	176	$9
16	SD *	554	73	4	42	23	257	300	290	352	642	769	583	4	85	0.32	63	23	13	29	138	55	51	0%	172	27%	65%	3	33%	67%	3.35	-21.5	47	134	$15
1st Half		329	44	3	23	16	255	251	292	346	638			5	88	0.42				28		50			155	31%	64%				3.28		49	140	$19
2nd Half		225	30	1	19	7	259	292	286	361	647	769	583	4	82	0.21	63	23	13	31	133	61	51	0%	164	20%	67%	3	33%	67%	3.46	-7.0	35	100	$9
17	**Proj**	**365**	**47**	**2**	**32**	**20**	**259**	**268**	**298**	**361**	**659**	**810**	**576**	**5**	**85**	**0.35**	**47**	**22**	**30**	**30**	**120**	**65**	**46**	**2%**	**149**	**34%**	**70%**				**3.60**	**-10.0**	**46**	**132**	**$14**

ROB CARROLL

Marisnick,Jake

Age: 26	Bats: R	Pos: CF LF	Health	A	LIMA Plan	D
Ht: 6' 3"	Wt: 223		PT/Exp	D	Rand Var	+2
			Consist	B	MM	2401

5-21-.209 with 10 SB in 287 AB at HOU. At this point, has career .220 xBA, 70 HctX, 70 xPX in 956 AB, so if you're looking for something more than a handful of SB, you've come to the wrong place. Even occasional pop vL (career 109 PX) isn't enough to add appeal, given .667 OPS vs. them. Once a prospect, now a suspect.

Yr	Tm	AB	R	HR	RBI	SB	BA	xBA	OBP	SLG	OPS	vL	vR	bb%	ct%	Eye	G	L	F	h%	HctX	PX	xPX	hr/f	Spd	SBO	SB%	#Wk	DOM	DIS	RC/G	RAR	BPV	BPX	R$
12	aa	223	21	2	12	12	221		251	319	569			4	79	0.19				27		69			118	37%	73%				2.58		14	35	$2
13	MIA *	374	43	10	45	12	245	244	285	383	668	431	498	5	73	0.21	42	25	33	31	73	98	55	4%	119	24%	62%	9	22%	67%	3.51	-6.6	20	50	$10
14	2 TM *	564	55	9	46	27	237	223	263	334	597	738	568	3	75	0.14	39	22	39	30	74	75	73	5%	121	31%	74%	12	25%	67%	2.90	-16.0	7	19	$15
15	HOU	339	46	9	36	24	236	223	281	383	665	669	662	5	69	0.17	42	20	38	32	72	107	93	10%	128	47%	73%	25	32%	48%	3.40	-11.6	12	32	$13
16	HOU *	314	42	5	22	11	204	224	244	320	564	701	519	5	70	0.18	45	19	36	28	75	90	68	7%	106	31%	63%	26	19%	54%	2.39	-19.8	-4	-11	$2
1st Half		137	18	1	8	5	168	189	217	245	463	562	436	6	69	0.20	38	17	45	24	83	67	92	3%	96	38%	53%	13	8%	62%	1.48	-14.1	-29	-83	-$2
2nd Half		177	24	4	14	6	232	249	273	379	651	787	569	4	71	0.15	50	21	29	31	69	107	53	11%	107	25%	75%	13	31%	46%	3.30	-6.5	11	31	$5
17	Proj	**200**	**25**	**4**	**17**	**9**	**221**	**228**	**263**	**348**	**611**	**689**	**567**	**5**	**71**	**0.17**	**43**	**20**	**37**	**29**	**74**	**89**	**74**	**8%**	**113**	**35%**	**69%**				**2.83**	**-10.6**	**6**	**17**	**$3**

Markakis,Nick

Age: 33	Bats: L	Pos: RF	Health	A	LIMA Plan	B+
Ht: 6' 2"	Wt: 215		PT/Exp	A	Rand Var	-1
			Consist	A	MM	1035

Consistent double-digit value built on high AB totals and outperforming xBA, and last year, also took best RBI total since 2011 (fueled by .308 BA w/RISP) to make it happen. Appeared to trade ct% for power, though PX questions whether we can really call it that. 2nd half may be a siren song; be careful not to crash on the rocks.

Yr	Tm	AB	R	HR	RBI	SB	BA	xBA	OBP	SLG	OPS	vL	vR	bb%	ct%	Eye	G	L	F	h%	HctX	PX	xPX	hr/f	Spd	SBO	SB%	#Wk	DOM	DIS	RC/G	RAR	BPV	BPX	R$
12	BAL	420	59	13	54	1	298	303	363	471	834	877	816	9	88	0.82	42	27	31	31	126	105	111	11%	90	2%	50%	18	78%	11%	6.15	11.6	83	208	$15
13	BAL	634	89	10	59	1	271	259	329	356	685	651	704	8	88	0.72	47	23	31	30	104	56	71	6%	88	2%	33%	27	44%	19%	4.07	-9.8	41	103	$15
14	BAL	642	81	14	50	4	276	258	342	386	729	673	751	9	87	0.74	46	20	34	30	103	74	85	7%	100	3%	67%	27	41%	11%	4.60	9.1	56	151	$18
15	ATL	612	73	3	53	2	296	261	370	376	746	635	795	10	86	0.84	52	21	27	34	97	60	55	2%	91	1%	67%	27	41%	19%	5.00	2.4	44	119	$16
16	ATL	599	67	13	89	0	269	259	346	397	744	613	800	11	83	0.70	43	22	35	31	111	82	105	7%	59	1%	0%	27	44%	19%	4.73	0.9	39	111	$13
1st Half		308	32	2	42	0	253	249	332	344	677	574	733	11	83	0.73	46	21	33	30	112	66	109	2%	68	0%	0%	14	36%	29%	3.92	-7.0	30	86	$8
2nd Half		291	35	11	47	0	285	271	361	454	815	674	860	10	83	0.68	40	23	38	31	110	98	100	12%	54	2%	0%	13	54%	8%	5.67	8.0	49	140	$19
17	Proj	**567**	**68**	**10**	**68**	**1**	**275**	**263**	**348**	**389**	**737**	**637**	**779**	**10**	**85**	**0.73**	**45**	**22**	**33**	**31**	**107**	**71**	**87**	**7%**	**74**	**2%**	**38%**				**4.70**	**0.0**	**30**	**86**	**$16**

Marte,Jefry

Age: 26	Bats: R	Pos: 1B LF 3B	Health	A	LIMA Plan	D+
Ht: 6' 1"	Wt: 190		PT/Exp	C	Rand Var	+1
			Consist	A	MM	4231

15-44-.252 in 258 AB at LAA. FB%, HctX held up nicely in first extended stint in majors, though disparity between 135 MLB PX and xPX suggests he may give back a few HR. Improvement vR, including 79% contact, may help him avoid platoon fate. Doesn't have skills of rising star, but nothing here says he can't stick in bigs.

Yr	Tm	AB	R	HR	RBI	SB	BA	xBA	OBP	SLG	OPS	vL	vR	bb%	ct%	Eye	G	L	F	h%	HctX	PX	xPX	hr/f	Spd	SBO	SB%	#Wk	DOM	DIS	RC/G	RAR	BPV	BPX	R$
12	aa	462	50	8	47	7	220		274	314	588			7	82	0.41				25		62			96	12%	57%				2.73		21	53	$3
13	aa	245	26	1	22	6	243		300	329	630			8	78	0.37				31		73			95	12%	85%				3.41		16	40	$3
14	aa	405	39	7	41	7	222		285	313	598			8	81	0.48				26		67			82	10%	68%				2.90		22	59	$4
15	DET *	437	46	15	60	6	233	266	285	409	694	920	506	7	79	0.35	46	19	35	26	114	115	102	20%	93	13%	52%	11	45%	36%	3.72	-9.0	52	141	$8
16	LAA *	420	53	17	60	4	236	245	292	416	708	783	793	7	76	0.32	46	15	39	27	111	113	109	19%	84	11%	42%	21	48%	29%	3.86	-5.2	35	100	$8
1st Half		254	25	6	28	2	217	234	274	346	620	229	770	7	73	0.29	44	21	35	27	101	88	112	17%	87	12%	31%	8	38%	38%	2.87	-12.6	6	17	$4
2nd Half		166	28	11	32	2	265	278	330	524	854	927	810	7	80	0.38	47	12	41	27	120	148	108	20%	88	8%	67%	13	54%	23%	5.71	6.1	79	226	$13
17	Proj	**227**	**28**	**11**	**32**	**3**	**238**	**268**	**298**	**448**	**746**	**839**	**694**	**7**	**78**	**0.36**	**46**	**17**	**37**	**26**	**113**	**124**	**107**	**17%**	**93**	**12%**	**54%**				**4.24**	**-5.9**	**50**	**143**	**$7**

Marte,Ketel

Age: 23	Bats: B	Pos: SS	Health	B	LIMA Plan	C+
Ht: 6' 1"	Wt: 180		PT/Exp	C	Rand Var	0
			Consist	C	MM	1425

1-33-.259 with 11 SB in 437 AB at SEA. While ankle sprain, case of mono sent 2nd half south, they also highlighted risk he carries: with few walks and no power, even modest BA hinges on ct%, LD%. If those dry up, so does OBP. Still young enough to achieve skill growth, but right now, not a single sign of it in sight.

Yr	Tm	AB	R	HR	RBI	SB	BA	xBA	OBP	SLG	OPS	vL	vR	bb%	ct%	Eye	G	L	F	h%	HctX	PX	xPX	hr/f	Spd	SBO	SB%	#Wk	DOM	DIS	RC/G	RAR	BPV	BPX	R$
12																																			
13																																			
14	a/a	523	59	3	41	22	263		289	347	636			4	83	0.22				31		67			104	27%	66%				3.34		26	70	$16
15	SEA *	487	58	4	39	24	279	266	333	375	708	720	780	8	84	0.50	52	22	26	33	82	66	45	4%	139	23%	71%	11	55%	18%	4.35	-0.6	46	124	$19
16	SEA *	465	59	1	35	13	254	253	284	318	602	525	651	4	82	0.23	52	22	26	31	71	47	41	1%	115	16%	72%	22	14%	45%	3.07	-17.0	9	26	$9
1st Half		272	37	1	17	10	266	270	293	350	644	610	688	4	83	0.23	49	25	26	32	78	58	49	2%	129	21%	70%	12	17%	33%	3.52	-7.6	27	77	$13
2nd Half		193	22	0	18	3	237	223	271	272	543	382	606	4	80	0.23	56	17	26	30	62	30	30	0%	97	8%	75%	10	10%	60%	2.48	-11.6	-17	-49	$3
17	Proj	**498**	**60**	**2**	**40**	**18**	**261**	**256**	**298**	**336**	**634**	**581**	**665**	**5**	**82**	**0.31**	**53**	**21**	**26**	**31**	**74**	**51**	**41**	**2%**	**118**	**20%**	**71%**				**3.44**	**-15.1**	**16**	**44**	**$15**

Marte,Starling

Age: 28	Bats: R	Pos: LF	Health	A	LIMA Plan	D+
Ht: 6' 2"	Wt: 170		PT/Exp	B	Rand Var	-3
			Consist	B	MM	2545

Three things to note about steep hr/f drop: 1) fluky 32% rate in 1H of 2015; 2) 10% rate from July 2015-June 2016; 3) 2H power last year likely undercut by back spasms. Skills say he's not a .300 hitter, and had to max out SBO, SB% to reach 47 SB, so expect regression. But AB rebound may push R$ upward anyway.

Yr	Tm	AB	R	HR	RBI	SB	BA	xBA	OBP	SLG	OPS	vL	vR	bb%	ct%	Eye	G	L	F	h%	HctX	PX	xPX	hr/f	Spd	SBO	SB%	#Wk	DOM	DIS	RC/G	RAR	BPV	BPX	R$
12	PIT *	555	71	14	68	29	255	262	294	430	723	1042	627	5	73	0.21	57	18	25	32	98	112	83	18%	191	40%	61%	9	33%	44%	3.94	-13.3	53	133	$20
13	PIT	510	83	12	35	41	280	259	343	441	784	1053	724	5	73	0.18	51	22	28	36	98	116	98	12%	201	47%	73%	24	29%	33%	4.73	10.0	56	140	$30
14	PIT	495	73	13	56	30	291	264	356	453	808	781	814	6	74	0.25	47	23	29	37	105	125	113	13%	174	32%	73%	26	50%	35%	5.33	21.8	61	165	$28
15	PIT	579	84	19	81	30	287	283	337	444	780	717	798	4	79	0.22	54	24	23	34	101	103	94	19%	126	28%	75%	27	48%	19%	4.98	4.3	46	124	$32
16	PIT	489	71	9	46	47	311	274	362	456	818	730	837	4	79	0.22	48	23	28	38	111	95	98	8%	156	46%	80%	25	36%	32%	5.79	15.9	49	140	$35
1st Half		289	45	6	31	23	322	271	368	478	845	615	916	4	77	0.16	48	24	28	40	112	101	108	10%	160	39%	79%	14	36%	29%	6.21	13.9	45	129	$40
2nd Half		200	26	3	15	24	295	277	353	425	778	1097	741	6	82	0.32	48	23	29	35	109	87	83	7%	139	58%	80%	11	36%	36%	5.22	4.4	51	146	$28
17	Proj	**564**	**81**	**14**	**60**	**40**	**295**	**276**	**350**	**451**	**801**	**816**	**900**	**5**	**78**	**0.24**	**50**	**23**	**27**	**36**	**106**	**99**	**96**	**12%**	**155**	**38%**	**75%**				**5.29**	**13.5**	**45**	**128**	**$36**

Martin,Leonys

Age: 29	Bats: L	Pos: CF	Health	A	LIMA Plan	C+
Ht: 6' 1"	Wt: 180		PT/Exp	B	Rand Var	-3
			Consist	C	MM	1505

Sudden surge in xPX, hr/f lasted only two months; after 6/1, posted 68 xPX, 7% hr/f, much like he always has, and 2H FB% regressed with it. Expended ct% to buy that power, too; better hope he kept the receipt, because xBA, BPV trends suggest he's teetering on brink of statistical ruin. Pay for SB, short everything else.

Yr	Tm	AB	R	HR	RBI	SB	BA	xBA	OBP	SLG	OPS	vL	vR	bb%	ct%	Eye	G	L	F	h%	HctX	PX	xPX	hr/f	Spd	SBO	SB%	#Wk	DOM	DIS	RC/G	RAR	BPV	BPX	R$
12	TEX *	277	40	10	35	10	291	294	341	496	837	500	624	7	80	0.37	47	24	29	34	88	135	55	0%	101	30%	49%	12	42%	42%	5.39	4.3	74	185	$12
13	TEX	457	66	8	49	36	260	255	313	385	698	573	749	6	77	0.27	51	21	28	32	79	88	61	8%	139	40%	80%	27	30%	33%	4.09	-1.9	35	88	$23
14	TEX	533	68	7	40	31	274	242	325	364	689	581	725	7	79	0.34	50	22	28	34	88	60	68	6%	158	27%	72%	27	30%	44%	4.08	2.9	26	70	$23
15	TEX *	325	31	6	28	15	221	230	266	325	591	566	582	6	77	0.27	52	15	33	27	80	74	62	7%	92	31%	71%	19	21%	63%	2.78	-17.5	9	24	$6
16	SEA	518	72	15	47	24	247	224	306	378	684	684	684	8	71	0.30	43	20	37	32	85	84	79	11%	133	22%	80%	25	36%	56%	3.98	-6.0	10	29	$17
1st Half		231	31	11	26	9	251	217	319	420	739	780	722	9	70	0.32	43	14	43	31	89	104	92	17%	115	21%	69%	13	31%	62%	4.41	-0.7	18	51	$17
2nd Half		287	41	4	21	15	244	228	295	345	640	623	650	7	72	0.28	43	24	33	33	82	68	70	6%	138	23%	88%	12	42%	50%	3.64	-7.5	0	0	$17
17	Proj	**488**	**60**	**9**	**39**	**24**	**243**	**230**	**298**	**352**	**650**	**618**	**665**	**7**	**75**	**0.30**	**47**	**19**	**34**	**31**	**84**	**69**	**71**	**8%**	**126**	**26%**	**75%**				**3.51**	**-14.7**	**7**	**20**	**$16**

Martin,Russell

Age: 34	Bats: R	Pos: CA	Health	A	LIMA Plan	B
Ht: 5' 10"	Wt: 215		PT/Exp	B	Rand Var	-1
			Consist	B	MM	3125

Said early-season neck stiffness kept him from turning head toward pitcher the way he prefers—can see the difference after 6/1: .820 OPS, 139 PX, 22% hr/f. Not saying that's sustainable, particularly at his age, and especially with ct% slide that lasted all year. But if you're chasing after upside, think HR, not BA.

Yr	Tm	AB	R	HR	RBI	SB	BA	xBA	OBP	SLG	OPS	vL	vR	bb%	ct%	Eye	G	L	F	h%	HctX	PX	xPX	hr/f	Spd	SBO	SB%	#Wk	DOM	DIS	RC/G	RAR	BPV	BPX	R$
12	NYY	422	50	21	53	6	211	264	311	403	713	880	643	11	77	0.56	48	19	33	22	101	121	107	20%	47	7%	86%	27	52%	22%	3.93	-2.7	45	113	$6
13	PIT	438	51	15	55	9	226	244	327	377	703	610	729	12	75	0.54	51	17	33	27	103	108	104	14%	58	12%	64%	26	38%	35%	3.86	1.9	30	75	$9
14	PIT	379	45	11	67	4	290	255	402	430	832	693	865	13	79	0.76	49	19	32	34	109	102	91	11%	71	6%	50%	23	39%	39%	5.81	26.6	49	132	$16
15	TOR	441	76	23	77	4	240	272	329	458	787	937	747	11	76	0.50	51	16	33	27	97	140	113	21%	79	8%	44%	27	48%	26%	4.77	13.8	63	170	$14
16	TOR	455	62	20	74	2	231	223	335	398	733	700	743	12	67	0.43	46	18	36	30	92	111	129	18%	55	2%	67%	27	33%	44%	4.28	5.7	2	6	$8
1st Half		227	28	7	34	1	225	203	313	339	652	699	634	10	66	0.32	42	22	36	31	90	77	124	13%	55	3%	50%	14	29%	64%	3.33	-5.7	-38	-109	$5
2nd Half		228	34	13	40	1	237	243	357	456	813	701	840	15	69	0.56	50	14	35	28	94	143	133	23%	61	1%	100%	13	38%	23%	5.34	8.2	41	117	$11
17	Proj	**430**	**61**	**20**	**71**	**3**	**241**	**247**	**345**	**429**	**775**	**770**	**776**	**12**	**72**	**0.51**	**48**	**17**	**34**	**29**	**97**	**118**	**117**	**19%**	**66**	**5%**	**57%**				**4.77**	**8.1**	**27**	**77**	**$13**

BRANDON KRUSE

Martinez,J.D.

Age: 29	Bats: R	Pos: RF	Health C	LIMA Plan B	
Ht: 6' 3"	Wt: 200		PT/Exp B	Rand Var -4	
			Consist B	MM 4235	

22-68-.307 in 460 AB at DET. PRO: Continued Eye growth; power skills still elite; typically out-hits xBA. CON: Didn't keep 2015 FB gains; won't repeat 41% 2H hit rate, so won't out-hit xBA by as much; injury bug returned. Bottom line: Despite HR dip, still a legit power threat. But set baseline at 25-30 HR, not 35-40.

Yr Tm	AB	R	HR	RBI	SB	BA	xBA	OBP	SLG	OPS	vL	vR	bb%	ct%	Eye	G	L	F	h%	HctX	PX	xPX	hr/f	Spd	SBO	SB%	#Wk	DOM	DIS	RC/G	RAR	BPV	BPX	R$
12 HOU *	485	38	11	58	0	230	224	292	349	641	690	683	8	76	0.37	52	17	32	28	87	81	79	12%	102	3%	0%	22	36%	32%	3.28	-23.2	18	45	$3
13 HOU	296	24	7	36	2	250	236	272	378	650	621	664	3	72	0.12	44	22	34	32	102	103	108	9%	90	3%	100%	18	33%	61%	3.57	-6.1	7	18	$4
14 DET *	506	69	30	92	7	308	287	349	568	917	1003	880	6	71	0.22	40	23	37	38	134	196	159	19%	116	9%	71%	24	54%	33%	7.23	46.2	91	246	$31
15 DET	596	93	38	102	3	282	265	344	535	879	915	870	8	70	0.30	34	22	43	34	131	175	183	21%	102	3%	60%	27	56%	30%	6.42	27.8	69	186	$28
16 DET *	496	71	22	72	2	301	266	365	517	882	861	925	9	72	0.35	42	21	36	38	119	147	144	18%	97	3%	47%	21	48%	14%	6.80	28.5	53	151	$20
1st Half	252	36	12	39	1	286	272	358	520	878	875	879	10	73	0.39	40	22	38	35	116	153	157	17%	101	3%	50%	11	55%	9%	6.51	12.9	65	186	$19
2nd Half	244	35	10	33	1	316	258	375	515	889	846	983	9	70	0.32	45	21	34	41	123	140	128	20%	94	2%	44%	10	40%	20%	7.10	15.9	41	117	$22
17 Proj	**546**	**76**	**27**	**84**	**3**	**292**	**263**	**351**	**513**	**864**	**849**	**869**	**8**	**71**	**0.31**	**41**	**22**	**37**	**37**	**122**	**146**	**149**	**18%**	**101**	**4%**	**58%**				**6.42**	**26.3**	**40**	**114**	**$23**

Martinez,Victor

Age: 38	Bats: B	Pos: DH	Health C	LIMA Plan B+	
Ht: 6' 2"	Wt: 195		PT/Exp A	Rand Var -2	
			Consist F	MM 2045	

Managed to fight through chronic knee issues to post yet another excellent season—not 2014-other-worldly excellent, but still great. And as long as his hitting base is strong enough, these skills say he'll keep raking. But those knees aren't going to hold up for much longer, and 2015 shows it'll get pretty ugly when they go.

Yr Tm	AB	R	HR	RBI	SB	BA	xBA	OBP	SLG	OPS	vL	vR	bb%	ct%	Eye	G	L	F	h%	HctX	PX	xPX	hr/f	Spd	SBO	SB%	#Wk	DOM	DIS	RC/G	RAR	BPV	BPX	R$
12																																		
13 DET	605	68	14	83	0	301	275	355	430	785	735	813	8	90	0.87	42	23	35	32	143	84	126	7%	82	1%	0%	26	65%	8%	5.54	17.2	69	173	$22
14 DET	561	87	32	103	3	335	320	409	565	974	1123	923	11	93	1.67	41	21	38	32	158	135	147	16%	91	3%	60%	26	88%	4%	8.79	69.7	129	349	$38
15 DET	440	39	11	64	0	245	256	301	366	667	870	616	7	88	0.60	40	21	39	26	116	73	110	7%	66	0%	0%	23	43%	26%	3.65	-23.3	46	124	$6
16 DET	553	65	27	86	0	289	276	351	476	826	812	832	8	84	0.56	37	23	39	31	132	100	132	15%	68	0%	0%	27	48%	30%	5.94	6.8	54	154	$20
1st Half	286	34	16	50	0	318	297	362	531	894	915	886	6	84	0.42	36	26	38	33	141	114	158	17%	70	0%	0%	14	57%	14%	7.17	12.8	64	183	$25
2nd Half	267	31	11	36	0	258	253	339	416	755	700	774	10	83	0.69	39	21	40	27	123	85	104	12%	73	0%	0%	13	38%	46%	4.80	-5.5	45	129	$14
17 Proj	**513**	**59**	**21**	**79**	**0**	**273**	**275**	**336**	**439**	**776**	**822**	**759**	**8**	**87**	**0.68**	**39**	**22**	**39**	**28**	**132**	**89**	**125**	**12%**	**72**	**1%**	**48%**				**5.13**	**-5.4**	**45**	**128**	**$18**

Mauer,Joe

Age: 34	Bats: L	Pos: 1B DH	Health B	LIMA Plan B+	
Ht: 6' 4"	Wt: 215		PT/Exp A	Rand Var +3	
			Consist A	MM 1255	

Has hit a plateau of, well, Mauer-like consistency. Sure, there are fluctuations in a stat here, a skill there. But at this point, there are no surprises. He's going to hit somewhere around .260-.280, probably get 10-ish HR, knock in 50-60, and walk a lot. It's all very bland and boring, and very predictable. But that's a good thing, right?

Yr Tm	AB	R	HR	RBI	SB	BA	xBA	OBP	SLG	OPS	vL	vR	bb%	ct%	Eye	G	L	F	h%	HctX	PX	xPX	hr/f	Spd	SBO	SB%	#Wk	DOM	DIS	RC/G	RAR	BPV	BPX	R$
12 MIN	545	81	10	85	8	319	286	416	446	861	754	918	14	84	1.02	53	25	22	37	136	83	113	10%	96	5%	67%	27	59%	7%	6.89	23.5	61	153	$25
13 MIN	445	62	11	47	0	324	288	404	476	880	882	879	12	80	0.69	47	28	25	39	125	115	113	12%	92	1%	0%	21	57%	29%	7.22	30.9	66	165	$18
14 MIN	455	60	4	55	3	277	269	361	371	732	654	776	12	79	0.63	51	27	22	34	96	79	70	5%	87	2%	100%	22	45%	32%	4.78	8.2	30	81	$12
15 MIN	592	69	10	66	2	265	276	338	380	718	720	718	10	81	0.60	56	24	20	31	108	80	81	10%	83	2%	67%	26	38%	27%	4.47	-7.9	36	97	$12
16 MIN	494	68	11	49	2	261	283	363	389	752	610	793	14	81	0.85	52	27	21	30	103	75	76	13%	102	1%	100%	26	38%	35%	4.90	0.5	45	129	$9
1st Half	287	36	7	26	1	258	271	362	369	731	615	772	14	80	0.81	49	28	23	30	108	62	88	13%	116	1%	100%	14	43%	36%	4.62	-4.0	34	97	$10
2nd Half	207	32	4	23	1	266	302	364	415	779	600	819	13	83	0.91	55	25	20	30	96	93	60	12%	85	2%	100%	12	33%	33%	5.29	1.1	61	174	$9
17 Proj	**522**	**70**	**10**	**58**	**2**	**271**	**284**	**360**	**395**	**755**	**672**	**787**	**12**	**81**	**0.75**	**53**	**26**	**21**	**32**	**105**	**78**	**78**	**11%**	**90**	**2%**	**84%**				**5.01**	**-1.4**	**35**	**99**	**$15**

Maybin,Cameron

Age: 30	Bats: R	Pos: CF	Health F	LIMA Plan B	
Ht: 6' 4"	Wt: 210		PT/Exp C	Rand Var -4	
			Consist C	MM 1535	

4-43-.315 with 15 SB in 349 AB at DET. It's getting easier to list the body parts he hasn't hurt (not many) than those he has (in 2016: shoulder, wrist, thumb, quad). Otherwise, with that speed and now an improving walk rate, OBP is up to an exciting level. Exciting as in... UP: 40 SB, if healthy (heh, yeah right).

Yr Tm	AB	R	HR	RBI	SB	BA	xBA	OBP	SLG	OPS	vL	vR	bb%	ct%	Eye	G	L	F	h%	HctX	PX	xPX	hr/f	Spd	SBO	SB%	#Wk	DOM	DIS	RC/G	RAR	BPV	BPX	R$
12 SD	507	67	8	45	26	243	242	306	349	656	630	666	8	78	0.40	55	16	28	30	107	71	88	7%	135	25%	79%	27	37%	33%	3.62	-18.9	29	73	$14
13 SD *	97	11	4	8	5	176	252	255	304	560	435	481	10	79	0.51	55	19	26	18	77	79	45	9%	95	31%	68%	5	20%	60%	2.33	-5.6	28	70	-$1
14 SD *	304	28	2	18	5	226	242	280	319	599	575	646	7	77	0.33	57	17	26	29	97	72	60	2%	140	11%	60%	20	15%	55%	2.88	-8.8	25	68	$1
15 ATL	505	65	10	59	23	267	266	327	370	697	711	692	8	80	0.44	58	22	20	32	75	67	46	12%	101	19%	79%	26	31%	38%	4.28	-3.2	21	57	$20
16 DET *	434	76	6	52	18	283	271	353	394	747	802	801	10	79	0.53	57	22	22	35	80	70	48	7%	143	18%	71%	19	32%	26%	4.90	6.6	38	109	$19
1st Half	238	40	3	31	12	285	273	359	377	736	1035	735	10	82	0.63	61	20	19	34	73	61	27	4%	122	22%	70%	8	38%	38%	4.75	1.7	36	103	$22
2nd Half	196	36	3	21	6	281	265	356	413	769	513	844	9	77	0.43	52	23	24	35	84	81	66	8%	151	14%	75%	11	27%	18%	5.08	3.2	37	106	$15
17 Proj	**448**	**66**	**6**	**47**	**17**	**263**	**262**	**330**	**368**	**698**	**681**	**705**	**9**	**79**	**0.45**	**57**	**21**	**23**	**32**	**82**	**65**	**52**	**8%**	**137**	**18%**	**74%**				**4.16**	**-4.6**	**25**	**73**	**$17**

Mazara,Nomar

Age: 22	Bats: L	Pos: RF LF	Health A	LIMA Plan B	
Ht: 6' 4"	Wt: 215		PT/Exp C	Rand Var +1	
			Consist B	MM 2125	

Didn't turn 21 until after he'd collected his first three-hit game (of course, that was his first MLB game). So keep that in mind. Otherwise, must make adjustments, because clearly the league did. Still a bright talent, but 2nd half, struggles vL suggest he could fall into a platoon, or worse... DN: 300 AB, more minors time.

Yr Tm	AB	R	HR	RBI	SB	BA	xBA	OBP	SLG	OPS	vL	vR	bb%	ct%	Eye	G	L	F	h%	HctX	PX	xPX	hr/f	Spd	SBO	SB%	#Wk	DOM	DIS	RC/G	RAR	BPV	BPX	R$
12																																		
13																																		
14 aa	85	9	3	14	0	293		352	484	837			8	73	0.34				37		152			96	0%	0%				6.16		63	170	$2
15 a/a	490	56	11	57	2	272		333	398	731			8	78	0.42				33		85			91	1%	100%				4.67		27	73	$12
16 TEX	516	59	20	64	0	266	254	320	419	739	548	791	7	78	0.35	49	21	30	30	91	84	77	16%	115	1%	0%	26	38%	35%	4.53	3.8	31	89	$12
1st Half	282	35	11	35	0	287	269	337	433	769	577	847	7	82	0.40	44	25	31	32	84	79	71	15%	100	1%	0%	13	46%	23%	5.13	5.4	35	100	$16
2nd Half	234	24	9	29	0	239	241	301	402	702	465	736	7	74	0.30	55	16	29	28	100	91	84	18%	126	2%	0%	13	31%	46%	3.88	-4.0	24	69	$7
17 Proj	**518**	**58**	**19**	**63**	**1**	**254**	**255**	**315**	**410**	**725**	**531**	**770**	**8**	**78**	**0.37**	**51**	**20**	**29**	**29**	**94**	**89**	**79**	**16%**	**108**	**2%**	**41%**				**4.32**	**-5.7**	**16**	**46**	**$13**

McCann,Brian

Age: 33	Bats: L	Pos: CA DH	Health A	LIMA Plan B	
Ht: 6' 3"	Wt: 210		PT/Exp B	Rand Var 0	
			Consist A	MM 2225	

Consistent FB%, HctX, health all mean you can ink in those 20 homers. Or can you? Gradual contact erosion means he's hitting fewer of those FB, even if the rate is the same. So any further ct% dip puts those 20 in jeopardy. Otherwise, it's steady as she goes.

Yr Tm	AB	R	HR	RBI	SB	BA	xBA	OBP	SLG	OPS	vL	vR	bb%	ct%	Eye	G	L	F	h%	HctX	PX	xPX	hr/f	Spd	SBO	SB%	#Wk	DOM	DIS	RC/G	RAR	BPV	BPX	R$
12 ATL	439	44	20	67	3	230	252	300	399	698	673	711	9	83	0.58	40	19	41	24	118	98	131	13%	63	3%	100%	27	48%	37%	4.00	-11.7	48	120	$8
13 ATL	356	43	20	57	0	256	273	336	461	796	616	869	10	81	0.59	35	22	42	26	119	125	150	16%	75	1%	0%	21	67%	29%	5.13	6.6	70	175	$11
14 NYY	495	57	23	75	0	232	266	286	406	692	850	633	6	84	0.42	33	22	45	23	113	106	127	12%	69	0%	0%	26	62%	23%	3.76	-4.2	58	157	$11
15 NYY	465	68	26	94	0	232	248	320	437	756	753	757	10	79	0.54	36	17	47	24	111	120	131	15%	68	0%	0%	27	52%	30%	4.49	-13.4	55	149	$12
16 NYY	429	56	20	58	1	242	242	335	413	748	662	770	11	77	0.55	34	21	44	27	111	97	120	14%	74	1%	100%	27	44%	41%	4.56	-11.9	32	91	$8
1st Half	215	34	13	35	0	233	245	340	447	787	749	797	13	77	0.62	33	18	48	24	113	120	142	16%	70	0%	0%	14	64%	21%	4.89	-4.0	51	146	$9
2nd Half	214	22	7	23	1	252	241	331	379	709	558	744	10	77	0.47	35	25	40	30	109	74	98	11%	85	2%	100%	13	23%	62%	4.22	-8.0	15	43	$7
17 Proj	**441**	**56**	**21**	**68**	**1**	**239**	**247**	**323**	**414**	**737**	**708**	**746**	**10**	**79**	**0.53**	**35**	**21**	**44**	**26**	**112**	**97**	**124**	**13%**	**71**	**1%**	**93%**				**4.38**	**3.2**	**28**	**80**	**$12**

McCann,James

Age: 27	Bats: R	Pos: CA	Health A	LIMA Plan D+	
Ht: 6' 2"	Wt: 210		PT/Exp D	Rand Var 0	
			Consist B	MM 2113	

12-48-.221 in 344 AB at DET. Opened up his swing and went for the fences. What the resulting FB spike gaveth in a few HR, it (and the massive ct% nosedive) tooketh away in the form of an ugly BA collapse. Still, he's got precious little to offer otherwise, so the power upside at least keeps him on our radar.

Yr Tm	AB	R	HR	RBI	SB	BA	xBA	OBP	SLG	OPS	vL	vR	bb%	ct%	Eye	G	L	F	h%	HctX	PX	xPX	hr/f	Spd	SBO	SB%	#Wk	DOM	DIS	RC/G	RAR	BPV	BPX	R$
12 aa	220	12	2	15	2	180		202	250	453			3	79	0.14				22		56			81	11%	43%				1.51		-4	-10	-$5
13 aa	441	40	6	43	2	246		285	355	639			5	79	0.26				30		84			86	6%	42%				3.32		23	58	$5
14 DET *	429	40	6	42	8	256	323	289	366	655	333	833	4	77	0.20	20	60	20	32	33	95	10	0%	75	11%	78%	3	33%	33%	3.64	4.0	17	46	$9
15 DET	401	32	7	41	0	264	254	297	387	683	916	609	4	78	0.18	50	23	27	33	90	82	63	8%	103	1%	0%	27	33%	48%	3.87	1.6	16	43	$6
16 DET *	366	33	12	50	0	212	204	267	341	608	848	511	7	68	0.24	41	18	41	28	94	83	112	13%	95	1%	0%	25	20%	56%	2.91	-10.8	-15	-43	$1
1st Half	177	15	5	23	0	191	196	251	298	549	845	416	7	67	0.25	42	20	39	25	81	66	112	12%	107	0%	0%	12	17%	58%	2.36	-10.0	-28	-80	-$2
2nd Half	189	18	7	27	0	233	210	286	381	667	852	580	6	69	0.22	41	17	42	30	105	98	112	13%	92	2%	0%	13	23%	54%	3.49	-3.7	-2	-6	$3
17 Proj	**365**	**32**	**10**	**43**	**1**	**234**	**232**	**277**	**368**	**645**	**860**	**551**	**5**	**73**	**0.20**	**45**	**20**	**35**	**29**	**93**	**86**	**92**	**11%**	**93**	**3%**	**48%**				**3.32**	**-9.0**	**-10**	**-28**	**$5**

ROD TRUESDELL

McCutchen,Andrew

Age: 30	Bats: R	Pos: CF	Health	B	LIMA Plan B+
Ht: 5' 11"	Wt: 175		PT/Exp	A	Rand Var +1
			Consist	D	MM 3335

Disclosed a thumb injury in June, which probably nagged him for much of 2016. That's two years in a row apparently affected by injuries. Showed his old self in Sept/Oct (.886 OPS, 152 xPX, 0.90 Eye); can he recapture pre-2015 glory? Maybe, but four injured body parts in two seasons should give you pause.

Yr Tm	AB	R	HR	RBI	SB	BA	xBA	OBP	SLG	OPS	vL	vR	bb%	ct%	Eye	G	L	F	h%	HctX	PX	xPX	hr/f	Spd	SBO	SB%	#Wk	DOM	DIS	RC/G	RAR	BPV	BPX	R$
12 PIT	593	107	31	96	20	327	281	400	553	953	1144	900	11	78	0.53	44	22	34	38	126	140	147	19%	146	16%	63%	27	56%	19%	7.99	53.3	90	225	$40
13 PIT	583	97	21	84	27	317	289	404	508	911	1130	864	12	83	0.77	41	24	35	36	138	125	123	12%	136	19%	73%	26	69%	12%	7.44	53.3	97	243	$40
14 PIT	548	89	25	83	18	314	284	410	542	952	912	962	13	79	0.73	40	19	41	36	139	159	155	14%	134	11%	86%	26	65%	12%	8.27	65.9	112	303	$36
15 PIT	566	91	23	96	11	292	268	401	488	889	918	881	15	77	0.74	38	24	38	35	131	132	159	14%	113	8%	69%	27	59%	30%	6.88	41.0	77	208	$28
16 PIT	598	81	24	79	6	256	249	336	430	766	741	772	10	76	0.48	36	22	42	30	111	104	134	13%	114	8%	46%	27	41%	30%	4.73	1.5	44	126	$16
1st Half	309	45	12	32	2	239	235	313	411	724	666	742	9	73	0.37	32	22	46	29	99	110	138	12%	110	9%	29%	14	36%	29%	4.00	-4.8	32	91	$12
2nd Half	289	36	12	47	4	273	264	360	450	810	886	799	12	80	0.64	39	23	37	31	123	99	130	14%	119	7%	67%	13	46%	31%	5.59	9.0	58	166	$20
17 Proj	**553**	**82**	**23**	**83**	**11**	**282**	**262**	**374**	**473**	**847**	**871**	**842**	**12**	**77**	**0.62**	**38**	**22**	**40**	**33**	**124**	**114**	**143**	**13%**	**122**	**9%**	**65%**				**6.11**	**25.2**	**54**	**155**	**$24**

Meadows,Austin

Age: 22	Bats: L	Pos: OF	Health	A	LIMA Plan D+
Ht: 6' 3"	Wt: 200		PT/Exp	F	Rand Var 0
			Consist	F	MM 4421

Top PIT prospect rebounded from broken orbital bone to dominate AA, then strained a hammy after promotion to AAA and never quite got it together there. So plainly, he needs some additional minors time, and is probably at least a year away. But as high-minors power/speed indexes show, he has an exciting tool kit.

Yr Tm	AB	R	HR	RBI	SB	BA	xBA	OBP	SLG	OPS	vL	vR	bb%	ct%	Eye	G	L	F	h%	HctX	PX	xPX	hr/f	Spd	SBO	SB%	#Wk	DOM	DIS	RC/G	RAR	BPV	BPX	R$
12																																		
13																																		
14																																		
15 aa	25	4	0	1	1	340		381	597	979			6	79	0.33				43		150			144	14%	100%				9.08		96	259	-$1
16 a/a	293	45	10	43	15	252		317	489	806			9	77	0.41				30		143			125	34%	74%				5.17		78	223	$12
1st Half	213	36	7	26	10	278		328	532	861			7	81	0.40				32		146			138	34%	70%				5.94		99	283	$16
2nd Half	80	8	3	16	5	184		287	375	662			13	65	0.42				23		132			104	35%	84%				3.49		26	74	$1
17 Proj	**156**	**20**	**4**	**26**	**7**	**223**	**249**	**306**	**414**	**719**	**719**	**719**	**11**	**71**	**0.42**	**42**	**20**	**38**	**29**		**125**		**10%**	**119**	**26%**	**74%**				**4.12**		**50**	**143**	**$5**

Mercer,Jordy

Age: 30	Bats: R	Pos: SS	Health	A	LIMA Plan C+
Ht: 6' 3"	Wt: 205		PT/Exp	B	Rand Var 0
			Consist	C	MM 1125

Usual assault on LHP ebbed late, but xBA shows 2nd half swoon wasn't skills-related. 2nd half notwithstanding, a prime candidate for DFS platoon (career .855 OPS vL, .645 vR). Otherwise, there's just not much to recommend, with mediocrity across the board. Roto value depends on AB totals, so hope health grade holds.

Yr Tm	AB	R	HR	RBI	SB	BA	xBA	OBP	SLG	OPS	vL	vR	bb%	ct%	Eye	G	L	F	h%	HctX	PX	xPX	hr/f	Spd	SBO	SB%	#Wk	DOM	DIS	RC/G	RAR	BPV	BPX	R$
12 PIT *	271	29	4	27	2	236	249	287	356	643	367	690	7	76	0.30	47	22	31	30	61	91	86	7%	88	15%	26%	17	24%	53%	3.07	-8.6	19	48	$2
13 PIT *	429	41	9	41	5	282	269	330	418	748	1152	654	7	81	0.37	47	23	30	33	113	97	117	10%	109	7%	62%	23	52%	30%	4.83	16.1	49	123	$12
14 PIT	506	56	12	55	4	255	264	305	387	693	803	658	6	82	0.39	48	20	32	29	90	94	89	9%	104	4%	80%	27	37%	33%	4.03	10.9	51	138	$11
15 PIT *	419	36	4	36	3	240	238	288	317	605	738	580	6	81	0.35	49	21	31	29	89	58	87	3%	84	5%	60%	23	26%	52%	3.03	-9.2	11	30	$3
16 PIT	519	66	11	59	1	256	257	328	374	701	829	669	9	84	0.61	49	20	32	29	86	68	60	8%	114	1%	50%	26	31%	15%	4.12	-7.6	45	129	$9
1st Half	270	35	5	29	1	274	248	359	374	733	943	669	11	84	0.75	49	19	32	31	86	58	73	7%	106	1%	100%	14	29%	14%	4.67	1.5	37	106	$11
2nd Half	249	31	6	30	0	237	267	291	373	665	645	668	7	84	0.46	48	20	32	26	86	78	45	9%	118	2%	0%	12	33%	17%	3.53	-7.0	51	146	$6
17 Proj	**518**	**58**	**9**	**54**	**2**	**250**	**255**	**310**	**363**	**673**	**783**	**644**	**7**	**83**	**0.46**	**48**	**20**	**31**	**29**	**87**	**69**	**73**	**7%**	**106**	**3%**	**52%**				**3.74**	**-11.2**	**20**	**58**	**$10**

Merrifield,Whit

Age: 28	Bats: R	Pos: 2B	Health	A	LIMA Plan C+
Ht: 6' 0"	Wt: 195		PT/Exp	B	Rand Var 0
			Consist	C	MM 1425

2-29-.283 with 8 SB in 311 AB at KC. Parlayed a red-hot first month-plus into a half-season's worth of AB, but predictably came back to earth. Skills history doesn't support the solid HctX; career PX likely a more accurate picture. Wheels would be his ticket, but poor OBP limits SB opps. Still, with enough AB... UP: 25 SB

Yr Tm	AB	R	HR	RBI	SB	BA	xBA	OBP	SLG	OPS	vL	vR	bb%	ct%	Eye	G	L	F	h%	HctX	PX	xPX	hr/f	Spd	SBO	SB%	#Wk	DOM	DIS	RC/G	RAR	BPV	BPX	R$
12 aa	96	9	1	6	2	231		277	293	570			6	79	0.30				29		39			118	18%	51%				2.52		-4	-10	-$1
13 aa	322	24	2	33	13	240		278	345	624			5	81	0.27				29		76			114	30%	62%				3.05		30	75	$6
14 a/a	483	57	6	36	12	269		309	391	700			5	82	0.31				32		96			103	22%	47%				3.86		47	127	$13
15 aaa	544	63	4	29	24	226		266	310	576			5	86	0.39				26		57			121	30%	70%				2.67		39	105	$9
16 KC *	585	76	7	49	22	251	256	292	363	654	891	657	5	77	0.25	45	26	30	32	111	80	87	3%	120	21%	80%	17	24%	47%	3.65	-18.8	19	54	$15
1st Half	313	43	5	27	16	269	279	301	394	695	885	716	4	78	0.21	47	29	24	33	113	86	96	6%	124	26%	88%	8	25%	63%	4.29	-4.6	30	86	$23
2nd Half	272	33	2	22	6	230	229	281	327	608	896	584	7	75	0.28	42	22	37	30	108	73	77	0%	106	15%	64%	9	22%	33%	2.98	-15.2	4	11	$6
17 Proj	**430**	**51**	**3**	**32**	**16**	**254**	**252**	**294**	**347**	**641**	**798**	**587**	**6**	**80**	**0.29**	**44**	**24**	**32**	**31**	**110**	**65**	**85**	**3%**	**123**	**21%**	**73%**				**3.49**	**-16.8**	**20**	**57**	**$12**

Mesoraco,Devin

Age: 29	Bats: R	Pos: CA	Health	F	LIMA Plan D
Ht: 6' 1"	Wt: 225		PT/Exp	F	Rand Var +5
			Consist	F	MM 2023

Has now undergone three labrum surgeries (two hip joints, left shoulder) in two years—which certainly implies something genetically deficient in the Mesoraco family's labra. Prior to his injury woes, he was breaking out into a real power source. Likely still owns that power skill, but now he's an end-game "Hey, why not?"

Yr Tm	AB	R	HR	RBI	SB	BA	xBA	OBP	SLG	OPS	vL	vR	bb%	ct%	Eye	G	L	F	h%	HctX	PX	xPX	hr/f	Spd	SBO	SB%	#Wk	DOM	DIS	RC/G	RAR	BPV	BPX	R$
12 CIN	165	17	5	14	1	212	238	288	352	640	803	590	9	80	0.52	45	17	38	24	85	92	80	10%	66	5%	50%	22	45%	32%	3.19	-5.5	34	85	-$1
13 CIN	323	31	9	42	0	238	246	287	362	649	874	576	7	81	0.39	45	21	34	27	88	83	78	10%	56	3%	0%	27	41%	37%	3.43	-2.5	24	60	$4
14 CIN	384	54	25	80	1	273	287	359	534	893	925	883	10	73	0.40	34	23	43	31	123	192	166	20%	56	4%	25%	24	54%	25%	6.25	30.9	85	230	$18
15 CIN	45	2	0	2	1	178	192	275	244	519	481	536	10	80	0.56	42	14	44	22	67	40	67	0%	102	9%	100%	7	43%	43%	2.07	-2.4	4	11	-$3
16 CIN	50	2	0	1	0	140	214	218	160	378	507	320	9	80	0.50	48	23	30	18	49	17	7	0%	96	9%	0%	4	25%	50%	0.93	-5.9	-16	-46	-$4
1st Half	50	2	0	1	0	140	214	218	160	378	507	320	9	80	0.50	48	23	30	18	49	17	7	0%	96	9%	0%	4	25%	50%	0.93	-5.5	-17	-49	-$4
2nd Half																																		
17 Proj	**288**	**30**	**10**	**35**	**0**	**247**	**247**	**313**	**388**	**700**	**844**	**652**	**8**	**79**	**0.44**	**44**	**21**	**35**	**28**	**83**	**84**	**75**	**12%**	**69**	**5%**	**12%**				**3.90**	**-2.1**	**9**	**27**	**$6**

Miller,Bradley

Age: 27	Bats: L	Pos: SS 1B	Health	A	LIMA Plan B+
Ht: 6' 2"	Wt: 185		PT/Exp	B	Rand Var +1
			Consist	B	MM 3335

That doubling in hr/f not supported by HctX nor xPX, so don't go assuming he's now a 30-HR guy. Really, skills last season not much different than recent years; with shaky finish vL keeping a platoon in play, AB (and thus counting stats) are the iffiest part of this projection. Sim note: RAR is at 1B; he's a relative goldmine at SS.

Yr Tm	AB	R	HR	RBI	SB	BA	xBA	OBP	SLG	OPS	vL	vR	bb%	ct%	Eye	G	L	F	h%	HctX	PX	xPX	hr/f	Spd	SBO	SB%	#Wk	DOM	DIS	RC/G	RAR	BPV	BPX	R$
12 aa	147	19	3	11	4	284		371	411	782			12	79	0.67				34		82			115	9%	76%				5.45		43	108	$3
13 SEA *	563	82	17	77	10	269	264	329	424	753	674	767	8	81	0.46	46	22	32	31	96	97	79	10%	140	11%	56%	15	53%	13%	4.70	1.6	61	153	$21
14 SEA	367	47	10	36	4	221	236	288	365	653	542	692	8	74	0.36	42	19	39	27	98	105	105	10%	128	7%	67%	27	37%	52%	3.40	-8.3	38	103	$4
15 SEA	438	44	11	46	13	258	254	329	402	730	513	803	10	77	0.47	48	20	31	31	107	97	98	10%	118	14%	76%	27	22%	37%	4.57	-4.7	42	114	$12
16 TAM	548	73	30	81	6	243	268	304	482	786	682	812	8	73	0.32	45	19	37	28	104	147	116	20%	110	9%	60%	26	62%	19%	4.81	-0.7	60	171	$15
1st Half	262	31	11	28	4	244	265	294	450	745	785	738	7	76	0.31	49	17	35	28	100	121	109	16%	115	13%	57%	14	64%	14%	4.34	-6.0	52	149	$11
2nd Half	286	42	19	53	2	241	270	313	510	824	623	889	9	70	0.32	41	21	39	28	107	172	123	24%	109	5%	67%	12	58%	25%	5.26	1.4	69	197	$18
17 Proj	**511**	**64**	**21**	**66**	**8**	**247**	**258**	**314**	**439**	**753**	**611**	**797**	**9**	**74**	**0.38**	**45**	**20**	**35**	**29**	**103**	**118**	**107**	**15%**	**115**	**10%**	**69%**				**4.60**	**2.0**	**42**	**119**	**$16**

Molina,Yadier

Age: 34	Bats: R	Pos: CA	Health	B	LIMA Plan B
Ht: 5' 11"	Wt: 205		PT/Exp	B	Rand Var -3
			Consist	C	MM 1145

Guess that thumb finally healed up, huh? Roared to finish with vintage line-drive stroke, and hr/f rebound suggests he was fully healthy in 2nd half for the first time in years. Of course, catchers are an oft-abused lot, so there are no guarantees he stays that way. But we can invest with a little more confidence again.

Yr Tm	AB	R	HR	RBI	SB	BA	xBA	OBP	SLG	OPS	vL	vR	bb%	ct%	Eye	G	L	F	h%	HctX	PX	xPX	hr/f	Spd	SBO	SB%	#Wk	DOM	DIS	RC/G	RAR	BPV	BPX	R$
12 STL	505	65	22	76	12	315	300	373	501	874	1021	833	8	89	0.82	40	25	35	32	124	107	112	14%	75	10%	80%	27	74%	0%	6.93	36.2	83	208	$26
13 STL	505	68	12	80	3	319	301	359	477	836	883	823	6	89	0.55	42	24	34	34	129	109	111	8%	71	4%	60%	26	65%	23%	6.32	35.5	78	195	$24
14 STL	404	40	7	38	1	282	271	333	386	719	795	695	6	86	0.51	51	23	27	31	115	75	95	7%	68	2%	50%	20	45%	25%	4.48	11.6	41	111	$10
15 STL	488	34	4	61	3	270	254	310	350	660	577	689	6	88	0.54	48	20	32	30	99	54	79	3%	72	3%	75%	25	32%	32%	3.87	0.6	31	84	$9
16 STL	534	56	8	58	3	307	282	360	427	787	776	790	7	88	0.62	48	22	30	34	111	75	88	6%	72	3%	60%	27	48%	26%	5.52	16.2	50	143	$17
1st Half	274	28	1	27	2	259	255	327	332	659	646	664	9	87	0.74	53	18	29	29	109	50	82	1%	75	4%	67%	14	43%	36%	3.68	-3.6	31	89	$9
2nd Half	260	28	7	31	1	358	311	396	527	923	941	917	5	89	0.46	44	25	31	38	114	102	94	10%	74	3%	50%	13	54%	15%	8.03	25.6	72	206	$25
17 Proj	**458**	**45**	**8**	**53**	**3**	**285**	**279**	**335**	**403**	**737**	**731**	**739**	**7**	**88**	**0.58**	**47**	**22**	**30**	**31**	**111**	**72**	**90**	**6%**	**72**	**3%**	**65%**				**4.74**	**7.8**	**39**	**112**	**$14**

ROD TRUESDELL

Moncada,Yoan

Age: 22 Bats: B Pos: 3B	Health A	LIMA Plan D	
Ht: 6' 2" Wt: 205	PT/Exp F	Rand Var -2	
	Consist F	MM 3411	

0-1-.211 in 19 AB at BOS. Exciting youngster struggled in Sept with big club, but this was a fine growth season. Power starting to emerge to complement fine speed, and he held his own after June promotion to AA. Needs—and likely will get—more time on the farm, but one of baseball's top hitting prospects.

Yr	Tm	AB	R	HR	RBI	SB	BA	xBA	OBP	SLG	OPS	vL	vR	bb%	ct%	Eye	G	L	F	h%	HctX	PX	xPX	hr/f	Spd	SBO	SB%	#Wk	DOM	DIS	RC/G	RAR	BPV	BPX	R$
12	for	138	25	1	15	12	263		340	328	668			10	76	0.49				34		45			122	37%	68%				3.74	-3.4	0	0	$5
13	for	165	31	2	13	7	254		320	386	707			9	81	0.50				31		84			163	31%	52%				3.77	-0.9	58	145	$4
14																																			
15																																			
16	BOS *	196	35	9	25	8	259	269	339	457	796	500	517	11	59	0.30	71	29	0	39	69	146	12	0%	125	21%	64%	3	0%	67%	5.11	1.8	15	43	$7
1st Half		52	8	2	9	2	279	277	302	545	847			3	71	0.11				35		164			120	19%	100%				6.02		62	177	$2
2nd Half		144	26	6	16	6	251	243	352	425	776	500	517	13	55	0.34	71	29	0	41	63	138	12	0%	118	22%	58%	3	0%	67%	4.78	-0.5	-7	-20	$9
17	Proj	191	31	5	21	6	261	240	329	431	760	760	760	9	70	0.34	46	20	34	34		106		12%	137	23%	52%				4.49	-2.3	26	75	$6

Mondesi,Raul

Age: 21 Bats: B Pos: 2B	Health A	LIMA Plan D+	
Ht: 6' 1" Wt: 165	PT/Exp F	Rand Var -1	
	Consist B	MM 1503	

2-13-.185 with 9 SB in 135 AB at KC. Speed demon's bat isn't MLB-ready yet, as skills plainly show. But there are some nuggets : xPX gives hope for power upside as he matures, SB% shows he knows how to use his turbo wheels. But low OBP squashing running chances for now, so don't mine for bigger SB upside yet.

Yr	Tm	AB	R	HR	RBI	SB	BA	xBA	OBP	SLG	OPS	vL	vR	bb%	ct%	Eye	G	L	F	h%	HctX	PX	xPX	hr/f	Spd	SBO	SB%	#Wk	DOM	DIS	RC/G	RAR	BPV	BPX	R$
12																																			
13																																			
14																																			
15	aa	304	30	5	27	16	230		264	344	608			4	71	0.15				31		80			128	35%	71%				2.94		-4	-11	$7
16	KC *	307	40	7	35	27	229	207	272	371	643	434	546	6	68	0.18	49	12	39	32	86	88	137	7%	176	44%	93%	10	20%	80%	3.65	-6.1	8	23	$12
1st Half		104	15	4	13	10	239	251	287	427	714			6	72	0.24				29		119			125	51%	90%				4.39		36	103	$9
2nd Half		203	26	3	22	18	228	191	270	351	621	434	546	5	66	0.17	49	12	39	33	83	74	137	7%	193	42%	95%	10	20%	80%	3.48	-6.1	-7	-20	$14
17	Proj	299	36	5	31	23	232	204	279	354	633	515	685	5	69	0.17	49	12	39	32	75	79	123	6%	164	41%	86%				3.35	-13.3	3	8	$12

Montero,Miguel

Age: 33 Bats: L Pos: CA	Health B	LIMA Plan D	
Ht: 5' 11" Wt: 190	PT/Exp C	Rand Var +3	
	Consist B	MM 2113	

Back injury bothered him most of the year, and it shows in big HctX and xPX dips, GB spike. With health, still owns the power upside that appeared to be peaking coming into the 2016 season. Now faces uncertain playing time, but watch his role: if he somehow finds 400 AB again, there's still this... UP: 20 HR

Yr	Tm	AB	R	HR	RBI	SB	BA	xBA	OBP	SLG	OPS	vL	vR	bb%	ct%	Eye	G	L	F	h%	HctX	PX	xPX	hr/f	Spd	SBO	SB%	#Wk	DOM	DIS	RC/G	RAR	BPV	BPX	R$
12	ARI	486	65	15	88	0	286	239	391	438	829	767	859	13	73	0.56	43	21	36	36	99	108	121	12%	105	0%	0%	27	41%	41%	5.94	22.4	39	98	$17
13	ARI	413	44	11	42	0	230	224	318	344	662	492	719	11	73	0.46	47	21	31	29	103	83	106	11%	73	0%	0%	23	22%	48%	3.58	-1.3	6	15	$3
14	ARI	489	40	13	72	0	243	241	329	370	699	563	735	10	80	0.58	46	21	33	28	112	92	124	10%	66	3%	0%	27	44%	33%	3.87	6.0	37	100	$8
15	CHC	347	36	15	53	1	248	242	345	409	754	786	749	12	70	0.48	40	26	34	31	102	110	150	18%	74	2%	50%	24	29%	46%	4.69	9.0	18	49	$7
16	CHC	241	33	8	33	1	216	236	327	357	684	439	727	14	76	0.66	50	17	33	25	83	84	115	13%	87	1%	100%	26	42%	54%	3.77	-4.7	26	74	$1
1st Half		133	17	4	17	1	195	226	314	323	638	360	688	15	73	0.64	55	15	30	24	72	76	93	14%	92	2%	100%	13	46%	46%	3.26	-3.7	12	34	$0
2nd Half		108	16	4	16	0	241	248	344	398	742	544	776	12	80	0.68	44	19	37	27	98	93	141	13%	85	0%	0%	13	38%	62%	4.46	1.0	45	129	$3
17	Proj	245	29	9	35	1	236	241	337	381	718	580	746	12	75	0.58	46	20	34	28	96	89	128	14%	80	1%	53%				4.18	0.3	12	35	$5

Morales,Kendrys

Age: 34 Bats: B Pos: DH	Health A	LIMA Plan B+	
Ht: 6' 1" Wt: 220	PT/Exp B	Rand Var -1	
	Consist F	MM 3035	

Opened up swing and netted most HR since 2009, but that free swinging (and odd flip in platoon splits) shaved enough points off BA to actually hurt overall value. Despite the season-to-season variability (and save that awful 2014 holdout season), he's earned consistently. Bid to $15 with assurance; above that is gravy.

Yr	Tm	AB	R	HR	RBI	SB	BA	xBA	OBP	SLG	OPS	vL	vR	bb%	ct%	Eye	G	L	F	h%	HctX	PX	xPX	hr/f	Spd	SBO	SB%	#Wk	DOM	DIS	RC/G	RAR	BPV	BPX	R$
12	LAA	484	61	22	73	0	273	267	320	467	787	761	791	6	76	0.27	51	20	28	32	118	129	109	21%	65	1%	0%	27	48%	37%	5.14	3.4	41	103	$15
13	SEA	602	64	23	80	0	277	259	336	449	785	794	780	8	81	0.43	49	19	33	31	123	115	134	14%	69	0%	0%	27	56%	30%	5.25	12.7	54	135	$19
14	2 AL	367	28	8	42	0	218	238	274	338	612	661	584	7	81	0.40	49	18	33	25	106	89	102	8%	62	0%	0%	17	41%	41%	2.99	-11.8	31	84	$1
15	KC	569	81	22	106	0	290	282	362	485	847	771	901	9	82	0.56	45	20	35	32	126	126	134	13%	65	0%	0%	27	63%	11%	6.20	11.8	68	184	$23
16	KC	558	65	30	93	0	263	262	327	468	795	930	730	8	78	0.40	44	20	36	29	131	117	140	19%	40	0%	0%	27	37%	26%	5.21	-4.6	37	106	$16
1st Half		273	33	14	45	0	264	259	328	465	793	1019	718	8	78	0.40	44	19	37	29	124	118	136	18%	51	0%	0%	14	29%	21%	5.21	-2.3	40	114	$15
2nd Half		285	32	16	48	0	263	266	326	470	796	876	745	8	79	0.40	44	21	35	28	138	116	143	20%	40	0%	0%	13	46%	31%	5.21	-2.4	38	109	$17
17	Proj	547	64	24	88	0	264	265	328	451	779	825	754	8	80	0.43	46	20	34	29	126	109	131	16%	53	0%	0%				5.05	-7.1	33	94	$18

Moreland,Mitch

Age: 31 Bats: L Pos: 1B	Health D	LIMA Plan C+	
Ht: 6' 2" Wt: 240	PT/Exp C	Rand Var +2	
	Consist D	MM 3125	

Took step back in a contract year, with a small drop in power (as highlighted by HctX, xPX). Still managed his 20+ HR, but that's no longer a given now that he's on the wrong side of 30. Since power is all you're buying here, this is not a good thing. Hit 9 of 22 HR to LCF; keep that in mind if he lands in new home park.

Yr	Tm	AB	R	HR	RBI	SB	BA	xBA	OBP	SLG	OPS	vL	vR	bb%	ct%	Eye	G	L	F	h%	HctX	PX	xPX	hr/f	Spd	SBO	SB%	#Wk	DOM	DIS	RC/G	RAR	BPV	BPX	R$
12	TEX	327	41	15	50	1	275	262	321	468	789	737	798	7	78	0.32	42	20	38	31	119	125	128	15%	68	3%	50%	22	41%	27%	5.26	-0.1	49	123	$10
13	TEX	462	60	23	60	0	232	255	299	437	736	701	752	9	75	0.38	43	17	39	26	115	143	138	17%	64	0%	0%	26	50%	31%	4.35	-3.5	52	130	$9
14	TEX	167	18	2	23	0	246	235	297	347	644	374	692	7	74	0.28	45	22	33	32	136	86	143	5%	66	0%	0%	10	30%	60%	3.48	-3.2	1	3	$1
15	TEX	471	51	23	85	1	278	265	330	482	812	681	876	6	76	0.29	46	20	35	32	120	135	131	18%	52	1%	100%	26	38%	38%	5.53	7.9	43	116	$17
16	TEX	460	49	22	60	1	233	252	298	422	720	799	700	7	74	0.30	42	21	37	27	110	116	111	17%	52	1%	100%	26	35%	31%	4.03	-11.4	22	63	$7
1st Half		249	28	11	34	0	229	241	297	410	706	648	724	8	73	0.32	45	19	35	27	104	115	96	17%	58	0%	0%	14	36%	29%	3.95	-8.7	18	51	$6
2nd Half		211	21	11	26	1	237	262	300	436	736	1050	674	6	76	0.26	37	23	40	26	117	117	128	17%	55	2%	100%	12	33%	33%	4.12	-6.2	29	83	$7
17	Proj	457	49	19	66	1	249	254	308	428	736	726	900	7	75	0.29	43	21	36	29	118	111	125	15%	54	1%	93%				4.36	-10.0	17	50	$12

Morrison,Logan

Age: 29 Bats: L Pos: 1B	Health D	LIMA Plan B	
Ht: 6' 3" Wt: 215	PT/Exp C	Rand Var 0	
	Consist B	MM 3135	

Wrist surgery ended year early, and it would've been interesting to see if he could keep up 2nd half power spike. He should be ready by spring, but his health grade and overall skills arrow is trending down. Contact dip is a concern, too. Young enough to turn things around, but the window out to bigger expectations is closing.

Yr	Tm	AB	R	HR	RBI	SB	BA	xBA	OBP	SLG	OPS	vL	vR	bb%	ct%	Eye	G	L	F	h%	HctX	PX	xPX	hr/f	Spd	SBO	SB%	#Wk	DOM	DIS	RC/G	RAR	BPV	BPX	R$
12	MIA	296	30	11	36	1	230	252	308	399	707	659	723	9	80	0.53	41	18	41	25	111	107	117	11%	73	1%	100%	17	47%	29%	4.01	-7.7	50	125	$3
13	MIA *	326	36	7	42	0	233	254	316	364	680	491	778	11	81	0.65	48	20	32	27	112	85	97	8%	113	0%	0%	17	41%	41%	3.82	-6.6	51	128	$3
14	SEA *	401	49	13	43	6	257	272	310	407	717	846	695	7	83	0.44	40	24	36	28	113	104	92	11%	71	8%	76%	20	35%	20%	4.33	3.3	52	141	$11
15	SEA	457	47	17	54	8	225	249	302	383	685	500	767	9	82	0.58	45	16	39	24	110	91	120	12%	95	10%	67%	27	48%	37%	3.70	-24.4	51	138	$8
16	TAM	353	45	14	43	4	238	256	319	414	733	739	731	9	75	0.42	44	21	35	28	104	110	100	15%	73	7%	67%	22	41%	41%	4.26	-13.1	30	86	$6
1st Half		249	30	8	28	4	233	240	313	365	679	822	652	10	75	0.44	49	20	31	28	98	83	81	14%	77	9%	67%	14	43%	43%	3.73	-13.4	10	29	$8
2nd Half		104	15	6	15	0	250	291	333	529	862	601	937	8	75	0.35	33	23	44	28	117	176	145	18%	72	0%	0%	8	38%	38%	5.57	0.2	80	229	$3
17	Proj	415	51	17	51	4	240	264	316	426	743	632	778	9	79	0.45	41	21	38	27	110	111	114	14%	75	6%	69%				4.35	-9.3	45	129	$10

Moss,Brandon

Age: 33 Bats: L Pos: 1B LF RF	Health B	LIMA Plan B	
Ht: 6' 1" Wt: 180	PT/Exp B	Rand Var +1	
	Consist B	MM 4215	

One-trick pony got his trick back, nearly reaching 30 HR despite missing almost a month with a bad ankle and, figuratively at least, limping to the finish line (.099 BA, 3 HR in Sept/Oct). Good thing, too; after all, you're not looking for steals or BA here, right? With a full season of health, power skills say 30 is well within reach.

Yr	Tm	AB	R	HR	RBI	SB	BA	xBA	OBP	SLG	OPS	vL	vR	bb%	ct%	Eye	G	L	F	h%	HctX	PX	xPX	hr/f	Spd	SBO	SB%	#Wk	DOM	DIS	RC/G	RAR	BPV	BPX	R$
12	OAK *	461	68	29	73	4	254	259	314	505	819	770	1006	8	69	0.28	33	21	46	30	111	178	176	26%	86	4%	78%	18	61%	28%	5.42	-0.1	63	158	$16
13	OAK	446	73	30	87	4	256	255	337	522	859	649	904	10	69	0.36	30	18	52	30	114	193	174	19%	106	6%	67%	27	70%	15%	5.86	16.7	83	208	$20
14	OAK	500	70	25	81	1	234	242	334	438	772	792	768	12	69	0.44	30	21	49	29	100	156	136	15%	75	1%	100%	27	44%	41%	4.74	8.3	51	138	$14
15	2 TM	469	47	19	58	0	226	229	304	407	711	717	709	9	68	0.33	33	20	47	29	117	133	156	13%	100	1%	0%	27	52%	37%	3.98	-19.8	31	84	$5
16	STL	413	66	28	67	1	225	241	300	484	784	664	828	9	66	0.28	27	20	53	27	107	172	186	19%	94	1%	100%	24	67%	25%	4.67	-8.3	48	137	$9
1st Half		215	40	17	40	0	251	268	341	567	909	544	1046	10	65	0.32	29	22	49	30	107	214	195	25%	106	0%	0%	14	79%	14%	6.31	7.6	86	246	$14
2nd Half		198	26	11	27	1	197	212	252	394	646	800	592	7	67	0.23	25	19	56	23	107	128	177	14%	80	3%	100%	10	50%	40%	3.19	-11.9	9	26	$4
17	Proj	445	62	26	67	1	226	236	303	454	757	710	774	9	67	0.31	29	20	51	27	109	150	169	17%	90	2%	76%				4.44	-8.9	29	83	$11

ROD TRUESDELL

Moustakas,Mike

Age: 28	Bats: L	Pos: 3B	Health F	LIMA Plan A	
Ht: 5' 11"	Wt: 210		PT/Exp C	Rand Var +5	
			Consist D	MM 3045	

Sidelined for season in May w/torn ACL just as breakout was in sight. Steady gain in walks, dip in strikeouts confirm improved maturity at dish. Only reason BA took nosedive was a fluky h%; see xBA for upside there. Added 20 ft of flyball distance from 2015, so don't assume HR/F pullback. If healthy... UP: .300-30-100

Yr	Tm	AB	R	HR	RBI	SB	BA	xBA	OBP	SLG	OPS	vL	vR	bb%	ct%	Eye	G	L	F	h%	HctX	PX	xPX	hr/f	Spd	SBO	SB%	#Wk	DOM	DIS	RC/G	RAR	BPV	BPX	R$
12	KC	563	69	20	73	5	242	236	296	412	708	704	710	6	78	0.31	34	16	50	28	88	115	109	9%	68	6%	71%	27	44%	33%	4.01	-9.0	39	98	$12
13	KC	472	42	12	42	2	233	241	287	364	651	546	682	6	82	0.39	37	19	45	26	86	91	87	7%	59	6%	33%	26	46%	23%	3.30	-9.2	35	88	$4
14	KC *	488	47	16	57	1	217	258	272	365	638	554	653	7	83	0.46	39	20	41	23	114	100	120	9%	55	1%	100%	26	50%	27%	3.25	-6.2	46	124	$5
15	KC	549	73	22	82	1	284	274	348	470	817	823	814	7	86	0.57	40	19	41	30	117	112	114	11%	64	2%	33%	27	63%	19%	5.55	15.2	70	189	$20
16	KC	104	12	7	13	0	240	301	301	500	801	842	791	8	88	0.69	42	19	40	21	133	134	135	19%	72	5%	0%	7	71%	29%	4.84	0.1	97	277	$1
1st Half		104	12	7	13	0	240	301	301	500	801	842	791	8	88	0.69	42	19	40	21	133	134	135	19%	72	5%	0%	7	71%	29%	4.84	-0.2	97	277	$1
2nd Half																																			
17	**Proj**	**520**	**75**	**25**	**88**	**1**	**269**	**274**	**326**	**470**	**796**	**784**	**800**	**7**	**84**	**0.50**	**39**	**19**	**42**	**28**	**114**	**111**	**117**	**13%**	**59**	**3%**	**31%**				**5.18**	**4.3**	**56**	**161**	**$18**

Moya,Steven

Age: 25	Bats: L	Pos: RF	Health A	LIMA Plan D	
Ht: 6' 6"	Wt: 220		PT/Exp C	Rand Var -4	
			Consist D	MM 4223	

5-11-.255 in 94 AB at DET. Long, hulking slugger still a work in progress. PRO: Hard-hit and xPX metrics soaring, overall holes in swing a little smaller. CON: Still can't take a walk, 60% ct% w/DET. Ignore vL OPS, as it came in 5 AB. Still a young power target, but inability to adjust to MLB pitching cements wildcard profile.

Yr	Tm	AB	R	HR	RBI	SB	BA	xBA	OBP	SLG	OPS	vL	vR	bb%	ct%	Eye	G	L	F	h%	HctX	PX	xPX	hr/f	Spd	SBO	SB%	#Wk	DOM	DIS	RC/G	RAR	BPV	BPX	R$
12																																			
13																																			
14	DET *	523	60	26	75	11	238	276	261	449	710	0	857	3	67	0.10	67	17	17	31	96	170	27	0%	98	19%	72%	3	0%	67%	3.85	-0.6	40	108	$17
15	DET *	522	41	15	56	4	203	196	239	342	581	0	634	4	65	0.13	33	17	50	28	93	113	88	0%	88	9%	46%	5	20%	80%	2.52	-36.9	-13	-35	$1
16	DET *	503	60	22	67	3	255	261	281	454	735	1467	749	3	72	0.13	39	26	35	31	123	126	142	25%	95	4%	72%	12	25%	67%	4.35	-5.2	26	74	$12
1st Half		274	37	15	41	0	273	283	301	524	825	1350	874	4	73	0.15	36	28	36	32	140	153	156	24%	99	2%	0%	7	43%	43%	5.45	5.9	55	157	$16
2nd Half		229	23	7	27	3	232	233	256	371	627	2000	410	3	70	0.10	50	20	30	30	57	92	76	33%	100	6%	100%	5	0%	100%	3.21	-10.3	-9	-26	$7
17	**Proj**	**270**	**27**	**11**	**34**	**3**	**246**	**246**	**272**	**428**	**700**	**750**	**633**	**4**	**68**	**0.12**	**44**	**23**	**33**	**32**	**90**	**123**	**108**	**18%**	**92**	**8%**	**64%**				**3.91**	**-6.3**	**4**	**11**	**$7**

Muncy,Max

Age: 26	Bats: L	Pos: 2B	Health A	LIMA Plan D	
Ht: 6' 0"	Wt: 190		PT/Exp C	Rand Var +3	
			Consist A	MM 1301	

2-8-.186 in 113 AB at OAK. Proof that taking a walk can only take you so far, even in a Moneyball org. 2015 xPX was fueled by a FB stroke that he couldn't maintain, and given spotty power in minors, it likely was a fluke. Collapse in 2nd half a reflection of inability to adjust as pitchers adjusted to him. Just not an everyday guy.

Yr	Tm	AB	R	HR	RBI	SB	BA	xBA	OBP	SLG	OPS	vL	vR	bb%	ct%	Eye	G	L	F	h%	HctX	PX	xPX	hr/f	Spd	SBO	SB%	#Wk	DOM	DIS	RC/G	RAR	BPV	BPX	R$
12																																			
13	aa	172	17	3	18	0	214		292	343	635			10	78	0.50				26		96			105	3%	0%				3.16		42	105	-$2
14	aa	435	45	5	48	5	225		331	318	648			14	76	0.66				28		74			96	5%	70%				3.46		23	62	$4
15	OAK *	314	33	6	37	0	226	196	293	361	654	500	660	9	69	0.31	32	13	55	31	109	109	209	8%	85	2%	0%	17	29%	47%	3.43	-9.2	10	27	$1
16	OAK *	336	42	8	30	4	208	230	310	318	628	400	572	13	75	0.59	51	19	30	25	89	66	74	8%	117	4%	100%	15	13%	53%	3.24	-10.7	15	43	$1
1st Half		205	23	5	20	3	222	233	313	348	661	0	680	12	75	0.54	50	17	33	27	153	78	175	0%	99	6%	100%	5	20%	20%	3.66	-4.9	19	54	$3
2nd Half		131	18	3	10	1	186	218	305	271	576	400	520	15	74	0.65	52	20	29	23	52	47	20	13%	137	2%	100%	10	10%	70%	2.62	-7.7	5	14	-$3
17	**Proj**	**123**	**14**	**3**	**12**	**1**	**212**	**215**	**306**	**332**	**638**	**463**	**643**	**12**	**74**	**0.52**	**43**	**16**	**40**	**27**	**100**	**78**	**134**	**7%**	**107**	**3%**	**77%**				**3.31**	**-5.7**	**4**	**11**	**$1**

Murphy,Daniel

Age: 32	Bats: L	Pos: 2B 1B	Health B	LIMA Plan A	
Ht: 6' 2"	Wt: 205		PT/Exp A	Rand Var -5	
			Consist F	MM 3255	

A post-peak breakout that we saw coming, and then some. Concurrent upticks in FB% and hard contact have sent xPX soaring, making another 20+ HR well within reach. And steady xBA gains validate another .300+ BA, even if regression of that lofty hit rate makes another near-.350 mark unreachable. Now among the elite.

Yr	Tm	AB	R	HR	RBI	SB	BA	xBA	OBP	SLG	OPS	vL	vR	bb%	ct%	Eye	G	L	F	h%	HctX	PX	xPX	hr/f	Spd	SBO	SB%	#Wk	DOM	DIS	RC/G	RAR	BPV	BPX	R$
12	NYM	571	62	6	65	10	291	285	332	403	735	680	761	6	86	0.44	51	24	25	33	88	79	55	5%	89	8%	83%	27	48%	37%	4.86	8.2	46	115	$17
13	NYM	658	92	13	78	23	286	266	319	415	733	616	790	5	86	0.34	42	21	36	32	112	87	100	6%	104	16%	88%	27	52%	19%	4.84	21.9	54	135	$30
14	NYM	596	79	9	57	13	289	285	332	403	734	695	747	6	86	0.45	42	28	29	33	106	84	89	6%	99	11%	72%	26	50%	23%	4.77	23.1	53	143	$22
15	NYM	499	56	14	73	2	281	299	322	449	770	633	817	6	92	0.82	43	21	36	28	124	101	109	8%	68	3%	50%	24	67%	4%	5.07	12.7	85	230	$15
16	WAS	531	88	25	104	5	347	314	390	595	985	924	1010	6	89	0.61	36	22	42	35	138	135	138	12%	111	6%	63%	26	77%	0%	8.86	54.8	113	323	$34
1st Half		310	48	14	56	2	348	303	388	581	969	830	1030	5	89	0.49	34	23	43	36	133	123	140	12%	119	6%	40%	14	79%	0%	8.40	29.0	101	289	$36
2nd Half		221	40	11	48	3	344	331	393	615	1008	1069	985	8	90	0.82	39	20	41	35	145	152	135	13%	98	5%	100%	12	75%	0%	9.52	26.8	128	366	$31
17	**Proj**	**557**	**81**	**20**	**91**	**5**	**315**	**306**	**359**	**518**	**877**	**822**	**899**	**6**	**89**	**0.63**	**40**	**22**	**37**	**33**	**127**	**114**	**117**	**11%**	**93**	**5%**	**65%**				**6.85**	**30.9**	**86**	**247**	**$30**

Murphy,John

Age: 26	Bats: R	Pos: CA	Health A	LIMA Plan D	
Ht: 5' 10"	Wt: 170		PT/Exp F	Rand Var +3	
			Consist F	MM 1101	

1-3-.146 in 82 AB at MIN. PRO: Still owns those 2013 power skills; is showing a FB lean; still just 26, catchers figure it out late; subpar h% will normalize. CON: No hard contact in two of last three seasons; plate control middling at best; low vL OPS doesn't support value in platoon. Not ready to make an impact yet.

Yr	Tm	AB	R	HR	RBI	SB	BA	xBA	OBP	SLG	OPS	vL	vR	bb%	ct%	Eye	G	L	F	h%	HctX	PX	xPX	hr/f	Spd	SBO	SB%	#Wk	DOM	DIS	RC/G	RAR	BPV	BPX	R$
12	aa	147	19	4	13	0	212		277	372	649			8	77	0.39				25		116			96	0%	0%				3.33		48	120	-$1
13	NYY *	439	55	12	41	1	245	244	311	387	697	641	143	9	80	0.48	38	19	44	28	138	103	126	0%	89	2%	44%	5	0%	60%	4.03	4.0	49	123	$7
14	NYY *	260	20	6	30	0	234	240	273	348	622	686	690	5	73	0.20	36	27	37	30	54	91	53	5%	88	0%	0%	15	40%	53%	3.17	-1.1	4	11	$2
15	NYY	155	21	3	14	0	277	244	327	406	734	770	696	7	72	0.28	47	23	30	37	102	98	95	9%	120	0%	0%	26	35%	54%	4.72	4.3	20	54	$2
16	MIN *	345	25	3	36	0	197	197	246	273	519	481	381	6	78	0.30	38	16	46	24	83	54	63	3%	81	0%	0%	10	20%	60%	2.13	-18.8	-4	-11	-$4
1st Half		185	13	1	20	0	172	179	232	241	472	533	169	7	82	0.42	41	9	50	21	68	52	38	0%	81	0%	0%	5	20%	60%	1.72	-14.5	8	23	-$7
2nd Half		160	12	3	17	0	225	215	262	310	573	465	720	5	75	0.20	35	23	42	29	98	58	89	8%	94	0%	0%	5	20%	60%	2.68	-7.1	-15	-43	-$1
17	**Proj**	**131**	**12**	**2**	**13**	**0**	**229**	**228**	**276**	**337**	**613**	**668**	**572**	**6**	**76**	**0.28**	**41**	**21**	**38**	**29**	**87**	**73**	**76**	**6%**	**104**	**0%**	**50%**				**3.09**	**-4.1**	**-13**	**-36**	**$1**

Murphy,Tom

Age: 26	Bats: R	Pos: CA	Health A	LIMA Plan C+	
Ht: 6' 1"	Wt: 220		PT/Exp F	Rand Var -4	
			Consist D	MM 4233	

5-13-.273 in 44 AB at COL. Premium power prospect looked like frontline backstop during huge Sept. While power was real, so was 56% ct% in majors, and we can't expect him to come anywhere close to that crazy hr/f again. Continued poor plate metrics give little hope for near-term consistency. High-risk, high-reward.

Yr	Tm	AB	R	HR	RBI	SB	BA	xBA	OBP	SLG	OPS	vL	vR	bb%	ct%	Eye	G	L	F	h%	HctX	PX	xPX	hr/f	Spd	SBO	SB%	#Wk	DOM	DIS	RC/G	RAR	BPV	BPX	R$
12																																			
13	aa	69	7	3	7	0	279		311	469	780			4	77	0.20				33		138			93	0%	0%				5.16		57	143	$0
14	aa	94	12	4	11	0	199		280	378	658			10	70	0.38				23		136			93	0%	0%				3.37		39	105	-$1
15	COL *	429	44	19	54	4	232	228	273	433	705	417	1362	5	68	0.18	33	17	50	29	142	146	213	25%	91	9%	51%	4	50%	25%	3.81	0.0	30	81	$8
16	COL *	347	46	20	56	2	293	273	323	579	902	651	1157	4	71	0.15	28	24	48	36	139	181	225	42%	122	4%	60%	6	83%	17%	6.69	22.0	77	220	$14
1st Half		153	14	6	17	0	201	245	216	417	632			2	64	0.05				27		157			113	8%	0%				2.75		22	63	$0
2nd Half		194	32	15	38	2	367	304	406	708	1114	651	1157	6	77	0.28	28	24	48	42	150	197	225	42%	120	3%	100%	6	83%	17%	11.65	36.2	115	329	$26
17	**Proj**	**364**	**45**	**18**	**52**	**2**	**257**	**261**	**311**	**492**	**803**	**510**	**927**	**6**	**70**	**0.20**	**38**	**22**	**40**	**32**	**135**	**153**	**203**	**18%**	**114**	**5%**	**63%**				**4.98**	**8.9**	**45**	**129**	**$12**

Myers,Wil

Age: 26	Bats: R	Pos: 1B	Health F	LIMA Plan B	
Ht: 6' 3"	Wt: 190		PT/Exp C	Rand Var 0	
			Consist C	MM 3425	

On path to major breakout before crashing back to earth late. Early power boosted by hr/f that wasn't backed by FB distance. Given GB stroke, 2nd half power more realistic. Spd uptick supports most of SB boost... if green light continues. Durability issues were chronic pre-2016, so even 500 AB is no sure thing. DN: 2015 x2

Yr	Tm	AB	R	HR	RBI	SB	BA	xBA	OBP	SLG	OPS	vL	vR	bb%	ct%	Eye	G	L	F	h%	HctX	PX	xPX	hr/f	Spd	SBO	SB%	#Wk	DOM	DIS	RC/G	RAR	BPV	BPX	R$
12	a/a	522	75	26	83	5	278		337	497	833			8	71	0.31				34		147			106	6%	58%				5.81		52	130	$21
13	TAM *	587	86	24	100	11	275	255	338	463	801	821	834	9	71	0.33	46	20	34	35	115	143	120	15%	102	9%	78%	16	50%	25%	5.50	15.4	47	118	$26
14	TAM *	349	40	8	40	9	221	216	301	329	630	532	649	10	72	0.41	48	16	36	29	98	88	96	7%	109	10%	89%	16	25%	50%	3.33	-9.1	13	35	$6
15	SD	225	40	8	29	5	253	255	336	427	763	793	751	11	76	0.49	48	17	36	30	115	119	107	14%	115	11%	71%	12	50%	33%	4.82	-3.6	55	149	$7
16	SD	599	99	28	94	28	259	263	336	461	797	814	791	10	73	0.43	45	21	34	31	100	125	111	19%	124	21%	82%	27	52%	33%	5.37	0.6	53	151	$28
1st Half		308	55	19	57	13	286	288	353	536	888	927	873	10	78	0.50	44	20	36	31	115	145	145	22%	112	18%	87%	14	57%	21%	6.94	16.0	83	237	$36
2nd Half		291	44	9	37	15	230	236	318	381	700	641	713	10	68	0.37	46	23	31	31	83	100	69	15%	137	24%	79%	13	46%	46%	3.98	-10.0	17	49	$21
17	**Proj**	**523**	**82**	**19**	**74**	**18**	**254**	**249**	**331**	**424**	**755**	**746**	**757**	**10**	**73**	**0.41**	**46**	**20**	**34**	**31**	**103**	**109**	**103**	**15%**	**122**	**16%**	**80%**				**4.81**	**-4.4**	**37**	**105**	**$22**

STEPHEN NICKRAND

Napoli,Mike

Age: 35 Bats: R Pos: 1B DH	Health A	LIMA Plan B	
Ht: 6' 0" Wt: 220	PT/Exp B	Rand Var 0	
	Consist B	MM 4115	

Side-stepped injury bug (finally!) en route to his first 500 AB campaign EVER. Returns in xPX, HctX suggest 30-35 HR plateau is supportable; three-yr plummet in GB% backs it up. Big 2nd half characterized by bb%, Eye upticks and production vs. both platoon sides. Not getting any younger, so some regression must be expected.

Yr	Tm	AB	R	HR	RBI	SB	BA	xBA	OBP	SLG	OPS	vL	vR	bb%	ct%	Eye	G	L	F	h%	HctX	PX	xPX	hr/f	Spd	SBO	SB%	#Wk	DOM	DIS	RC/G	RAR	BPV	BPX	R$
12	TEX	352	53	24	56	1	227	239	343	469	812	706	861	14	64	0.45	40	19	41	28	95	169	157	26%	98	1%	100%	23	39%	48%	5.17	-1.1	52	130	$9
13	BOS	498	79	23	92	1	259	251	360	482	842	899	816	13	62	0.39	37	24	39	37	108	195	156	19%	69	1%	50%	27	56%	41%	5.84	17.8	54	135	$18
14	BOS	415	49	17	55	3	248	235	370	419	789	923	739	16	68	0.59	45	19	36	32	107	139	138	17%	60	3%	60%	23	48%	39%	5.18	12.8	35	95	$11
15	2 AL	407	46	18	50	3	224	233	324	410	734	954	603	12	71	0.48	42	16	42	27	89	131	117	15%	86	6%	50%	26	42%	38%	4.21	-9.0	41	111	$6
16	CLE	557	92	34	101	5	239	233	335	465	800	817	792	12	65	0.40	36	18	45	30	97	152	149	20%	76	4%	83%	27	48%	41%	5.19	5.6	32	91	$17
1st Half		292	46	16	53	3	233	226	302	449	751	734	758	9	61	0.26	37	20	43	32	102	157	167	21%	77	4%	100%	14	43%	43%	4.56	-4.7	14	40	$16
2nd Half		265	46	18	48	2	245	239	368	483	851	897	829	16	69	0.60	36	17	48	28	92	147	131	20%	75	3%	67%	13	54%	38%	5.89	6.3	51	146	$18
17	**Proj**	**497**	**72**	**27**	**79**	**3**	**240**	**234**	**345**	**448**	**793**	**882**	**752**	**13**	**67**	**0.47**	**39**	**18**	**43**	**30**	**96**	**138**	**138**	**19%**	**78**	**3%**	**59%**				**5.08**	**-0.3**	**25**	**71**	**$13**

Naquin,Tyler

Age: 26 Bats: L Pos: CF	Health A	LIMA Plan B	
Ht: 6' 3" Wt: 190	PT/Exp D	Rand Var -5	
	Consist B	MM 4435	

14-43-.296 in 321 AB at CLE. Impressed in MLB debut, but inflated h% and poor ct% suggest a BA regression. Power was surprising given minors history, though PX/HctX say there was decent pop in his bat. Ugly SB% despite solid Spd likely caps SB potential. Too many small sample anamolies. Show us again before we commit.

Yr	Tm	AB	R	HR	RBI	SB	BA	xBA	OBP	SLG	OPS	vL	vR	bb%	ct%	Eye	G	L	F	h%	HctX	PX	xPX	hr/f	Spd	SBO	SB%	#Wk	DOM	DIS	RC/G	RAR	BPV	BPX	R$
12																																			
13	aa	80	7	1	5	1	193		229	254	483			4	69	0.15				27		54			101	26%	19%				1.48		-38	-95	-$3
14	aa	304	43	3	24	11	274		324	361	685			7	73	0.28				36		69			123	16%	77%				4.14		1	3	$10
15	a/a	327	44	6	24	11	279		347	416	764			9	76	0.44				35		106			99	16%	77%				5.13		39	105	$11
16	CLE *	391	57	15	50	7	289	252	359	485	844	775	898	10	67	0.33	46	23	30	40	105	134	127	22%	134	11%	56%	26	50%	46%	6.04	18.5	37	106	$15
1st Half		210	28	7	24	3	295	254	355	494	850	957	939	9	70	0.31	43	24	33	39	119	126	138	20%	142	10%	46%	13	62%	38%	6.05	9.2	41	117	$15
2nd Half		181	29	8	26	4	282	247	368	475	844	568	868	11	64	0.35	49	23	28	40	93	144	119	24%	111	11%	67%	13	38%	54%	6.01	7.8	29	83	$16
17	**Proj**	**444**	**63**	**16**	**46**	**10**	**264**	**261**	**339**	**448**	**787**	**685**	**798**	**9**	**71**	**0.36**	**48**	**23**	**29**	**34**	**103**	**124**	**127**	**18%**	**128**	**13%**	**67%**				**5.09**	**7.5**	**34**	**96**	**$16**

Navarro,Dioner

Age: 33 Bats: B Pos: CA	Health B	LIMA Plan D	
Ht: 5' 9" Wt: 215	PT/Exp D	Rand Var +4	
	Consist B	MM 1013	

Chalked up lowest BPV of career. Ct%, HctX both bottomed out in lock-step, and LD trend suggests serious BA downside. Not only that, but OPS vs. RHP in steady decline and on-base skills (bb%, Eye) both abandoned him. With limited PT, no carrying skill and BPV history, the return on investment here won't be much.

Yr	Tm	AB	R	HR	RBI	SB	BA	xBA	OBP	SLG	OPS	vL	vR	bb%	ct%	Eye	G	L	F	h%	HctX	PX	xPX	hr/f	Spd	SBO	SB%	#Wk	DOM	DIS	RC/G	RAR	BPV	BPX	R$
12	CIN *	276	23	6	35	0	262	280	307	380	687	750	754	6	85	0.42	34	31	34	29	119	74	96	10%	47	0%	0%	9	22%	33%	4.03	-1.9	26	65	$4
13	CHC	240	31	13	34	0	300	289	365	492	856	1123	764	9	85	0.64	41	25	34	31	104	110	91	19%	62	1%	0%	26	50%	31%	6.36	17.5	66	165	$9
14	TOR	481	40	12	69	3	274	263	317	395	712	725	707	6	84	0.42	40	24	36	31	97	83	94	8%	48	2%	100%	26	35%	46%	4.48	15.7	32	86	$14
15	TOR	171	17	5	20	0	246	248	307	374	682	894	625	9	83	0.59	37	22	41	27	108	80	123	8%	48	0%	0%	20	40%	50%	3.97	1.2	31	84	$1
16	2 AL	304	26	6	35	1	207	224	265	322	587	659	557	7	77	0.32	35	21	44	25	81	73	99	6%	69	5%	33%	26	23%	62%	2.66	-11.5	2	6	-$1
1st Half		161	17	4	21	1	224	256	274	379	653	619	667	6	78	0.31	39	24	38	26	104	95	105	8%	70	6%	50%	14	29%	50%	3.33	-4.0	25	71	$1
2nd Half		143	9	2	14	0	189	185	255	259	514	699	426	8	75	0.33	30	18	52	24	55	47	91	4%	65	3%	0%	12	17%	75%	1.98	-9.9	-26	-74	-$4
17	**Proj**	**259**	**23**	**7**	**31**	**1**	**232**	**239**	**289**	**353**	**642**	**751**	**602**	**8**	**80**	**0.41**	**36**	**22**	**42**	**27**	**90**	**73**	**103**	**7%**	**58**	**2%**	**38%**				**3.36**	**-6.1**	**7**	**19**	**$3**

Nieuwenhuis,Kirk

Age: 29 Bats: L Pos: CF RF	Health A	LIMA Plan D	
Ht: 6' 3" Wt: 215	PT/Exp D	Rand Var -1	
	Consist A	MM 4101	

Snagged regular PT vs. RHP, setting career-bests in HR and OPS. Consistently poor ct%, inability to hit LHP, xBA downside give little hope for overall BA value. Power skills are there (see xPX, hr/f), but will require consistent AB to fully manifest, which isn't guaranteed. Lack of other skills limits overall impact potential.

Yr	Tm	AB	R	HR	RBI	SB	BA	xBA	OBP	SLG	OPS	vL	vR	bb%	ct%	Eye	G	L	F	h%	HctX	PX	xPX	hr/f	Spd	SBO	SB%	#Wk	DOM	DIS	RC/G	RAR	BPV	BPX	R$
12	NYM	282	40	7	28	4	252	222	315	376	691	515	740	8	65	0.26	51	22	27	36	80	99	90	14%	94	11%	50%	17	18%	71%	3.85	-7.0	-12	-30	$5
13	NYM *	377	45	12	36	6	181	215	252	320	572	111	661	9	65	0.27	46	19	35	24	72	110	100	14%	103	10%	69%	11	27%	64%	2.49	-19.5	0	0	$0
14	NYM *	323	35	9	33	6	211	256	266	383	649	522	855	7	65	0.22	41	31	28	29	113	155	157	14%	74	16%	60%	16	56%	38%	3.19	-6.4	24	65	$3
15	2 TM *	233	34	9	32	3	216	248	268	416	684	182	680	7	67	0.21	44	21	36	28	125	153	166	14%	104	13%	62%	19	37%	58%	3.55	-5.4	37	100	$3
16	MIL	335	38	13	44	8	209	220	324	385	709	526	732	14	60	0.42	46	20	34	30	86	138	129	19%	63	18%	47%	25	24%	40%	3.71	-9.9	1	3	$4
1st Half		183	21	5	25	6	219	228	322	388	710	488	733	13	61	0.39	46	22	32	33	102	143	160	14%	68	21%	60%	14	21%	36%	3.91	-3.5	6	17	$6
2nd Half		152	17	8	19	2	197	207	326	382	708	555	730	16	60	0.46	47	17	36	27	67	132	90	26%	70	15%	29%	11	27%	45%	3.49	-5.1	-1	-3	$2
17	**Proj**	**218**	**27**	**8**	**27**	**4**	**210**	**230**	**300**	**386**	**686**	**437**	**714**	**11**	**63**	**0.33**	**45**	**21**	**33**	**29**	**96**	**132**	**134**	**18%**	**79**	**16%**	**48%**				**3.48**	**-7.2**	**6**	**17**	**$4**

Nimmo,Brandon

Age: 24 Bats: L Pos: LF	Health A	LIMA Plan D	
Ht: 6' 3" Wt: 185	PT/Exp D	Rand Var -5	
	Consist B	MM 1221	

1-6-.274 in 73 AB at NYM. Nearly led PCL in BA, but returned only pedestrian production in two MLB recalls. Posted average ct%, bb%, Eye skills in small sample, along with below-avg overall power ability. No guarantee for consistent AB. Almost dealt in the Jay Bruce trade so the Mets were not so committed to him either.

Yr	Tm	AB	R	HR	RBI	SB	BA	xBA	OBP	SLG	OPS	vL	vR	bb%	ct%	Eye	G	L	F	h%	HctX	PX	xPX	hr/f	Spd	SBO	SB%	#Wk	DOM	DIS	RC/G	RAR	BPV	BPX	R$
12																																			
13																																			
14	aa	240	28	5	19	4	200		280	320	600			10	75	0.43				25		91			116	8%	77%				2.87		28	76	$0
15	a/a	360	35	4	19	4	237		304	324	628			9	76	0.41				30		61			121	11%	37%				3.09		11	30	$2
16	NYM *	465	62	9	48	5	287	266	341	414	755	661	667	8	77	0.36	42	30	28	36	88	79	79	7%	134	10%	34%	10	20%	50%	4.70	0.3	29	83	$14
1st Half		279	33	4	29	3	269	273	327	399	726	0	780	8	78	0.39	46	29	25	33	105	79	90	17%	132	15%	30%	2	0%	50%	4.09	-5.1	32	91	$13
2nd Half		186	29	4	19	1	314	261	363	437	799	1100	593	7	76	0.31	38	31	31	40	74	80	70	0%	124	4%	54%	8	25%	50%	5.79	5.5	20	57	$14
17	**Proj**	**161**	**20**	**2**	**13**	**2**	**260**	**257**	**330**	**365**	**695**	**736**	**690**	**8**	**76**	**0.38**	**41**	**30**	**29**	**33**	**86**	**68**	**78**	**7%**	**130**	**9%**	**41%**				**3.85**	**-2.9**	**2**	**7**	**$4**

Norris,Derek

Age: 28 Bats: R Pos: CA	Health A	LIMA Plan D+	
Ht: 6' 0" Wt: 230	PT/Exp B	Rand Var +4	
	Consist C	MM 3203	

Career-worsts almost across the board. PRO: Despite h% blow, was on career-best HR pace supported by 1H power skills, and quad/elbow injuries perhaps contributed to 2H dive. CON: Still doesn't make much contact; OPS vL on three-year slide. If he's healthy, peak years could mean cheap HRs, albeit with BA downside.

Yr	Tm	AB	R	HR	RBI	SB	BA	xBA	OBP	SLG	OPS	vL	vR	bb%	ct%	Eye	G	L	F	h%	HctX	PX	xPX	hr/f	Spd	SBO	SB%	#Wk	DOM	DIS	RC/G	RAR	BPV	BPX	R$
12	OAK *	427	47	13	61	9	212	235	274	359	633	618	630	8	74	0.32	40	22	39	26	94	102	93	13%	87	12%	80%	16	31%	63%	3.20	-14.4	20	50	$5
13	OAK	264	41	9	30	5	246	241	345	409	754	990	445	12	73	0.52	36	21	43	30	97	124	95	11%	71	6%	100%	12	46%	46%	4.81	8.7	40	100	$6
14	OAK	385	46	10	55	2	270	243	361	403	763	863	699	12	78	0.63	46	19	35	33	101	99	94	9%	86	3%	50%	26	42%	31%	5.00	17.1	42	114	$11
15	SD	515	65	14	62	4	250	238	305	404	709	810	678	6	75	0.27	42	17	41	31	94	112	105	9%	96	4%	80%	27	41%	41%	4.10	4.3	31	84	$11
16	SD	415	50	14	42	9	186	212	255	328	583	628	565	8	67	0.26	35	22	43	24	93	100	103	12%	49	13%	82%	26	23%	54%	2.60	-24.0	-20	-57	$1
1st Half		237	33	10	28	4	207	244	265	384	649	726	616	7	73	0.26	38	21	41	24	108	115	114	14%	55	9%	100%	14	36%	29%	3.28	-6.3	14	40	$5
2nd Half		178	17	4	14	5	157	172	242	253	495	481	500	10	58	0.26	30	23	47	24	73	77	84	8%	57	18%	71%	12	8%	83%	1.83	-13.8	-66	-189	-$4
17	**Proj**	**319**	**38**	**10**	**36**	**5**	**236**	**223**	**308**	**384**	**692**	**781**	**653**	**9**	**70**	**0.32**	**38**	**20**	**42**	**31**	**92**	**101**	**98**	**11%**	**72**	**8%**	**77%**				**3.91**	**-2.2**	**2**	**5**	**$8**

Nunez,Eduardo

Age: 30 Bats: R Pos: 3B SS	Health B	LIMA Plan B	
Ht: 6' 0" Wt: 155	PT/Exp D	Rand Var -3	
	Consist B	MM 1535	

With health and regular PT for first time, returned top dollar. Trio of underlying speed skills say SB impact should be repeatable, while returns in FB% and xPX suggest at least some of HR boost has a chance to stick. Steady ct% and yearly BPX each show great overall stability. A low-risk power-speed combo to invest in.

Yr	Tm	AB	R	HR	RBI	SB	BA	xBA	OBP	SLG	OPS	vL	vR	bb%	ct%	Eye	G	L	F	h%	HctX	PX	xPX	hr/f	Spd	SBO	SB%	#Wk	DOM	DIS	RC/G	RAR	BPV	BPX	R$
12	NYY *	252	28	3	23	23	229	216	262	299	562	860	539	4	83	0.26	44	16	39	27	89	46	90	3%	141	50%	81%	12	33%	50%	2.72	-14.7	20	50	$7
13	NYY	304	38	3	28	10	260	250	307	372	679	652	693	6	83	0.39	41	21	38	30	89	78	81	3%	153	17%	77%	20	45%	35%	3.93	-0.5	56	140	$7
14	MIN *	253	32	5	28	10	251	265	274	377	651	586	716	3	83	0.19	56	16	27	29	80	78	42	9%	164	25%	78%	20	45%	40%	3.52	-1.4	52	141	$7
15	MIN	188	23	4	20	8	282	284	327	431	758	649	809	6	85	0.41	57	16	27	32	93	100	68	10%	117	26%	67%	24	50%	25%	4.78	0.5	67	181	$7
16	2 TM	553	73	16	67	40	288	264	325	432	758	750	760	5	84	0.33	50	17	34	32	95	80	85	10%	159	35%	80%	26	50%	27%	5.04	0.9	60	171	$32
1st Half		288	42	11	34	19	319	273	345	486	832	900	808	3	86	0.24	50	15	35	34	101	90	90	13%	149	31%	79%	14	57%	14%	6.21	10.4	68	194	$38
2nd Half		265	31	5	33	21	253	254	304	374	678	578	709	7	82	0.40	49	18	33	29	88	70	79	7%	159	39%	81%	12	42%	42%	3.96	-7.4	48	137	$26
17	**Proj**	**564**	**71**	**12**	**64**	**32**	**273**	**269**	**312**	**407**	**719**	**670**	**742**	**5**	**84**	**0.34**	**52**	**18**	**31**	**31**	**91**	**77**	**74**	**9%**	**150**	**29%**	**78%**				**4.43**	**-7.5**	**49**	**140**	**$28**

ALEC DOPP

Nunez,Renato

Age: 23	Bats: R	Pos: 3B	Health A	LIMA Plan D	
Ht: 6' 1"	Wt: 220		PT/Exp D	Rand Var 0	
			Consist B	MM 2311	

0-1-.133 in 15 AB at OAK. Boasts plus raw power and bat speed. However, poor pitch recognition and unwillingness to take a walk are worrisome traits. Probably needs more seasoning in minors, but he's an intriguing option in keeper leagues, particularly if the glove can progress enough to stick at 3B.

Yr	Tm	AB	R	HR	RBI	SB	BA	xBA	OBP	SLG	OPS	vL	vR	bb%	ct%	Eye	G	L	F	h%	HctX	PX	xPX	hr/f	Spd	SBO	SB%	#Wk	DOM	DIS	RC/G	RAR	BPV	BPX	R$
12																																			
13																																			
14																																			
15	aa	381	47	13	46	1	243		283	398	681			5	82	0.30				27		100			82	1%	100%				3.80		43	116	$7
16	OAK *	520	56	19	69	2	212	277	253	371	624	333	0	5	76	0.23	75	17	8	24	26	95	-3	0%	83	2%	100%	3	0%	100%	3.05	-28.0	16	46	$3
1st Half		300	33	10	42	2	227	256	266	389	655			5	79	0.25				26		95			96	3%	100%				3.44		32	91	$6
2nd Half		220	23	9	28	0	191	242	236	345	582	333	0	6	71	0.20	75	17	8	22	24	95	-3	0%	72	0%	0%	3	0%	100%	2.57	-16.2	-4	-11	-$1
17	Proj	**199**	**23**	**6**	**25**	**1**	**236**	**242**	**278**	**376**	**654**	**654**	**654**	**5**	**77**	**0.26**	**38**	**22**	**40**	**28**		**86**		**10%**	**82**	**1%**	**100%**				**3.50**	**-8.3**	**5**	**15**	**$2**

O Brien,Peter

Age: 26	Bats: R	Pos: LF	Health A	LIMA Plan D	
Ht: 6' 3"	Wt: 215		PT/Exp C	Rand Var -1	
			Consist B	MM 5101	

5-9-.141 in 64 AB at ARI. Combo of mammoth power and high FB% is exciting. However, horrendous ct%, unsightly BA and lack of defensive ability (best suited for DH) are major stumbling blocks. Until he reins in the swing-at-everything mindset a bit, his chances of finding success and steady PT in MLB aren't good.

Yr	Tm	AB	R	HR	RBI	SB	BA	xBA	OBP	SLG	OPS	vL	vR	bb%	ct%	Eye	G	L	F	h%	HctX	PX	xPX	hr/f	Spd	SBO	SB%	#Wk	DOM	DIS	RC/G	RAR	BPV	BPX	R$
12																																			
13																																			
14	aa	287	37	20	42	0	223		256	481	738			4	68	0.14				25		195			89	0%	0%				4.05		65	176	$7
15	ARI *	500	49	17	69	1	233	287	264	427	690	3333	393	4	70	0.14	40	40	20	30	60	140	134	####	112	5%	15%	4	50%	25%	3.61	-16.7	34	92	$7
16	ARI *	470	48	21	59	1	197	185	227	389	616	719	491	4	57	0.09	46	3	51	29	88	148	198	26%	101	2%	100%	10	30%	60%	2.82	-26.7	-13	-37	$1
1st Half		269	34	15	43	1	241	216	265	482	747	753	352	3	63	0.09	44	3	53	32	97	164	210	24%	109	2%	100%	6	17%	83%	4.30	-1.2	26	74	$9
2nd Half		201	15	6	16	1	141	148	178	268	446	0	1333	4	49	0.09	60	0	40	25	79	120	125	50%	99	3%	100%	4	50%	25%	1.43	-20.5	-69	-197	-$10
17	Proj	**101**	**10**	**7**	**13**	**0**	**205**	**228**	**235**	**481**	**717**	**1020**	**540**	**4**	**62**	**0.11**	**44**	**3.1**	**53**	**25**	**87**	**193**	**189**	**21%**	**103**	**5%**	**51%**				**3.59**	**-2.7**	**34**	**98**	**$2**

O Malley,Shawn

Age: 29	Bats: B	Pos: SS	Health A	LIMA Plan D	
Ht: 5' 10"	Wt: 160		PT/Exp D	Rand Var -1	
			Consist B	MM 1411	

2-17-.229 with 6 SB in 210 AB at SEA. Amassed a .365 OBP in 926 lifetime AB at Triple-A, but power has been nearly non-existent, even in the PCL. Sketchy ct% prevents him from utilizing his best asset: above-average Spd. Speed and defensive versatility give him a shot at possibly earning a utilityman gig in real-life MLB.

Yr	Tm	AB	R	HR	RBI	SB	BA	xBA	OBP	SLG	OPS	vL	vR	bb%	ct%	Eye	G	L	F	h%	HctX	PX	xPX	hr/f	Spd	SBO	SB%	#Wk	DOM	DIS	RC/G	RAR	BPV	BPX	R$
12	a/a	337	41	1	18	14	199		256	253	510			7	74	0.30				26		35			148	23%	75%				2.10		-13	-33	$0
13	aa	321	40	2	24	18	216		270	298	569			7	77	0.33				27		57			147	28%	84%				2.75		15	38	$6
14	LAA *	366	45	2	29	11	243	290	297	332	630	800	182	7	80	0.38	88	13	0	30	0	65	-15	0%	163	17%	69%	4	0%	75%	3.29	1.2	36	97	$7
15	SEA *	352	41	4	31	16	223	244	272	298	570	739	805	6	78	0.31	48	26	26	27	44	49	12	14%	136	28%	63%	5	20%	80%	2.54	-20.5	8	22	$6
16	SEA *	292	34	3	26	9	232	231	296	321	617	635	602	8	72	0.32	51	22	27	32	55	64	44	6%	124	17%	74%	21	24%	57%	3.17	-10.1	-6	-17	$4
1st Half		148	15	1	14	5	235	260	300	322	622	553	631	9	69	0.30	50	35	15	33	69	69	13	0%	98	18%	81%	8	13%	75%	3.30	-5.3	-18	-51	$4
2nd Half		144	19	2	12	4	229	220	306	319	626	669	589	8	74	0.34	52	17	32	30	50	60	57	7%	136	16%	67%	13	31%	46%	3.05	-6.3	2	6	$4
17	Proj	**162**	**19**	**1**	**14**	**6**	**229**	**242**	**296**	**310**	**605**	**615**	**595**	**8**	**75**	**0.33**	**51**	**24**	**25**	**30**	**58**	**53**	**39**	**4%**	**132**	**20%**	**70%**				**2.92**	**-7.7**	**-4**	**-11**	**$3**

Odor,Rougned

Age: 23	Bats: L	Pos: 2B	Health A	LIMA Plan B+	
Ht: 5' 11"	Wt: 195		PT/Exp B	Rand Var 0	
			Consist B	MM 4235	

Opened up swing to chase power, as evidenced by ct%/bb%/Eye deterioration. We usually consider this a bad thing, but he made it work (per xBA, xPX, HctX), so maybe it can stick. Average-ish Spd, low OBP and poor SB% may result in fewer green lights on basepaths. Strong keeper option, but a full repeat isn't a lock.

Yr	Tm	AB	R	HR	RBI	SB	BA	xBA	OBP	SLG	OPS	vL	vR	bb%	ct%	Eye	G	L	F	h%	HctX	PX	xPX	hr/f	Spd	SBO	SB%	#Wk	DOM	DIS	RC/G	RAR	BPV	BPX	R$
12																																			
13	aa	134	18	6	17	4	309		349	529	878			6	82	0.34				34		139			115	19%	69%				6.61		88	220	$5
14	TEX *	515	57	14	62	9	260	249	292	404	695	626	727	4	82	0.24	49	15	36	29	90	90	68	8%	129	16%	47%	22	41%	23%	3.78	6.0	48	130	$15
15	TEX *	534	76	20	77	9	273	277	316	486	802	781	781	6	83	0.37	46	15	40	30	106	126	102	12%	127	14%	51%	22	55%	18%	5.14	13.3	86	232	$21
16	TEX	605	89	33	88	14	271	269	296	502	798	763	811	3	78	0.14	40	18	42	30	112	135	131	17%	85	19%	67%	26	54%	19%	5.00	4.8	52	149	$25
1st Half		305	52	15	39	7	262	259	283	469	752	812	726	2	79	0.11	40	16	43	29	108	120	126	15%	88	16%	78%	14	57%	21%	4.49	-2.7	44	126	$23
2nd Half		300	37	18	49	7	280	279	309	537	846	697	888	4	77	0.17	40	19	41	31	116	150	136	19%	86	21%	58%	12	50%	17%	5.55	6.5	62	177	$27
17	Proj	**670**	**92**	**30**	**95**	**11**	**274**	**269**	**314**	**489**	**803**	**766**	**818**	**4**	**80**	**0.22**	**43**	**16**	**40**	**30**	**107**	**121**	**112**	**14%**	**104**	**13%**	**63%**				**5.11**	**6.0**	**62**	**176**	**$29**

Olson,Matt

Age: 23	Bats: L	Pos: RF	Health A	LIMA Plan D	
Ht: 6' 4"	Wt: 236		PT/Exp D	Rand Var 0	
			Consist A	MM 3211	

0-0-.095 in 21 AB at OAK. Displayed power and patience throughout minor league career (103 HR, 15% bb%), but not without warts. Swings and misses far too often, leaving him with a horrid BA. And history of struggles vL might limit him to a platoon role from the start. Needs more polish, but time is on his side.

Yr	Tm	AB	R	HR	RBI	SB	BA	xBA	OBP	SLG	OPS	vL	vR	bb%	ct%	Eye	G	L	F	h%	HctX	PX	xPX	hr/f	Spd	SBO	SB%	#Wk	DOM	DIS	RC/G	RAR	BPV	BPX	R$
12																																			
13																																			
14																																			
15	aa	466	62	12	57	4	217		331	366	697			15	68	0.54				29		123			81	4%	78%				3.96		28	76	$5
16	OAK *	485	67	14	55	1	217	210	319	382	701	0	527	13	71	0.51	47	6	47	28	51	119	-9	0%	79	1%	100%	4	50%	25%	3.97	-13.1	31	89	$3
1st Half		266	35	7	30	1	207	231	310	366	675			13	66	0.44				29		124			83	1%	100%				3.66		17	49	$2
2nd Half		219	32	8	25	0	229	214	330	402	732	0	527	13	77	0.65	47	6	47	26	55	113	-9	0%	79	0%	0%	4	50%	25%	4.38	-4.7	49	140	$4
17	Proj	**181**	**25**	**5**	**21**	**1**	**218**	**240**	**325**	**379**	**704**	**704**	**900**	**14**	**71**	**0.54**	**37**	**22**	**41**	**28**		**117**		**10%**	**80**	**2%**	**84%**				**4.03**	**-3.7**	**21**	**59**	**$2**

O Neill,Tyler

Age: 22	Bats: R	Pos: OF	Health A	LIMA Plan F	
Ht: 5' 11"	Wt: 210		PT/Exp F	Rand Var 0	
			Consist F	MM 1301	

SEA prospect owns terrific bat speed and power; added a much more patient approach in 2016. Average Spd, but chooses spots wisely. There's still work to be done (see ct%), but it's encouraging to see him making adjustments. Fine keeper league option, though consolidation likely another year away.

Yr	Tm	AB	R	HR	RBI	SB	BA	xBA	OBP	SLG	OPS	vL	vR	bb%	ct%	Eye	G	L	F	h%	HctX	PX	xPX	hr/f	Spd	SBO	SB%	#Wk	DOM	DIS	RC/G	RAR	BPV	BPX	R$
12																																			
13																																			
14																																			
15																																			
16	aa	492	67	23	101	12	282		359	487	846			11	66	0.36				38		141			90	10%	85%				6.28		29	83	$23
1st Half		305	42	13	59	6	291		354	502	856			9	70	0.32				38		142			89	8%	85%				6.43		40	114	$26
2nd Half		187	26	10	41	6	268		368	462	830			14	60	0.40				39		138			89	11%	85%				6.01		8	23	$17
17	Proj	**154**	**21**	**0**	**32**	**4**	**277**	**0**	**364**	**333**	**697**	**697**	**697**	**12**	**64**	**0.38**	**0**	**0**	**0**	**43**		**52**		**0%**	**91**	**9%**	**86%**				**4.39**		**-46**	**-133**	**$6**

Orlando,Paulo

Age: 31	Bats: R	Pos: RF CF	Health A	LIMA Plan D	
Ht: 6' 3"	Wt: 185		PT/Exp C	Rand Var -5	
			Consist C	MM 1521	

Injuries in the KC outfield opened the door for far more PT than expected. Extremely fortunate h% artificially inflated BA (see xBA). Unwillingness to take a walk puts a damper on his best asset: Spd. High GB% stifles what little power he has. He can be somewhat useful vL, but there aren't enough of those around to sustain him.

Yr	Tm	AB	R	HR	RBI	SB	BA	xBA	OBP	SLG	OPS	vL	vR	bb%	ct%	Eye	G	L	F	h%	HctX	PX	xPX	hr/f	Spd	SBO	SB%	#Wk	DOM	DIS	RC/G	RAR	BPV	BPX	R$
12	aa	420	39	4	29	15	226		263	299	562			5	84	0.32				26		48			99	23%	67%				2.53		16	40	$4
13	aaa	293	30	3	33	6	226		266	304	569			5	77	0.24				28		53			120	14%	61%				2.59		0	0	$2
14	aaa	501	38	4	39	21	228		264	307	571			5	79	0.23				28		57			119	29%	65%				2.56		8	22	$8
15	KC *	411	45	9	39	9	236	257	255	387	642	705	718	3	77	0.11	43	22	34	28	107	102	121	11%	134	18%	76%	21	52%	24%	3.27	-18.6	39	105	$7
16	KC	457	52	5	43	14	302	254	329	405	734	817	697	3	77	0.12	52	22	26	38	91	70	67	6%	150	14%	82%	26	27%	54%	4.81	1.2	17	49	$18
1st Half		187	16	1	16	5	326	241	352	422	775	770	776	3	78	0.12	51	19	30	41	84	63	61	2%	157	11%	83%	13	31%	54%	5.56	4.3	17	49	$14
2nd Half		270	36	4	27	9	285	262	313	393	706	841	636	3	76	0.13	53	24	23	36	96	75	72	9%	134	17%	82%	13	23%	54%	4.33	-2.8	13	37	$20
17	Proj	**203**	**21**	**4**	**19**	**6**	**267**	**256**	**298**	**390**	**688**	**726**	**668**	**3**	**78**	**0.15**	**49**	**22**	**29**	**33**	**97**	**78**	**89**	**8%**	**144**	**18%**	**75%**				**3.92**	**-4.6**	**16**	**44**	**$7**

GREG PYRON

Ortega,Rafael

Age: 26 Bats: L Pos: LF | Ht: 5' 11" Wt: 160

Health A | PT/Exp C | Consist A | LIMA Plan D | Rand Var +1 | MM 0421

1-16-.232 with 8 SB in 202 AB at LAA. Best way to improve prospect stock? Join LAA, especially if you're buried in a deep STL system. A defense-and-speed 4th OF type. On the high end, could ride a gaudy h% to some BA success and SB volume, but a fringy 69% career success rate suggests a yellow light on the bases.

Yr	Tm	AB	R	HR	RBI	SB	BA	xBA	OBP	SLG	OPS	vL	vR	bb%	ct%	Eye	G	L	F	h%	HctX	PX	xPX	hr/f	Spd	SBO	SB%	#Wk	DOM	DIS	RC/G	RAR	BPV	BPX	R$
12	COL	4	0	0	0	1	500	107	667	500	1167	0	2000	20	50	0.50	100	0	0	100	0	0	-11	0%	126	33%	100%				19.51	1.2	-119	-298	-$2
13	aa	158	18	1	8	7	220		288	288	576			9	84	0.59				26		43			141	27%	63%				2.61		31	78	$0
14	a/a	379	45	5	24	13	213		278	285	563			8	82	0.50				25		48			125	25%	54%				2.38		23	62	$4
15	aaa	437	49	1	31	13	241		307	312	619			9	80	0.49				30		51			117	16%	65%				3.16		17	46	$6
16	LAA *	507	57	4	37	18	247	265	280	330	610	400	595	4	86	0.33	57	18	25	28	76	51	46	3%	124	26%	59%	14	57%	21%	2.93	-20.7	33	94	$10
1st Half		248	28	2	19	7	223	261	257	283	540	500	585	4	87	0.35	59	18	22	25	81	36	61	4%	128	23%	51%	8	63%	25%	2.19	-17.7	25	71	$6
2nd Half		259	29	2	19	11	270	263	302	376	678	250	613	4	85	0.31	54	16	30	31	67	66	20	0%	114	28%	65%	6	50%	17%	3.79	-5.1	39	111	$15
17	Proj	**164**	**19**	**1**	**11**	**6**	**240**	**247**	**288**	**308**	**595**	**426**	**616**	**6**	**84**	**0.41**	**56**	**17**	**27**	**28**	**73**	**44**	**36**	**2%**	**124**	**23%**	**60%**				**2.83**	**-8.2**	**16**	**46**	**$2**

Ortiz,David

Age: 41 Bats: L Pos: DH | Ht: 6' 4" Wt: 250

Health B | PT/Exp A | Consist C | LIMA Plan F | Rand Var 0 | MM 0000

After arguably the greatest final season and easily the best age-40 season ever, it's tough to watch Big Papi hang it up. But we don't have to put in the work that he does to ready himself. We'll miss the elite production that was always underrated in the fantasy market because he blocked precious DH/UT spot.

Yr	Tm	AB	R	HR	RBI	SB	BA	xBA	OBP	SLG	OPS	vL	vR	bb%	ct%	Eye	G	L	F	h%	HctX	PX	xPX	hr/f	Spd	SBO	SB%	#Wk	DOM	DIS	RC/G	RAR	BPV	BPX	R$
12	BOS	324	65	23	60	0	318	318	415	611	1026	985	1050	15	84	1.10	37	21	42	32	143	175	150	20%	57	1%	0%	17	82%	6%	9.46	39.8	126	315	$19
13	BOS	518	84	30	103	4	309	308	395	564	959	733	1092	13	83	0.86	39	23	39	33	154	162	173	18%	66	2%	100%	25	64%	12%	8.33	53.6	109	273	$31
14	BOS	518	59	35	104	0	263	282	355	517	873	893	863	13	82	0.79	37	18	46	26	159	164	187	18%	35	0%	0%	26	73%	12%	6.37	34.7	96	259	$22
15	BOS	528	73	37	108	0	273	308	360	553	913	703	1008	13	82	0.81	37	22	41	27	150	169	162	20%	39	1%	0%	27	85%	4%	7.03	23.9	102	276	$23
16	BOS	537	79	38	127	2	315	320	401	620	1021	867	1075	13	84	0.93	33	22	45	32	156	171	170	18%	33	1%	100%	27	74%	7%	9.34	55.5	111	317	$31
1st Half		269	38	19	65	2	338	341	434	677	1110	786	1202	14	85	1.13	35	21	44	34	153	193	158	19%	44	2%	100%	14	86%	0%	11.36	40.9	139	397	$34
2nd Half		268	41	19	62	0	291	302	368	563	931	932	936	12	83	0.76	30	23	46	29	159	148	182	18%	32	0%	0%	13	62%	15%	7.56	15.3	84	240	$28
17	Proj																																		

Owings,Christopher

Age: 25 Bats: R Pos: SS CF | Ht: 5' 11" Wt: 185

Health C | PT/Exp C | Consist C | LIMA Plan B+ | Rand Var -1 | MM 2535

Led MLB in triples and was top-30 speedster despite month lost to foot injury. Career best ct% and GB% allowed speed to shine. PRO: SB success rate; age; dual eligibility; hints of potential pop. CON: Non-factor vR; poor bb% leaves OBP reliant on h%; 1317 below-avg career AB suggests WYSIWYG. DN: 250 AB.

Yr	Tm	AB	R	HR	RBI	SB	BA	xBA	OBP	SLG	OPS	vL	vR	bb%	ct%	Eye	G	L	F	h%	HctX	PX	xPX	hr/f	Spd	SBO	SB%	#Wk	DOM	DIS	RC/G	RAR	BPV	BPX	R$
12	aa	297	28	5	23	3	246		267	350	617			3	75	0.12				31		70			116	10%	50%				3.04		0	0	$2
13	ARI *	601	72	8	57	15	282	262	305	397	701	250	932	3	80	0.16	47	24	29	34	67	83	63	0%	123	16%	65%	4	50%	25%	4.17	11.5	31	78	$20
14	ARI *	350	38	6	27	10	255	257	287	386	673	829	672	4	78	0.21	45	24	31	31	90	93	77	8%	162	14%	91%	18	33%	50%	3.89	6.1	45	122	$8
15	ARI	515	59	4	43	16	227	227	264	322	587	495	614	5	72	0.18	39	26	34	31	94	76	93	3%	116	19%	80%	27	30%	63%	2.85	-14.4	-4	-11	$7
16	ARI	437	52	5	49	21	277	273	315	416	731	826	700	4	80	0.23	50	23	27	34	97	84	75	5%	158	23%	91%	22	36%	27%	4.72	1.3	46	131	$17
1st Half		179	21	2	18	8	285	270	340	419	759	906	701	8	79	0.39	55	20	25	35	94	83	68	6%	150	16%	100%	10	40%	30%	5.38	4.6	44	126	$13
2nd Half		258	31	3	31	13	271	275	296	415	711	754	699	2	81	0.10	46	25	29	33	100	84	79	5%	153	29%	87%	12	33%	25%	4.25	-1.6	43	123	$20
17	Proj	**502**	**58**	**7**	**49**	**19**	**260**	**258**	**295**	**388**	**683**	**673**	**687**	**4**	**78**	**0.20**	**46**	**24**	**30**	**32**	**93**	**80**	**78**	**6%**	**149**	**20%**	**87%**				**4.00**	**-6.8**	**30**	**87**	**$17**

Ozuna,Marcell

Age: 26 Bats: R Pos: CF | Ht: 6' 2" Wt: 220

Health A | PT/Exp A | Consist B | LIMA Plan B+ | Rand Var 0 | MM 3135

Return to 2014 level loses steam considering the league-wide HR surge, and his sharp ct% gains should have yielded higher BA. Was headed for breakout, but lingering June wrist injury derailed it. Pre-inj: 16 HR, .948 OPS; post-inj: 7 HR, .605 OPS. Glove protects AB vR. If he can finish the job in 2017, then ... UP: 30 HR

Yr	Tm	AB	R	HR	RBI	SB	BA	xBA	OBP	SLG	OPS	vL	vR	bb%	ct%	Eye	G	L	F	h%	HctX	PX	xPX	hr/f	Spd	SBO	SB%	#Wk	DOM	DIS	RC/G	RAR	BPV	BPX	R$
12																																			
13	MIA *	317	36	7	45	6	270	266	304	426	730	838	647	5	79	0.23	46	21	33	32	106	110	88	4%	121	10%	85%	13	31%	38%	4.56	4.2	51	128	$9
14	MIA	565	72	23	85	3	269	252	317	455	772	728	783	7	71	0.25	49	18	34	34	117	140	133	17%	127	3%	75%	26	42%	38%	5.05	19.7	49	132	$20
15	MIA *	579	64	14	53	3	263	255	310	402	712	888	646	6	77	0.29	48	21	31	32	115	102	106	9%	80	4%	48%	23	30%	43%	4.24	-1.1	26	70	$12
16	MIA	557	75	23	76	0	266	262	321	452	773	923	732	7	79	0.37	44	20	37	30	121	105	121	14%	135	2%	0%	26	38%	31%	4.89	3.8	58	166	$14
1st Half		302	50	17	47	0	311	272	362	550	911	1202	826	7	78	0.36	43	19	38	35	117	130	125	19%	168	1%	0%	14	43%	21%	7.27	22.6	82	234	$25
2nd Half		255	25	6	29	0	212	250	272	337	610	550	624	7	81	0.40	45	20	34	24	125	76	115	8%	89	4%	0%	12	33%	42%	2.80	-13.6	28	80	$2
17	Proj	**569**	**69**	**22**	**71**	**2**	**271**	**263**	**321**	**456**	**777**	**904**	**744**	**7**	**78**	**0.31**	**45**	**20**	**35**	**31**	**118**	**110**	**115**	**14%**	**113**	**4%**	**45%**				**5.00**	**8.0**	**34**	**98**	**$19**

Pagan,Angel

Age: 35 Bats: B Pos: LF | Ht: 6' 1" Wt: 195

Health F | PT/Exp B | Consist C | LIMA Plan B | Rand Var 0 | MM 1445

Age and health have diminished his once-appealing wheels, but a career-best hr/f allowed him to get in on the HR bonanza with a new season's high. Hasn't avoided the DL since 2012, but rock solid ct% offers useful BA floor and any double-digit SB output has value in today's speed-starved environs. Best used as fill-in OF.

Yr	Tm	AB	R	HR	RBI	SB	BA	xBA	OBP	SLG	OPS	vL	vR	bb%	ct%	Eye	G	L	F	h%	HctX	PX	xPX	hr/f	Spd	SBO	SB%	#Wk	DOM	DIS	RC/G	RAR	BPV	BPX	R$
12	SF	605	95	8	56	29	288	270	338	440	778	736	799	7	84	0.49	42	23	35	33	102	95	96	4%	148	22%	81%	27	59%	19%	5.40	11.6	73	183	$26
13	SF	280	44	5	30	9	282	277	334	414	749	807	725	8	87	0.64	43	23	33	31	88	86	77	6%	129	17%	69%	14	64%	0%	4.87	6.5	73	183	$10
14	SF	383	56	3	27	16	300	276	342	389	731	626	790	6	86	0.47	45	27	28	34	86	67	53	3%	119	19%	73%	18	39%	33%	4.82	11.1	48	130	$17
15	SF	512	55	3	37	12	262	237	303	332	635	714	604	6	82	0.34	43	23	34	31	83	50	68	2%	105	12%	75%	25	16%	48%	3.51	-18.0	13	35	$11
16	SF	495	71	12	55	15	277	283	331	418	750	717	766	8	87	0.64	43	25	32	30	86	78	56	9%	121	14%	79%	25	56%	16%	4.94	4.4	63	180	$18
1st Half		190	31	3	28	7	284	277	333	400	733	743	728	7	84	0.50	43	27	30	32	91	72	53	6%	104	15%	88%	12	42%	25%	4.93	2.6	42	120	$15
2nd Half		305	40	9	27	8	272	286	330	430	760	696	788	8	88	0.75	43	24	34	28	82	81	59	10%	129	13%	73%	13	69%	8%	4.95	4.3	75	214	$20
17	Proj	**456**	**62**	**7**	**43**	**14**	**271**	**270**	**320**	**385**	**705**	**692**	**711**	**7**	**85**	**0.50**	**43**	**25**	**32**	**30**	**86**	**67**	**62**	**6%**	**118**	**15%**	**77%**				**4.34**	**-1.5**	**46**	**133**	**$17**

Panik,Joe

Age: 26 Bats: L Pos: 2B | Ht: 6' 1" Wt: 190

Health C | PT/Exp B | Consist F | LIMA Plan A | Rand Var +4 | MM 1345

Lost a month to a concussion and numbers suggest it lingered, but a closer look points to bad luck more than anything else. The 1H/2H split matches pre/post concussion periods: xBA was flat, bb% and ct% both improved, and yet h% tumbled from already-low level. Rebound BA candidate still has .300+ potential.

Yr	Tm	AB	R	HR	RBI	SB	BA	xBA	OBP	SLG	OPS	vL	vR	bb%	ct%	Eye	G	L	F	h%	HctX	PX	xPX	hr/f	Spd	SBO	SB%	#Wk	DOM	DIS	RC/G	RAR	BPV	BPX	R$
12																																			
13	aa	522	47	3	42	7	217		277	289	566			8	85	0.56				25		53			104	10%	57%				2.55		32	80	$1
14	SF *	562	64	4	48	2	281	263	323	358	680	839	655	6	87	0.48	50	23	27	32	90	53	51	2%	137	3%	46%	17	24%	24%	4.04	10.3	46	124	$13
15	SF	382	59	8	37	3	312	288	378	455	833	769	852	9	89	0.90	43	23	34	33	115	91	89	7%	107	4%	60%	18	72%	11%	6.24	21.5	81	219	$15
16	SF	464	67	10	62	5	239	270	315	379	695	595	734	10	90	1.06	45	18	37	25	94	73	87	6%	123	4%	100%	24	67%	13%	4.04	-11.3	76	217	$8
1st Half		273	45	7	36	5	256	268	321	407	728	653	763	9	89	0.84	44	18	38	27	95	75	85	8%	139	7%	100%	13	62%	15%	4.59	-1.7	76	217	$14
2nd Half		191	22	3	26	0	215	268	308	340	648	483	699	11	92	1.50	48	16	36	22	91	70	89	5%	102	0%	0%	11	73%	9%	3.34	-8.6	77	220	$0
17	Proj	**542**	**77**	**9**	**64**	**4**	**282**	**273**	**349**	**405**	**754**	**693**	**775**	**9**	**89**	**0.91**	**46**	**20**	**34**	**30**	**100**	**69**	**83**	**6%**	**113**	**3%**	**71%**				**4.97**	**2.5**	**59**	**168**	**$18**

Park,Byung Ho

Age: 30 Bats: R Pos: DH 1B | Ht: 6' 1" Wt: 220

Health A | PT/Exp B | Consist F | LIMA Plan C | Rand Var +5 | MM 3103

12-24-.191 in 215 AB at MIN. Back-to-back 50+ HR seasons in Korea (MLEs here) converted to some nice MLB pop, but not enough to offset ct% issues. AAA was more feast-or-famine before a finger injury ended his season in August. Some players make the cultural transition better than others. Give him a cautious mulligan.

Yr	Tm	AB	R	HR	RBI	SB	BA	xBA	OBP	SLG	OPS	vL	vR	bb%	ct%	Eye	G	L	F	h%	HctX	PX	xPX	hr/f	Spd	SBO	SB%	#Wk	DOM	DIS	RC/G	RAR	BPV	BPX	R$
12	for	469	74	19	102	18	270		352	461	813			11	78	0.56				31		131			73	21%	64%				5.44	1.2	61	153	$23
13	for	450	89	22	114	9	296		396	482	878			14	80	0.82				33		117			79	7%	80%				6.94	29.3	67	168	$29
14	for	459	123	31	121	7	282		386	535	921			14	71	0.58				33		179			106	7%	68%				7.26	40.4	89	241	$33
15	for	528	126	32	142	9	319		392	572	964			11	71	0.41				40		176			84	8%	73%				8.34	45.3	74	200	$40
16	MIN *	331	42	19	39	1	187	231	245	409	655	656	693	7	64	0.22	41	17	42	22	96	152	144	21%	78	2%	100%	13	46%	38%	3.16	-17.8	18	51	$0
1st Half		221	29	12	24	1	193	223	268	406	673	656	693	9	62	0.27	41	17	42	24	93	151	144	21%	85	2%	100%	13	46%	38%	3.45	-11.5	15	43	$2
2nd Half		110	13	7	15	0	175	254	197	417	614			3	68	0.09				17		154			75	0%	0%				2.54		26	74	-$2
17	Proj	**351**	**63**	**15**	**68**	**1**	**250**	**228**	**325**	**429**	**754**	**716**	**767**	**9**	**69**	**0.31**	**41**	**17**	**42**	**32**	**84**	**119**	**130**	**15%**	**70**	**1%**	**69%**				**4.60**	**-9.3**	**13**	**37**	**$12**

PAUL SPORER

Parker,Jarrett

Age: 28 **Bats:** L **Pos:** RF
Ht: 6' 4" **Wt:** 210

Health	A	LIMA Plan	F
PT/Exp	C	Rand Var	+1
Consist	A	MM	3201

5-14-.236 in 127 AB at SF. Six HR as a Sept 2015 call-up got our attention, but we have since lost interest due to strikeouts and GB. Walk rate a plus, but 64% SB% at AA/AAA has curtailed opportunities in majors. Mighty platoon splits limit his value for now.

Yr	Tm	AB	R	HR	RBI	SB	BA	xBA	OBP	SLG	OPS	vL	vR	bb%	ct%	Eye	G	L	F	h%	HctX	PX	xPX	hr/f	Spd	SBO	SB%	#Wk	DOM	DIS	RC/G	RAR	BPV	BPX	R$
12																																			
13	aa	444	52	11	41	9	202		273	330	602			9	58	0.23				32		114			120	22%	43%				2.60		-18	-45	$3
14	a/a	442	46	9	48	9	223		286	352	639			8	66	0.26				32		111			108	15%	55%				3.17		4	11	$6
15	SF *	483	64	20	67	15	236	211	308	417	725	1456	1026	9	54	0.22	39	29	32	39	92	165	216	67%	107	20%	61%	7	43%	43%	4.10	-9.1	0	0	$15
16	SF *	321	55	15	40	1	224	227	308	414	722	370	895	11	61	0.31	52	20	28	32	86	134	76	22%	121	4%	25%	16	25%	69%	4.09	-5.2	10	29	$5
1st Half		222	34	13	33	1	243	244	323	459	782	448	1040	11	63	0.32	53	21	26	32	106	145	98	33%	107	5%	25%	8	38%	50%	4.81	2.4	24	69	$8
2nd Half		99	21	2	7	0	183	187	275	313	588	182	593	11	55	0.28	52	16	32	31	45	105	26	0%	134	0%	0%	8	13%	88%	2.69	-5.6	-32	-91	-$4
17	Proj	158	24	4	18	2	216	199	327	343	670	331	792	10	58	0.26	52	18	30	34	69	101	55	13%	112	10%	54%				3.18	-7.4	-29	-84	$0

Parra,Gerardo

Age: 30 **Bats:** L **Pos:** LF
Ht: 5' 11" **Wt:** 195

Health	B	LIMA Plan	B
PT/Exp	B	Rand Var	+3
Consist	D	MM	2243

7-39-.253 with 6 SB in 368 AB at COL. No (positive) Coors effect here! Lost 8 weeks to ankle sprain; came back as a bench OF/1B. Plate impatience closed his Eye; 2nd half ct% and lingering ankle aches (likely) to blame for BA/xBA freefall. Pedestrian HctX, xPX, Spd should produce more, but bb%, GB dampen the results.

Yr	Tm	AB	R	HR	RBI	SB	BA	xBA	OBP	SLG	OPS	vL	vR	bb%	ct%	Eye	G	L	F	h%	HctX	PX	xPX	hr/f	Spd	SBO	SB%	#Wk	DOM	DIS	RC/G	RAR	BPV	BPX	R$
12	ARI	385	58	7	36	15	273	267	335	392	727	631	754	8	80	0.43	53	22	24	33	108	83	101	9%	101	22%	63%	27	30%	33%	4.34	-4.4	35	88	$13
13	ARI	601	79	10	48	10	268	283	323	403	726	501	820	7	83	0.48	55	20	25	31	112	97	97	8%	100	13%	50%	27	52%	19%	4.30	4.3	58	145	$16
14	2 NL	529	64	9	40	9	261	266	308	369	677	554	704	6	81	0.32	54	22	24	31	96	76	85	9%	106	12%	56%	28	25%	43%	3.72	-0.9	31	84	$13
15	2 TM	547	83	14	51	14	291	287	328	452	780	658	809	5	83	0.30	47	24	29	33	109	104	98	11%	116	14%	78%	27	44%	22%	5.27	8.5	62	168	$23
16	COL *	394	47	7	41	6	247	271	265	384	648	634	684	2	79	0.12	55	19	26	29	103	90	100	9%	95	14%	60%	19	53%	37%	3.34	-15.2	25	71	$6
1st Half		243	32	5	27	6	263	296	274	424	698	768	673	2	84	0.10	58	18	24	30	104	101	94	10%	95	24%	60%	11	64%	18%	3.84	-4.4	49	140	$11
2nd Half		151	15	2	14	0	220	230	248	319	567	382	703	4	73	0.14	48	22	30	29	102	70	113	7%	96	0%	0%	8	38%	63%	2.58	-8.6	-14	-40	-$2
17	Proj	401	51	10	37	7	262	273	298	409	707	573	747	4	80	0.23	51	21	27	31	104	92	100	11%	101	12%	65%				4.08	-4.4	33	93	$12

Paulsen,Benjamin

Age: 29 **Bats:** L **Pos:** 1B
Ht: 6' 4" **Wt:** 205

Health	A	LIMA Plan	D
PT/Exp	C	Rand Var	+4
Consist	B	MM	3111

1-11-.217 in 92 AB at COL. Curious struggles against RHP stripped away previous plus skills, though 2-year erosion of power, HctX point to a larger (flukish?) cause. Whatever it is, the timing couldn't have been worse, as COL dropped him from 40-man roster. Sub-.700 OPS away from Coors makes him unworthy of speculation.

Yr	Tm	AB	R	HR	RBI	SB	BA	xBA	OBP	SLG	OPS	vL	vR	bb%	ct%	Eye	G	L	F	h%	HctX	PX	xPX	hr/f	Spd	SBO	SB%	#Wk	DOM	DIS	RC/G	RAR	BPV	BPX	R$
12	aa	436	47	13	43	1	240		288	382	670			6	73	0.25				30		97			102	5%	15%				3.53		14	35	$5
13	aaa	459	36	12	45	1	234		267	397	663			4	69	0.14				32		127			117	4%	32%				3.44		22	55	$4
14	COL *	498	52	17	54	2	246	255	296	428	725	1417	803	7	68	0.22	43	25	32	33	127	149	156	29%	102	8%	28%	10	50%	30%	4.08	-1.5	37	100	$10
15	COL *	450	53	13	58	2	257	249	306	425	731	554	815	7	71	0.25	45	22	33	33	99	121	110	14%	105	3%	44%	21	33%	33%	4.40	-12.7	28	76	$10
16	COL *	380	37	5	37	1	226	223	266	342	608	875	533	5	74	0.21	52	14	34	29	55	78	53	5%	123	1%	100%	9	22%	78%	3.01	-26.7	7	20	$0
1st Half		226	20	2	23	1	223	233	271	332	603	1750	611	6	77	0.28	54	15	31	28	71	73	64	7%	124	1%	100%	6	33%	67%	2.97	-14.7	17	49	$0
2nd Half		154	17	4	14	0	232	201	259	357	617	0	310	4	70	0.12	47	12	41	31	17	86	20	0%	109	0%	0%	3	0%	100%	3.08	-9.4	-10	-29	$1
17	Proj	198	21	5	21	1	240	234	284	391	675	702	672	6	71	0.21	47	18	35	31	73	101	81	11%	110	3%	44%				3.65	-8.6	3	8	$3

Pearce,Steve

Age: 34 **Bats:** R **Pos:** 1B
Ht: 5' 11" **Wt:** 205

Health	D	LIMA Plan	C+
PT/Exp	D	Rand Var	-3
Consist	F	MM	4033

Underappreciated: Consistent history of triple-digit HctX/PX/xPX; double-digit bb% and hr/f; and single-digit draft-day acquisition cost. Perfect for your last roster spot or first injury sub. Keep tabs on health (Sept forearm surgery), know the ABs are only part-time, but a useful piece when expectations are kept in check.

Yr	Tm	AB	R	HR	RBI	SB	BA	xBA	OBP	SLG	OPS	vL	vR	bb%	ct%	Eye	G	L	F	h%	HctX	PX	xPX	hr/f	Spd	SBO	SB%	#Wk	DOM	DIS	RC/G	RAR	BPV	BPX	R$
12	3 TM *	351	42	13	47	3	247	240	325	420	745	760	657	10	77	0.49	38	17	45	29	127	117	128	7%	76	7%	49%	15	40%	40%	4.51	-0.6	45	113	$7
13	BAL	119	14	4	13	1	261	243	362	420	782	802	749	11	79	0.60	39	17	44	30	120	112	129	10%	75	3%	100%	19	47%	37%	5.03	3.6	53	133	$1
14	BAL	338	51	21	49	5	293	294	373	556	930	1109	856	11	78	0.53	35	19	46	32	116	188	130	18%	70	5%	100%	26	62%	35%	7.48	35.5	105	284	$18
15	BAL	294	42	15	40	1	218	252	289	422	711	623	765	7	77	0.33	34	20	46	23	101	129	132	14%	77	3%	50%	22	50%	36%	3.73	-6.0	49	132	$4
16	2 AL	264	35	13	35	0	288	266	374	492	867	1022	798	11	80	0.63	43	19	38	32	112	117	118	16%	107	4%	0%	21	48%	38%	6.23	14.6	69	197	$8
1st Half		174	23	9	25	0	322	276	393	540	933	1239	818	10	82	0.63	43	19	38	35	116	121	124	16%	114	4%	0%	12	50%	33%	7.62	14.9	80	229	$12
2nd Half		90	12	4	10	0	222	247	340	400	740	719	751	13	76	0.64	44	19	37	25	104	108	104	16%	81	4%	0%	9	44%	44%	4.10	-1.0	42	120	$0
17	Proj	314	43	15	41	1	268	259	353	470	823	852	807	10	78	0.52	39	19	42	30	109	120	121	15%	88	4%	36%				5.50	3.6	43	122	$11

Pederson,Joc

Age: 25 **Bats:** L **Pos:** CF
Ht: 6' 1" **Wt:** 220

Health	A	LIMA Plan	B
PT/Exp	B	Rand Var	0
Consist	B	MM	5125

What we think we know after his second full MLB season: elite power and bb%; infrequent contact. What we don't know: real degree of platoon splits, where his hit rate will stabilize, and thus BA expecations. While we're in information-gathering mode, he's a very good one-trick pony (or two-trick, in OBP leagues).

Yr	Tm	AB	R	HR	RBI	SB	BA	xBA	OBP	SLG	OPS	vL	vR	bb%	ct%	Eye	G	L	F	h%	HctX	PX	xPX	hr/f	Spd	SBO	SB%	#Wk	DOM	DIS	RC/G	RAR	BPV	BPX	R$
12																																			
13	aa	439	73	20	52	28	260		350	456	806			12	72	0.49				32		142			105	28%	76%				5.48		59	148	$24
14	LA *	473	68	22	49	19	239	217	335	416	751	167	561	13	61	0.37	35	24	41	34	73	148	103	0%	91	23%	56%	5	20%	80%	4.34	7.5	17	46	$18
15	LA	480	67	26	54	4	210	225	346	417	763	691	784	16	65	0.54	42	16	42	26	104	152	147	20%	80	7%	36%	27	41%	37%	4.34	0.5	38	103	$7
16	LA	406	64	25	68	6	246	261	352	495	847	469	918	13	68	0.48	40	21	40	30	107	169	134	23%	73	7%	75%	25	56%	36%	5.81	14.0	58	166	$13
1st Half		229	34	13	33	4	236	264	328	476	804	541	838	12	71	0.47	39	19	41	27	99	159	115	20%	76	11%	67%	13	62%	31%	5.11	4.2	61	174	$13
2nd Half		177	30	12	35	2	260	257	380	520	900	419	1032	15	64	0.50	40	22	38	34	117	183	161	29%	75	4%	100%	12	50%	42%	6.76	11.6	57	163	$14
17	Proj	421	65	26	61	9	240	246	353	475	828	568	893	14	66	0.48	41	19	40	30	107	161	144	23%	77	12%	64%				5.40	11.4	44	126	$16

Pedroia,Dustin

Age: 33 **Bats:** R **Pos:** 2B
Ht: 5' 9" **Wt:** 180

Health	C	LIMA Plan	B+
PT/Exp	A	Rand Var	-3
Consist	B	MM	1255

What keeps this Energizer bunny going? HctX and LD% recovery fueled BA triumph over xBA, while ever-ready bb% ensured OBP kept pace to deliver a drumbeat of runs atop MLB's most prolific offense. Solid plate approach and consistent contact show no signs of age, so expect him to keep going in 2017.

Yr	Tm	AB	R	HR	RBI	SB	BA	xBA	OBP	SLG	OPS	vL	vR	bb%	ct%	Eye	G	L	F	h%	HctX	PX	xPX	hr/f	Spd	SBO	SB%	#Wk	DOM	DIS	RC/G	RAR	BPV	BPX	R$
12	BOS	563	81	15	65	20	290	288	347	449	797	848	775	8	89	0.80	46	20	35	30	123	98	108	9%	99	17%	77%	26	62%	12%	5.56	22.2	83	208	$24
13	BOS	641	91	9	84	17	301	284	372	415	787	937	722	10	88	0.97	50	22	28	33	116	80	82	6%	114	10%	77%	26	62%	27%	5.67	34.4	74	185	$29
14	BOS	551	72	7	53	6	278	276	337	376	712	727	707	8	86	0.68	48	24	28	31	112	75	89	5%	87	7%	50%	24	46%	13%	4.37	15.4	51	138	$16
15	BOS	381	46	12	42	2	291	270	356	441	797	834	785	9	87	0.75	50	18	32	31	97	90	92	11%	111	3%	50%	19	58%	16%	5.56	13.7	72	195	$12
16	BOS	633	105	15	74	7	318	295	376	449	825	812	827	9	88	0.84	49	24	27	34	115	75	82	10%	99	5%	64%	27	52%	4%	6.26	26.1	63	180	$28
1st Half		324	51	7	32	5	302	290	366	435	801	594	841	9	86	0.73	48	24	28	33	107	80	75	9%	108	6%	83%	14	57%	7%	5.88	9.6	61	174	$26
2nd Half		309	54	8	42	2	333	299	386	463	849	985	812	8	91	1.00	50	24	26	35	123	71	90	11%	86	5%	40%	13	46%	0%	6.68	15.4	65	186	$31
17	Proj	608	90	14	70	6	305	285	364	435	798	829	789	9	88	0.79	49	22	29	33	111	75	88	9%	102	5%	56%				5.71	15.3	50	143	$26

Pence,Hunter

Age: 34 **Bats:** R **Pos:** RF
Ht: 6' 4" **Wt:** 210

Health	F	LIMA Plan	B
PT/Exp	C	Rand Var	-4
Consist	A	MM	3235

13-57-.289 in 395 AB at SF. Effects of June-July hamstring strain were evident in 2nd half LD, HctX, xPX. Hit rate spike pushed BA beyond xBA, but gradual ct% decline threatens BA's edge. Average contact, power, speed combo still generates positive BPX, but age and health ask "for how long?"

Yr	Tm	AB	R	HR	RBI	SB	BA	xBA	OBP	SLG	OPS	vL	vR	bb%	ct%	Eye	G	L	F	h%	HctX	PX	xPX	hr/f	Spd	SBO	SB%	#Wk	DOM	DIS	RC/G	RAR	BPV	BPX	R$
12	2 NL	617	87	24	104	5	253	254	319	425	743	731	748	8	76	0.39	51	17	32	29	101	110	96	16%	118	4%	71%	27	44%	37%	4.55	-10.8	48	120	$18
13	SF	629	91	27	99	22	283	280	339	483	822	976	769	8	82	0.45	47	17	36	31	116	128	112	15%	118	15%	88%	27	48%	15%	5.92	23.2	82	205	$34
14	SF	650	106	20	74	13	277	264	332	445	777	770	779	7	80	0.40	52	14	34	32	97	112	88	11%	164	11%	68%	27	59%	26%	5.11	18.8	76	205	$27
15	SF	207	30	9	40	4	275	279	327	478	806	570	861	7	77	0.33	54	17	29	32	119	135	118	20%	90	10%	80%	11	73%	9%	5.52	3.9	59	159	$8
16	SF *	419	62	15	62	1	290	258	356	460	816	821	802	9	76	0.43	55	17	28	35	93	108	79	15%	104	2%	50%	20	40%	35%	5.85	13.6	44	126	$15
1st Half		181	27	7	36	0	298	274	375	486	861	895	844	11	78	0.59	54	19	27	35	105	114	95	18%	103	0%	0%	9	44%	22%	6.67	9.8	60	171	$14
2nd Half		238	35	8	26	1	284	244	339	440	779	748	768	8	75	0.33	55	15	30	35	83	103	64	13%	105	3%	50%	11	36%	45%	5.25	3.7	30	86	$15
17	Proj	449	67	16	69	3	283	263	342	458	800	769	811	8	77	0.40	54	16	30	33	101	108	91	16%	111	4%	61%				5.52	10.5	37	106	$18

MATT DODGE

Peralta,David

Age: 29	Bats: L	Pos: RF	Health	D	LIMA Plan	B+
Ht: 6' 2"	Wt: 210		PT/Exp	C	Rand Var	+4
			Consist	F	MM	3355

4-15-.251 with 2 SB in 171 AB at ARI. A lost season. Three DL trips; two were right wrist injuries that led to August surgery. Recovery from hand injuries can take time and affect power, so a repeat of 2015's elevated h% and hr/f is now even less likely. March results could give a clue into how quickly he rebounds.

Yr Tm	AB	R	HR	RBI	SB	BA	xBA	OBP	SLG	OPS	vL	vR	bb%	ct%	Eye	G	L	F	h%	HctX	PX	xPX	hr/f	Spd	SBO	SB%	#Wk	DOM	DIS	RC/G	RAR	BPV	BPX	R$
12																																		
13																																		
14 ARI *	531	64	13	69	7	271	282	309	430	739	510	848	5	84	0.34	48	21	31	30	110	104	90	10%	109	8%	71%	17	59%	18%	4.61	7.8	64	173	$17
15 ARI	462	61	17	78	9	312	286	371	522	893	686	936	9	77	0.41	52	21	27	38	119	133	115	18%	121	10%	69%	26	46%	15%	7.08	28.1	69	186	$24
16 ARI *	206	28	4	17	2	243	269	281	414	695	717	731	5	76	0.22	51	21	28	30	107	107	99	11%	115	8%	61%	10	30%	30%	3.86	-5.0	36	103	$2
1st Half	153	22	4	16	2	253	263	296	430	725	664	778	6	73	0.22	51	23	26	32	99	108	91	14%	120	6%	100%	8	25%	38%	4.41	-1.3	26	74	$4
2nd Half	53	5	0	1	0	215	268	235	369	603	1333	476	3	85	0.18	50	10	40	25	139	105	138	0%	102	22%	0%	2	50%	0%	2.46	-3.8	63	180	-$5
17 Proj	428	52	12	45	6	277	289	324	471	796	686	827	6	79	0.31	50	22	28	33	108	117	97	12%	108	9%	66%				5.24	6.6	60	171	$13

Peralta,Jhonny

Age: 35	Bats: R	Pos: 3B	Health	D	LIMA Plan	C+
Ht: 6' 1"	Wt: 195		PT/Exp	B	Rand Var	+2
			Consist	A	MM	2033

Left thumb surgery delayed season start to June and effectiveness to August, although struggled vL all season. Contact rate still strong, but 2nd half drops in HctX and xPX could indicate the start of age-related decline. Regaining in-season SS eligibility would be an added bonus, but still a competent contributor at the corner.

Yr Tm	AB	R	HR	RBI	SB	BA	xBA	OBP	SLG	OPS	vL	vR	bb%	ct%	Eye	G	L	F	h%	HctX	PX	xPX	hr/f	Spd	SBO	SB%	#Wk	DOM	DIS	RC/G	RAR	BPV	BPX	R$
12 DET	531	58	13	63	1	239	257	305	384	689	692	688	8	80	0.47	41	22	37	28	107	98	124	8%	86	2%	33%	27	56%	33%	3.85	-4.0	44	110	$7
13 DET	409	50	11	55	3	303	263	358	457	815	964	750	8	76	0.36	39	25	36	38	111	119	136	10%	81	5%	50%	21	57%	24%	5.87	26.7	41	103	$16
14 STL	560	61	21	75	3	263	278	336	443	779	879	751	9	80	0.52	39	23	38	30	117	131	132	12%	73	3%	60%	26	65%	12%	5.04	28.4	68	184	$17
15 STL	579	64	17	71	1	275	265	334	411	745	737	748	8	81	0.45	44	25	31	31	118	87	107	11%	83	3%	20%	27	33%	22%	4.68	15.1	36	97	$16
16 STL	289	37	8	29	0	260	267	307	408	715	541	778	6	81	0.36	41	24	35	30	105	92	103	10%	93	0%	0%	17	29%	12%	4.32	-2.4	39	111	$4
1st Half	88	9	3	11	0	239	275	277	409	686	345	821	5	82	0.31	34	25	41	26	114	104	130	10%	97	0%	0%	5	40%	0%	3.83	-1.7	52	149	$0
2nd Half	201	28	5	18	0	269	265	320	408	728	635	760	7	80	0.38	44	24	33	31	102	86	91	9%	92	0%	0%	12	25%	17%	4.54	0.5	33	94	$6
17 Proj	389	46	11	45	1	263	267	318	414	733	651	762	7	80	0.40	41	24	35	30	111	93	113	10%	87	2%	38%				4.51	-4.3	26	75	$10

Peraza,Jose

Age: 23	Bats: R	Pos: SS	Health	A	LIMA Plan	B
Ht: 6' 0"	Wt: 165		PT/Exp	D	Rand Var	-3
			Consist	C	MM	0545

3-25-.324 with 21 SB in 241 AB at CIN. Rode AAA shuttle until mid Aug, then .871 OPS in full-time play for rest of year. Needs continued HctX growth to unlock further BA potential in LD swing, and better SB efficiency to justify ever-green light. Combined OF eligibility in some leagues a plus. Invest for SB, and hope BA follows.

Yr Tm	AB	R	HR	RBI	SB	BA	xBA	OBP	SLG	OPS	vL	vR	bb%	ct%	Eye	G	L	F	h%	HctX	PX	xPX	hr/f	Spd	SBO	SB%	#Wk	DOM	DIS	RC/G	RAR	BPV	BPX	R$
12																																		
13																																		
14 aa	185	30	1	14	21	315		336	391	727			3	91	0.35				34		49			130	55%	71%				4.61		50	135	$13
15 LA *	503	54	3	35	30	255	231	276	324	599	779	125	3	90	0.28	37	21	42	28	37	40	37	0%	144	31%	79%	5	40%	20%	3.11	-9.7	41	111	$16
16 CIN *	529	62	5	44	30	294	269	328	382	710	793	754	5	85	0.33	43	28	29	34	73	54	55	5%	157	32%	63%	18	28%	33%	4.23	-6.0	40	114	$24
1st Half	284	34	1	15	15	258	258	296	316	612	429	555	5	84	0.33	48	26	26	31	52	36	46	0%	157	30%	67%	6	0%	67%	3.11	-11.6	23	66	$19
2nd Half	245	28	4	29	15	335	285	366	458	823	922	820	5	86	0.33	42	28	30	38	81	73	58	6%	144	34%	60%	12	42%	17%	5.80	9.1	55	157	$30
17 Proj	538	65	5	44	35	279	276	317	365	682	702	676	4	87	0.33	44	27	28	31	69	49	53	4%	169	36%	70%				3.81	-10.3	39	112	$26

Perez,Carlos

Age: 26	Bats: R	Pos: CA	Health	A	LIMA Plan	D
Ht: 6' 0"	Wt: 195		PT/Exp	D	Rand Var	+2
			Consist	B	MM	1113

5-31-.209 in 268 AB at LAA. If you knew to start him on May 22, July 2, July 26 and Oct 2, congratulations! (14-for-18, three HR, five 2B, 14 RBI.) Otherwise, h% drove BA far below Mendoza line (.176) with a .276 SLG. Glimmers of hope (ct%, 1H FB) could yet mold him into a 2018 target, but watch from afar in 2017.

Yr Tm	AB	R	HR	RBI	SB	BA	xBA	OBP	SLG	OPS	vL	vR	bb%	ct%	Eye	G	L	F	h%	HctX	PX	xPX	hr/f	Spd	SBO	SB%	#Wk	DOM	DIS	RC/G	RAR	BPV	BPX	R$
12																																		
13 a/a	317	27	2	29	1	236		287	308	595			7	82	0.39				28		58			83	2%	41%				2.92		14	35	$0
14 aaa	301	23	4	24	2	213		263	311	574			6	79	0.32				26		74			96	3%	100%				2.68		18	49	-$1
15 LAA *	332	27	5	29	3	258	243	307	364	671	461	713	7	83	0.41	42	20	38	30	75	75	63	5%	93	3%	100%	23	26%	52%	3.89	1.5	33	89	$4
16 LAA *	307	31	7	38	1	218	239	249	349	598	547	573	4	81	0.22	41	17	42	25	85	84	65	5%	78	6%	29%	25	32%	40%	2.74	-10.7	25	71	$1
1st Half	178	16	4	22	1	208	239	239	337	576	616	568	4	81	0.24	37	19	44	24	83	84	76	6%	80	3%	100%	14	43%	43%	2.65	-8.2	25	71	$0
2nd Half	129	15	3	16	0	233	240	260	365	625	410	584	4	81	0.20	49	13	37	27	89	85	42	4%	86	10%	0%	11	18%	36%	2.86	-5.1	29	83	$1
17 Proj	298	28	5	31	1	232	233	273	336	610	492	642	5	81	0.30	43	17	39	27	82	70	59	5%	89	5%	49%				2.99	-10.4	8	22	$3

Perez,Hernan

Age: 26	Bats: R	Pos: 3B RF	Health	A	LIMA Plan	C+
Ht: 6' 0"	Wt: 160		PT/Exp	C	Rand Var	-4
			Consist	C	MM	2525

13-56-.272 with 34 SB in 404 AB at MIL. Breakout season could be hard to top. Streaky power (10 HR in Jul-Aug) driven by 19% hr/f. Speed turned some GB to hits, but league average ct%, low bb%, xBA all say BA/OBP should drop. Which is a shame, since games played at seven positions kept him in lineup collecting PAs.

Yr Tm	AB	R	HR	RBI	SB	BA	xBA	OBP	SLG	OPS	vL	vR	bb%	ct%	Eye	G	L	F	h%	HctX	PX	xPX	hr/f	Spd	SBO	SB%	#Wk	DOM	DIS	RC/G	RAR	BPV	BPX	R$
12 DET	2	1	0	0	0	500	277	500	500	1000	0	2000	0	100	0.00	100	0	0	50	0	0	-11	0%	125	0%	0%	2	0%	0%	12.75	0.3	39	98	-$2
13 DET *	495	53	3	37	25	266	254	289	356	646	501	388	3	85	0.22	47	20	33	31	66	67	54	0%	138	29%	77%	12	8%	67%	3.59	-1.0	45	113	$17
14 DET *	552	56	5	42	17	258	207	297	363	659	0	833	5	87	0.43	50	0	50	29	189	72	-15	0%	151	18%	72%	4	25%	75%	3.66	4.3	65	176	$14
15 2 TM	263	14	1	21	5	243	233	257	327	584	635	552	2	78	0.08	43	22	34	31	102	66	98	1%	112	12%	83%	26	27%	54%	2.87	-10.1	2	5	$1
16 MIL *	466	57	14	64	35	274	249	304	424	728	787	699	4	77	0.19	43	20	36	33	100	91	97	12%	139	39%	84%	24	42%	29%	4.64	-3.0	34	97	$26
1st Half	185	17	4	25	11	274	244	301	392	692	660	712	4	79	0.18	43	22	35	33	105	71	104	9%	148	32%	79%	11	36%	36%	4.17	-3.4	27	77	$15
2nd Half	281	40	10	39	24	274	254	305	445	750	887	695	4	76	0.19	44	20	37	33	97	105	94	13%	129	44%	86%	13	46%	23%	4.96	1.3	38	109	$33
17 Proj	473	47	11	51	25	264	251	288	399	687	732	900	4	79	0.17	44	21	35	32	96	83	91	8%	136	29%	81%				4.05	-11.6	28	81	$20

Perez,Roberto

Age: 28	Bats: R	Pos: CA	Health	C	LIMA Plan	D
Ht: 6' 0"	Wt: 220		PT/Exp	F	Rand Var	+5
			Consist	C	MM	3101

Defense-first backup showed enouraging ct% gain, after April concussion and broken thumb wiped out first half. Power was slow to come back, but Sept G/L/F profile (44%/22%/34%), with 140 xPX, lends hope for return to 2014-15 levels. Power history worth $1 at the draft; additional playing time could make it profitable.

Yr Tm	AB	R	HR	RBI	SB	BA	xBA	OBP	SLG	OPS	vL	vR	bb%	ct%	Eye	G	L	F	h%	HctX	PX	xPX	hr/f	Spd	SBO	SB%	#Wk	DOM	DIS	RC/G	RAR	BPV	BPX	R$
12 aa	283	28	1	28	0	192		298	265	563			13	73	0.57				26		63			92	1%	0%				2.45		0	0	-$4
13 a/a	280	20	1	26	1	166		271	234	505			13	65	0.41				25		72			80	4%	25%				1.88		-31	-78	-$7
14 CLE *	259	31	7	36	1	257	217	324	397	721	397	786	9	66	0.29	45	17	38	36	85	125	123	5%	79	1%	100%	13	31%	62%	4.42	8.3	7	19	$5
15 CLE	184	30	7	21	0	228	237	348	402	751	841	715	15	65	0.52	53	20	27	31	89	134	121	21%	92	0%	0%	26	38%	50%	4.59	4.7	28	76	$1
16 CLE	153	14	3	17	0	183	213	285	294	579	683	528	13	71	0.52	54	15	31	24	72	75	94	9%	84	0%	0%	15	33%	53%	2.66	-5.8	-1	-3	-$3
1st Half	8	2	0	1	0	0	0	400	0	400	333	417	43	75	3.00	43	14	43	0	87	0	190	0%	95	0%	0%	3	67%	33%	0.00	-1.3	16	46	-$4
2nd Half	145	12	3	16	0	193	215	274	310	585	697	530	10	71	0.40	54	16	30	25	71	79	87	10%	81	0%	0%	12	25%	58%	2.72	-6.5	-5	-14	-$3
17 Proj	155	17	5	18	0	218	223	308	365	673	629	691	12	68	0.41	50	17	32	29	81	104	110	14%	81	1%	51%				3.65	-2.3	-5	-15	$2

Perez,Salvador

Age: 27	Bats: R	Pos: CA	Health	A	LIMA Plan	B+
Ht: 6' 3"	Wt: 175		PT/Exp	A	Rand Var	0
			Consist	A	MM	3335

Debuted a new plate approach heavy on FB, which kept 20 HR status at the expense of ct% and BA. In 2H, LD turned to GB, h% collapsed, and xBA cried even more. Nagging injuries (wrist, knee, hamstring) may have contributed, but still caught 128 G and avoided the DL. With full health, should return to double-digit value.

Yr Tm	AB	R	HR	RBI	SB	BA	xBA	OBP	SLG	OPS	vL	vR	bb%	ct%	Eye	G	L	F	h%	HctX	PX	xPX	hr/f	Spd	SBO	SB%	#Wk	DOM	DIS	RC/G	RAR	BPV	BPX	R$
12 KC *	339	46	11	44	0	301	291	327	450	778	1021	711	4	90	0.41	44	24	32	31	118	87	116	13%	106	0%	0%	16	75%	13%	5.37	11.5	73	183	$12
13 KC	496	48	13	79	0	292	272	323	433	757	867	714	4	87	0.33	47	21	33	31	109	88	96	9%	109	0%	0%	25	52%	20%	5.02	17.8	62	155	$17
14 KC	578	57	17	70	1	260	265	289	403	692	632	710	4	85	0.26	39	21	40	28	115	95	106	9%	97	1%	100%	27	56%	15%	3.99	11.1	56	151	$14
15 KC	531	52	21	70	1	260	268	280	426	706	560	775	2	85	0.16	42	21	37	27	88	99	87	12%	89	1%	100%	27	56%	22%	4.08	5.2	51	138	$13
16 KC	514	57	22	64	0	247	246	288	438	725	763	710	4	77	0.18	35	18	47	28	105	116	107	12%	91	0%	0%	27	48%	26%	4.12	3.8	38	109	$9
1st Half	263	29	12	37	0	281	253	315	490	806	687	839	4	75	0.16	29	22	49	34	107	130	124	13%	110	0%	0%	14	57%	21%	5.40	9.3	45	129	$14
2nd Half	251	28	10	27	0	211	235	258	382	641	809	542	4	79	0.21	40	15	46	23	104	102	90	11%	81	0%	0%	13	38%	31%	3.02	-8.7	33	94	$4
17 Proj	540	57	22	68	0	257	258	289	437	727	735	723	4	81	0.19	39	19	42	28	103	105	100	12%	93	0%	100%				4.25	1.8	27	78	$14

MATT DODGE

Peterson,Jace

Age: 27 Bats: L Pos: 2B | Ht: 6' 0" Wt: 205
Health A | PT/Exp C | Consist A | LIMA Plan D+ | Rand Var +1 | MM 1223

7-29-.254 in 350 AB at ATL. Dispatched to AAA after horrible April, he blistered the ball upon June return, but then quickly leveled off. Did take a step up in plate skills, led by that 2nd half walk rate. Yet tendency to pile up the CS wastes his OBP gains, and mostly punchless bat severely dampens his outlook. Nah.

Yr	Tm	AB	R	HR	RBI	SB	BA	xBA	OBP	SLG	OPS	vL	vR	bb%	ct%	Eye	G	L	F	h%	HctX	PX	xPX	hr/f	Spd	SBO	SB%	#Wk	DOM	DIS	RC/G	RAR	BPV	BPX	R$
12																																			
13																																			
14	SD *	375	40	2	32	13	227	241	298	316	614	607	168	9	76	0.42	63	14	23	29	80	73	57	0%	94	24%	55%	11	0%	82%	2.90	-5.7	11	30	$5
15	ATL	528	55	6	52	12	239	238	314	335	649	510	682	10	77	0.47	46	22	32	30	87	68	76	5%	106	15%	55%	27	22%	48%	3.35	-13.2	17	46	$8
16	ATL *	447	51	7	34	7	233	254	325	332	657	571	740	12	80	0.70	58	19	24	28	82	62	69	10%	104	10%	47%	23	30%	39%	3.43	-19.6	29	83	$4
1st Half		224	26	3	19	3	228	261	297	323	620	498	828	9	80	0.48	48	26	26	27	97	61	106	12%	111	13%	33%	10	30%	50%	2.90	-13.3	21	60	$4
2nd Half		223	25	4	15	4	238	249	350	341	691	649	696	15	81	0.93	63	14	23	28	74	63	49	10%	98	8%	67%	13	31%	31%	3.98	-5.5	36	103	$5
17	Proj	**374**	**41**	**5**	**32**	**8**	**234**	**249**	**321**	**335**	**656**	**574**	**673**	**11**	**79**	**0.58**	**54**	**19**	**27**	**28**	**84**	**64**	**71**	**7%**	**101**	**13%**	**54%**				**3.41**	**-16.0**	**16**	**45**	**$5**

Petit,Gregorio

Age: 32 Bats: R Pos: 2B SS | Ht: 5' 10" Wt: 200
Health B | PT/Exp F | Consist C | LIMA Plan F | Rand Var -3 | MM 1111

2-17-.245 in 204 AB in LAA. Tininess, thou art everywhere: the plethora of 1s and 2s in the Eye ratio column; the nine negative RAR/BPV/BPX values; the .643 MLB career OPS; the R$ value string; the 3-year range of xBA. But the descriptive quality of his surname? Enormous.

Yr	Tm	AB	R	HR	RBI	SB	BA	xBA	OBP	SLG	OPS	vL	vR	bb%	ct%	Eye	G	L	F	h%	HctX	PX	xPX	hr/f	Spd	SBO	SB%	#Wk	DOM	DIS	RC/G	RAR	BPV	BPX	R$
12	aaa	377	35	7	31	1	201		241	306	547			5	75	0.21				25		80			81	5%	22%				2.28		0	0	-$2
13	aaa	503	33	2	37	3	205		241	261	502			5	79	0.23				25		44			95	7%	43%				1.96		-7	-18	-$4
14	HOU *	414	43	9	36	1	231	246	256	350	606	1124	551	3	77	0.14	44	22	33	28	106	93	89	8%	86	7%	11%	11	45%	45%	2.80	-4.8	17	46	$4
15	NYY *	216	21	2	16	0	179	234	213	253	466	392	563	4	79	0.21	56	19	26	22	49	58	58	0%	64	0%	0%	8	13%	88%	1.67	-18.9	-5	-14	-$5
16	LAA *	259	25	2	19	2	244	236	293	333	627	617	660	7	73	0.26	50	22	28	32	80	69	70	5%	85	5%	69%	22	14%	45%	3.29	-7.8	-9	-26	$1
1st Half		170	21	2	16	1	266	250	307	384	691	671	780	6	73	0.22	45	25	30	35	97	90	101	8%	89	3%	100%	9	33%	22%	4.14	-1.6	4	11	$4
2nd Half		89	4	0	3	1	202	200	268	236	504	584	441	8	74	0.35	56	18	26	27	58	30	29	0%	78	9%	50%	13	0%	62%	1.97	-7.1	-37	-106	-$4
17	Proj	**198**	**17**	**2**	**14**	**1**	**214**	**235**	**264**	**302**	**566**	**695**	**504**	**6**	**76**	**0.25**	**49**	**22**	**30**	**27**	**87**	**63**	**71**	**5%**	**80**	**5%**	**48%**				**2.48**	**-14.3**	**-16**	**-46**	**$0**

Pham,Thomas

Age: 29 Bats: R Pos: CF LF | Ht: 6' 1" Wt: 210
Health D | PT/Exp D | Consist C | LIMA Plan D | Rand Var -2 | MM 3313

9-17-.226 in 159 AB at STL. One AB on Opening Day, then an oblique injury kept him out until June. Upon his return, a plethora of swings/misses and basketful of HR were strange bedfellows. xPX, HctX shows he has some pop, if ct% allows him to get to it. Expect a better BA and fewer HR, but the same ol' fight for playing time.

Yr	Tm	AB	R	HR	RBI	SB	BA	xBA	OBP	SLG	OPS	vL	vR	bb%	ct%	Eye	G	L	F	h%	HctX	PX	xPX	hr/f	Spd	SBO	SB%	#Wk	DOM	DIS	RC/G	RAR	BPV	BPX	R$
12	aa	39	2	1	2	0	125		187	221	408			7	46	0.14				25		116			95	0%	0%				1.21		-79	-198	-$3
13	a/a	269	24	5	30	6	234		287	357	644			7	71	0.25				31		90			129	17%	55%				3.25		10	25	$3
14	STL *	348	43	7	30	14	259	225	309	376	685	0	0	7	72	0.26	44	20	36	34	0	91	-15	0%	129	18%	85%	4	0%	100%	4.10	2.7	14	38	$11
15	STL *	324	48	9	45	8	262	258	334	427	761	783	833	10	73	0.40	51	21	27	33	120	111	119	16%	109	9%	100%	12	42%	33%	5.09	7.3	34	92	$11
16	STL *	283	39	12	30	8	212	224	299	379	678	734	784	11	60	0.31	45	25	30	30	104	126	126	35%	99	19%	57%	18	33%	56%	3.49	-10.3	-4	-11	$4
1st Half		156	19	5	15	6	198	241	282	329	611	600	852	10	66	0.34	40	35	25	27	76	90	101	40%	97	24%	60%	5	40%	40%	2.81	-8.6	-14	-40	$4
2nd Half		127	20	7	15	2	228	218	329	441	770	771	769	12	54	0.29	47	22	31	36	102	179	134	33%	95	12%	50%	13	31%	62%	4.45	-0.2	12	34	$5
17	Proj	**284**	**39**	**9**	**32**	**8**	**236**	**235**	**318**	**390**	**708**	**648**	**740**	**10**	**65**	**0.31**	**47**	**25**	**28**	**33**	**103**	**108**	**120**	**17%**	**116**	**15%**	**68%**				**3.98**	**-4.6**	**3**	**8**	**$8**

Phillips,Brandon

Age: 36 Bats: R Pos: 2B | Ht: 6' 0" Wt: 200
Health B | PT/Exp A | Consist B | LIMA Plan B | Rand Var -1 | MM 1245

It's what we all hope for: to age well. Sure, the bb% and SB% wrinkles are accumulating, and power isn't what it once was, but ct% and LD% remain in good health. The upshot is a plus-BA expectation, along with plenty of AB to rack up counting numbers. But at this point, don't ignore the yearly check-up.

Yr	Tm	AB	R	HR	RBI	SB	BA	xBA	OBP	SLG	OPS	vL	vR	bb%	ct%	Eye	G	L	F	h%	HctX	PX	xPX	hr/f	Spd	SBO	SB%	#Wk	DOM	DIS	RC/G	RAR	BPV	BPX	R$
12	CIN	580	86	18	77	15	281	277	321	429	750	741	754	5	86	0.35	47	21	32	30	99	90	79	11%	88	12%	88%	27	52%	19%	4.87	8.5	55	138	$23
13	CIN	606	80	18	103	5	261	258	310	396	706	746	689	6	84	0.40	46	19	34	29	99	85	92	10%	91	5%	63%	26	58%	23%	4.13	8.2	45	113	$19
14	CIN	462	44	8	51	2	266	258	306	372	678	594	704	5	84	0.31	44	22	34	30	104	79	79	6%	69	4%	40%	22	32%	32%	3.81	5.5	31	84	$10
15	CIN	588	69	12	70	23	294	273	328	395	723	710	727	4	88	0.40	45	25	30	32	94	58	66	8%	93	16%	88%	27	33%	37%	4.78	10.0	39	105	$27
16	CIN	550	74	11	64	14	291	278	320	416	736	654	761	3	88	0.26	46	21	32	32	95	75	66	7%	86	17%	64%	26	38%	23%	4.54	-5.1	45	129	$21
1st Half		298	38	6	30	4	252	263	292	369	661	716	639	4	86	0.32	47	19	34	27	95	69	75	7%	86	15%	40%	14	21%	43%	3.29	-13.5	36	103	$14
2nd Half		252	36	5	34	10	337	296	354	472	826	533	888	2	89	0.19	45	24	31	36	95	82	57	7%	90	18%	83%	12	58%	0%	6.43	10.8	56	160	$29
17	Proj	**539**	**65**	**11**	**62**	**12**	**288**	**276**	**320**	**407**	**727**	**652**	**750**	**4**	**87**	**0.30**	**45**	**23**	**32**	**31**	**97**	**70**	**69**	**7%**	**86**	**12%**	**76%**				**4.59**	**-3.2**	**40**	**114**	**$22**

Pillar,Kevin

Age: 28 Bats: R Pos: CF | Ht: 6' 0" Wt: 200
Health A | PT/Exp B | Consist A | LIMA Plan B+ | Rand Var 0 | MM 1335

Call it Kevin Kiermaier Disease: When highlight-reel defense lures you into assuming equal talent with the bat. The offensive game is more "meh" than "Wow!", though 2nd half OBP, LD% provide a glimmer. Prognosis: A breadth of skills that relies on AB total to drive value. Without a standout tool, likely to become chronic.

Yr	Tm	AB	R	HR	RBI	SB	BA	xBA	OBP	SLG	OPS	vL	vR	bb%	ct%	Eye	G	L	F	h%	HctX	PX	xPX	hr/f	Spd	SBO	SB%	#Wk	DOM	DIS	RC/G	RAR	BPV	BPX	R$
12																																			
13	TOR *	607	67	10	56	17	259	237	291	391	682	680	534	4	82	0.25	36	17	47	30	59	96	55	9%	107	26%	52%	8	25%	50%	3.60	-11.6	47	118	$17
14	TOR *	521	64	11	54	22	285	285	312	445	757	783	631	4	84	0.24	51	16	33	32	98	122	82	7%	100	29%	72%	12	17%	42%	4.82	13.9	72	195	$23
15	TOR	586	76	12	56	25	278	261	314	399	713	684	723	5	85	0.33	41	22	37	31	92	78	72	7%	107	20%	86%	27	33%	19%	4.51	0.0	48	130	$24
16	TOR	548	59	7	53	14	266	259	303	376	679	709	668	4	84	0.27	46	20	34	31	92	72	73	5%	99	16%	70%	25	32%	28%	3.83	-8.5	32	91	$14
1st Half		322	34	7	33	7	255	257	285	394	679	691	674	3	82	0.16	46	17	36	29	95	86	89	7%	116	16%	70%	14	29%	29%	3.65	-8.2	40	114	$15
2nd Half		226	25	0	20	7	283	263	328	350	677	746	660	6	85	0.45	45	25	31	33	88	52	51	0%	76	16%	70%	11	36%	27%	4.04	-3.1	20	57	$12
17	Proj	**568**	**66**	**8**	**54**	**16**	**269**	**262**	**306**	**386**	**692**	**731**	**900**	**5**	**84**	**0.30**	**44**	**20**	**35**	**31**	**89**	**76**	**69**	**5%**	**98**	**17%**	**72%**				**4.02**	**-8.1**	**38**	**110**	**$19**

Pinder,Chad

Age: 25 Bats: R Pos: 2B | Ht: 6' 2" Wt: 195
Health A | PT/Exp D | Consist B | LIMA Plan D | Rand Var 0 | MM 2201

1-4-.235 in 51 AB at OAK. Has shown life in his stick as he's worked his way up the ladder, but MLB pitching exposed the holes in his swing in his first cup of coffee. Given ability to handle either MI slot, it's a bat to watch if his contact comes around. Triple-A is likely to provide another opportunity.

Yr	Tm	AB	R	HR	RBI	SB	BA	xBA	OBP	SLG	OPS	vL	vR	bb%	ct%	Eye	G	L	F	h%	HctX	PX	xPX	hr/f	Spd	SBO	SB%	#Wk	DOM	DIS	RC/G	RAR	BPV	BPX	R$
12																																			
13																																			
14																																			
15	aa	477	53	10	64	5	272		302	403	706			4	76	0.18				34		96			85	10%	48%				4.10		18	49	$13
16	OAK *	477	68	12	49	4	236	230	274	380	654	810	448	5	73	0.19	50	13	37	30	132	98	173	7%	112	6%	80%	8	38%	38%	3.48	-17.8	14	40	$6
1st Half		293	43	7	33	3	237	236	270	381	651			4	72	0.16				31		99			115	7%	70%				3.42		11	31	$8
2nd Half		184	25	5	16	2	233	232	280	380	660	810	448	6	74	0.25	50	13	37	29	135	96	173	7%	111	5%	100%	8	38%	38%	3.59	-6.7	21	60	$3
17	Proj	**167**	**21**	**3**	**19**	**2**	**250**	**224**	**281**	**370**	**651**	**811**	**460**	**5**	**74**	**0.19**	**50**	**13**	**37**	**32**	**122**	**84**	**156**	**6%**	**103**	**7%**	**64%**				**3.55**	**-6.2**	**2**	**5**	**$4**

Piscotty,Stephen

Age: 26 Bats: R Pos: RF | Ht: 6' 3" Wt: 210
Health A | PT/Exp B | Consist C | LIMA Plan B+ | Rand Var -2 | MM 3235

Solid first full season in the majors, the type that often serves as a springboard to even bigger things. But 2nd half hiccup would seem to delay that expectation—plate skills, xPX, HctX all took a small step back. Consider his first half as his current upside—but know that it's too early to pay for it.

Yr	Tm	AB	R	HR	RBI	SB	BA	xBA	OBP	SLG	OPS	vL	vR	bb%	ct%	Eye	G	L	F	h%	HctX	PX	xPX	hr/f	Spd	SBO	SB%	#Wk	DOM	DIS	RC/G	RAR	BPV	BPX	R$
12																																			
13	aa	184	13	4	18	5	259		314	371	684			7	89	0.70				27		71			85	17%	62%				3.86		54	135	$3
14	aaa	500	50	6	50	8	244		288	339	626			6	86	0.45				27		71			81	12%	58%				3.20		40	108	$8
15	STL *	553	69	15	69	6	259	264	326	428	753	887	841	9	76	0.42	45	21	34	31	127	119	136	12%	132	10%	42%	12	50%	33%	4.57	-4.7	60	162	$14
16	STL	582	86	22	85	7	273	264	343	457	800	952	748	8	77	0.38	44	20	36	32	100	114	105	13%	112	8%	58%	27	48%	19%	5.21	8.8	52	149	$20
1st Half		289	48	10	44	4	298	274	377	481	858	1126	769	10	80	0.54	45	19	35	34	104	114	118	12%	107	11%	44%	14	57%	7%	6.06	11.1	66	189	$24
2nd Half		293	38	12	41	3	249	253	308	433	742	783	727	6	74	0.26	42	21	37	30	97	114	91	15%	117	5%	100%	13	38%	31%	4.43	-2.3	37	106	$16
17	Proj	**549**	**69**	**20**	**71**	**8**	**262**	**268**	**325**	**438**	**764**	**863**	**730**	**8**	**79**	**0.40**	**44**	**21**	**35**	**30**	**111**	**107**	**116**	**13%**	**116**	**10%**	**57%**				**4.68**	**-0.2**	**43**	**124**	**$18**

BRENT HERSHEY

Plouffe,Trevor

Age: 31 Bats: R Pos: 3B		Health	D	LIMA Plan	B
Ht: 6' 1"	Wt: 195	PT/Exp	B	Rand Var	0
		Consist	A	MM	2225

Ruin Your Health Grade in 5 Easy Steps: Sprained/strained intercostal, knee, groin, rib and oblique between Apr-Sept. Good news: Rate stats didn't suffer, minus a bit of pop. Bad news: In this HR environment, he's no longer above replacement level. Even if health and power rebound, profit margins remain small.

Yr	Tm	AB	R	HR	RBI	SB	BA	xBA	OBP	SLG	OPS	vL	vR	bb%	ct%	Eye	G	L	F	h%	HctX	PX	xPX	hr/f	Spd	SBO	SB%	#Wk	DOM	DIS	RC/G	RAR	BPV	BPX	R$
12	MIN	422	56	24	55	1	235	262	301	455	756	911	691	8	78	0.40	38	18	44	25	112	136	114	17%	90	4%	25%	24	58%	33%	4.36	-2.3	67	168	$9
13	MIN	477	44	14	52	2	254	249	309	392	701	826	663	7	77	0.30	39	25	37	30	105	98	113	10%	102	3%	67%	25	44%	32%	4.05	1.4	30	75	$9
14	MIN	520	69	14	80	2	258	266	328	423	751	783	738	9	79	0.49	38	21	40	30	113	127	133	8%	100	2%	67%	24	58%	17%	4.73	16.0	68	184	$15
15	MIN	573	74	22	86	2	244	260	307	435	742	780	727	8	78	0.40	41	18	41	28	115	124	129	12%	96	2%	67%	26	58%	15%	4.46	-1.8	59	159	$13
16	MIN	319	35	12	47	1	260	256	303	420	723	781	705	6	81	0.32	42	20	38	29	109	90	99	12%	82	1%	100%	17	47%	35%	4.39	-3.7	35	100	$7
1st Half		218	23	7	27	1	252	250	283	399	682	721	669	4	81	0.19	42	20	38	28	106	84	90	10%	89	2%	100%	12	42%	42%	3.82	-6.9	26	74	$7
2nd Half		101	12	5	20	0	277	264	345	465	810	910	781	10	82	0.61	43	20	37	29	115	103	118	16%	80	0%	0%	5	60%	20%	5.72	2.4	57	163	$5
17	Proj	419	50	15	66	1	258	257	318	424	742	803	720	8	80	0.43	41	20	39	29	112	98	117	12%	88	2%	69%				4.60	-3.5	33	94	$10

Polanco,Gregory

Age: 25 Bats: L Pos: RF LF		Health	A	LIMA Plan	B+
Ht: 6' 4"	Wt: 220	PT/Exp	A	Rand Var	0
		Consist	B	MM	3345

The Health grade says "A", but his body is unlikely to concur. Played through non-DL issues with knee, shoulder, hamstring and face (thanks to a Sept wall). Yet, this is a step up for a still-young player, as legit power materialized and hard LD stroke now points to BA upside. With health ... UP: 30 HR, .280 BA.

Yr	Tm	AB	R	HR	RBI	SB	BA	xBA	OBP	SLG	OPS	vL	vR	bb%	ct%	Eye	G	L	F	h%	HctX	PX	xPX	hr/f	Spd	SBO	SB%	#Wk	DOM	DIS	RC/G	RAR	BPV	BPX	R$
12																																			
13	a/a	252	30	4	33	11	233		311	344	655			10	85	0.76				26		74			100	27%	60%				3.34		52	130	$6
14	PIT *	551	89	12	72	26	258	252	320	377	697	466	727	8	80	0.45	50	19	31	31	84	85	86	10%	101	25%	69%	17	35%	41%	4.05	-0.7	35	95	$24
15	PIT	593	83	9	52	27	256	250	320	381	701	528	747	8	80	0.45	45	20	35	31	103	87	95	6%	115	24%	73%	27	41%	22%	4.14	-12.6	42	114	$20
16	PIT	527	79	22	86	17	258	274	323	463	786	781	786	9	77	0.45	39	24	37	30	112	125	110	14%	84	18%	74%	26	58%	23%	5.13	7.1	55	157	$21
1st Half		281	48	10	47	9	295	286	373	502	875	713	927	12	76	0.57	41	27	33	36	108	136	109	14%	88	16%	64%	14	71%	14%	6.67	15.7	66	189	$27
2nd Half		246	31	12	39	8	215	261	260	419	678	943	643	6	79	0.29	37	21	42	23	117	114	111	15%	86	20%	89%	12	42%	33%	3.62	-8.1	46	131	$14
17	Proj	544	81	22	79	20	263	271	324	454	778	688	801	9	79	0.45	40	22	37	30	105	112	101	14%	93	21%	71%				5.01	5.1	60	172	$26

Polanco,Jorge

Age: 23 Bats: B Pos: SS		Health	A	LIMA Plan	B
Ht: 5' 11"	Wt: 165	PT/Exp	D	Rand Var	0
		Consist	B	MM	1335

4-27-.282 with 4 SB in 245 AB at MIN. Up for good after the Nunez trade, made solid first impression with heavy LD approach and solid contact. Triple-A MLE (most of 1st half) shows that average power could show up, too. Speed, though, is muted by poor approach. Interesting second-tier SS.

Yr	Tm	AB	R	HR	RBI	SB	BA	xBA	OBP	SLG	OPS	vL	vR	bb%	ct%	Eye	G	L	F	h%	HctX	PX	xPX	hr/f	Spd	SBO	SB%	#Wk	DOM	DIS	RC/G	RAR	BPV	BPX	R$
12																																			
13																																			
14	MIN *	152	13	1	16	6	262	252	304	335	639	1000	1262	6	79	0.30	50	25	25	33	86	59	172	0%	118	22%	64%	3	67%	33%	3.40	1.0	14	38	$3
15	MIN *	492	52	5	45	17	266	269	313	350	662	1333	476	6	84	0.43	56	22	22	31	41	56	-16	0%	115	20%	60%	2	50%	0%	3.63	-11.1	31	84	$14
16	MIN *	538	53	12	62	8	271	273	322	424	746	857	718	7	82	0.41	33	30	37	31	78	89	64	5%	115	12%	54%	16	50%	25%	4.59	4.4	48	137	$14
1st Half		234	25	6	26	4	265	278	331	449	780	523	937	9	84	0.63	42	21	38	29	100	101	59	11%	123	12%	53%	5	80%	0%	4.96	3.4	75	214	$11
2nd Half		304	28	6	36	5	275	262	314	406	720	904	693	5	79	0.28	32	32	37	33	73	79	65	5%	112	12%	54%	11	36%	36%	4.31	-1.4	27	77	$16
17	Proj	426	42	8	45	11	269	262	322	397	719	689	733	6	82	0.38	36	27	37	31	84	76	63	6%	109	17%	60%				4.19	-3.4	35	99	$14

Pollock,A.J.

Age: 29 Bats: R Pos: CF		Health	F	LIMA Plan	B+
Ht: 6' 2"	Wt: 205	PT/Exp	D	Rand Var	0
		Consist	F	MM	3545

The injury risk is real: fractured right hand in 2014; fractured elbow in 2010 and 2016; and groin strain ended his 2016 comeback in early Sept. Power/speed combo paired with plus hit tool and growing ability to take a walk fueled his monstrous 2015. But 2015 PT stands out here as a stark outlier. High risk/high reward.

Yr	Tm	AB	R	HR	RBI	SB	BA	xBA	OBP	SLG	OPS	vL	vR	bb%	ct%	Eye	G	L	F	h%	HctX	PX	xPX	hr/f	Spd	SBO	SB%	#Wk	DOM	DIS	RC/G	RAR	BPV	BPX	R$
12	ARI *	509	47	4	39	14	250	253	289	334	623	808	535	5	86	0.37	50	20	30	29	123	57	110	10%	94	20%	54%	10	40%	20%	3.07	-24.8	28	70	$8
13	ARI	443	64	8	38	12	269	262	322	409	730	811	678	7	81	0.40	48	18	34	31	126	98	112	7%	137	14%	80%	27	48%	22%	4.58	6.1	61	153	$14
14	ARI *	314	43	7	29	14	274	281	318	447	764	953	828	6	84	0.40	52	14	34	31	109	116	97	9%	169	23%	82%	15	67%	13%	5.04	11.0	93	251	$13
15	ARI	609	111	20	76	39	315	299	367	498	865	881	860	8	85	0.60	50	21	29	34	129	111	99	13%	122	26%	85%	27	67%	19%	7.02	45.0	85	230	$44
16	ARI	41	9	2	4	4	244	209	326	390	716	425	788	11	80	0.63	42	9	48	26	89	71	119	13%	118	31%	100%	3	33%	33%	4.88	0.3	38	109	$1
1st Half																																			
2nd Half		41	9	2	4	4	244	209	326	390	716	425	788	11	80	0.63	42	9	48	26	89	71	119	13%	118	31%	100%	3	33%	33%	4.88	0.5	38	109	$1
17	Proj	522	76	17	51	22	281	275	330	466	796	778	802	7	84	0.45	48	15	37	31	111	105	108	11%	148	21%	79%				5.45	14.0	74	212	$26

Pompey,Dalton

Age: 24 Bats: B Pos: LF		Health	A	LIMA Plan	D+
Ht: 6' 1"	Wt: 170	PT/Exp	D	Rand Var	+2
		Consist	B	MM	1501

0-0-.000 with 2 SB and 3 R in 2 AB at TOR. Placed 2d in SB and R for all batters with .000 BA in 2016 (Darn you, Terrance Gore). A bit of a forgotten player after ~100 MLB AB in 2015; still has youth, raw speed and some punch in his bat. But sloppy ct%, OBP and SB% are all in need of polish before he gets another shot.

Yr	Tm	AB	R	HR	RBI	SB	BA	xBA	OBP	SLG	OPS	vL	vR	bb%	ct%	Eye	G	L	F	h%	HctX	PX	xPX	hr/f	Spd	SBO	SB%	#Wk	DOM	DIS	RC/G	RAR	BPV	BPX	R$
12																																			
13																																			
14	TOR *	204	34	4	18	13	285	241	343	439	782	259	1010	8	79	0.42	31	23	46	35	151	109	177	8%	155	32%	70%	5	20%	60%	5.19	7.7	67	181	$10
15	TOR *	480	79	9	41	25	275	229	342	391	733	859	611	9	80	0.51	43	17	40	33	108	72	80	8%	147	25%	68%	10	40%	40%	4.56	0.7	43	116	$22
16	TOR *	339	46	4	25	18	248	253	319	330	649	0	0	9	75	0.42	100	0	0	32	0	57	-24	0%	116	27%	67%	3	0%	100%	3.48	-9.1	3	9	$10
1st Half		168	20	1	12	9	258	216	323	318	641			9	77	0.41				33		46			111	28%	61%				3.34		-3	-9	$10
2nd Half		171	25	3	12	9	239	262	316	341	657	0	0	10	74	0.44	100	0	0	31	0	69	-24	0%	124	25%	74%	3	0%	100%	3.62	-4.7	11	31	$10
17	Proj	222	33	5	17	12	262	229	342	386	727	983	658	9	78	0.45	43	17	40	32	97	76	72	7%	132	27%	69%				4.27	-1.2	29	82	$10

Posey,Buster

Age: 30 Bats: R Pos: CA		Health	A	LIMA Plan	B+
Ht: 6' 2"	Wt: 195	PT/Exp	A	Rand Var	0
		Consist	B	MM	2255

A down year on the R$ scale, but no worry—most metrics well within range of normal variation. Traded some FB for GB, and 2H hr/f depressed HR output (nagging catcher dings a likely factor), but that's about it. Still a LD/BA godsend out of the CA cesspool; stability of HctX, xBA an xPX point to another season in the mid-$20s.

Yr	Tm	AB	R	HR	RBI	SB	BA	xBA	OBP	SLG	OPS	vL	vR	bb%	ct%	Eye	G	L	F	h%	HctX	PX	xPX	hr/f	Spd	SBO	SB%	#Wk	DOM	DIS	RC/G	RAR	BPV	BPX	R$
12	SF	530	78	24	103	1	336	301	408	549	957	1262	822	12	82	0.72	47	25	29	38	113	137	104	19%	93	1%	50%	27	70%	15%	8.65	60.3	90	225	$30
13	SF	520	61	15	72	2	294	279	371	450	821	891	792	10	87	0.86	47	20	33	32	118	103	116	10%	91	2%	67%	27	59%	7%	5.95	32.6	78	195	$19
14	SF	547	72	22	89	0	311	298	364	490	854	875	844	8	87	0.68	42	24	34	32	131	113	121	13%	90	1%	0%	27	70%	19%	6.57	46.2	85	230	$27
15	SF	557	74	19	95	2	318	288	379	470	849	854	847	9	91	1.08	44	22	34	33	137	87	113	11%	66	1%	100%	27	67%	7%	6.71	43.1	72	195	$27
16	SF	539	82	14	80	6	288	289	362	434	796	899	752	11	87	0.94	49	22	30	31	128	84	111	10%	99	4%	86%	27	63%	11%	5.68	19.2	70	200	$19
1st Half		272	47	9	39	4	290	307	358	467	825	938	773	10	86	0.78	48	25	28	31	134	102	104	14%	90	5%	100%	14	64%	0%	6.12	15.0	75	214	$22
2nd Half		267	35	5	41	2	285	267	365	401	766	855	731	12	88	1.13	50	18	32	31	123	67	117	6%	108	3%	67%	13	62%	23%	5.23	8.2	65	186	$17
17	Proj	535	75	16	85	3	301	288	371	454	825	902	794	10	88	0.94	46	22	32	32	129	86	113	11%	91	2%	80%				6.18	29.9	61	175	$24

Prado,Martin

Age: 33 Bats: R Pos: 3B		Health	B	LIMA Plan	B+
Ht: 6' 0"	Wt: 170	PT/Exp	A	Rand Var	-1
		Consist	A	MM	1255

On the one hand, he's a line-drive machine, and with that steady HctX, he'll remain a BA asset. On the other hand, his power (via xPX) is slowly beginning to leak, and a steady HctX will do little to reverse his HR decline. But this is as stable a skill set as you'll find, right down to the slugger-like vL platoon split. Rinse/repeat.

Yr	Tm	AB	R	HR	RBI	SB	BA	xBA	OBP	SLG	OPS	vL	vR	bb%	ct%	Eye	G	L	F	h%	HctX	PX	xPX	hr/f	Spd	SBO	SB%	#Wk	DOM	DIS	RC/G	RAR	BPV	BPX	R$
12	ATL	617	81	10	70	17	301	291	359	438	796	864	760	9	89	0.84	48	23	29	33	110	86	76	6%	130	11%	81%	27	63%	7%	5.82	20.7	82	205	$25
13	ARI	609	70	14	82	3	282	290	333	417	750	852	716	7	91	0.89	48	22	30	29	112	85	89	8%	94	5%	38%	27	67%	4%	4.81	14.1	78	195	$19
14	2 TM	536	62	12	58	3	282	276	321	412	733	979	668	5	85	0.33	49	22	29	31	102	88	78	9%	127	3%	75%	26	46%	27%	4.61	13.5	60	162	$16
15	MIA	500	52	9	63	1	288	267	338	394	732	856	695	7	86	0.54	47	23	30	32	103	66	69	7%	96	1%	100%	23	43%	30%	4.77	1.2	43	116	$14
16	MIA	600	70	8	75	2	305	288	359	417	775	1068	695	8	89	0.71	47	25	28	33	102	68	67	5%	116	2%	50%	27	52%	19%	5.42	7.2	60	171	$19
1st Half		309	35	2	28	0	320	270	364	405	769	899	729	7	87	0.56	53	22	25	36	92	53	47	3%	135	1%	0%	14	43%	21%	5.48	4.9	48	137	$18
2nd Half		291	35	6	47	2	289	305	353	430	782	1275	661	8	90	0.90	41	28	31	31	112	83	87	7%	95	4%	67%	13	62%	15%	5.35	3.7	73	209	$20
17	Proj	553	63	9	70	3	294	284	345	411	757	991	689	7	88	0.61	47	24	29	32	104	69	73	7%	111	3%	65%				5.08	3.0	42	121	$19

BRENT HERSHEY

Profar,Jurickson

Age: 24 Bats: B Pos: 3B	Health	F	LIMA Plan	C
Ht: 5' 11" Wt: 190	PT/Exp	F	Rand Var	0
	Consist	F	MM	2235

5-20-.239 with 2 SB in 272 AB at TEX. Team WANTS him to succeed—trumpeted bigger role when Odor suspended, and again when Fielder retired. But came up mostly empty; sure looks like shoulder injury sapped punch from his bat. Plate skills intact, and still a pup, but those two lost years? Valuable development time.

Yr	Tm	AB	R	HR	RBI	SB	BA	xBA	OBP	SLG	OPS	vL	vR	bb%	ct%	Eye	G	L	F	h%	HctX	PX	xPX	hr/f	Spd	SBO	SB%	#Wk	DOM	DIS	RC/G	RAR	BPV	BPX	R$
12	TEX *	497	66	14	55	14	276	255	349	447	796	0	846	10	83	0.67	54	8	38	31	112	105	123	20%	111	12%	77%	4	25%	75%	5.50	22.6	73	183	$17
13	TEX *	430	52	9	41	7	244	247	313	359	671	541	696	9	80	0.49	41	23	35	29	96	79	88	8%	96	10%	57%	19	26%	37%	3.68	3.3	30	75	$8
14																																			
15																																			
16	TEX *	441	58	9	41	5	243	247	311	350	661	461	728	9	80	0.49	53	19	28	29	77	62	47	8%	114	8%	55%	20	25%	65%	3.58	-9.5	23	66	$6
1st Half		272	41	7	32	3	281	270	331	409	740	432	1047	7	83	0.43	52	21	26	32	64	72	59	14%	124	10%	43%	7	43%	43%	4.55	0.7	41	117	$13
2nd Half		169	17	2	9	2	183	216	292	254	547	487	563	12	75	0.55	53	17	30	23	83	45	39	5%	104	4%	100%	13	15%	77%	2.29	-11.8	-6	-17	-$5
17	Proj	**411**	**50**	**13**	**37**	**6**	**250**	**258**	**330**	**392**	**722**	**530**	**802**	**10**	**79**	**0.52**	**48**	**21**	**31**	**29**	**85**	**82**	**64**	**12%**	**103**	**8%**	**66%**				**4.25**	**-7.9**	**31**	**87**	**$9**

Puig,Yasiel

Age: 26 Bats: R Pos: RF	Health	C	LIMA Plan	B
Ht: 6' 3" Wt: 235	PT/Exp	C	Rand Var	0
	Consist	B	MM	3235

11-45-.263 with 5 SB in 334 AB at LA. Lost MLB AB due to: separate L and R hamstring issues; perceived lack of hustle; knee; AAA demotion. Yet he puts together this 2nd half (w/ .828 MLB OPS) and his mostly three-digit power and speed metrics remind us of his game-changing skills. Just know he's frustration personified.

Yr	Tm	AB	R	HR	RBI	SB	BA	xBA	OBP	SLG	OPS	vL	vR	bb%	ct%	Eye	G	L	F	h%	HctX	PX	xPX	hr/f	Spd	SBO	SB%	#Wk	DOM	DIS	RC/G	RAR	BPV	BPX	R$
12																																			
13	LA *	529	89	26	74	22	309	285	368	533	900	1001	897	8	76	0.38	50	19	31	37	119	154	106	22%	127	24%	62%	18	56%	28%	6.82	32.7	82	205	$35
14	LA	558	92	16	69	11	296	272	382	480	863	736	901	11	78	0.54	52	15	33	36	116	134	110	11%	139	11%	61%	28	54%	29%	6.29	34.3	84	227	$26
15	LA	282	30	11	38	3	255	249	322	436	758	924	704	8	77	0.39	44	17	39	30	107	114	89	13%	105	8%	50%	18	39%	22%	4.60	-2.0	48	130	$7
16	LA *	403	54	14	54	5	268	252	316	428	745	784	715	7	79	0.34	48	16	35	31	100	92	90	12%	102	8%	61%	22	27%	32%	4.63	-0.5	36	103	$12
1st Half		224	27	6	25	4	259	234	311	384	695	658	708	5	79	0.25	47	17	36	31	102	70	80	10%	117	9%	80%	12	17%	33%	3.94	-5.0	18	51	$11
2nd Half		179	27	8	29	1	280	274	340	484	824	900	739	8	80	0.46	51	16	33	31	97	120	111	17%	87	7%	31%	10	40%	30%	5.57	4.5	61	174	$12
17	Proj	**419**	**58**	**16**	**57**	**6**	**275**	**261**	**340**	**460**	**800**	**858**	**770**	**8**	**78**	**0.39**	**49**	**17**	**35**	**32**	**106**	**109**	**99**	**14%**	**113**	**10%**	**57%**				**5.22**	**6.3**	**45**	**128**	**$17**

Pujols,Albert

Age: 37 Bats: R Pos: DH 1B	Health	B	LIMA Plan	B+
Ht: 6' 3" Wt: 240	PT/Exp	A	Rand Var	0
	Consist	A	MM	2145

Battled a recurrence of his plantar fasciitis down the stretch—though you'd never know it from these numbers. While the otherworldly xPX and Eye figures have long since scrolled off the page, his still-elite HctX serves as the foundation for everything else, with nary a skills crack despite his age. Next up: HR #600.

Yr	Tm	AB	R	HR	RBI	SB	BA	xBA	OBP	SLG	OPS	vL	vR	bb%	ct%	Eye	G	L	F	h%	HctX	PX	xPX	hr/f	Spd	SBO	SB%	#Wk	DOM	DIS	RC/G	RAR	BPV	BPX	R$
12	LAA	607	85	30	105	8	285	303	343	516	859	926	836	8	87	0.68	41	19	40	29	128	140	126	14%	53	6%	89%	27	78%	11%	6.32	24.5	96	240	$27
13	LAA	391	49	17	64	1	258	270	330	437	767	690	790	9	86	0.73	38	20	42	26	130	109	135	12%	62	2%	50%	17	59%	12%	4.88	4.3	70	175	$11
14	LAA	633	89	28	105	5	272	299	324	466	790	737	807	7	89	0.68	46	19	35	27	139	122	110	14%	54	4%	83%	27	70%	0%	5.29	22.3	85	230	$26
15	LAA	602	85	40	95	5	244	286	307	480	787	753	799	8	88	0.69	42	16	42	22	127	125	131	18%	52	6%	63%	27	67%	11%	4.83	-11.0	85	230	$21
16	LAA	593	71	31	119	4	268	269	323	457	780	811	770	8	87	0.65	44	17	40	26	129	94	132	15%	52	3%	100%	26	50%	23%	5.20	-5.0	58	166	$21
1st Half		306	33	15	56	3	252	268	328	435	763	910	716	10	87	0.90	49	15	36	25	125	93	119	15%	51	3%	100%	14	50%	29%	4.92	-5.2	61	174	$18
2nd Half		287	38	16	63	1	286	268	317	481	798	699	827	5	87	0.39	39	18	43	28	134	96	147	15%	61	1%	100%	12	50%	17%	5.50	0.0	56	160	$25
17	Proj	**584**	**76**	**29**	**97**	**3**	**265**	**273**	**320**	**456**	**776**	**759**	**781**	**7**	**88**	**0.64**	**43**	**17**	**40**	**26**	**131**	**98**	**130**	**14%**	**55**	**3%**	**76%**				**5.04**	**-7.7**	**60**	**172**	**$22**

Quinn,Roman

Age: 24 Bats: B Pos: LF	Health	A	LIMA Plan	C+
Ht: 5' 10" Wt: 170	PT/Exp	F	Rand Var	0
	Consist	A	MM	1503

0-6-.263 with 5 SB in 57 AB. Elite speedster who has battled injuries every step of the way. PRO: Wheels; solid bb%; more umph in swing than small frame would suggest. CON: Sub-par contact; staying healthy; limited high-minors experience. Worthy of a late-round dart throw due to SB upside.

Yr	Tm	AB	R	HR	RBI	SB	BA	xBA	OBP	SLG	OPS	vL	vR	bb%	ct%	Eye	G	L	F	h%	HctX	PX	xPX	hr/f	Spd	SBO	SB%	#Wk	DOM	DIS	RC/G	RAR	BPV	BPX	R$
12																																			
13																																			
14																																			
15	aa	232	35	4	12	23	272		314	378	692			6	79	0.30				33		62			164	53%	67%				3.82		29	78	$12
16	PHI *	343	57	5	26	30	256	253	321	378	698	911	633	9	71	0.33	57	22	22	34	51	83	50	0%	168	43%	75%	3	33%	33%	4.13	-5.3	22	63	$17
1st Half		205	36	3	13	20	255	218	310	367	677			7	70	0.27				35		78			144	50%	75%				3.87		3	9	$20
2nd Half		138	21	3	13	10	258	264	335	393	728	911	633	10	74	0.44	57	22	22	33	52	91	50	0%	150	33%	75%	3	33%	33%	4.53	0.1	35	100	$11
17	Proj	**323**	**51**	**6**	**28**	**29**	**263**	**226**	**338**	**382**	**720**	**983**	**624**	**8**	**75**	**0.33**	**42**	**20**	**39**	**33**	**47**	**74**	**45**	**6%**	**179**	**45%**	**72%**				**4.08**	**-3.7**	**25**	**71**	**$19**

Ramirez,Alexei

Age: 35 Bats: R Pos: SS	Health	A	LIMA Plan	B
Ht: 6' 3" Wt: 170	PT/Exp	A	Rand Var	+3
	Consist	B	MM	1343

Not exactly #BeliEVEN, but his contact rate pattern is something—and uncharacterstically strong, given the rest. Among the lowlights: non-existent power, slight LD dip in the 2nd half, more CS than SB—his 3-yr R$ string is not kind. RandVar says there might be a rebound but contact alone doesn't win championships.

Yr	Tm	AB	R	HR	RBI	SB	BA	xBA	OBP	SLG	OPS	vL	vR	bb%	ct%	Eye	G	L	F	h%	HctX	PX	xPX	hr/f	Spd	SBO	SB%	#Wk	DOM	DIS	RC/G	RAR	BPV	BPX	R$
12	CHW	593	59	9	73	20	265	254	287	364	651	724	631	3	87	0.21	46	20	34	29	85	61	69	5%	134	20%	74%	27	37%	33%	3.56	-6.0	44	110	$17
13	CHW	637	68	6	48	30	284	278	313	380	693	701	691	4	89	0.38	49	22	29	31	86	68	51	4%	129	24%	77%	27	56%	15%	4.23	14.7	60	150	$25
14	CHW	622	82	15	74	21	273	278	305	408	713	744	703	4	87	0.30	47	20	33	29	88	92	64	8%	125	18%	84%	26	50%	12%	4.37	21.2	69	186	$26
15	CHW	583	54	10	62	17	249	277	285	357	642	707	623	5	88	0.46	49	22	29	27	81	71	61	7%	97	18%	71%	27	56%	11%	3.43	-16.9	51	138	$14
16	2 TM	478	38	6	48	8	241	265	277	333	610	769	549	4	87	0.33	52	20	28	27	83	56	51	5%	109	16%	47%	27	41%	41%	2.85	-21.2	35	100	$5
1st Half		292	26	3	28	6	240	263	270	322	592	688	557	3	86	0.24	51	21	27	27	88	51	53	4%	106	21%	46%	14	29%	43%	2.62	-16.6	25	71	$7
2nd Half		186	12	3	20	2	242	266	288	349	637	886	536	6	88	0.50	52	18	29	26	74	62	48	6%	113	9%	50%	13	54%	38%	3.23	-6.9	49	140	$2
17	Proj	**414**	**37**	**7**	**44**	**10**	**251**	**271**	**288**	**356**	**644**	**770**	**601**	**5**	**88**	**0.38**	**50**	**20**	**30**	**27**	**82**	**63**	**56**	**6%**	**111**	**16%**	**64%**				**3.37**	**-13.6**	**35**	**100**	**$10**

Ramirez,Hanley

Age: 33 Bats: R Pos: 1B	Health	C	LIMA Plan	B
Ht: 6' 3" Wt: 195	PT/Exp	B	Rand Var	-1
	Consist	D	MM	3245

Impressive on the surface, but less so the deeper you look. Portions of his 1st half look suspiciously like his underwhelming 2015. One level down, an unconscious Sept/Oct (11 HR, 41% hr/f, 1.045 OPS) drove "rebound" season. Conclusion: He's beyond that 2015 fog, but asking for a full repeat is wishful thinking.

Yr	Tm	AB	R	HR	RBI	SB	BA	xBA	OBP	SLG	OPS	vL	vR	bb%	ct%	Eye	G	L	F	h%	HctX	PX	xPX	hr/f	Spd	SBO	SB%	#Wk	DOM	DIS	RC/G	RAR	BPV	BPX	R$
12	2 NL	604	79	24	92	21	257	262	322	437	759	794	745	8	78	0.41	47	18	34	29	114	115	115	15%	108	18%	75%	27	52%	33%	4.73	-9.9	55	138	$23
13	LA	304	62	20	57	10	345	326	402	638	1040	1142	1001	8	83	0.52	41	22	37	37	160	186	164	21%	115	14%	83%	18	72%	22%	9.94	42.0	133	333	$25
14	LA	449	64	13	71	14	283	281	369	448	817	869	801	11	81	0.67	45	21	34	32	115	124	115	10%	93	14%	74%	25	60%	16%	5.74	20.4	76	205	$21
15	BOS	401	59	19	53	6	249	277	291	426	717	710	720	5	82	0.30	50	20	30	26	111	101	84	19%	105	10%	67%	20	50%	25%	4.09	-10.1	53	143	$12
16	BOS	549	81	30	111	9	286	278	361	505	866	1097	796	10	78	0.50	48	19	33	32	118	127	109	21%	98	8%	75%	27	63%	19%	6.40	23.8	65	186	$26
1st Half		293	43	8	47	5	283	258	355	427	781	1041	713	9	78	0.46	51	19	31	34	111	90	99	11%	111	8%	71%	14	57%	21%	5.25	1.2	39	111	$22
2nd Half		256	38	22	64	4	289	301	369	594	963	1148	899	11	78	0.54	46	19	36	29	126	170	120	31%	81	7%	80%	13	69%	15%	7.79	19.3	95	271	$31
17	Proj	**511**	**76**	**24**	**90**	**6**	**278**	**273**	**347**	**471**	**818**	**923**	**782**	**9**	**79**	**0.47**	**47**	**20**	**33**	**31**	**119**	**112**	**108**	**18%**	**98**	**7%**	**63%**				**5.61**	**7.4**	**48**	**137**	**$23**

Ramirez,Jose

Age: 24 Bats: B Pos: 3B LF	Health	A	LIMA Plan	B+
Ht: 5' 9" Wt: 165	PT/Exp	B	Rand Var	-5
	Consist	C	MM	2445

Double Your Earnings in Five Easy Steps: 1) Bring speed, near-elite contact ability to the table; 2) Win an everyday lineup spot; 3) Surround yourself with strong supporting cast (runs/RBI opps); 4) Hit more LDs, and hit them harder; 5) Improve in most aspects in the 2H. A broad skills base that should continue to grow.

Yr	Tm	AB	R	HR	RBI	SB	BA	xBA	OBP	SLG	OPS	vL	vR	bb%	ct%	Eye	G	L	F	h%	HctX	PX	xPX	hr/f	Spd	SBO	SB%	#Wk	DOM	DIS	RC/G	RAR	BPV	BPX	R$
12																																			
13	CLE *	494	65	2	29	29	240	220	285	302	587	650	1069	6	90	0.66	50	10	40	26	76	39	135	0%	159	37%	61%	4	25%	50%	2.67	-19.7	54	135	$14
14	CLE *	482	57	6	40	25	265	274	312	366	677	676	632	6	86	0.47	47	24	28	30	86	72	71	4%	116	30%	66%	15	40%	27%	3.77	1.5	50	135	$18
15	CLE *	489	76	7	38	23	240	264	306	355	661	574	655	9	90	0.96	48	16	36	25	94	71	69	6%	131	25%	74%	20	35%	20%	3.63	-13.9	76	205	$14
16	CLE	565	84	11	76	22	312	290	363	462	825	841	818	7	89	0.71	41	23	36	34	97	91	77	6%	106	18%	76%	27	78%	7%	6.15	21.0	77	220	$30
1st Half		260	39	4	32	10	296	276	352	423	775	698	803	7	88	0.68	37	25	39	32	88	79	83	5%	116	18%	77%	14	71%	7%	5.35	3.4	67	191	$24
2nd Half		305	45	7	44	12	325	302	372	495	867	942	832	7	90	0.74	44	21	34	34	104	101	73	7%	97	19%	75%	13	85%	8%	6.88	16.4	85	243	$35
17	Proj	**584**	**84**	**13**	**62**	**26**	**280**	**281**	**333**	**424**	**757**	**755**	**759**	**7**	**89**	**0.70**	**43**	**21**	**36**	**30**	**95**	**83**	**73**	**7%**	**113**	**24%**	**71%**				**4.89**	**0.0**	**73**	**209**	**$28**

BRENT HERSHEY

Ramos,Wilson

Age: 29 Bats: R Pos: CA	Health C	LIMA Plan D
Ht: 6' 1" Wt: 235	PT/Exp B	Rand Var -4
	Consist F	MM 2031

Unofficial spring spokesman for LASIK enjoyed HctX surge as 1H ct% soared to new highs. Early bb%, hr/f, h% all followed suit, creating perfect storm. 2H pullback was inevitable; Sept ACL tear will shelve him into next summer. Despite GB%, contact skills have value if/when healthy. Check your expectations.

Yr	Tm	AB	R	HR	RBI	SB	BA	xBA	OBP	SLG	OPS	vL	vR	bb%	ct%	Eye	G	L	F	h%	HctX	PX	xPX	hr/f	Spd	SBO	SB%	#Wk	DOM	DIS	RC/G	RAR	BPV	BPX	R$
12	WAS	83	11	3	10	0	265	224	354	398	752	762	748	13	77	0.63	66	14	20	31	114	82	96	23%	65	0%	0%	6	33%	33%	4.94	1.5	21	53	$0
13	WAS	287	29	16	59	0	272	279	307	470	777	700	803	5	85	0.36	57	20	24	27	145	114	109	28%	60	1%	0%	18	61%	17%	4.99	10.7	62	155	$10
14	WAS	341	32	11	47	0	267	263	299	399	698	820	661	5	83	0.30	55	22	23	29	99	86	88	17%	48	0%	0%	22	32%	50%	4.18	7.1	28	76	$9
15	WAS	475	41	15	68	0	229	240	258	358	616	620	615	4	79	0.21	55	20	25	26	93	81	84	16%	54	0%	0%	26	27%	42%	3.10	-10.2	6	16	$5
16	WAS	482	58	22	80	0	307	280	354	496	850	1008	806	7	84	0.44	54	20	25	33	120	105	97	21%	54	0%	0%	26	62%	23%	6.46	26.8	50	143	$20
1st Half		245	38	13	46	0	343	317	394	567	961	885	986	8	87	0.66	53	23	24	36	121	122	90	25%	64	0%	0%	14	79%	14%	8.69	28.7	82	234	$26
2nd Half		237	20	9	34	0	270	235	311	422	733	1171	631	6	80	0.30	56	17	27	30	119	87	104	17%	52	0%	0%	12	42%	33%	4.58	3.0	19	54	$13
17	Proj	**211**	**22**	**8**	**33**	**0**	**274**	**262**	**314**	**433**	**746**	**859**	**715**	**6**	**82**	**0.34**	**56**	**20**	**25**	**30**	**111**	**89**	**94**	**19%**	**56**	**0%**	**0%**				**4.79**	**3.9**	**19**	**55**	**$5**

Rasmus,Colby

Age: 30 Bats: L Pos: LF CF	Health B	LIMA Plan D+
Ht: 6' 1" Wt: 175	PT/Exp C	Rand Var +3
	Consist C	MM 3203

Fast start yielded 7 HR in April, 45% h% fueled .313 BA in June. But chronic contact woes led to too many extended funks. Ongoing ear issues resulted in 2nd half DL stint, surgery, and late-season pine time. Power should rebound at least a tad, and his lefthandedness helps. But he's platoon BA-killer at best.

Yr	Tm	AB	R	HR	RBI	SB	BA	xBA	OBP	SLG	OPS	vL	vR	bb%	ct%	Eye	G	L	F	h%	HctX	PX	xPX	hr/f	Spd	SBO	SB%	#Wk	DOM	DIS	RC/G	RAR	BPV	BPX	R$
12	TOR	565	75	23	75	4	223	237	289	400	689	554	740	8	74	0.32	38	20	42	26	114	115	123	13%	116	6%	57%	27	37%	33%	3.66	-15.7	39	98	$10
13	TOR	417	57	22	66	0	276	253	338	501	840	712	893	8	68	0.27	33	22	45	36	109	175	148	17%	104	1%	0%	22	64%	27%	5.85	22.2	60	150	$16
14	TOR *	369	45	18	41	4	218	241	276	427	703	684	752	7	63	0.22	34	23	42	29	111	180	170	19%	91	6%	100%	21	52%	43%	3.90	2.3	42	114	$7
15	HOU	432	67	25	61	2	238	235	314	475	789	835	770	10	64	0.31	28	20	52	31	97	178	149	18%	88	3%	67%	27	41%	30%	4.95	7.2	48	130	$12
16	HOU	369	38	15	54	4	206	213	286	355	641	454	694	10	67	0.36	36	21	43	26	96	98	119	14%	80	5%	80%	22	18%	50%	3.31	-11.1	-5	-14	$3
1st Half		262	28	10	40	4	252	228	332	405	737	665	755	11	68	0.39	36	25	39	33	103	103	117	14%	85	6%	80%	14	14%	50%	4.65	1.5	4	11	$8
2nd Half		107	10	5	14	0	93	173	169	234	403	34	530	9	65	0.27	35	13	52	8	79	84	123	14%	94	0%	0%	8	25%	50%	1.12	-12.7	-24	-69	-$10
17	Proj	**400**	**48**	**18**	**55**	**2**	**220**	**214**	**292**	**397**	**690**	**553**	**736**	**9**	**66**	**0.30**	**34**	**19**	**47**	**28**	**96**	**119**	**137**	**15%**	**86**	**3%**	**78%**				**3.81**	**-8.0**	**-3**	**-10**	**$8**

Realmuto,Jacob

Age: 26 Bats: R Pos: CA	Health A	LIMA Plan B
Ht: 6' 1" Wt: 215	PT/Exp C	Rand Var -5
	Consist B	MM 2335

BA soared from the get-go thanks to season-long h% surprise. AB hike aided HR repeat, despite GB uptick. Add in double-digit SB with SBO/SB% support, and you end up with hard-to-find production from the catcher spot. Plate skills, HctX and xBA say he's not a .300 hitter. But age and health suggest he'll do just fine.

Yr	Tm	AB	R	HR	RBI	SB	BA	xBA	OBP	SLG	OPS	vL	vR	bb%	ct%	Eye	G	L	F	h%	HctX	PX	xPX	hr/f	Spd	SBO	SB%	#Wk	DOM	DIS	RC/G	RAR	BPV	BPX	R$
12																																			
13	aa	368	35	4	33	8	221		282	321	603			8	80	0.43				27		75			105	10%	88%				3.03		30	75	$2
14	MIA *	404	54	5	56	14	258	291	313	386	699	2000	563	7	82	0.44	43	33	24	30	101	91	57	0%	119	19%	71%	6	17%	67%	4.10	7.7	53	143	$13
15	MIA	441	49	10	47	8	259	269	290	406	696	791	671	4	84	0.27	45	21	34	29	107	88	105	8%	118	13%	67%	25	44%	16%	3.96	1.8	53	143	$11
16	MIA	509	60	11	48	12	303	261	343	428	771	617	806	5	80	0.28	49	20	30	36	97	82	86	9%	96	11%	75%	26	27%	38%	5.29	12.4	28	80	$20
1st Half		264	29	5	25	6	314	254	344	432	776	488	850	4	83	0.24	52	16	32	36	101	76	92	7%	99	11%	75%	14	29%	50%	5.47	9.5	32	91	$21
2nd Half		245	31	6	23	6	290	266	342	424	767	795	761	6	78	0.31	46	25	29	35	94	90	79	11%	92	12%	75%	12	25%	25%	5.10	6.6	25	71	$19
17	Proj	**496**	**58**	**12**	**51**	**12**	**275**	**269**	**318**	**421**	**739**	**712**	**746**	**6**	**81**	**0.31**	**47**	**21**	**32**	**32**	**101**	**88**	**93**	**10%**	**112**	**13%**	**73%**				**4.63**	**7.0**	**39**	**111**	**$18**

Reddick,Josh

Age: 30 Bats: L Pos: RF	Health C	LIMA Plan B+
Ht: 6' 2" Wt: 195	PT/Exp C	Rand Var -1
	Consist B	MM 2335

10-37-.281 in 398 AB at OAK/LA. More DL time, as fractured thumb and 6 weeks off from May-June didn't help declining power. Contact skills, speed were evident in 2nd half, but h%, SB% hurt his bottom line. Fragility, effort vL point to platoon profile. 2015 says there's still upside from here if he can stay on the field.

Yr	Tm	AB	R	HR	RBI	SB	BA	xBA	OBP	SLG	OPS	vL	vR	bb%	ct%	Eye	G	L	F	h%	HctX	PX	xPX	hr/f	Spd	SBO	SB%	#Wk	DOM	DIS	RC/G	RAR	BPV	BPX	R$
12	OAK	611	85	32	85	11	242	249	305	463	768	751	778	8	75	0.36	29	21	50	27	103	141	131	14%	115	9%	92%	28	61%	21%	4.82	-5.9	67	168	$19
13	OAK	385	54	12	56	9	226	240	307	379	686	667	695	11	78	0.53	36	20	44	26	89	106	110	9%	103	11%	82%	24	58%	25%	3.90	-8.3	50	125	$9
14	OAK	363	53	12	54	1	264	250	316	446	763	533	849	7	83	0.44	33	18	50	29	103	115	118	8%	135	2%	50%	21	62%	14%	4.87	8.0	79	214	$11
15	OAK	526	67	20	77	10	272	276	333	449	781	654	826	9	88	0.75	38	21	41	28	99	100	93	11%	109	8%	83%	26	58%	12%	5.29	6.4	82	222	$20
16	2 TM *	423	55	11	38	8	270	259	333	393	727	366	871	9	85	0.63	41	22	37	30	105	70	90	8%	117	9%	73%	22	50%	27%	4.57	-1.3	51	146	$11
1st Half		191	23	6	20	4	285	260	358	416	774	423	984	10	84	0.70	44	21	35	32	97	75	79	10%	104	6%	100%	9	56%	0%	5.45	4.1	48	137	$12
2nd Half		232	32	5	18	4	259	258	312	375	687	316	793	7	86	0.56	39	22	39	28	110	66	97	7%	125	11%	57%	13	46%	46%	3.90	-5.5	51	146	$11
17	Proj	**417**	**56**	**15**	**49**	**7**	**265**	**260**	**325**	**432**	**757**	**505**	**846**	**8**	**85**	**0.58**	**37**	**20**	**43**	**28**	**102**	**91**	**98**	**10%**	**117**	**8%**	**75%**				**4.87**	**2.2**	**57**	**164**	**$15**

Reed,A.J.

Age: 24 Bats: L Pos: 1B	Health A	LIMA Plan D+
Ht: 6' 4" Wt: 275	PT/Exp F	Rand Var 0
	Consist F	MM 3003

3-8-.164 in 122 AB at HOU. Acclaimed power prospect off fine 2015 AA campaign struggled at higher levels. Found AAA footing in June, but never got untracked in HOU. Problematic contact hidden by 2015 h%, but now in full view along with GB%, vL issues. Age helps, but this could take some time.

Yr	Tm	AB	R	HR	RBI	SB	BA	xBA	OBP	SLG	OPS	vL	vR	bb%	ct%	Eye	G	L	F	h%	HctX	PX	xPX	hr/f	Spd	SBO	SB%	#Wk	DOM	DIS	RC/G	RAR	BPV	BPX	R$
12																																			
13																																			
14																																			
15	aa	205	30	9	36	0	298		364	506	871			9	73	0.38				37		144			90	0%	0%				6.71		54	146	$8
16	HOU *	383	42	15	45	0	223	216	299	402	702	243	572	10	67	0.33	49	12	39	29	87	127	119	10%	62	0%	0%	15	13%	73%	3.95	-10.5	10	29	$3
1st Half		244	26	10	28	0	216	218	285	409	694	0	505	9	68	0.30	25	17	58	28	91	138	184	14%	66	0%	0%	3	33%	67%	3.79	-9.8	20	57	$3
2nd Half		139	16	5	17	0	238	196	325	392	717	322	586	11	67	0.39	54	11	35	32	86	107	106	9%	64	0%	0%	12	8%	75%	4.26	-3.5	-4	-11	$2
17	Proj	**315**	**40**	**9**	**45**	**0**	**231**	**212**	**307**	**373**	**680**	**364**	**719**	**10**	**69**	**0.35**	**54**	**11**	**35**	**31**	**77**	**102**	**95**	**11%**	**62**	**0%**	**0%**				**3.80**	**-12.4**	**-7**	**-20**	**$5**

Refsnyder,Rob

Age: 26 Bats: R Pos: 1B RF	Health A	LIMA Plan D
Ht: 6' 0" Wt: 200	PT/Exp C	Rand Var 0
	Consist A	MM 1441

0-12-.250, 2 SB in 152 AB at NYY. Career .293 minor league hitter with decent plate skills (.379 OBP) and a smatter of running game struggled with MLB consistency off the bench. Previous power flashes were a 2016 no-show, though recent xBA history still intrigues. Former 2B with sub-par glove now seeks a utility role.

Yr	Tm	AB	R	HR	RBI	SB	BA	xBA	OBP	SLG	OPS	vL	vR	bb%	ct%	Eye	G	L	F	h%	HctX	PX	xPX	hr/f	Spd	SBO	SB%	#Wk	DOM	DIS	RC/G	RAR	BPV	BPX	R$
12																																			
13																																			
14	a/a	515	64	12	49	7	278		334	426	760			8	77	0.36				34		115			101	12%	41%				4.71		46	124	$16
15	NYY *	493	60	11	53	12	249	281	320	377	697	667	1308	9	82	0.57	67	17	17	29	98	86	74	33%	87	11%	85%	6	33%	17%	4.17	-11.1	42	114	$12
16	NYY *	361	47	2	30	7	271	272	333	342	675	725	575	8	82	0.52	53	26	21	33	88	50	56	0%	123	8%	88%	17	24%	41%	4.08	-8.0	24	69	$8
1st Half		201	26	2	17	6	270	304	324	369	693	792	649	7	84	0.51	48	33	19	31	120	65	91	0%	97	12%	100%	7	43%	29%	4.38	-4.1	35	100	$10
2nd Half		160	21	0	13	1	273	232	344	308	652	669	524	10	79	0.52	56	21	23	34	63	30	29	0%	131	4%	50%	10	10%	50%	3.67	-6.6	2	6	$5
17	Proj	**191**	**24**	**3**	**18**	**4**	**265**	**275**	**329**	**364**	**693**	**789**	**626**	**9**	**81**	**0.51**	**53**	**26**	**21**	**32**	**86**	**66**	**54**	**8%**	**124**	**8%**	**75%**				**4.18**	**-5.1**	**18**	**51**	**$5**

Renda,Tony

Age: 26 Bats: R Pos: 2B	Health A	LIMA Plan D
Ht: 5' 10" Wt: 170	PT/Exp D	Rand Var +1
	Consist B	MM 0341

0-3-.183, 0 SB in 60 AB at CIN. 2nd-rounder in 2012 hit .326 with 90% ct% and 17 SB in 366 AB between AA and AAA. Unfortunately, these skills were no-shows in his small-sample MLB debut. Even if they re-surface, deficient power and just average defense make him a long shot for everyday playing time.

Yr	Tm	AB	R	HR	RBI	SB	BA	xBA	OBP	SLG	OPS	vL	vR	bb%	ct%	Eye	G	L	F	h%	HctX	PX	xPX	hr/f	Spd	SBO	SB%	#Wk	DOM	DIS	RC/G	RAR	BPV	BPX	R$
12																																			
13																																			
14																																			
15	aa	480	64	3	39	21	243		299	324	623			7	91	0.86				26		55			98	22%	76%				3.29		53	143	$12
16	CIN *	426	48	3	36	15	270	288	313	371	684	357	492	6	87	0.50	56	21	23	30	69	65	38	0%	115	18%	77%	9	22%	44%	4.08	-6.7	49	140	$12
1st Half		291	37	2	28	14	288	280	318	407	726			4	90	0.47				31		76			112	23%	93%				4.87		67	191	$19
2nd Half		135	11	1	8	1	230	240	304	292	596	357	492	10	80	0.54	56	21	23	28	64	39	38	0%	121	11%	21%	9	22%	44%	2.67	-7.5	10	29	-$4
17	Proj	**194**	**22**	**0**	**15**	**6**	**250**	**271**	**306**	**314**	**620**	**526**	**645**	**7**	**87**	**0.61**	**56**	**21**	**23**	**29**	**58**	**45**	**34**	**0%**	**113**	**17%**	**69%**				**3.23**	**-9.1**	**30**	**86**	**$5**

JOCK THOMPSON

Rendon,Anthony

Age: 27 | Bats: R | Pos: 3B | Ht: 6' 0" | Wt: 190

Health C | PT/Exp B | Consist D | LIMA Plan B+ | Rand Var 0 | MM 2335

Nice rebound from injury-plagued 2015, even if short of 2014 excellence. SBs a nice surprise, but running game declined as expected and looks constrained going forward. 2H power uptick fueled by FB spike; hr/f and xPX aren't quite as hopeful. Age and stable HctX, plate skills make this a solid-not-spectacular 3B option.

Yr	Tm	AB	R	HR	RBI	SB	BA	xBA	OBP	SLG	OPS	vL	vR	bb%	ct%	Eye	G	L	F	h%	HctX	PX	xPX	hr/f	Spd	SBO	SB%	#Wk	DOM	DIS	RC/G	RAR	BPV	BPX	R$
12	aa	68	11	2	2	0	148		242	320	562			11	76	0.51				15		111			124	0%	0%				2.31		52	130	-$3
13	WAS *	478	55	12	54	2	267	272	343	421	764	830	682	10	79	0.55	41	26	34	32	122	113	115	7%	113	2%	64%	20	45%	20%	5.01	14.0	64	160	$12
14	WAS	613	111	21	83	17	287	279	351	473	824	825	824	9	83	0.56	40	20	40	32	136	126	146	10%	120	12%	85%	27	67%	11%	5.97	38.9	88	238	$32
15	WAS *	335	44	5	25	1	261	238	337	361	698	750	697	10	78	0.52	45	21	33	32	111	76	104	6%	105	3%	33%	16	19%	44%	4.11	-5.5	26	70	$5
16	WAS	567	91	20	85	12	270	258	348	450	797	817	792	10	79	0.56	36	21	44	31	117	111	116	10%	106	11%	67%	26	58%	12%	5.33	5.7	61	174	$21
1st Half		298	52	8	31	9	258	253	347	409	756	871	724	12	78	0.63	41	22	37	31	128	95	116	9%	124	15%	64%	14	43%	14%	4.80	-0.8	50	143	$20
2nd Half		269	39	12	54	3	283	266	349	494	843	740	864	8	81	0.46	30	19	51	31	106	128	116	11%	92	6%	75%	12	75%	8%	5.94	8.0	73	209	$22
17	Proj	569	85	16	75	8	271	257	346	429	775	798	768	10	80	0.53	39	21	40	32	118	99	117	9%	106	8%	68%				5.08	3.2	46	131	$19

Renfroe,Hunter

Age: 25 | Bats: R | Pos: RF | Ht: 6' 1" | Wt: 220

Health A | PT/Exp C | Consist B | LIMA Plan D+ | Rand Var -1 | MM 4213

4-14-.371 in 35 AB at SD. Prototypical corner OF raked in Triple-A bandbox until over-aggressiveness showed up late in BA. Free-swinger thrived in Sept MLB call-up, but aversion to walks is a looming issue. Power is legit and ct% isn't gawd-awful. With adjustment... UP: .250 BA, 25 HR. If not... DN: Back to Triple-A.

Yr	Tm	AB	R	HR	RBI	SB	BA	xBA	OBP	SLG	OPS	vL	vR	bb%	ct%	Eye	G	L	F	h%	HctX	PX	xPX	hr/f	Spd	SBO	SB%	#Wk	DOM	DIS	RC/G	RAR	BPV	BPX	R$
12																																			
13																																			
14	aa	224	14	4	19	2	202		271	301	572			9	73	0.35				26		82			82	5%	60%				2.58		3	8	-$2
15	a/a	511	48	15	57	4	231		271	380	651			5	70	0.18				30		108			96	5%	77%				3.41		6	16	$6
16	SD *	568	73	25	85	3	256	244	277	456	732	1178	1192	3	75	0.11	43	13	43	30	81	124	125	31%	86	6%	59%	3	100%	0%	4.26	-6.8	31	89	$15
1st Half		336	44	14	48	2	272	268	293	470	763			3	77	0.13				32		122			93	5%	64%				4.78		40	114	$18
2nd Half		232	28	12	37	1	234	235	253	436	689	1178	1192	2	71	0.09	43	13	43	28	77	127	125	31%	80	7%	54%	3	100%	0%	3.60	-7.7	18	51	$9
17	Proj	331	35	17	42	2	235	241	276	449	725	797	694	5	72	0.21	43	13	43	27	69	133	113	17%	85	5%	67%				4.10	-5.9	27	77	$8

Revere,Ben

Age: 29 | Bats: L | Pos: CF LF | Ht: 5' 9" | Wt: 175

Health C | PT/Exp B | Consist C | LIMA Plan B | Rand Var +5 | MM 0555

Strained oblique in first game of the season; things snowballed from there. With the exception of June, hitting stroke proved elusive. FB% spike and unfortunate h% shaved 90 points off his BA and cost him his job. Elite ct%, speed look entrenched. With opportunity, a rebound candidate and... UP: .290 BA, 30+ SB.

Yr	Tm	AB	R	HR	RBI	SB	BA	xBA	OBP	SLG	OPS	vL	vR	bb%	ct%	Eye	G	L	F	h%	HctX	PX	xPX	hr/f	Spd	SBO	SB%	#Wk	DOM	DIS	RC/G	RAR	BPV	BPX	R$
12	MIN *	605	78	0	37	45	294	278	330	337	667	676	675	5	90	0.53	67	19	15	33	73	26	23	0%	151	30%	80%	24	21%	21%	4.15	-9.1	38	95	$27
13	PHI	315	37	0	17	22	305	277	338	352	691	858	641	5	89	0.44	59	23	17	34	85	32	31	0%	144	30%	73%	15	20%	33%	4.34	2.1	35	88	$15
14	PHI	601	71	2	28	49	306	293	325	361	686	763	653	2	92	0.27	65	21	14	33	64	33	23	3%	166	33%	86%	27	22%	15%	4.51	11.2	50	135	$34
15	2 TM	592	84	2	45	31	306	291	342	377	719	638	747	5	89	0.50	55	26	19	34	72	44	35	2%	150	21%	82%	27	30%	15%	4.83	8.6	49	132	$29
16	WAS	350	44	2	24	14	217	271	260	300	560	550	562	5	90	0.53	55	18	27	24	74	41	56	2%	155	25%	74%	24	38%	29%	2.49	-23.5	52	149	$4
1st Half		191	23	1	15	10	225	266	275	293	569	794	524	6	90	0.63	53	20	27	25	86	34	79	2%	138	28%	77%	11	36%	27%	2.66	-11.0	43	123	$7
2nd Half		159	21	1	9	4	208	278	241	308	549	274	608	4	91	0.40	58	16	26	22	61	50	28	3%	152	21%	67%	13	38%	31%	2.29	-11.2	57	163	$0
17	Proj	435	56	2	28	22	271	283	307	345	652	636	657	4	90	0.48	58	21	22	30	71	39	39	2%	156	24%	78%				3.72	-10.0	46	133	$17

Reyes,Jose

Age: 34 | Bats: B | Pos: 3B | Ht: 6' 1" | Wt: 175

Health B | PT/Exp B | Consist A | LIMA Plan B | Rand Var 0 | MM 1525

8-24-.267 with 9 SB in 255 AB at NYM. Not everything returned after 1H suspension: once-elite ct%, SS eligibility two big no-shows. Otherwise, some positives: HctX, bb% and power metrics made healthy rebounds from 2015 levels, and running game still shows some life. Speed should help BA decline gently; health is key.

Yr	Tm	AB	R	HR	RBI	SB	BA	xBA	OBP	SLG	OPS	vL	vR	bb%	ct%	Eye	G	L	F	h%	HctX	PX	xPX	hr/f	Spd	SBO	SB%	#Wk	DOM	DIS	RC/G	RAR	BPV	BPX	R$
12	MIA	642	86	11	57	40	287	291	347	433	780	753	792	9	91	1.13	46	22	32	30	109	84	83	6%	136	27%	78%	27	78%	4%	5.46	24.8	93	233	$29
13	TOR	382	58	10	37	15	296	275	353	427	780	705	804	8	88	0.72	46	21	33	32	96	84	81	9%	108	18%	71%	17	59%	24%	5.38	20.2	69	173	$18
14	TOR	610	94	9	51	30	287	268	328	398	726	709	732	6	88	0.52	42	23	36	31	89	77	66	5%	140	19%	94%	26	46%	4%	4.93	28.0	70	189	$29
15	2 TM	481	57	7	53	24	274	257	310	378	688	700	683	5	87	0.42	44	20	36	30	73	67	58	5%	113	24%	80%	24	46%	25%	4.20	6.0	48	130	$20
16	NYM *	317	53	9	27	12	251	249	315	408	722	1196	664	9	82	0.51	35	22	43	28	96	88	101	9%	141	18%	78%	12	67%	25%	4.38	-2.1	58	166	$10
1st Half		58	8	1	3	3	200	233	281	281	561			10	84	0.70				22		42			111	24%	66%	1	100%	0%	2.46		25	71	-$4
2nd Half		259	45	8	24	9	263	255	323	436	759	1196	664	8	81	0.47	35	22	43	30	95	99	101	9%	139	17%	82%	11	64%	27%	4.92	3.4	64	183	$13
17	Proj	454	67	10	40	21	261	255	315	385	699	777	673	7	84	0.50	41	22	37	29	91	72	79	7%	131	21%	81%				4.26	-8.5	48	137	$18

Reynolds,Mark

Age: 33 | Bats: R | Pos: 1B | Ht: 6' 1" | Wt: 200

Health B | PT/Exp C | Consist B | LIMA Plan D+ | Rand Var -5 | MM 3113

If he made a conscious plate approach adjustment, it worked—for now. Coors Field, a ct% uptick, LD spike and some h% luck helped produce career-high BA, despite HctX near career lows. Even .255 road BA was improved. But power ebbed again, and xPX isn't hopeful for a reversal. Skills history and age bet against a repeat.

Yr	Tm	AB	R	HR	RBI	SB	BA	xBA	OBP	SLG	OPS	vL	vR	bb%	ct%	Eye	G	L	F	h%	HctX	PX	xPX	hr/f	Spd	SBO	SB%	#Wk	DOM	DIS	RC/G	RAR	BPV	BPX	R$
12	BAL	457	65	23	69	1	221	236	335	429	763	722	778	14	65	0.46	37	20	42	28	100	161	138	18%	75	3%	25%	25	32%	44%	4.50	-12.9	42	105	$8
13	2 AL	445	55	21	67	3	220	217	306	393	699	725	684	10	65	0.33	39	18	42	29	94	132	125	17%	78	4%	75%	27	44%	48%	3.86	-9.8	13	33	$9
14	MIL	378	47	22	45	5	196	223	287	394	681	573	719	11	68	0.39	38	14	48	22	94	146	155	18%	91	7%	83%	26	46%	38%	3.58	-7.2	39	105	$6
15	STL	382	35	13	48	2	230	229	315	398	713	753	697	10	68	0.36	41	19	40	30	92	126	117	13%	91	5%	40%	27	48%	41%	3.98	-16.1	24	65	$4
16	COL	393	61	14	53	1	282	256	356	450	806	673	865	10	72	0.38	42	26	33	36	84	115	99	15%	95	3%	33%	23	48%	48%	5.53	2.2	28	80	$12
1st Half		253	40	8	33	0	285	262	351	451	802	652	870	9	72	0.36	44	26	30	37	81	118	97	15%	83	1%	0%	14	57%	36%	5.55	3.2	26	74	$14
2nd Half		140	21	6	20	1	279	246	365	450	815	710	856	10	71	0.40	37	25	38	35	90	110	103	16%	114	5%	50%	9	33%	67%	5.50	1.6	30	86	$9
17	Proj	314	41	13	42	2	243	237	327	417	744	678	900	10	70	0.37	40	21	39	31	90	117	116	15%	98	4%	51%				4.44	-6.2	9	25	$8

Rickard,Joey

Age: 26 | Bats: R | Pos: RF LF | Ht: 6' 1" | Wt: 183

Health C | PT/Exp D | Consist F | LIMA Plan D | Rand Var -2 | MM 1501

Rule 5 pick with career .390 OBP parlayed fine March into starting job on Opening Day. Struggles vR eventually landed him on the bench until torn thumb ligament ended his season in late July. If bb% can't translate, profile offers a few SB, no plus tools. And only a handful of AB.

Yr	Tm	AB	R	HR	RBI	SB	BA	xBA	OBP	SLG	OPS	vL	vR	bb%	ct%	Eye	G	L	F	h%	HctX	PX	xPX	hr/f	Spd	SBO	SB%	#Wk	DOM	DIS	RC/G	RAR	BPV	BPX	R$
12																																			
13																																			
14	aa	206	26	1	13	7	208		286	252	538			10	78	0.51				26		39			99	20%	62%				2.27		-3	-8	$1
15	a/a	325	43	2	35	16	287		365	406	770			11	77	0.54				37		87			120	20%	78%				5.35		39	105	$13
16	BAL	257	32	5	19	4	268	240	319	377	696	861	618	7	79	0.33	42	21	37	32	83	72	83	7%	127	7%	80%	16	25%	25%	4.19	-0.6	27	77	$5
1st Half		231	32	5	16	4	264	243	320	381	701	865	618	7	78	0.36	41	22	37	32	80	77	80	8%	126	8%	80%	14	21%	21%	4.21	-1.6	29	83	$6
2nd Half		26	0	0	3	0	308	153	308	346	654	800	619	0	85	0.00	48	14	38	36	115	30	106	0%	123	0%	0%	2	50%	50%	3.92	-0.4	1	3	-$5
17	Proj	223	29	2	17	7	247	223	317	331	648	819	590	9	78	0.46	45	17	38	31	101	58	96	3%	163	16%	71%				3.53	-7.8	10	30	$6

Rivera,Rene

Age: 33 | Bats: R | Pos: CA | Ht: 5' 10" | Wt: 210

Health A | PT/Exp D | Consist F | LIMA Plan D | Rand Var -1 | MM 2001

6-26-.222 in 185 AB at NYM. Prototypical example of the current state of MLB catching depth. Lifetime .213 hitter is still finding plenty of opportunity despite offering positive R$ just twice in parts of eight MLB seasons. Late-career power flashes may be keeping him alive, but there's no reason for him to live on your roster.

Yr	Tm	AB	R	HR	RBI	SB	BA	xBA	OBP	SLG	OPS	vL	vR	bb%	ct%	Eye	G	L	F	h%	HctX	PX	xPX	hr/f	Spd	SBO	SB%	#Wk	DOM	DIS	RC/G	RAR	BPV	BPX	R$
12	aaa	288	23	7	25	0	179		239	296	535			7	73	0.30				22		83			87	2%	0%				2.15		2	5	-$4
13	SD *	318	26	3	30	0	242	202	270	325	595	529	618	4	76	0.16	48	13	38	31	126	67	144	0%	75	4%	0%	10	10%	50%	2.84	-8.1	-9	-23	$1
14	SD	294	27	11	44	0	252	252	319	432	751	881	684	8	74	0.36	35	21	44	30	107	138	138	11%	66	0%	0%	27	48%	37%	4.63	10.1	46	124	$6
15	TAM	298	16	5	26	0	178	193	213	275	489	457	503	4	71	0.13	38	17	45	23	83	77	117	5%	41	0%	0%	26	12%	62%	1.77	-19.6	-31	-84	-$6
16	NYM *	210	14	6	29	0	218	209	278	327	604	943	556	8	72	0.30	47	21	32	27	92	67	96	14%	51	0%	0%	22	23%	55%	2.96	-9.3	-24	-69	$0
1st Half		95	7	3	16	0	199	217	255	311	566	850	543	7	69	0.25	48	24	28	25	84	71	90	23%	51	0%	0%	11	18%	64%	2.53	-4.8	-34	-97	-$1
2nd Half		115	7	3	13	0	235	204	299	339	638	1029	563	8	75	0.34	47	20	33	29	98	64	99	10%	62	0%	0%	11	27%	45%	3.35	-2.7	-13	-37	$0
17	Proj	229	16	7	28	0	214	218	271	340	611	741	566	7	73	0.25	43	19	37	26	96	82	112	11%	53	0%	0%				2.91	-8.7	-23	-67	$1

JOCK THOMPSON

Rivera,T.J.

Age: 28 Bats: R Pos: 2B	Health A	LIMA Plan D+	
Ht: 6' 1" Wt: 205	PT/Exp D	Rand Var -1	
	Consist B	MM 1131	

3-16-.333 in 105 AB at NYM. Despite aversion to walks, career .324 minor league hitter hiked power, won PCL batting crown, didn't miss a beat in MLB debut. Speed and glove are nothing special. Even with limitations, versatility and bat-to-ball skills suggest he'll have an MLB career. With the right opportunity, perhaps more.

Yr	Tm	AB	R	HR	RBI	SB	BA	xBA	OBP	SLG	OPS	vL	vR	bb%	ct%	Eye	G	L	F	h%	HctX	PX	xPX	hr/f	Spd	SBO	SB%	#Wk	DOM	DIS	RC/G	RAR	BPV	BPX	R$
12																																			
13																																			
14	aa	201	19	1	19	1	281		307	343	650			4	83	0.22				34		54			85	1%	100%				3.76		9	24	$3
15	a/a	403	45	5	34	1	254		279	349	628			3	85	0.23				29		66			89	2%	36%				3.29		29	78	$5
16	NYM *	510	52	10	69	2	275	263	299	394	692	457	997	3	83	0.20	42	24	34	32	91	74	92	10%	100	5%	32%	8	25%	25%	4.01	-14.1	28	80	$12
1st Half		250	27	4	33	1	256	243	283	359	642			4	82	0.21				29		64			87	8%	14%				3.24		17	49	$9
2nd Half		260	25	6	36	1	293	269	315	427	742	457	997	3	83	0.18	42	24	34	34	91	83	92	10%	102	2%	100%	8	25%	25%	4.88	-0.1	36	103	$15
17	Proj	**203**	**21**	**5**	**23**	**1**	**271**	**270**	**292**	**404**	**696**	**371**	**852**	**3**	**84**	**0.21**	**42**	**24**	**34**	**30**	**82**	**80**	**83**	**9%**	**102**	**3%**	**47%**				**4.12**	**-4.0**	**22**	**62**	**$3**

Rizzo,Anthony

Age: 27 Bats: L Pos: 1B	Health A	LIMA Plan C	
Ht: 6' 3" Wt: 220	PT/Exp A	Rand Var 0	
	Consist A	MM 4155	

2015 SB spike was obviously a one-off, and he lost some of his recent luster vL, but these are quibbles. Three consecutive seasons of 30+ HR and .380+ OBP backed up by rock-solid peripherals put him in elite company among the game's most reliable producers. Age, health and consistency cement Top 20 ADP status.

Yr	Tm	AB	R	HR	RBI	SB	BA	xBA	OBP	SLG	OPS	vL	vR	bb%	ct%	Eye	G	L	F	h%	HctX	PX	xPX	hr/f	Spd	SBO	SB%	#Wk	DOM	DIS	RC/G	RAR	BPV	BPX	R$
12	CHC *	594	80	32	94	4	290	291	340	510	849	599	892	7	79	0.37	45	24	30	32	112	136	119	18%	89	6%	51%	15	60%	20%	6.09	10.9	69	173	$26
13	CHC	606	71	23	80	6	233	269	323	419	742	625	796	11	79	0.60	43	20	38	26	112	130	124	13%	73	7%	55%	27	63%	7%	4.34	-4.5	66	165	$13
14	CHC	524	89	32	78	5	286	286	386	527	913	928	907	12	78	0.63	36	22	42	31	106	164	135	19%	79	6%	56%	25	72%	4%	6.90	40.2	93	251	$28
15	CHC	586	94	31	101	17	278	285	387	512	899	881	905	12	82	0.74	35	22	44	29	121	143	131	15%	81	14%	74%	27	70%	15%	6.51	19.1	93	251	$31
16	CHC	583	94	32	109	3	292	293	385	544	928	832	970	11	81	0.69	38	20	41	31	113	145	120	16%	78	5%	38%	27	78%	7%	7.07	28.4	90	257	$26
1st Half		280	47	20	61	2	282	299	401	571	973	807	1055	14	83	0.96	36	18	45	28	116	158	122	19%	73	6%	40%	14	79%	7%	7.54	19.5	110	314	$27
2nd Half		303	47	12	48	1	300	288	368	518	886	861	895	8	80	0.47	40	23	37	34	111	132	117	13%	86	4%	33%	13	77%	8%	6.64	12.9	71	203	$26
17	Proj	**593**	**96**	**33**	**105**	**5**	**288**	**289**	**381**	**533**	**914**	**849**	**940**	**11**	**81**	**0.63**	**38**	**21**	**41**	**31**	**114**	**140**	**125**	**17%**	**79**	**6%**	**50%**				**6.82**	**28.8**	**80**	**230**	**$30**

Rodriguez,Alex

Age: 41 Bats: R Pos: DH	Health D	LIMA Plan F	
Ht: 6' 3" Wt: 230	PT/Exp D	Rand Var +4	
	Consist F	MM 2201	

Contact and BA were lost in 2015. Now, disintegration of patience and power, and annual DL stint (hamstring this time) would ordinarily be a career-ender for any other 41-year-old. Cut by NYY in August, we still await a retirement decision. We'll project some token AB now, but it'll either be 2-3 times this, or zero.

Yr	Tm	AB	R	HR	RBI	SB	BA	xBA	OBP	SLG	OPS	vL	vR	bb%	ct%	Eye	G	L	F	h%	HctX	PX	xPX	hr/f	Spd	SBO	SB%	#Wk	DOM	DIS	RC/G	RAR	BPV	BPX	R$
12	NYY	463	74	18	57	13	272	250	353	430	783	924	717	10	75	0.44	45	22	32	33	108	103	118	16%	92	10%	93%	22	45%	32%	5.33	5.8	32	80	$18
13	NYY *	177	24	9	24	4	243	247	342	442	784	585	856	13	71	0.52	40	20	40	29	131	142	166	16%	78	11%	67%	8	50%	50%	5.01	2.7	48	120	$4
14																																			
15	NYY	523	83	33	86	4	250	261	356	486	842	926	806	14	72	0.58	43	18	39	28	111	154	147	22%	74	3%	100%	27	48%	19%	5.90	7.0	64	173	$19
16	NYY	225	19	9	31	3	200	225	247	351	598	647	573	6	70	0.21	46	19	35	24	83	96	90	16%	64	7%	100%	17	24%	53%	2.82	-18.8	-8	-23	$0
1st Half		180	18	8	28	3	222	229	259	383	642	780	578	5	69	0.16	45	20	35	27	88	102	99	18%	64	8%	100%	12	25%	58%	3.34	-11.9	-10	-29	$2
2nd Half		45	1	1	3	0	111	169	200	222	422	248	549	10	73	0.42	48	15	36	13	63	76	59	8%	75	0%	0%	5	20%	40%	1.28	-6.6	-1	-3	-$8
17	Proj	**130**	**13**	**4**	**16**	**1**	**227**	**218**	**283**	**369**	**653**	**594**	**684**	**7**	**68**	**0.23**	**45**	**18**	**37**	**30**	**95**	**97**	**111**	**14%**	**75**	**6%**	**86%**				**3.44**	**-8.2**	**-18**	**-50**	**$2**

Rodriguez,Sean

Age: 32 Bats: R Pos: 1B 2B SS	Health A	LIMA Plan D	
Ht: 6' 1" Wt: 198	PT/Exp D	Rand Var -5	
	Consist D	MM 4213	

Poster boy for productive bench players in The Year of The Home Run. Has always flashed power, but newfound patience and hr/f spike took it to the next level. Inflated h% and surprising surge vR added to his playing time. Entrenched ct% woes point to regression. If he was 5 years younger, UP: 20 HR. Now, a dart throw.

Yr	Tm	AB	R	HR	RBI	SB	BA	xBA	OBP	SLG	OPS	vL	vR	bb%	ct%	Eye	G	L	F	h%	HctX	PX	xPX	hr/f	Spd	SBO	SB%	#Wk	DOM	DIS	RC/G	RAR	BPV	BPX	R$
12	TAM	301	36	6	32	5	213	220	281	326	607	655	575	8	75	0.36	47	15	38	26	86	82	76	7%	103	7%	100%	25	20%	48%	3.01	-22.4	15	38	$1
13	TAM	195	21	5	23	1	246	227	320	385	704	745	545	8	70	0.29	36	23	41	33	83	110	81	9%	90	8%	25%	27	33%	44%	3.76	-4.8	12	30	$2
14	TAM	237	30	12	41	2	211	262	258	443	701	729	666	4	72	0.15	39	17	44	24	108	170	137	16%	110	9%	67%	27	52%	30%	3.44	-5.4	68	184	$4
15	PIT	224	25	4	17	2	246	232	281	362	642	655	634	2	72	0.08	48	20	32	32	81	90	106	8%	105	9%	50%	27	22%	52%	3.10	-15.1	-2	-5	$2
16	PIT	300	49	18	56	2	270	258	349	510	859	934	831	10	66	0.32	40	24	36	35	115	164	167	25%	87	4%	67%	26	46%	46%	6.06	6.2	43	123	$11
1st Half		146	27	6	25	2	260	252	347	479	827	903	785	10	64	0.33	42	22	36	36	95	167	136	18%	93	6%	100%	14	43%	50%	5.66	2.4	42	120	$9
2nd Half		154	22	12	31	0	279	266	351	539	890	986	866	9	68	0.32	38	26	36	34	135	161	195	32%	82	2%	0%	12	50%	42%	6.45	5.9	44	126	$13
17	Proj	**294**	**39**	**12**	**41**	**2**	**252**	**243**	**312**	**435**	**747**	**766**	**735**	**7**	**69**	**0.23**	**42**	**22**	**36**	**32**	**104**	**123**	**141**	**16%**	**96**	**6%**	**57%**				**4.40**	**-6.1**	**12**	**35**	**$9**

Rojas,Miguel

Age: 28 Bats: R Pos: 2B 1B SS	Health A	LIMA Plan D	
Ht: 5' 11" Wt: 195	PT/Exp D	Rand Var 0	
	Consist C	MM 1131	

Defense-first SS qualified at all four infield positions (in 2016), but that's not in and of itself a fantasy asset. Now he's a garden variety utility infielder with plus contact and none of the other accessories necessary to make it work. Anemic pop and average speed make him unlikely to grow beyond his current bench role. Pass.

Yr	Tm	AB	R	HR	RBI	SB	BA	xBA	OBP	SLG	OPS	vL	vR	bb%	ct%	Eye	G	L	F	h%	HctX	PX	xPX	hr/f	Spd	SBO	SB%	#Wk	DOM	DIS	RC/G	RAR	BPV	BPX	R$
12	a/a	272	19	1	14	2	177		229	200	429			6	86	0.50				20		16			95	8%	33%				1.35		2	5	-$6
13	aa	420	38	4	27	9	206		264	268	532			7	87	0.59				23		40			107	13%	65%				2.25		28	70	$0
14	LA *	308	32	4	17	4	205	221	243	271	515	283	516	5	82	0.29	68	8	24	24	50	50	35	4%	94	12%	53%	18	6%	56%	2.05	-16.2	10	27	-$1
15	MIA *	391	39	3	35	2	268	290	307	369	676	327	768	5	88	0.47	55	24	21	30	88	64	42	4%	107	9%	19%	16	38%	31%	3.67	-11.6	49	132	$6
16	MIA	194	27	1	14	2	247	267	288	325	613	697	579	5	86	0.41	54	20	26	28	70	55	37	2%	95	7%	67%	27	37%	44%	3.15	-10.5	29	83	$1
1st Half		100	14	0	9	1	250	255	287	300	587	848	483	6	86	0.43	58	19	24	29	65	39	29	0%	84	4%	100%	14	29%	50%	3.04	-5.4	14	40	$1
2nd Half		94	13	1	5	1	245	278	290	351	641	536	682	5	86	0.38	50	22	28	28	75	72	46	5%	109	10%	50%	13	46%	38%	3.24	-4.7	47	134	$1
17	Proj	**166**	**20**	**1**	**12**	**2**	**240**	**267**	**283**	**319**	**602**	**507**	**631**	**5**	**86**	**0.41**	**56**	**20**	**24**	**27**	**74**	**52**	**40**	**3%**	**102**	**9%**	**48%**				**2.92**	**-9.4**	**20**	**58**	**$2**

Romine,Austin

Age: 28 Bats: R Pos: CA	Health B	LIMA Plan D	
Ht: 6' 1" Wt: 220	PT/Exp F	Rand Var 0	
	Consist B	MM 1221	

Maintained good contact through increased playing time to drive career-year to date—albeit in another small sample. Too impatient, too many GBs to unlock above average power, but even these metrics ticked upward. Despite age, none of this likely makes a difference. Minus big tools, it's a backup profile until further notice.

Yr	Tm	AB	R	HR	RBI	SB	BA	xBA	OBP	SLG	OPS	vL	vR	bb%	ct%	Eye	G	L	F	h%	HctX	PX	xPX	hr/f	Spd	SBO	SB%	#Wk	DOM	DIS	RC/G	RAR	BPV	BPX	R$
12	aaa	61	5	3	7	0	189		265	350	615			9	82	0.57				19		93			91	0%	0%				2.92		50	125	-$2
13	NYY *	177	19	2	13	1	229	232	275	312	588	576	540	6	71	0.22	55	23	22	31	88	74	61	5%	74	2%	100%	19	26%	53%	2.87	-4.4	-18	-45	-$1
14	NYY *	298	25	5	24	1	196	247	240	292	532	3000	333	5	77	0.25	56	22	22	24	184	78	152	0%	70	1%	100%	5	20%	60%	2.24	-10.1	3	8	-$2
15	NYY *	340	30	6	39	0	219	355	258	321	579	0	0	5	81	0.28	50	50	0	25	0	70	-16	0%	65	2%	0%	1	0%	0%	2.66	-11.2	11	30	$0
16	NYY	165	17	4	26	1	242	260	269	382	650	725	551	4	81	0.23	47	19	33	28	88	90	100	9%	75	3%	100%	26	38%	42%	3.54	-1.5	30	86	$1
1st Half		90	4	2	14	0	256	212	266	400	666	663	669	2	84	0.14	56	17	27	28	82	92	70	10%	79	0%	0%	14	50%	36%	3.72	-1.1	42	120	$1
2nd Half		75	13	2	12	1	227	240	272	360	632	802	419	6	77	0.29	36	22	41	27	96	86	139	8%	78	6%	100%	12	25%	50%	3.33	-1.8	16	46	$2
17	Proj	**166**	**18**	**4**	**21**	**1**	**238**	**247**	**274**	**357**	**631**	**728**	**545**	**5**	**79**	**0.24**	**47**	**20**	**33**	**28**	**89**	**78**	**91**	**8%**	**71**	**3%**	**87%**				**3.30**	**-4.2**	**4**	**13**	**$3**

Rosario,Eddie

Age: 25 Bats: L Pos: LF CF	Health A	LIMA Plan B	
Ht: 6' 0" Wt: 170	PT/Exp C	Rand Var -2	
	Consist B	MM 3425	

10-32-.269, 5 SB in 335 AB at MIN. Inability to keep BA above .200 led to May demotion. Enjoyed h%-fueled .306 BA after July return. Plenty of tools here, including sneaky power, speed, defensive chops—and both age, handedness work in his favor. But poor pitch selection and free-swinging ways cap their potential.

Yr	Tm	AB	R	HR	RBI	SB	BA	xBA	OBP	SLG	OPS	vL	vR	bb%	ct%	Eye	G	L	F	h%	HctX	PX	xPX	hr/f	Spd	SBO	SB%	#Wk	DOM	DIS	RC/G	RAR	BPV	BPX	R$
12																																			
13	aa	289	31	3	30	5	254		294	362	656			5	75	0.22				33		87			105	15%	55%				3.49		14	35	$5
14	aa	316	32	6	28	6	213		245	347	592			4	77	0.18				26		103			103	20%	59%				2.64		31	84	$2
15	MIN *	548	69	15	60	12	259	242	284	438	722	811	727	3	75	0.14	39	20	41	32	96	110	110	10%	172	17%	62%	22	41%	27%	4.13	-10.3	49	132	$16
16	MIN *	495	74	16	54	9	275	257	300	439	739	594	752	3	76	0.15	46	19	34	33	93	106	102	12%	127	14%	63%	18	28%	50%	4.51	-2.8	36	103	$16
1st Half		279	37	9	32	7	251	257	274	410	684	472	557	3	79	0.15	51	15	34	29	78	102	79	10%	109	21%	68%	8	25%	63%	3.73	-8.1	37	106	$16
2nd Half		216	37	7	22	2	306	252	336	477	813	660	859	4	73	0.15	44	22	34	39	98	112	114	13%	142	7%	50%	10	30%	40%	5.67	5.8	33	94	$17
17	Proj	**438**	**59**	**13**	**46**	**8**	**264**	**250**	**292**	**433**	**725**	**680**	**738**	**4**	**75**	**0.16**	**44**	**19**	**37**	**32**	**92**	**105**	**104**	**11%**	**140**	**14%**	**61%**				**4.24**	**-2.7**	**31**	**88**	**$15**

JOCK THOMPSON

Rua,Ryan

Age: 27 Bats: R Pos: LF 1B	Health B	LIMA Plan D
Ht: 6' 2" Wt: 180	PT/Exp D	Rand Var -5
	Consist F	MM 2501

Intriguing 1st half fueled by h%, hr/f before opportunity dried up. PRO: Rising patience helped tap into his power; Spd and running game were revelations. CON: Contact rate, GB% issues look entrenched, capping BA and HR upside. Versatility helps, handedness and track record vR don't. Bench bat until something changes.

Yr	Tm	AB	R	HR	RBI	SB	BA	xBA	OBP	SLG	OPS	vL	vR	bb%	ct%	Eye	G	L	F	h%	HctX	PX	xPX	hr/f	Spd	SBO	SB%	#Wk	DOM	DIS	RC/G	RAR	BPV	BPX	R$
12																																			
13	aa	86	16	3	8	1	218		269	356	625			6	70	0.23				28		94			132	4%	100%				3.17		11	28	-$1
14	TEX *	576	58	15	68	5	266	266	313	403	716	922	664	6	78	0.31	52	23	25	32	97	101	86	9%	104	8%	48%	6	33%	33%	4.25	1.7	37	100	$16
15	TEX *	225	24	9	24	2	175	195	234	329	562	658	556	7	63	0.21	51	8	41	23	75	122	92	19%	91	6%	100%	11	27%	55%	2.41	-18.3	-5	-14	-$2
16	TEX	240	40	8	22	9	258	233	331	400	731	754	714	8	68	0.28	52	19	28	35	90	94	57	17%	148	14%	100%	27	30%	56%	4.60	-1.7	11	31	$8
1st Half		148	30	7	19	6	284	258	363	486	850	1026	727	9	70	0.32	55	15	30	36	87	130	66	23%	142	15%	100%	14	43%	50%	6.26	4.8	47	134	$13
2nd Half		92	10	1	3	3	217	198	277	261	538	346	692	7	65	0.22	47	27	27	32	96	31	42	6%	133	12%	100%	13	15%	62%	2.48	-7.4	-58	-166	-$1
17	**Proj**	**227**	**29**	**7**	**21**	**5**	**222**	**218**	**287**	**354**	**641**	**638**	**644**	**7**	**67**	**0.24**	**51**	**17**	**32**	**30**	**87**	**90**	**71**	**14%**	**123**	**10%**	**93%**				**3.34**	**-7.8**	**-15**	**-43**	**$3**

Rupp,Cameron

Age: 28 Bats: R Pos: CA	Health A	LIMA Plan D+
Ht: 6' 1" Wt: 240	PT/Exp D	Rand Var -4
	Consist D	MM 3003

Impressive season-long hr/f highlighted above-average power, despite GB% hike. But overall, that 1st half was a h%-fueled mirage. 2nd half regression combined with ongoing contact woes dragged him down and reaffirmed his issues vR. HR and defense make him a better bet than most #2 catchers, but the risks are obvious.

Yr	Tm	AB	R	HR	RBI	SB	BA	xBA	OBP	SLG	OPS	vL	vR	bb%	ct%	Eye	G	L	F	h%	HctX	PX	xPX	hr/f	Spd	SBO	SB%	#Wk	DOM	DIS	RC/G	RAR	BPV	BPX	R$
12																																			
13	PHI *	338	27	11	35	1	219	199	259	358	617	650	778	5	67	0.17	56	11	33	29	93	112	152	0%	61	3%	38%	2	0%	50%	2.99	-7.3	-11	-28	$1
14	PHI *	254	17	5	19	0	144	155	204	241	444	0	546	7	56	0.17	43	13	45	23	60	104	123	0%	58	0%	0%	6	0%	67%	1.46	-16.9	-60	-162	-$7
15	PHI	270	24	9	28	0	233	225	301	374	675	915	597	8	74	0.34	43	19	38	28	92	93	97	12%	74	1%	0%	27	37%	48%	3.62	-1.5	10	27	$2
16	PHI	389	36	16	54	1	252	248	303	447	750	993	699	6	71	0.21	48	17	34	32	99	134	108	17%	69	1%	100%	27	37%	33%	4.52	1.2	24	69	$7
1st Half		191	19	8	22	1	288	272	323	508	831	883	819	4	73	0.14	48	19	34	36	98	148	102	17%	71	3%	100%	14	50%	21%	5.73	8.5	42	120	$10
2nd Half		198	17	8	32	0	217	215	284	389	673	1124	590	8	68	0.27	49	16	35	28	100	119	113	17%	71	0%	0%	13	23%	46%	3.54	-3.7	7	20	$4
17	**Proj**	**404**	**35**	**13**	**48**	**1**	**225**	**219**	**283**	**376**	**659**	**853**	**614**	**7**	**69**	**0.23**	**45**	**17**	**37**	**29**	**91**	**106**	**107**	**13%**	**68**	**1%**	**52%**				**3.42**	**-8.9**	**-15**	**-42**	**$5**

Russell,Addison

Age: 23 Bats: R Pos: SS	Health A	LIMA Plan B+
Ht: 6' 0" Wt: 195	PT/Exp C	Rand Var +2
	Consist B	MM 3225

Still figuring things out. Ditched patience for more aggressive approach in 2nd half; HR output spiked and contact /BA metrics improved at the same time. Consistent hr/f speaks to legit power, though xPX and age say it's still in growth mode. xBA indicates BA is slowly coming around despite volatile plate skills. More baby steps likely.

Yr	Tm	AB	R	HR	RBI	SB	BA	xBA	OBP	SLG	OPS	vL	vR	bb%	ct%	Eye	G	L	F	h%	HctX	PX	xPX	hr/f	Spd	SBO	SB%	#Wk	DOM	DIS	RC/G	RAR	BPV	BPX	R$
12																																			
13																																			
14	aa	241	31	10	35	4	277		316	466	782			5	80	0.29				31		130			89	15%	48%				4.90		64	173	$9
15	CHC *	519	66	14	61	5	246	226	303	393	696	527	746	8	70	0.27	41	18	41	33	83	115	105	10%	95	6%	61%	25	36%	40%	3.98	3.2	17	46	$11
16	CHC	525	67	21	95	5	238	251	321	417	738	801	715	9	74	0.41	41	21	38	28	88	111	96	14%	108	5%	83%	27	52%	33%	4.35	-4.1	39	111	$12
1st Half		260	30	8	42	2	235	239	334	381	715	562	773	12	70	0.47	47	23	31	30	77	95	85	14%	122	3%	100%	14	57%	43%	4.20	-2.0	20	57	$9
2nd Half		265	37	13	53	3	242	264	307	453	760	1048	659	7	78	0.33	36	20	44	26	99	125	105	14%	95	7%	75%	13	46%	23%	4.43	-0.2	56	160	$15
17	**Proj**	**548**	**71**	**23**	**85**	**6**	**247**	**252**	**316**	**436**	**752**	**759**	**750**	**8**	**74**	**0.33**	**41**	**20**	**39**	**29**	**87**	**120**	**100**	**14%**	**101**	**7%**	**66%**				**4.50**	**0.5**	**32**	**92**	**$17**

Saladino,Tyler

Age: 27 Bats: R Pos: 2B SS	Health A	LIMA Plan D
Ht: 5' 11" Wt: 190	PT/Exp D	Rand Var -4
	Consist C	MM 1431

Versatility helped open the door when opportunity knocked. Provided a little bit of everything thanks to inflated 1st half hr/f, fortunate 2nd half h%, and season-long green light on bases. Young enough to get more chances, but this 2016 confluence isn't a good bet for a repeat. Absence of any standout skill limits his upside.

Yr	Tm	AB	R	HR	RBI	SB	BA	xBA	OBP	SLG	OPS	vL	vR	bb%	ct%	Eye	G	L	F	h%	HctX	PX	xPX	hr/f	Spd	SBO	SB%	#Wk	DOM	DIS	RC/G	RAR	BPV	BPX	R$
12	a/a	467	66	4	37	32	214		320	285	605			13	74	0.60				28		53			115	27%	79%				3.11		2	5	$10
13	aa	424	39	5	44	23	200		277	274	552			10	76	0.45				25		56			95	29%	71%				2.43		1	3	$6
14	aaa	294	27	6	28	5	248		293	373	666			6	79	0.31				29		89			103	8%	79%				3.72		33	89	$5
15	CHW *	432	55	7	43	28	219	257	270	322	592	650	585	7	79	0.33	54	23	23	26	61	63	32	9%	127	32%	86%	14	43%	50%	3.00	-20.9	19	51	$12
16	CHW	298	33	8	38	11	282	257	315	409	725	799	698	4	79	0.21	51	20	29	33	81	79	58	12%	90	21%	69%	25	20%	36%	4.41	-3.2	17	49	$11
1st Half		111	15	5	20	4	252	260	292	414	706	575	759	4	77	0.19	48	22	29	29	68	92	46	20%	81	24%	67%	14	14%	29%	3.86	-3.4	15	43	$8
2nd Half		187	18	3	18	7	299	254	330	406	736	952	664	4	81	0.22	53	19	28	36	89	72	65	7%	102	20%	70%	11	27%	45%	4.75	-0.7	21	60	$13
17	**Proj**	**165**	**19**	**4**	**19**	**7**	**253**	**258**	**300**	**372**	**672**	**729**	**652**	**6**	**79**	**0.28**	**52**	**21**	**27**	**30**	**73**	**73**	**47**	**11%**	**104**	**23%**	**77%**				**3.77**	**-5.1**	**16**	**45**	**$6**

Saltalamacchia,Jarrod

Age: 32 Bats: B Pos: CA	Health A	LIMA Plan F
Ht: 6' 3" Wt: 195	PT/Exp D	Rand Var +4
	Consist A	MM 4001

After six HR in April, a black hole the rest of the way. Historical power and patience remain intact, but career-long contact problems fell through the floor. HctX and h% followed in lock-step, dragging average down to unplayable levels. Should rebound some, but BA woes and volatility say the HR may not be worth it.

Yr	Tm	AB	R	HR	RBI	SB	BA	xBA	OBP	SLG	OPS	vL	vR	bb%	ct%	Eye	G	L	F	h%	HctX	PX	xPX	hr/f	Spd	SBO	SB%	#Wk	DOM	DIS	RC/G	RAR	BPV	BPX	R$
12	BOS	405	55	25	59	0	222	242	288	454	742	494	779	9	66	0.27	31	23	47	27	95	168	160	20%	91	1%	0%	27	48%	33%	4.26	1.4	43	108	$8
13	BOS	425	68	14	65	4	273	260	338	466	804	628	873	9	67	0.31	33	29	39	38	110	170	154	13%	80	5%	80%	27	52%	26%	5.56	22.3	50	125	$15
14	MIA	373	43	11	44	0	220	212	320	362	681	600	705	13	62	0.38	37	22	40	32	114	134	163	12%	84	1%	0%	25	32%	52%	3.75	4.8	7	19	$3
15	2 NL *	232	27	10	28	0	212	227	286	407	694	979	684	9	63	0.28	31	21	48	29	98	161	175	14%	69	0%	0%	21	57%	38%	3.77	-0.2	22	59	$1
16	DET	246	30	12	38	0	171	181	284	346	630	528	664	14	58	0.39	31	15	54	23	88	127	162	15%	106	0%	0%	25	32%	64%	3.07	-6.3	-4	-11	-$2
1st Half		131	21	8	24	0	206	206	325	443	768	547	825	15	56	0.42	18	21	61	29	84	181	192	17%	109	0%	0%	14	36%	64%	4.68	2.2	37	106	$2
2nd Half		115	9	4	14	0	130	134	237	235	472	510	456	13	59	0.36	45	8	46	17	91	69	130	12%	96	0%	0%	11	27%	64%	1.67	-9.7	-52	-149	-$6
17	**Proj**	**185**	**22**	**8**	**25**	**0**	**207**	**197**	**301**	**373**	**674**	**653**	**900**	**12**	**61**	**0.35**	**34**	**18**	**48**	**29**	**96**	**124**	**161**	**14%**	**88**	**0%**	**42%**				**3.62**	**-3.0**	**-21**	**-60**	**$2**

Sanchez,Carlos

Age: 25 Bats: B Pos: 2B	Health A	LIMA Plan D
Ht: 5' 11" Wt: 175	PT/Exp C	Rand Var +1
	Consist A	MM 1211

4-21-.208 in 154 AB at CHW. All four HR came in Sept, when FB% hike, .888 OPS in 71 AB was an improvement. But Sept ct%, bb% and h% all say it's unsustainable. Bigger picture shows a one-time contact-and-moderate-speed profile regressing at warp speed. Only age and versatility look attractive from here.

Yr	Tm	AB	R	HR	RBI	SB	BA	xBA	OBP	SLG	OPS	vL	vR	bb%	ct%	Eye	G	L	F	h%	HctX	PX	xPX	hr/f	Spd	SBO	SB%	#Wk	DOM	DIS	RC/G	RAR	BPV	BPX	R$
12	a/a	158	18	0	12	6	328		368	407	775			6	81	0.32				41		66			97	23%	54%				5.21		18	45	$5
13	aaa	432	41	0	23	13	218		264	267	531			6	81	0.31				27		43			105	21%	64%				2.24		2	5	$2
14	CHW *	537	48	5	45	12	248	240	288	331	619	867	423	5	77	0.25	42	26	32	31	84	64	87	0%	124	13%	69%	8	25%	75%	3.20	-3.1	11	30	$9
15	CHW *	520	54	7	45	6	244	261	276	349	624	606	591	4	78	0.20	54	23	23	30	76	79	48	7%	90	10%	59%	23	22%	57%	3.18	-17.0	13	35	$7
16	CHW *	389	40	11	44	8	214	230	252	356	608	405	662	5	72	0.18	39	21	40	27	67	93	75	9%	102	19%	59%	17	35%	53%	2.79	-23.5	6	17	$4
1st Half		239	24	5	20	6	214	234	262	332	594	667	374	6	71	0.23	40	27	33	28	34	80	42	0%	101	20%	65%	6	33%	67%	2.74	-15.4	-7	-20	$4
2nd Half		150	16	6	24	2	216	248	235	396	631	385	737	2	75	0.10	39	20	41	25	74	113	80	11%	104	17%	43%	11	36%	45%	2.84	-9.2	28	80	$3
17	**Proj**	**134**	**14**	**2**	**14**	**3**	**232**	**242**	**268**	**334**	**602**	**622**	**595**	**4**	**76**	**0.18**	**45**	**23**	**32**	**29**	**68**	**70**	**62**	**6%**	**103**	**15%**	**60%**				**2.84**	**-8.0**	**-4**	**-11**	**$2**

Sanchez,Gary

Age: 24 Bats: R Pos: CA	Health A	LIMA Plan B+
Ht: 6' 3" Wt: 235	PT/Exp C	Rand Var 0
	Consist C	MM 4145

20-42-.299 in 201 AB at NYY. Slow-maturing power, arm and makeup finally arrived with 2H bang. Torched AL pitching, posted 11% bb and 41% CS in extended debut. Late contact, BA fades (66%; .225 BA over final 102 AB) and receiving skills suggest work-in-progress. But plus tools and age point to bright future. Invest.

Yr	Tm	AB	R	HR	RBI	SB	BA	xBA	OBP	SLG	OPS	vL	vR	bb%	ct%	Eye	G	L	F	h%	HctX	PX	xPX	hr/f	Spd	SBO	SB%	#Wk	DOM	DIS	RC/G	RAR	BPV	BPX	R$
12																																			
13	aa	92	10	2	9	0	232		316	354	670			11	81	0.66				27		89			94	0%	0%				3.71		49	123	-$2
14	aa	429	39	12	53	1	245		303	367	669			8	76	0.35				29		90			78	2%	43%				3.72		18	49	$7
15	NYY *	367	44	18	55	6	255	164	304	459	763	0	0	7	76	0.29	0	0	100	29	0	135	-16	0%	66	10%	74%	2	0%	50%	4.74	10.8	47	127	$12
16	NYY *	485	70	30	88	7	277	289	337	533	870	868	1093	8	78	0.40	49	16	34	30	132	151	159	40%	68	7%	87%	11	45%	36%	6.37	34.5	71	203	$21
1st Half		223	25	8	32	5	251	354	281	439	719	0	0	4	82	0.23	67	33	0	27	111	112	59	0%	74	11%	100%	1	0%	100%	4.30	1.0	51	146	$11
2nd Half		262	45	22	56	3	300	294	381	613	994	934	1093	12	74	0.50	49	16	35	33	126	187	161	40%	68	5%	72%	10	50%	30%	8.45	31.2	91	260	$29
17	**Proj**	**449**	**55**	**26**	**67**	**5**	**255**	**276**	**319**	**489**	**809**	**690**	**849**	**8**	**77**	**0.40**	**47**	**17**	**36**	**27**	**113**	**139**	**145**	**21%**	**68**	**6%**	**78%**				**5.29**	**15.2**	**56**	**160**	**$16**

JOCK THOMPSON

Sanchez,Hector

Age: 27 Bats: B Pos: CA	Health	B	LIMA Plan	F
Ht: 5' 11" Wt: 185	PT/Exp	F	Rand Var	0
	Consist	C	MM	3011

3-8-.265 in 49 AB at CHW, SD. Anemic switch-hitter powered up vR, but small MLB sample isn't meaningful. Set career highs in BA, BB, 2B, HR in just 146 Triple-A AB—but notoriously hitter-friendly El Paso was his home. Sub-par plate skills add to skepticism—but age, xPX flashes, MLB catching shortage keeps us watching.

Yr Tm	AB	R	HR	RBI	SB	BA	xBA	OBP	SLG	OPS	vL	vR	bb%	ct%	Eye	G	L	F	h%	HctX	PX	xPX	hr/f	Spd	SBO	SB%	#Wk	DOM	DIS	RC/G	RAR	BPV	BPX	R$
12 SF	218	22	3	34	0	280	237	295	390	685	727	661	2	76	0.10	44	22	34	36	85	88	101	5%	81	0%	0%	25	36%	44%	4.09	-1.2	6	15	$4
13 SF *	214	15	5	26	0	235	247	286	337	623	860	552	7	78	0.33	43	27	31	28	84	71	74	10%	85	0%	0%	19	16%	42%	3.21	-3.0	11	28	$0
14 SF	163	8	3	28	0	196	198	237	301	538	531	540	5	66	0.15	34	21	46	28	95	96	150	6%	78	3%	0%	17	29%	71%	2.16	-6.6	-22	-59	-$2
15 SF *	195	18	3	15	0	205	212	238	302	540	458	533	4	77	0.19	52	14	33	25	62	71	49	7%	82	0%	0%	11	36%	55%	2.31	-9.1	0	0	-$3
16 2 TM *	253	20	13	35	0	236	246	286	446	732	286	886	6	73	0.25	33	21	46	27	106	134	91	17%	65	0%	0%	12	42%	42%	4.26	-1.1	32	91	$3
1st Half	69	6	6	13	0	221	266	303	513	816	0	935	10	74	0.45	22	17	61	21	117	171	128	9%	83	0%	0%	8	38%	38%	5.08	2.0	82	234	$1
2nd Half	184	14	7	22	0	242	251	279	421	700	667	842	5	72	0.18	43	24	33	30	97	120	59	29%	74	0%	0%	4	50%	50%	3.95	-1.0	17	49	$4
17 Proj	132	10	5	17	0	223	239	278	381	658	625	670	6	73	0.23	43	21	36	27	86	103	86	13%	81	0%	0%				3.33	-3.3	-6	-18	$0

Sandoval,Pablo

Age: 30 Bats: B Pos: 3B	Health	F	LIMA Plan	B
Ht: 5' 11" Wt: 240	PT/Exp	C	Rand Var	+5
	Consist	F	MM	1035

Few players have been in more need of a reset. Followed up 2015 AL debut disaster with abysmal March before shoulder surgery aborted his season. Conditioning is a constant concern and he may no longer be playable vL. But pre-2015, he still owned plus contact skills and solid production vR. If he's healthy in March, speculate.

Yr Tm	AB	R	HR	RBI	SB	BA	xBA	OBP	SLG	OPS	vL	vR	bb%	ct%	Eye	G	L	F	h%	HctX	PX	xPX	hr/f	Spd	SBO	SB%	#Wk	DOM	DIS	RC/G	RAR	BPV	BPX	R$
12 SF	396	59	12	63	1	283	274	342	447	789	745	809	9	85	0.64	43	20	37	31	120	103	117	10%	62	2%	50%	21	48%	24%	5.45	10.1	61	153	$13
13 SF	525	52	14	79	0	278	262	341	417	758	686	786	8	85	0.59	41	21	37	31	103	90	92	8%	53	0%	0%	25	44%	20%	4.97	15.2	46	115	$15
14 SF	588	68	16	73	0	279	263	324	415	739	563	824	6	86	0.46	43	21	37	30	114	89	111	9%	75	0%	0%	27	48%	30%	4.75	17.9	50	135	$18
15 BOS	470	43	10	47	0	245	253	292	366	658	465	744	5	84	0.34	49	19	32	27	88	79	69	8%	50	0%	0%	25	36%	32%	3.49	-14.9	28	76	$5
16 BOS	6	0	0	0	0	0	0	143	0	143	0	143	14	33	0.25	0	0	100	0	0	0	-24	0%	71	0%	0%	2	0%	100%	0.00	-1.0	-214	-611	-$2
1st Half	6	0	0	0	0	0	0	143	0	143	0	143	14	33	0.25	0	0	100	0	0	0	-24	0%	71	0%	0%	2	0%	100%	0.00	-1.2	-215	-614	-$2
2nd Half																																		
17 Proj	423	46	11	56	0	269	262	323	405	728	602	783	7	85	0.50	44	20	36	30	103	79	93	8%	56	0%	50%				4.51	-4.6	32	90	$11

Sano,Miguel

Age: 24 Bats: R Pos: 3B RF DH	Health	B	LIMA Plan	B
Ht: 6' 3" Wt: 235	PT/Exp	D	Rand Var	-1
	Consist	C	MM	5215

25-66-.236 in 437 AB at MIN. Struggled out of the gate with contact and glove at new position. Lost June to hamstring injury; nagged by elbow/back woes and work ethic questions in 2nd half. Through it all, immense power and patience still shine. BA concerns will depress his value, but with health... UP: 40 HR.

Yr Tm	AB	R	HR	RBI	SB	BA	xBA	OBP	SLG	OPS	vL	vR	bb%	ct%	Eye	G	L	F	h%	HctX	PX	xPX	hr/f	Spd	SBO	SB%	#Wk	DOM	DIS	RC/G	RAR	BPV	BPX	R$
12																																		
13 aa	233	28	14	44	2	213		299	477	776			11	64	0.34				26		209			102	6%	60%				4.57		77	193	$4
14																																		
15 MIN *	520	88	29	89	5	257	249	357	496	853	881	929	14	63	0.43	33	25	42	35	122	188	175	26%	94	5%	70%	15	60%	20%	6.04	25.0	61	165	$20
16 MIN *	462	60	27	68	1	231	224	317	458	776	818	771	11	59	0.31	34	20	46	32	96	173	157	21%	85	1%	100%	24	38%	42%	4.83	7.7	25	71	$9
1st Half	213	32	14	32	1	224	227	340	454	794	1080	760	15	60	0.44	31	22	47	30	104	166	176	22%	79	2%	100%	11	45%	36%	5.10	4.2	30	86	$9
2nd Half	249	28	13	36	0	237	222	295	462	757	696	780	8	58	0.20	36	18	45	35	91	179	142	20%	91	0%	0%	13	31%	46%	4.57	0.9	21	60	$9
17 Proj	494	70	31	80	3	238	242	327	491	818	836	812	12	61	0.34	34	22	44	32	107	186	164	23%	94	3%	74%				5.37	7.1	41	117	$16

Santana,Carlos

Age: 31 Bats: B Pos: DH 1B	Health	A	LIMA Plan	A
Ht: 5' 11" Wt: 190	PT/Exp	A	Rand Var	+1
	Consist	C	MM	3235

Shaking off typically depressed h% in 2H to own RHP keyed career year. Convergence of FB%, ct% bumps with rock-solid bb% also added fuel to HR, BA spikes. Early HctX surge never let up. LD-challenged profile will keep a lid on his average but power+patience combo sets a floor. OBP leaguers should be OK with the volatility.

Yr Tm	AB	R	HR	RBI	SB	BA	xBA	OBP	SLG	OPS	vL	vR	bb%	ct%	Eye	G	L	F	h%	HctX	PX	xPX	hr/f	Spd	SBO	SB%	#Wk	DOM	DIS	RC/G	RAR	BPV	BPX	R$
12 CLE	507	72	18	76	3	252	256	365	420	785	808	772	15	80	0.90	43	19	38	28	107	108	104	12%	90	5%	38%	26	50%	27%	5.10	3.2	66	165	$13
13 CLE	541	75	20	74	3	268	277	377	455	832	864	815	15	80	0.85	42	22	36	30	106	131	99	13%	78	2%	75%	27	67%	4%	5.95	22.4	78	195	$18
14 CLE	541	68	27	85	5	231	262	365	427	792	864	757	17	77	0.91	40	19	40	25	117	136	125	16%	73	4%	71%	27	59%	22%	5.15	17.9	76	205	$15
15 CLE	550	72	19	85	11	231	253	357	395	752	755	750	16	78	0.89	45	18	37	26	101	108	95	12%	79	8%	79%	27	59%	22%	4.71	-12.3	56	151	$14
16 CLE	582	89	34	87	5	259	281	366	498	865	742	915	15	83	1.00	43	16	41	26	122	129	123	17%	86	4%	71%	27	74%	7%	6.28	13.2	92	263	$20
1st Half	302	47	18	44	4	245	278	342	480	822	618	903	13	84	0.96	41	16	44	24	126	124	131	16%	83	6%	80%	14	79%	0%	5.57	0.7	90	257	$19
2nd Half	280	42	16	43	1	275	283	392	518	910	865	929	16	81	1.04	45	17	38	29	118	135	112	18%	91	2%	50%	13	69%	15%	7.08	12.7	95	271	$20
17 Proj	532	75	26	81	6	250	268	367	456	822	787	839	16	80	0.94	43	18	39	27	114	118	112	15%	82	5%	72%				5.67	2.6	69	197	$18

Santana,Danny

Age: 26 Bats: B Pos: CF	Health	C	LIMA Plan	D
Ht: 5' 11" Wt: 175	PT/Exp	D	Rand Var	+1
	Consist	C	MM	1523

Chronic hamstring woes shelved one-trick speedster for most of April and June. Failure to launch afterward cut into his playing time, before shoulder sprain finished him in late Aug. Swiped 8 bases in healthy/active May—his only valuable stretch—as broader skill set continued to stagnate. And he no longer has SS eligibility.

Yr Tm	AB	R	HR	RBI	SB	BA	xBA	OBP	SLG	OPS	vL	vR	bb%	ct%	Eye	G	L	F	h%	HctX	PX	xPX	hr/f	Spd	SBO	SB%	#Wk	DOM	DIS	RC/G	RAR	BPV	BPX	R$
12																																		
13 aa	539	50	1	34	23	263		287	339	625			3	81	0.18				32		53			142	29%	61%				3.15		17	43	$14
14 MIN *	502	82	7	46	23	304	265	335	448	783	786	841	5	74	0.18	46	26	28	40	85	115	63	9%	149	22%	82%	20	45%	35%	5.56	33.1	46	124	$26
15 MIN *	413	50	2	34	13	243	249	263	347	611	624	494	3	77	0.12	54	20	26	31	88	72	56	0%	141	25%	64%	22	9%	50%	2.95	-18.1	15	41	$7
16 MIN	233	29	2	14	12	240	246	279	326	606	404	658	5	76	0.22	53	22	25	31	93	58	76	5%	129	39%	57%	19	26%	58%	2.73	-11.4	3	9	$5
1st Half	148	19	2	12	11	243	246	285	338	623	354	691	5	78	0.24	53	20	27	30	94	61	75	7%	122	51%	61%	11	36%	55%	2.85	-7.5	9	26	$9
2nd Half	85	10	0	2	1	235	245	270	306	576	488	599	4	74	0.18	54	25	21	32	91	53	78	0%	127	16%	33%	8	13%	63%	2.50	-5.2	-12	-34	-$2
17 Proj	269	34	1	17	12	252	249	285	342	627	593	900	4	76	0.17	53	22	25	33	90	61	67	3%	134	31%	64%				3.11	-11.4	6	17	$8

Santana,Domingo

Age: 24 Bats: R Pos: RF	Health	C	LIMA Plan	C+
Ht: 6' 5" Wt: 220	PT/Exp	C	Rand Var	-2
	Consist	B	MM	4125

Couldn't sustain Mar/Apr promise. Shoulder/elbow woes and sub-par ct% took hold during May through Aug, as DL stints held him to 69 AB. Offered Sept upside reminder with 70% ct%, 129 HctX, 6 HR, .926 OPS in 88 AB. Still owns big-time power+patience, but health now a factor. With it and Sept contact... UP: .265 BA, 30 HR.

Yr Tm	AB	R	HR	RBI	SB	BA	xBA	OBP	SLG	OPS	vL	vR	bb%	ct%	Eye	G	L	F	h%	HctX	PX	xPX	hr/f	Spd	SBO	SB%	#Wk	DOM	DIS	RC/G	RAR	BPV	BPX	R$
12																																		
13 aa	416	58	21	51	10	228		292	437	728			8	63	0.24				31		170			98	17%	64%				4.09		35	88	$12
14 HOU *	460	47	12	60	4	245	224	317	384	701	100	0	10	60	0.26	33	33	33	38	86	133	235	0%	91	7%	50%	3	0%	100%	4.00	-1.2	-5	-14	$10
15 2 TM *	514	74	21	81	5	271	237	347	457	803	950	681	10	64	0.32	52	19	29	39	92	146	135	28%	110	8%	45%	11	55%	36%	5.33	7.0	28	76	$19
16 MIL	246	34	11	32	2	256	252	345	447	792	937	726	12	63	0.35	44	30	26	36	98	143	107	28%	83	7%	40%	17	29%	47%	5.04	2.6	16	46	$6
1st Half	128	19	4	13	0	234	239	347	391	737	948	635	14	59	0.40	53	30	17	36	89	132	87	31%	90	5%	0%	9	22%	44%	4.19	-2.0	0	0	$3
2nd Half	118	15	7	19	2	280	266	344	508	852	917	823	9	67	0.28	36	30	34	36	109	154	126	26%	88	10%	67%	8	38%	50%	6.04	4.5	36	103	$9
17 Proj	471	63	23	66	5	252	249	337	457	794	948	723	10	63	0.31	46	26	28	35	97	150	120	28%	92	9%	49%				4.95	3.6	15	41	$16

Sardinas,Luis

Age: 24 Bats: B Pos: SS	Health	A	LIMA Plan	D+
Ht: 6' 1" Wt: 180	PT/Exp	D	Rand Var	0
	Consist	A	MM	0423

4-18-.244 in 180 AB at SEA/SD. Speedy utility infielder is slowly improving anemic HctX, even turned a few more fly balls into some HR. But though age is on his side, he's still a long way from becoming productive. Spd+SBO combo has never turned into much of a running game, and BA/contact skills remain stagnant. Pass.

Yr Tm	AB	R	HR	RBI	SB	BA	xBA	OBP	SLG	OPS	vL	vR	bb%	ct%	Eye	G	L	F	h%	HctX	PX	xPX	hr/f	Spd	SBO	SB%	#Wk	DOM	DIS	RC/G	RAR	BPV	BPX	R$
12																																		
13 aa	135	11	1	13	4	253		273	304	577			3	84	0.17				29		37			92	20%	68%				2.77		1	3	$1
14 TEX *	464	51	1	36	13	253	274	274	319	592	824	552	3	84	0.18	63	21	16	30	41	55	25	0%	110	18%	66%	14	29%	50%	2.91	-5.3	19	51	$9
15 MIL *	487	45	1	28	12	236	234	267	288	555	364	482	4	83	0.24	62	14	25	28	68	37	49	0%	126	14%	72%	10	10%	70%	2.57	-17.7	8	22	$4
16 2 TM *	362	40	4	30	10	226	231	267	295	561	835	552	5	79	0.27	54	18	28	27	85	44	60	11%	129	19%	59%	19	26%	63%	2.48	-23.9	3	9	$4
1st Half	176	19	2	13	4	193	206	213	237	450	796	293	2	79	0.12	64	10	26	23	74	25	29	18%	113	19%	68%	9	11%	67%	1.57	-16.3	-24	-69	$0
2nd Half	186	21	2	17	5	256	249	315	349	664	861	668	8	80	0.42	49	21	29	31	91	62	74	8%	134	19%	53%	10	40%	60%	3.54	-5.2	27	77	$7
17 Proj	334	34	4	26	9	238	245	275	318	593	741	533	5	81	0.25	59	16	25	28	72	50	49	6%	123	17%	65%				2.82	-16.7	4	10	$6

JOCK THOMPSON

Saunders,Michael

Age: 30 Bats: L Pos: LF RF | Ht: 6' 4" Wt: 210

Health F | PT/Exp D | Consist F | LIMA Plan B | Rand Var -1 | MM 4225

Avoided DL and lived up to PX/xPX promise with first 20+ HR effort in otherwise uneven season. Chronic contact issues and big h% swings were heartburn for H2Hers, as 2H BA slump and GB spike cut into his PT. Big 1H vL came in 81 AB, with 68% ct%. But with more health, solid power+patience say repeat is do-able.

Yr	Tm	AB	R	HR	RBI	SB	BA	xBA	OBP	SLG	OPS	vL	vR	bb%	ct%	Eye	G	L	F	h%	HctX	PX	xPX	hr/f	Spd	SBO	SB%	#Wk	DOM	DIS	RC/G	RAR	BPV	BPX	R$
12	SEA	507	71	19	57	21	247	259	306	432	738	774	718	8	74	0.33	45	20	35	30	111	130	136	15%	107	22%	84%	28	39%	32%	4.54	-0.3	50	125	$17
13	SEA	406	59	12	46	13	236	241	323	397	720	654	751	12	71	0.46	41	22	37	30	103	123	129	11%	108	16%	72%	25	48%	44%	4.29	3.9	40	100	$11
14	SEA *	286	45	9	40	4	267	246	348	428	776	680	836	11	72	0.45	42	22	36	34	116	121	112	13%	129	10%	44%	18	39%	28%	4.92	10.4	49	132	$10
15	TOR	31	2	0	3	0	194	151	306	194	499	1417	393	14	68	0.50	75	15	10	29	56	0	59	0%	113	0%	0%	3	0%	67%	1.87	-2.4	-64	-173	-$3
16	TOR	490	70	24	57	1	253	257	338	478	815	927	783	11	68	0.38	41	22	37	32	103	154	130	20%	93	2%	33%	27	44%	37%	5.36	15.6	46	131	$11
1st Half		279	43	15	37	0	294	274	370	552	922	998	891	10	69	0.35	37	24	40	38	108	177	138	19%	104	3%	0%	14	57%	14%	7.02	20.1	71	203	$18
2nd Half		211	27	9	20	1	199	236	295	379	674	719	667	12	66	0.41	46	21	33	25	97	123	120	20%	85	2%	100%	13	31%	62%	3.60	-5.7	15	43	$2
17	**Proj**	**437**	**63**	**18**	**52**	**6**	**247**	**249**	**329**	**439**	**768**	**770**	**768**	**11**	**70**	**0.41**	**42**	**22**	**36**	**31**	**106**	**128**	**125**	**16%**	**101**	**8%**	**62%**				**4.82**	**4.8**	**33**	**96**	**$11**

Schebler,Scott

Age: 26 Bats: L Pos: RF | Ht: 6' 1" Wt: 208

Health A | PT/Exp C | Consist D | LIMA Plan C+ | Rand Var -2 | MM 2223

9-40-.265 in 257 AB at CIN. Strikeouts and GB% spike punched May Triple-A ticket after 65 AB. Improved in odd-but-intriguing 2nd half return—six Aug HR, .337 Sept BA were fueled by 20% hr/f and 40% h%, respectively. Offers strong-side platoon upside, but needs more FBs and more patience to fully unlock his power.

Yr	Tm	AB	R	HR	RBI	SB	BA	xBA	OBP	SLG	OPS	vL	vR	bb%	ct%	Eye	G	L	F	h%	HctX	PX	xPX	hr/f	Spd	SBO	SB%	#Wk	DOM	DIS	RC/G	RAR	BPV	BPX	R$
12																																			
13																																			
14	aa	489	57	21	51	7	229		273	425	698			6	73	0.23				27		137			124	12%	60%				3.73		54	146	$11
15	LA *	468	48	13	41	13	201	215	249	335	584	200	905	6	74	0.25	52	9	39	24	125	87	136	33%	122	18%	80%	7	43%	43%	2.68	-32.1	16	43	$4
16	CIN *	546	70	21	77	4	271	271	316	469	785	608	791	6	76	0.27	53	18	29	32	103	118	78	16%	111	6%	48%	15	47%	20%	5.06	5.9	46	131	$16
1st Half		262	23	9	30	1	242	231	280	428	708	167	627	5	74	0.20	57	5	39	30	115	117	140	6%	110	4%	50%	5	60%	40%	3.98	-5.6	33	94	$7
2nd Half		284	47	13	46	3	298	288	348	507	855	671	851	7	78	0.35	51	22	26	34	101	119	60	20%	111	7%	47%	10	40%	10%	6.19	11.9	57	163	$25
17	**Proj**	**362**	**44**	**11**	**43**	**4**	**256**	**253**	**314**	**418**	**732**	**574**	**758**	**6**	**75**	**0.26**	**49**	**20**	**31**	**31**	**107**	**98**	**92**	**13%**	**115**	**8%**	**57%**				**4.23**	**-4.9**	**21**	**61**	**$10**

Schimpf,Ryan

Age: 29 Bats: L Pos: 2B | Ht: 5' 9" Wt: 190

Health A | PT/Exp C | Consist C | LIMA Plan C | Rand Var -1 | MM 5013

20-51-.217 in 276 AB at SD. Minor league lifer with .249 career BA posts 15 HR, .349 BA in AAA to earn MLB debut. Mashed 16 HR with .260 BA in July/Aug before Sept fade (4 HR, .179 BA in 78 AB). He's no kid, and legit power comes with big issues. Woeful ct% and struggles vL (.157 BA in SD) point to platoon bat at best.

Yr	Tm	AB	R	HR	RBI	SB	BA	xBA	OBP	SLG	OPS	vL	vR	bb%	ct%	Eye	G	L	F	h%	HctX	PX	xPX	hr/f	Spd	SBO	SB%	#Wk	DOM	DIS	RC/G	RAR	BPV	BPX	R$
12	aa	111	17	7	12	2	251		355	503	857			14	68	0.49				31		186			92	11%	68%				5.98		76	190	$2
13	aa	442	48	18	46	2	178		270	349	618			11	63	0.34				23		139			101	6%	38%				2.84		19	48	-$1
14	a/a	397	49	20	44	2	198		270	410	681			9	65	0.28				25		176			93	5%	66%				3.51		49	132	$4
15	a/a	368	44	20	51	2	219		300	449	749			10	75	0.45				24		156			76	7%	31%				4.25		69	186	$6
16	SD *	442	71	30	81	1	237	242	321	531	852	698	907	11	66	0.37	20	16	65	28	107	199	202	18%	81	3%	30%	17	59%	29%	5.59	9.5	72	206	$12
1st Half		204	28	11	32	0	244	240	311	483	793	575	578	9	73	0.36	32	11	57	28	116	158	163	6%	62	3%	0%	4	50%	25%	4.92	0.8	57	163	$8
2nd Half		238	43	19	49	1	231	245	344	571	915	707	964	13	61	0.37	17	16	66	29	98	242	210	20%	103	4%	50%	13	62%	31%	6.17	9.9	94	269	$16
17	**Proj**	**343**	**49**	**21**	**53**	**2**	**225**	**233**	**328**	**484**	**811**	**690**	**836**	**11**	**68**	**0.38**	**23**	**14**	**63**	**27**	**105**	**174**	**191**	**14%**	**78**	**5%**	**42%**				**4.82**	**0.2**	**55**	**158**	**$9**

Schoop,Jonathan

Age: 25 Bats: R Pos: 2B | Ht: 6' 2" Wt: 195

Health C | PT/Exp B | Consist D | LIMA Plan B | Rand Var 0 | MM 3125

Future looks bright as HR+RBI surge, rising ct% and two-year xBA now suggest a decent BA floor. But the foundation has cracks. AB drove counting stats; FB%, xPX, HctX suggest his power may have a low ceiling. 2nd half BA deteriorated with h% regression. Age is a plus, but he has work to do.

Yr	Tm	AB	R	HR	RBI	SB	BA	xBA	OBP	SLG	OPS	vL	vR	bb%	ct%	Eye	G	L	F	h%	HctX	PX	xPX	hr/f	Spd	SBO	SB%	#Wk	DOM	DIS	RC/G	RAR	BPV	BPX	R$
12	aa	485	54	12	45	4	226		285	352	637			8	77	0.37				27		86			88	6%	55%				3.24		22	55	$4
13	BAL *	284	30	9	29	1	238	253	268	371	639	1167	750	4	79	0.19	67	17	17	27	137	88	69	50%	92	5%	27%	2	50%	0%	3.22	-4.3	22	55	$3
14	BAL	455	48	16	45	2	209	228	244	354	598	529	625	3	73	0.11	49	14	37	25	82	109	96	13%	88	3%	100%	27	33%	41%	2.65	-10.4	14	38	$4
15	BAL *	330	36	18	44	2	274	264	295	493	788	573	892	3	74	0.11	43	19	38	32	115	147	123	17%	78	3%	100%	15	53%	27%	5.14	8.1	45	122	$11
16	BAL	615	82	25	82	1	267	266	298	454	752	688	772	3	78	0.15	45	20	35	31	84	116	74	15%	94	2%	33%	27	44%	22%	4.53	-3.5	40	114	$17
1st Half		302	47	13	47	1	301	275	332	510	842	791	858	4	78	0.20	45	18	37	35	96	130	77	15%	112	3%	50%	14	50%	21%	6.08	10.6	61	174	$23
2nd Half		313	35	12	35	0	233	257	265	399	665	587	689	2	77	0.11	46	21	33	27	72	102	70	15%	79	2%	0%	13	38%	23%	3.30	-14.2	22	63	$10
17	**Proj**	**597**	**71**	**22**	**73**	**2**	**257**	**250**	**289**	**424**	**713**	**596**	**758**	**3**	**76**	**0.13**	**45**	**19**	**36**	**30**	**93**	**105**	**94**	**14%**	**86**	**3%**	**60%**				**4.05**	**-13.1**	**13**	**37**	**$16**

Schwarber,Kyle

Age: 24 Bats: L Pos: LF | Ht: 6' 0" Wt: 235

Health F | PT/Exp F | Consist F | LIMA Plan B+ | Rand Var 0 | MM 4125

Blew out ACL and season in the third game of the year, expected to be fully recovered by the spring. Big left-handed power+patience (16 HR, 13% bb% in 232 AB) on display in 2015 MLB debut should return. Contact and struggles vL will be works in progress. And whither his work behind the plate? Big risk, big reward.

Yr	Tm	AB	R	HR	RBI	SB	BA	xBA	OBP	SLG	OPS	vL	vR	bb%	ct%	Eye	G	L	F	h%	HctX	PX	xPX	hr/f	Spd	SBO	SB%	#Wk	DOM	DIS	RC/G	RAR	BPV	BPX	R$
12																																			
13																																			
14																																			
15	CHC *	489	88	29	82	4	271	247	368	505	873	481	953	13	68	0.48	40	17	42	34	117	164	157	24%	89	4%	56%	14	57%	21%	6.41	23.8	58	157	$21
16	CHC	4	0	0	0	0	0	0	200	0	200	0	200	20	50	0.50	100	0	0	0	203	0	-24	0%	84	0%	0%	1	0%	100%	0.00	-0.6	-132	-377	-$2
1st Half		4	0	0	0	0	0	0	200	0	200	0	200	20	50	0.50	100	0	0	0	203	0	-24	0%	84	0%	0%	1	0%	100%	0.00	-0.7	-133	-380	-$2
2nd Half																																			
17	**Proj**	**431**	**70**	**28**	**65**	**3**	**243**	**254**	**342**	**489**	**831**	**474**	**900**	**12**	**71**	**0.47**	**40**	**17**	**42**	**28**	**105**	**150**	**141**	**22%**	**90**	**5%**	**57%**				**5.43**	**12.6**	**52**	**150**	**$16**

Seager,Corey

Age: 23 Bats: L Pos: SS | Ht: 6' 4" Wt: 215

Health A | PT/Exp C | Consist B | LIMA Plan B+ | Rand Var -1 | MM 3255

Owned RHP in outstanding ROY-worthy effort. HR surge tailed off with 2nd half hr/f regression, but xPX remained optimistic. Season-long BA excellence fueled by ongoing LD, h% spikes, as HctX stayed elite. Plate skills, performance vL faded in Sept and have room for improvement. But age says he's just getting started.

Yr	Tm	AB	R	HR	RBI	SB	BA	xBA	OBP	SLG	OPS	vL	vR	bb%	ct%	Eye	G	L	F	h%	HctX	PX	xPX	hr/f	Spd	SBO	SB%	#Wk	DOM	DIS	RC/G	RAR	BPV	BPX	R$
12																																			
13																																			
14	aa	148	21	2	21	1	304		337	457	793			5	70	0.17				42		142			97	5%	41%				5.49		36	97	$4
15	LA *	599	86	20	82	5	280	296	328	462	790	926	1028	7	83	0.42	53	20	27	31	168	118	139	19%	90	5%	83%	6	83%	17%	5.39	27.4	69	186	$22
16	LA	627	105	26	72	3	308	290	365	512	877	722	948	8	79	0.41	46	24	29	36	127	122	130	18%	110	3%	50%	27	59%	19%	6.75	36.4	64	183	$27
1st Half		323	56	17	40	1	303	298	362	536	898	771	940	8	80	0.46	47	23	30	34	127	134	132	22%	109	4%	25%	14	57%	7%	6.87	21.5	78	223	$28
2nd Half		304	49	9	32	2	313	282	369	487	855	686	958	7	78	0.35	45	26	28	38	127	110	128	13%	108	2%	100%	13	62%	31%	6.60	17.5	48	137	$26
17	**Proj**	**620**	**96**	**22**	**75**	**4**	**301**	**289**	**353**	**494**	**847**	**743**	**904**	**7**	**79**	**0.34**	**49**	**23**	**28**	**35**	**143**	**119**	**133**	**16%**	**102**	**4%**	**65%**				**6.24**	**30.3**	**53**	**152**	**$28**

Seager,Kyle

Age: 29 Bats: L Pos: 3B | Ht: 5' 10" Wt: 215

Health A | PT/Exp A | Consist B | LIMA Plan B+ | Rand Var 0 | MM 3145

Few make hard contact like the Seagers. Rock-solid HctX and patience uptick set stage for hr/f bump and HR peak. 2nd half rebound vL fueled BA high and early Sept .300 flirtation before late fade. Limits imposed by ebbing speed is a minor quibble. He's wringing it all out of a solid skill set, with no end in sight.

Yr	Tm	AB	R	HR	RBI	SB	BA	xBA	OBP	SLG	OPS	vL	vR	bb%	ct%	Eye	G	L	F	h%	HctX	PX	xPX	hr/f	Spd	SBO	SB%	#Wk	DOM	DIS	RC/G	RAR	BPV	BPX	R$
12	SEA	594	62	20	86	13	259	259	316	423	738	658	783	7	81	0.42	36	22	42	29	109	106	115	10%	62	13%	72%	28	36%	21%	4.51	-0.6	46	115	$18
13	SEA	615	79	22	69	9	260	252	338	426	764	690	808	10	80	0.56	34	21	45	29	98	111	106	10%	71	7%	75%	27	56%	26%	4.90	17.0	53	133	$19
14	SEA	590	71	25	96	7	268	268	334	454	788	661	862	8	80	0.44	37	22	41	30	131	124	141	13%	72	8%	58%	27	52%	30%	5.07	23.9	59	159	$23
15	SEA	623	85	26	74	6	266	281	328	451	779	835	747	8	84	0.55	35	24	41	28	122	113	112	12%	68	8%	50%	27	70%	15%	4.95	6.9	66	178	$20
16	SEA	597	89	30	99	3	278	282	359	499	859	728	932	10	82	0.64	36	22	42	30	129	125	135	15%	59	2%	75%	27	63%	11%	6.21	24.0	68	194	$22
1st Half		307	49	16	54	1	270	285	355	511	867	612	1002	11	83	0.71	35	20	46	28	133	136	151	14%	57	3%	50%	14	71%	0%	6.18	11.4	82	234	$22
2nd Half		290	40	14	45	2	286	278	364	486	850	843	854	10	81	0.57	38	24	38	31	124	113	119	16%	67	2%	100%	13	54%	23%	6.25	11.1	55	157	$23
17	**Proj**	**603**	**83**	**29**	**90**	**5**	**273**	**279**	**346**	**482**	**828**	**763**	**864**	**9**	**82**	**0.57**	**36**	**23**	**41**	**29**	**124**	**118**	**126**	**14%**	**64**	**5%**	**64%**				**5.69**	**13.9**	**63**	**181**	**$25**

JOCK THOMPSON

Segura,Jean

Age: 27	Bats: R	Pos: 2B SS	Health A	LIMA Plan	B
Ht: 5' 11"	Wt: 160		PT/Exp A	Rand Var	-4
			Consist D	MM	1545

Just when we thought 2013 was long gone, he goes all-world on us in second half. Problem is, that power was driven by a hr/f we've never seen from him before, and xPX adds more sobering news. While Spd confirms he's a burner, that inflated hit rate drove opps way up, and BA with it. Be cautious when pushing the bidding.

Yr	Tm	AB	R	HR	RBI	SB	BA	xBA	OBP	SLG	OPS	vL	vR	bb%	ct%	Eye	G	L	F	h%	HctX	PX	xPX	hr/f	Spd	SBO	SB%	#Wk	DOM	DIS	RC/G	RAR	BPV	BPX	R$
12	2 TM *	555	66	7	50	38	274	263	318	365	683	290	756	6	84	0.39	66	15	19	32	82	54	57	0%	178	33%	71%	10	30%	40%	3.98	-5.9	45	113	$23
13	MIL	588	74	12	49	44	294	282	329	423	752	865	716	4	86	0.30	59	18	23	33	99	76	69	10%	196	37%	77%	26	46%	23%	4.91	21.0	73	183	$35
14	MIL	513	61	5	31	20	246	265	289	326	614	511	643	5	86	0.40	59	18	23	28	79	51	51	5%	182	22%	69%	27	41%	33%	3.07	-4.9	53	143	$12
15	MIL	560	57	6	50	25	257	252	281	336	616	679	594	2	83	0.14	59	17	24	30	71	49	48	5%	150	24%	81%	26	23%	27%	3.21	-15.7	24	65	$17
16	ARI	637	102	20	64	33	319	296	368	499	867	763	900	6	84	0.39	53	19	28	35	101	103	93	14%	165	25%	77%	27	48%	11%	6.63	30.6	82	234	$39
1st Half		331	47	5	34	13	308	283	355	432	787	715	810	6	85	0.42	54	20	26	35	97	73	75	7%	164	19%	72%	14	36%	7%	5.45	6.0	63	180	$33
2nd Half		306	55	15	30	20	330	311	383	572	954	818	996	6	83	0.36	52	18	30	36	106	138	113	20%	160	32%	80%	13	62%	15%	7.99	26.3	103	294	$46
17	Proj	613	84	12	55	32	290	277	333	418	750	685	771	5	84	0.32	56	18	26	33	90	73	75	9%	165	26%	77%				4.86	1.0	49	139	$30

Semien,Marcus

Age: 26	Bats: R	Pos: SS	Health A	LIMA Plan	B+
Ht: 6' 0"	Wt: 190		PT/Exp A	Rand Var	+1
			Consist A	MM	3425

That 2015 xPX hinted at a power breakout, and sure enough, it happened. Will it stick? Flyball distance only increased 3 ft, so big hr/f jump not likely to stick, and therefore neither will his homers. As for BA, even if h% regression sends it north, stagnant plate skills cap his upside there. Expect modest overall regression.

Yr	Tm	AB	R	HR	RBI	SB	BA	xBA	OBP	SLG	OPS	vL	vR	bb%	ct%	Eye	G	L	F	h%	HctX	PX	xPX	hr/f	Spd	SBO	SB%	#Wk	DOM	DIS	RC/G	RAR	BPV	BPX	R$
12																																			
13	CHW *	587	97	20	61	22	256	249	354	428	782	783	643	13	79	0.71	27	25	48	30	96	118	95	9%	129	16%	74%	5	40%	60%	5.18	30.6	76	190	$24
14	CHW *	534	68	17	62	8	224	245	301	383	684	735	637	10	74	0.42	40	21	39	27	78	119	75	10%	134	8%	77%	15	33%	53%	3.79	10.0	53	143	$10
15	OAK	556	65	15	45	11	257	242	310	405	715	879	653	7	76	0.32	38	23	39	31	98	96	119	9%	137	11%	69%	27	37%	30%	4.24	-2.5	39	105	$14
16	OAK	568	72	27	75	10	238	249	300	435	735	813	707	8	76	0.37	39	18	43	27	88	119	114	15%	109	9%	83%	27	41%	22%	4.40	1.5	48	137	$14
1st Half		282	40	17	43	5	245	252	307	475	783	1004	710	8	76	0.38	42	14	44	27	86	131	116	18%	130	9%	83%	14	50%	21%	4.97	4.3	65	186	$17
2nd Half		286	32	10	32	5	231	247	293	395	688	641	705	8	76	0.36	37	21	42	27	89	107	112	11%	91	9%	83%	13	31%	23%	3.87	-5.2	33	94	$10
17	Proj	576	73	21	65	11	242	245	307	412	719	801	687	9	76	0.39	38	21	42	28	90	104	107	12%	122	11%	77%				4.25	-3.7	36	103	$16

Shaffer,Richie

Age: 26	Bats: R	Pos: 1B	Health A	LIMA Plan	D
Ht: 6' 3"	Wt: 218		PT/Exp C	Rand Var	-1
			Consist C	MM	4201

1-4-.250 in 48 AB at TAM. The anatomy of a budding AAAAer: flashes of power muted by big holes in swing. Stats and skills tanked in second tour of AAA too, which means MLB growing pains could get ugly. Sure, that first-round pedigree will give him some more chances, but at age 26, he should be much farther along.

Yr	Tm	AB	R	HR	RBI	SB	BA	xBA	OBP	SLG	OPS	vL	vR	bb%	ct%	Eye	G	L	F	h%	HctX	PX	xPX	hr/f	Spd	SBO	SB%	#Wk	DOM	DIS	RC/G	RAR	BPV	BPX	R$
12																																			
13																																			
14	aa	427	46	14	51	3	190		267	360	626			9	68	0.33				24		139			98	4%	100%				3.05		35	95	$1
15	TAM *	467	62	24	64	3	221	221	301	436	737	521	1099	10	62	0.30	37	14	49	30	81	171	129	19%	76	5%	60%	9	33%	11%	4.24	-9.9	31	84	$9
16	TAM *	476	46	10	44	3	199	190	288	323	610	782	738	11	63	0.33	45	13	42	29	66	104	40	8%	86	5%	61%	9	56%	44%	2.93	-28.9	-15	-43	-$2
1st Half		282	26	5	27	2	210	199	295	307	602			11	65	0.35				30		78			80	2%	100%				2.96		-29	-83	-$1
2nd Half		194	20	5	17	2	184	203	277	345	622	782	738	11	59	0.31	45	13	42	28	62	146	40	8%	90	10%	44%	9	56%	44%	2.88	-13.9	5	14	-$3
17	Proj	188	21	6	21	1	203	207	292	372	664	566	744	10	63	0.32	42	13	45	28	70	132	76	12%	91	6%	63%				3.38	-10.1	-3	-9	$2

Shaw,Travis

Age: 27	Bats: L	Pos: 3B 1B	Health A	LIMA Plan	C
Ht: 6' 4"	Wt: 230		PT/Exp B	Rand Var	0
			Consist A	MM	3115

Spring sensation carried it over into Apr/May, but as pitchers adjusted, the bad outweighed the good. Power at risk for further erosion, as HctX dipped each of last three months. And holes in swing were getting bigger and bigger before late bottom-out, so that BA won't get any better. Moderate risk, marginal upside. DN: 10 HR

Yr	Tm	AB	R	HR	RBI	SB	BA	xBA	OBP	SLG	OPS	vL	vR	bb%	ct%	Eye	G	L	F	h%	HctX	PX	xPX	hr/f	Spd	SBO	SB%	#Wk	DOM	DIS	RC/G	RAR	BPV	BPX	R$
12	aa	110	11	2	10	1	223		329	413	743			14	68	0.49				31		174			84	7%	44%				4.35		64	160	-$1
13	aa	444	44	12	38	5	200		293	341	633			12	71	0.46				25		107			107	8%	62%				3.14		28	70	$1
14	a/a	490	61	16	61	6	252		315	415	730			8	78	0.41				30		121			87	7%	62%				4.39		52	141	$14
15	BOS *	515	56	17	61	0	248	237	302	397	699	975	723	7	77	0.34	37	20	43	29	98	98	129	18%	83	2%	0%	16	31%	38%	3.99	-8.8	28	76	$9
16	BOS	480	63	16	71	5	242	240	306	421	726	599	762	8	72	0.32	36	19	45	30	98	123	122	10%	76	6%	83%	26	35%	38%	4.32	-6.8	29	83	$10
1st Half		286	39	8	45	3	266	249	331	444	775	533	843	8	74	0.35	37	20	42	33	105	123	117	9%	85	6%	75%	14	36%	29%	5.03	1.2	38	109	$14
2nd Half		194	24	8	26	2	206	227	268	387	654	697	642	8	70	0.29	35	17	48	25	87	123	129	12%	69	5%	100%	12	33%	50%	3.40	-9.0	18	51	$3
17	Proj	417	47	14	51	3	236	239	301	408	709	753	692	8	74	0.34	36	19	44	29	96	114	126	11%	75	5%	70%				4.07	-10.3	24	69	$9

Shuck,J.B.

Age: 30	Bats: L	Pos: CF	Health A	LIMA Plan	D
Ht: 5' 11"	Wt: 205		PT/Exp D	Rand Var	+5
			Consist D	MM	0231

4-14-.205 in 224 AB at CHW. Combo of walks and decent legs gave him upside on the basepaths heading into 2016. But both tanked, and don't mean much when you can barely muster a .500 OPS vR. Deflated h% contributed, but it was bad in 2014 too. Nothing to suggest pitchers won't keep knocking bat out of his hands.

Yr	Tm	AB	R	HR	RBI	SB	BA	xBA	OBP	SLG	OPS	vL	vR	bb%	ct%	Eye	G	L	F	h%	HctX	PX	xPX	hr/f	Spd	SBO	SB%	#Wk	DOM	DIS	RC/G	RAR	BPV	BPX	R$
12	aaa	315	33	0	22	8	238		297	280	577			8	92	1.08				26		28			111	19%	46%				2.54		42	105	$2
13	LAA	437	60	2	39	8	293	264	331	366	697	745	682	6	88	0.50	55	20	25	33	73	52	44	2%	117	9%	67%	27	44%	26%	4.36	0.9	41	103	$14
14	2 AL *	516	48	5	41	7	213	226	251	286	537	310	394	5	90	0.51	57	8	34	23	55	45	27	6%	100	13%	48%	11	9%	45%	2.21	-27.3	38	103	$1
15	CHW	143	15	0	15	7	266	273	340	350	689	661	694	10	89	1.00	57	18	25	30	61	57	31	0%	106	27%	58%	25	44%	24%	3.85	-3.9	55	149	$3
16	CHW *	378	41	6	26	6	215	258	256	308	563	802	505	5	90	0.53	53	16	31	23	79	49	46	6%	91	14%	51%	21	29%	29%	2.44	-26.8	38	109	$1
1st Half		252	24	5	22	4	232	270	268	350	618	1500	606	5	90	0.47	47	20	33	24	100	62	76	10%	83	14%	52%	8	38%	25%	2.97	-13.3	44	126	$3
2nd Half		126	17	1	4	2	183	233	237	222	459	637	414	6	90	0.67	58	13	29	19	63	22	23	3%	91	14%	50%	13	23%	31%	1.53	-13.0	21	60	-$5
17	Proj	163	18	2	12	4	226	258	279	308	587	688	900	7	90	0.70	55	16	29	24	70	45	38	4%	97	19%	54%				2.66	-9.4	40	114	$2

Simmons,Andrelton

Age: 27	Bats: R	Pos: SS	Health B	LIMA Plan	B+
Ht: 6' 2"	Wt: 170		PT/Exp B	Rand Var	-1
			Consist B	MM	1445

On surface, status quo. But that 2H reminds us he has 20 SB in him if green light ever cooperates, as Spd returned to pre-2015 levels. And that ct% keeps raising BA floor, so don't expect regression there. Just know that double-digit HR ain't coming back; see dwindling HctX, xPX. Still, this is a place for post-hype BA/SB profit.

Yr	Tm	AB	R	HR	RBI	SB	BA	xBA	OBP	SLG	OPS	vL	vR	bb%	ct%	Eye	G	L	F	h%	HctX	PX	xPX	hr/f	Spd	SBO	SB%	#Wk	DOM	DIS	RC/G	RAR	BPV	BPX	R$
12	ATL *	340	41	5	37	9	278	271	335	396	731	796	726	8	87	0.66	56	17	27	31	85	72	45	8%	136	12%	81%	11	45%	18%	4.74	6.1	65	163	$10
13	ATL	606	76	17	59	6	248	272	296	396	692	692	691	6	91	0.73	42	18	39	25	102	86	89	8%	146	8%	55%	27	59%	7%	3.85	7.7	91	228	$13
14	ATL	540	44	7	46	4	244	250	286	331	617	679	603	6	89	0.53	52	16	31	26	102	56	87	5%	139	7%	44%	26	54%	19%	3.11	-1.1	55	149	$6
15	ATL	535	60	4	44	5	265	279	321	338	660	565	683	7	91	0.81	56	22	22	29	92	47	61	4%	116	5%	63%	27	56%	11%	3.67	-11.2	52	141	$10
16	LAA	448	48	4	44	10	281	282	324	366	690	752	671	6	92	0.74	55	20	26	30	87	51	54	4%	118	9%	91%	23	48%	4%	4.30	0.0	56	160	$12
1st Half		176	14	1	13	2	250	273	276	318	594	607	589	4	93	0.58	54	20	26	26	82	44	47	2%	96	7%	67%	10	60%	0%	2.99	-7.7	46	131	$2
2nd Half		272	34	3	31	8	301	284	354	397	751	872	718	7	90	0.81	55	20	25	33	90	55	59	5%	134	9%	100%	13	38%	8%	5.30	6.2	62	177	$19
17	Proj	558	59	6	52	12	284	277	329	371	700	726	693	6	91	0.71	54	19	26	31	91	50	62	4%	124	9%	82%				4.39	-1.3	46	132	$19

Smith,Mallex

Age: 24	Bats: L	Pos: CF LF	Health C	LIMA Plan	C+
Ht: 5' 9"	Wt: 170		PT/Exp F	Rand Var	0
			Consist A	MM	1523

3-22-.238 with 16 SB in 189 AB at ATL. Extreme groundball slap hitter who can't hit lefties, which puts a cap on his potential as a full-timer. But yes, superb wheels can give you the runs... and steals. If bb% growth nets a MLB platoon role, there is this... UP: 40 SB

Yr	Tm	AB	R	HR	RBI	SB	BA	xBA	OBP	SLG	OPS	vL	vR	bb%	ct%	Eye	G	L	F	h%	HctX	PX	xPX	hr/f	Spd	SBO	SB%	#Wk	DOM	DIS	RC/G	RAR	BPV	BPX	R$
12																																			
13																																			
14																																			
15	a/a	484	75	2	31	51	283		346	353	699			9	80	0.48				35		47			147	41%	78%				4.49		21	57	$30
16	ATL *	220	36	3	26	20	260	254	332	393	725	299	819	10	74	0.41	61	16	23	34	60	81	59	11%	144	45%	68%	15	27%	40%	4.25	-2.6	25	71	$11
1st Half		184	29	3	21	15	247	259	311	396	707	288	838	8	75	0.37	61	14	25	32	63	92	65	11%	142	48%	68%	11	27%	36%	3.92	-3.4	34	97	$13
2nd Half		36	7	0	5	5	321	268	429	369	797	400	656	16	70	0.62	64	36	0	46	38	23	-1	0%	122	39%	69%	4	25%	50%	5.79	1.3	-32	-91	$1
17	Proj	353	55	4	33	30	260	255	326	385	711	291	865	8	77	0.39	61	14	25	33	57	76	59	7%	148	44%	71%				4.12	-4.2	36	103	$19

STEPHEN NICKRAND

Smith,Seth

Age: 34 Bats: L Pos: RF LF	Health A	LIMA Plan D+
Ht: 6' 3" Wt: 215	PT/Exp B	Rand Var 0
	Consist A	MM 3133

There aren't many platoon guys who consistently generate profit at $5; this is one. Those with skeptical eye might dismiss HR uptick due to lucky hr/f. Turns out he added 25 ft of FB distance, so it can stick. Just know that path to 400+ AB blocked by deepening vL struggles, and he's at an age where it's not likely to change.

Yr	Tm	AB	R	HR	RBI	SB	BA	xBA	OBP	SLG	OPS	vL	vR	bb%	ct%	Eye	G	L	F	h%	HctX	PX	xPX	hr/f	Spd	SBO	SB%	#Wk	DOM	DIS	RC/G	RAR	BPV	BPX	R$
12	OAK	383	55	14	52	2	240	258	333	420	754	521	805	12	74	0.51	41	23	36	29	107	126	130	14%	78	4%	50%	26	58%	35%	4.56	-3.3	47	118	$8
13	OAK	368	49	8	40	0	253	243	329	391	721	621	748	10	74	0.41	45	20	35	32	91	113	102	8%	82	0%	0%	27	33%	41%	4.33	0.5	34	85	$6
14	SD	443	55	12	48	1	266	281	367	440	807	744	815	13	80	0.79	47	21	32	31	115	126	115	11%	93	1%	50%	27	59%	26%	5.56	21.2	79	214	$11
15	SEA	395	54	12	42	0	248	264	330	443	773	571	801	11	75	0.47	42	20	38	30	118	139	122	11%	94	0%	0%	27	52%	22%	4.93	1.9	62	168	$7
16	SEA	378	62	16	63	0	249	257	342	415	758	476	782	11	76	0.54	48	22	30	29	105	99	108	18%	76	0%	0%	26	38%	42%	4.70	0.0	32	91	$9
1st Half		211	36	10	38	0	280	256	370	455	825	427	866	11	79	0.60	49	19	32	31	112	99	108	19%	88	0%	0%	14	43%	36%	5.82	6.7	45	129	$13
2nd Half		167	26	6	25	0	210	258	307	365	673	573	679	11	74	0.48	47	25	28	25	96	100	109	17%	67	0%	0%	12	33%	50%	3.51	-6.1	19	54	$3
17	**Proj**	**373**	**55**	**13**	**51**	**0**	**245**	**262**	**336**	**419**	**755**	**579**	**776**	**11**	**76**	**0.53**	**46**	**22**	**33**	**29**	**108**	**109**	**114**	**14%**	**82**	**0%**	**50%**				**4.67**	**-0.3**	**34**	**96**	**$7**

Smoak,Justin

Age: 30 Bats: B Pos: 1B	Health A	LIMA Plan D
Ht: 6' 3" Wt: 200	PT/Exp D	Rand Var 0
	Consist B	MM 4013

Former top prospect now on wrong side of 30 with no signs of being able to nail down a full-time job. Eroding ct% bottomed out in 2nd half, muting the good power he still carries and putting even a part-time role in jeopardy. Only twinge of hope is in that LD% trend, but it won't matter if the Ks keep piling up.

Yr	Tm	AB	R	HR	RBI	SB	BA	xBA	OBP	SLG	OPS	vL	vR	bb%	ct%	Eye	G	L	F	h%	HctX	PX	xPX	hr/f	Spd	SBO	SB%	#Wk	DOM	DIS	RC/G	RAR	BPV	BPX	R$
12	SEA *	549	56	19	54	2	213	224	291	352	643	703	627	10	76	0.46	40	18	42	25	96	90	116	12%	79	1%	100%	26	38%	50%	3.33	-33.1	22	55	$3
13	SEA *	475	54	20	51	0	235	234	326	405	731	548	839	12	74	0.51	35	20	46	28	112	120	152	13%	89	0%	0%	25	44%	36%	4.41	-2.7	43	108	$8
14	SEA *	453	46	11	55	0	224	223	292	349	641	618	611	9	73	0.37	42	18	39	28	116	101	145	10%	68	3%	0%	18	33%	33%	3.23	-12.6	15	41	$4
15	TOR	296	44	18	59	0	226	274	299	470	768	839	757	9	71	0.34	43	24	34	26	112	166	141	25%	76	0%	0%	27	56%	33%	4.57	-3.2	59	159	$7
16	TOR	299	33	14	34	1	217	224	314	391	705	621	738	12	63	0.36	30	27	42	29	99	123	144	18%	84	1%	100%	26	27%	58%	3.97	-8.1	0	0	$2
1st Half		197	22	9	23	1	234	235	329	411	740	629	787	12	64	0.39	31	28	40	31	107	125	135	18%	93	2%	100%	14	21%	64%	4.49	-3.6	12	34	$4
2nd Half		102	11	5	11	0	186	204	284	353	637	600	648	11	59	0.31	28	25	47	25	84	120	163	18%	85	0%	0%	12	33%	50%	3.08	-6.6	-19	-54	-$2
17	**Proj**	**251**	**30**	**12**	**34**	**0**	**227**	**234**	**311**	**414**	**725**	**676**	**742**	**10**	**67**	**0.35**	**36**	**24**	**41**	**29**	**102**	**125**	**146**	**18%**	**78**	**1%**	**47%**				**4.18**	**-7.0**	**0**	**-1**	**$5**

Smolinski,Jacob

Age: 28 Bats: R Pos: CF RF	Health B	LIMA Plan D+
Ht: 6' 0" Wt: 215	PT/Exp D	Rand Var +4
	Consist C	MM 2233

7-27-.238 in 290 AB at OAK. This is the kind of player who produces more value to you the less he plays. Righties carve him up, so hope for FT impact is fool's gold. Both production and plate control much better vL, but even his platoon value was fading late in season. Subpar Spd, poor xPX give no latent hope. Heed RAR.

Yr	Tm	AB	R	HR	RBI	SB	BA	xBA	OBP	SLG	OPS	vL	vR	bb%	ct%	Eye	G	L	F	h%	HctX	PX	xPX	hr/f	Spd	SBO	SB%	#Wk	DOM	DIS	RC/G	RAR	BPV	BPX	R$
12	aa	408	57	5	33	7	228		337	333	669			14	78	0.76				28		76			105	9%	62%				3.65		36	90	$4
13	a/a	370	36	6	29	7	219		298	316	614			10	79	0.53				26		69			107	8%	87%				3.13		24	60	$2
14	TEX *	382	47	10	41	4	249	261	301	398	700	1357	757	7	76	0.31	40	26	34	30	122	114	106	14%	93	7%	64%	6	50%	50%	4.03	1.6	38	103	$8
15	2AL *	297	44	13	51	3	248	271	314	454	767	833	454	9	81	0.49	45	15	40	27	96	131	93	12%	88	9%	43%	22	32%	45%	4.64	1.1	73	197	$8
16	OAK *	435	45	9	39	6	229	257	276	345	622	796	557	6	84	0.40	43	22	35	25	100	67	69	8%	88	9%	65%	21	24%	29%	3.12	-16.5	29	83	$4
1st Half		215	28	6	28	5	250	264	294	410	704	1263	572	6	84	0.38	41	19	41	27	96	95	69	15%	88	13%	81%	8	50%	0%	4.12	-2.5	52	149	$10
2nd Half		220	17	3	11	1	209	242	281	282	563	583	553	6	84	0.42	43	23	33	24	101	41	69	5%	99	6%	33%	13	8%	46%	2.28	-15.4	12	34	-$2
17	**Proj**	**259**	**30**	**7**	**28**	**3**	**246**	**259**	**312**	**393**	**704**	**890**	**576**	**7**	**81**	**0.43**	**43**	**21**	**36**	**28**	**101**	**87**	**83**	**10%**	**90**	**8%**	**61%**				**3.95**	**-4.3**	**34**	**96**	**$6**

Solarte,Yangervis

Age: 29 Bats: B Pos: 3B	Health B	LIMA Plan B+
Ht: 5' 11" Wt: 176	PT/Exp B	Rand Var -2
	Consist B	MM 2145

Biggest challenge of year for him was overcoming family tragedy, so everything else in perspective. Early hamstring issue prevented him from delivering on 20-HR upside. Contact skill sets a nice BA floor that protects his value, while xPX suggests a cap on recent PX gains. But we'll be rooting for him.

Yr	Tm	AB	R	HR	RBI	SB	BA	xBA	OBP	SLG	OPS	vL	vR	bb%	ct%	Eye	G	L	F	h%	HctX	PX	xPX	hr/f	Spd	SBO	SB%	#Wk	DOM	DIS	RC/G	RAR	BPV	BPX	R$
12	aaa	518	47	9	37	2	244		283	340	623			5	90	0.56				26		60			84	3%	64%				3.23		47	118	$4
13	aaa	526	47	9	53	2	231		270	334	604			5	85	0.35				26		72			79	2%	100%				3.01		33	83	$4
14	2TM	469	56	10	48	0	260	254	336	369	705	760	673	10	88	0.91	45	19	35	28	99	72	71	7%	92	1%	0%	26	42%	12%	4.23	7.0	58	157	$10
15	SD	526	63	14	63	1	270	280	320	428	748	667	771	6	89	0.61	44	19	37	28	119	94	96	8%	101	1%	100%	27	63%	15%	4.71	0.4	77	208	$13
16	SD	405	55	15	71	1	286	282	341	467	808	772	819	7	84	0.48	41	22	37	31	112	104	91	12%	77	2%	50%	22	45%	18%	5.56	6.5	60	171	$14
1st Half		143	20	5	24	0	301	279	387	483	869	1082	786	11	84	0.78	39	22	39	33	116	110	95	11%	74	0%	0%	9	67%	22%	6.67	7.0	70	200	$8
2nd Half		262	35	10	47	1	279	283	314	458	772	542	835	4	85	0.30	43	22	35	30	110	101	89	13%	86	3%	50%	13	31%	15%	4.96	0.5	56	160	$17
17	**Proj**	**521**	**65**	**16**	**74**	**1**	**274**	**276**	**329**	**430**	**760**	**737**	**767**	**7**	**86**	**0.55**	**44**	**21**	**36**	**29**	**113**	**89**	**90**	**10%**	**85**	**1%**	**56%**				**4.88**	**-0.1**	**49**	**141**	**$17**

Soler,Jorge

Age: 25 Bats: R Pos: LF	Health D	LIMA Plan C+
Ht: 6' 3" Wt: 205	PT/Exp D	Rand Var +2
	Consist D	MM 3215

12-31-.238 in 227 AB at CHC. Just when it looked like breakout was around corner, this happened. Lack of consistency chronic (.984 OPS, 76% ct% in Aug; .671 OPS, 55% ct% in Sept). So too are nagging injuries. Combined with erosions in HctX and xPX, he's truly a high-risk/high-reward wild card now.

Yr	Tm	AB	R	HR	RBI	SB	BA	xBA	OBP	SLG	OPS	vL	vR	bb%	ct%	Eye	G	L	F	h%	HctX	PX	xPX	hr/f	Spd	SBO	SB%	#Wk	DOM	DIS	RC/G	RAR	BPV	BPX	R$
12																																			
13																																			
14	CHC *	264	38	16	59	1	296	312	365	594	960	701	964	10	73	0.41	52	12	36	35	128	230	131	21%	96	3%	47%	6	67%	33%	7.76	29.1	128	346	$14
15	CHC	366	39	10	47	3	262	236	324	399	723	730	720	8	67	0.26	42	28	30	37	110	107	123	14%	102	4%	75%	20	30%	50%	4.43	-2.9	2	5	$8
16	CHC *	264	40	12	32	0	224	215	325	394	719	812	749	13	68	0.47	40	17	43	28	86	112	91	17%	90	0%	0%	19	47%	37%	4.20	-3.3	17	49	$3
1st Half		130	24	5	13	0	223	230	322	377	699	685	709	12	72	0.47	34	22	44	27	89	98	88	12%	101	0%	0%	10	40%	40%	3.87	-2.3	23	66	$2
2nd Half		134	16	7	19	0	225	191	336	411	747	1099	791	14	64	0.46	47	10	43	29	84	127	97	24%	89	0%	0%	9	56%	33%	4.54	0.3	15	43	$3
17	**Proj**	**405**	**53**	**16**	**52**	**1**	**248**	**231**	**331**	**420**	**750**	**774**	**900**	**11**	**68**	**0.38**	**44**	**19**	**37**	**32**	**101**	**118**	**109**	**15%**	**97**	**2%**	**69%**				**4.68**	**2.8**	**6**	**18**	**$11**

Souza,Steven

Age: 28 Bats: R Pos: RF	Health C	LIMA Plan C+
Ht: 6' 3" Wt: 220	PT/Exp C	Rand Var 0
	Consist B	MM 3205

As xPX warned, that 1st half power surge didn't stick. Even if we chalk it up to hip issue that flared up in mid-season, those ups-and-downs are likely to continue given huge holes in his swing. HctX dip, Spd surge give legs more upside than thump, but late-season hip surgery clouds outlook for 2017.

Yr	Tm	AB	R	HR	RBI	SB	BA	xBA	OBP	SLG	OPS	vL	vR	bb%	ct%	Eye	G	L	F	h%	HctX	PX	xPX	hr/f	Spd	SBO	SB%	#Wk	DOM	DIS	RC/G	RAR	BPV	BPX	R$
12																																			
13	aa	273	43	12	35	16	265		341	476	817			10	69	0.38				34		168			92	32%	70%				5.43		62	155	$14
14	WAS *	369	48	14	57	19	284	254	356	465	820	2071	105	10	75	0.44	50	13	38	35	122	136	141	33%	75	25%	70%	9	22%	78%	5.72	17.3	53	143	$21
15	TAM	373	59	16	40	12	225	220	318	399	717	730	712	11	61	0.32	45	20	35	32	92	138	101	21%	101	18%	67%	21	24%	48%	3.98	-9.0	10	27	$10
16	TAM	430	58	17	49	7	247	225	303	409	713	664	731	7	63	0.19	41	25	34	35	83	118	110	18%	115	13%	54%	24	25%	58%	3.95	-9.7	-2	-6	$10
1st Half		219	26	10	25	3	251	234	310	434	743	796	725	7	61	0.20	46	25	28	36	85	137	106	26%	101	10%	60%	13	23%	62%	4.40	-1.9	1	3	$10
2nd Half		211	32	7	24	4	242	213	297	384	681	541	737	6	65	0.19	36	24	40	34	81	99	114	13%	125	16%	50%	11	27%	55%	3.51	-7.6	-9	-26	$10
17	**Proj**	**481**	**66**	**18**	**57**	**10**	**242**	**229**	**313**	**405**	**718**	**683**	**731**	**8**	**65**	**0.27**	**42**	**23**	**35**	**33**	**86**	**117**	**107**	**16%**	**108**	**15%**	**59%**				**4.01**	**-9.9**	**-1**	**-2**	**$15**

Span,Denard

Age: 33 Bats: L Pos: CF	Health D	LIMA Plan A
Ht: 6' 0" Wt: 205	PT/Exp B	Rand Var +1
	Consist C	MM 1355

On surface, went back to being multi-category contributor after injury-marred 2015, even doubling his prior power output in the process. But that xPX tempers any optimism that it will stick. Swiftly declining Spd, age put double-digit swipes in jeopardy too. His upside now is as an empty BA contributor.

Yr	Tm	AB	R	HR	RBI	SB	BA	xBA	OBP	SLG	OPS	vL	vR	bb%	ct%	Eye	G	L	F	h%	HctX	PX	xPX	hr/f	Spd	SBO	SB%	#Wk	DOM	DIS	RC/G	RAR	BPV	BPX	R$
12	MIN	516	71	4	41	17	283	290	342	395	738	739	737	8	88	0.76	54	21	24	32	80	78	48	4%	109	16%	74%	26	58%	23%	4.81	1.7	66	165	$16
13	WAS	610	75	4	47	20	279	285	327	380	707	539	765	6	87	0.55	54	23	23	31	68	65	41	3%	151	15%	77%	26	46%	12%	4.39	5.0	62	155	$20
14	WAS	610	94	5	37	31	302	288	355	416	771	694	802	8	89	0.77	46	24	30	33	98	80	52	3%	132	21%	82%	27	56%	7%	5.49	28.2	78	211	$30
15	WAS	246	38	5	22	11	301	301	365	431	796	542	880	9	89	0.96	50	24	26	32	95	84	72	9%	101	14%	100%	13	54%	23%	6.07	11.9	76	205	$11
16	SF	572	70	11	53	12	266	282	331	381	712	566	781	8	86	0.67	53	23	25	29	87	64	51	9%	94	11%	63%	27	52%	30%	4.25	-6.6	43	123	$15
1st Half		304	38	4	30	8	253	273	335	352	687	617	728	10	85	0.74	54	22	24	29	84	57	46	7%	97	14%	62%	14	50%	36%	3.86	-5.9	36	103	$15
2nd Half		268	32	7	23	4	280	291	326	414	741	485	833	6	88	0.56	51	23	26	30	90	71	57	12%	88	8%	67%	13	54%	23%	4.71	1.5	50	143	$15
17	**Proj**	**515**	**70**	**8**	**44**	**13**	**283**	**289**	**342**	**398**	**739**	**575**	**805**	**8**	**88**	**0.71**	**51**	**23**	**26**	**31**	**90**	**67**	**57**	**7%**	**103**	**12%**	**76%**				**4.82**	**4.5**	**55**	**157**	**$19**

STEPHEN NICKRAND

Spangenberg,Cory

Age: 26 **Bats:** L **Pos:** 2B **Ht:** 6' 0" **Wt:** 185
Health F **PT/Exp** F **Consist** A
LIMA Plan C **Rand Var** +2 **MM** 1523

Sidelined for nearly entire season due to torn quad. Pre-injury profile as line-drive hitter with good wheels makes him worth a look again. Rising Spd, improved SB% in 2015 keeps 20 SB in play. Just cap your expectations given so-so plate control, which also reduces hope he'll be anything more than a mid-level BA contributor.

Yr	Tm	AB	R	HR	RBI	SB	BA	xBA	OBP	SLG	OPS	vL	vR	bb%	ct%	Eye	G	L	F	h%	HctX	PX	xPX	hr/f	Spd	SBO	SB%	#Wk	DOM	DIS	RC/G	RAR	BPV	BPX	R$
12																																			
13	aa	287	30	2	17	16	259		294	325	620			5	75	0.21				34		50			132	37%	57%				2.95		-6	-15	$8
14	SD *	343	38	4	27	15	291	250	320	415	735	667	795	4	75	0.17	45	26	30	38	86	93	113	14%	137	32%	56%	5	20%	40%	4.30	9.1	24	65	$14
15	SD *	341	42	5	24	12	260	262	321	385	706	703	738	8	76	0.38	50	25	25	33	84	86	74	8%	145	17%	75%	20	40%	40%	4.25	0.8	36	97	$9
16	SD	48	6	1	8	1	229	251	302	354	656	1074	448	8	73	0.31	69	16	16	29	51	72	15	20%	123	8%	100%	3	33%	67%	3.49	-1.9	3	9	-$1
1st Half		48	6	1	8	1	229	251	302	354	656	1074	448	8	73	0.31	69	16	16	29	51	72	15	20%	123	8%	100%	3	33%	67%	3.49	-1.9	3	9	-$1
2nd Half																																			
17	**Proj**	**328**	**38**	**6**	**33**	**14**	**262**	**255**	**313**	**388**	**701**	**831**	**654**	**6**	**75**	**0.26**	**54**	**22**	**24**	**34**	**73**	**77**	**69**	**10%**	**138**	**26%**	**64%**				**3.93**	**-8.5**	**15**	**43**	**$10**

Springer,George

Age: 27 **Bats:** R **Pos:** RF **Ht:** 6' 3" **Wt:** 200
Health D **PT/Exp** B **Consist** B
LIMA Plan B **Rand Var** +1 **MM** 4325

Three reasons not to expect another step up in 2017: 1) All of his thump still comes vL; 2) holes in swing remain large; 3) GB tilt, marginal HctX put power at risk. Those issues were glossed over by high volume of ABs. Health grade makes repeat there unlikely, so he'll be overvalued. For profit, stop when bidding hits $20.

Yr	Tm	AB	R	HR	RBI	SB	BA	xBA	OBP	SLG	OPS	vL	vR	bb%	ct%	Eye	G	L	F	h%	HctX	PX	xPX	hr/f	Spd	SBO	SB%	#Wk	DOM	DIS	RC/G	RAR	BPV	BPX	R$
12	aa	73	6	2	4	3	186		233	284	518			6	61	0.16				28		86			96	37%	57%				1.89		-45	-113	-$2
13	a/a	492	81	29	82	34	262		346	501	847			11	61	0.34				36		194			102	32%	79%				5.99		56	140	$33
14	HOU *	346	57	22	57	8	239	241	328	475	802	774	811	12	62	0.34	45	15	39	32	105	191	161	28%	133	11%	80%	14	57%	36%	5.23	13.8	65	176	$14
15	HOU	388	59	16	41	16	276	261	367	459	826	936	767	11	72	0.46	45	24	30	35	106	127	112	19%	123	17%	80%	19	63%	32%	5.84	11.9	51	138	$18
16	HOU	644	116	29	82	9	261	260	359	457	815	945	769	12	72	0.49	48	20	31	32	99	122	111	20%	128	10%	47%	27	41%	26%	5.27	10.7	52	149	$22
1st Half		331	59	18	49	6	260	264	359	468	827	858	818	12	75	0.54	53	17	30	30	93	120	93	24%	127	12%	50%	14	50%	21%	5.35	6.4	58	166	$25
2nd Half		313	57	11	33	3	262	253	359	444	803	1015	713	12	70	0.46	43	24	33	34	105	123	131	15%	125	8%	43%	13	31%	31%	5.19	4.5	42	120	$19
17	**Proj**	**525**	**89**	**23**	**68**	**10**	**260**	**249**	**357**	**448**	**804**	**911**	**759**	**12**	**69**	**0.43**	**46**	**21**	**32**	**33**	**103**	**123**	**121**	**19%**	**128**	**10%**	**64%**				**5.25**	**8.6**	**32**	**93**	**$21**

Stanton,Giancarlo

Age: 27 **Bats:** R **Pos:** RF **Ht:** 6' 5" **Wt:** 242
Health F **PT/Exp** B **Consist** C
LIMA Plan B **Rand Var** +2 **MM** 5235

A $40 player trapped in a $5 body. Hip, groin, ribs were maladies this go-around. When he hits, he mashes, as confirmed by top-tier power skills. But that two-year slide vR adds to his risk. First 40+ HR season requires health, reversal of vR trend, and reduction in Ks, all of which are chronic issues. Bring a rabbit's foot.

Yr	Tm	AB	R	HR	RBI	SB	BA	xBA	OBP	SLG	OPS	vL	vR	bb%	ct%	Eye	G	L	F	h%	HctX	PX	xPX	hr/f	Spd	SBO	SB%	#Wk	DOM	DIS	RC/G	RAR	BPV	BPX	R$
12	MIA	449	75	37	86	6	290	288	361	608	969	1024	950	9	68	0.32	36	22	42	35	132	226	163	29%	77	7%	75%	23	61%	17%	7.72	32.3	97	243	$25
13	MIA	425	62	24	62	1	249	253	365	480	845	1006	789	15	67	0.53	43	18	38	31	109	180	139	22%	77	1%	100%	22	45%	27%	5.90	16.1	67	168	$13
14	MIA	539	89	37	105	13	288	278	395	555	950	1075	920	15	68	0.55	41	20	39	36	120	206	146	26%	75	8%	93%	24	75%	13%	7.94	58.0	93	251	$35
15	MIA	279	47	27	67	4	265	282	346	606	952	1172	893	11	66	0.36	35	20	45	30	142	236	210	32%	85	9%	67%	12	67%	25%	7.14	18.5	102	276	$16
16	MIA	413	56	27	74	0	240	243	326	489	815	947	779	11	66	0.36	40	17	43	29	115	167	156	23%	79	0%	0%	24	46%	46%	5.28	7.4	45	129	$10
1st Half		256	34	15	40	0	219	221	316	441	758	839	734	12	61	0.35	42	16	42	29	95	159	132	22%	92	0%	0%	14	36%	50%	4.51	-1.5	26	74	$9
2nd Half		157	22	12	34	0	274	278	343	567	910	1132	849	9	74	0.37	38	18	44	30	149	179	189	23%	70	0%	0%	10	60%	40%	6.71	9.0	79	226	$12
17	**Proj**	**466**	**70**	**35**	**94**	**4**	**262**	**265**	**349**	**545**	**893**	**1058**	**848**	**11**	**68**	**0.40**	**38**	**19**	**43**	**31**	**129**	**183**	**173**	**26%**	**78**	**4%**	**78%**				**6.50**	**24.4**	**61**	**174**	**$23**

Story,Trevor

Age: 24 **Bats:** R **Pos:** SS **Ht:** 6' 1" **Wt:** 180
Health C **PT/Exp** C **Consist** D
LIMA Plan B+ **Rand Var** -2 **MM** 5325

On pace for explosive debut before torn ligament in thumb sidelined him for final two months. With a 150+ xPX each month, we can put 30 HR in stone w/health, especially given xFB tilt and #1 FB+HR distance in MLB. And wheels support double-digit bags. Risk is volatilty, since holes in swing were big. Take it. UP: 40 HR

Yr	Tm	AB	R	HR	RBI	SB	BA	xBA	OBP	SLG	OPS	vL	vR	bb%	ct%	Eye	G	L	F	h%	HctX	PX	xPX	hr/f	Spd	SBO	SB%	#Wk	DOM	DIS	RC/G	RAR	BPV	BPX	R$
12																																			
13																																			
14	aa	205	23	8	16	2	192		269	356	625			10	59	0.26				28		147			108	8%	69%				3.00		8	22	$0
15	a/a	512	60	16	58	16	259		309	463	771			7	73	0.26				33		144			116	18%	83%				4.96		56	151	$17
16	COL	372	67	27	72	8	272	259	341	567	909	975	883	9	65	0.27	29	24	47	34	119	199	191	24%	122	15%	62%	17	53%	12%	6.41	19.3	75	214	$18
1st Half		293	47	19	50	5	266	256	333	549	883	849	896	8	64	0.26	31	23	45	35	117	196	184	22%	125	13%	63%	14	50%	14%	6.11	14.0	70	200	$21
2nd Half		79	20	8	22	3	291	272	371	633	1004	1625	841	9	68	0.32	22	24	54	33	126	210	216	28%	105	25%	60%	3	67%	0%	7.57	7.1	93	266	$8
17	**Proj**	**547**	**91**	**36**	**92**	**11**	**260**	**255**	**331**	**531**	**862**	**1085**	**792**	**8**	**68**	**0.27**	**30**	**23**	**47**	**32**	**122**	**177**	**203**	**20%**	**126**	**15%**	**62%**				**5.67**	**19.4**	**65**	**186**	**$27**

Suarez,Eugenio

Age: 25 **Bats:** R **Pos:** 3B **Ht:** 5' 11" **Wt:** 205
Health A **PT/Exp** B **Consist** A
LIMA Plan B+ **Rand Var** -1 **MM** 3215

Chances of building upon this mini-breakout? PRO: Concurrent 2H upticks in bb%, ct%; hard contact on rise, especially late; mashes LH now. CON: Power at mercy of hr/f, which tanked down stretch, and only-decent FB distance and xPX make 1H repeat unlikely; not that good vR. Still young, but for now, pay only for a repeat.

Yr	Tm	AB	R	HR	RBI	SB	BA	xBA	OBP	SLG	OPS	vL	vR	bb%	ct%	Eye	G	L	F	h%	HctX	PX	xPX	hr/f	Spd	SBO	SB%	#Wk	DOM	DIS	RC/G	RAR	BPV	BPX	R$
12																																			
13	aa	442	43	7	36	7	231		290	347	638			8	77	0.36				29		85			112	18%	38%				3.03		27	68	$4
14	DET *	442	57	10	50	10	246	231	306	379	685	656	650	8	74	0.33	35	22	43	31	87	107	109	5%	96	13%	70%	17	29%	59%	3.88	2.2	26	70	$11
15	CIN *	575	67	21	69	7	263	248	310	429	739	819	744	6	75	0.28	41	21	38	32	95	111	105	12%	107	9%	54%	18	39%	39%	4.47	-3.4	37	100	$17
16	CIN	565	78	21	70	11	248	241	317	411	728	882	683	8	73	0.33	41	22	38	31	103	104	105	13%	93	11%	69%	27	30%	37%	4.26	-12.0	20	57	$15
1st Half		292	39	14	39	6	233	233	301	408	709	919	632	8	70	0.28	42	21	37	28	91	103	108	18%	127	14%	60%	14	21%	43%	3.81	-9.7	19	54	$15
2nd Half		273	39	7	31	5	264	250	334	414	748	823	732	9	75	0.40	39	22	39	33	115	105	103	9%	76	8%	83%	13	38%	31%	4.77	-0.9	27	77	$15
17	**Proj**	**580**	**74**	**19**	**67**	**10**	**251**	**242**	**317**	**408**	**725**	**804**	**700**	**8**	**74**	**0.33**	**40**	**21**	**39**	**31**	**99**	**101**	**106**	**11%**	**98**	**11%**	**64%**				**4.23**	**-11.4**	**22**	**62**	**$17**

Susac,Andrew

Age: 27 **Bats:** R **Pos:** CA **Ht:** 6' 2" **Wt:** 210
Health B **PT/Exp** F **Consist** B
LIMA Plan D **Rand Var** +3 **MM** 3303

1-2-.235 in 17 AB at MIL. The makings of an intriguing second catcher speculation... 1) xPX has consistently outperformed PX; 2) former 2nd round pick hidden in past by Posey; 3) prior thumb, wrist injuries zapped that upside. He's at the right age now to take another step up in new org. With opportunity, health... UP: 15 HR

Yr	Tm	AB	R	HR	RBI	SB	BA	xBA	OBP	SLG	OPS	vL	vR	bb%	ct%	Eye	G	L	F	h%	HctX	PX	xPX	hr/f	Spd	SBO	SB%	#Wk	DOM	DIS	RC/G	RAR	BPV	BPX	R$
12																																			
13	aa	262	24	8	34	1	213		297	359	656			11	71	0.40				27		116			79	1%	100%				3.47		23	58	$1
14	SF *	301	36	9	40	0	227	223	298	363	661	1011	668	9	71	0.35	37	20	43	29	103	111	156	12%	86	0%	0%	12	42%	42%	3.57	1.0	19	51	$3
15	SF *	161	18	4	15	0	225	224	296	377	673	824	578	9	66	0.29	47	19	34	32	95	121	123	10%	110	0%	0%	17	29%	47%	3.68	-0.6	13	35	-$1
16	MIL *	266	24	7	29	0	203	237	259	325	585	5000	528	7	71	0.26	17	33	50	26	96	84	184	17%	86	0%	0%	4	75%	0%	2.70	-14.1	-7	-20	-$2
1st Half		127	8	1	14	0	190	205	267	273	540			9	72	0.37				25		65			82	0%	0%				2.29		-15	-43	-$4
2nd Half		139	15	5	15	0	215	236	252	373	625	5000	528	5	70	0.16	17	33	50	27	94	102	184	17%	99	0%	0%	4	75%	0%	3.06	-4.6	2	6	$0
17	**Proj**	**258**	**26**	**9**	**36**	**0**	**233**	**229**	**298**	**397**	**695**	**867**	**599**	**8**	**69**	**0.29**	**43**	**19**	**38**	**30**	**98**	**110**	**136**	**13%**	**98**	**0%**	**100%**				**3.89**	**-1.9**	**-3**	**-9**	**$5**

Suzuki,Ichiro

Age: 43 **Bats:** L **Pos:** RF **Ht:** 5' 9" **Wt:** 175
Health A **PT/Exp** C **Consist** D
LIMA Plan D+ **Rand Var** -1 **MM** 0543

Hard to find a more consistent 5th OF target in deep leagues than this one. Nothing here to suggest he'll stop producing a BA that won't hurt you or double-digit steals, since his Spd STILL hasn't dipped below 120 in career and pitch recognition actually keeps getting better. Bid $5, take $5 or so profit into bank.

Yr	Tm	AB	R	HR	RBI	SB	BA	xBA	OBP	SLG	OPS	vL	vR	bb%	ct%	Eye	G	L	F	h%	HctX	PX	xPX	hr/f	Spd	SBO	SB%	#Wk	DOM	DIS	RC/G	RAR	BPV	BPX	R$
12	2 AL	629	77	9	55	29	283	292	307	390	696	649	724	3	90	0.36	51	25	24	30	70	63	40	7%	123	23%	81%	28	57%	14%	4.31	-15.0	57	143	$24
13	NYY	520	57	7	35	20	262	264	297	342	639	753	590	5	88	0.41	52	21	27	29	58	50	34	6%	129	18%	83%	26	38%	27%	3.59	-15.4	42	105	$15
14	NYY	359	42	1	22	15	284	255	324	340	664	807	632	6	81	0.31	58	22	20	35	67	45	22	2%	126	17%	83%	27	22%	48%	4.03	-0.6	11	30	$12
15	MIA	398	45	1	21	11	229	251	282	279	561	723	514	7	87	0.61	58	18	23	26	52	26	28	1%	168	15%	69%	27	22%	44%	2.61	-27.4	36	97	$3
16	MIA	327	48	1	22	10	291	286	354	376	730	859	700	8	87	0.71	48	28	24	33	77	51	50	1%	129	12%	83%	27	41%	22%	4.82	1.3	47	134	$10
1st Half		161	25	0	12	7	335	290	410	385	795	763	802	12	91	1.40	50	29	22	37	85	32	44	0%	116	13%	78%	14	57%	21%	6.18	6.3	48	137	$15
2nd Half		166	23	1	10	3	247	281	296	367	664	969	604	5	84	0.33	47	27	27	29	69	71	57	3%	123	8%	100%	13	23%	23%	3.65	-5.1	41	117	$5
17	**Proj**	**261**	**34**	**1**	**16**	**8**	**268**	**274**	**321**	**344**	**665**	**798**	**630**	**7**	**86**	**0.54**	**52**	**24**	**24**	**31**	**67**	**44**	**40**	**2%**	**131**	**14%**	**80%**				**3.88**	**-6.1**	**34**	**97**	**$8**

STEPHEN NICKRAND

Suzuki,Kurt

Age: 33 Bats: R Pos: CA	Health	A	LIMA Plan	D+	Sure, there's still value in catchers like this who won't hurt you. Just don't mine here for mid-30s backstop upside. Subpar and declining xPX, chronic mediocrity vR cap his appeal. His BA, with sturdy ct% by his side, does have a decent floor. Still, there's no profit above $5.
Ht: 6' 0" Wt: 195	PT/Exp	C	Rand Var	0	
	Consist	C	MM	1133	

Yr	Tm	AB	R	HR	RBI	SB	BA	xBA	OBP	SLG	OPS	vL	vR	bb%	ct%	Eye	G	L	F	h%	HctX	PX	xPX	hr/f	Spd	SBO	SB%	#Wk	DOM	DIS	RC/G	RAR	BPV	BPX	R$
12	2 TM	408	36	6	43	2	235	223	276	328	605	628	598	5	82	0.27	41	17	42	27	112	66	102	4%	84	2%	100%	28	21%	46%	2.99	-13.9	18	45	$3
13	2 TM	285	25	5	32	2	232	255	290	337	627	653	619	7	88	0.63	37	23	40	25	106	69	100	5%	92	3%	100%	26	38%	31%	3.24	-4.0	50	125	$2
14	MIN	452	37	3	61	0	288	268	345	383	727	810	695	7	90	0.74	44	22	34	32	100	76	82	2%	74	1%	0%	27	59%	15%	4.58	15.9	58	157	$11
15	MIN	433	36	5	50	0	240	230	296	314	610	658	587	6	86	0.49	43	19	38	27	100	50	84	4%	81	0%	0%	26	38%	35%	3.03	-9.0	24	65	$3
16	MIN	345	34	8	49	0	258	270	301	403	704	745	685	5	86	0.38	40	21	39	28	103	88	79	7%	63	0%	0%	26	54%	27%	4.08	2.1	46	131	$5
1st Half		180	13	4	25	0	278	269	316	411	727	797	693	4	83	0.26	39	25	36	32	100	81	70	8%	74	0%	0%	14	43%	36%	4.48	1.7	29	83	$6
2nd Half		165	21	4	24	0	236	274	285	394	679	684	676	6	90	0.59	41	17	41	24	107	95	89	6%	63	0%	0%	12	67%	17%	3.68	-2.3	67	191	$4
17	Proj	**363**	**34**	**6**	**48**	**0**	**253**	**259**	**303**	**369**	**672**	**717**	**653**	**6**	**87**	**0.48**	**42**	**20**	**38**	**28**	**103**	**72**	**84**	**5%**	**72**	**0%**	**64%**				**3.73**	**-4.3**	**29**	**84**	**$5**

Swanson,Dansby

Age: 23 Bats: R Pos: SS	Health	A	LIMA Plan	B+	3-17-.302 in 129 AB at ATL. Top 2015 pick enjoyed swift ascent through minors. Pedigree of elite pitch recognition should ease MLB transition. Package of pop and speed flashed in Sept gives hope for more. He's still plenty green though, so we can't rule out more time in high minors. A gem among young SS investments.
Ht: 6' 1" Wt: 190	PT/Exp	F	Rand Var	-1	
	Consist	F	MM	2525	

Yr	Tm	AB	R	HR	RBI	SB	BA	xBA	OBP	SLG	OPS	vL	vR	bb%	ct%	Eye	G	L	F	h%	HctX	PX	xPX	hr/f	Spd	SBO	SB%	#Wk	DOM	DIS	RC/G	RAR	BPV	BPX	R$
12																																			
13																																			
14																																			
15																																			
16	ATL *	462	74	11	62	10	266	250	336	401	737	1015	771	10	75	0.43	46	23	31	33	106	84	97	10%	150	9%	82%	8	25%	63%	4.73	1.5	35	100	$15
1st Half		210	36	5	25	3	257	246	326	397	723			9	79	0.48				31		80			156	7%	74%				4.44		46	131	$11
2nd Half		252	38	6	37	7	273	243	344	405	749	1015	771	10	73	0.40	46	23	31	35	102	87	97	10%	129	11%	87%	8	25%	63%	4.98	3.7	21	60	$18
17	Proj	**538**	**76**	**11**	**65**	**12**	**262**	**248**	**328**	**393**	**721**	**985**	**681**	**10**	**75**	**0.42**	**46**	**23**	**31**	**33**	**92**	**83**	**87**	**9%**	**153**	**9%**	**84%**				**4.57**	**1.6**	**25**	**70**	**$18**

Swihart,Blake

Age: 25 Bats: B Pos: LF	Health	F	LIMA Plan	D+	0-5-.258 in 62 AB at BOS. Ankle injury stopped sophomore campaign in June. PRO: Concurrent gains in bb%, ct%; Spd now at impact level. CON: RHers handcuff him; power in freefall, no longer CA-eligible in many leagues. In short, a profile worth stashing as a catcher, but as an OF? Not so much.
Ht: 6' 1" Wt: 200	PT/Exp	D	Rand Var	0	
	Consist	B	MM	1323	

Yr	Tm	AB	R	HR	RBI	SB	BA	xBA	OBP	SLG	OPS	vL	vR	bb%	ct%	Eye	G	L	F	h%	HctX	PX	xPX	hr/f	Spd	SBO	SB%	#Wk	DOM	DIS	RC/G	RAR	BPV	BPX	R$
12																																			
13																																			
14	a/a	416	44	10	53	7	279		321	433	754			6	80	0.30				33		116			92	8%	86%				4.95		52	141	$14
15	BOS *	369	54	5	40	5	281	249	323	384	708	603	754	6	74	0.24	46	27	28	37	91	81	71	9%	101	8%	61%	22	23%	41%	4.33	-0.7	7	19	$11
16	BOS *	165	21	1	13	2	246	230	353	325	678	1657	629	14	78	0.77	46	22	33	31	83	46	95	0%	141	7%	48%	5	20%	40%	3.76	-2.5	23	66	$1
1st Half		165	21	1	13	2	246	230	353	325	678	1657	629	14	78	0.77	46	22	33	31	83	46	95	0%	141	7%	48%	5	20%	40%	3.76	-3.4	23	66	$1
2nd Half																																			
17	Proj	**256**	**32**	**4**	**27**	**4**	**253**	**248**	**316**	**373**	**690**	**963**	**637**	**9**	**78**	**0.43**	**44**	**23**	**34**	**31**	**86**	**77**	**85**	**6%**	**114**	**8%**	**66%**				**4.02**	**-3.3**	**21**	**60**	**$6**

Szczur,Matthew

Age: 27 Bats: R Pos: LF	Health	A	LIMA Plan	D	When looking for a fourth or fifth OF, it's best to identify some latent skills worth speculating on. Let's try it out. Power? Zilch. Pitch recognition? Marginal at best. Speed? Now there's something...at least until lack of walks and subpar OBP wipe hope away. Lefty-masher? Nope. Consonant rate in surname? Ding ding!
Ht: 6' 1" Wt: 195	PT/Exp	D	Rand Var	-2	
	Consist	B	MM	1311	

Yr	Tm	AB	R	HR	RBI	SB	BA	xBA	OBP	SLG	OPS	vL	vR	bb%	ct%	Eye	G	L	F	h%	HctX	PX	xPX	hr/f	Spd	SBO	SB%	#Wk	DOM	DIS	RC/G	RAR	BPV	BPX	R$
12	aa	143	19	2	5	3	188		247	311	558			7	77	0.35				23		80			145	20%	59%				2.32		34	85	-$2
13	aa	512	59	2	33	17	245		298	317	615			7	83	0.46				29		55			113	22%	55%				2.99		27	68	$10
14	CHC *	476	43	3	22	22	219	210	259	272	531	909	427	5	78	0.25	46	18	36	27	40	45	50	11%	106	27%	73%	6	50%	33%	2.31	-22.0	-6	-16	$6
15	CHC *	339	34	7	30	16	237	208	283	352	635	725	492	6	77	0.29	34	16	50	29	85	79	118	4%	87	28%	73%	14	36%	36%	3.29	-14.7	13	35	$8
16	CHC	185	30	5	24	2	259	247	312	400	712	671	737	7	79	0.33	43	20	38	30	72	86	56	9%	123	13%	33%	26	42%	54%	3.91	-3.9	36	103	$4
1st Half		87	15	3	16	1	276	239	315	425	741	801	704	5	77	0.25	37	23	40	33	78	82	76	12%	128	13%	33%	13	38%	62%	4.32	-0.3	25	71	$5
2nd Half		98	15	2	8	1	245	251	308	378	686	558	767	8	81	0.42	47	17	36	29	66	89	40	7%	116	13%	33%	13	46%	46%	3.57	-2.7	46	131	$2
17	Proj	**164**	**22**	**4**	**16**	**4**	**242**	**233**	**291**	**370**	**662**	**723**	**615**	**6**	**79**	**0.32**	**40**	**18**	**42**	**29**	**71**	**79**	**76**	**7%**	**117**	**20%**	**58%**				**3.44**	**-5.1**	**23**	**64**	**$4**

Tapia,Raimel

Age: 23 Bats: L Pos: CF	Health	A	LIMA Plan	C	0-3-.263 in 38 AB at COL. Came into 2016 as a solid toolsy prospect. Left it as a top-50 prospect behind big reduction in strikeouts in high minors. Will it stick? Early MLB returns are pessimistic, but if it does, those legs will give him value. Just don't expect power for now; xPX confirms there's none here yet. UP: 30 SB
Ht: 6' 2" Wt: 160	PT/Exp	F	Rand Var	-2	
	Consist	F	MM	1541	

Yr	Tm	AB	R	HR	RBI	SB	BA	xBA	OBP	SLG	OPS	vL	vR	bb%	ct%	Eye	G	L	F	h%	HctX	PX	xPX	hr/f	Spd	SBO	SB%	#Wk	DOM	DIS	RC/G	RAR	BPV	BPX	R$
12																																			
13																																			
14																																			
15																																			
16	COL *	566	80	7	42	22	318	291	346	438	784	500	570	4	88	0.34	37	33	30	35	76	64	59	0%	176	25%	55%	6	0%	67%	5.18	8.7	65	186	$27
1st Half		318	50	6	22	11	334	270	371	464	835			6	89	0.53				36		70			158	25%	45%				5.74		72	206	$32
2nd Half		248	32	2	21	11	308	284	325	423	747	500	570	2	86	0.18	37	33	30	35	75	61	59	0%	177	24%	72%	6	0%	67%	4.96	3.5	54	154	$22
17	Proj	**202**	**28**	**2**	**16**	**10**	**293**	**277**	**311**	**419**	**730**	**855**	**695**	**4**	**82**	**0.21**	**37**	**33**	**30**	**35**	**68**	**71**	**53**	**5%**	**168**	**33%**	**61%**				**4.41**	**-0.6**	**40**	**113**	**$10**

Taylor,Michael

Age: 26 Bats: R Pos: CF	Health	A	LIMA Plan	D	7-16-.231 with 14 SB in 221 AB at WAS. Power/speed package still tantalizes at times, but he's clearly at a crossroads. Holes in swing are firmly chronic and relegate speed to back burner. Dwindling PX makes that 2nd half collapse even more worrisome. Age 26 is the dividing line between prospect and suspect. Be forewarned.
Ht: 6' 2" Wt: 190	PT/Exp	C	Rand Var	+3	
	Consist	B	MM	3503	

Yr	Tm	AB	R	HR	RBI	SB	BA	xBA	OBP	SLG	OPS	vL	vR	bb%	ct%	Eye	G	L	F	h%	HctX	PX	xPX	hr/f	Spd	SBO	SB%	#Wk	DOM	DIS	RC/G	RAR	BPV	BPX	R$
12																																			
13																																			
14	WAS *	467	65	17	52	27	258	240	323	417	739	1095	553	9	63	0.25	55	23	23	38	49	139	65	20%	117	31%	69%	6	17%	50%	4.45	8.7	16	43	$22
15	WAS *	498	52	15	66	18	235	219	290	364	654	667	633	7	66	0.23	46	22	32	33	90	96	115	15%	112	18%	81%	26	19%	54%	3.58	-11.0	-8	-22	$14
16	WAS *	338	43	8	24	20	215	228	269	335	604	755	596	7	66	0.22	44	27	30	30	86	89	81	17%	109	33%	83%	22	18%	64%	3.03	-17.0	-14	-40	$8
1st Half		191	25	6	12	10	225	240	266	372	638	805	559	5	66	0.16	44	27	29	31	82	108	80	17%	102	35%	77%	14	21%	50%	3.21	-7.7	-5	-14	$9
2nd Half		147	18	2	12	10	203	203	276	287	562	598	1064	9	66	0.30	41	24	35	29	111	65	93	17%	125	31%	90%	8	13%	88%	2.76	-8.1	-25	-71	$5
17	Proj	**259**	**31**	**9**	**26**	**14**	**227**	**228**	**286**	**377**	**662**	**627**	**686**	**8**	**66**	**0.24**	**44**	**24**	**32**	**31**	**95**	**105**	**99**	**16%**	**117**	**28%**	**82%**				**3.61**	**-7.2**	**-1**	**-4**	**$9**

Teixeira,Mark

Age: 37 Bats: B Pos: 1B	Health	F	LIMA Plan	F	Taking relatively early path to retirement as nagging injuries continue to mount. After eight seasons of 500+ AB in first nine, never reached that threshold in last five. Still, one of five switch-hitters with 400 HR in career, and his 12.6 HR/AB in 2015 was 9th best all-time among bats age 35 or older. Lots of good years.
Ht: 6' 3" Wt: 215	PT/Exp	B	Rand Var	+3	
	Consist	F	MM	0000	

Yr	Tm	AB	R	HR	RBI	SB	BA	xBA	OBP	SLG	OPS	vL	vR	bb%	ct%	Eye	G	L	F	h%	HctX	PX	xPX	hr/f	Spd	SBO	SB%	#Wk	DOM	DIS	RC/G	RAR	BPV	BPX	R$
12	NYY	451	66	24	84	2	251	281	332	475	807	865	770	11	82	0.65	41	19	39	26	122	137	120	16%	66	3%	67%	24	67%	21%	5.32	0.4	79	198	$14
13	NYY	53	5	3	12	0	151	239	270	340	609	935	432	13	64	0.42	29	29	43	16	77	139	128	20%	68	0%	0%	3	33%	67%	2.68	-3.3	16	40	-$2
14	NYY	440	56	22	62	1	216	254	313	398	711	691	718	12	75	0.53	41	21	37	24	114	125	119	18%	60	2%	50%	25	36%	40%	3.95	-2.5	44	119	$8
15	NYY	392	57	31	79	2	255	296	357	548	906	787	958	13	78	0.69	39	19	42	25	123	179	137	23%	63	2%	100%	21	67%	14%	6.65	19.6	104	281	$16
16	NYY	387	43	15	44	2	204	241	292	362	654	685	640	11	73	0.45	43	21	35	24	95	100	106	15%	64	2%	100%	25	36%	48%	3.39	-17.6	14	40	$1
1st Half		198	21	7	17	1	192	226	276	323	599	594	602	10	71	0.38	49	21	31	23	84	82	90	16%	72	2%	100%	12	17%	67%	2.81	-14.4	-8	-23	-$1
2nd Half		189	22	8	27	1	217	257	309	402	711	840	672	12	75	0.53	38	22	40	25	106	118	121	14%	66	2%	100%	13	54%	31%	4.07	-6.0	40	114	$3
17	Proj																																		

STEPHEN NICKRAND

Thompson,Trayce

Age: 26 Bats: R Pos: CF RF LF | Ht: 6' 3" Wt: 225
Health C | LIMA Plan D+ | PT/Exp C | Rand Var +4 | Consist B | MM 3223

1st half emergence was halted by two season-ending fractures in his lower back. Pre-injury growth in patience and Eye point to a more complete hitter; xBA agrees. But HR outburst was driven by lofty hr/f that masked worm-killing GB%, xPX confirms he was out over his skis a bit. Nice 4th OF, just don't chase "1H HR x 2".

Yr	Tm	AB	R	HR	RBI	SB	BA	xBA	OBP	SLG	OPS	vL	vR	bb%	ct%	Eye	G	L	F	h%	HctX	PX	xPX	hr/f	Spd	SBO	SB%	#Wk	DOM	DIS	RC/G	RAR	BPV	BPX	R$
12	a/a	68	9	3	5	3	238		331	435	766			12	65	0.39				32		146			113	13%	100%				5.05		35	88	$0
13	aa	507	65	14	61	21	210		288	352	640			10	70	0.36				27		108			108	24%	71%				3.23		19	48	$12
14	aa	518	63	13	43	15	203		275	349	623			9	67	0.30				28		126			108	18%	72%				3.04		20	54	$6
15	CHW *	510	60	16	48	10	243	271	289	416	704	998	811	6	77	0.28	39	29	32	29	100	114	99	16%	100	15%	64%	10	80%	20%	3.94	-11.9	42	114	$11
16	LA	236	31	13	32	5	225	258	302	436	738	708	749	10	72	0.39	52	16	32	25	91	133	105	24%	71	11%	83%	15	47%	47%	4.36	-1.8	38	109	$5
1st Half		211	31	13	32	5	242	271	322	474	796	717	825	11	74	0.46	50	17	32	26	96	139	104	25%	73	11%	83%	14	50%	43%	5.17	4.5	54	154	$6
2nd Half		25	0	0	0	0	80	69	115	120	235	619	105	4	52	0.08	69	8	23	15	49	51	110	0%	87	0%	0%	1	0%	100%	0.38	-3.7	-115	-329	-$12
17	**Proj**	**286**	**37**	**10**	**32**	**8**	**248**	**247**	**317**	**417**	**734**	**941**	**631**	**9**	**71**	**0.35**	**47**	**20**	**33**	**31**	**81**	**111**	**104**	**15%**	**88**	**15%**	**72%**				**4.44**	**-0.6**	**25**	**72**	**$7**

Toles,Andrew

Age: 25 Bats: L Pos: LF | Ht: 5' 10" Wt: 185
Health A | LIMA Plan D+ | PT/Exp F | Rand Var 0 | Consist F | MM 3351

3-16-.314 in 105 AB at LA. Tolesy—err, toolsy OF was dulled by behavioral issues in minors; eventually discarded by TAM. But flashed as-advertised plus athleticism in MLB debut. Speed is the highlight, but early returns show enough ct%, HctX, and pop to form broad skill set. Lots of paths to value; well worth a late flyer.

Yr	Tm	AB	R	HR	RBI	SB	BA	xBA	OBP	SLG	OPS	vL	vR	bb%	ct%	Eye	G	L	F	h%	HctX	PX	xPX	hr/f	Spd	SBO	SB%	#Wk	DOM	DIS	RC/G	RAR	BPV	BPX	R$
12																																			
13																																			
14																																			
15																																			
16	LA *	336	47	9	41	13	291	286	329	470	799	692	893	5	80	0.28	48	22	30	34	104	114	90	13%	110	30%	56%	11	27%	45%	5.09	4.3	55	157	$15
1st Half		192	24	4	19	12	267	267	304	424	728			5	82	0.29				31		97			103	42%	68%	1	100%	0%	4.23		47	134	$16
2nd Half		144	23	5	22	1	323	291	362	531	893	692	893	6	77	0.27	48	22	30	39	100	139	90	13%	105	15%	18%	10	20%	50%	6.42	7.6	64	183	$13
17	**Proj**	**198**	**29**	**5**	**26**	**6**	**298**	**284**	**340**	**472**	**812**	**631**	**836**	**6**	**79**	**0.28**	**48**	**22**	**30**	**36**	**90**	**115**	**81**	**10%**	**109**	**22%**	**55%**				**5.39**	**5.3**	**53**	**153**	**$10**

Tomas,Yasmany

Age: 26 Bats: R Pos: RF LF | Ht: 6' 2" Wt: 230
Health A | LIMA Plan B | PT/Exp C | Rand Var +1 | Consist B | MM 4145

This is how you renovate a skill set: boosted FB% (albeit from sub-basement to ground floor) and power blossomed. Best of all, didn't compromise other features: LD% steady, ct% improved in-season, and it all came together in 2H. xBA loved the new look. But unless he blows the roof of FB%, this is a near-term ceiling

Yr	Tm	AB	R	HR	RBI	SB	BA	xBA	OBP	SLG	OPS	vL	vR	bb%	ct%	Eye	G	L	F	h%	HctX	PX	xPX	hr/f	Spd	SBO	SB%	#Wk	DOM	DIS	RC/G	RAR	BPV	BPX	R$
12	for	272	45	12	49	4	278		310	476	787			5	80	0.24				31		124			93	10%	62%				5.11	0.8	59	148	$10
13	for	277	44	9	59	1	269		335	465	800			9	82	0.56				30		127			114	6%	21%				5.19	6.0	85	213	$10
14	for	241	27	4	35	5	267		317	403	720			7	81	0.38				32		102			102	20%	45%				4.06	0.4	51	138	$6
15	ARI *	427	41	10	50	5	267	250	297	395	692	797	673	4	73	0.16	55	22	23	35	98	92	77	13%	95	7%	71%	25	24%	40%	4.07	-9.7	4	11	$10
16	ARI	530	72	31	83	2	272	279	313	508	820	1112	724	6	74	0.23	48	21	31	31	124	145	129	25%	64	5%	33%	27	48%	33%	5.38	10.8	46	131	$18
1st Half		266	36	13	31	2	259	267	308	462	770	1046	662	6	73	0.25	49	22	29	31	120	130	119	23%	58	7%	50%	14	50%	43%	4.76	0.5	28	80	$14
2nd Half		264	36	18	52	0	284	289	318	553	871	1203	782	5	76	0.20	46	21	34	31	128	159	139	27%	80	4%	0%	13	46%	23%	6.05	10.2	66	189	$22
17	**Proj**	**530**	**66**	**28**	**86**	**3**	**277**	**280**	**317**	**504**	**821**	**1041**	**746**	**5**	**76**	**0.24**	**48**	**20**	**31**	**32**	**116**	**136**	**109**	**22%**	**84**	**7%**	**44%**				**5.45**	**11.4**	**45**	**130**	**$22**

Tomlinson,Kelby

Age: 27 Bats: R Pos: 2B | Ht: 6' 2" Wt: 180
Health B | LIMA Plan D | PT/Exp C | Rand Var 0 | Consist C | MM 0531

0-6-.292 with 5 SB in 106 AB at SF. Give credit where it's due—has only one plus skill (Spd), and plays to it: plenty of contact, but almost never in the air. Takes walks; runs aggressively when he gets on. But can't drive the ball at all, and shaky SB% caps SB upside. One-trick pony, and the trick is only good, not elite.

Yr	Tm	AB	R	HR	RBI	SB	BA	xBA	OBP	SLG	OPS	vL	vR	bb%	ct%	Eye	G	L	F	h%	HctX	PX	xPX	hr/f	Spd	SBO	SB%	#Wk	DOM	DIS	RC/G	RAR	BPV	BPX	R$
12																																			
13	aa	96	9	0	3	2	166		256	211	467			11	69	0.39				24		49			104	14%	66%				1.65		-30	-75	-$4
14	aa	433	50	1	25	39	233		292	281	573			8	78	0.38				30		34			150	43%	74%				2.77		3	8	$15
15	SF *	567	74	4	55	22	286	277	333	373	706	913	682	7	81	0.37	56	28	17	35	63	58	28	9%	140	22%	60%	10	50%	40%	4.20	0.5	26	70	$22
16	SF *	291	34	0	21	14	258	269	325	302	627	728	640	9	83	0.59	51	29	20	31	91	32	29	0%	125	20%	76%	15	27%	47%	3.44	-12.3	15	43	$7
1st Half		76	9	0	3	5	289	264	379	329	708	825	533	12	83	0.77	56	25	19	35	95	32	27	0%	116	21%	83%	10	30%	50%	4.64	-0.4	17	49	$4
2nd Half		215	25	0	18	9	247	275	308	292	600	555	1500	8	83	0.52	40	36	24	30	81	33	36	0%	127	20%	72%	5	20%	40%	3.06	-11.3	15	43	$8
17	**Proj**	**192**	**23**	**1**	**13**	**10**	**255**	**270**	**323**	**320**	**643**	**634**	**655**	**9**	**80**	**0.48**	**50**	**30**	**20**	**31**	**77**	**43**	**31**	**3%**	**133**	**24%**	**72%**				**3.50**	**-7.5**	**8**	**23**	**$6**

Torreyes,Ronald

Age: 24 Bats: R Pos: 3B | Ht: 5' 9" Wt: 140
Health A | LIMA Plan D | PT/Exp D | Rand Var 0 | Consist B | MM 1541

Scrawny slap hitter does the right things to play up his wheels: lots of contact, lots of GBs. What's missing is the OBP to get him on base more often, along with the SBO/SB% to turn those opps into actual SBs. Still young enough for those to snap into place, but not worth chasing until we see some evidence of that growth.

Yr	Tm	AB	R	HR	RBI	SB	BA	xBA	OBP	SLG	OPS	vL	vR	bb%	ct%	Eye	G	L	F	h%	HctX	PX	xPX	hr/f	Spd	SBO	SB%	#Wk	DOM	DIS	RC/G	RAR	BPV	BPX	R$
12																																			
13	aa	375	41	2	30	4	244		287	332	619			6	91	0.70				26		57			125	6%	79%				3.23		62	155	$3
14	aaa	460	48	2	34	9	257		286	322	607			4	94	0.62				27		44			115	17%	47%				2.93		53	143	$8
15	LA *	424	51	3	31	4	230	242	268	305	573	0	1100	5	90	0.49	40	20	40	25	0	48	-16	0%	133	9%	48%	4	25%	50%	2.61	-20.1	49	132	$2
16	NYY	155	20	1	12	2	258	280	305	374	680	495	745	6	87	0.50	55	20	26	29	79	63	50	3%	175	8%	67%	25	28%	52%	3.86	-3.9	65	186	$1
1st Half		63	7	0	5	0	222	266	290	302	591	581	595	9	84	0.60	66	19	15	26	58	38	28	0%	174	0%	0%	13	15%	54%	2.87	-3.7	39	111	-$2
2nd Half		92	13	1	7	2	283	286	316	424	740	426	841	4	89	0.40	48	20	32	31	94	79	65	4%	158	14%	67%	12	42%	50%	4.61	-0.5	78	223	$3
17	**Proj**	**166**	**20**	**1**	**13**	**4**	**262**	**278**	**304**	**354**	**658**	**490**	**900**	**5**	**89**	**0.52**	**55**	**20**	**25**	**29**	**80**	**52**	**50**	**2%**	**157**	**13%**	**73%**				**3.67**	**-5.9**	**46**	**132**	**$4**

Travis,Devon

Age: 26 Bats: R Pos: 2B | Ht: 5' 9" Wt: 183
Health F | LIMA Plan B+ | PT/Exp D | Rand Var -4 | Consist B | MM 2335

11-50-.300 in 410 AB at TOR. Recovery from 2015 shoulder injury kept him out til late May. 2015 PX/xPX now looks flukish when compared to larger 2016 sample. Big 2H BA fueled by silly h%: xBA rightfully notes that you can't sustain that BA with average-ish HctX, LD%, and Spd. RandVar seals the case for regression.

Yr	Tm	AB	R	HR	RBI	SB	BA	xBA	OBP	SLG	OPS	vL	vR	bb%	ct%	Eye	G	L	F	h%	HctX	PX	xPX	hr/f	Spd	SBO	SB%	#Wk	DOM	DIS	RC/G	RAR	BPV	BPX	R$
12																																			
13																																			
14	aa	396	49	7	37	11	259		306	391	697			6	84	0.42				29		86			129	17%	67%				4.02		57	154	$11
15	TOR *	260	42	8	36	4	282	277	340	447	787	974	812	8	79	0.42	50	22	28	33	95	116	109	16%	89	7%	79%	12	58%	8%	5.41	8.4	52	141	$9
16	TOR *	432	56	11	53	4	297	261	329	448	776	617	838	4	79	0.22	46	19	34	35	94	98	81	10%	109	5%	80%	20	25%	25%	5.35	7.4	39	111	$15
1st Half		154	21	5	22	3	269	266	301	432	733	396	936	4	82	0.26	46	18	36	30	83	99	68	13%	100	9%	100%	7	29%	14%	4.65	-0.7	49	140	$9
2nd Half		278	35	6	31	1	313	256	344	457	800	800	800	4	78	0.21	47	20	33	39	99	97	87	8%	112	3%	50%	13	23%	31%	5.76	7.3	33	94	$18
17	**Proj**	**527**	**74**	**15**	**66**	**8**	**276**	**268**	**320**	**434**	**754**	**681**	**779**	**6**	**80**	**0.31**	**47**	**20**	**33**	**32**	**93**	**100**	**91**	**11%**	**109**	**8%**	**76%**				**4.86**	**0.9**	**40**	**115**	**$20**

Trout,Mike

Age: 25 Bats: R Pos: CF | Ht: 6' 1" Wt: 235
Health A | LIMA Plan C | PT/Exp A | Rand Var -3 | Consist B | MM 4445

We've seen multiple versions of this guy over the years, but 2016 gives clarity on what the still-approaching-prime-years version will look like: PX has settled where xPX has been beckoning. Strong HctX and h% ensure a lofty BA. SBs determined by SBO; how much he wants to run. R$ shows he has the highest floor in the game.

Yr	Tm	AB	R	HR	RBI	SB	BA	xBA	OBP	SLG	OPS	vL	vR	bb%	ct%	Eye	G	L	F	h%	HctX	PX	xPX	hr/f	Spd	SBO	SB%	#Wk	DOM	DIS	RC/G	RAR	BPV	BPX	R$
12	LAA *	636	144	31	92	53	328	276	398	555	953	862	999	10	75	0.47	44	23	33	40	108	144	113	22%	144	28%	90%	24	63%	13%	8.75	66.1	82	205	$54
13	LAA	589	109	27	97	33	323	287	432	557	988	954	1000	16	77	0.81	41	23	36	38	122	159	133	16%	144	18%	83%	27	74%	11%	9.11	77.6	112	280	$47
14	LAA	602	115	36	111	16	287	272	377	561	939	910	948	12	69	0.45	34	19	47	36	115	209	151	18%	137	10%	89%	27	67%	11%	7.61	62.8	112	303	$38
15	LAA	575	104	41	90	11	299	289	402	590	991	1032	978	14	73	0.58	37	24	38	35	129	190	153	25%	114	10%	61%	27	70%	11%	8.27	60.4	106	286	$35
16	LAA	549	123	29	100	30	315	276	441	550	991	971	996	17	75	0.85	41	22	37	38	127	142	142	19%	110	17%	81%	27	59%	19%	8.99	69.4	84	240	$42
1st Half		302	59	17	54	13	325	293	426	573	999	862	1041	15	79	0.83	43	21	36	37	129	145	139	20%	85	13%	93%	14	71%	7%	9.47	39.9	89	254	$43
2nd Half		247	64	12	46	17	304	255	457	522	979	1104	942	20	70	0.86	39	23	38	39	124	138	146	18%	136	21%	74%	13	46%	31%	8.44	27.4	76	217	$40
17	**Proj**	**561**	**119**	**32**	**98**	**20**	**306**	**273**	**421**	**558**	**978**	**986**	**976**	**16**	**73**	**0.68**	**39**	**22**	**39**	**37**	**124**	**154**	**145**	**20%**	**126**	**12%**	**80%**				**8.53**	**62.1**	**88**	**251**	**$40**

RAY MURPHY

Trumbo,Mark

Age: 31	Bats: R	Pos: RF DH	Health B	LIMA Plan B+
Ht: 6' 4"	Wt: 235		PT/Exp B	Rand Var 0
			Consist B	MM 4125

Cobbled together a career year by maxing out his AB, FB%, and hr/f at same time. Beyond those metrics, nothing really out of line with what we've seen before. Inevitable hr/f pullback tells us to set expectations at mid-30s HR rather than mid-40s. And he's a free agent, so be sure to account for potential new park.

Yr	Tm	AB	R	HR	RBI	SB	BA	xBA	OBP	SLG	OPS	vL	vR	bb%	ct%	Eye	G	L	F	h%	HctX	PX	xPX	hr/f	Spd	SBO	SB%	#Wk	DOM	DIS	RC/G	RAR	BPV	BPX	R$
12	LAA	544	66	32	95	4	268	248	317	491	808	808	808	6	72	0.24	45	16	39	32	114	144	132	21%	88	7%	44%	27	52%	37%	5.20	5.3	44	110	$21
13	LAA	620	85	34	100	5	234	256	294	453	747	923	685	8	70	0.29	46	17	37	28	105	158	132	21%	79	5%	71%	27	52%	26%	4.43	2.8	49	123	$19
14	ARI	328	37	14	61	2	235	241	293	415	707	796	679	8	73	0.31	45	15	40	28	111	133	135	14%	81	7%	40%	18	39%	44%	3.94	0.4	40	108	$8
15	2 TM	508	62	22	64	0	262	244	310	449	759	856	709	7	74	0.27	42	18	40	31	107	124	122	14%	110	0%	0%	27	52%	30%	4.82	0.7	43	116	$13
16	BAL	613	94	47	108	2	256	268	316	533	850	608	932	8	72	0.30	40	17	43	28	115	166	147	25%	76	2%	100%	27	52%	30%	5.75	18.6	62	177	$22
1st Half		324	47	24	62	1	281	268	329	556	884	796	914	6	72	0.23	41	18	42	32	109	167	138	25%	85	1%	100%	14	50%	21%	6.41	15.7	60	171	$26
2nd Half		289	47	23	46	1	228	268	303	509	812	394	952	9	73	0.38	38	17	45	23	122	165	157	24%	70	2%	100%	13	54%	38%	5.08	3.3	66	189	$18
17	**Proj**	**557**	**77**	**34**	**90**	**2**	**250**	**255**	**307**	**483**	**791**	**708**	**822**	**7**	**73**	**0.30**	**41**	**17**	**42**	**28**	**113**	**141**	**139**	**20%**	**87**	**2%**	**63%**				**5.01**	**5.2**	**39**	**110**	**$18**

Tucker,Preston

Age: 26	Bats: L	Pos: DH	Health B	LIMA Plan D
Ht: 6' 0"	Wt: 215		PT/Exp C	Rand Var +1
			Consist B	MM 3011

4-8-.164 in 134 AB at HOU. Supposed bat-first OF hasn't shown much over two years in HOU (.219/.274/.403 over 434 MLB AB). Virtually every column in this box shows that his interesting minors profile has been utterly absent in The Show. Likely to get a few more looks, but we're in "show me first" mode now.

Yr	Tm	AB	R	HR	RBI	SB	BA	xBA	OBP	SLG	OPS	vL	vR	bb%	ct%	Eye	G	L	F	h%	HctX	PX	xPX	hr/f	Spd	SBO	SB%	#Wk	DOM	DIS	RC/G	RAR	BPV	BPX	R$
12																																			
13	aa	237	28	8	23	0	229		293	391	683			8	78	0.40				26		112			99	2%	0%				3.70		49	123	$1
14	a/a	536	57	18	68	4	235		290	392	682			7	73	0.29				29		122			76	6%	51%				3.71		31	84	$11
15	HOU *	429	48	21	57	1	242	258	289	441	730	466	807	6	77	0.29	47	18	36	27	106	129	104	16%	69	3%	25%	22	41%	32%	4.20	-15.9	46	124	$9
16	HOU *	364	37	10	31	1	207	224	249	364	613	421	570	5	69	0.18	45	16	39	27	96	108	98	11%	90	3%	37%	11	27%	45%	2.88	-29.7	4	11	-$1
1st Half		237	22	8	20	1	219	243	259	397	656	0	624	5	71	0.19	49	17	34	27	122	117	120	15%	95	5%	37%	7	14%	43%	3.29	-16.2	18	51	$1
2nd Half		127	14	2	10	0	182	188	224	294	518	727	461	5	67	0.16	37	14	49	26	54	86	61	6%	86	0%	0%	4	50%	50%	2.05	-14.1	-26	-74	-$5
17	**Proj**	**165**	**18**	**6**	**17**	**0**	**217**	**233**	**276**	**384**	**660**	**562**	**682**	**6**	**72**	**0.23**	**44**	**16**	**40**	**26**	**92**	**110**	**93**	**12%**	**83**	**3%**	**44%**				**3.26**	**-11.4**	**9**	**26**	**$2**

Tulowitzki,Troy

Age: 32	Bats: R	Pos: SS	Health D	LIMA Plan B
Ht: 6' 3"	Wt: 205		PT/Exp B	Rand Var +3
			Consist F	MM 3235

1st-half quad injury cost him three weeks; also played through late-season thumb injury. Plate skills recovered nicely from rough 1H, while season-long symmetry of BA/xBA and PX/xPX establish a nice baseline for his post-Coors profile. That profile won't disappoint, as long as you price it for fewer than 500 AB.

Yr	Tm	AB	R	HR	RBI	SB	BA	xBA	OBP	SLG	OPS	vL	vR	bb%	ct%	Eye	G	L	F	h%	HctX	PX	xPX	hr/f	Spd	SBO	SB%	#Wk	DOM	DIS	RC/G	RAR	BPV	BPX	R$
12	COL *	208	35	10	31	2	286	288	348	501	849	671	918	9	88	0.76	46	17	37	29	103	118	98	13%	125	7%	50%	9	67%	0%	6.05	11.5	101	253	$8
13	COL	446	72	25	82	1	312	288	391	540	931	906	938	11	81	0.67	42	21	38	34	124	148	147	18%	86	1%	100%	24	75%	17%	7.82	52.8	93	233	$25
14	COL	315	71	21	52	1	340	310	432	603	1035	1348	930	14	82	0.88	38	23	39	36	150	170	164	21%	102	2%	50%	16	75%	13%	9.94	55.4	124	335	$23
15	2 TM	486	77	17	70	1	280	254	337	440	777	940	735	7	77	0.33	41	22	37	34	126	110	126	12%	84	1%	100%	25	44%	36%	5.19	10.9	36	97	$17
16	TOR	492	54	24	79	1	254	257	318	443	761	767	759	8	79	0.43	41	19	40	28	110	108	113	15%	75	1%	100%	25	52%	24%	4.77	6.6	45	129	$12
1st Half		220	25	14	37	1	232	238	309	459	768	671	804	9	75	0.42	42	12	46	25	103	132	144	18%	88	2%	100%	12	33%	42%	4.67	1.3	53	151	$9
2nd Half		272	29	10	42	0	272	273	325	430	756	882	727	7	83	0.43	39	25	36	30	116	90	90	12%	69	0%	0%	13	69%	8%	4.85	3.0	41	117	$14
17	**Proj**	**479**	**69**	**22**	**75**	**1**	**279**	**266**	**346**	**470**	**816**	**908**	**789**	**9**	**80**	**0.47**	**41**	**21**	**39**	**31**	**121**	**110**	**124**	**15%**	**85**	**1%**	**72%**				**5.68**	**16.5**	**41**	**117**	**$20**

Turner,Justin

Age: 32	Bats: R	Pos: 3B	Health B	LIMA Plan B+
Ht: 6' 0"	Wt: 200		PT/Exp C	Rand Var +2
			Consist B	MM 3255

Answered the last question about his relatively late-career breakout by sustaining it over a full season. Reverse platoon split is an oddity; may actually be one of the only areas of possible improvement here. Rest of his profile is near-flawless. Good contact, lots of liners, now with some FB tilt. Pay for a repeat.

Yr	Tm	AB	R	HR	RBI	SB	BA	xBA	OBP	SLG	OPS	vL	vR	bb%	ct%	Eye	G	L	F	h%	HctX	PX	xPX	hr/f	Spd	SBO	SB%	#Wk	DOM	DIS	RC/G	RAR	BPV	BPX	R$
12	NYM	171	20	2	19	1	269	283	319	392	711	650	768	5	86	0.38	47	24	29	30	92	86	68	5%	94	5%	50%	25	40%	20%	4.10	-2.4	53	133	$2
13	NYM	200	12	2	16	0	280	257	319	385	704	668	735	5	83	0.32	46	22	32	33	120	80	132	4%	94	2%	0%	22	45%	32%	4.24	1.4	37	93	$1
14	LA	288	46	7	43	6	340	283	404	493	897	911	890	9	80	0.48	49	23	28	41	115	117	105	11%	100	7%	86%	26	50%	31%	7.67	29.6	63	170	$17
15	LA	385	55	16	60	5	294	291	370	491	861	751	904	9	82	0.51	36	28	36	33	113	126	118	14%	76	7%	71%	25	40%	28%	6.23	16.7	69	186	$17
16	LA	556	79	27	90	4	275	283	339	493	832	640	919	8	81	0.45	36	24	40	30	123	125	123	15%	93	4%	80%	27	59%	22%	5.77	12.6	69	197	$20
1st Half		275	35	11	40	1	262	275	340	444	783	688	810	9	83	0.57	34	24	41	28	130	103	126	11%	85	3%	50%	14	50%	29%	4.97	0.6	59	169	$14
2nd Half		281	44	16	50	3	288	291	339	541	880	613	1058	7	79	0.35	38	23	39	32	117	148	119	18%	99	5%	100%	13	69%	15%	6.62	13.5	79	226	$25
17	**Proj**	**580**	**82**	**23**	**89**	**3**	**282**	**283**	**347**	**474**	**822**	**688**	**888**	**8**	**81**	**0.45**	**39**	**25**	**36**	**32**	**117**	**115**	**116**	**13%**	**91**	**3%**	**64%**				**5.67**	**12.8**	**55**	**157**	**$24**

Turner,Trea

Age: 24	Bats: R	Pos: CF 2B	Health A	LIMA Plan D+
Ht: 6' 1"	Wt: 185		PT/Exp D	Rand Var -3
			Consist D	MM 3545

13-40-.342 with 33 SB in 307 AB at WAS. Immediate impact on the bases was no surprise, but MLEs did not foretell the pop in his bat. And yet, HctX and xPX fully back the 2H power surge. Ct% uptick another nice surprise, and mutes BA downside even as h% regression pushes BA back toward xBA. He's legit.

Yr	Tm	AB	R	HR	RBI	SB	BA	xBA	OBP	SLG	OPS	vL	vR	bb%	ct%	Eye	G	L	F	h%	HctX	PX	xPX	hr/f	Spd	SBO	SB%	#Wk	DOM	DIS	RC/G	RAR	BPV	BPX	R$
12																																			
13																																			
14																																			
15	WAS *	494	64	7	48	27	295	248	345	405	750	819	570	7	77	0.33	50	21	29	37	36	79	11	13%	115	24%	76%	8	13%	50%	5.06	18.1	21	57	$25
16	WAS *	638	109	18	71	56	313	276	362	494	856	751	985	7	79	0.36	43	25	32	37	111	107	122	17%	193	35%	87%	14	64%	21%	6.91	40.1	74	211	$48
1st Half		315	51	4	30	21	291	345	364	425	789	2500	2000	10	76	0.48	33	67	0	37	103	90	59	0%	150	24%	91%	1	100%	0%	5.89	12.6	44	126	$36
2nd Half		323	59	14	41	35	333	294	359	561	920	684	981	4	81	0.21	43	25	32	38	115	123	123	17%	201	49%	85%	13	62%	23%	7.89	29.7	93	266	$59
17	**Proj**	**555**	**90**	**19**	**56**	**42**	**299**	**276**	**346**	**490**	**836**	**606**	**900**	**7**	**78**	**0.33**	**43**	**25**	**32**	**35**	**104**	**112**	**111**	**14%**	**187**	**34%**	**83%**				**6.29**	**27.7**	**66**	**189**	**$39**

Upton,Justin

Age: 29	Bats: R	Pos: LF	Health A	LIMA Plan B
Ht: 6' 3"	Wt: 205		PT/Exp A	Rand Var 0
			Consist B	MM 4325

Spent the entire season working off a dreadful April/May (3-11-.217), and it took a big September (13-28-.292) to finish the job. 2nd half skills quell any lingering concerns about that slow start, restoring stability to overall profile. Holding 2015's FB% gains opens the door to... UP: 40 HR (after all, 40 is the new 30).

Yr	Tm	AB	R	HR	RBI	SB	BA	xBA	OBP	SLG	OPS	vL	vR	bb%	ct%	Eye	G	L	F	h%	HctX	PX	xPX	hr/f	Spd	SBO	SB%	#Wk	DOM	DIS	RC/G	RAR	BPV	BPX	R$
12	ARI	554	107	17	67	18	280	250	355	430	785	830	766	10	78	0.52	44	21	36	33	105	96	107	11%	126	15%	69%	27	48%	22%	5.29	11.4	50	125	$24
13	ATL	558	94	27	70	8	263	254	354	464	818	994	762	12	71	0.47	41	22	38	32	89	145	110	18%	108	5%	89%	27	56%	33%	5.69	27.7	59	148	$22
14	ATL	566	77	29	102	8	270	262	342	491	833	981	794	10	70	0.35	40	20	40	34	115	173	159	18%	94	8%	67%	26	62%	19%	5.77	33.9	67	181	$26
15	SD	542	85	26	81	19	251	240	336	454	790	558	848	11	71	0.43	39	17	44	31	108	140	131	15%	126	16%	79%	26	50%	38%	5.19	12.7	57	154	$23
16	DET	570	81	31	87	9	246	243	310	465	775	754	783	8	69	0.28	39	18	43	30	106	144	126	18%	96	10%	69%	27	44%	48%	4.76	8.1	37	106	$17
1st Half		303	37	8	36	5	231	217	287	373	660	743	624	7	66	0.22	37	22	41	32	91	107	101	10%	100	9%	83%	14	29%	57%	3.56	-8.2	-4	-11	$11
2nd Half		267	44	23	51	4	262	274	336	569	905	767	956	9	72	0.36	41	15	45	28	123	183	151	27%	94	11%	57%	13	62%	38%	6.29	14.4	81	231	$25
17	**Proj**	**571**	**86**	**30**	**90**	**10**	**255**	**246**	**328**	**473**	**801**	**756**	**816**	**9**	**70**	**0.35**	**39**	**18**	**42**	**31**	**109**	**139**	**133**	**18%**	**106**	**10%**	**68%**				**5.20**	**12.5**	**41**	**117**	**$24**

Upton,Melvin

Age: 32	Bats: R	Pos: LF CF	Health C	LIMA Plan C+
Ht: 6' 3"	Wt: 180		PT/Exp C	Rand Var -2
			Consist B	MM 3505

Turned late-2015 flashes of life into a full-blown resurrection, at least for 1st half. Batted .256 w/SD, then .196 after July 25 trade to TOR. Seems to be only one metric that matters here: ct%. If he's at or near 70%, that unlocks the power and speed. Under 65% and it's back into the abyss where he lived the previous 3 years.

Yr	Tm	AB	R	HR	RBI	SB	BA	xBA	OBP	SLG	OPS	vL	vR	bb%	ct%	Eye	G	L	F	h%	HctX	PX	xPX	hr/f	Spd	SBO	SB%	#Wk	DOM	DIS	RC/G	RAR	BPV	BPX	R$
12	TAM	573	79	28	78	31	246	246	298	454	752	792	737	7	71	0.27	40	19	41	30	87	145	105	17%	125	29%	84%	25	48%	28%	4.70	2.2	52	130	$24
13	ATL	391	30	9	26	12	184	190	268	289	557	449	598	10	61	0.29	45	19	36	27	80	93	112	10%	97	18%	71%	25	12%	72%	2.40	-19.9	-28	-70	$0
14	ATL	519	67	12	35	20	208	209	287	333	620	566	633	10	67	0.33	43	18	39	29	95	102	129	9%	163	21%	74%	26	27%	31%	3.08	-10.0	19	51	$8
15	SD *	255	29	6	21	11	247	236	310	397	707	792	736	8	69	0.30	41	24	34	34	101	111	112	10%	135	23%	79%	18	39%	44%	4.20	-3.9	25	68	$6
16	2 TM	492	64	20	61	27	238	231	291	402	693	874	634	7	68	0.24	49	18	34	31	84	105	103	17%	130	30%	77%	27	30%	56%	3.91	-5.4	13	37	$18
1st Half		297	40	13	39	19	263	242	313	438	750	818	726	7	71	0.25	46	20	34	33	98	106	119	18%	132	32%	79%	14	36%	36%	4.73	2.4	25	71	$27
2nd Half		195	24	7	22	8	200	213	257	349	606	975	501	8	64	0.23	53	14	33	27	61	103	78	17%	120	27%	73%	13	23%	77%	2.86	-9.9	-8	-23	$5
17	**Proj**	**450**	**55**	**15**	**45**	**21**	**227**	**225**	**290**	**380**	**670**	**789**	**626**	**8**	**67**	**0.28**	**46**	**19**	**35**	**30**	**86**	**103**	**105**	**14%**	**137**	**25%**	**76%**				**3.65**	**-11.2**	**9**	**26**	**$14**

RAY MURPHY

Utley,Chase

Age: 38 Bats: L Pos: 2B	Health: C	LIMA Plan: D+
Ht: 6' 1" Wt: 200	PT/Exp: B	Rand Var: 0
	Consist: C	MM: 2133

Mustered a late-30s rebound season thanks to better treatment from h% and hr/f, but a wider-lens look at this profile shows acceleration of overall decline: xPX reached league average, ct% took another hit, 2nd half Eye shows how he's lost all control of the strike zone. Formerly robust profile now looking threadbare.

Yr	Tm	AB	R	HR	RBI	SB	BA	xBA	OBP	SLG	OPS	vL	vR	bb%	ct%	Eye	G	L	F	h%	HctX	PX	xPX	hr/f	Spd	SBO	SB%	#Wk	DOM	DIS	RC/G	RAR	BPV	BPX	R$
12	PHI	301	48	11	45	11	256	278	365	429	793	679	869	13	86	1.00	42	21	36	27	129	102	110	12%	89	13%	92%	15	60%	13%	5.29	8.3	78	195	$11
13	PHI	476	73	18	69	8	284	269	348	475	823	754	855	9	83	0.57	38	20	43	31	121	119	126	11%	113	8%	73%	24	67%	21%	5.80	28.9	82	205	$21
14	PHI	589	74	11	78	10	270	276	339	407	746	682	775	8	86	0.62	39	25	36	30	113	95	106	6%	99	7%	91%	27	67%	22%	4.77	23.3	66	178	$19
15	2 NL	373	37	8	39	4	212	257	286	343	629	557	655	8	83	0.50	44	20	36	24	112	86	106	7%	84	5%	100%	22	45%	45%	3.10	-12.3	43	116	$1
16	LA	512	79	14	52	2	252	255	319	396	716	470	768	7	78	0.35	44	22	34	30	118	90	100	11%	94	3%	50%	27	26%	33%	4.09	-11.7	27	77	$10
1st Half		266	40	5	25	1	252	252	338	368	706	523	741	9	79	0.48	44	24	32	30	128	72	95	7%	104	4%	33%	14	21%	36%	3.93	-6.9	25	71	$8
2nd Half		246	39	9	27	1	252	259	298	427	725	419	795	5	76	0.22	44	21	35	30	108	110	107	14%	82	2%	100%	13	31%	31%	4.24	-4.1	29	83	$11
17	Proj	**324**	**44**	**8**	**36**	**1**	**246**	**258**	**315**	**385**	**700**	**562**	**743**	**8**	**81**	**0.42**	**43**	**22**	**35**	**28**	**115**	**85**	**105**	**8%**	**90**	**2%**	**62%**				**3.94**	**-8.2**	**31**	**89**	**$5**

Valbuena,Luis

Age: 31 Bats: L Pos: 3B	Health: C	LIMA Plan: C+
Ht: 5' 10" Wt: 215	PT/Exp: B	Rand Var: -3
	Consist: B	MM: 3123

July hamstring injury ended his season, eventually required surgery. Pre-injury, BA was playing back to xBA's level while power remained his best asset. Still, longer-term erosion of ct%, HctX, xPX, FB% all suggest that power is getting tougher and tougher to sustain. Return to 20 HR plausible, but don't pay for it.

Yr	Tm	AB	R	HR	RBI	SB	BA	xBA	OBP	SLG	OPS	vL	vR	bb%	ct%	Eye	G	L	F	h%	HctX	PX	xPX	hr/f	Spd	SBO	SB%	#Wk	DOM	DIS	RC/G	RAR	BPV	BPX	R$
12	CHC *	476	52	9	49	1	228	242	309	361	670	624	657	10	75	0.47	43	21	35	28	87	102	82	5%	62	3%	17%	17	29%	29%	3.59	-14.7	25	63	$3
13	CHC	331	34	12	37	1	218	239	331	378	708	647	715	14	81	0.84	40	16	45	23	109	104	131	10%	68	5%	20%	22	59%	27%	3.84	-1.1	57	143	$2
14	CHC	478	68	16	51	1	249	255	341	435	776	610	811	12	76	0.58	31	20	48	30	120	140	155	9%	82	2%	33%	27	52%	22%	4.94	17.9	68	184	$11
15	HOU	434	62	25	56	1	224	256	310	438	748	581	808	10	76	0.47	34	21	45	24	109	136	147	17%	64	1%	100%	27	41%	33%	4.38	-2.4	53	143	$8
16	HOU	292	38	13	40	1	260	250	357	459	816	741	841	13	72	0.54	37	21	42	32	105	129	134	15%	57	2%	50%	17	47%	29%	5.60	6.8	38	109	$7
1st Half		228	29	9	28	0	254	241	355	443	798	782	802	13	69	0.50	37	21	43	33	106	134	134	14%	53	1%	0%	14	43%	29%	5.27	2.5	29	83	$8
2nd Half		64	9	4	12	1	281	277	365	516	880	663	1030	12	83	0.82	36	23	42	29	100	113	136	18%	87	5%	100%	3	67%	33%	6.88	3.6	74	211	$3
17	Proj	**370**	**50**	**18**	**52**	**2**	**251**	**257**	**340**	**451**	**791**	**653**	**842**	**12**	**77**	**0.58**	**36**	**21**	**43**	**28**	**106**	**117**	**138**	**14%**	**70**	**3%**	**71%**				**5.19**	**3.3**	**47**	**135**	**$12**

Valencia,Danny

Age: 32 Bats: R Pos: 3B RF	Health: B	LIMA Plan: B
Ht: 6' 2" Wt: 210	PT/Exp: C	Rand Var: -4
	Consist: D	MM: 3135

1st half was a more-than-worthy followup to 2015, then everything cratered in 2nd half. Possible explanations abound: mid-season position change? Possible injury? Fallout from August clubhouse altercation? 2H 2015 + 1H 2016 was an interesting profile; if that version returns... UP: 25 HR. But odds are low for 32-year-old.

Yr	Tm	AB	R	HR	RBI	SB	BA	xBA	OBP	SLG	OPS	vL	vR	bb%	ct%	Eye	G	L	F	h%	HctX	PX	xPX	hr/f	Spd	SBO	SB%	#Wk	DOM	DIS	RC/G	RAR	BPV	BPX	R$
12	2 AL *	471	39	9	55	1	210	228	237	326	563	592	448	3	79	0.16	43	18	39	25	118	82	114	6%	78	8%	11%	13	23%	62%	2.34	-32.7	13	33	$0
13	BAL *	423	48	19	59	1	257	278	291	470	761	1031	672	5	78	0.22	38	22	40	29	119	148	142	15%	94	5%	18%	17	47%	35%	4.53	7.2	70	175	$11
14	2 AL	264	20	4	30	1	258	251	296	371	667	835	540	5	77	0.23	45	24	31	32	111	93	105	6%	87	3%	50%	22	36%	50%	3.72	0.3	19	51	$3
15	2 AL	345	59	18	66	2	290	285	345	519	864	834	881	8	77	0.36	52	17	30	33	117	151	110	22%	85	5%	50%	27	63%	26%	6.31	16.9	71	192	$16
16	OAK	471	72	17	51	1	287	257	346	446	792	924	742	8	76	0.36	45	23	32	35	97	99	94	15%	109	1%	50%	25	28%	36%	5.45	8.5	32	91	$15
1st Half		234	36	11	30	0	308	272	358	500	858	1076	783	7	78	0.33	45	23	32	36	119	111	119	19%	115	0%	0%	13	31%	31%	6.53	10.4	50	143	$18
2nd Half		237	36	6	21	1	266	242	335	392	727	792	700	9	73	0.38	45	23	32	34	75	86	67	11%	100	3%	50%	12	25%	42%	4.49	-2.7	13	37	$12
17	Proj	**455**	**64**	**16**	**59**	**2**	**276**	**261**	**329**	**444**	**772**	**862**	**725**	**7**	**76**	**0.32**	**46**	**22**	**32**	**33**	**104**	**106**	**100**	**15%**	**96**	**3%**	**45%**				**5.05**	**2.1**	**22**	**64**	**$16**

Van Slyke,Scott

Age: 30 Bats: R Pos: LF	Health: F	LIMA Plan: D
Ht: 6' 5" Wt: 195	PT/Exp: F	Rand Var: +5
	Consist: F	MM: 2211

1-7-.225 in 102 AB at LA. Injuries (back in 1st half, wrist in 2nd) once again kept us from finding out if his plus-profile power could scale to a larger role. Now, with his last power display sliding deeper into the rear-view mirror, and further opportunities perhaps not available as he enters his 30s, we may never know.

Yr	Tm	AB	R	HR	RBI	SB	BA	xBA	OBP	SLG	OPS	vL	vR	bb%	ct%	Eye	G	L	F	h%	HctX	PX	xPX	hr/f	Spd	SBO	SB%	#Wk	DOM	DIS	RC/G	RAR	BPV	BPX	R$
12	LA *	412	45	13	47	4	234	249	285	396	681	538	483	7	77	0.31	44	18	38	27	93	115	85	13%	89	9%	51%	7	43%	14%	3.65	-13.4	42	105	$6
13	LA *	333	49	15	50	6	257	233	356	460	816	764	850	13	66	0.45	36	17	47	35	93	166	147	16%	100	10%	64%	18	44%	44%	5.52	14.3	54	135	$11
14	LA	212	32	11	29	4	297	252	386	524	910	1045	767	12	67	0.39	35	20	45	40	109	185	176	17%	120	9%	67%	28	46%	46%	7.09	19.5	75	203	$10
15	LA	222	19	6	30	3	239	228	317	383	700	784	633	9	72	0.37	39	19	42	31	107	110	130	9%	93	7%	75%	23	48%	39%	3.98	-4.8	25	68	$3
16	LA *	131	14	2	11	2	210	235	247	302	549	739	529	5	77	0.21	39	24	37	26	99	65	102	3%	97	15%	46%	12	33%	67%	2.27	-9.6	0	0	-$1
1st Half		76	9	2	10	1	179	199	203	310	513	976	407	3	74	0.12	20	17	63	22	112	93	182	5%	97	8%	100%	7	43%	57%	1.98	-6.0	9	26	-$1
2nd Half		55	5	0	1	1	255	264	339	291	630	594	655	7	80	0.36	55	30	16	32	89	30	38	0%	106	19%	33%	5	20%	80%	2.66	-3.0	-9	-26	-$1
17	Proj	**161**	**17**	**4**	**16**	**3**	**242**	**234**	**319**	**382**	**701**	**817**	**617**	**8**	**74**	**0.33**	**38**	**21**	**41**	**30**	**102**	**95**	**118**	**9%**	**101**	**12%**	**52%**				**3.71**	**-3.6**	**7**	**21**	**$4**

Vargas,Kennys

Age: 26 Bats: B Pos: 1B	Health: A	LIMA Plan: D+
Ht: 6' 5" Wt: 275	PT/Exp: C	Rand Var: +2
	Consist: A	MM: 4013

10-20-.230 in 152 AB at MIN. Third straight season with a couple-hundred AB in the DH/1B mix; this was his best showing. Newly-discovered FB tilt helped unlock his power; xPX certainly approved. But combo of ct% problems and struggles vR (career .693 OPS, 66% ct% in MLB) likely pin him to a bad-side platoon role.

Yr	Tm	AB	R	HR	RBI	SB	BA	xBA	OBP	SLG	OPS	vL	vR	bb%	ct%	Eye	G	L	F	h%	HctX	PX	xPX	hr/f	Spd	SBO	SB%	#Wk	DOM	DIS	RC/G	RAR	BPV	BPX	R$
12																																			
13																																			
14	MIN *	571	65	22	87	0	256	248	311	418	729	602	899	7	76	0.33	47	19	34	30	101	117	109	17%	61	2%	0%	10	40%	50%	4.38	5.5	32	86	$16
15	MIN *	419	49	15	53	0	242	240	320	384	704	869	514	10	68	0.36	51	26	23	32	83	99	56	18%	59	0%	0%	16	13%	69%	4.13	-16.3	-6	-16	$7
16	MIN *	482	61	22	69	1	213	221	322	407	729	1262	654	14	68	0.50	38	15	48	26	114	133	152	22%	57	1%	100%	12	50%	33%	4.26	-18.4	24	69	$5
1st Half		285	32	11	44	1	206	236	311	373	683			13	71	0.52				25		108			64	1%	100%	1	100%	0%	3.74		16	46	$5
2nd Half		197	30	11	24	0	222	229	338	456	795	1262	654	15	63	0.48	38	15	48	29	107	175	152	22%	62	0%	0%	11	45%	36%	5.06	-2.6	43	123	$5
17	Proj	**309**	**39**	**14**	**42**	**0**	**231**	**237**	**322**	**422**	**745**	**833**	**696**	**12**	**68**	**0.42**	**45**	**19**	**36**	**29**	**99**	**128**	**111**	**19%**	**61**	**0%**	**57%**				**4.50**	**-5.6**	**14**	**39**	**$7**

Vazquez,Christian

Age: 26 Bats: R Pos: CA	Health: F	LIMA Plan: D+
Ht: 5' 9" Wt: 200	PT/Exp: F	Rand Var: +2
	Consist: A	MM: 1133

1-12-.227 in 172 AB at BOS. Missed 2015 due to TJ surgery, came back with his hitting "skills" fully intact. For most other hitters, that would be good news, but not here. Elite defense will buy time for the bat to develop, but there isn't even a foundational skill present: ct% shaky, power absent, typical CA speed. Stay clear.

Yr	Tm	AB	R	HR	RBI	SB	BA	xBA	OBP	SLG	OPS	vL	vR	bb%	ct%	Eye	G	L	F	h%	HctX	PX	xPX	hr/f	Spd	SBO	SB%	#Wk	DOM	DIS	RC/G	RAR	BPV	BPX	R$
12	aa	73	9	0	4	0	199		266	257	523			8	87	0.70				23		48			97	0%	0%				2.18		34	85	-$3
13	a/a	345	37	4	37	5	262		332	355	687			10	86	0.76				30		67			89	11%	49%				3.90		46	115	$7
14	BOS *	419	42	3	36	0	249	230	308	335	643	539	638	8	78	0.39	57	17	26	31	82	77	58	3%	71	1%	0%	12	25%	42%	3.46	1.7	14	38	$4
15																																			
16	BOS *	324	38	3	27	2	240	270	292	328	620	804	527	7	77	0.32	60	25	15	30	87	65	53	5%	84	2%	100%	16	13%	56%	3.24	-6.0	1	3	$2
1st Half		177	21	1	14	1	241	268	305	320	625	771	539	8	78	0.42	60	25	15	30	90	57	55	5%	92	2%	100%	12	17%	58%	3.31	-4.4	4	11	$2
2nd Half		147	17	2	13	1	239	252	275	338	612	1000	0	5	76	0.21	67	17	17	30	52	74	17	0%	80	3%	100%	4	0%	50%	3.14	-4.4	0	0	$2
17	Proj	**325**	**36**	**2**	**29**	**2**	**246**	**257**	**303**	**328**	**631**	**685**	**617**	**7**	**79**	**0.37**	**59**	**22**	**20**	**31**	**87**	**61**	**56**	**4%**	**75**	**3%**	**61%**				**3.32**	**-7.9**	**-3**	**-7**	**$4**

Villar,Jonathan

Age: 26 Bats: B Pos: SS 3B	Health: A	LIMA Plan: D+
Ht: 6' 1" Wt: 205	PT/Exp: B	Rand Var: -5
	Consist: D	MM: 2525

Dusted last year's "UP: 40 SB" by early August, on his way to an epic season. Sustainable? Just-average xPX, outlier hr/f and lofty GB% all say power was a mirage. Improved bb%, HctX should prop OBP, and OBP means chances to run. SBO says he'll keep taking those chances even amid some likely h% slippage.

Yr	Tm	AB	R	HR	RBI	SB	BA	xBA	OBP	SLG	OPS	vL	vR	bb%	ct%	Eye	G	L	F	h%	HctX	PX	xPX	hr/f	Spd	SBO	SB%	#Wk	DOM	DIS	RC/G	RAR	BPV	BPX	R$
12	aa	326	41	9	38	30	230		289	339	628			8	70	0.28				30		73			108	45%	77%				3.30		-11	-28	$13
13	HOU *	549	63	8	40	42	246	249	308	361	669	673	627	8	68	0.28	66	20	14	35	82	91	54	6%	138	40%	73%	11	18%	64%	3.70	3.4	5	13	$22
14	HOU *	453	55	9	46	34	213	218	279	325	604	644	608	8	67	0.27	51	19	30	30	84	91	108	13%	101	41%	76%	19	21%	47%	2.96	-4.7	-10	-27	$14
15	HOU *	396	58	6	33	31	242	240	293	356	649	761	742	7	70	0.24	57	20	23	33	75	85	44	10%	140	45%	71%	15	33%	40%	3.41	-4.3	5	14	$16
16	MIL	589	92	19	63	62	285	264	369	457	826	930	786	12	70	0.45	56	20	24	38	101	120	101	20%	111	43%	78%	27	44%	48%	6.04	24.4	37	106	$43
1st Half		294	40	6	30	26	296	252	382	422	804	879	773	13	69	0.46	59	22	19	41	86	94	82	16%	104	33%	74%	14	36%	57%	5.83	11.6	10	29	$38
2nd Half		295	52	13	33	36	275	276	356	492	848	982	798	11	72	0.45	52	19	29	34	115	144	121	22%	115	55%	80%	13	54%	38%	6.19	15.1	61	174	$47
17	Proj	**569**	**86**	**12**	**55**	**53**	**270**	**249**	**340**	**404**	**745**	**789**	**721**	**10**	**70**	**0.36**	**56**	**20**	**24**	**36**	**91**	**94**	**85**	**13%**	**118**	**42%**	**76%**				**4.80**	**5.7**	**21**	**61**	**$36**

RAY MURPHY

Vogelbach,Daniel

Age: 24	Bats: L	Pos: 1B	Health	A	LIMA Plan D+
Ht: 6' 0"	Wt: 250		PT/Exp	F	Rand Var 0
			Consist	A	MM 3011

0-0-.083 in 12 AB at SEA. Dealt from CHC to SEA mid-season, hung a .417 OBP and 0.97 Eye (40% FB) in AAA. MLEs understandably punish those PCL numbers, but this is a budding patience-and-power profile. Defensive shortcomings could impact PT, but this is a bat worthy of a late-round flyer in deeper leagues.

Yr	Tm	AB	R	HR	RBI	SB	BA	xBA	OBP	SLG	OPS	vL	vR	bb%	ct%	Eye	G	L	F	h%	HctX	PX	xPX	hr/f	Spd	SBO	SB%	#Wk	DOM	DIS	RC/G	RAR	BPV	BPX	R$
12																																			
13																																			
14																																			
15	aa	254	32	6	31	1	241		356	371	727			15	73	0.66				31		98			91	2%	41%				4.39		29	78	$3
16	SEA *	471	61	17	74	0	242	249	345	403	748	0	258	14	73	0.58	67	17	17	30	0	103	-24	0%	51	0%	0%	4	0%	75%	4.67	-2.5	19	54	$8
1st Half		269	36	11	44	0	254	244	344	439	783			12	71	0.47				32		122			57	0%	0%				5.17		25	71	$11
2nd Half		202	25	6	30	0	226	245	346	355	700	0	258	15	76	0.75	67	17	17	27	0	78	-24	0%	59	0%	0%	4	0%	75%	4.04	-6.5	16	46	$4
17	Proj	**210**	**28**	**7**	**33**	**0**	**253**	**241**	**360**	**415**	**775**	**775**	**775**	**14**	**73**	**0.63**	**38**	**22**	**40**	**31**		**103**		**12%**	**64**	**1%**	**50%**				**5.08**	**-0.1**	**22**	**62**	**$4**

Vogt,Stephen

Age: 32	Bats: L	Pos: CA DH	Health	A	LIMA Plan B
Ht: 6' 3"	Wt: 225		PT/Exp	C	Rand Var +1
			Consist	B	MM 2035

Gave back 2015's bb% gains; HctX dipped despite ct% gains, which signals decline in quality of contact. Related, increased FB% didn't translate into more HR as hr/f regressed toward lifetime 9% hr/f. Stable xBA and xPX hint at small recovery. Troubles vL could force a strict platoon, which may actually be a good thing.

Yr	Tm	AB	R	HR	RBI	SB	BA	xBA	OBP	SLG	OPS	vL	vR	bb%	ct%	Eye	G	L	F	h%	HctX	PX	xPX	hr/f	Spd	SBO	SB%	#Wk	DOM	DIS	RC/G	RAR	BPV	BPX	R$
12	TAM *	374	35	6	31	1	197	168	261	300	561	0	80	8	79	0.40	26	9	65	23	30	68	54	0%	90	1%	100%	9	11%	33%	2.50	-19.2	14	35	-$3
13	OAK *	431	53	11	52	0	242	247	296	386	682	667	698	7	80	0.38	30	24	46	28	102	98	111	8%	102	2%	0%	13	38%	46%	3.75	0.4	44	110	$6
14	OAK *	357	37	11	46	2	275	254	315	428	744	647	770	6	86	0.42	33	20	47	30	123	97	144	8%	105	2%	100%	17	53%	35%	4.78	14.8	67	181	$11
15	OAK	445	58	18	71	0	261	259	341	443	783	631	832	11	78	0.58	38	22	40	30	96	115	110	13%	90	2%	0%	25	48%	32%	5.15	18.3	56	151	$12
16	OAK	490	54	14	56	0	251	260	305	406	711	549	748	7	83	0.42	30	23	46	28	90	93	106	7%	73	0%	0%	27	52%	26%	4.16	4.2	44	126	$7
1st Half		243	26	6	23	0	263	258	305	416	721	586	743	5	84	0.33	32	21	46	29	92	94	106	6%	76	0%	0%	14	57%	21%	4.33	1.3	44	126	$7
2nd Half		247	28	8	33	0	239	262	304	397	700	527	752	8	83	0.51	28	25	47	26	89	92	105	8%	75	0%	0%	13	46%	31%	4.00	-1.0	45	129	$7
17	Proj	**452**	**52**	**15**	**60**	**0**	**257**	**258**	**316**	**420**	**736**	**595**	**770**	**8**	**82**	**0.46**	**32**	**23**	**45**	**29**	**98**	**95**	**113**	**9%**	**83**	**1%**	**42%**				**4.52**	**5.1**	**36**	**103**	**$12**

Votto,Joey

Age: 33	Bats: L	Pos: 1B	Health	C	LIMA Plan C
Ht: 6' 3"	Wt: 235		PT/Exp	B	Rand Var -4
			Consist	D	MM 4155

Rebounded from slow 1st half, by his standards, with second straight monster 2nd half (2015+2016= 30-99-.372). Swung more often (yay, RBI!) yet maintained trademark lofty LD%, HctX and ct%. This is clearly one of the most skilled hitters in the game. If he ever gets in that 2nd half groove for full season, UP: .350 BA.

Yr	Tm	AB	R	HR	RBI	SB	BA	xBA	OBP	SLG	OPS	vL	vR	bb%	ct%	Eye	G	L	F	h%	HctX	PX	xPX	hr/f	Spd	SBO	SB%	#Wk	DOM	DIS	RC/G	RAR	BPV	BPX	R$
12	CIN	374	59	14	56	5	337	311	474	567	1041	887	1109	20	77	1.11	38	30	32	41	134	171	161	15%	66	5%	63%	21	76%	10%	10.12	46.1	108	270	$20
13	CIN	581	101	24	73	6	305	279	435	491	926	824	977	19	76	0.98	44	27	29	37	120	128	128	18%	102	4%	67%	27	63%	0%	7.80	51.2	78	195	$29
14	CIN	220	32	6	23	1	255	276	390	409	799	969	736	18	78	0.96	41	27	33	30	109	122	146	11%	59	2%	50%	11	64%	18%	5.35	7.5	63	170	$4
15	CIN	545	95	29	80	11	314	285	459	541	1000	1009	997	21	75	1.06	42	25	33	37	126	151	150	22%	72	6%	79%	27	59%	22%	9.20	56.7	87	235	$33
16	CIN	556	101	29	97	8	326	298	434	550	985	861	1033	16	78	0.90	43	27	30	37	123	133	134	22%	76	4%	89%	27	56%	22%	9.13	55.9	77	220	$33
1st Half		277	45	14	40	6	253	266	382	455	837	632	919	16	71	0.67	41	27	31	31	125	131	164	23%	59	7%	86%	14	43%	36%	5.89	6.4	40	114	$22
2nd Half		279	56	15	57	2	398	330	487	645	1132	1103	1143	16	86	1.38	44	27	28	43	122	134	111	21%	89	2%	100%	13	69%	8%	13.62	56.1	112	320	$44
17	Proj	**547**	**96**	**29**	**92**	**7**	**319**	**298**	**440**	**548**	**988**	**949**	**1003**	**18**	**78**	**0.99**	**42**	**27**	**31**	**37**	**122**	**138**	**140**	**22%**	**70**	**4%**	**80%**				**9.04**	**57.8**	**82**	**235**	**$34**

Walker,Neil

Age: 31	Bats: B	Pos: 2B	Health	B	LIMA Plan B+
Ht: 6' 2"	Wt: 215		PT/Exp	B	Rand Var -3
			Consist	B	MM 3235

Back pain (herniated disc) bothered him for most of the 2nd half and ultimately resulted in season-ending surgery (expected ready for spring training). Career best HR/AB was supported by a rise in xPX and FB%. Vastly better production vL, albeit in a small sample. If those gains stick and back cooperates (big IF)... UP: 30 HR.

Yr	Tm	AB	R	HR	RBI	SB	BA	xBA	OBP	SLG	OPS	vL	vR	bb%	ct%	Eye	G	L	F	h%	HctX	PX	xPX	hr/f	Spd	SBO	SB%	#Wk	DOM	DIS	RC/G	RAR	BPV	BPX	R$
12	PIT	472	62	14	69	7	280	259	342	426	768	602	824	9	78	0.45	42	24	34	33	104	101	115	11%	78	9%	58%	25	44%	28%	5.08	9.8	36	90	$16
13	PIT *	499	62	16	54	1	252	268	322	415	738	518	805	9	82	0.59	39	23	39	28	116	106	115	11%	93	2%	33%	22	50%	27%	4.50	12.3	63	158	$10
14	PIT	512	74	23	76	2	271	282	342	467	809	727	831	8	83	0.51	38	23	39	29	102	126	105	14%	72	3%	50%	26	65%	12%	5.33	28.5	72	195	$20
15	PIT	543	69	16	71	4	269	261	328	427	756	575	793	7	80	0.40	42	21	37	31	112	105	113	10%	87	4%	80%	27	41%	22%	4.83	10.3	46	124	$16
16	NYM	412	57	23	55	3	282	255	347	476	823	1001	766	9	80	0.50	35	21	43	30	116	102	136	16%	92	3%	75%	21	52%	24%	5.87	11.6	48	137	$15
1st Half		273	34	15	35	1	264	240	323	451	774	992	718	8	77	0.39	33	20	47	29	118	102	151	15%	81	3%	50%	14	36%	29%	4.99	1.5	33	94	$15
2nd Half		139	23	8	20	2	317	285	392	525	918	1011	874	11	84	0.82	40	24	36	33	113	103	109	19%	105	4%	100%	7	86%	14%	7.85	11.4	76	217	$14
17	Proj	**510**	**70**	**23**	**68**	**4**	**272**	**266**	**340**	**457**	**797**	**827**	**788**	**9**	**81**	**0.52**	**39**	**22**	**39**	**30**	**112**	**101**	**118**	**14%**	**89**	**4%**	**77%**				**5.40**	**8.7**	**48**	**136**	**$20**

Wallace,Brett

Age: 30	Bats: L	Pos: 3B 1B	Health	A	LIMA Plan F
Ht: 6' 1"	Wt: 260		PT/Exp	D	Rand Var +5
			Consist	B	MM 2001

Played sparingly in April, logging just 23 AB. Hit a HR on May 3, which earned him a run of PT for a couple weeks. He responded with a .943 OPS from May 3-18, and then completely went in the tank again. How many more chances will the one-time top prospect get? The BPX column paints a bleak picture.

Yr	Tm	AB	R	HR	RBI	SB	BA	xBA	OBP	SLG	OPS	vL	vR	bb%	ct%	Eye	G	L	F	h%	HctX	PX	xPX	hr/f	Spd	SBO	SB%	#Wk	DOM	DIS	RC/G	RAR	BPV	BPX	R$
12	HOU *	539	59	20	61	0	243	232	290	399	688	711	757	6	66	0.20	38	27	35	33	115	118	138	16%	51	1%	0%	12	25%	33%	3.85	-25.3	-10	-25	$9
13	HOU *	495	61	21	62	2	241	230	291	434	725	450	787	7	61	0.18	41	22	37	35	78	165	118	22%	62	3%	63%	17	41%	47%	4.23	-5.3	11	28	$11
14	aaa	472	46	14	43	0	233		283	354	636			6	65	0.19				33		102			82	1%	0%				3.29		-19	-51	$5
15	SD *	335	34	10	38	1	244	241	295	380	675	752	950	7	68	0.23	40	29	31	33	104	104	157	25%	48	1%	100%	16	44%	38%	3.79	-15.6	-14	-38	$5
16	SD	217	19	6	20	0	189	203	309	318	627	687	615	12	62	0.35	51	21	28	27	87	102	79	16%	47	0%	0%	26	15%	73%	2.84	-17.1	-31	-89	-$3
1st Half		148	15	5	14	0	209	216	346	372	718	707	720	15	65	0.50	58	17	25	29	104	124	88	21%	49	0%	0%	14	29%	64%	3.93	-5.4	5	14	-$1
2nd Half		69	4	1	6	0	145	176	221	203	424	663	345	4	55	0.10	33	31	36	24	52	48	59	7%	61	0%	0%	12	0%	83%	1.09	-9.3	-113	-323	-$6
17	Proj	**129**	**12**	**4**	**13**	**0**	**206**	**215**	**285**	**333**	**618**	**624**	**900**	**8**	**63**	**0.22**	**41**	**26**	**33**	**30**	**86**	**96**	**106**	**15%**	**53**	**1%**	**65%**				**2.83**	**-8.3**	**-48**	**-137**	**$0**

Wendle,Joe

Age: 27	Bats: L	Pos: 2B	Health	A	LIMA Plan D
Ht: 6' 1"	Wt: 190		PT/Exp	B	Rand Var 0
			Consist	A	MM 1431

1-11-.260 with 2 SB in 96 AB at OAK. Plus Spd is a foundational element that could play with just-average other skills, but at least right now, those other skills don't quite reach that threshold. Take a wait-and-see approach. Perhaps your patience will somehow rub off on him and his approach at the plate.

Yr	Tm	AB	R	HR	RBI	SB	BA	xBA	OBP	SLG	OPS	vL	vR	bb%	ct%	Eye	G	L	F	h%	HctX	PX	xPX	hr/f	Spd	SBO	SB%	#Wk	DOM	DIS	RC/G	RAR	BPV	BPX	R$
12																																			
13																																			
14	aa	336	36	6	39	3	216		259	342	601			6	81	0.30				25		92			100	8%	58%				2.82		39	105	$2
15	aaa	577	64	7	45	10	252		274	380	654			3	78	0.14				31		93			112	11%	81%				3.56		27	73	$10
16	OAK *	587	80	10	63	14	249	261	283	381	664	745	572	5	76	0.20	54	21	25	31	94	84	65	5%	143	15%	75%	6	0%	50%	3.65	-18.8	24	69	$13
1st Half		304	38	5	29	4	223	232	256	356	612			4	72	0.16				29		91			119	8%	100%				3.06		6	17	$7
2nd Half		283	42	5	34	10	277	271	312	408	720	745	572	5	80	0.26	54	21	25	33	99	77	65	5%	146	20%	67%	6	0%	50%	4.36	-3.6	37	106	$20
17	Proj	**235**	**29**	**2**	**23**	**5**	**248**	**259**	**274**	**356**	**630**	**778**	**602**	**4**	**78**	**0.19**	**54**	**21**	**25**	**31**	**89**	**72**	**59**	**5%**	**132**	**13%**	**74%**				**3.35**	**-10.2**	**16**	**45**	**$5**

Werth,Jayson

Age: 38	Bats: R	Pos: LF	Health	D	LIMA Plan B
Ht: 6' 4"	Wt: 225		PT/Exp	B	Rand Var +1
			Consist	D	MM 3215

Managed to avoid the DL for just 2nd time in five years, thus shedding his former "F" Health grade. Skills erosion now evident (see ct%, xPX); no surprise at this age. Big year vL masked some of that deterioration, but newfound struggles vR are glaring. The snowball only gathers speed as it heads down the slope.

Yr	Tm	AB	R	HR	RBI	SB	BA	xBA	OBP	SLG	OPS	vL	vR	bb%	ct%	Eye	G	L	F	h%	HctX	PX	xPX	hr/f	Spd	SBO	SB%	#Wk	DOM	DIS	RC/G	RAR	BPV	BPX	R$
12	WAS *	321	45	5	34	8	292	249	381	428	809	1037	755	13	80	0.73	42	19	39	35	104	96	88	5%	120	9%	80%	16	69%	13%	5.93	10.7	61	153	$11
13	WAS	462	84	25	82	10	318	281	398	532	931	1092	884	11	78	0.59	36	26	38	36	131	142	142	18%	78	7%	91%	22	64%	14%	8.01	49.0	74	185	$31
14	WAS	534	85	16	82	9	292	262	394	455	849	933	823	13	79	0.73	40	20	40	35	134	123	142	9%	88	5%	90%	26	69%	15%	6.44	39.3	69	186	$25
15	WAS *	354	52	12	46	1	227	240	303	384	687	771	658	10	76	0.45	34	22	44	27	114	107	137	11%	64	2%	43%	16	31%	44%	3.81	-9.7	29	78	$5
16	WAS	525	84	21	69	5	244	238	335	417	752	1031	668	12	74	0.51	41	17	42	29	107	112	116	13%	76	4%	83%	26	46%	35%	4.72	1.4	32	91	$12
1st Half		268	41	10	40	2	250	236	337	422	758	1135	608	12	73	0.50	42	17	42	31	122	114	127	12%	79	4%	67%	14	50%	36%	4.83	3.0	33	94	$13
2nd Half		257	43	11	29	3	237	240	333	412	746	856	723	12	74	0.52	41	18	41	28	92	110	106	14%	78	4%	100%	12	42%	33%	4.60	1.1	33	94	$12
17	Proj	**464**	**73**	**15**	**62**	**5**	**241**	**241**	**332**	**399**	**731**	**897**	**683**	**12**	**75**	**0.54**	**41**	**18**	**41**	**29**	**112**	**102**	**124**	**11%**	**78**	**4%**	**83%**				**4.45**	**-0.1**	**31**	**89**	**$13**

GREG PYRON

White,Tyler

Age: 26	Bats: R	Pos: 1B	Health	A	LIMA Plan D
Ht: 5' 11"	Wt: 225		PT/Exp	D	Rand Var +2
			Consist	D	MM 2111

8-28-.217 in 249 AB at HOU. Former Rd-33 pick had a productive minor league career with tremendous Eye (0.98) and solid LD% (often ~23%). But aside from his 10-for-15, 3 HR first week of the season, the MLB results didn't translate. Some value in his average power skills—but at 26, his window is closing quickly.

Yr	Tm	AB	R	HR	RBI	SB	BA	xBA	OBP	SLG	OPS	vL	vR	bb%	ct%	Eye	G	L	F	h%	HctX	PX	xPX	hr/f	Spd	SBO	SB%	#Wk	DOM	DIS	RC/G	RAR	BPV	BPX	R$
12																																			
13																																			
14																																			
15	a/a	403	50	11	70	1	268		363	404	766			13	78	0.67				32		92			81	1%	37%				5.06		37	100	$11
16	HOU *	423	43	18	48	2	208	244	267	383	650	798	591	7	76	0.33	43	18	39	23	96	106	105	11%	69	3%	59%	21	33%	38%	3.27	-20.9	26	74	$2
1st Half		218	21	9	24	1	206	231	280	380	660	624	710	9	73	0.38	40	17	43	24	94	108	125	13%	77	2%	100%	11	27%	36%	3.44	-11.3	21	60	$2
2nd Half		205	22	8	24	1	211	262	253	385	638	1095	314	5	79	0.27	48	19	33	23	96	103	65	5%	68	5%	37%	10	40%	40%	3.07	-12.9	33	94	$2
17	Proj	204	23	5	28	1	232	236	304	363	668	941	507	9	77	0.44	45	18	37	28	95	83	89	9%	71	3%	59%				3.63	-9.0	11	31	$1

Wieters,Matt

Age: 31	Bats: B	Pos: CA	Health	D	LIMA Plan B
Ht: 6' 5"	Wt: 225		PT/Exp	D	Rand Var +2
			Consist	C	MM 2035

First full season since 2013 provided peeks of past promise in ct%, xBA, and 2nd half power bump. Still hits the ball hard, and post-June h% affected BA dip. Another healthy year might be asking a lot, but the skills pieces—if assembled correctly—are in place for... UP: .275, 25 HR. Of course, that's a refrain we've heard before.

Yr	Tm	AB	R	HR	RBI	SB	BA	xBA	OBP	SLG	OPS	vL	vR	bb%	ct%	Eye	G	L	F	h%	HctX	PX	xPX	hr/f	Spd	SBO	SB%	#Wk	DOM	DIS	RC/G	RAR	BPV	BPX	R$
12	BAL	526	67	23	83	3	249	265	329	435	764	908	715	10	79	0.54	44	20	35	28	110	119	113	16%	67	2%	100%	27	59%	26%	4.85	11.0	53	133	$14
13	BAL	523	59	22	79	2	235	256	287	417	704	872	628	8	80	0.41	39	18	44	25	105	122	126	12%	71	2%	100%	26	62%	27%	4.10	5.9	56	140	$11
14	BAL	104	13	5	18	0	308	292	339	500	839	799	849	5	82	0.32	28	30	43	34	138	127	160	14%	83	4%	0%	6	67%	33%	6.11	8.0	66	178	$4
15	BAL	258	24	8	25	0	267	255	319	422	742	728	746	8	74	0.31	43	25	32	33	101	109	113	13%	78	0%	0%	19	53%	37%	4.74	7.4	24	65	$4
16	BAL	423	48	17	66	1	243	261	302	409	711	645	733	7	80	0.38	36	24	40	27	107	94	113	13%	81	1%	100%	27	41%	44%	4.10	2.9	35	100	$8
1st Half		205	23	9	37	1	268	258	321	444	765	509	853	8	76	0.35	43	22	35	31	98	106	109	17%	90	2%	100%	14	21%	57%	5.05	5.3	33	94	$11
2nd Half		218	25	8	29	0	220	264	285	376	661	779	623	6	83	0.42	31	26	44	23	116	84	116	10%	76	0%	0%	13	62%	31%	3.33	-5.4	39	111	$5
17	Proj	488	54	19	69	1	257	264	311	425	736	725	739	7	79	0.36	37	25	38	29	111	99	121	13%	76	1%	50%				4.49	5.0	23	66	$14

Williams,Nick

Age: 23	Bats: L	Pos: OF	Health	A	LIMA Plan D
Ht: 6' 3"	Wt: 195		PT/Exp	C	Rand Var 0
			Consist	D	MM 2201

PHI prospect disappointed in first tour of Triple-A, giving back 2015's gains in plate skills. Blessed with quick hands, good bat speed and moderate power, it's all stymied by poor plate discipline. Likewise, above-average Spd is done in by poor SB%. Many tools in dire need of polish. You'll need patience as much as he does.

Yr	Tm	AB	R	HR	RBI	SB	BA	xBA	OBP	SLG	OPS	vL	vR	bb%	ct%	Eye	G	L	F	h%	HctX	PX	xPX	hr/f	Spd	SBO	SB%	#Wk	DOM	DIS	RC/G	RAR	BPV	BPX	R$
12																																			
13																																			
14	aa	62	3	0	3	1	208		229	266	494			3	64	0.07				32		53			115	16%	43%				1.82		-58	-157	-$2
15	aa	475	61	15	43	10	270		310	432	742			6	77	0.25				32		106			113	17%	54%				4.42		38	103	$15
16	aaa	497	75	14	61	6	246		273	415	688			4	69	0.12				33		119			106	11%	57%				3.73		13	37	$11
1st Half		286	43	9	38	5	277		317	456	773			5	69	0.19				37		124			115	12%	60%				4.94		23	66	$17
2nd Half		211	32	5	23	1	204		211	360	571			1	69	0.03				27		112			113	8%	47%				2.37		4	11	$1
17	Proj	101	14	2	11	1	248	230	277	370	647	647	647	4	72	0.14	44	20	36	33		86		6%	114	13%	55%				3.35		2	4	$2

Williamson,Mac

Age: 26	Bats: R	Pos: RF	Health	B	LIMA Plan D+
Ht: 6' 4"	Wt: 235		PT/Exp	F	Rand Var +1
			Consist	A	MM 3113

6-15-.223 in 112 AB at SF. Two DL stints (strained left shoulder and strained quad) cost him a month. In minors, had plus power and would take a walk. But sketchy and stagnant ct% strangles his BA, while high GB% keeps us from getting overly excited about the thump. Play it cool.

Yr	Tm	AB	R	HR	RBI	SB	BA	xBA	OBP	SLG	OPS	vL	vR	bb%	ct%	Eye	G	L	F	h%	HctX	PX	xPX	hr/f	Spd	SBO	SB%	#Wk	DOM	DIS	RC/G	RAR	BPV	BPX	R$
12																																			
13																																			
14																																			
15	SF *	480	63	9	60	3	231	246	293	350	643	321	690	8	72	0.31	52	24	24	31	124	89	74	0%	88	4%	73%	3	0%	67%	3.40	-21.1	2	5	$6
16	SF *	320	41	13	47	2	219	238	270	388	658	722	731	7	69	0.22	56	17	27	27	105	114	76	29%	68	6%	41%	18	28%	39%	3.33	-13.2	2	6	$3
1st Half		216	28	9	34	2	223	253	262	401	662	857	549	5	72	0.19	57	16	27	27	103	117	70	30%	72	7%	56%	9	22%	33%	3.38	-8.7	16	46	$6
2nd Half		104	13	4	13	0	210	208	286	361	647	583	856	10	62	0.28	55	18	28	29	101	107	82	27%	79	4%	0%	9	33%	44%	3.20	-4.9	-21	-60	-$1
17	Proj	322	41	13	43	2	222	240	294	397	691	676	711	8	69	0.28	56	17	27	28	102	117	77	22%	77	5%	47%				3.63	-10.6	3	9	$6

Winker,Jesse

Age: 23	Bats: L	Pos: OF	Health	A	LIMA Plan D+
Ht: 6' 2"	Wt: 215		PT/Exp	D	Rand Var 0
			Consist	C	MM 2123

Wrist injury cost CIN prospect a month in 1st half and could have sapped power all year. Excellent Eye ensures a good BA/OBP while we wait to see if he can learn to drive the ball. Strong 2015 2H (.426 OBP and 10 HR in 225 AB) at AA provided a glimpse of his potential. Still has questions to answer, but a fine keeper league asset.

Yr	Tm	AB	R	HR	RBI	SB	BA	xBA	OBP	SLG	OPS	vL	vR	bb%	ct%	Eye	G	L	F	h%	HctX	PX	xPX	hr/f	Spd	SBO	SB%	#Wk	DOM	DIS	RC/G	RAR	BPV	BPX	R$
12																																			
13																																			
14	aa	77	12	2	6	0	186		288	316	604			13	68	0.45				25		116			99	0%	0%				2.85		21	57	-$2
15	aa	443	60	13	48	7	264		359	407	766			13	78	0.69				31		96			95	8%	62%				4.98		46	124	$13
16	aaa	380	35	3	41	0	284		375	363	738			13	82	0.81				34		56			80	0%	0%				4.84		24	69	$7
1st Half		199	15	2	22	0	268		367	347	714			13	81	0.83				32		54			78	0%	0%				4.43		21	60	$5
2nd Half		181	20	1	19	0	300		384	381	764			12	83	0.78				36		59			82	0%	0%				5.32		28	80	$8
17	Proj	306	34	8	33	2	277	255	368	415	783	783	900	13	81	0.75	46	20	34	32		86		10%	82	3%	64%				5.36		31	88	$9

Wolters,Tony

Age: 25	Bats: L	Pos: CA	Health	A	LIMA Plan D
Ht: 5' 10"	Wt: 200		PT/Exp	D	Rand Var -2
			Consist	C	MM 2221

Began career at 2B before moving to C in 2013. Now settled defensively at CA, already had the "hit like a backup catcher" role down pat. Hints of still-developing plate skills and line-drive stroke are the only reasons for even mild optimism here, and those are pretty flimsy. Until further notice, has backup CA ceiling.

Yr	Tm	AB	R	HR	RBI	SB	BA	xBA	OBP	SLG	OPS	vL	vR	bb%	ct%	Eye	G	L	F	h%	HctX	PX	xPX	hr/f	Spd	SBO	SB%	#Wk	DOM	DIS	RC/G	RAR	BPV	BPX	R$
12																																			
13																																			
14	aa	341	29	1	28	2	221		279	276	556			7	76	0.33				29		50			95	5%	53%				2.49		-10	-27	-$1
15	aa	239	21	2	15	3	198		256	263	518			7	72	0.28				27		49			111	9%	55%				2.09		-21	-57	-$3
16	COL	205	27	3	30	4	259	258	327	395	723	579	757	9	74	0.40	48	23	29	34	64	98	72	7%	98	9%	80%	25	36%	48%	4.48	0.4	25	71	$4
1st Half		114	15	1	15	3	211	249	297	316	613	232	696	11	76	0.52	50	20	30	27	59	83	59	4%	89	11%	100%	13	38%	31%	3.17	-3.4	22	63	$2
2nd Half		91	12	2	15	1	319	266	367	495	862	955	837	7	71	0.27	44	28	28	43	69	118	90	12%	105	8%	50%	12	33%	67%	6.58	6.0	28	80	$6
17	Proj	193	21	4	21	3	240	249	300	363	663	627	672	8	73	0.32	47	25	29	31	65	84	78	9%	101	8%	66%				3.61	-3.1	5	15	$4

Wong,Kolten

Age: 26	Bats: L	Pos: 2B	Health	A	LIMA Plan B
Ht: 5' 9"	Wt: 190		PT/Exp	C	Rand Var 0
			Consist	D	MM 1425

5-23-.240 with 7 SB in 313 AB at STL. Rough start earned brief AAA stint, but 2nd half rebound was sturdy. Problems vL could prevent return to 500 AB, but bb% gains could merit a return to top of lineup, which is key to an SBO% recovery. 2014 wasn't that long ago, so there's still room for... UP: 20 HR/20 SB.

Yr	Tm	AB	R	HR	RBI	SB	BA	xBA	OBP	SLG	OPS	vL	vR	bb%	ct%	Eye	G	L	F	h%	HctX	PX	xPX	hr/f	Spd	SBO	SB%	#Wk	DOM	DIS	RC/G	RAR	BPV	BPX	R$
12	aa	523	62	7	40	16	251		298	344	642			6	85	0.43				29		59			113	21%	57%				3.29		34	85	$11
13	STL *	471	58	7	35	18	247	272	299	357	656	0	410	7	83	0.44	61	17	22	28	74	72	18	0%	132	16%	94%	8	0%	75%	3.79	1.8	46	115	$12
14	STL *	477	63	14	51	24	257	262	294	395	689	790	656	5	83	0.30	47	19	34	28	93	90	82	11%	100	25%	86%	23	39%	30%	4.10	9.9	45	122	$20
15	STL	557	71	11	61	15	262	262	321	386	707	552	772	6	83	0.38	45	22	33	30	98	80	87	7%	100	17%	65%	27	30%	30%	3.99	-2.9	40	108	$17
16	STL *	341	46	8	31	8	249	252	322	383	705	653	689	10	82	0.62	46	20	34	28	87	67	79	6%	148	8%	100%	26	35%	38%	4.33	-5.4	49	140	$7
1st Half		194	28	4	17	4	252	245	322	359	680	509	642	9	82	0.57	52	18	30	29	71	52	49	2%	149	6%	100%	14	29%	50%	4.05	-4.3	35	100	$8
2nd Half		147	18	4	14	4	245	263	337	415	752	770	747	10	83	0.68	39	22	39	27	105	88	114	9%	126	10%	100%	12	42%	25%	4.69	-0.5	63	180	$6
17	Proj	420	54	7	41	13	253	255	322	373	695	649	708	8	83	0.49	46	20	33	29	92	66	80	6%	123	13%	83%				4.02	-9.6	42	120	$13

GREG PYRON

Wright,David

Age: 34 Bats: R Pos: 3B | Ht: 6' 0" Wt: 200

Health F | LIMA Plan D+ | PT/Exp D | Rand Var 0 | Consist C | MM 3223

Mets fans continue to hang on to hope - heck, he's ONLY 34 - but he has failed to log 40 games in each of past two seasons. Underwent neck surgery (cervical discectomy and fusion) in June. Still has chronic back issue (stenosis). Small sample 2016 seemed like a desperate sell-out for power. DN: Retirement.

Yr	Tm	AB	R	HR	RBI	SB	BA	xBA	OBP	SLG	OPS	vL	vR	bb%	ct%	Eye	G	L	F	h%	HctX	PX	xPX	hr/f	Spd	SBO	SB%	#Wk	DOM	DIS	RC/G	RAR	BPV	BPX	R$
12	NYM	581	91	21	93	15	306	278	391	492	883	917	867	12	81	0.72	42	22	35	35	116	123	134	13%	92	13%	60%	27	59%	19%	6.83	36.0	75	188	$30
13	NYM	430	63	18	58	17	307	280	390	514	904	1072	836	11	82	0.70	38	23	39	34	124	130	141	13%	145	14%	85%	21	62%	5%	7.40	40.2	99	248	$26
14	NYM	535	54	8	63	8	269	245	324	374	698	921	634	7	79	0.37	40	23	37	33	116	84	113	5%	81	9%	62%	24	38%	46%	4.13	6.4	24	65	$15
15	NYM	152	24	5	17	2	289	247	379	434	814	1023	746	13	76	0.61	37	24	39	35	120	98	133	11%	85	6%	67%	9	22%	44%	5.86	5.1	36	97	$4
16	NYM	137	18	7	14	3	226	228	350	438	788	714	814	16	60	0.47	23	28	49	32	116	165	228	18%	77	12%	60%	8	38%	50%	4.91	-0.2	28	80	$2
1st Half		137	18	7	14	3	226	228	350	438	788	714	814	16	60	0.47	23	28	49	32	116	165	228	18%	77	12%	60%	8	38%	50%	4.91	0.1	28	80	$2
2nd Half																																			
17	**Proj**	**246**	**33**	**9**	**29**	**5**	**258**	**247**	**348**	**427**	**775**	**876**	**740**	**12**	**73**	**0.51**	**34**	**25**	**41**	**32**	**118**	**111**	**158**	**12%**	**92**	**11%**	**67%**				**5.01**	**0.9**	**31**	**88**	**$7**

Yelich,Christian

Age: 25 Bats: L Pos: LF CF | Ht: 6' 4" Wt: 189

Health B | LIMA Plan B | PT/Exp A | Rand Var -2 | Consist B | MM 3345

Mechanical adjustments aimed to help him drive the ball paid huge dividends in 2nd half, as FB%/xPX rose. His hr/f is likely unsustainable, but may not slip far (3rd in MLB in avg. FB distance). Speed decline perplexing, but did move to the middle of the lineup. In growth mode; still hasn't reached his ceiling.

Yr	Tm	AB	R	HR	RBI	SB	BA	xBA	OBP	SLG	OPS	vL	vR	bb%	ct%	Eye	G	L	F	h%	HctX	PX	xPX	hr/f	Spd	SBO	SB%	#Wk	DOM	DIS	RC/G	RAR	BPV	BPX	R$
12																																			
13	MIA *	433	62	9	41	14	276	276	356	427	782	476	941	11	72	0.44	63	23	14	37	103	114	83	17%	154	15%	73%	10	30%	20%	5.31	15.6	49	123	$16
14	MIA	582	94	9	54	21	284	271	362	402	764	819	747	11	76	0.51	61	21	18	36	113	91	97	12%	138	15%	75%	25	44%	16%	5.16	22.9	44	119	$25
15	MIA	476	63	7	44	16	300	282	366	416	782	703	812	9	79	0.47	62	23	15	37	115	85	82	13%	123	14%	76%	25	52%	32%	5.52	10.6	40	108	$20
16	MIA	578	78	21	98	9	298	289	376	483	859	716	908	11	76	0.52	57	23	20	36	117	118	97	24%	94	7%	69%	27	52%	22%	6.52	30.4	51	146	$25
1st Half		279	38	6	40	4	315	295	399	473	872	775	906	12	77	0.59	59	25	16	39	118	107	81	17%	96	7%	57%	14	50%	29%	6.81	17.9	50	143	$23
2nd Half		299	40	15	58	5	281	284	355	492	847	655	910	10	75	0.47	54	22	24	33	117	129	112	28%	96	7%	83%	13	54%	15%	6.25	15.2	55	157	$27
17	**Proj**	**596**	**83**	**20**	**79**	**15**	**292**	**282**	**367**	**469**	**836**	**698**	**887**	**10**	**76**	**0.49**	**54**	**23**	**23**	**35**	**115**	**111**	**93**	**19%**	**112**	**11%**	**74%**				**6.15**	**28.4**	**47**	**133**	**$29**

Young,Chris

Age: 33 Bats: R Pos: LF | Ht: 6' 2" Wt: 190

Health D | LIMA Plan D+ | PT/Exp D | Rand Var -3 | Consist B | MM 4221

9-24-.276 in 203 AB at BOS. June hamstring strain cost him two months, but the gains in LD%, HctX and xPX were notable. Continued to love left-handed pitching. Spd on the decline, which isn't surprising given his age. Best suited for short side of a platoon, so value accordingly.

Yr	Tm	AB	R	HR	RBI	SB	BA	xBA	OBP	SLG	OPS	vL	vR	bb%	ct%	Eye	G	L	F	h%	HctX	PX	xPX	hr/f	Spd	SBO	SB%	#Wk	DOM	DIS	RC/G	RAR	BPV	BPX	R$
12	ARI	325	36	14	41	8	231	259	311	434	745	810	707	10	76	0.46	31	22	47	26	106	143	136	12%	76	15%	73%	24	46%	38%	4.38	-1.7	62	155	$7
13	OAK	335	46	12	40	10	200	231	280	379	659	712	614	10	72	0.39	29	22	50	24	83	131	120	10%	116	19%	77%	26	46%	31%	3.36	-6.5	50	125	$5
14	2 TM *	352	45	13	43	9	229	244	297	403	699	561	720	9	77	0.42	29	20	52	26	94	129	109	8%	105	15%	74%	23	43%	48%	3.93	2.6	62	168	$9
15	NYY	318	53	14	42	3	252	253	320	453	773	972	585	9	77	0.41	36	17	47	29	97	134	105	12%	107	5%	75%	26	50%	35%	4.87	4.4	67	181	$9
16	BOS *	226	31	9	26	4	268	261	332	475	807	999	766	9	74	0.37	25	25	50	32	112	142	127	12%	84	11%	67%	19	47%	32%	5.41	7.4	55	157	$6
1st Half		130	16	6	15	2	277	269	338	508	846	1042	734	8	75	0.33	21	26	54	33	122	155	138	12%	87	7%	100%	12	58%	25%	6.07	5.9	66	189	$7
2nd Half		96	15	3	11	2	255	253	330	431	762	919	820	10	73	0.42	34	23	43	32	96	125	109	13%	88	16%	50%	7	29%	43%	4.59	0.4	42	120	$4
17	**Proj**	**223**	**32**	**9**	**27**	**4**	**249**	**254**	**326**	**449**	**775**	**889**	**705**	**9**	**75**	**0.40**	**31**	**22**	**48**	**29**	**101**	**132**	**116**	**11%**	**94**	**12%**	**66%**				**4.76**	**2.1**	**48**	**136**	**$7**

Zimmer,Bradley

Age: 24 Bats: L Pos: DH | Ht: 6' 4" Wt: 185

Health A | LIMA Plan D | PT/Exp F | Rand Var | Consist B | MM 2503

First-rounder from 2014 draft took a step back, as contact rate—previously not a problem—collapsed. Possesses secondary skills (moderate power; plus speed) to be an impact player, but clearly has to make more contact to reach his full potential. His pedigree calls for patience in keeper leagues.

Yr	Tm	AB	R	HR	RBI	SB	BA	xBA	OBP	SLG	OPS	vL	vR	bb%	ct%	Eye	G	L	F	h%	HctX	PX	xPX	hr/f	Spd	SBO	SB%	#Wk	DOM	DIS	RC/G	RAR	BPV	BPX	R$
12																																			
13																																			
14																																			
15	aa	187	22	6	22	11	208		270	354	624			8	70	0.28				27		108			95	33%	83%				3.18		11	30	$4
16	a/a	468	65	13	53	32	229		322	382	704			12	61	0.35				35		121			107	37%	67%				3.90		-2	-6	$17
1st Half		284	40	11	39	24	219		309	428	737			12	62	0.34				31		158			125	56%	64%				3.90		35	100	$24
2nd Half		184	24	2	14	9	244		339	309	648			13	59	0.35				40		61			112	17%	79%				3.65		-55	-157	$7
17	**Proj**	**250**	**32**	**6**	**27**	**15**	**224**	**209**	**307**	**353**	**660**	**660**	**660**	**11**	**64**	**0.33**	**42**	**21**	**37**	**33**		**99**		**10%**	**115**	**31%**	**76%**				**3.59**	**-14.9**	**-6**	**-17**	**$9**

Zimmerman,Ryan

Age: 32 Bats: R Pos: 1B | Ht: 6' 2" Wt: 225

Health F | LIMA Plan B | PT/Exp C | Rand Var +4 | Consist C | MM 3225

It's now 3 years south of 500 AB. Injuries (plantar fasciitis, rib cage, wrist) were again a major issue. Quality of contact declined sharply (HctX/xPX) as patience eroded. RandVar/xBA suggest at least a mild rebound. Remnants of vintage skills remain as a low-odds upside but huge health risk hovers. If you're willing to gamble...

Yr	Tm	AB	R	HR	RBI	SB	BA	xBA	OBP	SLG	OPS	vL	vR	bb%	ct%	Eye	G	L	F	h%	HctX	PX	xPX	hr/f	Spd	SBO	SB%	#Wk	DOM	DIS	RC/G	RAR	BPV	BPX	R$
12	WAS	578	93	25	95	5	282	274	346	478	824	861	810	9	80	0.49	48	18	33	32	139	126	144	16%	83	4%	71%	25	60%	20%	5.85	6.9	65	163	$24
13	WAS	568	84	26	79	6	275	267	344	465	809	850	794	10	77	0.45	45	21	34	32	128	127	144	18%	96	4%	100%	25	48%	24%	5.69	17.8	58	145	$23
14	WAS	214	26	5	38	0	280	284	342	449	790	779	794	9	83	0.59	44	21	35	32	121	128	115	8%	70	0%	0%	13	69%	15%	5.52	8.1	75	203	$6
15	WAS	346	43	16	73	1	249	275	308	465	773	1058	672	9	77	0.42	48	17	35	28	124	146	141	16%	66	1%	100%	17	47%	35%	4.97	-3.9	65	176	$10
16	WAS	427	60	15	46	4	218	243	272	370	642	683	632	6	76	0.28	49	17	35	25	106	94	99	13%	80	6%	80%	24	46%	46%	3.24	-27.5	17	49	$4
1st Half		270	42	11	36	1	219	247	282	396	679	752	655	8	75	0.34	50	14	35	25	107	109	98	15%	86	4%	50%	14	64%	29%	3.58	-12.7	31	89	$7
2nd Half		157	18	4	10	3	217	234	253	325	578	465	595	4	76	0.16	45	21	34	26	105	67	100	10%	73	10%	100%	10	20%	70%	2.68	-11.7	-9	-26	$1
17	**Proj**	**454**	**59**	**16**	**64**	**4**	**241**	**257**	**296**	**405**	**702**	**808**	**900**	**7**	**77**	**0.35**	**47**	**18**	**35**	**28**	**115**	**103**	**117**	**13%**	**71**	**4%**	**90%**				**4.06**	**-14.1**	**31**	**89**	**$11**

Zobrist,Ben

Age: 36 Bats: B Pos: 2B LF RF | Ht: 6' 3" Wt: 200

Health B | LIMA Plan A | PT/Exp A | Rand Var 0 | Consist B | MM 2255

Patience and batting eye remain elite, but what happens after contact—hard-hit, LD%, power and speed—is all merely average and/or starting to wilt. The plate skills can prop that up, but there is still reason to be at least a little cautious, particularly at an age where declining AB totals may eat into counting stats.

Yr	Tm	AB	R	HR	RBI	SB	BA	xBA	OBP	SLG	OPS	vL	vR	bb%	ct%	Eye	G	L	F	h%	HctX	PX	xPX	hr/f	Spd	SBO	SB%	#Wk	DOM	DIS	RC/G	RAR	BPV	BPX	R$
12	TAM	560	88	20	74	14	270	285	377	471	848	879	835	15	82	0.94	43	22	35	30	109	128	114	13%	110	13%	61%	27	67%	19%	6.03	27.5	93	233	$21
13	TAM	612	77	12	71	11	275	260	354	402	756	643	812	11	85	0.79	43	20	37	31	103	87	98	6%	106	7%	79%	27	67%	19%	4.98	23.1	65	163	$20
14	TAM	570	83	10	52	10	272	267	354	395	749	873	703	12	85	0.89	49	18	33	30	103	88	89	6%	113	8%	67%	25	60%	16%	4.88	24.5	71	192	$18
15	2 AL	467	76	13	56	3	276	293	359	450	809	926	753	12	88	1.11	49	19	32	29	107	108	85	10%	106	5%	43%	23	65%	9%	5.58	18.9	96	259	$15
16	CHC	523	94	18	76	6	272	288	386	446	831	856	823	16	84	1.17	48	22	30	29	111	99	94	13%	99	5%	60%	27	52%	19%	5.92	15.8	79	226	$18
1st Half		277	55	11	43	3	296	284	404	473	877	900	866	15	84	1.11	45	22	33	32	120	102	118	14%	99	5%	60%	14	57%	14%	6.83	15.7	79	226	$23
2nd Half		246	39	7	33	3	244	293	366	415	781	792	777	16	85	1.24	51	21	28	26	102	97	67	12%	96	6%	60%	13	46%	23%	5.01	1.5	80	229	$12
17	**Proj**	**513**	**84**	**15**	**65**	**6**	**269**	**286**	**370**	**435**	**805**	**861**	**783**	**14**	**85**	**1.09**	**48**	**20**	**32**	**29**	**107**	**96**	**89**	**11%**	**103**	**6%**	**59%**				**5.53**	**10.8**	**74**	**210**	**$19**

Zunino,Mike

Age: 26 Bats: R Pos: CA | Ht: 6' 2" Wt: 220

Health A | LIMA Plan D+ | PT/Exp C | Rand Var -3 | Consist C | MM 4005

12-31-.207 in 164 AB at SEA. Prodigious power/FB% combo persists. However, dreadful ct%/BA has limited his PT. Was much more selective at the plate in 2016, swinging at 6% fewer pitches outside the zone and doubling his bb%. It's a step in the right direction. Improving ct% is key to more PT and ... UP: 30 HR.

Yr	Tm	AB	R	HR	RBI	SB	BA	xBA	OBP	SLG	OPS	vL	vR	bb%	ct%	Eye	G	L	F	h%	HctX	PX	xPX	hr/f	Spd	SBO	SB%	#Wk	DOM	DIS	RC/G	RAR	BPV	BPX	R$
12	aa	51	6	2	7	0	303		363	520	884			9	84	0.60				32		134			89	0%	0%				6.92		90	225	$0
13	SEA *	376	49	12	44	1	201	219	256	350	606	650	609	7	67	0.22	43	19	39	26	92	117	108	10%	91	1%	100%	12	33%	67%	2.87	-9.9	5	13	$2
14	SEA	438	51	22	60	0	199	226	254	404	658	722	632	4	64	0.11	34	17	49	25	86	170	143	16%	85	5%	0%	27	30%	37%	2.83	-6.8	27	73	$5
15	SEA *	391	33	13	33	0	183	186	224	315	539	522	534	5	64	0.15	33	17	50	25	81	102	121	10%	75	1%	0%	21	14%	62%	2.17	-19.6	-28	-76	-$4
16	SEA *	444	52	25	74	0	225	223	299	435	734	835	769	10	66	0.31	29	18	53	28	94	141	155	23%	86	1%	0%	14	29%	43%	4.23	4.9	25	71	$7
1st Half		252	32	13	42	0	237	222	297	435	732	0	2600	8	70	0.28	0	25	75	29	142	127	225	67%	73	2%	0%	2	50%	50%	4.23	0.7	21	60	$9
2nd Half		192	19	11	33	0	210	219	301	434	736	835	706	12	62	0.34	31	18	52	27	86	162	152	20%	89	0%	0%	12	25%	42%	4.22	0.5	28	80	$4
17	**Proj**	**410**	**44**	**21**	**57**	**0**	**230**	**223**	**323**	**426**	**749**	**815**	**723**	**10**	**68**	**0.35**	**34**	**17**	**49**	**28**	**86**	**129**	**136**	**15%**	**80**	**1%**	**10%**				**4.28**	**1.7**	**5**	**14**	**$8**

GREG PYRON

THE NEXT TIER · Batters

The preceding section provided player boxes and analysis for 441 batters. As we know, far more than 441 batters will play in the major leagues in 2017. Many of those additional hitters are covered in the minor league section, but that still leaves a gap: established major leaguers who don't play enough, or well enough, to merit a player box.

This section looks to fill that gap. Here, you will find "The Next Tier" of batters who are mostly past their growth years, but who are likely to see some playing time in 2017. We are including their 2015-16 MLB stats here for reference for you to do your own analysis. This way, if Chase D'Arnaud stumbles into some playing time in June, a quick check would show that his Spd skills were an asset even in 2016. Or if you're looking for a short-term backup catcher, Josh Phegley's bit of pop might stand out.

Batter	Yr	B	Age	Pos	AB	R	HR	RBI	SB	BA	xBA	OPS	vL	vR	bb%	ct%	Eye	GLF	HctX	PX	xPX	Spd	SBO	SB%	BPV
Aviles, Mike	15	R	34	o	290	37	5	17	3	231	240	599	542	650	6	87	0.53	49/16/35	88	54	71	90	6	75	33
	16	R	35		167	17	1	6	2	74	243	269	480	558	5	84	0.33	53/19/28	86	37	51	112	11	50	11
Blanco, Andres	15	B	31	45	233	32	7	25	1	292	295	863	798	974	8	81	0.48	46/20/34	88	143	102	100	4	50	87
	16	B	32		190	26	4	21	2	77	271	405	551	764	5	78	0.27	52/19/29	87	103	68	88	13	40	35
Butera, Drew	15	R	31	2	107	9	1	5	0	196	186	505	476	586	5	76	0.23	33/19/49	66	43	57	88	4	0	-23
	16	R	32		123	18	4	16	0	34	256	480	555	883	6	71	0.22	40/22/38	71	138	95	102	0	0	38
Cabrera, Ramon	15	B	25	2	30	4	1	3	0	367	254	867	909	750	0	83	0.00	64/16/20	59	80	25	119	0	0	35
	16	B	26		171	11	3	23	1	59	249	357	558	658	4	82	0.27	41/22/38	80	72	64	56	5	50	15
Colabello, Chris	15	R	31	3	333	55	15	54	2	321	271	886	868	935	6	71	0.23	48/25/27	98	142	94	97	2	100	42
	16	R	32		29	0	0	1	0	12	76	069	0	333	6	69	0.22	60/10/30	70	0	76	72	0	0	-87
Colon, Christian	15	R	26	4	107	8	0	6	3	290	252	692	666	746	9	84	0.65	44/27/29	57	40	32	99	14	60	19
	16	R	27		147	13	1	13	0	57	223	293	648	557	7	79	0.35	50/20/30	63	45	43	101	3	0	-1
Conger, Hank	15	B	27	2	201	25	11	33	0	229	250	759	892	618	10	69	0.37	35/22/44	75	159	110	65	2	0	44
	16	B	28		124	6	3	10	0	37	182	306	708	562	9	68	0.30	44/18/38	100	82	106	68	0	0	-22
Crawford, Carl	15	L	33	o	181	19	4	16	10	265	255	707	712	678	5	77	0.24	43/24/33	105	93	108	98	28	83.3	26
	16	L	34		81	8	0	6	0	42	275	235	167	514	5	86	0.36	59/24/17	40	29	14	99	6	0	10
D Arnaud, Chase	15	R	28	6	17	2	0	0	0	176	164	516	200	615	6	59	0.14	50/10/40	26	73	10	137	33	0	-51
	16	R	29		233	24	1	21	9	76	241	335	681	635	9	79	0.46	42/23/35	84	65	71	129	19	75	25
De Aza, Alejandro	15	L	31	o	325	51	7	35	7	262	245	755	800	470	9	74	0.37	39/23/38	85	109	104	146	14	58.3	47
	16	L	32		234	31	6	25	4	56	231	321	581	625	10	71	0.39	34/28/38	127	78	157	76	12	57.1	-6
De Jesus, Ivan	15	R	28	46	201	15	4	28	0	244	247	684	667	728	9	73	0.35	50/23/27	74	95	78	92	4	0	13
	16	R	29		221	21	1	20	3	81	246	312	533	646	7	77	0.33	48/27/25	72	46	60	70	6	75	-17
Drew, Stephen	15	L	32	4	383	43	17	44	0	201	245	652	642	690	9	81	0.52	38/16/47	77	109	95	90	3	0	60
	16	L	33		143	24	8	21	0	37	284	524	485	910	10	78	0.52	32/22/47	132	155	187	93	3	0	87
Ellis, A.J.	15	R	34	2	181	24	7	21	0	238	257	758	642	913	15	79	0.84	44/21/35	103	108	108	84	0	0	60
	16	R	35		171	11	2	22	2	58	238	298	566	620	10	82	0.61	41/22/36	102	55	92	75	7	66.7	16
Gimenez, Chris	15	R	32	2	98	19	5	14	2	255	284	820	711	1095	9	81	0.53	42/18/41	86	145	86	87	9	100	85
	16	R	33		139	17	4	11	0	48	223	331	736	557	7	70	0.24	49/21/30	94	75	113	78	0	0	-18
Gose, Anthony	15	L	24	o	485	73	5	26	23	254	238	688	713	546	8	70	0.31	54/21/25	77	87	54	160	26	67.6	17
	16	L	25		91	11	2	7	0	30	204	341	361	730	9	58	0.24	58/19/23	76	95	77	139	5	0	-28
Hanigan, Ryan	15	R	34	2	174	28	2	16	0	247	247	664	587	895	10	78	0.51	52/24/24	82	62	47	88	0	0	9
	16	R	35		105	9	1	14	0	42	219	238	245	548	6	74	0.26	54/21/26	70	49	65	64	0	0	-29
Heisey, Chris	15	R	30	o	55	8	2	9	0	182	182	674	974	570	21	69	0.88	21/13/67	91	105	119	92	5	0	33
	16	R	31		139	18	9	17	0	29	231	446	764	722	9	68	0.30	31/19/50	81	139	124	104	3	0	35
Infante, Omar	15	R	33	4	440	39	2	44	2	220	246	552	548	561	2	84	0.13	41/21/38	87	66	72	116	5	50	31
	16	R	34		134	16	0	11	0	43	235	321	604	598	6	83	0.39	38/20/42	101	60	99	116	0	0	29
Kratz, Erik	15	R	35	2	26	3	0	3	0	192	218	484	336	600	4	81	0.20	45/14/41	97	69	132	69	0	0	9
	16	R	36		85	3	1	4	0	20	129	153	607	102	1	62	0.03	41/8/51	98	47	108	67	0	0	-88
Mathis, Jeff	15	R	32	2	93	9	2	12	0	161	227	504	476	676	7	74	0.29	41/20/39	91	89	97	84	0	0	9
	16	R	33		126	12	2	15	0	36	194	333	845	498	3	71	0.11	41/16/43	76	63	101	108	0	0	-22
McGehee, Casey	15	R	32	5	237	14	2	20	1	198	230	538	508	645	8	79	0.42	57/19/25	78	60	53	47	4	50	-3
	16	R	33		92	4	0	1	0	41	173	239	700	412	3	85	0.21	53/14/33	110	9	104	85	0	0	-19
Morneau, Justin	15	L	34	0	168	19	3	15	0	310	272	821	813	849	7	85	0.52	48/19/33	129	93	122	123	0	0	68
	16	L	35		203	16	6	25	0	76	253	429	798	717	6	74	0.23	50/20/31	85	113	88	84	0	0	26
Nava, Daniel	15	B	32	o	139	13	1	10	1	194	194	560	548	597	13	74	0.56	45/18/37	93	41	112	90	2	100	-16
	16	B	33		130	11	1	13	0	39	241	292	1167	579	7	77	0.33	38/28/34	109	52	97	70	0	0	-12
Paredes, Jimmy	15	B	26	o	363	46	10	42	4	275	242	726	740	651	5	69	0.17	49/23/28	104	105	101	114	9	50	8
	16	B	27		158	15	5	19	0	61	228	367	402	694	4	70	0.15	55/17/27	83	102	94	94	3	0	0

THE NEXT TIER

Batters

Batter	Yr	B	Age	Pos	AB	R	HR	RBI	SB	BA	xBA	OPS	vL	vR	bb%	ct%	Eye	GLF	HctX	PX	xPX	Spd	SBO	SB%	BPV
Pennington, Cliff	15	B	31	4	210	24	3	21	3	210	228	578	618	427	11	77	0.55	44/24/32	96	51	88	68	5	100	-6
	16	B	32		172	18	3	10	1	46	202	308	190	624	7	68	0.24	40/22/38	67	64	65	121	3	100	-23
Phegley, Josh	15	R	26	2	225	27	9	34	0	249	266	749	709	788	6	77	0.27	37/21/43	101	137	120	69	0	0	53
	16	R	37		78	11	1	10	0	26	250	372	658	709	6	83	0.38	39/20/41	108	80	108	83	0	0	36
Pierzynski, A.J.	15	L	38	2	407	38	9	49	0	300	294	769	799	655	4	91	0.51	47/25/29	104	80	75	69	2	0	59
	16	L	39		247	15	2	23	1	111	261	304	216	604	2	88	0.21	50/20/30	94	57	69	51	2	100	21
Plawecki, Kevin	15	R	23	2	233	18	3	21	0	219	209	576	609	411	7	74	0.28	46/20/34	92	60	87	91	0	0	-11
	16	R	33		132	6	1	11	0	55	187	265	651	530	11	75	0.52	56/17/27	58	52	44	88	0	0	-6
Raburn, Ryan	15	R	34	o	173	22	8	29	0	301	290	936	467	1004	12	75	0.52	44/22/35	131	175	152	96	0	0	92
	16	R	35		223	30	9	30	0	67	220	404	835	615	11	64	0.35	46/16/38	100	130	148	113	0	0	19
Recker, Anthony	15	R	31	2	80	6	2	5	1	125	174	452	326	756	12	56	0.31	40/24/36	88	73	101	72	6	100	-68
	16	R	32		90	6	2	15	1	21	247	433	872	812	15	76	0.73	30/22/48	119	113	182	51	3	100	40
Reimold, Nolan	15	R	31	o	170	24	6	20	0	247	225	738	691	791	12	72	0.49	49/16/35	88	97	94	117	0	0	28
	16	R	32		203	25	6	15	1	64	227	365	565	768	10	69	0.35	45/20/35	71	97	83	118	6	33.3	12
Robinson, Clint	15	L	30	3	309	44	10	34	0	272	274	782	757	985	11	83	0.71	41/25/34	105	95	111	89	0	0	59
	16	L	31		196	16	5	26	0	77	206	332	653	634	9	81	0.53	47/16/37	96	54	75	65	0	0	6
Robinson, Shane	15	R	30	o	180	28	0	16	6	250	237	621	641	592	6	84	0.41	52/16/32	83	48	77	154	15	85.7	35
	16	R	31		98	16	1	10	3	37	228	235	556	411	9	83	0.59	46/19/35	65	39	79	104	22	60	14
Rollins, Jimmy	15	B	36	6	517	71	13	41	12	224	245	643	610	762	8	83	0.51	38/19/43	93	84	106	109	17	60	51
	16	B	37		149	25	2	8	5	56	234	329	1311	502	10	78	0.48	48/16/36	65	72	55	117	18	71.4	25
Romine, Andrew	15	L	29	35o	184	25	2	15	10	255	229	622	613	640	6	75	0.24	58/20/22	46	45	39	118	29	66.7	-14
	16	L	30		174	21	2	16	8	70	258	322	611	630	7	78	0.34	52/26/22	73	52	53	120	18	100	6
Rosales, Adam	15	R	32	45	114	14	3	7	4	228	219	638	684	608	8	74	0.33	49/15/36	77	80	95	108	28	50	9
	16	R	33		214	37	13	35	4	48	235	495	843	789	12	59	0.33	37/17/46	88	200	145	134	8	100	62
Ruf, Darin	15	R	28	3	268	30	12	39	1	235	251	714	483	1107	7	74	0.30	45/20/35	115	120	129	51	2	100	25
	16	R	29		83	8	3	9	0	25	215	337	695	511	5	70	0.16	42/20/38	71	84	113	82	6	0	-16
Ruiz, Carlos	15	R	36	2	284	23	2	22	1	211	246	575	501	886	9	85	0.65	44/22/33	60	53	52	82	3	50	26
	16	R	37		201	21	3	15	3	77	246	348	793	668	12	84	0.82	46/21/33	115	53	71	68	6	75	23
Soto, Geovany	15	R	32	2	187	20	9	21	0	219	234	708	676	780	10	66	0.33	37/23/40	98	139	163	69	2	0	19
	16	R	33		78	11	4	9	0	21	290	487	952	729	7	73	0.29	37/32/32	111	141	129	72	0	0	43
Stewart, Chris	15	R	33	2	159	9	0	15	0	289	231	659	657	667	4	82	0.21	54/22/24	64	45	29	85	0	0	-1
	16	R	34		98	10	1	7	0	40	225	286	778	563	11	85	0.80	49/17/34	70	46	70	90	0	0	27
Tejada, Ruben	15	R	25	5	360	36	3	28	2	261	258	688	675	731	10	81	0.54	40/27/33	94	71	101	91	3	66.7	27
	16	R	26		66	9	0	5	0	23	233	242	742	265	10	80	0.54	42/20/38	74	63	80	97	0	0	22
Thole, Josh	15	L	28	2	49	5	0	2	0	204	229	495	466	583	6	82	0.33	48/23/30	54	36	47	84	0	0	-5
	16	L	29		118	7	1	7	0	35	203	220	563	440	10	76	0.46	38/22/40	72	35	83	61	0	0	-26
Uribe, Juan	15	R	36	5	360	40	14	43	2	253	251	737	685	893	9	78	0.43	45/19/36	96	108	100	55	2	100	33
	16	R	37		238	19	7	25	0	88	236	332	472	645	6	79	0.31	46/20/34	102	75	106	33	0	0	1
Weeks, Rickie	15	R	31	o	84	7	2	9	0	167	145	513	290	691	10	70	0.36	52/5/43	52	55	67	60	0	0	-35
	16	R	31		180	29	9	27	5	57	251	450	1010	639	10	70	0.37	45/18/37	114	137	151	98	11	100	41
Wilson, Bobby	15	R	32	2	132	8	1	14	0	189	199	505	590	296	8	70	0.28	50/20/30	68	53	59	49	3	0	-43
	16	R	33		228	25	7	33	0	69	226	355	739	589	5	72	0.17	41/24/35	73	74	71	45	0	0	-27

The following section contains player boxes for every pitcher who had significant playing time in 2016 and/or is expected to get fantasy roster-worthy innings in 2017. In most cases, high-end prospects who have yet to make their major league debuts will not appear here; you can find scouting reports for them in the Prospects section.

Snapshot Section

The top band of each player box contains the following information:

Age as of Opening Day 2017.

Throws right (R) or left (L).

Role: Starters (SP) are those projected to face 20+ batters per game; the rest are relievers (RP).

Ht/Wt: Each batter's height and weight.

Type evaluates the extent to which a pitcher allows the ball to be put into play and his ground ball or fly ball tendency. CON (contact) represents pitchers who allow the ball to be put into play a great deal. PWR (power) represents those with high strikeout and/or walk totals who keep the ball out of play. GB are those who have a ground ball rate more than 50%; xGB are those who have a GB rate more than 55%. FB are those who have a fly ball rate more than 40%; xFB are those who have a FB rate more than 45%.

Reliability Grades analyze each pitcher's forecast risk, on an A-F scale. High grades go to those who have accumulated few disabled list days (Health), have a history of substantial and regular major league playing time (PT/Exp) and have displayed consistent performance over the past three years, using xERA (Consist).

LIMA Plan Grade evaluates how well that pitcher would be a good fit for a team using the LIMA Plan draft strategy. Best grades go to pitchers who have excellent base skills and had a 2016 dollar value less than $20. Lowest grades will go to poor skills and values more than $20.

Random Variance Score (Rand Var) measures the impact random variance had on the pitcher's 2016 stats and the probability that his 2017 performance will exceed or fall short of 2016. The variables tracked are those prone to regression—H%, S%, hr/f and xERA to ERA variance. Players are rated on a scale of –5 to +5 with positive scores indicating rebounds and negative scores indicating corrections. Note that this score is computer-generated and the projections will override it on occasion.

Mayberry Method (MM) acknowledges the imprecision of the forecasting process by projecting player performance in broad strokes. The four digits of MM each represent a fantasy-relevant skill—ERA, strikeout rate, saves potential and playing time (IP)—and are all on a scale of 0 to 5.

Commentaries for each pitcher provide a brief analysis of his skills and the potential impact on performance in 2017. MLB statistics are listed first for those who played only a portion of 2016 at the major league level. Note that these commentaries generally look at performance related issues only. Role and playing time expectations may impact these analyses, so you will have to adjust accordingly. Upside (UP) and downside (DN) statistical potential appears for some players; these are less grounded in hard data and more speculative of skills potential.

Player Stat Section

The past five years' statistics represent the total accumulated in the majors as well as in Triple-A, Double-A ball and various foreign leagues during each year. All non-major league stats have been converted to a major league equivalent (MLE) performance level. Minor league levels below Double-A are not included.

Nearly all baseball publications separate a player's statistical experiences in the major leagues from the minor leagues and outside leagues. While this may be appropriate for official record-keeping purposes, it is not an easy-to-analyze snapshot of a player's complete performance for a given year.

Bill James has proven that minor league statistics (converted to MLEs), at Double-A level or above, provide as accurate a record of a player's performance as Major league statistics. Other researchers have also devised conversion factors for foreign leagues. Since these are adequate barometers, we include them in the pool of historical data for each year.

Team designations: An asterisk (*) appearing with a team name means that Triple-A and/or Double-A numbers are included in that year's stat line. Any stints of less than 10 IP are not included (to screen out most rehab appearances). A designation of "a/a" means the stats were accumulated at both AA and AAA levels that year. "for" represents a foreign or independent league. The designation "2TM" appears whenever a player was on more than one major league team, crossing leagues, in a season. "2AL" and "2NL" represent more than one team in the same league. Players who were cut during the season and finished 2016 as a free agent are designated as FAA (Free agent, AL) and FAN (Free agent, NL).

Stats: Descriptions of all the categories appear in the Encyclopedia.

- The leading decimal point has been suppressed on some categories to conserve space.
- Data for platoons (vL, vR), balls-in-play (G/L/F) and consistency (Wk#, DOM, DIS) are for major league performance only.
- Formulas that use BIP data, like xERA and BPV, are used for years in which G/L/F data is available. Where feasible, older versions of these formulas are used otherwise.

Earned run average is presented alongside skills-based xERA. WHIP appears next, followed by opponents' overall OPS (oOPS). OPS splits vs. left-handed and right-handed batters appear to the right of oOPS. Batters faced per game (BF/G) provide a quick view of a pitcher's role—starters will generally have levels over 20.

Basic pitching skills are measured with Control, or walk rate (Ctl), Dominance, or strikeout rate (Dom), and Command, or strikeout-to-walk rate (Cmd). First-pitch strike rate (FpK) and Swinging strikeout rate (SwK) are also presented with these basic skills. Our research shows that FpK serves as a useful tool for validating Ctl, and SwK serves as a similar check on Dom.

Once the ball leaves the bat, it will either be a (G)round ball, (L)ine drive or (F)ly ball.

Random variance indicators include hit rate (H%)—often referred to as batting average on balls-in-play (BABIP)—which tends to regress to 30%. Normal strand rates (S%) fall within the tolerances of 65% to 80%. The ratio of home runs to fly balls (hr/f) is another sanity check; levels far from 10% are prone to regression.

In looking at consistency for starting pitchers, we track games started (GS), average pitch counts (APC) for all outings (for starters and relievers), the percentage of DOMinating starts (PQS 4 or 5) and DISaster starts (PQS 0 or 1). The larger the variance between DOM and DIS, the greater the consistency.

For relievers, we look at their saves success rate (Sv%) and Leverage Index (LI). A Doug Dennis study showed little correlation between saves success and future opportunity. However, you can increase your odds by prospecting for pitchers who have *both* a high saves percentage (80% or better) *and* high skills. Relievers with LI levels over 1.0 are being used more often by managers to win ballgames.

The final section includes several overall performance measures: runs above replacement (RAR), Base performance value (BPV), Base performance index (BPX, which is BPV indexed to each year's league average) and the Rotisserie value (R$).

2017 Projections

Forecasts are computed from a player's trends over the past five years. Adjustments were made for leading indicators and variances between skill and statistical output. After reviewing the leading indicators, you might opt to make further adjustments.

Although each year's numbers include all playing time at the Double-A level or above, the 2017 forecast only represents potential playing time at the major league level, and again is highly preliminary.

Note that the projected Rotisserie values in this book will not necessarily align with each player's historical actuals. Since we currently have no idea who is going to close games for the Reds, or whether Tyler Glasnow is going to break camp with the Pirates, it is impossible to create a finite pool of playing time, something which is required for valuation. So the projections are roughly based on a 12-team AL/NL league, and include an inflated number of innings, league-wide. This serves to flatten the spread of values and depress individual player dollar projections. In truth, a $25 player in this book might actually be worth $21, or $28. This level of precision is irrelevant in a process that is driven by market forces anyway. So, don't obsess over it.

Be aware of other sources that publish perfectly calibrated Rotisserie values over the winter. They are likely making arbitrary decisions as to where free agents are going to sign and who is going to land jobs in the spring. We do not make those leaps of faith here.

Bottom line… It is far too early to be making definitive projections for 2017, especially on playing time. Focus on the skill levels and trends, then consult BaseballHQ.com for playing time revisions as players change teams and roles become more defined. A free projections update will be available online in March.

Do-it-yourself analysis

Here are some data points you can look at in doing your own player analysis:

- Variance between vLH and vRH opposition OPS
- Variance in 2016 hr/f rate from 10%
- Variance in 2016 hit rate (H%) from 30%
- Variance in 2016 strand rate (S%) to tolerances (65% - 80%)
- Variance between ERA and xERA each year
- Growth or decline in Base Performance Value (BPV)
- Spikes in innings pitched
- Trends in average pitch counts (APC)
- Trends in DOM/DIS splits
- Trends in saves success rate (Sv%)
- Variance between Dom changes and corresponding SwK levels
- Variance between Ctl changes and corresponding FpK levels

Adleman,Timothy

Age: 29 | Th: R | Role: RP | Ht: 6' 5" | Wt: 225 | Type: FB

Health: D | PT/Exp: D | Consist: A | LIMA Plan: C | Rand Var: 0 | MM: 0101

4-4, 4.00 ERA in 70 IP at CIN. Former indy leaguer already exceeding expectations by cracking majors. While lack of strikeouts, FB tilt, age, 90-mph fastball, and no pedigree all conspire against him, tuck away that SwK and FpK combo and watch from a distance. There might be a buck worth spending here.

Yr Tm	W	L	Sv	IP	K	ERA	xERA	WHIP	oOPS	vL	vR	BF/G	Ctl	Dom	Cmd	FpK	SwK	G	L	F	H%	S%	hr/f	GS	APC	DOM%	DIS%	Sv%	LI	RAR	BPV	BPX	R$
12																																	
13																																	
14 aa	3	8	0	79	57	3.53	4.51	1.36				11.0	2.5	6.5	2.6						31%	78%								2.0	61	73	-$1
15 aa	9	10	0	150	91	3.77	4.87	1.57				24.4	3.5	5.5	1.6						33%	77%								3.5	43	51	-$4
16 CIN *	7	5	0	126	77	3.90	4.77	1.34	779	787	773	22.9	2.3	5.5	2.4	65%	10%	36	18	45	30%	77%	14%	13	85	15%	69%			4.6	40	48	$2
1st Half	3	1	0	36	26	5.11	4.40	1.39	764	1028	515	21.8	3.5	6.5	1.9	67%	10%	46	15	39	29%	65%	14%	4	84	0%	75%			-4.1	47	56	-$4
2nd Half	4	4	0	90	51	3.40	4.91	1.33	785	686	864	23.3	1.9	5.1	2.7	65%	10%	33	19	48	30%	82%	14%	9	86	22%	67%			8.7	41	49	$4
17 Proj	**5**	**5**	**0**	**87**	**67**	**3.91**	**4.73**	**1.36**	**789**	**837**	**747**	**19.7**	**2.9**	**6.9**	**2.4**	**66%**	**10%**	**38**	**18**	**44**	**31%**	**75%**	**9%**	**18**						**3.0**	**64**	**76**	**$0**

Alcantara,Raul

Age: 24 | Th: R | Role: SP | Ht: 6' 4" | Wt: 220 | Type: Con xFB

Health: A | PT/Exp: D | Consist: F | LIMA Plan: C | Rand Var: +5 | MM: 0001

1-3, 7.25 ERA in 22 IP at OAK. Command artist (32/3 K/BB in 45 IP at AAA), but inability to miss bats gives no hope for more strikeouts. Without a GB tilt, he'll be pounded into submission; see hit and hr/f rates for evidence. And pinpoint control not fully supported by FpK, so it's no sure thing. Speculate elsewhere.

Yr Tm	W	L	Sv	IP	K	ERA	xERA	WHIP	oOPS	vL	vR	BF/G	Ctl	Dom	Cmd	FpK	SwK	G	L	F	H%	S%	hr/f	GS	APC	DOM%	DIS%	Sv%	LI	RAR	BPV	BPX	R$
12																																	
13																																	
14 aa	2	0	0	20	8	2.50	2.70	1.19				26.3	2.2	3.9	1.7						28%	77%								3.0	65	77	-$1
15																																	
16 OAK *	10	9	0	158	98	4.91	5.31	1.46	1067	958	1189	22.5	2.0	5.6	2.8	61%	6%	40	17	43	33%	69%	26%	5	76	0%	60%			-14.0	49	59	-$4
1st Half	5	5	0	74	46	5.53	6.02	1.64				23.7	2.9	5.6	1.9						35%	68%	0%	0						-12.3	26	31	-$12
2nd Half	5	4	0	84	53	3.97	4.34	1.25	1067	958	1189	21.3	1.1	5.7	5.1	61%	6%	40	17	43	31%	71%	26%	5	76	0%	60%			2.2	107	128	$2
17 Proj	**5**	**8**	**0**	**116**	**73**	**4.62**	**4.98**	**1.40**	**728**	**663**	**801**	**22.2**	**1.8**	**5.6**	**3.1**	**61%**	**6%**	**40**	**17**	**43**	**33%**	**70%**	**8%**	**22**						**-6.1**	**70**	**84**	**-$4**

Allen,Cody

Age: 28 | Th: R | Role: RP | Ht: 6' 1" | Wt: 210 | Type: Pwr FB

Health: A | PT/Exp: A | Consist: A | LIMA Plan: C | Rand Var: -3 | MM: 4530

With three straight years of top-flight skills, he's firmly among the closing elite now. Eroding FB rate gives hope for even further upside. But he does carry a twinge of risk, since FpK decline suggests those early-season walks could return, especially since Ctl has been borderline for a while. Enjoy, but monitor that risk.

Yr Tm	W	L	Sv	IP	K	ERA	xERA	WHIP	oOPS	vL	vR	BF/G	Ctl	Dom	Cmd	FpK	SwK	G	L	F	H%	S%	hr/f	GS	APC	DOM%	DIS%	Sv%	LI	RAR	BPV	BPX	R$
12 CLE *	3	3	3	68	65	3.05	3.18	1.19	710	776	654	4.9	3.2	8.5	2.7	53%	10%	39	24	37	28%	78%	6%	0	20			50	0.44	8.2	91	119	$5
13 CLE	6	1	2	70	88	2.43	3.48	1.25	679	691	669	3.9	3.3	11.3	3.4	55%	12%	30	25	45	33%	85%	9%	0	16			50	1.11	12.4	121	158	$7
14 CLE	6	4	24	70	91	2.07	3.08	1.06	601	451	757	3.7	3.4	11.8	3.5	63%	14%	36	15	48	28%	87%	9%	0	15			86	1.43	14.4	135	161	$18
15 CLE	2	5	34	69	99	2.99	3.01	1.17	596	512	676	4.1	3.2	12.9	4.0	60%	14%	33	26	41	36%	73%	3%	0	16			89	1.23	8.3	155	184	$18
16 CLE	3	5	32	68	87	2.51	3.08	1.00	584	677	501	3.9	3.6	11.5	3.2	55%	14%	46	18	36	24%	82%	15%	0	17			91	1.25	14.0	135	160	$21
1st Half	2	3	17	35	42	3.12	3.52	1.15	638	744	542	4.1	4.4	10.9	2.5	60%	14%	48	17	35	25%	78%	14%	0	18			89	1.44	4.6	103	123	$19
2nd Half	1	2	15	33	45	1.89	2.66	0.84	522	600	456	3.7	2.7	12.2	4.5	50%	14%	42	20	38	22%	88%	16%	0	16			94	1.05	9.5	166	198	$23
17 Proj	**3**	**4**	**32**	**65**	**85**	**2.93**	**3.22**	**1.10**	**616**	**614**	**619**	**3.9**	**3.3**	**11.8**	**3.5**	**57%**	**14%**	**39**	**21**	**40**	**30%**	**77%**	**10%**	**0**						**10.1**	**139**	**166**	**$18**

Altavilla,Dan

Age: 24 | Th: R | Role: RP | Ht: 5' 11" | Wt: 200 | Type: Pwr

Health: A | PT/Exp: F | Consist: F | LIMA Plan: B | Rand Var: -5 | MM: 3310

0-0, 0.73 ERA in 12 IP at SEA. Starter-turned-reliever now an intriguing end-gamer. With competencies in missing bats, inducing groundballs, keeping both lefties and righties honest, and packing triple-digit heat, he's got the makings of a future closer. At minimum, a LIMA gem. With opportunity... UP: 20 Sv

Yr Tm	W	L	Sv	IP	K	ERA	xERA	WHIP	oOPS	vL	vR	BF/G	Ctl	Dom	Cmd	FpK	SwK	G	L	F	H%	S%	hr/f	GS	APC	DOM%	DIS%	Sv%	LI	RAR	BPV	BPX	R$
12																																	
13																																	
14																																	
15																																	
16 SEA *	7	3	16	69	66	2.21	2.94	1.21	560	552	563	4.8	3.1	8.6	2.8	69%	12%	50	25	25	30%	83%	0%	0	11			76	0.61	16.9	104	124	$14
1st Half	4	2	9	33	31	3.65	4.69	1.52				5.5	4.3	8.6	2.0						33%	79%	0%	0						2.2	65	77	$9
2nd Half	3	1	7	36	35	0.90	1.37	0.93	560	552	563	4.3	2.0	8.7	4.2	69%	12%	50	25	25	28%	89%	0%	0	11			78	0.61	14.7	156	186	$18
17 Proj	**4**	**2**	**2**	**65**	**62**	**2.72**	**3.68**	**1.17**				**4.7**	**3.0**	**8.6**	**2.9**	**0%**	**0%**	**44**	**22**	**33**	**30%**	**79%**	**8%**	**0**						**11.9**	**98**	**117**	**$5**

Alvarez,Dario

Age: 28 | Th: L | Role: RP | Ht: 6' 1" | Wt: 170 | Type: Pwr FB

Health: A | PT/Exp: F | Consist: F | LIMA Plan: C | Rand Var: +5 | MM: 2500

3-1, 5.06 ERA in 27 IP at TEX/ATL. On surface, a LOOGY who had nearly 2x as many IP against righties and flopped. But skills were good against both; blame hit and hr/f rates for that inflated OPS vR. His unavoidable risk is walks though, and with horrible FpK, it's not going away. For now, too risky to roster.

Yr Tm	W	L	Sv	IP	K	ERA	xERA	WHIP	oOPS	vL	vR	BF/G	Ctl	Dom	Cmd	FpK	SwK	G	L	F	H%	S%	hr/f	GS	APC	DOM%	DIS%	Sv%	LI	RAR	BPV	BPX	R$
12																																	
13																																	
14 NYM	0	0	0	1	1	13.50	5.68	3.00	1500	1750	1250	2.0	0.0	6.8	0.0	63%	26%	43	14	43	52%	67%	33%	0	8			0	1.68	-1.6	143	170	-$4
15 NYM *	4	2	0	46	52	4.06	3.18	1.27	1178	964	1571	3.5	4.4	10.3	2.4	45%	7%	15	15	69	29%	69%	22%	0	12			0	0.96	-0.5	99	117	-$1
16 2 TM *	5	2	1	58	80	6.49	6.21	1.68	803	693	866	4.6	4.1	12.4	3.0	46%	14%	39	21	40	42%	64%	24%	0	18			100	0.98	-16.4	81	97	-$7
1st Half	2	2	0	31	46	7.37	6.28	1.86	560	651	466	4.4	5.9	13.6	2.3	52%	20%	45	9	45	45%	61%	20%	0	15			0	1.23	-12.0	84	100	-$10
2nd Half	3	0	1	27	34	5.49	6.12	1.49	888	718	966	4.9	2.1	11.1	5.2	43%	12%	37	24	39	39%	70%	25%	0	19			100	0.87	-4.4	108	129	-$5
17 Proj	**4**	**1**	**0**	**44**	**53**	**4.62**	**4.07**	**1.42**	**637**	**538**	**682**	**4.0**	**4.5**	**11.0**	**2.4**	**43%**	**12%**	**37**	**24**	**39**	**32%**	**71%**	**14%**	**0**						**-2.3**	**91**	**108**	**-$2**

Alvarez,Jose

Age: 28 | Th: L | Role: RP | Ht: 5' 10" | Wt: 190 | Type:

Health: A | PT/Exp: D | Consist: C | LIMA Plan: C | Rand Var: 0 | MM: 1100

When you play in a deep league, any arm who posts decent stats is on the table. Discount that sub-2 ERA and good skills in 2nd half as that was done over a tiny sample and there's little in history to support it. FB that barely cracks 90 mph cements it. Spend your dollar elsewhere.

Yr Tm	W	L	Sv	IP	K	ERA	xERA	WHIP	oOPS	vL	vR	BF/G	Ctl	Dom	Cmd	FpK	SwK	G	L	F	H%	S%	hr/f	GS	APC	DOM%	DIS%	Sv%	LI	RAR	BPV	BPX	R$
12 aa	6	9	0	136	63	5.15	4.43	1.40				23.0	1.9	4.2	2.2						32%	62%								-19.1	51	66	-$8
13 DET *	9	11	1	167	123	4.14	4.33	1.33	866	851	872	19.8	2.3	6.6	2.9	55%	11%	40	23	37	31%	72%	16%	6	50	0%	50%	100	1.22	-5.6	68	89	$1
14 LAA *	0	2	0	31	15	5.64	5.65	1.53	667	0	2000	17.0	3.5	4.3	1.2	67%	20%	50	0	50	29%	67%	0%	0	5			0	1.79	-7.3	0	0	-$7
15 LAA	4	3	0	67	59	3.49	3.74	1.21	642	575	690	4.4	3.1	7.9	2.6	69%	11%	51	19	30	29%	72%	9%	0	16			0	0.89	3.9	88	105	$2
16 LAA	1	3	0	57	51	3.45	4.24	1.50	745	671	811	4.0	2.4	8.0	3.4	64%	10%	44	24	32	38%	78%	7%	0	15			0	0.94	5.2	103	122	-$2
1st Half	1	2	0	37	35	4.38	4.16	1.59	802	663	928	4.1	2.9	8.5	2.9	64%	10%	45	23	31	39%	73%	8%	0	15			0	1.01	-0.9	98	116	-$3
2nd Half	0	1	0	20	16	1.77	4.39	1.33	645	684	611	3.8	1.3	7.1	5.3	63%	10%	41	25	34	36%	88%	4%	0	13			0	0.82	6.1	110	132	-$1
17 Proj	**1**	**3**	**0**	**58**	**45**	**3.61**	**4.26**	**1.39**	**725**	**680**	**760**	**4.9**	**2.5**	**7.0**	**2.8**	**64%**	**11%**	**45**	**22**	**32**	**33%**	**76%**	**9%**	**0**						**4.2**	**82**	**98**	**-$2**

Anderson,Brett

Age: 29 | Th: L | Role: SP | Ht: 6' 4" | Wt: 215 | Type: xGB

Health: F | PT/Exp: C | Consist: C | LIMA Plan: C | Rand Var: +5 | MM: 3101

Just when 2015 gave a glimmer of hope, he went under knife again, reminding us the one constant here is his lack-of-health grade. Long history of xERA in mid-3s tells us he can have value in doses. But you can't buy health. Still, this is the perfect, easily fungible end-gamer that could make a difference one year.

Yr Tm	W	L	Sv	IP	K	ERA	xERA	WHIP	oOPS	vL	vR	BF/G	Ctl	Dom	Cmd	FpK	SwK	G	L	F	H%	S%	hr/f	GS	APC	DOM%	DIS%	Sv%	LI	RAR	BPV	BPX	R$
12 OAK *	5	3	0	58	40	3.28	3.47	1.20	565	515	581	21.3	1.8	6.2	3.4	62%	9%	60	24	17	30%	74%	6%	6	88	33%	17%			5.3	91	118	$2
13 OAK	1	4	3	45	46	6.04	3.36	1.61	794	853	774	12.5	4.2	9.3	2.2	58%	9%	63	16	21	37%	63%	18%	5	48	40%	40%	100	0.78	-12.0	94	122	-$7
14 COL	1	3	0	43	29	2.91	3.55	1.32	688	724	675	22.5	2.7	6.0	2.2	62%	9%	61	17	22	32%	77%	3%	8	83	25%	25%			4.5	75	89	-$1
15 LA	10	9	0	180	116	3.69	3.53	1.33	726	698	737	24.2	2.3	5.8	2.5	58%	8%	66	15	19	31%	75%	17%	31	88	13%	39%			6.0	86	103	$5
16 LA	1	2	0	11	5	11.91	6.27	2.56	1208	1267	1178	15.5	3.2	4.0	1.3	67%	6%	50	29	21	44%	56%	36%	3	52	0%	100%	0	0.71	-10.8	14	16	-$9
1st Half																																	
2nd Half	1	2	0	11	5	11.91	6.27	2.56	1208	1267	1178	15.5	3.2	4.0	1.3	67%	6%	50	29	21	44%	56%	36%	3	52	0%	100%	0	0.71	-10.8	14	16	-$9
17 Proj	**6**	**4**	**0**	**87**	**69**	**3.88**	**3.66**	**1.34**	**695**	**706**	**690**	**21.2**	**3.0**	**7.1**	**2.4**	**59%**	**9%**	**63**	**17**	**20**	**31%**	**72%**	**12%**	**15**						**3.4**	**88**	**105**	**$1**

STEPHEN NICKRAND

Anderson,Chase

Age: 29	Th: R	Role: SP	Health	B	LIMA Plan	B+
Ht: 6' 0"	Wt: 190	Type:	PT/Exp	B	Rand Var	+1
			Consist	A	MM	1103

Proof that not all guys with starting roles are worth your time. This one has lucked into IP by being on bad teams last two seasons. As FpK keeps declining, SwK won't help him push his strikeout needle, so Cmd will erode further. He's already getting hit hard enough as it is. Risk far outweighs reward.

Yr Tm	W	L	Sv	IP	K	ERA	xERA	WHIP	oOPS	vL	vR	BF/G	Ctl	Dom	Cmd	FpK	SwK	G	L	F	H%	S%	hr/f	GS	APC	DOM%	DIS%	Sv%	LI	RAR	BPV	BPX	R$
12 aa	5	4	0	104	79	3.70	4.23	1.31				20.5	2.2	6.8	3.0						32%	75%								4.1	76	99	$1
13 aaa	4	7	0	88	63	5.76	5.84	1.67				15.2	3.1	6.4	2.0						36%	66%								-20.6	41	53	-$12
14 ARI *	13	9	0	153	135	3.23	3.79	1.25	779	714	831	23.1	2.7	7.9	2.9	63%	10%	40	24	36	30%	78%	14%	21	90	10%	33%			9.7	82	98	$9
15 ARI	6	6	0	153	111	4.30	4.16	1.30	754	746	761	23.7	2.4	6.5	2.8	62%	8%	42	24	34	30%	69%	11%	27	91	11%	26%			-6.4	74	88	$0
16 MIL	9	11	0	152	120	4.39	4.75	1.37	819	664	935	20.9	3.1	7.1	2.3	58%	9%	36	23	41	29%	74%	15%	30	85	13%	47%	0	0.78	-3.8	57	68	$1
1st Half	4	9	0	82	62	5.49	4.90	1.38	835	660	1005	22.3	3.1	6.8	2.2	58%	8%	36	23	41	29%	66%	16%	16	90	19%	50%			-13.1	54	64	-$3
2nd Half	5	2	0	70	58	3.10	4.59	1.36	798	672	869	19.4	3.2	7.5	2.3	57%	9%	36	23	41	30%	85%	13%	14	80	7%	43%	0	0.76	9.4	62	74	$7
17 Proj	**8**	**10**	**0**	**160**	**126**	**4.40**	**4.50**	**1.35**	**785**	**700**	**850**	**23.1**	**2.9**	**7.1**	**2.5**	**60%**	**9%**	**39**	**23**	**38**	**30%**	**71%**	**13%**	**26**						**-4.1**	**67**	**80**	**$0**

Anderson,Cody

Age: 26	Th: R	Role: RP	Health	A	LIMA Plan	C
Ht: 6' 4"	Wt: 240	Type:	PT/Exp	D	Rand Var	+5
			Consist	F	MM	1101

2-5, 6.68 ERA in 61 IP at CLE. Strong 2015 MLB debut indeed turned out to be a fluke, as that 1st half shows. But 120+ BPV in 2nd half out of the bullpen suggests there's still something rosterable. Rising SwK supports late K surge. As long as he's in the pen, call him an "end-of-staff filler that won't hurt you."

Yr Tm	W	L	Sv	IP	K	ERA	xERA	WHIP	oOPS	vL	vR	BF/G	Ctl	Dom	Cmd	FpK	SwK	G	L	F	H%	S%	hr/f	GS	APC	DOM%	DIS%	Sv%	LI	RAR	BPV	BPX	R$
12																																	
13																																	
14 aa	4	11	0	126	68	6.34	5.97	1.63				22.4	3.1	4.9	1.6						33%	62%								-40.3	16	19	-$19
15 CLE *	11	6	0	163	87	2.90	3.34	1.19	647	715	594	23.3	2.2	4.8	2.2	61%	8%	46	21	34	28%	78%	9%	15	86	13%	27%			21.4	60	71	$13
16 CLE *	2	7	1	93	85	6.15	6.52	1.62	935	930	941	12.9	2.3	8.2	3.5	58%	12%	40	26	34	38%	66%	19%	9	52	11%	56%	100	0.70	-22.4	60	71	-$12
1st Half	1	5	0	63	53	7.42	7.50	1.71	953	987	914	21.8	2.4	7.6	3.1	57%	12%	40	26	34	37%	61%	22%	8	79	13%	63%	0	0.97	-25.0	29	34	-$16
2nd Half	1	2	1	30	32	3.52	4.49	1.43	889	776	1008	6.8	2.1	9.5	4.4	59%	13%	40	27	33	39%	76%	12%	1	28	0%	0%	100	0.46	2.5	127	152	-$2
17 Proj	**3**	**4**	**0**	**73**	**55**	**4.15**	**4.30**	**1.35**	**769**	**769**	**769**	**13.0**	**2.3**	**6.8**	**2.9**	**59%**	**11%**	**42**	**24**	**33**	**32%**	**72%**	**11%**	**7**						**0.3**	**79**	**94**	**-$2**

Anderson,Tyler

Age: 27	Th: L	Role: SP	Health	C	LIMA Plan	B
Ht: 6' 4"	Wt: 210	Type: GB	PT/Exp	D	Rand Var	0
			Consist	A	MM	2103

5-6, 3.54 ERA in 114 IP at COL. Former first rounder finally shook off arm woes and looked good in MLB debut. That command came with full underlying support, so don't dismiss it. And GB profile gives him a higher floor than you'd expect from a thin-air pitcher. Very rosterable as long as shoulder, elbow stay attached.

Yr Tm	W	L	Sv	IP	K	ERA	xERA	WHIP	oOPS	vL	vR	BF/G	Ctl	Dom	Cmd	FpK	SwK	G	L	F	H%	S%	hr/f	GS	APC	DOM%	DIS%	Sv%	LI	RAR	BPV	BPX	R$
12																																	
13																																	
14 aa	7	4	0	118	83	2.94	3.64	1.38				21.6	3.4	6.3	1.8						31%	78%								11.7	68	81	$3
15																																	
16 COL *	7	8	0	141	116	3.47	4.07	1.31	742	607	783	24.3	2.4	7.4	3.1	64%	11%	51	20	29	32%	76%	12%	19	94	16%	11%			12.5	84	100	$6
1st Half	2	4	0	51	41	2.93	3.94	1.37	697	625	722	23.6	2.6	7.3	2.8	66%	11%	60	22	18	34%	79%	8%	4	99	25%	0%			7.9	89	106	$3
2nd Half	5	4	0	91	75	3.77	3.94	1.28	754	602	798	25.2	2.3	7.4	3.3	63%	11%	49	20	31	31%	74%	13%	15	93	13%	13%			4.7	99	118	$8
17 Proj	**8**	**8**	**0**	**160**	**123**	**3.26**	**4.01**	**1.34**	**718**	**618**	**750**	**23.1**	**2.8**	**7.0**	**2.5**	**65%**	**11%**	**53**	**21**	**26**	**32%**	**77%**	**9%**	**29**						**18.3**	**80**	**95**	**$7**

Andriese,Matt

Age: 27	Th: R	Role: RP	Health	A	LIMA Plan	B+
Ht: 6' 3"	Wt: 210	Type:	PT/Exp	D	Rand Var	0
			Consist	A	MM	2203

8-8, 4.37 ERA in 128 IP at TAM. On surface, these are stats you don't want. But 3 reasons he should be one of your top speculative targets... 1) Huge skill growth in 2nd half supported by FpK, SwK; 2) Fluky H%, S%, hr/f kept that growth hidden; 3) good skills vs. LH and RH says he can stick as a SP. UP: 3.00 ERA, 200 K

Yr Tm	W	L	Sv	IP	K	ERA	xERA	WHIP	oOPS	vL	vR	BF/G	Ctl	Dom	Cmd	FpK	SwK	G	L	F	H%	S%	hr/f	GS	APC	DOM%	DIS%	Sv%	LI	RAR	BPV	BPX	R$
12																																	
13 a/a	11	7	0	135	91	3.36	3.52	1.28				20.4	1.8	6.1	3.4						33%	73%								8.4	97	127	$7
14 aaa	11	8	0	162	107	4.83	4.94	1.46				24.8	2.9	5.9	2.1						32%	69%								-21.8	44	53	-$7
15 TAM *	6	8	2	131	105	3.59	4.31	1.36	728	785	677	14.4	2.0	7.3	3.7	59%	9%	48	17	35	35%	75%	11%	8	44	13%	50%	100	0.77	6.0	97	115	$3
16 TAM *	9	10	1	162	144	4.45	4.20	1.27	720	706	732	18.9	1.8	8.0	4.4	66%	11%	43	19	38	33%	67%	11%	19	68	11%	26%	100	0.81	-5.2	108	128	$5
1st Half	7	4	0	94	76	3.66	3.32	1.24	597	559	622	20.0	2.3	7.3	3.2	64%	10%	46	20	34	32%	70%	3%	8	69	13%	25%	0	0.95	6.1	101	121	$11
2nd Half	2	6	1	68	68	5.53	3.85	1.30	815	792	840	18.1	1.2	9.0	7.6	68%	12%	40	18	42	34%	64%	17%	11	68	9%	27%	100	0.69	-11.3	147	176	-$3
17 Proj	**9**	**9**	**0**	**152**	**136**	**3.63**	**3.89**	**1.25**	**706**	**718**	**695**	**17.8**	**2.0**	**8.0**	**3.9**	**63%**	**10%**	**45**	**18**	**37**	**32%**	**75%**	**11%**	**27**						**10.5**	**113**	**134**	**$8**

Archer,Chris

Age: 28	Th: R	Role: SP	Health	A	LIMA Plan	B
Ht: 6' 3"	Wt: 200	Type: Pwr	PT/Exp	A	Rand Var	+2
			Consist	A	MM	3405

Just when we thought he was an ace, he sabotaged many rotations in 1st half. Fortunately, that blowup was fueled by H% and hr/f, both of which regressed, pushing ERA back to where it should be. And that late skill rejuvenation is the best we've ever seen from him. There's plenty of profit here now. UP: Cy Young

Yr Tm	W	L	Sv	IP	K	ERA	xERA	WHIP	oOPS	vL	vR	BF/G	Ctl	Dom	Cmd	FpK	SwK	G	L	F	H%	S%	hr/f	GS	APC	DOM%	DIS%	Sv%	LI	RAR	BPV	BPX	R$
12 TAM *	8	12	0	157	154	4.19	3.21	1.32	624	915	435	21.0	4.2	8.8	2.1	62%	10%	44	18	38	30%	68%	11%	4	82	50%	0%	0	0.99	-3.3	90	118	$3
13 TAM *	14	10	0	179	144	3.64	3.79	1.27	660	801	455	22.1	3.1	7.3	2.4	58%	9%	47	19	34	29%	75%	12%	23	91	26%	30%			5.1	66	87	$10
14 TAM	10	9	0	195	173	3.33	3.68	1.28	650	624	685	25.7	3.3	8.0	2.4	57%	10%	47	22	31	31%	75%	7%	32	99	31%	19%			9.9	79	94	$9
15 TAM	12	13	0	212	252	3.23	3.12	1.14	613	604	622	25.5	2.8	10.7	3.8	64%	13%	46	20	34	31%	74%	10%	34	101	44%	15%			19.2	141	168	$22
16 TAM	9	19	0	201	233	4.02	3.50	1.24	703	698	708	25.8	3.0	10.4	3.5	58%	13%	48	18	35	31%	73%	16%	33	103	36%	27%			4.1	133	158	$12
1st Half	4	11	0	104	127	4.50	3.73	1.43	766	755	776	25.4	4.0	11.0	2.8	57%	12%	46	21	33	34%	73%	18%	18	102	22%	44%			-4.0	114	136	$4
2nd Half	5	8	0	97	106	3.51	3.25	1.04	631	637	625	26.1	1.9	9.8	5.0	60%	13%	50	14	36	28%	72%	14%	15	104	53%	7%			8.1	152	181	$20
17 Proj	**13**	**11**	**0**	**203**	**221**	**3.21**	**3.42**	**1.15**	**625**	**632**	**619**	**24.1**	**2.9**	**9.8**	**3.4**	**60%**	**12%**	**47**	**19**	**34**	**30%**	**75%**	**11%**	**33**						**24.6**	**124**	**147**	**$21**

Arrieta,Jake

Age: 31	Th: R	Role: SP	Health	B	LIMA Plan	D+
Ht: 6' 4"	Wt: 225	Type: Pwr GB	PT/Exp	A	Rand Var	-2
			Consist	B	MM	3305

Nobody expected a repeat of 2015 breakout, but 1st half line would have been fine had he been able to keep it up. Regression in control was foretold by FpK, which gives it the look of a potentially chronic issue. Late fade raises workload concerns given 2015 IP spike and prior arm issues. For 2017, call him a cautionary ace.

Yr Tm	W	L	Sv	IP	K	ERA	xERA	WHIP	oOPS	vL	vR	BF/G	Ctl	Dom	Cmd	FpK	SwK	G	L	F	H%	S%	hr/f	GS	APC	DOM%	DIS%	Sv%	LI	RAR	BPV	BPX	R$
12 BAL *	8	13	0	171	151	6.13	4.74	1.47	763	846	664	21.5	3.6	8.0	2.2	56%	8%	44	24	32	33%	58%	15%	18	82	28%	22%	0	0.79	-44.6	62	81	-$15
13 2 TM *	12	9	0	155	120	5.06	4.43	1.49	718	664	775	22.2	4.4	7.0	1.6	60%	7%	40	25	34	31%	67%	12%	14	90	14%	29%			-22.8	50	65	-$7
14 CHC	10	5	0	157	167	2.53	2.79	0.99	535	553	520	24.6	2.4	9.6	4.1	59%	11%	49	22	28	28%	74%	4%	25	97	60%	12%			23.4	136	162	$20
15 CHC	22	6	0	229	236	1.77	2.62	0.86	507	449	557	26.4	1.9	9.3	4.9	60%	11%	56	21	23	25%	81%	8%	33	104	67%	3%			62.0	150	179	$51
16 CHC	18	8	0	197	190	3.10	3.60	1.08	583	612	557	25.6	3.5	8.7	2.5	59%	11%	53	20	28	25%	74%	11%	31	101	42%	19%			26.5	93	111	$26
1st Half	12	3	0	108	115	2.33	3.33	1.06	538	629	463	25.6	3.5	9.6	2.7	59%	11%	54	19	26	26%	79%	7%	17	103	47%	18%			24.9	110	131	$34
2nd Half	6	5	0	89	75	4.04	3.94	1.11	638	593	676	25.6	3.4	7.6	2.2	59%	10%	51	20	30	23%	67%	15%	14	98	36%	21%			1.6	73	86	$16
17 Proj	**16**	**9**	**0**	**203**	**196**	**3.32**	**3.50**	**1.13**	**617**	**615**	**619**	**25.0**	**3.2**	**8.7**	**2.7**	**59%**	**11%**	**52**	**21**	**27**	**28%**	**72%**	**10%**	**32**						**21.7**	**100**	**120**	**$21**

Axford,John

Age: 34	Th: R	Role: RP	Health	A	LIMA Plan	B+
Ht: 6' 5"	Wt: 195	Type: Pwr GB	PT/Exp	C	Rand Var	0
			Consist	A	MM	2400

He'll keep getting attention as plan B closer, since he's been in the mix for awhile now and has gotten full-time shot two of last five years. But skills simply don't support end-game work. What Dom and GB gives him, chronic wildness takes away. Inability to get strike one (FpK) says that's not changing any time soon.

Yr Tm	W	L	Sv	IP	K	ERA	xERA	WHIP	oOPS	vL	vR	BF/G	Ctl	Dom	Cmd	FpK	SwK	G	L	F	H%	S%	hr/f	GS	APC	DOM%	DIS%	Sv%	LI	RAR	BPV	BPX	R$
12 MIL	5	8	35	69	93	4.67	3.42	1.44	717	671	767	4.1	5.1	12.1	2.4	54%	11%	46	24	30	33%	71%	19%	0	19			80	1.22	-5.6	105	136	$12
13 2 NL	7	7	0	65	65	4.02	3.74	1.52	796	838	761	3.9	3.6	9.0	2.5	53%	10%	45	24	31	35%	79%	17%	0	16			0	1.11	-1.2	88	114	-$2
14 2 TM	2	4	10	55	63	3.95	3.77	1.45	691	630	743	3.9	5.9	10.4	1.8	57%	10%	54	14	33	29%	75%	13%	0	17			77	1.07	-1.4	59	70	$1
15 COL	4	5	25	56	62	4.20	3.84	1.58	704	671	731	4.2	5.2	10.0	1.9	51%	11%	56	17	27	35%	74%	10%	0	18			81	1.16	-1.7	75	89	$6
16 OAK	6	4	3	66	60	3.97	4.17	1.45	711	671	744	4.3	4.1	8.2	2.0	51%	11%	54	19	27	32%	74%	12%	0	18			30	1.01	1.7	69	82	$1
1st Half	3	2	1	33	27	5.51	4.49	1.59	833	832	832	4.1	3.3	7.4	2.3	51%	10%	51	17	32	35%	68%	15%	0	17			20	1.12	-5.3	74	88	-$4
2nd Half	3	2	2	33	33	2.45	3.84	1.30	578	486	647	4.4	4.9	9.0	1.8	51%	12%	58	20	22	29%	81%	5%	0	19			40	0.88	7.1	65	78	$5
17 Proj	**4**	**5**	**1**	**58**	**60**	**4.07**	**4.00**	**1.47**	**698**	**657**	**733**	**4.0**	**4.7**	**9.3**	**2.0**	**52%**	**11%**	**54**	**18**	**28**	**32%**	**74%**	**12%**	**0**						**0.8**	**71**	**85**	**-$2**

STEPHEN NICKRAND

Baez,Pedro

Health: C | LIMA Plan: B+
Age: 29 | Th: R | Role: RP | PT/Exp: D | Rand Var: -1
Ht: 6' 2" | Wt: 195 | Type: Pwr FB | Consist: A | MM: 3411

It's easy to dismiss setup guys who don't get a sniff at finishing games. But this one now has back-to-back seasons of elite peripherals, and with strong SwK/FpK support, they're no fluke. Steady reduction in FB% says he hasn't peaked yet. A LIMA gem without opportunity. With it, a legit stopper. UP: 30 Saves

Yr Tm	W	L	Sv	IP	K	ERA	xERA	WHIP	oOPS	vL	vR	BF/G	Ctl	Dom	Cmd	FpK	SwK	G	L	F	H%	S%	hr/f	GS	APC	DOM%	DIS%	Sv%	LI	RAR	BPV	BPX	R$
12																																	
13 aa	1	1	0	23	19	5.47	6.30	1.71				6.6	3.2	7.3	2.3						37%	71%								-4.6	41	53	-$6
14 LA *	2	1	12	66	49	3.28	3.40	1.16	537	578	501	4.4	2.2	6.7	3.0	61%	10%	37	15	49	28%	75%	9%	0	18			100	0.46	3.7	81	97	$6
15 LA	4	2	0	51	60	3.35	3.27	1.14	693	735	678	4.0	1.9	10.6	5.5	66%	16%	38	19	44	34%	72%	7%	0	16			0	1.20	3.8	154	184	$2
16 LA	3	2	0	74	83	3.04	3.39	1.00	615	553	649	4.0	2.7	10.1	3.8	63%	15%	43	20	38	25%	78%	16%	0	16			0	1.02	10.5	130	155	$7
1st Half	1	2	0	37	44	3.68	3.17	1.01	627	608	636	4.0	2.9	10.8	3.7	65%	16%	47	20	33	23%	73%	24%	0	16			0	1.14	2.3	139	166	$5
2nd Half	2	0	0	37	39	2.41	3.59	0.99	604	502	663	4.1	2.4	9.4	3.9	62%	14%	39	19	42	26%	82%	10%	0	16			0	0.90	8.2	121	144	$9
17 Proj	**4**	**2**	**4**	**73**	**78**	**3.12**	**3.48**	**1.07**	**653**	**615**	**671**	**4.0**	**2.3**	**9.7**	**4.2**	**64%**	**15%**	**40**	**19**	**40**	**29%**	**76%**	**11%**	**0**						**9.5**	**130**	**155**	**$7**

Bailey,Andrew

Health: D | LIMA Plan: D+
Age: 33 | Th: R | Role: RP | PT/Exp: F | Rand Var: +2
Ht: 6' 3" | Wt: 245 | Type: Pwr FB | Consist: A | MM: 0200

3-1, 5.36 ERA with 6 Sv in 44 IP at PHI/LAA. Proof that too many arms keep getting save opps even when they don't deserve them. Couldn't keep up 1st half momentum, and with health woes, that shouldn't have been a surprise. Late struggles confirm he'll get exposed even when healthy. No longer worthy of speculation.

Yr Tm	W	L	Sv	IP	K	ERA	xERA	WHIP	oOPS	vL	vR	BF/G	Ctl	Dom	Cmd	FpK	SwK	G	L	F	H%	S%	hr/f	GS	APC	DOM%	DIS%	Sv%	LI	RAR	BPV	BPX	R$
12 BOS	1	1	6	15	14	7.04	5.33	1.89	862	1084	636	3.9	4.7	8.2	1.8	55%	7%	33	23	44	39%	63%	9%	0	16			67	1.20	-5.7	32	42	-$5
13 BOS	3	1	8	29	39	3.77	3.32	1.22	761	661	872	3.9	3.8	12.2	3.3	56%	12%	22	24	54	28%	82%	21%	0	16			62	1.21	0.3	119	155	$2
14																																	
15 NYY *	1	1	6	35	28	2.85	4.20	1.43	812	433	1021	5.0	4.1	7.3	1.8	51%	13%	41	14	45	30%	84%	15%	0	17			86	0.38	4.8	57	68	$0
16 2 TM *	6	2	7	59	58	4.52	3.91	1.30	757	651	824	4.2	3.4	9.0	2.6	65%	10%	40	18	42	31%	68%	13%	0	18			78	0.92	-2.4	82	98	$3
1st Half	3	0	0	27	28	4.39	3.76	1.05	674	593	715	4.3	3.0	9.5	3.1	65%	11%	40	17	43	24%	63%	14%	0	18			0	1.09	-0.7	106	127	$6
2nd Half	0	1	6	17	13	6.88	5.73	1.76	864	708	990	4.2	4.2	6.9	1.6	63%	9%	40	20	40	35%	63%	13%	0	17			100	0.71	-5.6	28	33	$0
17 Proj	**2**	**1**	**0**	**44**	**37**	**4.63**	**4.78**	**1.45**	**761**	**643**	**843**	**4.3**	**3.9**	**7.6**	**2.0**	**64%**	**10%**	**40**	**19**	**41**	**31%**	**72%**	**12%**	**0**						**-2.3**	**51**	**60**	**-$4**

Bailey,Homer

Health: F | LIMA Plan: B+
Age: 31 | Th: R | Role: SP | PT/Exp: D | Rand Var: +2
Ht: 6' 3" | Wt: 205 | Type: Pwr | Consist: F | MM: 2203

2-3, 6.65 ERA in 26 IP at CIN. On road back to full health after May 2015 TJS. Bad finish, lack of usable skills shouldn't come as a surprise given lingering biceps tenderness. There was a lot to like pre-surgery, including rising GB% and solid command-related skills. If healthy in spring, there's still a $15 pitcher here.

Yr Tm	W	L	Sv	IP	K	ERA	xERA	WHIP	oOPS	vL	vR	BF/G	Ctl	Dom	Cmd	FpK	SwK	G	L	F	H%	S%	hr/f	GS	APC	DOM%	DIS%	Sv%	LI	RAR	BPV	BPX	R$
12 CIN	13	10	0	208	168	3.68	3.92	1.24	718	682	747	26.5	2.3	7.3	3.2	66%	10%	45	20	35	30%	75%	12%	33	101	36%	36%			8.6	93	121	$12
13 CIN	11	12	0	209	199	3.49	3.29	1.12	660	746	575	26.5	2.3	8.6	3.7	64%	11%	46	19	34	29%	72%	10%	32	103	38%	22%			9.7	115	150	$16
14 CIN	9	5	0	146	124	3.71	3.46	1.23	703	750	666	26.3	2.8	7.7	2.8	62%	11%	51	21	29	29%	73%	13%	23	99	35%	26%			0.6	92	109	$5
15 CIN	0	1	0	11	3	5.56	5.64	1.76	1009	1424	707	25.5	3.2	2.4	0.8	63%	7%	52	17	31	31%	76%	23%	2	86	0%	100%			-2.2	-13	-15	-$6
16 CIN *	3	6	0	51	44	7.67	9.53	2.16	816	968	706	18.1	3.8	7.8	2.1	54%	10%	45	30	25	43%	69%	11%	6	76	17%	33%			-21.9	-5	-5	-$15
1st Half	0	2	0	11	9	8.38	14.43	2.80				15.0	4.4	7.2	1.6						48%	80%	0%	0						-5.5	-86	-102	-$9
2nd Half	3	4	0	40	36	7.49	8.24	1.99	816	968	706	19.4	3.6	7.9	2.2	54%	10%	45	30	25	41%	65%	11%	6	76	17%	33%			-16.4	18	22	-$16
17 Proj	**8**	**8**	**0**	**131**	**116**	**4.03**	**3.96**	**1.35**	**723**	**798**	**661**	**22.8**	**2.8**	**8.0**	**2.9**	**61%**	**11%**	**47**	**23**	**31**	**32%**	**73%**	**13%**	**24**						**2.6**	**94**	**112**	**$2**

Barnes,Jacob

Health: C | LIMA Plan: C
Age: 27 | Th: R | Role: RP | PT/Exp: D | Rand Var: -4
Ht: 6' 2" | Wt: 220 | Type: Pwr | Consist: D | MM: 2200

0-1, 2.70 ERA in 27 IP at MIL. Elbow issues cut season short, but there's something really good here. Top-tier SwK supports double-digit K rate, and few pitchers were filthier vR than this one (19/1 K/BB in 15 IP). With health and an out pitch vL, expect higher leverage to follow, meaning he could get into late-game mix.

Yr Tm	W	L	Sv	IP	K	ERA	xERA	WHIP	oOPS	vL	vR	BF/G	Ctl	Dom	Cmd	FpK	SwK	G	L	F	H%	S%	hr/f	GS	APC	DOM%	DIS%	Sv%	LI	RAR	BPV	BPX	R$
12																																	
13																																	
14 aa	2	6	0	106	63	5.25	4.56	1.43				19.5	3.5	5.4	1.6						30%	64%								-19.6	35	42	-$9
15 aa	4	5	0	75	68	4.85	5.20	1.73				8.7	4.1	8.2	2.0						39%	70%								-8.2	74	88	-$8
16 MIL *	2	2	2	52	47	2.10	2.62	1.12	612	820	437	4.3	2.4	8.3	3.4	62%	16%	49	21	31	30%	82%	5%	0	15			67	0.55	13.3	118	141	$5
1st Half	2	2	1	34	33	2.51	2.97	1.19	746	862	588	4.8	3.0	8.7	2.9	67%	16%	58	19	23	30%	81%	14%	0	17			50	0.31	7.1	105	126	$5
2nd Half	0	0	1	17	14	1.04	1.49	0.90	491	757	348	3.6	1.0	7.4	7.1	57%	15%	41	22	37	28%	87%	0%	0	13			100	0.74	6.7	205	244	$3
17 Proj	**1**	**2**	**0**	**44**	**39**	**3.51**	**4.00**	**1.24**				**5.8**	**2.8**	**8.0**	**2.8**	**0%**	**0%**	**45**	**20**	**35**	**30%**	**74%**	**9%**	**0**						**3.6**	**90**	**107**	**-$1**

Barnes,Matt

Health: A | LIMA Plan: C
Age: 27 | Th: R | Role: RP | PT/Exp: D | Rand Var: 0
Ht: 6' 4" | Wt: 205 | Type: Pwr | Consist: F | MM: 1301

Skills finally showed signs of life after giving up starting for good. While the 5+ ERA might suggest otherwise, his 2nd half triple-digit peripherals were backed by a big surge in both FpK and SwK, and he did it in high-leverage spots. Blame an aberrant H% for that ERA spike. If 2H gains stick... UP: double-digit saves

Yr Tm	W	L	Sv	IP	K	ERA	xERA	WHIP	oOPS	vL	vR	BF/G	Ctl	Dom	Cmd	FpK	SwK	G	L	F	H%	S%	hr/f	GS	APC	DOM%	DIS%	Sv%	LI	RAR	BPV	BPX	R$
12																																	
13 a/a	6	10	0	113	119	5.01	5.09	1.59				20.0	3.8	9.4	2.5						38%	70%								-16.0	78	101	-$8
14 BOS *	8	9	0	137	93	4.98	4.57	1.50	861	1000	762	21.1	3.3	6.1	1.8	67%	13%	31	21	48	33%	66%	7%	0	31			0	0.27	-21.0	54	64	-$9
15 BOS *	4	5	0	81	72	5.68	6.34	1.77	887	800	959	7.6	4.5	8.1	1.8	58%	10%	39	22	40	37%	71%	16%	2	25	0%	100%	0	0.88	-17.1	37	44	-$12
16 BOS	4	3	1	67	71	4.05	4.03	1.40	711	741	693	4.6	4.2	9.6	2.3	58%	11%	46	21	33	32%	72%	10%	0	19			50	1.08	1.1	84	99	$0
1st Half	2	3	0	39	38	3.20	4.31	1.35	722	879	643	5.5	4.1	8.7	2.1	55%	10%	43	23	35	30%	80%	11%	0	22			0	0.81	4.8	66	79	$2
2nd Half	2	0	1	27	33	5.27	3.62	1.46	696	593	778	3.8	4.3	10.9	2.5	62%	13%	50	19	31	36%	63%	9%	0	16			50	1.35	-3.6	108	129	-$3
17 Proj	**4**	**4**	**0**	**73**	**71**	**3.90**	**4.16**	**1.37**	**688**	**656**	**712**	**6.0**	**3.9**	**8.9**	**2.3**	**59%**	**11%**	**44**	**21**	**35**	**31%**	**74%**	**11%**	**0**						**2.6**	**77**	**92**	**$0**

Barnette,Tony

Health: A | LIMA Plan: B
Age: 33 | Th: R | Role: RP | PT/Exp: C | Rand Var: -5
Ht: 6' 1" | Wt: 190 | Type: Pwr | Consist: F | MM: 3300

After finding success as a stopper in Japan, got first taste of majors on wrong side of age 30 and held his own. Sophomore follow-up dependent largely on control. It was wobbly in past, and with subpar FpK and its late fade, we need to err on the side of caution. Still, a worthy LIMA end-staff stash in very deep leagues.

Yr Tm	W	L	Sv	IP	K	ERA	xERA	WHIP	oOPS	vL	vR	BF/G	Ctl	Dom	Cmd	FpK	SwK	G	L	F	H%	S%	hr/f	GS	APC	DOM%	DIS%	Sv%	LI	RAR	BPV	BPX	R$
12 for	1	2	33	54	49	2.28	3.37	1.13				3.7	2.3	8.2	3.6						28%	87%								11.6	100	130	$17
13 for	1	8	7	40	59	7.55	4.95	1.56				3.7	5.3	13.2	2.5						37%	52%								-18.2	91	119	-$7
14 for	1	2	14	32	40	4.19	4.67	1.33				4.0	3.8	11.2	2.9						31%	77%								-1.8	79	94	$3
15 for	3	1	41	63	53	1.42	1.59	1.00				4.1	3.4	7.6	2.3						23%	87%								19.8	104	124	$25
16 TEX	7	3	0	60	49	2.09	3.83	1.16	638	777	523	4.6	2.4	7.3	3.1	57%	12%	46	25	29	29%	85%	8%	0	17			0	1.16	15.6	91	108	$7
1st Half	5	3	0	37	27	2.70	4.23	1.34	677	861	519	4.7	2.7	6.6	2.5	59%	11%	44	30	26	32%	81%	7%	0	17			0	1.47	6.7	68	81	$6
2nd Half	2	0	0	24	22	1.14	3.25	0.89	574	626	530	4.6	1.9	8.4	4.4	54%	13%	51	16	33	24%	95%	10%	0	18			0	0.65	8.9	128	153	$8
17 Proj	**5**	**3**	**0**	**65**	**62**	**3.34**	**3.68**	**1.19**	**667**	**800**	**558**	**4.3**	**2.9**	**8.5**	**2.9**	**56%**	**12%**	**48**	**22**	**30**	**29%**	**75%**	**11%**	**0**						**6.9**	**99**	**118**	**$3**

Barraclough,Kyle

Health: A | LIMA Plan: B+
Age: 27 | Th: R | Role: RP | PT/Exp: D | Rand Var: -2
Ht: 6' 3" | Wt: 225 | Type: Pwr GB | Consist: A | MM: 5511

The makings of a future bullpen stud... 1) Lofty Dom comes with full SwK support; 2) Got strike one much more often in 2H, so further Ctl improvement in cards; 3) Newfound GB lean limits the blowup potential of those walks anyway. Tweak vL final piece to back-end (1.7 Cmd vL). With gains there... UP: 30 Sv

Yr Tm	W	L	Sv	IP	K	ERA	xERA	WHIP	oOPS	vL	vR	BF/G	Ctl	Dom	Cmd	FpK	SwK	G	L	F	H%	S%	hr/f	GS	APC	DOM%	DIS%	Sv%	LI	RAR	BPV	BPX	R$
12																																	
13																																	
14																																	
15 MIA *	4	1	10	53	59	3.12	2.74	1.44	563	656	497	4.3	6.9	10.1	1.5	48%	15%	32	26	42	28%	77%	5%	0	19			83	1.15	5.5	102	122	$4
16 MIA	6	3	0	73	113	2.85	2.87	1.22	538	584	492	4.1	5.4	14.0	2.6	57%	14%	52	21	27	32%	75%	3%	0	18			0	1.21	12.0	135	160	$7
1st Half	4	2	0	33	56	3.03	2.88	1.41	629	716	569	4.0	6.6	15.4	2.3	51%	13%	54	18	28	37%	78%	6%	0	18			0	1.17	4.7	131	157	$5
2nd Half	2	1	0	40	57	2.70	2.86	1.08	460	504	401	4.2	4.5	12.8	2.9	62%	15%	51	23	27	29%	72%	0%	0	18			0	1.24	7.3	138	165	$9
17 Proj	**6**	**2**	**4**	**73**	**100**	**2.93**	**3.01**	**1.18**	**536**	**583**	**488**	**4.0**	**4.8**	**12.4**	**2.6**	**57%**	**14%**	**52**	**21**	**27**	**30%**	**73%**	**3%**	**0**						**11.3**	**122**	**145**	**$8**

STEPHEN NICKRAND

Barrett,Jake

Age: 25 | Th: R | Role: RP | Ht: 6' 2" | Wt: 220 | Type: Pwr
Health: A | PT/Exp: D | Consist: C
LIMA Plan: B | Rand Var: -2 | MM: 0210

BPV by month from May to Sept (106, 33, 152, -127, 104) underscores that consistency isn't exactly his forte. Reason for the yo-yo peripherals was spotty control, and given late FpK dip, we can't expect resolution there, meaning he'll keep being relegated to low-leverage work. Not an attractive profile.

Yr Tm	W	L	Sv	IP	K	ERA	xERA	WHIP	oOPS	vL	vR	BF/G	Ctl	Dom	Cmd	FpK	SwK	G	L	F	H%	S%	hr/f	GS	APC	DOM%	DIS%	Sv%	LI	RAR	BPV	BPX	R$
12																																	
13 aa	1	1	14	25	19	0.49	2.84	1.00				3.9	1.1	6.9	6.1						27%	105%								10.3	150	195	$7
14 a/a	2	2	28	55	40	3.38	3.66	1.39				4.2	4.1	6.5	1.6						29%	76%								2.5	61	73	$9
15 a/a	4	3	15	53	42	5.17	5.45	1.72				5.1	3.8	7.2	1.9						38%	69%								-7.9	59	70	-$1
16 ARI	1	2	4	59	56	3.49	4.35	1.26	682	790	601	3.7	4.2	8.5	2.0	58%	13%	45	18	37	27%	75%	10%	0	14			44	1.01	5.1	61	73	$2
1st Half	1	0	1	30	28	3.30	4.22	1.27	739	794	703	3.8	3.3	8.4	2.5	63%	13%	43	21	37	29%	79%	13%	0	14			25	1.17	3.3	83	99	$2
2nd Half	0	2	3	29	28	3.68	4.50	1.26	620	786	474	3.6	5.2	8.6	1.6	53%	12%	47	14	38	25%	71%	7%	0	14			60	0.86	1.8	39	47	$2
17 Proj	2	3	2	58	50	4.22	4.64	1.44	758	865	674	4.1	4.1	7.7	1.9	57%	13%	45	17	38	32%	71%	7%	0						-0.2	51	60	-$3

Bauer,Trevor

Age: 26 | Th: R | Role: SP | Ht: 6' 1" | Wt: 175 | Type: Pwr
Health: A | PT/Exp: A | Consist: A
LIMA Plan: B | Rand Var: 0 | MM: 1205

Haphazard pattern of skills and results showing no signs of becoming predictable for former top prospect. GB% growth was nice, but SwK, FpK stagnation will prevent him from moving needle further on Cmd. Without gains there, he'll continue to be a true SP wildcard, as shown by DOM/DIS%. Hope for move to pen.

Yr Tm	W	L	Sv	IP	K	ERA	xERA	WHIP	oOPS	vL	vR	BF/G	Ctl	Dom	Cmd	FpK	SwK	G	L	F	H%	S%	hr/f	GS	APC	DOM%	DIS%	Sv%	LI	RAR	BPV	BPX	R$
12 ARI *	13	4	0	147	154	2.91	3.41	1.32	795	851	729	23.4	4.1	9.4	2.3	64%	7%	45	25	30	31%	80%	15%	4	81	25%	75%			20.0	93	121	$13
13 CLE *	7	9	0	138	104	5.04	5.44	1.72	840	908	778	24.2	5.7	6.8	1.2	57%	7%	35	20	45	32%	73%	13%	4	88	0%	50%			-20.1	30	40	-$14
14 CLE *	9	9	0	199	181	3.77	3.97	1.33	737	729	744	25.0	3.3	8.2	2.5	56%	9%	35	23	41	31%	74%	9%	26	100	31%	38%			-0.7	77	91	$4
15 CLE	11	12	0	176	170	4.55	4.21	1.31	713	705	721	24.0	4.0	8.7	2.2	59%	10%	39	20	41	28%	68%	12%	30	93	40%	27%	0	0.76	-12.8	64	77	$2
16 CLE	12	8	0	190	168	4.26	4.11	1.31	712	690	732	23.2	3.3	8.0	2.4	60%	9%	49	20	31	30%	69%	12%	28	88	25%	39%	0	0.74	-1.7	81	96	$7
1st Half	7	2	0	95	87	3.02	3.84	1.16	627	627	626	20.6	3.1	8.2	2.6	57%	10%	51	17	32	28%	76%	8%	12	81	42%	33%	0	0.71	13.7	92	110	$18
2nd Half	5	6	0	95	81	5.51	4.40	1.46	794	747	837	26.3	3.5	7.7	2.2	62%	9%	47	23	30	32%	64%	15%	16	97	13%	44%			-15.5	69	82	-$5
17 Proj	11	10	0	189	171	4.36	4.30	1.35	727	710	744	23.5	3.7	8.2	2.2	59%	9%	43	21	36	30%	70%	11%	34						-3.9	69	82	$3

Bedrosian,Cam

Age: 25 | Th: R | Role: RP | Ht: 6' 0" | Wt: 205 | Type: Pwr
Health: D | PT/Exp: D | Consist: D
LIMA Plan: A | Rand Var: -5 | MM: 3530

Former 1st-rounder finally blossomed into impact reliever, thanks in part due to new slider grip. Then blood clot in pitching arm cut season short after being anointed stopper. New GB tilt, elimination of LH/RH splits, late SwK and FpK surges all point to a future dominant closer if he's fully healthy. UP: 40 Sv

Yr Tm	W	L	Sv	IP	K	ERA	xERA	WHIP	oOPS	vL	vR	BF/G	Ctl	Dom	Cmd	FpK	SwK	G	L	F	H%	S%	hr/f	GS	APC	DOM%	DIS%	Sv%	LI	RAR	BPV	BPX	R$
12																																	
13																																	
14 LAA *	2	2	17	59	78	3.66	2.05	1.10	801	1055	531	4.2	4.0	11.9	3.0	61%	11%	41	21	38	29%	66%	9%	0	24			81	0.67	0.6	139	166	$8
15 LAA *	2	1	3	69	70	3.99	4.18	1.52	833	1047	719	5.2	4.1	9.1	2.2	55%	7%	43	23	34	36%	73%	9%	0	19			60	0.73	-0.3	90	107	-$3
16 LAA	2	0	1	40	51	1.12	2.94	1.09	532	583	485	3.6	3.1	11.4	3.6	62%	11%	49	21	29	32%	91%	4%	0	15			50	0.78	15.3	147	175	$5
1st Half	1	0	0	29	30	1.24	3.31	1.10	551	583	527	3.6	2.8	9.3	3.3	58%	10%	54	19	27	30%	90%	5%	0	14			0	0.76	10.5	124	148	$6
2nd Half	1	0	1	11	21	0.79	2.17	1.06	480	583	307	3.7	4.0	16.7	4.2	73%	14%	29	29	41	39%	92%	0%	0	16			50	0.83	4.7	200	239	$3
17 Proj	2	1	27	58	67	2.92	3.37	1.21	584	657	537	4.1	3.6	10.3	2.9	57%	9%	49	21	30	31%	76%	6%	0						9.1	116	138	$13

Benoit,Joaquin

Age: 39 | Th: R | Role: RP | Ht: 6' 3" | Wt: 220 | Type: Pwr FB
Health: C | PT/Exp: C | Consist: B
LIMA Plan: B+ | Rand Var: -4 | MM: 2400

Dumped by many after rough 1st half, but blame shoulder inflammation for those issues, as he rebounded when healthy. Still, he's hanging on to LIMA reliever status by a thread: rising xERA, declining LI are proof that his days of pitching meaningful innings might be coming to an end, especially as he nears 40.

Yr Tm	W	L	Sv	IP	K	ERA	xERA	WHIP	oOPS	vL	vR	BF/G	Ctl	Dom	Cmd	FpK	SwK	G	L	F	H%	S%	hr/f	GS	APC	DOM%	DIS%	Sv%	LI	RAR	BPV	BPX	R$
12 DET	5	3	2	71	84	3.68	3.36	1.14	720	721	720	3.9	2.8	10.6	3.8	58%	18%	36	20	44	28%	78%	18%	0	17			33	1.05	3.0	130	170	$5
13 DET	4	1	24	67	73	2.01	3.17	1.03	575	524	645	4.0	3.0	9.8	3.3	63%	15%	42	20	38	27%	84%	8%	0	16			92	1.19	15.3	117	152	$17
14 SD	4	2	11	54	64	1.49	2.98	0.77	459	480	440	3.9	2.3	10.6	4.6	63%	19%	35	15	50	22%	85%	5%	0	15			92	1.25	15.1	141	168	$13
15 SD	6	5	2	65	63	2.34	3.48	0.90	547	612	471	3.8	3.2	8.7	2.7	54%	17%	46	17	36	19%	81%	12%	0	15			33	1.17	13.1	95	113	$10
16 2 AL	3	1	1	48	52	2.81	4.24	1.27	624	701	559	4.0	4.5	9.8	2.2	58%	15%	39	22	39	28%	82%	10%	0	16			25	1.08	8.2	71	84	$2
1st Half	1	1	0	20	21	5.03	4.86	1.47	675	686	661	4.6	5.9	9.6	1.6	56%	13%	43	22	35	27%	69%	16%	0	19			0	1.11	-2.0	33	39	-$4
2nd Half	2	0	1	28	31	1.27	3.84	1.13	583	715	492	3.6	3.5	9.8	2.8	59%	15%	37	21	42	28%	93%	7%	0	15			50	1.07	10.2	98	116	$6
17 Proj	3	3	0	58	62	3.41	3.92	1.22	672	736	610	3.9	3.7	9.7	2.6	58%	16%	40	19	40	29%	76%	11%	0						5.6	93	111	$2

Berrios,Jose

Age: 23 | Th: R | Role: SP | Ht: 6' 0" | Wt: 185 | Type: Pwr FB
Health: A | PT/Exp: D | Consist: B
LIMA Plan: B+ | Rand Var: +3 | MM: 1201

3-7, 8.02 ERA in 58 IP at MIN. By any measure, a horrible debut for this top prospect. Was it nerves? Lights-out in AAA (2.51 ERA, 0.99 WHIP, 125/36 K/BB in 111 IP). With nearly 200 IP at AAA under his belt by age 23, the foundation for growth is there, but you'll need a bench for him until he proves he can make the leap.

Yr Tm	W	L	Sv	IP	K	ERA	xERA	WHIP	oOPS	vL	vR	BF/G	Ctl	Dom	Cmd	FpK	SwK	G	L	F	H%	S%	hr/f	GS	APC	DOM%	DIS%	Sv%	LI	RAR	BPV	BPX	R$
12																																	
13																																	
14 a/a	3	5	0	44	27	5.36	3.71	1.35				20.2	3.0	5.5	1.9						31%	58%								-8.7	61	73	-$4
15 a/a	14	5	0	166	147	3.41	3.11	1.14				24.4	2.0	7.9	4.0						30%	72%								11.4	118	140	$15
16 MIN *	13	12	0	170	153	4.98	4.29	1.39	932	837	1034	23.0	3.8	8.1	2.1	55%	9%	38	22	40	30%	66%	16%	14	82	7%	50%			-16.6	63	75	$0
1st Half	9	4	0	93	86	4.41	3.59	1.27	1102	1007	1206	23.7	3.9	8.4	2.2	57%	11%	35	23	43	28%	68%	29%	4	80	0%	25%			-2.5	73	87	$8
2nd Half	4	8	0	77	66	5.67	5.13	1.53	873	778	975	22.3	3.8	7.8	2.1	54%	8%	39	22	39	33%	65%	12%	10	82	10%	60%			-14.1	51	61	-$10
17 Proj	8	9	0	116	98	4.59	4.44	1.31	686	622	755	24.0	3.0	7.6	2.5	55%	9%	37	22	40	31%	66%	8%	19						-5.7	71	84	$0

Betances,Dellin

Age: 29 | Th: R | Role: RP | Ht: 6' 8" | Wt: 260 | Type: Pwr GB
Health: A | PT/Exp: C | Consist: A
LIMA Plan: B+ | Rand Var: +5 | MM: 5531

Hard to imagine that he could get even better, but rising GB%, SwK% suggest he hasn't peaked yet. Still, there is some concern. After backing into the closer role, FpK dropped and Ctl spiked. Walks are the bane of the effective closer; how many others survive with a 5.3 bb/9? So don't assume anything.

Yr Tm	W	L	Sv	IP	K	ERA	xERA	WHIP	oOPS	vL	vR	BF/G	Ctl	Dom	Cmd	FpK	SwK	G	L	F	H%	S%	hr/f	GS	APC	DOM%	DIS%	Sv%	LI	RAR	BPV	BPX	R$
12 a/a	6	9	0	131	102	8.28	7.13	2.11				24.0	7.1	7.0	1.0						37%	60%								-69.1	18	24	-$41
13 NYY *	6	4	5	89	98	4.16	3.25	1.40	965	1339	804	8.5	5.0	9.9	2.0	65%	9%	36	36	29	32%	69%	25%	0	20			100	0.28	-3.3	98	127	$1
14 NYY	5	0	1	90	135	1.40	2.03	0.78	442	405	482	4.9	2.4	13.5	5.6	66%	13%	47	20	33	26%	85%	7%	0	20			20	1.19	26.0	203	242	$18
15 NYY	6	4	9	84	131	1.50	2.43	1.01	510	454	558	4.5	4.3	14.0	3.3	59%	15%	48	21	32	27%	90%	12%	0	19			69	1.42	25.5	163	194	$19
16 NYY	3	6	12	73	126	3.08	2.09	1.12	577	634	532	4.1	3.5	15.5	4.5	61%	16%	54	19	27	38%	74%	13%	0	17			71	1.19	10.0	218	260	$12
1st Half	2	4	0	41	74	2.63	1.70	0.98	555	637	498	3.9	2.0	16.2	8.2	63%	16%	51	20	29	40%	76%	14%	0	17			0	1.27	7.9	268	320	$11
2nd Half	1	2	12	32	52	3.66	2.68	1.31	602	627	579	4.3	5.3	14.6	2.7	59%	16%	57	18	25	35%	73%	13%	0	18			80	1.09	2.1	154	184	$13
17 Proj	4	5	31	87	135	2.83	2.52	1.13	573	571	574	4.5	4.0	14.0	3.5	61%	15%	51	20	29	33%	77%	12%	0						14.6	172	205	$21

Bettis,Chad

Age: 28 | Th: R | Role: RP | Ht: 6' 1" | Wt: 193 | Type:
Health: B | PT/Exp: C | Consist: A
LIMA Plan: C | Rand Var: +2 | MM: 1103

Exhibit A of why W-L record isn't an accurate barometer of value. This one got more run support in the NL than any starting pitcher not named Arrieta. While skill foundation is getting stronger, BPX tells us it's still subpar. And that DOM/DIS% reveals his blowup risk, especially given gopheritis vR. Speculate elsewhere.

Yr Tm	W	L	Sv	IP	K	ERA	xERA	WHIP	oOPS	vL	vR	BF/G	Ctl	Dom	Cmd	FpK	SwK	G	L	F	H%	S%	hr/f	GS	APC	DOM%	DIS%	Sv%	LI	RAR	BPV	BPX	R$
12																																	
13 COL *	4	7	0	108	82	5.46	5.75	1.54	859	812	906	16.8	2.9	6.9	2.4	61%	8%	47	21	32	34%	69%	12%	8	49	0%	63%	0	0.91	-21.2	38	49	-$11
14 COL *	3	6	3	80	56	5.37	4.87	1.58	1020	901	1138	8.6	3.5	6.3	1.8	50%	6%	46	24	30	35%	65%	14%	0	24			60	0.70	-16.1	53	64	-$8
15 COL *	11	8	0	157	125	4.29	4.79	1.46	771	737	806	24.1	3.2	7.1	2.3	58%	10%	49	22	28	33%	73%	11%	20	94	20%	40%			-6.4	58	69	-$2
16 COL	14	8	0	186	138	4.79	4.31	1.41	775	694	854	25.4	2.9	6.7	2.3	63%	9%	51	22	27	32%	68%	14%	32	95	19%	44%			-13.8	72	86	$0
1st Half	6	6	0	95	73	5.85	4.20	1.52	817	734	881	25.2	2.3	6.9	3.0	66%	9%	51	23	26	36%	62%	15%	17	94	12%	47%			-19.6	92	110	-$9
2nd Half	8	2	0	91	65	3.67	4.44	1.30	727	659	813	25.7	3.5	6.5	1.9	58%	9%	51	21	28	28%	75%	13%	15	97	27%	40%			5.8	51	61	$8
17 Proj	11	9	0	174	130	4.70	4.35	1.45	794	734	857	18.4	3.1	6.7	2.2	60%	9%	50	22	28	32%	69%	13%	34						-10.9	66	78	-$3

STEPHEN NICKRAND

Biagini,Joe

Age: 27	Th: R	Role: RP	Health: A	LIMA Plan: B+
Ht: 6' 5"	Wt: 240	Type: GB	PT/Exp: D	Rand Var: -1
			Consist: A	MM: 2110

Thrust into important innings late (see 2nd half LI) and handled it intrepidly. Those late Ctl gains can stick given his top-tier FpK, and concurrent surge in SwK also supports another increase in strikeouts. With GB tilt and lack of big LH/RH splits, he's got the makings of a good setup guy. Or, with opportunity... UP: 20 Sv

Yr Tm	W	L	Sv	IP	K	ERA	xERA	WHIP	oOPS	vL	vR	BF/G	Ctl	Dom	Cmd	FpK	SwK	G	L	F	H%	S%	hr/f	GS	APC	DOM%	DIS%	Sv%	LI	RAR	BPV	BPX	R$
12																																	
13																																	
14																																	
15 aa	10	7	0	130	70	3.35	3.89	1.38				23.8	2.6	4.8	1.8						31%	75%								9.8	55	66	$4
16 TOR	4	3	1	68	62	3.06	3.75	1.30	678	725	644	4.9	2.5	8.2	3.3	69%	12%	52	21	26	34%	76%	6%	0	19			33	0.91	9.4	110	131	$3
1st Half	3	2	1	30	26	3.00	4.41	1.53	689	723	663	4.8	3.3	7.8	2.4	66%	11%	54	17	29	37%	78%	0%	0	19			50	0.66	4.4	83	99	$2
2nd Half	1	1	0	38	36	3.11	3.25	1.12	668	724	628	5.0	1.9	8.6	4.5	72%	13%	50	26	24	31%	74%	12%	0	18			0	1.15	5.0	132	157	$4
17 Proj	4	3	2	65	50	3.33	3.88	1.25	665	709	634	6.8	2.5	6.9	2.7	70%	12%	52	22	26	31%	74%	7%	0						6.9	85	102	$2

Blair,Aaron

Age: 25	Th: R	Role: SP	Health: B	LIMA Plan: D+
Ht: 6' 4"	Wt: 250	Type:	PT/Exp: D	Rand Var: +5
			Consist: D	MM: 0101

2-7, 7.59 ERA in 70 IP at ATL. Blasted in MLB debut, which shouldn't come as a surprise given steady skill erosion. Waning Cmd doesn't suggest an easy solution is in sight, and lack of DOM starts means he's a long way from helping your team. Late SwK surge keeps the door open just a crack, but don't dare use him yet.

Yr Tm	W	L	Sv	IP	K	ERA	xERA	WHIP	oOPS	vL	vR	BF/G	Ctl	Dom	Cmd	FpK	SwK	G	L	F	H%	S%	hr/f	GS	APC	DOM%	DIS%	Sv%	LI	RAR	BPV	BPX	R$
12																																	
13																																	
14 aa	4	1	0	46	40	2.36	2.72	1.08				22.6	3.0	7.7	2.5						25%	84%								7.9	85	102	$3
15 a/a	13	5	0	160	102	3.23	3.51	1.24				25.0	2.7	5.7	2.1						28%	76%								14.5	62	73	$11
16 ATL *	7	11	0	142	108	6.70	5.83	1.70	920	1033	815	22.9	4.3	6.8	1.6	56%	10%	40	22	38	35%	61%	16%	15	81	0%	67%			-43.9	34	40	-$20
1st Half	3	6	0	79	56	6.30	5.09	1.61	907	957	858	21.8	4.8	6.4	1.3	58%	9%	41	21	37	31%	61%	12%	11	81	0%	73%			-20.5	35	42	-$17
2nd Half	4	5	0	63	52	7.21	6.75	1.82	952	1239	702	24.4	3.7	7.4	2.0	52%	13%	35	25	40	39%	61%	25%	4	80	0%	50%			-23.5	35	41	-$24
17 Proj	4	5	0	73	54	4.87	4.94	1.47	793	949	652	23.8	3.5	6.7	1.9	55%	11%	38	24	39	32%	68%	9%	13						-6.1	42	50	-$5

Blanton,Joe

Age: 36	Th: R	Role: RP	Health: A	LIMA Plan: C+
Ht: 6' 2"	Wt: 240	Type: Pwr	PT/Exp: D	Rand Var: -5
			Consist: A	MM: 2301

Finally found home in bullpen in mid-30s after frustrating owners for a decade prior. The relief version pumped up Ks with backing of SwK, and strong FpK suggests his control could get even better. But unless GB tilt returns, his prior blowup potential remains, as reflected by mediocre xERA. An end-staff stash.

Yr Tm	W	L	Sv	IP	K	ERA	xERA	WHIP	oOPS	vL	vR	BF/G	Ctl	Dom	Cmd	FpK	SwK	G	L	F	H%	S%	hr/f	GS	APC	DOM%	DIS%	Sv%	LI	RAR	BPV	BPX	R$
12 2 NL	10	13	0	191	166	4.71	3.61	1.26	759	799	718	26.0	1.6	7.8	4.9	62%	10%	45	23	32	32%	67%	15%	30	94	40%	20%	0	0.83	-16.4	121	157	$2
13 LAA	2	14	0	133	108	6.04	4.14	1.61	904	844	976	21.8	2.3	7.3	3.2	64%	10%	44	22	33	36%	68%	19%	20	79	20%	40%	0	0.69	-35.5	92	119	-$18
14																																	
15 2 TM *	10	4	2	115	100	3.78	4.06	1.24	668	790	558	10.9	2.2	7.8	3.6	62%	13%	49	20	31	31%	74%	11%	4	32	0%	50%	100	0.52	2.7	90	107	$7
16 LA	7	2	0	80	80	2.48	3.97	1.01	573	546	587	4.2	2.9	9.0	3.1	65%	15%	33	22	46	25%	80%	7%	0	17			0	0.96	16.9	94	112	$11
1st Half	3	2	0	43	44	2.32	3.61	0.77	500	586	453	4.1	2.7	9.3	3.4	64%	15%	34	17	48	16%	79%	10%	0	17			0	1.03	9.8	105	126	$14
2nd Half	4	0	0	37	36	2.65	4.40	1.29	646	508	721	4.3	3.1	8.7	2.8	65%	15%	31	26	43	32%	80%	4%	0	17			0	0.88	7.1	80	96	$7
17 Proj	5	4	0	80	73	3.57	3.99	1.22	701	725	684	6.6	2.5	8.3	3.3	64%	13%	39	22	39	30%	75%	11%	0						6.1	98	117	$3

Blazek,Michael

Age: 28	Th: R	Role: RP	Health: D	LIMA Plan: D+
Ht: 6' 0"	Wt: 200	Type: Pwr	PT/Exp: D	Rand Var: +3
			Consist: F	MM: 0200

The benefit of pitching on a bad team is you can still have a job even if you are bad yourself. This reliever fits that to a tee, as he was allowed to post 40 IP of terrible stats and skills before they finally stopped using him late. Inflated hit rate didn't help, but health, consistency grades serve as reminders to stay far away.

Yr Tm	W	L	Sv	IP	K	ERA	xERA	WHIP	oOPS	vL	vR	BF/G	Ctl	Dom	Cmd	FpK	SwK	G	L	F	H%	S%	hr/f	GS	APC	DOM%	DIS%	Sv%	LI	RAR	BPV	BPX	R$
12 a/a	5	9	0	83	70	4.73	3.85	1.29				8.2	3.8	7.6	2.0						27%	66%								-7.4	60	79	-$2
13 2 NL *	1	3	9	63	57	3.12	3.04	1.35	759	833	711	4.9	5.5	8.1	1.5	57%	11%	44	11	45	26%	78%	12%	0	19			82	0.56	5.8	76	99	$3
14 aaa	4	4	1	102	72	5.11	5.65	1.66				12.4	3.8	6.3	1.7						35%	71%								-17.2	35	42	-$11
15 MIL	5	3	0	47	47	2.43	3.75	1.04	557	551	561	4.9	2.9	7.6	2.6	62%	11%	47	19	34	25%	78%	6%	0	19			0	0.57	10.6	83	99	$5
16 MIL	3	1	0	41	36	5.66	5.84	1.91	932	890	957	4.9	5.9	7.8	1.3	58%	10%	41	20	40	36%	74%	13%	0	20			0	0.95	-7.5	1	2	-$8
1st Half	3	1	0	29	24	4.97	5.97	1.83	855	847	860	4.5	6.2	7.4	1.2	60%	10%	37	24	38	34%	74%	9%	0	19			0	1.05	-2.8	-18	-22	-$6
2nd Half	0	0	0	12	12	7.30	5.55	2.11	1102	1000	1149	6.3	5.1	8.8	1.7	52%	10%	48	10	43	40%	73%	22%	0	24			0	0.65	-4.7	45	54	-$12
17 Proj	2	3	0	51	41	4.73	5.04	1.56	788	779	795	5.8	4.6	7.3	1.6	61%	10%	41	22	37	32%	71%	8%	0						-3.4	27	33	-$5

Blevins,Jerry

Age: 33	Th: L	Role: RP	Health: F	LIMA Plan: A
Ht: 6' 6"	Wt: 175	Type: Pwr	PT/Exp: D	Rand Var: -2
			Consist: D	MM: 3510

Relevant again after spending recent seasons on scrap heap. While we can't bet on that 2H Dom repeating, his SwK did surge to upper-tier levels late, so he can stick as a double-digit Dom guy. Now two years removed from a fly ball tilt too, and GB% jump in 2H should make it three. With health, a LOOGY LIMA gem.

Yr Tm	W	L	Sv	IP	K	ERA	xERA	WHIP	oOPS	vL	vR	BF/G	Ctl	Dom	Cmd	FpK	SwK	G	L	F	H%	S%	hr/f	GS	APC	DOM%	DIS%	Sv%	LI	RAR	BPV	BPX	R$
12 OAK	5	1	1	65	54	2.48	4.10	1.07	637	575	693	4.1	3.4	7.4	2.2	52%	11%	38	18	44	23%	83%	9%	0	16			100	0.92	12.4	57	74	$7
13 OAK	5	0	0	60	52	3.15	4.00	1.07	651	741	581	3.7	2.6	7.8	3.1	58%	10%	31	19	50	25%	75%	8%	0	15			0	0.97	5.3	81	105	$4
14 WAS	2	3	0	57	66	4.87	3.37	1.24	623	419	821	3.8	3.6	10.4	2.9	68%	12%	39	24	37	32%	59%	6%	0	15			0	0.94	-8.0	106	126	-$2
15 NYM	1	0	0	5	4	0.00	1.77	0.00	0	0	0	2.1	0.0	7.2	0.0	60%	9%	55	36	9	0%	0%	0%	0	8			0	1.50	2.4	163	194	-$2
16 NYM	4	2	2	42	52	2.79	3.46	1.21	627	636	611	2.4	3.2	11.1	3.5	61%	11%	46	17	37	33%	81%	10%	0	10			67	1.31	7.3	138	164	$3
1st Half	2	0	0	23	22	2.35	3.92	1.00	548	605	431	2.5	2.7	8.6	3.1	59%	9%	41	16	43	25%	81%	8%	0	10			0	1.23	5.2	100	119	$4
2nd Half	2	2	2	19	30	3.32	2.85	1.47	711	672	772	2.4	3.8	14.2	3.8	63%	14%	52	17	30	43%	81%	14%	0	10			67	1.40	2.0	184	219	$2
17 Proj	3	2	2	44	51	3.40	3.58	1.22	642	601	695	2.8	3.3	10.5	3.2	62%	12%	42	19	39	31%	75%	9%	0						4.2	119	142	$2

Bolsinger,Michael

Age: 29	Th: R	Role: RP	Health: C	LIMA Plan: C
Ht: 6' 2"	Wt: 200	Type: Pwr	PT/Exp: D	Rand Var: +5
			Consist: F	MM: 1200

1-4, 6.83 ERA in 28 IP at LA. Well, that was a mess. SP like this have razor thin margins of error. When one skill deteriorates (GB%) and they get struck with some bad luck (H%, S%, hr/f), it all can go bust. That 2015 looks like a clear outlier now. Dangerous low floor/ceiling combo confirmed by DOM/DIS%. Pass.

Yr Tm	W	L	Sv	IP	K	ERA	xERA	WHIP	oOPS	vL	vR	BF/G	Ctl	Dom	Cmd	FpK	SwK	G	L	F	H%	S%	hr/f	GS	APC	DOM%	DIS%	Sv%	LI	RAR	BPV	BPX	R$
12 aa	4	3	0	78	53	4.85	5.62	1.76				23.7	4.5	6.1	1.4						36%	73%								-8.0	38	50	-$10
13 a/a	11	7	0	144	103	4.72	5.10	1.58				24.4	3.3	6.4	1.9						35%	71%								-15.2	49	64	-$8
14 ARI *	9	9	0	144	118	4.61	4.82	1.49	872	906	843	23.0	3.0	7.4	2.5	67%	9%	52	21	26	35%	70%	16%	9	85	22%	33%	0	0.83	-15.4	68	82	-$6
15 LA *	9	9	0	156	146	3.35	3.52	1.29	705	793	636	20.7	3.6	8.4	2.3	55%	9%	53	18	29	30%	76%	12%	21	85	24%	43%			11.7	84	100	$8
16 LA *	4	9	0	82	73	6.99	7.23	1.84	908	961	876	15.3	3.7	8.0	2.1	61%	10%	34	28	39	39%	65%	22%	6	78	0%	50%			-28.3	28	33	-$15
1st Half	2	4	0	42	37	5.52	6.11	1.58	908	961	876	15.3	3.2	7.9	2.5	61%	10%	34	28	39	34%	70%	22%		78	0%	50%			-6.9	39	46	-$8
2nd Half	2	5	0	40	36	8.51	8.38	2.10				15.3	4.3	8.0	1.9						43%	60%	0%							-21.5	19	23	-$23
17 Proj	2	4	0	44	38	4.85	4.36	1.48	796	849	756	17.1	3.6	7.8	2.2	62%	9%	46	23	31	32%	70%	15%	8						-3.5	67	80	-$4

Bowman,Matthew

Age: 26	Th: R	Role: RP	Health: A	LIMA Plan: B+
Ht: 6' 0"	Wt: 175	Type: xGB	PT/Exp: D	Rand Var: 0
			Consist: F	MM: 2000

As an extreme GBer with decent command, this one can carve out a nice career as a middleman. Increasing LI during season might indicate possible future save opps, but metrics tailed in higher leverage outings. So-so SwK for a reliever doesn't support further growth, so view him as a low-upside LIMA stash.

Yr Tm	W	L	Sv	IP	K	ERA	xERA	WHIP	oOPS	vL	vR	BF/G	Ctl	Dom	Cmd	FpK	SwK	G	L	F	H%	S%	hr/f	GS	APC	DOM%	DIS%	Sv%	LI	RAR	BPV	BPX	R$
12																																	
13																																	
14 a/a	10	8	0	135	108	2.85	3.51	1.26				22.9	2.1	7.2	3.5						33%	78%								14.9	104	124	$8
15 aaa	7	16	0	140	65	5.35	5.96	1.71				22.6	3.0	4.2	1.4						35%	69%								-24.0	18	21	-$17
16 STL	2	5	0	68	52	3.46	3.63	1.17	623	570	651	4.8	2.7	6.9	2.6	62%	10%	62	19	19	28%	71%	10%	0	18			0	0.81	6.1	93	110	$2
1st Half	1	2	0	32	22	3.41	3.39	0.98	557	567	552	5.1	2.0	6.3	3.1	63%	10%	67	15	19	24%	68%	17%	0	19			0	0.47	3.0	103	123	$4
2nd Half	1	3	0	36	30	3.50	3.84	1.33	678	573	737	4.5	3.3	7.5	2.3	62%	10%	57	23	20	32%	72%	5%	0	17			0	1.05	3.1	83	98	$0
17 Proj	3	6	0	65	44	3.75	3.94	1.38	737	649	785	7.8	2.7	6.0	2.2	62%	10%	61	19	20	32%	73%	11%	0						3.5	74	88	-$2

STEPHEN NICKRAND

Boxberger,Brad

Age: 29	Th: R	Role	RP	Health	F	LIMA Plan	C
Ht: 6' 2"	Wt: 220	Type	Pwr FB	PT/Exp	C	Rand Var	0
				Consist	D	MM	2510

Quite the skills slide over the past two seasons. The 2016 version couldn't find home plate at all, and with history of wildness and subpar FpK, we can't bank on improvement there. Abdomen, oblique issues limited IP and serve as a reminder of spotty health. Still owns 2012-2014, but a true wildcard now.

Yr	Tm	W	L	Sv	IP	K	ERA	xERA	WHIP	oOPS	vL	vR	BF/G	Ctl	Dom	Cmd	FpK	SwK	G	L	F	H%	S%	hr/f	GS	APC	DOM%	DIS%	Sv%	LI	RAR	BPV	BPX	R$
12	SD *	2	2	5	71	86	2.43	2.98	1.31	734	820	659	4.8	4.4	11.0	2.5	45%	12%	40	13	46	33%	82%	10%	0	24			71	0.73	13.9	116	152	$6
13	SD *	2	5	6	79	100	3.24	3.28	1.27	760	495	948	5.4	3.4	11.3	3.3	62%	13%	42	17	40	35%	76%	14%	0	22			75	0.66	6.1	125	163	$4
14	TAM	5	2	2	65	104	2.37	2.08	0.84	538	402	659	3.9	2.8	14.5	5.2	67%	15%	41	17	42	24%	82%	19%	0	17			40	1.23	11.0	204	243	$11
15	TAM	4	10	41	63	74	3.71	3.98	1.37	703	657	759	3.9	4.6	10.6	2.3	56%	13%	36	21	43	30%	78%	13%	0	17			87	1.58	1.9	81	96	$17
16	TAM	4	3	0	24	22	4.81	5.64	1.73	728	750	711	4.2	7.0	8.1	1.2	58%	10%	48	15	37	30%	74%	12%	0	17			0	1.15	-1.9	-17	-21	-$4
1st Half		0	0	0	1	0	27.00	18.41	4.50	1850	3500	333	6.0	13.5	0.0	0.0	83%	0%	0	50	50	35%	50%	50%	0	16			0	0.12	-1.9	-387	-461	-$7
2nd Half		4	3	0	24	22	4.18	5.34	1.65	677	615	727	4.2	6.8	8.4	1.2	56%	10%	51	13	36	30%	76%	8%	0	18			0	1.19	0.0	-5	-7	-$4
17	Proj	**5**	**5**	**2**	**58**	**71**	**3.79**	**3.91**	**1.33**	**650**	**566**	**729**	**4.2**	**4.9**	**11.0**	**2.2**	**59%**	**13%**	**43**	**17**	**40**	**30%**	**74%**	**11%**	**0**						**2.9**	**87**	**103**	**$2**

Boyd,Matt

Age: 26	Th: L	Role	SP	Health	A	LIMA Plan	B+
Ht: 6' 3"	Wt: 215	Type	xFB	PT/Exp	D	Rand Var	0
				Consist	D	MM	1203

6-5, 4.53 ERA in 97 IP at DET. While stats and skills scream plateau, three reasons to speculate on a breakout... 1) Huge skill growth in 2H supported by FpK, SwK gains; 2) better vR as season went along; 3) at the right age for another step up. With continued reduction in FB%... UP: 3.50 ERA, 180 K

Yr	Tm	W	L	Sv	IP	K	ERA	xERA	WHIP	oOPS	vL	vR	BF/G	Ctl	Dom	Cmd	FpK	SwK	G	L	F	H%	S%	hr/f	GS	APC	DOM%	DIS%	Sv%	LI	RAR	BPV	BPX	R$
12																																		
13																																		
14	aa	1	4	0	43	39	8.72	7.05	1.82				19.8	2.8	8.2	2.9						42%	51%								-26.2	56	67	-$13
15	2 AL *	10	8	0	172	128	3.84	3.77	1.17	979	1134	913	21.5	2.5	6.7	2.6	59%	9%	32	16	52	26%	73%	18%	12	77	0%	50%	0	0.74	2.6	63	74	$9
16	DET *	8	10	0	161	126	4.00	4.45	1.33	765	598	800	21.6	2.8	7.0	2.5	63%	10%	38	17	45	30%	75%	13%	18	84	22%	44%	0	0.87	3.8	58	69	$4
1st Half		2	7	0	93	65	4.21	4.58	1.41	803	497	842	23.2	3.1	6.3	2.1	58%	8%	40	20	39	31%	73%	14%	5	82	20%	40%	0	0.80	-0.2	48	57	$0
2nd Half		6	3	0	68	61	3.71	4.35	1.22	748	624	779	20.2	2.4	8.1	3.4	65%	11%	37	16	48	29%	77%	13%	13	85	23%	46%	0	0.90	4.1	96	115	$9
17	Proj	**10**	**10**	**0**	**174**	**148**	**4.08**	**4.50**	**1.31**	**762**	**794**	**753**	**20.8**	**2.4**	**7.7**	**3.2**	**60%**	**9%**	**36**	**17**	**47**	**31%**	**74%**	**11%**	**35**						**2.4**	**87**	**103**	**$4**

Brach,Brad

Age: 31	Th: R	Role	RP	Health	A	LIMA Plan	B
Ht: 6' 6"	Wt: 210	Type	Pwr	PT/Exp	C	Rand Var	-5
				Consist	A	MM	3401

Easy to view him as a middleman who has tapped out his potential. But small signs of more: another year of more Ks backed by more swinging strikes, and steady increase in FpK validates recent control gains. Problems vL (career 1.7 Cmd) preclude Sv opps, but LI shows he's still a trusted asset.

Yr	Tm	W	L	Sv	IP	K	ERA	xERA	WHIP	oOPS	vL	vR	BF/G	Ctl	Dom	Cmd	FpK	SwK	G	L	F	H%	S%	hr/f	GS	APC	DOM%	DIS%	Sv%	LI	RAR	BPV	BPX	R$
12	SD	2	4	0	67	75	3.78	3.97	1.25	674	718	646	4.2	4.5	10.1	2.3	55%	11%	35	20	45	26%	76%	15%	0	17			0	1.17	1.9	75	98	$1
13	SD *	5	3	3	75	67	2.95	4.72	1.52	819	647	972	5.0	3.9	8.0	2.1	54%	9%	38	23	39	34%	84%	9%	0	19			100	0.62	8.5	63	83	$1
14	BAL *	10	2	1	86	86	3.47	3.63	1.30	640	776	543	5.6	3.3	9.1	2.7	58%	13%	36	19	45	32%	75%	8%	0	23			50	0.82	2.9	95	113	$4
15	BAL	5	3	1	79	89	2.72	3.61	1.20	627	534	729	5.2	4.3	10.1	2.3	58%	14%	45	19	36	27%	81%	10%	0	21			50	0.99	12.1	88	105	$7
16	BAL	10	4	2	79	92	2.05	3.35	1.04	578	784	399	4.4	2.8	10.5	3.7	60%	15%	41	21	38	28%	85%	10%	0	18			29	1.05	20.8	131	155	$14
1st Half		5	1	2	45	50	1.01	3.32	0.81	471	601	355	4.6	2.6	10.1	3.8	60%	16%	40	16	43	21%	94%	7%	0	20			40	1.09	17.5	129	154	$20
2nd Half		5	3	0	34	42	3.41	3.37	1.34	704	1000	449	4.1	3.1	11.0	3.5	59%	15%	43	26	31	35%	79%	14%	0	17			0	1.00	3.3	134	160	$6
17	Proj	**8**	**4**	**1**	**73**	**81**	**3.01**	**3.67**	**1.20**	**644**	**746**	**554**	**4.6**	**3.4**	**10.1**	**2.9**	**59%**	**14%**	**41**	**21**	**38**	**30%**	**78%**	**10%**	**0**						**10.5**	**108**	**129**	**$6**

Bracho,Silvino

Age: 24	Th: R	Role	RP	Health	A	LIMA Plan	C+
Ht: 5' 11"	Wt: 179	Type	Pwr xFB	PT/Exp	F	Rand Var	+5
				Consist	F	MM	1300

0-2, 7.30 ERA in 25 IP at ARI. AA closer flopped in transition to MLB. Much of damage inflicted by fluke hit, strand, and hr/f rates, so he won't be this bad again. But as an extreme FB pitcher, he's at the mercy of which way the wind is blowing, and low LI tells us MLB clubs don't trust him yet either. Monitor from afar.

Yr	Tm	W	L	Sv	IP	K	ERA	xERA	WHIP	oOPS	vL	vR	BF/G	Ctl	Dom	Cmd	FpK	SwK	G	L	F	H%	S%	hr/f	GS	APC	DOM%	DIS%	Sv%	LI	RAR	BPV	BPX	R$
12																																		
13																																		
14																																		
15	ARI *	2	1	17	57	67	2.15	3.04	1.10	680	988	486	4.5	2.1	10.6	5.0	52%	16%	18	25	57	32%	86%	13%	0	17			89	0.55	12.8	151	180	$12
16	ARI *	0	4	15	58	53	6.13	5.34	1.48	951	920	970	4.0	2.7	8.1	3.0	62%	11%	29	21	51	35%	60%	16%	0	18			88	0.57	-14.0	66	78	-$2
1st Half		0	3	14	35	33	4.59	3.62	1.28	993	600	1234	4.2	3.0	8.5	2.8	67%	9%	20	23	57	31%	64%	10%	0	22			93	1.08	-1.7	91	109	$6
2nd Half		0	1	1	23	20	8.43	7.91	1.78	920	1106	793	3.8	2.3	7.6	3.3	59%	12%	35	19	46	39%	55%	21%	0	16			50	0.31	-12.2	30	36	-$15
17	Proj	**0**	**1**	**0**	**29**	**29**	**5.01**	**4.33**	**1.39**	**700**	**867**	**586**	**4.1**	**2.4**	**9.1**	**3.8**	**59%**	**12%**	**35**	**19**	**46**	**35%**	**67%**	**10%**	**0**						**-2.9**	**111**	**132**	**-$4**

Bradley,Archie

Age: 24	Th: R	Role	SP	Health	D	LIMA Plan	D+
Ht: 6' 4"	Wt: 235	Type	Pwr GB	PT/Exp	D	Rand Var	+2
				Consist	B	MM	1203

8-9, 5.02 ERA in 142 IP at ARI. Top prospect finally turned upside into strikeouts, but with only modest SwK backing, will they stick? And chronic wildness, mediocre FpK don't foretell control gains. Reversal of prior vL/vR splits confirms volatility, as underscored by that ugly DOM/DIS%. Don't roster without a bench.

Yr	Tm	W	L	Sv	IP	K	ERA	xERA	WHIP	oOPS	vL	vR	BF/G	Ctl	Dom	Cmd	FpK	SwK	G	L	F	H%	S%	hr/f	GS	APC	DOM%	DIS%	Sv%	LI	RAR	BPV	BPX	R$
12																																		
13	aa	12	5	0	123	103	2.60	3.41	1.38				24.7	4.4	7.5	1.7						30%	82%								19.3	74	97	$9
14	a/a	3	7	0	79	60	4.76	3.83	1.53				20.2	5.0	6.8	1.3						31%	66%								-9.9	66	78	-$6
15	ARI *	3	3	0	57	40	4.70	4.90	1.57	768	587	985	20.8	4.2	6.3	1.5	55%	6%	58	14	28	32%	71%	10%	8	81	0%	63%			-5.2	41	49	-$6
16	ARI *	13	10	0	182	182	4.39	4.25	1.47	802	936	666	23.7	4.2	9.0	2.2	57%	9%	45	25	30	33%	71%	13%	26	99	15%	38%			-4.4	78	93	$2
1st Half		8	4	0	93	92	3.48	3.27	1.28	763	914	628	23.7	4.1	8.9	2.2	62%	10%	47	23	31	29%	75%	18%	9	99	22%	33%			8.1	86	103	$13
2nd Half		5	6	0	90	90	5.32	4.41	1.66	823	946	689	24.3	4.2	9.0	2.1	54%	8%	44	26	29	38%	68%	10%	17	99	12%	41%			-12.5	71	85	-$9
17	Proj	**10**	**9**	**0**	**160**	**139**	**4.46**	**4.42**	**1.51**	**753**	**754**	**750**	**22.4**	**4.3**	**7.9**	**1.8**	**56%**	**8%**	**50**	**21**	**29**	**33%**	**71%**	**9%**	**31**						**-5.3**	**54**	**64**	**-$3**

Brault,Steven

Age: 25	Th: L	Role	SP	Health	A	LIMA Plan	D+
Ht: 6' 0"	Wt: 190	Type	Pwr	PT/Exp	D	Rand Var	+3
				Consist	F	MM	1201

0-3, 4.86 ERA in 33 IP at PIT. Model case for looking at xERA when a SP unexpectedly starts season strong. Those who heeded his 1st half xERA avoided predictable 2n half blowup. Even if it was exacerbated by H%, S%, and hr/f damage, inability to get strike one will keep walks a major concern, making him unrosterable.

Yr	Tm	W	L	Sv	IP	K	ERA	xERA	WHIP	oOPS	vL	vR	BF/G	Ctl	Dom	Cmd	FpK	SwK	G	L	F	H%	S%	hr/f	GS	APC	DOM%	DIS%	Sv%	LI	RAR	BPV	BPX	R$
12																																		
13																																		
14																																		
15	aa	9	3	0	90	65	2.32	2.46	1.11				23.6	1.8	6.5	3.5						30%	78%								18.3	117	139	$11
16	PIT *	2	10	0	105	93	5.23	5.73	1.73	893	828	902	19.9	4.7	8.0	1.7	48%	10%	45	26	29	36%	71%	15%	7	83	0%	71%	0	0.71	-13.4	48	58	-$11
1st Half		2	3	0	35	35	3.55	5.31	1.70				19.8	4.1	9.0	2.2						39%	80%	0%	0						2.8	76	91	-$1
2nd Half		0	7	0	70	58	6.07	5.94	1.75	893	828	902	19.9	5.0	7.6	1.5	48%	10%	45	26	29	35%	67%	15%	7	83	0%	71%	0	0.71	-16.2	35	42	-$17
17	Proj	**4**	**5**	**0**	**73**	**60**	**4.44**	**4.58**	**1.52**	**661**	**652**	**660**	**21.3**	**3.8**	**7.5**	**1.9**	**48%**	**10%**	**45**	**26**	**29**	**34%**	**71%**	**7%**	**15**						**-2.3**	**54**	**64**	**-$4**

Britton,Zach

Age: 29	Th: L	Role	RP	Health	A	LIMA Plan	C
Ht: 6' 2"	Wt: 172	Type	Pwr xGB	PT/Exp	A	Rand Var	-5
				Consist	A	MM	5430

The most dominant closer since Mariano? Surging SwK makes him a good bet for double-digit Dom again, and when batters do make contact, they pound the ball into the ground at an amazing *80%* clip. Sure, we probably won't see that H%/S% again, so his ERA will go up. But he's the game's top closer now. UP: 50 Sv

Yr	Tm	W	L	Sv	IP	K	ERA	xERA	WHIP	oOPS	vL	vR	BF/G	Ctl	Dom	Cmd	FpK	SwK	G	L	F	H%	S%	hr/f	GS	APC	DOM%	DIS%	Sv%	LI	RAR	BPV	BPX	R$
12	BAL *	10	5	0	124	92	5.34	4.77	1.53	756	714	778	23.4	4.2	6.7	1.6	51%	10%	61	16	23	32%	66%	14%	11	89	36%	45%	0	0.73	-20.2	45	59	-$9
13	BAL *	8	8	0	143	77	5.48	5.89	1.81	837	849	832	24.6	4.2	4.8	1.1	54%	7%	58	20	22	36%	69%	13%	7	83	14%	71%	0	0.75	-28.5	23	31	-$19
14	BAL	3	2	37	76	62	1.65	2.44	0.90	500	386	559	4.0	2.7	7.3	2.7	55%	13%	75	13	12	22%	85%	17%	0	15			90	1.41	19.7	111	133	$24
15	BAL	4	1	36	66	79	1.92	1.75	0.99	547	325	636	4.0	1.9	10.8	5.6	64%	17%	79	11	9	31%	82%	20%	0	14			90	1.17	16.5	200	238	$23
16	BAL	2	1	47	67	74	0.54	2.03	0.84	430	495	410	3.7	2.4	9.9	4.1	56%	18%	80	11	9	24%	95%	7%	0	15			100	1.31	30.2	172	204	$32
1st Half		2	1	23	34	41	0.80	1.66	0.77	425	288	465	3.7	2.1	11.0	5.1	54%	19%	81	14	5	24%	92%	25%	0	15			100	1.40	14.1	199	237	$32
2nd Half		0	0	24	33	33	0.27	2.42	0.90	434	690	356	3.7	2.7	8.9	3.3	57%	16%	79	9	12	25%	97%	0%	0	15			100	1.22	16.1	145	172	$33
17	Proj	**3**	**1**	**45**	**65**	**68**	**1.92**	**2.21**	**0.94**	**507**	**482**	**516**	**3.9**	**2.3**	**9.4**	**4.1**	**57%**	**16%**	**77**	**12**	**11**	**27%**	**80%**	**13%**	**0**						**18.3**	**163**	**194**	**$26**

STEPHEN NICKRAND

Broxton,Jonathan

Age: 33	Th: R	Role RP	Health D	LIMA Plan C	
Ht: 6' 3"	Wt: 295	Type Pwr	PT/Exp C	Rand Var +2	
			Consist A	MM 2301	

Current version still shows roster-worthy flashes (see 2nd half), but barely average skills in 2 of 3 years confirm that late-game upside is long gone, a fact that MLB managers fully agree with now (see plummeting LI). Even if prior stopper pedigree keeps teams interested in him, that doesn't mean that you should.

Yr Tm	W	L	Sv	IP	K	ERA	xERA	WHIP	oOPS	vL	vR	BF/G	Ctl	Dom	Cmd	FpK	SwK	G	L	F	H%	S%	hr/f	GS	APC	DOM%	DIS%	Sv%	LI	RAR	BPV	BPX	R$
12 2 TM	4	5	27	58	45	2.48	3.55	1.26	676	628	715	4.0	2.6	7.0	2.6	57%	9%	54	22	24	31%	80%	5%	0	16			82	1.33	11.0	86	113	$14
13 CIN	2	2	0	31	25	4.11	4.09	1.27	712	779	656	3.9	3.5	7.3	2.1	53%	13%	46	16	37	27%	71%	12%	0	15			0	1.24	-0.9	61	79	-$3
14 2 NL	4	3	7	59	49	2.30	3.74	1.02	569	564	572	3.7	2.9	7.5	2.6	61%	11%	46	10	44	24%	80%	6%	0	15			47	1.34	10.4	81	96	$8
15 2 NL	4	5	0	60	63	4.62	3.42	1.38	766	833	721	3.9	3.3	9.4	2.9	60%	12%	53	20	28	34%	68%	16%	0	15			0	0.90	-4.9	112	133	-$3
16 STL	4	2	0	61	57	4.30	3.97	1.25	673	708	650	3.9	3.6	8.5	2.4	59%	10%	48	24	28	28%	68%	15%	0	15			0	0.69	-0.8	82	98	$0
1st Half	1	0	0	33	25	3.51	4.68	1.17	564	765	447	3.9	4.9	6.8	1.4	63%	9%	48	24	28	22%	70%	8%	0	16			0	0.67	2.8	16	19	$1
2nd Half	3	2	0	27	32	5.27	3.22	1.35	788	643	894	4.0	2.0	10.5	5.3	55%	13%	48	24	28	37%	66%	23%	0	14			0	0.71	-3.6	162	194	-$2
17 Proj	4	5	0	73	70	4.11	3.74	1.26	701	710	694	3.8	3.1	8.7	2.8	59%	11%	49	20	31	30%	70%	13%	0						0.7	99	118	$0

Buchholz,Clay

Age: 32	Th: R	Role RP	Health F	LIMA Plan C	
Ht: 6' 3"	Wt: 190	Type	PT/Exp A	Rand Var -1	
			Consist C	MM 1103	

Hard to find a starting pitcher who struggles more with putting together good back-to-back seasons. Touch of SwK, FpK erosion supported Cmd decline, but not this much. Getting strike one at a top clip in 2nd half fueled his rebound, and given 2015 mark, we can't dismiss it. Since 2017 is an odd year... (No! Don't go there!)

Yr Tm	W	L	Sv	IP	K	ERA	xERA	WHIP	oOPS	vL	vR	BF/G	Ctl	Dom	Cmd	FpK	SwK	G	L	F	H%	S%	hr/f	GS	APC	DOM%	DIS%	Sv%	LI	RAR	BPV	BPX	R$
12 BOS	11	8	0	189	129	4.56	4.27	1.33	757	761	751	27.7	3.0	6.1	2.0	63%	9%	48	20	33	29%	69%	13%	29	100	31%	31%			-12.8	54	71	$0
13 BOS	12	1	0	108	96	1.74	3.31	1.02	546	536	560	26.0	3.0	8.0	2.7	60%	10%	48	21	32	25%	84%	5%	16	102	50%	6%			28.3	89	116	$18
14 BOS	8	11	0	170	132	5.34	3.99	1.39	751	793	696	26.3	2.9	7.0	2.4	60%	9%	47	19	34	32%	62%	9%	28	98	29%	32%			-33.5	74	88	-$9
15 BOS	7	7	0	113	107	3.26	3.36	1.21	664	610	725	26.1	1.8	8.5	4.7	65%	11%	48	21	31	34%	73%	6%	18	95	50%	17%			9.9	130	154	$7
16 BOS	8	10	0	139	93	4.78	5.11	1.33	742	788	695	15.9	3.6	6.0	1.7	62%	10%	41	16	43	27%	68%	11%	21	60	14%	48%	0	0.72	-10.1	31	37	-$1
1st Half	3	9	0	81	53	5.91	5.42	1.49	830	908	757	19.6	4.1	5.9	1.4	58%	10%	42	16	42	27%	65%	16%	13	76	8%	62%	0	0.74	-17.1	15	18	-$8
2nd Half	5	1	0	59	40	3.22	4.70	1.11	612	628	593	12.4	2.8	6.1	2.2	69%	10%	39	16	45	26%	72%	5%	8	46	25%	25%	0	0.70	7.0	53	63	$9
17 Proj	9	8	0	145	111	4.08	4.38	1.26	696	706	685	18.4	2.8	6.9	2.4	64%	10%	44	18	38	29%	69%	9%	27						2.0	70	83	$5

Buchter,Ryan

Age: 30	Th: L	Role RP	Health A	LIMA Plan C+	
Ht: 6' 4"	Wt: 215	Type Pwr xFB	PT/Exp D	Rand Var -5	
			Consist C	MM 0410	

It's amazing how much a friendly hit rate can hide. In this case, it covers up his chronic control woes, and poor FpK gives little hope for improvement. Plus, those baserunners are more likely to turn into ER given xFB profile. Even if double-digit Dom sticks (no sure thing), risk far outweighs his reward.

Yr Tm	W	L	Sv	IP	K	ERA	xERA	WHIP	oOPS	vL	vR	BF/G	Ctl	Dom	Cmd	FpK	SwK	G	L	F	H%	S%	hr/f	GS	APC	DOM%	DIS%	Sv%	LI	RAR	BPV	BPX	R$
12 a/a	3	3	4	49	46	3.39	3.72	1.58				4.9	6.9	8.4	1.2						29%	78%								3.8	74	96	-$2
13 aaa	4	0	5	62	84	3.44	3.68	1.58				5.3	7.9	12.2	1.5						30%	80%								3.3	97	126	$0
14 ATL *	4	3	1	64	52	3.76	4.42	1.60	333	1000	0	5.7	6.0	7.4	1.2	67%	8%	100	0	0	30%	78%	0%	0	12			20	2.46	-0.2	53	63	-$3
15 aaa	2	0	3	51	48	2.24	3.11	1.43				5.0	4.9	8.5	1.7						32%	83%								10.8	95	113	$1
16 SD	3	0	1	63	78	2.86	4.02	1.03	559	489	597	3.7	4.4	11.1	2.5	55%	10%	21	21	58	23%	74%	5%	0	17			50	0.92	10.4	80	95	$6
1st Half	1	0	1	36	52	2.75	3.68	1.17	622	500	698	3.8	4.8	13.0	2.7	56%	11%	20	26	54	30%	78%	5%	0	17			50	0.85	6.4	104	124	$7
2nd Half	2	0	0	27	26	3.00	4.48	0.85	469	466	469	3.6	4.0	8.7	2.2	52%	9%	21	16	63	15%	67%	5%	0	16			0	1.03	4.0	47	56	$6
17 Proj	3	2	5	65	69	4.05	5.04	1.40	792	697	840	4.5	4.7	9.5	2.0	54%	10%	21	20	59	30%	74%	7%	0						1.1	41	49	$0

Bumgarner,Madison

Age: 27	Th: L	Role SP	Health A	LIMA Plan D+	
Ht: 6' 4"	Wt: 225	Type Pwr	PT/Exp A	Rand Var -2	
			Consist A	MM 4405	

Last two seasons have solidified him as a sure-fire ace. Flies in ointment? Steady GB% dip adds twinge of risk, but pinpoint control and SwK-backed Dom afford plenty of room for error. A bit of H% and S% help kept surface stats extra shiny, so his ERA is headed north a bit. That's nitpicking though. Now a $25+ lock.

Yr Tm	W	L	Sv	IP	K	ERA	xERA	WHIP	oOPS	vL	vR	BF/G	Ctl	Dom	Cmd	FpK	SwK	G	L	F	H%	S%	hr/f	GS	APC	DOM%	DIS%	Sv%	LI	RAR	BPV	BPX	R$
12 SF	16	11	0	208	191	3.37	3.44	1.11	670	581	694	26.5	2.1	8.3	3.9	62%	10%	48	19	33	29%	74%	12%	32	102	34%	22%			16.6	117	153	$23
13 SF	13	9	0	201	199	2.77	3.25	1.03	577	487	602	25.9	2.8	8.9	3.2	60%	11%	47	18	35	26%	76%	8%	31	103	48%	6%			27.2	110	144	$26
14 SF	18	10	0	217	219	2.98	3.08	1.09	653	539	684	26.5	1.8	9.1	5.1	66%	12%	44	20	36	31%	76%	10%	33	102	48%	15%			20.4	137	163	$23
15 SF	18	9	0	218	234	2.93	3.10	1.01	612	539	627	27.2	1.6	9.6	6.0	64%	13%	42	23	36	30%	75%	10%	32	104	59%	6%			27.9	150	179	$32
16 SF	15	9	0	227	251	2.74	3.48	1.03	619	513	645	26.8	2.1	10.0	4.6	65%	12%	40	19	41	28%	79%	11%	34	105	56%	9%			40.5	140	166	$34
1st Half	9	4	0	115	126	2.20	3.46	1.02	609	496	635	27.1	2.3	9.9	4.3	67%	12%	40	21	39	28%	85%	10%	17	107	65%	6%			28.2	134	160	$37
2nd Half	6	5	0	112	125	3.29	3.50	1.04	630	528	655	26.6	2.0	10.0	5.0	63%	12%	39	17	43	29%	74%	11%	17	103	47%	12%			12.4	144	172	$31
17 Proj	15	9	0	210	225	2.91	3.35	1.04	624	527	648	25.7	2.0	9.6	4.9	64%	12%	42	20	39	29%	77%	11%	32						33.1	140	166	$28

Bundy,Dylan

Age: 24	Th: R	Role RP	Health A	LIMA Plan B+	
Ht: 6' 1"	Wt: 200	Type Pwr FB	PT/Exp D	Rand Var 0	
			Consist B	MM 1303	

Finally on road back after elbow, shoulder issues derailed development of this top prospect. That second half gives a glimpse of his upside, as strikeouts surged behind SwK uptick while he got stretched back out as a starter. But that ugly DOM/DIS% highlights downside, so view him as a speculation only in keeper leagues.

Yr Tm	W	L	Sv	IP	K	ERA	xERA	WHIP	oOPS	vL	vR	BF/G	Ctl	Dom	Cmd	FpK	SwK	G	L	F	H%	S%	hr/f	GS	APC	DOM%	DIS%	Sv%	LI	RAR	BPV	BPX	R$
12 BAL *	2	0	0	18	11	3.40	3.57	1.37	533	1000	250	15.4	4.3	5.6	1.3	50%	10%	20	0	80	27%	76%	0%	0	15			0	0.40	1.4	51	66	-$3
13																																	
14																																	
15 aa	0	3	0	22	21	4.91	3.74	1.39				11.6	2.1	8.5	4.0						38%	61%								-2.6	131	156	-$5
16 BAL	10	6	0	110	104	4.02	4.51	1.38	766	756	776	13.2	3.4	8.5	2.5	61%	11%	36	22	42	31%	77%	13%	14	54	14%	43%	0	0.82	2.3	75	89	$3
1st Half	2	1	0	36	25	3.28	5.04	1.49	775	704	849	7.4	2.5	6.3	2.5	62%	10%	32	23	45	35%	80%	6%	0	30			0	0.85	4.0	56	66	-$2
2nd Half	8	5	0	74	79	4.38	4.25	1.32	762	782	739	21.3	3.9	9.6	2.5	61%	12%	38	21	40	28%	75%	18%	14	88	14%	43%	0	0.79	-1.7	84	100	$6
17 Proj	13	8	0	145	140	3.94	4.40	1.39	767	751	784	11.8	3.3	8.7	2.6	61%	11%	36	22	42	32%	77%	13%	9						4.5	79	94	$5

Burgos,Enrique

Age: 26	Th: R	Role RP	Health B	LIMA Plan D+	
Ht: 6' 4"	Wt: 200	Type Pwr	PT/Exp F	Rand Var 0	
			Consist B	MM 1510	

1-2, 5.66 ERA in 41 IP at ARI. Power arm continues to flash upside (144 BPV in Aug), but as long as he can't find the plate, it won't matter. Inability to get strike one got worse as season went along, so we can't bank on that happening anytime soon. This isn't a place to speculate for saves, even on a bad team.

Yr Tm	W	L	Sv	IP	K	ERA	xERA	WHIP	oOPS	vL	vR	BF/G	Ctl	Dom	Cmd	FpK	SwK	G	L	F	H%	S%	hr/f	GS	APC	DOM%	DIS%	Sv%	LI	RAR	BPV	BPX	R$
12																																	
13																																	
14																																	
15 ARI *	2	3	13	51	70	4.47	5.08	1.72	709	822	629	4.2	6.1	12.2	2.0	55%	16%	34	27	39	39%	76%	8%	0	17			76	1.00	-3.2	89	106	-$1
16 ARI *	4	2	2	69	66	4.29	4.21	1.52	779	836	726	4.5	5.2	8.6	1.6	52%	12%	42	21	38	31%	73%	13%	0	17			29	1.05	-0.8	68	81	-$2
1st Half	3	1	1	37	29	3.37	3.99	1.53	811	1029	701	4.9	5.4	7.1	1.3	59%	11%	35	19	46	30%	78%	8%	0	18			33	0.44	3.7	60	72	$1
2nd Half	1	1	1	32	37	5.34	4.11	1.50	770	803	734	4.1	5.1	10.4	2.1	50%	12%	44	21	35	33%	66%	14%	0	17			25	1.21	-4.6	72	86	-$5
17 Proj	2	2	5	44	50	4.55	4.48	1.60	715	736	692	4.3	5.6	10.3	1.9	50%	12%	44	21	35	34%	73%	9%	0						-1.9	57	68	-$3

Bush,Matt

Age: 31	Th: R	Role RP	Health A	LIMA Plan B	
Ht: 5' 10"	Wt: 185	Type Pwr	PT/Exp F	Rand Var -1	
			Consist F	MM 4311	

7-2, 2.48 ERA in 62 IP at TEX. Former 1st overall pick would be potential closer fodder if he was 5 years younger. Still: 1) Shaved Ctl in half late behind uptick in FpK; 2) SwK, upper-90s heat foretell more Ks; 3) added GB tilt in 2H. And he's deadly to both LH and RH (4.0+ Cmd vL/R). Can still be LIMA fodder.

Yr Tm	W	L	Sv	IP	K	ERA	xERA	WHIP	oOPS	vL	vR	BF/G	Ctl	Dom	Cmd	FpK	SwK	G	L	F	H%	S%	hr/f	GS	APC	DOM%	DIS%	Sv%	LI	RAR	BPV	BPX	R$
12																																	
13																																	
14																																	
15																																	
16 TEX *	7	4	6	79	74	2.81	2.20	0.96	525	636	458	4.2	2.2	8.5	3.9	66%	13%	42	25	32	25%	74%	8%	0	16			67	1.10	13.4	124	147	$12
1st Half	3	3	5	40	38	3.24	2.52	1.05	521	548	506	4.3	2.9	8.5	2.9	64%	13%	35	24	41	25%	72%	4%	0	16			83	1.08	4.7	101	120	$12
2nd Half	4	1	1	38	36	2.35	3.08	0.86	527	677	422	4.3	1.4	8.5	6.0	67%	13%	47	26	26	25%	77%	11%	0	16			33	1.12	8.7	139	166	$13
17 Proj	7	3	8	73	68	2.75	3.35	0.93	540	653	472	4.2	2.0	8.5	4.2	66%	13%	42	25	32	25%	74%	10%	0						12.9	118	141	$12

STEPHEN NICKRAND

Butler,Eddie

Age: 26	Th: R	Role SP		Health	B	LIMA Plan	D
Ht: 6' 2"	Wt: 180	Type Con		PT/Exp	D	Rand Var	+5
				Consist	B	MM	0001

2-5, 7.17 ERA in 64 IP at COL. It's never good when your ERA could be a Boeing aircraft model. Of course, it'd be helpful if he would miss a bat now and again. With that Dom, and without a large GB tilt, home park is irrelevant—he'll get hit in the mountains, to the prairies, to the oceans, white... well, you get the idea.

Yr Tm	W	L	Sv	IP	K	ERA	xERA	WHIP	oOPS	vL	vR	BF/G	Ctl	Dom	Cmd	FpK	SwK	G	L	F	H%	S%	hr/f	GS	APC	DOM%	DIS%	Sv%	LI	RAR	BPV	BPX	R$
12																																	
13 aa	1	0	0	28	20	0.90	0.70	0.80				16.7	2.1	6.5	3.2						21%	88%								10.1	127	165	$2
14 COL *	7	11	0	129	57	5.08	5.24	1.52	973	1310	760	25.5	3.0	4.0	1.3	49%	5%	52	25	23	31%	68%	13%	3	86	0%	100%			-21.4	16	19	-$11
15 COL *	5	16	0	143	72	6.21	6.32	1.77	952	1073	831	24.3	4.3	4.5	1.1	57%	7%	50	22	28	33%	66%	17%	16	85	0%	69%			-39.5	3	4	-$24
16 COL *	10	8	0	153	73	6.69	6.42	1.67	944	894	977	21.5	2.9	4.3	1.5	58%	8%	46	25	30	33%	62%	20%	9	63	11%	67%	0	0.78	-47.1	1	2	-$21
1st Half	4	5	0	76	46	6.63	6.64	1.68	939	946	934	21.5	2.6	5.5	2.1	59%	8%	45	25	31	36%	63%	21%	9	74	11%	67%	0	0.88	-23.0	19	23	-$19
2nd Half	6	3	0	77	27	6.74	6.20	1.66	963	641	1197	21.5	3.3	3.1	0.9	57%	9%	52	24	24	31%	61%	13%	0	38			0	0.54	-24.1	-13	-15	-$23
17 Proj	**5**	**7**	**0**	**87**	**41**	**6.25**	**5.48**	**1.68**	**909**	**964**	**864**	**22.9**	**3.4**	**4.2**	**1.2**	**58%**	**8%**	**47**	**24**	**30**	**33%**	**64%**	**14%**	**17**						**-22.1**	**8**	**10**	**-$14**

Cabrera,Mauricio

Age: 23	Th: R	Role RP		Health	A	LIMA Plan	B
Ht: 6' 2"	Wt: 245	Type Pwr xGB		PT/Exp	F	Rand Var	-1
				Consist	D	MM	1311

5-1, 2.82 ERA in 38 IP at ATL. Flamethrower went from having absolutely no clue where his 100-mph heater was going to at least a marginal idea. Ks dipped too—especially late (5.6 Sept Dom). Still figuring things out in MLB—but you can't teach 100 mph. Ctl says don't go all in, but with opportunity... UP: 25 Sv

Yr Tm	W	L	Sv	IP	K	ERA	xERA	WHIP	oOPS	vL	vR	BF/G	Ctl	Dom	Cmd	FpK	SwK	G	L	F	H%	S%	hr/f	GS	APC	DOM%	DIS%	Sv%	LI	RAR	BPV	BPX	R$
12																																	
13																																	
14																																	
15 aa	0	1	0	17	23	7.00	4.45	1.86				6.2	9.6	11.8	1.2						33%	60%								-6.5	91	108	-$7
16 ATL *	8	4	10	72	63	3.65	2.72	1.39	587	691	498	4.6	5.5	7.9	1.4	57%	12%	49	18	33	29%	71%	0%	0	16			71	1.21	4.8	89	106	$6
1st Half	3	3	5	37	32	4.22	2.75	1.44	473	400	533	5.4	6.3	7.9	1.3	42%	7%	33	11	56	28%	67%	0%	0	11			63	0.52	-0.2	87	104	$4
2nd Half	5	1	5	35	31	3.06	4.41	1.33	596	714	496	4.1	4.6	7.9	1.7	58%	12%	51	18	31	30%	74%	0%	0	16			83	1.29	4.9	47	56	$9
17 Proj	**4**	**2**	**5**	**73**	**68**	**3.50**	**4.39**	**1.35**	**542**	**649**	**451**	**4.4**	**5.1**	**8.5**	**1.7**	**58%**	**12%**	**51**	**18**	**31**	**30%**	**71%**	**0%**	**0**						**6.1**	**45**	**54**	**$2**

Cahill,Trevor

Age: 29	Th: R	Role RP		Health	D	LIMA Plan	C
Ht: 6' 3"	Wt: 195	Type Pwr xGB		PT/Exp	D	Rand Var	-1
				Consist	A	MM	2301

4-4, 2.72 ERA in 66 IP at CHC. Numbers skewed by a couple of poor rehab outings; overall MLB skills closer to 1H numbers. All-in-all, consolidated the gains made late in 2015, including revived Dom, strong GB tilt. Walks are still an issue, and value is marginal out of the pen, but he's back from the dead.

Yr Tm	W	L	Sv	IP	K	ERA	xERA	WHIP	oOPS	vL	vR	BF/G	Ctl	Dom	Cmd	FpK	SwK	G	L	F	H%	S%	hr/f	GS	APC	DOM%	DIS%	Sv%	LI	RAR	BPV	BPX	R$
12 ARI	13	12	0	200	156	3.78	3.60	1.29	706	696	718	26.2	3.3	7.0	2.1	63%	10%	61	16	23	29%	72%	12%	32	99	31%	31%			5.8	75	98	$9
13 ARI *	8	12	0	163	112	4.18	4.16	1.43	745	769	719	23.9	4.0	6.2	1.5	60%	8%	56	20	24	29%	72%	12%	25	91	16%	36%	0	0.85	-6.3	47	61	-$3
14 ARI *	5	14	1	139	126	5.21	4.77	1.58	791	929	657	16.1	4.8	8.2	1.7	57%	11%	48	24	27	33%	67%	10%	17	60	18%	35%	50	0.67	-25.2	60	72	-$11
15 2 NL *	2	6	0	80	55	5.72	4.86	1.55	725	684	751	9.4	3.9	6.2	1.6	59%	10%	63	19	18	32%	63%	17%	3	26	0%	100%	0	0.63	-17.3	44	52	-$11
16 CHC *	4	7	0	85	85	3.44	4.50	1.51	621	660	594	6.6	5.1	9.0	1.8	54%	12%	57	22	22	31%	81%	18%	1	23	0%	0%	0	0.70	7.9	62	74	$0
1st Half	1	2	0	38	41	2.37	3.87	1.29	613	667	577	5.4	4.7	9.7	2.1	52%	13%	54	21	25	27%	87%	15%	0	22			0	0.69	8.5	79	94	$5
2nd Half	3	5	0	47	44	4.31	5.45	1.68	632	651	619	8.5	5.4	8.4	1.6	57%	10%	60	23	16	33%	78%	25%	1	25	0%	0%	0	0.73	-0.7	45	54	-$3
17 Proj	**3**	**6**	**0**	**73**	**73**	**3.66**	**3.72**	**1.38**	**674**	**710**	**648**	**8.5**	**4.6**	**9.0**	**2.0**	**57%**	**11%**	**58**	**21**	**21**	**30%**	**75%**	**15%**	**0**						**4.8**	**74**	**88**	**$0**

Cain,Matt

Age: 32	Th: R	Role RP		Health	F	LIMA Plan	C
Ht: 6' 3"	Wt: 245	Type Pwr		PT/Exp	C	Rand Var	+3
				Consist	C	MM	0201

Is a role change in order? Was simply awful again as a SP, with three more DL stints tossed in for good measure. Then returned in September as a reliever and pitched well—albeit only 5.2 IP (4 H, 2 ER, 1 BB, 6 K). After three injured years and at 32, one wonders if the pen would be a better home.

Yr Tm	W	L	Sv	IP	K	ERA	xERA	WHIP	oOPS	vL	vR	BF/G	Ctl	Dom	Cmd	FpK	SwK	G	L	F	H%	S%	hr/f	GS	APC	DOM%	DIS%	Sv%	LI	RAR	BPV	BPX	R$
12 SF	16	5	0	219	193	2.79	3.71	1.04	635	711	563	27.4	2.1	7.9	3.8	62%	10%	37	21	42	27%	77%	8%	32	105	53%	13%			33.1	101	132	$32
13 SF	8	10	0	184	158	4.00	3.87	1.16	678	644	704	25.3	2.7	7.7	2.9	63%	9%	38	22	40	27%	69%	11%	30	97	37%	20%			-3.1	82	107	$8
14 SF	2	7	0	90	70	4.18	3.96	1.25	725	737	713	24.9	3.2	7.0	2.2	62%	9%	45	19	36	27%	71%	14%	15	96	20%	40%			-4.9	62	74	-$2
15 SF *	3	6	0	84	59	5.47	5.44	1.48	897	960	840	19.0	2.8	6.3	2.3	59%	9%	36	24	40	32%	66%	15%	11	76	9%	45%	0	0.68	-15.7	37	44	-$9
16 SF	4	8	0	89	72	5.64	4.81	1.51	864	901	836	18.9	3.2	7.3	2.3	63%	9%	37	24	39	33%	66%	15%	17	75	6%	53%	0	0.71	-16.0	59	70	-$8
1st Half	1	5	0	57	41	5.34	5.01	1.52	846	911	791	23.1	2.8	6.4	2.3	65%	9%	35	25	40	34%	67%	11%	11	90	9%	45%			-8.1	53	63	-$8
2nd Half	3	3	0	32	31	6.19	4.44	1.50	898	880	908	14.3	3.9	8.7	2.2	59%	10%	41	22	37	31%	65%	24%	6	58	0%	67%	0	0.67	-7.9	70	83	-$7
17 Proj	**4**	**7**	**0**	**87**	**71**	**5.26**	**4.61**	**1.42**	**832**	**859**	**810**	**8.2**	**3.2**	**7.3**	**2.3**	**61%**	**10%**	**39**	**23**	**39**	**31%**	**67%**	**15%**	**0**						**-11.5**	**63**	**75**	**-$6**

Caminero,Arquimedes

Age: 30	Th: R	Role RP		Health	B	LIMA Plan	D+
Ht: 6' 4"	Wt: 185	Type Pwr		PT/Exp	D	Rand Var	-3
				Consist	D	MM	1200

Home plate is this fireballer's personal desert mirage—at times snapping into sharp focus, but mostly dancing blurrily and tantalizingly 60 feet away. With his stuff, he'll keep getting chances, and could still could tap into previous year's Cmd. But managers don't hand the ninth inning to an arm they can't trust.

Yr Tm	W	L	Sv	IP	K	ERA	xERA	WHIP	oOPS	vL	vR	BF/G	Ctl	Dom	Cmd	FpK	SwK	G	L	F	H%	S%	hr/f	GS	APC	DOM%	DIS%	Sv%	LI	RAR	BPV	BPX	R$
12 aa	0	0	2	18	15	3.88	4.47	1.74				6.7	5.8	7.5	1.3						36%	75%								0.3	71	93	-$5
13 MIA *	6	2	5	67	66	4.30	2.93	1.18	603	841	422	4.8	3.5	8.9	2.5	54%	10%	25	17	58	27%	64%	10%	0	16			63	0.51	-3.6	93	121	$3
14 MIA *	4	2	10	70	68	5.81	5.91	1.75	943	583	1093	6.6	4.4	8.8	2.0	56%	16%	37	5	58	38%	67%	18%	0	19			83	0.97	-17.8	58	69	-$7
15 PIT	5	1	0	75	73	3.62	3.67	1.23	661	681	649	4.4	3.5	8.8	2.5	62%	13%	48	24	29	29%	73%	12%	0	15			0	0.86	3.2	90	107	$2
16 2 TM	2	3	1	61	50	3.56	5.27	1.65	830	835	824	4.9	4.9	7.4	1.5	55%	10%	43	19	38	33%	82%	10%	0	19			33	0.78	4.7	22	27	-$3
1st Half	0	2	1	30	25	3.60	5.41	1.90	906	928	883	5.3	5.7	7.5	1.3	52%	9%	46	22	32	37%	83%	10%	0	21			50	0.55	2.2	5	6	-$5
2nd Half	2	1	0	31	25	3.52	5.14	1.40	751	727	768	4.6	4.1	7.3	1.8	59%	11%	40	16	44	29%	79%	10%	0	18			0	0.99	2.5	40	47	-$1
17 Proj	**4**	**2**	**0**	**65**	**59**	**3.98**	**4.56**	**1.49**	**773**	**786**	**763**	**4.8**	**4.3**	**8.1**	**1.9**	**58%**	**11%**	**45**	**21**	**35**	**32%**	**76%**	**11%**	**0**						**1.7**	**53**	**64**	**-$3**

Carrasco,Carlos

Age: 30	Th: R	Role SP		Health	D	LIMA Plan	B
Ht: 6' 3"	Wt: 215	Type Pwr		PT/Exp	A	Rand Var	+1
				Consist	A	MM	4405

Strained hammy, broken pinkie took chunks out of what was otherwise another superb season, his third straight with elite skills. Of course, it's also two straight with injury time (plus TJS in 2012), so that health grade has to be a factor. It all means you can't draft him as your #1, but he's a terrific next-tier option.

Yr Tm	W	L	Sv	IP	K	ERA	xERA	WHIP	oOPS	vL	vR	BF/G	Ctl	Dom	Cmd	FpK	SwK	G	L	F	H%	S%	hr/f	GS	APC	DOM%	DIS%	Sv%	LI	RAR	BPV	BPX	R$
12																																	
13 CLE *	4	5	1	118	94	5.15	4.76	1.50	864	980	745	16.5	3.1	7.2	2.3	67%	9%	50	22	28	35%	66%	9%	7	52	14%	71%	100	0.59	-18.8	64	83	-$9
14 CLE	8	7	1	134	140	2.55	2.73	0.99	543	516	566	13.2	1.9	9.4	4.8	63%	14%	53	20	28	29%	75%	7%	14	49	43%	0%	100	0.63	19.6	148	176	$17
15 CLE	14	12	0	184	216	3.63	2.75	1.07	646	639	651	24.3	2.1	10.6	5.0	67%	14%	51	19	30	31%	69%	13%	30	93	57%	20%			7.6	163	194	$19
16 CLE	11	8	0	146	150	3.32	3.41	1.15	711	739	688	24.0	2.1	9.2	4.4	62%	13%	49	20	31	30%	78%	16%	25	90	32%	20%			15.7	137	162	$15
1st Half	4	2	0	63	63	2.56	3.16	1.06	678	657	694	24.8	2.1	9.0	4.2	59%	12%	53	20	28	27%	86%	22%	10	92	40%	10%			12.7	134	160	$15
2nd Half	7	6	0	83	87	3.90	3.60	1.22	734	798	683	23.4	2.1	9.4	4.6	63%	13%	46	20	34	33%	72%	13%	15	88	27%	27%			2.9	138	164	$14
17 Proj	**14**	**10**	**0**	**189**	**197**	**3.44**	**3.24**	**1.14**	**669**	**693**	**649**	**20.1**	**2.2**	**9.4**	**4.3**	**64%**	**13%**	**50**	**20**	**30**	**31%**	**73%**	**13%**	**37**						**17.4**	**138**	**165**	**$18**

Cashner,Andrew

Age: 30	Th: R	Role SP		Health	F	LIMA Plan	C
Ht: 6' 6"	Wt: 200	Type Pwr		PT/Exp	A	Rand Var	+2
				Consist	B	MM	1203

Peripherals on an ominous four-year slide, and it's across the board—walks and FB rate up; FpK, SwK, and strikeouts all down. Let's not even talk about that failing grade in health. Just now reaching peak age, so there's still hope he can recapture former glory/promise. But with further erosion... DN: mid-year DFA

Yr Tm	W	L	Sv	IP	K	ERA	xERA	WHIP	oOPS	vL	vR	BF/G	Ctl	Dom	Cmd	FpK	SwK	G	L	F	H%	S%	hr/f	GS	APC	DOM%	DIS%	Sv%	LI	RAR	BPV	BPX	R$
12 SD *	5	5	0	70	77	3.58	3.15	1.22	688	525	815	7.2	3.1	9.9	3.2	55%	13%	53	23	24	32%	72%	17%	5	24	40%	20%	0	1.25	3.7	116	151	$3
13 SD	10	9	0	175	128	3.09	3.56	1.13	639	703	578	22.8	2.4	6.6	2.7	60%	9%	53	19	29	28%	74%	8%	26	87	31%	15%	0	0.73	16.8	84	110	$14
14 SD	5	7	0	123	93	2.55	3.60	1.13	623	675	573	26.6	2.1	6.8	3.2	63%	8%	48	20	31	29%	79%	6%	19	95	32%	26%			18.1	91	108	$10
15 SD	6	16	0	185	165	4.34	3.95	1.44	772	896	669	25.9	3.2	8.0	2.5	62%	9%	47	23	30	34%	72%	12%	31	100	23%	26%			-8.6	83	99	-$4
16 2 NL	5	11	0	132	112	5.25	4.65	1.53	849	903	794	21.0	4.1	7.6	1.9	55%	8%	46	20	33	32%	68%	15%	27	85	11%	37%	0	1.05	-17.3	51	61	-$8
1st Half	3	6	0	59	42	4.42	4.74	1.44	803	716	903	21.8	3.7	6.4	1.8	56%	6%	50	19	31	30%	72%	12%	12	88	0%	33%			-1.7	44	53	-$2
2nd Half	2	5	0	73	70	5.92	4.58	1.60	886	1072	716	20.4	4.4	8.6	1.9	54%	9%	44	22	35	34%	66%	16%	15	82	20%	40%	0	1.27	-15.6	57	68	-$13
17 Proj	**6**	**11**	**0**	**145**	**129**	**4.15**	**4.23**	**1.43**	**780**	**849**	**715**	**24.4**	**3.6**	**8.0**	**2.2**	**58%**	**8%**	**47**	**21**	**31**	**32%**	**74%**	**12%**	**25**						**0.7**	**73**	**87**	**-$1**

ROD TRUESDELL

Casilla,Santiago

Age: 36 Th: R Role: RP | Health: D | LIMA Plan: B
Ht: 6' 0" Wt: 200 Type: Pwr | PT/Exp: B | Rand Var: +1
Consist: A | MM: 3310

Overall, a solid year, with career-best strikeout rate. But that obscures late problems—started skidding a bit in July, then really went off the road in Sept (4.60 xERA, 1.7 Cmd), losing closer's job. Struggles vL continue to mount as well. Still a decent LIMA option, but far from a lock to regain the ninth anywhere.

Yr Tm	W	L	Sv	IP	K	ERA	xERA	WHIP	oOPS	vL	vR	BF/G	Ctl	Dom	Cmd	FpK	SwK	G	L	F	H%	S%	hr/f	GS	APC	DOM%	DIS%	Sv%	LI	RAR	BPV	BPX	R$
12 SF	7	6	25	63	55	2.84	3.78	1.22	656	727	608	3.7	3.1	7.8	2.5	53%	10%	55	15	30	28%	83%	14%	0	14			81	1.37	9.2	89	116	$15
13 SF	7	2	2	50	38	2.16	4.03	1.28	627	652	611	3.6	4.5	6.8	1.5	54%	10%	54	17	29	26%	84%	5%	0	14			67	1.66	10.5	34	44	$4
14 SF	3	3	19	58	45	1.70	3.07	0.86	493	539	461	4.0	2.3	6.9	3.0	57%	11%	56	15	29	21%	83%	7%	0	16			83	1.37	14.7	96	115	$15
15 SF	4	2	38	58	62	2.79	3.51	1.28	680	841	531	3.6	3.6	9.6	2.7	57%	11%	46	24	30	31%	82%	13%	0	14			86	1.47	8.4	101	120	$18
16 SF	2	5	31	58	65	3.57	3.46	1.19	710	849	622	3.9	2.9	10.1	3.4	54%	11%	48	16	36	30%	75%	15%	0	15			78	1.79	4.4	128	152	$14
1st Half	1	2	19	33	42	3.03	3.04	1.29	722	891	609	3.9	3.3	11.6	3.5	52%	11%	53	16	30	34%	82%	17%	0	16			83	1.88	4.7	150	179	$17
2nd Half	1	3	12	25	23	4.26	3.99	1.07	694	789	637	3.8	2.5	8.2	3.3	55%	12%	41	16	43	25%	65%	14%	0	14			71	1.67	-0.2	99	118	$10
17 Proj	**3**	**4**	**9**	**58**	**58**	**3.09**	**3.63**	**1.15**	**663**	**782**	**580**	**3.7**	**3.0**	**8.9**	**3.0**	**55%**	**11%**	**48**	**18**	**34**	**28%**	**78%**	**13%**	**0**						**7.9**	**106**	**126**	**$6**

Cecil,Brett

Age: 30 Th: L Role: RP | Health: D | LIMA Plan: B
Ht: 6' 1" Wt: 235 Type: Pwr | PT/Exp: D | Rand Var: +5
Consist: A | MM: 5500

A first half to forget. Lost 5 games in April (think about that: it's REALLY hard for a setup man to lose 5 games in a month), then tore a lat muscle in May and missed a month-plus. Came back to pitch really well in 2nd half, with awful hr/f luck sabotaging ERA. FpK, Ctl gains a great sign. Rand Var agrees—he'll rebound.

Yr Tm	W	L	Sv	IP	K	ERA	xERA	WHIP	oOPS	vL	vR	BF/G	Ctl	Dom	Cmd	FpK	SwK	G	L	F	H%	S%	hr/f	GS	APC	DOM%	DIS%	Sv%	LI	RAR	BPV	BPX	R$
12 TOR *	6	8	0	144	104	4.50	4.78	1.46	855	603	934	17.1	2.8	6.5	2.4	52%	10%	37	22	41	33%	71%	14%	9	49	0%	33%	0	0.72	-8.5	58	76	-$5
13 TOR	5	1	1	61	70	2.82	2.96	1.10	594	458	736	4.2	3.4	10.4	3.0	58%	12%	51	20	29	28%	76%	9%	0	15			33	0.89	7.8	124	161	$5
14 TOR	2	3	5	53	76	2.70	2.68	1.37	627	714	569	3.5	4.6	12.8	2.8	54%	17%	54	25	22	37%	80%	7%	0	14			71	1.22	6.8	140	167	$3
15 TOR	5	5	5	54	70	2.48	2.49	0.96	562	539	576	3.4	2.2	11.6	5.4	60%	15%	52	19	29	30%	77%	11%	0	13			63	1.01	9.9	181	215	$9
16 TOR	1	7	0	37	45	3.93	3.14	1.28	742	673	799	2.9	2.0	11.0	5.6	66%	13%	42	28	30	36%	76%	20%	0	10			0	1.08	1.2	166	197	-$2
1st Half	0	5	0	12	10	4.63	4.78	1.71	842	766	906	3.1	2.3	7.7	3.3	66%	10%	40	23	38	41%	74%	7%	0	11			0	1.57	-0.6	94	113	-$5
2nd Half	1	2	0	25	35	3.60	2.45	1.08	688	625	739	2.8	1.8	12.6	7.0	66%	14%	43	32	25	32%	77%	33%	0	10			0	0.84	1.8	200	238	$0
17 Proj	**3**	**4**	**0**	**58**	**74**	**2.97**	**2.67**	**1.08**	**630**	**583**	**664**	**3.4**	**2.1**	**11.5**	**5.4**	**59%**	**14%**	**48**	**25**	**27**	**33%**	**77%**	**16%**	**0**						**8.7**	**176**	**210**	**$4**

Cedeno,Xavier

Age: 30 Th: L Role: RP | Health: A | LIMA Plan: A
Ht: 6' 1" Wt: 205 Type: Pwr | PT/Exp: D | Rand Var: 0
Consist: A | MM: 3310

Stiff neck ended season in late Aug. Otherwise, another solid season for this consistent lefty-killer. Of course, that lefty-killing is a double-edged sword, since it means he's likely to stay in a setup role. Even so, he's a terrific LIMA pick, and delivers a bushel-basket of holds, too (if that helps you).

Yr Tm	W	L	Sv	IP	K	ERA	xERA	WHIP	oOPS	vL	vR	BF/G	Ctl	Dom	Cmd	FpK	SwK	G	L	F	H%	S%	hr/f	GS	APC	DOM%	DIS%	Sv%	LI	RAR	BPV	BPX	R$
12 HOU *	2	1	2	59	56	3.12	3.86	1.41	704	616	797	3.8	3.5	8.7	2.5	50%	11%	50	15	35	34%	78%	10%	0	13			29	1.05	6.5	92	120	$0
13 2 TM *	2	0	4	47	43	2.90	3.55	1.43	811	603	1039	3.6	4.7	8.3	1.8	62%	10%	60	15	25	31%	80%	0%	0	14			57	0.61	5.5	80	105	$0
14 WAS *	5	1	4	46	47	3.05	2.82	1.09	833	1067	600	4.1	2.5	9.1	3.6	47%	8%	38	33	29	28%	75%	14%	0	12			57	0.94	3.9	117	139	$4
15 2 TM	4	1	1	46	47	2.35	3.16	1.17	614	490	768	2.9	2.7	9.2	3.4	54%	15%	53	21	26	30%	84%	13%	0	11			33	1.28	9.2	123	146	$3
16 TAM	3	4	0	41	43	3.70	3.57	1.19	597	483	705	3.2	2.8	9.4	3.3	63%	13%	47	24	29	32%	68%	6%	0	13			0	1.30	2.5	117	139	$0
1st Half	3	2	0	28	28	3.86	3.62	1.18	608	503	705	3.5	2.9	9.0	3.1	68%	13%	47	26	27	31%	66%	5%	0	13			0	1.60	1.1	109	130	$2
2nd Half	0	2	0	13	15	3.38	3.48	1.20	574	442	706	2.8	2.7	10.1	3.8	52%	13%	47	19	33	33%	73%	8%	0	12			0	0.81	1.3	135	161	-$3
17 Proj	**4**	**2**	**2**	**51**	**50**	**3.14**	**3.60**	**1.21**	**618**	**520**	**722**	**3.4**	**3.1**	**8.9**	**2.9**	**57%**	**13%**	**50**	**20**	**30**	**31%**	**75%**	**8%**	**0**						**6.5**	**105**	**125**	**$3**

Cervenka,Hunter

Age: 27 Th: L Role: RP | Health: A | LIMA Plan: D
Ht: 6' 1" Wt: 245 Type: Pwr | PT/Exp: D | Rand Var: -3
Consist: F | MM: 0300

The quintessential LOOGY (68 games, 43 IP). Now, we aren't saying a good LOOGY, necessarily. Sure, he might be fine if he could find the plate, but a 45% FpK won't cut it. Even subracting 5 IBB, still put up a 4.8 Ctl, and that's not cutting it either. Avoid until he reduces the walks.

Yr Tm	W	L	Sv	IP	K	ERA	xERA	WHIP	oOPS	vL	vR	BF/G	Ctl	Dom	Cmd	FpK	SwK	G	L	F	H%	S%	hr/f	GS	APC	DOM%	DIS%	Sv%	LI	RAR	BPV	BPX	R$
12																																	
13 aa	5	1	1	38	28	3.68	3.27	1.41				5.4	4.9	6.6	1.3						29%	73%								0.9	67	88	-$1
14 aa	4	4	1	62	55	4.32	2.78	1.32				5.3	4.6	8.0	1.7						29%	64%								-4.4	91	108	-$2
15 a/a	2	1	1	38	47	5.31	6.15	2.04				5.8	7.0	11.1	1.6						43%	73%								-6.3	77	91	-$8
16 2 NL	1	0	0	43	42	3.53	4.61	1.36	667	624	720	2.7	5.8	8.7	1.5	45%	11%	47	17	36	26%	75%	8%	0	11			0	1.08	3.5	25	30	-$2
1st Half	0	0	0	25	31	2.55	3.66	1.18	570	528	615	2.8	5.8	11.3	1.9	39%	13%	52	13	35	24%	79%	6%	0	12			0	1.00	5.0	76	91	$1
2nd Half	1	0	0	19	11	4.82	5.96	1.61	784	728	864	2.6	5.8	5.3	0.9	52%	9%	42	20	38	28%	71%	10%	0	10			0	1.17	-1.5	-41	-49	-$6
17 Proj	**1**	**3**	**0**	**51**	**48**	**4.29**	**4.98**	**1.57**	**752**	**706**	**811**	**3.6**	**5.9**	**8.5**	**1.4**	**47%**	**10%**	**46**	**17**	**37**	**31%**	**72%**	**6%**	**0**						**-0.6**	**18**	**22**	**-$5**

Cessa,Luis

Age: 25 Th: R Role: SP | Health: A | LIMA Plan: C
Ht: 6' 0" Wt: 205 Type: | PT/Exp: D | Rand Var: +2
Consist: B | MM: 0101

4-4, 4.35 ERA in 70 IP at NYY. A decent debut for the former OF, who shows good command with his 95-mph heater and swing-and-miss breaking stuff. Dom/SwK discrepancy suggests he's still learning the art of pitching, and hints at some K upside. Could be a good one in time, but likely needs a bit more seasoning.

Yr Tm	W	L	Sv	IP	K	ERA	xERA	WHIP	oOPS	vL	vR	BF/G	Ctl	Dom	Cmd	FpK	SwK	G	L	F	H%	S%	hr/f	GS	APC	DOM%	DIS%	Sv%	LI	RAR	BPV	BPX	R$
12																																	
13																																	
14																																	
15 a/a	8	10	0	139	96	5.35	5.21	1.60				24.6	2.4	6.2	2.6						38%	65%								-23.8	68	81	-$13
16 NYY *	10	7	0	148	104	4.39	4.69	1.28	744	766	728	18.9	2.4	6.4	2.6	58%	11%	43	20	37	28%	73%	20%	9	62	11%	33%	0	0.53	-3.7	44	52	$4
1st Half	3	1	0	51	31	4.80	5.04	1.42	773	563	983	15.5	3.9	5.4	1.4	55%	11%	38	15	47	26%	72%	25%	0	34			0	0.15	-3.9	12	14	-$4
2nd Half	7	6	0	96	74	4.17	4.50	1.20	739	813	689	21.5	1.7	6.9	4.1	58%	11%	44	20	35	29%	73%	18%	9	74	11%	33%	0	0.69	0.2	79	94	$8
17 Proj	**7**	**6**	**0**	**116**	**81**	**4.64**	**4.69**	**1.42**	**720**	**771**	**686**	**20.6**	**2.5**	**6.3**	**2.5**	**58%**	**11%**	**44**	**20**	**35**	**32%**	**70%**	**11%**	**24**						**-6.5**	**67**	**80**	**-$3**

Chacin,Jhoulys

Age: 29 Th: R Role: SP | Health: F | LIMA Plan: D+
Ht: 6' 3" Wt: 225 Type: | PT/Exp: C | Rand Var: +1
Consist: B | MM: 1103

Can he keep this new and improved Dom rate? An unimproved SwK says probably not. What's more, that PQS DOM%-DIS% ratio shows there's not much upside overall, and lots of downside. Health grade certainly doesn't help matters either. There are plenty of better places to speculate.

Yr Tm	W	L	Sv	IP	K	ERA	xERA	WHIP	oOPS	vL	vR	BF/G	Ctl	Dom	Cmd	FpK	SwK	G	L	F	H%	S%	hr/f	GS	APC	DOM%	DIS%	Sv%	LI	RAR	BPV	BPX	R$
12 COL *	4	7	0	92	54	4.66	5.32	1.56	821	910	720	22.3	3.9	5.3	1.4	59%	8%	39	24	37	31%	73%	12%	14	83	7%	64%			-7.3	21	27	-$8
13 COL	14	10	0	197	126	3.47	4.02	1.26	685	722	650	26.3	2.8	5.7	2.1	61%	8%	47	25	29	29%	73%	6%	31	96	29%	29%			9.7	53	69	$10
14 COL	1	7	0	63	42	5.40	4.56	1.44	790	751	821	24.7	4.0	6.0	1.5	63%	9%	43	22	35	29%	64%	12%	11	93	9%	73%			-13.0	21	25	-$7
15 ARI *	9	7	0	155	89	3.39	3.82	1.35	729	982	497	25.9	3.1	5.2	1.7	55%	10%	47	19	33	30%	76%	15%	4	85	50%	50%	0	0.84	11.0	51	61	$4
16 2 TM	6	8	0	144	119	4.81	4.36	1.44	745	762	728	18.6	3.4	7.4	2.2	61%	8%	48	23	29	33%	68%	11%	22	70	18%	59%	0	0.68	-11.1	67	80	-$4
1st Half	3	7	0	80	58	5.87	4.75	1.58	824	829	819	24.1	3.7	6.6	1.8	62%	8%	51	21	28	34%	63%	13%	15	88	20%	67%			-16.6	46	55	-$11
2nd Half	3	1	0	64	61	3.50	3.90	1.27	642	669	617	14.2	3.1	8.5	2.8	61%	9%	45	25	30	31%	74%	9%	7	57	14%	43%	0	0.61	5.5	93	111	$4
17 Proj	**6**	**8**	**0**	**145**	**106**	**4.46**	**4.55**	**1.39**	**731**	**746**	**716**	**20.0**	**3.4**	**6.6**	**2.0**	**61%**	**8%**	**45**	**23**	**31**	**31%**	**69%**	**9%**	**30**						**-4.9**	**51**	**61**	**-$2**

Chapman,Aroldis

Age: 29 Th: L Role: RP | Health: B | LIMA Plan: C+
Ht: 6' 4" Wt: 195 Type: Pwr | PT/Exp: A | Rand Var: -4
Consist: B | MM: 5530

Utterly dominant once again following 30-game suspension. The trade of a few strikeouts for markedly better Ctl was a net win. Even continued to build on the GB profile that began in 2015 2H, meaning fewer chances to give up the odd HR (or ANY runs, for that matter). Next up—breaking the elusive 40-save barrier.

Yr Tm	W	L	Sv	IP	K	ERA	xERA	WHIP	oOPS	vL	vR	BF/G	Ctl	Dom	Cmd	FpK	SwK	G	L	F	H%	S%	hr/f	GS	APC	DOM%	DIS%	Sv%	LI	RAR	BPV	BPX	R$
12 CIN	5	5	38	72	122	1.51	2.12	0.81	450	330	501	4.1	2.9	15.3	5.3	53%	18%	37	20	43	28%	85%	7%	0	18			88	1.42	22.2	213	278	$32
13 CIN	4	5	38	64	112	2.54	2.30	1.04	544	379	592	3.8	4.1	15.8	3.9	59%	17%	34	24	42	31%	81%	15%	0	16			88	1.38	10.4	186	243	$23
14 CIN	0	3	36	54	106	2.00	1.52	0.83	406	372	415	3.7	4.0	17.7	4.4	58%	21%	43	22	35	30%	75%	4%	0	17			95	1.44	11.6	231	275	$21
15 CIN	4	4	33	66	116	1.63	2.55	1.15	527	451	554	4.3	4.5	15.7	3.5	56%	20%	37	22	41	36%	88%	6%	0	18			92	1.24	19.1	177	211	$23
16 2 TM	4	1	36	58	90	1.55	2.24	0.86	452	462	448	3.8	2.8	14.0	5.0	57%	19%	46	25	29	29%	83%	6%	0	17			92	1.39	18.9	200	238	$25
1st Half	2	0	16	22	33	2.86	2.57	0.95	567	400	589	3.6	1.6	13.5	8.3	57%	18%	39	20	41	34%	74%	10%	0	15			94	1.26	3.6	216	257	$16
2nd Half	2	1	20	36	57	0.75	2.03	0.81	373	479	339	3.9	3.5	14.3	4.1	58%	20%	52	28	20	25%	90%	0%	0	17			91	1.47	15.3	192	228	$31
17 Proj	**4**	**3**	**43**	**64**	**108**	**1.71**	**2.21**	**0.94**	**472**	**433**	**483**	**3.7**	**3.4**	**15.1**	**4.4**	**57%**	**19%**	**43**	**23**	**34**	**31%**	**83%**	**7%**	**0**						**19.6**	**200**	**238**	**$28**

ROD TRUESDELL

Chargois,J.T.

Age: 26	Th: R	Role: RP		Health: A	LIMA Plan: C		
Ht: 6' 3"	Wt: 200	Type: Pwr xGB		PT/Exp: F	Rand Var: -5		
				Consist: A	MM: 2210		

1-1, 4.70 ERA in 23 IP at MIN. Minor league closer posted a 1.35 ERA in AA/AAA but saw low-leverage time in late-season debut. Mid-90s heater and a plus slider are MLB quality, but Dom dip with MIN hints at some work yet to do. But if 1st half Dom surfaces in the Show and electric Sept was no fluke... UP: 20 Sv

Yr Tm	W	L	Sv	IP	K	ERA	xERA	WHIP	oOPS	vL	vR	BF/G	Ctl	Dom	Cmd	FpK	SwK	G	L	F	H%	S%	hr/f	GS	APC	DOM%	DIS%	Sv%	LI	RAR	BPV	BPX	R$
12																																	
13																																	
14																																	
15 aa	1	1	11	33	26	3.20	3.68	1.51				4.5	5.4	7.2	1.3						30%	78%								3.1	69	82	$1
16 MIN *	3	2	16	70	59	2.80	3.58	1.37	752	758	745	4.6	3.4	7.6	2.3	59%	9%	55	23	22	33%	79%	0%	0	15			100	0.69	11.9	86	103	$8
1st Half	2	0	12	34	32	2.82	3.70	1.34	1350	2000	1000	4.7	3.4	8.6	2.5	63%	0%	40	60	0	32%	81%	0%	0	30			100	0.01	5.7	89	106	$12
2nd Half	1	2	4	36	27	2.79	3.46	1.40	706	674	725	4.5	3.3	6.7	2.0	59%	10%	56	20	23	33%	78%	0%	0	14			100	0.72	6.2	84	101	$5
17 Proj	2	1	2	44	37	3.42	3.86	1.33	685	669	694	4.4	3.4	7.8	2.3	59%	10%	56	20	23	31%	76%	10%	0						4.1	83	99	-$1

Chatwood,Tyler

Age: 27	Th: R	Role: SP	Health: F	LIMA Plan: C+	
Ht: 5' 11"	Wt: 175	Type: Pwr xGB	PT/Exp: C	Rand Var: 0	
			Consist: B	MM: 1103	

Fooled some with a quick start, but it wasn't skills-supported, and things tailed off in 2nd half—not surprising given he's just one season post-TJS. Return of xGB tilt a plus, but Cmd still poor, and it was his back that acted up this time. Former first-round pick will keep getting chances, but still too risky to depend on.

Yr Tm	W	L	Sv	IP	K	ERA	xERA	WHIP	oOPS	vL	vR	BF/G	Ctl	Dom	Cmd	FpK	SwK	G	L	F	H%	S%	hr/f	GS	APC	DOM%	DIS%	Sv%	LI	RAR	BPV	BPX	R$
12 COL *	6	9	1	126	83	5.80	5.84	1.72	836	890	774	17.9	4.3	5.9	1.4	54%	6%	56	21	23	34%	67%	19%	12	61	0%	67%	100	0.62	-27.7	27	35	-$18
13 COL *	10	6	0	145	91	3.13	3.90	1.42	711	729	697	23.7	2.9	5.7	1.9	55%	7%	59	21	21	32%	77%	7%	20	89	15%	45%			13.1	64	84	$4
14 COL	1	0	0	24	20	4.50	3.56	1.21	711	472	1015	25.3	3.0	7.5	2.5	50%	10%	46	29	26	26%	68%	22%	4	89	25%	50%			-2.2	78	93	-$3
15																																	
16 COL	12	9	0	158	117	3.87	4.31	1.37	723	751	693	24.8	4.0	6.7	1.7	54%	8%	57	17	26	29%	74%	12%	27	94	22%	37%			6.2	47	56	$5
1st Half	8	4	0	86	53	3.15	4.14	1.23	671	584	741	24.9	3.0	5.6	1.8	55%	8%	58	17	24	27%	76%	10%	14	93	29%	36%			11.0	54	65	$13
2nd Half	4	5	0	72	64	4.73	4.52	1.55	781	887	616	24.7	5.1	8.0	1.6	54%	9%	56	17	27	31%	72%	16%	13	96	15%	38%			-4.8	39	47	-$3
17 Proj	9	10	0	145	103	4.02	4.39	1.46	748	791	704	22.9	3.8	6.4	1.7	55%	8%	57	19	24	31%	74%	11%	27						3.0	47	56	-$1

Chavez,Jesse

Age: 33	Th: R	Role: RP	Health: B	LIMA Plan: C	
Ht: 6' 1"	Wt: 170	Type: Pwr	PT/Exp: B	Rand Var: +2	
			Consist: A	MM: 1201	

Didn't fare as well after trade to LA, with an xERA over 4.50 in the NL. Otherwise, the move back to bullpen suited him—not that it helped anyone fanalytically. He'll likely continue to toil in pitching's No Man's Land: A swingman who's more valuable to his big league club than to you.

Yr Tm	W	L	Sv	IP	K	ERA	xERA	WHIP	oOPS	vL	vR	BF/G	Ctl	Dom	Cmd	FpK	SwK	G	L	F	H%	S%	hr/f	GS	APC	DOM%	DIS%	Sv%	LI	RAR	BPV	BPX	R$
12 2AL *	9	6	2	130	101	5.37	4.97	1.44	983	1144	888	16.2	2.4	7.0	2.9	62%	11%	36	29	35	34%	64%	26%	2	36	0%	50%	100	0.66	-21.7	65	85	-$6
13 OAK *	4	6	1	87	74	3.64	3.71	1.35	620	630	605	9.1	2.6	7.6	2.9	61%	10%	43	17	39	34%	72%	5%	0	27			50	0.93	2.4	95	124	$0
14 OAK	8	8	0	146	136	3.45	3.72	1.31	692	663	729	19.4	3.0	8.4	2.8	63%	9%	42	23	35	31%	78%	11%	21	75	29%	24%	0	0.66	5.2	89	106	$5
15 OAK	7	15	1	157	136	4.18	4.04	1.35	730	825	616	22.4	2.8	7.8	2.8	61%	9%	43	23	34	32%	72%	11%	26	86	23%	38%	100	0.74	-4.3	87	104	$1
16 2 TM	2	2	0	67	63	4.43	4.05	1.33	779	836	740	4.5	2.4	8.5	3.5	64%	10%	43	18	39	32%	73%	15%	0	18			0	0.90	-2.0	108	128	-$2
1st Half	0	2	0	32	34	3.62	3.76	1.24	732	738	724	4.3	2.8	9.5	3.4	69%	10%	46	15	39	30%	79%	17%	0	17			0	0.98	2.3	119	142	$0
2nd Half	2	0	0	35	29	5.19	4.33	1.41	820	946	753	4.8	2.1	7.5	3.6	59%	10%	40	20	39	34%	67%	14%	0	19			0	0.81	-4.3	98	117	-$4
17 Proj	4	4	0	87	78	4.29	4.12	1.34	755	799	716	7.2	2.6	8.1	3.1	62%	10%	43	20	37	32%	72%	13%	0						-1.1	97	115	-$1

Chen,Wei-Yin

Age: 31	Th: L	Role: SP	Health: D	LIMA Plan: C+	
Ht: 6' 0"	Wt: 200	Type:	PT/Exp: A	Rand Var: +3	
			Consist: A	MM: 2103	

Missed two months with an elbow sprain, then pitched pretty well out of the 'pen late. Beset by gopheritis once again, and with his middling SwK and low GB%, we just have to accept that as part of the package. The steady xERA is all you need to set 2017 expectations, with that health grade as a caveat.

Yr Tm	W	L	Sv	IP	K	ERA	xERA	WHIP	oOPS	vL	vR	BF/G	Ctl	Dom	Cmd	FpK	SwK	G	L	F	H%	S%	hr/f	GS	APC	DOM%	DIS%	Sv%	LI	RAR	BPV	BPX	R$
12 BAL	12	11	0	193	154	4.02	4.33	1.26	729	682	747	25.6	2.7	7.2	2.7	60%	10%	37	21	42	29%	73%	12%	32	98	22%	31%			-0.1	73	95	$8
13 BAL	7	7	0	137	104	4.07	4.19	1.32	761	689	783	24.9	2.6	6.8	2.7	59%	8%	34	25	41	31%	73%	10%	23	95	13%	17%			-3.5	66	86	$1
14 BAL	16	6	0	186	136	3.54	3.86	1.23	727	670	746	24.9	1.7	6.6	3.9	61%	8%	41	22	38	30%	76%	10%	31	96	23%	29%			4.6	92	109	$10
15 BAL	11	8	0	191	153	3.34	4.01	1.22	758	576	815	25.5	1.9	7.2	3.7	68%	9%	40	20	39	30%	79%	12%	31	97	26%	19%			14.7	95	114	$13
16 MIA	5	5	0	123	100	4.96	4.23	1.28	789	778	791	23.6	1.8	7.3	4.2	64%	10%	40	21	38	31%	66%	15%	22	87	27%	27%			-11.8	102	121	-$1
1st Half	4	3	0	92	74	5.11	4.37	1.32	803	806	803	24.4	2.1	7.3	3.5	63%	9%	39	22	38	31%	66%	14%	16	90	31%	38%			-10.4	92	110	-$1
2nd Half	1	2	0	32	26	4.55	3.83	1.17	746	665	758	21.7	0.9	7.4	8.7	66%	10%	44	18	37	31%	68%	16%	6	81	17%	0%			-1.4	132	158	-$3
17 Proj	9	8	0	174	138	4.16	4.09	1.23	758	668	780	23.3	1.7	7.2	4.3	65%	9%	41	20	39	30%	72%	14%	30						0.7	103	122	$6

Cingrani,Tony

Age: 27	Th: L	Role: RP	Health: D	LIMA Plan: B	
Ht: 6' 4"	Wt: 215	Type: Pwr	PT/Exp: C	Rand Var: -2	
			Consist: A	MM: 0310	

Why he won't close again: 1) Horrendous Ctl makes every save opp an adventure; 2) A couple-of-mph speed bump to his fastball only made him MORE hittable; 3) He's (still) left-handed. Still owns that 2013 somewhere, but it's getting farther in the rear-view. A LOOGY role may be looming.

Yr Tm	W	L	Sv	IP	K	ERA	xERA	WHIP	oOPS	vL	vR	BF/G	Ctl	Dom	Cmd	FpK	SwK	G	L	F	H%	S%	hr/f	GS	APC	DOM%	DIS%	Sv%	LI	RAR	BPV	BPX	R$
12 CIN *	5	3	0	94	96	2.81	3.47	1.26	623	533	700	20.3	4.1	9.2	2.2	55%	13%	64	0	36	28%	83%	25%	0	34			0	0.86	14.0	81	105	$7
13 CIN *	10	4	0	136	162	2.60	2.46	1.06	649	533	693	18.2	3.6	10.7	3.0	57%	11%	34	21	45	25%	81%	13%	18	79	33%	28%	0	0.93	21.2	113	147	$18
14 CIN	2	8	0	63	61	4.55	4.51	1.53	811	613	862	21.5	5.0	8.7	1.7	54%	9%	35	22	44	30%	76%	15%	11	86	9%	64%	0	0.85	-6.3	35	41	-$5
15 CIN *	0	4	0	58	66	4.33	4.67	1.62	811	915	751	5.9	5.8	10.2	1.8	50%	12%	38	27	35	34%	75%	10%	1	19	0%	100%	0	1.24	-2.6	75	89	-$7
16 CIN	2	5	17	63	49	4.14	5.11	1.44	719	674	743	4.2	5.3	7.0	1.3	55%	9%	47	16	38	28%	72%	7%	0	17			74	1.16	0.4	8	10	$4
1st Half	1	2	9	37	27	3.38	5.27	1.31	693	746	656	4.1	5.1	6.5	1.3	54%	9%	43	14	43	23%	78%	9%	0	17			64	1.30	3.8	1	2	$7
2nd Half	1	3	8	26	22	5.26	4.87	1.64	756	526	842	4.2	5.6	7.7	1.4	56%	8%	52	18	30	33%	66%	5%	0	17			89	0.96	-3.4	17	21	$0
17 Proj	2	6	5	65	61	4.29	4.83	1.50	761	711	783	5.7	5.3	8.5	1.6	54%	10%	42	20	37	30%	73%	9%	0						-0.8	30	35	-$2

Cishek,Steve

Age: 31	Th: R	Role: RP	Health: B	LIMA Plan: C+	
Ht: 6' 5"	Wt: 200	Type: Pwr	PT/Exp: B	Rand Var: -2	
			Consist: C	MM: 3410	

Underwent hip labrum surgery in October, and appears likely to start 2017 on DL. That he pitched so well after suffering the injury is impressive—as was this entire bounce-back season, really. Will have a tough time regaining a closer job with the late start, but if opportunity knocks... UP: 20 Sv

Yr Tm	W	L	Sv	IP	K	ERA	xERA	WHIP	oOPS	vL	vR	BF/G	Ctl	Dom	Cmd	FpK	SwK	G	L	F	H%	S%	hr/f	GS	APC	DOM%	DIS%	Sv%	LI	RAR	BPV	BPX	R$
12 MIA	5	2	15	64	68	2.69	3.55	1.30	663	787	548	4.0	4.1	9.6	2.3	57%	10%	52	16	31	31%	80%	6%	0	16			79	1.20	10.4	92	120	$10
13 MIA	4	6	34	70	74	2.33	2.96	1.08	568	664	459	4.1	2.8	9.6	3.4	63%	10%	53	18	29	29%	79%	6%	0	16			94	1.23	13.2	126	165	$20
14 MIA	4	5	39	65	84	3.17	2.84	1.21	643	586	713	4.1	2.9	11.6	4.0	67%	10%	43	26	31	35%	74%	6%	0	17			91	1.61	4.6	151	180	$18
15 2 NL	2	6	4	55	48	3.58	4.42	1.48	720	754	696	4.1	4.4	7.8	1.8	64%	10%	46	22	32	32%	77%	8%	0	16			44	0.91	2.6	46	55	-$1
16 SEA	4	6	25	64	76	2.81	3.35	1.02	600	728	498	4.2	3.0	10.7	3.6	61%	12%	44	17	39	26%	79%	13%	0	17			78	1.52	10.9	135	160	$17
1st Half	2	4	20	38	46	2.39	3.26	0.98	558	765	364	4.4	3.1	11.0	3.5	63%	12%	44	20	36	24%	84%	15%	0	19			83	1.59	8.4	136	162	$24
2nd Half	2	2	5	26	30	3.42	3.48	1.06	661	659	660	3.8	2.7	10.3	3.8	60%	11%	44	13	44	28%	72%	11%	0	16			63	1.43	2.5	132	158	$7
17 Proj	3	4	5	51	56	3.12	3.59	1.19	649	698	610	3.9	3.3	9.9	3.0	63%	11%	45	19	36	30%	77%	10%	0						6.7	112	133	$4

Claudio,Alexander

Age: 25	Th: L	Role: RP	Health: F	LIMA Plan: B+	
Ht: 6' 3"	Wt: 180	Type: Con xGB	PT/Exp: D	Rand Var: -3	
			Consist: D	MM: 3000	

4-1, 2.79 ERA in 52 IP at TEX. Handled thankless long-man role with aplomb. But lefty sidearm motion means platoon split is a given, and mid-to-upper-80s fastball (not to mention upper-60s change) doesn't exactly light up the radar gun. Thus, he's unlikely to step into a high-leverage role. But he's fun to watch.

Yr Tm	W	L	Sv	IP	K	ERA	xERA	WHIP	oOPS	vL	vR	BF/G	Ctl	Dom	Cmd	FpK	SwK	G	L	F	H%	S%	hr/f	GS	APC	DOM%	DIS%	Sv%	LI	RAR	BPV	BPX	R$
12																																	
13 aa	1	5	0	32	25	3.77	4.21	1.42				6.4	3.3	7.0	2.1						32%	75%								0.4	65	85	-$3
14 TEX *	2	3	0	55	38	2.63	2.82	1.13	693	465	855	8.7	1.3	6.2	4.8	46%	12%	58	25	17	31%	75%	0%	0	14			0	0.41	7.5	137	163	$2
15 TEX *	4	2	0	56	42	3.38	4.48	1.35	762	716	813	4.9	2.2	6.8	3.1	65%	11%	51	16	33	33%	79%	27%	0	14			0	1.16	4.0	75	89	-$1
16 TEX *	4	1	1	68	41	2.28	2.78	1.14	662	449	752	6.0	1.9	5.4	2.8	65%	11%	63	17	20	29%	80%	6%	0	20			100	0.72	16.0	89	106	$6
1st Half	1	1	1	33	18	2.77	2.94	1.19	816	1000	760	7.4	2.2	4.7	2.1	68%	10%	53	23	23	28%	76%	7%	0	22			100	0.77	5.8	69	83	$4
2nd Half	3	0	0	35	23	1.82	2.64	1.10	575	242	747	5.0	1.6	6.0	3.8	63%	11%	68	13	19	29%	84%	5%	0	20			0	0.69	10.1	114	136	$8
17 Proj	3	2	0	51	34	3.05	3.59	1.21	645	473	715	5.9	2.0	6.1	3.1	65%	11%	62	17	21	30%	75%	8%	0						7.1	97	116	$1

ROD TRUESDELL

Clemens,Paul

Age: 29	Th: R	Role RP	Health A	LIMA Plan D
Ht: 6' 3"	Wt: 195	Type Pwr FB	PT/Exp D	Rand Var +1
			Consist F	MM 0001

4-5, 4.04 ERA in 71 IP at MIA/SD. Got a long look in 2nd half, earning, shall we say, mixed reviews. If not for a 79% strand rate, his usual five-plus ERA would have been in play (see xERA). Flyball tilt, subpar SwK make for a volatile pairing, and the latter didn't support 2nd half Dom uptick. Let's put it this way: He's no Roger.

Yr Tm	W	L	Sv	IP	K	ERA	xERA	WHIP	oOPS	vL	vR	BF/G	Ctl	Dom	Cmd	FpK	SwK	G	L	F	H%	S%	hr/f	GS	APC	DOM%	DIS%	Sv%	LI	RAR	BPV	BPX	R$
12 a/a	11	10	0	143	90	6.04	6.55	1.70				24.0	2.6	5.6	2.2						36%	67%								-35.8	25	33	-$20
13 HOU *	7	9	0	103	62	5.36	5.12	1.46	865	871	859	10.8	3.2	5.4	1.7	58%	8%	35	16	48	30%	67%	13%	5	33	0%	40%	0	0.90	-19.0	22	29	-$8
14 HOU *	6	4	1	71	50	5.02	4.74	1.50	862	770	971	9.6	4.6	6.3	1.4	55%	6%	41	21	38	29%	69%	16%	0	32			100	0.60	-11.2	34	40	-$5
15 a/a	2	5	1	47	26	7.97	7.08	2.01				14.1	5.9	5.1	0.9						35%	60%								-23.1	0	0	-$15
16 2 NL *	10	9	0	147	102	5.23	5.11	1.51	818	662	926	19.8	3.7	6.3	1.7	59%	7%	40	18	43	31%	68%	15%	14	66	7%	57%	0	0.97	-18.8	33	40	-$7
1st Half	7	4	0	85	55	6.35	5.54	1.61	1162	886	1336	23.6	4.0	5.8	1.5	60%	6%	37	13	50	32%	62%	33%	2	91	0%	100%			-22.7	24	29	-$12
2nd Half	3	5	0	61	47	3.67	4.92	1.37	762	628	856	16.7	3.4	6.9	2.0	59%	7%	40	18	41	29%	79%	11%	12	63	8%	50%	0	1.00	3.9	51	61	$0
17 Proj	**5**	**7**	**0**	**87**	**58**	**5.16**	**5.65**	**1.61**	**843**	**774**	**899**	**14.9**	**4.2**	**6.0**	**1.4**	**59%**	**7%**	**38**	**17**	**44**	**32%**	**71%**	**10%**	**13**						**-10.4**	**10**	**11**	**-$8**

Clevinger,Michael

Age: 26	Th: R	Role SP	Health A	LIMA Plan D+
Ht: 6' 4"	Wt: 210	Type Pwr xFB	PT/Exp D	Rand Var 0
			Consist B	MM 0203

0-3, 5.26 ERA in 53 IP at CLE. PRO: Nice Dom uptick in second full year back from TJS; vL splits; a winner in minors (11-1 W-L). CON: Ctl also spiked; vR splits; and flyball lean led to serious HR issues (1.4 hr/9 in MLB). Some skills, but inexperienced (just 150 IP pre-2015). For 2017, let him learn on your pal's roster.

Yr Tm	W	L	Sv	IP	K	ERA	xERA	WHIP	oOPS	vL	vR	BF/G	Ctl	Dom	Cmd	FpK	SwK	G	L	F	H%	S%	hr/f	GS	APC	DOM%	DIS%	Sv%	LI	RAR	BPV	BPX	R$
12																																	
13																																	
14																																	
15 aa	9	8	0	158	114	3.95	3.82	1.31				24.2	2.5	6.5	2.6						32%	70%								0.3	76	91	$3
16 CLE *	14	4	0	146	125	4.63	4.76	1.50	768	505	976	18.5	4.2	7.7	1.8	61%	10%	38	22	40	32%	72%	13%	10	57	0%	60%	0	0.84	-8.0	52	62	$0
1st Half	8	1	0	84	72	4.68	4.61	1.48	849	575	1127	22.7	4.1	7.6	1.9	55%	11%	42	20	38	32%	70%	18%	3	91	0%	67%			-5.1	56	67	$1
2nd Half	6	3	0	62	53	4.56	4.96	1.52	735	472	925	14.9	4.3	7.8	1.8	63%	9%	36	22	41	31%	74%	11%	7	50	0%	57%	0	0.85	-2.8	46	55	-$2
17 Proj	**7**	**5**	**0**	**131**	**105**	**4.33**	**4.94**	**1.43**	**708**	**463**	**884**	**22.7**	**3.5**	**7.2**	**2.0**	**63%**	**9%**	**36**	**22**	**41**	**31%**	**72%**	**8%**	**22**						**-2.2**	**49**	**58**	**-$2**

Clippard,Tyler

Age: 32	Th: R	Role RP	Health A	LIMA Plan B+
Ht: 6' 4"	Wt: 170	Type Pwr xFB	PT/Exp C	Rand Var 0
			Consist C	MM 1410

Skills-wise, he actually had a better year than 2015. But hr/f luck finally ended, and with his flyball ways, that meant a HR spike. The big question: Can he earn enough trust to close again? Only if his hr/f fortune is a repeatable skill; otherwise, Ctl, FB% suggest the blow-up can always resurface. Heed the xERA range.

Yr Tm	W	L	Sv	IP	K	ERA	xERA	WHIP	oOPS	vL	vR	BF/G	Ctl	Dom	Cmd	FpK	SwK	G	L	F	H%	S%	hr/f	GS	APC	DOM%	DIS%	Sv%	LI	RAR	BPV	BPX	R$
12 WAS	2	6	32	73	84	3.72	4.03	1.16	621	519	725	4.1	3.6	10.4	2.9	62%	12%	30	14	57	28%	70%	7%	0	17			86	1.25	2.7	98	128	$16
13 WAS	6	3	0	71	73	2.41	3.68	0.86	517	507	527	3.8	3.0	9.3	3.0	59%	15%	28	16	56	18%	81%	9%	0	16			0	1.10	12.8	90	118	$10
14 WAS	7	4	1	70	82	2.18	3.26	1.00	541	642	423	3.7	2.9	10.5	3.6	63%	15%	37	14	49	27%	82%	6%	0	15			14	1.34	13.6	124	148	$10
15 2 TM	5	4	19	71	64	2.92	4.96	1.13	599	468	745	4.4	3.9	8.1	2.1	56%	12%	21	18	61	23%	79%	7%	0	18			76	1.25	9.2	39	46	$13
16 2 TM	4	6	3	63	72	3.57	4.15	1.27	716	753	679	3.8	3.7	10.3	2.8	57%	13%	31	19	50	29%	79%	13%	0	15			50	1.05	4.8	94	112	$3
1st Half	2	3	1	31	37	3.16	3.62	1.24	747	782	708	3.7	2.9	10.6	3.7	51%	14%	32	24	45	32%	82%	15%	0	15			33	1.23	4.0	123	147	$4
2nd Half	2	3	2	32	35	3.98	4.69	1.29	687	723	654	3.9	4.5	9.9	2.2	63%	12%	30	15	55	27%	75%	11%	0	16			67	0.88	0.8	65	77	$2
17 Proj	**5**	**5**	**2**	**65**	**70**	**3.32**	**4.26**	**1.17**	**644**	**635**	**654**	**3.8**	**3.7**	**9.7**	**2.6**	**59%**	**13%**	**29**	**17**	**54**	**27%**	**77%**	**10%**	**0**						**7.0**	**82**	**98**	**$4**

Cobb,Alex

Age: 29	Th: R	Role SP	Health F	LIMA Plan B+
Ht: 6' 2"	Wt: 195	Type Pwr xGB	PT/Exp C	Rand Var +5
			Consist F	MM 2203

1-2, 8.59 ERA in 22 IP at TAM. Struggled, perhaps predictably, in those tentative first steps back from May 2015 TJS. Entering that season, we were touting him as a potential breakout star, and he had the skills to back it up. He surely still owns those skills, but probably needs at least a half-season to find them again.

Yr Tm	W	L	Sv	IP	K	ERA	xERA	WHIP	oOPS	vL	vR	BF/G	Ctl	Dom	Cmd	FpK	SwK	G	L	F	H%	S%	hr/f	GS	APC	DOM%	DIS%	Sv%	LI	RAR	BPV	BPX	R$
12 TAM *	12	13	0	178	142	4.19	3.82	1.34	690	735	633	23.8	2.9	7.2	2.5	62%	8%	59	20	21	32%	69%	13%	23	94	35%	35%			-3.8	79	103	$3
13 TAM	11	3	0	143	134	2.76	3.04	1.15	644	677	592	26.3	2.8	8.4	3.0	59%	10%	56	22	23	28%	80%	15%	22	101	36%	14%			19.5	109	142	$15
14 TAM	10	9	0	166	149	2.87	3.16	1.14	619	590	646	25.2	2.5	8.1	3.2	59%	11%	56	16	27	29%	76%	9%	27	97	44%	22%			17.9	110	132	$14
15																																	
16 TAM *	1	3	0	37	24	9.00	9.13	2.09	968	1206	737	20.2	3.1	5.8	1.8	65%	8%	53	19	29	41%	59%	22%	5	77	20%	60%			-22.0	-13	-16	-$14
1st Half																																	
2nd Half	1	2	0	22	16	8.59	4.81	1.77	968	1206	737	20.8	2.9	6.5	2.3	65%	8%	53	19	29	37%	53%	22%	5	77	20%	60%			-11.9	71	85	-$14
17 Proj	**8**	**7**	**0**	**131**	**113**	**3.92**	**3.69**	**1.30**	**709**	**777**	**629**	**22.8**	**2.8**	**7.8**	**2.8**	**61%**	**9%**	**55**	**20**	**25**	**31%**	**72%**	**14%**	**24**						**4.3**	**98**	**117**	**$4**

Cole,A.J.

Age: 25	Th: R	Role SP	Health A	LIMA Plan C
Ht: 6' 4"	Wt: 180	Type xFB	PT/Exp D	Rand Var +3
			Consist B	MM 0101

1-1, 5.17 ERA in 38 IP at WAS. Flashes of good things are in there: 9.2 Dom in his 8 starts with WAS, improving command overall. But he's allowed a .463 Slg in the majors, and xFB profile means when they hit 'em, they tend to hit 'em far. Still a work in progress, and appears at least a year away... but watch him.

Yr Tm	W	L	Sv	IP	K	ERA	xERA	WHIP	oOPS	vL	vR	BF/G	Ctl	Dom	Cmd	FpK	SwK	G	L	F	H%	S%	hr/f	GS	APC	DOM%	DIS%	Sv%	LI	RAR	BPV	BPX	R$
12																																	
13 aa	4	2	0	45	41	2.57	2.21	0.97				24.6	1.9	8.2	4.4						27%	76%								7.3	135	176	$4
14 a/a	13	3	0	134	93	3.39	4.49	1.41				22.7	2.0	6.2	3.1						35%	77%								5.8	80	96	$3
15 WAS *	5	6	1	115	72	4.25	4.35	1.40	812	935	571	20.2	2.9	5.6	1.9	43%	10%	36	27	36	31%	71%	8%	1	52	0%	100%	100	0.48	-4.1	49	58	-$3
16 WAS *	9	10	0	163	128	5.92	5.85	1.58	779	783	773	23.9	3.0	7.0	2.4	58%	11%	32	13	55	35%	65%	11%	8	84	13%	38%			-34.8	42	50	-$13
1st Half	6	4	0	86	59	6.22	6.32	1.76				24.5	3.1	6.1	2.0						38%	65%	0%	0						-21.4	36	43	-$17
2nd Half	3	6	0	77	69	5.58	5.33	1.38	779	783	773	23.2	2.8	8.0	2.8	58%	11%	32	13	55	31%	65%	11%	8	84	13%	38%			-13.3	50	59	-$10
17 Proj	**6**	**7**	**0**	**116**	**88**	**4.73**	**5.32**	**1.42**	**743**	**755**	**728**	**22.7**	**2.7**	**6.8**	**2.5**	**58%**	**11%**	**32**	**13**	**55**	**33%**	**69%**	**7%**	**22**						**-7.8**	**60**	**72**	**-$4**

Cole,Gerrit

Age: 26	Th: R	Role SP	Health F	LIMA Plan A
Ht: 6' 4"	Wt: 240	Type Pwr	PT/Exp B	Rand Var 0
			Consist B	MM 2203

Finally shut down in Sept with an inflamed elbow. Also lost time to a strained triceps, but from news reports—and the palpable skills decline—it was the elbow that likely bothered him for a good chunk of the season. With health, the budding star we saw in 2015 still lurks. But that F in health drops him a tier.

Yr Tm	W	L	Sv	IP	K	ERA	xERA	WHIP	oOPS	vL	vR	BF/G	Ctl	Dom	Cmd	FpK	SwK	G	L	F	H%	S%	hr/f	GS	APC	DOM%	DIS%	Sv%	LI	RAR	BPV	BPX	R$
12 a/a	4	6	0	65	55	3.58	3.68	1.39				21.0	3.1	7.6	2.4						34%	73%								3.5	90	117	-$1
13 PIT *	15	10	0	185	138	3.27	2.80	1.15	638	614	658	23.7	2.7	6.7	2.5	63%	10%	49	25	26	28%	72%	8%	19	91	32%	16%			13.7	86	112	$16
14 PIT *	14	6	0	160	151	3.44	3.33	1.21	693	729	659	24.9	2.5	8.5	3.4	62%	10%	49	19	32	31%	73%	9%	22	100	45%	14%			6.0	107	128	$10
15 PIT	19	8	0	208	202	2.60	3.16	1.09	623	597	648	26.0	1.9	8.7	4.6	62%	11%	48	22	30	31%	77%	7%	32	101	59%	13%			35.0	132	157	$30
16 PIT	7	10	0	116	98	3.88	4.17	1.44	754	870	652	24.1	2.8	7.6	2.7	60%	9%	46	25	29	35%	73%	7%	21	92	24%	29%			4.4	85	102	$1
1st Half	5	4	0	68	55	2.77	4.20	1.32	677	771	606	24.1	2.6	7.2	2.8	60%	8%	43	26	31	33%	79%	5%	12	96	33%	25%			12.0	80	96	$8
2nd Half	2	6	0	48	43	5.48	4.11	1.62	859	978	728	24.1	3.0	8.1	2.7	60%	9%	49	25	26	38%	66%	10%	9	88	11%	33%			-7.6	92	110	-$9
17 Proj	**12**	**13**	**0**	**174**	**156**	**3.34**	**3.75**	**1.26**	**697**	**755**	**643**	**23.6**	**2.6**	**8.1**	**3.1**	**61%**	**10%**	**48**	**24**	**29**	**32%**	**75%**	**9%**	**30**						**18.3**	**101**	**120**	**$12**

Colome,Alexander

Age: 28	Th: R	Role RP	Health D	LIMA Plan C
Ht: 6' 2"	Wt: 220	Type Pwr	PT/Exp C	Rand Var -4
			Consist B	MM 4530

We'd do a "starter or reliever—you decide" thing here, but it would be WAY too easy. Spectacular follow-up to 2015 2nd half explosion that came after switch to pen. Lost some time to biceps tendinitis, and history of arm issues is all that stands between him and full-fledged "super-closer" status (assuming that's a thing).

Yr Tm	W	L	Sv	IP	K	ERA	xERA	WHIP	oOPS	vL	vR	BF/G	Ctl	Dom	Cmd	FpK	SwK	G	L	F	H%	S%	hr/f	GS	APC	DOM%	DIS%	Sv%	LI	RAR	BPV	BPX	R$
12 a/a	8	4	0	92	78	3.74	3.56	1.41				22.8	4.0	7.6	1.9						32%	72%								3.1	81	106	$1
13 TAM *	5	7	0	86	73	3.33	4.08	1.43	715	685	739	21.6	3.9	7.6	1.9	61%	12%	43	22	35	32%	79%	12%	3	88	33%	67%			5.7	67	87	$0
14 TAM *	9	6	0	110	73	4.36	4.12	1.49	590	566	612	23.6	3.5	6.0	1.7	67%	9%	38	22	41	33%	69%	3%	3	77	67%	0%	0	0.68	-8.4	64	76	-$4
15 TAM	8	5	0	110	88	3.94	4.06	1.30	698	736	658	10.6	2.5	7.2	2.8	62%	11%	40	25	35	32%	71%	8%	13	40	8%	38%	0	1.06	0.3	79	94	$2
16 TAM	2	4	37	57	71	1.91	2.85	1.02	572	479	638	4.0	2.4	11.3	4.7	63%	16%	47	23	30	29%	88%	15%	0	15			93	1.23	16.0	164	194	$22
1st Half	1	2	19	31	38	1.76	2.75	1.11	569	716	472	4.2	3.2	11.2	3.5	62%	15%	54	25	21	30%	88%	13%	0	16			100	1.41	9.2	146	174	$22
2nd Half	1	2	18	26	33	2.08	2.96	0.92	574	240	843	3.7	1.4	11.4	8.3	65%	17%	39	21	39	28%	90%	15%	0	14			86	1.05	6.8	186	221	$22
17 Proj	**3**	**4**	**39**	**58**	**69**	**2.66**	**3.13**	**1.09**	**583**	**534**	**626**	**5.9**	**2.6**	**10.7**	**4.1**	**63%**	**15%**	**43**	**24**	**33**	**30%**	**79%**	**11%**	**0**						**11.0**	**143**	**170**	**$20**

ROD TRUESDELL

Colon,Bartolo

Age: 44	Th: R	Role SP	Health B	LIMA Plan C
Ht: 5' 11"	Wt: 245	Type Con	PT/Exp A	Rand Var 0
			Consist A	MM 1003

Shades of Methuselah. But as his ERA seems to show continued life, xERA tells a different story. There are small signs of erosion all over the place, but we said the same thing last year. When (if?) he finally retires, he can regale friends with tall tales of being on that team with Julio Franco and Babe Ruth.

Yr Tm	W	L	Sv	IP	K	ERA	xERA	WHIP	oOPS	vL	vR	BF/G	Ctl	Dom	Cmd	FpK	SwK	G	L	F	H%	S%	hr/f	GS	APC	DOM%	DIS%	Sv%	LI	RAR	BPV	BPX	R$
12 OAK	10	9	0	152	91	3.43	4.23	1.21	692	782	587	26.5	1.4	5.4	4.0	67%	5%	46	18	36	30%	75%	9%	24	89	33%	25%			11.0	84	110	$9
13 OAK	18	6	0	190	117	2.65	4.00	1.17	659	681	636	25.6	1.4	5.5	4.0	65%	7%	42	21	38	30%	80%	6%	30	93	30%	33%			28.6	83	108	$21
14 NYM	15	13	0	202	151	4.09	3.82	1.23	716	681	755	27.3	1.3	6.7	5.0	66%	6%	39	22	39	32%	69%	9%	31	97	52%	39%			-8.8	102	121	$6
15 NYM	14	13	0	195	136	4.16	4.05	1.24	741	735	748	24.7	1.1	6.3	5.7	66%	7%	42	21	37	32%	70%	11%	31	82	29%	35%	0	0.76	-4.8	103	123	$7
16 NYM	15	8	0	192	128	3.43	4.26	1.21	729	795	664	23.3	1.5	6.0	4.0	63%	6%	43	23	34	30%	76%	11%	33	84	24%	30%	0	0.78	18.0	89	105	$15
1st Half	7	4	0	94	63	2.87	4.18	1.17	679	739	620	22.5	1.6	6.0	3.7	61%	6%	42	25	32	29%	80%	11%	16	81	19%	25%	0	0.79	15.3	85	101	$18
2nd Half	8	4	0	98	65	3.96	4.34	1.25	776	847	704	24.1	1.4	6.0	4.3	65%	6%	44	20	36	31%	73%	12%	17	87	29%	35%			2.7	93	110	$13
17 Proj	**12**	**10**	**0**	**174**	**118**	**4.13**	**4.25**	**1.23**	**731**	**762**	**698**	**23.9**	**1.5**	**6.1**	**4.2**	**65%**	**6%**	**42**	**22**	**37**	**31%**	**70%**	**10%**	**29**						**1.2**	**90**	**108**	**$7**

Conley,Adam

Age: 27	Th: L	Role SP	Health C	LIMA Plan B
Ht: 6' 3"	Wt: 200	Type Pwr FB	PT/Exp C	Rand Var -1
			Consist B	MM 0203

Pitched little after middle-finger tendinitis in Aug. PRO: Kept Dom gains from late in 2015; FpK says Ctl should've been better; continued success vR. CON: He's lost former GB tilt; SwK says Dom will regress; serious stamina problems (oOPS per time thru order: .685, .707, .842). xERA confirms: too risky.

Yr Tm	W	L	Sv	IP	K	ERA	xERA	WHIP	oOPS	vL	vR	BF/G	Ctl	Dom	Cmd	FpK	SwK	G	L	F	H%	S%	hr/f	GS	APC	DOM%	DIS%	Sv%	LI	RAR	BPV	BPX	R$
12																																	
13 aa	11	7	0	139	108	4.11	3.76	1.35				22.2	2.5	7.0	2.8						33%	69%								-4.2	87	114	$2
14 aaa	3	5	0	60	39	6.12	4.57	1.57				21.9	3.7	5.9	1.6						34%	58%								-17.6	55	65	-$9
15 MIA *	13	4	0	174	123	3.51	3.72	1.35	723	767	714	21.3	3.3	6.4	1.9	58%	11%	41	19	41	30%	75%	9%	11	73	18%	36%	0	0.72	9.6	65	77	$7
16 MIA	8	6	0	133	124	3.85	4.67	1.40	738	759	731	23.4	4.2	8.4	2.0	64%	10%	38	21	41	31%	75%	8%	25	91	24%	32%			5.6	54	64	$3
1st Half	5	5	0	94	87	3.65	4.45	1.32	709	734	700	23.8	3.7	8.4	2.2	61%	10%	39	21	40	30%	74%	8%	17	93	35%	29%			6.2	66	79	$7
2nd Half	3	1	0	40	37	4.31	5.20	1.59	804	823	798	22.4	5.2	8.4	1.6	69%	11%	36	20	43	32%	76%	10%	8	86	0%	38%			-0.6	24	29	-$5
17 Proj	**9**	**7**	**0**	**152**	**124**	**4.23**	**4.90**	**1.45**	**760**	**800**	**749**	**22.0**	**3.9**	**7.4**	**1.9**	**63%**	**11%**	**39**	**20**	**41**	**31%**	**72%**	**8%**	**30**						**-0.8**	**43**	**51**	**-$1**

Corbin,Patrick

Age: 27	Th: L	Role SP	Health F	LIMA Plan C
Ht: 6' 2"	Wt: 165	Type Pwr GB	PT/Exp C	Rand Var +5
			Consist A	MM 2203

Although skills were better than that 5-plus ERA, was still a big disappointment—as a SP. Moved to bullpen in Sept and suddenly was terrific, with a 10.8 Dom and 2 mph more on his fastball. Of course, that calls his 2017 role into question, as do L/R splits. Don't draft until role is defined and Ctl returns to pre-2016 range.

Yr Tm	W	L	Sv	IP	K	ERA	xERA	WHIP	oOPS	vL	vR	BF/G	Ctl	Dom	Cmd	FpK	SwK	G	L	F	H%	S%	hr/f	GS	APC	DOM%	DIS%	Sv%	LI	RAR	BPV	BPX	R$
12 ARI *	11	10	1	186	154	3.90	4.26	1.34	783	780	784	22.1	2.2	7.4	3.3	58%	9%	46	23	31	33%	73%	13%	17	73	24%	47%	100	0.77	2.6	88	114	$6
13 ARI	14	8	0	208	178	3.41	3.48	1.17	671	560	703	26.9	2.3	7.7	3.3	70%	11%	47	22	31	29%	73%	10%	32	96	34%	28%			11.6	100	131	$16
14																																	
15 ARI *	7	5	0	101	87	3.63	4.07	1.28	743	574	788	21.9	2.0	7.7	3.9	61%	11%	47	23	30	33%	74%	12%	16	78	25%	19%			4.2	100	119	$3
16 ARI	5	13	1	156	131	5.15	4.39	1.56	825	743	851	19.5	3.8	7.6	2.0	57%	10%	54	19	27	33%	70%	18%	24	71	21%	42%	100	0.89	-18.4	65	78	-$9
1st Half	4	6	0	101	74	4.90	4.37	1.45	814	843	805	25.7	3.2	6.6	2.1	56%	10%	53	20	27	31%	71%	20%	17	93	29%	35%			-8.9	63	75	-$6
2nd Half	1	7	1	55	57	5.60	4.41	1.77	845	599	931	13.9	4.9	9.4	1.9	58%	11%	56	19	26	38%	70%	16%	7	51	0%	57%	100	0.96	-9.5	69	82	-$15
17 Proj	**7**	**12**	**0**	**160**	**141**	**4.47**	**4.05**	**1.45**	**778**	**646**	**818**	**20.5**	**3.2**	**8.0**	**2.5**	**60%**	**10%**	**51**	**21**	**28**	**33%**	**72%**	**14%**	**30**						**-5.6**	**86**	**102**	**-$3**

Cosart,Jarred

Age: 27	Th: R	Role SP	Health B	LIMA Plan D
Ht: 6' 3"	Wt: 180	Type Pwr xGB	PT/Exp C	Rand Var 0
			Consist B	MM 0001

0-4, 6.00 ERA in 57 IP at MIA/SD. Suffered from hammy and groin strains, a blister, and elbow bone spurs—all in 2nd half. No excuse for ghoulish 1st half though, nor the 4-year skills decline. Subpar FpK, SwK give little hope for Cmd rebound, and that's ultimately been his undoing all along. Why are we still talking about him?

Yr Tm	W	L	Sv	IP	K	ERA	xERA	WHIP	oOPS	vL	vR	BF/G	Ctl	Dom	Cmd	FpK	SwK	G	L	F	H%	S%	hr/f	GS	APC	DOM%	DIS%	Sv%	LI	RAR	BPV	BPX	R$
12 a/a	6	7	0	115	82	3.31	3.55	1.40				23.1	3.7	6.4	1.7						31%	75%								10.0	71	93	$2
13 HOU *	8	5	0	153	114	3.00	3.32	1.39	631	489	849	23.0	4.9	6.7	1.4	52%	6%	55	21	24	27%	79%	7%	10	102	10%	40%			16.3	63	82	$6
14 2 TM	13	11	0	180	115	3.69	4.12	1.36	671	684	657	25.5	3.6	5.7	1.6	58%	7%	54	19	26	29%	73%	6%	30	98	30%	37%			1.1	37	44	$3
15 MIA *	2	6	0	91	61	5.00	4.89	1.54	762	742	781	20.9	4.8	6.0	1.3	54%	8%	55	18	27	29%	70%	18%	13	84	0%	54%	0	0.73	-11.7	29	34	-$9
16 2 NL *	3	8	0	108	61	5.89	6.12	1.85	751	683	818	21.9	5.6	5.1	0.9	54%	7%	61	21	18	33%	69%	12%	13	84	0%	46%			-22.6	12	15	-$17
1st Half	2	4	0	54	28	6.21	6.72	2.03	776	716	863	23.7	6.3	4.7	0.7	50%	5%	65	29	6	35%	70%	0%	3	103	0%	33%			-13.4	7	9	-$19
2nd Half	1	4	0	54	33	5.58	5.52	1.67	741	664	806	20.2	4.9	5.5	1.1	56%	7%	59	18	23	31%	68%	13%	10	79	0%	50%			-9.3	18	22	-$15
17 Proj	**4**	**7**	**0**	**102**	**63**	**5.02**	**5.14**	**1.63**	**796**	**739**	**853**	**21.9**	**4.9**	**5.6**	**1.1**	**56%**	**7%**	**56**	**19**	**25**	**31%**	**70%**	**12%**	**21**						**-10.4**	**2**	**2**	**-$10**

Cotton,Jharel

Age: 25	Th: R	Role RP	Health A	LIMA Plan B
Ht: 5' 11"	Wt: 195	Type Pwr xFB	PT/Exp D	Rand Var +4
			Consist B	MM 1303

2-0, 2.15 ERA in 29 IP at OAK. Change-up specialist dynamite after trade from LA, both at Triple-A (2.82 ERA at Nashville) and in late-season audition. xFB lean is his one weakness (4 HR allowed with OAK, 24 in 165 IP overall). Improving cutter could help mitigate that; if so, and FB% drops... UP: 3.50 ERA

Yr Tm	W	L	Sv	IP	K	ERA	xERA	WHIP	oOPS	vL	vR	BF/G	Ctl	Dom	Cmd	FpK	SwK	G	L	F	H%	S%	hr/f	GS	APC	DOM%	DIS%	Sv%	LI	RAR	BPV	BPX	R$
12																																	
13																																	
14																																	
15 a/a	5	2	0	70	68	2.99	3.30	1.24				17.8	2.7	8.8	3.3						32%	77%								8.4	109	130	$4
16 OAK *	13	6	0	165	148	5.23	4.07	1.21	538	441	617	20.2	2.5	8.1	3.2	66%	13%	38	14	48	29%	60%	10%	5	88	20%	20%			-21.2	77	91	$3
1st Half	7	4	0	75	73	6.27	4.64	1.34				17.3	3.4	8.8	2.6						30%	56%	0%	0						-19.1	62	74	-$3
2nd Half	6	2	0	90	74	4.38	3.60	1.11	538	441	617	23.7	1.8	7.4	4.1	66%	13%	38	14	48	28%	65%	10%	5	88	20%	20%			-2.1	98	117	$8
17 Proj	**11**	**5**	**0**	**145**	**133**	**3.97**	**4.38**	**1.22**	**629**	**546**	**694**	**19.3**	**2.6**	**8.3**	**3.2**	**66%**	**13%**	**38**	**14**	**48**	**30%**	**71%**	**8%**	**28**						**3.9**	**96**	**114**	**$8**

Coulombe,Daniel

Age: 27	Th: L	Role RP	Health A	LIMA Plan C
Ht: 5' 10"	Wt: 185	Type Pwr xGB	PT/Exp D	Rand Var +5
			Consist A	MM 3300

3-1, 4.53 ERA in 48 IP at OAK. Career reliever tops out at 90 mph. But he gets tons of GB, and an outstanding curve piles up the swings-and-misses, making for an intriguing skills mix. That said, periodic control issues, something of a vR split, and the lack of big heat will likely condemn him to LH specialist role.

Yr Tm	W	L	Sv	IP	K	ERA	xERA	WHIP	oOPS	vL	vR	BF/G	Ctl	Dom	Cmd	FpK	SwK	G	L	F	H%	S%	hr/f	GS	APC	DOM%	DIS%	Sv%	LI	RAR	BPV	BPX	R$
12																																	
13																																	
14 LA *	0	0	1	25	30	2.87	3.90	1.40	768	819	731	4.6	3.9	10.5	2.7	64%	14%	44	31	25	35%	82%	25%	0	16			25	0.54	2.7	103	123	-$2
15 2 TM *	3	1	1	57	44	4.28	3.93	1.55	742	548	921	4.8	4.9	6.9	1.4	56%	8%	56	21	23	32%	70%	0%	0	19			25	0.59	-2.3	68	81	-$4
16 OAK *	3	1	0	73	80	3.51	3.00	1.17	634	557	692	5.3	3.0	10.0	3.4	61%	14%	62	17	21	31%	72%	24%	0	21			0	0.47	6.1	117	139	$4
1st Half	1	1	0	41	41	2.94	3.75	1.25	786	815	768	5.4	2.4	8.9	3.8	59%	12%	60	15	25	33%	80%	31%	0	21			0	0.51	6.3	109	131	$4
2nd Half	2	0	0	32	40	4.26	2.03	1.06	535	416	635	5.1	3.7	11.3	3.0	63%	16%	64	18	18	27%	59%	17%	0	21			0	0.44	-0.3	132	158	$3
17 Proj	**2**	**1**	**0**	**44**	**43**	**3.90**	**3.39**	**1.30**	**633**	**594**	**661**	**5.0**	**3.8**	**9.0**	**2.3**	**61%**	**14%**	**62**	**17**	**21**	**31%**	**69%**	**10%**	**0**						**1.6**	**98**	**117**	**-$1**

Cueto,Johnny

Age: 31	Th: R	Role SP	Health D	LIMA Plan D+
Ht: 5' 10"	Wt: 215	Type	PT/Exp A	Rand Var -1
			Consist B	MM 3205

A nice rebound from 2015 second-half swoon. Threw fewer four-seamers and more off-speed stuff, and the result was a career-best FpK and Cmd, plus a nice GB% regression. And despite nagging injuries, keeps taking the post, too; 200 IP looks like his new baseline. Once again among the elite.

Yr Tm	W	L	Sv	IP	K	ERA	xERA	WHIP	oOPS	vL	vR	BF/G	Ctl	Dom	Cmd	FpK	SwK	G	L	F	H%	S%	hr/f	GS	APC	DOM%	DIS%	Sv%	LI	RAR	BPV	BPX	R$
12 CIN	19	9	0	217	170	2.78	3.59	1.17	667	708	620	26.9	2.0	7.1	3.5	63%	9%	49	22	29	30%	78%	8%	33	105	48%	21%			33.1	99	129	$26
13 CIN	5	2	0	61	51	2.82	3.27	1.05	607	561	644	22.0	2.7	7.6	2.8	61%	11%	51	25	24	25%	79%	17%	11	87	18%	27%			7.8	93	121	$5
14 CIN	20	9	0	244	242	2.25	3.07	0.96	574	561	585	28.3	2.4	8.9	3.7	63%	10%	46	19	35	25%	82%	10%	34	108	56%	6%			44.7	120	143	$38
15 2 TM	11	13	0	212	176	3.44	3.76	1.13	675	598	743	27.1	2.0	7.5	3.8	63%	10%	43	22	36	29%	73%	9%	32	102	34%	28%			13.7	103	122	$17
16 SF	18	5	0	220	198	2.79	3.43	1.09	633	670	601	27.5	1.8	8.1	4.4	68%	10%	50	21	29	30%	76%	8%	32	103	53%	16%			38.0	124	148	$30
1st Half	12	1	0	122	107	2.57	3.31	1.02	598	671	547	28.5	1.7	7.9	4.7	69%	10%	52	21	27	29%	76%	7%	17	106	65%	12%			24.4	126	150	$36
2nd Half	6	4	0	97	91	3.05	3.57	1.18	676	669	683	26.5	2.0	8.4	4.1	68%	10%	48	21	31	31%	77%	10%	15	100	40%	20%			13.7	123	146	$22
17 Proj	**15**	**8**	**0**	**203**	**181**	**2.91**	**3.55**	**1.10**	**642**	**634**	**649**	**26.2**	**2.0**	**8.0**	**4.0**	**66%**	**10%**	**47**	**21**	**32**	**29%**	**76%**	**10%**	**30**						**32.1**	**115**	**137**	**$24**

ROD TRUESDELL

Darvish,Yu

Age: 30	Th: R	Role SP	Health	F	LIMA Plan	C+
Ht: 6' 5"	Wt: 225	Type Pwr	PT/Exp	C	Rand Var	+1
			Consist	A	MM	3505

7-5, 3.41 ERA in 100 IP at TEX. Other than a brief hiccup with a sore shoulder, a strong post-TJS season. Cmd better than ever in 2H, with a bit of a FB% spike the only skills issue. Of course, flyballs (and thus HR) are part of the package, as well as (at least) nagging ailments. So riskier than most aces—but still an ace.

Yr Tm	W	L	Sv	IP	K	ERA	xERA	WHIP	oOPS	vL	vR	BF/G	Ctl	Dom	Cmd	FpK	SwK	G	L	F	H%	S%	hr/f	GS	APC	DOM%	DIS%	Sv%	LI	RAR	BPV	BPX	R$
12 TEX	16	9	0	191	221	3.90	3.48	1.28	659	674	640	28.1	4.2	10.4	2.5	58%	13%	46	22	32	31%	70%	9%	29	109	59%	17%			2.6	98	128	$13
13 TEX	13	9	0	210	277	2.83	2.86	1.07	611	655	543	26.3	3.4	11.9	3.5	57%	13%	41	21	38	27%	80%	14%	32	108	56%	9%			26.7	140	183	$27
14 TEX	10	7	0	144	182	3.06	3.18	1.26	679	721	605	27.5	3.1	11.3	3.7	62%	11%	36	23	41	35%	79%	9%	22	105	50%	9%			12.2	136	162	$10
15																																	
16 TEX *	8	7	0	127	154	3.41	3.20	1.16	636	607	662	21.1	3.1	10.9	3.6	58%	13%	40	20	40	30%	75%	12%	17	93	47%	12%			12.3	119	142	$12
1st Half	3	1	0	36	34	2.00	2.17	1.06	597	688	484	17.3	3.4	8.6	2.5	48%	12%	46	23	31	25%	84%	8%	3	82	33%	0%			9.6	104	124	$8
2nd Half	5	6	0	92	120	3.96	3.60	1.20	643	588	688	23.0	2.9	11.8	4.0	60%	13%	39	19	42	33%	71%	13%	14	95	50%	14%			2.6	127	151	$14
17 Proj	**13**	**8**	**0**	**189**	**229**	**3.16**	**3.41**	**1.17**	**640**	**666**	**607**	**25.4**	**3.2**	**10.9**	**3.4**	**58%**	**12%**	**41**	**21**	**38**	**31%**	**76%**	**11%**	**30**						**23.9**	**128**	**152**	**$20**

Davies,Zachary

Age: 24	Th: R	Role SP	Health	A	LIMA Plan	B
Ht: 6' 0"	Wt: 155	Type GB	PT/Exp	C	Rand Var	0
			Consist	A	MM	2103

PRO: Consistent strike-thrower with a GB lean, not much of a platoon split, few DIS starts. CON: Marginal SwK likely caps K rate, few DOM starts. As that DOM%/DIS% and his xERA shows, the "low ceiling, high floor" label does seem to fit here. But there's draft-day value in that predictability.

Yr Tm	W	L	Sv	IP	K	ERA	xERA	WHIP	oOPS	vL	vR	BF/G	Ctl	Dom	Cmd	FpK	SwK	G	L	F	H%	S%	hr/f	GS	APC	DOM%	DIS%	Sv%	LI	RAR	BPV	BPX	R$
12																																	
13																																	
14 aa	10	7	0	110	94	3.70	3.98	1.32				21.7	2.5	7.7	3.1						33%	73%								0.6	90	107	$3
15 MIL *	9	10	0	162	112	3.53	3.71	1.36	614	434	740	22.6	3.2	6.2	1.9	60%	11%	58	21	21	31%	74%	10%	6	90	33%	50%			8.7	67	80	$4
16 MIL	11	7	0	163	135	3.97	3.98	1.25	728	768	691	24.4	2.1	7.4	3.6	62%	9%	45	22	33	31%	72%	12%	28	92	25%	29%			4.5	100	119	$8
1st Half	5	4	0	79	68	4.22	4.00	1.24	751	834	670	23.6	2.6	7.7	3.0	60%	8%	46	21	33	29%	71%	16%	14	92	29%	36%			-0.2	93	111	$7
2nd Half	6	3	0	84	67	3.74	3.97	1.26	707	705	709	25.1	1.6	7.2	4.5	63%	9%	45	23	32	33%	72%	9%	14	93	21%	21%			4.7	108	129	$10
17 Proj	**12**	**9**	**0**	**174**	**136**	**3.76**	**3.98**	**1.30**	**724**	**679**	**761**	**23.1**	**2.5**	**7.0**	**2.8**	**61%**	**10%**	**50**	**22**	**28**	**31%**	**73%**	**10%**	**31**						**9.3**	**87**	**103**	**$7**

Davis,Wade

Age: 31	Th: R	Role RP	Health	D	LIMA Plan	B
Ht: 6' 5"	Wt: 225	Type Pwr	PT/Exp	C	Rand Var	-5
			Consist	B	MM	4530

His owners collectively sighed in relief when he returned from elbow strain with a dominant last month (10 IP, 15/1 K/BB). Lost a mph off his fastball, though, and xERA highlights the skills erosion. Add the health issues, and there's plenty of risk here. But we know what he can do when he's right. UP: 40 Sv

Yr Tm	W	L	Sv	IP	K	ERA	xERA	WHIP	oOPS	vL	vR	BF/G	Ctl	Dom	Cmd	FpK	SwK	G	L	F	H%	S%	hr/f	GS	APC	DOM%	DIS%	Sv%	LI	RAR	BPV	BPX	R$
12 TAM	3	0	0	70	87	2.43	3.31	1.09	570	464	654	5.3	3.7	11.1	3.0	57%	13%	39	22	40	28%	81%	8%	0	23			0	0.85	13.7	117	153	$7
13 KC	8	11	0	135	114	5.32	4.38	1.68	822	910	721	19.9	3.9	7.6	2.0	59%	8%	41	27	32	37%	69%	11%	24	80	21%	50%	0	0.85	-24.3	51	67	-$13
14 KC	9	2	3	72	109	1.00	2.08	0.85	408	513	298	3.9	2.9	13.6	4.7	61%	15%	48	22	30	29%	87%	0%	0	17			50	1.23	24.3	194	231	$17
15 KC	8	1	17	67	78	0.94	3.04	0.79	451	453	449	3.6	2.7	10.4	3.9	61%	12%	38	21	41	21%	92%	5%	0	15			94	1.22	25.1	131	157	$23
16 KC	2	1	27	43	47	1.87	3.47	1.13	537	489	586	3.9	3.3	9.8	2.9	53%	13%	49	18	33	30%	82%	0%	0	16			90	1.00	12.4	113	134	$14
1st Half	1	0	19	29	28	1.23	3.68	1.02	462	447	480	3.9	3.7	8.6	2.3	59%	13%	52	15	33	25%	87%	0%	0	16			90	1.10	10.7	85	102	$19
2nd Half	1	1	8	14	19	3.21	3.06	1.36	679	596	736	4.0	2.6	12.2	4.8	40%	12%	42	25	33	42%	74%	0%	0	17			89	0.80	1.7	170	203	$4
17 Proj	**5**	**1**	**32**	**65**	**75**	**2.67**	**3.34**	**1.08**	**544**	**570**	**515**	**4.5**	**3.3**	**10.3**	**3.1**	**60%**	**13%**	**45**	**21**	**34**	**29%**	**75%**	**4%**	**0**						**12.2**	**120**	**142**	**$19**

Dayton,Grant

Age: 29	Th: L	Role RP	Health	A	LIMA Plan	A
Ht: 6' 1"	Wt: 205	Type Pwr xFB	PT/Exp	D	Rand Var	+3
			Consist	D	MM	3510

0-1, 2.05 ERA in 26 IP at LA. Late bloomer exploded at two minor league levels and simply kept blowing hitters away in MLB. Misses bats with his darting fastball despite its average speed. xFB profile means gopheritis can strike at any time, but if newly minted Dom doesn't fade, there's closer-worthy stuff here.

Yr Tm	W	L	Sv	IP	K	ERA	xERA	WHIP	oOPS	vL	vR	BF/G	Ctl	Dom	Cmd	FpK	SwK	G	L	F	H%	S%	hr/f	GS	APC	DOM%	DIS%	Sv%	LI	RAR	BPV	BPX	R$
12																																	
13 aa	4	4	1	38	44	3.19	4.56	1.45				5.4	3.2	10.4	3.3						37%	82%								3.1	101	132	$0
14 a/a	2	3	4	72	60	3.61	5.11	1.52				6.2	3.3	7.5	2.2						34%	80%								1.1	56	67	-$2
15 a/a	3	4	1	57	50	5.29	3.89	1.36				5.7	2.4	7.8	3.3						35%	59%								-9.4	103	123	-$5
16 LA *	5	3	5	78	107	2.94	1.95	0.91	495	428	552	4.6	2.0	12.3	6.0	58%	16%	26	21	53	29%	71%	14%	0	19			63	1.05	12.1	194	230	$12
1st Half	5	2	2	39	50	3.58	2.72	1.17				5.3	2.5	11.7	4.7						36%	68%	0%	0						2.9	167	199	$9
2nd Half	0	1	3	40	57	2.31	1.21	0.66	495	428	552	4.1	1.6	12.9	8.1	58%	16%	26	21	53	20%	77%	14%	0	19			60	1.05	9.2	236	282	$15
17 Proj	**3**	**3**	**2**	**58**	**70**	**3.25**	**3.43**	**1.02**	**538**	**490**	**579**	**5.0**	**2.1**	**10.8**	**5.2**	**58%**	**16%**	**33**	**21**	**46**	**30%**	**71%**	**8%**	**0**						**6.7**	**149**	**177**	**$5**

De La Cruz,Joel

Age: 28	Th: R	Role RP	Health	A	LIMA Plan	D+
Ht: 6' 1"	Wt: 240	Type Con	PT/Exp	D	Rand Var	+1
			Consist	A	MM	0000

0-7, 4.88 ERA in 63 IP at ATL. With a sub-tipping-point strikeout rate, he has no margin for error. But as consistently poor xERAs show all too well, he's been far from error-free at the higher levels. Let's put it this way: If you could somehow bid minus-five dollars for him, you'd still lose money.

Yr Tm	W	L	Sv	IP	K	ERA	xERA	WHIP	oOPS	vL	vR	BF/G	Ctl	Dom	Cmd	FpK	SwK	G	L	F	H%	S%	hr/f	GS	APC	DOM%	DIS%	Sv%	LI	RAR	BPV	BPX	R$
12																																	
13																																	
14 a/a	7	9	0	122	64	5.27	5.44	1.60				19.2	2.9	4.7	1.7						34%	67%								-22.9	31	37	-$12
15 a/a	8	2	0	84	34	4.73	5.46	1.57				16.1	2.7	3.6	1.4						33%	71%								-8.0	14	17	-$6
16 ATL *	1	10	0	120	73	5.55	5.51	1.60	792	774	809	12.4	3.7	5.5	1.5	57%	9%	43	22	34	32%	67%	14%	9	46	0%	67%	0	0.57	-20.2	24	28	-$13
1st Half	1	4	0	64	37	6.11	6.18	1.79	820	857	764	13.3	4.0	5.2	1.3	56%	4%	32	27	41	36%	66%	11%	1	85	0%	100%			-15.1	20	24	-$17
2nd Half	0	6	0	57	36	4.92	5.07	1.39	789	763	813	12.0	3.3	5.7	1.7	57%	10%	44	22	34	28%	69%	14%	8	44	0%	63%	0	0.56	-5.1	35	42	-$9
17 Proj	**2**	**3**	**0**	**51**	**27**	**5.30**	**5.38**	**1.57**	**783**	**761**	**805**	**14.1**	**3.2**	**4.7**	**1.5**	**57%**	**10%**	**44**	**22**	**34**	**32%**	**68%**	**9%**	**7**						**-7.0**	**22**	**27**	**-$7**

de la Rosa,Jorge

Age: 36	Th: L	Role SP	Health	D	LIMA Plan	D+
Ht: 6' 1"	Wt: 210	Type Pwr	PT/Exp	A	Rand Var	+4
			Consist	B	MM	1203

The "Coors Field Syndrome" is a dreaded malady where a pitcher, exposed endlessly to thin COL air, eventually just can't take it anymore. This poor guy has managed to hold it together until recently and is now seeing a complete skills collapse. There is no cure but research is ongoing. Let's have a "Save Jorge" telethon.

Yr Tm	W	L	Sv	IP	K	ERA	xERA	WHIP	oOPS	vL	vR	BF/G	Ctl	Dom	Cmd	FpK	SwK	G	L	F	H%	S%	hr/f	GS	APC	DOM%	DIS%	Sv%	LI	RAR	BPV	BPX	R$
12 COL	0	2	0	11	6	9.28	5.98	1.78	1065	250	1219	17.7	1.7	5.1	3.0	62%	13%	34	14	52	33%	57%	22%	3	68	0%	100%			-6.9	58	75	-$8
13 COL	16	6	0	168	112	3.49	4.14	1.38	721	510	770	23.8	3.3	6.0	1.8	60%	10%	47	25	28	31%	76%	8%	30	92	17%	47%			7.8	43	57	$7
14 COL	14	11	0	184	139	4.10	3.79	1.24	707	532	760	24.0	3.3	6.8	2.1	55%	10%	52	18	31	27%	70%	13%	32	96	13%	38%			-8.2	64	76	$6
15 COL	9	7	0	149	134	4.17	3.88	1.36	739	670	759	24.4	3.9	8.1	2.1	58%	12%	52	21	27	30%	72%	15%	26	95	23%	31%			-3.8	70	83	$2
16 COL	8	9	0	134	108	5.51	4.90	1.64	861	849	865	22.7	4.2	7.3	1.7	55%	11%	47	21	32	33%	70%	17%	24	87	8%	50%	0	0.74	-21.8	41	49	-$11
1st Half	5	5	0	56	53	5.98	4.44	1.60	849	769	879	19.5	4.5	8.6	1.9	57%	12%	52	17	31	32%	67%	22%	10	76	10%	40%	0	0.69	-12.3	62	74	-$7
2nd Half	3	4	0	78	55	5.17	5.23	1.67	869	914	855	25.8	4.0	6.3	1.6	53%	10%	44	23	32	34%	72%	14%	14	97	7%	57%			-9.5	28	33	-$13
17 Proj	**9**	**8**	**0**	**131**	**105**	**4.75**	**4.51**	**1.48**	**796**	**740**	**814**	**22.9**	**3.9**	**7.3**	**1.9**	**56%**	**11%**	**49**	**21**	**30**	**31%**	**71%**	**15%**	**25**						**-9.1**	**52**	**62**	**-$4**

De La Rosa,Rubby

Age: 28	Th: R	Role RP	Health	F	LIMA Plan	C
Ht: 6' 0"	Wt: 170	Type Pwr	PT/Exp	B	Rand Var	+3
			Consist	A	MM	1201

Red flag alert: At this writing, had recently received a stem cell injection into his elbow (ouch) to try to avoid a second TJS, as rest/rehab didn't work. Too bad, as early skills bump was encouraging. Now, of course, looms the risk of surgery. UP: Stem cells work, takes a step up. DN: Out for 2017, part of 2018.

Yr Tm	W	L	Sv	IP	K	ERA	xERA	WHIP	oOPS	vL	vR	BF/G	Ctl	Dom	Cmd	FpK	SwK	G	L	F	H%	S%	hr/f	GS	APC	DOM%	DIS%	Sv%	LI	RAR	BPV	BPX	R$
12 LA	0	0	0	1	0	27.00	30.13	3.00	500	500	500	4.0	27.0	0.0	0.0	50%	5%	0	0	100	0%	0%	0%	0	20			0	0.14	-1.9	-751	-980	-$5
13 BOS *	3	5	0	92	68	5.33	4.80	1.56	877	646	994	11.5	5.0	6.7	1.3	64%	11%	48	14	38	30%	67%	13%	0	17			0	0.50	-16.6	36	48	-$10
14 BOS *	6	12	0	162	120	4.46	4.53	1.48	814	832	792	22.4	3.5	6.7	1.9	52%	9%	46	22	32	33%	70%	12%	18	92	11%	56%	0	0.74	-14.3	58	69	-$7
15 ARI	14	9	0	189	150	4.67	4.13	1.36	781	949	611	25.3	3.0	7.2	2.4	57%	12%	49	18	33	30%	71%	17%	32	94	25%	38%			-16.6	75	89	$0
16 ARI	4	5	0	51	54	4.26	3.76	1.24	696	656	725	17.1	3.6	9.6	2.7	53%	11%	51	18	30	28%	71%	19%	10	66	20%	50%	0	0.98	-0.5	106	126	$0
1st Half	4	5	0	48	49	4.15	3.58	1.15	673	591	738	18.6	2.8	9.3	3.3	55%	11%	53	18	30	28%	69%	18%	8	70	25%	50%	0	1.02	0.2	121	144	$1
2nd Half	0	0	0	3	5	6.00	8.27	2.67	1016	1667	536	8.5	15.0	15.0	1.0	29%	9%	29	29	43	37%	86%	33%	2	44	0%	50%			-0.7	-128	-153	-$10
17 Proj	**6**	**8**	**0**	**102**	**85**	**4.54**	**4.23**	**1.37**	**745**	**778**	**710**	**18.4**	**3.4**	**7.5**	**2.2**	**55%**	**10%**	**49**	**20**	**31**	**30%**	**70%**	**13%**	**19**						**-4.3**	**71**	**84**	**-$2**

ROD TRUESDELL

De Leon,Jose

Age: 24 | Th: R | Role: RP | Ht: 6' 2" | Wt: 190 | Type: Pwr xFB
Health: A | PT/Exp: D | Consist: B
LIMA Plan: B+ | Rand Var: +5 | MM: 2503

2-0, 6.35 ERA in 17 IP at LA. Missed two months in 1st half due to shoulder inflammation and sprained ankle. Dominated Triple-A (hitter-friendly PCL) with an 11.6 Dom, 2.1 Ctl and 2.61 ERA in 86.1 IP. Three above-average pitches makes for a tremendous keeper option.

Yr Tm	W	L	Sv	IP	K	ERA	xERA	WHIP	oOPS	vL	vR	BF/G	Ctl	Dom	Cmd	FpK	SwK	G	L	F	H%	S%	hr/f	GS	APC	DOM%	DIS%	Sv%	LI	RAR	BPV	BPX	R$
12																																	
13																																	
14																																	
15 aa	2	6	0	77	90	4.59	4.35	1.30				19.7	3.2	10.5	3.3						32%	70%								-5.9	91	108	-$2
16 LA *	9	1	0	103	108	3.93	3.54	1.12	937	658	1220	20.4	2.2	9.4	4.2	60%	11%	40	18	42	29%	70%	24%	4	76	0%	75%			3.3	113	135	$8
1st Half	1	0	0	23	29	3.65	3.50	1.16				15.5	2.9	11.3	3.9						31%	74%	0%	0						1.6	121	144	-$2
2nd Half	8	1	0	80	79	4.01	3.55	1.11	937	658	1220	22.5	2.0	8.8	4.3	60%	11%	40	18	42	29%	69%	24%	4	76	0%	75%			1.8	112	133	$11
17 Proj	**7**	**5**	**0**	**131**	**147**	**3.91**	**3.73**	**1.20**	**652**	**475**	**832**	**19.2**	**2.7**	**10.1**	**3.8**	**60%**	**11%**	**40**	**18**	**42**	**31%**	**73%**	**13%**	**25**						**4.5**	**128**	**152**	**$7**

deGrom,Jacob

Age: 29 | Th: R | Role: SP | Ht: 6' 4" | Wt: 185 | Type: Pwr
Health: B | PT/Exp: B | Consist: A
LIMA Plan: B | Rand Var: -1 | MM: 3303

Couldn't quite match amazing 2015 campaign, but this remains a strong skill set. Underwent Sept surgery to reposition ulnar nerve in right arm and "should" be ready by March. 2nd half fade due mostly to his final three outings (16 ER in 14.2 IP). Health is the biggest obstacle to a third straight strong year.

Yr Tm	W	L	Sv	IP	K	ERA	xERA	WHIP	oOPS	vL	vR	BF/G	Ctl	Dom	Cmd	FpK	SwK	G	L	F	H%	S%	hr/f	GS	APC	DOM%	DIS%	Sv%	LI	RAR	BPV	BPX	R$
12																																	
13 a/a	6	7	0	136	90	4.52	4.76	1.51				24.5	2.7	6.0	2.2						35%	70%								-10.9	59	77	-$7
14 NYM *	13	6	0	179	168	2.59	2.83	1.16	613	639	594	24.5	2.6	8.4	3.2	63%	12%	45	23	31	30%	79%	6%	22	102	50%	18%			25.4	113	135	$18
15 NYM	14	8	0	191	205	2.54	3.04	0.98	574	663	475	25.0	1.8	9.7	5.4	68%	13%	44	21	35	29%	78%	9%	30	99	63%	13%			33.4	148	176	$30
16 NYM	7	8	0	148	143	3.04	3.57	1.20	685	624	749	25.2	2.2	8.7	4.0	64%	11%	46	23	32	32%	79%	12%	24	98	38%	13%			21.0	121	144	$13
1st Half	4	4	0	86	84	2.62	3.40	1.10	633	603	667	24.7	2.1	8.8	4.2	65%	11%	47	23	30	30%	80%	10%	14	97	29%	14%			16.7	127	151	$18
2nd Half	3	4	0	62	59	3.63	3.81	1.34	753	654	848	25.8	2.3	8.6	3.7	62%	12%	44	22	34	34%	77%	13%	10	100	50%	10%			4.3	113	135	$5
17 Proj	**10**	**7**	**0**	**160**	**153**	**3.08**	**3.62**	**1.19**	**673**	**671**	**675**	**24.7**	**2.2**	**8.6**	**3.9**	**65%**	**12%**	**45**	**22**	**33**	**31%**	**77%**	**10%**	**26**						**21.7**	**118**	**140**	**$14**

Delgado,Randall

Age: 27 | Th: R | Role: RP | Ht: 6' 3" | Wt: 200 | Type: Pwr
Health: D | PT/Exp: C | Consist: A
LIMA Plan: C | Rand Var: 0 | MM: 1300

The 2015 xERA foretold the regression, but that proved to be a false floor. Continued weak Ctl and some SwK/Dom erosion pushed Cmd into danger zone. Cmd vL (2013-16: 3.2, 1.9, 1.6, 1.2), xERA and BPX collectively going in the wrong direction. These issues all preclude him from higher leverage work.

Yr Tm	W	L	Sv	IP	K	ERA	xERA	WHIP	oOPS	vL	vR	BF/G	Ctl	Dom	Cmd	FpK	SwK	G	L	F	H%	S%	hr/f	GS	APC	DOM%	DIS%	Sv%	LI	RAR	BPV	BPX	R$
12 ATL *	8	12	0	137	121	4.40	4.47	1.48	727	744	711	22.6	4.1	8.0	2.0	60%	9%	50	22	28	32%	72%	11%	17	90	18%	47%	0	0.80	-6.6	63	83	-$3
13 ARI *	7	12	0	180	127	4.73	4.73	1.33	793	765	819	22.7	2.7	6.3	2.4	60%	9%	42	20	38	29%	70%	17%	19	91	16%	37%	0	0.75	-19.1	41	53	-$4
14 ARI	4	4	0	78	86	4.87	3.89	1.36	701	690	710	7.2	4.1	10.0	2.5	56%	14%	35	21	44	33%	64%	7%	4	31	0%	75%	0	0.82	-10.8	83	99	-$3
15 ARI	8	4	1	72	73	3.25	4.13	1.33	679	688	671	4.8	4.1	9.1	2.2	63%	13%	41	18	41	30%	79%	9%	1	20	0%	100%	33	1.07	6.3	72	86	$4
16 ARI	5	2	0	75	68	4.44	4.85	1.51	777	867	715	4.3	4.3	8.2	1.9	63%	10%	41	21	38	32%	72%	9%	0	17			0	0.88	-2.3	49	59	-$3
1st Half	1	1	0	43	39	3.56	4.73	1.47	759	973	626	5.4	4.4	8.2	1.9	60%	10%	43	20	37	31%	79%	11%	0	22			0	0.75	3.3	49	59	-$1
2nd Half	4	1	0	32	29	5.63	5.00	1.56	800	748	839	3.4	4.2	8.2	1.9	66%	10%	39	23	38	34%	64%	8%	0	13			0	0.97	-5.7	50	60	-$5
17 Proj	**5**	**3**	**0**	**58**	**55**	**4.40**	**4.51**	**1.44**	**747**	**769**	**729**	**4.7**	**4.1**	**8.6**	**2.1**	**62%**	**12%**	**40**	**21**	**39**	**32%**	**71%**	**9%**	**0**						**-1.5**	**61**	**73**	**-$2**

DeSclafani,Anthony

Age: 27 | Th: R | Role: SP | Ht: 6' 2" | Wt: 195 | Type:
Health: D | PT/Exp: C | Consist: A
LIMA Plan: B | Rand Var: 0 | MM: 1205

9-5, 3.28 ERA in 123 IP at CIN. Oblique strain shelved him until June. Maintained 2015's Dom gains, but improved Ctl shouldn't last given FpK decline. Better Cmd vL with revised pitch mix (2015: 2.0; 2016: 4.6), but they hit him hard (11 HR). Still evolving, not yet primed for a step forward. DN: 4.50 ERA.

Yr Tm	W	L	Sv	IP	K	ERA	xERA	WHIP	oOPS	vL	vR	BF/G	Ctl	Dom	Cmd	FpK	SwK	G	L	F	H%	S%	hr/f	GS	APC	DOM%	DIS%	Sv%	LI	RAR	BPV	BPX	R$
12																																	
13 aa	5	4	0	75	52	4.25	4.42	1.36				24.1	1.8	6.2	3.5						34%	70%								-3.6	84	109	-$2
14 MIA *	8	9	0	135	104	4.63	3.86	1.31	801	893	710	16.9	2.3	6.9	3.0	66%	9%	36	24	40	32%	64%	9%	5	42	20%	60%	0	0.40	-14.8	87	103	-$2
15 CIN	9	13	0	185	151	4.05	4.04	1.35	742	783	697	25.3	2.7	7.4	2.7	63%	10%	45	21	34	32%	72%	9%	31	94	29%	23%			-1.9	83	99	$2
16 CIN *	9	6	0	140	118	3.97	4.48	1.23	723	837	585	23.7	2.0	7.6	3.8	58%	10%	42	23	35	30%	75%	13%	20	98	25%	30%			3.9	79	94	$7
1st Half	2	1	0	47	36	4.34	5.38	1.30	732	860	536	21.7	1.9	6.9	3.6	55%	9%	41	21	38	29%	77%	6%	5	102	60%	40%			-0.9	51	61	-$1
2nd Half	7	5	0	93	82	3.77	3.89	1.19	719	829	596	25.5	2.0	7.9	3.9	59%	10%	42	23	35	30%	74%	15%	15	97	13%	27%			4.8	108	129	$11
17 Proj	**11**	**10**	**0**	**189**	**152**	**3.80**	**4.15**	**1.29**	**764**	**857**	**656**	**22.5**	**2.2**	**7.3**	**3.3**	**61%**	**10%**	**42**	**22**	**36**	**31%**	**75%**	**12%**	**34**						**9.0**	**91**	**109**	**$8**

Devenski,Christopher

Age: 26 | Th: R | Role: RP | Ht: 6' 3" | Wt: 210 | Type: Pwr FB
Health: A | PT/Exp: D | Consist: B
LIMA Plan: C+ | Rand Var: -4 | MM: 2301

Minor league SP moved to pen and thrived. Lacks overpowering fastball, but leans heavily on superb change-up (21% SwK). Pinpoint Ctl backed by FpK and willingness to throw strikes. Replaced middling curve with new slider (23% SwK) in 2nd half. Starter or reliever in 2017? We're intrigued either way.

Yr Tm	W	L	Sv	IP	K	ERA	xERA	WHIP	oOPS	vL	vR	BF/G	Ctl	Dom	Cmd	FpK	SwK	G	L	F	H%	S%	hr/f	GS	APC	DOM%	DIS%	Sv%	LI	RAR	BPV	BPX	R$
12																																	
13																																	
14 aa	5	3	0	41	32	4.50	4.56	1.34				17.2	3.9	6.9	1.7						26%	73%								-3.9	34	41	-$2
15 aa	7	4	2	120	87	3.54	4.76	1.42				21.1	2.5	6.5	2.6						33%	79%								6.2	60	71	$2
16 HOU	4	4	1	108	104	2.16	3.48	0.91	551	639	465	8.5	1.7	8.6	5.2	64%	14%	33	26	41	27%	77%	4%	5	33	40%	40%	100	0.91	27.1	122	145	$17
1st Half	0	2	1	55	45	2.45	4.12	1.11	623	548	686	10.2	2.3	7.4	3.2	63%	12%	30	29	41	29%	78%	3%	4	39	25%	50%	100	0.46	11.8	79	94	$11
2nd Half	4	2	0	53	59	1.86	2.88	0.71	472	724	191	7.1	1.0	10.0	9.8	66%	15%	37	22	40	25%	75%	4%	1	28	100%	0%	0	1.26	15.4	167	199	$23
17 Proj	**6**	**4**	**0**	**102**	**98**	**3.24**	**3.80**	**1.11**	**690**	**859**	**520**	**8.2**	**2.1**	**8.7**	**4.2**	**65%**	**14%**	**35**	**23**	**42**	**30%**	**74%**	**8%**	**0**						**11.9**	**114**	**136**	**$8**

Diaz,Edwin

Age: 23 | Th: R | Role: RP | Ht: 6' 3" | Wt: 165 | Type: Pwr
Health: A | PT/Exp: D | Consist: B
LIMA Plan: C+ | Rand Var: +2 | MM: 5530

0-4, 2.79 ERA with 18 Sv in 52 IP at SEA. Opened 2016 as SP at AA before converting to RP in May. Made June MLB debut and became closer on Aug 2. Fastball (13% SwK)/slider (34% SwK) combo was devastating as he pounded the zone and limited walks. BPX/xERA/Cmd/GB% point to a top-tier closer.

Yr Tm	W	L	Sv	IP	K	ERA	xERA	WHIP	oOPS	vL	vR	BF/G	Ctl	Dom	Cmd	FpK	SwK	G	L	F	H%	S%	hr/f	GS	APC	DOM%	DIS%	Sv%	LI	RAR	BPV	BPX	R$
12																																	
13																																	
14																																	
15 aa	5	10	0	104	93	4.88	3.76	1.36				21.8	2.9	8.1	2.8						34%	62%								-11.8	96	114	-$4
16 SEA *	3	7	19	92	137	2.80	3.10	1.13	627	604	643	5.6	2.1	13.3	6.2	58%	19%	47	23	31	37%	79%	15%	0	17			86	1.34	15.8	193	229	$17
1st Half	3	4	1	56	78	2.53	3.41	1.17	704	461	822	7.4	1.9	12.5	6.5	59%	17%	42	21	36	37%	83%	17%	0	18			100	0.98	11.5	189	226	$14
2nd Half	0	3	18	36	59	3.22	2.20	1.07	591	650	543	4.2	2.5	14.6	5.9	57%	20%	49	23	28	37%	72%	14%	0	16			86	1.48	4.3	223	266	$22
17 Proj	**5**	**3**	**41**	**65**	**83**	**3.05**	**2.97**	**1.16**	**598**	**553**	**628**	**7.3**	**2.7**	**11.5**	**4.3**	**58%**	**19%**	**46**	**22**	**31**	**34%**	**75%**	**9%**	**0**						**9.2**	**159**	**189**	**$21**

Dickey,R.A.

Age: 42 | Th: R | Role: SP | Ht: 6' 2" | Wt: 220 | Type:
Health: B | PT/Exp: A | Consist: A
LIMA Plan: B | Rand Var: +1 | MM: 1103

Aside from some SwK and Dom recovery, not much went right for him in 2016. Among the warning signs: Ctl decline, worst ERA/xERA since 2009, troubling xERA trend, issues with HR (1.5 hr/9), crumbling DOM% and well below-average BPX. He's 42; even knuckleballers reach the end of the line.

Yr Tm	W	L	Sv	IP	K	ERA	xERA	WHIP	oOPS	vL	vR	BF/G	Ctl	Dom	Cmd	FpK	SwK	G	L	F	H%	S%	hr/f	GS	APC	DOM%	DIS%	Sv%	LI	RAR	BPV	BPX	R$
12 NYM	20	6	0	234	230	2.73	3.22	1.05	640	682	605	27.3	2.1	8.9	4.3	62%	13%	46	20	34	28%	79%	11%	33	99	45%	18%	0	0.76	36.9	127	166	$36
13 TOR	14	13	0	225	177	4.21	4.11	1.24	728	777	672	27.7	2.8	7.1	2.5	61%	10%	40	19	40	27%	71%	13%	34	103	29%	32%			-9.4	69	90	$7
14 TOR	14	13	0	216	173	3.71	4.01	1.23	705	659	740	26.9	3.1	7.2	2.3	63%	11%	42	20	38	27%	74%	11%	34	103	29%	24%			0.7	67	79	$9
15 TOR	11	11	0	214	126	3.91	4.54	1.19	708	664	747	26.8	2.6	5.3	2.1	59%	9%	42	21	37	26%	71%	10%	33	99	21%	30%			1.5	46	55	$9
16 TOR	10	15	0	170	126	4.46	4.75	1.37	788	790	787	24.3	3.3	6.7	2.0	62%	11%	42	22	36	29%	73%	15%	29	91	14%	28%	0	0.83	-5.6	50	60	$1
1st Half	5	9	0	103	70	4.21	4.66	1.32	796	877	735	25.5	3.1	6.1	2.0	59%	10%	46	20	34	27%	75%	17%	17	97	12%	29%			-0.2	51	61	$4
2nd Half	5	6	0	67	56	4.84	4.88	1.43	777	657	864	22.7	3.8	7.5	2.0	66%	13%	36	24	40	31%	69%	11%	12	84	17%	25%	0	0.90	-5.3	48	57	-$2
17 Proj	**9**	**10**	**0**	**145**	**108**	**4.55**	**4.58**	**1.31**	**755**	**720**	**782**	**24.6**	**3.1**	**6.7**	**2.2**	**62%**	**11%**	**41**	**22**	**37**	**29%**	**69%**	**12%**	**24**						**-6.4**	**56**	**67**	**$0**

GREG PYRON

Diekman,Jake

Age: 30 Th: L Role RP	Health B	LIMA Plan B+
Ht: 6' 4" Wt: 205 Type Pwr	PT/Exp C	Rand Var -2
	Consist A	MM 2510

Locked in on the strike zone for half a season, producing an interesting/usable skill set, but then Ctl went poof again. Above-average SwK/Dom, success both vL and vR makes him a quality RP in real-life. Wildness precludes higher-leverage work and even makes him a sketchy option in holds leagues.

Yr Tm	W	L	Sv	IP	K	ERA	xERA	WHIP	oOPS	vL	vR	BF/G	Ctl	Dom	Cmd	FpK	SwK	G	L	F	H%	S%	hr/f	GS	APC	DOM%	DIS%	Sv%	LI	RAR	BPV	BPX	R$
12 PHI *	2	2	7	54	65	3.10	3.53	1.53	696	590	774	4.1	5.7	10.9	1.9	53%	13%	52	25	23	35%	78%	6%	0	17			70	1.18	6.1	107	140	$1
13 PHI *	2	4	11	68	71	4.53	4.30	1.65	598	368	765	4.1	5.5	9.3	1.7	59%	14%	51	29	20	36%	71%	5%	0	14			79	0.92	-5.6	84	110	-$2
14 PHI	5	5	0	71	100	3.80	2.99	1.42	692	577	748	4.3	4.4	12.7	2.9	55%	14%	43	26	30	38%	73%	8%	0	18			0	1.14	-0.5	129	154	$0
15 2 TM	2	1	0	58	69	4.01	3.54	1.44	689	729	660	3.9	4.8	10.6	2.2	59%	12%	56	15	28	33%	73%	11%	0	16			0	0.86	-0.4	96	115	-$3
16 TEX	4	2	4	53	59	3.40	3.76	1.17	594	625	578	3.3	4.4	10.0	2.3	53%	11%	48	20	32	26%	72%	9%	0	14			80	1.08	5.2	87	104	$4
1st Half	1	1	2	32	35	2.81	3.46	0.97	537	517	545	3.3	3.4	9.8	2.9	52%	10%	47	17	36	22%	75%	11%	0	14			100	1.22	5.4	111	133	$6
2nd Half	3	1	2	21	24	4.29	4.25	1.48	674	740	627	3.4	6.0	10.3	1.7	55%	14%	49	24	27	31%	70%	7%	0	14			67	0.90	-0.2	50	60	$1
17 Proj	**4**	**2**	**5**	**58**	**65**	**3.80**	**3.71**	**1.33**	**649**	**643**	**652**	**3.5**	**4.6**	**10.2**	**2.2**	**56%**	**13%**	**50**	**21**	**29**	**31%**	**72%**	**9%**	**0**						**2.8**	**87**	**104**	**$2**

Doolittle,Sean

Age: 30 Th: L Role RP	Health F	LIMA Plan A
Ht: 6' 2" Wt: 190 Type Pwr xFB	PT/Exp C	Rand Var 0
	Consist B	MM 3410

Missed two months in 2nd half with shoulder strain. Excellent Cmd fully backed by FpK and SwK. Extreme FB% hasn't hurt him in past due to depressed hr/f, but luck ran out as hr/f regressed. Durability remains chief concern, but the skills themselves remain closer-worthy.

Yr Tm	W	L	Sv	IP	K	ERA	xERA	WHIP	oOPS	vL	vR	BF/G	Ctl	Dom	Cmd	FpK	SwK	G	L	F	H%	S%	hr/f	GS	APC	DOM%	DIS%	Sv%	LI	RAR	BPV	BPX	R$
12 OAK	2	1	1	47	60	3.04	3.17	1.08	611	794	509	4.3	2.1	11.4	5.5	66%	13%	35	15	50	33%	73%	5%	0	18			50	1.38	5.7	162	211	$3
13 OAK	5	5	2	69	60	3.13	3.55	0.96	573	516	603	3.8	1.7	7.8	4.6	65%	12%	33	20	47	27%	68%	5%	0	15			29	1.21	6.3	106	138	$7
14 OAK	2	4	22	63	89	2.73	2.61	0.73	459	276	550	3.9	1.1	12.8	11.1	72%	17%	23	18	59	27%	66%	6%	0	15			85	1.29	7.8	200	238	$17
15 OAK	1	0	4	14	15	3.95	3.99	1.24	651	1065	531	4.8	3.3	9.9	3.0	65%	10%	32	19	49	32%	69%	6%	0	21			80	0.75	0.0	99	118	-$2
16 OAK	2	3	4	39	45	3.23	3.65	1.05	705	584	798	3.5	1.8	10.4	5.6	70%	16%	29	16	55	29%	77%	12%	0	14			67	1.18	4.6	144	171	$3
1st Half	2	2	4	31	35	2.93	3.70	1.04	699	475	854	3.5	2.3	10.3	4.4	71%	16%	30	16	53	27%	81%	13%	0	13			80	1.15	4.7	130	155	$5
2nd Half	0	1	0	8	10	4.32	3.49	1.08	727	882	563	3.8	0.0	10.8	0.0	65%	16%	27	14	59	37%	63%	8%	0	14			0	1.31	-0.1	200	238	-$6
17 Proj	**3**	**3**	**5**	**51**	**57**	**3.33**	**3.57**	**1.00**	**615**	**519**	**669**	**3.7**	**1.8**	**10.1**	**5.5**	**69%**	**14%**	**30**	**18**	**52**	**29%**	**69%**	**7%**	**0**						**5.4**	**140**	**167**	**$5**

Duffey,Tyler

Age: 26 Th: R Role SP	Health A	LIMA Plan B+
Ht: 6' 3" Wt: 225 Type	PT/Exp D	Rand Var +5
	Consist D	MM 1103

9-12, 6.43 ERA in 133 IP at MIN. Often around the plate, but with a 90 mph fastball and just one decent swing-and-miss offering (13% SwK on curve), his margin for error is small. Unlucky H%, S% and hr/f hint at some gains to come and 2015 shows the upside. Too early to give up on, so speculate cautiously.

Yr Tm	W	L	Sv	IP	K	ERA	xERA	WHIP	oOPS	vL	vR	BF/G	Ctl	Dom	Cmd	FpK	SwK	G	L	F	H%	S%	hr/f	GS	APC	DOM%	DIS%	Sv%	LI	RAR	BPV	BPX	R$
12																																	
13																																	
14 a/a	10	3	0	127	80	4.84	4.79	1.33				25.1	1.8	5.7	3.1						31%	67%								-17.2	58	69	-$3
15 MIN *	12	9	0	196	148	3.20	3.33	1.28	702	664	738	25.1	2.3	6.8	2.9	64%	10%	50	19	31	33%	74%	8%	10	91	50%	20%			18.3	97	115	$12
16 MIN *	10	13	0	164	133	6.03	5.71	1.49	876	714	1038	22.8	2.5	7.3	2.9	64%	9%	48	23	29	34%	63%	20%	26	88	23%	42%			-37.2	51	60	-$11
1st Half	4	6	0	89	69	5.08	5.48	1.47	829	725	917	24.0	2.2	6.9	3.2	61%	9%	48	23	29	34%	69%	19%	13	95	31%	46%			-9.8	60	72	-$7
2nd Half	6	7	0	74	64	7.18	6.00	1.51	933	702	1222	21.5	2.9	7.8	2.7	67%	9%	48	22	30	33%	55%	20%	13	80	15%	38%			-27.4	41	48	-$17
17 Proj	**9**	**8**	**0**	**131**	**101**	**4.31**	**4.12**	**1.36**	**780**	**662**	**902**	**23.5**	**2.4**	**6.9**	**2.9**	**64%**	**9%**	**49**	**21**	**30**	**32%**	**72%**	**13%**	**23**						**-1.9**	**87**	**103**	**$0**

Duffy,Danny

Age: 28 Th: L Role RP	Health C	LIMA Plan C+
Ht: 6' 2" Wt: 185 Type Pwr FB	PT/Exp A	Rand Var 0
	Consist B	MM 2305

Post-hype prospect finally stayed healthy and delivered on his promise. New focus on pounding the strike zone led to vastly improved Ctl, backed by FpK. SwK/Dom surged, in part, due to upgraded slider (20% SwK). He got the FB% under control in 2nd half, so if health cooperates, then ... UP: 3.00 ERA.

Yr Tm	W	L	Sv	IP	K	ERA	xERA	WHIP	oOPS	vL	vR	BF/G	Ctl	Dom	Cmd	FpK	SwK	G	L	F	H%	S%	hr/f	GS	APC	DOM%	DIS%	Sv%	LI	RAR	BPV	BPX	R$
12 KC	2	2	0	28	28	3.90	4.80	1.59	771	491	859	20.2	5.9	9.1	1.6	52%	10%	35	21	44	32%	76%	6%	6	88	0%	17%			0.4	19	25	-$4
13 KC *	5	2	0	93	90	4.26	4.48	1.54	608	692	571	19.4	4.4	8.7	2.0	54%	11%	32	27	41	34%	73%	0%	5	94	20%	20%			-4.5	72	94	-$4
14 KC	9	12	0	149	113	2.53	4.24	1.11	605	386	670	19.5	3.2	6.8	2.1	59%	8%	36	18	46	25%	81%	6%	25	78	32%	24%	0	0.87	22.3	50	60	$14
15 KC	7	8	1	137	102	4.08	4.56	1.39	746	593	785	19.6	3.5	6.7	1.9	57%	9%	39	25	36	30%	73%	10%	24	79	8%	29%	100	0.75	-2.0	44	52	$0
16 KC	12	3	0	180	188	3.51	3.72	1.14	710	449	760	17.4	2.1	9.4	4.5	62%	13%	36	21	43	30%	76%	13%	26	64	38%	15%	0	0.72	15.1	127	151	$17
1st Half	4	1	0	75	87	3.11	3.41	1.05	682	387	753	11.6	1.9	10.4	5.4	63%	15%	34	20	45	29%	78%	13%	10	42	40%	10%	0	0.70	10.1	148	176	$17
2nd Half	8	2	0	104	101	3.80	3.96	1.21	730	509	764	26.9	2.2	8.7	3.9	62%	12%	38	21	41	30%	75%	13%	16	100	38%	19%			5.1	112	134	$18
17 Proj	**13**	**7**	**0**	**196**	**190**	**3.35**	**3.94**	**1.20**	**703**	**494**	**751**	**18.0**	**2.5**	**8.7**	**3.5**	**60%**	**11%**	**37**	**22**	**41**	**30%**	**77%**	**11%**	**35**						**20.2**	**105**	**125**	**$16**

Duke,Zach

Age: 34 Th: L Role RP	Health A	LIMA Plan A
Ht: 6' 1" Wt: 205 Type Pwr xGB	PT/Exp C	Rand Var -4
	Consist B	MM 3400

Heavy GB%/elite Dom provide a terrific foundation. Ctl was marginally better and FpK suggests additional upside. Good fortune with hr/f and S% gave ERA some artificial luster, so there should be some pullback there, but he's still worthy of a spot in Holds formats.

Yr Tm	W	L	Sv	IP	K	ERA	xERA	WHIP	oOPS	vL	vR	BF/G	Ctl	Dom	Cmd	FpK	SwK	G	L	F	H%	S%	hr/f	GS	APC	DOM%	DIS%	Sv%	LI	RAR	BPV	BPX	R$
12 WAS *	16	5	0	178	76	4.42	5.82	1.61	556	646	520	23.2	2.3	3.8	1.7	54%	11%	40	28	33	34%	75%	0%	0	27			0	0.37	-8.8	18	24	-$9
13 2 NL *	3	2	2	59	44	4.11	4.41	1.38	806	728	854	4.8	2.4	6.7	2.7	56%	10%	50	21	29	32%	72%	9%	1	20	0%	100%	100	1.09	-1.8	68	89	-$2
14 MIL	5	1	0	59	74	2.45	2.32	1.13	578	569	586	3.2	2.6	11.4	4.4	63%	13%	58	22	20	33%	79%	10%	0	13			0	1.11	9.3	170	202	$5
15 CHW	3	6	1	61	66	3.41	3.39	1.30	724	604	799	3.6	4.7	9.8	2.1	55%	11%	58	17	25	27%	80%	24%	0	15			33	1.47	4.1	84	100	$1
16 2 TM	2	1	2	61	68	2.36	3.38	1.26	612	580	635	3.2	4.3	10.0	2.3	59%	11%	59	18	24	31%	81%	6%	0	13			40	1.20	13.8	102	121	$4
1st Half	2	0	1	26	30	3.08	3.23	1.33	682	723	629	2.8	3.8	10.3	2.7	59%	12%	58	22	20	34%	76%	7%	0	11			25	1.30	3.6	119	142	$3
2nd Half	0	1	1	35	38	1.82	3.50	1.21	556	424	639	3.5	4.7	9.9	2.1	59%	10%	60	14	26	28%	85%	5%	0	14			100	1.10	10.1	89	106	$6
17 Proj	**3**	**2**	**0**	**58**	**62**	**2.81**	**3.39**	**1.27**	**653**	**592**	**697**	**3.4**	**4.0**	**9.7**	**2.4**	**58%**	**11%**	**58**	**18**	**24**	**30%**	**80%**	**12%**	**0**						**9.9**	**103**	**123**	**$2**

Dull,Ryan

Age: 27 Th: R Role RP	Health A	LIMA Plan C+
Ht: 5' 11" Wt: 175 Type Pwr xFB	PT/Exp D	Rand Var -5
	Consist D	MM 1301

Throws three pitches, but relies heavily on 91 mph fastball and hard slider (20% SwK). Significant 2nd half progress in curbing FBs was a big key to growth, LI shows he was rewarded accordingly. Looming correction to H%/S% will push ERA toward xERA, but end result remains highly playable.

Yr Tm	W	L	Sv	IP	K	ERA	xERA	WHIP	oOPS	vL	vR	BF/G	Ctl	Dom	Cmd	FpK	SwK	G	L	F	H%	S%	hr/f	GS	APC	DOM%	DIS%	Sv%	LI	RAR	BPV	BPX	R$
12																																	
13																																	
14 aa	5	5	6	56	49	3.34	4.28	1.34				5.9	2.5	7.8	3.1						33%	78%								2.8	84	100	$3
15 OAK *	4	4	13	78	72	1.62	2.41	1.04	713	875	594	5.0	2.6	8.3	3.2	50%	11%	41	14	45	26%	89%	20%	0	20			93	1.13	22.6	109	130	$16
16 OAK	5	5	3	74	73	2.42	3.89	0.87	577	687	517	4.1	1.8	8.8	4.9	64%	13%	33	16	51	23%	82%	10%	0	17			50	1.13	16.2	121	144	$12
1st Half	2	2	0	41	43	2.18	3.80	0.75	515	580	487	4.3	1.7	9.4	5.4	67%	13%	31	13	56	20%	81%	8%	0	18			0	0.86	10.3	131	156	$13
2nd Half	3	3	3	33	30	2.73	4.01	1.03	653	780	562	3.9	1.9	8.2	4.3	59%	12%	35	18	46	26%	83%	12%	0	17			50	1.43	6.0	109	130	$11
17 Proj	**5**	**5**	**0**	**73**	**68**	**3.07**	**4.16**	**1.11**	**652**	**806**	**561**	**4.6**	**2.5**	**8.4**	**3.4**	**62%**	**13%**	**34**	**16**	**50**	**28%**	**77%**	**8%**	**0**						**10.0**	**96**	**114**	**$5**

Dyson,Sam

Age: 29 Th: R Role RP	Health A	LIMA Plan C
Ht: 6' 2" Wt: 205 Type xGB	PT/Exp C	Rand Var -2
	Consist B	MM 3130

Induces groundballs at an amazing rate. Had four pitches generate a 10% SwK or better in 2015, but only one pitch—the change-up (17% SwK)—held that distinction in 2016. That Dom loss makes him a mid-tier closer at best. At worst, the 2H Ctl/Cmd and BPX wasn't even closer worthy, opening door to... DN: 15 Sv.

Yr Tm	W	L	Sv	IP	K	ERA	xERA	WHIP	oOPS	vL	vR	BF/G	Ctl	Dom	Cmd	FpK	SwK	G	L	F	H%	S%	hr/f	GS	APC	DOM%	DIS%	Sv%	LI	RAR	BPV	BPX	R$
12 TOR *	2	2	9	46	19	3.62	4.23	1.46	1750	2000	1667	5.6	3.4	3.8	1.1	63%	4%	80	20	0	30%	75%	0%	0	13			90	0.17	2.2	31	40	$0
13 MIA *	4	12	0	117	51	3.97	4.16	1.50	959	1014	919	19.5	3.3	3.9	1.2	48%	6%	69	5	26	32%	72%	18%	1	35	0%	100%	0	0.79	-1.5	39	51	-$6
14 MIA *	5	2	1	67	49	2.33	3.20	1.33	653	781	553	6.3	3.3	6.5	2.0	60%	11%	63	19	18	31%	81%	4%	0	22			33	0.68	11.7	80	96	$3
15 2 TM	5	4	2	75	71	2.63	2.74	1.14	603	557	633	4.1	2.5	8.5	3.4	60%	13%	69	17	14	30%	78%	13%	0	15			50	1.02	12.4	132	157	$7
16 TEX	3	2	38	70	55	2.43	3.38	1.22	658	740	593	3.9	2.9	7.0	2.4	61%	9%	65	19	16	29%	83%	16%	0	14			88	1.32	15.3	90	107	$20
1st Half	1	2	17	40	31	2.72	3.23	1.08	645	769	558	3.7	2.3	7.0	3.1	65%	10%	61	21	18	27%	78%	15%	0	13			89	1.43	7.2	104	124	$19
2nd Half	2	0	21	31	24	2.05	3.58	1.40	675	708	642	4.2	3.8	7.0	1.8	56%	8%	70	16	13	31%	88%	17%	0	15			88	1.18	8.1	72	86	$21
17 Proj	**4**	**2**	**31**	**65**	**51**	**2.82**	**3.44**	**1.27**	**652**	**696**	**618**	**4.5**	**3.1**	**7.0**	**2.3**	**60%**	**11%**	**67**	**18**	**15**	**30%**	**79%**	**12%**	**0**						**11.0**	**88**	**105**	**$15**

GREG PYRON

Edwards,Carl

Age: 25 Th: R Role RP	Health A	LIMA Plan A	
Ht: 6' 2" Wt: 155 Type Pwr xGB	PT/Exp D	Rand Var +5	
	Consist A	MM 5500	

1-2, 3.75 ERA with 2 Sv in 36 IP at CHC. 48th-rd pick from 2011 thrived in first extended time in MLB (2.52 xERA and 13.0 Dom). Though Ctl in minors was brutal, FpK backs 3.5 Ctl in MLB. SwK/Dom/GB% and ability vL are exciting. Needs to prove he's curbed the walks, but seeds here are impressive.

Yr Tm	W	L	Sv	IP	K	ERA	xERA	WHIP	oOPS	vL	vR	BF/G	Ctl	Dom	Cmd	FpK	SwK	G	L	F	H%	S%	hr/f	GS	APC	DOM%	DIS%	Sv%	LI	RAR	BPV	BPX	R$
12																																	
13																																	
14 aa	1	2	0	48	40	2.72	2.04	1.13				19.0	3.9	7.4	1.9						25%	75%								6.0	94	112	$1
15 CHC *	5	3	6	60	67	3.30	2.02	1.30	566	929	350	6.0	6.8	10.1	1.5	63%	10%	58	25	17	24%	73%	0%	0	14			67	0.19	4.9	109	130	$4
16 CHC *	1	2	3	61	81	4.29	2.07	1.08	456	425	475	4.0	4.7	11.9	2.6	56%	18%	50	21	29	24%	61%	19%	0	17			75	0.95	-0.7	124	147	$2
1st Half	1	1	1	32	39	4.23	2.64	1.25	342	282	385	4.5	5.2	10.9	2.1	52%	21%	38	15	46	27%	66%	17%	0	21			100	0.75	-0.2	107	128	$1
2nd Half	0	1	2	29	42	4.34	2.59	0.90	481	463	489	3.7	4.0	13.0	3.2	57%	18%	53	22	25	20%	52%	20%	0	17			67	0.99	-0.6	156	186	$4
17 Proj	**2**	**2**	**0**	**58**	**74**	**3.56**	**2.94**	**1.03**	**462**	**464**	**459**	**5.0**	**4.1**	**11.5**	**2.8**	**57%**	**18%**	**53**	**22**	**25**	**25%**	**65%**	**9%**	**0**						**4.5**	**126**	**150**	**$3**

Eflin,Zach

Age: 23 Th: R Role SP	Health D	LIMA Plan D+	
Ht: 6' 6" Wt: 215 Type Con FB	PT/Exp D	Rand Var +5	
	Consist B	MM 0001	

3-5, 5.54 ERA in 63 IP at PHI. Limits walks, but doesn't get enough groundballs or miss enough bats (8% SwK% at Triple-A). Diagnosed in Aug with stress fracture in right foot and patellar tendinopathy in both knees. Underwent knee surgeries (Aug and Sept). Expected ready for spring training but needs to prove his worth.

Yr Tm	W	L	Sv	IP	K	ERA	xERA	WHIP	oOPS	vL	vR	BF/G	Ctl	Dom	Cmd	FpK	SwK	G	L	F	H%	S%	hr/f	GS	APC	DOM%	DIS%	Sv%	LI	RAR	BPV	BPX	R$
12																																	
13																																	
14																																	
15 aa	8	6	0	132	62	4.09	4.31	1.29				23.5	1.5	4.2	2.8						30%	70%								-2.0	54	64	$1
16 PHI *	8	7	0	132	80	4.84	3.74	1.19	828	939	723	24.0	2.0	5.5	2.8	62%	6%	36	24	40	28%	61%	13%	11	90	18%	64%			-10.5	64	76	$1
1st Half	5	4	0	89	58	4.54	3.27	1.14	809	749	863	23.4	1.6	5.9	3.6	66%	5%	38	22	40	29%	60%	13%	4	88	0%	50%			-3.9	95	113	$5
2nd Half	3	3	0	43	22	5.44	5.25	1.30	838	1039	644	25.4	2.7	4.6	1.7	60%	7%	35	24	41	26%	63%	14%	7	92	29%	71%			-6.6	22	27	-$6
17 Proj	**4**	**5**	**0**	**73**	**38**	**4.69**	**4.89**	**1.26**	**755**	**821**	**693**	**24.1**	**2.0**	**4.8**	**2.4**	**62%**	**6%**	**36**	**23**	**40**	**28%**	**65%**	**10%**	**12**						**-4.4**	**47**	**56**	**-$3**

Eickhoff,Jerad

Age: 26 Th: R Role SP	Health A	LIMA Plan C	
Ht: 6' 4" Wt: 200 Type FB	PT/Exp B	Rand Var 0	
	Consist A	MM 1205	

Solid first full season in MLB, but there are reasons for concern. Strong Cmd, but FpK suggests Ctl gains won't last; severe issues vL persist. FB% jumped in 2nd half, putting him at risk for HR and at whims of hr/f. Worth keeping an eye on, but not much upside just yet.

Yr Tm	W	L	Sv	IP	K	ERA	xERA	WHIP	oOPS	vL	vR	BF/G	Ctl	Dom	Cmd	FpK	SwK	G	L	F	H%	S%	hr/f	GS	APC	DOM%	DIS%	Sv%	LI	RAR	BPV	BPX	R$
12																																	
13 aa	1	1	0	29	11	10.19	8.29	1.97				23.1	4.8	3.3	0.7						32%	50%								-22.6	-53	-70	-$14
14 aa	10	9	0	154	118	5.11	4.30	1.34				23.8	3.2	6.9	2.2						30%	64%								-26.1	55	66	-$5
15 PHI *	15	8	0	184	155	4.14	4.08	1.27	621	830	458	24.3	2.6	7.6	2.9	65%	11%	38	22	40	30%	71%	9%	8	92	50%	13%			-4.1	75	89	$7
16 PHI	11	14	0	197	167	3.65	4.06	1.16	740	822	645	24.6	1.9	7.6	4.0	61%	10%	41	20	39	29%	75%	13%	33	92	24%	24%			13.2	104	124	$15
1st Half	5	9	0	96	83	3.38	4.00	1.24	747	763	730	25.1	2.3	7.8	3.5	62%	10%	44	22	34	31%	78%	12%	16	97	25%	31%			9.6	101	120	$14
2nd Half	6	5	0	101	84	3.91	4.12	1.09	733	875	558	24.1	1.6	7.5	4.7	60%	10%	38	18	44	27%	72%	14%	17	87	24%	18%			3.5	107	127	$17
17 Proj	**11**	**12**	**0**	**189**	**157**	**4.07**	**4.19**	**1.22**	**750**	**898**	**601**	**24.0**	**2.3**	**7.5**	**3.2**	**62%**	**10%**	**39**	**21**	**40**	**29%**	**71%**	**12%**	**32**						**2.8**	**89**	**106**	**$8**

Estrada,Marco

Age: 33 Th: R Role SP	Health D	LIMA Plan C	
Ht: 5' 11" Wt: 180 Type Pwr xFB	PT/Exp A	Rand Var -3	
	Consist A	MM 1203	

A tale of two halves: H%/S% gave success in 1st half and took it away in 2nd. Skills stayed virtually the same throughout, despite July diagnosis of a herniated disc in back. Has long used high popup rate to outpitch skills, but wide gap between xERA and ERA is instructive, as is the modest BPX column.

Yr Tm	W	L	Sv	IP	K	ERA	xERA	WHIP	oOPS	vL	vR	BF/G	Ctl	Dom	Cmd	FpK	SwK	G	L	F	H%	S%	hr/f	GS	APC	DOM%	DIS%	Sv%	LI	RAR	BPV	BPX	R$
12 MIL	5	7	0	138	143	3.64	3.59	1.14	703	728	681	19.4	1.9	9.3	4.9	62%	11%	34	20	45	31%	73%	10%	23	77	26%	22%	0	0.71	6.3	129	168	$9
13 MIL	7	4	0	128	118	3.87	3.60	1.08	670	651	687	24.4	2.0	8.3	4.1	60%	11%	38	18	44	27%	70%	12%	21	95	43%	29%			0.0	110	144	$8
14 MIL	7	6	0	151	127	4.36	4.15	1.20	752	719	781	16.0	2.6	7.6	2.9	61%	11%	33	18	50	27%	71%	13%	18	65	11%	50%	0	0.63	-11.5	77	91	$2
15 TOR	13	8	0	181	131	3.13	4.61	1.04	633	638	626	21.3	2.7	6.5	2.4	57%	10%	32	16	52	22%	76%	9%	28	86	21%	29%	0	0.76	18.5	53	64	$20
16 TOR	9	9	0	176	165	3.48	4.46	1.12	639	602	680	24.9	3.3	8.4	2.5	59%	11%	33	18	48	25%	74%	10%	29	98	34%	17%			15.5	73	87	$16
1st Half	5	3	0	104	99	2.93	4.26	0.99	582	624	539	25.7	3.4	8.5	2.5	61%	11%	34	17	49	20%	78%	11%	16	101	38%	6%			16.2	75	90	$23
2nd Half	4	6	0	72	66	4.27	4.74	1.31	714	576	886	24.0	3.3	8.3	2.5	56%	12%	32	20	47	30%	71%	9%	13	95	31%	31%			-0.7	71	85	$5
17 Proj	**9**	**8**	**0**	**160**	**139**	**3.85**	**4.41**	**1.14**	**672**	**630**	**719**	**20.9**	**2.9**	**7.8**	**2.7**	**59%**	**11%**	**33**	**18**	**49**	**26%**	**71%**	**10%**	**30**						**6.7**	**73**	**87**	**$10**

Familia,Jeurys

Age: 27 Th: R Role RP	Health D	LIMA Plan C	
Ht: 6' 4" Wt: 185 Type Pwr xGB	PT/Exp A	Rand Var -3	
	Consist B	MM 4431	

Tweak to pitch mix led to uptick in GB%, as he essentially phased out the splitter in favor of more four-seam fastballs. Eye-catching Ctl backslide, but FpK implies it shouldn't have been quite as sharp. Favorable hr/f helped him to a sub-3.00. Not quite in the elite tier of closers, but this is a fine skill set.

Yr Tm	W	L	Sv	IP	K	ERA	xERA	WHIP	oOPS	vL	vR	BF/G	Ctl	Dom	Cmd	FpK	SwK	G	L	F	H%	S%	hr/f	GS	APC	DOM%	DIS%	Sv%	LI	RAR	BPV	BPX	R$
12 NYM *	9	9	0	149	122	5.10	4.73	1.64	644	751	560	18.5	4.7	7.3	1.6	42%	9%	48	18	33	35%	68%	0%	1	26	0%	0%	0	0.13	-19.9	61	79	-$12
13 NYM	0	0	1	11	8	4.22	5.79	1.97	908	889	918	5.8	7.6	6.8	0.9	52%	7%	52	15	33	31%	84%	18%	0	22			100	0.69	-0.5	-54	-70	-$5
14 NYM	2	5	5	77	73	2.21	3.36	1.18	587	821	377	4.2	3.7	8.5	2.3	53%	13%	57	15	28	28%	82%	5%	0	16			50	1.18	14.6	87	104	$7
15 NYM	2	2	43	78	86	1.85	2.62	1.00	569	616	531	4.1	2.2	9.9	4.5	61%	16%	58	20	22	28%	86%	14%	0	15			90	1.29	20.4	155	185	$27
16 NYM	3	4	51	78	84	2.55	3.08	1.21	574	629	526	4.1	3.6	9.7	2.7	57%	15%	63	18	19	31%	77%	3%	0	16			91	1.22	15.7	119	142	$27
1st Half	2	1	28	39	38	2.75	3.16	1.19	581	677	497	4.0	3.0	8.7	2.9	56%	16%	63	19	19	32%	74%	0%	0	15			100	1.22	7.0	117	139	$28
2nd Half	1	3	23	38	46	2.35	3.00	1.23	567	579	556	4.2	4.2	10.8	2.6	58%	15%	64	16	20	31%	80%	6%	0	18			82	1.21	8.7	122	146	$26
17 Proj	**2**	**4**	**43**	**73**	**76**	**2.81**	**3.15**	**1.20**	**595**	**673**	**529**	**4.4**	**3.4**	**9.5**	**2.8**	**58%**	**15%**	**61**	**18**	**21**	**31%**	**76%**	**7%**	**0**						**12.4**	**117**	**139**	**$21**

Farmer,Buck

Age: 26 Th: R Role RP	Health A	LIMA Plan D+	
Ht: 6' 3" Wt: 220 Type	PT/Exp D	Rand Var +2	
	Consist B	MM 0101	

0-1, 4.60 ERA in 29 IP at DET. Tallied a 3.96 ERA, 8.3 Dom, 2.5 Ctl and 47% GB% in 100 IP as a starter at Triple-A around numerous brief MLB stints. Trouble vL wasn't evident in minors, perhaps just a sample size quirk. GB% is the starting point of a playable skill set, but the second component is not yet in evidence.

Yr Tm	W	L	Sv	IP	K	ERA	xERA	WHIP	oOPS	vL	vR	BF/G	Ctl	Dom	Cmd	FpK	SwK	G	L	F	H%	S%	hr/f	GS	APC	DOM%	DIS%	Sv%	LI	RAR	BPV	BPX	R$
12																																	
13																																	
14 DET *	2	2	0	29	21	8.12	6.03	1.70	1054	1189	880	16.2	4.1	6.7	1.6	70%	11%	33	15	52	35%	51%	14%	2	49	0%	100%	0	0.42	-15.5	30	35	-$8
15 DET *	7	7	0	127	84	5.70	5.29	1.53	986	1067	920	18.4	3.0	5.9	2.0	60%	8%	45	15	40	33%	64%	18%	5	50	0%	80%	0	0.58	-27.2	38	45	-$12
16 DET *	5	7	0	129	99	5.28	5.72	1.63	771	903	604	16.9	3.6	6.9	1.9	60%	11%	52	11	37	35%	70%	13%	1	36	0%	100%	0	0.28	-17.4	38	45	-$11
1st Half	1	4	0	54	38	7.27	7.19	1.78	594	733	423	13.1	3.3	6.4	1.9	56%	10%	50	12	38	37%	62%	8%	0	22			0	0.20	-20.6	12	14	-$20
2nd Half	4	3	0	75	60	3.85	4.67	1.52	903	1027	745	21.8	3.9	7.2	1.9	64%	11%	53	10	37	33%	76%	17%	1	61	0%	100%	0	0.40	3.1	57	68	-$4
17 Proj	**3**	**4**	**0**	**73**	**52**	**4.82**	**4.93**	**1.59**	**876**	**947**	**802**	**17.5**	**3.4**	**6.5**	**1.9**	**62%**	**10%**	**50**	**12**	**38**	**34%**	**72%**	**11%**	**14**						**-5.6**	**53**	**63**	**-$7**

Farquhar,Daniel

Age: 30 Th: R Role RP	Health A	LIMA Plan C	
Ht: 5' 11" Wt: 180 Type Pwr	PT/Exp D	Rand Var +4	
	Consist B	MM 2300	

1-0, 3.06 ERA in 35 IP at TAM. Good chunk of 1H was spent at Triple-A, most of 2H was in MLB with great success. Dom/SwK spike in that 2H brought us back to his halcyon days of 2013-14. But in this sequel, Ctl wasn't along for the ride. Resulting Cmd remains far from peak levels and merely tolerable in today's game.

Yr Tm	W	L	Sv	IP	K	ERA	xERA	WHIP	oOPS	vL	vR	BF/G	Ctl	Dom	Cmd	FpK	SwK	G	L	F	H%	S%	hr/f	GS	APC	DOM%	DIS%	Sv%	LI	RAR	BPV	BPX	R$
12 a/a	3	3	9	68	60	2.85	2.42	1.11				6.1	2.8	7.9	2.8						28%	74%								9.7	107	140	$8
13 SEA *	0	4	22	76	104	3.74	2.59	1.18	586	485	695	5.0	3.1	12.3	4.0	55%	14%	42	25	33	35%	67%	5%	0	20			81	1.18	1.2	157	205	$10
14 SEA	3	1	1	71	81	2.66	2.98	1.13	607	641	578	4.4	2.8	10.3	3.7	59%	12%	42	27	31	31%	79%	9%	0	17			33	0.85	9.5	130	154	$5
15 SEA *	2	9	4	89	80	4.25	4.69	1.39	818	676	938	5.4	2.7	8.1	3.0	58%	11%	39	22	40	33%	73%	15%	0	19			57	0.91	-3.2	76	91	-$2
16 TAM *	5	2	2	73	64	3.97	4.75	1.41	786	774	792	4.6	3.1	7.9	2.5	54%	14%	38	29	33	32%	76%	27%	0	19			67	0.99	2.0	62	73	$0
1st Half	3	1	1	35	24	6.49	6.66	1.64	1099	1857	774	4.6	2.6	6.1	2.4	64%	11%	25	31	44	35%	64%	38%	0	19			100	0.37	-10.0	20	24	-$7
2nd Half	2	1	1	38	41	1.64	2.97	1.19	628	373	801	4.6	3.7	9.6	2.6	49%	16%	47	27	25	28%	91%	14%	0	19			50	1.28	12.0	101	120	$7
17 Proj	**2**	**2**	**0**	**44**	**42**	**3.56**	**3.88**	**1.32**	**737**	**616**	**837**	**4.8**	**3.0**	**8.7**	**2.9**	**55%**	**13%**	**43**	**26**	**31**	**32%**	**76%**	**13%**	**0**						**3.4**	**96**	**115**	**-$1**

GREG PYRON

Feldman,Scott

Age: 34	Th: R	Role RP	Health D	LIMA Plan B+	
Ht: 6' 5"	Wt: 210	Type Con	PT/Exp B	Rand Var 0	
			Consist A	MM 1001	

We weren't terribly enamored with the SP version, how about as a reliever? Increased GB% and Dom in RP role (though still subpar 7.1 Dom). Ctl and GB% continue to be his only above-average attributes. The xERA column tells us not to expect another sub-4.00 ERA. Interest level: Unchanged.

Yr Tm	W	L	Sv	IP	K	ERA	xERA	WHIP	oOPS	vL	vR	BF/G	Ctl	Dom	Cmd	FpK	SwK	G	L	F	H%	S%	hr/f	GS	APC	DOM%	DIS%	Sv%	LI	RAR	BPV	BPX	R$
12 TEX	6	11	0	124	96	5.09	4.12	1.38	745	752	736	18.5	2.3	7.0	3.0	61%	8%	42	26	32	33%	64%	11%	21	73	19%	38%	0	0.71	-16.5	83	108	-$6
13 2 TM	12	12	0	182	132	3.86	3.85	1.18	671	672	670	25.3	2.8	6.5	2.4	56%	8%	50	19	32	27%	70%	11%	30	100	30%	40%			0.0	71	92	$9
14 HOU	8	12	0	180	107	3.74	4.13	1.30	725	715	737	26.4	2.5	5.3	2.1	61%	7%	47	22	31	30%	73%	9%	29	102	10%	34%			0.0	54	64	$2
15 HOU	5	5	0	108	61	3.90	4.26	1.31	739	664	824	25.1	2.2	5.1	2.3	61%	7%	49	24	28	29%	74%	13%	18	98	28%	44%			0.8	58	69	$0
16 2 AL	7	4	0	77	56	3.97	4.32	1.38	782	891	707	8.5	2.2	6.5	2.9	60%	8%	50	20	30	32%	75%	13%	5	33	0%	60%	0	0.71	2.0	86	102	$1
1st Half	5	3	0	49	34	2.76	4.48	1.29	728	874	627	10.1	2.4	6.2	2.6	60%	7%	46	23	31	30%	83%	10%	5	38	0%	60%	0	0.91	8.7	72	86	$5
2nd Half	2	1	0	28	22	6.11	4.03	1.54	872	920	839	6.6	1.9	7.1	3.7	61%	8%	57	16	27	36%	63%	20%	0	27			0	0.48	-6.6	110	131	-$8
17 Proj	**5**	**4**	**0**	**73**	**49**	**4.37**	**4.25**	**1.37**	**773**	**783**	**765**	**8.2**	**2.2**	**6.1**	**2.7**	**60%**	**8%**	**50**	**21**	**29**	**32%**	**71%**	**14%**	**0**						**-1.6**	**77**	**92**	**-$2**

Feliz,Michael

Age: 24	Th: R	Role RP	Health A	LIMA Plan A	
Ht: 6' 4"	Wt: 230	Type Pwr	PT/Exp D	Rand Var +5	
			Consist A	MM 4511	

Minor league SP quickly adjusted to bullpen. Ability to miss bats and rack up boatloads of Ks makes him one to watch. FpK, especially in 2nd half, suggests that Ctl problems could be even worse than he advertised here. xERA endorses this skill set; electric stuff is always appealing. But FpK/Ctl urge caution.

Yr Tm	W	L	Sv	IP	K	ERA	xERA	WHIP	oOPS	vL	vR	BF/G	Ctl	Dom	Cmd	FpK	SwK	G	L	F	H%	S%	hr/f	GS	APC	DOM%	DIS%	Sv%	LI	RAR	BPV	BPX	R$
12																																	
13																																	
14																																	
15 HOU *	6	3	1	87	69	2.91	2.50	1.03	884	868	898	16.7	2.4	7.2	3.0	66%	13%	38	31	31	25%	75%	25%	0	35			100	0.05	11.2	95	114	$9
16 HOU	8	1	0	65	95	4.43	2.94	1.18	659	705	619	5.7	3.0	13.2	4.3	51%	14%	42	21	37	34%	67%	18%	0	24			0	0.99	-1.9	175	207	$4
1st Half	5	1	0	38	53	3.52	2.70	0.94	559	646	483	6.8	2.3	12.4	5.3	52%	14%	45	19	36	28%	68%	16%	0	30			0	1.12	3.2	184	219	$9
2nd Half	3	0	0	27	42	5.74	3.27	1.54	786	779	792	4.8	4.1	14.2	3.5	49%	15%	38	24	38	42%	67%	20%	0	20			0	0.87	-5.1	162	193	-$4
17 Proj	**6**	**3**	**2**	**73**	**88**	**3.68**	**3.35**	**1.18**	**634**	**661**	**611**	**7.1**	**3.0**	**10.9**	**3.7**	**50%**	**15%**	**41**	**22**	**37**	**31%**	**74%**	**14%**	**0**						**4.6**	**136**	**162**	**$5**

Feliz,Neftali

Age: 29	Th: R	Role RP	Health F	LIMA Plan B+	
Ht: 6' 3"	Wt: 180	Type Pwr FB	PT/Exp D	Rand Var 0	
			Consist C	MM 1310	

Flashed career-best skills in 1st half; faded in 2nd half and missed final month with right arm discomfort (no structural damage). Encouraging that he was able to maintain stellar SwK/Dom and 1.5 mph uptick in velocity all year. Health grade depicts risk, but enough progress to maybe rekindle the closer-in-waiting talk.

Yr Tm	W	L	Sv	IP	K	ERA	xERA	WHIP	oOPS	vL	vR	BF/G	Ctl	Dom	Cmd	FpK	SwK	G	L	F	H%	S%	hr/f	GS	APC	DOM%	DIS%	Sv%	LI	RAR	BPV	BPX	R$
12 TEX	3	1	0	43	37	3.16	4.61	1.20	623	616	631	21.9	4.9	7.8	1.6	53%	10%	37	15	48	22%	78%	9%	7	92	29%	29%	0	0.74	4.5	24	32	$1
13 TEX	0	0	0	5	4	0.00	4.72	1.50	659	629	665	3.5	3.9	7.7	2.0	38%	9%	21	29	50	35%	100%	0%	0	18			0	0.75	2.2	34	44	-$4
14 TEX *	3	2	20	60	45	2.69	3.11	1.00	586	513	663	4.3	2.8	6.8	2.4	66%	10%	27	22	51	20%	86%	11%	0	16			87	1.44	7.8	57	68	$12
15 2 AL	3	4	10	48	39	6.38	4.58	1.56	821	768	876	4.4	3.4	7.3	2.2	57%	10%	38	26	37	35%	59%	9%	0	17			59	1.23	-14.3	57	67	-$4
16 PIT	4	2	2	54	61	3.52	3.71	1.14	696	641	742	3.5	3.5	10.2	2.9	59%	15%	38	23	39	25%	78%	19%	0	15			50	1.19	4.4	105	125	$3
1st Half	2	0	0	31	35	2.90	3.12	0.87	591	508	667	3.2	2.0	10.2	5.0	62%	15%	42	16	41	23%	74%	13%	0	14			0	1.18	4.9	148	177	$6
2nd Half	2	2	2	23	26	4.37	4.61	1.50	826	823	827	4.0	5.6	10.3	1.9	57%	15%	32	31	37	27%	82%	27%	0	17			100	1.20	-0.5	46	55	$0
17 Proj	**4**	**3**	**2**	**58**	**56**	**3.74**	**4.33**	**1.29**	**735**	**688**	**779**	**4.2**	**3.8**	**8.7**	**2.3**	**59%**	**13%**	**35**	**24**	**41**	**27%**	**78%**	**15%**	**0**						**3.2**	**67**	**80**	**$1**

Fernandez,Jose

Age: 24	Th: R	Role RP	Health F	LIMA Plan F	
Ht: 6' 3"	Wt: 240	Type ####	PT/Exp C	Rand Var +1	
			Consist A	MM ####	

Tragically passed away in a late-Sept boating accident. Showcased immense talent in parts of four MLB seasons, accumulating a dominant 2.58 ERA, 1.05 WHIP, 11.2 Dom, 2.7 Ctl and 151 BPV in 471 career IP. Truly one of the game's elite and most gifted young performers. Rest in peace, Jose.

Yr Tm	W	L	Sv	IP	K	ERA	xERA	WHIP	oOPS	vL	vR	BF/G	Ctl	Dom	Cmd	FpK	SwK	G	L	F	H%	S%	hr/f	GS	APC	DOM%	DIS%	Sv%	LI	RAR	BPV	BPX	R$
12																																	
13 MIA	12	6	0	173	187	2.19	3.06	0.98	522	546	494	24.3	3.0	9.7	3.2	62%	11%	45	22	33	25%	80%	7%	28	93	39%	18%			35.7	117	152	$28
14 MIA	4	2	0	52	70	2.44	2.45	0.95	536	672	393	25.6	2.3	12.2	5.4	65%	15%	49	17	35	30%	78%	10%	8	98	63%	0%			8.3	185	221	$6
15 MIA	6	1	0	65	79	2.92	2.90	1.16	638	860	446	24.1	1.9	11.0	5.6	61%	14%	40	29	31	36%	76%	8%	11	90	55%	9%			8.3	163	194	$5
16 MIA	16	8	0	182	253	2.86	2.79	1.12	624	693	543	25.4	2.7	12.5	4.6	61%	15%	40	28	32	34%	76%	10%	29	101	48%	3%			29.8	169	201	$27
1st Half	10	4	0	100	146	2.69	2.57	1.03	576	687	458	24.7	2.8	13.1	4.7	61%	15%	42	26	32	32%	76%	10%	16	101	50%	0%			18.5	180	215	$32
2nd Half	6	4	0	82	107	3.07	3.07	1.23	679	699	652	26.3	2.6	11.7	4.5	61%	14%	39	30	31	36%	77%	10%	13	102	46%	8%			11.3	157	187	$20
17 Proj																																	

Fiers,Mike

Age: 32	Th: R	Role SP	Health A	LIMA Plan B+	
Ht: 6' 3"	Wt: 190	Type Pwr	PT/Exp B	Rand Var +2	
			Consist B	MM 1203	

Evolution of a junk-baller: After allowing 19 HR via a 90 mph four-seam fastball in 2015, scaled back and threw change/curve/cutter more. This helped cut down FB%, but hr/f jumped instead and came with a Dom/SwK cost. End result was a slight net loss (xERA, BPV). Now for deep leagues only.

Yr Tm	W	L	Sv	IP	K	ERA	xERA	WHIP	oOPS	vL	vR	BF/G	Ctl	Dom	Cmd	FpK	SwK	G	L	F	H%	S%	hr/f	GS	APC	DOM%	DIS%	Sv%	LI	RAR	BPV	BPX	R$
12 MIL *	10	13	0	183	174	4.45	4.23	1.34	694	690	698	23.0	2.8	8.6	3.1	60%	9%	33	28	39	33%	69%	9%	22	94	41%	23%	0	0.74	-9.7	87	113	$2
13 MIL *	2	6	0	51	38	4.68	5.82	1.50	972	999	930	13.8	3.4	6.8	2.0	60%	9%	35	26	39	30%	77%	26%	3	37	0%	67%	0	1.02	-5.1	19	25	-$5
14 MIL *	14	10	0	174	174	2.90	3.07	1.08	531	517	542	21.9	1.9	9.0	4.7	58%	10%	33	20	47	29%	78%	8%	10	80	60%	0%	0	0.74	18.0	131	156	$19
15 2 TM	7	10	0	180	180	3.69	4.00	1.25	713	664	756	24.5	3.2	9.0	2.8	60%	10%	38	20	42	30%	75%	11%	30	98	20%	20%	0	0.78	6.0	91	109	$8
16 HOU	11	8	0	169	134	4.48	4.25	1.36	801	749	843	23.4	2.2	7.2	3.2	63%	9%	42	26	32	32%	71%	15%	30	89	30%	40%	0	0.76	-6.1	88	105	$2
1st Half	6	3	0	90	60	4.12	4.32	1.33	790	724	845	23.8	1.9	6.0	3.2	59%	9%	42	29	29	31%	74%	15%	15	89	27%	40%	0	0.74	0.8	77	92	$5
2nd Half	5	5	0	79	74	4.90	4.16	1.39	814	779	839	22.9	2.6	8.4	3.2	66%	9%	42	23	35	33%	69%	15%	15	89	33%	40%			-6.9	101	121	-$1
17 Proj	**10**	**10**	**0**	**174**	**156**	**4.10**	**4.13**	**1.30**	**762**	**719**	**798**	**22.0**	**2.6**	**8.1**	**3.2**	**62%**	**10%**	**39**	**23**	**38**	**31%**	**73%**	**13%**	**33**						**1.9**	**93**	**111**	**$5**

Finnegan,Brandon

Age: 24	Th: L	Role RP	Health A	LIMA Plan C+	
Ht: 5' 11"	Wt: 180	Type Pwr	PT/Exp C	Rand Var -1	
			Consist C	MM 1305	

Converted RP showed signs of growth. Are we buying? PRO: SwK/Dom and BPX jumped in 2nd half, while FpK hints at further Ctl gains. CON: More FBs led to major HR problems, especially vR (27 HR allowed vR). VERDICT: Worth watching for signs of further progress, but gopheritis a stubborn stain right now.

Yr Tm	W	L	Sv	IP	K	ERA	xERA	WHIP	oOPS	vL	vR	BF/G	Ctl	Dom	Cmd	FpK	SwK	G	L	F	H%	S%	hr/f	GS	APC	DOM%	DIS%	Sv%	LI	RAR	BPV	BPX	R$
12																																	
13																																	
14 KC	0	1	0	7	10	1.29	1.90	1.00	546	778	433	4.0	1.3	12.9	10.0	64%	14%	59	18	24	38%	86%	0%	0	17			0	0.67	2.1	234	278	-$2
15 2 TM *	5	8	1	105	102	5.51	4.88	1.55	713	765	695	11.8	5.0	8.7	1.7	58%	10%	54	17	29	32%	66%	22%	4	38	25%	50%	50	0.85	-20.2	54	65	-$9
16 CIN	10	11	0	172	145	3.98	4.87	1.36	748	633	781	23.7	4.4	7.6	1.7	54%	10%	38	23	39	26%	77%	15%	31	93	13%	39%			4.5	34	40	$5
1st Half	3	7	0	96	69	4.48	5.21	1.39	738	730	740	24.5	4.6	6.4	1.4	50%	9%	39	24	37	26%	72%	13%	17	96	12%	41%			-3.5	10	12	$0
2nd Half	7	4	0	76	76	3.33	4.46	1.32	760	482	830	22.6	4.2	9.0	2.2	59%	11%	36	20	43	27%	85%	17%	14	89	14%	36%			8.0	65	77	$11
17 Proj	**11**	**13**	**0**	**189**	**173**	**4.27**	**4.43**	**1.37**	**763**	**695**	**784**	**16.3**	**4.3**	**8.3**	**1.9**	**56%**	**10%**	**44**	**20**	**36**	**28%**	**74%**	**16%**	**31**						**-1.8**	**55**	**66**	**$3**

Fister,Doug

Age: 33	Th: R	Role SP	Health D	LIMA Plan C	
Ht: 6' 8"	Wt: 200	Type Con	PT/Exp A	Rand Var 0	
			Consist B	MM 0003	

At his peak, he relied upon pounding strike zone, limiting walks and getting plenty of GB. Each of those areas has shown erosion, especially Ctl. Puny SwK/Dom has long been an issue, so any Ctl/GB% degradation is magnified. Negative trends in xERA, Ctl, Cmd, DIS% and BPX paint a bleak picture.

Yr Tm	W	L	Sv	IP	K	ERA	xERA	WHIP	oOPS	vL	vR	BF/G	Ctl	Dom	Cmd	FpK	SwK	G	L	F	H%	S%	hr/f	GS	APC	DOM%	DIS%	Sv%	LI	RAR	BPV	BPX	R$
12 DET	10	10	0	162	137	3.45	3.45	1.19	683	734	611	25.9	2.1	7.6	3.7	63%	8%	51	22	27	31%	74%	12%	26	97	46%	27%			11.2	111	144	$12
13 DET	14	9	0	209	159	3.67	3.38	1.31	710	687	738	26.7	1.9	6.9	3.6	59%	8%	54	21	24	33%	73%	9%	32	102	31%	22%	0	0.80	5.1	104	136	$8
14 WAS	16	6	0	164	98	2.41	3.75	1.08	654	690	618	26.5	1.3	5.4	4.1	65%	6%	49	17	34	27%	84%	10%	25	99	36%	36%			26.8	88	105	$19
15 WAS	5	7	1	103	63	4.19	4.49	1.40	796	738	860	18.0	2.1	5.5	2.6	62%	6%	45	21	34	32%	74%	12%	15	66	20%	47%	100	0.86	-3.0	65	78	-$3
16 HOU	12	13	0	180	115	4.64	4.89	1.43	788	946	606	24.3	3.1	5.7	1.9	60%	6%	45	20	34	30%	70%	12%	32	94	22%	47%			-10.0	43	51	-$1
1st Half	8	5	0	98	64	3.66	4.56	1.28	744	930	553	25.6	3.0	5.9	1.9	59%	6%	49	18	33	27%	77%	15%	16	98	25%	31%			6.4	51	61	$9
2nd Half	4	8	0	82	51	5.82	5.28	1.60	837	962	673	23.1	3.2	5.6	1.8	60%	6%	41	22	36	34%	64%	9%	16	89	19%	63%			-16.5	34	41	-$14
17 Proj	**9**	**11**	**0**	**174**	**111**	**4.55**	**4.60**	**1.38**	**775**	**844**	**694**	**22.1**	**2.5**	**5.8**	**2.3**	**61%**	**6%**	**46**	**20**	**34**	**31%**	**70%**	**11%**	**33**						**-7.8**	**61**	**72**	**-$2**

GREG PYRON

Flynn,Brian

Age: 27	Th: L	Role: RP	Health	F	LIMA Plan	D+
Ht: 6' 8"	Wt: 240	Type: Pwr GB	PT/Exp	D	Rand Var	0
			Consist	F	MM	1100

1-2, 2.60 ERA in 55 IP at KC. Imposing lefty looks the part, but skills don't move the needle. MLB ERA largely a function of 23% hit rate, and while GB% is nice, FpK offers little hope of Ctl bump. Historical struggles vL discourage situational work, so middle relief it is. No reason for you to go all-in on Flynn.

Yr Tm	W	L	Sv	IP	K	ERA	xERA	WHIP	oOPS	vL	vR	BF/G	Ctl	Dom	Cmd	FpK	SwK	G	L	F	H%	S%	hr/f	GS	APC	DOM%	DIS%	Sv%	LI	RAR	BPV	BPX	R$
12 aa	3	1	0	50	32	5.16	5.30	1.59				24.5	2.9	5.8	2.0						35%	68%								-7.1	47	62	-$8
13 MIA *	7	14	0	179	139	3.83	4.26	1.43	1068	1326	999	24.5	2.9	7.0	2.4	57%	10%	38	33	29	34%	74%	24%	4	85	0%	75%			0.8	72	93	-$1
14 MIA *	8	11	0	147	91	4.37	5.48	1.66	929	667	987	24.3	3.1	5.6	1.8	60%	4%	50	27	23	36%	74%	0%	1	70	0%	100%	0	0.61	-11.5	44	52	-$10
15																																	
16 KC *	3	3	0	79	66	2.93	3.15	1.26	598	585	605	7.2	4.0	7.5	1.9	55%	11%	55	18	27	27%	79%	13%	1	23	0%	100%	0	0.87	12.3	74	87	$4
1st Half	3	1	0	45	40	3.37	3.72	1.38	625	496	695	9.9	3.9	8.0	2.1	59%	12%	54	22	24	31%	77%	14%	0	32			0	0.82	4.5	77	92	$4
2nd Half	0	2	0	34	26	2.36	4.13	1.11	580	643	546	5.2	4.2	6.8	1.6	53%	11%	55	15	30	21%	83%	12%	1	19	0%	100%	0	0.88	7.8	43	51	$4
17 Proj	**2**	**3**	**0**	**58**	**43**	**3.89**	**4.31**	**1.39**	**753**	**726**	**767**	**10.5**	**3.5**	**6.7**	**1.9**	**55%**	**11%**	**55**	**18**	**27**	**31%**	**73%**	**9%**	**1**						**2.2**	**58**	**69**	**-$2**

Foltynewicz,Mike

Age: 25	Th: R	Role: SP	Health	C	LIMA Plan	B+
Ht: 6' 4"	Wt: 200	Type: Pwr	PT/Exp	D	Rand Var	+1
			Consist	D	MM	1203

9-5, 4.31 ERA in 123 IP at ATL. Mediocre results cloaked fireballer's steady skills growth, but he closed with a flourish as Ctl improved and Dom spiked, backed by SwK. Blood clot delayed start of season; elbow woes arose in June. If health holds, breakout within reach... UP: 3.50 ERA, 175 K

Yr Tm	W	L	Sv	IP	K	ERA	xERA	WHIP	oOPS	vL	vR	BF/G	Ctl	Dom	Cmd	FpK	SwK	G	L	F	H%	S%	hr/f	GS	APC	DOM%	DIS%	Sv%	LI	RAR	BPV	BPX	R$
12																																	
13 aa	5	3	3	103	85	3.22	3.19	1.29				18.4	4.4	7.4	1.7						26%	77%								8.3	68	89	$5
14 HOU *	7	8	0	121	103	5.36	4.77	1.53	864	1062	659	14.3	4.2	7.6	1.8	52%	10%	29	21	51	33%	66%	9%	0	20			0	0.38	-24.2	55	66	-$9
15 ATL *	5	12	0	143	132	5.26	5.96	1.62	896	950	843	22.7	3.6	8.3	2.3	63%	10%	33	23	44	36%	72%	14%	15	82	13%	40%	0	0.99	-22.9	46	55	-$13
16 ATL *	10	7	0	150	132	3.92	3.86	1.27	761	775	750	22.8	3.0	7.9	2.6	63%	10%	41	21	37	30%	73%	13%	22	96	23%	32%			5.1	76	90	$8
1st Half	3	4	0	63	51	3.04	3.34	1.22	802	1062	626	21.3	3.6	7.3	2.0	66%	9%	39	23	38	26%	79%	17%	7	91	29%	57%			9.0	67	80	$9
2nd Half	7	3	0	87	81	4.55	4.10	1.31	744	674	808	24.7	2.6	8.4	3.2	63%	11%	42	21	37	32%	68%	12%	15	99	20%	20%			-3.9	101	120	$7
17 Proj	**9**	**9**	**0**	**160**	**143**	**4.07**	**4.31**	**1.35**	**734**	**785**	**691**	**22.2**	**3.2**	**8.1**	**2.5**	**63%**	**10%**	**40**	**22**	**38**	**31%**	**74%**	**12%**	**30**						**2.4**	**76**	**91**	**$3**

Friedrich,Christian

Age: 29	Th: L	Role: SP	Health	C	LIMA Plan	D+
Ht: 6' 4"	Wt: 215	Type: Pwr	PT/Exp	C	Rand Var	0
			Consist	C	MM	0101

Through 6 GS (2.12 ERA), leaving thin air behind seemed to be panacea. Hardly. Cmd shows he was the same unrosterable guy, drop in SwK offers little hope of Dom improvement, and FpK says, "Don't believe 2nd half Ctl improvement." Say something nice? RHB crushed him less; GB rate limits HR. You can do better.

Yr Tm	W	L	Sv	IP	K	ERA	xERA	WHIP	oOPS	vL	vR	BF/G	Ctl	Dom	Cmd	FpK	SwK	G	L	F	H%	S%	hr/f	GS	APC	DOM%	DIS%	Sv%	LI	RAR	BPV	BPX	R$
12 COL *	7	9	0	115	95	5.47	4.86	1.42	860	816	872	23.1	2.7	7.4	2.8	52%	9%	42	23	35	33%	63%	15%	16	87	19%	44%			-20.5	65	85	-$7
13																																	
14 COL *	2	13	1	116	89	8.14	7.44	1.87	782	400	943	12.6	4.0	6.9	1.7	55%	14%	39	25	36	37%	58%	12%	3	25	0%	67%	100	0.97	-62.8	10	12	-$29
15 COL	0	4	0	58	45	5.25	4.67	1.71	820	659	965	4.0	3.9	6.9	1.8	54%	11%	47	23	29	37%	69%	9%	0	14			0	0.89	-9.2	46	55	-$10
16 SD	5	12	0	129	100	4.80	4.82	1.41	732	676	748	23.6	3.6	7.0	1.9	60%	9%	45	19	36	31%	67%	9%	23	89	26%	39%	0	0.74	-9.8	51	60	-$4
1st Half	4	3	0	50	43	3.96	4.95	1.54	723	683	735	25.1	4.9	7.7	1.6	61%	9%	48	19	34	31%	76%	10%	9	98	33%	44%			1.4	34	40	$0
2nd Half	1	9	0	79	57	5.33	4.74	1.34	737	671	754	22.7	2.8	6.5	2.3	60%	9%	43	19	38	30%	60%	8%	14	84	21%	36%	0	0.72	-11.2	61	73	-$6
17 Proj	**5**	**8**	**0**	**116**	**90**	**4.55**	**4.63**	**1.45**	**749**	**652**	**793**	**21.4**	**3.6**	**7.0**	**1.9**	**57%**	**10%**	**45**	**21**	**34**	**31%**	**71%**	**11%**	**18**						**-5.1**	**51**	**61**	**-$4**

Fulmer,Carson

Age: 23	Th: R	Role: SP	Health	A	LIMA Plan	D+
Ht: 6' 1"	Wt: 190	Type: Pwr	PT/Exp	F	Rand Var	+5
			Consist	F	MM	0301

0-2, 8.49 ERA in 12 IP at CHW. After 17 AA starts (1.7 Cmd in 87 IP), top prospect got feet wet in majors as reliever. SwK, GB% showed potential, but Ctl not quite there yet, as FpK attests. Closed with competent 14 IP in AAA, where he likely starts 2017. One to watch in keeper leagues, but that's it for now.

Yr Tm	W	L	Sv	IP	K	ERA	xERA	WHIP	oOPS	vL	vR	BF/G	Ctl	Dom	Cmd	FpK	SwK	G	L	F	H%	S%	hr/f	GS	APC	DOM%	DIS%	Sv%	LI	RAR	BPV	BPX	R$
12																																	
13																																	
14																																	
15																																	
16 CHW *	6	12	0	115	102	5.79	4.95	1.64	873	828	924	17.7	5.3	8.0	1.5	51%	10%	44	26	29	33%	65%	20%	0	27			0	0.43	-22.7	54	64	-$11
1st Half	4	8	0	82	70	5.71	5.11	1.70				23.1	5.6	7.7	1.4						33%	66%	0%	0						-15.4	49	58	-$12
2nd Half	2	4	0	33	31	5.97	4.51	1.51	874	828	924	10.9	4.3	8.6	2.0	51%	10%	44	26	29	33%	60%	20%	0	27			0	0.43	-7.2	69	82	-$9
17 Proj	**8**	**9**	**0**	**116**	**106**	**4.99**	**4.89**	**1.56**				**42.5**	**4.9**	**8.2**	**1.7**	**55%**	**9%**	**42**	**20**	**38**	**32%**	**69%**	**10%**	**21**						**-11.4**	**36**	**42**	**-$6**

Fulmer,Michael

Age: 24	Th: R	Role: SP	Health	B	LIMA Plan	C+
Ht: 6' 3"	Wt: 210	Type:	PT/Exp	D	Rand Var	0
			Consist	A	MM	2205

11-7, 3.06 ERA in 159 IP at DET. Rookie burst onto scene with 2.25 ERA through first 19 starts, then S% fortune caught up with him—but it wasn't all luck. In 2nd half, traded a bit of Dom for Ctl, but SwK still good enough to rack up Ks. Robust GB rate provides a nice foundation. Should be a solid investment.

Yr Tm	W	L	Sv	IP	K	ERA	xERA	WHIP	oOPS	vL	vR	BF/G	Ctl	Dom	Cmd	FpK	SwK	G	L	F	H%	S%	hr/f	GS	APC	DOM%	DIS%	Sv%	LI	RAR	BPV	BPX	R$
12																																	
13																																	
14																																	
15 aa	10	3	0	118	95	2.53	3.32	1.22				22.6	2.3	7.3	3.1						31%	81%								20.8	96	115	$11
16 DET *	12	8	0	174	148	3.28	3.42	1.16	652	621	684	24.0	2.5	7.6	3.1	61%	11%	49	19	32	28%	76%	11%	26	95	35%	31%			19.6	88	104	$16
1st Half	9	3	0	86	86	2.77	3.30	1.19	598	519	664	23.0	3.2	9.0	2.8	59%	12%	49	19	32	28%	82%	10%	12	95	33%	17%			15.0	92	110	$21
2nd Half	3	5	0	88	62	3.77	3.97	1.14	693	686	702	25.7	1.7	6.3	3.6	63%	10%	49	19	31	28%	70%	12%	14	96	36%	43%			4.6	94	112	$12
17 Proj	**14**	**7**	**0**	**189**	**154**	**3.47**	**3.87**	**1.21**	**689**	**662**	**719**	**23.6**	**2.4**	**7.4**	**3.1**	**61%**	**11%**	**49**	**19**	**31**	**30%**	**74%**	**10%**	**32**						**16.9**	**96**	**114**	**$14**

Gallardo,Yovani

Age: 31	Th: R	Role: SP	Health	D	LIMA Plan	D+
Ht: 6' 3"	Wt: 220	Type: Pwr	PT/Exp	A	Rand Var	0
			Consist	B	MM	0103

Missed two months with shoulder injury after rough April, but things hardly improved upon return. Posted career-worst Cmd, BPV, and xERA, while FpK continues to speak to strained relationship with strike zone. The pitcher you remember from 2009-12 no longer exists. It's time to move on.

Yr Tm	W	L	Sv	IP	K	ERA	xERA	WHIP	oOPS	vL	vR	BF/G	Ctl	Dom	Cmd	FpK	SwK	G	L	F	H%	S%	hr/f	GS	APC	DOM%	DIS%	Sv%	LI	RAR	BPV	BPX	R$
12 MIL	16	9	0	204	204	3.66	3.66	1.30	706	759	654	26.1	3.6	9.0	2.5	56%	8%	48	21	31	30%	76%	15%	33	105	33%	18%			8.9	92	119	$13
13 MIL	12	10	0	181	144	4.18	3.85	1.36	720	729	713	24.9	3.3	7.2	2.2	56%	7%	49	23	28	31%	71%	12%	31	98	26%	35%			-7.1	67	88	$2
14 MIL	8	11	0	192	146	3.51	3.72	1.29	698	637	742	25.5	2.5	6.8	2.7	57%	7%	51	20	29	31%	76%	12%	32	101	28%	28%			5.5	84	100	$5
15 TEX	13	11	0	184	121	3.42	4.46	1.42	729	765	694	24.0	3.3	5.9	1.8	59%	7%	49	22	29	31%	78%	9%	33	98	6%	42%			12.4	44	52	$5
16 BAL	6	8	0	118	85	5.42	5.36	1.58	813	808	815	22.9	4.7	6.5	1.4	54%	7%	43	20	37	31%	68%	12%	23	92	9%	52%			-17.8	12	14	-$9
1st Half	3	1	0	34	23	5.77	5.54	1.57	833	966	714	21.6	4.2	6.0	1.4	53%	7%	36	23	41	32%	64%	9%	7	88	0%	57%			-6.7	9	11	-$5
2nd Half	3	7	0	84	62	5.27	5.28	1.59	804	735	852	23.4	4.8	6.7	1.4	54%	7%	46	19	35	30%	69%	13%	16	93	13%	50%			-11.2	14	16	-$11
17 Proj	**8**	**10**	**0**	**160**	**115**	**4.51**	**4.81**	**1.47**	**767**	**779**	**756**	**23.3**	**3.8**	**6.5**	**1.7**	**56%**	**7%**	**46**	**21**	**33**	**31%**	**72%**	**11%**	**29**						**-6.3**	**37**	**45**	**-$4**

Gant,John

Age: 24	Th: R	Role: RP	Health	D	LIMA Plan	D+
Ht: 6' 5"	Wt: 200	Type: Pwr	PT/Exp	D	Rand Var	+3
			Consist	B	MM	0201

1-4, 4.86 ERA in 50 IP at ATL. Shuttled between AAA and majors, bullpen and rotation, active roster and DL (oblique). So perhaps judgment should be reserved, especially given evident Dom ability. Lost strike zone in Sept (5.4 Ctl, 48% FpK), and will need to prove he can get out RHB, but too young to give up on.

Yr Tm	W	L	Sv	IP	K	ERA	xERA	WHIP	oOPS	vL	vR	BF/G	Ctl	Dom	Cmd	FpK	SwK	G	L	F	H%	S%	hr/f	GS	APC	DOM%	DIS%	Sv%	LI	RAR	BPV	BPX	R$
12																																	
13																																	
14																																	
15 aa	8	5	0	100	76	4.28	4.28	1.53				24.2	3.8	6.9	1.8						34%	71%								-3.9	69	82	-$4
16 ATL *	4	7	0	106	99	5.07	5.21	1.58	831	765	909	14.6	3.8	8.4	2.2	60%	10%	42	24	34	36%	69%	14%	7	47	14%	29%	0	0.46	-11.5	62	74	-$7
1st Half	4	2	0	73	73	4.16	4.15	1.41	801	823	768	16.3	3.0	8.9	2.9	66%	10%	39	24	37	35%	71%	10%	4	49	25%	25%	0	0.52	0.3	96	115	-$2
2nd Half	0	5	0	33	26	7.12	7.61	1.96	874	658	1064	12.0	5.4	7.1	1.3	51%	10%	47	24	29	36%	67%	22%	3	45	0%	33%	0	0.39	-11.8	0	0	-$20
17 Proj	**5**	**8**	**0**	**102**	**84**	**4.92**	**4.85**	**1.65**	**840**	**733**	**955**	**16.2**	**4.2**	**7.5**	**1.8**	**57%**	**10%**	**43**	**24**	**32**	**35%**	**71%**	**10%**	**17**						**-9.2**	**43**	**51**	**-$9**

KRISTOPHER OLSON

Garcia,Jaime

Age: 30	Th: L	Role SP	Health F	LIMA Plan B+
Ht: 6' 1"	Wt: 200	Type Pwr xGB	PT/Exp B	Rand Var +4
			Consist A	MM 2203

Did you wonder what would happen "if he could just stay healthy for a full year"? Wonder no more. Reality didn't live up to fantasy. Too many runners did him in: Ctl regressed to match historical FpK; H% got in on the correction game too. Hr/f brought them all around. Expect ERA back under 4.00, IP back under 150.

Yr	Tm	W	L	Sv	IP	K	ERA	xERA	WHIP	oOPS	vL	vR	BF/G	Ctl	Dom	Cmd	FpK	SwK	G	L	F	H%	S%	hr/f	GS	APC	DOM%	DIS%	Sv%	LI	RAR	BPV	BPX	R$
12	STL *	8	8	0	137	113	4.08	4.06	1.34	730	649	750	24.8	2.2	7.4	3.4	63%	12%	54	20	26	34%	70%	7%	20	88	40%	25%			-1.1	96	125	$2
13	STL	5	2	0	55	43	3.58	3.35	1.30	725	905	666	26.0	2.4	7.0	2.9	68%	12%	63	14	23	31%	76%	15%	9	92	22%	22%			2.0	101	132	$0
14	STL	3	1	0	44	39	4.12	2.89	1.05	696	881	631	25.3	1.4	8.0	5.6	60%	13%	55	20	25	28%	65%	19%	7	90	43%	14%			-2.1	139	165	$0
15	STL	10	6	0	130	97	2.43	3.25	1.05	574	630	557	25.5	2.1	6.7	3.2	59%	9%	61	16	22	27%	78%	7%	20	93	50%	10%			24.5	104	124	$17
16	STL	10	13	0	172	150	4.67	3.83	1.37	779	702	798	23.2	3.0	7.9	2.6	60%	10%	57	18	25	31%	70%	20%	30	81	17%	40%	0	0.74	-10.1	96	114	$1
1st Half		6	6	0	96	81	3.84	3.81	1.34	691	684	693	25.7	3.1	7.6	2.5	58%	9%	58	20	22	32%	73%	12%	16	90	25%	38%			4.1	89	106	$7
2nd Half		4	7	0	76	69	5.71	3.85	1.41	889	730	923	20.6	2.9	8.2	2.9	62%	10%	55	16	28	31%	66%	28%	14	71	7%	43%	0	0.70	-14.2	104	124	-$7
17	**Proj**	**9**	**8**	**0**	**138**	**116**	**3.89**	**3.72**	**1.30**	**708**	**707**	**709**	**23.4**	**2.9**	**7.6**	**2.6**	**61%**	**10%**	**58**	**18**	**25**	**31%**	**72%**	**13%**	**24**						**5.0**	**94**	**112**	**$5**

Garrett,Amir

Age: 25	Th: L	Role SP	Health A	LIMA Plan B
Ht: 6' 5"	Wt: 210	Type Pwr	PT/Exp F	Rand Var 0
			Consist F	MM 0101

Big lefty still new to pitching (3rd season on mound). Ctl shows he's still working it out mechanically, and move to AAA in 2nd half proved to be a challenge, as big fastball wasn't generating Dom on its own anymore. He's just a few more adjustments away from reaching Cincinnati as a high-Dom mid-rotation type.

Yr	Tm	W	L	Sv	IP	K	ERA	xERA	WHIP	oOPS	vL	vR	BF/G	Ctl	Dom	Cmd	FpK	SwK	G	L	F	H%	S%	hr/f	GS	APC	DOM%	DIS%	Sv%	LI	RAR	BPV	BPX	R$
12																																		
13																																		
14																																		
15																																		
16	a/a	7	8	0	145	116	3.74	3.43	1.35				24.1	4.2	7.2	1.7						29%	73%								8.0	70	83	$4
1st Half		5	4	0	90	76	2.65	2.48	1.27				24.4	4.2	7.7	1.8						29%	77%								17.0	95	114	$13
2nd Half		2	4	0	55	40	5.52	4.98	1.49				23.7	4.4	6.5	1.5						29%	66%								-9.0	28	34	-$9
17	**Proj**	**4**	**6**	**0**	**94**	**73**	**4.38**	**4.75**	**1.40**				**24.0**	**4.3**	**7.0**	**1.6**	**58%**	**9%**	**46**	**20**	**34**	**28%**	**71%**	**12%**	**17**						**-2.2**	**33**	**39**	**-$3**

Garza,Matt

Age: 33	Th: R	Role SP	Health F	LIMA Plan C
Ht: 6' 4"	Wt: 205	Type	PT/Exp B	Rand Var 0
			Consist A	MM 1103

Lat strain cost him a big chunk of 1st half, not that he was missed. Played with his pitch mix, boosting GB%. But that's just shuffling deck chairs on a doomed ocean liner. There just aren't any plus offerings in his arsenal anymore. Velocity in multi-year decline, secondary stuff increasingly getting tattooed. Bad scene.

Yr	Tm	W	L	Sv	IP	K	ERA	xERA	WHIP	oOPS	vL	vR	BF/G	Ctl	Dom	Cmd	FpK	SwK	G	L	F	H%	S%	hr/f	GS	APC	DOM%	DIS%	Sv%	LI	RAR	BPV	BPX	R$
12	CHC	5	7	0	104	96	3.91	3.54	1.18	693	745	643	23.6	2.8	8.3	3.0	62%	11%	47	19	33	28%	72%	16%	18	94	33%	22%			1.4	100	130	$4
13	2 TM *	11	7	0	171	144	3.63	3.76	1.23	712	733	687	24.7	2.5	7.6	3.1	64%	10%	39	23	38	30%	74%	12%	24	101	38%	21%			5.0	83	108	$9
14	MIL	8	8	0	163	126	3.64	3.90	1.18	644	634	652	25.2	2.8	6.9	2.5	64%	9%	43	21	36	28%	70%	7%	27	94	33%	26%			2.1	72	85	$7
15	MIL	6	14	0	149	104	5.63	4.73	1.57	832	862	804	25.6	3.5	6.3	1.8	61%	8%	45	22	33	33%	67%	14%	25	92	8%	52%	0	0.83	-30.6	43	51	-$15
16	MIL	6	8	0	102	70	4.51	4.67	1.50	774	825	727	24.3	3.2	6.2	1.9	59%	8%	55	17	28	33%	72%	11%	19	90	5%	42%			-4.1	58	70	-$4
1st Half		1	1	0	22	14	3.74	4.97	1.66	801	718	891	25.3	2.9	5.8	2.0	62%	6%	51	19	31	38%	75%	0%	4	85	0%	25%			1.2	55	65	-$4
2nd Half		5	7	0	80	56	4.73	4.59	1.46	766	858	687	24.0	3.3	6.3	1.9	59%	9%	56	17	27	31%	71%	15%	15	92	7%	47%			-5.3	59	71	-$4
17	**Proj**	**7**	**10**	**0**	**145**	**104**	**4.74**	**4.54**	**1.46**	**787**	**810**	**766**	**24.0**	**3.1**	**6.5**	**2.1**	**61%**	**8%**	**49**	**20**	**31**	**32%**	**70%**	**13%**	**26**						**-9.9**	**60**	**71**	**-$5**

Gausman,Kevin

Age: 26	Th: R	Role SP	Health D	LIMA Plan B
Ht: 6' 4"	Wt: 185	Type Pwr	PT/Exp C	Rand Var 0
			Consist B	MM 2305

From a skills perspective, maybe not quite the long-awaited breakout, but some consolidation in evidence: Dom finally caught up to strong SwK, while Ctl and GB tilt held steady. It took until final two months (2.83 ERA in Aug/Sept) for all of that to translate to results, and positions him for... UP: 3.00 ERA, 200 K.

Yr	Tm	W	L	Sv	IP	K	ERA	xERA	WHIP	oOPS	vL	vR	BF/G	Ctl	Dom	Cmd	FpK	SwK	G	L	F	H%	S%	hr/f	GS	APC	DOM%	DIS%	Sv%	LI	RAR	BPV	BPX	R$
12																																		
13	BAL *	6	11	0	130	119	4.71	4.11	1.30	792	811	772	14.8	1.9	8.3	4.4	61%	10%	42	25	33	34%	65%	19%	5	40	0%	40%	0	0.80	-13.4	115	150	-$2
14	BAL *	8	10	0	157	125	3.60	3.92	1.35	685	700	662	21.1	3.2	7.2	2.2	57%	9%	41	23	35	31%	75%	6%	20	98	35%	25%			2.8	71	85	$2
15	BAL *	4	9	0	130	118	4.28	4.42	1.25	739	643	843	18.2	2.5	8.2	3.3	55%	12%	44	17	38	30%	72%	13%	17	75	35%	24%	0	0.72	-5.2	74	88	$0
16	BAL	9	12	0	180	174	3.61	3.84	1.28	742	659	812	25.2	2.4	8.7	3.7	57%	11%	44	21	35	32%	78%	15%	30	104	30%	20%			12.9	115	137	$11
1st Half		1	6	0	82	76	3.97	3.89	1.27	758	632	853	24.9	2.0	8.4	4.2	56%	11%	44	22	35	32%	76%	16%	14	102	29%	21%			2.2	119	142	$4
2nd Half		8	6	0	98	98	3.31	3.80	1.29	728	680	773	25.6	2.7	9.0	3.4	58%	12%	45	21	35	32%	80%	14%	16	106	31%	19%			10.7	113	134	$16
17	**Proj**	**12**	**10**	**0**	**189**	**177**	**3.64**	**3.86**	**1.26**	**730**	**672**	**787**	**20.8**	**2.5**	**8.5**	**3.4**	**57%**	**11%**	**44**	**21**	**35**	**31%**	**77%**	**14%**	**37**						**12.9**	**107**	**127**	**$11**

Gearrin,Cory

Age: 31	Th: R	Role RP	Health B	LIMA Plan B+
Ht: 6' 3"	Wt: 200	Type Pwr xGB	PT/Exp D	Rand Var +2
			Consist A	MM 2210

Missed six weeks in 2nd half with sore shoulder. Before you write him off as another non-descript reliever, look at lofty LI (manager trusts him), elite SwK (especially in small Sept sample when shoulder was fresh), GB tilt/LD avoidance. In unsettled pen, some Save opps aren't out of the realm.

Yr	Tm	W	L	Sv	IP	K	ERA	xERA	WHIP	oOPS	vL	vR	BF/G	Ctl	Dom	Cmd	FpK	SwK	G	L	F	H%	S%	hr/f	GS	APC	DOM%	DIS%	Sv%	LI	RAR	BPV	BPX	R$
12	ATL *	3	4	9	75	74	2.50	2.92	1.28	642	992	411	5.0	3.4	8.9	2.7	63%	13%	55	23	23	33%	79%	8%	0	13			82	0.88	13.9	112	146	$8
13	ATL	2	1	1	31	23	3.77	4.09	1.48	754	629	826	3.6	4.6	6.7	1.4	54%	10%	51	25	24	30%	75%	10%	0	13			33	0.71	0.3	24	31	-$3
14																																		
15	SF *	2	2	0	47	40	3.35	3.94	1.36	237	0	282	4.9	3.1	7.7	2.5	62%	18%	86	14	0	32%	77%	0%	0	7			0	0.98	3.5	79	94	-$2
16	SF	3	2	3	48	45	4.28	3.52	1.16	654	655	654	3.5	2.6	8.4	3.2	58%	12%	56	15	28	29%	63%	10%	0	13			43	1.40	-0.6	114	136	$1
1st Half		3	0	2	36	29	2.97	3.56	1.05	584	648	564	3.6	2.7	7.2	2.6	59%	10%	59	17	24	25%	72%	8%	0	13			50	1.32	5.5	93	111	$4
2nd Half		0	2	1	12	16	8.25	3.39	1.50	840	670	900	3.3	2.3	12.0	5.3	57%	17%	47	12	41	42%	44%	14%	0	13			33	1.61	-6.0	180	215	-$9
17	**Proj**	**3**	**1**	**2**	**44**	**36**	**3.25**	**3.93**	**1.30**	**686**	**669**	**694**	**4.0**	**3.6**	**7.4**	**2.1**	**57%**	**10%**	**56**	**20**	**24**	**30%**	**76%**	**8%**	**0**						**5.1**	**70**	**84**	**$0**

Gee,Dillon

Age: 31	Th: R	Role SP	Health D	LIMA Plan C
Ht: 6' 1"	Wt: 200	Type	PT/Exp B	Rand Var +1
			Consist C	MM 0001

At least in first half, tried to join the league-wide strikeout party. But he could only mingle and make polite conversation for so long before retreating to his well-established low-Dom ways. Worked as both a spot starter and out of the bullpen, but splits don't indicate hidden value in either role. Decline his next RSVP.

Yr	Tm	W	L	Sv	IP	K	ERA	xERA	WHIP	oOPS	vL	vR	BF/G	Ctl	Dom	Cmd	FpK	SwK	G	L	F	H%	S%	hr/f	GS	APC	DOM%	DIS%	Sv%	LI	RAR	BPV	BPX	R$
12	NYM	6	7	0	110	97	4.10	3.54	1.25	697	770	610	27.2	2.4	8.0	3.3	59%	11%	50	20	30	31%	70%	13%	17	103	41%	6%			-1.2	107	140	$2
13	NYM	12	11	0	199	142	3.62	4.07	1.28	738	822	666	26.3	2.1	6.4	3.0	62%	10%	43	20	38	31%	76%	10%	32	93	25%	31%			6.1	79	103	$8
14	NYM	7	8	0	137	94	4.00	4.12	1.25	715	719	711	25.9	2.8	6.2	2.2	60%	8%	44	18	38	27%	72%	12%	22	96	14%	36%			-4.3	57	68	$2
15	NYM *	8	7	0	134	76	5.49	5.91	1.65	879	1058	690	26.1	2.2	5.1	2.3	67%	10%	51	20	29	37%	67%	12%	7	77	14%	43%	0	0.70	-25.4	42	50	-$15
16	KC	8	9	0	125	89	4.68	4.85	1.46	815	835	795	16.7	2.7	6.4	2.4	61%	8%	41	21	38	32%	74%	15%	14	62	14%	36%	0	0.73	-7.6	62	74	-$3
1st Half		3	2	0	53	46	4.05	4.68	1.56	849	872	822	14.1	3.2	7.8	2.4	64%	10%	42	20	38	34%	82%	17%	4	54	25%	0%	0	0.60	0.9	73	87	-$2
2nd Half		5	7	0	72	43	5.15	4.98	1.40	789	803	777	19.5	2.3	5.4	2.4	59%	7%	41	21	38	30%	68%	14%	10	71	10%	50%	0	0.86	-8.5	55	65	-$4
17	**Proj**	**5**	**6**	**0**	**87**	**59**	**4.71**	**4.68**	**1.46**	**803**	**870**	**737**	**20.0**	**2.5**	**6.1**	**2.4**	**62%**	**9%**	**45**	**20**	**35**	**32%**	**71%**	**13%**	**19**						**-5.6**	**64**	**76**	**-$4**

Gibson,Kyle

Age: 29	Th: R	Role SP	Health D	LIMA Plan C
Ht: 6' 6"	Wt: 215	Type GB	PT/Exp A	Rand Var +3
			Consist A	MM 1103

Couldn't build on promise from 2015, though maybe not all his fault. Team defense was a huge problem all year long (see H%), and organizational allergy to strikeouts may explain SwK/Dom disconnect. With new regime in town, he's worth one more shot in the end-game. UP: 3.50 ERA (still)

Yr	Tm	W	L	Sv	IP	K	ERA	xERA	WHIP	oOPS	vL	vR	BF/G	Ctl	Dom	Cmd	FpK	SwK	G	L	F	H%	S%	hr/f	GS	APC	DOM%	DIS%	Sv%	LI	RAR	BPV	BPX	R$
12																																		
13	MIN *	9	9	0	153	97	4.50	4.44	1.46	874	875	869	24.2	3.2	5.7	1.8	52%	8%	50	21	28	32%	70%	13%	10	90	0%	70%			-12.0	49	64	-$5
14	MIN	13	12	0	179	107	4.47	4.01	1.31	679	705	650	24.4	2.9	5.4	1.9	57%	9%	54	19	27	29%	65%	8%	31	90	19%	35%			-16.0	51	61	-$1
15	MIN	11	11	0	195	145	3.84	3.94	1.29	698	702	693	25.7	3.0	6.7	2.2	61%	10%	53	20	27	29%	72%	11%	32	101	31%	31%			3.0	71	84	$7
16	MIN	6	11	0	147	104	5.07	4.70	1.56	820	886	760	26.1	3.4	6.4	1.9	59%	10%	49	23	29	33%	70%	14%	25	99	16%	56%			-16.0	51	60	-$9
1st Half		2	5	0	52	35	4.82	4.62	1.43	756	843	676	25.4	3.4	6.0	1.8	60%	10%	54	19	27	30%	68%	13%	9	98	22%	56%			-4.0	47	56	-$3
2nd Half		4	6	0	95	69	5.21	4.74	1.63	854	908	803	26.5	3.3	6.5	2.0	59%	10%	46	25	29	35%	71%	15%	16	99	13%	56%			-12.0	52	62	-$12
17	**Proj**	**7**	**10**	**0**	**145**	**105**	**4.29**	**4.38**	**1.44**	**757**	**794**	**719**	**25.1**	**3.2**	**6.5**	**2.1**	**58%**	**10%**	**51**	**21**	**28**	**32%**	**72%**	**12%**	**25**						**-1.8**	**61**	**72**	**-$2**

RAY MURPHY

Giles,Kenneth

Age:	26	Th:	R	Role	RP	Health	A
Ht:	6' 2"	Wt:	190	Type	Pwr	PT/Exp	C
						Consist	C

LIMA Plan	A
Rand Var	+5
MM	5530

Unceremoniously relegated to setup role in 1st half. Fought off initial struggles, then just started blowing it by everyone. 2nd half Dom/SwK are just video-game silly; team had no choice but to give him closer role. 6-ER blowup in final week wrecked 2nd half ERA, but overall 2nd half skills showcased elite-closer stuff. Pay up.

Yr	Tm	W	L	Sv	IP	K	ERA	xERA	WHIP	oOPS	vL	vR	BF/G	Ctl	Dom	Cmd	FpK	SwK	G	L	F	H%	S%	hr/f	GS	APC	DOM%	DIS%	Sv%	LI	RAR	BPV	BPX	R$
12																																		
13																																		
14	PHI *	5	1	13	74	97	1.56	1.22	0.94	450	436	461	4.1	2.9	11.7	4.0	63%	16%	44	15	41	28%	83%	3%	0	16			93	1.15	20.0	170	203	$17
15	PHI	6	3	15	70	87	1.80	3.24	1.20	569	574	565	4.3	3.2	11.2	3.5	60%	15%	45	22	33	34%	85%	3%	0	17			75	1.15	18.7	138	164	$14
16	HOU	2	5	15	66	102	4.11	2.96	1.29	709	590	823	4.1	3.4	14.0	4.1	64%	20%	40	25	36	38%	71%	15%	0	16			75	1.25	0.6	177	210	$7
1st Half		0	3	1	34	44	4.76	3.62	1.41	757	709	803	4.0	2.9	11.6	4.0	68%	17%	33	30	37	38%	70%	15%	0	15			25	1.21	-2.4	142	170	-$2
2nd Half		2	2	14	32	58	3.41	2.26	1.17	653	457	847	4.3	4.0	16.5	4.1	60%	23%	49	16	34	39%	74%	14%	0	18			88	1.30	3.0	216	258	$16
17	Proj	4	3	41	65	94	2.84	2.90	1.19	624	555	684	4.0	3.3	13.0	3.9	62%	18%	44	21	35	35%	78%	9%	0						10.8	165	196	$21

Giolito,Lucas

Age:	22	Th:	R	Role	SP	Health	A
Ht:	6' 6"	Wt:	255	Type	Pwr	PT/Exp	D
						Consist	A

LIMA Plan	D+
Rand Var	+5
MM	1203

0-1, 6.75 ERA in 21 IP at WAS. Top SP prospect knocked around in MLB cameo. In minors work, he showed good progress: fared a lot better in late-season AAA stint (4.0 Cmd, 9.6 Dom in 37 IP) than in earlier-season AA work. If those late-season gains stick, he could come very quickly. UP: 12 Wins, 3.50 ERA.

Yr	Tm	W	L	Sv	IP	K	ERA	xERA	WHIP	oOPS	vL	vR	BF/G	Ctl	Dom	Cmd	FpK	SwK	G	L	F	H%	S%	hr/f	GS	APC	DOM%	DIS%	Sv%	LI	RAR	BPV	BPX	R$
12																																		
13																																		
14																																		
15	aa	4	2	0	47	38	4.63	4.44	1.52				25.7	3.3	7.3	2.2						36%	68%								-3.9	76	90	-$4
16	WAS *	6	6	0	130	106	4.28	4.89	1.57	988	881	1112	21.1	4.1	7.3	1.8	55%	6%	41	27	32	34%	74%	29%	4	66	0%	75%	0	0.68	-1.4	54	64	-$4
1st Half		5	3	0	75	62	3.91	4.24	1.58	298	347	200	22.0	4.6	7.4	1.6	57%	4%	55	9	36	34%	74%	0%	1	45	0%	0%			2.6	71	85	-$1
2nd Half		1	3	0	55	44	4.62	5.64	1.52	1098	990	1212	19.8	3.4	7.2	2.1	55%	7%	38	30	32	32%	76%	35%	3	71	0%	100%	0	0.67	-2.9	34	40	-$7
17	Proj	8	6	0	138	114	4.10	4.57	1.44	648	583	717	21.9	3.4	7.4	2.2	55%	7%	38	30	32	32%	74%	10%	27						1.5	58	69	-$1

Givens,Mychal

Age:	27	Th:	R	Role	RP	Health	A
Ht:	6' 1"	Wt:	207	Type	Pwr	PT/Exp	D
						Consist	D

LIMA Plan	B+
Rand Var	-1
MM	3501

Profile of a future closer got a bit tarnished by Ctl problems, especially in 1st half. FpK confirms the in-season recovery, but also caps optimism for further near-term improvement. Problems vL also limit his role. Still a work in progress, but for now treat him as a 100-K LIMA option rather than a sleeper saves source.

Yr	Tm	W	L	Sv	IP	K	ERA	xERA	WHIP	oOPS	vL	vR	BF/G	Ctl	Dom	Cmd	FpK	SwK	G	L	F	H%	S%	hr/f	GS	APC	DOM%	DIS%	Sv%	LI	RAR	BPV	BPX	R$
12																																		
13																																		
14	aa	0	0	0	25	23	4.53	3.92	1.77				6.5	8.2	8.2	1.0						31%	72%								-2.5	78	93	-$6
15	BAL *	6	2	15	87	101	2.19	2.07	1.05	538	555	527	5.9	2.4	10.4	4.3	63%	13%	39	30	31	31%	79%	5%	0	21			88	0.79	19.0	157	187	$18
16	BAL	8	2	0	75	96	3.13	3.64	1.27	664	1025	504	4.7	4.3	11.6	2.7	59%	15%	35	25	39	32%	78%	9%	0	20			0	1.10	9.7	104	124	$6
1st Half		5	1	0	36	47	3.72	4.07	1.51	756	1139	585	5.2	5.0	11.6	2.4	57%	14%	33	29	38	36%	78%	11%	0	22			0	1.24	2.1	86	103	$3
2nd Half		3	1	0	38	49	2.58	3.25	1.04	567	904	417	4.3	3.8	11.5	3.1	61%	17%	38	21	41	27%	76%	6%	0	18			0	0.97	7.6	122	145	$9
17	Proj	5	3	0	73	89	2.95	3.41	1.17	633	844	527	5.0	3.5	11.1	3.1	61%	14%	37	27	36	31%	75%	6%	0						11.1	119	142	$6

Glasnow,Tyler

Age:	23	Th:	R	Role	SP	Health	C
Ht:	6' 7"	Wt:	195	Type	Pwr GB	PT/Exp	D
						Consist	A

LIMA Plan	B+
Rand Var	-1
MM	2403

0-2, 4.24 ERA in 23 IP at PIT. In-season, seemed at times like PIT was being super-cautious in not promoting top SP prospect. Here, the reason seems obvious: they saw this emerging Ctl issue; as 13 BB in 23 MLB IP confirms. SwK and GB% tilt are in place, just needs more strikes. That's last piece of this puzzle.

Yr	Tm	W	L	Sv	IP	K	ERA	xERA	WHIP	oOPS	vL	vR	BF/G	Ctl	Dom	Cmd	FpK	SwK	G	L	F	H%	S%	hr/f	GS	APC	DOM%	DIS%	Sv%	LI	RAR	BPV	BPX	R$
12																																		
13																																		
14																																		
15	a/a	7	4	0	104	108	2.78	2.52	1.19				20.8	3.4	9.3	2.7						30%	76%								15.2	116	138	$9
16	PIT *	8	5	0	140	141	2.76	2.91	1.33	774	810	744	20.0	5.3	9.1	1.7	61%	12%	48	21	32	28%	80%	10%	4	63	0%	50%	0	0.55	24.6	90	106	$11
1st Half		7	2	0	96	92	2.41	2.73	1.29				23.2	5.1	8.6	1.7						27%	82%	0%	0						21.1	89	106	$17
2nd Half		1	3	0	44	49	3.82	3.67	1.49	775	810	744	15.8	6.0	10.1	1.7	61%	12%	48	21	32	31%	75%	10%	4	63	0%	50%	0	0.55	2.0	87	103	-$1
17	Proj	8	6	0	145	151	3.95	3.96	1.30	658	674	645	22.6	4.2	9.4	2.2	61%	12%	48	21	32	30%	71%	10%	21						4.4	81	96	$5

Glover,Koda

Age:	24	Th:	R	Role	RP	Health	B
Ht:	6' 5"	Wt:	225	Type	Pwr FB	PT/Exp	F
						Consist	F

LIMA Plan	A
Rand Var	+2
MM	2300

2-0, 5.03 ERA in 20 IP at WAS. Quick-moving protoypical bullpen prospect (8th rd. pick in 2015 draft) pairs mid-90s fastball with nasty slider and aggressive demeanor. First stint in MLB was bumpy (2.3 Cmd, 65 BPV), but has raw materials to work his way up bullpen pecking order. Worth tucking away for 2018 and beyond.

Yr	Tm	W	L	Sv	IP	K	ERA	xERA	WHIP	oOPS	vL	vR	BF/G	Ctl	Dom	Cmd	FpK	SwK	G	L	F	H%	S%	hr/f	GS	APC	DOM%	DIS%	Sv%	LI	RAR	BPV	BPX	R$
12																																		
13																																		
14																																		
15																																		
16	WAS *	5	1	6	66	58	4.12	3.32	1.17	664	635	687	5.1	2.4	8.0	3.2	66%	11%	42	17	41	29%	66%	13%	0	16			75	0.86	0.6	96	114	$4
1st Half		2	0	4	29	27	3.44	3.05	1.21				5.3	2.4	8.3	3.5						32%	71%	0%	0						2.6	117	139	$5
2nd Half		3	1	2	37	32	4.63	3.52	1.14	664	635	687	4.9	2.5	7.7	3.1	66%	11%	42	17	41	27%	63%	13%	0	16			50	0.86	-2.0	81	96	$4
17	Proj	3	2	0	44	41	3.72	4.00	1.16	633	600	660	5.0	2.5	8.4	3.4	66%	11%	42	17	41	29%	72%	9%	0						2.5	106	126	$0

Godley,Zachary

Age:	27	Th:	R	Role	RP	Health	A
Ht:	6' 3"	Wt:	235	Type	GB	PT/Exp	D
						Consist	D

LIMA Plan	D+
Rand Var	+5
MM	1100

5-4, 6.39 ERA in 75 IP at ARI. We said last year "Not overpowering, and when his command is off, he can be hit hard", and that's pretty much what happened here. Even 2nd half Dom increase is a red herring, as it was really a result of elevated H%: Ks per batter faced were flat. Nothing to see here.

Yr	Tm	W	L	Sv	IP	K	ERA	xERA	WHIP	oOPS	vL	vR	BF/G	Ctl	Dom	Cmd	FpK	SwK	G	L	F	H%	S%	hr/f	GS	APC	DOM%	DIS%	Sv%	LI	RAR	BPV	BPX	R$
12																																		
13																																		
14																																		
15	ARI *	7	2	0	61	44	4.10	3.90	1.36	688	528	809	15.9	4.1	6.5	1.6	58%	12%	46	22	32	27%	72%	13%	6	64	50%	33%	0	0.74	-1.0	50	59	-$1
16	ARI *	9	10	0	157	115	5.49	5.48	1.55	844	891	804	16.3	3.0	6.6	2.2	55%	12%	54	18	28	34%	67%	19%	9	43	0%	56%	0	0.85	-25.2	43	51	-$10
1st Half		5	6	0	84	54	4.71	5.13	1.54	698	231	857	20.3	3.2	5.8	1.8	57%	12%	53	13	34	33%	71%	18%	1	30	0%	100%	0	0.99	-5.3	40	47	-$6
2nd Half		4	4	0	73	61	6.40	5.88	1.57	867	946	791	13.4	2.9	7.5	2.6	55%	12%	54	19	27	35%	61%	20%	8	45	0%	50%	0	0.82	-19.9	48	58	-$16
17	Proj	3	2	0	44	32	5.08	4.50	1.48	810	814	805	15.7	3.5	6.7	1.9	56%	12%	51	20	29	32%	68%	13%	7						-4.8	56	66	-$5

Goeddel,Erik

Age:	28	Th:	R	Role	RP	Health	D
Ht:	6' 3"	Wt:	185	Type	Pwr FB	PT/Exp	D
						Consist	C

LIMA Plan	C
Rand Var	0
MM	1300

2-2, 4.54 ERA in 36 IP at NYM. He packs mid-90s heat, but in today's game that isn't at all distinguishing. 3.5 Ctl in MLB is consistent with FpK, and pairs reasonably with borderline double-digit Dom. That sounds good, but even if you accept the 2nd half skill as baseline, eye over to 2nd half BPX: dead average. Just another guy.

Yr	Tm	W	L	Sv	IP	K	ERA	xERA	WHIP	oOPS	vL	vR	BF/G	Ctl	Dom	Cmd	FpK	SwK	G	L	F	H%	S%	hr/f	GS	APC	DOM%	DIS%	Sv%	LI	RAR	BPV	BPX	R$
12																																		
13	aa	9	7	0	134	106	4.76	4.95	1.55				23.4	3.8	7.1	1.9						33%	71%								-14.8	50	65	-$7
14	NYM *	3	2	0	70	58	4.42	4.76	1.57	406	583	307	5.6	3.9	7.5	1.9	54%	15%	31	31	38	35%	72%	0%	0	16			0	0.18	-5.8	64	76	-$6
15	NYM	1	1	0	33	34	2.43	3.38	0.99	553	520	568	3.8	2.4	9.2	3.8	52%	13%	41	20	39	28%	75%	3%	0	14			0	0.71	6.3	119	141	$1
16	NYM *	3	3	1	64	62	4.38	4.37	1.45	710	690	719	4.6	4.0	8.7	2.2	62%	12%	28	25	46	33%	72%	10%	0	18			33	0.68	-1.5	71	85	-$2
1st Half		2	1	1	33	27	4.21	4.35	1.49	546	968	310	4.9	4.4	7.5	1.7	75%	13%	33	19	48	32%	73%	8%	0	17			50	0.80	-0.1	58	71	-$1
2nd Half		1	2	0	32	35	4.55	4.39	1.40	760	608	849	4.3	3.7	10.0	2.7	58%	11%	27	28	46	34%	70%	11%	0	18			0	0.64	-1.4	86	102	-$3
17	Proj	2	2	0	44	44	3.95	4.36	1.35	709	608	763	4.8	3.6	9.0	2.5	56%	12%	32	25	43	32%	72%	7%	0						1.3	77	91	-$2

RAY MURPHY

Gomez,Jeanmar

Age: 29	Th: R	Role RP	Health A	LIMA Plan C+	
Ht: 6' 4"	Wt: 215	Type GB	PT/Exp C	Rand Var 0	
			Consist A	MM 1021	

Third choice at closer in April lasted all season, but September's Chaconian meltdown (17 ER, 19 hits, 5 BB in 8 IP) may force a change. GB increase was helpful, but substandard FpK and SwK leave no margin for error. Research says that closers with <75 BPV rarely get a second 20 save season. You have been warned.

Yr	Tm	W	L	Sv	IP	K	ERA	xERA	WHIP	oOPS	vL	vR	BF/G	Ctl	Dom	Cmd	FpK	SwK	G	L	F	H%	S%	hr/f	GS	APC	DOM%	DIS%	Sv%	LI	RAR	BPV	BPX	R$
12	CLE *	11	13	0	160	92	5.53	4.92	1.44	810	822	800	22.0	2.8	5.2	1.8	56%	8%	48	19	33	31%	63%	15%	17	73	0%	53%	0	0.68	-30.0	32	42	-$10
13	PIT	3	0	0	81	53	3.35	3.83	1.15	617	621	614	9.8	3.1	5.9	1.9	63%	9%	55	19	26	25%	72%	10%	8	36	0%	38%	0	0.69	5.2	55	72	$2
14	PIT	2	2	1	62	38	3.19	4.35	1.50	810	1065	646	6.1	3.3	5.5	1.7	65%	9%	47	25	28	32%	82%	11%	0	22			100	0.62	4.2	34	41	-$2
15	PHI	2	3	0	75	50	3.01	4.11	1.33	697	700	695	4.9	2.0	6.0	2.9	62%	9%	49	22	29	33%	78%	6%	0	18			0	0.71	8.7	80	95	$0
16	PHI	3	5	37	69	47	4.85	4.40	1.46	762	837	706	4.2	2.9	6.2	2.1	56%	8%	52	22	26	33%	67%	10%	0	16			86	1.28	-5.6	63	75	$10
1st Half		3	2	22	39	25	2.75	4.15	1.14	655	813	536	4.3	2.3	5.7	2.5	55%	9%	52	20	29	27%	79%	9%	0	16			92	1.46	7.0	71	84	$21
2nd Half		0	3	15	29	22	7.67	4.73	1.88	886	865	902	4.2	3.7	6.8	1.8	57%	7%	52	24	23	40%	58%	13%	0	17			79	1.08	-12.6	53	63	-$4
17	**Proj**	**2**	**4**	**14**	**73**	**49**	**4.53**	**4.47**	**1.48**	**769**	**829**	**725**	**4.9**	**2.9**	**6.1**	**2.1**	**59%**	**8%**	**50**	**22**	**27**	**33%**	**70%**	**9%**	**0**						**-3.0**	**60**	**71**	**$0**

Gonzalez,Gio

Age: 31	Th: L	Role SP	Health B	LIMA Plan B+	
Ht: 5' 11"	Wt: 185	Type Pwr	PT/Exp A	Rand Var +1	
			Consist A	MM 2305	

Hitters caught on to 4th consecutive year of fastball velocity decline (now down to 90.8) as hr/f spike helped drive first big ERA/xERA miss since 2009. Concurrent 2nd half drops in SwK/FpK show declining quality of his stuff. 30+ starts again, but now at league average ERA, WHIP.

Yr	Tm	W	L	Sv	IP	K	ERA	xERA	WHIP	oOPS	vL	vR	BF/G	Ctl	Dom	Cmd	FpK	SwK	G	L	F	H%	S%	hr/f	GS	APC	DOM%	DIS%	Sv%	LI	RAR	BPV	BPX	R$
12	WAS	21	8	0	199	207	2.89	3.40	1.13	582	659	561	25.7	3.4	9.3	2.7	59%	10%	48	22	30	28%	75%	6%	32	100	47%	13%			27.7	102	132	$28
13	WAS	11	8	0	196	192	3.36	3.60	1.25	668	568	696	25.6	3.5	8.8	2.5	61%	10%	44	23	33	30%	75%	10%	32	104	41%	28%			12.3	87	113	$12
14	WAS	10	10	0	159	162	3.57	3.41	1.20	647	628	653	24.2	3.2	9.2	2.9	58%	11%	45	19	37	30%	71%	7%	27	97	41%	26%			3.3	103	122	$9
15	WAS	11	8	0	176	169	3.79	3.66	1.42	711	641	732	24.5	3.5	8.7	2.4	60%	10%	54	20	27	35%	73%	6%	31	95	23%	29%			3.7	92	110	$4
16	WAS	11	11	0	177	171	4.57	3.87	1.34	730	633	756	23.9	3.0	8.7	2.9	57%	10%	48	23	30	33%	68%	13%	32	97	28%	31%			-8.3	101	120	$3
1st Half		4	7	0	92	97	4.81	3.78	1.39	735	611	767	25.3	3.1	9.5	3.0	61%	11%	48	22	31	34%	67%	13%	16	100	31%	25%			-7.0	112	134	$1
2nd Half		7	4	0	86	74	4.31	3.97	1.30	724	655	744	22.5	2.8	7.8	2.7	54%	9%	47	24	28	31%	69%	12%	16	95	25%	38%			-1.2	89	106	$6
17	**Proj**	**12**	**10**	**0**	**181**	**175**	**3.95**	**3.81**	**1.32**	**702**	**635**	**722**	**23.4**	**3.2**	**8.7**	**2.7**	**58%**	**10%**	**49**	**21**	**30**	**32%**	**71%**	**10%**	**32**						**5.3**	**97**	**115**	**$7**

Gonzalez,Miguel

Age: 33	Th: R	Role SP	Health D	LIMA Plan B+	
Ht: 6' 1"	Wt: 165	Type	PT/Exp B	Rand Var -1	
			Consist A	MM 1103	

5-8, 3.73 ERA in 135 IP at CHW. Spent most of April in AAA then 4-week DL trip in Aug-Sep for groin strain. Skills had been barely roster-worthy until that 2nd half. Do we believe? Ctl not supported by FpK. hr/f not supported by FB rate. The planets of random luck aligned for 77 IP; it was a gift. At 33, it won't keep giving.

Yr	Tm	W	L	Sv	IP	K	ERA	xERA	WHIP	oOPS	vL	vR	BF/G	Ctl	Dom	Cmd	FpK	SwK	G	L	F	H%	S%	hr/f	GS	APC	DOM%	DIS%	Sv%	LI	RAR	BPV	BPX	R$
12	BAL *	12	6	1	150	117	3.03	3.02	1.13	694	701	685	18.5	2.8	7.0	2.5	66%	9%	35	22	43	26%	77%	10%	15	94	33%	33%	100	0.69	18.2	78	102	$17
13	BAL	11	8	0	171	120	3.78	4.28	1.23	713	689	736	23.7	2.8	6.3	2.3	59%	9%	39	21	40	27%	74%	11%	28	90	18%	36%	0	0.75	1.8	55	72	$7
14	BAL	10	9	0	159	111	3.23	4.36	1.30	751	772	724	24.9	2.9	6.3	2.2	61%	9%	37	21	42	28%	82%	12%	26	95	19%	38%	0	0.75	10.1	50	60	$6
15	BAL	9	12	0	145	109	4.91	4.45	1.40	795	831	761	23.9	3.2	6.8	2.1	62%	9%	40	24	36	30%	69%	15%	26	94	27%	50%			-17.0	54	65	-$4
16	CHW *	6	9	0	156	114	4.09	4.32	1.33	686	675	697	22.4	2.3	6.6	2.9	61%	8%	40	22	38	31%	72%	7%	23	88	26%	30%	0	0.77	1.9	69	82	$2
1st Half		2	4	0	80	62	4.62	4.91	1.47	762	720	796	21.4	3.5	7.0	2.0	61%	10%	43	21	36	32%	72%	10%	11	84	9%	36%	0	0.76	-4.2	46	55	-$3
2nd Half		4	5	0	77	52	3.55	3.71	1.18	617	641	587	23.6	1.1	6.1	5.8	61%	7%	38	23	39	31%	72%	4%	12	91	42%	25%			6.1	136	162	$8
17	**Proj**	**8**	**9**	**0**	**145**	**105**	**4.34**	**4.54**	**1.31**	**755**	**762**	**747**	**22.8**	**2.5**	**6.5**	**2.6**	**61%**	**9%**	**39**	**22**	**38**	**30%**	**70%**	**11%**	**26**						**-2.8**	**67**	**80**	**$1**

Graveman,Kendall

Age: 26	Th: R	Role SP	Health D	LIMA Plan B+	
Ht: 6' 2"	Wt: 195	Type Con GB	PT/Exp C	Rand Var 0	
			Consist B	MM 1005	

First full MLB season featured impressive 2nd half FpK growth while staying in the game longer (+1.3 IP/G) and maintaining strong GB tilt. But 2nd half hit rate and SwK declines will cause more wobbles on the low Dom / low Ctl tightrope. Worth consideration as you're fishing through the discount bin.

Yr	Tm	W	L	Sv	IP	K	ERA	xERA	WHIP	oOPS	vL	vR	BF/G	Ctl	Dom	Cmd	FpK	SwK	G	L	F	H%	S%	hr/f	GS	APC	DOM%	DIS%	Sv%	LI	RAR	BPV	BPX	R$
12																																		
13																																		
14	TOR *	4	2	0	49	26	2.51	3.58	1.26	556	625	500	16.7	1.3	4.9	3.6	78%	13%	64	29	7	32%	80%	0%	0	12			0	0.36	7.5	96	115	$1
15	OAK *	8	10	0	140	88	3.75	4.56	1.41	761	724	794	23.7	3.1	5.7	1.9	59%	8%	50	22	29	30%	77%	14%	21	90	19%	43%			3.7	42	50	$1
16	OAK	10	11	0	186	108	4.11	4.42	1.31	734	751	714	25.4	2.3	5.2	2.3	65%	8%	52	20	27	29%	71%	13%	31	91	16%	26%			1.8	63	74	$5
1st Half		3	6	0	80	55	4.84	4.61	1.54	843	874	808	23.8	3.0	6.2	2.0	60%	9%	52	19	29	33%	72%	16%	15	87	7%	33%			-6.4	59	70	-$6
2nd Half		7	5	0	106	53	3.57	4.28	1.13	646	657	632	26.8	1.7	4.5	2.7	68%	6%	52	21	26	27%	71%	11%	16	95	25%	19%			8.2	66	78	$13
17	**Proj**	**11**	**11**	**0**	**189**	**111**	**3.97**	**4.40**	**1.33**	**724**	**724**	**724**	**25.0**	**2.4**	**5.3**	**2.2**	**62%**	**8%**	**51**	**21**	**28**	**30%**	**72%**	**11%**	**31**						**5.2**	**60**	**72**	**$4**

Gray,Jonathan

Age: 25	Th: R	Role SP	Health B	LIMA Plan B	
Ht: 6' 4"	Wt: 255	Type Pwr	PT/Exp C	Rand Var +3	
			Consist D	MM 2305	

Blame hr/f (1H), h% (2H) and S% (all year) for the elevated ERA, and hope no one else noticed the skills supporting xERA. Dom fully backed by strong SwK, and FpK gains point to Ctl improvement on the horizon. BPX and oOPS say invest despite home ballpark, and with a bullpen... UP: sub-4 ERA.

Yr	Tm	W	L	Sv	IP	K	ERA	xERA	WHIP	oOPS	vL	vR	BF/G	Ctl	Dom	Cmd	FpK	SwK	G	L	F	H%	S%	hr/f	GS	APC	DOM%	DIS%	Sv%	LI	RAR	BPV	BPX	R$
12																																		
13																																		
14	aa	10	5	0	124	92	5.58	4.70	1.44				22.1	3.2	6.6	2.1						32%	62%								-28.2	51	60	-$8
15	COL *	6	8	0	155	123	5.35	5.68	1.67	856	755	949	23.2	3.2	7.1	2.2	58%	10%	42	25	33	37%	68%	10%	9	76	22%	33%			-26.5	55	65	-$16
16	COL	10	10	0	168	185	4.61	3.60	1.26	703	694	712	24.6	3.2	9.9	3.1	62%	12%	44	24	32	32%	65%	13%	29	96	41%	34%			-8.7	115	137	$6
1st Half		5	4	0	82	87	4.81	3.47	1.20	713	706	720	24.4	3.0	9.5	3.2	62%	12%	48	22	30	29%	63%	18%	14	94	43%	43%			-6.3	118	141	$6
2nd Half		5	6	0	86	98	4.41	3.72	1.32	693	685	703	24.7	3.4	10.3	3.1	63%	13%	39	27	34	34%	66%	8%	15	99	40%	27%			-2.4	111	133	$6
17	**Proj**	**10**	**10**	**0**	**189**	**178**	**4.42**	**4.02**	**1.33**	**725**	**679**	**772**	**22.7**	**3.2**	**8.5**	**2.6**	**61%**	**12%**	**43**	**25**	**32**	**32%**	**68%**	**11%**	**35**						**-5.3**	**86**	**103**	**$3**

Gray,Sonny

Age: 27	Th: R	Role SP	Health D	LIMA Plan C	
Ht: 5' 10"	Wt: 190	Type Pwr GB	PT/Exp A	Rand Var +5	
			Consist A	MM 2205	

Neck, shoulder and forearm injuries affected playing time (10 weeks over 2 DL trips). Ctl and hr/f ballooned sending ERA, WHIP, oOPS soaring. Even so, Dom, FpK and GB% stayed solid, giving hope that with health, 2016 can be forgotten. Hit and strand rate regression will also make 2017 look better.

Yr	Tm	W	L	Sv	IP	K	ERA	xERA	WHIP	oOPS	vL	vR	BF/G	Ctl	Dom	Cmd	FpK	SwK	G	L	F	H%	S%	hr/f	GS	APC	DOM%	DIS%	Sv%	LI	RAR	BPV	BPX	R$
12	a/a	6	9	0	152	84	4.43	4.26	1.48				24.2	3.3	5.0	1.5						32%	69%								-7.8	48	62	-$7
13	OAK *	15	10	0	182	165	3.20	3.29	1.28	570	622	499	23.4	2.8	8.1	2.9	60%	10%	53	20	28	32%	75%	8%	10	83	40%	20%	0	0.66	15.1	101	132	$13
14	OAK	14	10	0	219	183	3.08	3.36	1.19	627	639	614	27.2	3.0	7.5	2.5	58%	9%	56	18	26	28%	76%	9%	33	100	36%	21%			17.8	87	104	$16
15	OAK	14	7	0	208	169	2.73	3.62	1.08	590	579	601	26.8	2.6	7.3	2.9	59%	10%	53	17	31	26%	78%	9%	31	99	42%	23%			31.7	94	112	$26
16	OAK	5	11	0	117	94	5.69	4.30	1.50	818	757	880	23.5	3.2	7.2	2.2	61%	8%	54	19	27	33%	64%	17%	22	89	9%	45%			-21.7	75	89	-$9
1st Half		3	7	0	85	67	5.42	4.28	1.45	804	709	891	24.8	3.2	7.1	2.2	62%	8%	54	18	28	32%	65%	16%	15	92	13%	40%			-12.9	75	89	-$8
2nd Half		2	4	0	32	27	6.40	4.34	1.61	855	861	846	20.7	3.3	7.5	2.3	59%	8%	52	21	27	35%	63%	21%	7	80	0%	57%			-8.8	75	90	-$12
17	**Proj**	**13**	**12**	**0**	**203**	**167**	**3.64**	**3.90**	**1.29**	**678**	**670**	**686**	**26.8**	**2.9**	**7.4**	**2.6**	**60%**	**9%**	**53**	**19**	**28**	**30%**	**74%**	**11%**	**31**						**13.7**	**87**	**103**	**$11**

Green,Chad

Age: 26	Th: R	Role SP	Health B	LIMA Plan B+	
Ht: 6' 3"	Wt: 210	Type Pwr FB	PT/Exp D	Rand Var +1	
			Consist D	MM 1301	

2-4, 4.73 ERA in 46 IP at NYY. Swingman debut ended with Sept forearm strain. The 94 innings at AAA were very good, but less than 250 total IP at upper minors says we need to see a bit more of that SwK, Dom and Cmd before investing. Potential reserve stash.

Yr	Tm	W	L	Sv	IP	K	ERA	xERA	WHIP	oOPS	vL	vR	BF/G	Ctl	Dom	Cmd	FpK	SwK	G	L	F	H%	S%	hr/f	GS	APC	DOM%	DIS%	Sv%	LI	RAR	BPV	BPX	R$
12																																		
13																																		
14																																		
15	aa	5	14	0	149	108	4.84	5.48	1.65				24.6	2.8	6.5	2.4						38%	70%								-16.2	61	73	-$13
16	NYY *	9	10	1	140	135	3.07	3.96	1.26	852	1014	704	20.5	2.5	8.6	3.4	60%	13%	41	21	38	32%	81%	25%	8	70	25%	38%	100	0.68	19.3	95	113	$12
1st Half		7	7	0	93	82	2.52	3.42	1.23	794	1176	564	22.1	2.2	8.0	3.6	59%	12%	45	24	31	32%	82%	33%	2	54	0%	0%	0	0.54	19.1	108	129	$17
2nd Half		2	3	1	48	53	4.15	5.00	1.33	870	974	760	18.0	3.1	10.0	3.2	61%	13%	40	20	40	31%	78%	23%	6	75	33%	50%	100	0.72	0.2	71	85	$2
17	**Proj**	**4**	**5**	**0**	**87**	**80**	**3.71**	**4.27**	**1.32**	**650**	**698**	**601**	**22.0**	**2.7**	**8.3**	**3.0**	**61%**	**13%**	**40**	**20**	**40**	**32%**	**76%**	**10%**	**13**						**5.1**	**94**	**112**	**$1**

MATT DODGE

Greene,Shane			Health	C	LIMA Plan	C
Age: 28	Th: R	Role: RP	PT/Exp	D	Rand Var	+5
Ht: 6' 3"	Wt: 200	Type: Pwr	Consist	C	MM	2301

Standard pitching career path #3: Ineffective starter moved to pen, simplified pitch mix (in this case, slider + cutter replaced curve + change), and found some skills growth. SwK and Dom rose nicely, but S% and 2nd half H% ruined results. With that xERA and Dom, color us interested once his luck reverses.

Yr Tm	W	L	Sv	IP	K	ERA	xERA	WHIP	oOPS	vL	vR	BF/G	Ctl	Dom	Cmd	FpK	SwK	G	L	F	H%	S%	hr/f	GS	APC	DOM%	DIS%	Sv%	LI	RAR	BPV	BPX	R$
12																																	
13 aa	8	4	0	79	55	4.25	6.14	1.72				25.7	2.5	6.3	2.5						39%	77%								-3.8	50	65	-$6
14 NYY *	10	6	0	145	127	4.53	5.05	1.59	715	765	661	21.3	3.5	7.9	2.3	59%	11%	50	22	28	37%	72%	13%	14	90	36%	36%	0	0.70	-14.1	69	82	-$7
15 DET *	5	9	0	119	66	6.29	5.60	1.58	897	1017	757	20.9	3.0	5.0	1.7	62%	7%	44	23	33	33%	61%	14%	16	74	25%	56%	0	0.70	-34.1	24	28	-$17
16 DET	5	4	2	60	59	5.82	3.87	1.33	680	788	586	5.1	3.3	8.8	2.7	58%	13%	48	21	32	33%	53%	6%	3	20	0%	33%	67	1.26	-12.1	96	114	-$3
1st Half	1	2	1	29	28	4.91	3.95	1.16	561	627	507	6.2	3.7	8.6	2.3	58%	13%	45	18	37	29%	53%	0%	3	24	0%	33%	100	1.06	-2.6	78	93	$0
2nd Half	4	2	1	31	31	6.68	3.79	1.48	780	917	655	4.5	2.9	9.0	3.1	58%	13%	50	23	27	37%	53%	12%	0	17			50	1.39	-9.5	112	133	-$5
17 Proj	**6**	**5**	**0**	**73**	**69**	**3.92**	**3.87**	**1.32**	**705**	**809**	**601**	**7.8**	**3.1**	**8.6**	**2.8**	**59%**	**11%**	**47**	**22**	**31**	**32%**	**71%**	**9%**	**0**						**2.4**	**95**	**113**	**$1**

Gregerson,Luke			Health	B	LIMA Plan	B
Age: 33	Th: R	Role: RP	PT/Exp	B	Rand Var	0
Ht: 6' 3"	Wt: 205	Type: Pwr xGB	Consist	A	MM	5410

Closer in Apr-May, but fantasy asset all year. Top-notch skills (SwK, Dom, FpK, GB%) ensured ERA, WHIP, K scoring contributions. A few warts appeared in 2H (with oblique DL trip) as Ctl reacted to FpK drop and hr/f spiked (1.2 hr/9), but results still OK. A fine holds source and late round bargain.

Yr Tm	W	L	Sv	IP	K	ERA	xERA	WHIP	oOPS	vL	vR	BF/G	Ctl	Dom	Cmd	FpK	SwK	G	L	F	H%	S%	hr/f	GS	APC	DOM%	DIS%	Sv%	LI	RAR	BPV	BPX	R$
12 SD	2	0	9	72	72	2.39	3.30	1.09	612	663	578	3.8	2.6	9.0	3.4	60%	16%	50	18	32	28%	83%	11%	0	14			69	1.19	14.4	120	156	$10
13 SD	6	8	4	66	64	2.71	3.27	1.01	572	624	521	3.7	2.4	8.7	3.6	60%	14%	45	20	35	27%	73%	5%	0	13			44	1.26	9.4	113	148	$8
14 OAK	5	5	3	72	59	2.12	3.24	1.01	604	526	663	3.9	1.9	7.3	3.9	60%	14%	52	15	33	26%	84%	9%	0	14			27	1.31	14.5	112	133	$9
15 HOU	7	3	31	61	59	3.10	2.71	0.95	573	606	537	3.7	1.5	8.7	5.9	67%	16%	60	16	23	28%	70%	13%	0	14			86	1.23	6.5	155	184	$19
16 HOU	4	3	15	58	67	3.28	2.84	0.97	589	746	439	3.9	2.8	10.5	3.7	63%	20%	60	14	26	26%	69%	14%	0	14			71	1.23	6.5	150	179	$11
1st Half	3	1	13	35	42	3.57	2.52	0.91	588	831	379	3.9	2.0	10.7	5.3	66%	21%	60	18	23	28%	60%	11%	0	14			72	1.22	2.7	175	209	$16
2nd Half	1	2	2	22	25	2.82	3.37	1.07	589	627	546	4.0	4.0	10.1	2.5	58%	19%	61	9	30	22%	81%	18%	0	15			67	1.23	3.8	111	133	$3
17 Proj	**4**	**4**	**2**	**58**	**60**	**3.22**	**3.05**	**1.03**	**606**	**667**	**547**	**3.7**	**2.5**	**9.3**	**3.7**	**62%**	**18%**	**58**	**15**	**28**	**27%**	**72%**	**13%**	**0**						**7.0**	**136**	**162**	**$5**

Greinke,Zack			Health	D	LIMA Plan	B+
Age: 33	Th: R	Role: SP	PT/Exp	A	Rand Var	+1
Ht: 6' 2"	Wt: 185	Type: Pwr	Consist	B	MM	2205

His luck-fueled 2015 was followed by an expected regression in the 1st half, but 2nd half crash took it too far. July oblique strain likely contributed, but FpK stayed strong all year so Ctl should rebound. Risk now elevated, but pay for a modest recovery. This is a 2017 buying opportunity.

Yr Tm	W	L	Sv	IP	K	ERA	xERA	WHIP	oOPS	vL	vR	BF/G	Ctl	Dom	Cmd	FpK	SwK	G	L	F	H%	S%	hr/f	GS	APC	DOM%	DIS%	Sv%	LI	RAR	BPV	BPX	R$
12 2 TM	15	5	0	212	200	3.48	3.34	1.20	663	691	635	25.5	2.3	8.5	3.7	59%	9%	49	22	29	31%	73%	10%	34	100	41%	21%			14.1	118	154	$18
13 LA	15	4	0	178	148	2.63	3.43	1.11	647	733	568	25.6	2.3	7.5	3.2	58%	11%	46	24	31	28%	79%	9%	28	101	39%	21%			27.0	96	125	$21
14 LA	17	8	0	202	207	2.71	2.93	1.15	660	627	689	25.7	1.9	9.2	4.8	63%	12%	49	23	29	32%	80%	12%	32	100	41%	13%			25.6	141	168	$21
15 LA	19	3	0	223	200	1.66	3.14	0.84	507	535	482	26.3	1.6	8.1	5.0	64%	13%	48	19	33	24%	84%	7%	32	101	56%	3%			63.3	128	152	$49
16 ARI	13	7	0	159	134	4.37	4.10	1.27	750	745	756	25.7	2.3	7.6	3.3	68%	11%	46	20	35	31%	70%	14%	26	96	31%	35%			-3.5	98	116	$6
1st Half	10	3	0	109	91	3.62	3.87	1.16	697	728	662	26.4	1.7	7.5	4.3	68%	11%	48	18	34	30%	72%	11%	17	97	41%	35%			7.7	114	136	$14
2nd Half	3	4	0	49	43	6.02	4.65	1.52	863	777	1001	24.2	3.6	7.8	2.2	67%	10%	42	22	36	31%	66%	20%	9	95	11%	33%			-11.1	63	75	-$11
17 Proj	**13**	**9**	**0**	**189**	**169**	**3.37**	**3.79**	**1.20**	**697**	**694**	**701**	**24.9**	**2.5**	**8.1**	**3.3**	**65%**	**11%**	**46**	**21**	**33**	**29%**	**77%**	**13%**	**30**						**19.0**	**103**	**122**	**$15**

Griffin,A.J.			Health	F	LIMA Plan	C
Age: 29	Th: R	Role: SP	PT/Exp	D	Rand Var	+2
Ht: 6' 5"	Wt: 215	Type: Pwr xFB	Consist	F	MM	0203

Needed a Rust-Oleum break for May shoulder stiffness, otherwise pitched creakily in the rotation all season. Recent repairs (2104 TJS, 2015 shoulder) and poor results (PQS-DIS) kept run times short (5 IP/start). 2nd half struggles (LD% jump, 38% hard-hit balls) warn recovery still in progress.

Yr Tm	W	L	Sv	IP	K	ERA	xERA	WHIP	oOPS	vL	vR	BF/G	Ctl	Dom	Cmd	FpK	SwK	G	L	F	H%	S%	hr/f	GS	APC	DOM%	DIS%	Sv%	LI	RAR	BPV	BPX	R$
12 OAK *	14	4	0	184	139	3.03	2.92	1.07	630	629	631	22.4	1.8	6.8	3.8	62%	9%	37	24	39	27%	75%	10%	15	95	27%	33%			22.5	105	137	$22
13 OAK	14	10	0	200	171	3.83	4.10	1.13	688	666	713	25.7	2.4	7.7	3.2	60%	9%	32	18	49	26%	74%	13%	32	100	38%	19%			1.0	83	108	$14
14																																	
15																																	
16 TEX	7	4	0	119	107	5.07	4.80	1.36	833	978	697	22.1	3.5	8.1	2.3	57%	9%	29	23	48	28%	71%	17%	23	90	17%	52%			-12.9	59	70	-$2
1st Half	3	0	0	43	42	2.93	4.30	1.09	605	645	562	21.6	3.6	8.8	2.5	59%	9%	34	19	46	25%	77%	8%	8	92	25%	25%			6.7	74	89	$9
2nd Half	4	4	0	76	65	6.28	5.08	1.51	952	1172	760	22.4	3.4	7.7	2.2	56%	10%	27	25	49	29%	68%	21%	15	88	13%	67%			-19.6	50	60	-$9
17 Proj	**8**	**7**	**0**	**145**	**125**	**4.63**	**4.68**	**1.33**	**779**	**834**	**720**	**23.3**	**3.2**	**7.8**	**2.5**	**59%**	**9%**	**32**	**21**	**47**	**29%**	**71%**	**14%**	**26**						**-7.9**	**64**	**76**	**-$1**

Grilli,Jason			Health	F	LIMA Plan	B+
Age: 40	Th: R	Role: RP	PT/Exp	C	Rand Var	+1
Ht: 6' 5"	Wt: 225	Type: Pwr xFB	Consist	B	MM	2510

More walks, more fly balls and more hr/f a bad combination at the back end of the bullpen. Still a crazy-good Dom with his strong SwK, but Cmd not worthy of high leverage assignment. Both the Ctl and Age fields have a value that starts with a "4". Nothing else matters.

Yr Tm	W	L	Sv	IP	K	ERA	xERA	WHIP	oOPS	vL	vR	BF/G	Ctl	Dom	Cmd	FpK	SwK	G	L	F	H%	S%	hr/f	GS	APC	DOM%	DIS%	Sv%	LI	RAR	BPV	BPX	R$
12 PIT	1	6	2	59	90	2.91	2.88	1.14	635	485	767	3.8	3.4	13.8	4.1	57%	15%	31	24	45	33%	80%	12%	0	16			40	1.20	8.0	166	217	$5
13 PIT	0	2	33	50	74	2.70	2.57	1.06	595	707	496	3.7	2.3	13.3	5.7	62%	15%	33	25	42	35%	78%	9%	0	16			94	1.17	7.2	188	244	$16
14 2 TM	1	5	12	54	57	4.00	3.83	1.33	702	683	711	3.8	3.5	9.5	2.7	61%	11%	32	26	42	33%	71%	6%	0	15			71	1.10	-1.7	87	103	$2
15 ATL	3	4	24	34	45	2.94	3.34	1.13	620	598	636	3.9	2.7	12.0	4.5	61%	16%	27	26	47	34%	75%	5%	0	16			92	1.56	4.2	149	178	$11
16 2 TM	7	6	4	59	81	4.12	3.95	1.29	727	877	613	3.7	4.9	12.4	2.5	57%	14%	30	20	50	28%	74%	15%	0	16			50	1.19	0.5	99	117	$4
1st Half	2	2	3	29	44	4.08	4.03	1.50	712	822	630	3.8	5.7	13.8	2.4	57%	13%	25	25	51	37%	75%	9%	0	16			60	1.17	0.4	99	118	$2
2nd Half	5	4	1	30	37	4.15	3.87	1.09	741	926	594	3.7	4.2	11.0	2.6	56%	14%	34	16	50	20%	73%	20%	0	16			33	1.20	0.1	98	117	$5
17 Proj	**5**	**6**	**2**	**58**	**76**	**4.30**	**3.90**	**1.32**	**715**	**784**	**660**	**3.7**	**4.5**	**11.8**	**2.6**	**58%**	**14%**	**30**	**22**	**48**	**32%**	**71%**	**11%**	**0**						**-0.8**	**100**	**119**	**$1**

Grimm,Justin			Health	B	LIMA Plan	C+
Age: 28	Th: R	Role: RP	PT/Exp	D	Rand Var	+2
Ht: 6' 3"	Wt: 175	Type: Pwr	Consist	A	MM	3500

Found his niche in the 7th inning (1.35 ERA in 20 IP), but substandard FpK and elevated LD% relegated him to lower leverage situations where ERA, WHIP suffered. Worth a buck for the strikeouts (Dom fully supported by SwK); maybe more if he can combine the 2nd half Cmd with the 1st half GBs.

Yr Tm	W	L	Sv	IP	K	ERA	xERA	WHIP	oOPS	vL	vR	BF/G	Ctl	Dom	Cmd	FpK	SwK	G	L	F	H%	S%	hr/f	GS	APC	DOM%	DIS%	Sv%	LI	RAR	BPV	BPX	R$
12 TEX *	12	7	0	149	96	4.06	4.06	1.36	935	1006	855	20.7	2.1	5.8	2.8	61%	8%	44	29	27	33%	69%	8%	2	50	0%	50%	0	0.33	-0.8	78	102	$2
13 2 TM *	10	12	0	146	113	5.78	5.37	1.61	846	860	830	17.9	3.4	6.9	2.1	58%	8%	43	21	36	35%	64%	13%	17	61	12%	59%	0	0.80	-34.4	49	64	-$14
14 CHC	5	2	0	69	70	3.78	3.49	1.25	632	528	684	4.0	3.5	9.1	2.6	61%	11%	49	16	35	31%	70%	6%	0	16			0	0.87	-0.4	96	115	$1
15 CHC	3	5	3	50	67	1.99	3.09	1.15	575	507	608	3.3	4.7	12.1	2.6	59%	14%	45	25	30	27%	87%	12%	0	14			50	1.04	12.1	114	136	$6
16 CHC	2	1	0	53	65	4.10	3.67	1.33	679	732	639	3.3	3.9	11.1	2.8	57%	13%	41	23	36	33%	71%	10%	0	13			0	0.67	0.6	113	134	-$1
1st Half	0	0	0	28	31	5.79	4.23	1.54	775	905	695	3.4	4.5	10.0	2.2	58%	11%	45	23	33	34%	64%	15%	0	13			0	0.54	-5.5	81	96	-$5
2nd Half	2	1	0	25	34	2.19	3.10	1.09	556	557	552	3.2	3.3	12.4	3.8	56%	14%	36	24	40	32%	81%	5%	0	13			0	0.84	6.1	149	178	$4
17 Proj	**3**	**2**	**0**	**44**	**52**	**3.58**	**3.57**	**1.26**	**641**	**649**	**636**	**3.6**	**3.9**	**10.8**	**2.8**	**58%**	**12%**	**43**	**22**	**35**	**32%**	**73%**	**9%**	**0**						**3.3**	**110**	**131**	**$0**

Gsellman,Robert			Health	A	LIMA Plan	B+
Age: 23	Th: R	Role: SP	PT/Exp	D	Rand Var	-1
Ht: 6' 4"	Wt: 205	Type: xGB	Consist	A	MM	2001

4-2, 2.42 ERA with 42 K in 45 IP at NYM. Strong debut for a GB-inducing rookie in a playoff chase, with a Dom higher than the 6.0 he posted in his 207 IP in the upper minors. He will need punchouts to continue to exceed those MLEs in order to merit sleeper sixth-starter consideration. Expect some pullback.

Yr Tm	W	L	Sv	IP	K	ERA	xERA	WHIP	oOPS	vL	vR	BF/G	Ctl	Dom	Cmd	FpK	SwK	G	L	F	H%	S%	hr/f	GS	APC	DOM%	DIS%	Sv%	LI	RAR	BPV	BPX	R$
12																																	
13																																	
14																																	
15 aa	7	7	0	92	43	4.01	3.82	1.35				24.0	2.5	4.2	1.7						30%	69%								-0.5	48	58	-$1
16 NYM *	8	11	0	160	118	3.60	3.66	1.29	639	589	682	23.4	2.5	6.6	2.7	61%	10%	54	23	23	31%	73%	4%	7	89	29%	14%	0	1.01	11.6	81	96	$7
1st Half	3	5	0	69	42	3.30	3.29	1.25				23.5	2.1	5.5	2.7						31%	72%	0%	0						7.6	83	99	$6
2nd Half	5	6	0	90	76	3.83	3.94	1.31	640	589	682	23.3	2.8	7.5	2.7	61%	10%	54	23	23	31%	73%	4%	7	89	29%	14%	0	1.01	4.0	79	94	$8
17 Proj	**7**	**5**	**0**	**102**	**69**	**3.91**	**4.08**	**1.32**	**653**	**573**	**719**	**23.7**	**2.5**	**6.1**	**2.4**	**61%**	**10%**	**54**	**23**	**23**	**31%**	**70%**	**7%**	**18**						**3.5**	**75**	**89**	**$1**

MATT DODGE

Guerra,Deolis

Age: 28	Th: R	Role	RP	Health	D	LIMA Plan	B+
Ht: 6' 5"	Wt: 250	Type		PT/Exp	D	Rand Var	-1
				Consist	B	MM	1100

Has now logged 70 IP worth of 1.3 Ctl, 5.3 Cmd in majors, but FpK casts a lot of doubt on sustainability of that low walk rate, and if that goes, so does any hope at success. High LD%, hr/f should regress, but when viewed in conjuction with mediocre Dom, suggest a pitcher who's simply not fooling anybody.

Yr Tm	W	L	Sv	IP	K	ERA	xERA	WHIP	oOPS	vL	vR	BF/G	Ctl	Dom	Cmd	FpK	SwK	G	L	F	H%	S%	hr/f	GS	APC	DOM%	DIS%	Sv%	LI	RAR	BPV	BPX	R$
12 a/a	4	3	1	70	59	5.01	4.33	1.38				8.2	2.9	7.6	2.6						33%	65%								-8.6	74	96	-$4
13																																	
14 aaa	2	2	0	52	43	5.71	5.31	1.58				6.3	3.3	7.4	2.2						35%	64%								-12.6	56	67	-$8
15 PIT *	4	1	4	53	45	3.17	3.79	1.20	1077	599	1328	6.1	2.0	7.6	3.9	52%	11%	37	27	35	31%	78%	28%	0	31			80	0.78	5.2	99	118	$3
16 LAA	3	0	0	53	36	3.21	4.11	1.11	671	541	802	5.0	1.2	6.1	5.1	55%	10%	42	26	32	29%	75%	11%	0	20			0	0.74	6.5	97	116	$2
1st Half	1	0	0	23	18	2.35	3.24	0.78	488	333	636	5.8	0.0	7.0	0.0	52%	10%	41	29	29	27%	71%	5%	0	23			0	0.62	5.2	146	174	$5
2nd Half	2	0	0	30	18	3.86	4.81	1.35	795	675	921	4.6	2.1	5.3	2.6	57%	10%	43	24	33	30%	78%	14%	0	19			0	0.80	1.2	61	73	$0
17 Proj	**2**	**2**	**0**	**58**	**44**	**3.94**	**4.20**	**1.29**	**718**	**579**	**858**	**5.6**	**2.4**	**6.8**	**2.8**	**55%**	**10%**	**42**	**26**	**32**	**31%**	**72%**	**12%**	**0**						**1.8**	**78**	**93**	**-$1**

Guerra,Junior

Age: 32	Th: R	Role	RP	Health	C	LIMA Plan	C+
Ht: 5' 11"	Wt: 215	Type	Pwr	PT/Exp	D	Rand Var	-1
				Consist	D	MM	1203

9-3, 2.81 ERA in 122 IP at MIL. Converted infielder spent years in minors, independent ball, Mexico, and Italy before dropping this surprise. But that's the thing; there's a reason no one expected this, and skills agree—MLB xERA was 4.18, Cmd fell to 1.8 in 2nd half. Your draft day mantra: Look away from that ERA.

Yr Tm	W	L	Sv	IP	K	ERA	xERA	WHIP	oOPS	vL	vR	BF/G	Ctl	Dom	Cmd	FpK	SwK	G	L	F	H%	S%	hr/f	GS	APC	DOM%	DIS%	Sv%	LI	RAR	BPV	BPX	R$
12																																	
13																																	
14																																	
15 CHW *	4	7	7	87	83	4.63	4.59	1.49	1033	1000	1044	11.1	4.4	8.6	1.9	63%	11%	57	21	21	32%	71%	33%	0	22			88	0.22	-7.2	62	74	-$2
16 MIL *	9	5	0	148	118	3.25	2.90	1.16	633	618	645	23.6	3.4	7.2	2.1	58%	11%	45	19	36	26%	74%	8%	20	93	30%	20%			17.2	77	91	$12
1st Half	5	3	0	93	77	3.94	3.05	1.14	640	641	637	24.5	3.0	7.5	2.5	59%	12%	43	19	38	26%	68%	10%	11	93	36%	9%			2.9	80	95	$12
2nd Half	4	2	0	56	41	2.10	2.66	1.20	624	579	651	22.4	3.9	6.7	1.7	58%	11%	48	19	33	25%	84%	6%	9	94	22%	33%			14.3	74	88	$13
17 Proj	**9**	**8**	**0**	**160**	**135**	**3.87**	**4.40**	**1.32**	**712**	**687**	**730**	**16.0**	**3.9**	**7.6**	**2.0**	**58%**	**11%**	**46**	**19**	**35**	**29%**	**72%**	**9%**	**25**						**6.3**	**56**	**67**	**$5**

Gustave,Jandel

Age: 24	Th: R	Role	RP	Health	A	LIMA Plan	D+
Ht: 6' 2"	Wt: 210	Type	Pwr FB	PT/Exp	F	Rand Var	+3
				Consist	B	MM	0200

1-0, 3.52 ERA in 15 IP at HOU. Small sample size, for sure, but FpK, SwK, and 9.4 MLB Dom gave a taste of upside for righty whose fastball can hit triple digits. But we can't just set aside the MLEs, and they're preaching caution and patience. For now, he's one to watch rather than own.

Yr Tm	W	L	Sv	IP	K	ERA	xERA	WHIP	oOPS	vL	vR	BF/G	Ctl	Dom	Cmd	FpK	SwK	G	L	F	H%	S%	hr/f	GS	APC	DOM%	DIS%	Sv%	LI	RAR	BPV	BPX	R$
12																																	
13																																	
14																																	
15 aa	5	2	20	59	43	2.43	3.56	1.39				5.4	3.7	6.6	1.8						31%	83%								11.1	70	83	$10
16 HOU *	4	3	3	72	63	4.03	3.03	1.25	676	625	711	4.8	3.3	7.8	2.4	67%	12%	40	23	38	30%	66%	13%	0	17			75	0.44	1.4	93	110	$2
1st Half	1	2	1	35	31	5.38	3.57	1.44				5.0	3.5	7.9	2.3						35%	58%	0%	0						-5.1	96	114	-$3
2nd Half	3	1	2	37	32	2.77	2.53	1.08	676	625	711	4.7	3.1	7.8	2.5	67%	12%	40	23	38	25%	77%	13%	0	17			100	0.44	6.5	91	108	$8
17 Proj	**3**	**2**	**0**	**44**	**35**	**4.17**	**4.64**	**1.34**	**694**	**659**	**715**	**5.1**	**3.5**	**7.3**	**2.1**	**61%**	**11%**	**40**	**23**	**38**	**29%**	**73%**	**11%**	**0**						**0.1**	**56**	**67**	**-$2**

Hader,Joshua

Age: 23	Th: L	Role	SP	Health	A	LIMA Plan	B+
Ht: 6' 3"	Wt: 185	Type	Pwr	PT/Exp	D	Rand Var	+2
				Consist	A	MM	1401

Tall, lanky southpaw has a fastball that can hit high 90s and Dom to match, but Ctl remains a work in progress. Came very close to late-season call-up to Milwaukee, which suggests he should be a candidate to make his MLB debut at some point in 2017. Fantasy impact may take another year.

Yr Tm	W	L	Sv	IP	K	ERA	xERA	WHIP	oOPS	vL	vR	BF/G	Ctl	Dom	Cmd	FpK	SwK	G	L	F	H%	S%	hr/f	GS	APC	DOM%	DIS%	Sv%	LI	RAR	BPV	BPX	R$
12																																	
13																																	
14 aa	1	1	0	20	22	6.74	4.30	1.60				17.7	6.7	9.9	1.5						30%	57%								-7.4	71	85	-$5
15 aa	4	7	1	104	104	4.07	4.06	1.36				18.1	3.2	9.0	2.8						33%	72%								-1.4	89	106	$0
16 a/a	3	8	0	126	139	4.07	3.54	1.38				21.2	4.1	9.9	2.4						34%	70%								1.8	102	121	$1
1st Half	2	3	0	81	90	3.17	3.36	1.35				21.1	3.8	10.0	2.6						34%	76%								10.2	109	130	$6
2nd Half	1	5	0	45	49	5.70	3.85	1.43				21.2	4.5	9.8	2.2						33%	59%								-8.4	90	107	-$8
17 Proj	**3**	**5**	**0**	**87**	**89**	**4.46**	**4.17**	**1.38**				**22.3**	**3.8**	**9.2**	**2.4**	**59%**	**9%**	**40**	**23**	**37**	**32%**	**69%**	**10%**	**16**						**-2.9**	**80**	**96**	**-$3**

Hahn,Jesse

Age: 27	Th: R	Role	SP	Health	B	LIMA Plan	D+
Ht: 6' 4"	Wt: 215	Type	GB	PT/Exp	C	Rand Var	+4
				Consist	D	MM	0001

2-4, 6.02 ERA in 46 IP at OAK. Chose not to have second TJS after forearm, elbow pain in 2015, but looking at these skills, can't help but wonder if that was a mistake. And if that's not the explanation, then declining Dom/Cmd, rising xERA are even more alarming. Either way, best to give him a wide berth.

Yr Tm	W	L	Sv	IP	K	ERA	xERA	WHIP	oOPS	vL	vR	BF/G	Ctl	Dom	Cmd	FpK	SwK	G	L	F	H%	S%	hr/f	GS	APC	DOM%	DIS%	Sv%	LI	RAR	BPV	BPX	R$
12																																	
13																																	
14 SD *	9	5	0	116	102	2.76	2.88	1.24	623	656	583	17.4	3.7	7.9	2.1	60%	11%	50	22	27	29%	78%	8%	12	84	33%	25%	0	0.89	14.0	90	108	$8
15 OAK	6	6	0	97	64	3.35	3.83	1.17	623	735	502	25.4	2.3	6.0	2.6	61%	8%	53	25	23	28%	71%	7%	16	96	25%	19%			7.3	75	90	$5
16 OAK *	3	11	0	113	58	6.19	6.44	1.86	860	1069	685	22.1	4.6	4.6	1.0	66%	6%	49	23	28	35%	67%	18%	9	79	11%	67%			-27.9	8	9	-$20
1st Half	3	8	0	74	37	6.08	6.92	1.98	897	1121	701	22.1	5.1	4.5	0.9	69%	6%	54	23	23	36%	70%	21%	7	76	0%	71%			-17.2	3	4	-$21
2nd Half	0	3	0	39	21	6.38	5.55	1.65	738	874	637	22.0	3.8	4.7	1.2	55%	7%	33	22	44	33%	61%	13%	2	89	50%	50%			-10.6	18	22	-$16
17 Proj	**3**	**5**	**0**	**73**	**45**	**4.73**	**4.66**	**1.49**	**754**	**863**	**644**	**21.8**	**3.6**	**5.6**	**1.6**	**63%**	**8%**	**52**	**23**	**25**	**32%**	**68%**	**9%**	**14**						**-4.8**	**35**	**42**	**-$6**

Hamels,Cole

Age: 33	Th: L	Role	SP	Health	B	LIMA Plan	C
Ht: 6' 4"	Wt: 190	Type	Pwr	PT/Exp	A	Rand Var	0
				Consist	A	MM	2305

Still chugging along with his 7th straight 200+ IP season, BUT: worst Ctl, Cmd of career; notable drop in FpK; first time BPV has ever fallen below 100. W-L record will be tough to repeat, and when you add in ERA/xERA difference, he's at risk for R$ regression. He's still great, just not flawless.

Yr Tm	W	L	Sv	IP	K	ERA	xERA	WHIP	oOPS	vL	vR	BF/G	Ctl	Dom	Cmd	FpK	SwK	G	L	F	H%	S%	hr/f	GS	APC	DOM%	DIS%	Sv%	LI	RAR	BPV	BPX	R$
12 PHI	17	6	0	215	216	3.05	3.32	1.12	661	629	673	28.0	2.2	9.0	4.2	63%	14%	43	22	35	30%	78%	12%	31	107	45%	3%			25.6	125	163	$27
13 PHI	8	14	0	220	202	3.60	3.46	1.16	699	712	695	27.4	2.0	8.3	4.0	63%	13%	43	21	37	31%	71%	9%	33	104	45%	15%			7.2	115	149	$13
14 PHI	9	9	0	205	198	2.46	3.20	1.15	641	636	641	27.6	2.6	8.7	3.4	61%	13%	46	22	31	30%	81%	8%	30	105	57%	10%			32.3	111	132	$20
15 2 TM	13	8	0	212	215	3.65	3.39	1.19	669	646	675	27.5	2.6	9.1	3.5	61%	14%	48	21	31	30%	72%	12%	32	104	44%	19%			8.3	119	142	$16
16 TEX	15	5	0	201	200	3.32	3.83	1.31	699	605	722	26.5	3.5	9.0	2.6	57%	13%	50	20	31	31%	79%	14%	32	102	34%	25%			21.6	96	114	$16
1st Half	9	2	0	108	105	2.93	3.80	1.28	705	610	730	26.8	3.4	8.8	2.6	57%	13%	51	20	29	29%	84%	17%	17	101	29%	24%			16.8	94	112	$20
2nd Half	6	3	0	93	95	3.77	3.86	1.33	692	594	713	26.1	3.5	9.2	2.6	58%	13%	49	19	32	32%	74%	11%	15	102	40%	27%			4.8	98	117	$12
17 Proj	**12**	**8**	**0**	**203**	**202**	**3.55**	**3.76**	**1.29**	**697**	**643**	**711**	**26.6**	**3.2**	**9.0**	**2.8**	**59%**	**13%**	**48**	**20**	**32**	**31%**	**75%**	**12%**	**31**						**16.0**	**101**	**120**	**$12**

Hammel,Jason

Age: 34	Th: R	Role	SP	Health	C	LIMA Plan	C+
Ht: 6' 6"	Wt: 200	Type	Pwr	PT/Exp	A	Rand Var	0
				Consist	A	MM	2303

Left off postseason roster because of elbow tightness, which only adds to concerns raised by Dom and Cmd slip, and backslide in xERA. That said, R$ consistency last three years has been impressive, and Ctl could be stabilizing influence. Can be an underrated asset if you accept his limitations.

Yr Tm	W	L	Sv	IP	K	ERA	xERA	WHIP	oOPS	vL	vR	BF/G	Ctl	Dom	Cmd	FpK	SwK	G	L	F	H%	S%	hr/f	GS	APC	DOM%	DIS%	Sv%	LI	RAR	BPV	BPX	R$
12 BAL	8	6	0	118	113	3.43	3.48	1.24	637	586	692	24.7	3.2	8.6	2.7	57%	11%	53	19	28	30%	74%	10%	20	97	35%	25%			8.5	100	130	$7
13 BAL	7	8	1	139	96	4.97	4.52	1.46	813	881	716	23.5	3.1	6.2	2.0	56%	8%	40	22	38	31%	70%	13%	23	89	9%	57%	100	0.77	-19.0	46	60	-$7
14 2 TM	10	11	0	176	158	3.47	3.53	1.12	680	691	670	23.8	2.2	8.1	3.6	57%	10%	40	22	38	28%	74%	12%	29	93	48%	21%	0	0.75	5.9	103	122	$12
15 CHC	10	7	0	171	172	3.74	3.57	1.16	714	696	728	22.9	2.1	9.1	4.3	61%	11%	38	25	37	30%	73%	13%	31	89	32%	23%			4.6	122	146	$12
16 CHC	15	10	0	167	144	3.83	4.20	1.21	729	797	679	23.1	2.9	7.8	2.7	60%	11%	42	20	38	27%	74%	14%	30	87	33%	30%			7.3	83	98	$13
1st Half	7	5	0	91	73	3.45	4.24	1.15	707	876	576	23.4	2.9	7.2	2.5	57%	10%	43	19	37	25%	76%	13%	16	88	31%	25%			8.3	74	88	$15
2nd Half	8	5	0	75	71	4.30	4.15	1.27	755	701	793	22.7	2.9	8.5	3.0	64%	12%	41	20	39	30%	71%	14%	14	87	36%	36%			-1.0	94	112	$9
17 Proj	**13**	**10**	**0**	**174**	**159**	**3.91**	**3.97**	**1.21**	**721**	**737**	**709**	**22.4**	**2.6**	**8.2**	**3.1**	**60%**	**11%**	**41**	**21**	**38**	**29%**	**72%**	**13%**	**31**						**6.0**	**96**	**114**	**$11**

BRANDON KRUSE

Hand,Brad

Hand,Brad				Health	B	LIMA Plan	B+
Age: 27	Th: L	Role	RP	PT/Exp	C	Rand Var	0
Ht: 6' 2"	Wt: 185	Type	Pwr	Consist	B	MM	4511

Tamed righties and had his best season as a liberally deployed RP. Led RP in appearances and IP, finished 4th in Ks. Slider usage surged to 30% and fastball velocity sat at a career-high 94 mph. H% and S% could regress, but SwK justifies the Dom bump and 2nd half showed significant growth. UP: 15 Sv

Yr Tm	W	L	Sv	IP	K	ERA	xERA	WHIP	oOPS	vL	vR	BF/G	Ctl	Dom	Cmd	FpK	SwK	G	L	F	H%	S%	hr/f	GS	APC	DOM%	DIS%	Sv%	LI	RAR	BPV	BPX	R$
12 MIA *	11	8	0	152	133	4.96	4.62	1.55	1169	1850	962	23.7	5.1	7.9	1.6	43%	3%	50	0	50	31%	69%	14%	1	96	0%	100%			-17.6	54	71	-$8
13 MIA *	4	6	0	102	83	4.03	3.96	1.46	553	530	564	19.9	4.9	7.3	1.5	52%	9%	42	20	37	29%	74%	9%	2	43	0%	50%	0	0.73	-2.1	58	76	-$3
14 MIA *	5	8	1	133	85	4.21	4.00	1.34	732	594	789	15.4	3.2	5.7	1.8	59%	7%	50	18	32	29%	70%	9%	16	56	13%	31%	100	0.58	-7.6	50	60	-$2
15 MIA	4	7	0	93	67	5.30	4.39	1.49	784	512	887	10.7	3.1	6.5	2.1	52%	9%	46	23	30	33%	65%	10%	12	41	8%	50%	0	0.60	-15.4	57	68	-$8
16 SD	4	4	1	89	111	2.92	3.34	1.11	589	421	689	4.4	3.6	11.2	3.1	59%	13%	47	17	36	28%	77%	10%	0	18			14	1.30	14.0	128	153	$9
1st Half	2	2	0	45	54	3.38	4.10	1.32	631	470	745	5.1	4.8	10.7	2.3	60%	11%	44	17	39	31%	75%	7%	0	20			0	1.17	4.6	86	102	$5
2nd Half	2	2	1	44	57	2.45	2.62	0.89	540	347	633	3.9	2.5	11.7	4.8	57%	14%	51	18	32	25%	79%	16%	0	16			25	1.43	9.4	172	205	$14
17 Proj	**3**	**4**	**8**	**73**	**87**	**3.32**	**3.26**	**1.18**	**644**	**443**	**738**	**6.4**	**3.2**	**10.7**	**3.4**	**56%**	**11%**	**48**	**20**	**33**	**31%**	**75%**	**12%**	**0**						**7.8**	**133**	**158**	**$7**

Happ,J.A.

Happ,J.A.				Health	D	LIMA Plan	D+
Age: 34	Th: L	Role	SP	PT/Exp	A	Rand Var	-1
Ht: 6' 6"	Wt: 195	Type	Pwr	Consist	A	MM	1203

Gave back small velocity gains from PIT, but maintained new mix: heavy fastball/slider; sprinkled in curve/change. But outside of wacky win total, not much else changed. Age, ERA/xERA gap, decline in BPV, and just average Cmd should temper his price even with a positive SwK trend. Will come back to the pack.

Yr Tm	W	L	Sv	IP	K	ERA	xERA	WHIP	oOPS	vL	vR	BF/G	Ctl	Dom	Cmd	FpK	SwK	G	L	F	H%	S%	hr/f	GS	APC	DOM%	DIS%	Sv%	LI	RAR	BPV	BPX	R$
12 2 TM	10	11	0	145	144	4.79	3.98	1.40	787	730	807	22.4	3.5	9.0	2.6	64%	10%	44	17	39	33%	68%	12%	24	91	25%	21%	0	0.73	-13.8	89	116	-$2
13 TOR	5	7	0	93	77	4.56	4.83	1.47	734	802	708	23.1	4.4	7.5	1.7	60%	8%	36	18	46	31%	71%	8%	18	96	28%	44%			-8.0	31	40	-$5
14 TOR	11	11	0	158	133	4.22	4.03	1.34	770	874	743	22.4	2.9	7.6	2.6	62%	8%	41	20	40	31%	72%	12%	26	90	23%	31%	0	0.82	-9.2	77	92	$1
15 2 TM	11	8	0	172	151	3.61	3.83	1.27	698	680	705	22.4	2.4	7.9	3.4	60%	9%	42	24	34	32%	74%	9%	31	89	23%	26%	0	0.78	7.5	99	117	$9
16 TOR	20	4	0	195	163	3.18	4.13	1.17	665	651	669	24.9	2.8	7.5	2.7	60%	10%	42	22	35	27%	77%	11%	32	95	31%	25%			24.2	81	96	$22
1st Half	11	3	0	107	80	3.54	4.29	1.20	708	737	701	25.6	2.6	6.8	2.6	57%	10%	43	21	36	28%	75%	12%	17	94	35%	35%			8.5	72	86	$20
2nd Half	9	1	0	88	83	2.75	3.93	1.13	613	573	626	24.1	3.0	8.5	2.9	63%	11%	42	23	35	27%	80%	10%	15	96	27%	13%			15.7	92	110	$25
17 Proj	**15**	**9**	**0**	**174**	**151**	**3.59**	**4.11**	**1.24**	**693**	**693**	**693**	**22.9**	**2.8**	**7.8**	**2.8**	**61%**	**9%**	**42**	**22**	**36**	**29%**	**75%**	**11%**	**31**						**12.9**	**84**	**100**	**$12**

Harris,Will

Harris,Will				Health	A	LIMA Plan	B
Age: 32	Th: R	Role	RP	PT/Exp	C	Rand Var	-3
Ht: 6' 4"	Wt: 250	Type	Pwr GB	Consist	A	MM	4410

Why did ARI cut him again?! SwK, FpK and GB surges yielded another great year, including a stint as closer. Lost job after rough month (allowed 10 of his 16 ER), but skills held firm despite massive H% during those 8 IP. Had 1.04 ERA, 20 Ks in 17.3 IP after job loss. Offers value even without Sv opps.

Yr Tm	W	L	Sv	IP	K	ERA	xERA	WHIP	oOPS	vL	vR	BF/G	Ctl	Dom	Cmd	FpK	SwK	G	L	F	H%	S%	hr/f	GS	APC	DOM%	DIS%	Sv%	LI	RAR	BPV	BPX	R$
12 COL *	5	2	1	70	66	4.34	4.17	1.36	922	724	1073	4.6	2.7	8.5	3.2	54%	12%	37	23	40	34%	69%	13%	0	17			50	0.65	-2.8	94	122	-$1
13 ARI	4	1	0	53	53	2.91	3.18	1.23	661	509	759	3.6	2.6	9.1	3.5	58%	11%	47	23	29	33%	77%	7%	0	14			0	1.01	6.2	119	155	$2
14 ARI *	3	5	1	75	67	2.37	3.58	1.30	740	721	757	4.3	3.6	8.1	2.3	55%	11%	35	25	40	30%	85%	10%	0	17			33	0.76	12.6	80	95	$3
15 HOU	5	5	2	71	68	1.90	3.25	0.90	525	455	586	4.1	2.8	8.6	3.1	60%	9%	51	20	30	20%	88%	15%	0	17			33	1.28	18.0	109	130	$12
16 HOU	1	2	12	64	69	2.25	2.91	1.05	560	513	603	3.9	2.1	9.7	4.6	64%	14%	58	17	25	31%	80%	7%	0	16			80	1.17	15.3	154	183	$11
1st Half	0	1	7	36	35	0.76	2.88	0.90	435	464	413	3.9	1.5	8.8	5.8	65%	14%	61	13	26	28%	91%	0%	0	16			100	1.15	15.1	158	188	$15
2nd Half	1	1	5	28	34	4.13	2.95	1.24	710	562	875	3.8	2.9	10.8	3.8	62%	14%	53	23	23	33%	69%	18%	0	16			63	1.19	0.2	149	177	$5
17 Proj	**3**	**3**	**2**	**65**	**67**	**2.73**	**3.21**	**1.10**	**607**	**519**	**683**	**3.9**	**2.7**	**9.3**	**3.5**	**61%**	**12%**	**53**	**20**	**27**	**29%**	**78%**	**11%**	**0**						**11.8**	**126**	**150**	**$6**

Harvey,Matt

Harvey,Matt				Health	F	LIMA Plan	C+
Age: 28	Th: R	Role	SP	PT/Exp	C	Rand Var	+2
Ht: 6' 4"	Wt: 225	Type	Pwr	Consist	C	MM	3303

Thoracic outlet syndrome surgery ended season early and its symptoms played a role in near-5.00 ERA. With limited sample, TOS is in nascent stages in terms of projectable recovery and results are spotty. Pay attention to spring velocity readings and endurance. If a severe discount isn't there, let someone else take the risk.

Yr Tm	W	L	Sv	IP	K	ERA	xERA	WHIP	oOPS	vL	vR	BF/G	Ctl	Dom	Cmd	FpK	SwK	G	L	F	H%	S%	hr/f	GS	APC	DOM%	DIS%	Sv%	LI	RAR	BPV	BPX	R$
12 NYM *	10	10	0	169	168	3.50	3.41	1.29	631	662	592	23.2	3.8	8.9	2.4	60%	13%	38	24	37	30%	75%	10%	10	98	40%	20%			10.8	89	115	$10
13 NYM	9	5	0	178	191	2.27	2.73	0.93	530	456	603	26.5	1.6	9.6	6.2	64%	13%	48	20	33	29%	76%	5%	26	104	65%	4%			35.1	157	205	$28
14																																	
15 NYM	13	8	0	189	188	2.71	3.25	1.02	609	676	544	26.0	1.8	8.9	5.1	68%	12%	46	18	36	29%	78%	10%	29	96	55%	14%			29.2	137	164	$26
16 NYM	4	10	0	93	76	4.86	4.36	1.47	797	864	724	23.6	2.4	7.4	3.0	66%	11%	41	25	34	36%	67%	8%	17	89	18%	41%			-7.6	86	103	-$5
1st Half	4	10	0	89	72	4.55	4.39	1.40	780	876	667	23.8	2.5	7.3	2.9	66%	11%	40	25	35	34%	68%	8%	16	90	19%	44%			-4.0	81	96	-$4
2nd Half	0	0	0	4	4	12.27	3.52	3.00	1095	400	1313	21.0	0.0	9.8	0.0	62%	11%	59	29	12	63%	55%	0%	1	75	0%	0%			-3.7	214	255	-$13
17 Proj	**10**	**9**	**0**	**160**	**154**	**3.57**	**3.61**	**1.14**	**667**	**697**	**633**	**24.4**	**2.2**	**8.7**	**3.9**	**65%**	**12%**	**44**	**22**	**35**	**30%**	**71%**	**9%**	**26**						**12.3**	**118**	**140**	**$12**

Heaney,Andrew

Heaney,Andrew				Health	B	LIMA Plan	C
Age: 26	Th: L	Role	SP	PT/Exp	D	Rand Var	+5
Ht: 6' 2"	Wt: 195	Type	FB	Consist	B	MM	0100

Season ended before it even started as flexor strain gave way to TJS after 3 months of rehab didn't work. With surgery in early July, could lose his 2017 as well. The once-promising prospect is now looking at his first full season coming at age 27 in 2018. Even dynasty leaguers should be looking elsewhere.

Yr Tm	W	L	Sv	IP	K	ERA	xERA	WHIP	oOPS	vL	vR	BF/G	Ctl	Dom	Cmd	FpK	SwK	G	L	F	H%	S%	hr/f	GS	APC	DOM%	DIS%	Sv%	LI	RAR	BPV	BPX	R$
12																																	
13 aa	4	1	0	34	20	3.65	3.83	1.34				23.3	2.5	5.3	2.1						31%	73%								0.9	61	79	-$2
14 MIA *	9	9	0	167	139	3.89	3.59	1.22	847	611	944	21.7	2.2	7.5	3.4	60%	10%	45	19	35	31%	70%	18%	5	68	0%	60%	0	0.66	-3.1	95	113	$5
15 LAA *	12	6	0	184	141	3.94	3.92	1.35	679	568	723	24.0	2.5	6.9	2.8	62%	9%	38	22	40	33%	71%	7%	18	91	22%	28%			0.5	84	100	$4
16 LAA	0	1	0	6	7	6.00	3.11	1.17	840	833	842	25.0	0.0	10.5	0.0	60%	14%	44	17	39	34%	60%	29%	1	87	0%	0%			-1.3	211	251	-$4
1st Half	0	1	0	6	7	6.00	3.11	1.17	840	833	842	25.0	0.0	10.5	0.0	60%	14%	44	17	39	34%	60%	29%	1	87	0%	0%			-1.3	211	252	-$4
2nd Half																																	
17 Proj	**1**	**1**	**0**	**15**	**10**	**3.86**	**4.68**	**1.31**	**664**	**565**	**702**	**23.1**	**2.4**	**6.4**	**2.7**	**62%**	**9%**	**38**	**22**	**40**	**32%**	**71%**	**5%**	**3**						**0.6**	**67**	**80**	**-$3**

Hellickson,Jeremy

Hellickson,Jeremy				Health	D	LIMA Plan	C+
Age: 30	Th: R	Role	SP	PT/Exp	B	Rand Var	0
Ht: 6' 1"	Wt: 185	Type		Consist	C	MM	1205

Improvements not outwardly obvious in profile despite ERA nearly a run better than 2015. Leaning on changeup yielded big results, particularly vR; altered pitch mix and return of Cmd aided H% gains reminiscent of 2010-2012 glory days. Career HR issue is a reminder that this can blow up quickly, though.

Yr Tm	W	L	Sv	IP	K	ERA	xERA	WHIP	oOPS	vL	vR	BF/G	Ctl	Dom	Cmd	FpK	SwK	G	L	F	H%	S%	hr/f	GS	APC	DOM%	DIS%	Sv%	LI	RAR	BPV	BPX	R$
12 TAM	10	11	0	177	124	3.10	4.39	1.25	710	703	717	23.9	3.0	6.3	2.1	60%	9%	42	21	37	27%	82%	12%	31	97	26%	35%			19.9	52	68	$12
13 TAM	12	10	0	174	135	5.17	4.16	1.35	775	785	763	23.0	2.6	7.0	2.7	60%	10%	40	20	40	31%	64%	11%	31	90	16%	42%	0	1.04	-28.0	74	96	-$4
14 TAM *	2	9	0	88	75	5.36	6.12	1.71	759	585	966	21.1	2.7	7.7	2.8	63%	10%	36	23	41	40%	69%	10%	13	91	8%	46%			-17.6	67	79	-$12
15 ARI	9	12	0	146	121	4.62	4.22	1.33	781	790	774	23.6	2.7	7.5	2.8	63%	11%	42	21	36	31%	69%	13%	27	92	11%	37%			-11.9	83	98	-$1
16 PHI	12	10	0	189	154	3.71	4.02	1.15	709	751	672	24.1	2.1	7.3	3.4	61%	11%	41	25	34	28%	72%	13%	32	91	34%	31%			11.1	93	111	$15
1st Half	6	6	0	100	90	4.06	3.83	1.21	780	875	712	24.2	2.3	8.1	3.6	62%	12%	42	24	33	30%	72%	17%	17	93	41%	35%			1.6	106	126	$12
2nd Half	6	4	0	89	64	3.32	4.24	1.09	629	642	614	24.1	2.0	6.4	3.2	60%	10%	39	25	35	27%	72%	8%	15	90	27%	27%			9.5	79	94	$18
17 Proj	**10**	**12**	**0**	**181**	**146**	**4.19**	**4.24**	**1.29**	**747**	**733**	**760**	**22.7**	**2.4**	**7.2**	**3.0**	**61%**	**11%**	**40**	**23**	**36**	**31%**	**71%**	**11%**	**33**						**0.0**	**84**	**100**	**$5**

Hembree,Heath

Hembree,Heath				Health	B	LIMA Plan	B+
Age: 28	Th: R	Role	RP	PT/Exp	D	Rand Var	-5
Ht: 6' 4"	Wt: 210	Type	Pwr FB	Consist	B	MM	1200

Severe platoon split as MLBer could be pushing him toward the rare ROOGY role. Nothing in the profile supports the gaudy ERA so heed xERA, unless he starts facing fewer lefties. With a mid-20s LD% and 40-ish FB% history, and lack of one outstanding skill, the former closer-of-the-future talk seems a bit foolhardy.

Yr Tm	W	L	Sv	IP	K	ERA	xERA	WHIP	oOPS	vL	vR	BF/G	Ctl	Dom	Cmd	FpK	SwK	G	L	F	H%	S%	hr/f	GS	APC	DOM%	DIS%	Sv%	LI	RAR	BPV	BPX	R$
12 aaa	1	1	15	38	31	4.27	2.56	1.21				3.9	4.1	7.3	1.8						26%	63%								-1.2	84	109	$4
13 SF *	1	4	31	63	64	3.40	3.40	1.21	392	375	396	4.0	2.4	9.2	3.9	55%	17%	53	13	33	32%	74%	0%	0	15			86	0.37	3.6	119	155	$13
14 BOS *	1	4	20	56	50	4.80	5.40	1.62	846	962	799	4.6	3.9	8.1	2.0	75%	10%	28	22	50	36%	72%	6%	0	29			83	0.81	-7.3	56	66	$1
15 BOS *	2	5	8	57	40	3.47	4.06	1.33	795	862	741	4.6	3.3	6.4	2.0	63%	9%	27	25	48	29%	77%	13%	0	18			73	0.45	3.5	54	64	$2
16 BOS	4	1	0	51	47	2.65	4.54	1.33	695	890	591	5.9	3.0	8.3	2.8	59%	10%	36	24	40	32%	85%	10%	0	23			0	0.93	9.7	82	98	$2
1st Half	4	0	0	34	35	2.10	4.17	1.31	667	1114	420	7.1	2.6	9.2	3.5	55%	9%	37	25	38	34%	88%	8%	0	28			0	0.83	8.9	109	130	$5
2nd Half	0	1	0	17	12	3.78	5.35	1.38	755	390	936	4.3	3.8	6.5	1.7	66%	11%	36	21	43	27%	80%	13%	0	17			0	1.04	0.8	28	34	-$5
17 Proj	**2**	**2**	**0**	**44**	**36**	**3.74**	**4.55**	**1.33**	**703**	**686**	**711**	**4.6**	**3.0**	**7.4**	**2.5**	**62%**	**10%**	**36**	**22**	**41**	**30%**	**76%**	**10%**	**0**						**2.4**	**67**	**80**	**-$2**

PAUL SPORER

Hendricks,Kyle

Age: 27	Th: R	Role SP	Health A	LIMA Plan D+	
Ht: 6' 2"	Wt: 165	Type	PT/Exp A	Rand Var -5	
			Consist A	MM 3205	

Brilliant effort benefited from elite H% and S%, but FpK and SwK gains underscore command and ability to induce swings/misses. MLB-best defense helped, too, but xERA is the reality check. Dallas Keuchel showed volatility of contact-based approach even with plus skills. Could easily swing to ... DN: 3.70 ERA.

Yr Tm	W	L	Sv	IP	K	ERA	xERA	WHIP	oOPS	vL	vR	BF/G	Ctl	Dom	Cmd	FpK	SwK	G	L	F	H%	S%	hr/f	GS	APC	DOM%	DIS%	Sv%	LI	RAR	BPV	BPX	R$
12																																	
13 a/a	13	4	0	166	106	2.46	3.17	1.22				24.9	1.9	5.7	2.9						31%	80%								28.9	90	117	$16
14 CHC *	17	7	0	183	127	3.45	3.42	1.23	610	584	633	24.7	1.9	6.3	3.3	64%	8%	48	19	33	31%	72%	5%	13	89	31%	23%			6.5	94	112	$11
15 CHC	8	7	0	180	167	3.95	3.28	1.16	677	797	580	23.1	2.2	8.4	3.9	63%	9%	51	22	27	30%	68%	13%	32	87	31%	22%			0.3	121	144	$9
16 CHC	16	8	0	190	170	2.13	3.48	0.98	581	616	555	24.0	2.1	8.1	3.9	68%	10%	48	20	31	26%	82%	9%	30	93	33%	7%	0	0.76	48.2	115	136	$34
1st Half	6	6	0	91	83	2.76	3.56	1.05	605	656	570	24.7	2.5	8.2	3.3	69%	9%	52	19	30	27%	77%	11%	15	93	27%	13%			16.1	110	132	$24
2nd Half	10	2	0	99	87	1.55	3.41	0.91	558	579	540	23.4	1.7	7.9	4.6	68%	11%	45	22	33	25%	88%	8%	15	93	40%	0%	0	0.76	32.1	120	143	$43
17 Proj	**14**	**7**	**0**	**189**	**159**	**3.10**	**3.60**	**1.11**	**645**	**702**	**600**	**23.5**	**2.0**	**7.6**	**3.7**	**66%**	**10%**	**49**	**21**	**30**	**29%**	**74%**	**9%**	**31**						**25.4**	**109**	**130**	**$20**

Hendriks,Liam

Age: 28	Th: R	Role RP	Health C	LIMA Plan C+	
Ht: 6' 0"	Wt: 200	Type Pwr	PT/Exp C	Rand Var +2	
			Consist A	MM 3400	

Popular LIMA target repeated newfound Dom, but improvements vL couldn't negate regression vR. Triceps injury likely played a role. He had an 8.27 ERA before his DL stint in early May, then a 2.23 ERA when he returned, but never got a crack at closing. Skills and mid-90s heat still offer hope.

Yr Tm	W	L	Sv	IP	K	ERA	xERA	WHIP	oOPS	vL	vR	BF/G	Ctl	Dom	Cmd	FpK	SwK	G	L	F	H%	S%	hr/f	GS	APC	DOM%	DIS%	Sv%	LI	RAR	BPV	BPX	R$
12 MIN *	10	11	0	192	119	4.03	4.19	1.31	890	768	1020	24.7	2.6	5.6	2.1	54%	5%	41	24	35	29%	72%	17%	16	91	6%	63%			-0.3	49	64	$4
13 MIN *	5	11	0	146	84	5.83	5.73	1.55	907	929	879	24.5	1.8	5.2	2.9	59%	9%	37	22	42	35%	63%	14%	8	89	0%	63%	0	0.64	-35.3	49	63	-$17
14 2AL *	13	4	0	176	121	3.18	3.21	1.13	786	814	762	21.7	1.0	6.2	6.2	70%	8%	39	25	37	31%	72%	8%	6	61	17%	50%	0	0.75	12.2	153	183	$13
15 TOR	5	0	0	65	71	2.92	2.95	1.08	605	746	499	4.5	1.5	9.9	6.5	69%	12%	46	23	31	33%	73%	5%	0	18			0	0.91	8.3	161	191	$5
16 OAK	0	4	0	65	71	3.76	3.67	1.28	704	608	766	5.2	1.9	9.9	5.1	65%	12%	40	21	39	36%	73%	8%	0	20			0	0.95	3.4	143	170	$0
1st Half	0	1	0	26	26	5.88	3.73	1.58	816	863	789	6.4	1.0	9.0	8.7	66%	10%	40	28	32	43%	63%	11%	0	25			0	0.60	-5.4	152	181	-$7
2nd Half	0	3	0	39	45	2.33	3.64	1.09	622	450	747	4.5	2.6	10.5	4.1	65%	13%	40	16	44	30%	82%	7%	0	18			0	1.13	8.9	138	164	$4
17 Proj	**2**	**3**	**0**	**65**	**69**	**3.30**	**3.47**	**1.22**	**682**	**677**	**686**	**6.0**	**1.7**	**9.6**	**5.5**	**66%**	**11%**	**41**	**22**	**37**	**35%**	**75%**	**8%**	**0**						**7.2**	**145**	**172**	**$2**

Hernandez,David

Age: 32	Th: R	Role RP	Health F	LIMA Plan C	
Ht: 6' 2"	Wt: 230	Type Pwr FB	PT/Exp D	Rand Var +1	
			Consist A	MM 1401	

Hasn't been the same since 2014 TJS. Walks and homers have continually capped his upside, and his inability to wrest wide-open closer role likely puts to rest any chance of it ever happening. Meanwhile, the Ks don't overcome the xERA and health risks. Nothing to see here.

Yr Tm	W	L	Sv	IP	K	ERA	xERA	WHIP	oOPS	vL	vR	BF/G	Ctl	Dom	Cmd	FpK	SwK	G	L	F	H%	S%	hr/f	GS	APC	DOM%	DIS%	Sv%	LI	RAR	BPV	BPX	R$
12 ARI	2	3	4	68	98	2.50	2.94	1.02	544	683	415	3.9	2.9	12.9	4.5	64%	15%	31	22	46	32%	77%	6%	0	15			40	1.04	12.7	163	213	$10
13 ARI	5	6	2	62	66	4.48	3.85	1.19	702	847	578	4.2	3.5	9.5	2.8	63%	13%	32	21	47	27%	67%	13%	0	17			25	1.14	-4.7	88	115	$1
14																																	
15 ARI	1	5	0	34	33	4.28	3.94	1.31	778	739	803	3.6	2.9	8.8	3.0	55%	11%	39	19	41	30%	74%	15%	0	15			0	0.86	-1.3	96	115	-$3
16 PHI	3	4	1	73	80	3.84	4.24	1.50	785	852	730	4.6	4.0	9.9	2.5	58%	12%	37	25	38	35%	80%	14%	0	18			33	0.85	3.1	86	103	-$1
1st Half	1	2	1	40	50	4.76	3.81	1.46	786	847	742	4.6	3.6	11.3	3.1	57%	14%	37	25	38	36%	73%	17%	0	18			50	0.99	-2.8	121	145	-$2
2nd Half	2	2	0	33	30	2.73	4.81	1.55	785	855	713	4.6	4.4	8.2	1.9	59%	11%	38	25	38	33%	87%	11%	0	18			0	0.70	6.0	45	54	$0
17 Proj	**3**	**6**	**0**	**73**	**78**	**4.01**	**4.12**	**1.36**	**749**	**810**	**698**	**4.0**	**3.6**	**9.6**	**2.7**	**59%**	**12%**	**36**	**23**	**41**	**32%**	**75%**	**13%**	**0**						**1.6**	**91**	**109**	**-$1**

Hernandez,Felix

Age: 31	Th: R	Role SP	Health D	LIMA Plan B	
Ht: 6' 3"	Wt: 230	Type Pwr GB	PT/Exp A	Rand Var 0	
			Consist B	MM 2205	

Three years of sinking velocity, Dom, and IP have paired with rising Ctl, HR, ERA, and WHIP to severely curb hopes of return to glory. Modest 3 mph split between fastball and change-up has hurt the former more; increased secondary usage could be an answer, but adjust expectations. Name value could inflate price.

Yr Tm	W	L	Sv	IP	K	ERA	xERA	WHIP	oOPS	vL	vR	BF/G	Ctl	Dom	Cmd	FpK	SwK	G	L	F	H%	S%	hr/f	GS	APC	DOM%	DIS%	Sv%	LI	RAR	BPV	BPX	R$
12 SEA	13	9	0	232	223	3.06	3.19	1.14	629	643	608	28.5	2.2	8.7	4.0	63%	11%	49	22	29	31%	74%	8%	33	104	55%	15%			27.2	124	162	$25
13 SEA	12	10	0	204	216	3.04	2.83	1.13	643	671	610	26.5	2.0	9.5	4.7	62%	11%	51	21	27	32%	75%	10%	31	102	61%	13%			20.8	146	190	$20
14 SEA	15	6	0	236	248	2.14	2.54	0.92	546	519	584	26.8	1.8	9.5	5.4	65%	13%	56	18	26	27%	80%	10%	34	101	65%	9%			46.7	157	187	$38
15 SEA	18	9	0	202	191	3.53	3.25	1.18	682	699	665	26.6	2.6	8.5	3.3	63%	11%	56	17	27	29%	74%	15%	31	98	61%	16%			10.8	118	140	$18
16 SEA	11	8	0	153	122	3.82	4.35	1.32	718	739	702	26.2	3.8	7.2	1.9	59%	10%	50	21	29	28%	75%	15%	25	98	16%	40%			7.1	54	64	$7
1st Half	4	4	0	63	53	2.86	4.05	1.22	642	657	627	26.6	3.7	7.6	2.0	61%	9%	53	19	27	27%	80%	13%	10	100	20%	20%			10.4	67	80	$10
2nd Half	7	4	0	90	69	4.48	4.57	1.39	771	808	745	25.9	3.9	6.9	1.8	58%	11%	48	21	31	28%	72%	16%	15	97	13%	53%			-3.3	45	54	$4
17 Proj	**13**	**9**	**0**	**203**	**179**	**3.56**	**3.74**	**1.22**	**682**	**688**	**677**	**25.8**	**3.0**	**7.9**	**2.6**	**61%**	**11%**	**53**	**19**	**28**	**29%**	**74%**	**14%**	**32**						**15.9**	**92**	**109**	**$14**

Herrera,Kelvin

Age: 27	Th: R	Role RP	Health B	LIMA Plan B	
Ht: 5' 10"	Wt: 162	Type Pwr	PT/Exp C	Rand Var 0	
			Consist B	MM 4411	

Gaudy SwK in 2014-15 suggested better Dom, gave credence to elite results as we waited for base skills to catch up. Double-digit Dom and big Ctl gains finally yielded a premium season. Shone brightly in closer chance: 1.69 ERA, 0.75 WHIP, 23.0 Cmd in 21 IP. With opportunity, easy UP: 30 Sv.

Yr Tm	W	L	Sv	IP	K	ERA	xERA	WHIP	oOPS	vL	vR	BF/G	Ctl	Dom	Cmd	FpK	SwK	G	L	F	H%	S%	hr/f	GS	APC	DOM%	DIS%	Sv%	LI	RAR	BPV	BPX	R$
12 KC	4	3	3	84	77	2.35	3.16	1.19	643	742	580	4.5	2.2	8.2	3.7	59%	12%	56	20	25	32%	81%	7%	0	17			75	1.20	17.3	121	158	$9
13 KC *	5	8	4	76	96	3.23	2.90	1.09	701	738	661	4.2	3.2	11.3	3.5	56%	15%	48	18	34	28%	76%	18%	0	17			67	1.19	6.0	121	157	$8
14 KC	4	3	0	70	59	1.41	3.43	1.14	561	617	508	4.1	3.3	7.6	2.3	55%	13%	49	27	24	28%	86%	0%	0	16			0	1.14	20.1	73	87	$7
15 KC	4	3	0	70	64	2.71	3.79	1.12	578	470	677	4.0	3.4	8.3	2.5	61%	14%	45	23	33	26%	78%	8%	0	15			0	1.17	10.7	81	97	$5
16 KC	2	6	12	72	86	2.75	2.86	0.96	590	557	625	3.9	1.5	10.8	7.2	65%	16%	44	23	33	30%	75%	10%	0	15			80	1.22	12.8	175	208	$13
1st Half	1	1	0	39	49	1.40	2.68	0.85	517	665	373	3.8	1.6	11.4	7.0	69%	18%	46	19	36	29%	87%	6%	0	14			0	1.13	13.3	185	220	$12
2nd Half	1	5	12	33	37	4.32	3.09	1.08	670	447	925	4.1	1.4	10.0	7.4	60%	13%	43	26	31	32%	63%	14%	0	16			92	1.32	-0.5	164	196	$13
17 Proj	**3**	**5**	**8**	**73**	**76**	**2.74**	**3.25**	**1.06**	**599**	**544**	**653**	**3.9**	**2.3**	**9.5**	**4.0**	**61%**	**14%**	**46**	**23**	**31**	**29%**	**77%**	**9%**	**0**						**12.9**	**131**	**156**	**$9**

Hill,Rich

Age: 37	Th: L	Role SP	Health F	LIMA Plan C	
Ht: 6' 4"	Wt: 185	Type Pwr	PT/Exp D	Rand Var -4	
			Consist A	MM 2401	

Sits 2nd to only Kershaw in ERA and WHIP since 2015 (min. 130 IP), but he's 164th of 173 in IP during that time. Skills aren't in question, even at 37 years old, but how much will he pitch? This one area where community slant toward ageism could pay off, because IP uncertainty is built into cost. A worthy gamble.

Yr Tm	W	L	Sv	IP	K	ERA	xERA	WHIP	oOPS	vL	vR	BF/G	Ctl	Dom	Cmd	FpK	SwK	G	L	F	H%	S%	hr/f	GS	APC	DOM%	DIS%	Sv%	LI	RAR	BPV	BPX	R$
12 BOS	1	0	0	20	21	1.83	3.96	1.42	685	674	697	3.3	5.0	9.6	1.9	62%	7%	43	24	33	33%	86%	0%	0	14			0	1.10	5.3	58	76	-$2
13 CLE	1	2	0	39	51	6.28	4.13	1.73	719	696	749	2.9	6.8	11.9	1.8	48%	10%	42	20	38	38%	63%	8%	0	12			0	1.28	-11.5	51	67	-$8
14 2AL *	3	3	2	48	50	3.69	3.51	1.51	801	679	1125	4.6	4.9	9.3	1.9	41%	14%	38	31	31	35%	73%	0%	0	7			67	1.07	0.3	100	119	-$2
15 BOS *	7	5	0	83	81	3.53	3.57	1.36	410	358	423	10.2	4.6	8.8	1.9	61%	12%	48	16	35	29%	76%	9%	4	109	50%	0%			4.4	77	92	$2
16 2 TM	12	5	0	110	129	2.12	3.18	1.00	530	522	532	22.0	2.7	10.5	3.9	60%	11%	45	19	36	29%	79%	4%	20	91	40%	10%			28.2	140	166	$20
1st Half	8	3	0	70	80	2.31	3.37	1.11	567	469	597	24.0	3.3	10.3	3.1	58%	11%	50	16	34	30%	79%	3%	12	100	42%	8%			16.2	123	146	$21
2nd Half	4	2	0	40	49	1.79	2.86	0.79	460	653	418	18.9	1.6	10.9	7.0	65%	11%	37	24	39	26%	80%	6%	8	77	38%	13%			12.0	170	202	$18
17 Proj	**9**	**6**	**0**	**109**	**120**	**3.08**	**3.73**	**1.20**	**582**	**635**	**552**	**20.4**	**3.7**	**10.0**	**2.7**	**59%**	**10%**	**42**	**21**	**37**	**30%**	**75%**	**5%**	**14**						**14.9**	**99**	**118**	**$10**

Hochevar,Luke

Age: 33	Th: R	Role RP	Health F	LIMA Plan A	
Ht: 6' 5"	Wt: 215	Type Pwr xFB	PT/Exp D	Rand Var +1	
			Consist A	MM 3400	

Hit hard on his off days: three 3-ER outings were 56% of 16 ER all season. A 7.84 ERA in final 10 IP ballooned the bottom line before season-ending thoracic outlet surgery. Injuries have continually limited him and TOS has spotty track record for returns. Base skills are there, will health be? Worth $1 in AL-only leagues.

Yr Tm	W	L	Sv	IP	K	ERA	xERA	WHIP	oOPS	vL	vR	BF/G	Ctl	Dom	Cmd	FpK	SwK	G	L	F	H%	S%	hr/f	GS	APC	DOM%	DIS%	Sv%	LI	RAR	BPV	BPX	R$
12 KC	8	16	0	185	144	5.73	4.23	1.42	818	877	749	25.0	3.0	7.0	2.4	59%	9%	43	22	35	32%	61%	14%	32	94	19%	28%			-39.2	67	87	-$13
13 KC	5	2	2	70	82	1.92	2.89	0.82	533	607	452	4.5	2.2	10.5	4.8	69%	14%	35	19	46	22%	86%	11%	0	18			40	0.92	16.9	143	187	$12
14																																	
15 KC	1	1	1	51	49	3.73	4.14	1.28	737	748	730	4.4	2.8	8.7	3.1	63%	10%	36	18	46	31%	76%	10%	0	18			50	0.87	1.4	94	112	-$1
16 KC	2	3	0	37	40	3.86	3.74	1.07	703	524	823	3.8	2.2	9.6	4.4	62%	14%	36	15	48	28%	71%	13%	0	15			0	1.21	1.5	129	153	$0
1st Half	1	1	0	31	35	2.90	3.59	0.94	641	446	764	3.7	2.0	10.2	5.0	59%	15%	34	13	53	26%	76%	10%	0	14			0	1.18	4.9	140	167	$2
2nd Half	1	2	0	6	5	8.53	4.59	1.74	970	808	1110	4.1	2.8	7.1	2.5	76%	11%	45	25	30	35%	56%	33%	0	16			0	1.33	-3.4	74	88	-$9
17 Proj	**2**	**2**	**0**	**44**	**46**	**3.36**	**3.68**	**1.04**	**654**	**644**	**663**	**4.7**	**2.4**	**9.5**	**4.0**	**63%**	**13%**	**36**	**17**	**46**	**27%**	**73%**	**11%**	**0**						**4.5**	**121**	**144**	**$1**

PAUL SPORER

Hoffman,Jeff

Age: 24	Th: R	Role	SP	Health	A	LIMA Plan	D+
Ht: 6' 5"	Wt: 225	Type	Pwr GB	PT/Exp	D	Rand Var	+5
				Consist	F	MM	1101

0-4, 4.88 ERA in 31 IP at COL. Overall Ctl woes and gaudy OPS vR tanked results, but some intrigue: solid Dom vR, diverse arsenal with 4 velocity levels, and plus GB rate. Velocity alone isn't enough as his fastball sorely lacks command, but there is a foundation here. There will be bumps, but monitor this top prospect.

Yr	Tm	W	L	Sv	IP	K	ERA	xERA	WHIP	oOPS	vL	vR	BF/G	Ctl	Dom	Cmd	FpK	SwK	G	L	F	H%	S%	hr/f	GS	APC	DOM%	DIS%	Sv%	LI	RAR	BPV	BPX	R$
12																																		
13																																		
14																																		
15	aa	2	2	0	48	29	4.02	3.44	1.20				21.4	2.4	5.5	2.3						28%	68%								-0.3	61	73	-$2
16	COL *	6	13	0	150	118	5.37	5.72	1.63	881	858	906	22.2	3.8	7.1	1.8	58%	7%	50	22	28	34%	70%	23%	6	70	17%	83%	0	0.61	-21.8	37	44	-$12
1st Half		4	6	0	94	72	4.73	5.20	1.52				25.4	3.2	7.0	2.2						34%	72%	0%	0						-6.2	49	59	-$7
2nd Half		2	7	0	56	45	6.43	6.57	1.81	882	858	906	18.6	4.9	7.2	1.5	58%	7%	50	22	28	35%	67%	23%	6	70	17%	83%	0	0.61	-15.5	20	24	-$20
17	**Proj**	**6**	**8**	**0**	**116**	**88**	**4.83**	**4.55**	**1.50**	**695**	**684**	**707**	**21.1**	**3.5**	**6.8**	**1.9**	**58%**	**7%**	**50**	**22**	**28**	**32%**	**70%**	**13%**	**24**						**-9.2**	**56**	**67**	**-$6**

Holland,Derek

Age: 30	Th: L	Role	SP	Health	F	LIMA Plan	C
Ht: 6' 2"	Wt: 185	Type		PT/Exp	C	Rand Var	0
				Consist	B	MM	0103

Lost another tick off fastball, saw Dom sink further, and had no fantasy viability. Has just 203 IP over last three yrs since 2013 breakout. Previous HR issues have returned with vR work the main culprit. Path back to success is daunting, shift to multi-IP relief work might be on the way. Best hope? Recapturing velocity.

Yr	Tm	W	L	Sv	IP	K	ERA	xERA	WHIP	oOPS	vL	vR	BF/G	Ctl	Dom	Cmd	FpK	SwK	G	L	F	H%	S%	hr/f	GS	APC	DOM%	DIS%	Sv%	LI	RAR	BPV	BPX	R$
12	TEX	12	7	0	175	145	4.67	4.08	1.22	745	656	770	25.2	2.7	7.4	2.8	59%	8%	43	17	40	27%	68%	15%	27	95	30%	22%	0	0.81	-14.2	83	108	$4
13	TEX	10	9	0	213	189	3.42	3.78	1.29	711	671	722	27.1	2.7	8.0	3.0	63%	10%	41	23	36	32%	76%	9%	33	99	39%	21%			11.6	90	117	$10
14	TEX *	4	1	0	57	45	2.90	4.38	1.37	601	618	596	20.0	2.5	7.1	2.8	66%	10%	41	17	41	33%	82%	0%	5	95	80%	0%	0	0.66	5.9	74	89	$1
15	TEX	4	3	0	59	41	4.91	4.25	1.30	828	740	848	24.5	2.6	6.3	2.4	63%	7%	42	23	35	28%	68%	17%	10	91	20%	50%			-6.9	63	75	-$3
16	TEX	7	9	0	107	67	4.95	5.15	1.41	770	578	812	21.0	2.9	5.6	1.9	62%	8%	38	22	40	30%	68%	11%	20	83	15%	50%	0	0.74	-10.0	38	45	-$3
1st Half		5	5	0	73	43	5.20	5.44	1.42	773	530	829	22.5	3.1	5.3	1.7	61%	7%	36	22	42	30%	66%	10%	14	92	7%	43%			-9.1	26	32	-$3
2nd Half		2	4	0	35	24	4.41	4.56	1.38	763	696	778	18.3	2.6	6.2	2.4	64%	10%	43	22	35	31%	72%	13%	6	68	33%	67%	0	0.61	-1.0	63	75	-$4
17	**Proj**	**9**	**9**	**0**	**138**	**97**	**4.62**	**4.64**	**1.35**	**782**	**674**	**808**	**23.7**	**2.7**	**6.3**	**2.4**	**63%**	**9%**	**41**	**21**	**38**	**30%**	**70%**	**12%**	**24**						**-7.2**	**60**	**72**	**-$1**

Holland,Greg

Age: 31	Th: R	Role	RP	Health	B	LIMA Plan	B+
Ht: 5' 11"	Wt: 200	Type	Pwr	PT/Exp	C	Rand Var	-5
				Consist	D	MM	4520

Out since late Sept 2015 with TJS, but should be ready for 2017. Lost some velocity ahead of injury and command fell apart, but SwK held at elite level. Ks are enough to hold some value even as non-closer, but without return of mid-90s fastball, there isn't much to see here. Speculate, but don't pay for past results.

Yr	Tm	W	L	Sv	IP	K	ERA	xERA	WHIP	oOPS	vL	vR	BF/G	Ctl	Dom	Cmd	FpK	SwK	G	L	F	H%	S%	hr/f	GS	APC	DOM%	DIS%	Sv%	LI	RAR	BPV	BPX	R$
12	KC	7	4	16	67	91	2.96	3.31	1.37	653	577	712	4.3	4.6	12.2	2.7	50%	13%	45	18	36	36%	78%	3%	0	17			80	1.41	8.8	120	156	$10
13	KC	2	1	47	67	103	1.21	2.10	0.87	479	512	439	3.8	2.4	13.8	5.7	58%	17%	39	27	33	30%	89%	7%	0	16			94	1.34	22.0	201	262	$31
14	KC	1	3	46	62	90	1.44	2.29	0.91	472	494	444	3.7	2.9	13.0	4.5	57%	15%	48	17	35	28%	87%	7%	0	15			96	1.21	17.7	182	217	$26
15	KC	3	2	32	45	49	3.83	3.88	1.46	692	777	615	4.0	5.2	9.9	1.9	63%	15%	49	22	29	32%	73%	6%	0	15			86	1.23	0.7	63	75	$11
16																																		
1st Half																																		
2nd Half																																		
17	**Proj**	**3**	**2**	**10**	**58**	**73**	**3.08**	**3.20**	**1.13**	**572**	**594**	**549**	**3.8**	**3.7**	**11.3**	**3.1**	**58%**	**16%**	**45**	**22**	**33**	**30%**	**72%**	**6%**	**0**						**7.9**	**127**	**151**	**$7**

Hoyt,James

Age: 30	Th: R	Role	RP	Health	A	LIMA Plan	C+
Ht: 6' 5"	Wt: 220	Type	Pwr xGB	PT/Exp	D	Rand Var	+5
				Consist	C	MM	4500

1-1, 4.50 ERA in 22 IP at HOU. Grinded 5 yrs in MiLB, independent, and winter lgs to make MLB. Filthy mid-80s slider is primary pitch and drives big Dom seen in debut. Aug HR trouble (4 in 9 IP) quelled in Sept. (1 in 13) as slider was unhittable. If 94-95 mph fastball develops, setup is an option and maybe more.

Yr	Tm	W	L	Sv	IP	K	ERA	xERA	WHIP	oOPS	vL	vR	BF/G	Ctl	Dom	Cmd	FpK	SwK	G	L	F	H%	S%	hr/f	GS	APC	DOM%	DIS%	Sv%	LI	RAR	BPV	BPX	R$
12																																		
13	aa	0	1	1	33	26	3.44	2.08	1.13				5.9	4.1	7.3	1.8						24%	68%								1.7	87	114	-$2
14	a/a	3	3	7	60	61	3.95	5.18	1.62				5.1	3.9	9.3	2.4						38%	77%								-1.5	76	91	-$1
15	aaa	0	1	9	49	50	4.06	4.07	1.42				4.4	2.1	9.3	4.3						39%	69%								-0.6	136	162	-$1
16	HOU *	5	4	29	77	98	2.74	2.44	1.07	707	702	709	4.2	3.5	11.5	3.3	62%	15%	54	17	29	27%	79%	33%	0	17			88	0.63	13.8	128	152	$21
1st Half		3	3	20	39	53	2.28	1.91	1.05				4.4	4.0	12.1	3.0						27%	81%	0%	0						9.3	139	165	$26
2nd Half		2	1	9	38	45	3.22	3.00	1.08	707	702	709	4.1	2.9	10.8	3.7	62%	15%	54	17	29	28%	76%	33%	0	17			82	0.63	4.5	119	142	$15
17	**Proj**	**2**	**2**	**0**	**44**	**55**	**3.35**	**3.10**	**1.25**	**602**	**612**	**594**	**4.5**	**3.2**	**11.3**	**3.5**	**62%**	**15%**	**54**	**17**	**29**	**34%**	**75%**	**9%**	**0**						**4.5**	**148**	**176**	**$0**

Hudson,Daniel

Age: 30	Th: R	Role	RP	Health	B	LIMA Plan	C
Ht: 6' 4"	Wt: 220	Type	Pwr	PT/Exp	D	Rand Var	+4
				Consist	A	MM	2320

An impossibly-bad mid-season stretch (26 ER in 9.7 IP) did irreparable damage to ERA, but showed lingering 9th inning upside otherwise (1.60 ERA in 50.7 IP; 8.5 Dom). In fact, Dom/SwK in the 2nd half alone shows why we care. Bottom line will scare many, but worth a $1 look.

Yr	Tm	W	L	Sv	IP	K	ERA	xERA	WHIP	oOPS	vL	vR	BF/G	Ctl	Dom	Cmd	FpK	SwK	G	L	F	H%	S%	hr/f	GS	APC	DOM%	DIS%	Sv%	LI	RAR	BPV	BPX	R$
12	ARI	3	2	0	45	37	7.35	4.34	1.63	910	994	807	22.4	2.4	7.3	3.1	56%	10%	37	27	36	37%	57%	17%	9	89	22%	33%			-18.6	83	108	-$11
13																																		
14	ARI	0	1	0	3	2	13.50	4.22	1.50	769	500	1200	4.3	0.0	6.8	0.0	54%	8%	45	18	36	42%	0%	0%	0	16			0	0.68	-3.2	145	172	-$4
15	ARI	4	3	4	68	71	3.86	3.78	1.32	691	624	743	4.5	3.3	9.4	2.8	57%	13%	43	22	35	32%	73%	10%	1	18	0%	0%	67	1.11	0.9	101	121	$1
16	ARI	3	2	5	60	58	5.22	4.22	1.44	753	791	719	3.8	3.3	8.7	2.6	56%	12%	41	27	32	34%	64%	10%	0	16			71	1.16	-7.7	86	102	-$2
1st Half		1	1	1	32	25	3.69	4.34	1.07	585	689	486	3.8	3.1	7.1	2.3	57%	11%	44	20	35	25%	66%	6%	0	16			100	1.11	1.9	66	78	$2
2nd Half		2	1	4	29	33	6.91	4.08	1.85	913	895	928	3.9	3.5	10.4	3.0	55%	14%	38	34	28	44%	63%	16%	0	16			67	1.21	-9.6	109	130	-$7
17	**Proj**	**3**	**2**	**16**	**51**	**50**	**3.84**	**3.92**	**1.32**	**702**	**716**	**689**	**4.4**	**3.2**	**8.9**	**2.8**	**56%**	**13%**	**41**	**26**	**33**	**32%**	**74%**	**13%**	**0**						**2.2**	**94**	**112**	**$5**

Hughes,Phil

Age: 31	Th: R	Role	SP	Health	F	LIMA Plan	C
Ht: 6' 5"	Wt: 230	Type	Con FB	PT/Exp	A	Rand Var	+3
				Consist	B	MM	1101

Shoulder surgery mercifully ended season in June. HR suppression drove 2014, but they're back in full force since. Fading fastball velocity has pushed him to the cutter, which yields same SwK and weaker contact. Health plus even more cutter usage could be key to any hope, but heed career 4.53 ERA as starter. No thanks.

Yr	Tm	W	L	Sv	IP	K	ERA	xERA	WHIP	oOPS	vL	vR	BF/G	Ctl	Dom	Cmd	FpK	SwK	G	L	F	H%	S%	hr/f	GS	APC	DOM%	DIS%	Sv%	LI	RAR	BPV	BPX	R$
12	NYY	16	13	0	191	165	4.19	4.30	1.26	765	610	928	25.5	2.2	7.8	3.6	66%	9%	32	20	48	30%	74%	12%	32	101	25%	28%			-4.1	91	119	$9
13	NYY	4	14	0	146	121	5.19	4.44	1.46	832	863	793	21.4	2.6	7.5	2.9	71%	9%	31	23	46	34%	68%	11%	29	85	24%	34%	0	0.76	-23.8	74	96	-$10
14	MIN	16	10	0	210	186	3.52	3.39	1.13	674	619	733	26.7	0.7	8.0	11.6	73%	9%	36	23	40	34%	70%	6%	32	95	47%	9%			5.7	139	166	$15
15	MIN	11	9	0	155	94	4.40	4.42	1.29	812	761	869	24.1	0.9	5.4	5.9	72%	6%	35	24	40	31%	73%	13%	25	84	8%	24%	0	0.73	-8.5	86	102	$1
16	MIN	1	7	0	59	34	5.95	5.24	1.51	851	956	797	21.6	2.0	5.2	2.6	70%	7%	35	24	41	33%	64%	13%	11	76	0%	64%	0	0.72	-12.8	53	63	-$8
1st Half		1	7	0	59	34	5.95	5.24	1.51	851	956	797	21.6	2.0	5.2	2.6	70%	7%	35	24	41	33%	64%	13%	11	76	0%	64%	0	0.72	-12.8	53	63	-$8
2nd Half																																		
17	**Proj**	**5**	**8**	**0**	**102**	**74**	**4.74**	**4.51**	**1.34**	**789**	**767**	**807**	**22.9**	**1.6**	**6.5**	**4.2**	**71%**	**8%**	**35**	**23**	**42**	**33%**	**69%**	**11%**	**18**						**-6.9**	**88**	**105**	**-$3**

Hutchison,Drew

Age: 26	Th: R	Role	SP	Health	D	LIMA Plan	C
Ht: 6' 2"	Wt: 165	Type	Pwr FB	PT/Exp	B	Rand Var	+3
				Consist	B	MM	0201

1-0, 5.25 ERA in 24 IP at TOR/PIT. Just 11 IP at PIT so this episode of The Ray Searage Renaissance is incomplete. Still has a live arm that can miss bats (SwK firm despite Dom drop), but HRs were key even before the league went HR-wild. Too young to ignore, but must prove something before going beyond $1-2.

Yr	Tm	W	L	Sv	IP	K	ERA	xERA	WHIP	oOPS	vL	vR	BF/G	Ctl	Dom	Cmd	FpK	SwK	G	L	F	H%	S%	hr/f	GS	APC	DOM%	DIS%	Sv%	LI	RAR	BPV	BPX	R$
12	TOR *	7	4	0	75	59	4.18	4.31	1.33	756	750	763	22.4	2.7	7.1	2.6	54%	9%	45	25	30	31%	72%	15%	11	90	18%	27%			-1.5	65	85	$0
13	a/a	0	4	0	27	26	7.16	6.09	1.75				17.4	2.7	8.7	3.3						42%	57%								-10.8	85	111	-$9
14	TOR	11	13	0	185	184	4.48	3.84	1.26	723	811	615	24.6	2.9	9.0	3.1	59%	11%	36	19	45	31%	67%	10%	32	95	28%	34%			-16.9	96	115	$2
15	TOR	13	5	0	150	129	5.57	4.22	1.48	825	750	906	22.1	2.6	7.7	2.9	64%	10%	40	24	36	35%	65%	13%	28	84	29%	46%	0	0.73	-29.8	86	102	-$8
16	2 TM *	8	6	0	162	127	5.18	5.14	1.48	903	957	866	20.5	3.5	7.1	2.0	59%	11%	35	22	43	32%	68%	19%	3	45	0%	0%	0	0.47	-19.7	42	50	-$7
1st Half		7	3	0	94	79	4.11	3.93	1.33	957	875	1061	23.0	3.6	7.6	2.1	55%	7%	35	20	45	29%	72%	22%	1	58	0%	0%	0	0.90	1.0	65	78	$4
2nd Half		1	3	0	68	48	6.66	6.80	1.69	882	1011	820	18.0	3.3	6.4	1.9	61%	13%	35	23	42	34%	65%	18%	2	41	0%	0%	0	0.35	-20.7	11	13	-$22
17	**Proj**	**6**	**7**	**0**	**116**	**95**	**4.52**	**4.70**	**1.47**	**821**	**854**	**791**	**20.9**	**3.1**	**7.4**	**2.4**	**60%**	**11%**	**38**	**22**	**40**	**33%**	**74%**	**12%**	**24**						**-4.7**	**65**	**78**	**-$4**

PAUL SPORER

Iglesias,Raisel

Age: 27	Th: R	Role: RP	Health: D	LIMA Plan: B+
Ht: 6' 2"	Wt: 185	Type: Pwr	PT/Exp: D	Rand Var: -4
			Consist: A	MM: 2321

More shoulder woes DL'd him in May, joined pen in June return an effort to stay whole. PRO: Multi-inning force with stellar 2nd half ERA/WHIP and save opps; velocity uptick, dominance vR, BPV all suggest closer-in-waiting. CON: Volatile Ctl, lucky 2nd half H%/S% say he's not yet this good. Yet. With health he could soar.

Yr Tm	W	L	Sv	IP	K	ERA	xERA	WHIP	oOPS	vL	vR	BF/G	Ctl	Dom	Cmd	FpK	SwK	G	L	F	H%	S%	hr/f	GS	APC	DOM%	DIS%	Sv%	LI	RAR	BPV	BPX	R$
12 for	4	9	12	83	70	3.77	3.63	1.38				11.6	4.0	7.6	1.9						31%	73%								2.5	74	97	$4
13																																	
14																																	
15 CIN *	4	10	0	124	122	4.26	3.75	1.21	682	753	618	20.9	2.7	8.8	3.3	62%	13%	47	21	32	30%	68%	14%	16	87	38%	25%	0	0.72	-4.6	93	110	$2
16 CIN	3	2	6	78	83	2.53	3.77	1.14	623	777	483	8.8	3.0	9.5	3.2	54%	12%	41	21	38	29%	82%	9%	5	34	20%	20%	75	1.01	16.1	110	131	$9
1st Half	1	1	0	36	36	3.03	4.05	1.32	745	801	679	16.7	2.5	9.1	3.6	46%	10%	36	23	41	33%	83%	12%	5	64	20%	20%	0	0.94	5.1	109	130	$2
2nd Half	2	1	6	43	47	2.11	3.52	0.98	514	749	343	6.3	3.4	9.9	2.9	60%	14%	45	19	36	25%	80%	5%	0	24			75	1.04	10.9	111	132	$16
17 Proj	**3**	**5**	**20**	**87**	**87**	**3.30**	**3.76**	**1.19**	**664**	**793**	**549**	**10.9**	**3.1**	**9.0**	**3.0**	**57%**	**12%**	**44**	**21**	**35**	**29%**	**75%**	**10%**	**3**						**9.5**	**102**	**121**	**$12**

Iwakuma,Hisashi

Age: 36	Th: R	Role: SP	Health: F	LIMA Plan: B+
Ht: 6' 3"	Wt: 210	Type:	PT/Exp: A	Rand Var: 0
			Consist: B	MM: 2105

Health fueled IP rebound as wins kept R$ afloat, but that's the good news. FpK and SwK off all season, cutting into once-elite Cmd. Lost GB% touch as H% rose; 1.3 hr/9 a career-worst. More velocity decline, age leave him closer to the edge. Pitchability points to an uptick, but... DN: 4.50 ERA, more DL time.

Yr Tm	W	L	Sv	IP	K	ERA	xERA	WHIP	oOPS	vL	vR	BF/G	Ctl	Dom	Cmd	FpK	SwK	G	L	F	H%	S%	hr/f	GS	APC	DOM%	DIS%	Sv%	LI	RAR	BPV	BPX	R$
12 SEA	9	5	2	125	101	3.16	3.74	1.28	718	716	720	17.3	3.1	7.3	2.3	60%	10%	52	20	27	28%	81%	17%	16	64	19%	38%	100	0.59	13.2	77	101	$9
13 SEA	14	6	0	220	185	2.66	3.29	1.01	630	599	667	26.2	1.7	7.6	4.4	63%	11%	49	18	34	26%	80%	12%	33	94	48%	21%			32.6	117	152	$29
14 SEA	15	9	0	179	154	3.52	3.00	1.05	642	702	573	25.3	1.1	7.7	7.3	66%	10%	50	21	29	30%	70%	13%	28	91	43%	14%			4.9	139	165	$16
15 SEA	9	5	0	130	111	3.54	3.34	1.06	674	703	645	25.8	1.5	7.7	5.3	68%	11%	50	18	31	28%	73%	15%	20	93	40%	25%			6.7	127	152	$11
16 SEA	16	12	0	199	147	4.12	4.43	1.33	776	766	785	25.3	2.1	6.6	3.2	64%	8%	41	21	38	31%	73%	12%	33	90	24%	30%			1.8	82	98	$8
1st Half	8	6	0	108	77	4.43	4.59	1.35	811	876	755	26.8	2.0	6.4	3.2	63%	9%	39	21	40	31%	72%	13%	17	93	18%	29%			-3.2	78	93	$6
2nd Half	8	6	0	91	70	3.74	4.24	1.30	734	630	820	23.8	2.2	6.9	3.2	65%	8%	43	22	35	32%	74%	10%	16	88	31%	31%			5.0	87	104	$10
17 Proj	**14**	**9**	**0**	**181**	**145**	**3.71**	**3.89**	**1.20**	**716**	**711**	**720**	**24.3**	**1.8**	**7.2**	**4.0**	**65%**	**9%**	**46**	**20**	**34**	**30%**	**74%**	**13%**	**30**						**10.7**	**104**	**124**	**$12**

Jackson,Edwin

Age: 33	Th: R	Role: RP	Health: D	LIMA Plan: D+
Ht: 6' 2"	Wt: 205	Type: Pwr	PT/Exp: C	Rand Var: +2
			Consist: B	MM: 0101

Stuff is long gone. Now a well-travelled journeyman / innings-eater for non-contending rotations that have been savaged by injuries and need 2nd half help. But regardless of the trend your eyes land on—Ctl, Cmd, OPS vR, DOM%/DIS%—the "Suitcase" nickname has been well-earned.

Yr Tm	W	L	Sv	IP	K	ERA	xERA	WHIP	oOPS	vL	vR	BF/G	Ctl	Dom	Cmd	FpK	SwK	G	L	F	H%	S%	hr/f	GS	APC	DOM%	DIS%	Sv%	LI	RAR	BPV	BPX	R$
12 WAS	10	11	0	190	168	4.03	3.80	1.22	719	758	677	25.5	2.8	8.0	2.9	62%	13%	47	17	36	29%	70%	12%	31	96	35%	32%			-0.4	94	123	$9
13 CHC	8	18	0	175	135	4.98	3.98	1.46	775	816	741	25.1	3.0	6.9	2.3	56%	9%	51	20	28	33%	66%	10%	31	95	16%	35%			-24.1	72	94	-$9
14 CHC	6	15	0	141	123	6.33	4.32	1.64	869	930	816	22.6	4.0	7.9	2.0	55%	11%	39	26	35	35%	62%	12%	27	89	11%	56%	0	0.77	-45.0	50	59	-$19
15 2 NL	4	3	1	56	40	3.07	4.41	1.17	622	565	657	4.9	3.4	6.5	1.9	54%	11%	41	22	37	25%	75%	7%	0	19			50	0.77	6.1	44	52	$2
16 2 NL	5	7	0	84	61	5.89	5.36	1.58	857	786	914	17.8	4.4	6.5	1.5	53%	10%	40	21	39	31%	66%	14%	13	67	15%	54%	0	0.78	-17.6	17	20	-$9
1st Half	0	1	0	11	7	5.91	6.20	1.78	917	757	999	5.9	5.1	5.9	1.2	60%	9%	35	12	53	32%	71%	11%	0	24			0	0.81	-2.3	-17	-20	-$5
2nd Half	5	6	0	73	54	5.89	5.24	1.55	848	789	898	25.1	4.3	6.6	1.5	52%	10%	41	22	37	30%	65%	14%	13	93	15%	54%			-15.4	22	27	-$9
17 Proj	**5**	**9**	**0**	**102**	**80**	**4.94**	**4.69**	**1.45**	**787**	**791**	**783**	**13.6**	**3.7**	**7.1**	**1.9**	**55%**	**11%**	**43**	**22**	**35**	**31%**	**68%**	**11%**	**11**						**-9.4**	**48**	**57**	**-$5**

Jansen,Kenley

Age: 29	Th: R	Role: RP	Health: C	LIMA Plan: C
Ht: 6' 6"	Wt: 260	Type: Pwr xFB	PT/Exp: A	Rand Var: -3
			Consist: A	MM: 5530

Same dominant self. Nothing changed besides H% luck and health, as more IP and save opps drove R$ into the stratosphere. 2015 FB% spike held, but outstanding command again held HR damage in check. ERA looks regression-bound, still a one-pitch wonder, still a DL risk. And still elite.

Yr Tm	W	L	Sv	IP	K	ERA	xERA	WHIP	oOPS	vL	vR	BF/G	Ctl	Dom	Cmd	FpK	SwK	G	L	F	H%	S%	hr/f	GS	APC	DOM%	DIS%	Sv%	LI	RAR	BPV	BPX	R$
12 LA	5	3	25	65	99	2.35	2.63	0.85	504	518	490	3.9	3.0	13.7	4.5	61%	15%	33	19	48	24%	78%	10%	0	16			78	1.31	13.3	175	229	$22
13 LA	4	3	28	77	111	1.88	2.29	0.86	509	531	494	3.9	2.1	13.0	6.2	64%	16%	37	24	39	29%	83%	10%	0	17			88	1.33	18.8	192	251	$24
14 LA	2	3	44	65	101	2.76	2.43	1.13	610	710	521	3.9	2.6	13.9	5.3	67%	17%	35	28	37	38%	78%	9%	0	16			90	1.27	7.9	193	230	$21
15 LA	2	1	36	52	80	2.41	2.46	0.78	513	566	459	3.7	1.4	13.8	10.0	70%	18%	35	11	54	29%	77%	10%	0	15			95	1.22	10.0	223	266	$22
16 LA	3	2	47	69	104	1.83	2.48	0.67	446	542	352	3.5	1.4	13.6	9.5	68%	18%	30	15	55	26%	76%	6%	0	14			89	1.21	19.9	214	255	$33
1st Half	3	2	24	34	42	1.34	2.97	0.68	435	514	362	3.5	1.3	11.2	8.4	67%	17%	31	15	54	24%	82%	3%	0	13			89	1.47	11.8	175	208	$33
2nd Half	0	0	23	35	62	2.31	2.06	0.66	456	568	343	3.6	1.5	15.9	10.3	69%	19%	29	16	55	28%	70%	9%	0	15			88	0.96	8.1	253	301	$33
17 Proj	**3**	**2**	**43**	**65**	**98**	**2.46**	**2.62**	**0.86**	**539**	**627**	**454**	**3.6**	**1.7**	**13.5**	**7.8**	**68%**	**18%**	**32**	**17**	**51**	**31%**	**75%**	**8%**	**0**						**13.9**	**207**	**246**	**$26**

Jeffress,Jeremy

Age: 29	Th: R	Role: RP	Health: B	LIMA Plan: C+
Ht: 6' 1"	Wt: 205	Type: Pwr xGB	PT/Exp: C	Rand Var: -4
			Consist: B	MM: 3210

Nailed all but one save opp before losing 9th-inning role at July trade deadline. Kept runs off the board despite deteriorating 2nd half Ctl until late Aug DUI arrest shelved him for a month. Sub-par Dom, ERA/xERA gap put closer-worthiness in question. Killer sinker, ERA history, sucesss vR keep him roster-worthy.

Yr Tm	W	L	Sv	IP	K	ERA	xERA	WHIP	oOPS	vL	vR	BF/G	Ctl	Dom	Cmd	FpK	SwK	G	L	F	H%	S%	hr/f	GS	APC	DOM%	DIS%	Sv%	LI	RAR	BPV	BPX	R$
12 KC *	5	4	3	73	63	5.80	4.59	1.62	838	594	1029	6.3	4.8	7.9	1.6	53%	9%	48	26	26	35%	62%	0%	0	22			43	0.64	-16.0	66	87	-$9
13 TOR *	2	0	7	38	35	1.78	3.43	1.43	592	284	829	4.6	4.5	8.3	1.8	60%	12%	69	23	8	32%	88%	50%	0	19			88	0.67	9.7	86	113	$3
14 2 TM *	5	2	5	74	65	2.33	3.68	1.44	709	967	509	5.1	3.7	7.9	2.1	60%	7%	59	26	16	34%	83%	7%	0	16			63	0.85	12.9	90	107	$4
15 MIL	5	0	0	68	67	2.65	3.08	1.26	666	752	617	4.0	2.9	8.9	3.0	56%	12%	58	24	18	32%	81%	15%	0	15			0	1.15	11.0	117	139	$4
16 2 TM	3	2	27	58	42	2.33	3.64	1.26	656	906	475	4.1	2.8	6.5	2.3	61%	10%	60	24	16	30%	82%	7%	0	15			96	1.08	13.3	80	95	$14
1st Half	1	2	21	35	26	2.60	3.63	1.30	712	938	466	4.1	2.1	6.8	3.3	62%	11%	56	25	19	33%	81%	10%	0	14			95	1.20	6.8	99	119	$18
2nd Half	2	0	6	23	16	1.93	3.66	1.20	566	802	482	4.0	3.9	6.2	1.6	58%	8%	67	21	12	27%	82%	0%	0	15			100	0.89	6.5	52	62	$7
17 Proj	**4**	**2**	**8**	**65**	**54**	**2.48**	**3.57**	**1.30**	**652**	**848**	**535**	**4.2**	**3.3**	**7.4**	**2.2**	**58%**	**10%**	**61**	**23**	**16**	**31%**	**81%**	**8%**	**0**						**13.7**	**82**	**98**	**$6**

Jenkins,Tyrell

Age: 24	Th: R	Role: SP	Health: A	LIMA Plan: D
Ht: 6' 4"	Wt: 180	Type: GB	PT/Exp: D	Rand Var: 0
			Consist: B	MM: 0000

2-4, 5.88 in 52 IP at ATL. Athletic prospect with improving repertoire stymied again in effort to miss more bats. Maintained historical GB tilt following June MLB debut. But velocity dropped all season, as deficient Dom and suspect Ctl continued in wrong direction. He has time, but looks like a marginal bullpen arm for now.

Yr Tm	W	L	Sv	IP	K	ERA	xERA	WHIP	oOPS	vL	vR	BF/G	Ctl	Dom	Cmd	FpK	SwK	G	L	F	H%	S%	hr/f	GS	APC	DOM%	DIS%	Sv%	LI	RAR	BPV	BPX	R$
12																																	
13																																	
14																																	
15 a/a	8	9	0	138	78	4.03	4.44	1.55				24.2	4.2	5.1	1.2						31%	74%								-1.2	41	48	-$5
16 ATL *	11	7	0	136	74	4.17	5.39	1.68	893	884	895	19.7	4.7	4.9	1.1	49%	6%	48	18	34	32%	77%	19%	8	64	0%	63%	0	0.59	0.3	20	24	-$5
1st Half	6	4	0	74	45	3.92	5.49	1.70	953	1027	913	18.7	3.8	5.5	1.4	52%	5%	48	23	29	35%	78%	22%	0	40			0	0.47	2.4	36	43	-$3
2nd Half	5	3	0	61	29	4.48	5.27	1.64	879	852	891	21.0	5.7	4.2	0.7	49%	7%	48	17	35	27%	77%	19%	8	74	0%	63%	0	0.65	-2.2	3	4	-$7
17 Proj	**3**	**2**	**0**	**44**	**24**	**4.38**	**5.75**	**1.62**	**751**	**754**	**747**	**21.4**	**4.6**	**4.9**	**1.1**	**49%**	**7%**	**48**	**17**	**35**	**31%**	**74%**	**7%**	**9**						**-1.0**	**-10**	**-12**	**-$5**

Jennings,Dan

Age: 30	Th: L	Role: RP	Health: C	LIMA Plan: B+
Ht: 6' 3"	Wt: 190	Type: Pwr xGB	PT/Exp: D	Rand Var: -5
			Consist: A	MM: 2200

Already extreme GBer has become more extreme over the past two seasons. Rode season-long S% to ERA excellence, as ability to smother HR damage and contain LHBs and RHBs alike kept him in innings. 2nd half Dom and Ctl improvement was interesting; history says they're fleeting. Watch for now.

Yr Tm	W	L	Sv	IP	K	ERA	xERA	WHIP	oOPS	vL	vR	BF/G	Ctl	Dom	Cmd	FpK	SwK	G	L	F	H%	S%	hr/f	GS	APC	DOM%	DIS%	Sv%	LI	RAR	BPV	BPX	R$
12 MIA *	2	3	2	71	50	3.34	4.23	1.47	771	788	753	4.7	3.7	6.3	1.7	48%	7%	45	20	35	32%	78%	9%	0	15			50	0.62	5.9	58	76	-$1
13 MIA *	6	6	1	66	58	3.24	3.42	1.39	714	745	675	4.2	3.9	7.9	2.0	53%	11%	49	20	32	32%	76%	3%	0	14			25	1.24	5.0	86	112	$1
14 MIA	0	2	0	40	38	1.34	3.92	1.54	738	753	724	3.9	3.8	8.5	2.2	52%	12%	49	20	32	36%	95%	8%	0	15			0	0.75	12.0	77	92	-$1
15 CHW	2	3	0	56	46	3.99	3.68	1.40	664	635	687	4.6	3.8	7.3	1.9	57%	9%	65	16	19	32%	71%	9%	0	18			0	0.77	-0.2	72	85	-$3
16 CHW	4	3	1	61	46	2.08	4.31	1.40	679	654	694	4.0	4.2	6.8	1.6	53%	9%	54	24	22	31%	85%	3%	0	16			33	0.95	15.8	43	51	$3
1st Half	3	1	0	34	20	1.85	4.87	1.44	690	672	698	5.2	4.8	5.3	1.1	49%	7%	54	25	21	29%	86%	0%	0	21			0	0.81	9.8	-2	-2	$4
2nd Half	1	2	1	27	26	2.36	3.66	1.35	664	636	688	3.2	3.4	8.8	2.6	59%	11%	54	22	24	34%	83%	6%	0	12			50	1.07	6.0	99	118	$3
17 Proj	**3**	**3**	**0**	**58**	**48**	**3.38**	**4.09**	**1.42**	**704**	**692**	**714**	**3.9**	**3.9**	**7.5**	**1.9**	**55%**	**10%**	**55**	**21**	**24**	**32%**	**77%**	**8%**	**0**						**5.8**	**64**	**76**	**-$1**

JOCK THOMPSON

Jepsen,Kevin

Age:	32	Th:	R	Role	RP	PT/Exp	C	Rand Var	+2
Ht:	6' 3"	Wt:	230	Type	Pwr	Consist	C	MM	0200
						Health	C	LIMA Plan	D+

Stepped in as closer a week into season, but ineffectiveness led to his removal in early June. Red flags abound: SwK, Dom, velocity dropped noticeably for second straight year; he uncharacteristically struggled vR; GB% plummeted. Unlikely to be that bad again, but doubtful he gets another shot at saves.

Yr Tm	W	L	Sv	IP	K	ERA	xERA	WHIP	oOPS	vL	vR	BF/G	Ctl	Dom	Cmd	FpK	SwK	G	L	F	H%	S%	hr/f	GS	APC	DOM%	DIS%	Sv%	LI	RAR	BPV	BPX	R$
12 LAA *	5	4	4	70	65	3.08	2.72	1.14	647	744	552	3.8	2.6	8.4	3.2	52%	9%	35	23	42	30%	73%	6%	0	14			67	1.16	8.0	112	146	$7
13 LAA	1	3	0	36	36	4.50	4.10	1.53	769	865	679	3.6	3.5	9.0	2.6	53%	9%	40	20	39	37%	71%	7%	0	15			0	1.12	-2.8	86	111	-$5
14 LAA	0	2	2	65	75	2.63	2.93	1.05	547	628	470	3.5	3.2	10.4	3.3	65%	13%	48	20	33	27%	77%	8%	0	14			50	1.04	8.9	127	151	$5
15 2 AL	3	6	15	70	59	2.33	4.03	1.13	560	653	449	3.8	3.5	7.6	2.2	57%	11%	46	20	35	25%	82%	7%	0	16			75	1.45	14.1	67	80	$11
16 2 AL	2	6	7	50	35	5.98	5.61	1.67	939	1086	854	3.9	3.8	6.3	1.7	57%	9%	31	26	43	32%	70%	17%	0	15			64	1.00	-11.0	20	24	-$6
1st Half	2	5	7	31	22	6.16	5.59	1.76	978	1100	908	4.3	3.5	6.5	1.8	57%	8%	30	28	42	35%	70%	16%	0	16			64	1.17	-7.5	29	35	-$3
2nd Half	0	1	0	19	13	5.68	5.64	1.53	871	1064	758	3.3	4.3	6.2	1.4	57%	9%	33	23	44	27%	71%	19%	0	13			0	0.78	-3.5	7	8	-$9
17 Proj	**2**	**5**	**0**	**58**	**48**	**4.14**	**4.66**	**1.38**	**743**	**827**	**678**	**3.6**	**3.6**	**7.5**	**2.1**	**58%**	**10%**	**38**	**23**	**39**	**30%**	**74%**	**12%**	**0**						**0.4**	**53**	**63**	**-$3**

Jimenez,Ubaldo

Age:	33	Th:	R	Role	SP	PT/Exp	A	Rand Var	+1
Ht:	6' 4"	Wt:	200	Type	Pwr	Consist	B	MM	1203
						Health	B	LIMA Plan	D+

Suffered through brutal 1st half, as he couldn't get ball over the plate, and H% didn't help. Ended season on high note, with 2.45 ERA, 3.0 Cmd over final 7 GS, but he's teased us before with these flashes. Shaky Ctl, high DIS% show he's extremely flammable, which more than offsets Dom potential.

Yr Tm	W	L	Sv	IP	K	ERA	xERA	WHIP	oOPS	vL	vR	BF/G	Ctl	Dom	Cmd	FpK	SwK	G	L	F	H%	S%	hr/f	GS	APC	DOM%	DIS%	Sv%	LI	RAR	BPV	BPX	R$
12 CLE	9	17	0	177	143	5.40	5.03	1.61	817	854	778	26.0	4.8	7.3	1.5	52%	8%	38	23	38	30%	69%	12%	31	101	13%	48%			-30.2	16	21	-$16
13 CLE	13	9	0	183	194	3.30	3.66	1.33	684	661	708	24.3	3.9	9.6	2.4	58%	9%	44	20	36	31%	78%	9%	32	99	28%	25%			12.7	88	114	$11
14 BAL	6	9	0	125	116	4.81	4.47	1.52	737	779	683	22.1	5.5	8.3	1.5	55%	7%	41	22	37	29%	70%	11%	22	92	14%	50%	0	0.74	-16.5	20	23	-$7
15 BAL	12	10	0	184	168	4.11	3.81	1.36	728	702	756	24.7	3.3	8.2	2.5	60%	8%	49	22	29	32%	72%	13%	32	96	22%	25%			-3.3	85	101	$4
16 BAL	8	12	1	142	125	5.44	4.73	1.56	772	885	690	22.0	4.6	7.9	1.7	58%	9%	49	18	33	33%	66%	11%	25	86	12%	48%	100	0.73	-21.9	46	55	-$8
1st Half	5	8	0	80	72	6.95	5.18	1.92	883	997	797	22.9	5.4	8.1	1.5	56%	8%	50	21	30	38%	64%	13%	16	89	6%	69%	0	0.76	-27.3	28	33	-$20
2nd Half	3	4	1	62	53	3.48	4.17	1.10	599	697	533	20.8	3.5	7.7	2.2	60%	10%	48	14	38	24%	71%	9%	9	82	22%	11%	100	0.69	5.4	70	84	$7
17 Proj	**7**	**9**	**0**	**131**	**117**	**4.62**	**4.44**	**1.43**	**730**	**781**	**685**	**22.2**	**4.2**	**8.1**	**1.9**	**58%**	**8%**	**47**	**19**	**34**	**31%**	**69%**	**11%**	**25**						**-6.9**	**56**	**67**	**-$2**

Johnson,Jim

Age:	34	Th:	R	Role	RP	PT/Exp	C	Rand Var	0
Ht:	6' 5"	Wt:	250	Type	Pwr xGB	Consist	B	MM	2220
						Health	C	LIMA Plan	C+

Thrust into closer role in mid-July, and successfully converted final 18 Sv chances. Closer experience, ability to keep ball down work in his favor, though consistently below-average SwK indicates he won't sustain Dom gains. Recent ERA history shows that when strikeouts disappear, he walks a pretty thin line.

Yr Tm	W	L	Sv	IP	K	ERA	xERA	WHIP	oOPS	vL	vR	BF/G	Ctl	Dom	Cmd	FpK	SwK	G	L	F	H%	S%	hr/f	GS	APC	DOM%	DIS%	Sv%	LI	RAR	BPV	BPX	R$
12 BAL	2	1	51	69	41	2.49	3.41	1.02	556	581	526	3.8	2.0	5.4	2.7	57%	7%	62	16	21	25%	76%	7%	0	14			94	1.29	12.9	84	109	$27
13 BAL	3	8	50	70	56	2.94	3.17	1.28	699	740	653	3.9	2.3	7.2	3.1	61%	9%	58	20	21	32%	79%	11%	0	15			85	1.39	8.0	103	134	$22
14 2 AL	5	2	2	53	42	7.09	4.66	1.95	861	941	776	4.9	5.9	7.1	1.2	63%	8%	58	20	22	37%	63%	14%	0	18			67	0.60	-22.0	4	5	-$12
15 2 NL	2	6	10	67	50	4.46	3.67	1.46	743	675	793	4.0	2.7	6.8	2.5	61%	8%	62	17	21	34%	70%	11%	0	15			59	1.41	-4.1	89	106	-$1
16 ATL	2	6	20	65	68	3.06	3.17	1.19	631	590	671	4.1	2.8	9.5	3.4	57%	8%	55	22	23	32%	74%	8%	0	16			87	1.29	9.0	128	152	$11
1st Half	1	4	1	28	26	4.55	3.15	1.23	691	797	591	4.1	2.6	8.5	3.3	54%	8%	57	27	16	32%	63%	17%	0	16			50	1.23	-1.2	117	139	-$2
2nd Half	1	2	19	37	42	1.95	3.18	1.16	587	441	733	4.1	2.9	10.2	3.5	59%	8%	54	19	28	32%	83%	4%	0	17			90	1.34	10.2	137	163	$21
17 Proj	**3**	**5**	**22**	**65**	**55**	**3.94**	**3.78**	**1.37**	**696**	**674**	**717**	**4.1**	**3.2**	**7.6**	**2.4**	**59%**	**8%**	**58**	**20**	**22**	**33%**	**71%**	**9%**	**0**						**2.0**	**86**	**103**	**$7**

Jones,Nate

Age:	31	Th:	R	Role	RP	PT/Exp	D	Rand Var	-3
Ht:	6' 5"	Wt:	185	Type	Pwr	Consist	C	MM	5511
						Health	F	LIMA Plan	B

Nasty stuff on display all year, but reached new heights in 2nd half, when FpK and GB% also took a step forward. Combination of elite Dom, stellar Ctl, and GB tilt ensure that, at the very least, should be top-notch LIMA option, with potential for massive value. If ninth inning gig were to come available... UP: 30 Sv

Yr Tm	W	L	Sv	IP	K	ERA	xERA	WHIP	oOPS	vL	vR	BF/G	Ctl	Dom	Cmd	FpK	SwK	G	L	F	H%	S%	hr/f	GS	APC	DOM%	DIS%	Sv%	LI	RAR	BPV	BPX	R$
12 CHW	8	0	0	72	65	2.39	4.00	1.38	686	528	774	4.6	4.0	8.2	2.0	55%	11%	46	23	32	31%	84%	6%	0	18			0	1.19	14.4	62	81	$5
13 CHW	4	5	0	78	89	4.15	2.87	1.22	659	710	621	4.5	3.0	10.3	3.4	61%	14%	51	21	28	33%	66%	9%	0	18			0	1.36	-2.8	133	173	$1
14 CHW	0	0	0	0	0	0.00	0.00	0.00		3000	2000	2.5	0.0	0.0	0.0						0%	20%	0%	0	15			0	1.50	0.0	-22	-26	-$5
15 CHW	2	2	0	19	27	3.32	2.51	0.95	695	567	770	3.8	2.8	12.8	4.5	59%	16%	46	14	41	21%	85%	33%	0	15			0	1.17	1.5	177	211	-$1
16 CHW	5	3	3	71	80	2.29	2.97	0.89	552	667	477	3.9	1.9	10.2	5.3	64%	15%	46	21	33	26%	80%	12%	0	14			25	1.53	16.5	156	185	$12
1st Half	4	2	2	38	36	2.61	3.40	0.82	524	709	421	3.7	1.7	8.5	5.1	59%	13%	40	22	38	23%	71%	8%	0	13			33	1.43	7.4	127	151	$13
2nd Half	1	1	1	33	44	1.93	2.46	0.96	583	628	547	4.0	2.2	12.1	5.5	69%	16%	53	20	27	29%	89%	20%	0	15			17	1.65	9.1	190	227	$10
17 Proj	**5**	**3**	**6**	**73**	**85**	**2.91**	**3.02**	**1.06**	**600**	**646**	**569**	**4.1**	**2.6**	**10.5**	**4.0**	**62%**	**14%**	**49**	**21**	**30**	**29%**	**75%**	**11%**	**0**						**11.4**	**145**	**172**	**$9**

Karns,Nathan

Age:	29	Th:	R	Role	SP	PT/Exp	B	Rand Var	+3
Ht:	6' 5"	Wt:	230	Type	Pwr	Consist	C	MM	1401
						Health	B	LIMA Plan	C

Started strong, with 3.43 ERA, 2.7 Cmd through 10 GS. Ctl soon escaped him though, and helped cost his rotation spot, even before back strain effectively ended season in late July. Has proven to be solid source of Dom, but health history, inability to find strike zone suggest betting against return to sub-4.00 ERA.

Yr Tm	W	L	Sv	IP	K	ERA	xERA	WHIP	oOPS	vL	vR	BF/G	Ctl	Dom	Cmd	FpK	SwK	G	L	F	H%	S%	hr/f	GS	APC	DOM%	DIS%	Sv%	LI	RAR	BPV	BPX	R$
12																																	
13 WAS *	10	7	0	145	130	4.48	4.73	1.43	1060	1266	845	23.6	3.5	8.1	2.3	64%	10%	36	31	33	32%	73%	36%	3	82	0%	67%			-10.9	59	77	-$2
14 TAM *	10	10	0	157	134	6.62	5.65	1.65	661	384	859	24.3	4.2	7.7	1.8	49%	10%	43	13	43	35%	60%	23%	2	103	50%	50%			-55.9	44	53	-$21
15 TAM	7	5	0	147	145	3.67	3.89	1.28	699	690	708	23.0	3.4	8.9	2.6	58%	10%	42	22	37	30%	76%	13%	26	90	15%	27%	0	0.80	5.2	87	104	$6
16 SEA	6	2	1	94	101	5.15	4.32	1.48	760	628	875	19.0	4.3	9.6	2.2	57%	11%	40	23	37	34%	67%	11%	15	76	40%	27%	100	0.62	-11.2	76	90	-$4
1st Half	6	2	1	86	92	4.50	4.24	1.43	737	631	834	22.1	4.1	9.6	2.4	57%	11%	40	24	37	33%	70%	10%	15	89	40%	27%	100	0.68	-3.3	81	96	-$2
2nd Half	0	0	0	8	9	11.88	5.17	2.04	971	583	1177	8.4	6.5	9.7	1.5	57%	15%	48	20	32	38%	40%	25%	0	34			0	0.43	-7.9	26	31	-$17
17 Proj	**8**	**5**	**0**	**123**	**127**	**4.35**	**4.18**	**1.41**	**750**	**679**	**818**	**22.6**	**3.9**	**9.3**	**2.4**	**58%**	**10%**	**40**	**23**	**37**	**32%**	**72%**	**12%**	**23**						**-2.4**	**81**	**96**	**$0**

Kazmir,Scott

Age:	33	Th:	L	Role	SP	PT/Exp	A	Rand Var	+2
Ht:	6' 0"	Wt:	195	Type	Pwr	Consist	A	MM	2303
						Health	D	LIMA Plan	B+

Spent most of year racking up strikeouts, but for third straight season, skills fell off dramatically in 2nd half. Posted ugly 4.7 Dom, 7% SwK in four Aug starts before landing on DL with neck pain. Positive hr/f regression should help him bounce back, though it's clear he can't be counted on for full season of production.

Yr Tm	W	L	Sv	IP	K	ERA	xERA	WHIP	oOPS	vL	vR	BF/G	Ctl	Dom	Cmd	FpK	SwK	G	L	F	H%	S%	hr/f	GS	APC	DOM%	DIS%	Sv%	LI	RAR	BPV	BPX	R$
12																																	
13 CLE	10	9	0	158	162	4.04	3.53	1.32	735	573	794	23.2	2.7	9.2	3.4	61%	11%	41	23	36	34%	73%	12%	29	95	28%	34%			-3.5	113	147	$4
14 OAK	15	9	0	190	164	3.55	3.60	1.16	648	673	641	24.3	2.4	7.8	3.3	62%	10%	44	19	37	29%	71%	8%	32	93	50%	22%			4.6	98	116	$13
15 2 AL	7	11	0	183	155	3.10	4.03	1.21	678	774	645	24.6	2.9	7.6	2.6	61%	11%	43	20	37	28%	79%	10%	31	95	35%	29%			19.5	80	95	$13
16 LA	10	6	0	136	134	4.56	4.20	1.36	762	647	805	22.7	3.4	8.8	2.6	60%	10%	41	23	36	31%	71%	15%	26	92	23%	42%			-6.1	86	102	$2
1st Half	7	3	0	95	101	4.37	3.95	1.27	718	619	763	23.9	3.4	9.6	2.8	60%	11%	41	21	37	30%	70%	15%	17	96	29%	29%			-2.1	100	119	$6
2nd Half	3	3	0	42	33	4.97	4.80	1.56	856	751	880	20.4	3.5	7.1	2.1	60%	8%	40	27	34	33%	72%	16%	9	85	11%	67%			-4.0	53	63	-$8
17 Proj	**9**	**8**	**0**	**145**	**135**	**4.08**	**4.08**	**1.30**	**721**	**671**	**737**	**23.8**	**3.1**	**8.4**	**2.7**	**61%**	**10%**	**42**	**22**	**36**	**30%**	**72%**	**12%**	**25**						**2.0**	**87**	**104**	**$4**

Kela,Keone

Age:	24	Th:	R	Role	RP	PT/Exp	D	Rand Var	+5
Ht:	6' 1"	Wt:	215	Type	Pwr	Consist	B	MM	3510
						Health	D	LIMA Plan	C+

April elbow injury required surgery, which cost him three months. Upon return, had a few blowups and shaky Ctl, but swing-and-miss stuff was still there. Bad luck severely inflated ERA, which, combined with injury, will suppress his price tag. That should create buying opportunity for an intriguing high-upside arm.

Yr Tm	W	L	Sv	IP	K	ERA	xERA	WHIP	oOPS	vL	vR	BF/G	Ctl	Dom	Cmd	FpK	SwK	G	L	F	H%	S%	hr/f	GS	APC	DOM%	DIS%	Sv%	LI	RAR	BPV	BPX	R$
12																																	
13																																	
14 aa	2	1	5	39	47	2.22	2.45	1.34				4.5	6.3	11.1	1.8						28%	83%								7.3	114	135	$2
15 TEX	7	5	1	60	68	2.39	3.01	1.16	615	739	527	3.6	2.7	10.1	3.8	58%	14%	51	21	29	32%	82%	9%	0	15			25	1.21	11.7	139	166	$7
16 TEX	5	1	0	34	45	6.09	3.57	1.38	779	577	872	4.3	4.5	11.9	2.6	55%	12%	44	22	34	32%	59%	21%	0	18			0	0.84	-8.0	115	137	-$3
1st Half	1	0	0	6	12	7.11	2.59	1.58	982	585	1228	4.3	4.3	17.1	4.0	53%	12%	43	21	36	41%	71%	60%	0	20			0	0.72	-2.3	213	254	-$4
2nd Half	4	1	0	28	33	5.86	3.82	1.34	727	569	792	4.3	4.6	10.7	2.4	55%	12%	44	22	34	31%	56%	13%	0	18			0	0.87	-5.7	92	110	-$3
17 Proj	**6**	**3**	**2**	**58**	**69**	**3.58**	**3.45**	**1.21**	**624**	**590**	**641**	**4.0**	**4.0**	**10.7**	**2.7**	**56%**	**13%**	**47**	**21**	**32**	**30%**	**71%**	**8%**	**0**						**4.4**	**109**	**129**	**$4**

BRIAN RUDD

Kelley,Shawn

Age: 33 | Th: R | Role: RP | Ht: 6' 2" | Wt: 215 | Type: Pwr xFB
Health: C | PT/Exp: C | Consist: A | LIMA Plan: B+ | Rand Var: -1 | MM: 4511

Q: How does a 49% FB% pitcher with a 14% hr/f fire a sub-2.75 ERA? A: Lots and lots of strike ones and strike threes. xERA/BPV trends are peaking about as high as we can expect for a 33-year-old. Along with health grade, be skeptical of a full repeat, but he'll remain plenty valuable.

Yr Tm	W	L	Sv	IP	K	ERA	xERA	WHIP	oOPS	vL	vR	BF/G	Ctl	Dom	Cmd	FpK	SwK	G	L	F	H%	S%	hr/f	GS	APC	DOM%	DIS%	Sv%	LI	RAR	BPV	BPX	R$
12 SEA *	4	4	6	64	65	2.52	2.83	1.12	717	747	701	4.2	2.7	9.1	3.4	60%	12%	29	20	51	29%	81%	8%	0	16			67	1.00	11.8	115	150	$8
13 NYY	4	2	0	53	71	4.39	3.42	1.31	729	760	707	4.0	3.9	12.0	3.1	65%	12%	33	21	46	33%	71%	13%	0	17			0	1.33	-3.4	122	159	-$1
14 NYY	3	6	4	52	67	4.53	3.30	1.26	663	612	709	3.7	3.5	11.7	3.4	61%	15%	34	23	44	34%	65%	9%	0	15			57	1.33	-5.0	128	152	$0
15 SD	2	2	0	51	63	2.45	3.04	1.09	596	667	536	3.9	2.6	11.0	4.2	72%	15%	43	19	38	31%	81%	9%	0	15			0	0.88	9.5	149	177	$3
16 WAS	3	2	7	58	80	2.64	2.92	0.90	635	792	539	3.3	1.7	12.4	7.3	66%	16%	36	14	49	28%	81%	14%	0	14			78	1.23	11.1	191	227	$10
1st Half	1	1	4	31	46	2.90	2.58	0.94	661	639	673	3.5	1.7	13.4	7.7	68%	16%	39	18	43	31%	76%	14%	0	14			80	1.25	4.9	210	251	$10
2nd Half	2	1	3	27	34	2.33	3.31	0.85	605	930	363	3.2	1.7	11.3	6.8	63%	16%	34	11	55	24%	89%	14%	0	13			75	1.21	6.2	171	204	$10
17 Proj	**4**	**4**	**7**	**73**	**94**	**3.04**	**3.16**	**1.03**	**630**	**735**	**555**	**3.4**	**2.4**	**11.6**	**4.9**	**66%**	**15%**	**37**	**17**	**46**	**29%**	**76%**	**12%**	**0**						**10.3**	**161**	**191**	**$10**

Kelly,Joe

Age: 29 | Th: R | Role: RP | Ht: 6' 1" | Wt: 175 | Type: Pwr
Health: D | PT/Exp: C | Consist: A | LIMA Plan: A | Rand Var: +4 | MM: 4401

4-0, 5.18 ERA in 40 IP at BOS. Most important number in this box? Column: GS; Row: 2nd Half. Career splits concur with the entire row—as a RP, he more consistently gets ahead of hitters, strikes them out, and walks less than as starter. Health is key, but could be a bullpen force. UP: 80 IP, 100 K

Yr Tm	W	L	Sv	IP	K	ERA	xERA	WHIP	oOPS	vL	vR	BF/G	Ctl	Dom	Cmd	FpK	SwK	G	L	F	H%	S%	hr/f	GS	APC	DOM%	DIS%	Sv%	LI	RAR	BPV	BPX	R$
12 STL *	7	12	0	179	112	3.35	4.17	1.40	740	917	607	21.0	2.8	5.6	2.0	60%	8%	52	21	27	32%	77%	11%	16	71	13%	44%	0	0.78	14.6	57	74	$3
13 STL	10	5	0	124	79	2.69	4.17	1.35	694	691	696	14.4	3.2	5.7	1.8	55%	8%	51	21	28	30%	83%	9%	15	53	0%	47%	0	0.87	18.1	46	60	$7
14 2 TM	6	4	0	96	66	4.20	4.00	1.35	693	689	695	24.4	3.9	6.2	1.6	57%	7%	55	21	24	28%	70%	11%	17	93	18%	35%			-5.5	38	45	-$2
15 BOS *	11	7	0	153	124	4.76	4.53	1.44	768	702	836	22.5	3.3	7.3	2.2	62%	8%	46	25	29	32%	68%	12%	25	95	8%	40%			-15.2	61	73	-$3
16 BOS *	5	1	2	75	83	4.02	4.90	1.57	828	899	791	8.9	3.8	10.0	2.6	52%	11%	47	28	25	38%	76%	18%	6	37	17%	67%	67	1.11	1.6	88	105	-$1
1st Half	3	1	0	41	43	6.47	6.93	1.97	1001	1112	942	19.8	5.3	9.4	1.8	49%	11%	49	26	26	41%	68%	22%	6	79	17%	67%			-11.6	47	56	-$10
2nd Half	2	0	2	34	40	1.00	2.42	1.09	558	568	552	4.9	2.0	10.7	5.3	57%	11%	44	33	23	34%	92%	10%	0	19			67	1.25	13.2	175	209	$10
17 Proj	**5**	**3**	**0**	**73**	**78**	**3.25**	**3.25**	**1.21**	**666**	**666**	**666**	**7.7**	**2.5**	**9.6**	**3.8**	**56%**	**9%**	**48**	**26**	**26**	**33%**	**75%**	**11%**	**0**						**8.4**	**131**	**156**	**$4**

Kennedy,Ian

Age: 32 | Th: R | Role: SP | Ht: 6' 0" | Wt: 195 | Type: Pwr FB
Health: B | PT/Exp: A | Consist: A | LIMA Plan: C+ | Rand Var: 0 | MM: 1305

The vanilla ice cream of starters: consistent, durable, but never spectacular. Flyball jump, 2nd half Dom slide could be the initial soft spots, but he's got the time/tools (FpK, K history) to stave off a full meltdown. In the right context—a hot afternoon; the end game—one can count on him to still hit the spot.

Yr Tm	W	L	Sv	IP	K	ERA	xERA	WHIP	oOPS	vL	vR	BF/G	Ctl	Dom	Cmd	FpK	SwK	G	L	F	H%	S%	hr/f	GS	APC	DOM%	DIS%	Sv%	LI	RAR	BPV	BPX	R$
12 ARI	15	12	0	208	187	4.02	4.06	1.30	775	790	759	27.2	2.4	8.1	3.4	65%	11%	37	21	42	32%	73%	11%	33	102	42%	27%			-0.1	96	126	$9
13 2 NL	7	10	0	181	163	4.91	4.14	1.40	781	828	736	25.6	3.6	8.1	2.2	62%	10%	38	23	39	31%	68%	13%	31	100	26%	35%			-23.4	64	83	-$6
14 SD	13	13	0	201	207	3.63	3.56	1.29	698	689	706	25.6	3.1	9.3	3.0	64%	11%	40	23	38	32%	73%	8%	33	103	33%	15%			2.8	100	119	$9
15 SD	9	15	0	168	174	4.28	3.74	1.30	815	842	788	23.8	2.8	9.3	3.3	61%	11%	38	23	39	31%	74%	17%	30	97	13%	27%			-6.5	108	129	$4
16 KC	11	11	0	196	184	3.68	4.40	1.22	722	709	735	24.8	3.0	8.5	2.8	62%	10%	33	20	47	28%	77%	13%	33	102	30%	27%			12.3	81	97	$14
1st Half	6	7	0	94	93	4.04	4.30	1.22	741	745	736	24.5	3.1	8.9	2.9	63%	10%	33	18	48	27%	77%	16%	16	100	44%	31%			1.8	89	106	$12
2nd Half	5	4	0	102	91	3.35	4.50	1.23	705	678	735	25.1	3.0	8.0	2.7	61%	10%	33	21	46	28%	78%	10%	17	105	18%	24%			10.5	75	89	$16
17 Proj	**11**	**12**	**0**	**189**	**183**	**3.87**	**4.17**	**1.26**	**746**	**747**	**746**	**24.0**	**3.0**	**8.7**	**2.9**	**62%**	**10%**	**36**	**21**	**43**	**30%**	**75%**	**13%**	**32**						**7.4**	**90**	**108**	**$9**

Kershaw,Clayton

Age: 29 | Th: L | Role: SP | Ht: 6' 3" | Wt: 215 | Type: Pwr
Health: D | PT/Exp: A | Consist: A | LIMA Plan: C | Rand Var: -4 | MM: 5505

That 1st half pace was nothing short of stunning, as 2015's otherwordly numbers only got BETTER. But then back woes hit, sidelined him for 2+ months, and cost him some swing-and-miss upon his return. Age, track record are impeccable, though health grade can't be ignored. Atop 2017's High Risk/High Reward chart.

Yr Tm	W	L	Sv	IP	K	ERA	xERA	WHIP	oOPS	vL	vR	BF/G	Ctl	Dom	Cmd	FpK	SwK	G	L	F	H%	S%	hr/f	GS	APC	DOM%	DIS%	Sv%	LI	RAR	BPV	BPX	R$
12 LA	14	9	0	228	229	2.53	3.23	1.02	593	570	599	27.3	2.5	9.1	3.6	65%	11%	47	19	34	27%	78%	8%	33	105	67%	6%			41.7	121	157	$36
13 LA	16	9	0	236	232	1.83	2.93	0.92	521	477	532	27.5	2.0	8.8	4.5	65%	12%	46	23	31	26%	82%	6%	33	104	67%	3%			59.2	130	169	$44
14 LA	21	3	0	198	239	1.77	2.27	0.86	521	477	531	27.7	1.4	10.8	7.7	69%	15%	52	19	29	29%	81%	7%	27	101	81%	4%			48.2	187	223	$40
15 LA	16	7	0	233	301	2.13	2.31	0.88	521	554	511	27.0	1.6	11.6	7.2	68%	16%	50	22	28	29%	79%	10%	33	103	76%	3%			52.6	194	231	$47
16 LA	12	4	0	149	172	1.69	2.43	0.72	472	309	529	25.9	0.7	10.4	15.6	70%	16%	49	20	30	26%	80%	8%	21	98	76%	5%			45.9	196	233	$35
1st Half	11	2	0	121	145	1.79	2.32	0.73	475	349	516	27.6	0.7	10.8	16.1	70%	17%	50	21	29	27%	78%	7%	16	104	81%	6%			35.9	204	243	$43
2nd Half	1	2	0	28	27	1.29	2.94	0.71	459	182	595	20.6	0.6	8.7	13.5	69%	13%	48	18	34	24%	89%	8%	5	78	60%	0%			10.0	165	197	$4
17 Proj	**15**	**6**	**0**	**189**	**216**	**2.00**	**2.67**	**0.86**	**518**	**375**	**566**	**24.5**	**1.5**	**10.3**	**7.1**	**68%**	**15%**	**49**	**20**	**31**	**28%**	**80%**	**8%**	**28**						**51.0**	**174**	**207**	**$38**

Keuchel,Dallas

Age: 29 | Th: L | Role: SP | Ht: 6' 3" | Wt: 205 | Type: xGB
Health: B | PT/Exp: A | Consist: B | LIMA Plan: A | Rand Var: +3 | MM: 3205

Death by paper cuts? Small shifts in Ctl, Dom, GB%, hr/f and S% added up to a cool $34 loss from 2015 earnings. Began to recover some in 2nd half, until shoulder barked and he missed Sept. Steady FpK, SwK and elite xGB profile provide apt foundation that should lead to at least a partial rebound if health cooperates.

Yr Tm	W	L	Sv	IP	K	ERA	xERA	WHIP	oOPS	vL	vR	BF/G	Ctl	Dom	Cmd	FpK	SwK	G	L	F	H%	S%	hr/f	GS	APC	DOM%	DIS%	Sv%	LI	RAR	BPV	BPX	R$
12 HOU *	9	12	0	178	81	4.56	4.48	1.40	823	750	844	23.4	2.9	4.1	1.4	55%	6%	52	17	31	29%	69%	16%	16	87	13%	63%			-12.0	25	33	-$5
13 HOU	6	10	0	154	123	5.15	3.72	1.54	812	750	832	22.0	3.0	7.2	2.4	63%	9%	56	21	23	35%	69%	17%	22	81	18%	36%	0	0.90	-24.4	81	106	-$11
14 HOU	12	9	0	200	146	2.93	3.07	1.18	655	595	674	27.9	2.2	6.6	3.0	65%	9%	64	17	19	30%	76%	10%	29	104	41%	17%			20.1	102	121	$15
15 HOU	20	8	0	232	216	2.48	2.80	1.02	575	461	606	27.6	2.0	8.4	4.2	61%	11%	62	19	20	28%	79%	14%	33	106	42%	6%			42.3	137	164	$37
16 HOU	9	12	0	168	144	4.55	3.65	1.29	736	603	772	27.0	2.6	7.7	3.0	63%	10%	57	19	24	31%	67%	16%	26	103	35%	19%			-7.5	104	124	$3
1st Half	5	9	0	107	93	5.13	3.77	1.42	789	663	826	27.2	2.9	7.8	2.7	63%	10%	57	20	23	33%	66%	19%	17	103	24%	24%			-12.4	99	118	-$1
2nd Half	4	3	0	61	51	3.54	3.45	1.05	635	472	674	26.6	2.1	7.5	3.6	63%	10%	56	17	27	27%	69%	13%	9	102	56%	11%			4.9	113	135	$10
17 Proj	**12**	**10**	**0**	**181**	**150**	**3.63**	**3.45**	**1.18**	**672**	**561**	**702**	**26.2**	**2.3**	**7.5**	**3.2**	**63%**	**10%**	**59**	**18**	**23**	**29%**	**71%**	**14%**	**28**						**12.4**	**109**	**129**	**$13**

Kimbrel,Craig

Age: 29 | Th: R | Role: RP | Ht: 6' 0" | Wt: 205 | Type: Pwr
Health: B | PT/Exp: A | Consist: A | LIMA Plan: B | Rand Var: -1 | MM: 5530

Torn meniscus required July surgery, wasn't the same after. Couldn't find the plate (2nd half Ctl) and was squared up mercilessly when he did (LD%, hr/f). But Dom remained strong, better FpK points to fewer walks, and FB% spike due largely to horrific April. That smell? Could well be a buying opportunity.

Yr Tm	W	L	Sv	IP	K	ERA	xERA	WHIP	oOPS	vL	vR	BF/G	Ctl	Dom	Cmd	FpK	SwK	G	L	F	H%	S%	hr/f	GS	APC	DOM%	DIS%	Sv%	LI	RAR	BPV	BPX	R$
12 ATL	3	1	42	63	116	1.01	1.43	0.65	358	331	387	3.7	2.0	16.7	8.3	71%	20%	49	19	32	28%	89%	10%	0	15			93	1.29	23.3	273	356	$34
13 ATL	4	3	50	67	98	1.21	2.12	0.88	487	574	393	3.8	2.7	13.2	4.9	56%	14%	47	24	29	28%	91%	10%	0	15			93	1.30	22.0	189	247	$32
14 ATL	0	3	47	62	95	1.61	2.36	0.91	430	425	436	3.9	3.8	13.9	3.7	58%	17%	41	23	35	26%	83%	5%	0	17			92	1.44	16.2	166	198	$26
15 SD	4	2	39	59	87	2.58	2.61	1.04	569	629	508	3.9	3.3	13.2	4.0	61%	16%	46	20	34	30%	80%	14%	0	17			91	1.49	10.1	171	204	$22
16 BOS	2	6	31	53	83	3.40	3.33	1.09	539	514	559	3.9	5.1	14.1	2.8	68%	15%	29	23	48	27%	70%	8%	0	16			94	1.50	5.2	123	146	$16
1st Half	1	3	17	32	48	2.53	3.03	0.94	504	528	483	3.9	3.4	13.5	4.0	71%	16%	30	19	52	27%	75%	6%	0	17			89	1.36	6.5	160	190	$20
2nd Half	1	3	14	21	35	4.71	3.86	1.33	587	476	689	3.8	7.7	15.0	1.9	65%	14%	29	29	42	25%	65%	13%	0	16			100	1.68	-1.4	69	82	$10
17 Proj	**2**	**5**	**38**	**58**	**91**	**2.92**	**2.63**	**0.96**	**510**	**500**	**519**	**3.5**	**3.7**	**14.1**	**3.8**	**64%**	**16%**	**37**	**23**	**40**	**27%**	**72%**	**11%**	**0**						**9.1**	**169**	**201**	**$21**

Kintzler,Brandon

Age: 32 | Th: R | Role: RP | Ht: 6' 0" | Wt: 185 | Type: Con xGB
Health: F | PT/Exp: D | Consist: F | LIMA Plan: C+ | Rand Var: 0 | MM: 2030

0-2, 3.15 ERA with 17 Sv in 54 IP at MIL. Jim Johnson once notched two 50-Sv seasons with this same dance. Can he? PRO: Improved FpK makes Ctl believable; elite GB%. CON: SwK/Dom unconvincing; skills history inconsistent; age + health outlook cloudy. Might have the role, but don't bank on him keeping it.

Yr Tm	W	L	Sv	IP	K	ERA	xERA	WHIP	oOPS	vL	vR	BF/G	Ctl	Dom	Cmd	FpK	SwK	G	L	F	H%	S%	hr/f	GS	APC	DOM%	DIS%	Sv%	LI	RAR	BPV	BPX	R$
12 MIL *	3	3	9	64	38	3.94	4.46	1.53	732	744	717	5.3	3.3	5.4	1.6	70%	10%	51	27	22	34%	73%	9%	0	21			90	0.64	0.6	53	69	-$1
13 MIL	3	3	0	77	58	2.69	3.03	1.06	567	540	586	4.3	1.9	6.8	3.6	60%	9%	57	24	18	29%	74%	5%	0	15			0	1.05	11.2	107	139	$5
14 MIL	3	3	0	58	31	3.24	3.87	1.34	781	648	859	3.7	2.5	4.8	1.9	60%	7%	57	18	25	29%	81%	17%	0	14			0	1.04	3.6	54	65	-$1
15 MIL *	1	2	0	26	17	6.46	6.58	1.94	1021	1017	1000	5.4	3.3	6.0	1.8	56%	9%	63	29	8	42%	64%	50%	0	21			0	0.59	-8.0	47	56	-$9
16 MIN *	4	3	17	70	43	3.69	4.18	1.32	705	673	730	4.5	1.5	5.5	3.7	65%	7%	62	18	20	33%	73%	14%	0	15			81	1.01	4.3	88	105	$7
1st Half	4	1	4	39	24	3.59	3.90	1.20	677	627	702	4.6	1.3	5.5	4.2	61%	8%	65	11	24	30%	73%	24%	0	15			80	0.81	2.9	94	112	$7
2nd Half	0	2	13	31	19	3.82	3.86	1.47	725	694	754	4.4	1.8	5.6	3.2	68%	6%	60	23	17	36%	73%	6%	0	16			81	1.17	1.4	90	108	$7
17 Proj	**3**	**3**	**28**	**58**	**36**	**3.49**	**3.94**	**1.33**	**723**	**661**	**767**	**4.3**	**2.0**	**5.5**	**2.7**	**63%**	**7%**	**59**	**19**	**21**	**32%**	**75%**	**10%**	**0**						**5.0**	**82**	**98**	**$10**

BRENT HERSHEY

Kluber,Corey

Age: 31	Th: R	Role SP	Health B	LIMA Plan C	
Ht: 6' 4"	Wt: 215	Type Pwr	PT/Exp A	Rand Var 0	
			Consist A	MM 3405	

Early-season "struggle" due to depressed S%, quickly cured by the arrival of Andrew Miller (note 20% spike in 2nd half). That's not to say that his ERA is an illusion, just a bit bullpen-aided to help erase those littered baserunners. This is one of the safest, highly skilled elite starters out there.

Yr	Tm	W	L	Sv	IP	K	ERA	xERA	WHIP	oOPS	vL	vR	BF/G	Ctl	Dom	Cmd	FpK	SwK	G	L	F	H%	S%	hr/f	GS	APC	DOM%	DIS%	Sv%	LI	RAR	BPV	BPX	R$
12	CLE *	13	12	0	188	157	4.53	4.91	1.52	834	860	801	24.7	3.2	7.5	2.3	57%	12%	45	22	33	35%	71%	13%	12	90	8%	42%			-12.1	64	84	-$5
13	CLE	11	5	0	147	136	3.85	3.25	1.26	729	751	704	23.4	2.0	8.3	4.1	60%	11%	46	26	29	33%	72%	12%	24	88	33%	25%	0	0.73	0.3	119	155	$6
14	CLE	18	9	0	236	269	2.44	2.74	1.09	624	687	553	28.0	1.9	10.3	5.3	64%	12%	48	21	31	33%	80%	7%	34	103	62%	12%			37.7	158	189	$30
15	CLE	9	16	0	222	245	3.49	3.07	1.05	650	740	549	27.7	1.8	9.9	5.4	63%	13%	42	22	36	30%	70%	11%	32	102	47%	13%			13.0	150	178	$22
16	CLE	18	9	0	215	227	3.14	3.45	1.06	631	648	615	26.9	2.4	9.5	4.0	62%	13%	44	19	36	28%	74%	11%	32	100	59%	16%			27.8	129	153	$29
1st Half		8	8	0	114	114	3.79	3.39	1.04	603	614	593	26.9	2.1	9.0	4.2	64%	12%	49	19	32	29%	65%	9%	17	98	59%	18%			5.6	131	157	$24
2nd Half		10	1	0	101	113	2.41	3.51	1.07	663	684	642	26.8	2.7	10.1	3.8	61%	14%	39	19	42	27%	85%	12%	15	101	60%	13%			22.2	126	151	$35
17	**Proj**	**16**	**10**	**0**	**218**	**233**	**3.26**	**3.36**	**1.10**	**652**	**698**	**604**	**26.2**	**2.2**	**9.6**	**4.3**	**62%**	**13%**	**44**	**21**	**35**	**30%**	**74%**	**11%**	**33**						**24.9**	**135**	**161**	**$25**

Knebel,Corey

Age: 25	Th: R	Role RP	Health D	LIMA Plan C+	
Ht: 6' 3"	Wt: 220	Type Pwr	PT/Exp D	Rand Var +2	
			Consist B	MM 3410	

An off-season saves dark horse, he missed most of the 1st half with an oblique injury and then took a while to shake off the rust. Big Dom not fully supported by SwK and has a funky reverse platoon split, but 2nd half return of Ctl via gains in FpK and mid-90s fastball bode well. Watchable.

Yr	Tm	W	L	Sv	IP	K	ERA	xERA	WHIP	oOPS	vL	vR	BF/G	Ctl	Dom	Cmd	FpK	SwK	G	L	F	H%	S%	hr/f	GS	APC	DOM%	DIS%	Sv%	LI	RAR	BPV	BPX	R$
12																																		
13																																		
14	DET *	5	1	3	54	64	3.06	2.28	1.13	776	733	826	5.1	4.1	10.6	2.6	59%	9%	48	16	36	27%	74%	0%	0	21			50	0.37	4.6	119	142	$4
15	MIL *	1	2	6	66	76	3.67	3.92	1.27	744	764	728	4.2	3.3	10.4	3.2	58%	10%	49	20	31	32%	76%	20%	0	17			75	0.49	2.3	99	118	$2
16	MIL	1	4	2	33	38	4.68	4.13	1.47	708	510	909	4.1	4.4	10.5	2.4	61%	8%	42	21	37	35%	69%	9%	0	17			50	1.00	-2.0	89	106	-$3
1st Half		0	1	0	4	6	8.31	7.76	2.77	853	607	1136	4.8	12.5	12.5	1.0	50%	7%	42	8	50	49%	67%	0%	0	20			0	0.63	-2.2	-92	-110	-$8
2nd Half		1	3	2	28	32	4.13	3.72	1.27	679	488	868	4.0	3.2	10.2	3.2	64%	9%	42	23	35	32%	70%	11%	0	17			50	1.06	0.2	118	140	-$2
17	**Proj**	**3**	**3**	**2**	**58**	**62**	**3.57**	**3.58**	**1.19**	**643**	**537**	**737**	**4.3**	**3.3**	**9.7**	**2.9**	**61%**	**9%**	**45**	**22**	**33**	**29%**	**72%**	**11%**	**0**						**4.4**	**108**	**129**	**$2**

Koehler,Tom

Age: 31	Th: R	Role SP	Health A	LIMA Plan D+	
Ht: 6' 2"	Wt: 225	Type Pwr	PT/Exp A	Rand Var 0	
			Consist A	MM 0103	

Credited with a "quality start" in 53 of 96 GS over the past three seasons, yet according to BPX, he's never come close to being a league-average pitcher. In fact, since 2014, ERA/xERA/WHIP have been on a steady climb; Cmd and BPV just the opposite. Perhaps—preaching/choir, etc.—we need a new definition.

Yr	Tm	W	L	Sv	IP	K	ERA	xERA	WHIP	oOPS	vL	vR	BF/G	Ctl	Dom	Cmd	FpK	SwK	G	L	F	H%	S%	hr/f	GS	APC	DOM%	DIS%	Sv%	LI	RAR	BPV	BPX	R$
12	MIA *	12	12	0	164	130	5.28	5.74	1.67	896	818	941	19.9	4.0	7.1	1.8	61%	5%	24	27	49	35%	70%	20%	1	26	0%	100%	0	0.70	-25.6	41	53	-$15
13	MIA *	5	12	0	166	106	4.31	3.99	1.37	754	706	796	21.1	3.7	5.7	1.6	59%	8%	48	22	30	28%	70%	10%	23	78	13%	43%	0	0.72	-9.2	45	59	-$4
14	MIA	10	10	0	191	153	3.81	4.06	1.30	691	649	737	25.1	3.3	7.2	2.2	59%	9%	43	18	39	29%	72%	7%	32	92	25%	34%			-1.6	60	72	$4
15	MIA	11	14	0	187	137	4.08	4.52	1.37	739	760	717	25.0	3.7	6.6	1.8	58%	8%	46	18	36	29%	73%	11%	31	93	16%	35%	0	0.77	-2.8	43	51	$2
16	MIA	9	13	0	177	147	4.33	4.79	1.47	764	772	755	23.5	4.2	7.5	1.8	59%	10%	42	23	34	30%	73%	12%	33	94	21%	42%			-3.1	41	48	-$1
1st Half		6	7	0	87	73	4.45	4.91	1.54	755	843	669	24.2	4.9	7.6	1.6	58%	9%	44	23	33	32%	71%	7%	16	95	13%	25%			-2.8	27	32	-$1
2nd Half		3	6	0	90	74	4.22	4.68	1.39	772	712	849	22.8	3.6	7.4	2.1	61%	11%	41	23	36	29%	76%	16%	17	92	29%	59%			-0.3	55	65	$0
17	**Proj**	**9**	**12**	**0**	**174**	**137**	**4.49**	**4.68**	**1.42**	**755**	**747**	**763**	**23.2**	**3.9**	**7.1**	**1.8**	**59%**	**9%**	**44**	**21**	**35**	**30%**	**71%**	**11%**	**32**						**-6.3**	**45**	**54**	**-$2**

Krol,Ian

Age: 26	Th: L	Role RP	Health A	LIMA Plan A	
Ht: 6' 1"	Wt: 180	Type Pwr	PT/Exp D	Rand Var +2	
			Consist B	MM 3400	

Added a tick on his fastball that quietly propelled a nice growth season. SwK/Dom felt immediate effect, but FpK improved, too, and more ground balls helped to reduce blow-up potential. With some positive H% regression, could become deep-league relevant bullpen arm.

Yr	Tm	W	L	Sv	IP	K	ERA	xERA	WHIP	oOPS	vL	vR	BF/G	Ctl	Dom	Cmd	FpK	SwK	G	L	F	H%	S%	hr/f	GS	APC	DOM%	DIS%	Sv%	LI	RAR	BPV	BPX	R$
12																																		
13	WAS *	3	2	1	57	52	2.61	2.85	1.07	785	593	957	3.8	2.4	8.2	3.4	57%	7%	39	20	41	27%	81%	14%	0	15			20	1.18	8.8	103	134	$4
14	DET	0	0	1	33	28	4.96	4.34	1.68	906	764	1048	3.4	3.6	7.7	2.2	53%	8%	40	29	31	36%	76%	18%	0	14			25	1.24	-4.9	60	72	-$6
15	DET *	3	4	1	59	53	4.17	3.85	1.45	847	884	822	4.1	4.6	8.0	1.7	56%	9%	45	23	32	31%	71%	15%	0	16			20	0.87	-1.5	72	85	-$3
16	ATL	2	0	0	51	56	3.18	3.09	1.31	701	721	686	3.4	2.3	9.9	4.3	60%	11%	56	21	23	36%	78%	12%	0	14			0	1.22	6.4	150	178	$0
1st Half		1	0	0	22	26	2.86	2.84	1.23	688	476	829	3.5	2.9	10.6	3.7	67%	12%	53	26	21	33%	80%	18%	0	14			0	1.09	3.6	145	173	$2
2nd Half		1	0	0	29	30	3.41	3.29	1.38	709	864	576	3.4	1.9	9.3	5.0	55%	10%	58	17	25	38%	76%	9%	0	15			0	1.31	2.8	153	183	$0
17	**Proj**	**2**	**1**	**0**	**58**	**59**	**3.17**	**3.39**	**1.23**	**631**	**615**	**644**	**3.4**	**2.8**	**9.2**	**3.3**	**57%**	**10%**	**49**	**24**	**26**	**32%**	**75%**	**8%**	**0**						**7.3**	**119**	**141**	**$1**

Kuhl,Chad

Age: 24	Th: R	Role SP	Health B	LIMA Plan B+	
Ht: 6' 3"	Wt: 215	Type Con GB	PT/Exp D	Rand Var -1	
			Consist C	MM 1003	

5-4, 4.20 ERA in 71 IP at PIT. Threw strikes and didn't embarrass himself in debut as PIT covered some injury issues. Without a heavy GB lean, will need more swings/misses—as well as an out pitch against lefties—before a full endorsement. But youth, solid skills foundation a good starting point.

Yr	Tm	W	L	Sv	IP	K	ERA	xERA	WHIP	oOPS	vL	vR	BF/G	Ctl	Dom	Cmd	FpK	SwK	G	L	F	H%	S%	hr/f	GS	APC	DOM%	DIS%	Sv%	LI	RAR	BPV	BPX	R$
12																																		
13																																		
14																																		
15	aa	11	5	0	153	82	2.87	3.52	1.25				23.9	2.3	4.8	2.1						29%	78%								20.6	58	69	$11
16	PIT *	11	7	0	154	106	3.69	4.57	1.37	757	854	676	21.5	2.2	6.2	2.8	57%	9%	44	20	36	32%	76%	9%	14	82	21%	36%			9.4	64	76	$6
1st Half		7	2	0	88	54	3.63	5.05	1.43	748	774	708	23.3	2.2	5.5	2.6	67%	8%	31	17	51	33%	79%	6%	2	86	0%	50%			6.1	48	57	$6
2nd Half		4	5	0	67	52	3.78	3.93	1.28	758	873	672	19.5	2.2	7.0	3.2	55%	9%	47	20	33	32%	72%	10%	12	81	25%	33%			3.4	86	103	$5
17	**Proj**	**9**	**6**	**0**	**131**	**87**	**3.72**	**4.46**	**1.30**	**696**	**798**	**620**	**22.0**	**2.2**	**6.0**	**2.7**	**55%**	**9%**	**47**	**20**	**33**	**31%**	**73%**	**8%**	**24**						**7.5**	**72**	**86**	**$4**

Lackey,John

Age: 38	Th: R	Role SP	Health C	LIMA Plan D+	
Ht: 6' 6"	Wt: 245	Type Pwr	PT/Exp A	Rand Var -1	
			Consist A	MM 2203	

Surely we're not going to question this old dog, who keeps sniffing out success wherever he goes. He throws strikes, gets whiffs (with additional SwK support in 2016), and limits baserunners. At some point the snarl will eclipse the stuff, but no signs of that yet. A loyal and reliable fantasy friend.

Yr	Tm	W	L	Sv	IP	K	ERA	xERA	WHIP	oOPS	vL	vR	BF/G	Ctl	Dom	Cmd	FpK	SwK	G	L	F	H%	S%	hr/f	GS	APC	DOM%	DIS%	Sv%	LI	RAR	BPV	BPX	R$
12																																		
13	BOS	10	13	0	189	161	3.52	3.50	1.16	703	657	760	26.8	1.9	7.7	4.0	64%	10%	47	18	35	29%	75%	13%	29	99	38%	14%			8.1	111	145	$12
14	2 TM	14	10	0	198	164	3.82	3.67	1.28	730	719	742	26.9	2.1	7.5	3.5	68%	10%	44	22	34	32%	74%	12%	31	99	35%	23%			-1.9	99	117	$6
15	STL	13	10	0	218	175	2.77	3.81	1.21	679	749	620	27.2	2.2	7.2	3.3	71%	10%	46	21	33	30%	81%	10%	33	95	33%	18%			32.2	95	113	$21
16	CHC	11	8	0	188	180	3.35	3.68	1.06	645	694	609	25.8	2.5	8.6	3.4	68%	12%	41	23	36	26%	73%	13%	29	98	41%	17%			19.6	105	125	$21
1st Half		7	4	0	105	107	3.27	3.55	1.04	640	677	610	25.8	2.5	9.2	3.7	69%	12%	39	22	38	27%	72%	11%	16	98	50%	19%			11.9	116	138	$24
2nd Half		4	4	0	84	73	3.44	3.85	1.08	652	717	608	25.8	2.6	7.9	3.0	66%	11%	43	23	34	25%	74%	16%	13	99	31%	15%			7.7	93	110	$17
17	**Proj**	**10**	**8**	**0**	**174**	**152**	**3.56**	**3.88**	**1.20**	**704**	**742**	**672**	**26.1**	**2.3**	**7.9**	**3.4**	**68%**	**11%**	**44**	**22**	**35**	**30%**	**74%**	**12%**	**27**						**13.5**	**101**	**120**	**$12**

Law,Derek

Age: 26	Th: R	Role RP	Health B	LIMA Plan B+	
Ht: 6' 3"	Wt: 220	Type GB	PT/Exp D	Rand Var -3	
			Consist F	MM 4220	

Hard thrower with closing experience in minors, showed the goods in first full season for the job—elite Ctl, good Dom, xGB lean, flat platoon split. Need to keep tabs on Sept elbow injury that resulted in DL time, but could be rounded into a bullpen force very quickly. With health and opportunity ... UP: 30 Sv

Yr	Tm	W	L	Sv	IP	K	ERA	xERA	WHIP	oOPS	vL	vR	BF/G	Ctl	Dom	Cmd	FpK	SwK	G	L	F	H%	S%	hr/f	GS	APC	DOM%	DIS%	Sv%	LI	RAR	BPV	BPX	R$
12																																		
13																																		
14	aa	2	0	13	28	24	2.90	2.66	1.27				4.2	4.6	7.8	1.7						27%	76%								2.9	87	103	$4
15	aa	0	1	13	26	27	6.32	6.28	1.87				4.3	3.2	9.6	3.0						46%	64%								-7.5	95	113	-$3
16	SF	4	2	1	55	50	2.13	3.24	0.96	570	523	598	3.5	1.5	8.2	5.6	63%	11%	50	22	28	28%	80%	7%	0	13			50	0.90	14.0	136	161	$7
1st Half		3	1	1	29	29	3.10	3.19	1.10	657	591	697	4.1	1.2	9.0	7.3	67%	10%	46	27	26	34%	71%	5%	0	14			100	0.85	3.9	153	182	$6
2nd Half		1	1	0	26	21	1.04	3.29	0.81	461	439	474	3.0	1.7	7.3	4.2	57%	12%	55	14	30	21%	95%	10%	0	12			0	0.94	10.1	117	140	$8
17	**Proj**	**3**	**2**	**14**	**44**	**38**	**2.69**	**3.24**	**0.99**	**581**	**536**	**609**	**3.4**	**1.5**	**8.0**	**5.2**	**61%**	**11%**	**52**	**20**	**29**	**28%**	**74%**	**8%**	**0**						**8.0**	**131**	**157**	**$8**

BRENT HERSHEY

Leake,Mike

Age: 29 | Th: R | Role: SP | Ht: 6' 1" | Wt: 180 | Type: Con GB
Health: B | PT/Exp: A | Consist: A | LIMA Plan: B+ | Rand Var: +2 | MM: 2105

Very disappointing first year in STL on the surface, including 6.03 ERA in final 11 GS. But look deeper and you see 2H surge in Dom and SwK, career-best Ctl and BPV, along with typical high GB%. Five straight seasons with 30-plus starts shows reliability, and when luck turns around, could be a bargain in 2017.

Yr	Tm	W	L	Sv	IP	K	ERA	xERA	WHIP	oOPS	vL	vR	BF/G	Ctl	Dom	Cmd	FpK	SwK	G	L	F	H%	S%	hr/f	GS	APC	DOM%	DIS%	Sv%	LI	RAR	BPV	BPX	R$
12	CIN	8	9	0	179	116	4.58	4.00	1.35	805	806	803	25.2	2.1	5.8	2.8	63%	7%	49	25	27	31%	70%	17%	30	90	27%	30%			-12.4	76	100	-$3
13	CIN	14	7	0	192	122	3.37	3.93	1.25	719	717	721	25.8	2.2	5.7	2.5	59%	7%	49	21	30	29%	77%	12%	31	94	29%	35%			11.8	69	90	$11
14	CIN	11	13	0	214	164	3.70	3.45	1.25	730	801	674	27.3	2.1	6.9	3.3	60%	8%	53	20	26	31%	73%	13%	33	97	30%	27%			1.2	98	117	$7
15	2 NL	11	10	0	192	119	3.70	3.95	1.16	686	727	635	25.9	2.3	5.6	2.4	61%	7%	52	22	27	26%	72%	14%	30	92	27%	33%			6.1	68	81	$11
16	STL	9	12	0	177	125	4.69	3.93	1.32	756	761	752	25.2	1.5	6.4	4.2	62%	7%	54	21	25	33%	66%	14%	30	89	23%	33%			-10.8	105	125	$1
1st Half		5	6	0	98	63	4.13	4.12	1.21	723	784	675	25.8	1.6	5.8	3.7	61%	6%	51	21	28	29%	70%	15%	16	90	31%	25%			0.7	91	109	$7
2nd Half		4	6	0	79	62	5.38	3.68	1.45	796	736	850	24.6	1.5	7.1	4.8	63%	10%	57	21	22	37%	62%	11%	14	87	14%	43%			-11.5	122	146	-$7
17	Proj	10	11	0	181	127	3.97	3.89	1.29	742	754	730	25.0	1.9	6.3	3.4	62%	8%	53	21	26	31%	72%	13%	30						4.9	94	112	$5

Lester,Jon

Age: 33 | Th: L | Role: SP | Ht: 6' 2" | Wt: 190 | Type: Pwr
Health: A | PT/Exp: A | Consist: A | LIMA Plan: D+ | Rand Var: -4 | MM: 3305

Spring diagnosis of bone chips in elbow had no effect on performance, as he posted career-best ERA and topped 200 IP for 8th time in 9 years. Got a little help from H% and S%, but skills—specifically Ctl, Dom, and SwK—are both strong and remarkably consistent. ERA will probably rise a bit, but keep riding him.

Yr	Tm	W	L	Sv	IP	K	ERA	xERA	WHIP	oOPS	vL	vR	BF/G	Ctl	Dom	Cmd	FpK	SwK	G	L	F	H%	S%	hr/f	GS	APC	DOM%	DIS%	Sv%	LI	RAR	BPV	BPX	R$
12	BOS	9	14	0	205	166	4.82	3.92	1.38	773	738	785	26.5	3.0	7.3	2.4	58%	9%	49	22	29	32%	67%	14%	33	104	30%	24%			-20.4	77	101	-$4
13	BOS	15	8	0	213	177	3.75	3.88	1.29	702	670	711	27.4	2.8	7.5	2.6	61%	9%	45	20	35	31%	73%	8%	33	108	45%	21%			2.9	81	106	$9
14	2 AL	16	11	0	220	220	2.46	3.19	1.10	635	697	617	27.7	2.0	9.0	4.6	61%	10%	42	21	37	31%	81%	7%	32	109	59%	9%			34.8	129	154	$26
15	CHC	11	12	0	205	207	3.34	3.13	1.12	661	658	662	25.9	2.1	9.1	4.4	61%	11%	49	22	29	31%	72%	10%	32	100	44%	16%			15.8	135	161	$19
16	CHC	19	5	0	203	197	2.44	3.42	1.02	602	540	620	24.9	2.3	8.7	3.8	63%	11%	47	20	33	26%	82%	12%	32	99	50%	16%			43.7	120	143	$34
1st Half		9	4	0	108	105	2.67	3.43	1.05	637	584	652	25.1	2.1	8.8	4.2	62%	11%	47	19	34	27%	82%	15%	17	99	41%	18%			20.1	126	151	$31
2nd Half		10	1	0	95	92	2.18	3.41	0.98	561	488	582	24.7	2.6	8.7	3.4	63%	11%	47	21	31	25%	81%	9%	15	99	60%	13%			23.6	113	135	$38
17	Proj	17	7	0	203	200	3.04	3.39	1.07	630	605	637	25.0	2.2	8.9	4.0	62%	11%	47	21	32	29%	75%	10%	32						28.7	125	149	$26

Lewis,Colby

Age: 37 | Th: R | Role: SP | Ht: 6' 4" | Wt: 240 | Type: xFB
Health: F | PT/Exp: A | Consist: A | LIMA Plan: B | Rand Var: -3 | MM: 0103

Was a pleasant surprise before June lat stain knocked him out for a few months, but early success not supported by skills. Still pounding the strike zone, but xERA history, Health grade, declining velocity/Dom, and extreme fly ball tendencies should be more than enough red flags. He's an ERA time bomb.

Yr	Tm	W	L	Sv	IP	K	ERA	xERA	WHIP	oOPS	vL	vR	BF/G	Ctl	Dom	Cmd	FpK	SwK	G	L	F	H%	S%	hr/f	GS	APC	DOM%	DIS%	Sv%	LI	RAR	BPV	BPX	R$
12	TEX	6	6	0	105	93	3.43	3.77	1.08	715	771	641	26.7	1.2	8.0	6.6	69%	9%	33	21	46	29%	75%	11%	16	102	44%	25%			7.6	122	159	$9
13	a/a	0	2	0	24	14	11.14	10.50	2.30				17.5	3.7	5.1	1.4						41%	53%								-21.5	-48	-63	-$15
14	TEX	10	14	0	170	133	5.18	4.48	1.52	840	853	823	26.3	2.5	7.0	2.8	66%	8%	33	23	44	35%	69%	10%	29	97	14%	38%			-30.2	69	82	-$11
15	TEX	17	9	0	205	142	4.66	4.49	1.24	738	756	717	26.1	1.8	6.2	3.4	63%	9%	34	22	44	30%	65%	9%	33	96	30%	30%			-17.7	75	89	$5
16	TEX	6	5	0	116	73	3.71	4.89	1.13	696	679	712	24.8	2.2	5.6	2.6	66%	8%	34	19	47	25%	74%	11%	19	92	32%	47%			6.8	55	66	$7
1st Half		6	1	0	98	61	3.21	4.59	1.02	641	671	611	25.7	1.7	5.6	3.2	67%	8%	36	18	46	24%	75%	9%	15	95	40%	40%			11.8	68	81	$11
2nd Half		0	4	0	18	12	6.38	6.53	1.69	952	724	1098	21.8	4.4	5.9	1.3	63%	7%	25	22	53	29%	72%	18%	4	83	0%	75%			-5.0	-10	-12	-$15
17	Proj	7	15	0	152	107	4.61	4.87	1.32	787	739	834	23.4	2.3	6.3	2.7	65%	8%	32	21	46	29%	71%	12%	27						-7.8	61	72	-$1

Liberatore,Adam

Age: 30 | Th: L | Role: RP | Ht: 6' 3" | Wt: 225 | Type: Pwr
Health: B | PT/Exp: D | Consist: B | LIMA Plan: B+ | Rand Var: -2 | MM: 2400

Luck was clearly on his side early on, but season took turn for the worse in 2nd half due to H% and S% overcorrection, plus elbow injury that required off-season surgery. SwK seems low for 9.0+ Dom, so may be hard-pressed to maintain gains; without that, there's not much reason to have him on your radar.

Yr	Tm	W	L	Sv	IP	K	ERA	xERA	WHIP	oOPS	vL	vR	BF/G	Ctl	Dom	Cmd	FpK	SwK	G	L	F	H%	S%	hr/f	GS	APC	DOM%	DIS%	Sv%	LI	RAR	BPV	BPX	R$
12	a/a	4	5	9	73	40	2.80	4.36	1.49				6.4	3.4	4.9	1.4						32%	82%								10.9	44	57	$3
13	a/a	5	3	1	62	58	4.18	3.34	1.39				6.0	3.7	8.4	2.3						34%	67%								-2.4	97	127	-$1
14	aaa	6	1	4	65	68	2.22	2.29	1.10				4.7	2.3	9.4	4.1						32%	79%								12.2	146	174	$8
15	LA *	2	3	3	51	43	4.36	3.79	1.30	671	671	671	3.6	3.3	7.5	2.3	65%	11%	41	22	37	29%	68%	10%	0	12			75	1.13	-2.5	70	84	-$2
16	LA	2	2	0	43	47	3.38	3.85	1.20	630	494	782	3.0	3.6	9.9	2.8	60%	10%	39	21	40	30%	71%	5%	0	12			0	1.13	4.3	99	117	$0
1st Half		1	0	0	27	28	0.68	3.54	0.94	504	435	603	3.0	3.4	9.5	2.8	51%	10%	42	21	37	24%	92%	0%	0	13			0	1.12	11.6	99	118	$6
2nd Half		1	2	0	16	19	7.88	4.33	1.63	807	608	958	3.1	3.9	10.7	2.7	72%	11%	35	22	43	39%	50%	10%	0	12			0	1.14	-7.3	99	118	-$8
17	Proj	3	3	0	51	53	3.92	4.00	1.31	715	525	898	3.5	3.4	9.4	2.8	64%	10%	40	21	39	32%	73%	10%	0						1.7	95	113	-$1

Light,Pat

Age: 26 | Th: R | Role: RP | Ht: 6' 5" | Wt: 220 | Type: Pwr
Health: A | PT/Exp: F | Consist: A | LIMA Plan: D | Rand Var: +5 | MM: 0200

0-1, 11.34 ERA in 17 IP at BOS/MIN. Battled Ctl issues for second straight year, and though it was small sample, MLB-worst FpK is not an encouraging sign. Has shown ability to keep ball down and miss some bats, but until he finds strike zone on a consistent basis, can safely be ignored.

Yr	Tm	W	L	Sv	IP	K	ERA	xERA	WHIP	oOPS	vL	vR	BF/G	Ctl	Dom	Cmd	FpK	SwK	G	L	F	H%	S%	hr/f	GS	APC	DOM%	DIS%	Sv%	LI	RAR	BPV	BPX	R$
12																																		
13																																		
14																																		
15	a/a	3	5	5	63	56	5.25	4.54	1.60				5.9	5.7	8.0	1.4						31%	67%								-10.0	57	67	-$6
16	2 AL *	2	2	9	55	49	5.83	4.92	1.69	956	675	1099	5.1	6.0	8.0	1.3	38%	9%	54	19	26	32%	65%	27%	0	21			90	0.58	-11.0	52	62	-$4
1st Half		0	1	5	29	27	4.85	4.12	1.43	1563	833	1731	5.6	4.7	8.4	1.8	28%	2%	50	21	29	30%	68%	50%	0	24			100	0.00	-2.4	63	76	-$1
2nd Half		2	1	4	26	22	6.93	5.82	1.97	790	652	873	4.7	7.6	7.6	1.0	41%	10%	56	19	26	35%	64%	18%	0	21			80	0.66	-8.7	44	52	-$9
17	Proj	1	2	0	29	26	4.89	5.18	1.69				5.3	6.2	8.0	1.3	0%	0%	48	20	32	32%	72%	10%	0						-2.5	4	5	-$5

Liriano,Francisco

Age: 33 | Th: L | Role: SP | Ht: 6' 2" | Wt: 215 | Type: Pwr GB
Health: C | PT/Exp: A | Consist: B | LIMA Plan: C | Rand Var: +3 | MM: 2403

Resurfacing of Ctl issues, along with lofty hr/f, sent ERA skyrocketing, but after trade to TOR, posted 2.9 Ctl, 2.92 ERA. Eased concerns about 1st half SwK dip with 2nd half rebound, and consistently high GB% suggests HR issues won't carry over. A little riskier than in years past, but after down year, offers good profit potential.

Yr	Tm	W	L	Sv	IP	K	ERA	xERA	WHIP	oOPS	vL	vR	BF/G	Ctl	Dom	Cmd	FpK	SwK	G	L	F	H%	S%	hr/f	GS	APC	DOM%	DIS%	Sv%	LI	RAR	BPV	BPX	R$
12	2 AL	6	12	0	157	167	5.34	4.12	1.47	741	603	784	20.4	5.0	9.6	1.9	54%	13%	44	21	35	31%	65%	13%	28	80	29%	39%	0	0.83	-25.7	60	78	-$9
13	PIT *	18	9	0	180	182	3.36	3.15	1.26	611	321	689	24.4	3.4	9.1	2.7	58%	14%	50	24	25	31%	74%	8%	26	96	38%	27%			11.1	102	133	$15
14	PIT	7	10	0	162	175	3.38	3.33	1.30	644	735	622	23.8	4.5	9.7	2.2	56%	14%	54	19	27	29%	76%	12%	29	94	28%	28%			7.2	85	102	$6
15	PIT	12	7	0	187	205	3.38	3.21	1.21	631	592	641	24.9	3.4	9.9	2.9	57%	15%	51	22	26	30%	74%	12%	31	96	45%	13%			13.5	116	138	$15
16	2 TM	8	13	0	163	168	4.69	4.21	1.48	773	739	783	23.6	4.7	9.3	2.0	56%	12%	52	18	30	31%	73%	19%	29	90	24%	45%	0	0.74	-10.1	70	83	-$2
1st Half		5	8	0	88	85	5.34	4.84	1.64	807	662	852	25.3	5.6	8.7	1.5	52%	11%	49	19	32	32%	71%	18%	16	96	13%	50%			-12.4	32	38	-$8
2nd Half		3	5	0	75	83	3.94	3.53	1.30	732	839	703	21.7	3.6	9.9	2.8	60%	13%	55	16	28	30%	76%	21%	13	84	38%	38%	0	0.70	2.3	115	137	$4
17	Proj	11	9	0	174	185	3.78	3.73	1.35	688	674	691	23.7	4.1	9.6	2.3	57%	13%	52	19	29	31%	74%	13%	29						8.8	91	108	$7

Locke,Jeff

Age: 29 | Th: L | Role: RP | Ht: 6' 1" | Wt: 215 | Type:
Health: A | PT/Exp: B | Consist: B | LIMA Plan: D+ | Rand Var: +1 | MM: 0003

Transition to more four-seamers, fewer sinkers and curves apparently wasn't the answer, as he lost Dom, GB%, and eventually his rotation spot. Inflated H% partially to blame for 2nd half troubles, but just getting to 2.0 Cmd has proven a major challenge. R$ trend shows whatever value he once offered is gone.

Yr	Tm	W	L	Sv	IP	K	ERA	xERA	WHIP	oOPS	vL	vR	BF/G	Ctl	Dom	Cmd	FpK	SwK	G	L	F	H%	S%	hr/f	GS	APC	DOM%	DIS%	Sv%	LI	RAR	BPV	BPX	R$
12	PIT *	11	8	0	176	135	3.60	4.22	1.38	749	836	716	23.1	2.8	6.9	2.5	62%	9%	49	15	36	32%	76%	17%	6	70	0%	17%	0	0.64	9.0	70	92	$5
13	PIT	10	7	0	166	125	3.52	4.11	1.38	686	748	667	23.7	4.5	6.8	1.5	58%	9%	53	21	26	28%	75%	9%	30	91	10%	30%			7.2	30	39	$4
14	PIT *	10	7	0	181	117	4.12	4.33	1.37	722	521	776	25.3	3.0	5.8	1.9	58%	10%	51	20	30	30%	72%	13%	21	93	29%	38%			-8.4	46	55	-$1
15	PIT	8	11	0	168	129	4.49	4.07	1.42	735	792	718	24.5	3.2	6.9	2.2	62%	9%	51	24	25	32%	69%	11%	30	93	17%	37%			-11.0	67	79	-$4
16	PIT	9	8	0	127	73	5.44	5.09	1.53	841	752	876	18.8	3.1	5.2	1.7	61%	9%	47	20	32	32%	66%	12%	19	70	26%	63%	0	0.75	-19.7	34	40	-$8
1st Half		8	5	0	95	49	5.13	5.04	1.36	786	680	825	25.1	2.9	4.7	1.6	62%	9%	47	19	34	28%	65%	12%	16	92	31%	63%			-11.0	30	35	-$5
2nd Half		1	3	0	33	24	6.34	5.21	2.02	977	903	1012	11.6	3.6	6.6	1.8	61%	9%	47	25	28	42%	69%	12%	3	45	0%	67%	0	0.70	-8.7	47	56	-$19
17	Proj	8	10	0	160	110	4.91	4.63	1.53	802	766	816	17.4	3.2	6.2	2.0	61%	9%	49	22	29	33%	69%	12%	29						-14.2	53	63	-$8

BRIAN RUDD

Lopez,Reynaldo

Age: 23	Th: R	Role: SP	Health: A	LIMA Plan: B+
Ht: 6' 0"	Wt: 185	Type: Pwr	PT/Exp: D	Rand Var: 0
			Consist: F	MM: 1301

5-3, 4.91 ERA in 44 IP at WAS. High-upside prospect struggled with FpK, Ctl (4.5) in MLB debut, but upper-90s fastball translated just fine (8.6 Dom). Cmd, BPV from 1st half in AA showcase long-term potential. However, 2017 may be more about exercising patience as he fine-tunes his skills.

Yr Tm	W	L	Sv	IP	K	ERA	xERA	WHIP	oOPS	vL	vR	BF/G	Ctl	Dom	Cmd	FpK	SwK	G	L	F	H%	S%	hr/f	GS	APC	DOM%	DIS%	Sv%	LI	RAR	BPV	BPX	R$
12																																	
13																																	
14																																	
15																																	
16 WAS *	10	10	0	153	149	4.48	4.41	1.40	772	666	885	21.6	3.5	8.7	2.5	56%	10%	41	23	35	33%	71%	9%	6	73	17%	50%	0	0.62	-5.6	74	88	$2
1st Half	3	5	0	82	88	4.11	4.36	1.43				23.3	3.4	9.6	2.8						35%	73%	0%	0						0.8	92	110	$2
2nd Half	7	5	0	71	61	4.92	4.46	1.37	772	666	885	19.8	3.6	7.7	2.1	56%	10%	41	23	35	29%	68%	9%	6	73	17%	50%	0	0.62	-6.4	54	64	$1
17 Proj	**5**	**4**	**0**	**87**	**82**	**4.11**	**4.15**	**1.30**	**667**	**605**	**733**	**23.3**	**3.2**	**8.5**	**2.7**	**59%**	**10%**	**41**	**23**	**35**	**30%**	**72%**	**12%**	**15**						**0.9**	**86**	**103**	**$1**

Lorenzen,Michael

Age: 25	Th: R	Role: RP	Health: D	LIMA Plan: A
Ht: 6' 3"	Wt: 195	Type: Pwr xGB	PT/Exp: D	Rand Var: +3
			Consist: D	MM: 3221

Talk about finding one's calling: move to pen ramped up velocity, Dom (though lack of big SwK gain adds touch of skepticism), boosted FpK, and transformed him into GB% machine. FB% was so low that 23% hr/f didn't even hurt ERA. Still talk of move back to SP, where he had 4.98 xERA last year, but skills say RP=R$.

Yr Tm	W	L	Sv	IP	K	ERA	xERA	WHIP	oOPS	vL	vR	BF/G	Ctl	Dom	Cmd	FpK	SwK	G	L	F	H%	S%	hr/f	GS	APC	DOM%	DIS%	Sv%	LI	RAR	BPV	BPX	R$
12																																	
13																																	
14 aa	4	6	0	121	76	3.50	4.16	1.38				21.1	3.2	5.7	1.8						30%	77%								3.6	48	58	-$1
15 CIN *	8	11	0	156	100	4.59	5.12	1.52	882	1007	784	20.5	3.8	5.8	1.5	57%	9%	41	28	31	31%	73%	16%	21	74	0%	57%	0	0.69	-12.1	28	33	-$8
16 CIN	2	1	0	50	48	2.88	2.87	1.08	630	548	708	5.8	2.3	8.6	3.7	63%	10%	63	21	16	28%	78%	23%	0	22			0	0.84	8.1	133	158	$3
1st Half	0	0	0	7	7	4.05	2.24	0.90	896	673	1046	6.8	0.0	9.5	0.0	54%	10%	56	28	17	25%	75%	67%	0	23			0	0.11	0.1	204	243	-$5
2nd Half	2	1	0	43	41	2.70	2.97	1.11	588	533	644	5.6	2.7	8.5	3.2	64%	10%	64	20	16	28%	78%	16%	0	21			0	0.94	8.0	122	146	$4
17 Proj	**3**	**3**	**18**	**73**	**66**	**3.13**	**3.41**	**1.22**	**680**	**683**	**677**	**6.6**	**2.7**	**8.2**	**3.0**	**61%**	**10%**	**56**	**21**	**22**	**30%**	**78%**	**15%**	**0**						**9.5**	**109**	**130**	**$10**

Lugo,Seth

Age: 27	Th: R	Role: RP	Health: A	LIMA Plan: C
Ht: 6' 4"	Wt: 225	Type: FB	PT/Exp: D	Rand Var: 0
			Consist: B	MM: 0101

5-2, 2.67 ERA in 64 IP at NYM. Not a breakout, just a lucky MLB H%/S% combo (24%/81%), the flip side of fortunes in AAA. Fared better as RP (8.5 Dom, 2.7 Cmd) than SP (5.6, 1.9), and FpK could present path forward, but reality is he's a late bloomer who didn't arrive 'til 26; may disappear as fast as he came.

Yr Tm	W	L	Sv	IP	K	ERA	xERA	WHIP	oOPS	vL	vR	BF/G	Ctl	Dom	Cmd	FpK	SwK	G	L	F	H%	S%	hr/f	GS	APC	DOM%	DIS%	Sv%	LI	RAR	BPV	BPX	R$
12																																	
13																																	
14																																	
15 a/a	8	7	0	136	103	4.27	4.41	1.39				23.9	2.3	6.8	2.9						34%	70%								-5.3	77	92	-$1
16 NYM *	8	6	0	137	94	4.72	5.02	1.47	666	672	661	15.5	2.6	6.2	2.3	64%	10%	43	19	38	33%	70%	10%	8	57	13%	38%	0	0.65	-8.9	50	60	-$4
1st Half	3	4	0	71	46	6.37	6.84	1.78	583	1000	452	16.2	2.2	5.8	2.6	44%	9%	50	33	17	39%	65%	0%	0	33			0	0.01	-19.0	39	47	-$16
2nd Half	5	2	0	67	49	2.97	3.09	1.15	669	666	672	14.7	3.1	6.6	2.1	64%	10%	43	18	39	25%	78%	10%	8	58	13%	38%	0	0.69	10.0	66	79	$9
17 Proj	**5**	**4**	**0**	**87**	**63**	**4.35**	**4.75**	**1.40**	**778**	**744**	**808**	**17.9**	**2.6**	**6.5**	**2.5**	**64%**	**10%**	**43**	**18**	**39**	**33%**	**71%**	**7%**	**16**						**-1.7**	**69**	**82**	**-$2**

Lyles,Jordan

Age: 26	Th: R	Role: RP	Health: F	LIMA Plan: D+
Ht: 6' 4"	Wt: 185	Type: GB	PT/Exp: C	Rand Var: +3
			Consist: C	MM: 0001

4-5, 5.83 ERA in 59 IP at COL. Received Sept vote of confidence from manager Walt Weiss, less than a month before COL chose not to renew Weiss's contact. If that doesn't tell you something, maybe xERA will. Or do you prefer lousy Cmd? A declining BPV? Perhaps an F health grade is your thing. He's got it all!

Yr Tm	W	L	Sv	IP	K	ERA	xERA	WHIP	oOPS	vL	vR	BF/G	Ctl	Dom	Cmd	FpK	SwK	G	L	F	H%	S%	hr/f	GS	APC	DOM%	DIS%	Sv%	LI	RAR	BPV	BPX	R$
12 HOU *	10	12	0	182	128	4.72	4.60	1.37	772	886	683	23.9	2.4	6.3	2.6	61%	7%	54	17	29	32%	68%	15%	25	95	8%	44%			-15.8	59	77	-$3
13 HOU *	9	11	1	165	103	5.64	5.11	1.53	801	751	859	21.8	3.0	5.6	1.9	56%	7%	48	21	30	33%	64%	12%	25	91	8%	40%	50	1.01	-36.2	39	50	-$14
14 COL	7	4	0	127	90	4.33	3.90	1.37	750	844	654	24.8	3.3	6.4	2.0	57%	8%	52	23	26	30%	70%	12%	22	95	5%	32%			-9.3	57	68	-$2
15 COL	2	5	0	49	30	5.14	4.45	1.49	751	797	697	21.2	3.5	5.5	1.6	58%	8%	50	26	25	32%	63%	5%	10	77	0%	30%			-7.1	33	39	-$6
16 COL *	8	7	1	103	53	6.73	6.49	1.86	790	902	713	10.1	4.2	4.6	1.1	60%	7%	51	24	25	36%	63%	8%	5	24	20%	80%	25	0.98	-32.4	10	12	-$17
1st Half	5	4	0	70	37	7.84	7.53	2.03	861	983	768	20.1	4.4	4.7	1.1	62%	7%	47	27	26	38%	61%	9%	5	47	20%	80%	0	0.74	-31.7	0	0	-$23
2nd Half	3	3	1	33	16	4.36	5.16	1.48	732	825	669	4.7	3.8	4.4	1.1	59%	8%	55	21	24	30%	70%	7%	0	17			25	1.05	-0.7	8	10	-$4
17 Proj	**5**	**5**	**0**	**73**	**42**	**5.32**	**4.94**	**1.57**	**797**	**876**	**730**	**10.3**	**3.6**	**5.2**	**1.4**	**59%**	**8%**	**51**	**23**	**25**	**33%**	**66%**	**9%**	**1**						**-10.1**	**24**	**29**	**-$7**

Lynn,Lance

Age: 30	Th: R	Role: SP	Health: F	LIMA Plan: B
Ht: 6' 5"	Wt: 280	Type: Pwr	PT/Exp: B	Rand Var: 0
			Consist: A	MM: 2301

Had Tommy John surgery in Nov 2015, made three minor league rehab starts in Aug, but he and STL decided to shut it down. Pitched through pain for most of 2nd half of 2015, so it's worth remembering what he did in 1H: 9.5 Dom, 3.1 Cmd, 108 BPV, 3.66 xERA. Buy low, hope that he can once again soar high.

Yr Tm	W	L	Sv	IP	K	ERA	xERA	WHIP	oOPS	vL	vR	BF/G	Ctl	Dom	Cmd	FpK	SwK	G	L	F	H%	S%	hr/f	GS	APC	DOM%	DIS%	Sv%	LI	RAR	BPV	BPX	R$
12 STL	18	7	0	176	180	3.78	3.58	1.32	728	841	624	21.3	3.3	9.2	2.8	61%	10%	44	24	32	32%	73%	10%	29	86	34%	34%	0	0.83	5.0	99	130	$11
13 STL	15	10	0	202	198	3.97	3.63	1.31	701	765	652	25.9	3.4	8.8	2.6	63%	10%	43	23	34	32%	70%	7%	33	102	52%	27%			-2.6	88	115	$8
14 STL	15	10	0	204	181	2.74	3.81	1.26	662	697	635	26.2	3.2	8.0	2.5	60%	9%	44	20	36	30%	80%	6%	33	105	30%	18%			25.2	80	95	$16
15 STL	12	11	0	175	167	3.03	3.95	1.37	708	809	623	24.2	3.5	8.6	2.5	56%	9%	44	22	34	33%	80%	8%	31	98	32%	29%			20.2	82	98	$11
16																																	
1st Half																																	
2nd Half																																	
17 Proj	**8**	**6**	**0**	**109**	**104**	**3.41**	**4.03**	**1.32**	**699**	**777**	**636**	**24.0**	**3.4**	**8.6**	**2.6**	**60%**	**10%**	**44**	**22**	**34**	**32%**	**75%**	**8%**	**19**						**10.4**	**87**	**103**	**$5**

Lyons,Tyler

Age: 29	Th: L	Role: RP	Health: D	LIMA Plan: A
Ht: 6' 2"	Wt: 195	Type: Pwr	PT/Exp: D	Rand Var: 0
			Consist: B	MM: 3300

First full year in bullpen was going great until knee injury ended season in Aug. Elite FpK could mean return of sub-2.0 Ctl, posted 3.6 Cmd vR (7 HR suggests bulk of unlucky hr/f happened there, too), and 1st half BPV, xERA show he may even merit some saves consideration. Excellent LIMA pick for second year in a row.

Yr Tm	W	L	Sv	IP	K	ERA	xERA	WHIP	oOPS	vL	vR	BF/G	Ctl	Dom	Cmd	FpK	SwK	G	L	F	H%	S%	hr/f	GS	APC	DOM%	DIS%	Sv%	LI	RAR	BPV	BPX	R$
12 a/a	9	13	0	153	117	4.50	4.45	1.38				23.7	2.2	6.9	3.2						34%	68%								-9.2	82	107	-$2
13 STL *	9	6	0	153	112	4.08	3.21	1.18	725	630	762	21.1	2.1	6.6	3.2	59%	9%	47	19	33	30%	65%	10%	8	66	25%	25%	0	0.97	-4.0	93	121	$6
14 STL *	8	6	0	120	97	4.87	4.99	1.45	682	280	806	19.7	2.2	7.3	3.3	62%	11%	43	16	40	35%	68%	10%	4	49	0%	25%	0	0.54	-16.7	79	95	-$6
15 STL *	12	6	0	155	138	3.75	5.12	1.37	751	746	752	19.7	1.7	8.1	4.8	60%	10%	39	25	36	35%	79%	19%	8	56	13%	25%	0	0.61	4.1	102	121	$5
16 STL	2	0	0	48	46	3.38	3.68	1.02	667	464	788	6.2	2.6	8.6	3.3	72%	11%	40	24	36	23%	78%	20%	0	23			0	0.59	4.8	102	122	$2
1st Half	2	0	0	37	37	3.68	3.37	1.06	712	368	903	6.2	2.5	9.1	3.7	72%	9%	44	25	31	24%	77%	28%	0	23			0	0.53	2.3	119	142	$3
2nd Half	0	0	0	11	9	2.38	4.69	0.88	515	728	348	6.3	3.2	7.1	2.3	73%	14%	27	20	53	18%	78%	6%	0	23			0	0.78	2.5	48	57	-$2
17 Proj	**3**	**2**	**0**	**44**	**42**	**3.50**	**3.63**	**1.16**	**706**	**443**	**807**	**7.1**	**2.1**	**8.7**	**4.0**	**67%**	**10%**	**43**	**21**	**35**	**29%**	**76%**	**15%**	**0**						**3.7**	**119**	**142**	**$0**

Madson,Ryan

Age: 36	Th: R	Role: RP	Health: F	LIMA Plan: C+
Ht: 6' 6"	Wt: 200	Type: GB	PT/Exp: C	Rand Var: 0
			Consist: C	MM: 2230

Surprise 30-Sv season made for some happy owners, but red flags abound: sharp Dom drop, especially in 2H; FpK, SwK also collapsed; BPV, xERA not closer-worthy. Complained of dead arm in Aug 2015, has been worked pretty hard for a guy who missed three years rebuilding elbow. DN: Another extended absence.

Yr Tm	W	L	Sv	IP	K	ERA	xERA	WHIP	oOPS	vL	vR	BF/G	Ctl	Dom	Cmd	FpK	SwK	G	L	F	H%	S%	hr/f	GS	APC	DOM%	DIS%	Sv%	LI	RAR	BPV	BPX	R$
12																																	
13																																	
14																																	
15 KC	1	2	3	63	58	2.13	3.17	0.96	573	547	597	3.6	2.0	8.2	4.1	66%	14%	55	13	32	26%	82%	9%	0	13			60	1.12	14.3	128	152	$7
16 OAK	6	7	30	65	49	3.62	4.24	1.28	701	695	706	4.3	2.8	6.8	2.5	56%	12%	46	23	31	30%	75%	12%	0	16			81	1.38	4.6	72	85	$14
1st Half	3	2	15	34	29	2.91	4.24	1.29	705	770	660	4.2	3.2	7.7	2.4	60%	14%	40	27	33	30%	83%	13%	0	15			83	1.24	5.4	71	84	$15
2nd Half	3	5	15	31	20	4.40	4.25	1.27	696	634	771	4.4	2.3	5.9	2.5	52%	10%	53	19	29	30%	67%	11%	0	17			79	1.53	-0.8	73	87	$12
17 Proj	**4**	**6**	**25**	**65**	**53**	**3.54**	**4.04**	**1.28**	**698**	**674**	**720**	**4.1**	**2.8**	**7.3**	**2.6**	**58%**	**12%**	**50**	**19**	**31**	**30%**	**75%**	**10%**	**0**						**5.3**	**83**	**99**	**$11**

BRANDON KRUSE

Maeda,Kenta

Age: 29	Th: R	Role SP	Health A	LIMA Plan C+	
Ht: 6' 1"	Wt: 175	Type Pwr	PT/Exp B	Rand Var 0	
			Consist B	MM 2305	

Some may look at half-season ERA splits and think that opponents figured him out, but there's nothing in skills to back that up. 2nd half ERA increase was largely driven by hr/f; in fact, xERA, Cmd, and BPV all say he got better. Okay, he struggled vL (2.0 Cmd). Don't let that stop you from buying a repeat.

Yr Tm	W	L	Sv	IP	K	ERA	xERA	WHIP	oOPS	vL	vR	BF/G	Ctl	Dom	Cmd	FpK	SwK	G	L	F	H%	S%	hr/f	GS	APC	DOM%	DIS%	Sv%	LI	RAR	BPV	BPX	R$
12																																	
13																																	
14																																	
15 for	15	8	0	176	170	4.32	4.37	1.27				24.8	3.2	8.7	2.7						28%	73%								-7.7	65	77	$7
16 LA	16	11	0	176	179	3.48	3.63	1.14	649	730	580	22.4	2.6	9.2	3.6	61%	12%	44	20	36	29%	73%	12%	32	92	25%	19%			15.3	118	140	$19
1st Half	7	5	0	93	89	2.82	3.72	1.09	605	609	600	23.3	2.7	8.6	3.2	61%	12%	44	20	36	27%	77%	9%	16	93	31%	13%			15.7	104	125	$22
2nd Half	9	6	0	83	90	4.23	3.53	1.19	697	860	558	21.5	2.4	9.8	4.1	62%	12%	43	21	35	31%	69%	15%	16	90	19%	25%			-0.4	133	158	$15
17 Proj	**16**	**10**	**0**	**181**	**182**	**3.55**	**3.71**	**1.20**	**668**	**771**	**580**	**22.8**	**2.8**	**9.1**	**3.3**	**61%**	**12%**	**44**	**21**	**36**	**30%**	**74%**	**12%**	**32**						**14.2**	**110**	**130**	**$16**

Manaea,Sean

Age: 25	Th: L	Role SP	Health B	LIMA Plan B	
Ht: 6' 5"	Wt: 245	Type Pwr	PT/Exp D	Rand Var 0	
			Consist A	MM 2303	

7-9, 3.86 ERA in 145 IP at OAK. Lots to like from this debut: Elite Cmd, especially in 2nd half; FpK supports Ctl gains, while SwK, 2015 MLE suggest some Dom upside; more GB% as season went on. 17 of 20 HR came vR, though hr/f suggests bad luck played a role. Poised to take a step up.

Yr Tm	W	L	Sv	IP	K	ERA	xERA	WHIP	oOPS	vL	vR	BF/G	Ctl	Dom	Cmd	FpK	SwK	G	L	F	H%	S%	hr/f	GS	APC	DOM%	DIS%	Sv%	LI	RAR	BPV	BPX	R$
12																																	
13																																	
14																																	
15 aa	6	1	0	50	51	2.49	3.59	1.33				22.9	3.6	9.2	2.6						32%	84%								9.0	95	114	$3
16 OAK *	9	9	0	163	141	3.66	3.83	1.21	713	526	754	23.4	2.3	7.8	3.4	65%	12%	44	21	35	30%	74%	14%	24	87	33%	29%	0	0.78	10.7	88	104	$11
1st Half	5	4	0	73	61	4.57	4.70	1.40	799	492	889	23.7	2.6	7.5	2.9	64%	12%	41	22	37	33%	70%	13%	10	84	20%	30%			-3.5	70	83	$1
2nd Half	4	5	0	90	80	2.91	3.60	1.05	656	560	673	23.7	2.0	8.0	4.0	65%	13%	47	20	33	26%	79%	15%	14	89	43%	29%	0	0.80	14.1	115	137	$18
17 Proj	**14**	**7**	**0**	**174**	**162**	**3.38**	**3.75**	**1.21**	**701**	**512**	**744**	**24.6**	**2.3**	**8.4**	**3.6**	**65%**	**12%**	**45**	**20**	**35**	**31%**	**76%**	**11%**	**29**						**17.4**	**111**	**132**	**$14**

Marinez,Jhan

Age: 28	Th: R	Role RP	Health A	LIMA Plan D+	
Ht: 6' 1"	Wt: 165	Type Pwr GB	PT/Exp D	Rand Var -2	
			Consist C	MM 1200	

Pitched in more games (24) in July/Aug than rest of year combined, so 2nd half Dom drop seems more like burnout or hitters adjusting than injury. 1st half Dom looks like small sample 24 IP outlier. Ctl gains have been nice, but FpK decline raises concern he may backslide. Too much skill inconsistency to safely invest.

Yr Tm	W	L	Sv	IP	K	ERA	xERA	WHIP	oOPS	vL	vR	BF/G	Ctl	Dom	Cmd	FpK	SwK	G	L	F	H%	S%	hr/f	GS	APC	DOM%	DIS%	Sv%	LI	RAR	BPV	BPX	R$
12 CHW *	4	2	4	66	57	3.99	3.77	1.39	650	933	400	6.6	5.4	7.7	1.4	73%	3%	43	43	14	26%	74%	0%	0	18			67	1.24	0.2	56	73	$0
13 aaa	2	4	2	28	22	8.00	7.58	1.81				6.5	6.1	7.0	1.2						28%	63%								-14.3	-28	-37	-$9
14 a/a	8	3	0	40	37	6.35	5.59	1.79				5.6	6.3	8.3	1.3						34%	65%								-13.0	46	55	-$6
15 a/a	4	1	7	67	57	2.91	3.65	1.34				5.6	3.9	7.6	1.9						29%	81%								8.7	70	83	$4
16 2 TM	0	1	0	62	50	3.18	4.09	1.33	710	717	705	5.8	3.0	7.2	2.4	56%	9%	50	24	26	32%	77%	8%	0	21			0	0.57	7.8	76	90	$0
1st Half	0	0	0	24	27	3.00	3.27	1.46	770	868	652	6.6	3.0	10.1	3.4	60%	11%	51	30	19	38%	82%	15%	0	25			0	0.51	3.5	130	155	-$1
2nd Half	0	1	0	38	23	3.29	4.62	1.25	670	561	729	5.4	3.1	5.4	1.8	53%	8%	50	20	30	28%	74%	6%	0	19			0	0.59	4.3	43	51	$0
17 Proj	**3**	**1**	**0**	**58**	**49**	**3.66**	**4.21**	**1.41**	**729**	**744**	**718**	**5.7**	**4.0**	**7.6**	**1.9**	**56%**	**9%**	**50**	**24**	**26**	**31%**	**76%**	**11%**	**0**						**3.8**	**58**	**69**	**-$1**

Martinez,Carlos

Age: 25	Th: R	Role SP	Health A	LIMA Plan D+	
Ht: 6' 0"	Wt: 190	Type Pwr GB	PT/Exp A	Rand Var -1	
			Consist A	MM 3305	

Whiff rate on change-up went from 24% in 2015 to 15% in 1st half amid speculation he was tipping the pitch, so perhaps that explains Dom, SwK fluctuations (2H change-up whiff rate was 19%). ERA likely to regress a bit, and still needs to improve vL (career 1.7 Cmd), but at 25, we probably haven't seen his best yet.

Yr Tm	W	L	Sv	IP	K	ERA	xERA	WHIP	oOPS	vL	vR	BF/G	Ctl	Dom	Cmd	FpK	SwK	G	L	F	H%	S%	hr/f	GS	APC	DOM%	DIS%	Sv%	LI	RAR	BPV	BPX	R$
12 aa	4	3	0	71	50	3.05	3.32	1.21				19.2	2.6	6.3	2.4						29%	77%								8.5	74	97	$3
13 STL *	8	4	1	108	86	3.24	3.09	1.25	704	764	661	11.9	2.9	7.1	2.4	62%	10%	52	19	29	30%	74%	4%	1	23	0%	100%	100	0.75	8.3	88	115	$6
14 STL	2	4	1	89	84	4.03	3.54	1.41	713	849	609	6.8	3.6	8.5	2.3	58%	14%	51	22	27	34%	70%	6%	7	24	14%	14%	17	1.34	-3.2	83	99	-$3
15 STL	14	7	0	180	184	3.01	3.28	1.29	687	756	623	24.4	3.2	9.2	2.9	63%	11%	54	20	25	32%	78%	11%	29	92	41%	21%	0	0.82	21.2	113	134	$15
16 STL	16	9	0	195	174	3.04	3.69	1.22	643	730	540	26.1	3.2	8.0	2.5	62%	10%	56	18	26	29%	77%	11%	31	98	32%	23%			27.7	91	108	$20
1st Half	7	5	0	95	73	2.83	3.80	1.11	579	723	397	25.8	2.9	6.9	2.4	61%	9%	58	16	26	26%	76%	9%	15	95	33%	13%			16.0	81	97	$21
2nd Half	9	4	0	100	101	3.24	3.58	1.33	701	736	662	26.4	3.5	9.1	2.6	63%	11%	55	19	26	32%	78%	13%	16	100	31%	31%			11.7	102	121	$19
17 Proj	**15**	**8**	**0**	**203**	**188**	**3.21**	**3.66**	**1.28**	**671**	**751**	**591**	**25.3**	**3.2**	**8.4**	**2.6**	**62%**	**11%**	**55**	**19**	**26**	**31%**	**76%**	**10%**	**33**						**24.6**	**95**	**114**	**$16**

Matz,Steven

Age: 26	Th: L	Role SP	Health D	LIMA Plan B	
Ht: 6' 2"	Wt: 195	Type Pwr	PT/Exp C	Rand Var +1	
			Consist A	MM 3303	

Spent 2016 checking off nearly every skill gain box we could hope for: Increased Dom and Cmd? Uh-huh. Growth in FpK and SwK? Yup. More GB%? Indeed. Only item missing was health, and with shoulder issues, bone spurs in elbow, it was a big one. Can't ignore that risk, but with full season IP, $20 is within reach.

Yr Tm	W	L	Sv	IP	K	ERA	xERA	WHIP	oOPS	vL	vR	BF/G	Ctl	Dom	Cmd	FpK	SwK	G	L	F	H%	S%	hr/f	GS	APC	DOM%	DIS%	Sv%	LI	RAR	BPV	BPX	R$
12																																	
13																																	
14 aa	6	5	0	71	60	2.25	2.97	1.15				23.6	1.6	7.6	4.7						32%	81%								13.1	137	164	$6
15 NYM *	12	4	0	137	122	2.13	2.75	1.12	650	650	644	23.5	2.7	8.0	2.9	62%	9%	46	21	34	28%	84%	12%	6	96	17%	17%			31.1	100	119	$19
16 NYM	9	8	0	132	129	3.40	3.39	1.21	689	698	686	24.9	2.1	8.8	4.2	65%	10%	51	21	28	32%	75%	14%	22	98	36%	23%			12.9	130	154	$10
1st Half	7	3	0	82	79	3.40	3.42	1.23	689	684	690	24.4	2.0	8.7	4.4	66%	10%	53	19	28	33%	75%	12%	14	95	36%	36%			8.0	134	160	$13
2nd Half	2	5	0	50	50	3.40	3.36	1.17	689	720	678	25.8	2.3	8.9	3.8	63%	10%	48	25	27	30%	75%	17%	8	103	38%	0%			4.9	124	148	$6
17 Proj	**10**	**8**	**0**	**145**	**135**	**3.15**	**3.55**	**1.16**	**635**	**656**	**628**	**24.0**	**2.3**	**8.4**	**3.6**	**63%**	**10%**	**48**	**22**	**30**	**30%**	**76%**	**11%**	**24**						**18.7**	**114**	**136**	**$13**

Maurer,Brandon

Age: 26	Th: R	Role RP	Health C	LIMA Plan B+	
Ht: 6' 5"	Wt: 200	Type Pwr	PT/Exp C	Rand Var 0	
			Consist A	MM 2220	

Half-season splits give clear example of relationship between FpK and Ctl. Bulk of 2nd half Ctl growth came vL, as he raised Cmd from 1.9 to 4.3. But you should still hedge your bets on full season of saves because of elevated FB rate, and lack of shut-it-down strand rate. Don't ignore his xERA.

Yr Tm	W	L	Sv	IP	K	ERA	xERA	WHIP	oOPS	vL	vR	BF/G	Ctl	Dom	Cmd	FpK	SwK	G	L	F	H%	S%	hr/f	GS	APC	DOM%	DIS%	Sv%	LI	RAR	BPV	BPX	R$
12 aa	9	2	0	138	106	3.71	3.88	1.43				24.4	3.2	6.9	2.2						34%	73%								5.2	80	104	$1
13 SEA *	8	12	0	137	111	5.95	5.38	1.57	883	919	835	18.8	3.3	7.3	2.2	59%	10%	44	19	37	35%	63%	15%	14	70	21%	43%	0	0.74	-35.2	50	65	-$14
14 SEA *	2	4	3	89	75	4.23	4.06	1.34	705	631	759	7.4	2.6	7.6	2.9	63%	10%	39	18	43	33%	69%	6%	7	30	0%	43%	75	0.72	-5.4	84	100	-$2
15 SD	7	4	0	51	39	3.00	3.83	1.06	568	427	711	3.9	2.6	6.9	2.6	61%	13%	48	22	30	26%	73%	7%	0	15			0	1.15	6.1	78	93	$4
16 SD	0	5	13	70	72	4.52	4.16	1.26	686	648	722	4.2	3.0	9.3	3.1	60%	12%	38	20	42	32%	65%	8%	0	17			68	1.02	-2.9	103	123	$3
1st Half	0	2	1	39	47	5.82	4.07	1.45	793	714	868	4.4	4.2	10.9	2.6	53%	13%	39	23	39	34%	62%	15%	0	18			20	0.92	-7.8	100	120	-$4
2nd Half	0	3	12	31	25	2.90	4.26	1.03	546	561	530	4.1	1.5	7.3	5.0	69%	11%	37	18	45	29%	71%	2%	0	16			86	1.15	4.9	106	127	$12
17 Proj	**3**	**5**	**23**	**65**	**58**	**3.90**	**4.04**	**1.20**	**646**	**598**	**694**	**4.6**	**2.5**	**7.9**	**3.2**	**62%**	**11%**	**41**	**20**	**39**	**30%**	**68%**	**7%**	**0**						**2.3**	**94**	**112**	**$10**

May,Trevor

Age: 27	Th: R	Role RP	Health D	LIMA Plan C+	
Ht: 6' 5"	Wt: 215	Type Pwr FB	PT/Exp C	Rand Var +5	
			Consist A	MM 2500	

H%, S%, hr/f, LD killed his ERA, but pitched entire season with stress fracture in his back, which makes these skills even more remarkable. SwK supports Dom jump, FpK suggests Ctl may rebound, and BPV, LI paint a pretty saves-friendly picture. Still a possibility he returns to rotation, but if not... UP: 3.50 ERA, 25 Sv

Yr Tm	W	L	Sv	IP	K	ERA	xERA	WHIP	oOPS	vL	vR	BF/G	Ctl	Dom	Cmd	FpK	SwK	G	L	F	H%	S%	hr/f	GS	APC	DOM%	DIS%	Sv%	LI	RAR	BPV	BPX	R$
12 aa	10	13	0	150	129	5.53	5.19	1.55				23.4	4.6	7.8	1.7						31%	67%								-27.9	40	52	-$12
13 aa	9	9	0	152	129	5.18	4.74	1.55				24.6	3.9	7.7	2.0						34%	67%								-24.6	61	80	-$10
14 MIN *	11	12	0	144	118	5.06	4.42	1.49	900	892	907	22.2	4.0	7.4	1.9	62%	10%	36	23	41	33%	66%	12%	9	84	0%	44%	0	0.70	-23.4	62	74	-$7
15 MIN	8	9	0	115	110	4.00	3.86	1.33	752	759	743	10.3	2.0	8.6	4.2	63%	11%	39	21	40	35%	72%	8%	16	39	25%	31%	0	0.87	-0.6	117	140	$2
16 MIN	2	2	0	43	60	5.27	3.57	1.31	757	547	872	4.3	3.6	12.7	3.5	62%	14%	31	26	43	35%	63%	15%	0	19			0	1.18	-5.7	140	166	-$3
1st Half	0	2	0	27	40	6.08	3.56	1.50	837	561	966	4.2	3.4	13.5	4.0	61%	15%	28	30	42	42%	63%	17%	0	19			0	1.26	-6.2	158	189	-$5
2nd Half	2	0	0	16	20	3.94	3.59	1.00	601	526	653	4.3	3.9	11.3	2.9	64%	11%	38	19	43	22%	64%	13%	0	20			0	1.04	0.5	112	134	$0
17 Proj	**5**	**4**	**0**	**65**	**78**	**4.14**	**3.75**	**1.31**	**730**	**670**	**776**	**6.3**	**3.4**	**10.8**	**3.2**	**63%**	**12%**	**36**	**23**	**41**	**33%**	**72%**	**12%**	**0**						**0.4**	**117**	**139**	**$0**

BRANDON KRUSE

McAllister,Zach

Age: 29 | Th: R | Role: RP | Ht: 6' 5" | Wt: 230 | Type: Pwr

Health: D | PT/Exp: C | Consist: B | LIMA Plan: C | Rand Var: -2 | MM: 1300

Held ERA in check despite volatile peripherals and July DL stint (hip) that cut into his IP. But 2015 now looks like a ceiling. Ctl spike and gopheritis hurt as RHBs torched him in 1st half. Restored order and GB% in 2nd half rebound, but lofty H% returned as Dom drifted all year. Needs more consistency to restore LIMA luster.

Yr Tm	W	L	Sv	IP	K	ERA	xERA	WHIP	oOPS	vL	vR	BF/G	Ctl	Dom	Cmd	FpK	SwK	G	L	F	H%	S%	hr/f	GS	APC	DOM%	DIS%	Sv%	LI	RAR	BPV	BPX	R$
12 CLE *	11	10	0	189	153	3.97	4.53	1.37	767	724	820	23.9	2.7	7.3	2.7	61%	9%	41	19	40	32%	75%	12%	22	96	9%	23%			1.1	66	86	$4
13 CLE	9	9	0	134	101	3.75	4.46	1.36	739	737	741	24.1	3.3	6.8	2.1	61%	7%	37	22	41	30%	75%	8%	24	96	21%	42%			1.9	48	63	$2
14 CLE *	11	8	0	155	121	4.04	3.95	1.34	750	789	715	19.5	2.5	7.0	2.9	62%	8%	42	21	37	33%	70%	7%	15	66	13%	47%	0	0.91	-5.6	84	100	$2
15 CLE	4	4	1	69	84	3.00	3.37	1.35	702	632	764	4.9	3.0	11.0	3.7	57%	11%	43	21	36	36%	81%	10%	1	20	0%	0%	50	0.87	8.2	137	163	$2
16 CLE	3	2	0	52	54	3.44	4.59	1.45	742	692	788	4.4	4.0	9.3	2.3	60%	10%	36	22	43	33%	80%	9%	2	18	0%	50%	0	0.96	4.8	74	88	-$1
1st Half	2	2	0	26	28	4.10	5.08	1.48	772	561	969	4.1	4.8	9.6	2.0	59%	12%	27	22	51	31%	77%	11%	1	16	0%	100%	0	1.12	0.3	48	57	-$1
2nd Half	1	0	0	26	26	2.77	4.11	1.42	712	828	609	4.7	3.1	9.0	2.9	60%	9%	44	22	35	35%	83%	7%	1	19	0%	0%	0	0.76	4.6	99	119	-$1
17 Proj	3	3	0	58	59	3.39	4.16	1.40	724	702	743	4.9	3.3	9.1	2.8	59%	10%	40	21	39	34%	79%	9%	0						5.7	92	110	$0

McCarthy,Brandon

Age: 33 | Th: R | Role: SP | Ht: 6' 7" | Wt: 200 | Type:

Health: F | PT/Exp: C | Consist: B | LIMA Plan: C | Rand Var: +1 | MM: 1101

Fine July—2.39/3.12 ERA/xERA, 11.3 Dom, 3.1 Ctl in 26 IP over 5 starts—14 months after TJS. But calf injury slowed him, hip woes DL'd him, and he logged 14 IP (15 runs) afterward. Plenty of recent skills, with historical Ctl and 2014 standing out. But the risk is obvious, and age, inactivity will eventually chip away.

Yr Tm	W	L	Sv	IP	K	ERA	xERA	WHIP	oOPS	vL	vR	BF/G	Ctl	Dom	Cmd	FpK	SwK	G	L	F	H%	S%	hr/f	GS	APC	DOM%	DIS%	Sv%	LI	RAR	BPV	BPX	R$
12 OAK	8	6	0	111	73	3.24	4.23	1.25	706	769	636	26.1	1.9	5.9	3.0	67%	7%	41	24	35	30%	77%	8%	18	92	22%	39%			10.6	73	95	$6
13 ARI	5	11	0	135	76	4.53	3.95	1.35	759	716	807	26.2	1.4	5.1	3.6	68%	6%	48	25	27	33%	67%	10%	22	91	18%	36%			-11.1	79	103	-$4
14 2 TM	10	15	0	200	175	4.05	3.11	1.28	746	751	741	26.1	1.5	7.9	5.3	67%	9%	53	23	25	34%	72%	16%	32	95	28%	25%			-7.6	133	158	$3
15 LA	3	0	0	23	29	5.87	2.99	1.22	898	691	1124	23.5	1.6	11.3	7.3	66%	12%	38	22	40	29%	68%	38%	4	92	50%	25%			-5.4	178	212	-$3
16 LA	2	3	0	40	44	4.95	4.53	1.38	642	720	587	17.1	5.9	9.9	1.7	60%	8%	35	27	38	28%	62%	6%	9	70	33%	22%	0	0.83	-3.8	33	40	-$3
1st Half	1	0	0	5	8	0.00	1.50	0.60	284	250	311	18.0	1.8	14.4	8.0	61%	15%	67	11	22	25%	100%	0%	1	72	100%	0%			2.6	255	304	$2
2nd Half	1	3	0	35	36	5.66	5.06	1.49	689	786	620	17.0	6.4	9.3	1.4	60%	7%	31	29	40	29%	60%	6%	8	70	25%	25%	0	0.84	-6.3	2	3	-$4
17 Proj	4	6	0	87	68	4.58	4.35	1.36	730	751	710	21.9	3.0	7.0	2.3	65%	7%	43	26	32	31%	67%	9%	17						-4.2	66	78	-$3

McCullers,Lance

Age: 23 | Th: R | Role: SP | Ht: 6' 1" | Wt: 205 | Type: Pwr GB

Health: F | PT/Exp: D | Consist: B | LIMA Plan: A | Rand Var: +2 | MM: 4501

Ominous ending to promising return. Sore shoulder shelved him until mid-May, dominated in July before Aug elbow strain ended his year. Even with elevated H%, season-long Dom+GB spike hint at sky-high ceiling. Ctl a work-in-progress, but health now the big issue. Even if he stays whole, an IP limit is likely.

Yr Tm	W	L	Sv	IP	K	ERA	xERA	WHIP	oOPS	vL	vR	BF/G	Ctl	Dom	Cmd	FpK	SwK	G	L	F	H%	S%	hr/f	GS	APC	DOM%	DIS%	Sv%	LI	RAR	BPV	BPX	R$
12																																	
13																																	
14																																	
15 HOU *	9	8	1	158	172	2.70	2.69	1.14	659	590	729	21.5	3.2	9.8	3.0	57%	10%	46	22	32	29%	79%	9%	22	96	36%	18%			24.6	115	137	$18
16 HOU	6	5	0	81	106	3.22	3.24	1.54	736	751	722	25.1	5.0	11.8	2.4	57%	13%	57	22	21	38%	80%	12%	14	96	21%	14%			9.7	112	133	$2
1st Half	3	2	0	46	56	3.91	3.75	1.67	745	719	764	26.0	5.7	11.0	1.9	59%	13%	57	22	21	39%	75%	4%	8	98	13%	13%			1.6	79	94	-$1
2nd Half	3	3	0	35	50	2.31	2.64	1.37	724	786	645	24.0	4.1	12.9	3.1	53%	14%	58	21	22	37%	89%	24%	6	93	33%	17%			8.1	156	186	$5
17 Proj	8	7	0	116	144	3.02	3.20	1.28	654	643	665	23.2	4.1	11.2	2.7	56%	12%	53	22	25	32%	78%	12%	21						16.8	120	143	$9

McGee,Jake

Age: 30 | Th: L | Role: RP | Ht: 6' 3" | Wt: 190 | Type: Pwr FB

Health: D | PT/Exp: C | Consist: C | LIMA Plan: A | Rand Var: +3 | MM: 2410

Scuffled early before rebounding in May. Lost 3 weeks to June knee strain, then lost closer role after being lit up in July return. Coors Field (6.38 ERA, 6 HR in 24 IP) didn't help. Previous Dom, SwK were nowhere to be found, but FpK surge hints at a Ctl return. Comeback candidate with uncertain role.

Yr Tm	W	L	Sv	IP	K	ERA	xERA	WHIP	oOPS	vL	vR	BF/G	Ctl	Dom	Cmd	FpK	SwK	G	L	F	H%	S%	hr/f	GS	APC	DOM%	DIS%	Sv%	LI	RAR	BPV	BPX	R$
12 TAM	5	2	0	55	73	1.95	2.49	0.80	452	665	291	3.1	1.8	11.9	6.6	62%	14%	44	19	37	27%	78%	7%	0	13			0	1.39	14.1	187	244	$10
13 TAM	5	3	1	63	75	4.02	3.20	1.18	659	678	648	3.7	3.2	10.8	3.4	63%	12%	43	19	39	30%	70%	13%	0	16			20	1.16	-1.2	130	169	$2
14 TAM	5	2	19	71	90	1.89	2.68	0.90	486	572	452	3.8	2.0	11.4	5.6	65%	14%	38	19	43	29%	79%	3%	0	16			83	1.38	16.3	166	198	$18
15 TAM	1	2	6	37	48	2.41	2.95	0.94	544	607	513	3.8	1.9	11.6	6.0	62%	13%	39	16	46	30%	78%	7%	0	16			60	1.30	7.1	173	206	$5
16 COL	2	3	15	46	38	4.73	4.76	1.58	887	821	922	3.6	3.2	7.5	2.4	66%	9%	40	22	38	34%	76%	16%	0	15			79	0.78	-3.0	68	80	$1
1st Half	0	2	15	22	16	5.32	5.10	1.64	881	1114	802	4.0	2.9	6.5	2.3	67%	8%	37	24	39	36%	70%	10%	0	17			83	0.91	-3.1	56	67	$6
2nd Half	2	1	0	24	22	4.18	4.44	1.52	894	657	1077	3.3	3.4	8.4	2.4	65%	10%	43	19	38	32%	83%	22%	0	13			0	0.68	0.0	79	95	-$3
17 Proj	3	3	9	51	54	3.50	3.78	1.25	720	712	724	3.5	2.6	9.5	3.6	64%	11%	40	19	41	32%	77%	12%	0						4.3	119	142	$4

McHugh,Collin

Age: 30 | Th: R | Role: SP | Ht: 6' 2" | Wt: 195 | Type: Pwr

Health: A | PT/Exp: A | Consist: B | LIMA Plan: A | Rand Var: +2 | MM: 2205

Solid Cmd fed by stable SwK, Dom uptick. FpK trajectory says Ctl drift isn't an issue. But increasingly elevated H% suggests that 2014 was a fluke, as more FBs and newfound HR issues helped fuel mediocre DOM%/DIS%. Could rebound slightly, but his upside is less interesting than it was a year ago.

Yr Tm	W	L	Sv	IP	K	ERA	xERA	WHIP	oOPS	vL	vR	BF/G	Ctl	Dom	Cmd	FpK	SwK	G	L	F	H%	S%	hr/f	GS	APC	DOM%	DIS%	Sv%	LI	RAR	BPV	BPX	R$
12 NYM *	7	13	0	170	130	3.81	3.94	1.30	1044	1192	937	21.2	2.8	6.9	2.4	60%	9%	33	28	39	30%	73%	19%	4	50	25%	75%	0	1.17	4.2	68	88	$5
13 2 NL *	6	9	0	139	85	5.41	5.62	1.60	1053	1252	914	22.8	2.2	5.5	2.5	54%	9%	40	28	32	36%	67%	18%	5	62	0%	80%	0	0.56	-26.5	49	64	-$15
14 HOU *	11	9	0	174	167	2.91	2.49	1.05	588	609	556	22.4	2.4	8.7	3.5	58%	11%	42	24	34	27%	74%	9%	25	99	40%	12%			17.8	118	141	$18
15 HOU	19	7	0	204	171	3.89	3.90	1.28	705	648	755	26.8	2.3	7.6	3.2	62%	11%	45	20	35	32%	71%	9%	32	101	41%	25%			1.8	96	114	$12
16 HOU	13	10	0	185	177	4.34	4.15	1.41	790	804	777	24.1	2.6	8.6	3.3	67%	11%	41	21	38	34%	73%	12%	33	96	27%	27%			-3.4	103	123	$4
1st Half	5	6	0	96	91	4.50	4.19	1.45	806	851	767	24.6	2.6	8.5	3.3	66%	12%	44	19	38	36%	72%	11%	17	97	29%	24%			-3.7	104	124	$1
2nd Half	8	4	0	89	86	4.16	4.10	1.36	772	755	789	23.6	2.6	8.7	3.3	68%	11%	39	22	39	33%	74%	13%	16	94	25%	31%			0.3	103	122	$7
17 Proj	14	9	0	181	164	3.97	4.00	1.30	736	719	753	23.7	2.4	8.1	3.4	64%	11%	43	21	36	33%	73%	11%	32						4.9	103	123	$8

Mejia,Adalberto

Age: 24 | Th: L | Role: SP | Ht: 6' 3" | Wt: 195 | Type:

Health: A | PT/Exp: D | Consist: C | LIMA Plan: C | Rand Var: -3 | MM: 0101

0-0, 7.71 ERA in 2 IP at MIN. Prospect with decent repertoire and pitchability was shut down shortly after late-Aug MLB debut due to innings limit. Impressive—3.00 ERA, 126/30 K/BB in 132 IP—at AA/AAA levels, should get 2017 chances. Back-of-the-rotation upside with no GB tilt. Watch for now.

Yr Tm	W	L	Sv	IP	K	ERA	xERA	WHIP	oOPS	vL	vR	BF/G	Ctl	Dom	Cmd	FpK	SwK	G	L	F	H%	S%	hr/f	GS	APC	DOM%	DIS%	Sv%	LI	RAR	BPV	BPX	R$
12																																	
13																																	
14 aa	7	9	0	108	72	5.00	4.58	1.46				21.0	2.5	6.0	2.4						34%	65%								-16.8	65	77	-$7
15 aa	5	2	0	51	33	3.20	2.99	1.25				17.4	3.3	5.9	1.8						28%	74%								4.8	69	82	$1
16 MIN *	9	5	0	134	102	3.97	4.26	1.32	1098	2500	808	24.2	2.1	6.9	3.3	62%	5%	33	25	42	32%	72%	0%	0	42			0	0.05	3.6	81	96	$4
1st Half	4	2	0	82	62	3.56	3.69	1.25				23.9	2.2	6.8	3.0						31%	73%	0%	0						6.4	84	101	$8
2nd Half	5	3	0	52	41	4.63	5.17	1.44	1098	2500	808	24.6	1.9	7.0	3.6	62%	5%	33	25	42	35%	71%	0%	0	42			0	0.05	-2.8	78	92	-$1
17 Proj	4	6	0	73	52	4.10	4.61	1.34				21.0	2.5	6.4	2.5	0%	0%	38	24	38	31%	73%	10%	14						0.8	63	74	-$1

Melancon,Mark

Age: 32 | Th: R | Role: RP | Ht: 6' 2" | Wt: 215 | Type: xGB

Health: A | PT/Exp: A | Consist: A | LIMA Plan: C | Rand Var: -5 | MM: 5231

More top-shelf consistency with some luck from MLB's best soft-tossing closer. 1st half Ctl and GB% not quite vintage—but fortunate S% and hr/f stinginess more than compensated. Ended with season-high 3.29 ERA in Sept. Light Dom points to risk and eventual downside. All nits; he's still elite until further notice.

Yr Tm	W	L	Sv	IP	K	ERA	xERA	WHIP	oOPS	vL	vR	BF/G	Ctl	Dom	Cmd	FpK	SwK	G	L	F	H%	S%	hr/f	GS	APC	DOM%	DIS%	Sv%	LI	RAR	BPV	BPX	R$
12 BOS *	0	2	12	67	62	4.59	3.82	1.21	754	875	655	4.3	2.1	8.3	4.0	62%	10%	50	24	26	31%	64%	22%	0	18			92	0.62	-4.7	105	137	$2
13 PIT	3	2	16	71	70	1.39	2.33	0.96	511	357	638	3.9	1.0	8.9	8.8	65%	12%	60	24	16	31%	85%	3%	0	14			76	1.31	21.6	170	222	$16
14 PIT	3	5	33	71	71	1.90	2.50	0.87	473	415	524	3.8	1.4	9.0	6.5	69%	14%	57	20	23	27%	78%	5%	0	14			89	1.37	16.1	159	190	$22
15 PIT	3	2	51	77	62	2.23	3.00	0.93	541	380	673	3.8	1.6	7.3	4.4	62%	12%	58	20	23	26%	78%	8%	0	14			96	1.35	16.4	123	146	$30
16 2 NL	2	2	47	71	65	1.64	3.01	0.90	511	560	471	3.6	1.5	8.2	5.4	66%	11%	54	21	25	26%	84%	6%	0	14			92	1.04	22.4	139	165	$29
1st Half	0	1	24	33	28	1.35	3.74	1.02	530	581	487	3.7	2.2	7.6	3.5	69%	10%	47	20	33	27%	88%	3%	0	13			96	1.04	11.7	103	122	$26
2nd Half	2	1	23	38	37	1.89	2.39	0.79	494	538	457	3.5	0.9	8.8	9.3	63%	12%	61	21	18	25%	79%	12%	0	14			88	1.04	10.8	172	205	$32
17 Proj	2	2	43	73	66	2.10	2.90	0.91	521	494	544	3.6	1.5	8.2	5.5	65%	12%	56	21	23	27%	78%	7%	0						18.6	141	168	$26

JOCK THOMPSON

Mengden,Daniel

Age: 24	Th: R	Role SP	Health A	LIMA Plan C
Ht: 6' 2"	Wt: 190	Type Pwr	PT/Exp D	Rand Var 0
			Consist F	MM 1200

2-9, 6.50 ERA in 72 IP at OAK. Strike-thrower with plus change-up zipped thru high minors (1.46 ERA, 4 HR allowed, 95/29 K/BB in 98 IP). Found rougher sledding in MLB debut. Lost GB tilt as RHBs solved him with regularity. Poor 2nd half H%/S% luck didn't help. Back-of-the-rotation arm with work to do.

Yr	Tm	W	L	Sv	IP	K	ERA	xERA	WHIP	oOPS	vL	vR	BF/G	Ctl	Dom	Cmd	FpK	SwK	G	L	F	H%	S%	hr/f	GS	APC	DOM%	DIS%	Sv%	LI	RAR	BPV	BPX	R$
12																																		
13																																		
14																																		
15																																		
16	OAK *	12	11	0	170	149	3.79	3.71	1.33	819	824	815	22.8	3.3	7.9	2.4	61%	10%	40	24	36	31%	72%	11%	14	94	21%	36%			8.3	81	96	$8
1st Half		6	5	0	99	86	2.10	2.65	1.14	685	876	503	24.6	3.2	7.8	2.4	62%	11%	42	25	33	27%	84%	11%	5	103	40%	20%			25.7	93	110	$21
2nd Half		6	6	0	71	63	6.17	5.19	1.58	909	787	1016	20.8	3.4	8.0	2.3	61%	9%	38	24	39	36%	61%	12%	9	88	11%	44%			-17.3	65	78	-$10
17	Proj	5	5	0	65	57	4.15	4.32	1.32	683	688	678	21.7	3.3	7.9	2.4	61%	9%	40	24	36	31%	70%	8%	12						0.3	70	84	-$1

Meyer,Alex

Age: 27	Th: R	Role RP	Health C	LIMA Plan D+
Ht: 6' 9"	Wt: 220	Type Pwr xFB	PT/Exp D	Rand Var 0
			Consist F	MM 0301

1-3, 5.68 ERA in 25 IP at MIN/LAA. Control- and health-challenged, but still throws gas. Flashed the goods early at AAA and late in MLB (16/7 K/BB in final 3 GS) despite May-Aug DL stint for shoulder. FpK suggests long road ahead, and SwK belies career 10+ Dom. But age, arm keep the flame.

Yr	Tm	W	L	Sv	IP	K	ERA	xERA	WHIP	oOPS	vL	vR	BF/G	Ctl	Dom	Cmd	FpK	SwK	G	L	F	H%	S%	hr/f	GS	APC	DOM%	DIS%	Sv%	LI	RAR	BPV	BPX	R$
12																																		
13	aa	4	3	0	70	70	3.62	3.40	1.35				22.5	3.6	9.0	2.5						33%	72%								2.2	100	130	$0
14	aaa	7	7	0	130	123	4.55	4.76	1.58				21.3	4.6	8.5	1.8						34%	72%								-13.0	66	79	-$7
15	MIN *	4	5	0	95	81	6.98	6.46	1.97	1409	1500	1333	11.3	5.2	7.7	1.5	40%	5%	13	0	88	40%	63%	29%	0	33			0	0.91	-35.2	47	55	-$22
16	2 AL *	2	4	1	47	49	3.50	3.20	1.29	828	1023	705	17.5	4.0	9.5	2.4	45%	9%	38	18	44	31%	74%	10%	6	68	0%	33%	100	0.71	4.0	98	117	$0
1st Half		1	2	1	21	21	3.05	3.50	1.34	1259	1429	1146	17.5	3.4	8.8	2.6	43%	10%	36	29	36	33%	77%	20%	1	47	0%	100%	100	0.61	2.9	99	118	$1
2nd Half		1	2	0	26	29	3.86	2.95	1.26	724	933	585	17.4	4.6	10.1	2.2	46%	9%	39	16	46	28%	70%	8%	5	77	0%	20%			1.1	99	119	-$1
17	Proj	4	6	0	87	87	4.54	4.86	1.51	747	971	597	15.9	4.4	8.9	2.0	46%	9%	39	16	46	34%	70%	5%	14						-3.7	59	70	-$4

Miley,Wade

Age: 30	Th: L	Role SP	Health A	LIMA Plan C
Ht: 6' 2"	Wt: 190	Type Pwr	PT/Exp A	Rand Var +4
			Consist A	MM 1203

2nd half Cmd fueled by Dom spike over final 9 weeks with only slight SwK uptick. Except for July, bottom line was awful. RHBs owned him; career-worst 1.4 hr/9 and another shaky H%/S% combo didn't help. Better than this, but he's teased with 2nd half xERA/BPV surges before. Historical DOM%/DIS% points to low ceiling.

Yr	Tm	W	L	Sv	IP	K	ERA	xERA	WHIP	oOPS	vL	vR	BF/G	Ctl	Dom	Cmd	FpK	SwK	G	L	F	H%	S%	hr/f	GS	APC	DOM%	DIS%	Sv%	LI	RAR	BPV	BPX	R$
12	ARI	16	11	0	195	144	3.33	3.89	1.18	685	544	723	25.2	1.7	6.7	3.9	60%	9%	43	23	34	31%	73%	7%	29	94	38%	34%	0	0.82	16.5	95	123	$17
13	ARI	10	10	0	203	147	3.55	3.79	1.32	727	704	732	25.7	2.9	6.5	2.2	59%	8%	52	21	27	30%	76%	13%	33	98	30%	30%			7.8	68	89	$7
14	ARI	8	12	0	201	183	4.34	3.59	1.40	746	727	752	26.2	3.4	8.2	2.4	63%	10%	51	21	28	32%	71%	14%	33	97	24%	24%			-14.8	86	102	-$3
15	BOS	11	11	0	194	147	4.46	4.16	1.37	740	674	760	26.0	3.0	6.8	2.3	61%	9%	49	21	30	32%	68%	9%	32	100	34%	28%			-11.9	70	83	-$1
16	2 AL	9	13	0	166	137	5.37	4.14	1.42	808	671	842	23.7	2.7	7.4	2.8	60%	9%	47	23	30	33%	65%	16%	30	91	13%	37%			-24.1	87	103	-$6
1st Half		6	4	0	81	59	5.58	4.57	1.40	813	809	814	24.6	2.7	6.6	2.5	61%	9%	44	20	36	31%	64%	15%	14	94	7%	29%			-13.8	68	81	-$4
2nd Half		3	9	0	85	78	5.17	3.73	1.44	804	524	868	22.9	2.6	8.2	3.1	59%	9%	51	25	24	35%	66%	18%	16	88	19%	44%			-10.3	106	126	-$7
17	Proj	8	10	0	145	119	4.78	4.11	1.39	772	664	800	24.3	2.8	7.4	2.6	61%	9%	49	22	29	32%	68%	13%	25						-10.5	84	100	-$3

Miller,Andrew

Age: 32	Th: L	Role RP	Health D	LIMA Plan C+
Ht: 6' 6"	Wt: 205	Type Pwr GB	PT/Exp B	Rand Var -2
			Consist A	MM 5521

Career-best Ctl and season-long GB spike fueled ridiculous command and ERA gains, even as FpK backed off. Allowed more than a run only once in 70 appearances. Coughed up 8 HR, but if you didn't take him deep, you didn't take him. Potential $20 reliever even without a single save. Can regress and still be filthy.

Yr	Tm	W	L	Sv	IP	K	ERA	xERA	WHIP	oOPS	vL	vR	BF/G	Ctl	Dom	Cmd	FpK	SwK	G	L	F	H%	S%	hr/f	GS	APC	DOM%	DIS%	Sv%	LI	RAR	BPV	BPX	R$
12	BOS	3	2	0	40	51	3.35	3.32	1.19	588	429	829	3.2	4.5	11.4	2.6	54%	10%	43	23	34	28%	73%	9%	0	13			0	1.17	3.3	105	137	$1
13	BOS	1	2	0	31	48	2.64	2.47	1.37	624	725	526	3.6	5.0	14.1	2.8	59%	14%	56	21	23	36%	85%	20%	0	15			0	0.81	4.6	153	199	-$1
14	2 AL	5	5	1	62	103	2.02	1.80	0.80	456	467	446	3.3	2.5	14.9	6.1	59%	15%	47	22	31	29%	77%	9%	0	14			50	1.54	13.2	226	270	$11
15	NYY	3	2	36	62	100	2.04	2.14	0.86	475	602	444	4.1	2.9	14.6	5.0	66%	18%	48	18	33	27%	81%	13%	0	16			95	1.22	14.6	210	250	$24
16	2 AL	10	1	12	74	123	1.45	1.63	0.69	487	523	474	3.9	1.1	14.9	13.7	62%	17%	54	17	29	28%	91%	20%	0	16			86	1.23	25.1	271	322	$25
1st Half		5	1	7	37	66	1.47	1.45	0.68	495	564	472	3.8	1.2	16.2	13.2	60%	18%	56	14	30	29%	95%	26%	0	15			88	1.24	12.3	292	348	$25
2nd Half		5	0	5	38	57	1.43	1.81	0.69	480	487	476	4.1	1.0	13.6	14.3	64%	16%	53	19	27	28%	87%	14%	0	17			83	1.21	12.8	251	299	$25
17	Proj	7	2	14	73	117	2.09	1.89	0.81	493	530	476	3.6	2.1	14.5	6.9	62%	16%	51	19	30	29%	80%	16%	0						18.8	233	277	$20

Miller,Shelby

Age: 26	Th: R	Role SP	Health B	LIMA Plan C
Ht: 6' 3"	Wt: 225	Type Pwr	PT/Exp A	Rand Var +3
			Consist B	MM 1103

3-12, 6.15 ERA in 101 IP at ARI. Wheels fell off early as Ctl vanished, Cmd fell to unrosterable levels and LHBs took him apart. Horrid start fueled late-May DL stint (sprained finger?), then AAA demotion. Sept finish (12 scoreless IP at ARI) is noise. xERA scan is his reality. Key '16 stat: 20 starts, 1 PQS-DOM.

Yr	Tm	W	L	Sv	IP	K	ERA	xERA	WHIP	oOPS	vL	vR	BF/G	Ctl	Dom	Cmd	FpK	SwK	G	L	F	H%	S%	hr/f	GS	APC	DOM%	DIS%	Sv%	LI	RAR	BPV	BPX	R$
12	STL *	12	10	0	150	153	4.58	4.54	1.37	463	485	445	19.1	3.1	9.1	3.0	57%	13%	42	15	42	33%	70%	0%	1	33	100%	0%	0	0.88	-10.5	81	106	$1
13	STL	15	9	0	173	169	3.06	3.73	1.21	670	761	588	23.3	3.0	8.8	3.0	62%	10%	38	20	41	29%	79%	10%	31	96	23%	35%			17.2	94	123	$16
14	STL	10	9	0	183	127	3.74	4.44	1.27	697	707	690	23.9	3.6	6.2	1.7	60%	7%	40	19	41	26%	74%	10%	31	89	23%	42%	0	0.75	0.1	33	40	$5
15	ATL	6	17	0	205	171	3.02	4.02	1.25	663	732	594	26.1	3.2	7.5	2.3	61%	10%	48	18	34	29%	77%	6%	33	98	30%	24%			23.7	75	89	$13
16	ARI *	8	13	0	152	114	5.59	5.57	1.60	867	943	767	23.9	3.1	6.7	2.2	59%	8%	42	23	35	35%	66%	12%	20	87	5%	50%			-26.2	47	56	-$12
1st Half		2	8	0	64	45	6.85	5.50	1.76	911	992	809	22.8	4.6	6.3	1.4	59%	8%	42	24	34	33%	63%	17%	13	87	8%	62%			-21.1	9	11	-$19
2nd Half		6	5	0	87	69	4.65	4.89	1.49	792	865	689	25.1	2.0	7.1	3.6	60%	7%	41	21	38	37%	68%	4%	7	86	0%	29%			-5.0	92	110	-$6
17	Proj	7	11	0	145	114	4.46	4.59	1.43	766	841	681	23.8	3.1	7.1	2.3	60%	8%	43	20	37	32%	70%	9%	26						-4.9	63	75	-$3

Miranda,Ariel

Age: 28	Th: L	Role SP	Health A	LIMA Plan D+
Ht: 6' 2"	Wt: 190	Type xFB	PT/Exp D	Rand Var +1
			Consist B	MM 0103

5-2, 3.88 ERA in 58 IP at SEA. Cuban import debuted in 2nd half with intriguing Sept bottom line—2.62 ERA, 0.87 WHIP over 34 IP in 6 starts—from MLB rotation. Ridiculous 19% H% says it's not sustainable. Overall, the odds against an ex-FBer without an elite Dom finding extended MLB success are prohibitive.

Yr	Tm	W	L	Sv	IP	K	ERA	xERA	WHIP	oOPS	vL	vR	BF/G	Ctl	Dom	Cmd	FpK	SwK	G	L	F	H%	S%	hr/f	GS	APC	DOM%	DIS%	Sv%	LI	RAR	BPV	BPX	R$
12	for	8	6	0	128	83	4.19	4.43	1.37				26.8	3.6	5.9	1.6						28%	74%								-2.8	35	46	-$1
13	for	5	4	0	78	76	3.87	4.22	1.35				25.0	3.9	8.8	2.3						30%	77%								0.0	66	86	$0
14																																		
15	aa	5	2	0	45	32	5.11	4.52	1.59				24.8	4.0	6.4	1.6						35%	66%								-6.4	60	72	-$6
16	2 AL *	9	9	0	159	110	5.36	5.44	1.47	738	859	707	21.9	3.1	6.3	2.0	60%	8%	31	18	51	31%	68%	14%	10	76	10%	30%	0	0.86	-22.9	27	33	-$8
1st Half		3	7	0	80	59	6.59	6.15	1.65	1000	1143	750	22.3	3.2	6.6	2.1	64%	6%	43	14	43	35%	62%	0%	0	50			0	0.61	-23.6	32	38	-$17
2nd Half		6	2	0	79	51	4.13	4.72	1.28	724	804	706	21.6	3.0	5.9	2.0	60%	9%	31	18	52	25%	77%	14%	10	78	10%	30%	0	0.88	0.6	24	28	$2
17	Proj	9	7	0	145	106	4.85	5.51	1.46	790	929	760	23.5	3.5	6.6	1.9	60%	9%	31	18	52	30%	72%	10%	26						-11.8	33	39	-$5

Mitchell,Bryan

Age: 26	Th: R	Role RP	Health F	LIMA Plan D+
Ht: 6' 2"	Wt: 205	Type Pwr GB	PT/Exp D	Rand Var -3
			Consist A	MM 0101

1-2, 3.24 ERA in 25 IP at NYY. Hard-thrower with GB tilt was set to open in MLB pen. Fractured toe intervened in late March; didn't pitch until August. A starter for most of his career, held his own in 5 Sept starts (3.29 ERA) despite poor peripherals. Shaky Ctl and SwK tab him as a reliever. Avoid for now.

Yr	Tm	W	L	Sv	IP	K	ERA	xERA	WHIP	oOPS	vL	vR	BF/G	Ctl	Dom	Cmd	FpK	SwK	G	L	F	H%	S%	hr/f	GS	APC	DOM%	DIS%	Sv%	LI	RAR	BPV	BPX	R$
12																																		
13	aa	0	0	0	19	14	2.43	2.37	1.15				24.7	2.5	6.7	2.7						30%	77%								3.3	103	135	-$2
14	NYY *	6	8	0	114	88	4.73	5.21	1.58	751	1013	554	19.3	3.8	7.0	1.8	59%	10%	55	26	19	34%	72%	0%	1	52	0%	100%	0	0.30	-13.9	47	56	-$8
15	NYY *	5	7	1	105	81	4.83	4.64	1.63	817	757	861	13.3	4.8	6.9	1.4	57%	9%	50	28	22	34%	69%	19%	2	30	0%	100%	100	0.57	-11.2	57	68	-$9
16	NYY *	1	3	0	41	28	3.67	4.49	1.53	741	750	735	19.7	3.9	6.1	1.5	53%	7%	48	19	33	32%	77%	4%	5	78	0%	60%			2.6	51	61	-$4
1st Half																																		
2nd Half		1	3	0	41	28	3.67	4.49	1.53	742	750	735	19.7	3.9	6.1	1.5	53%	7%	48	19	33	32%	77%	4%	5	78	0%	60%			2.6	51	61	-$4
17	Proj	5	8	0	116	86	4.42	4.98	1.57	748	726	761	17.4	4.1	6.7	1.6	53%	7%	48	19	33	33%	73%	7%	22						-3.2	36	42	-$6

JOCK THOMPSON

Montas,Frankie

Age: 24	Th: R	Role RP	Health F
Ht: 6' 2"	Wt: 255	Type Pwr	PT/Exp F
LIMA Plan C	Rand Var 0	Consist A	MM 2400

High-octane arm again unable to stay off the DL. Looked great in small sample May/June effort following Feb rib surgery, but subsequent oblique problems made for a lost season. 100 mph fastball is calling card; lagging secondary pitches, inconsistent delivery raise role questions. Better conditioning is critical.

Yr Tm	W	L	Sv	IP	K	ERA	xERA	WHIP	oOPS	vL	vR	BF/G	Ctl	Dom	Cmd	FpK	SwK	G	L	F	H%	S%	hr/f	GS	APC	DOM%	DIS%	Sv%	LI	RAR	BPV	BPX	R$
12																																	
13																																	
14																																	
15 CHW *	5	7	0	127	117	3.85	3.47	1.41	699	921	560	17.9	4.3	8.3	1.9	53%	13%	38	16	46	32%	71%	6%	2	41	0%	50%	0	0.31	1.8	86	102	$0
16 a/a	0	0	0	16	19	2.76	3.46	1.19				9.2	1.6	10.6	6.7						36%	79%								2.8	186	222	-$2
1st Half	0	0	0	16	19	2.76	3.46	1.19				9.2	1.6	10.6	6.7						36%	79%								2.8	186	222	-$2
2nd Half																																	
17 Proj	1	1	0	44	47	4.25	4.00	1.39				11.8	3.8	9.7	2.6	11%	58%	42	21	37	33%	71%	10%	3						-0.3	93	111	-$3

Montgomery,Michael

Age: 28	Th: L	Role RP	Health A
Ht: 6' 5"	Wt: 215	Type Pwr xGB	PT/Exp C
LIMA Plan B	Rand Var -1	Consist B	MM 2101

One-time SP prospect rediscovered velocity in the pen, suddenly gained relevance as a swingman. Year-long Dom, SwK spikes held up nicely. GB% surge also helped neutralize 2nd half gopheritis and control issues. FpK, S% point to a pullback. Hardly a rock-solid history; he's in the pen for a reason.

Yr Tm	W	L	Sv	IP	K	ERA	xERA	WHIP	oOPS	vL	vR	BF/G	Ctl	Dom	Cmd	FpK	SwK	G	L	F	H%	S%	hr/f	GS	APC	DOM%	DIS%	Sv%	LI	RAR	BPV	BPX	R$
12 a/a	5	12	0	150	91	6.70	6.33	1.73				25.2	3.7	5.5	1.5						35%	62%								-49.6	15	20	-$27
13 aaa	7	8	0	109	65	5.50	5.00	1.61				24.1	3.9	5.4	1.4						33%	65%								-21.9	35	45	-$11
14 aaa	10	5	0	126	81	5.49	4.72	1.53				21.9	3.7	5.8	1.6						33%	63%								-27.2	45	54	-$10
15 SEA *	8	9	0	155	112	4.33	3.95	1.34	754	841	725	24.0	3.1	6.5	2.1	63%	9%	51	20	29	30%	69%	13%	16	91	19%	50%			-7.1	62	73	-$1
16 2 TM	4	5	0	100	92	2.52	3.42	1.17	652	570	691	8.4	3.4	8.3	2.4	56%	12%	58	23	19	27%	82%	16%	7	31	0%	14%	0	0.75	20.6	93	110	$9
1st Half	2	3	0	46	42	2.33	3.24	1.08	578	470	639	6.4	2.9	8.2	2.8	55%	11%	60	20	20	28%	78%	4%	0	23			0	0.80	10.6	106	127	$10
2nd Half	2	2	0	54	50	2.68	3.58	1.25	715	677	729	11.4	3.9	8.4	2.2	56%	13%	57	25	18	27%	85%	27%	7	42	0%	14%	0	0.69	10.0	82	97	$9
17 Proj	5	5	0	102	81	3.79	3.95	1.32	716	694	725	9.7	3.5	7.2	2.1	59%	11%	55	22	23	30%	73%	13%	0						5.0	69	83	$1

Moore,Matt

Age: 28	Th: L	Role SP	Health F
Ht: 6' 2"	Wt: 205	Type Pwr FB	PT/Exp C
LIMA Plan B	Rand Var 0	Consist B	MM 1303

Finally healthy, ex-top prospect ate innings as Ks, wins fueled fantasy value. PRO: Dominance over final 8 starts (5 PQS-DOM; 9.3 Dom in 45 IP); FpK with room for Ctl gains. CON: DOM%/DIS% and game-to-game volatility; 2H Ctl fade; mid-90s mph still MIA; light GB%. Consistency is critical to a step up.

Yr Tm	W	L	Sv	IP	K	ERA	xERA	WHIP	oOPS	vL	vR	BF/G	Ctl	Dom	Cmd	FpK	SwK	G	L	F	H%	S%	hr/f	GS	APC	DOM%	DIS%	Sv%	LI	RAR	BPV	BPX	R$
12 TAM	11	11	0	177	175	3.81	4.24	1.35	706	685	712	24.5	4.1	8.9	2.2	60%	12%	37	20	43	30%	74%	9%	31	98	23%	19%			4.6	64	83	$7
13 TAM	17	4	0	150	143	3.29	4.23	1.30	655	617	672	23.8	4.5	8.6	1.9	51%	10%	39	18	42	27%	77%	8%	27	97	26%	22%			10.6	48	63	$12
14 TAM	0	2	0	10	6	2.70	4.75	1.50	777	1010	703	22.0	4.5	5.4	1.2	44%	7%	45	27	27	29%	86%	11%	2	92	0%	50%			1.3	-1	-2	-$3
15 TAM *	5	7	0	103	93	5.12	5.22	1.48	839	785	866	23.4	3.1	8.1	2.6	60%	10%	39	22	39	34%	69%	11%	12	88	17%	67%			-14.7	59	71	-$7
16 2 TM	13	12	0	198	178	4.08	4.47	1.29	694	654	706	25.4	3.3	8.1	2.5	62%	11%	38	20	42	29%	72%	10%	33	100	36%	33%			2.6	73	87	$9
1st Half	4	5	0	96	90	4.67	4.24	1.32	752	686	773	25.6	2.6	8.4	3.2	62%	11%	38	20	41	31%	69%	14%	16	101	31%	31%			-5.7	97	116	$3
2nd Half	9	7	0	102	88	3.53	4.70	1.26	638	616	644	25.2	3.9	7.8	2.0	61%	10%	38	19	43	28%	74%	7%	17	98	41%	35%			8.3	51	61	$15
17 Proj	12	10	0	174	159	4.05	4.40	1.33	716	685	727	23.9	3.4	8.2	2.4	59%	11%	39	20	41	30%	73%	10%	30						3.0	72	86	$6

Morgan,Adam

Age: 27	Th: L	Role SP	Health A
Ht: 6' 1"	Wt: 200	Type FB	PT/Exp D
LIMA Plan D+	Rand Var +4	Consist A	MM 0103

2-1, 6.04 ERA in 113 IP at PHI. Dom soared and Cmd improved as he added a few ticks of velocity. Brought already good Ctl down to exquisite levels, even threw fewer FBs. None of this mattered, as MLB RHBs teed off on soft-tosser all season and HRs decimated him again. Can only improve, but needs a new wrinkle.

Yr Tm	W	L	Sv	IP	K	ERA	xERA	WHIP	oOPS	vL	vR	BF/G	Ctl	Dom	Cmd	FpK	SwK	G	L	F	H%	S%	hr/f	GS	APC	DOM%	DIS%	Sv%	LI	RAR	BPV	BPX	R$
12 aa	4	1	0	36	25	3.93	3.84	1.34				24.7	2.7	6.4	2.4						32%	71%								0.4	73	95	-$2
13 aaa	2	7	0	71	42	4.66	6.24	1.69				20.1	3.3	5.3	1.6						34%	76%								-7.0	15	20	-$9
14																																	
15 PHI *	5	13	0	153	77	5.16	5.53	1.51	775	617	820	23.6	2.7	4.5	1.7	66%	10%	31	20	49	31%	69%	10%	15	83	0%	33%			-22.5	17	20	-$13
16 PHI *	8	12	0	164	137	5.65	5.63	1.47	878	726	927	22.6	2.3	7.5	3.3	60%	11%	37	25	38	34%	65%	16%	21	85	14%	38%	0	0.72	-29.4	62	73	-$9
1st Half	2	7	0	79	68	6.15	6.40	1.61	915	862	931	21.9	2.4	7.7	3.3	59%	11%	35	24	40	37%	65%	16%	11	83	9%	27%	0	0.68	-19.1	55	66	-$14
2nd Half	6	5	0	85	69	5.18	4.91	1.33	834	573	923	23.4	2.1	7.4	3.4	61%	12%	40	26	35	31%	65%	17%	10	87	20%	50%			-10.3	68	82	-$4
17 Proj	7	10	0	131	91	5.18	4.98	1.49	846	685	895	22.7	2.6	6.3	2.5	63%	11%	35	23	42	33%	69%	11%	25						-15.9	57	68	-$8

Morin,Michael

Age: 26	Th: R	Role RP	Health C
Ht: 6' 4"	Wt: 218	Type Pwr FB	PT/Exp D
LIMA Plan C+	Rand Var 0	Consist B	MM 2310

Early Dom slide and victimization by 1H S% helped put him on mid-season Anaheim-to-Salt Lake shuttle. Even after this passed, 2H h% did him no favors—and 2014 GB% hasn't returned. Seems like we should be getting more from change-up artist with plus Cmd and consistent FpK, SwK history. But don't wait up.

Yr Tm	W	L	Sv	IP	K	ERA	xERA	WHIP	oOPS	vL	vR	BF/G	Ctl	Dom	Cmd	FpK	SwK	G	L	F	H%	S%	hr/f	GS	APC	DOM%	DIS%	Sv%	LI	RAR	BPV	BPX	R$
12																																	
13 aa	0	2	10	31	29	2.39	2.95	1.10				4.7	1.4	8.4	6.0						32%	81%								5.7	164	214	$3
14 LAA	4	4	0	59	54	2.90	3.67	1.19	629	737	511	4.1	2.9	8.2	2.8	63%	12%	44	17	39	30%	76%	5%	0	15			0	1.07	6.1	92	110	$3
15 LAA *	8	4	2	53	57	6.25	4.81	1.45	720	687	740	3.7	2.5	9.8	4.0	63%	16%	39	18	43	38%	56%	7%	0	12			67	0.70	-14.9	110	131	-$4
16 LAA	2	2	0	56	49	4.37	4.12	1.20	677	731	645	3.8	2.4	7.9	3.3	67%	13%	39	21	40	30%	66%	9%	0	14			0	0.90	-1.2	94	112	-$1
1st Half	1	1	0	35	29	4.93	4.19	1.13	644	610	661	4.0	2.6	7.5	2.9	67%	14%	41	17	42	27%	57%	10%	0	15			0	0.75	-3.2	84	100	$0
2nd Half	1	1	0	21	20	3.43	4.00	1.33	729	923	619	3.5	2.1	8.6	4.0	67%	11%	35	27	37	35%	77%	9%	0	13			0	1.11	2.0	110	131	-$2
17 Proj	4	3	2	58	55	4.26	3.99	1.27	710	765	673	3.8	2.3	8.6	3.7	65%	14%	39	21	40	33%	68%	8%	0						-0.5	108	129	$0

Musgrove,Joe

Age: 24	Th: R	Role SP	Health A
Ht: 6' 5"	Wt: 230	Type	PT/Exp D
LIMA Plan B+	Rand Var 0	Consist A	MM 2103

4-4, 4.06 ERA in 62 IP at HOU. SP prospect posted 2.74 ERA, 87/10 K/BB over 85 IP between AA-AAA prior to Aug MLB debut. Lost big minor league GB tilt in the transition, as DOM%/DIS% highlights growing pains. But 8.4 Cmd, 2.3 Ctl in HOU speak to legit skills. An investable future with mid-rotation upside.

Yr Tm	W	L	Sv	IP	K	ERA	xERA	WHIP	oOPS	vL	vR	BF/G	Ctl	Dom	Cmd	FpK	SwK	G	L	F	H%	S%	hr/f	GS	APC	DOM%	DIS%	Sv%	LI	RAR	BPV	BPX	R$
12																																	
13																																	
14																																	
15 aa	4	0	1	45	29	2.49	3.47	1.00				21.5	1.2	5.8	4.9						24%	88%								8.2	99	118	$4
16 HOU *	11	8	0	147	129	3.52	3.92	1.18	758	822	710	21.8	1.6	7.9	5.0	62%	10%	43	21	36	31%	75%	14%	10	89	30%	30%	0	0.78	12.1	119	142	$12
1st Half	5	4	0	66	56	3.41	4.13	1.19				20.5	1.2	7.5	6.2						32%	77%	0%	0						6.4	140	167	$10
2nd Half	6	4	0	81	74	3.62	3.75	1.18	758	822	710	23.1	1.9	8.2	4.3	62%	10%	43	21	36	31%	74%	14%	10	89	30%	30%	0	0.78	5.7	111	132	$13
17 Proj	10	7	0	160	126	3.88	4.00	1.18	719	775	678	22.2	1.4	7.1	4.9	62%	10%	43	21	36	30%	73%	12%	29						6.1	110	131	$8

Neal,Zachary

Age: 28	Th: R	Role RP	Health A
Ht: 6' 3"	Wt: 220	Type Con GB	PT/Exp D
LIMA Plan C	Rand Var 0	Consist C	MM 0000

2-4, 4.24 ERA in 70 IP at OAK. Journeyman minor leaguer with 3.78 career ERA made May MLB debut, ate innings as swingman. Exquisite control and ability to generate GBs have brought him this far; durability and broad repertoire are plusses. But strikeout-challenged profile offers little upside. Avoid.

Yr Tm	W	L	Sv	IP	K	ERA	xERA	WHIP	oOPS	vL	vR	BF/G	Ctl	Dom	Cmd	FpK	SwK	G	L	F	H%	S%	hr/f	GS	APC	DOM%	DIS%	Sv%	LI	RAR	BPV	BPX	R$
12 aa	4	6	0	69	40	4.73	5.10	1.52				14.2	1.8	5.2	3.0						36%	68%								-6.1	68	88	-$6
13 aa	8	12	0	166	78	4.98	4.76	1.41				25.0	2.0	4.2	2.1						32%	66%								-22.9	37	49	-$9
14 a/a	10	7	0	150	82	3.65	4.64	1.35				25.1	1.2	4.9	4.0						33%	75%								1.6	84	100	$1
15 a/a	10	13	0	168	75	5.74	5.92	1.63				26.6	2.0	4.0	2.0						35%	65%								-36.8	27	33	-$19
16 OAK *	9	6	2	132	51	4.50	4.61	1.30	722	667	778	15.5	1.1	3.5	3.3	61%	9%	53	17	30	30%	68%	12%	6	39	17%	83%	67	0.46	-5.0	54	64	$1
1st Half	7	2	1	67	24	4.86	5.26	1.42	985	1158	767	16.8	0.9	3.2	3.4	69%	7%	54	21	25	33%	67%	25%	1	26	0%	100%	100	0.14	-5.6	51	61	$0
2nd Half	2	4	1	64	26	4.12	3.93	1.18	636	479	781	14.3	1.2	3.7	3.2	59%	10%	53	15	32	28%	68%	8%	5	46	20%	80%	50	0.62	0.6	58	69	$2
17 Proj	3	3	0	58	25	4.65	4.60	1.39	799	797	802	18.7	1.4	3.9	2.9	63%	9%	53	17	29	32%	68%	10%	11						-3.3	65	77	-$4

JOCK THOMPSON

Nelson,Jimmy

Age: 28	Th: R	Role SP	Health A	LIMA Plan D+	
Ht: 6' 5"	Wt: 250	Type Pwr	PT/Exp A	Rand Var +1	
			Consist B	MM 1203	

It's a trap! Fast start—2.88 ERA, 1.17 WHIP, 5 wins in 72 IP thru May—paved over mediocre peripherals before the collapse. Stagnant Dom, disintegrating control and ballooning hr/f led the way down; stable GB% couldn't stem the tide. FpK, SwK are pessimistic on Cmd rebound. DOM%/DIS% says he's unrosterable.

Yr	Tm	W	L	Sv	IP	K	ERA	xERA	WHIP	oOPS	vL	vR	BF/G	Ctl	Dom	Cmd	FpK	SwK	G	L	F	H%	S%	hr/f	GS	APC	DOM%	DIS%	Sv%	LI	RAR	BPV	BPX	R$
12	aa	2	4	0	46	37	4.88	4.28	1.72				20.9	7.6	7.2	0.9						29%	71%								-4.9	55	72	-$8
13	MIL *	10	10	0	162	147	3.67	3.79	1.43	286	473	63	22.3	4.0	8.2	2.0	49%	11%	42	33	25	33%	74%	0%	1	36	0%	0%	0	0.28	4.0	81	105	$3
14	MIL *	12	11	0	180	151	3.01	3.14	1.21	793	804	782	23.5	2.7	7.6	2.8	63%	10%	48	20	32	30%	76%	8%	12	79	25%	42%	0	0.83	16.3	96	114	$13
15	MIL	11	13	0	177	148	4.11	3.90	1.29	704	876	568	25.1	3.3	7.5	2.3	60%	10%	51	20	29	29%	70%	12%	30	93	43%	30%			-3.3	75	89	$5
16	MIL	8	16	0	179	140	4.62	4.80	1.52	791	779	802	25.2	4.3	7.0	1.6	58%	8%	49	19	31	31%	73%	15%	32	93	9%	50%			-9.5	37	44	-$5
1st Half		5	7	0	101	74	3.65	4.62	1.37	748	776	722	25.5	3.9	6.6	1.7	57%	8%	48	21	31	28%	77%	13%	17	93	12%	35%			6.7	39	46	$5
2nd Half		3	9	0	78	66	5.86	5.04	1.71	841	783	883	24.9	4.8	7.6	1.6	59%	8%	51	18	31	34%	69%	16%	15	93	7%	67%			-16.1	35	42	-$17
17	**Proj**	**9**	**13**	**0**	**160**	**131**	**4.39**	**4.48**	**1.45**	**749**	**794**	**710**	**23.8**	**4.0**	**7.4**	**1.8**	**60%**	**9%**	**50**	**19**	**31**	**31%**	**72%**	**12%**	**29**						**-4.0**	**51**	**61**	**-$2**

Neris,Hector

Age: 28	Th: R	Role RP	Health A	LIMA Plan B+	
Ht: 6' 2"	Wt: 175	Type Pwr	PT/Exp D	Rand Var -2	
			Consist C	MM 3511	

Stunning workhorse effort out of the pen, with 100 Ks to boot. PRO: Consistent Dom, Ctl and velocity throughout; whiffs supported by elite SwK; no platoon issues. CON: FpK says Ctl will rise from here; GB% is nothing special. He's roster-worthy with closer upside, but history says don't overpay.

Yr	Tm	W	L	Sv	IP	K	ERA	xERA	WHIP	oOPS	vL	vR	BF/G	Ctl	Dom	Cmd	FpK	SwK	G	L	F	H%	S%	hr/f	GS	APC	DOM%	DIS%	Sv%	LI	RAR	BPV	BPX	R$
12																																		
13	aa	6	4	0	97	79	5.12	4.80	1.43				9.0	3.6	7.3	2.0						30%	68%								-15.0	45	59	-$6
14	PHI *	7	3	2	78	60	4.16	3.92	1.30	0	0	0	6.6	3.4	6.9	2.0	100%	22%	50	0	50	28%	71%	0%	0	9			40	1.97	-4.0	57	68	$1
15	PHI *	3	5	1	78	70	4.21	5.00	1.56	772	770	772	5.8	4.2	8.1	1.9	52%	14%	39	15	46	34%	76%	15%	0	21			33	0.69	-2.4	56	67	-$5
16	PHI	4	4	2	80	102	2.58	3.22	1.11	620	632	607	4.2	3.4	11.4	3.4	52%	16%	42	25	34	29%	83%	14%	0	17			33	1.11	16.0	135	160	$9
1st Half		2	3	1	44	53	2.66	3.18	1.07	611	630	593	4.1	3.3	10.8	3.3	50%	16%	46	21	33	27%	81%	15%	0	17			33	1.10	8.3	130	156	$10
2nd Half		2	1	1	36	49	2.48	3.27	1.16	631	633	628	4.2	3.5	12.1	3.5	54%	16%	38	28	34	31%	84%	13%	0	18			33	1.11	7.7	140	167	$9
17	**Proj**	**4**	**3**	**10**	**73**	**84**	**3.20**	**3.68**	**1.23**	**678**	**682**	**674**	**4.9**	**3.6**	**10.5**	**2.9**	**52%**	**15%**	**40**	**21**	**39**	**30%**	**79%**	**12%**	**0**						**8.9**	**109**	**130**	**$7**

Neshek,Pat

Age: 36	Th: R	Role RP	Health A	LIMA Plan A	
Ht: 6' 3"	Wt: 205	Type Pwr xFB	PT/Exp C	Rand Var -3	
			Consist A	MM 2300	

Competent performance from consistent middle reliever fueled by outstanding Ctl, stable Dom and ability to contain H%. Soft-tosser's inability to induce GBs keeps xERA suspect, and age adds more risk to his profile. But with FpK cooperation, should continue providing ERA and WHIP help as a do-no-harm RP.

Yr	Tm	W	L	Sv	IP	K	ERA	xERA	WHIP	oOPS	vL	vR	BF/G	Ctl	Dom	Cmd	FpK	SwK	G	L	F	H%	S%	hr/f	GS	APC	DOM%	DIS%	Sv%	LI	RAR	BPV	BPX	R$
12	OAK *	5	3	11	64	52	3.39	4.08	1.33	530	1108	369	4.5	2.1	7.3	3.5	63%	13%	35	17	48	34%	76%	12%	0	14			69	1.21	4.9	96	125	$5
13	OAK	2	1	0	40	29	3.35	4.90	1.36	738	922	644	3.9	3.3	6.5	1.9	54%	11%	33	19	48	29%	82%	10%	0	15			0	0.39	2.6	37	48	-$2
14	STL	7	2	6	67	68	1.87	3.21	0.79	480	541	442	3.6	1.2	9.1	7.6	67%	13%	35	11	54	25%	80%	4%	0	14			60	1.38	15.5	144	172	$14
15	HOU	3	6	1	55	51	3.62	3.87	1.12	709	768	673	3.4	2.0	8.4	4.3	69%	11%	32	22	46	28%	74%	11%	0	13			25	1.32	2.3	108	128	$2
16	HOU	2	2	0	47	43	3.06	4.00	0.94	606	967	463	3.1	2.1	8.2	3.9	71%	11%	33	21	46	23%	74%	10%	0	12			0	1.20	6.5	102	122	$3
1st Half		2	1	0	25	23	2.84	4.03	0.87	659	1330	389	3.0	2.1	8.2	3.8	70%	11%	29	20	51	20%	78%	12%	0	12			0	1.42	4.2	97	115	$5
2nd Half		0	1	0	22	20	3.32	3.97	1.02	551	574	542	3.1	2.1	8.3	4.0	72%	11%	38	21	41	27%	70%	8%	0	11			0	0.94	2.3	109	130	$1
17	**Proj**	**3**	**3**	**0**	**58**	**53**	**3.40**	**3.96**	**1.06**	**661**	**838**	**575**	**3.2**	**2.0**	**8.3**	**4.1**	**68%**	**11%**	**34**	**20**	**47**	**27%**	**74%**	**10%**	**0**						**5.7**	**107**	**127**	**$3**

Nicasio,Juan

Age: 30	Th: R	Role RP	Health C	LIMA Plan A	
Ht: 6' 3"	Wt: 190	Type Pwr	PT/Exp C	Rand Var +4	
			Consist C	MM 3401	

Glow from stellar March, rotation return vanished quickly—but 2H relief work was a revelation. Velocity ticked up, GB% spiked, Ctl and HR issues subsided as he became a swing-and-miss machine. Only H% marred the effort, though 2H FpK is skeptical about control gains. Scary inconsistency, scary bullpen upside. UP: 20 Sv

Yr	Tm	W	L	Sv	IP	K	ERA	xERA	WHIP	oOPS	vL	vR	BF/G	Ctl	Dom	Cmd	FpK	SwK	G	L	F	H%	S%	hr/f	GS	APC	DOM%	DIS%	Sv%	LI	RAR	BPV	BPX	R$
12	COL	2	3	0	58	54	5.28	4.19	1.62	861	902	825	23.4	3.4	8.4	2.5	60%	8%	40	25	36	37%	69%	11%	11	93	18%	36%			-9.0	77	100	-$8
13	COL	9	9	0	158	119	5.14	4.41	1.47	785	737	827	22.7	3.7	6.8	1.9	57%	8%	45	21	34	32%	66%	10%	31	92	16%	65%			-24.7	47	61	-$9
14	COL *	9	8	1	129	89	5.50	6.06	1.59	860	900	827	13.3	3.3	6.2	1.9	59%	8%	46	20	34	33%	70%	18%	14	49	7%	50%	100	0.76	-28.0	21	25	-$12
15	LA	1	3	1	58	65	3.86	4.04	1.56	742	969	634	4.9	4.9	10.0	2.0	62%	12%	43	25	32	37%	73%	2%	1	20	0%	100%	33	1.05	0.8	68	81	-$4
16	PIT	10	7	0	118	138	4.50	3.70	1.37	774	934	638	9.9	3.4	10.5	3.1	63%	11%	44	22	35	34%	70%	14%	12	42	25%	50%	0	0.89	-4.5	119	141	$3
1st Half		6	6	0	68	67	5.40	4.43	1.43	831	1049	609	18.7	3.8	8.8	2.3	67%	9%	41	21	39	31%	66%	16%	12	77	25%	50%	0	0.95	-10.2	74	89	-$1
2nd Half		4	1	0	50	71	3.26	2.77	1.29	695	733	671	5.9	2.9	12.9	4.4	57%	14%	48	24	28	39%	75%	9%	0	26			0	0.86	5.7	180	214	$7
17	**Proj**	**5**	**4**	**0**	**87**	**95**	**3.75**	**3.68**	**1.31**	**715**	**831**	**634**	**7.4**	**3.4**	**9.8**	**2.9**	**61%**	**11%**	**45**	**23**	**33**	**32%**	**74%**	**11%**	**0**						**4.7**	**107**	**128**	**$2**

Nicolino,Justin

Age: 25	Th: L	Role SP	Health A	LIMA Plan D+	
Ht: 6' 3"	Wt: 195	Type Con	PT/Exp C	Rand Var +1	
			Consist B	MM 0001	

3-6, 4.99 ERA in 79 IP at MIA. Improved already very good control, added incrementally to Dom and GB%, but the sum wasn't enough to move the needle. ERA/xERA combo—along with pretty much everything else—says nothing has changed other than an unfortunate S%. Entrenched SwK still dominates the profile.

Yr	Tm	W	L	Sv	IP	K	ERA	xERA	WHIP	oOPS	vL	vR	BF/G	Ctl	Dom	Cmd	FpK	SwK	G	L	F	H%	S%	hr/f	GS	APC	DOM%	DIS%	Sv%	LI	RAR	BPV	BPX	R$
12																																		
13	aa	3	2	0	45	27	6.16	6.49	1.88				23.7	2.5	5.3	2.1						41%	65%								-12.8	48	62	-$11
14	aa	14	4	0	170	67	3.29	3.48	1.18				24.4	1.0	3.5	3.4						30%	72%								9.4	80	95	$9
15	MIA *	12	11	0	189	74	4.36	5.16	1.51	758	722	768	25.6	2.4	3.5	1.5	65%	5%	44	18	38	32%	73%	9%	12	87	0%	50%			-9.4	18	22	-$7
16	MIA *	10	12	0	164	76	5.36	5.17	1.46	798	687	837	22.0	1.9	4.2	2.2	63%	5%	47	22	32	33%	64%	9%	13	67	0%	69%	0	0.93	-23.8	34	40	-$8
1st Half		5	7	0	99	46	4.78	4.74	1.42	829	667	880	24.7	2.1	4.1	2.0	62%	6%	45	23	33	32%	67%	8%	11	84	0%	64%			-7.2	37	44	-$5
2nd Half		5	5	0	65	30	6.24	5.83	1.52	693	737	671	18.9	1.6	4.2	2.6	66%	5%	54	16	30	34%	60%	11%	2	41	0%	100%	0	1.10	-16.6	31	37	-$14
17	**Proj**	**4**	**5**	**0**	**73**	**32**	**5.03**	**5.03**	**1.49**	**865**	**838**	**874**	**22.7**	**1.9**	**4.0**	**2.1**	**64%**	**5%**	**48**	**19**	**33**	**33%**	**67%**	**8%**	**14**						**-7.5**	**46**	**55**	**-$6**

Niese,Jon

Age: 30	Th: L	Role RP	Health D	LIMA Plan D+	
Ht: 6' 4"	Wt: 215	Type	PT/Exp A	Rand Var +5	
			Consist B	MM 1101	

Inability to miss many bats leaves him dependent on control and GB skills. The former deserted him and the latter didn't help much, as HR onslaught began early and never let up. FpK says Ctl should retrace, even Dom uptick is a positive. But DOM%/DIS%, hr/f trends point to ceiling that looks irrelevant from here.

Yr	Tm	W	L	Sv	IP	K	ERA	xERA	WHIP	oOPS	vL	vR	BF/G	Ctl	Dom	Cmd	FpK	SwK	G	L	F	H%	S%	hr/f	GS	APC	DOM%	DIS%	Sv%	LI	RAR	BPV	BPX	R$
12	NYM	13	9	0	190	155	3.40	3.70	1.17	663	665	663	26.3	2.3	7.3	3.2	63%	8%	48	21	31	28%	75%	13%	30	101	30%	10%			14.3	95	124	$16
13	NYM	8	8	0	143	105	3.71	3.93	1.44	739	660	765	25.9	3.0	6.6	2.2	61%	8%	52	21	27	33%	75%	8%	24	98	17%	33%			2.7	67	88	$0
14	NYM	9	11	0	188	138	3.40	3.68	1.27	722	656	742	26.2	2.2	6.6	3.1	63%	8%	48	23	30	31%	76%	10%	30	93	27%	23%			7.8	87	103	$7
15	NYM	9	10	0	177	113	4.13	4.17	1.40	764	789	757	23.3	2.8	5.8	2.1	62%	6%	55	21	25	31%	73%	14%	29	82	21%	34%	0	0.77	-3.6	60	71	-$1
16	2 NL	8	7	0	121	88	5.50	4.71	1.59	884	887	883	18.8	3.5	6.5	1.9	63%	8%	51	20	28	32%	71%	22%	20	69	5%	45%	0	0.79	-19.6	52	62	-$9
1st Half		6	6	0	92	65	5.07	4.50	1.53	878	791	909	25.8	3.2	6.3	2.0	62%	8%	55	19	26	31%	73%	24%	16	94	6%	44%			-10.0	60	72	-$7
2nd Half		2	1	0	29	23	6.91	5.37	1.78	902	1202	804	10.3	4.4	7.2	1.6	63%	9%	39	25	36	35%	64%	18%	4	39	0%	50%	0	0.81	-9.6	28	34	-$14
17	**Proj**	**4**	**5**	**0**	**87**	**63**	**4.47**	**4.56**	**1.51**	**792**	**874**	**767**	**16.8**	**3.3**	**6.6**	**2.0**	**63%**	**8%**	**48**	**22**	**29**	**33%**	**73%**	**13%**	**15**						**-3.0**	**57**	**68**	**-$5**

Nola,Aaron

Age: 24	Th: R	Role SP	Health D	LIMA Plan A	
Ht: 6' 2"	Wt: 195	Type Pwr GB	PT/Exp C	Rand Var +5	
			Consist B	MM 3303	

Posted 2.65 ERA thru 12 starts, supported by sub-3 xERA, 85/15 K/BB. Terrific Dom, GB% remained intact during mysterious H%-and-BB-fueled collapse that followed. Season ended in late July DL stint, now rehabbing low-grade flexor tendon sprain with PRP injections. Health is the key; with it... UP: 3.25 ERA.

Yr	Tm	W	L	Sv	IP	K	ERA	xERA	WHIP	oOPS	vL	vR	BF/G	Ctl	Dom	Cmd	FpK	SwK	G	L	F	H%	S%	hr/f	GS	APC	DOM%	DIS%	Sv%	LI	RAR	BPV	BPX	R$
12																																		
13																																		
14	aa	2	0	0	24	14	2.86	5.09	1.32				19.9	1.8	5.1	2.8						29%	88%								2.6	38	46	-$2
15	PHI *	16	6	0	187	151	3.10	3.58	1.17	703	834	618	24.1	1.8	7.2	4.1	64%	9%	48	20	32	30%	77%	15%	13	86	31%	23%			19.9	105	126	$19
16	PHI	6	9	0	111	121	4.78	3.25	1.31	712	703	720	24.2	2.4	9.8	4.2	61%	10%	55	20	25	36%	64%	13%	20	90	35%	15%			-8.1	146	174	$0
1st Half		5	8	0	96	106	4.69	3.14	1.28	710	717	703	24.5	2.2	9.9	4.6	62%	10%	55	21	24	35%	65%	15%	17	91	35%	18%			-5.9	154	183	$2
2nd Half		1	1	0	15	15	5.40	3.92	1.47	728	595	822	22.3	3.6	9.0	2.5	54%	10%	56	14	30	37%	59%	0%	3	81	33%	0%			-2.2	99	118	-$9
17	**Proj**	**10**	**9**	**0**	**152**	**154**	**3.70**	**3.37**	**1.24**	**699**	**700**	**698**	**22.5**	**2.3**	**9.1**	**4.0**	**60%**	**10%**	**52**	**18**	**30**	**33%**	**72%**	**11%**	**27**						**9.1**	**133**	**159**	**$9**

JOCK THOMPSON

Nolasco,Ricky

Age: 34	Th: R	Role SP	Health F	LIMA Plan B+	
Ht: 6' 2"	Wt: 230	Type	PT/Exp B	Rand Var 0	
			Consist A	MM 1105	

Rebound from a lost 2015 (and elbow woes) went as well as could be expected. Stellar control emerged intact, as did sub-par Dom, HR issues. 1st half H% the result of still being around the plate with pedestrian stuff. 2nd half uptick fueled by 23% H% / 80% S% in September. History of both says that this will pass.

Yr Tm	W	L	Sv	IP	K	ERA	xERA	WHIP	oOPS	vL	vR	BF/G	Ctl	Dom	Cmd	FpK	SwK	G	L	F	H%	S%	hr/f	GS	APC	DOM%	DIS%	Sv%	LI	RAR	BPV	BPX	R$
12 MIA	12	13	0	191	125	4.48	4.27	1.37	755	809	696	26.8	2.2	5.9	2.7	63%	9%	47	22	32	32%	68%	9%	31	96	19%	35%			-10.9	71	93	-$1
13 2 NL	13	11	0	199	165	3.70	3.62	1.21	693	721	660	24.5	2.1	7.4	3.6	60%	11%	43	24	33	31%	71%	9%	33	94	33%	24%	0	0.75	4.0	99	129	$11
14 MIN	6	12	0	159	115	5.38	4.13	1.52	861	906	816	25.7	2.2	6.5	3.0	58%	9%	42	22	36	35%	67%	12%	27	98	19%	37%			-32.1	79	94	-$13
15 MIN	5	2	0	37	35	6.75	4.34	1.71	856	758	942	19.2	3.4	8.4	2.5	52%	10%	41	28	32	40%	59%	8%	8	74	13%	50%	0	0.71	-12.8	80	95	-$8
16 2 AL	8	14	0	198	144	4.42	4.35	1.24	744	711	770	25.5	2.0	6.6	3.3	61%	9%	43	19	38	30%	68%	11%	32	98	28%	34%			-5.5	85	101	$5
1st Half	3	6	0	97	79	5.31	4.28	1.38	814	794	831	25.8	1.8	7.4	4.2	63%	10%	43	19	39	34%	64%	12%	16	98	25%	25%			-13.3	105	126	-$4
2nd Half	5	8	0	101	65	3.56	4.42	1.12	671	625	707	25.3	2.2	5.8	2.6	59%	9%	44	19	38	26%	72%	10%	16	98	31%	44%			7.8	66	78	$13
17 Proj	**10**	**14**	**0**	**181**	**140**	**4.54**	**4.38**	**1.40**	**784**	**754**	**810**	**23.0**	**2.4**	**7.0**	**2.9**	**58%**	**9%**	**43**	**22**	**36**	**33%**	**70%**	**10%**	**33**						**-7.8**	**81**	**96**	**-$1**

Norris,Bud

Age: 32	Th: R	Role RP	Health D	LIMA Plan C	
Ht: 6' 0"	Wt: 215	Type Pwr	PT/Exp B	Rand Var +2	
			Consist A	MM 1201	

HR-plagued April cost him rotation spot. Found magic in LHB-neutralizing cutter that helped fuel Dom, GB spikes—and more SP work. Gopheritis returned to stay in July, control left in Aug following DL stint (back) as season left the tracks. The flashes keep him in opportunities, but Ctl, HR history are big red flags.

Yr Tm	W	L	Sv	IP	K	ERA	xERA	WHIP	oOPS	vL	vR	BF/G	Ctl	Dom	Cmd	FpK	SwK	G	L	F	H%	S%	hr/f	GS	APC	DOM%	DIS%	Sv%	LI	RAR	BPV	BPX	R$
12 HOU	7	13	0	168	165	4.65	4.10	1.37	751	782	720	25.3	3.5	8.8	2.5	58%	11%	39	21	40	31%	69%	12%	29	97	34%	38%			-13.2	81	105	-$2
13 2 AL	10	12	0	177	147	4.18	4.27	1.49	779	889	629	24.2	3.4	7.5	2.2	61%	10%	40	21	38	34%	74%	8%	30	94	23%	30%	0	0.88	-6.8	61	79	-$3
14 BAL	15	8	0	165	139	3.65	3.77	1.22	710	753	659	24.5	2.8	7.6	2.7	60%	8%	42	21	37	28%	74%	11%	28	98	29%	25%			1.9	80	95	$9
15 2 TM	3	11	0	83	71	6.72	4.42	1.58	895	899	890	9.9	3.4	7.7	2.3	58%	10%	43	23	34	34%	59%	17%	11	39	9%	64%	0	0.82	-28.3	69	82	-$14
16 2 NL	6	10	0	113	102	5.10	4.36	1.46	763	915	646	14.1	3.9	8.1	2.1	62%	10%	48	22	31	32%	67%	14%	19	57	26%	37%	0	0.75	-12.7	67	79	-$4
1st Half	4	7	0	76	68	3.89	4.02	1.30	679	821	572	14.0	3.4	8.0	2.3	61%	10%	49	22	29	30%	71%	10%	11	56	36%	36%	0	0.72	2.8	79	94	$2
2nd Half	2	3	0	37	34	7.61	5.08	1.80	918	1085	786	14.4	4.9	8.3	1.7	63%	9%	45	21	34	35%	60%	20%	8	60	13%	38%	0	0.80	-15.5	41	48	-$18
17 Proj	**4**	**7**	**0**	**87**	**77**	**4.49**	**4.34**	**1.45**	**784**	**867**	**703**	**16.5**	**3.5**	**8.0**	**2.3**	**61%**	**10%**	**44**	**22**	**34**	**33%**	**72%**	**13%**	**12**						**-3.2**	**73**	**87**	**-$4**

Norris,Daniel

Age: 24	Th: L	Role SP	Health D	LIMA Plan B+	
Ht: 6' 2"	Wt: 180	Type Pwr	PT/Exp D	Rand Var +2	
			Consist A	MM 1303	

4-2, 3.38 ERA in 69 IP at DET. A physical mess since Sept 2014 debut. Most recently, off-season surgery for thyroid cancer, fractured back in March, oblique strain in June. Return to health in late July coincided with 2nd half FpK, SwK spikes. Fine Sept (11.5 Dom, 2.4 Ctl, 2.73 ERA in 5 starts) points to... UP: 3.50 ERA, 150 Ks.

Yr Tm	W	L	Sv	IP	K	ERA	xERA	WHIP	oOPS	vL	vR	BF/G	Ctl	Dom	Cmd	FpK	SwK	G	L	F	H%	S%	hr/f	GS	APC	DOM%	DIS%	Sv%	LI	RAR	BPV	BPX	R$
12																																	
13																																	
14 TOR *	6	2	0	65	83	4.98	4.14	1.35	667	594	719	15.0	4.1	11.5	2.8	43%	7%	35	20	45	32%	66%	11%	1	28	0%	0%	0	0.85	-10.0	95	113	-$2
15 2 AL *	6	12	0	151	114	5.03	4.96	1.55	732	880	680	22.7	3.7	6.8	1.8	53%	9%	39	17	43	33%	68%	11%	13	80	15%	46%			-19.9	49	58	-$11
16 DET *	10	9	0	149	139	4.65	4.93	1.53	762	648	800	22.4	3.3	8.3	2.5	64%	11%	38	23	39	36%	71%	12%	13	85	23%	31%	0	0.72	-8.5	73	87	-$3
1st Half	5	6	0	69	64	6.00	5.59	1.74	901	1043	840	22.4	3.7	8.3	2.2	57%	7%	29	21	50	40%	64%	18%	2	63	0%	0%	0	0.52	-15.3	72	85	-$10
2nd Half	5	3	0	81	75	3.77	4.55	1.39	733	551	793	22.6	3.1	8.4	2.7	66%	12%	40	23	37	33%	77%	11%	11	91	27%	36%			4.2	73	87	$4
17 Proj	**9**	**9**	**0**	**145**	**136**	**3.98**	**4.24**	**1.34**	**721**	**672**	**737**	**24.3**	**3.3**	**8.4**	**2.6**	**61%**	**11%**	**41**	**20**	**39**	**31%**	**73%**	**10%**	**25**						**3.8**	**82**	**98**	**$4**

Nova,Ivan

Age: 30	Th: R	Role SP	Health F	LIMA Plan B	
Ht: 6' 5"	Wt: 225	Type GB	PT/Exp C	Rand Var +2	
			Consist A	MM 2105	

Leaving Yankee Stadium, AL East helped deflate horrendous 1st half hr/f and ERA. But July Dom surge touched off 2nd half recovery before Aug trade. Subsequent NL effort—3 walks in final 64 IP, 2.42 ERA in PNC Park—brought it home. A full season? Unlikely for light-Dom, HR-prone GBer. But watch where FA lands.

Yr Tm	W	L	Sv	IP	K	ERA	xERA	WHIP	oOPS	vL	vR	BF/G	Ctl	Dom	Cmd	FpK	SwK	G	L	F	H%	S%	hr/f	GS	APC	DOM%	DIS%	Sv%	LI	RAR	BPV	BPX	R$
12 NYY	12	8	0	170	153	5.02	3.95	1.47	860	848	872	26.7	3.0	8.1	2.7	58%	9%	45	22	32	34%	70%	17%	28	96	18%	32%			-21.1	89	116	-$6
13 NYY *	11	6	0	157	130	3.08	3.57	1.29	678	676	680	24.8	2.8	7.4	2.7	54%	10%	54	20	26	31%	78%	8%	20	91	40%	25%	0	0.77	15.2	86	112	$10
14 NYY	2	2	0	21	12	8.27	4.53	1.84	1033	764	1444	24.0	2.6	5.2	2.0	64%	5%	49	20	31	36%	59%	26%	4	82	0%	75%			-11.6	51	60	-$7
15 NYY	6	11	0	94	63	5.07	4.50	1.40	793	899	682	24.3	3.2	6.0	1.9	55%	8%	49	19	32	30%	66%	13%	17	90	18%	53%			-12.9	50	60	-$5
16 2 TM	12	8	1	162	127	4.17	3.74	1.25	778	857	716	21.4	1.6	7.1	4.5	62%	10%	54	19	28	32%	71%	16%	26	72	31%	42%	100	0.74	0.5	117	139	$8
1st Half	5	5	1	75	55	5.06	4.04	1.38	819	844	801	19.1	2.0	6.6	3.2	59%	9%	55	18	27	32%	68%	20%	11	66	18%	55%	100	0.73	-8.0	97	116	$0
2nd Half	7	3	0	87	72	3.40	3.49	1.15	741	868	633	23.9	1.1	7.4	6.5	64%	10%	52	20	29	31%	74%	14%	15	79	40%	33%			8.5	133	158	$14
17 Proj	**13**	**12**	**0**	**189**	**146**	**4.03**	**3.95**	**1.31**	**774**	**840**	**714**	**22.5**	**2.3**	**7.0**	**3.1**	**59%**	**9%**	**51**	**20**	**29**	**31%**	**73%**	**14%**	**35**						**3.7**	**94**	**112**	**$6**

Nuno,Vidal

Age: 29	Th: L	Role RP	Health A	LIMA Plan C	
Ht: 5' 11"	Wt: 195	Type FB	PT/Exp C	Rand Var -1	
			Consist A	MM 1200	

Solid FpK keeps Ctl in stellar territory but it's not enough. Even with all but 3 IP out of the pen, still unable to build on swing-and-miss promise from 2015. Soft-tosser has enough skill to stay employed, though HR-avoidance is hanging by a thread. More downside than up.

Yr Tm	W	L	Sv	IP	K	ERA	xERA	WHIP	oOPS	vL	vR	BF/G	Ctl	Dom	Cmd	FpK	SwK	G	L	F	H%	S%	hr/f	GS	APC	DOM%	DIS%	Sv%	LI	RAR	BPV	BPX	R$
12 aa	9	5	0	114	80	3.19	4.88	1.42				24.2	2.3	6.3	2.8						33%	82%								11.6	61	79	$3
13 NYY *	3	2	0	45	33	2.15	2.47	0.94	654	691	643	16.9	1.7	6.6	3.9	66%	4%	35	18	47	24%	85%	6%	3	63	0%	33%	0	1.03	9.5	105	137	$4
14 2 TM	2	12	0	162	129	4.56	4.08	1.26	745	582	793	21.9	2.6	7.2	2.8	67%	9%	38	19	43	29%	68%	12%	28	83	21%	29%	0	0.71	-16.4	76	91	-$3
15 2 TM *	5	8	0	146	118	3.71	4.47	1.27	772	562	836	13.5	1.9	7.3	3.9	65%	11%	42	17	41	31%	77%	14%	10	41	10%	60%	0	0.91	4.5	85	101	$4
16 SEA	1	1	0	59	51	3.53	4.15	1.33	811	809	812	4.5	1.7	7.8	4.6	63%	8%	36	24	40	33%	82%	15%	1	17	0%	100%	0	0.87	4.8	109	130	-$1
1st Half	0	1	0	33	33	3.27	3.83	1.21	773	787	765	4.8	1.9	9.0	4.7	59%	9%	37	23	40	31%	82%	16%	1	18	0%	100%	0	1.01	3.7	125	149	$1
2nd Half	1	0	0	26	18	3.86	4.58	1.48	858	839	867	4.2	1.4	6.3	4.5	69%	7%	35	25	40	35%	82%	15%	0	16			0	0.72	1.1	89	106	-$3
17 Proj	**2**	**2**	**0**	**58**	**47**	**3.85**	**4.29**	**1.31**	**788**	**716**	**818**	**6.8**	**1.8**	**7.2**	**3.9**	**65%**	**9%**	**38**	**21**	**41**	**32%**	**77%**	**13%**	**0**						**2.5**	**97**	**115**	**-$2**

O Day,Darren

Age: 34	Th: R	Role RP	Health F	LIMA Plan A	
Ht: 6' 4"	Wt: 225	Type Pwr FB	PT/Exp C	Rand Var +1	
			Consist A	MM 3510	

Top-shelf setup man started fine, struggled uncharacteristically with control and HR in May before injuries took over in early June. Lost 7+ weeks to a hamstring strain; Aug shoulder woes sidelined him for another 35 days. Elite Dom was untouched throughout. FB tendency and age elevate risk, but there's still value here.

Yr Tm	W	L	Sv	IP	K	ERA	xERA	WHIP	oOPS	vL	vR	BF/G	Ctl	Dom	Cmd	FpK	SwK	G	L	F	H%	S%	hr/f	GS	APC	DOM%	DIS%	Sv%	LI	RAR	BPV	BPX	R$
12 BAL	7	1	0	67	69	2.28	3.34	0.94	613	664	584	3.8	1.9	9.3	4.9	65%	12%	34	23	43	26%	81%	8%	0	15			0	1.10	14.3	128	167	$10
13 BAL	5	3	2	62	59	2.18	3.38	1.00	617	922	443	3.6	2.2	8.6	3.9	63%	12%	37	22	41	26%	85%	10%	0	14			33	1.22	12.9	110	144	$8
14 BAL	5	2	4	69	73	1.70	2.99	0.89	550	633	497	4.0	2.5	9.6	3.8	59%	14%	45	17	38	23%	87%	10%	0	16			50	1.33	17.3	128	152	$12
15 BAL	6	2	6	65	82	1.52	2.95	0.93	540	627	493	3.8	1.9	11.3	5.9	66%	15%	35	20	45	29%	89%	7%	0	16			55	1.21	19.7	164	196	$14
16 BAL	3	1	3	31	38	3.77	3.89	1.23	717	862	648	3.9	3.8	11.0	2.9	68%	15%	34	22	44	28%	78%	17%	0	16			60	1.09	1.6	109	129	$1
1st Half	2	1	2	20	25	3.15	3.86	1.35	815	816	813	4.0	4.1	11.3	2.8	69%	13%	35	27	38	29%	91%	25%	0	16			50	1.25	2.6	106	126	$2
2nd Half	1	0	1	11	13	4.91	3.93	1.00	525	970	357	3.7	3.3	10.6	3.3	66%	17%	33	11	56	25%	50%	7%	0	16			100	0.81	-1.0	114	136	-$2
17 Proj	**5**	**2**	**1**	**58**	**66**	**3.16**	**3.45**	**1.06**	**648**	**734**	**600**	**3.7**	**2.7**	**10.2**	**3.7**	**65%**	**13%**	**37**	**22**	**40**	**27%**	**77%**	**14%**	**0**						**7.4**	**126**	**150**	**$5**

Odorizzi,Jake

Age: 27	Th: R	Role SP	Health B	LIMA Plan C+	
Ht: 6' 2"	Wt: 175	Type Pwr FB	PT/Exp A	Rand Var 0	
			Consist A	MM 1205	

FB% ticked up again, HR were more persistent, and damage inflicted by RHBs is on the upswing. Yet despite unimpressive DOM%/DIS%, still managed to retain sub-4 ERA, eat innings, rack up Wins, Ks and more mid-rotation value. Control, upper hand vL keep his head above water, but this looks like a ceiling.

Yr Tm	W	L	Sv	IP	K	ERA	xERA	WHIP	oOPS	vL	vR	BF/G	Ctl	Dom	Cmd	FpK	SwK	G	L	F	H%	S%	hr/f	GS	APC	DOM%	DIS%	Sv%	LI	RAR	BPV	BPX	R$
12 KC *	15	6	0	153	117	3.36	3.89	1.32	820	899	400	22.6	3.0	6.9	2.3	56%	7%	27	27	46	30%	77%	8%	2	76	0%	100%			12.3	69	89	$10
13 TAM *	9	7	1	154	129	3.83	3.46	1.22	744	846	627	21.5	2.7	7.5	2.8	57%	8%	32	26	42	29%	71%	8%	4	76	0%	50%	100	0.80	0.7	83	108	$7
14 TAM	11	13	0	168	174	4.13	3.96	1.28	692	663	726	23.2	3.2	9.3	2.9	61%	10%	30	21	49	31%	71%	9%	31	98	35%	32%			-8.0	90	108	$4
15 TAM	9	9	0	169	150	3.35	3.99	1.15	680	630	745	25.0	2.4	8.0	3.3	60%	11%	37	22	41	29%	75%	9%	28	98	25%	11%			12.8	92	110	$13
16 TAM	10	6	0	188	166	3.69	4.33	1.19	715	578	814	23.4	2.6	8.0	3.1	58%	10%	37	19	44	28%	75%	12%	33	100	21%	42%			11.5	88	105	$13
1st Half	3	3	0	94	90	3.91	4.17	1.22	721	612	805	22.7	3.0	8.6	2.9	55%	10%	39	18	43	28%	74%	13%	17	103	24%	47%			3.2	92	110	$10
2nd Half	7	3	0	93	76	3.47	4.48	1.17	710	540	822	24.2	2.2	7.3	3.3	62%	10%	34	20	46	28%	77%	11%	16	98	19%	38%			8.3	84	101	$17
17 Proj	**11**	**9**	**0**	**189**	**170**	**3.73**	**4.19**	**1.21**	**709**	**619**	**793**	**23.7**	**2.5**	**8.1**	**3.2**	**60%**	**10%**	**36**	**20**	**44**	**29%**	**74%**	**10%**	**32**						**10.6**	**91**	**109**	**$12**

JOCK THOMPSON

Oh,Seung-Hwan

Age: 34	Th: R	Role RP	Health A	LIMA Plan C+	
Ht: 5' 10"	Wt: 205	Type Pwr FB	PT/Exp A	Rand Var -4	
			Consist D	MM 4531	

Quickly ascended from middle relief to closer role in stateside debut, and deserved it. Elite SwK/FpK should keep Cmd in the stratosphere, and he held a 140+ BPV each month. Sure, luck is involved in any sub-2.00 ERA (see 1H hr/f), and xERA reflects risk of FB%, but that's nitpicking. Encore should be just as good.

Yr	Tm	W	L	Sv	IP	K	ERA	xERA	WHIP	oOPS	vL	vR	BF/G	Ctl	Dom	Cmd	FpK	SwK	G	L	F	H%	S%	hr/f	GS	APC	DOM%	DIS%	Sv%	LI	RAR	BPV	BPX	R$
12	for	2	1	37	56	77	2.41	1.39	0.93				4.2	2.6	12.4	4.8						30%	73%								11.0	185	241	$22
13	for	4	1	28	52	51	2.16	2.36	0.93				4.0	2.2	8.9	4.1						23%	86%								10.9	121	158	$17
14	for	2	4	39	67	77	2.18	2.22	0.90				3.9	2.2	10.4	4.8						24%	85%								12.9	146	174	$23
15	for	2	3	41	69	63	3.39	4.23	1.28				4.5	2.6	8.1	3.2						31%	79%								4.9	79	94	$17
16	STL	6	3	19	80	103	1.92	2.96	0.92	510	455	555	4.1	2.0	11.6	5.7	67%	18%	40	19	41	29%	82%	7%	0	17			83	1.30	22.3	173	205	$22
1st Half		2	0	2	42	57	1.71	2.91	0.90	451	414	486	4.1	2.8	12.2	4.4	65%	19%	47	13	40	28%	81%	3%	0	17			67	0.93	12.8	170	203	$16
2nd Half		4	3	17	38	46	2.15	2.97	0.93	576	509	624	4.2	1.2	11.0	9.2	68%	18%	33	26	41	30%	84%	11%	0	17			85	1.75	9.5	176	210	$28
17	**Proj**	**4**	**3**	**36**	**73**	**89**	**2.38**	**3.10**	**1.01**	**583**	**511**	**640**	**4.1**	**2.1**	**11.0**	**5.2**	**67%**	**18%**	**38**	**21**	**41**	**30%**	**82%**	**10%**	**0**						**16.2**	**158**	**188**	**$23**

Osuna,Roberto

Age: 22	Th: R	Role RP	Health A	LIMA Plan C	
Ht: 6' 0"	Wt: 215	Type Pwr xFB	PT/Exp C	Rand Var -3	
			Consist A	MM 3431	

Second verse same as the first. Named closer in late March, never looked back in mirror image of breakout rookie season. Impeccable FpK suggests pinpoint Ctl is here to stay, while he produced whiffs with ease. Extreme FB% opens up HR risk, but should also suppress H%, WHIP. Already nearing "set and forget" status.

Yr	Tm	W	L	Sv	IP	K	ERA	xERA	WHIP	oOPS	vL	vR	BF/G	Ctl	Dom	Cmd	FpK	SwK	G	L	F	H%	S%	hr/f	GS	APC	DOM%	DIS%	Sv%	LI	RAR	BPV	BPX	R$
12																																		
13																																		
14																																		
15	TOR	1	6	20	70	75	2.58	3.41	0.92	591	638	537	4.0	2.1	9.7	4.7	63%	15%	34	20	46	25%	77%	9%	0	16			87	1.36	11.8	131	156	$15
16	TOR	4	3	36	74	82	2.68	3.45	0.93	603	729	480	4.0	1.7	10.0	5.9	70%	16%	33	20	47	27%	78%	10%	0	16			86	1.39	13.8	145	172	$24
1st Half		2	1	16	38	46	2.39	3.25	0.98	600	752	456	4.0	1.9	11.0	5.8	70%	17%	35	21	45	30%	79%	7%	0	16			89	1.18	8.4	159	190	$22
2nd Half		2	2	20	36	36	2.97	3.65	0.88	606	706	507	4.0	1.5	8.9	6.0	70%	14%	32	19	49	23%	77%	13%	0	16			83	1.61	5.5	130	155	$26
17	**Proj**	**3**	**4**	**43**	**73**	**78**	**2.67**	**3.42**	**0.92**	**599**	**688**	**504**	**3.8**	**1.8**	**9.7**	**5.3**	**67%**	**15%**	**33**	**20**	**47**	**26%**	**78%**	**10%**	**0**						**13.6**	**138**	**164**	**$25**

Ottavino,Adam

Age: 31	Th: R	Role RP	Health F	LIMA Plan A	
Ht: 6' 5"	Wt: 215	Type Pwr xGB	PT/Exp D	Rand Var +3	
			Consist B	MM 4430	

Activated in July—14 months after TJS—and became closer by Aug. Returned with xGB% tilt thanks to heavy sinker; Dom backed by SwK with minimal velocity loss. But underlying FpK hints at more BBs, and elbow hasn't been tested over full season. Skills in place to be effective stopper, but still some risk.

Yr	Tm	W	L	Sv	IP	K	ERA	xERA	WHIP	oOPS	vL	vR	BF/G	Ctl	Dom	Cmd	FpK	SwK	G	L	F	H%	S%	hr/f	GS	APC	DOM%	DIS%	Sv%	LI	RAR	BPV	BPX	R$
12	COL *	5	1	0	99	99	4.43	4.60	1.46	717	745	698	6.4	3.8	9.1	2.4	59%	12%	48	26	26	34%	72%	16%	0	25			0	0.64	-5.0	74	97	-$4
13	COL	1	3	0	78	78	2.64	3.62	1.33	672	853	544	6.6	3.6	9.0	2.5	61%	12%	46	22	33	32%	82%	7%	0	25			0	1.01	11.8	89	116	$2
14	COL	1	4	1	65	70	3.60	3.09	1.28	735	943	645	3.6	2.2	9.7	4.4	61%	12%	47	19	34	35%	74%	10%	0	14			17	1.31	1.1	140	166	$0
15	COL	1	0	3	10	13	0.00	1.89	0.48	265	321	217	3.5	1.7	11.3	6.5	51%	13%	63	5	32	16%	100%	0%	0	14			100	1.05	5.0	198	236	$1
16	COL	1	3	7	27	35	2.67	2.32	0.93	528	780	350	3.1	2.3	11.7	5.0	52%	11%	62	17	21	27%	77%	23%	0	13			58	1.28	5.1	187	222	$4
1st Half																																		
2nd Half		1	3	7	27	35	2.67	2.32	0.93	528	780	350	3.1	2.3	11.7	5.0	52%	11%	62	17	21	27%	77%	23%	0	13			58	1.28	5.1	187	223	$4
17	**Proj**	**1**	**3**	**30**	**55**	**61**	**3.28**	**3.10**	**1.22**	**657**	**837**	**542**	**4.3**	**3.0**	**9.9**	**3.4**	**58%**	**12%**	**57**	**19**	**24**	**32%**	**76%**	**15%**	**0**						**6.2**	**134**	**160**	**$13**

Owens,Henry

Age: 24	Th: L	Role SP	Health A	LIMA Plan D	
Ht: 6' 6"	Wt: 205	Type Pwr xFB	PT/Exp C	Rand Var +2	
			Consist C	MM 0200	

0-2, 6.95 ERA in 22 IP at BOS. Walked nearly a batter per inning in MLB cameo; not exactly a way to impress your future employer. Poor Ctl in minors, FpK suggest free passes will continue. Still gives up too many FB. Dom/SwK holds our interest with first-round pedigree, but immediate success a long shot.

Yr	Tm	W	L	Sv	IP	K	ERA	xERA	WHIP	oOPS	vL	vR	BF/G	Ctl	Dom	Cmd	FpK	SwK	G	L	F	H%	S%	hr/f	GS	APC	DOM%	DIS%	Sv%	LI	RAR	BPV	BPX	R$
12																																		
13	aa	3	1	0	30	40	2.08	2.58	1.14				20.0	4.3	11.8	2.8						27%	87%								6.7	118	154	$1
14	a/a	17	5	0	159	145	3.63	3.23	1.26				24.9	3.4	8.2	2.4						30%	72%								2.1	90	107	$9
15	BOS *	7	12	0	185	137	4.49	3.68	1.36	726	859	699	24.2	4.1	6.7	1.6	54%	13%	35	16	49	28%	67%	8%	11	96	18%	18%			-12.0	58	69	-$2
16	BOS *	10	9	0	160	133	5.83	5.58	1.76	1007	744	1093	25.2	6.5	7.5	1.2	52%	10%	31	20	49	31%	69%	17%	5	84	20%	80%			-32.3	32	38	-$16
1st Half		5	5	0	89	70	6.02	6.18	1.90	1049	952	1071	24.8	7.7	7.0	0.9	42%	7%	34	17	49	30%	71%	18%	3	81	0%	100%			-20.2	16	20	-$20
2nd Half		5	4	0	70	63	5.58	4.81	1.59	954	422	1120	25.8	5.0	8.1	1.6	66%	14%	25	25	50	33%	65%	17%	2	89	50%	50%			-12.0	56	67	-$12
17	**Proj**	**3**	**2**	**0**	**44**	**38**	**4.77**	**5.41**	**1.50**	**670**	**791**	**644**	**24.4**	**5.0**	**7.9**	**1.6**	**54%**	**13%**	**35**	**16**	**49**	**30%**	**69%**	**7%**	**8**						**-3.1**	**21**	**24**	**-$4**

Papelbon,Jonathan

Age: 36	Th: R	Role RP	Health C	LIMA Plan B+	
Ht: 6' 5"	Wt: 230	Type Pwr FB	PT/Exp B	Rand Var 0	
			Consist B	MM 1310	

Abrupt fall from grace, as he hit DL (ribs) in June, lost job in July, requested release in August. Skills took similar tumble, as FpK plunge (injury-related?) choked once-stable Ctl, while career-worst xERA, BPV paint ominous picture. Owns better skills, off-season recovery should help, but stranglehold on saves likely gone.

Yr	Tm	W	L	Sv	IP	K	ERA	xERA	WHIP	oOPS	vL	vR	BF/G	Ctl	Dom	Cmd	FpK	SwK	G	L	F	H%	S%	hr/f	GS	APC	DOM%	DIS%	Sv%	LI	RAR	BPV	BPX	R$
12	PHI	5	6	38	70	92	2.44	2.84	1.06	621	627	616	4.1	2.3	11.8	5.1	62%	13%	41	18	40	31%	83%	12%	0	16			90	1.24	13.6	169	221	$24
13	PHI	5	1	29	62	57	2.92	3.58	1.14	631	644	618	4.2	1.6	8.3	5.2	64%	11%	40	17	43	31%	78%	8%	0	16			81	1.18	7.2	124	162	$15
14	PHI	2	3	39	66	63	2.04	3.25	0.90	500	462	539	3.9	2.0	8.5	4.2	64%	13%	42	16	42	26%	78%	3%	0	15			91	1.42	14.0	119	142	$23
15	2 NL	4	3	24	63	56	2.13	3.41	1.03	640	786	495	4.4	1.7	8.0	4.7	66%	14%	50	15	35	27%	86%	11%	0	15			92	0.95	14.3	125	149	$17
16	WAS	2	4	19	35	31	4.37	4.83	1.46	754	777	728	4.1	3.6	8.0	2.2	57%	11%	35	21	44	33%	71%	7%	0	15			86	1.18	-0.8	59	70	$4
1st Half		1	2	16	25	19	3.28	4.75	1.34	738	750	723	4.1	2.9	6.9	2.4	62%	10%	35	21	44	31%	77%	6%	0	15			89	1.29	2.8	59	70	$9
2nd Half		1	2	3	10	12	6.97	4.98	1.74	786	829	732	4.2	5.2	10.5	2.0	48%	12%	37	20	43	39%	59%	8%	0	16			75	0.94	-3.5	62	74	-$7
17	**Proj**	**2**	**2**	**5**	**44**	**40**	**3.84**	**4.31**	**1.32**	**700**	**733**	**666**	**4.2**	**3.2**	**8.2**	**2.5**	**64%**	**12%**	**41**	**18**	**41**	**32%**	**72%**	**7%**	**0**						**1.9**	**80**	**95**	**$0**

Paulino,David

Age: 23	Th: R	Role RP	Health A	LIMA Plan A	
Ht: 6' 7"	Wt: 215	Type Pwr	PT/Exp F	Rand Var -3	
			Consist F	MM 2300	

0-1, 5.14 ERA in 7 IP at HOU. First prolonged glimpse of towering hurler, who rapidly rose from Gulf Coast League. Early returns were solid thanks to pinpoint Ctl, and he's missed bats at every level. Limited experience (203 career IP; TJS in 2014) suggests patience is needed, but keeper owners can get in line.

Yr	Tm	W	L	Sv	IP	K	ERA	xERA	WHIP	oOPS	vL	vR	BF/G	Ctl	Dom	Cmd	FpK	SwK	G	L	F	H%	S%	hr/f	GS	APC	DOM%	DIS%	Sv%	LI	RAR	BPV	BPX	R$
12																																		
13																																		
14																																		
15																																		
16	HOU *	5	5	1	85	84	2.63	2.68	1.10	665	770	393	16.7	2.0	8.9	4.4	59%	6%	43	13	43	31%	77%	0%	1	42	0%	100%	100	0.36	16.4	139	165	$9
1st Half		4	2	1	58	59	2.12	2.19	1.00				17.1	1.7	9.1	5.5						30%	80%	0%	0						14.8	170	202	$15
2nd Half		1	3	0	27	25	3.89	3.97	1.35	665	770	393	16.1	2.9	8.4	2.9	59%	6%	43	13	43	33%	72%	0%	1	42	0%	100%	0	0.36	1.0	91	108	-$2
17	**Proj**	**3**	**5**	**0**	**58**	**56**	**3.73**	**3.86**	**1.23**				**16.5**	**2.5**	**8.7**	**3.5**	**0%**	**0%**	**42**	**20**	**38**	**31%**	**73%**	**10%**	**9**						**3.3**	**109**	**130**	**$0**

Paxton,James

Age: 28	Th: L	Role SP	Health F	LIMA Plan B	
Ht: 6' 4"	Wt: 220	Type Pwr	PT/Exp C	Rand Var +1	
			Consist B	MM 2205	

6-7, 3.79 ERA in 121 IP at SEA. Called up to rotation in June and stuck all year. Mediocre surface stats, but seeds of upside were planted: Dom growth came with SwK support, top-shelf FB velo; GB%, Ctl combo reduce DIS% risk. Health, IP spike prevent us from going all in, but 2nd half gains hint at... UP: 3.00 ERA

Yr	Tm	W	L	Sv	IP	K	ERA	xERA	WHIP	oOPS	vL	vR	BF/G	Ctl	Dom	Cmd	FpK	SwK	G	L	F	H%	S%	hr/f	GS	APC	DOM%	DIS%	Sv%	LI	RAR	BPV	BPX	R$
12	aa	9	4	0	106	96	3.68	4.34	1.58				22.3	4.8	8.1	1.7						34%	76%								4.4	72	95	-$2
13	SEA *	11	11	0	170	131	4.25	4.35	1.48	533	790	475	22.8	3.2	6.9	2.1	54%	10%	59	17	24	34%	71%	13%	4	96	25%	25%			-8.1	67	88	-$3
14	SEA	6	4	0	74	59	3.04	3.50	1.20	612	527	629	23.3	3.5	7.2	2.0	54%	8%	55	23	23	28%	74%	6%	13	91	23%	8%			6.4	67	80	$4
15	SEA	3	4	0	67	56	3.90	4.47	1.43	704	1054	606	22.8	3.9	7.5	1.9	53%	7%	48	17	34	31%	76%	11%	13	85	15%	38%			0.5	56	67	-$3
16	SEA *	10	10	0	172	159	3.95	4.07	1.31	717	733	714	22.9	2.1	8.3	4.1	62%	12%	48	22	30	34%	71%	8%	20	98	30%	15%			5.1	111	132	$8
1st Half		6	6	0	88	83	4.43	4.99	1.50	826	932	801	22.4	2.8	8.4	3.0	62%	12%	50	22	28	37%	72%	8%	7	104	14%	14%			-2.6	82	98	$2
2nd Half		4	4	0	84	76	3.44	3.10	1.10	655	576	668	23.5	1.3	8.2	6.4	63%	12%	47	22	31	32%	70%	8%	13	94	38%	15%			7.7	168	200	$14
17	**Proj**	**12**	**10**	**0**	**189**	**165**	**3.59**	**3.94**	**1.32**	**687**	**835**	**653**	**22.6**	**2.8**	**7.9**	**2.8**	**58%**	**10%**	**49**	**20**	**30**	**32%**	**74%**	**9%**	**34**						**13.9**	**92**	**109**	**$9**

RYAN BLOOMFIELD

Peacock,Brad

Age: 29	Th: R	Role SP	Health F	LIMA Plan D+	
Ht: 6' 1"	Wt: 175	Type Pwr xFB	PT/Exp C	Rand Var +2	
			Consist A	MM 0200	

0-1, 3.69 ERA in 32 IP at HOU. Stayed healthy all year, but skills in AAA were hardly a step forward. Walks remain an issue, stagnant Dom now subpar in today's K-friendly age, SwK hints it will stay that way. Late-season MLB "success" a product of LD% fluke. Recent xERAs confirm: former bright prospect has lost shine.

Yr Tm	W	L	Sv	IP	K	ERA	xERA	WHIP	oOPS	vL	vR	BF/G	Ctl	Dom	Cmd	FpK	SwK	G	L	F	H%	S%	hr/f	GS	APC	DOM%	DIS%	Sv%	LI	RAR	BPV	BPX	R$
12 aaa	12	9	0	135	115	6.17	5.28	1.65				21.5	4.3	7.7	1.8						35%	62%								-35.7	54	70	-$16
13 HOU *	11	8	0	162	141	4.21	4.23	1.31	779	919	594	21.0	3.3	7.8	2.4	56%	8%	37	19	45	29%	73%	14%	14	83	21%	29%	0	0.79	-7.0	60	78	$3
14 HOU	4	9	0	132	119	4.72	4.59	1.56	801	793	811	21.0	4.8	8.1	1.7	57%	9%	37	21	42	31%	74%	12%	24	85	13%	46%	0	0.81	-15.8	32	38	-$9
15 HOU	0	1	0	5	3	5.40	5.05	1.40	808	1167	422	22.0	3.6	5.4	1.5	68%	6%	31	31	38	31%	57%	0%	1	85	0%	100%			-0.9	9	11	-$5
16 HOU *	5	7	0	149	121	4.86	5.10	1.52	700	718	686	20.1	3.4	7.3	2.1	58%	9%	41	9	49	33%	70%	14%	5	49	20%	60%	0	0.40	-12.3	52	62	-$6
1st Half	2	4	0	77	58	6.20	6.40	1.79				23.6	3.7	6.8	1.8						38%	66%	0%	0						-19.1	35	42	-$18
2nd Half	3	3	0	72	63	3.43	3.71	1.22	700	718	686	17.1	3.1	7.9	2.6	58%	9%	41	9	49	28%	77%	14%	5	49	20%	60%	0	0.40	6.8	73	87	$6
17 Proj	**2**	**2**	**0**	**44**	**37**	**4.68**	**4.92**	**1.48**	**816**	**899**	**720**	**20.1**	**3.8**	**7.7**	**2.0**	**57%**	**8%**	**38**	**16**	**46**	**32%**	**71%**	**10%**	**9**						**-2.6**	**52**	**62**	**-$4**

Peavy,Jake

Age: 36	Th: R	Role RP	Health F	LIMA Plan C	
Ht: 6' 1"	Wt: 180	Type Pwr FB	PT/Exp B	Rand Var +4	
			Consist A	MM 1201	

Banished to bullpen in Aug, when nagging back issues re-surfaced. Dom/SwK recovered, but failed to hit 90 mph with FB for first time, and xERA continued to head wrong way. Health, age are severe hurdles, and while RandVar points to better numbers, you can improve from a 5.54 ERA and still be pretty bad.

Yr Tm	W	L	Sv	IP	K	ERA	xERA	WHIP	oOPS	vL	vR	BF/G	Ctl	Dom	Cmd	FpK	SwK	G	L	F	H%	S%	hr/f	GS	APC	DOM%	DIS%	Sv%	LI	RAR	BPV	BPX	R$
12 CHW	11	12	0	219	194	3.37	3.82	1.10	671	714	614	27.6	2.0	8.0	4.0	63%	10%	37	19	45	28%	74%	10%	32	109	50%	9%			17.4	104	136	$22
13 2 AL	12	5	0	145	121	4.17	4.00	1.15	697	731	659	25.7	2.2	7.5	3.4	66%	9%	33	21	47	28%	68%	10%	23	103	48%	30%			-5.4	86	112	$7
14 2 TM	7	13	0	203	158	3.73	4.12	1.28	742	766	719	26.6	2.8	7.0	2.5	64%	10%	38	20	42	29%	74%	9%	32	101	19%	25%			0.3	67	80	$4
15 SF *	8	9	0	143	99	4.42	4.10	1.27	684	650	720	23.4	2.2	6.2	2.8	63%	9%	38	17	45	30%	68%	8%	19	92	21%	32%			-8.1	67	80	$1
16 SF	5	9	0	119	102	5.54	4.73	1.43	838	921	774	16.8	2.7	7.7	2.8	64%	11%	36	19	44	33%	64%	11%	21	65	19%	24%	0	0.75	-19.7	80	94	-$7
1st Half	4	7	0	83	63	5.44	4.97	1.46	856	934	791	22.6	2.8	6.9	2.4	65%	11%	37	18	45	33%	64%	9%	16	86	19%	31%			-12.8	62	74	-$6
2nd Half	1	2	0	36	39	5.75	4.20	1.36	797	884	739	10.5	2.5	9.8	3.9	63%	11%	34	22	44	33%	63%	17%	5	43	20%	0%	0	0.74	-6.9	120	143	-$7
17 Proj	**5**	**7**	**0**	**116**	**99**	**4.85**	**4.44**	**1.32**	**782**	**816**	**754**	**16.8**	**2.5**	**7.7**	**3.1**	**64%**	**10%**	**36**	**19**	**44**	**31%**	**67%**	**11%**	**19**						**-9.5**	**85**	**101**	**-$3**

Pelfrey,Mike

Age: 33	Th: R	Role SP	Health F	LIMA Plan D+	
Ht: 6' 7"	Wt: 250	Type Con GB	PT/Exp B	Rand Var +2	
			Consist D	MM 0001	

He was paid $67K per inning to do this. Another brutal year; with with lowest Dom, Cmd of any MLB SP (min. 100 IP), and no signs of improvement from SwK or FpK. August back injury led to 'pen demotion, but hey, at least he kept ball on the ground. Owed another $8 million in 2017; guess the joke's on us.

Yr Tm	W	L	Sv	IP	K	ERA	xERA	WHIP	oOPS	vL	vR	BF/G	Ctl	Dom	Cmd	FpK	SwK	G	L	F	H%	S%	hr/f	GS	APC	DOM%	DIS%	Sv%	LI	RAR	BPV	BPX	R$
12 NYM	0	0	0	20	13	2.29	3.77	1.42	683	672	697	28.3	1.8	5.9	3.3	64%	9%	53	27	20	36%	82%	0%	3	102	33%	33%			4.2	89	116	-$3
13 MIN	5	13	0	153	101	5.19	4.59	1.55	789	762	821	23.4	3.1	6.0	1.9	55%	6%	43	21	36	34%	67%	7%	29	94	14%	48%			-24.9	44	57	-$13
14 MIN	0	3	0	24	10	7.99	6.83	1.99	924	648	1315	23.8	6.8	3.8	0.6	50%	5%	44	18	38	30%	62%	15%	5	91	0%	100%			-12.4	-94	-112	-$9
15 MIN	6	11	0	165	86	4.26	4.45	1.48	772	834	716	23.8	2.5	4.7	1.9	58%	6%	51	23	26	33%	71%	7%	30	89	20%	40%			-6.1	47	56	-$6
16 DET	4	10	0	119	56	5.07	5.31	1.73	877	923	828	22.5	3.5	4.2	1.2	58%	7%	52	22	26	34%	73%	14%	22	86	0%	73%	0	0.72	-12.9	12	15	-$13
1st Half	2	7	0	92	44	4.78	5.29	1.72	881	907	851	24.6	3.4	4.3	1.3	60%	7%	52	21	27	34%	75%	15%	16	92	0%	69%	0	0.73	-6.7	16	19	-$13
2nd Half	2	3	0	27	12	6.08	5.36	1.76	864	987	761	17.6	3.7	4.1	1.1	54%	5%	52	25	23	35%	64%	9%	6	70	0%	83%	0	0.68	-6.2	2	3	-$11
17 Proj	**3**	**6**	**0**	**73**	**37**	**5.05**	**5.08**	**1.62**	**824**	**881**	**770**	**21.4**	**3.1**	**4.6**	**1.5**	**57%**	**6%**	**50**	**23**	**27**	**34%**	**69%**	**9%**	**15**						**-7.7**	**27**	**32**	**-$8**

Peralta,Wily

Age: 28	Th: R	Role SP	Health D	LIMA Plan D+	
Ht: 6' 2"	Wt: 255	Type GB	PT/Exp B	Rand Var +3	
			Consist C	MM 1103	

7-11, 4.86 ERA in 128 IP at MIL. Awful start led to AAA demotion in June. Returned with some life, as increased use of slider led to 2nd half SwK, Dom gains, and held strong GB% all year. Ctl will remain an issue with subpar FpK, while xERA trend, DIS% keep expectations in check. Still a long road back to 2014.

Yr Tm	W	L	Sv	IP	K	ERA	xERA	WHIP	oOPS	vL	vR	BF/G	Ctl	Dom	Cmd	FpK	SwK	G	L	F	H%	S%	hr/f	GS	APC	DOM%	DIS%	Sv%	LI	RAR	BPV	BPX	R$
12 MIL *	9	12	0	176	146	5.34	5.17	1.71	601	639	564	23.4	4.8	7.5	1.6	61%	9%	55	21	24	36%	68%	0%	5	76	40%	20%	0	0.66	-28.7	56	72	-$18
13 MIL	11	15	0	183	129	4.37	4.17	1.42	722	753	692	25.1	3.6	6.3	1.8	58%	9%	51	21	28	30%	71%	12%	32	93	19%	53%			-11.4	46	60	-$2
14 MIL	17	11	0	199	154	3.53	3.62	1.30	714	820	606	26.2	2.8	7.0	2.5	58%	9%	54	19	28	30%	77%	14%	32	100	28%	31%			5.1	83	99	$9
15 MIL	5	10	0	109	60	4.72	4.67	1.54	844	889	796	23.9	3.1	5.0	1.6	57%	7%	52	20	28	32%	72%	13%	20	88	10%	55%			-10.2	37	44	-$8
16 MIL *	8	14	0	169	123	5.56	6.03	1.66	855	880	832	22.9	3.3	6.6	2.0	56%	9%	50	23	27	35%	69%	17%	23	93	13%	57%			-28.7	34	41	-$15
1st Half	4	9	0	80	52	7.55	8.03	2.00	999	954	1038	22.8	3.9	5.8	1.5	55%	7%	49	24	27	39%	64%	19%	13	91	0%	85%			-33.3	-2	-2	-$30
2nd Half	4	5	0	89	71	3.77	4.22	1.35	680	802	546	23.1	2.7	7.2	2.7	56%	11%	51	21	28	32%	75%	14%	10	95	30%	20%			4.6	72	86	-$1
17 Proj	**9**	**14**	**0**	**174**	**122**	**4.51**	**4.50**	**1.49**	**800**	**851**	**748**	**23.3**	**3.2**	**6.3**	**2.0**	**56%**	**9%**	**51**	**21**	**28**	**32%**	**72%**	**13%**	**32**						**-6.9**	**56**	**67**	**-$5**

Perdomo,Luis

Age: 24	Th: R	Role RP	Health A	LIMA Plan C	
Ht: 6' 2"	Wt: 160	Type xGB	PT/Exp D	Rand Var +5	
			Consist F	MM 2103	

Rule 5 pick weathered early storm (and 6 ER hurricane on Opening Day) after somehow getting rotation promotion in June. Heavy sinker drove xGB, and while stingy Ctl fueled 2nd half gains, he sacrificed Dom, SwK to do so. Worthy end-game option as 2nd half xERA point to improvement, but breakout odds are slim.

Yr Tm	W	L	Sv	IP	K	ERA	xERA	WHIP	oOPS	vL	vR	BF/G	Ctl	Dom	Cmd	FpK	SwK	G	L	F	H%	S%	hr/f	GS	APC	DOM%	DIS%	Sv%	LI	RAR	BPV	BPX	R$
12																																	
13																																	
14																																	
15																																	
16 SD	9	10	0	147	105	5.71	4.20	1.59	847	861	834	18.9	2.8	6.4	2.3	59%	9%	59	20	21	35%	67%	22%	20	68	10%	40%	0	0.65	-27.4	77	91	-$12
1st Half	2	3	0	53	48	8.49	4.69	2.06	977	973	979	13.4	4.4	8.2	1.8	55%	11%	56	23	21	42%	60%	25%	5	49	0%	80%	0	0.52	-28.1	61	73	-$27
2nd Half	7	7	0	94	57	4.13	3.91	1.32	761	785	741	26.3	1.9	5.5	2.9	62%	7%	61	17	21	31%	73%	20%	15	93	13%	27%			0.7	86	102	-$2
17 Proj	**8**	**9**	**0**	**131**	**93**	**4.50**	**4.07**	**1.44**	**724**	**719**	**729**	**17.2**	**3.1**	**6.4**	**2.1**	**59%**	**9%**	**59**	**20**	**21**	**32%**	**70%**	**14%**	**23**						**-4.9**	**70**	**83**	**-$3**

Perez,Martin

Age: 26	Th: L	Role SP	Health F	LIMA Plan D+	
Ht: 6' 0"	Wt: 180	Type Con GB	PT/Exp C	Rand Var 0	
			Consist B	MM 1003	

Crashed back to earth after H%/S%-fueled mirage in 1st half. Kept ball on ground, though not quite to 2015's degree, while FpK hints at Ctl improvement. Other signs are ominous, as he doesn't miss enough bats to reverse Dom slide, and poor xERA held steady all year. Lots and lots of bad innings.

Yr Tm	W	L	Sv	IP	K	ERA	xERA	WHIP	oOPS	vL	vR	BF/G	Ctl	Dom	Cmd	FpK	SwK	G	L	F	H%	S%	hr/f	GS	APC	DOM%	DIS%	Sv%	LI	RAR	BPV	BPX	R$
12 TEX *	8	10	0	165	83	4.95	4.68	1.51	819	596	924	21.0	3.7	4.5	1.2	60%	7%	49	21	30	30%	68%	8%	6	55	0%	67%	0	0.75	-19.0	28	36	-$11
13 TEX *	15	8	0	168	109	3.77	4.27	1.35	728	759	718	25.0	2.5	5.9	2.3	61%	10%	48	21	31	31%	75%	12%	20	93	35%	45%			2.0	56	72	$5
14 TEX	4	3	0	51	35	4.38	3.73	1.34	743	707	753	25.9	3.3	6.1	1.8	60%	8%	53	23	25	30%	67%	8%	8	97	13%	38%			-4.1	52	61	-$2
15 TEX *	3	7	0	104	68	4.73	4.69	1.49	729	537	777	22.5	2.3	5.9	2.5	65%	8%	60	18	22	35%	67%	5%	14	87	21%	50%			-9.9	66	79	-$8
16 TEX	10	11	0	199	103	4.39	4.92	1.41	741	537	786	25.9	3.4	4.7	1.4	64%	8%	53	20	26	29%	70%	10%	33	93	12%	48%			-5.0	22	26	-$1
1st Half	7	4	0	104	51	3.39	4.93	1.37	717	434	783	25.5	3.8	4.4	1.2	64%	7%	54	20	26	27%	78%	12%	17	97	6%	41%			10.3	9	11	$8
2nd Half	3	7	0	95	52	5.49	4.92	1.46	764	649	789	26.4	3.0	4.9	1.6	65%	9%	52	21	27	31%	62%	9%	16	90	19%	56%			-15.3	37	44	-$11
17 Proj	**8**	**11**	**0**	**174**	**102**	**4.45**	**4.56**	**1.43**	**757**	**604**	**796**	**24.5**	**3.1**	**5.3**	**1.7**	**64%**	**8%**	**54**	**20**	**25**	**31%**	**69%**	**9%**	**30**						**-5.6**	**44**	**53**	**-$4**

Perez,Williams

Age: 26	Th: R	Role SP	Health F	LIMA Plan D+	
Ht: 6' 0"	Wt: 240	Type xGB	PT/Exp D	Rand Var +5	
			Consist B	MM 1001	

2-3, 6.04 ERA in 54 IP at ATL. Broke camp with rotation gig, but injuries in May (rotator cuff), Sept (elbow) derailed year. GB%/Ctl combo has value, particularly given FpK spike, but brutal S% inflated ERA.That's the end of the good news. Inability to get whiffs is major obstacle that relegates him to a desperation pick.

Yr Tm	W	L	Sv	IP	K	ERA	xERA	WHIP	oOPS	vL	vR	BF/G	Ctl	Dom	Cmd	FpK	SwK	G	L	F	H%	S%	hr/f	GS	APC	DOM%	DIS%	Sv%	LI	RAR	BPV	BPX	R$
12																																	
13																																	
14 aa	7	6	0	133	84	3.41	3.47	1.31				21.1	2.6	5.7	2.2						31%	73%								5.4	73	86	$3
15 ATL *	10	7	1	155	104	3.97	4.58	1.48	809	865	748	21.6	3.6	6.0	1.7	57%	7%	51	20	29	32%	75%	12%	20	81	10%	50%	100	0.72	-0.2	47	55	-$1
16 ATL *	3	5	0	78	47	5.19	3.91	1.25	752	811	692	21.2	2.6	5.5	2.1	65%	6%	57	15	28	28%	60%	14%	11	78	9%	64%			-9.6	49	58	-$3
1st Half	3	4	0	68	37	4.50	3.54	1.23	666	762	570	23.0	2.7	5.0	1.8	66%	6%	58	16	26	27%	64%	10%	9	83	11%	56%			-2.6	49	58	-$2
2nd Half	0	1	0	10	10	9.90	6.44	1.41	1335	1143	1544	14.1	1.9	9.0	4.8	55%	6%	52	9	39	33%	28%	33%	2	54	0%	100%			-7.0	69	82	-$12
17 Proj	**4**	**5**	**0**	**87**	**53**	**4.34**	**4.47**	**1.40**	**752**	**831**	**670**	**22.2**	**2.9**	**5.5**	**1.9**	**62%**	**6%**	**55**	**18**	**27**	**31%**	**70%**	**10%**	**17**						**-1.6**	**53**	**63**	**-$3**

RYAN BLOOMFIELD

Perkins,Glen

Age: 34	Th: L	Role RP	Health F	LIMA Plan C+	
Ht: 5' 11"	Wt: 205	Type Pwr FB	PT/Exp C	Rand Var +5	
			Consist C	MM 2300	

Lost season thanks to torn labrum; June surgery with lengthy rehab casts cloud over 2017 outlook. Pre-injury trends were troubling, as BPV and xERA headed wrong way due to steady Dom decline. Strong Ctl on his side, but recovery road can take many wrong turns. Minimal impact until 2nd half, at best.

Yr Tm	W	L	Sv	IP	K	ERA	xERA	WHIP	oOPS	vL	vR	BF/G	Ctl	Dom	Cmd	FpK	SwK	G	L	F	H%	S%	hr/f	GS	APC	DOM%	DIS%	Sv%	LI	RAR	BPV	BPX	R$
12 MIN	3	1	16	70	78	2.56	3.12	1.04	631	488	721	4.0	2.0	10.0	4.9	63%	14%	42	19	39	29%	82%	12%	0	15			80	0.92	12.6	144	188	$14
13 MIN	2	0	36	63	77	2.30	2.67	0.93	562	544	568	3.9	2.2	11.1	5.1	70%	14%	36	26	38	28%	79%	9%	0	15			90	1.16	12.1	155	202	$21
14 MIN	4	3	34	62	66	3.65	3.34	1.18	720	772	700	4.1	1.6	9.6	6.0	65%	12%	35	23	42	34%	73%	9%	0	15			83	1.13	0.7	143	170	$15
15 MIN	3	5	32	57	54	3.32	3.90	1.19	701	850	648	4.0	1.6	8.5	5.4	64%	11%	34	22	45	31%	80%	12%	0	14			91	1.50	4.5	123	146	$14
16 MIN	0	0	0	2	3	9.00	5.44	3.00	1200	1200	1171	6.0	4.5	13.5	3.0	50%	17%	38	13	50	65%	67%	0%	0	24			0	0.62	-1.2	138	163	-$5
1st Half	0	0	0	2	3	9.00	5.44	3.00	1200	1200	1171	6.0	4.5	13.5	3.0	50%	17%	38	13	50	65%	67%	0%	0	24			0	0.62	-1.2	137	163	-$5
2nd Half																																	
17 Proj	1	1	0	29	29	3.53	3.74	1.18	703	734	691	4.0	1.9	8.9	4.8	66%	11%	36	23	41	32%	74%	10%	0						2.3	125	148	-$1

Phelps,David

Age: 30	Th: R	Role RP	Health F	LIMA Plan C+	
Ht: 6' 3"	Wt: 185	Type Pwr	PT/Exp B	Rand Var -3	
			Consist B	MM 2411	

Amazing what a few ticks on fastball can do, as 3 more mph lifted Dom to uncharted waters. But career-best ERA from swing role came with help from S%, and he hit DL for 4th straight year. Ctl remained an issue with FpK plunge, and while BPV, xERA confirm gains were made, we're looking at his peak.

Yr Tm	W	L	Sv	IP	K	ERA	xERA	WHIP	oOPS	vL	vR	BF/G	Ctl	Dom	Cmd	FpK	SwK	G	L	F	H%	S%	hr/f	GS	APC	DOM%	DIS%	Sv%	LI	RAR	BPV	BPX	R$
12 NYY	4	4	0	100	96	3.34	3.82	1.19	682	786	597	12.5	3.4	8.7	2.5	62%	7%	43	19	38	27%	78%	14%	11	51	27%	27%	0	0.83	8.3	84	110	$6
13 NYY	6	5	0	87	79	4.98	3.97	1.42	749	756	738	17.1	3.6	8.2	2.3	59%	7%	42	22	36	33%	65%	9%	12	68	17%	25%	0	0.92	-12.0	70	91	-$4
14 NYY	5	5	1	113	92	4.38	4.21	1.42	751	699	805	15.5	3.7	7.3	2.0	62%	6%	41	24	35	31%	72%	11%	17	60	18%	35%	100	0.86	-8.9	52	62	-$4
15 MIA	4	8	0	112	77	4.50	4.48	1.36	729	758	705	21.0	2.7	6.2	2.3	65%	5%	42	23	35	31%	68%	9%	19	81	16%	47%	0	0.72	-7.4	60	71	-$4
16 MIA	7	6	4	87	114	2.28	3.17	1.14	582	725	465	5.5	3.9	11.8	3.0	56%	10%	46	21	33	30%	83%	9%	5	23	20%	0%	40	1.18	20.4	131	155	$13
1st Half	4	4	3	44	54	2.25	3.03	0.98	533	708	400	4.3	2.5	11.0	4.5	58%	11%	43	20	38	29%	78%	5%	0	17			43	1.22	10.5	153	183	$16
2nd Half	3	2	1	43	60	2.32	3.31	1.31	631	739	534	7.5	5.5	12.7	2.3	53%	10%	50	21	29	30%	87%	15%	5	33	20%	0%	33	1.11	9.8	108	128	$11
17 Proj	7	7	2	116	122	3.34	3.82	1.27	666	736	603	8.6	3.7	9.5	2.6	59%	8%	44	22	34	30%	76%	10%	3						12.1	93	111	$8

Pineda,Michael

Age: 28	Th: R	Role SP	Health F	LIMA Plan A	
Ht: 6' 5"	Wt: 265	Type Pwr	PT/Exp B	Rand Var +5	
			Consist A	MM 3403	

Another year of skills looking vastly better than stats, as unfriendly H%-S%-hr/f from 2015 got even worse. Took Dom to new level with elite SwK and velocity uptick, and regained GB% in 2H, while FpK says not to worry about Ctl bump. Skills are there; if he can just limit gopheritis, we might see... UP: 3.25 ERA.

Yr Tm	W	L	Sv	IP	K	ERA	xERA	WHIP	oOPS	vL	vR	BF/G	Ctl	Dom	Cmd	FpK	SwK	G	L	F	H%	S%	hr/f	GS	APC	DOM%	DIS%	Sv%	LI	RAR	BPV	BPX	R$
12																																	
13 a/a	2	1	0	32	28	5.23	4.30	1.32				16.7	3.7	7.8	2.1						28%	64%								-5.5	52	68	-$4
14 NYY	5	5	0	76	59	1.89	3.39	0.83	526	533	518	22.3	0.8	7.0	8.4	67%	12%	39	19	42	25%	81%	5%	13	88	38%	23%			17.5	120	143	$11
15 NYY	12	10	0	161	156	4.37	3.21	1.23	752	741	762	24.7	1.2	8.7	7.4	64%	12%	48	22	30	34%	68%	15%	27	94	30%	37%			-8.1	152	180	$6
16 NYY	6	12	0	176	207	4.82	3.45	1.35	784	801	770	23.6	2.7	10.6	3.9	67%	15%	46	22	33	35%	68%	17%	32	94	9%	25%			-13.6	142	168	$1
1st Half	3	7	0	89	108	5.24	3.44	1.38	821	823	819	24.4	2.3	10.9	4.7	67%	15%	43	23	34	37%	66%	17%	16	97	0%	25%			-11.6	154	184	-$1
2nd Half	3	5	0	86	99	4.38	3.46	1.32	743	777	715	22.8	3.1	10.3	3.3	68%	14%	49	20	31	33%	71%	16%	16	91	19%	25%			-2.0	128	153	$3
17 Proj	9	11	0	174	179	3.85	3.48	1.23	716	721	711	22.1	2.2	9.3	4.3	66%	13%	46	21	33	33%	72%	13%	32						7.3	132	157	$9

Pomeranz,Drew

Age: 28	Th: L	Role SP	Health C	LIMA Plan C	
Ht: 6' 6"	Wt: 230	Type Pwr	PT/Exp B	Rand Var 0	
			Consist A	MM 2303	

Shot out of gate in SD rotation, dealt to BOS for playoff push, but limped to finish (6.61 Sept ERA, forearm issues). Relied heavily on knockout curve, which lends credence to SwK, Dom gains. Ctl still an issue, however, and subpar FpK hints it's not going away. 1H version not coming back; heed xERA for most likely outcome.

Yr Tm	W	L	Sv	IP	K	ERA	xERA	WHIP	oOPS	vL	vR	BF/G	Ctl	Dom	Cmd	FpK	SwK	G	L	F	H%	S%	hr/f	GS	APC	DOM%	DIS%	Sv%	LI	RAR	BPV	BPX	R$
12 COL *	6	13	0	147	122	4.31	5.15	1.59	775	464	864	20.3	4.2	7.5	1.8	56%	10%	44	20	36	34%	75%	14%	22	77	9%	59%			-5.3	49	64	-$7
13 COL *	8	6	0	113	95	5.86	5.64	1.69	951	405	1150	21.2	4.3	7.6	1.8	54%	8%	51	17	32	35%	66%	19%	4	52	0%	100%	0	0.78	-27.7	43	57	-$13
14 OAK *	8	5	0	115	106	2.90	3.48	1.24	586	664	563	16.7	3.3	8.3	2.5	52%	9%	46	18	36	29%	81%	10%	10	57	50%	20%	0	0.75	12.0	82	97	$7
15 OAK	5	6	3	86	82	3.66	3.84	1.19	651	438	749	6.7	3.2	8.6	2.6	58%	12%	43	21	36	28%	71%	9%	9	27	22%	33%	50	1.27	3.2	88	105	$5
16 2 TM	11	12	0	171	186	3.32	3.71	1.18	658	643	663	22.7	3.4	9.8	2.9	56%	12%	46	17	37	28%	77%	14%	30	92	30%	27%	0	0.83	18.3	108	128	$16
1st Half	7	7	0	95	109	2.65	3.55	1.09	571	607	555	24.1	3.7	10.3	2.8	55%	12%	47	16	37	26%	79%	10%	16	100	38%	19%			18.0	111	133	$24
2nd Half	4	5	0	76	77	4.16	3.92	1.30	761	693	782	21.2	3.1	9.2	3.0	57%	11%	45	17	38	30%	75%	18%	14	83	21%	36%	0	0.89	0.2	104	124	$7
17 Proj	11	11	0	174	173	3.63	3.94	1.25	689	592	724	22.2	3.4	9.0	2.6	56%	11%	45	18	37	29%	75%	12%	27						11.9	92	110	$10

Porcello,Rick

Age: 28	Th: R	Role SP	Health B	LIMA Plan D+	
Ht: 6' 5"	Wt: 195	Type	PT/Exp A	Rand Var -1	
			Consist A	MM 2205	

Exhibit A on how pitchers are at whims of randomness, as xERA has been flat for three years now. Took pinpoint Ctl to new level with FpK support, which keeps floor high. GBs continued to turn into FBs, though, and SwK suggests middling Dom is here to stay. Don't pay for repeat, but he's a reliable mid-rotation cog.

Yr Tm	W	L	Sv	IP	K	ERA	xERA	WHIP	oOPS	vL	vR	BF/G	Ctl	Dom	Cmd	FpK	SwK	G	L	F	H%	S%	hr/f	GS	APC	DOM%	DIS%	Sv%	LI	RAR	BPV	BPX	R$
12 DET	10	12	0	176	107	4.59	4.15	1.53	808	883	725	25.3	2.2	5.5	2.4	63%	8%	53	24	23	35%	71%	12%	31	91	10%	45%			-12.6	69	90	-$9
13 DET	13	8	0	177	142	4.32	3.32	1.28	709	808	602	23.0	2.1	7.2	3.4	60%	9%	55	21	24	32%	68%	14%	29	89	31%	31%	0	0.84	-10.0	105	137	$4
14 DET	15	13	0	205	129	3.43	3.74	1.23	712	732	686	26.3	1.8	5.7	3.1	64%	8%	49	22	29	30%	74%	9%	31	95	32%	32%	0	0.83	7.9	80	96	$10
15 BOS	9	15	0	172	149	4.92	3.77	1.36	787	815	751	26.3	2.0	7.8	3.9	60%	9%	46	22	33	34%	67%	14%	28	98	43%	32%			-20.3	111	132	-$4
16 BOS	22	4	0	223	189	3.15	3.72	1.01	635	600	672	27.0	1.3	7.6	5.9	64%	9%	43	19	38	28%	73%	9%	33	103	55%	9%			28.7	123	147	$32
1st Half	9	2	0	100	89	3.78	3.78	1.14	704	602	825	25.9	1.9	8.0	4.2	61%	8%	46	18	36	29%	71%	13%	16	102	44%	19%			5.1	117	140	$18
2nd Half	13	2	0	123	100	2.63	3.67	0.90	576	597	556	27.9	0.8	7.3	9.1	67%	9%	41	19	40	27%	74%	7%	17	105	65%	0%			23.6	129	153	$43
17 Proj	16	9	0	203	163	3.74	3.81	1.16	696	704	687	25.6	1.6	7.2	4.5	63%	9%	46	20	34	30%	71%	11%	32						11.4	110	131	$16

Pressly,Ryan

Age: 28	Th: R	Role RP	Health D	LIMA Plan B+	
Ht: 6' 3"	Wt: 175	Type Pwr	PT/Exp D	Rand Var -1	
			Consist A	MM 1211	

Former Rule 5 pick broke camp with bullpen gig, became MIN's go-to weapon. Skills suggest it was more of a butter knife, as ERA crept closer to stagnant xERA. More whiffs fueled career-high Dom, but Cmd is far from closer-worthy and he gave back GB%. Health grade an additional obstacle to higher leverage role. Pass.

Yr Tm	W	L	Sv	IP	K	ERA	xERA	WHIP	oOPS	vL	vR	BF/G	Ctl	Dom	Cmd	FpK	SwK	G	L	F	H%	S%	hr/f	GS	APC	DOM%	DIS%	Sv%	LI	RAR	BPV	BPX	R$
12 aa	2	2	0	28	17	4.04	4.27	1.43				8.4	3.5	5.6	1.6						30%	73%								-0.1	45	59	-$4
13 MIN	3	3	0	77	49	3.87	4.29	1.28	677	746	614	6.4	3.2	5.8	1.8	46%	8%	44	21	35	28%	70%	6%	0	24			0	0.70	-0.1	40	52	-$1
14 MIN *	3	4	6	89	63	3.65	4.26	1.47	779	887	715	6.3	3.1	6.3	2.0	59%	9%	47	27	26	34%	75%	12%	0	15			75	0.81	1.0	66	79	-$1
15 MIN	3	2	0	28	22	2.93	4.39	1.41	645	678	626	4.4	3.9	7.2	1.8	59%	9%	47	20	33	33%	77%	0%	0	16			0	0.93	3.5	48	58	-$2
16 MIN	6	7	1	75	67	3.70	4.36	1.35	725	659	767	4.6	2.7	8.0	2.9	57%	12%	39	24	36	33%	76%	10%	0	17			17	1.19	4.5	87	103	$2
1st Half	2	4	0	43	43	3.74	4.24	1.32	687	773	630	4.6	3.3	8.9	2.7	56%	12%	39	23	39	31%	75%	11%	0	17			0	0.98	2.4	88	104	$2
2nd Half	4	3	1	32	24	3.66	4.52	1.41	773	539	971	4.5	2.0	6.8	3.4	58%	12%	40	26	34	35%	78%	8%	0	17			20	1.46	2.1	87	103	$2
17 Proj	5	5	5	73	65	3.95	4.21	1.39	755	703	795	5.2	2.8	8.0	2.8	53%	11%	41	23	35	33%	74%	10%	0						2.1	87	104	$1

Price,David

Age: 31	Th: L	Role SP	Health B	LIMA Plan C+	
Ht: 6' 5"	Wt: 225	Type Pwr	PT/Exp A	Rand Var +1	
			Consist A	MM 3305	

Rocky start in BOS debut (6.75 ERA in 7 GS) due to nasty H%/S%, hr/f. Recent xERA trend may keep him from being cream of crop, but consider: Dom, Ctl stable and strong, both supported by sub-indicators; massive IP history, consistency scores elevate his floor; BPV firmly in ace territory. Still a fine rotation anchor.

Yr Tm	W	L	Sv	IP	K	ERA	xERA	WHIP	oOPS	vL	vR	BF/G	Ctl	Dom	Cmd	FpK	SwK	G	L	F	H%	S%	hr/f	GS	APC	DOM%	DIS%	Sv%	LI	RAR	BPV	BPX	R$
12 TAM	20	5	0	211	205	2.56	3.10	1.10	602	520	626	27.0	2.5	8.7	3.5	63%	9%	53	20	27	29%	80%	11%	31	107	58%	13%			37.9	120	157	$32
13 TAM	10	8	0	187	151	3.33	3.34	1.10	661	489	712	27.4	1.3	7.3	5.6	68%	8%	45	22	33	30%	72%	9%	27	100	56%	11%			12.4	119	155	$15
14 2 AL	15	12	0	248	271	3.26	3.00	1.08	647	657	644	29.7	1.4	9.8	7.1	70%	11%	41	21	38	32%	73%	10%	34	110	59%	3%			14.7	159	189	$23
15 2 AL	18	5	0	220	225	2.45	3.36	1.08	621	658	609	27.8	1.9	9.2	4.8	67%	12%	40	23	36	30%	80%	8%	32	106	63%	9%			41.1	132	157	$33
16 BOS	17	9	0	230	228	3.99	3.60	1.20	721	749	712	27.2	2.0	8.9	4.6	65%	12%	44	22	34	32%	71%	14%	35	103	40%	23%			5.6	130	154	$17
1st Half	8	5	0	108	120	4.74	3.40	1.24	735	743	733	26.8	2.1	10.0	4.8	64%	13%	43	25	32	34%	65%	15%	17	103	47%	18%			-7.3	144	172	$11
2nd Half	9	4	0	122	108	3.33	3.78	1.18	708	753	690	27.5	1.8	8.0	4.3	65%	11%	45	20	35	30%	77%	12%	18	102	33%	28%			12.9	116	139	$23
17 Proj	16	8	0	218	217	3.47	3.48	1.14	675	690	671	26.9	1.8	9.0	4.9	66%	12%	43	22	35	31%	73%	11%	32						19.4	133	158	$21

RYAN BLOOMFIELD

Quackenbush,Kevin

Age: 28 | Th: R | Role: RP | Ht: 6' 3" | Wt: 207 | Type: Pwr
Health: A | PT/Exp: C | Consist: B
LIMA Plan: B+ | Rand Var: -1 | MM: 1200

Early Cmd issues cemented middle relief role and several AAA tours—only real distinction was number of decisions he had. As for skills, middling FpK, SwK, xERA say sneaky fastball and crafty delivery weren't deceptive enough. Even with the 2nd half Dom recovery, not as intriguing as he seemed a few years back.

Yr	Tm	W	L	Sv	IP	K	ERA	xERA	WHIP	oOPS	vL	vR	BF/G	Ctl	Dom	Cmd	FpK	SwK	G	L	F	H%	S%	hr/f	GS	APC	DOM%	DIS%	Sv%	LI	RAR	BPV	BPX	R$
12																																		
13	a/a	10	2	17	65	72	1.74	2.60	1.25				4.6	3.9	9.9	2.6						32%	86%								17.0	119	155	$15
14	SD	3	3	6	54	56	2.48	3.40	1.10	568	512	633	4.0	3.0	9.3	3.1	64%	9%	37	27	36	29%	78%	4%	0	16			86	1.17	8.4	101	121	$6
15	SD	3	2	0	58	58	4.01	3.73	1.23	670	799	565	4.3	3.1	8.9	2.9	60%	9%	44	21	36	30%	70%	10%	0	18			0	0.47	-0.4	100	119	-$1
16	SD	7	7	2	60	42	3.92	5.08	1.29	743	827	690	4.2	3.3	6.3	1.9	57%	8%	35	22	43	27%	74%	10%	0	17			67	0.85	2.0	37	44	$2
1st Half		5	3	0	33	17	4.32	5.83	1.23	706	758	674	4.0	3.8	4.6	1.2	56%	7%	32	20	48	22%	69%	10%	0	16			0	0.82	-0.5	-9	-11	$2
2nd Half		2	4	2	26	25	3.42	4.19	1.37	787	899	711	4.5	2.7	8.5	3.1	58%	8%	39	24	37	34%	79%	10%	0	19			100	0.90	2.5	97	116	$2
17	**Proj**	**4**	**4**	**0**	**58**	**52**	**3.76**	**4.26**	**1.29**	**722**	**794**	**666**	**4.2**	**3.2**	**8.1**	**2.5**	**59%**	**9%**	**39**	**23**	**38**	**30%**	**74%**	**10%**	**0**						**3.1**	**77**	**92**	**$0**

Quintana,Jose

Age: 28 | Th: L | Role: SP | Ht: 6' 0" | Wt: 215 | Type:
Health: A | PT/Exp: A | Consist: A
LIMA Plan: D+ | Rand Var: -1 | MM: 2205

In the midst of a Mark Buehrle-esque run as the southside's proficient, easily-projected lefty. Continues to throw strikes with just enough swing-and-miss, with little regard to batters' handedness or batted ball outcomes. While this may be as good as it gets for him, enjoy another 200-inning dose of quiet reliability.

Yr	Tm	W	L	Sv	IP	K	ERA	xERA	WHIP	oOPS	vL	vR	BF/G	Ctl	Dom	Cmd	FpK	SwK	G	L	F	H%	S%	hr/f	GS	APC	DOM%	DIS%	Sv%	LI	RAR	BPV	BPX	R$
12	CHW *	7	9	0	185	117	3.68	4.06	1.35	754	700	775	22.7	2.8	5.7	2.0	61%	8%	47	22	31	30%	74%	11%	22	87	18%	50%	0	0.73	7.6	55	72	$3
13	CHW	9	7	0	200	164	3.51	3.85	1.22	695	717	687	25.2	2.5	7.4	2.9	66%	9%	43	20	37	29%	75%	10%	33	101	36%	21%			8.8	86	112	$10
14	CHW	9	11	0	200	178	3.32	3.51	1.24	662	686	653	25.9	2.3	8.0	3.4	66%	9%	45	22	33	33%	73%	5%	32	105	25%	19%			10.3	104	124	$9
15	CHW	9	10	0	206	177	3.36	3.60	1.27	722	663	740	26.9	1.9	7.7	4.0	69%	9%	47	23	30	33%	75%	9%	32	105	38%	16%			15.4	112	134	$11
16	CHW	13	12	0	208	181	3.20	3.98	1.16	687	650	698	26.2	2.2	7.8	3.6	65%	8%	40	21	39	30%	76%	10%	32	103	47%	19%			25.3	101	119	$21
1st Half		6	8	0	112	100	3.06	3.93	1.12	650	521	688	26.1	2.2	8.1	3.7	64%	9%	39	20	41	29%	75%	7%	17	103	59%	12%			15.5	103	123	$23
2nd Half		7	4	0	96	81	3.36	4.03	1.21	730	813	708	26.2	2.1	7.6	3.5	66%	8%	42	22	36	30%	78%	13%	15	102	33%	27%			9.8	98	117	$18
17	**Proj**	**14**	**11**	**0**	**203**	**173**	**3.32**	**3.94**	**1.22**	**701**	**684**	**706**	**25.7**	**2.2**	**7.7**	**3.5**	**66%**	**9%**	**43**	**22**	**35**	**31%**	**76%**	**9%**	**32**						**21.8**	**101**	**120**	**$16**

Ramirez,Erasmo

Age: 27 | Th: R | Role: RP | Ht: 5' 11" | Wt: 205 | Type:
Health: A | PT/Exp: B | Consist: B
LIMA Plan: B+ | Rand Var: 0 | MM: 1101

2016 move to bullpen was essentially a remix of 2015 in shorter takes. Lefties and long flies were more problematic even as GB% helped him—give a little, take a little. But aggregate is modest, and neither role has uncovered hidden Dom. At this point, it's hard to envision him as anything but just a pedestrian arm.

Yr	Tm	W	L	Sv	IP	K	ERA	xERA	WHIP	oOPS	vL	vR	BF/G	Ctl	Dom	Cmd	FpK	SwK	G	L	F	H%	S%	hr/f	GS	APC	DOM%	DIS%	Sv%	LI	RAR	BPV	BPX	R$
12	SEA *	7	6	0	136	101	3.35	3.11	1.14	616	612	622	17.4	1.8	6.6	3.6	64%	12%	40	24	36	29%	72%	10%	8	55	50%	13%	0	0.76	11.1	102	133	$10
13	SEA *	8	6	0	121	96	4.36	4.71	1.42	772	791	742	23.3	3.1	7.2	2.3	59%	9%	42	21	36	32%	73%	14%	13	91	0%	38%	0	0.74	-7.3	56	73	-$2
14	SEA *	7	11	0	162	117	4.34	4.66	1.38	815	790	848	21.2	2.5	6.5	2.6	61%	11%	38	19	43	32%	72%	13%	14	76	14%	50%	0	0.63	-12.0	59	70	-$4
15	TAM	11	6	0	163	126	3.75	3.76	1.13	655	567	753	19.6	2.2	6.9	3.2	65%	11%	48	21	32	28%	69%	10%	27	71	19%	33%	0	0.70	4.3	91	109	$11
16	TAM	7	11	2	91	63	3.77	4.26	1.28	766	905	685	5.9	2.6	6.3	2.4	63%	9%	53	15	32	28%	76%	16%	1	21	0%	0%	33	1.43	4.7	74	88	$4
1st Half		7	7	0	52	38	4.30	4.15	1.36	803	937	722	6.5	2.6	6.5	2.5	63%	9%	54	16	30	30%	73%	17%	1	23	0%	0%	0	1.56	-0.7	80	95	$4
2nd Half		0	4	2	38	25	3.05	4.42	1.17	714	857	635	5.2	2.6	5.9	2.3	64%	10%	50	15	35	25%	82%	15%	0	19			100	1.29	5.4	64	77	$3
17	**Proj**	**5**	**7**	**0**	**87**	**63**	**3.75**	**4.26**	**1.24**	**723**	**747**	**703**	**8.7**	**2.5**	**6.5**	**2.6**	**63%**	**10%**	**48**	**18**	**34**	**28%**	**74%**	**12%**	**0**						**4.7**	**75**	**90**	**$2**

Ramirez,J.C.

Age: 28 | Th: R | Role: RP | Ht: 6' 3" | Wt: 175 | Type: GB
Health: A | PT/Exp: D | Consist: A
LIMA Plan: B | Rand Var: +2 | MM: 1000

Adage about making a silk purse from a sow's ear comes to mind here. Actually proved hard to hit in 2nd half for LAA, his fourth team in two years. High-octane FB hasn't translated into strikeouts and Ctl is spotty, but he's of the "live arm" variety who will pique interest wherever he's allowed to air it out. Voila! Silk purse.

Yr	Tm	W	L	Sv	IP	K	ERA	xERA	WHIP	oOPS	vL	vR	BF/G	Ctl	Dom	Cmd	FpK	SwK	G	L	F	H%	S%	hr/f	GS	APC	DOM%	DIS%	Sv%	LI	RAR	BPV	BPX	R$
12	a/a	3	4	4	67	44	4.90	4.31	1.45				6.4	4.3	5.8	1.4						29%	67%								-7.3	39	51	-$4
13	PHI *	5	3	3	73	52	5.66	5.24	1.67	975	1019	944	6.3	5.0	6.5	1.3	53%	10%	39	22	40	32%	67%	18%	0	23			75	0.57	-16.1	34	44	-$9
14	a/a	2	3	3	44	24	3.67	4.84	1.45				5.4	3.9	4.8	1.2						28%	80%								0.4	16	19	-$2
15	2 TM *	2	4	1	67	45	3.61	4.02	1.41	764	571	901	4.9	3.6	6.1	1.7	59%	10%	44	17	39	30%	75%	10%	0	21			17	1.22	2.9	55	66	-$2
16	2 TM	3	4	2	79	59	4.35	4.07	1.26	713	659	763	4.8	2.5	6.8	2.7	61%	10%	55	17	28	29%	70%	17%	0	18			33	0.97	-1.5	87	103	$0
1st Half		1	3	1	37	34	6.08	3.74	1.38	776	820	735	5.2	2.4	8.3	3.4	63%	11%	58	13	29	33%	59%	21%	0	19			25	0.98	-8.6	119	142	-$4
2nd Half		2	1	1	42	25	2.81	4.37	1.15	654	514	788	4.5	2.6	5.4	2.1	59%	10%	52	20	28	25%	81%	14%	0	17			50	0.96	7.1	57	69	$4
17	**Proj**	**3**	**3**	**0**	**65**	**45**	**4.05**	**4.36**	**1.35**	**713**	**649**	**773**	**4.9**	**3.2**	**6.1**	**1.9**	**61%**	**10%**	**55**	**17**	**28**	**29%**	**74%**	**14%**	**0**						**1.1**	**56**	**67**	**-$2**

Ramos,A.J.

Age: 30 | Th: R | Role: RP | Ht: 5' 10" | Wt: 210 | Type: Pwr
Health: B | PT/Exp: B | Consist: B
LIMA Plan: C | Rand Var: -5 | MM: 2530

The high-wire act plays on. With ominous Ctl, GB/LD rates scattering in the wrong direction, it's a lot to ask of Dom/SwK to continue saving the day. (To the rescue: hr/f.) Fatigue was evident in 2nd half (also broke finger), but saves are saves. Have to wonder how long he can tiptoe that Cmd line without toppling, though.

Yr	Tm	W	L	Sv	IP	K	ERA	xERA	WHIP	oOPS	vL	vR	BF/G	Ctl	Dom	Cmd	FpK	SwK	G	L	F	H%	S%	hr/f	GS	APC	DOM%	DIS%	Sv%	LI	RAR	BPV	BPX	R$
12	MIA *	3	3	21	78	89	2.11	2.13	1.04	754	436	1056	4.6	3.3	10.2	3.1	65%	18%	32	23	45	26%	83%	20%	0	14			81	0.94	18.3	124	162	$19
13	MIA	3	4	0	80	86	3.15	3.97	1.26	603	740	484	5.0	4.8	9.7	2.0	61%	12%	39	19	43	28%	75%	5%	0	20			0	0.98	7.1	61	79	$3
14	MIA	7	0	0	64	73	2.11	3.89	1.23	543	522	555	4.0	6.0	10.3	1.7	57%	14%	42	19	39	25%	82%	2%	0	16			0	1.36	12.9	42	49	$6
15	MIA	2	4	32	70	87	2.30	3.10	1.01	562	602	529	3.9	3.3	11.1	3.3	59%	17%	43	16	40	26%	82%	9%	0	15			84	1.27	14.4	132	157	$21
16	MIA	1	4	40	64	73	2.81	4.24	1.36	600	578	627	4.1	4.9	10.3	2.1	60%	12%	36	26	38	32%	78%	2%	0	17			93	1.15	10.9	66	78	$18
1st Half		0	0	24	33	41	2.45	3.93	1.24	553	557	548	4.0	5.2	11.2	2.2	60%	13%	37	25	38	29%	80%	3%	0	16			96	1.08	7.1	76	91	$22
2nd Half		1	4	16	31	32	3.19	4.59	1.48	646	599	700	4.3	4.6	9.3	2.0	60%	11%	36	27	37	35%	76%	0%	0	18			89	1.23	3.8	56	67	$13
17	**Proj**	**2**	**4**	**32**	**65**	**75**	**3.02**	**3.95**	**1.26**	**620**	**619**	**621**	**4.0**	**4.6**	**10.3**	**2.3**	**60%**	**13%**	**39**	**22**	**39**	**29%**	**77%**	**7%**	**0**						**9.4**	**80**	**95**	**$15**

Ramos,Edubray

Age: 24 | Th: R | Role: RP | Ht: 6' 0" | Wt: 160 | Type: Pwr xFB
Health: A | PT/Exp: F | Consist: B
LIMA Plan: A | Rand Var: 0 | MM: 2311

1-3, 3.83 in 40 IP at PHI. Rookie's line included 40 punchouts and 15 holds after late June callup. Improved command got him there and MLB 2.5 Ctl/3.6 Cmd was convincing enough. Key stat: 10 HR allowed in 255 IP of U.S. professional ball. Sample size tempers enthusiasm, but seeds of an end-gamer are there.

Yr	Tm	W	L	Sv	IP	K	ERA	xERA	WHIP	oOPS	vL	vR	BF/G	Ctl	Dom	Cmd	FpK	SwK	G	L	F	H%	S%	hr/f	GS	APC	DOM%	DIS%	Sv%	LI	RAR	BPV	BPX	R$
12																																		
13																																		
14																																		
15	aa	1	2	0	20	16	4.04	3.25	1.42				4.8	4.4	7.0	1.6						31%	68%								-0.2	81	96	-$4
16	PHI *	3	4	10	79	75	2.72	2.65	1.03	687	794	572	4.5	1.8	8.6	4.9	59%	11%	37	25	38	29%	77%	12%	0	15			71	1.09	14.2	142	169	$12
1st Half		2	1	10	44	42	1.58	1.65	0.88	538	111	833	5.1	1.1	8.6	7.9	57%	12%	54	31	15	28%	83%	0%	0	14			83	1.22	14.3	221	264	$20
2nd Half		1	3	0	34	33	4.19	4.03	1.22	711	874	520	3.9	2.6	8.7	3.3	59%	11%	35	24	41	30%	70%	13%	0	15			0	1.07	0.0	98	116	$0
17	**Proj**	**3**	**4**	**5**	**73**	**69**	**3.41**	**3.92**	**1.14**	**598**	**716**	**461**	**4.3**	**2.0**	**8.6**	**4.3**	**59%**	**11%**	**35**	**24**	**41**	**31%**	**73%**	**8%**	**0**						**6.9**	**114**	**136**	**$5**

Ray,Robbie

Age: 25 | Th: L | Role: SP | Ht: 6' 2" | Wt: 170 | Type: Pwr
Health: A | PT/Exp: C | Consist: C
LIMA Plan: C | Rand Var: +5 | MM: 2403

Season of extreme numbers (Dom, H%) calls for some parsing. Half-season trends, 1H-2015 to 2H-2016: Dom: 7.2, 9.0, 10.5, 12.1. SwK: 8, 10, 11, 13. xERA: 4.13, 3.86, 3.80, 3.42. Tacked on bit of velocity, too. Success hinges on learning how to limit hard contact. When that happens... UP: 3.25 ERA.

Yr	Tm	W	L	Sv	IP	K	ERA	xERA	WHIP	oOPS	vL	vR	BF/G	Ctl	Dom	Cmd	FpK	SwK	G	L	F	H%	S%	hr/f	GS	APC	DOM%	DIS%	Sv%	LI	RAR	BPV	BPX	R$
12																																		
13	aa	5	2	0	58	50	4.42	4.27	1.44				22.4	3.1	7.8	2.5						34%	69%								-4.0	79	103	-$3
14	DET *	8	10	0	129	79	5.85	5.78	1.73	993	889	1038	20.2	4.0	5.5	1.4	54%	6%	35	24	41	35%	66%	12%	6	61	17%	50%	0	0.65	-33.5	30	36	-$17
15	ARI *	7	15	0	169	166	3.55	3.86	1.42	731	723	733	22.5	3.9	8.8	2.3	61%	9%	44	22	35	34%	75%	7%	23	98	22%	26%			8.6	88	104	$3
16	ARI	8	15	0	174	218	4.90	3.62	1.47	770	684	797	24.3	3.7	11.3	3.1	56%	12%	46	22	33	37%	69%	15%	32	99	22%	19%			-15.4	128	152	-$2
1st Half		4	7	0	92	108	4.78	3.80	1.55	796	662	840	24.6	3.6	10.5	2.9	55%	11%	46	24	30	38%	72%	15%	17	100	24%	12%			-6.7	116	138	-$3
2nd Half		4	8	0	82	110	5.05	3.42	1.38	739	711	748	23.8	3.7	12.1	3.2	57%	13%	46	19	36	36%	66%	16%	15	98	20%	27%			-8.7	140	167	-$1
17	**Proj**	**9**	**14**	**0**	**174**	**189**	**4.07**	**3.87**	**1.40**	**737**	**691**	**753**	**22.0**	**3.7**	**9.8**	**2.6**	**58%**	**11%**	**45**	**21**	**34**	**34%**	**73%**	**11%**	**33**						**2.6**	**98**	**117**	**$3**

ROB CARROLL

Reed,Addison

Age: 28	Th: R	Role RP	Health A	LIMA Plan B
Ht: 6' 4"	Wt: 215	Type Pwr	PT/Exp C	Rand Var -4
			Consist B	MM 3411

How to resurrect your career: 1) Embrace the new role; 2) Declare "0-1 Rule" via ridiculous FpK rate; 3) Get them flailing (Dom, SwK); 4) Instill positivity (career-best Cmd, Ctl, Dom); 5) Welcome the happy accident (S%). Regression lies in the weeds, but that's where 6) Mastering muscle memory comes in.

Yr Tm	W	L	Sv	IP	K	ERA	xERA	WHIP	oOPS	vL	vR	BF/G	Ctl	Dom	Cmd	FpK	SwK	G	L	F	H%	S%	hr/f	GS	APC	DOM%	DIS%	Sv%	LI	RAR	BPV	BPX	R$
12 CHW	3	2	29	55	54	4.75	4.13	1.36	753	773	737	3.8	2.9	8.8	3.0	66%	10%	33	24	43	34%	67%	9%	0	15			88	1.53	-5.0	91	118	$8
13 CHW	5	4	40	71	72	3.79	3.75	1.11	603	608	597	4.3	2.9	9.1	3.1	65%	12%	33	22	45	28%	67%	7%	0	17			83	1.19	0.7	96	125	$19
14 ARI	1	7	32	59	69	4.25	3.51	1.21	740	610	863	4.1	2.3	10.5	4.6	66%	14%	29	23	48	32%	72%	14%	0	16			84	1.25	-3.7	134	160	$11
15 2 NL	3	3	4	56	51	3.38	4.15	1.38	714	699	726	4.4	3.1	8.2	2.7	57%	9%	43	18	39	34%	76%	5%	0	17			50	1.18	4.1	86	103	$1
16 NYM	4	2	1	78	91	1.97	3.08	0.94	536	532	538	3.8	1.5	10.5	7.0	70%	12%	39	23	38	30%	81%	5%	0	15			20	1.23	21.3	166	197	$12
1st Half	2	2	1	38	48	2.37	2.97	1.00	539	591	501	3.8	2.1	11.4	5.3	70%	12%	46	19	35	31%	80%	9%	0	15			33	1.22	8.5	171	204	$11
2nd Half	2	0	0	40	43	1.59	3.15	0.88	534	476	577	3.8	0.9	9.8	10.8	70%	13%	33	26	41	30%	82%	2%	0	14			0	1.23	12.7	162	193	$14
17 Proj	**3**	**3**	**2**	**73**	**80**	**2.86**	**3.42**	**1.11**	**629**	**601**	**651**	**3.9**	**2.1**	**10.0**	**4.8**	**65%**	**12%**	**39**	**22**	**40**	**32%**	**77%**	**7%**	**0**						**11.9**	**139**	**166**	**$6**

Reed,Cody

Age: 24	Th: L	Role SP	Health B	LIMA Plan C
Ht: 6' 5"	Wt: 225	Type Pwr GB	PT/Exp D	Rand Var +5
			Consist F	MM 1203

0-7, 7.36 ERA in 48 IP at CIN. When not being victimized by big flies or issuing free passes, rookie showed aptitude for inducing GB and Ks before back spasms ended season early. Homers weren't a problem in minors, and MLB 4.48 xERA shows promise, but plan on usual growing pains if jumping on board now.

Yr Tm	W	L	Sv	IP	K	ERA	xERA	WHIP	oOPS	vL	vR	BF/G	Ctl	Dom	Cmd	FpK	SwK	G	L	F	H%	S%	hr/f	GS	APC	DOM%	DIS%	Sv%	LI	RAR	BPV	BPX	R$
12																																	
13																																	
14																																	
15 aa	8	4	0	78	72	3.32	3.53	1.29				24.8	2.9	8.3	2.9						32%	75%								6.2	96	115	$4
16 CIN *	6	11	0	121	101	5.49	6.11	1.62	968	782	1022	23.3	3.1	7.6	2.5	59%	10%	52	21	27	36%	70%	28%	10	88	10%	40%			-19.4	44	52	-$10
1st Half	6	5	0	81	77	5.34	5.65	1.50	1044	556	1114	24.9	2.7	8.5	3.2	61%	14%	44	23	33	35%	69%	38%	3	89	33%	0%			-11.4	65	78	-$6
2nd Half	0	6	0	40	25	5.80	7.04	1.88	929	832	966	20.9	3.9	5.6	1.4	58%	9%	55	21	24	37%	71%	22%	7	88	0%	57%			-7.9	10	12	-$18
17 Proj	**8**	**12**	**0**	**131**	**108**	**4.58**	**4.20**	**1.49**	**746**	**610**	**783**	**22.8**	**3.2**	**7.4**	**2.4**	**59%**	**11%**	**51**	**21**	**28**	**34%**	**72%**	**14%**	**25**						**-6.3**	**77**	**92**	**-$4**

Reyes,Alex

Age: 22	Th: R	Role SP	Health A	LIMA Plan B
Ht: 6' 3"	Wt: 175	Type Pwr xFB	PT/Exp F	Rand Var 0
			Consist D	MM 2503

4-1, 1.57 ERA in 46 IP at STL. With 50-game suspension (marijuana) behind him, showed what hoopla was all about—great stuff, including a heater that tops 100 mph and knee-buckling curve. Still needs to address chronic Ctl issues, but has shown glimpses of an ace-caliber skill set. Coming, but not quite yet.

Yr Tm	W	L	Sv	IP	K	ERA	xERA	WHIP	oOPS	vL	vR	BF/G	Ctl	Dom	Cmd	FpK	SwK	G	L	F	H%	S%	hr/f	GS	APC	DOM%	DIS%	Sv%	LI	RAR	BPV	BPX	R$
12																																	
13																																	
14																																	
15 aa	3	2	0	35	48	3.24	1.87	1.13				17.1	4.4	12.4	2.8						30%	70%								3.1	144	172	$1
16 STL *	6	4	1	111	136	3.77	3.54	1.39	578	672	509	18.0	4.3	11.0	2.5	56%	12%	43	15	41	35%	73%	2%	5	66	20%	0%	100	0.95	5.7	110	130	$4
1st Half	2	1	0	35	47	5.30	4.59	1.52				18.8	4.5	12.2	2.7						39%	66%	0%	0						-4.7	103	123	-$6
2nd Half	4	3	1	77	89	3.08	3.06	1.33	578	672	509	17.7	4.3	10.5	2.4	56%	12%	43	15	41	33%	76%	2%	5	66	20%	0%	100	0.95	10.5	113	134	$8
17 Proj	**10**	**7**	**0**	**152**	**186**	**3.55**	**3.85**	**1.27**	**603**	**660**	**562**	**21.2**	**4.3**	**11.0**	**2.5**	**56%**	**12%**	**43**	**15**	**41**	**31%**	**73%**	**7%**	**26**						**12.0**	**102**	**121**	**$10**

Richard,Clayton

Age: 33	Th: L	Role RP	Health D	LIMA Plan D+
Ht: 6' 5"	Wt: 240	Type Con xGB	PT/Exp D	Rand Var -2
			Consist F	MM 0001

Thought he disappeared a few years back, yet there he is with 2.41 ERA as SP in 2H. He's the same guy, though—a few strike-ones, but no strikeouts. And with all the walks and hits, thank goodness for that S%. Everything has to go right for him, but how often does THAT happen? Take your chances elsewhere.

Yr Tm	W	L	Sv	IP	K	ERA	xERA	WHIP	oOPS	vL	vR	BF/G	Ctl	Dom	Cmd	FpK	SwK	G	L	F	H%	S%	hr/f	GS	APC	DOM%	DIS%	Sv%	LI	RAR	BPV	BPX	R$
12 SD	14	14	0	219	107	3.99	4.17	1.23	739	591	784	27.6	1.7	4.4	2.5	63%	7%	54	18	28	28%	72%	15%	33	96	24%	39%			0.6	65	84	$8
13 SD	2	5	0	53	24	7.01	4.94	1.63	947	639	1050	19.9	3.6	4.1	1.1	54%	6%	52	21	27	29%	62%	25%	11	71	0%	82%	0	0.89	-20.4	7	9	-$12
14 a/a	1	2	0	21	6	7.45	9.82	2.27				27.1	2.3	2.5	1.1						42%	69%								-9.8	-37	-44	-$9
15 CHC *	9	4	0	105	44	2.99	4.13	1.34	714	534	820	13.3	1.9	3.7	2.0	61%	7%	59	26	15	31%	79%	14%	3	27	0%	33%	0	0.90	12.7	45	53	$4
16 2 NL	3	4	1	68	41	3.33	4.60	1.66	761	654	799	8.5	4.1	5.5	1.3	63%	9%	65	17	18	34%	81%	10%	9	30	11%	33%	100	0.64	7.2	30	35	-$3
1st Half	0	1	1	12	6	7.30	5.34	2.19	870	924	799	2.9	4.4	4.4	1.0	63%	6%	69	14	16	42%	63%	0%	0	10			100	0.67	-4.7	8	10	-$11
2nd Half	3	3	0	55	35	2.44	4.44	1.54	734	435	799	17.4	4.1	5.7	1.4	63%	10%	64	18	18	32%	86%	12%	9	62	11%	33%	0	0.60	11.9	35	41	-$1
17 Proj	**7**	**8**	**0**	**116**	**59**	**4.77**	**4.72**	**1.53**	**830**	**576**	**915**	**18.0**	**3.1**	**4.6**	**1.5**	**59%**	**7%**	**57**	**21**	**22**	**31%**	**72%**	**18%**	**22**						**-8.3**	**33**	**40**	**-$7**

Richards,Garrett

Age: 29	Th: R	Role SP	Health F	LIMA Plan C
Ht: 6' 3"	Wt: 215	Type Pwr GB	PT/Exp B	Rand Var -5
			Consist A	MM 2203

Tore ulnar collateral ligament in May and opted for stem-cell treatments over TJS. While early returns are encouraging, Health grade is party crasher in what should be peak years. When right (2015), induces lots of GB, empty swings with variety of pitches. Buying low could net nice return now, even more in 2018.

Yr Tm	W	L	Sv	IP	K	ERA	xERA	WHIP	oOPS	vL	vR	BF/G	Ctl	Dom	Cmd	FpK	SwK	G	L	F	H%	S%	hr/f	GS	APC	DOM%	DIS%	Sv%	LI	RAR	BPV	BPX	R$
12 LAA *	11	6	1	148	102	4.23	4.65	1.54	793	900	682	14.7	3.9	6.2	1.6	55%	11%	45	22	33	33%	73%	9%	9	40	22%	56%	33	0.95	-3.9	50	65	-$4
13 LAA	7	8	1	145	101	4.16	3.70	1.34	699	751	626	13.2	2.7	6.3	2.3	54%	9%	58	19	23	31%	70%	11%	17	50	18%	24%	50	0.78	-5.2	75	98	$0
14 LAA	13	4	0	169	164	2.61	3.08	1.04	529	519	542	26.1	2.7	8.8	3.2	55%	11%	51	21	28	28%	74%	4%	26	101	58%	8%			23.4	113	135	$21
15 LAA	15	12	0	207	176	3.65	3.75	1.24	664	628	707	27.0	3.3	7.6	2.3	60%	12%	55	17	28	28%	73%	12%	32	102	34%	31%			8.1	81	97	$13
16 LAA	1	3	0	35	34	2.34	4.03	1.33	683	483	858	24.7	3.9	8.8	2.3	57%	11%	46	25	29	31%	84%	7%	6	103	33%	0%			7.9	78	92	$0
1st Half	1	3	0	35	34	2.34	4.03	1.33	684	483	858	24.7	3.9	8.8	2.3	57%	11%	46	25	29	31%	84%	7%	6	103	33%	0%			7.9	78	93	$0
2nd Half																																	
17 Proj	**9**	**7**	**0**	**131**	**115**	**3.34**	**3.88**	**1.26**	**655**	**609**	**705**	**25.3**	**3.3**	**7.9**	**2.4**	**57%**	**11%**	**51**	**21**	**28**	**30%**	**74%**	**8%**	**21**						**13.7**	**82**	**98**	**$8**

Rivero,Felipe

Age: 25	Th: L	Role RP	Health B	LIMA Plan A
Ht: 6' 0"	Wt: 195	Type Pwr	PT/Exp D	Rand Var +1
			Consist B	MM 3411

Early trouble vL and June tailspin deemed him expendable, but Cmd issues didn't deter new employer, who referred to his arm as Chapman-esque. Mechanics are inconsistent, but heater played against all comers. With on-the-job training coming at major-league level, skills lag behind tools. Growth stock.

Yr Tm	W	L	Sv	IP	K	ERA	xERA	WHIP	oOPS	vL	vR	BF/G	Ctl	Dom	Cmd	FpK	SwK	G	L	F	H%	S%	hr/f	GS	APC	DOM%	DIS%	Sv%	LI	RAR	BPV	BPX	R$
12																																	
13																																	
14 aa	2	7	0	44	31	4.34	4.60	1.49				18.8	3.5	6.4	1.9						33%	72%								-3.2	54	65	-$4
15 WAS	2	1	2	48	43	2.79	3.41	0.95	544	486	600	3.9	2.0	8.0	3.9	63%	12%	45	21	33	26%	70%	5%	0	16			67	1.10	7.0	112	133	$4
16 2 NL	1	6	1	77	92	4.09	3.46	1.29	671	765	626	4.4	3.9	10.8	2.8	57%	15%	48	22	30	32%	70%	12%	0	17			25	1.04	0.9	115	137	$0
1st Half	0	3	1	39	44	5.35	3.22	1.16	670	815	581	4.1	3.0	10.2	3.4	58%	14%	50	20	30	30%	54%	14%	0	16			50	1.03	-5.6	131	156	-$1
2nd Half	1	3	0	38	48	2.82	3.70	1.41	671	697	662	4.7	4.7	11.3	2.4	57%	15%	46	23	31	34%	82%	10%	0	19			0	1.06	6.5	100	120	$2
17 Proj	**2**	**5**	**7**	**73**	**74**	**3.42**	**3.65**	**1.21**	**647**	**647**	**647**	**4.6**	**3.3**	**9.2**	**2.8**	**59%**	**14%**	**47**	**22**	**32**	**30%**	**73%**	**9%**	**0**						**6.9**	**102**	**122**	**$5**

Roark,Tanner

Age: 30	Th: R	Role RP	Health A	LIMA Plan D+
Ht: 6' 2"	Wt: 230	Type	PT/Exp A	Rand Var -2
			Consist A	MM 1103

It's his second time outmaneuvering pedestrian peripherals to put up good numbers. Those skills are fringe-average, he's now 30, and his control is regressing. Reliability grades notwithstanding, best to set your expectations (and bid) on the xERA foundation. Litmus test: offer him up in trade, see what you'd get.

Yr Tm	W	L	Sv	IP	K	ERA	xERA	WHIP	oOPS	vL	vR	BF/G	Ctl	Dom	Cmd	FpK	SwK	G	L	F	H%	S%	hr/f	GS	APC	DOM%	DIS%	Sv%	LI	RAR	BPV	BPX	R$
12 aaa	6	17	0	148	100	5.47	5.74	1.63				23.5	2.8	6.1	2.1						36%	67%								-26.5	43	57	-$17
13 WAS *	16	4	2	159	103	3.04	2.60	1.08	476	634	358	13.2	1.8	5.8	3.3	71%	7%	50	24	26	28%	72%	3%	5	54	40%	0%	100	0.95	16.3	99	129	$18
14 WAS	15	10	0	199	138	2.85	3.80	1.09	632	672	591	25.7	1.8	6.3	3.5	65%	9%	41	21	38	28%	77%	7%	31	97	29%	26%			21.7	84	100	$19
15 WAS	4	7	1	111	70	4.38	4.17	1.31	784	866	709	11.7	2.1	5.7	2.7	60%	8%	48	22	31	30%	71%	15%	12	45	17%	50%	50	0.90	-5.7	71	85	-$2
16 WAS	16	10	0	210	172	2.83	4.00	1.17	634	617	648	25.1	3.1	7.4	2.4	58%	9%	49	20	31	27%	79%	9%	33	99	36%	18%	0	0.81	35.3	75	89	$24
1st Half	7	5	0	107	93	2.93	3.66	1.23	644	581	700	26.0	2.9	7.8	2.7	58%	9%	53	22	25	30%	78%	9%	17	102	41%	24%			16.6	94	113	$21
2nd Half	9	5	0	103	79	2.72	4.35	1.11	622	657	592	24.3	3.4	6.9	2.0	57%	10%	44	18	38	24%	80%	9%	16	96	31%	13%	0	0.83	18.6	55	65	$28
17 Proj	**12**	**9**	**0**	**174**	**127**	**3.77**	**4.24**	**1.27**	**718**	**760**	**681**	**18.7**	**2.6**	**6.6**	**2.5**	**60%**	**9%**	**47**	**21**	**32**	**30%**	**73%**	**10%**	**33**						**9.1**	**73**	**87**	**$8**

ROB CARROLL

Robertson,David

Age: 32	Th: R	Role: RP	Health: B	LIMA Plan: C+
Ht: 5' 11"	Wt: 190	Type: Pwr	PT/Exp: A	Rand Var: -1
			Consist: B	MM: 4531

Tripled 2015 Ctl, but opponents mustered only .244 Slg against him in high-leverage situations. S%, GB% also pitched in to stave off challengers, but would be more convincing if he reclaimed influence vL and recaptured strike zone. Track record says he can, but having a Plan B is becoming more of a priority.

Yr	Tm	W	L	Sv	IP	K	ERA	xERA	WHIP	oOPS	vL	vR	BF/G	Ctl	Dom	Cmd	FpK	SwK	G	L	F	H%	S%	hr/f	GS	APC	DOM%	DIS%	Sv%	LI	RAR	BPV	BPX	R$
12	NYY	2	7	2	61	81	2.67	2.84	1.17	638	575	710	3.8	2.8	12.0	4.3	65%	10%	45	20	35	34%	80%	10%	0	15			40	1.15	10.1	163	213	$5
13	NYY	5	1	3	66	77	2.04	2.66	1.04	584	484	695	3.7	2.4	10.4	4.3	59%	10%	51	20	29	29%	84%	11%	0	15			60	1.19	15.0	151	197	$9
14	NYY	4	5	39	64	96	3.08	2.38	1.06	588	437	765	4.1	3.2	13.4	4.2	61%	13%	44	23	33	31%	75%	16%	0	17			89	1.67	5.3	177	211	$20
15	CHW	6	5	34	63	86	3.41	2.60	0.93	573	462	651	4.2	1.8	12.2	6.6	68%	14%	36	30	34	30%	67%	14%	0	16			83	1.35	4.3	184	219	$21
16	CHW	5	3	37	62	75	3.47	3.94	1.36	684	610	756	4.3	4.6	10.8	2.3	61%	13%	45	14	40	32%	77%	10%	0	17			84	1.44	5.6	93	111	$17
1st Half		0	1	23	36	42	3.28	4.16	1.40	645	566	719	4.6	5.0	10.6	2.1	63%	12%	47	13	40	32%	77%	6%	0	18			92	1.38	4.0	79	94	$18
2nd Half		5	2	14	27	33	3.71	3.66	1.31	737	667	811	4.0	4.1	11.1	2.8	59%	14%	44	16	41	31%	77%	15%	0	16			74	1.52	1.6	113	135	$15
17	**Proj**	**5**	**4**	**39**	**73**	**94**	**3.32**	**3.23**	**1.18**	**643**	**552**	**733**	**4.0**	**3.4**	**11.7**	**3.4**	**63%**	**13%**	**43**	**20**	**37**	**31%**	**76%**	**13%**	**0**						**7.8**	**138**	**164**	**$20**

Robles,Hansel

Age: 26	Th: R	Role: RP	Health: A	LIMA Plan: B+
Ht: 5' 11"	Wt: 185	Type: Pwr FB	PT/Exp: D	Rand Var: -1
			Consist: B	MM: 1401

Results had feel of season-long tinkering for sophomore reliever. Added changeup to repertoire to nice 1st half K effect, while ramping up fastball in 2nd half had opposite impact. Positive correlation between inducing GB and being used in more critical situations may pay off for him later, but for now, he's nothing special.

Yr	Tm	W	L	Sv	IP	K	ERA	xERA	WHIP	oOPS	vL	vR	BF/G	Ctl	Dom	Cmd	FpK	SwK	G	L	F	H%	S%	hr/f	GS	APC	DOM%	DIS%	Sv%	LI	RAR	BPV	BPX	R$
12																																		
13																																		
14	aa	7	6	0	111	91	4.36	4.18	1.39				15.5	3.3	7.4	2.3						32%	70%								-8.4	69	83	-$3
15	NYM	4	3	0	54	61	3.67	3.64	1.02	655	560	717	3.8	3.0	10.2	3.4	60%	13%	33	18	49	24%	70%	12%	0	16			0	1.02	2.0	113	135	$3
16	NYM	6	4	1	78	85	3.48	4.31	1.35	703	586	784	4.9	4.2	9.8	2.4	59%	12%	30	29	41	32%	77%	8%	0	20			33	1.07	6.8	73	86	$3
1st Half		2	3	0	39	48	3.20	4.33	1.37	731	547	851	4.8	4.3	11.0	2.5	56%	13%	23	29	49	32%	82%	10%	0	20			0	0.93	4.8	81	97	$3
2nd Half		4	1	1	38	37	3.76	4.29	1.33	675	624	712	4.9	4.0	8.7	2.2	63%	11%	37	29	34	31%	71%	6%	0	21			50	1.22	2.0	64	76	$4
17	**Proj**	**4**	**3**	**0**	**73**	**76**	**3.83**	**4.14**	**1.24**	**695**	**593**	**766**	**4.8**	**3.6**	**9.5**	**2.6**	**60%**	**12%**	**32**	**24**	**44**	**29%**	**72%**	**9%**	**0**						**3.2**	**83**	**99**	**$1**

Rodney,Fernando

Age: 40	Th: R	Role: RP	Health: B	LIMA Plan: C+
Ht: 5' 11"	Wt: 230	Type: Pwr GB	PT/Exp: B	Rand Var: 0
			Consist: B	MM: 2420

As SD closer, 1st half featured the most obscene numbers since his other-worldly 2012. As MIA set-up man, 2nd half featured his highest xERA, lowest BPV since 2011. At 40, what about saves going forward? With four teams in two years, you can't count on anything. If he backs into 9th inning work, it probably won't last.

Yr	Tm	W	L	Sv	IP	K	ERA	xERA	WHIP	oOPS	vL	vR	BF/G	Ctl	Dom	Cmd	FpK	SwK	G	L	F	H%	S%	hr/f	GS	APC	DOM%	DIS%	Sv%	LI	RAR	BPV	BPX	R$
12	TAM	2	2	48	75	76	0.60	2.58	0.78	417	435	394	3.7	1.8	9.2	5.1	61%	13%	58	17	25	23%	95%	4%	0	15			96	1.24	31.4	152	198	$37
13	TAM	5	4	37	67	82	3.38	3.24	1.34	634	716	538	4.3	4.9	11.1	2.3	56%	13%	51	25	25	32%	74%	7%	0	18			82	1.34	4.0	97	126	$17
14	SEA	1	6	48	66	76	2.85	3.19	1.34	646	726	530	4.1	3.8	10.3	2.7	60%	11%	49	24	27	34%	79%	6%	0	16			94	1.36	7.3	110	131	$19
15	2 TM	7	5	16	63	58	4.74	4.05	1.40	776	845	721	4.1	4.2	8.3	2.0	59%	10%	51	18	31	30%	70%	16%	0	16			70	1.22	-6.0	66	79	$4
16	2 NL	2	4	25	65	74	3.44	3.66	1.39	668	726	611	4.2	5.1	10.2	2.0	57%	13%	55	22	23	31%	77%	14%	0	17			89	1.13	6.0	79	94	$10
1st Half		0	1	17	31	35	0.29	2.90	0.85	390	423	363	3.9	3.8	10.3	2.7	63%	15%	58	15	26	20%	96%	0%	0	15			100	1.26	14.7	118	141	$24
2nd Half		2	3	8	35	39	6.23	4.39	1.88	871	911	824	4.5	6.2	10.1	1.6	53%	12%	53	27	20	38%	68%	25%	0	19			73	1.03	-8.7	45	54	-$2
17	**Proj**	**3**	**4**	**12**	**58**	**63**	**3.74**	**3.75**	**1.39**	**695**	**753**	**637**	**4.0**	**4.6**	**9.7**	**2.1**	**58%**	**12%**	**53**	**21**	**26**	**31%**	**75%**	**13%**	**0**						**3.2**	**83**	**98**	**$4**

Rodon,Carlos

Age: 24	Th: L	Role: SP	Health: B	LIMA Plan: B+
Ht: 6' 3"	Wt: 234	Type: Pwr	PT/Exp: B	Rand Var: +3
			Consist: A	MM: 2305

A year removed from all the hype, a quiet growth season. Intially looked like replay of 2015, but parlayed July misfortune (7.92 ERA, sprained wrist) into 7-2 Aug/Sept as fastball approached triple digits. FpK, Ctl trends were positive responses to increased workload. Step by step, inch by inch.

Yr	Tm	W	L	Sv	IP	K	ERA	xERA	WHIP	oOPS	vL	vR	BF/G	Ctl	Dom	Cmd	FpK	SwK	G	L	F	H%	S%	hr/f	GS	APC	DOM%	DIS%	Sv%	LI	RAR	BPV	BPX	R$
12																																		
13																																		
14																																		
15	CHW	9	6	0	139	139	3.75	4.00	1.44	725	524	799	23.3	4.6	9.0	2.0	53%	11%	47	23	30	32%	75%	10%	23	94	26%	26%	0	0.87	3.7	63	75	$2
16	CHW	9	10	0	165	168	4.04	3.96	1.39	763	609	799	25.5	2.9	9.2	3.1	54%	11%	44	21	35	34%	75%	14%	28	100	18%	25%			3.1	107	128	$4
1st Half		2	6	0	87	88	4.24	4.04	1.46	774	528	838	25.4	3.1	9.1	2.9	52%	10%	45	20	35	35%	75%	15%	15	99	7%	27%			-0.6	104	124	$0
2nd Half		7	4	0	78	80	3.81	3.86	1.32	750	719	756	25.7	2.8	9.2	3.3	56%	11%	43	22	35	33%	75%	13%	13	101	31%	23%			3.7	112	134	$9
17	**Proj**	**11**	**10**	**0**	**181**	**183**	**3.74**	**3.93**	**1.37**	**733**	**569**	**779**	**25.4**	**3.4**	**9.1**	**2.7**	**54%**	**11%**	**45**	**22**	**33**	**32%**	**76%**	**12%**	**30**						**10.0**	**94**	**112**	**$7**

Rodriguez,Eduardo

Age: 24	Th: L	Role: SP	Health: D	LIMA Plan: B
Ht: 6' 2"	Wt: 220	Type: Pwr FB	PT/Exp: D	Rand Var: 0
			Consist: A	MM: 1203

3-7, 4.71 ERA in 107 IP at BOS. 1st half washed out by dislocated kneecap that whacked mechanics, but 29 K in final 17 IP put strong coda on 2nd half rebound. SwK hike gives hope that some of that Dom may stick. All told, gives up less than a hit per inning, and a few more FpK could mean... UP: 3.50 ERA.

Yr	Tm	W	L	Sv	IP	K	ERA	xERA	WHIP	oOPS	vL	vR	BF/G	Ctl	Dom	Cmd	FpK	SwK	G	L	F	H%	S%	hr/f	GS	APC	DOM%	DIS%	Sv%	LI	RAR	BPV	BPX	R$
12																																		
13	aa	4	3	0	60	52	4.68	3.83	1.34				22.5	3.4	7.8	2.3						31%	66%								-6.0	74	97	-$3
14	aa	6	8	0	120	93	4.42	4.35	1.46				23.3	2.8	7.0	2.5						35%	69%								-10.0	77	92	-$5
15	BOS *	14	9	0	170	136	3.92	3.95	1.30	701	820	662	24.1	2.4	7.2	3.1	57%	9%	43	24	33	32%	71%	10%	21	96	33%	33%			0.9	84	100	$7
16	BOS *	3	11	0	145	120	4.74	4.48	1.31	726	711	730	22.2	3.0	7.5	2.5	59%	11%	32	22	46	29%	68%	11%	20	93	30%	35%			-9.8	56	67	-$2
1st Half		1	6	0	64	39	6.33	6.47	1.51	993	850	1019	23.2	2.6	5.4	2.1	64%	9%	31	22	47	30%	65%	18%	6	90	0%	67%			-17.0	-1	-1	-$13
2nd Half		2	5	0	81	82	3.47	2.90	1.15	611	672	592	21.4	3.3	9.1	2.8	57%	12%	32	22	45	28%	72%	7%	14	94	43%	21%			7.1	101	120	$8
17	**Proj**	**8**	**10**	**0**	**160**	**142**	**3.96**	**4.31**	**1.28**	**699**	**724**	**692**	**22.6**	**3.0**	**8.0**	**2.7**	**59%**	**10%**	**36**	**23**	**41**	**30%**	**72%**	**10%**	**29**						**4.6**	**79**	**94**	**$5**

Rodriguez,Francisco

Age: 35	Th: R	Role: RP	Health: A	LIMA Plan: D+
Ht: 6' 0"	Wt: 180	Type: Pwr	PT/Exp: A	Rand Var: -1
			Consist: B	MM: 3330

With fewer K in K-Rod, goes at it a bit differently these days. Commanded fastball-changeup differential, coaxing grounders at a career-best level; dug even deeper into toolbox in 2H. Dom fade, control loss are red flags, but he's shown that making adjustments is another of his skills. Good for another round.

Yr	Tm	W	L	Sv	IP	K	ERA	xERA	WHIP	oOPS	vL	vR	BF/G	Ctl	Dom	Cmd	FpK	SwK	G	L	F	H%	S%	hr/f	GS	APC	DOM%	DIS%	Sv%	LI	RAR	BPV	BPX	R$
12	MIL	2	7	3	72	72	4.38	3.87	1.33	708	723	684	3.9	3.9	9.0	2.3	61%	8%	42	26	33	30%	69%	12%	0	16			30	1.15	-3.2	77	101	-$1
13	2 TM	3	2	10	47	54	2.70	3.22	1.20	734	513	1003	4.0	2.7	10.4	3.9	60%	11%	36	25	39	31%	86%	15%	0	16			100	0.91	6.7	129	168	$6
14	MIL	5	5	44	68	73	3.04	2.99	0.99	648	526	772	3.9	2.4	9.7	4.1	59%	12%	44	21	35	23%	83%	23%	0	15			90	1.19	5.8	132	157	$23
15	MIL	1	3	38	57	62	2.21	2.76	0.86	547	538	558	3.6	1.7	9.8	5.6	63%	14%	46	24	30	24%	81%	14%	0	14			95	1.01	12.3	153	183	$22
16	DET	3	4	44	58	52	3.24	3.74	1.13	642	648	634	3.9	3.2	8.0	2.5	61%	12%	55	16	29	26%	75%	13%	0	15			90	1.46	6.8	90	107	$20
1st Half		0	0	23	30	29	3.03	3.56	1.11	642	671	617	3.7	3.0	8.8	2.9	56%	12%	50	21	29	28%	74%	9%	0	15			92	1.09	4.2	104	125	$20
2nd Half		3	4	21	29	23	3.45	3.92	1.15	643	626	649	4.0	3.5	7.2	2.1	66%	13%	59	11	30	24%	76%	17%	0	16			88	1.87	2.6	74	88	$21
17	**Proj**	**3**	**5**	**40**	**65**	**60**	**3.42**	**3.65**	**1.09**	**634**	**601**	**668**	**3.8**	**3.0**	**8.2**	**2.7**	**62%**	**13%**	**50**	**19**	**31**	**25%**	**74%**	**15%**	**0**						**6.2**	**94**	**112**	**$19**

Roe,Chaz

Age: 30	Th: R	Role: RP	Health: B	LIMA Plan: C
Ht: 6' 5"	Wt: 180	Type: Pwr GB	PT/Exp: D	Rand Var: 0
			Consist: B	MM: 2300

2-0, 3.64 ERA in 30 IP at BAL/ATL. Long string of MLEs paints him as a 'tweener—that's because he absolutely cannot get lefties out (.959 oOPS lifetime). For sure, some of his 2016 MLB skills look darn good (11.2 Dom, 69% FpK, 58% GB%), but four employers in four years can't all be wrong... can they?

Yr	Tm	W	L	Sv	IP	K	ERA	xERA	WHIP	oOPS	vL	vR	BF/G	Ctl	Dom	Cmd	FpK	SwK	G	L	F	H%	S%	hr/f	GS	APC	DOM%	DIS%	Sv%	LI	RAR	BPV	BPX	R$
12																																		
13	ARI *	1	1	8	47	42	2.63	2.87	1.19	726	991	599	4.1	3.3	8.0	2.4	55%	10%	57	13	30	28%	80%	18%	0	17			73	1.22	7.1	92	120	$4
14	NYY *	3	3	14	66	58	4.22	3.76	1.35	1239	1500	1111	5.5	3.3	7.9	2.4	62%	15%	17	17	67	32%	69%	0%	0	15			78	0.10	-3.9	82	98	$3
15	BAL *	8	3	2	67	54	4.06	4.09	1.45	798	912	716	5.3	3.8	7.2	1.9	61%	10%	52	20	28	33%	72%	12%	0	20			40	0.98	-0.8	69	82	$0
16	2 TM *	3	2	4	67	69	3.84	3.32	1.31	672	971	410	4.4	3.6	9.3	2.6	69%	13%	58	8	34	32%	70%	8%	0	16			80	1.01	2.9	102	121	$2
1st Half		1	2	4	40	36	4.25	4.19	1.46	1250	829	1933	4.9	3.8	8.3	2.2	75%	13%	50	0	50	34%	71%	50%	0	27			100	0.13	-0.3	78	93	$1
2nd Half		2	0	0	28	33	3.25	3.09	1.08	620	987	315	4.0	3.3	10.7	3.3	68%	13%	58	9	33	30%	69%	5%	0	15			0	1.07	3.2	142	169	$3
17	**Proj**	**2**	**3**	**0**	**51**	**49**	**3.74**	**3.83**	**1.30**	**720**	**990**	**508**	**4.6**	**3.5**	**8.7**	**2.5**	**65%**	**12%**	**53**	**16**	**31**	**32%**	**71%**	**7%**	**0**						**2.8**	**92**	**110**	**-$1**

ROB CARROLL

Rogers,Taylor

Age: 26 | Th: L | Role: RP | Ht: 6' 3" | Wt: 180 | Type:
Health: A | PT/Exp: D | Consist: B
LIMA Plan: C | Rand Var: +3 | MM: 1100

3-1, 3.96 ERA in 61 IP at MIN. Dom breakout was the difference-maker, but low FpK, SwK are Exhibits A and B in the case against a repeat. Minus all the Ks, he's barely average, and judging by vR results (6 of 7 HR allowed hit by RHB), may even be leaning toward LOOGY. Steer clear for now.

Yr	Tm	W	L	Sv	IP	K	ERA	xERA	WHIP	oOPS	vL	vR	BF/G	Ctl	Dom	Cmd	FpK	SwK	G	L	F	H%	S%	hr/f	GS	APC	DOM%	DIS%	Sv%	LI	RAR	BPV	BPX	R$
12																																		
13																																		
14	aa	11	6	0	145	91	4.09	4.45	1.48				26.0	2.4	5.6	2.4						35%	71%								-6.3	71	84	-$3
15	aaa	11	12	0	174	98	5.56	5.58	1.65				27.8	2.4	5.1	2.1						37%	65%								-34.3	46	55	-$18
16	MIN *	3	2	0	79	75	4.57	4.93	1.48	719	547	811	5.3	2.6	8.6	3.3	56%	8%	51	20	28	37%	71%	14%	0	18			0	0.84	-3.7	89	105	-$4
1st Half		3	1	0	41	34	4.84	6.36	1.70	794	480	968	6.7	2.3	7.5	3.2	57%	8%	49	19	32	40%	74%	17%	0	18			0	0.71	-3.3	65	78	-$5
2nd Half		0	1	0	38	41	4.26	3.31	1.24	669	589	710	4.5	2.8	9.7	3.4	56%	8%	53	21	26	33%	66%	11%	0	17			0	0.92	-0.3	129	154	-$2
17	**Proj**	**3**	**2**	**0**	**58**	**45**	**4.34**	**4.15**	**1.41**	**741**	**572**	**831**	**8.5**	**2.5**	**7.0**	**2.8**	**56%**	**8%**	**49**	**21**	**29**	**34%**	**70%**	**8%**	**0**						**-1.1**	**85**	**101**	**-$3**

Romo,Sergio

Age: 34 | Th: R | Role: RP | Ht: 5' 10" | Wt: 190 | Type: Pwr
Health: F | PT/Exp: C | Consist: B
LIMA Plan: A | Rand Var: -3 | MM: 4420

Bounced back from 1H forearm flexor strain to reclaim closer role in late Sept, and BPX says SF was right to hand it to him. Cmd, FpK, SwK all remain elite. But history of FB%, hr/f flare-ups makes it a little nerve-wracking to trust him. Bet you didn't expect we'd make you walk a mile in Bruce Bochy's shoes, huh?

Yr	Tm	W	L	Sv	IP	K	ERA	xERA	WHIP	oOPS	vL	vR	BF/G	Ctl	Dom	Cmd	FpK	SwK	G	L	F	H%	S%	hr/f	GS	APC	DOM%	DIS%	Sv%	LI	RAR	BPV	BPX	R$
12	SF	4	2	14	55	63	1.79	2.64	0.85	525	491	537	3.1	1.6	10.2	6.3	67%	16%	49	21	30	26%	86%	12%	0	12			93	1.43	15.2	168	219	$15
13	SF	5	8	38	60	58	2.54	3.39	1.08	614	745	511	3.8	1.8	8.7	4.8	69%	14%	41	24	36	30%	80%	8%	0	15			88	1.58	9.9	126	165	$21
14	SF	6	4	23	58	59	3.72	3.27	0.95	622	777	528	3.6	1.9	9.2	4.9	69%	15%	37	18	45	25%	67%	13%	0	14			82	1.26	0.1	130	154	$13
15	SF	0	5	2	57	71	2.98	2.70	1.06	622	929	467	3.3	1.6	11.1	7.1	70%	17%	45	23	32	35%	72%	7%	0	13			50	1.26	6.9	181	216	$3
16	SF	1	0	4	31	33	2.64	3.50	1.08	709	790	674	2.9	2.1	9.7	4.7	65%	15%	38	14	47	28%	86%	14%	0	12			100	1.27	5.9	135	160	$2
1st Half		0	0	0	3	1	2.70	5.68	0.60	530	1000	143	3.0	2.7	2.7	1.0	50%	10%	30	10	60	0%	0%	17%	0	13			0	1.20	0.6	-16	-19	-$6
2nd Half		1	0	4	27	32	2.63	3.25	1.13	730	751	720	2.9	2.0	10.5	5.3	67%	16%	39	15	45	32%	85%	13%	0	12			100	1.28	5.2	154	183	$3
17	**Proj**	**3**	**3**	**10**	**52**	**57**	**2.88**	**3.26**	**1.04**	**643**	**772**	**575**	**3.2**	**1.8**	**10.0**	**5.5**	**68%**	**15%**	**41**	**19**	**40**	**30%**	**78%**	**11%**	**0**						**8.3**	**150**	**179**	**$8**

Rondon,Bruce

Age: 26 | Th: R | Role: RP | Ht: 6' 2" | Wt: 190 | Type: Pwr FB
Health: F | PT/Exp: D | Consist: A
LIMA Plan: C | Rand Var: 0 | MM: 1500

5-2, 2.97 ERA in 36 IP at DET. Exhibited best Cmd of career in 2nd half, but FpK casts doubts on Ctl gain, and high FB% leaves little room for error should walks start piling up again. MLB ERA—aided by 24% H%, 77% S%—will convince some that he's arrived. Let them take the risk.

Yr	Tm	W	L	Sv	IP	K	ERA	xERA	WHIP	oOPS	vL	vR	BF/G	Ctl	Dom	Cmd	FpK	SwK	G	L	F	H%	S%	hr/f	GS	APC	DOM%	DIS%	Sv%	LI	RAR	BPV	BPX	R$
12	a/a	1	1	14	30	26	1.45	3.03	1.28				4.1	4.6	8.0	1.7						26%	93%								9.4	77	100	$6
13	DET *	2	3	15	58	63	2.68	2.58	1.18	720	873	608	3.9	3.8	9.6	2.6	47%	15%	47	24	29	29%	78%	9%	0	15			79	0.93	8.5	110	143	$9
14																																		
15	DET	1	0	5	31	36	5.81	4.31	1.61	770	865	696	4.1	5.5	10.5	1.9	54%	12%	41	25	34	35%	64%	10%	0	17			56	1.14	-7.1	58	69	-$5
16	DET *	7	4	9	58	68	3.88	4.12	1.44	583	416	781	4.2	4.8	10.5	2.2	59%	16%	32	17	51	33%	76%	12%	0	15			64	1.08	2.2	86	102	$4
1st Half		4	2	9	29	31	4.30	5.24	1.80	362	350	357	4.8	6.4	9.4	1.5	65%	18%	19	13	69	36%	77%	9%	0	16			69	1.29	-0.4	66	78	$5
2nd Half		3	2	0	29	37	3.45	3.41	1.08	633	427	908	3.8	3.1	11.6	3.7	57%	16%	35	18	46	28%	74%	13%	0	15			0	1.04	2.6	138	164	$4
17	**Proj**	**4**	**2**	**0**	**58**	**68**	**4.32**	**4.20**	**1.43**	**713**	**616**	**817**	**4.0**	**4.7**	**10.5**	**2.2**	**56%**	**14%**	**38**	**21**	**41**	**33%**	**71%**	**9%**	**0**						**-0.9**	**77**	**92**	**-$2**

Rondon,Hector

Age: 29 | Th: R | Role: RP | Ht: 6' 3" | Wt: 230 | Type: Pwr
Health: B | PT/Exp: B | Consist: A
LIMA Plan: B | Rand Var: +3 | MM: 4420

Ugly hr/f made this look like a step backward, but xERA indicates otherwise, and elite Cmd, FpK, BPX show he was better than ever. Triceps issue was likely cause of 2nd half Dom loss, HR explosion, and there's no shame in getting bumped by Aroldis Chapman. Skills say he deserves another shot at saves.

Yr	Tm	W	L	Sv	IP	K	ERA	xERA	WHIP	oOPS	vL	vR	BF/G	Ctl	Dom	Cmd	FpK	SwK	G	L	F	H%	S%	hr/f	GS	APC	DOM%	DIS%	Sv%	LI	RAR	BPV	BPX	R$
12																																		
13	CHC	2	1	0	55	44	4.77	4.39	1.41	737	546	908	5.4	4.1	7.2	1.8	54%	11%	43	22	35	29%	68%	10%	0	21			0	0.65	-6.1	40	52	-$5
14	CHC	4	4	29	63	63	2.42	2.99	1.06	526	616	454	4.0	2.1	9.0	4.2	65%	12%	49	23	28	30%	77%	4%	0	16			88	1.16	10.4	131	156	$17
15	CHC	6	4	30	70	69	1.67	3.04	1.00	568	640	503	3.9	1.9	8.9	4.6	63%	11%	52	20	27	28%	86%	8%	0	15			88	1.51	19.8	138	164	$23
16	CHC	2	3	18	51	58	3.53	2.95	0.98	641	743	569	3.7	1.4	10.2	7.3	72%	11%	46	20	34	28%	71%	18%	0	15			78	1.09	4.2	170	202	$10
1st Half		1	1	13	27	35	1.65	2.53	0.66	409	413	405	3.6	1.0	11.5	11.7	71%	10%	46	13	41	24%	81%	8%	0	13			81	1.15	8.6	205	244	$19
2nd Half		1	2	5	24	23	5.70	3.49	1.35	880	1007	770	3.8	1.9	8.7	4.6	74%	12%	46	26	28	32%	65%	32%	0	16			71	1.03	-4.4	130	155	$0
17	**Proj**	**3**	**3**	**25**	**58**	**62**	**2.99**	**3.14**	**1.09**	**647**	**712**	**595**	**3.8**	**2.0**	**9.7**	**4.9**	**67%**	**11%**	**48**	**21**	**31**	**30%**	**78%**	**15%**	**0**						**8.6**	**146**	**174**	**$14**

Rosenthal,Trevor

Age: 27 | Th: R | Role: RP | Ht: 6' 2" | Wt: 190 | Type: Pwr
Health: D | PT/Exp: A | Consist: B
LIMA Plan: C+ | Rand Var: +5 | MM: 3510

Battled hamstring, shoulder injuries in 2H, but damage was done long before then. Odd that Ctl issues resurfaced in spite of FpK improvement. Huge FB% drop was undermined by fluky hr/f, and 44% hit rate is ridiculous. This sure looks like year ruined by poor health; worth a rebound flyer, especially if he moves to SP.

Yr	Tm	W	L	Sv	IP	K	ERA	xERA	WHIP	oOPS	vL	vR	BF/G	Ctl	Dom	Cmd	FpK	SwK	G	L	F	H%	S%	hr/f	GS	APC	DOM%	DIS%	Sv%	LI	RAR	BPV	BPX	R$
12	STL *	8	8	0	132	114	3.06	2.40	1.09	513	395	597	13.2	3.2	7.8	2.4	58%	13%	54	13	33	26%	73%	11%	0	19			0	0.63	15.6	94	123	$14
13	STL	2	4	3	75	108	2.63	2.47	1.10	608	586	626	4.2	2.4	12.9	5.4	63%	15%	44	19	36	36%	77%	6%	0	17			38	1.21	11.5	190	247	$7
14	STL	2	6	45	70	87	3.20	3.69	1.41	641	523	738	4.3	5.4	11.1	2.1	56%	13%	38	25	37	33%	76%	3%	0	18			88	1.42	4.7	71	85	$17
15	STL	2	4	48	69	83	2.10	3.28	1.27	619	526	686	4.2	3.3	10.9	3.3	57%	12%	46	19	35	35%	85%	5%	0	18			94	1.66	15.8	131	156	$24
16	STL	2	4	14	40	56	4.46	3.92	1.91	792	800	785	4.4	6.5	12.5	1.9	61%	12%	52	25	22	44%	77%	13%	0	19			78	1.08	-1.4	80	95	$0
1st Half		2	3	14	27	39	5.67	4.02	2.11	871	886	860	4.1	7.3	13.0	1.8	60%	11%	58	21	22	46%	74%	19%	0	18			82	1.29	-4.9	72	85	$2
2nd Half		0	1	0	13	17	2.03	3.68	1.50	619	650	586	5.1	4.7	11.5	2.4	63%	14%	41	35	24	39%	85%	0%	0	21			0	0.52	3.6	98	117	-$5
17	**Proj**	**3**	**5**	**7**	**65**	**84**	**3.48**	**3.45**	**1.33**	**630**	**567**	**676**	**4.2**	**4.5**	**11.6**	**2.6**	**59%**	**12%**	**46**	**22**	**32**	**33%**	**74%**	**8%**	**0**						**5.7**	**112**	**134**	**$4**

Ross,Joe

Age: 24 | Th: R | Role: SP | Ht: 6' 3" | Wt: 185 | Type:
Health: D | PT/Exp: D | Consist: C
LIMA Plan: B | Rand Var: 0 | MM: 2203

Dealt with blister problem in April, shoulder inflammation in July-Aug, and yet, managed to keep skills stable. Two partial seasons add up to 182 MLB IP with 8.0 Dom, 3.2 Cmd, and 3.88 xERA. Health grade, struggles vL remind us we can't assume he'll deliver that, but it's certainly a reasonable upside goal.

Yr	Tm	W	L	Sv	IP	K	ERA	xERA	WHIP	oOPS	vL	vR	BF/G	Ctl	Dom	Cmd	FpK	SwK	G	L	F	H%	S%	hr/f	GS	APC	DOM%	DIS%	Sv%	LI	RAR	BPV	BPX	R$
12																																		
13																																		
14	aa	2	0	0	20	17	3.89	4.51	1.28				20.5	0.4	7.7	17.8						37%	72%								-0.4	388	462	-$2
15	WAS *	10	8	0	153	127	3.45	3.09	1.15	628	809	461	20.2	2.4	7.5	3.1	59%	12%	50	16	34	29%	72%	10%	13	72	38%	15%	0	0.71	9.6	96	115	$11
16	WAS	7	5	0	105	93	3.43	3.96	1.30	713	824	611	23.5	2.5	8.0	3.2	56%	11%	43	27	30	33%	76%	10%	19	90	26%	32%			9.9	97	116	$5
1st Half		7	4	0	95	79	3.49	3.99	1.26	705	816	600	25.0	2.5	7.5	3.0	56%	11%	44	26	30	31%	74%	10%	16	94	31%	31%			8.2	90	107	$7
2nd Half		0	1	0	10	14	2.79	3.69	1.76	778	895	685	15.7	2.8	13.0	4.7	60%	12%	28	34	38	50%	88%	9%	3	68	0%	33%			1.7	165	197	-$9
17	**Proj**	**11**	**7**	**0**	**160**	**132**	**3.49**	**3.90**	**1.22**	**680**	**821**	**549**	**22.5**	**2.4**	**7.5**	**3.1**	**57%**	**12%**	**46**	**22**	**31**	**30%**	**73%**	**9%**	**29**						**13.8**	**93**	**111**	**$11**

Ross,Robbie

Age: 28 | Th: L | Role: RP | Ht: 5' 11" | Wt: 185 | Type: Pwr GB
Health: A | PT/Exp: C | Consist: B
LIMA Plan: B+ | Rand Var: -2 | MM: 2200

With exception of 1st half, not enough Dom to offset backslides in Ctl and FpK, and SwK doesn't give reason to think that's gonna change. Splits aren't too bad, and low FB% is a plus, but BPV argues he's not quite saves-worthy; LI hints that teams agree. Alas, no one dreams of becoming a competent middle reliever.

Yr	Tm	W	L	Sv	IP	K	ERA	xERA	WHIP	oOPS	vL	vR	BF/G	Ctl	Dom	Cmd	FpK	SwK	G	L	F	H%	S%	hr/f	GS	APC	DOM%	DIS%	Sv%	LI	RAR	BPV	BPX	R$
12	TEX	6	0	0	65	47	2.22	3.52	1.20	624	613	632	4.6	3.2	6.5	2.0	58%	8%	62	18	20	28%	83%	8%	0	18			0	0.97	14.4	71	93	$6
13	TEX	4	2	0	62	58	3.03	3.43	1.32	684	950	523	4.1	2.7	8.4	3.1	68%	11%	45	28	26	33%	78%	8%	0	15			0	1.18	6.4	100	130	$1
14	TEX *	8	10	0	139	86	5.53	5.61	1.60	851	766	892	15.7	3.0	5.6	1.9	67%	7%	54	19	27	34%	66%	12%	12	50	0%	42%	0	0.75	-30.7	34	41	-$14
15	BOS	0	2	6	61	53	3.86	3.71	1.30	729	649	775	4.8	3.0	7.9	2.7	62%	10%	50	25	26	31%	74%	15%	0	19			75	0.90	0.8	89	106	$0
16	BOS	3	2	0	55	56	3.25	3.72	1.27	624	545	675	4.4	3.7	9.1	2.4	57%	11%	49	25	26	31%	74%	5%	0	18			0	1.00	6.4	90	107	$1
1st Half		0	1	0	26	31	5.26	3.40	1.36	636	470	718	5.0	3.9	10.9	2.8	61%	13%	51	25	25	36%	59%	6%	0	21			0	1.09	-3.4	120	143	-$3
2nd Half		3	1	0	30	25	1.52	3.99	1.18	612	595	625	4.0	3.6	7.6	2.1	53%	10%	48	25	28	27%	88%	5%	0	16			0	0.92	9.8	64	76	$6
17	**Proj**	**3**	**2**	**0**	**58**	**52**	**3.72**	**3.88**	**1.32**	**685**	**625**	**722**	**4.8**	**3.3**	**8.0**	**2.4**	**60%**	**10%**	**50**	**24**	**26**	**31%**	**72%**	**9%**	**0**						**3.4**	**82**	**97**	**-$1**

BRANDON KRUSE

Ross,Tyson

Age: 30	Th: R	Role	RP	Health	F	LIMA Plan	C
Ht: 6' 6"	Wt: 215	Type	Pwr xGB	PT/Exp	B	Rand Var	+5
				Consist	A	MM	3303

After awful Opening Day start, shoulder inflammation eventually led to thoracic outlet syndrome surgery at end of season. Possible he won't be ready by start of 2017, and probably wise to assume a few bumps in road no matter when he returns. Consistency of 2013-15 skills makes him still worthy of consideration.

Yr Tm	W	L	Sv	IP	K	ERA	xERA	WHIP	oOPS	vL	vR	BF/G	Ctl	Dom	Cmd	FpK	SwK	G	L	F	H%	S%	hr/f	GS	APC	DOM%	DIS%	Sv%	LI	RAR	BPV	BPX	R$
12 OAK *	8	13	0	152	98	4.76	4.73	1.56	870	974	759	20.2	3.9	5.8	1.5	55%	7%	50	23	27	33%	69%	10%	13	72	0%	46%	0	0.97	-13.9	45	59	-$10
13 SD	3	8	0	125	119	3.17	3.20	1.15	627	709	548	14.4	3.2	8.6	2.7	54%	12%	55	15	30	28%	74%	8%	16	57	44%	13%	0	1.09	10.8	102	133	$7
14 SD	13	14	0	196	195	2.81	3.02	1.21	634	635	632	26.2	3.3	9.0	2.7	58%	13%	57	21	22	30%	79%	11%	31	101	48%	23%			22.6	107	127	$16
15 SD	10	12	0	196	212	3.26	3.07	1.31	652	721	584	24.9	3.9	9.7	2.5	58%	13%	62	19	20	32%	75%	9%	33	98	33%	18%			17.0	111	132	$12
16 SD	0	1	0	5	5	11.81	3.68	1.88	986	1033	873	27.0	1.7	8.4	5.0	70%	15%	47	37	16	47%	30%	0%	1	94	0%	0%			-5.0	131	156	-$6
1st Half	0	1	0	5	5	11.81	3.68	1.88	986	1033	873	27.0	1.7	8.4	5.0	70%	15%	47	37	16	47%	30%	0%	1	94	0%	0%			-5.0	132	157	-$6
2nd Half																																	
17 Proj	**6**	**9**	**0**	**138**	**131**	**3.36**	**3.60**	**1.27**	**657**	**723**	**591**	**19.2**	**3.5**	**8.6**	**2.4**	**56%**	**12%**	**57**	**19**	**25**	**31%**	**74%**	**9%**	**27**						**14.1**	**94**	**112**	**$7**

Rusin,Chris

Age: 30	Th: L	Role	RP	Health	C	LIMA Plan	A
Ht: 6' 2"	Wt: 185	Type	Pwr GB	PT/Exp	C	Rand Var	0
				Consist	D	MM	2201

And just like that, a bullpen asset is born? PRO: SwK supports 2H Dom jump; went from 2.2 Cmd vR as SP to 3.4 as RP; recent trends in GB%/FB%. CON: FpK does not buy 2H Ctl improvement; 2H velocity topped out at 91. It's 30 elite IP vs. 295 disastrous IP, plus Coors. There are less risky longshots out there.

Yr Tm	W	L	Sv	IP	K	ERA	xERA	WHIP	oOPS	vL	vR	BF/G	Ctl	Dom	Cmd	FpK	SwK	G	L	F	H%	S%	hr/f	GS	APC	DOM%	DIS%	Sv%	LI	RAR	BPV	BPX	R$
12 CHC *	10	12	0	173	97	5.62	5.70	1.63	881	678	955	23.3	3.6	5.1	1.4	53%	10%	45	25	30	33%	67%	14%	7	72	14%	57%			-34.2	19	24	-$19
13 CHC *	10	13	0	187	90	4.21	4.41	1.40	750	521	819	24.7	2.6	4.3	1.6	58%	8%	48	23	29	30%	71%	13%	13	79	0%	54%			-8.0	34	44	-$3
14 CHC *	8	13	0	159	83	5.54	6.05	1.67	830	458	1128	26.4	2.7	4.7	1.8	59%	8%	48	18	34	35%	68%	7%	0	49			0	0.32	-35.3	24	28	-$19
15 COL *	9	12	0	166	98	6.00	6.61	1.72	867	867	867	24.3	2.9	5.3	1.8	67%	9%	52	21	27	36%	68%	15%	22	90	18%	50%	0	0.77	-41.8	15	18	-$23
16 COL	3	5	0	84	69	3.74	3.52	1.25	706	716	701	12.1	2.5	7.4	3.0	58%	10%	58	21	21	31%	70%	10%	7	44	0%	43%	0	0.75	4.7	102	122	$2
1st Half	2	4	0	55	39	4.12	3.85	1.34	729	855	682	19.3	2.8	6.4	2.3	59%	8%	59	23	18	32%	68%	7%	7	67	0%	43%	0	0.74	0.5	77	92	$1
2nd Half	1	1	0	30	30	3.03	2.98	1.08	661	514	745	6.9	1.8	9.1	5.0	54%	13%	57	17	26	30%	76%	15%	0	27			0	0.76	4.2	150	179	$3
17 Proj	**3**	**4**	**0**	**73**	**62**	**4.07**	**3.78**	**1.42**	**799**	**723**	**828**	**13.9**	**2.5**	**7.8**	**3.1**	**61%**	**10%**	**54**	**20**	**25**	**35%**	**74%**	**14%**	**9**						**1.1**	**104**	**123**	**-$2**

Ryan,Kyle

Age: 25	Th: L	Role	RP	Health	A	LIMA Plan	B
Ht: 6' 5"	Wt: 180	Type	Con GB	PT/Exp	C	Rand Var	-2
				Consist	B	MM	1000

Glance at his Dom and you need read no further. Help from H%, hr/f got him more IP than deserved, given xERA. Solid GB% gains, gets job done vL (3.4 Cmd), but that Dom! Are you still reading? Why? Okay, I guess it's finally safe to reveal the dark secret that will change your life: The truth is that [EDITED FOR SPACE]

Yr Tm	W	L	Sv	IP	K	ERA	xERA	WHIP	oOPS	vL	vR	BF/G	Ctl	Dom	Cmd	FpK	SwK	G	L	F	H%	S%	hr/f	GS	APC	DOM%	DIS%	Sv%	LI	RAR	BPV	BPX	R$
12																																	
13																																	
14 DET *	12	10	0	170	83	4.44	4.44	1.36	626	700	601	22.2	2.1	4.4	2.1	63%	7%	77	6	17	31%	68%	0%	1	27	0%	0%	0	1.06	-14.7	43	51	-$3
15 DET *	6	13	0	159	80	4.79	5.04	1.56	795	817	788	21.2	3.1	4.5	1.5	60%	8%	48	22	30	33%	69%	16%	6	56	0%	50%	0	1.07	-16.3	32	38	-$12
16 DET	4	2	0	56	35	3.07	4.05	1.13	636	630	640	4.0	2.4	5.7	2.3	62%	9%	56	18	26	27%	72%	4%	0	15			0	0.64	7.7	70	84	$3
1st Half	3	2	0	29	20	2.51	3.76	1.29	717	806	645	4.2	1.9	6.3	3.3	64%	9%	55	21	24	33%	81%	5%	0	15			0	0.96	5.9	95	114	$4
2nd Half	1	0	0	27	15	3.67	4.37	0.96	548	424	636	3.9	3.0	5.0	1.7	60%	9%	57	13	29	21%	60%	4%	0	15			0	0.33	1.7	44	53	$2
17 Proj	**3**	**3**	**0**	**58**	**32**	**3.95**	**4.49**	**1.30**	**711**	**682**	**727**	**6.8**	**2.7**	**5.0**	**1.9**	**61%**	**9%**	**53**	**19**	**28**	**29%**	**69%**	**6%**	**0**						**1.7**	**49**	**59**	**-$1**

Ryu,Hyun-Jin

Age: 30	Th: L	Role	SP	Health	F	LIMA Plan	C+
Ht: 6' 3"	Wt: 250	Type		PT/Exp	D	Rand Var	+5
				Consist	F	MM	2201

After shoulder issue ended 2014 early, and led to labrum surgery in May 2015, LA thought he'd be ready by start of 2016. Now, after Sept elbow surgery, they think he'll be ready by start of 2017. It's been said definition of insanity is doing same thing over and over, expecting different results. We'd still take a flyer.

Yr Tm	W	L	Sv	IP	K	ERA	xERA	WHIP	oOPS	vL	vR	BF/G	Ctl	Dom	Cmd	FpK	SwK	G	L	F	H%	S%	hr/f	GS	APC	DOM%	DIS%	Sv%	LI	RAR	BPV	BPX	R$
12 for	9	9	0	183	199	3.30	2.96	1.21				27.3	2.8	9.8	3.5						33%	72%								16.2	127	165	$15
13 LA	14	8	0	192	154	3.00	3.51	1.20	660	738	633	26.1	2.3	7.2	3.1	59%	9%	51	19	31	30%	77%	9%	30	102	33%	20%			20.5	97	126	$16
14 LA	14	7	0	152	139	3.38	3.23	1.19	658	665	656	24.3	1.7	8.2	4.8	62%	9%	47	22	30	33%	72%	6%	26	94	42%	27%			6.9	127	151	$11
15																																	
16 LA	0	1	0	5	4	11.57	5.53	2.14	1144	800	1238	24.0	3.9	7.7	2.0	54%	11%	41	24	35	43%	44%	17%	1	89	0%	100%			-4.2	54	64	-$6
1st Half																																	
2nd Half	0	1	0	5	4	11.57	5.53	2.14	1144	800	1238	24.0	3.9	7.7	2.0	54%	11%	41	24	35	43%	44%	17%	1	89	0%	100%			-4.2	54	64	-$6
17 Proj	**5**	**3**	**0**	**73**	**63**	**3.25**	**3.71**	**1.20**	**643**	**677**	**632**	**25.5**	**2.3**	**7.9**	**3.4**	**61%**	**9%**	**49**	**21**	**30**	**31%**	**73%**	**6%**	**11**						**8.4**	**106**	**126**	**$4**

Sabathia,CC

Age: 36	Th: L	Role	SP	Health	F	LIMA Plan	B
Ht: 6' 6"	Wt: 290	Type	Pwr	PT/Exp	B	Rand Var	0
				Consist	A	MM	1203

Past concerns about size, workload appear to have come to fruition over last three years. Follow trend in just about any skill—xERA, Ctl, Cmd, FpK, BPV/BPX—and find reason to worry. "Routine cleanup" of right knee after season ended doesn't add confidence. Add in age, and... DN: 5.00 ERA, less than 100 IP

Yr Tm	W	L	Sv	IP	K	ERA	xERA	WHIP	oOPS	vL	vR	BF/G	Ctl	Dom	Cmd	FpK	SwK	G	L	F	H%	S%	hr/f	GS	APC	DOM%	DIS%	Sv%	LI	RAR	BPV	BPX	R$
12 NYY	15	6	0	200	197	3.38	3.29	1.14	666	667	665	29.8	2.0	8.9	4.5	63%	12%	48	21	31	31%	74%	13%	28	108	57%	18%			15.8	132	172	$21
13 NYY	14	13	0	211	175	4.78	3.89	1.37	770	662	804	28.4	2.8	7.5	2.7	65%	10%	45	22	33	32%	68%	13%	32	104	28%	22%			-23.7	83	108	-$2
14 NYY	3	4	0	46	48	5.28	3.29	1.48	875	570	921	26.1	2.0	9.4	4.8	70%	11%	48	22	30	37%	71%	23%	8	100	13%	25%			-8.7	142	169	-$5
15 NYY	6	10	0	167	137	4.73	4.08	1.42	797	516	864	25.0	2.7	7.4	2.7	62%	9%	46	22	32	32%	71%	17%	29	93	17%	41%			-15.9	84	100	-$6
16 NYY	9	12	0	180	152	3.91	4.22	1.32	713	662	725	25.6	3.3	7.6	2.3	61%	10%	50	17	33	30%	74%	13%	30	97	23%	33%			6.3	77	92	$7
1st Half	5	5	0	77	61	3.17	4.49	1.29	648	723	634	25.2	3.5	7.2	2.0	63%	10%	46	19	35	30%	76%	5%	13	95	23%	23%			9.6	58	69	$10
2nd Half	4	7	0	103	91	4.46	4.03	1.34	759	628	797	25.9	3.1	8.0	2.6	60%	10%	53	16	31	30%	73%	19%	17	98	24%	41%			-3.4	92	109	$4
17 Proj	**8**	**11**	**0**	**160**	**135**	**4.35**	**4.20**	**1.39**	**767**	**620**	**801**	**25.2**	**3.1**	**7.6**	**2.4**	**63%**	**10%**	**48**	**19**	**32**	**31%**	**73%**	**15%**	**27**						**-3.2**	**79**	**95**	**-$1**

Salas,Fernando

Age: 32	Th: R	Role	RP	Health	C	LIMA Plan	A
Ht: 6' 2"	Wt: 210	Type	Pwr FB	PT/Exp	C	Rand Var	0
				Consist	A	MM	2310

Posted 7.54 ERA, 4.4 Ctl, 4.9 Dom, 58% FpK, 9% SwK in June-July; 2.53 ERA, 1.5 Ctl, 8.9 Dom, 69% FpK, 12% SwK rest of year. No reported injury, but sure looks like he was pitching through something. 6 Saves, LI history suggest teams view him as closer-ish, and BPV concurs; just mind the FB% risk.

Yr Tm	W	L	Sv	IP	K	ERA	xERA	WHIP	oOPS	vL	vR	BF/G	Ctl	Dom	Cmd	FpK	SwK	G	L	F	H%	S%	hr/f	GS	APC	DOM%	DIS%	Sv%	LI	RAR	BPV	BPX	R$
12 STL	1	4	0	59	60	4.30	4.13	1.41	720	681	747	3.9	4.1	9.2	2.2	67%	13%	38	24	38	33%	71%	8%	0	16			0	1.18	-2.0	70	91	-$4
13 STL *	1	5	12	52	38	3.48	2.88	1.09	715	829	645	4.1	2.0	6.6	3.3	69%	10%	32	15	53	28%	70%	7%	0	17			80	1.05	2.4	96	125	$5
14 LAA	5	0	0	59	61	3.38	3.41	1.09	637	510	771	4.2	2.1	9.4	4.4	64%	13%	29	30	42	30%	71%	8%	0	17			0	1.00	2.6	117	140	$3
15 LAA	5	2	0	64	74	4.24	3.37	1.15	716	729	707	3.7	1.7	10.5	6.2	66%	13%	35	22	43	33%	66%	11%	0	14			0	1.12	-2.2	155	185	$1
16 2 TM	3	7	6	74	64	3.91	4.12	1.11	699	682	714	3.9	2.3	7.8	3.4	66%	11%	39	17	44	26%	71%	13%	0	16			55	1.14	2.5	95	113	$5
1st Half	3	5	2	38	27	4.97	4.58	1.18	764	893	652	4.1	2.6	6.4	2.5	64%	11%	39	18	43	24%	65%	16%	0	17			33	1.44	-3.7	62	74	$2
2nd Half	0	2	4	36	37	2.78	3.66	1.04	631	475	783	3.7	2.0	9.3	4.6	67%	12%	39	17	44	28%	79%	10%	0	16			80	0.84	6.2	130	156	$8
17 Proj	**3**	**4**	**5**	**65**	**64**	**3.78**	**3.80**	**1.12**	**684**	**637**	**726**	**3.8**	**2.2**	**8.9**	**4.1**	**66%**	**12%**	**37**	**21**	**43**	**29%**	**71%**	**11%**	**0**						**3.3**	**116**	**138**	**$4**

Salazar,Danny

Age: 27	Th: R	Role	SP	Health	B	LIMA Plan	B+
Ht: 6' 0"	Wt: 190	Type	Pwr	PT/Exp	B	Rand Var	+1
				Consist	B	MM	2403

Parade of injuries that began in June reads like a big flashing caution sign: shoulder fatigue, elbow soreness, forearm tightness. Still managed to raise Dom, lower FB%, which only adds to tantalizing intrigue. Temptation is to think "Potential ace!", but he's yet to throw 200 IP or show Ctl issues are behind him.

Yr Tm	W	L	Sv	IP	K	ERA	xERA	WHIP	oOPS	vL	vR	BF/G	Ctl	Dom	Cmd	FpK	SwK	G	L	F	H%	S%	hr/f	GS	APC	DOM%	DIS%	Sv%	LI	RAR	BPV	BPX	R$
12 aa	4	0	0	34	20	2.44	2.62	1.12				22.3	2.2	5.3	2.5						27%	78%								6.6	82	107	$1
13 CLE *	8	8	1	145	176	3.08	2.86	1.11	655	588	733	18.4	2.4	10.9	4.6	67%	15%	34	26	40	32%	75%	14%	10	82	20%	0%			14.0	150	195	$14
14 CLE *	10	14	0	171	184	4.25	4.63	1.43	751	696	786	23.4	3.3	9.7	3.0	59%	12%	34	23	42	35%	73%	10%	20	93	30%	25%			-10.7	89	106	-$2
15 CLE	14	10	0	185	195	3.45	3.44	1.13	673	724	628	25.2	2.6	9.5	3.7	59%	12%	44	19	37	29%	74%	12%	30	102	33%	17%			11.6	123	147	$18
16 CLE	11	6	0	137	161	3.87	3.75	1.34	697	628	755	23.4	4.1	10.6	2.6	54%	12%	48	17	35	32%	74%	13%	25	96	36%	28%			5.5	104	124	$8
1st Half	10	3	0	93	107	2.22	3.61	1.11	569	499	626	25.0	4.1	10.3	2.5	53%	12%	47	16	36	26%	83%	7%	15	104	47%	7%			22.7	99	118	$21
2nd Half	1	3	0	44	54	7.36	4.03	1.82	925	854	984	20.9	4.1	11.0	2.7	55%	10%	49	19	33	42%	63%	23%	10	85	20%	60%			-17.2	115	137	-$20
17 Proj	**11**	**9**	**0**	**174**	**194**	**3.81**	**3.73**	**1.29**	**683**	**645**	**715**	**21.9**	**3.4**	**10.0**	**2.9**	**57%**	**12%**	**44**	**20**	**37**	**32%**	**74%**	**12%**	**33**						**8.1**	**110**	**131**	**$9**

BRANDON KRUSE

Sale,Chris

Age: 28	Th: L	Role SP	Health	B	LIMA Plan	C
Ht: 6' 5"	Wt: 170	Type Pwr	PT/Exp	A	Rand Var	0
			Consist	A	MM	4405

Chose to trade 2 mph of velocity and change-up for more sinkers in order to pitch deeper into games. Worked great for IP, less great for skills. But R$ says it didn't hurt value, and really, it's a matter of going from elite to very, very good. He'll be fine; just don't ask him to wear a throwback jersey.

Yr	Tm	W	L	Sv	IP	K	ERA	xERA	WHIP	oOPS	vL	vR	BF/G	Ctl	Dom	Cmd	FpK	SwK	G	L	F	H%	S%	hr/f	GS	APC	DOM%	DIS%	Sv%	LI	RAR	BPV	BPX	R$
12	CHW	17	8	0	192	192	3.05	3.27	1.14	660	601	682	25.7	2.4	9.0	3.8	57%	11%	45	23	32	30%	77%	12%	29	101	52%	21%	0	0.87	22.9	120	157	$24
13	CHW	11	14	0	214	226	3.07	2.94	1.07	636	360	699	28.9	1.9	9.5	4.9	63%	11%	47	21	32	30%	76%	13%	30	108	70%	10%			21.2	144	187	$23
14	CHW	12	4	0	174	208	2.17	2.81	0.97	567	393	608	26.3	2.0	10.8	5.3	67%	14%	41	18	41	29%	81%	8%	26	106	58%	4%			33.7	158	188	$27
15	CHW	13	11	0	209	274	3.41	2.74	1.09	649	610	657	27.5	1.8	11.8	6.5	67%	15%	43	22	35	34%	73%	13%	31	107	65%	10%			14.3	185	220	$23
16	CHW	17	10	0	227	233	3.34	3.42	1.04	651	585	663	28.3	1.8	9.3	5.2	62%	12%	41	21	38	29%	73%	12%	32	107	66%	13%			23.9	137	163	$29
1st Half		14	2	0	120	118	2.93	3.47	0.98	602	591	604	27.8	1.8	8.9	4.9	63%	11%	40	23	37	27%	76%	12%	17	108	76%	12%			18.7	129	154	$37
2nd Half		3	8	0	107	115	3.80	3.37	1.10	705	581	731	29.0	1.8	9.7	5.5	61%	13%	42	19	39	31%	69%	12%	15	107	53%	13%			5.2	147	175	$20
17	Proj	14	10	0	210	223	3.29	3.33	1.05	645	549	664	26.7	1.9	9.5	5.1	64%	13%	42	21	37	30%	73%	11%	30						23.3	141	168	$24

Samardzija,Jeff

Age: 32	Th: R	Role SP	Health	A	LIMA Plan	C+
Ht: 6' 6"	Wt: 220	Type	PT/Exp	A	Rand Var	0
			Consist	B	MM	2205

Seems like something was up in June-July (5.1 Dom, 8% SwK, 18% hr/f, 5.03 xERA in 10 GS), but if so, he and SF are keeping it quiet. Showed flashes of former peak in May (8.3 Dom, 129 BPV), Sept (10.3 Dom, 143 BPV), but these days, flashes are all you get. Health, IP boost value above league-average skills.

Yr	Tm	W	L	Sv	IP	K	ERA	xERA	WHIP	oOPS	vL	vR	BF/G	Ctl	Dom	Cmd	FpK	SwK	G	L	F	H%	S%	hr/f	GS	APC	DOM%	DIS%	Sv%	LI	RAR	BPV	BPX	R$
12	CHC	9	13	0	175	180	3.81	3.45	1.22	698	759	636	25.8	2.9	9.3	3.2	60%	13%	45	22	33	30%	72%	13%	28	99	46%	21%			4.3	112	146	$10
13	CHC	8	13	0	214	214	4.34	3.49	1.35	736	783	695	27.7	3.3	9.0	2.7	60%	11%	48	20	31	32%	70%	13%	33	105	33%	18%			-12.5	100	130	$1
14	2 TM	7	13	0	220	202	2.99	3.05	1.07	646	662	631	26.6	1.8	8.3	4.7	65%	12%	50	19	31	29%	75%	11%	33	101	58%	9%			20.3	129	154	$19
15	CHW	11	13	0	214	163	4.96	4.25	1.29	765	839	689	28.4	2.1	6.9	3.3	62%	10%	39	21	40	31%	64%	11%	32	104	28%	28%			-26.4	85	101	-$2
16	SF	12	11	0	203	167	3.81	4.00	1.20	710	780	639	25.9	2.4	7.4	3.1	63%	10%	46	20	34	29%	72%	12%	32	100	28%	34%			9.6	93	110	$14
1st Half		8	5	0	111	84	3.97	4.03	1.18	716	828	628	26.5	1.9	6.8	3.5	63%	10%	47	20	33	29%	70%	12%	17	101	35%	41%			3.0	95	113	$15
2nd Half		4	6	0	92	83	3.61	3.97	1.22	702	735	657	25.3	2.9	8.1	2.8	64%	10%	46	20	34	29%	74%	11%	15	98	20%	27%			6.6	91	108	$12
17	Proj	11	9	0	189	160	3.97	3.94	1.21	715	772	656	26.0	2.4	7.7	3.3	63%	10%	45	20	35	30%	70%	12%	29						5.0	97	116	$9

Sampson,Keyvius

Age: 26	Th: R	Role RP	Health	A	LIMA Plan	D+
Ht: 6' 0"	Wt: 185	Type Pwr	PT/Exp	D	Rand Var	0
			Consist	B	MM	0301

0-1, 4.35 ERA in 39 IP at CIN. Question of whether he starts or relieves is secondary to fact that skills suggest he can't fire a strike when needed. 2nd half improvements in FpK, SwK, FB% offer slight reasons for hope, but without Cmd growth, likely will continue to ride the minor league shuttle.

Yr	Tm	W	L	Sv	IP	K	ERA	xERA	WHIP	oOPS	vL	vR	BF/G	Ctl	Dom	Cmd	FpK	SwK	G	L	F	H%	S%	hr/f	GS	APC	DOM%	DIS%	Sv%	LI	RAR	BPV	BPX	R$
12	aa	8	11	0	122	111	4.67	3.35	1.30				19.4	3.8	8.1	2.2						30%	63%								-9.9	83	109	$0
13	a/a	12	7	0	141	122	3.51	3.34	1.26				20.6	3.6	7.8	2.2						28%	74%								6.2	77	100	$8
14	aaa	2	5	0	92	82	5.40	4.86	1.56				10.6	5.6	8.0	1.4						29%	68%								-18.7	44	52	-$10
15	CIN *	5	12	0	135	107	5.26	5.37	1.74	853	920	799	21.2	5.1	7.1	1.4	55%	9%	39	22	39	35%	70%	10%	12	80	0%	67%	0	0.73	-21.6	46	55	-$16
16	CIN *	3	4	0	102	95	3.34	4.08	1.38	830	767	859	11.9	4.5	8.4	1.9	53%	11%	38	18	43	28%	81%	18%	2	44	100%	0%	0	0.32	10.6	62	73	$2
1st Half		2	4	0	69	61	3.75	4.24	1.40	1140	949	1261	14.5	4.4	7.9	1.8	48%	8%	28	18	54	28%	78%	24%	0	45			0	0.44	3.7	55	65	$3
2nd Half		1	0	0	33	34	2.48	3.73	1.34	680	655	691	8.5	4.8	9.5	2.0	56%	12%	43	18	38	28%	87%	14%	2	44	100%	0%	0	0.26	6.9	76	90	$2
17	Proj	3	4	0	87	79	4.34	4.84	1.54	712	754	688	12.8	4.8	8.2	1.7	56%	11%	42	20	38	32%	74%	10%	8						-1.7	38	46	-$5

Sanchez,Aaron

Age: 25	Th: R	Role RP	Health	C	LIMA Plan	D+
Ht: 6' 4"	Wt: 190	Type Pwr xGB	PT/Exp	B	Rand Var	-1
			Consist	A	MM	2205

TOR wasn't able to slow down workload as much as hoped, so let's assume some of 2nd half skill decline was fatigue. FpK, SwK growth turned Cmd from poor to promising—next step will be restoring xGB%. But with W-L regression, ERA/xERA gap, leap to 200+ IP (including post-season), lots of reasons for caution.

Yr	Tm	W	L	Sv	IP	K	ERA	xERA	WHIP	oOPS	vL	vR	BF/G	Ctl	Dom	Cmd	FpK	SwK	G	L	F	H%	S%	hr/f	GS	APC	DOM%	DIS%	Sv%	LI	RAR	BPV	BPX	R$
12																																		
13																																		
14	TOR *	5	9	3	133	102	3.96	3.47	1.37	367	469	306	12.1	4.5	6.9	1.5	53%	7%	66	15	20	28%	71%	6%	0	19			100	1.17	-3.6	65	77	$0
15	TOR	7	6	0	92	61	3.22	4.08	1.28	666	878	435	9.3	4.3	5.9	1.4	53%	7%	61	18	22	25%	78%	16%	11	35	0%	45%	0	1.08	8.5	30	36	$4
16	TOR	15	2	0	192	161	3.00	3.77	1.17	625	657	592	26.3	3.0	7.5	2.6	61%	9%	54	20	25	28%	77%	11%	30	97	43%	17%			28.2	88	105	$21
1st Half		8	1	0	105	96	3.08	3.44	1.23	660	705	607	27.3	2.9	8.2	2.8	60%	9%	59	21	20	30%	78%	15%	16	100	50%	19%			14.5	106	126	$20
2nd Half		7	1	0	87	65	2.91	4.16	1.08	583	590	575	25.2	3.0	6.8	2.2	62%	9%	49	19	31	25%	75%	8%	14	94	36%	14%			13.7	68	81	$22
17	Proj	14	7	0	196	159	3.30	3.75	1.21	649	769	534	14.1	3.3	7.3	2.2	60%	9%	58	19	24	28%	75%	12%	23						21.4	79	94	$16

Sanchez,Anibal

Age: 33	Th: R	Role SP	Health	F	LIMA Plan	C
Ht: 5' 11"	Wt: 220	Type Pwr	PT/Exp	A	Rand Var	+5
			Consist	B	MM	1203

Cmd, xERA, BPV columns show how we got here, but real nail in coffin last two years has been FB%, hr/f. FpK suggests 2H Ctl was legit, and overall, post-All-Star work offers hope. But 4.08 xERA only sets upside clock back to 2015, and health/IP remain big issues. You wanna bet against third straight negative R$?

Yr	Tm	W	L	Sv	IP	K	ERA	xERA	WHIP	oOPS	vL	vR	BF/G	Ctl	Dom	Cmd	FpK	SwK	G	L	F	H%	S%	hr/f	GS	APC	DOM%	DIS%	Sv%	LI	RAR	BPV	BPX	R$
12	2 TM	9	13	0	196	167	3.86	3.70	1.27	716	645	797	26.5	2.2	7.7	3.5	66%	10%	46	21	32	32%	72%	11%	31	99	32%	26%			3.6	103	134	$8
13	DET	14	8	0	182	202	2.57	3.08	1.15	616	673	548	25.7	2.7	10.0	3.7	62%	13%	45	22	33	32%	79%	6%	29	103	55%	14%			29.1	131	170	$22
14	DET	8	5	0	126	102	3.43	3.58	1.10	597	562	648	23.4	2.1	7.3	3.4	60%	10%	46	19	35	29%	67%	3%	21	95	33%	10%	0	0.75	4.9	97	116	$8
15	DET	10	10	0	157	138	4.99	4.11	1.28	768	681	866	26.4	2.8	7.9	2.8	65%	10%	40	21	39	29%	66%	16%	25	101	40%	24%			-19.9	85	101	-$1
16	DET	7	13	0	153	135	5.87	4.59	1.46	828	771	888	19.1	3.1	7.9	2.5	67%	10%	40	19	41	32%	64%	16%	26	74	12%	38%	0	0.84	-31.8	77	91	-$10
1st Half		5	8	0	74	59	6.05	5.17	1.57	879	842	912	16.5	4.0	7.1	1.8	63%	9%	40	16	43	31%	66%	16%	12	64	8%	58%	0	0.91	-17.1	39	46	-$10
2nd Half		2	5	0	79	76	5.70	4.08	1.35	780	713	861	22.5	2.3	8.7	3.8	70%	10%	39	22	39	33%	61%	15%	14	86	14%	21%	0	0.74	-14.7	111	133	-$9
17	Proj	7	9	0	131	116	4.93	4.22	1.33	760	699	829	21.5	2.8	8.0	2.9	65%	10%	41	20	39	31%	66%	14%	25						-12.0	89	105	-$2

Santana,Ervin

Age: 34	Th: R	Role SP	Health	B	LIMA Plan	C+
Ht: 6' 2"	Wt: 160	Type	PT/Exp	A	Rand Var	-1
			Consist	A	MM	1203

What to make of all these skill fluctuations? PRO: Owned 2H Dom, SwK in 2014; posted 9.3 Dom over last 11 GS. CON: Lowest FpK since 2006; 2H surge was more about H%/S% than skills; sizable overall ERA/xERA gap. Age makes him more likely to go down than up; even 2nd half xERA suggests a near-4 ERA pitcher.

Yr	Tm	W	L	Sv	IP	K	ERA	xERA	WHIP	oOPS	vL	vR	BF/G	Ctl	Dom	Cmd	FpK	SwK	G	L	F	H%	S%	hr/f	GS	APC	DOM%	DIS%	Sv%	LI	RAR	BPV	BPX	R$
12	LAA	9	13	0	178	133	5.16	4.38	1.27	774	867	664	25.5	3.1	6.7	2.2	62%	9%	43	20	37	25%	66%	19%	30	95	27%	40%			-25.1	59	77	-$2
13	KC	9	10	0	211	161	3.24	3.66	1.14	668	675	659	26.8	2.2	6.9	3.2	66%	10%	46	21	33	27%	77%	12%	32	100	44%	16%			16.2	89	116	$15
14	ATL	14	10	0	196	179	3.95	3.57	1.31	724	763	676	26.4	2.9	8.2	2.8	63%	12%	43	25	33	32%	71%	9%	31	96	32%	29%			-5.0	91	108	$5
15	MIN *	10	5	0	129	90	3.79	4.09	1.31	729	804	651	26.6	2.9	6.3	2.2	61%	10%	41	22	38	29%	74%	10%	17	99	47%	35%			2.7	56	67	$4
16	MIN	7	11	0	181	149	3.38	4.20	1.22	682	667	697	24.9	2.6	7.4	2.8	59%	10%	43	22	36	29%	76%	10%	30	98	27%	27%			18.2	83	99	$12
1st Half		2	7	0	84	60	4.50	4.70	1.40	777	704	845	23.9	2.8	6.4	2.3	58%	9%	43	20	37	31%	71%	11%	15	94	13%	47%			-3.2	62	73	-$2
2nd Half		5	4	0	97	89	2.40	3.78	1.06	596	634	557	26.0	2.5	8.2	3.3	59%	12%	42	23	35	27%	81%	9%	15	102	40%	7%			21.4	101	120	$24
17	Proj	8	11	0	174	140	3.94	4.25	1.28	730	757	701	25.5	2.7	7.2	2.7	61%	10%	42	22	36	30%	73%	11%	28						5.4	77	92	$5

Santiago,Hector

Age: 29	Th: L	Role RP	Health	A	LIMA Plan	B
Ht: 6' 0"	Wt: 210	Type Pwr xFB	PT/Exp	A	Rand Var	-1
			Consist	A	MM	0203

Simply cannot combine this many fly balls with this many free passes and hope to succeed. 2H Dom drop can probably be blamed on K-averse MIN (5.4 after trade); even so, doesn't fan enough to save Cmd. H%/S% have shaved at least half a run off ERA each of last 5 years—if luck turns, things will get ugly fast.

Yr	Tm	W	L	Sv	IP	K	ERA	xERA	WHIP	oOPS	vL	vR	BF/G	Ctl	Dom	Cmd	FpK	SwK	G	L	F	H%	S%	hr/f	GS	APC	DOM%	DIS%	Sv%	LI	RAR	BPV	BPX	R$
12	CHW	4	1	4	70	79	3.33	4.11	1.34	680	592	744	7.3	5.1	10.1	2.0	56%	9%	38	20	42	27%	81%	14%	4	32	25%	25%	67	0.83	6.0	60	78	$3
13	CHW	4	9	0	149	137	3.56	4.38	1.40	739	686	762	19.3	4.3	8.3	1.9	57%	9%	36	20	44	30%	78%	9%	23	79	26%	35%	0	0.88	5.5	46	59	$1
14	LAA	6	9	0	127	108	3.75	4.53	1.36	698	606	732	18.1	3.7	7.6	2.0	56%	8%	31	19	50	29%	76%	8%	24	76	8%	50%	0	0.80	-0.1	45	54	$0
15	LAA	9	9	0	181	162	3.59	4.74	1.26	723	633	752	23.5	3.5	8.1	2.3	57%	9%	30	16	54	27%	78%	10%	32	96	19%	31%	0	0.74	8.4	58	69	$9
16	2 AL	13	10	0	182	144	4.70	5.26	1.36	774	750	780	23.8	3.9	7.1	1.8	55%	9%	34	16	50	27%	71%	12%	33	96	18%	48%			-11.4	35	41	$2
1st Half		5	4	0	91	77	4.93	4.88	1.34	767	612	818	22.9	3.9	7.6	1.9	54%	10%	39	15	46	26%	69%	14%	17	94	18%	47%			-8.3	48	57	$1
2nd Half		8	6	0	91	67	4.47	5.64	1.39	780	945	745	24.7	3.9	6.7	1.7	55%	8%	29	17	54	27%	74%	10%	16	98	19%	50%			-3.1	22	27	$3
17	Proj	11	10	0	174	147	4.44	5.05	1.40	773	721	789	19.8	3.9	7.6	2.0	56%	8%	32	17	50	29%	73%	11%	36						-5.3	43	51	$0

BRANDON KRUSE

Scheppers,Tanner

Age: 30	Th: R	Role: RP	Health: F	LIMA Plan: C
Ht: 6' 4"	Wt: 220	Type: Pwr	PT/Exp: F	Rand Var: -1
			Consist: A	MM: 1200

Yet another year almost entirely lost to injury. In 2016, it was "only" his knee—is that a positive? Hard to take away much from 9 IP in September, and we're now three seasons removed from 2013 competence, when skills were hardly eye-popping. Feel free to shred his one-time "closer of the future" tag.

Yr Tm	W	L	Sv	IP	K	ERA	xERA	WHIP	oOPS	vL	vR	BF/G	Ctl	Dom	Cmd	FpK	SwK	G	L	F	H%	S%	hr/f	GS	APC	DOM%	DIS%	Sv%	LI	RAR	BPV	BPX	R$
12 TEX *	2	3	12	63	54	4.34	5.57	1.51	908	949	881	4.2	1.9	7.7	4.2	53%	9%	43	20	37	37%	75%	15%	0	14			80	0.95	-2.6	89	116	$0
13 TEX	6	2	1	77	59	1.88	3.48	1.07	605	599	610	4.0	2.8	6.9	2.5	60%	10%	50	19	31	25%	87%	9%	0	14			33	1.26	18.8	77	100	$10
14 TEX	0	1	0	23	17	9.00	4.50	1.78	922	925	916	13.9	3.9	6.7	1.7	56%	7%	56	14	31	34%	51%	24%	4	52	25%	50%	0	0.76	-14.9	48	57	-$9
15 TEX *	4	3	2	58	46	4.55	4.62	1.58	778	768	786	4.2	5.6	7.2	1.3	55%	8%	40	19	40	30%	73%	13%	0	16			40	1.08	-4.2	46	55	-$4
16 TEX	1	1	1	9	5	4.15	4.81	1.04	570	333	622	3.5	3.1	5.2	1.7	66%	9%	48	15	37	24%	56%	0%	0	13			100	1.63	0.0	35	42	-$3
1st Half																																	
2nd Half	1	1	1	9	5	4.15	4.81	1.04	570	333	622	3.5	3.1	5.2	1.7	66%	9%	48	15	37	24%	56%	0%	0	13			100	1.63	0.0	35	42	-$3
17 Proj	**2**	**2**	**0**	**44**	**35**	**4.22**	**4.56**	**1.42**	**733**	**727**	**738**	**4.1**	**3.4**	**7.3**	**2.1**	**55%**	**9%**	**44**	**20**	**37**	**32%**	**73%**	**10%**	**0**						**-0.2**	**61**	**73**	**-$3**

Scherzer,Max

Age: 32	Th: R	Role: SP	Health: A	LIMA Plan: C
Ht: 6' 3"	Wt: 190	Type: Pwr xFB	PT/Exp: A	Rand Var: 0
			Consist: A	MM: 4505

Someday all the IP may catch up to him, but no sign yet. Ctl, FpK fell back in line with career norms, and he slid to "mere" 2.8 Cmd vL. High FB% will always leave him susceptible to bad hr/f turns, as happened in April and May. But enough nitpicking. SwK just one clear sign he's still a stud at the top of his game.

Yr Tm	W	L	Sv	IP	K	ERA	xERA	WHIP	oOPS	vL	vR	BF/G	Ctl	Dom	Cmd	FpK	SwK	G	L	F	H%	S%	hr/f	GS	APC	DOM%	DIS%	Sv%	LI	RAR	BPV	BPX	R$
12 DET	16	7	0	188	231	3.74	3.35	1.27	721	831	588	24.6	2.9	11.1	3.9	61%	13%	36	22	41	34%	75%	12%	32	102	34%	22%			6.3	136	177	$14
13 DET	21	3	0	214	240	2.90	3.16	0.97	583	645	494	26.1	2.4	10.1	4.3	64%	13%	36	19	45	27%	73%	8%	32	106	63%	3%			25.6	132	172	$33
14 DET	18	5	0	220	252	3.15	3.24	1.18	663	685	629	27.4	2.6	10.3	4.0	63%	12%	37	22	42	33%	76%	8%	33	110	39%	6%			16.2	131	156	$20
15 WAS	14	12	0	229	276	2.79	3.00	0.92	600	657	538	27.2	1.3	10.9	8.1	71%	16%	36	19	45	29%	76%	11%	33	102	58%	9%			32.9	173	207	$37
16 WAS	20	7	0	228	284	2.96	3.33	0.97	619	757	477	26.5	2.2	11.2	5.1	65%	16%	33	19	48	27%	77%	12%	34	105	65%	12%			34.7	153	182	$38
1st Half	9	5	0	115	148	3.30	3.15	0.96	635	761	496	26.3	2.3	11.6	5.1	64%	16%	34	19	47	26%	76%	16%	17	105	59%	18%			12.6	160	191	$34
2nd Half	11	2	0	114	136	2.61	3.50	0.98	603	751	460	26.8	2.1	10.8	5.0	66%	16%	32	20	49	28%	78%	8%	17	105	71%	6%			22.1	146	174	$43
17 Proj	**17**	**7**	**0**	**203**	**245**	**3.03**	**3.27**	**1.00**	**623**	**717**	**517**	**25.6**	**2.1**	**10.9**	**5.2**	**66%**	**15%**	**34**	**20**	**46**	**29%**	**75%**	**11%**	**30**						**28.9**	**152**	**181**	**$30**

Schugel,Andrew

Age: 28	Th: R	Role: RP	Health: D	LIMA Plan: C
Ht: 5' 11"	Wt: 185	Type: FB	PT/Exp: D	Rand Var: +5
			Consist: F	MM: 0101

2-2, 3.63 ERA in 52 IP at PIT. Journeyman minor-league SP found home in bullpen, albeit in low-leverage role. Placement on 60-day DL in mid-Sept had little to do with severity of shoulder injury, but speaks to continuing fringe status. MLB Dom (8.0) a pleasant surprise, but SwK casts doubt on sustainability. Yawn.

Yr Tm	W	L	Sv	IP	K	ERA	xERA	WHIP	oOPS	vL	vR	BF/G	Ctl	Dom	Cmd	FpK	SwK	G	L	F	H%	S%	hr/f	GS	APC	DOM%	DIS%	Sv%	LI	RAR	BPV	BPX	R$
12 aa	6	8	0	140	94	3.53	3.70	1.35				21.7	3.4	6.0	1.8						30%	74%								8.5	60	78	$3
13 aaa	4	6	0	89	64	6.23	5.76	1.66				21.1	2.8	6.4	2.3						37%	62%								-26.0	49	64	-$14
14 aa	6	4	0	148	95	4.48	4.37	1.52				24.7	3.2	5.8	1.8						34%	68%								-13.5	62	74	-$9
15 ARI *	9	9	0	124	68	5.65	6.27	1.75	1018	1282	786	21.9	2.7	4.9	1.8	67%	8%	61	17	22	37%	68%	22%	0	38			0	0.22	-25.8	29	34	-$16
16 PIT *	3	4	1	70	59	4.21	2.54	1.07	591	483	696	5.6	2.1	7.6	3.6	64%	9%	42	24	33	28%	59%	8%	0	23			33	0.70	-0.2	116	138	$2
1st Half	1	2	1	45	37	3.20	2.21	0.98	595	538	647	5.7	2.1	7.5	3.6	65%	9%	38	25	37	26%	69%	7%	0	23			50	0.66	5.5	116	139	$6
2nd Half	2	2	0	25	22	6.04	3.14	1.22	571	282	921	5.3	2.2	7.9	3.6	61%	7%	62	23	15	32%	46%	25%	0	21			0	0.80	-5.7	115	138	-$4
17 Proj	**4**	**4**	**0**	**73**	**53**	**5.05**	**4.68**	**1.37**	**702**	**638**	**761**	**9.1**	**2.5**	**6.6**	**2.6**	**65%**	**9%**	**38**	**25**	**37**	**32%**	**63%**	**7%**	**0**						**-7.7**	**66**	**79**	**-$4**

Severino,Luis

Age: 23	Th: R	Role: SP	Health: B	LIMA Plan: B+
Ht: 6' 2"	Wt: 215	Type: Pwr	PT/Exp: D	Rand Var: +5
			Consist: C	MM: 2301

2-3, 5.83 ERA in 71 IP at NYY. Many expected he'd build on rookie success, cement rotation spot, but 1H hr/f helped crush that idea. Seemed more at home in bullpen (0.39 ERA in 23 IP), but given youth, will get chance to fix issues, including lost effectiveness of change-up. In near term, more growing pains likely.

Yr Tm	W	L	Sv	IP	K	ERA	xERA	WHIP	oOPS	vL	vR	BF/G	Ctl	Dom	Cmd	FpK	SwK	G	L	F	H%	S%	hr/f	GS	APC	DOM%	DIS%	Sv%	LI	RAR	BPV	BPX	R$
12																																	
13																																	
14 aa	2	2	0	25	26	2.82	2.61	1.10				16.3	2.1	9.5	4.5						32%	75%								2.8	148	176	$0
15 NYY *	14	5	0	162	143	3.07	2.97	1.16	705	705	702	21.5	2.8	8.0	2.9	63%	10%	50	20	30	29%	75%	17%	11	93	9%	27%			17.7	97	115	$17
16 NYY *	11	9	0	148	135	5.35	4.82	1.45	812	747	872	18.1	2.7	8.2	3.0	59%	9%	45	24	31	35%	64%	16%	11	58	9%	64%	0	0.70	-21.2	79	94	-$4
1st Half	4	6	0	72	57	5.91	5.14	1.48	919	820	1031	23.8	2.7	7.1	2.6	58%	8%	49	27	24	34%	61%	27%	7	94	14%	71%			-15.3	58	69	-$8
2nd Half	7	3	0	76	78	4.82	4.52	1.42	693	647	726	14.7	2.7	9.2	3.4	60%	11%	40	20	40	36%	67%	8%	4	41	0%	50%	0	0.68	-5.9	99	118	-$1
17 Proj	**8**	**7**	**0**	**116**	**105**	**4.23**	**3.89**	**1.29**	**719**	**692**	**746**	**20.3**	**2.8**	**8.2**	**3.0**	**61%**	**10%**	**46**	**22**	**32**	**32%**	**69%**	**10%**	**22**						**-0.6**	**97**	**116**	**$2**

Shaw,Bryan

Age: 29	Th: R	Role: RP	Health: A	LIMA Plan: B+
Ht: 6' 1"	Wt: 220	Type: Pwr GB	PT/Exp: C	Rand Var: 0
			Consist: A	MM: 2300

Results—once early hr/f woes abated—look familiar, but some new wrinkles skills-wise. The good: spike in GB%, especially in 2H; uptick in SwK, which backed best-ever Dom. The bad: big dip in FpK, which showed up in Ctl. Only mystery may be which path he takes to end up at same place: steady, boring setup man.

Yr Tm	W	L	Sv	IP	K	ERA	xERA	WHIP	oOPS	vL	vR	BF/G	Ctl	Dom	Cmd	FpK	SwK	G	L	F	H%	S%	hr/f	GS	APC	DOM%	DIS%	Sv%	LI	RAR	BPV	BPX	R$
12 ARI	1	6	2	59	41	3.49	4.03	1.42	747	863	630	3.9	3.6	6.2	1.7	57%	9%	56	21	23	31%	76%	10%	0	15			50	0.78	3.8	48	62	-$2
13 CLE	7	3	1	75	73	3.24	3.58	1.17	586	678	506	4.5	3.4	8.8	2.6	57%	11%	43	25	33	29%	73%	6%	0	18			20	0.99	5.8	88	115	$5
14 CLE	5	5	2	76	64	2.59	3.62	1.09	602	776	493	3.9	2.6	7.5	2.9	59%	11%	46	18	36	27%	79%	8%	0	16			22	1.37	10.8	90	107	$7
15 CLE	3	3	2	64	54	2.95	3.81	1.22	693	673	704	3.6	2.7	7.6	2.8	62%	11%	46	24	31	29%	81%	14%	0	14			33	1.21	8.0	89	105	$3
16 CLE	2	5	1	67	69	3.24	3.59	1.26	686	756	637	3.7	3.8	9.3	2.5	53%	12%	54	19	27	29%	79%	17%	0	15			25	1.13	7.8	98	116	$2
1st Half	1	3	0	32	35	4.55	3.65	1.36	811	864	770	3.6	3.4	9.9	2.9	53%	12%	47	23	30	31%	75%	27%	0	16			0	1.26	-1.4	111	133	-$1
2nd Half	1	2	1	35	34	2.06	3.52	1.17	562	634	517	3.7	4.1	8.7	2.1	54%	12%	61	15	25	27%	83%	5%	0	15			50	1.01	9.2	85	101	$6
17 Proj	**3**	**4**	**0**	**65**	**61**	**3.13**	**3.79**	**1.25**	**680**	**750**	**632**	**3.7**	**3.3**	**8.4**	**2.5**	**57%**	**11%**	**51**	**20**	**29**	**29%**	**79%**	**13%**	**0**						**8.5**	**90**	**107**	**$2**

Shields,James

Age: 35	Th: R	Role: SP	Health: A	LIMA Plan: C
Ht: 6' 4"	Wt: 220	Type: Pwr	PT/Exp: A	Rand Var: +3
			Consist: B	MM: 1203

Aside from hot July (1.78 ERA), which itself featured mediocre 1.5 Cmd, this was a mess. Neither rise in walks (see FpK) nor drop in Dom (see SwK, lost velocity) were a fluke; uptick in FB% compounded by high hr/f. Even seeing if someone'll go to $2 on "Big Game James" is a dangerous game of chicken.

Yr Tm	W	L	Sv	IP	K	ERA	xERA	WHIP	oOPS	vL	vR	BF/G	Ctl	Dom	Cmd	FpK	SwK	G	L	F	H%	S%	hr/f	GS	APC	DOM%	DIS%	Sv%	LI	RAR	BPV	BPX	R$
12 TAM	15	10	0	228	223	3.52	3.23	1.17	678	706	645	28.6	2.3	8.8	3.8	61%	11%	52	19	29	30%	73%	13%	33	110	52%	12%			13.9	127	165	$21
13 KC	13	9	0	229	196	3.15	3.72	1.24	678	614	753	27.8	2.7	7.7	2.9	58%	10%	42	23	35	30%	77%	9%	34	108	32%	18%			20.2	87	113	$16
14 KC	14	8	0	227	180	3.21	3.56	1.18	702	698	706	27.6	1.7	7.1	4.1	63%	10%	45	21	34	30%	76%	10%	34	107	38%	21%			14.8	104	124	$15
15 SD	13	7	0	202	216	3.91	3.67	1.33	776	890	660	26.1	3.6	9.6	2.7	60%	13%	45	21	34	31%	77%	18%	33	101	30%	18%			1.2	99	117	$8
16 2 TM	6	19	0	182	135	5.85	5.26	1.60	891	866	915	24.9	4.1	6.7	1.6	54%	9%	40	21	38	31%	69%	18%	33	95	9%	42%			-37.1	29	34	-$17
1st Half	3	9	0	88	70	5.85	4.98	1.68	881	862	898	24.6	4.2	7.2	1.7	53%	10%	44	22	34	34%	68%	16%	16	95	13%	31%			-18.0	38	45	-$16
2nd Half	3	10	0	94	65	5.84	5.52	1.52	901	870	932	25.2	3.9	6.2	1.6	55%	9%	37	21	42	28%	69%	19%	17	95	6%	53%			-19.1	21	25	-$17
17 Proj	**8**	**12**	**0**	**174**	**147**	**4.72**	**4.49**	**1.42**	**816**	**825**	**806**	**25.2**	**3.4**	**7.6**	**2.2**	**58%**	**10%**	**43**	**21**	**36**	**30%**	**72%**	**16%**	**29**						**-11.3**	**65**	**77**	**-$4**

Shipley,Braden

Age: 25	Th: R	Role: SP	Health: A	LIMA Plan: D+
Ht: 6' 1"	Wt: 185	Type: Con	PT/Exp: D	Rand Var: +1
			Consist: A	MM: 0001

4-5, 5.27 ERA in 70 IP at ARI. Former first-rounder made majors on back of pinpoint control, despite lackluster Dom. At ARI, Ctl (3.6) got a bit shakier, Dom stayed low, and hr/f soared to make it a rough welcome. Additional seasoning would seem to be in order. Monitor from afar for now.

Yr Tm	W	L	Sv	IP	K	ERA	xERA	WHIP	oOPS	vL	vR	BF/G	Ctl	Dom	Cmd	FpK	SwK	G	L	F	H%	S%	hr/f	GS	APC	DOM%	DIS%	Sv%	LI	RAR	BPV	BPX	R$
12																																	
13																																	
14 aa	1	2	0	20	16	4.37	4.07	1.29				20.6	4.4	7.0	1.6						23%	72%								-1.5	38	46	-$3
15 aa	9	11	0	157	100	4.52	4.31	1.48				24.1	3.3	5.7	1.7						33%	69%								-10.7	55	65	-$6
16 ARI *	12	10	0	189	107	4.50	4.95	1.45	901	894	909	25.3	2.3	5.1	2.2	58%	8%	43	24	34	32%	71%	18%	11	91	9%	55%	0	0.76	-7.3	42	50	-$2
1st Half	6	4	0	99	55	4.17	4.45	1.39				26.1	1.6	5.0	3.2						34%	70%	0%	0						0.2	74	89	$2
2nd Half	6	6	0	90	52	4.87	5.50	1.51	901	894	909	24.4	3.2	5.2	1.6	58%	8%	43	24	34	31%	72%	18%	11	91	9%	55%	0	0.76	-7.5	17	21	-$6
17 Proj	**6**	**6**	**0**	**102**	**60**	**4.57**	**5.03**	**1.47**	**749**	**716**	**794**	**24.6**	**2.8**	**5.4**	**1.9**	**58%**	**8%**	**43**	**24**	**34**	**32%**	**70%**	**8%**	**18**						**-4.8**	**41**	**48**	**-$4**

KRISTOPHER OLSON

Shoemaker,Matthew

Age: 30 | Th: R | Role: SP | Ht: 6' 2" | Wt: 225 | Type:
Health: C | PT/Exp: B | Consist: A | LIMA Plan: B+ | Rand Var: 0 | MM: 2203

After rough April, newfound reliance on split-finger saved season. From May 21 on: 2.83 ERA, 7.1 Cmd in 130 IP (20 GS). Skills, particularly Dom, tailed off a bit after June, but FpK speaks to resilence of Ctl, and SwK raises hopes Dom could rebound as well. Sept skull fracture on comeback adds uncertainty, though.

Yr Tm	W	L	Sv	IP	K	ERA	xERA	WHIP	oOPS	vL	vR	BF/G	Ctl	Dom	Cmd	FpK	SwK	G	L	F	H%	S%	hr/f	GS	APC	DOM%	DIS%	Sv%	LI	RAR	BPV	BPX	R$
12 aaa	11	10	0	177	100	5.43	5.79	1.59				26.9	2.0	5.1	2.5						36%	67%								-30.8	44	57	-$17
13 LAA *	11	13	0	189	131	4.25	4.70	1.35	328	490	0	26.3	1.3	6.2	4.6	53%	10%	42	25	33	34%	71%	0%	1	93	0%	0%			-9.1	99	128	$0
14 LAA *	17	4	0	162	144	3.47	3.54	1.17	658	702	610	20.2	1.8	8.0	4.5	63%	11%	41	20	39	31%	73%	9%	20	78	35%	20%	0	0.81	5.3	121	144	$12
15 LAA	7	10	0	135	116	4.46	4.12	1.26	758	727	791	22.8	2.3	7.7	3.3	60%	10%	39	18	42	29%	71%	14%	24	84	38%	42%	0	0.76	-8.2	93	111	$1
16 LAA	9	13	0	160	143	3.88	3.91	1.23	723	705	745	24.7	1.7	8.0	4.8	68%	13%	40	24	36	32%	71%	10%	27	92	26%	30%			6.1	117	139	$9
1st Half	3	9	0	92	93	4.40	3.88	1.32	752	729	779	24.5	2.0	9.1	4.7	68%	14%	37	26	37	35%	69%	11%	16	94	31%	38%			-2.4	126	150	$5
2nd Half	6	4	0	68	50	3.18	3.94	1.10	682	673	693	25.1	1.3	6.6	5.0	70%	12%	44	21	35	29%	75%	10%	11	89	18%	18%			8.5	106	126	$14
17 Proj	**12**	**11**	**0**	**174**	**151**	**3.95**	**3.93**	**1.20**	**717**	**705**	**731**	**22.9**	**1.8**	**7.8**	**4.3**	**65%**	**12%**	**40**	**21**	**39**	**31%**	**71%**	**11%**	**31**						**5.2**	**110**	**131**	**$10**

Siegrist,Kevin

Age: 27 | Th: L | Role: RP | Ht: 6' 5" | Wt: 190 | Type: Pwr xFB
Health: D | PT/Exp: C | Consist: A | LIMA Plan: B | Rand Var: -5 | MM: 1410

Again outpitched xERA in high-lev setup role, but bypassed for closer in favor of RHP with stronger skills. It's not just handedness holding him back: FB% not a fit for 9th, and FpK suggests volatility. Velo also down 2 mph from 2013 debut. Probably safe as your last pitcher, but Rand Var even casts doubt on that.

Yr Tm	W	L	Sv	IP	K	ERA	xERA	WHIP	oOPS	vL	vR	BF/G	Ctl	Dom	Cmd	FpK	SwK	G	L	F	H%	S%	hr/f	GS	APC	DOM%	DIS%	Sv%	LI	RAR	BPV	BPX	R$
12 aa	1	2	0	32	23	3.92	3.37	1.15				16.0	2.4	6.3	2.6						26%	69%								0.4	69	90	-$2
13 STL *	5	2	1	67	86	1.14	0.74	0.84	432	388	479	3.9	3.7	11.5	3.1	61%	10%	39	24	37	20%	89%	3%	0	15			100	0.84	22.7	151	197	$14
14 STL	1	4	0	30	37	6.82	4.17	1.58	818	827	811	3.8	4.7	11.0	2.3	65%	10%	30	20	49	36%	58%	12%	0	16			0	1.32	-11.5	77	92	-$7
15 STL	7	1	6	75	90	2.17	3.83	1.17	605	811	511	3.9	4.1	10.8	2.6	63%	11%	31	21	48	29%	83%	5%	0	16			60	1.22	16.5	94	111	$11
16 STL	6	3	3	62	66	2.77	4.09	1.10	650	690	631	3.7	3.8	9.6	2.5	59%	11%	34	20	46	23%	84%	14%	0	16			38	1.42	10.8	83	99	$7
1st Half	5	2	1	32	34	2.78	3.92	0.96	632	732	588	3.6	3.1	9.5	3.1	60%	10%	33	15	51	20%	84%	15%	0	14			20	1.49	5.6	99	118	$10
2nd Half	1	1	2	29	32	2.76	4.28	1.26	667	651	676	3.8	4.6	9.8	2.1	58%	11%	35	24	41	26%	85%	13%	0	17			67	1.35	5.2	65	78	$5
17 Proj	**4**	**3**	**7**	**58**	**65**	**3.51**	**4.13**	**1.27**	**699**	**750**	**672**	**3.9**	**4.0**	**10.1**	**2.5**	**61%**	**11%**	**33**	**21**	**46**	**29%**	**77%**	**11%**	**0**						**4.9**	**84**	**100**	**$4**

Simmons,Shae

Age: 26 | Th: R | Role: RP | Ht: 5' 9" | Wt: 180 | Type: Pwr GB
Health: F | PT/Exp: F | Consist: B | LIMA Plan: C+ | Rand Var: -5 | MM: 4410

Road back from February 2015 Tommy John surgery not as smooth as he'd hoped. Finally made it back to major league mound in Sept with strong GB tilt intact. Next step is to recapture FpK, Dom that fed speculation about future ninth-inning work. Has to prove he can stay healthy, but keep him on your radar.

Yr Tm	W	L	Sv	IP	K	ERA	xERA	WHIP	oOPS	vL	vR	BF/G	Ctl	Dom	Cmd	FpK	SwK	G	L	F	H%	S%	hr/f	GS	APC	DOM%	DIS%	Sv%	LI	RAR	BPV	BPX	R$
12																																	
13																																	
14 ATL *	1	3	15	46	50	2.73	2.39	1.19	598	489	730	3.8	3.7	9.9	2.6	63%	12%	53	25	23	30%	76%	8%	0	14			100	1.36	5.7	121	144	$7
15																																	
16 ATL	0	0	0	7	3	1.35	3.20	0.90	560	286	909	3.6	0.0	4.1	0.0	52%	7%	62	24	14	28%	83%	0%	0	15			0	0.48	2.3	113	134	-$3
1st Half																																	
2nd Half	0	0	0	7	3	1.35	3.20	0.90	560	286	909	3.6	0.0	4.1	0.0	52%	7%	62	24	14	28%	83%	0%	0	15			0	0.48	2.3	113	135	-$3
17 Proj	**1**	**4**	**2**	**58**	**65**	**3.04**	**3.25**	**1.18**				**3.5**	**3.8**	**10.1**	**2.6**	**56%**	**11%**	**54**	**23**	**24**	**30%**	**74%**	**7%**	**0**						**8.3**	**110**	**131**	**$3**

Skaggs,Tyler

Age: 25 | Th: L | Role: SP | Ht: 6' 5" | Wt: 195 | Type: Pwr
Health: F | PT/Exp: D | Consist: A | LIMA Plan: B | Rand Var: 0 | MM: 2303

3-4, 4.17 ERA in 50 IP at LAA. Return from TJS delayed by April shoulder soreness. When team called him up, seemed due more to desperation than merit. Yet he reeled off 12 1/3 scoreless IP in first two starts and had other flashes of brilliance. Can he sustain Dom? SwK has doubts. But seeds of something good are here.

Yr Tm	W	L	Sv	IP	K	ERA	xERA	WHIP	oOPS	vL	vR	BF/G	Ctl	Dom	Cmd	FpK	SwK	G	L	F	H%	S%	hr/f	GS	APC	DOM%	DIS%	Sv%	LI	RAR	BPV	BPX	R$
12 ARI *	10	9	0	152	122	3.53	3.99	1.28	785	333	863	22.2	2.7	7.3	2.7	52%	10%	34	18	48	30%	76%	13%	6	87	0%	50%			9.0	71	93	$8
13 ARI *	8	13	0	143	127	4.48	4.16	1.40	780	710	799	23.2	3.1	8.0	2.6	62%	9%	45	20	35	34%	68%	17%	7	94	29%	43%			-10.9	82	107	-$2
14 LAA	5	5	0	113	86	4.30	3.59	1.21	674	742	655	25.8	2.4	6.8	2.9	64%	9%	50	19	31	30%	65%	9%	18	95	44%	22%			-7.8	87	103	$0
15																																	
16 LAA *	6	6	0	82	88	3.21	3.31	1.25	750	804	734	19.6	3.4	9.6	2.9	60%	9%	43	23	34	31%	76%	10%	10	88	30%	30%			9.9	103	123	$5
1st Half	0	2	0	15	13	3.20	4.02	1.29				15.1	2.9	8.2	2.8						31%	80%	0%	0						1.8	80	95	-$6
2nd Half	6	4	0	67	74	3.21	3.16	1.24	750	804	734	21.0	3.5	9.9	2.9	60%	9%	43	23	34	31%	76%	10%	10	88	30%	30%			8.1	108	129	$8
17 Proj	**8**	**12**	**0**	**145**	**133**	**3.74**	**3.99**	**1.30**	**701**	**722**	**695**	**22.7**	**3.0**	**8.2**	**2.8**	**62%**	**9%**	**46**	**21**	**34**	**31%**	**74%**	**10%**	**26**						**8.1**	**91**	**108**	**$6**

Smith,Joe

Age: 33 | Th: R | Role: RP | Ht: 6' 2" | Wt: 215 | Type: Pwr GB
Health: D | PT/Exp: C | Consist: B | LIMA Plan: B+ | Rand Var: 0 | MM: 2200

Righted himself after 1st half Dom and Ctl woes, though pitching in lower-leverage situations may have helped. Ability to induce groundballs ever-present, but when hitters did get ball aloft, it cleared fences at crazy rate. May continue to churn out quality innings, but days as anyone's Plan B closer may be over.

Yr Tm	W	L	Sv	IP	K	ERA	xERA	WHIP	oOPS	vL	vR	BF/G	Ctl	Dom	Cmd	FpK	SwK	G	L	F	H%	S%	hr/f	GS	APC	DOM%	DIS%	Sv%	LI	RAR	BPV	BPX	R$
12 CLE	7	4	0	67	53	2.96	3.68	1.16	594	585	600	3.9	3.4	7.1	2.1	57%	9%	58	17	25	26%	76%	8%	0	15			0	1.22	8.8	73	96	$5
13 CLE	6	2	3	63	54	2.29	3.59	1.22	643	698	592	3.7	3.3	7.7	2.3	59%	9%	49	21	30	28%	85%	10%	0	14			38	1.37	12.3	77	101	$6
14 LAA	7	2	15	75	68	1.81	2.67	0.80	491	584	385	3.8	1.8	8.2	4.5	66%	8%	59	15	26	22%	80%	8%	0	15			79	1.25	17.8	136	162	$18
15 LAA	5	5	5	65	57	3.58	3.49	1.27	684	786	587	3.9	2.6	7.9	3.0	63%	8%	52	23	25	32%	72%	9%	0	14			56	1.29	3.1	101	120	$3
16 2 TM	2	5	6	52	40	3.46	4.05	1.25	716	726	708	4.0	3.1	6.9	2.2	66%	9%	50	23	27	27%	79%	20%	0	15			67	0.90	4.7	69	81	$2
1st Half	1	3	6	27	18	4.61	4.62	1.35	716	745	684	4.4	4.0	5.9	1.5	57%	9%	51	22	27	27%	68%	14%	0	16			75	0.90	-1.4	29	35	$3
2nd Half	1	2	0	25	22	2.19	3.47	1.14	714	685	727	3.6	2.2	8.0	3.7	76%	9%	49	23	28	26%	96%	26%	0	14			0	0.91	6.1	113	134	$2
17 Proj	**4**	**4**	**0**	**58**	**49**	**3.47**	**3.78**	**1.25**	**711**	**751**	**678**	**3.9**	**2.7**	**7.5**	**2.8**	**65%**	**9%**	**52**	**21**	**26**	**30%**	**76%**	**15%**	**0**						**5.1**	**93**	**110**	**$1**

Smith,Will

Age: 27 | Th: L | Role: RP | Ht: 6' 5" | Wt: 240 | Type: Pwr
Health: D | PT/Exp: D | Consist: B | LIMA Plan: A | Rand Var: -1 | MM: 3510

Just when Sv opps were within reach, tore knee ligament in spring. After June debut, took about a month to get back to high-SwK, high-Dom self. FpK improved greatly, but failed to bring Ctl along for the ride. Pretend 2016 1st half isn't there and scan down BPV/BPX. If health, managerial whim align, still ... UP: 30 Sv

Yr Tm	W	L	Sv	IP	K	ERA	xERA	WHIP	oOPS	vL	vR	BF/G	Ctl	Dom	Cmd	FpK	SwK	G	L	F	H%	S%	hr/f	GS	APC	DOM%	DIS%	Sv%	LI	RAR	BPV	BPX	R$
12 KC *	10	13	0	179	120	4.56	5.28	1.54	853	897	835	25.2	2.7	6.0	2.2	57%	7%	42	23	35	35%	72%	11%	16	88	6%	50%			-12.0	48	63	-$8
13 KC *	8	5	4	122	123	3.65	3.77	1.24	631	557	684	10.6	2.3	9.0	3.8	63%	16%	43	16	41	32%	74%	19%	1	26	0%	0%	44	1.72	3.3	109	142	$7
14 MIL	1	3	1	66	86	3.70	3.15	1.42	737	516	872	3.7	4.2	11.8	2.8	53%	13%	44	23	33	36%	76%	11%	0	14			17	1.48	0.3	119	142	-$1
15 MIL	7	2	0	63	91	2.70	2.88	1.20	649	786	545	3.5	3.4	12.9	3.8	60%	16%	46	15	39	35%	80%	9%	0	14			0	1.15	9.9	165	196	$6
16 2 NL	2	4	0	40	48	3.35	3.78	1.21	637	627	645	3.2	4.0	10.7	2.7	70%	12%	35	25	40	30%	74%	8%	0	12			0	1.58	4.2	97	116	$0
1st Half	1	2	0	14	10	1.98	4.57	0.95	569	455	656	3.5	3.3	6.6	2.0	72%	7%	27	30	43	20%	83%	6%	0	13			0	1.36	3.7	35	41	$1
2nd Half	1	2	0	27	38	4.05	3.36	1.35	669	700	639	3.0	4.4	12.8	2.9	70%	14%	41	22	37	36%	71%	9%	0	12			0	1.67	0.5	131	156	$0
17 Proj	**3**	**3**	**5**	**58**	**73**	**3.22**	**3.41**	**1.24**	**653**	**626**	**672**	**3.9**	**3.7**	**11.3**	**3.1**	**61%**	**14%**	**43**	**20**	**37**	**32%**	**76%**	**10%**	**0**						**6.9**	**126**	**150**	**$4**

Smyly,Drew

Age: 28 | Th: L | Role: RP | Ht: 6' 3" | Wt: 190 | Type: Pwr xFB
Health: F | PT/Exp: B | Consist: B | LIMA Plan: A | Rand Var: +1 | MM: 2303

Tale of two seasons, each disappointing: In 1H, H%/S%, hr/f conspired to thwart strong skills. After stars aligned for 5 GS in July-Aug (2.25 ERA), results faltered again, due to sagging Dom, SwK. All this murkiness, but underlying skill is still there. Recency bias may suppress his draft price just enough to speculate.

Yr Tm	W	L	Sv	IP	K	ERA	xERA	WHIP	oOPS	vL	vR	BF/G	Ctl	Dom	Cmd	FpK	SwK	G	L	F	H%	S%	hr/f	GS	APC	DOM%	DIS%	Sv%	LI	RAR	BPV	BPX	R$
12 DET *	4	5	0	117	114	4.51	4.39	1.36	732	671	759	16.3	3.1	8.8	2.8	58%	9%	40	19	41	32%	70%	10%	18	76	6%	33%	0	0.83	-7.2	78	102	-$3
13 DET	6	0	2	76	81	2.37	3.06	1.04	601	471	699	4.8	2.0	9.6	4.8	59%	11%	43	18	39	30%	79%	5%	0	20			33	1.12	14.0	139	182	$10
14 2 AL	9	10	0	153	133	3.24	3.79	1.16	688	486	763	22.1	2.5	7.8	3.2	62%	10%	37	20	43	28%	77%	10%	25	93	28%	32%	0	0.73	9.5	89	106	$10
15 TAM	5	2	0	67	77	3.11	3.53	1.17	701	507	751	22.9	2.7	10.4	3.9	61%	12%	37	19	44	30%	82%	14%	12	95	25%	33%			7.0	129	154	$4
16 TAM	7	12	0	175	167	4.88	4.44	1.27	763	724	773	24.6	2.5	8.6	3.4	58%	11%	31	19	49	30%	67%	13%	30	96	27%	33%			-14.9	95	113	$2
1st Half	2	9	0	96	108	5.33	3.90	1.26	778	738	789	25.3	2.2	10.1	4.5	61%	13%	33	19	48	32%	63%	15%	16	99	38%	19%			-13.5	132	158	$0
2nd Half	5	3	0	79	59	4.33	5.13	1.29	744	706	752	23.8	2.8	6.7	2.4	56%	9%	29	20	51	28%	72%	10%	14	94	14%	50%			-1.4	52	61	$3
17 Proj	**9**	**10**	**0**	**174**	**174**	**3.97**	**4.09**	**1.23**	**727**	**607**	**762**	**19.0**	**2.6**	**9.0**	**3.4**	**59%**	**11%**	**34**	**19**	**46**	**30%**	**73%**	**12%**	**33**						**4.7**	**104**	**123**	**$8**

KRISTOPHER OLSON

Snell,Blake

Age: 24	Th: L	Role SP	Health A	LIMA Plan B
Ht: 6' 4"	Wt: 180	Type Pwr	PT/Exp D	Rand Var 0
			Consist F	MM 2503

6-8, 3.54 ERA in 78 IP at TAM. Top prospect brought big strikeout rate with him to majors, but strike-zone mastery? Not so much. Still, SwK is a nice building block, and greater success should follow as H%, LD% normalize. Perhaps not quite "there" yet, but on his way.

Yr Tm	W	L	Sv	IP	K	ERA	xERA	WHIP	oOPS	vL	vR	BF/G	Ctl	Dom	Cmd	FpK	SwK	G	L	F	H%	S%	hr/f	GS	APC	DOM%	DIS%	Sv%	LI	RAR	BPV	BPX	R$
12																																	
13																																	
14																																	
15 a/a	12	4	0	113	119	1.97	2.49	1.12				21.2	3.3	9.4	2.8						28%	85%								27.8	112	133	$18
16 TAM *	9	13	0	152	175	3.69	4.49	1.59	728	656	747	21.6	4.8	10.4	2.2	57%	12%	37	27	36	37%	77%	6%	19	90	26%	37%			9.3	91	108	$2
1st Half	4	8	0	89	97	3.90	4.60	1.60	716	721	713	23.0	4.5	9.8	2.2	57%	7%	40	23	37	37%	76%	3%	5	98	20%	60%			3.2	87	103	$1
2nd Half	5	5	0	63	78	3.41	4.23	1.58	733	616	759	20.1	5.1	11.1	2.2	57%	13%	35	29	36	37%	79%	7%	14	88	29%	29%			6.1	74	88	$3
17 Proj	**11**	**8**	**0**	**160**	**180**	**3.91**	**3.96**	**1.34**	**632**	**562**	**652**	**23.8**	**4.3**	**10.1**	**2.4**	**57%**	**11%**	**40**	**24**	**36**	**32%**	**71%**	**8%**	**28**						**5.4**	**85**	**101**	**$7**

Socolovich,Miguel

Age: 30	Th: R	Role RP	Health A	LIMA Plan C
Ht: 6' 1"	Wt: 205	Type Pwr xGB	PT/Exp D	Rand Var +1
			Consist C	MM 1200

1-0, 2.00 ERA in 18 IP at STL. For second year in a row, vet of seven orgs, Japan and TJS provided smattering of competent IP, albeit with next to nothing at stake. Maybe this year he'll get the chance to put decent GB% to sterner test. If so, celebrate persistence paying off, but don't feel pressure to roster him yourself.

Yr Tm	W	L	Sv	IP	K	ERA	xERA	WHIP	oOPS	vL	vR	BF/G	Ctl	Dom	Cmd	FpK	SwK	G	L	F	H%	S%	hr/f	GS	APC	DOM%	DIS%	Sv%	LI	RAR	BPV	BPX	R$
12 2 TM *	4	0	2	72	58	3.30	3.13	1.13	762	766	756	6.6	3.0	7.3	2.4	57%	7%	40	16	44	25%	75%	14%	0	24			67	0.80	6.4	74	96	$5
13																																	
14 aaa	2	2	3	59	53	3.26	4.75	1.49				5.0	2.6	8.1	3.1						37%	80%								3.6	89	105	-$1
15 STL *	6	3	0	62	55	2.49	2.34	1.14	568	410	673	5.0	3.4	8.0	2.4	67%	11%	48	17	35	27%	78%	3%	0	18			0	0.53	11.3	100	120	$6
16 STL *	3	6	5	70	61	3.45	2.83	1.17	380	589	229	4.6	3.0	7.9	2.7	48%	13%	53	7	40	29%	71%	12%	0	16			63	0.29	6.3	97	115	$5
1st Half	2	5	3	36	30	3.16	3.47	1.36				4.7	3.4	7.5	2.2						32%	76%	0%	0						4.6	87	103	$5
2nd Half	1	1	2	34	31	3.77	2.14	0.96	380	589	229	4.5	2.5	8.4	3.3	48%	13%	53	7	40	24%	62%	12%	0	16			67	0.29	1.7	111	133	$5
17 Proj	**2**	**2**	**0**	**44**	**38**	**3.60**	**4.17**	**1.26**	**704**	**1032**	**463**	**5.0**	**3.0**	**7.9**	**2.6**	**48%**	**13%**	**53**	**7**	**40**	**29%**	**74%**	**9%**	**0**						**3.1**	**92**	**110**	**-$1**

Soria,Joakim

Age: 33	Th: R	Role RP	Health F	LIMA Plan C+
Ht: 6' 2"	Wt: 170	Type Pwr	PT/Exp C	Rand Var +3
			Consist B	MM 3401

Overcame early mechanical struggles as SwK hit new heights in 2nd half, and FpK promised better Ctl. Bypassed when need in 9th arose mostly due to bad luck (H%, hr/f, LD%). Caveats include returning struggles vR after two-year hiatus, ever-present injury risk. Still, many will fail to see closer-worthy 2H skills.

Yr Tm	W	L	Sv	IP	K	ERA	xERA	WHIP	oOPS	vL	vR	BF/G	Ctl	Dom	Cmd	FpK	SwK	G	L	F	H%	S%	hr/f	GS	APC	DOM%	DIS%	Sv%	LI	RAR	BPV	BPX	R$
12																																	
13 TEX	1	0	0	24	28	3.80	3.43	1.35	624	316	943	3.9	5.3	10.6	2.0	56%	10%	52	18	30	29%	73%	12%	0	17			0	1.04	0.2	78	102	-$3
14 2 AL	2	4	18	44	48	3.25	2.93	0.99	605	675	503	3.8	1.2	9.7	8.0	63%	10%	43	22	35	32%	67%	5%	0	14			90	1.12	2.7	164	195	$9
15 2 TM	3	1	24	68	64	2.53	3.54	1.09	628	722	536	3.8	2.5	8.5	3.4	61%	10%	42	23	35	27%	83%	13%	0	16			80	1.35	12.0	105	125	$15
16 KC	5	8	1	67	68	4.05	3.96	1.46	800	669	931	4.2	3.6	9.2	2.5	63%	12%	50	20	30	33%	77%	18%	0	17			13	1.25	1.1	95	113	$0
1st Half	3	3	1	37	33	3.13	4.00	1.23	720	528	916	4.2	3.6	8.0	2.2	58%	10%	52	16	32	27%	79%	13%	0	17			25	0.98	4.9	76	90	$4
2nd Half	2	5	0	29	35	5.22	3.87	1.74	888	826	948	4.2	3.7	10.7	2.9	68%	14%	48	24	28	41%	76%	24%	0	17			0	1.56	-3.7	120	143	-$6
17 Proj	**4**	**6**	**0**	**73**	**75**	**3.44**	**3.69**	**1.30**	**717**	**704**	**731**	**3.8**	**2.9**	**9.3**	**3.2**	**63%**	**12%**	**46**	**21**	**33**	**32%**	**78%**	**13%**	**0**						**6.7**	**112**	**134**	**$2**

Stephenson,Robert

Age: 24	Th: R	Role SP	Health A	LIMA Plan D+
Ht: 6' 3"	Wt: 200	Type Pwr xFB	PT/Exp D	Rand Var +4
			Consist C	MM 0203

2-3, 6.08 ERA in 37 IP at CIN. Was fortunate (19% H%) to escape two April spot starts unscathed, but luck ran out in Sept return. Yes, hr/f may take turn for the better, but that won't cure all if he keeps falling behind hitters and getting hit this hard. Given work that remains, probably best to keep your distance for now.

Yr Tm	W	L	Sv	IP	K	ERA	xERA	WHIP	oOPS	vL	vR	BF/G	Ctl	Dom	Cmd	FpK	SwK	G	L	F	H%	S%	hr/f	GS	APC	DOM%	DIS%	Sv%	LI	RAR	BPV	BPX	R$
12																																	
13 aa	0	2	0	17	16	6.27	6.60	1.98				20.0	7.1	8.9	1.2						36%	71%								-5.0	32	41	-$7
14 aa	7	10	0	137	128	5.24	4.56	1.43				21.5	4.7	8.4	1.8						28%	67%								-25.3	51	61	-$7
15 a/a	8	11	0	134	128	4.84	4.05	1.46				22.9	5.0	8.6	1.7						30%	68%								-14.5	68	82	-$4
16 CIN *	10	12	0	174	139	6.10	5.67	1.62	893	958	824	24.1	5.1	7.2	1.4	53%	10%	34	24	41	30%	66%	19%	8	90	0%	63%			-41.0	22	26	-$16
1st Half	7	5	0	94	64	5.18	4.88	1.51	680	757	563	25.3	4.9	6.2	1.3	42%	8%	34	24	41	27%	69%	12%	2	96	0%	50%			-11.4	25	30	-$7
2nd Half	3	7	0	80	75	7.19	6.58	1.75	985	1064	913	22.8	5.3	8.4	1.6	58%	10%	35	24	41	33%	62%	23%	6	88	0%	67%			-29.6	18	22	-$26
17 Proj	**7**	**10**	**0**	**131**	**117**	**5.34**	**5.24**	**1.55**	**699**	**751**	**651**	**23.1**	**5.0**	**8.0**	**1.6**	**58%**	**10%**	**35**	**24**	**41**	**30%**	**69%**	**12%**	**25**						**-18.4**	**22**	**26**	**-$9**

Stewart,Brock

Age: 25	Th: R	Role SP	Health A	LIMA Plan B
Ht: 6' 3"	Wt: 210	Type xFB	PT/Exp F	Rand Var +1
			Consist F	MM 1203

2-2, 5.79 ERA in 28 IP at LA. Rocketed from High-A to majors by June, but sent back to minors after lackluster debut. Month later, returned to thankless assignment in Coors and hit groove (1.89 ERA in 19 IP, albeit with 1.9 Cmd). Few rough edges to smooth out, but little left to prove in AAA. May just need a chance.

Yr Tm	W	L	Sv	IP	K	ERA	xERA	WHIP	oOPS	vL	vR	BF/G	Ctl	Dom	Cmd	FpK	SwK	G	L	F	H%	S%	hr/f	GS	APC	DOM%	DIS%	Sv%	LI	RAR	BPV	BPX	R$
12																																	
13																																	
14																																	
15																																	
16 LA *	9	6	0	138	123	3.09	3.38	1.17	856	743	924	21.2	1.9	8.0	4.3	60%	11%	42	13	45	31%	76%	18%	5	69	20%	40%	0	0.69	18.7	119	141	$13
1st Half	6	4	0	80	80	2.43	2.67	1.06	1006	1278	801	23.9	1.5	9.0	5.8	57%	16%	50	21	29	31%	79%	25%	1	95	0%	0%			17.3	168	200	$20
2nd Half	3	2	0	58	43	4.00	4.35	1.31	821	600	949	18.4	2.3	6.6	2.9	61%	10%	41	11	49	31%	73%	17%	4	65	25%	50%	0	0.67	1.3	67	79	$3
17 Proj	**8**	**5**	**0**	**131**	**110**	**3.62**	**4.43**	**1.21**	**574**	**458**	**643**	**22.8**	**2.0**	**7.6**	**3.8**	**61%**	**10%**	**41**	**11**	**49**	**31%**	**74%**	**7%**	**23**						**9.2**	**101**	**120**	**$7**

Storen,Drew

Age: 29	Th: R	Role RP	Health C	LIMA Plan C+
Ht: 6' 2"	Wt: 190	Type Pwr	PT/Exp C	Rand Var +5
			Consist A	MM 3310

Lost effectiveness coincided with 2-mph velocity drop, but skills say he deserved better. Left-handed hitters killed him in 1H, helped drive him out of TOR. In SEA, results vL, skills improved, to the point where 2H bears strong resemblance to 2014. If velocity returns, GB rate holds, could return to prominence quickly.

Yr Tm	W	L	Sv	IP	K	ERA	xERA	WHIP	oOPS	vL	vR	BF/G	Ctl	Dom	Cmd	FpK	SwK	G	L	F	H%	S%	hr/f	GS	APC	DOM%	DIS%	Sv%	LI	RAR	BPV	BPX	R$
12 WAS	3	1	4	30	24	2.37	3.31	0.99	496	635	418	3.1	2.4	7.1	3.0	59%	14%	54	18	28	26%	73%	0%	0	11			80	1.21	6.1	96	125	$3
13 WAS	4	2	3	62	58	4.52	3.85	1.36	729	816	668	3.9	2.8	8.5	3.1	59%	10%	41	20	39	33%	69%	10%	0	14			38	1.09	-5.0	96	126	-$2
14 WAS	2	1	11	56	46	1.12	3.23	0.98	540	592	500	3.4	1.8	7.3	4.2	63%	11%	53	15	33	27%	91%	4%	0	12			79	1.21	18.2	116	138	$11
15 WAS	2	2	29	55	67	3.44	3.17	1.11	603	706	482	3.9	2.6	11.0	4.2	62%	13%	38	24	38	32%	70%	8%	0	15			85	1.13	3.6	143	170	$13
16 2 AL	4	3	3	52	48	5.23	3.86	1.34	779	979	667	4.0	2.3	8.4	3.7	65%	11%	49	20	32	33%	63%	14%	0	15			75	0.86	-6.6	116	138	-$2
1st Half	1	3	3	31	30	5.81	4.18	1.55	876	1172	677	4.1	2.6	8.7	3.3	63%	12%	45	21	33	37%	65%	15%	0	15			75	0.85	-6.2	110	131	-$3
2nd Half	3	0	0	21	18	4.35	3.38	1.02	615	523	652	3.8	1.7	7.8	4.5	67%	9%	54	17	29	27%	58%	12%	0	15			0	0.88	-0.4	126	151	$0
17 Proj	**4**	**2**	**5**	**58**	**56**	**3.84**	**3.52**	**1.16**	**660**	**755**	**594**	**3.6**	**2.2**	**8.7**	**3.9**	**64%**	**11%**	**48**	**19**	**33**	**31%**	**68%**	**10%**	**0**						**2.5**	**123**	**146**	**$3**

Strahm,Matt

Age: 25	Th: L	Role RP	Health A	LIMA Plan B+
Ht: 6' 4"	Wt: 180	Type Pwr GB	PT/Exp F	Rand Var -2
			Consist F	MM 2401

2-2, 1.23 ERA in 22 IP at KC. Seemed to have fixed Ctl issues prior to 7/31 callup, though FpK calls that into question. Things did get a bit loose late (7 BB in last 7 1/3 IP), but MLB 12.3 Dom, SwK, futility of RHB hint at significant upside, especially given reports he'll compete for SP role in spring. Keep an eye on him.

Yr Tm	W	L	Sv	IP	K	ERA	xERA	WHIP	oOPS	vL	vR	BF/G	Ctl	Dom	Cmd	FpK	SwK	G	L	F	H%	S%	hr/f	GS	APC	DOM%	DIS%	Sv%	LI	RAR	BPV	BPX	R$
12																																	
13																																	
14																																	
15																																	
16 KC *	5	10	0	124	114	4.14	4.91	1.43	484	641	411	12.3	2.6	8.3	3.2	53%	13%	47	24	29	35%	75%	0%	0	21			0	1.66	0.7	78	93	$0
1st Half	2	7	0	83	62	4.69	5.34	1.46				23.6	2.0	6.8	3.4						35%	71%	0%	0						-5.1	67	80	-$2
2nd Half	3	3	0	42	52	3.05	4.05	1.37	484	641	411	6.2	3.8	11.2	3.0	53%	13%	47	24	29	35%	82%	0%	0	21			0	1.66	5.9	104	124	$4
17 Proj	**5**	**8**	**0**	**102**	**106**	**3.69**	**3.94**	**1.47**	**774**	**1160**	**597**	**14.4**	**3.6**	**9.4**	**2.6**	**53%**	**13%**	**47**	**24**	**29**	**35%**	**79%**	**14%**	**19**						**6.3**	**96**	**114**	**$0**

KRISTOPHER OLSON

Straily,Dan

Age: 28 | Th: R | Role: SP | Ht: 6' 2" | Wt: 220 | Type: Pwr xFB
Health: A | PT/Exp: B | Consist: B | LIMA Plan: C+ | Rand Var: -2 | MM: 0203

Found surprising success in 2H when he made strides with FpK, Ctl, but got plenty of help from S%, H% (including 21% for year vL). FB tendencies led to NL-high 31 HR allowed, but luckily, 24 were solo shots. Issues with long ball aren't going away, and he'll be hard-pressed to post another sub-4.00 ERA in 2017.

Yr	Tm	W	L	Sv	IP	K	ERA	xERA	WHIP	oOPS	vL	vR	BF/G	Ctl	Dom	Cmd	FpK	SwK	G	L	F	H%	S%	hr/f	GS	APC	DOM%	DIS%	Sv%	LI	RAR	BPV	BPX	R$
12	OAK *	11	8	0	191	190	3.15	2.94	1.11	803	1047	640	23.5	2.7	8.9	3.3	51%	10%	30	15	55	28%	75%	17%	7	96	29%	29%			20.5	107	139	$21
13	OAK *	13	9	0	184	151	3.48	3.26	1.22	666	711	617	23.2	3.2	7.4	2.3	60%	12%	36	20	44	28%	74%	8%	27	91	22%	33%			8.7	76	99	$12
14	2 TM *	8	11	0	170	147	5.75	5.34	1.53	832	765	906	21.8	3.9	7.8	2.0	47%	12%	35	16	49	32%	65%	13%	8	63	13%	25%	0	0.60	-42.2	44	52	-$15
15	HOU *	10	10	0	139	113	5.31	5.66	1.57	747	796	681	23.5	2.1	7.3	3.4	47%	10%	42	21	38	38%	67%	10%	3	73	0%	67%	0	0.64	-23.2	75	89	-$10
16	CIN	14	8	0	191	162	3.76	4.72	1.19	712	645	763	23.3	3.4	7.6	2.2	61%	11%	32	20	48	25%	75%	12%	31	90	16%	16%	0	0.77	10.1	54	65	$15
1st Half		4	5	0	95	78	4.34	4.79	1.22	675	653	700	22.1	4.1	7.4	1.8	58%	10%	35	22	43	24%	67%	11%	15	89	13%	20%	0	0.76	-1.8	36	43	$8
2nd Half		10	3	0	96	84	3.19	4.65	1.16	747	631	805	24.6	2.8	7.9	2.8	64%	11%	29	18	53	25%	84%	13%	16	92	19%	13%			11.9	73	87	$22
17	Proj	**10**	**11**	**0**	**174**	**148**	**4.35**	**4.73**	**1.33**	**779**	**749**	**804**	**22.9**	**3.1**	**7.6**	**2.5**	**59%**	**11%**	**33**	**18**	**49**	**30%**	**72%**	**11%**	**32**						**-3.3**	**66**	**78**	**$3**

Strasburg,Stephen

Age: 28 | Th: R | Role: SP | Ht: 6' 4" | Wt: 235 | Type: Pwr
Health: D | PT/Exp: A | Consist: A | LIMA Plan: B | Rand Var: 0 | MM: 4503

Virtually unhittable for much of year, but posted 7.36 ERA over last seven starts. 49% H%, 45% S% deserve much of the blame, though sore elbow, which limited him to one start from mid-Aug on, and FB% jump likely played roles as well. 1H highlights massive upside, but you certainly can't bank on 200 IP.

Yr	Tm	W	L	Sv	IP	K	ERA	xERA	WHIP	oOPS	vL	vR	BF/G	Ctl	Dom	Cmd	FpK	SwK	G	L	F	H%	S%	hr/f	GS	APC	DOM%	DIS%	Sv%	LI	RAR	BPV	BPX	R$
12	WAS	15	6	0	159	197	3.16	2.96	1.15	649	714	578	23.3	2.7	11.1	4.1	62%	12%	44	23	33	32%	76%	11%	28	93	46%	21%			16.7	149	194	$19
13	WAS	8	9	0	183	191	3.00	2.98	1.05	587	629	550	24.4	2.8	9.4	3.4	59%	11%	52	17	31	27%	74%	11%	30	95	43%	10%			19.5	125	163	$19
14	WAS	14	11	0	215	242	3.14	2.78	1.12	672	653	687	25.5	1.8	10.1	5.6	65%	12%	46	23	31	32%	76%	13%	34	97	47%	9%			16.0	158	188	$20
15	WAS	11	7	0	127	155	3.46	2.94	1.11	653	572	737	22.7	1.8	11.0	6.0	66%	12%	42	23	34	33%	72%	12%	23	89	39%	22%			7.8	168	200	$13
16	WAS	15	4	0	148	183	3.60	3.30	1.10	637	615	658	24.9	2.7	11.2	4.2	65%	12%	40	21	39	31%	70%	11%	24	99	58%	13%			10.8	146	174	$17
1st Half		11	0	0	100	123	2.71	3.05	1.03	595	557	629	26.3	2.5	11.1	4.4	65%	12%	44	20	36	29%	78%	12%	15	104	67%	13%			18.2	154	183	$26
2nd Half		4	4	0	48	60	5.44	3.80	1.25	719	715	722	22.7	3.0	11.3	3.8	67%	11%	31	23	46	34%	56%	9%	9	92	44%	11%			-7.4	130	156	-$1
17	Proj	**14**	**8**	**0**	**160**	**193**	**3.48**	**3.18**	**1.12**	**658**	**633**	**683**	**22.9**	**2.2**	**10.9**	**4.9**	**65%**	**12%**	**40**	**22**	**37**	**32%**	**72%**	**11%**	**27**						**14.0**	**154**	**183**	**$17**

Street,Huston

Age: 33 | Th: R | Role: RP | Ht: 6' 0" | Wt: 205 | Type: Pwr FB
Health: F | PT/Exp: B | Consist: C | LIMA Plan: D+ | Rand Var: +3 | MM: 0220

Late April oblique strain cost him a month, and later, knee injury ended season two months early. Skills weren't closer-worthy even when he was healthy, taking turn for the worse across the board. RHB had their way with him, and with 88 mph "heat," can't count on SwK, Dom rebound. A very risky investment.

Yr	Tm	W	L	Sv	IP	K	ERA	xERA	WHIP	oOPS	vL	vR	BF/G	Ctl	Dom	Cmd	FpK	SwK	G	L	F	H%	S%	hr/f	GS	APC	DOM%	DIS%	Sv%	LI	RAR	BPV	BPX	R$
12	SD	2	1	23	39	47	1.85	2.76	0.72	425	384	461	3.6	2.5	10.8	4.3	63%	14%	42	20	38	19%	77%	6%	0	15			96	1.19	10.4	147	191	$15
13	SD	2	5	33	57	46	2.70	3.93	1.02	691	689	693	3.8	2.2	7.3	3.3	64%	12%	30	22	48	22%	89%	16%	0	15			94	1.22	8.1	79	104	$17
14	2 TM	2	2	41	59	57	1.37	3.36	0.94	521	482	561	3.8	2.1	8.6	4.1	64%	13%	36	20	43	26%	90%	6%	0	15			93	1.45	17.4	112	134	$23
15	LAA	3	3	40	62	57	3.18	4.13	1.16	641	758	522	4.1	2.9	8.2	2.9	56%	13%	34	20	45	27%	77%	9%	0	17			89	1.56	6.0	82	98	$19
16	LAA	3	2	9	22	14	6.45	6.28	1.93	975	675	1240	4.0	4.8	5.6	1.2	61%	9%	36	22	42	35%	71%	15%	0	15			75	1.02	-6.2	-15	-18	-$3
1st Half		3	1	7	16	10	4.96	6.27	1.84	826	697	951	4.0	5.5	5.5	1.0	57%	9%	40	22	38	35%	72%	5%	0	15			78	1.25	-1.6	-32	-38	$0
2nd Half		0	1	2	6	4	10.50	6.31	2.17	1337	606	1842	4.1	3.0	6.0	2.0	72%	8%	26	22	52	35%	67%	33%	0	16			67	0.39	-4.7	31	37	-$10
17	Proj	**5**	**3**	**11**	**58**	**47**	**3.67**	**4.67**	**1.33**	**734**	**694**	**772**	**3.9**	**3.3**	**7.3**	**2.2**	**60%**	**10%**	**37**	**21**	**42**	**29%**	**77%**	**10%**	**0**						**3.7**	**56**	**67**	**$5**

Strickland,Hunter

Age: 28 | Th: R | Role: RP | Ht: 6' 5" | Wt: 200 | Type: Pwr
Health: A | PT/Exp: D | Consist: C | LIMA Plan: A | Rand Var: -1 | MM: 3310

Increased sinker usage led to higher GB%, but SwK, FpK, Ctl all wavered. Furthermore, was less effective vL, as H% corrected, and Cmd dipped to 1.4. Still extremely tough vR, and looks like a solid LIMA option, though maybe not quite as attractive as he was heading into last year.

Yr	Tm	W	L	Sv	IP	K	ERA	xERA	WHIP	oOPS	vL	vR	BF/G	Ctl	Dom	Cmd	FpK	SwK	G	L	F	H%	S%	hr/f	GS	APC	DOM%	DIS%	Sv%	LI	RAR	BPV	BPX	R$
12	aa	2	2	1	41	25	5.53	6.19	1.71				8.1	3.0	5.5	1.8						36%	69%								-7.7	29	38	-$8
13																																		
14	SF *	2	1	12	43	48	1.98	2.10	0.90	440	500	400	3.4	0.9	10.0	11.2	84%	13%	56	25	19	30%	81%	0%	0	11			100	0.45	9.2	289	345	$9
15	SF *	4	4	5	73	70	2.28	1.63	0.87	543	509	562	3.8	1.6	8.6	5.3	65%	15%	40	20	40	25%	76%	8%	0	13			71	1.28	15.1	164	196	$12
16	SF	3	3	3	61	57	3.10	3.72	1.13	589	741	515	3.5	2.8	8.4	3.0	57%	12%	47	22	30	29%	74%	8%	0	14			38	1.29	8.2	101	120	$5
1st Half		3	1	1	31	29	2.90	3.76	1.10	586	748	522	3.2	2.9	8.4	2.9	59%	12%	46	20	33	27%	75%	7%	0	13			25	1.33	4.9	98	116	$6
2nd Half		0	2	2	30	28	3.30	3.68	1.17	592	736	506	3.8	2.7	8.4	3.1	54%	12%	48	25	27	30%	73%	9%	0	16			50	1.24	3.3	105	125	$3
17	Proj	**3**	**3**	**8**	**63**	**59**	**3.27**	**3.67**	**1.12**	**617**	**699**	**573**	**3.8**	**2.5**	**8.4**	**3.4**	**60%**	**13%**	**44**	**22**	**34**	**29%**	**72%**	**8%**	**0**						**7.1**	**106**	**127**	**$6**

Stripling,Ross

Age: 27 | Th: R | Role: RP | Ht: 6' 3" | Wt: 210 | Type: GB
Health: A | PT/Exp: D | Consist: B | LIMA Plan: C | Rand Var: 0 | MM: 1101

5-9, 3.96 ERA in 100 IP at LA. Injuries paved way for rotation spot early on, fired 7 1/3 no-hit innings in debut, but overall numbers in 14 GS rather uninspiring (4.52 ERA, 6.5 Dom). GB tilt, solid Ctl could make him viable back-end SP, but lack of swing-and-miss stuff leaves him with minimal upside.

Yr	Tm	W	L	Sv	IP	K	ERA	xERA	WHIP	oOPS	vL	vR	BF/G	Ctl	Dom	Cmd	FpK	SwK	G	L	F	H%	S%	hr/f	GS	APC	DOM%	DIS%	Sv%	LI	RAR	BPV	BPX	R$
12																																		
13	aa	6	4	1	94	70	3.51	4.03	1.36				18.7	1.8	6.7	3.6						35%	74%								4.2	100	130	$1
14																																		
15	aa	3	6	0	67	44	5.20	4.91	1.42				22.0	2.6	5.9	2.3						32%	65%								-10.3	45	54	-$6
16	LA *	5	11	0	117	87	4.08	4.12	1.31	709	656	752	17.8	2.5	6.7	2.7	64%	8%	51	20	29	31%	71%	11%	14	72	14%	50%	0	0.99	1.6	70	84	$1
1st Half		2	4	0	55	40	4.20	3.61	1.33	717	598	815	18.9	3.1	6.6	2.1	59%	8%	49	23	28	31%	68%	8%	8	85	25%	50%	0	0.97	-0.1	73	87	$0
2nd Half		3	7	0	62	47	3.96	4.56	1.29	702	707	697	17.0	1.9	6.8	3.6	68%	9%	52	18	30	31%	75%	14%	6	63	0%	50%	0	1.01	1.7	76	91	$2
17	Proj	**5**	**9**	**0**	**102**	**72**	**4.21**	**4.17**	**1.36**	**768**	**715**	**810**	**19.2**	**2.4**	**6.4**	**2.7**	**65%**	**9%**	**51**	**20**	**29**	**32%**	**71%**	**11%**	**15**						**-0.3**	**81**	**97**	**-$1**

Stroman,Marcus

Age: 26 | Th: R | Role: SP | Ht: 5' 9" | Wt: 185 | Type: Pwr xGB
Health: F | PT/Exp: C | Consist: A | LIMA Plan: A | Rand Var: +3 | MM: 4205

Breakout buzz quieted during rough 1H, though 2H likely to get hype train rolling again. Sinker usage dropped every month, but maintained elite GB% while generating more whiffs, and if not for crazy high hr/f, might've hit double-digit R$. ERA/xERA gap shows he deserved better, and 2H xERA reveals lofty ceiling.

Yr	Tm	W	L	Sv	IP	K	ERA	xERA	WHIP	oOPS	vL	vR	BF/G	Ctl	Dom	Cmd	FpK	SwK	G	L	F	H%	S%	hr/f	GS	APC	DOM%	DIS%	Sv%	LI	RAR	BPV	BPX	R$
12																																		
13	aa	9	5	0	112	114	3.70	3.81	1.20				22.5	2.1	9.2	4.4						32%	74%								2.3	117	153	$6
14	TOR *	13	10	1	166	151	3.70	3.23	1.20	633	646	620	20.3	2.0	8.1	4.0	58%	9%	54	18	28	33%	69%	6%	20	80	45%	35%	100	0.84	0.8	124	147	$9
15	TOR	4	0	0	27	18	1.67	3.13	0.96	554	514	646	25.8	2.0	6.0	3.0	66%	8%	64	18	18	24%	88%	14%	4	93	75%	25%			7.6	96	114	$2
16	TOR	9	10	0	204	166	4.37	3.55	1.29	720	741	698	26.7	2.4	7.3	3.1	61%	10%	60	20	20	31%	68%	17%	32	97	34%	31%			-4.5	106	125	$5
1st Half		6	4	0	108	77	5.08	3.96	1.39	758	808	707	27.2	2.7	6.4	2.4	59%	9%	59	20	21	32%	64%	14%	17	97	29%	35%			-11.9	81	96	-$1
2nd Half		3	6	0	96	89	3.56	3.11	1.18	675	660	689	26.1	2.1	8.3	4.0	63%	11%	61	19	20	31%	74%	20%	15	97	40%	27%			7.4	134	160	$11
17	Proj	**13**	**9**	**0**	**189**	**168**	**3.74**	**3.35**	**1.23**	**685**	**698**	**672**	**23.2**	**2.2**	**8.0**	**3.7**	**60%**	**10%**	**58**	**19**	**23**	**32%**	**71%**	**13%**	**33**						**10.5**	**122**	**145**	**$12**

Strop,Pedro

Age: 32 | Th: R | Role: RP | Ht: 6' 0" | Wt: 160 | Type: Pwr xGB
Health: D | PT/Exp: C | Consist: A | LIMA Plan: A | Rand Var: 0 | MM: 5500

Threw sliders on just over half his offerings, and why not, when it induces 25% SwK? FpK remains shaky, so probably won't duplicate career-best Ctl, and H% likely to rise as well. But elite Dom/GB combo well-established, and RHBs don't stand a chance, so he remains a prime LIMA option for the back of your staff.

Yr	Tm	W	L	Sv	IP	K	ERA	xERA	WHIP	oOPS	vL	vR	BF/G	Ctl	Dom	Cmd	FpK	SwK	G	L	F	H%	S%	hr/f	GS	APC	DOM%	DIS%	Sv%	LI	RAR	BPV	BPX	R$
12	BAL	5	2	3	66	58	2.44	3.72	1.34	613	674	556	4.0	5.0	7.9	1.6	53%	11%	64	16	20	28%	82%	6%	0	16			30	1.25	12.9	48	63	$5
13	2 TM	2	5	1	57	66	4.55	3.24	1.24	663	653	671	3.8	4.1	10.4	2.5	55%	13%	49	26	26	29%	64%	14%	0	15			25	1.25	-4.9	103	135	-$2
14	CHC	2	4	2	61	71	2.21	2.65	1.07	535	621	478	3.8	3.7	10.5	2.8	56%	16%	55	24	21	27%	79%	7%	0	14			33	1.12	11.5	122	145	$6
15	CHC	2	6	3	68	81	2.91	2.98	1.00	538	641	475	3.6	3.8	10.7	2.8	58%	17%	51	20	29	23%	73%	11%	0	14			60	1.30	8.8	118	141	$7
16	CHC	2	2	0	47	60	2.85	2.58	0.89	517	608	470	3.5	2.9	11.4	4.0	53%	16%	58	16	25	24%	71%	15%	0	14			0	0.98	7.8	164	195	$4
1st Half		1	2	0	31	43	2.90	2.31	0.87	515	600	479	3.5	2.6	12.5	4.8	55%	17%	58	16	25	25%	71%	18%	0	14			0	1.12	4.9	190	227	$6
2nd Half		1	0	0	16	17	2.76	3.15	0.92	521	612	437	3.5	3.3	9.4	2.8	48%	15%	59	15	26	22%	71%	10%	0	13			0	0.70	2.9	116	139	$1
17	Proj	**2**	**3**	**0**	**58**	**67**	**2.97**	**2.93**	**1.01**	**548**	**636**	**490**	**3.4**	**3.5**	**10.5**	**3.0**	**54%**	**16%**	**56**	**19**	**25**	**25%**	**72%**	**12%**	**0**						**8.7**	**128**	**153**	**$4**

BRIAN RUDD

Suarez,Albert

Age: 27	Th: R	Role RP	Health A	LIMA Plan D+
Ht: 6' 2"	Wt: 185	Type	PT/Exp D	Rand Var +1
			Consist B	MM 0000

3-5, 4.29 ERA in 84 IP at SF. Held his own splitting time between SP and RP, though skills were uninspiring in both roles. In 1st half, compensated for lack of Dom by keeping ball down and limiting walks, but both regressed in 2nd half. Mediocre Cmd, BPV histories offer no upside. Pass.

Yr Tm	W	L	Sv	IP	K	ERA	xERA	WHIP	oOPS	vL	vR	BF/G	Ctl	Dom	Cmd	FpK	SwK	G	L	F	H%	S%	hr/f	GS	APC	DOM%	DIS%	Sv%	LI	RAR	BPV	BPX	R$
12																																	
13																																	
14 aa	3	6	0	56	26	5.14	5.94	1.75				23.2	3.1	4.3	1.4						36%	70%								-9.7	24	28	-$9
15 aa	11	9	0	163	99	4.00	4.36	1.36				25.2	2.4	5.5	2.3						31%	73%								-0.9	53	63	$2
16 SF *	7	8	0	130	85	4.65	4.47	1.40	809	765	848	17.6	2.9	5.9	2.1	60%	9%	48	21	31	31%	68%	13%	12	62	8%	50%	0	0.72	-7.4	50	59	-$2
1st Half	4	3	0	73	45	3.66	3.49	1.22	726	768	692	17.4	2.4	5.5	2.3	58%	9%	52	19	29	28%	71%	12%	6	63	17%	17%	0	0.72	4.8	64	76	$5
2nd Half	3	5	0	56	40	5.94	5.74	1.62	912	762	1088	17.9	3.4	6.4	1.9	61%	9%	43	23	34	34%	65%	15%	6	62	0%	83%	0	0.72	-12.2	34	40	-$12
17 Proj	**3**	**3**	**0**	**44**	**27**	**4.49**	**4.71**	**1.40**	**838**	**766**	**910**	**14.1**	**2.9**	**5.6**	**1.9**	**60%**	**9%**	**47**	**21**	**32**	**30%**	**71%**	**12%**	**5**						**-1.6**	**48**	**57**	**-$4**

Syndergaard,Noah

Age: 24	Th: R	Role SP	Health A	LIMA Plan C
Ht: 6' 5"	Wt: 200	Type Pwr	PT/Exp C	Rand Var 0
			Consist B	MM 4405

Latest '16 ADP of the Mets' trio despite consensus he was the most skilled. So there! 1H skills elite, but gave owners a scare with mid-year bone spurs in elbow, followed by arm fatigue. Holding runners (48 SB allowed) is his only weakness. SwK, FpK, Ctl took step back in 2H, but overall skills still excellent. Your anchor now.

Yr Tm	W	L	Sv	IP	K	ERA	xERA	WHIP	oOPS	vL	vR	BF/G	Ctl	Dom	Cmd	FpK	SwK	G	L	F	H%	S%	hr/f	GS	APC	DOM%	DIS%	Sv%	LI	RAR	BPV	BPX	R$
12																																	
13 aa	6	1	0	54	63	3.04	3.42	1.09				19.2	1.8	10.4	5.7						31%	79%								5.5	151	197	$4
14 aaa	9	7	0	133	129	3.62	3.88	1.33				21.2	2.3	8.7	3.7						35%	73%								2.0	114	136	$3
15 NYM *	12	7	0	180	195	2.99	2.87	1.03	645	691	601	23.8	1.9	9.8	5.1	64%	13%	46	20	34	29%	76%	14%	24	99	42%	17%			21.5	145	173	$23
16 NYM	14	9	0	184	218	2.60	2.90	1.15	639	713	581	24.0	2.1	10.7	5.1	64%	15%	51	22	27	34%	79%	9%	30	95	50%	10%	0	0.78	36.1	164	195	$25
1st Half	9	3	0	101	123	2.41	2.58	1.06	603	700	522	23.6	1.3	11.0	8.2	67%	16%	53	21	26	35%	78%	8%	16	89	63%	6%	0	0.79	22.2	192	229	$31
2nd Half	5	6	0	83	95	2.83	3.31	1.26	681	730	646	24.4	3.0	10.3	3.4	60%	13%	49	22	29	34%	80%	10%	14	102	36%	14%			13.9	131	156	$19
17 Proj	**14**	**7**	**0**	**196**	**220**	**2.93**	**3.09**	**1.13**	**645**	**703**	**596**	**24.0**	**2.2**	**10.1**	**4.6**	**63%**	**14%**	**49**	**21**	**30**	**32%**	**77%**	**11%**	**30**						**30.4**	**149**	**178**	**$23**

Taillon,Jameson

Age: 25	Th: R	Role SP	Health B	LIMA Plan B
Ht: 6' 5"	Wt: 240	Type GB	PT/Exp D	Rand Var +1
			Consist F	MM 3205

5-4, 3.38 ERA in 104 IP at PIT. Excellent debut, especially considering he was coming off two lost seasons following TJ surgery. Lot of positive signs, from stellar Ctl to GB tilt to 9.6 Cmd vR. Top prospect pedigree, 2nd half rise in SwK and FpK hint at potential for higher Dom, so rise to ace status could happen quickly.

Yr Tm	W	L	Sv	IP	K	ERA	xERA	WHIP	oOPS	vL	vR	BF/G	Ctl	Dom	Cmd	FpK	SwK	G	L	F	H%	S%	hr/f	GS	APC	DOM%	DIS%	Sv%	LI	RAR	BPV	BPX	R$
12 aa	3	0	0	17	15	1.83	1.00	0.77				20.4	0.5	7.9	16.0						27%	74%								4.6	398	519	$1
13 a/a	5	10	0	147	117	4.16	3.94	1.39				23.9	3.0	7.2	2.4						33%	70%								-5.3	79	103	-$2
14																																	
15																																	
16 PIT *	9	6	0	166	133	3.19	3.15	1.08	702	731	671	23.1	1.3	7.2	5.6	62%	9%	52	20	27	29%	73%	15%	18	86	11%	28%			20.4	142	168	$17
1st Half	6	3	0	90	69	3.18	3.06	1.09	779	837	663	23.4	1.2	6.9	5.9	58%	7%	52	26	22	30%	72%	21%	5	86	20%	40%			11.1	151	180	$18
2nd Half	3	3	0	76	64	3.20	3.45	1.07	674	675	673	23.4	1.4	7.6	5.3	63%	9%	53	18	29	29%	75%	14%	13	86	8%	23%			9.3	129	154	$15
17 Proj	**11**	**9**	**0**	**181**	**146**	**3.58**	**3.64**	**1.20**	**692**	**738**	**637**	**23.4**	**2.0**	**7.2**	**3.7**	**61%**	**9%**	**52**	**21**	**27**	**31%**	**72%**	**10%**	**31**						**13.6**	**107**	**128**	**$12**

Tanaka,Masahiro

Age: 28	Th: R	Role SP	Health D	LIMA Plan C
Ht: 6' 3"	Wt: 215	Type	PT/Exp A	Rand Var 0
			Consist A	MM 3205

Struggles with long ball in 2015 may have prompted change in approach, as he threw way more sinkers for most of year. Dom, SwK, and xERA dropped off for second straight season, and Sept forearm strain a reminder of health risk. But while we can't count on ace level production, overall skills are worth investing in.

Yr Tm	W	L	Sv	IP	K	ERA	xERA	WHIP	oOPS	vL	vR	BF/G	Ctl	Dom	Cmd	FpK	SwK	G	L	F	H%	S%	hr/f	GS	APC	DOM%	DIS%	Sv%	LI	RAR	BPV	BPX	R$
12 for	10	4	0	173	160	2.33	2.97	1.13				31.1	1.2	8.3	6.8						34%	80%								36.0	185	242	$23
13 for	22	0	1	199	164	1.52	2.41	1.03				29.5	1.7	7.4	4.4						29%	88%								57.7	132	173	$38
14 NYY	13	5	0	136	141	2.77	2.76	1.06	657	632	687	27.1	1.4	9.3	6.7	62%	14%	47	24	29	31%	79%	14%	20	100	50%	5%			16.3	155	185	$16
15 NYY	12	7	0	154	139	3.51	3.34	0.99	674	697	654	25.4	1.6	8.1	5.1	63%	12%	47	19	34	25%	73%	17%	24	95	50%	21%			8.6	129	153	$17
16 NYY	14	4	0	200	165	3.07	3.68	1.08	645	655	635	26.0	1.6	7.4	4.6	64%	11%	48	21	31	28%	76%	12%	31	95	35%	16%			27.7	116	138	$24
1st Half	5	2	0	105	82	3.35	3.63	1.06	622	576	659	26.3	1.6	7.1	4.3	62%	12%	51	21	27	28%	71%	10%	16	95	38%	13%			10.8	112	133	$20
2nd Half	9	2	0	95	83	2.75	3.74	1.09	670	727	603	25.6	1.6	7.9	4.9	67%	11%	45	20	35	29%	82%	13%	15	94	33%	20%			16.9	121	144	$28
17 Proj	**13**	**7**	**0**	**189**	**167**	**3.36**	**3.47**	**1.08**	**678**	**692**	**663**	**25.7**	**1.6**	**8.0**	**5.1**	**64%**	**12%**	**47**	**21**	**32**	**29%**	**74%**	**14%**	**29**						**19.2**	**127**	**151**	**$19**

Tazawa,Junichi

Age: 31	Th: R	Role RP	Health B	LIMA Plan C+
Ht: 5' 11"	Wt: 180	Type Pwr	PT/Exp D	Rand Var +2
			Consist A	MM 2400

In peak form early on, with 1.37 ERA, 11.4 Dom, and 16% SwK through first 21 appearances. But posted 6.00 ERA rest of the way, and landed on DL in July with shoulder strain. H%, hr/f certainly factored into second straight poor 2nd half, and still looks like respectable source of Ks, but far from a lock for strong ratios.

Yr Tm	W	L	Sv	IP	K	ERA	xERA	WHIP	oOPS	vL	vR	BF/G	Ctl	Dom	Cmd	FpK	SwK	G	L	F	H%	S%	hr/f	GS	APC	DOM%	DIS%	Sv%	LI	RAR	BPV	BPX	R$
12 BOS *	4	3	5	86	89	2.56	3.10	1.23	558	519	583	5.6	2.5	9.3	3.7	67%	15%	49	24	27	34%	79%	3%	0	18			63	0.82	15.5	126	165	$9
13 BOS	5	4	0	68	72	3.16	3.31	1.20	744	790	704	4.0	1.6	9.5	6.0	62%	13%	34	27	39	34%	79%	12%	0	15			0	1.09	5.9	140	182	$3
14 BOS	4	3	0	63	64	2.86	3.42	1.19	660	615	702	3.7	2.4	9.1	3.8	60%	12%	37	28	36	32%	79%	8%	0	14			0	1.34	6.9	114	136	$3
15 BOS	2	7	3	59	56	4.14	3.81	1.33	751	808	710	4.0	2.0	8.6	4.3	64%	12%	40	19	40	35%	70%	7%	0	16			30	1.17	-1.3	119	141	-$1
16 BOS	3	2	0	50	54	4.17	3.81	1.23	730	628	807	3.9	2.5	9.8	3.9	62%	13%	40	19	41	31%	73%	16%	0	16			0	1.15	0.1	126	149	$0
1st Half	1	1	0	32	37	3.62	3.59	1.05	649	479	780	3.7	2.2	10.3	4.6	64%	14%	36	17	47	28%	72%	13%	0	15			0	1.14	2.3	139	166	$2
2nd Half	2	1	0	17	17	5.19	4.24	1.56	867	883	850	4.3	3.1	8.8	2.8	59%	13%	45	22	33	35%	74%	22%	0	17			0	1.16	-2.1	98	117	-$5
17 Proj	**3**	**3**	**0**	**58**	**59**	**3.88**	**3.83**	**1.31**	**737**	**718**	**751**	**4.0**	**2.4**	**9.2**	**3.7**	**62%**	**13%**	**41**	**21**	**38**	**34%**	**74%**	**12%**	**0**						**2.2**	**117**	**140**	**-$1**

Teheran,Julio

Age: 26	Th: R	Role SP	Health B	LIMA Plan C
Ht: 6' 2"	Wt: 205	Type FB	PT/Exp A	Rand Var -1
			Consist A	MM 1205

Combination of Ctl rebound, career-best Dom, and H% fortune added up to excellent 1H, but predictably, proved unsustainable. Despite WHIP fluctuations, skill set has been pretty consistent. Dominance vR, durability, history of stellar Cmd provide a pretty safe floor, but probably best to use 2H as baseline.

Yr Tm	W	L	Sv	IP	K	ERA	xERA	WHIP	oOPS	vL	vR	BF/G	Ctl	Dom	Cmd	FpK	SwK	G	L	F	H%	S%	hr/f	GS	APC	DOM%	DIS%	Sv%	LI	RAR	BPV	BPX	R$
12 ATL *	7	9	0	137	92	5.55	5.16	1.49	467	250	579	21.1	2.7	6.0	2.2	52%	8%	22	33	44	33%	64%	0%	1	50	100%	0%	0	0.71	-26.0	44	58	-$12
13 ATL	14	8	0	186	170	3.20	3.67	1.17	700	823	580	25.8	2.2	8.2	3.8	65%	11%	38	21	41	30%	78%	10%	30	96	27%	23%			15.3	105	137	$16
14 ATL	14	13	0	221	186	2.89	3.73	1.08	639	687	587	26.8	2.1	7.6	3.6	60%	11%	35	21	44	28%	77%	8%	33	99	55%	21%			23.2	93	111	$22
15 ATL	11	8	0	201	171	4.04	4.15	1.31	737	893	583	25.5	3.3	7.7	2.3	57%	11%	40	24	36	29%	73%	13%	33	99	36%	27%			-1.9	68	81	$6
16 ATL	7	10	0	188	167	3.21	3.95	1.05	650	756	564	25.3	2.0	8.0	4.1	62%	11%	39	19	42	27%	74%	10%	30	99	43%	23%			22.8	108	128	$20
1st Half	3	7	0	113	105	2.72	3.76	0.93	594	670	528	26.1	1.9	8.4	4.4	62%	11%	40	17	44	24%	79%	11%	17	103	53%	18%			20.5	117	140	$27
2nd Half	4	3	0	75	62	3.94	4.24	1.23	729	888	610	24.2	2.0	7.4	3.6	61%	11%	38	22	40	31%	70%	8%	13	94	31%	31%			2.3	95	113	$8
17 Proj	**10**	**9**	**0**	**189**	**161**	**3.75**	**4.14**	**1.19**	**704**	**826**	**596**	**25.3**	**2.4**	**7.7**	**3.2**	**61%**	**11%**	**38**	**21**	**40**	**29%**	**72%**	**10%**	**30**						**10.2**	**90**	**108**	**$11**

Thompson,Jake

Age: 23	Th: R	Role SP	Health A	LIMA Plan D+
Ht: 6' 4"	Wt: 235	Type GB	PT/Exp D	Rand Var +1
			Consist A	MM 0103

3-6, 5.70 ERA in 54 IP at PHI. Took a step back, as Dom slipped during first taste of AAA, and even further in majors. League-worst FpK led to higher than expected Ctl, was awful vL (0.8 Cmd), and not exactly dominant vR, either (1.7 Cmd). Still time for him to develop, but an extremely risky investment for 2017.

Yr Tm	W	L	Sv	IP	K	ERA	xERA	WHIP	oOPS	vL	vR	BF/G	Ctl	Dom	Cmd	FpK	SwK	G	L	F	H%	S%	hr/f	GS	APC	DOM%	DIS%	Sv%	LI	RAR	BPV	BPX	R$
12																																	
13																																	
14 aa	4	1	0	47	45	3.60	3.58	1.36				21.7	4.1	8.7	2.1						31%	74%								0.8	84	100	-$1
15 aa	11	7	0	133	102	4.13	4.05	1.34				23.0	2.7	6.9	2.5						32%	70%								-2.7	72	86	$2
16 PHI *	14	11	0	183	110	4.22	4.48	1.38	852	902	798	24.8	3.4	5.4	1.6	49%	7%	46	17	37	28%	73%	16%	10	92	10%	60%			-0.7	32	38	$4
1st Half	6	5	0	98	62	3.99	4.79	1.41				25.8	2.9	5.7	1.9						30%	76%	0%	0						2.4	38	45	$4
2nd Half	8	6	0	86	48	4.48	4.12	1.34	852	902	798	23.8	3.9	5.1	1.3	49%	7%	46	17	37	26%	70%	16%	10	92	10%	60%			-3.1	28	33	$3
17 Proj	**9**	**11**	**0**	**145**	**103**	**4.46**	**4.83**	**1.40**	**751**	**795**	**705**	**23.7**	**3.3**	**6.4**	**1.9**	**49%**	**7%**	**46**	**17**	**37**	**29%**	**72%**	**11%**	**26**						**-4.8**	**49**	**58**	**-$1**

BRIAN RUDD

Thornburg,Tyler

Age: 28	Th: R	Role RP	Health D	LIMA Plan C	
Ht: 6' 0"	Wt: 185	Type Pwr FB	PT/Exp D	Rand Var -5	
			Consist F	MM 1430	

Excelled in first full season as RP, and locked down closer role for final two months. Added velocity helped fuel Dom spike, including improvements vL. Had luck on his side in 2H, and with high FB%, shaky Ctl, and short track record, he's no sure thing. But ability to miss bats looks legit; he could evolve into top-tier closer.

Yr	Tm	W	L	Sv	IP	K	ERA	xERA	WHIP	oOPS	vL	vR	BF/G	Ctl	Dom	Cmd	FpK	SwK	G	L	F	H%	S%	hr/f	GS	APC	DOM%	DIS%	Sv%	LI	RAR	BPV	BPX	R$
12	MIL *	10	4	0	135	116	4.17	4.45	1.37	922	757	1071	19.5	3.1	7.8	2.5	53%	8%	42	20	38	31%	73%	32%	3	48	0%	67%	0	0.42	-2.5	66	86	$1
13	MIL *	3	10	0	141	121	4.43	4.64	1.50	575	479	684	18.5	3.6	7.7	2.2	60%	7%	36	24	39	34%	72%	1%	7	59	29%	29%	0	0.52	-9.8	64	84	-$7
14	MIL	3	1	0	30	28	4.25	4.91	1.52	670	458	808	4.9	6.4	8.5	1.3	54%	11%	36	19	45	29%	70%	3%	0	19			0	0.94	-1.9	-5	-6	-$3
15	MIL *	2	9	0	123	78	5.49	6.49	1.68	723	741	709	13.5	3.7	5.7	1.6	61%	10%	35	24	41	33%	72%	17%	0	27			0	0.73	-23.2	7	8	-$17
16	MIL	8	5	13	67	90	2.15	3.24	0.94	541	413	635	3.9	3.4	12.1	3.6	56%	13%	32	23	45	24%	82%	9%	0	17			62	1.51	16.9	137	163	$17
1st Half		3	2	2	32	44	2.84	3.02	0.92	567	353	762	3.8	3.1	12.5	4.0	56%	13%	38	20	42	22%	79%	17%	0	17			40	1.33	5.3	156	187	$10
2nd Half		5	3	11	35	46	1.53	3.43	0.96	516	482	537	4.1	3.6	11.7	3.3	57%	13%	28	25	47	26%	85%	3%	0	17			69	1.69	11.6	120	143	$23
17	Proj	4	4	32	58	60	3.48	4.11	1.25	696	624	751	4.4	3.5	9.4	2.7	59%	11%	34	23	43	30%	76%	10%	0						5.1	87	104	$14

Tillman,Chris

Age: 29	Th: R	Role SP	Health B	LIMA Plan C	
Ht: 6' 5"	Wt: 210	Type Pwr	PT/Exp A	Rand Var 0	
			Consist A	MM 1103	

Started strong, with 2.87 ERA, 8.7 Dom in 14 GS, but things quickly unraveled—whiffs fell back to career norms as velocity diminished from April to Oct, taking Cmd from passable to poor, and leading to 4.64 ERA over final 16 GS. Wins and ERA are tempting targets but xERA, FpK and SwK hold a scarier downside.

Yr	Tm	W	L	Sv	IP	K	ERA	xERA	WHIP	oOPS	vL	vR	BF/G	Ctl	Dom	Cmd	FpK	SwK	G	L	F	H%	S%	hr/f	GS	APC	DOM%	DIS%	Sv%	LI	RAR	BPV	BPX	R$
12	BAL *	17	12	0	179	143	4.02	3.95	1.31	639	601	701	23.0	2.9	7.2	2.4	55%	9%	35	21	44	30%	72%	11%	15	96	27%	27%			-0.1	70	91	$8
13	BAL	16	7	0	206	179	3.71	3.87	1.22	730	744	711	25.6	3.0	7.8	2.6	57%	9%	39	22	40	27%	76%	14%	33	105	24%	18%			4.0	77	101	$13
14	BAL	13	6	0	207	150	3.34	4.21	1.23	671	670	672	25.6	2.9	6.5	2.3	58%	8%	41	20	39	28%	76%	8%	34	100	29%	26%			10.2	59	70	$11
15	BAL	11	11	0	173	120	4.99	4.58	1.39	763	698	828	23.9	3.3	6.2	1.9	58%	8%	43	21	35	30%	65%	10%	31	95	16%	32%			-22.0	43	52	-$5
16	BAL	16	6	0	172	140	3.77	4.45	1.28	732	728	735	23.8	3.5	7.3	2.1	57%	9%	41	22	36	28%	74%	10%	30	98	30%	33%			9.0	58	68	$11
1st Half		10	2	0	99	91	3.71	4.16	1.25	736	798	673	24.1	3.3	8.2	2.5	56%	10%	42	20	38	28%	75%	13%	17	99	41%	35%			5.8	80	95	$15
2nd Half		6	4	0	73	49	3.84	4.88	1.33	725	606	803	23.5	3.7	6.1	1.6	58%	8%	41	25	34	28%	72%	7%	13	97	15%	31%			3.1	27	33	$6
17	Proj	14	8	0	174	134	4.03	4.56	1.31	729	693	764	24.2	3.3	6.9	2.1	57%	8%	41	22	37	29%	72%	10%	30						3.4	54	64	$6

Tolleson,Shawn

Age: 29	Th: R	Role RP	Health F	LIMA Plan C	
Ht: 6' 2"	Wt: 215	Type Pwr	PT/Exp C	Rand Var +5	
			Consist B	MM 2300	

Removed from closer role when sporting 10.12 ERA in late May, sent to AAA in July, where year ended due to back strain. Drop in Dom, struggles vL were his own doing, but H%/S%/hr/f show he was about as unlucky as could be. Good bet to bounce back a bit, but reclaiming 9th inning duties will be a challenge.

Yr	Tm	W	L	Sv	IP	K	ERA	xERA	WHIP	oOPS	vL	vR	BF/G	Ctl	Dom	Cmd	FpK	SwK	G	L	F	H%	S%	hr/f	GS	APC	DOM%	DIS%	Sv%	LI	RAR	BPV	BPX	R$
12	LA *	3	2	5	60	67	3.75	3.19	1.19	698	988	485	4.1	3.7	10.1	2.7	67%	12%	38	22	40	28%	72%	10%	0	16			100	0.65	1.9	99	129	$3
13	LA	0	0	0	0	0	0.00	0.00	0.00		0	1000	2.0	0.0	0.0	0.0						0%	100%	0%	0	11			0	0.70	0.0	-22	-29	-$5
14	TEX	3	1	0	72	69	2.76	3.80	1.17	659	643	672	4.6	3.5	8.7	2.5	56%	10%	40	18	42	26%	84%	12%	0	18			0	0.75	8.6	79	94	$4
15	TEX	6	4	35	72	76	2.99	3.40	1.15	675	705	638	4.1	2.1	9.5	4.5	66%	11%	42	21	37	31%	80%	12%	0	16			95	1.24	8.7	133	159	$20
16	TEX	2	2	11	36	29	7.68	4.36	1.73	904	954	867	4.5	2.5	7.2	2.9	61%	9%	52	22	26	38%	58%	24%	0	18			73	0.95	-15.6	92	110	-$5
1st Half		2	2	11	29	24	5.90	4.23	1.48	830	975	713	4.2	2.5	7.4	3.0	64%	10%	47	23	30	33%	65%	21%	0	17			73	1.06	-6.1	92	110	-$2
2nd Half		0	0	0	7	5	14.73	4.90	2.73	1129	875	1280	5.9	2.5	6.1	2.5	51%	6%	65	21	15	51%	44%	40%	0	21			0	0.49	-9.5	87	104	-$19
17	Proj	3	2	0	58	56	3.90	3.96	1.26	720	806	648	4.2	3.0	8.7	2.9	62%	10%	43	20	37	30%	75%	15%	0						2.1	97	115	$0

Tomlin,Josh

Age: 32	Th: R	Role SP	Health F	LIMA Plan B+	
Ht: 6' 1"	Wt: 195	Type Con	PT/Exp C	Rand Var +2	
			Consist A	MM 1103	

On the surface, strong 1H was followed by 2H collapse, but xERA shows skills were virtually unchanged. Has league-best Ctl working for him, but career-high GB% wasn't enough to slow HR barrage. Overdue for at least a little hr/f regression, but with velocity, SwK, and Dom headed in wrong direction, he's playing with fire.

Yr	Tm	W	L	Sv	IP	K	ERA	xERA	WHIP	oOPS	vL	vR	BF/G	Ctl	Dom	Cmd	FpK	SwK	G	L	F	H%	S%	hr/f	GS	APC	DOM%	DIS%	Sv%	LI	RAR	BPV	BPX	R$
12	CLE	5	8	0	103	56	6.36	4.82	1.46	860	945	768	21.5	2.2	4.9	2.2	64%	8%	42	21	37	31%	59%	13%	16	77	19%	63%	0	0.89	-29.9	49	64	-$13
13	CLE *	2	0	0	23	11	2.52	1.91	0.92	500	0	667	14.3	0.0	4.4	0.0	67%	8%	38	0	63	28%	69%	0%	0	36			0	0.23	3.8	0	0	$0
14	CLE *	8	10	0	144	119	4.24	4.54	1.24	781	718	848	18.8	1.6	7.4	4.8	68%	10%	37	27	36	31%	71%	15%	16	69	13%	38%	0	0.94	-8.9	100	119	$2
15	CLE *	8	4	0	90	71	3.79	4.11	1.08	642	448	838	23.3	1.0	7.1	6.8	66%	10%	38	16	46	28%	74%	15%	10	95	50%	10%			1.9	136	162	$6
16	CLE	13	9	0	174	118	4.40	4.22	1.19	778	685	845	24.2	1.0	6.1	5.9	68%	8%	44	21	35	29%	71%	18%	29	87	17%	28%	0	0.74	-4.4	104	123	$8
1st Half		9	1	0	95	64	3.21	4.20	1.09	742	731	748	25.9	0.9	6.0	6.4	65%	7%	41	22	37	27%	82%	17%	15	93	20%	20%			11.5	102	122	$18
2nd Half		4	8	0	79	54	5.83	4.24	1.31	820	640	970	22.5	1.1	6.2	5.4	71%	9%	47	20	33	31%	60%	19%	14	81	14%	36%	0	0.71	-16.0	106	126	-$5
17	Proj	12	11	0	174	125	4.46	4.11	1.20	776	668	871	23.9	1.2	6.4	5.2	67%	9%	41	21	38	29%	70%	16%	32						-5.9	102	122	$6

Tonkin,Michael

Age: 27	Th: R	Role RP	Health A	LIMA Plan C+	
Ht: 6' 7"	Wt: 220	Type Pwr FB	PT/Exp D	Rand Var +5	
			Consist C	MM 2301	

Newfound ability to miss bats lasted most of year, but he hit a wall and recorded 8% SwK, 11.45 ERA over final 12 games. Likely to bounce back and at least provide some Ks, but drop in GB%, ongoing struggles vL (13 HR in 209 career AB) are concerns, and will likely prevent him from taking on more prominent role.

Yr	Tm	W	L	Sv	IP	K	ERA	xERA	WHIP	oOPS	vL	vR	BF/G	Ctl	Dom	Cmd	FpK	SwK	G	L	F	H%	S%	hr/f	GS	APC	DOM%	DIS%	Sv%	LI	RAR	BPV	BPX	R$
12																																		
13	MIN *	2	4	21	68	64	3.45	3.49	1.30	528	490	579	4.6	2.5	8.4	3.4	55%	7%	41	24	35	34%	73%	0%	0	19			84	0.26	3.5	112	146	$8
14	MIN *	3	4	10	64	52	4.00	4.44	1.44	822	1024	708	4.3	2.6	7.3	2.8	60%	8%	43	25	32	35%	73%	11%	0	13			83	0.88	-2.1	81	97	$1
15	MIN *	2	1	14	64	54	2.26	2.88	1.05	699	1011	485	4.2	2.0	7.6	3.7	65%	7%	57	11	31	27%	84%	18%	0	14			82	0.68	13.5	106	126	$11
16	MIN	3	2	0	72	80	5.02	4.05	1.45	831	1061	710	4.8	3.0	10.0	3.3	60%	11%	34	26	40	35%	70%	16%	0	20			0	0.76	-7.4	111	132	-$4
1st Half		2	2	0	39	48	4.15	3.67	1.33	801	1067	680	4.7	3.0	11.1	3.7	63%	12%	33	26	42	35%	74%	14%	0	21			0	0.63	0.2	129	154	$0
2nd Half		1	0	0	33	32	6.06	4.52	1.59	866	1054	748	5.0	3.0	8.8	2.9	57%	11%	36	27	38	36%	67%	18%	0	19			0	0.91	-7.5	90	108	-$9
17	Proj	3	2	0	73	70	4.14	4.03	1.31	728	904	632	4.5	2.6	8.7	3.3	60%	11%	42	20	38	32%	72%	12%	0						0.4	105	125	-$1

Torres,Carlos

Age: 34	Th: R	Role RP	Health A	LIMA Plan B	
Ht: 6' 2"	Wt: 185	Type Pwr	PT/Exp C	Rand Var -4	
			Consist A	MM 2201	

Had 5.4 Ctl, 54% FpK through end of May, but settled down after, posting 2.2 Ctl, 64% FpK rest of way. Still missing enough bats to be decent source of Ks, but can't count on H% and S% cooperating again. xERA history, age, and inconsistent Ctl indicate another sub-3.00 ERA is a long shot.

Yr	Tm	W	L	Sv	IP	K	ERA	xERA	WHIP	oOPS	vL	vR	BF/G	Ctl	Dom	Cmd	FpK	SwK	G	L	F	H%	S%	hr/f	GS	APC	DOM%	DIS%	Sv%	LI	RAR	BPV	BPX	R$
12	COL *	10	7	0	114	83	5.20	4.97	1.59	723	660	768	11.2	4.2	6.5	1.5	57%	8%	44	27	29	33%	68%	5%	0	29			0	0.60	-16.6	45	58	-$9
13	NYM *	10	9	0	158	126	3.60	4.02	1.22	701	678	716	14.2	2.0	7.2	3.6	67%	11%	44	20	37	30%	76%	16%	9	40	11%	22%	0	1.04	5.3	84	109	$8
14	NYM	8	6	2	97	96	3.06	3.57	1.31	715	680	734	5.5	3.5	8.9	2.5	61%	12%	47	17	36	31%	81%	12%	1	22	100%	0%	40	1.07	8.1	90	107	$5
15	NYM	5	6	0	58	48	4.68	3.88	1.37	743	750	739	4.1	2.8	7.5	2.7	61%	10%	48	23	29	33%	66%	10%	0	16			0	1.09	-5.1	85	101	-$3
16	MIL	3	3	2	82	78	2.73	3.94	1.15	655	632	673	4.7	3.3	8.5	2.6	60%	12%	45	21	35	27%	80%	10%	0	18			40	1.05	14.8	88	104	$7
1st Half		1	1	2	41	43	3.29	4.21	1.29	719	755	688	5.0	4.2	9.4	2.3	56%	13%	39	22	39	29%	79%	12%	0	21			100	0.81	4.5	74	88	$5
2nd Half		2	2	0	41	35	2.18	3.68	1.02	588	515	654	4.4	2.4	7.6	3.2	64%	11%	50	19	31	26%	82%	9%	0	16			0	1.28	10.3	101	120	$9
17	Proj	4	4	0	73	65	3.63	3.96	1.24	694	664	715	4.8	3.1	8.1	2.6	61%	11%	46	21	33	29%	73%	10%	0						5.0	86	102	$2

Treinen,Blake

Age: 29	Th: R	Role RP	Health A	LIMA Plan B	
Ht: 6' 4"	Wt: 215	Type Pwr xGB	PT/Exp C	Rand Var -4	
			Consist A	MM 3300	

Seems to like bullpen role, as he proved previous year's Dom gains were no fluke, and nudged up already-elite GB%. Six IBB spiked Ctl (from 3.4 to 4.2), and more sliders held lefties in check. Unlikely to repeat, but xERA has been stable for two years running, and provides good idea of what to expect when S% corrects.

Yr	Tm	W	L	Sv	IP	K	ERA	xERA	WHIP	oOPS	vL	vR	BF/G	Ctl	Dom	Cmd	FpK	SwK	G	L	F	H%	S%	hr/f	GS	APC	DOM%	DIS%	Sv%	LI	RAR	BPV	BPX	R$
12																																		
13	aa	6	7	0	119	68	4.60	5.14	1.55				24.7	2.5	5.1	2.0						34%	71%								-10.7	43	56	-$8
14	WAS *	10	5	0	131	79	3.46	4.10	1.40	678	798	564	17.9	2.3	5.4	2.4	57%	8%	59	22	19	33%	75%	3%	7	49	0%	43%	0	0.56	4.5	69	82	$1
15	WAS	2	5	0	68	65	3.86	3.25	1.39	692	934	493	4.7	4.3	8.6	2.0	59%	11%	62	23	15	32%	72%	15%	0	17			0	0.93	0.9	81	96	-$2
16	WAS	4	1	1	67	63	2.28	3.32	1.22	648	737	600	3.6	4.2	8.5	2.0	57%	11%	66	14	20	27%	84%	15%	0	14			33	1.23	15.8	84	100	$6
1st Half		4	1	0	34	32	2.12	3.43	1.26	665	699	647	3.6	4.2	8.5	2.0	57%	11%	66	12	22	27%	88%	16%	0	14			0	1.10	8.7	82	98	$7
2nd Half		0	0	1	33	31	2.45	3.21	1.18	629	777	551	3.6	4.1	8.5	2.1	57%	11%	66	17	17	26%	81%	14%	0	13			33	1.35	7.1	86	102	$5
17	Proj	3	2	0	58	55	3.26	3.46	1.34	691	862	574	4.1	3.9	8.5	2.2	57%	11%	64	19	18	31%	77%	13%	0						6.7	89	106	$0

BRIAN RUDD

Triggs,Andrew

Age: 28	Th: R	Role: RP	Health: A	LIMA Plan: B+
Ht: 6' 4"	Wt: 220	Type: GB	PT/Exp: D	Rand Var: +3
			Consist: C	MM: 3201

1-1, 4.31 ERA in 56 IP at OAK. "Meh" debut from unheralded prospect who dealt with calf, back issues. Before you move on: Dom, GB% fueled skill set that exploded in 2nd half, and though FpK is skeptical of Ctl, he's held it in minors. With rotation gig, he's a shiny object at the dollar store.

Yr Tm	W	L	Sv	IP	K	ERA	xERA	WHIP	oOPS	vL	vR	BF/G	Ctl	Dom	Cmd	FpK	SwK	G	L	F	H%	S%	hr/f	GS	APC	DOM%	DIS%	Sv%	LI	RAR	BPV	BPX	R$
12																																	
13																																	
14 a/a	4	3	20	62	30	3.42	3.77	1.29				5.8	2.3	4.3	1.8						29%	74%								2.4	48	57	$7
15 aa	0	2	17	61	55	1.47	2.26	1.09				5.5	1.8	8.0	4.4						32%	85%								18.8	148	177	$12
16 OAK *	3	2	2	75	71	4.31	3.71	1.28	699	759	648	7.7	2.3	8.5	3.8	54%	10%	51	24	25	34%	66%	12%	6	39	17%	33%	67	0.46	-1.1	114	135	$0
1st Half	2	1	2	39	38	5.61	5.00	1.53	861	817	895	6.5	3.2	8.8	2.8	57%	10%	56	18	26	37%	64%	20%	1	32	0%	100%	67	0.34	-6.8	80	95	-$3
2nd Half	1	1	0	36	33	2.89	2.29	1.02	559	711	421	9.8	1.3	8.2	6.5	52%	11%	46	29	25	31%	70%	5%	5	46	20%	20%	0	0.61	5.7	186	222	$4
17 Proj	**3**	**4**	**0**	**116**	**100**	**3.52**	**3.50**	**1.18**	**677**	**743**	**619**	**6.6**	**2.0**	**7.7**	**3.9**	**54%**	**10%**	**50**	**24**	**25**	**31%**	**72%**	**11%**	**0**						**9.6**	**114**	**135**	**$5**

Uehara,Koji

Age: 42	Th: R	Role: RP	Health: F	LIMA Plan: A
Ht: 6' 1"	Wt: 190	Type: Pwr xFB	PT/Exp: C	Rand Var: +1
			Consist: B	MM: 4510

Rough June inflated ERA in another year of eye-popping skills, injury woes; this time a pec strain in July. SwK/FpK slipped, but they still lock in elite Cmd, while xFB profile keeps WHIP in check despite HR risk. Closer-worthy BPV if he gets another shot, but age, health are major obstacles.

Yr Tm	W	L	Sv	IP	K	ERA	xERA	WHIP	oOPS	vL	vR	BF/G	Ctl	Dom	Cmd	FpK	SwK	G	L	F	H%	S%	hr/f	GS	APC	DOM%	DIS%	Sv%	LI	RAR	BPV	BPX	R$
12 TEX	0	0	1	36	43	1.75	2.74	0.64	466	545	369	3.5	0.8	10.8	14.3	67%	19%	33	17	51	21%	84%	10%	0	14			100	0.66	10.1	184	240	$5
13 BOS	4	1	21	74	101	1.09	2.24	0.57	400	338	466	3.6	1.1	12.2	11.2	70%	20%	40	11	48	20%	89%	7%	0	14			88	1.34	25.5	209	272	$27
14 BOS	6	5	26	64	80	2.52	2.70	0.92	629	613	650	3.9	1.1	11.2	10.0	64%	20%	32	23	45	29%	84%	14%	0	15			84	1.48	9.7	181	216	$18
15 BOS	2	4	25	40	47	2.23	3.54	0.92	562	507	614	3.7	2.0	10.5	5.2	73%	20%	27	17	56	27%	79%	5%	0	15			93	1.38	8.6	140	166	$14
16 BOS	2	3	7	47	63	3.45	3.31	0.96	657	478	812	3.7	2.1	12.1	5.7	65%	16%	21	20	58	27%	73%	13%	0	15			78	0.94	4.3	159	189	$6
1st Half	2	3	2	31	45	4.60	3.42	1.05	692	597	765	3.8	2.6	12.9	5.0	64%	17%	18	19	63	29%	63%	14%	0	16			50	1.02	-1.6	159	189	$5
2nd Half	0	0	5	16	18	1.15	3.06	0.77	580	287	959	3.4	1.1	10.3	9.0	67%	14%	28	22	50	23%	100%	11%	0	15			100	0.77	5.9	161	192	$7
17 Proj	**2**	**2**	**2**	**44**	**54**	**3.38**	**3.27**	**0.94**	**668**	**531**	**811**	**3.6**	**1.6**	**11.1**	**6.9**	**68%**	**17%**	**27**	**20**	**53**	**27%**	**74%**	**14%**	**0**						**4.4**	**162**	**193**	**$3**

Urena,Jose

Age: 25	Th: R	Role: RP	Health: B	LIMA Plan: D+
Ht: 6' 2"	Wt: 195	Type:	PT/Exp: D	Rand Var: +3
			Consist: A	MM: 0001

4-9, 6.13 ERA in 84 IP at MIA. Rode AAA shuttle in first half; odometer likely to keep rolling. Soft-tossing Dom stifles upside, while FpK/Ctl cement shaky Cmd. Low S% didn't help, but xERA says there's still plenty of work to do. Stronger 2nd half says not to cross him off yet, but have the pen ready.

Yr Tm	W	L	Sv	IP	K	ERA	xERA	WHIP	oOPS	vL	vR	BF/G	Ctl	Dom	Cmd	FpK	SwK	G	L	F	H%	S%	hr/f	GS	APC	DOM%	DIS%	Sv%	LI	RAR	BPV	BPX	R$
12																																	
13																																	
14 aa	13	8	0	162	100	3.78	3.82	1.24				25.3	1.6	5.6	3.5						31%	71%								-0.7	87	104	$5
15 MIA *	7	6	0	129	61	4.32	4.75	1.52	818	871	777	18.1	3.2	4.3	1.4	58%	9%	48	20	32	32%	72%	7%	9	50	0%	56%	0	0.59	-5.7	31	37	-$6
16 MIA *	7	12	1	132	91	5.49	4.76	1.48	800	864	725	14.2	3.6	6.2	1.7	56%	9%	48	22	30	31%	64%	13%	12	51	8%	50%	33	0.90	-21.2	42	50	-$8
1st Half	2	3	1	50	31	6.50	5.58	1.72	860	758	948	9.5	4.8	5.6	1.2	53%	11%	49	25	25	33%	62%	11%	0	25			33	0.98	-14.3	25	30	-$14
2nd Half	5	9	0	82	60	4.87	4.25	1.33	778	895	629	21.2	2.8	6.6	2.3	57%	8%	47	21	32	30%	65%	14%	12	87	8%	50%			-6.8	57	68	-$4
17 Proj	**7**	**8**	**0**	**116**	**70**	**4.82**	**4.83**	**1.47**	**781**	**813**	**751**	**16.3**	**3.2**	**5.4**	**1.7**	**56%**	**9%**	**48**	**22**	**30**	**32%**	**68%**	**9%**	**19**						**-9.0**	**38**	**46**	**-$6**

Urias,Julio

Age: 20	Th: L	Role: SP	Health: A	LIMA Plan: B
Ht: 6' 0"	Wt: 160	Type: Pwr	PT/Exp: D	Rand Var: -1
			Consist: A	MM: 3303

5-2, 3.39 ERA in 77 IP at LA. Premier arm didn't disappoint at 19, as Cmd sub-indicators (FpK, SwK) showed he could hang. S%, hr/f were both on his side though, as xERA wasn't fully convinced. Limited IP suggests kid gloves might stay on for 2017, but once they come off? Look out.

Yr Tm	W	L	Sv	IP	K	ERA	xERA	WHIP	oOPS	vL	vR	BF/G	Ctl	Dom	Cmd	FpK	SwK	G	L	F	H%	S%	hr/f	GS	APC	DOM%	DIS%	Sv%	LI	RAR	BPV	BPX	R$
12																																	
13																																	
14																																	
15 a/a	3	5	0	73	72	4.04	3.14	1.19				19.4	2.2	9.0	4.0						33%	65%								-0.7	128	153	$0
16 LA *	10	3	0	122	128	2.71	3.27	1.25	728	740	725	17.1	2.8	9.4	3.4	63%	11%	44	27	30	33%	80%	8%	15	79	13%	33%	0	0.73	22.3	117	139	$13
1st Half	5	3	0	74	81	2.49	2.70	1.09	771	653	811	19.3	2.7	9.8	3.7	63%	10%	41	22	37	29%	81%	13%	7	87	14%	29%			15.5	125	149	$17
2nd Half	5	0	0	48	47	3.04	4.16	1.49	695	822	665	14.8	3.0	8.9	3.0	62%	11%	45	30	25	38%	78%	3%	8	73	13%	38%	0	0.72	6.8	107	128	$6
17 Proj	**10**	**5**	**0**	**145**	**147**	**3.32**	**3.48**	**1.17**	**632**	**686**	**617**	**21.3**	**2.6**	**9.1**	**3.5**	**63%**	**11%**	**44**	**27**	**29**	**31%**	**73%**	**10%**	**27**						**15.5**	**115**	**137**	**$12**

Vargas,Jason

Age: 34	Th: L	Role: SP	Health: F	LIMA Plan: C
Ht: 6' 0"	Wt: 215	Type:	PT/Exp: C	Rand Var: 0
			Consist: B	MM: 1103

0-0, 2.25 ERA in 12 IP at KC. Returned from 14-month TJS hiatus with SwK surge and a career-high BPV! Gotta love small samples. History of subpar xERA, Dom now comes with workload, health risks in mid-30s. Ctl makes him serviceable if recent hr/f holds, but don't expect late-career surge.

Yr Tm	W	L	Sv	IP	K	ERA	xERA	WHIP	oOPS	vL	vR	BF/G	Ctl	Dom	Cmd	FpK	SwK	G	L	F	H%	S%	hr/f	GS	APC	DOM%	DIS%	Sv%	LI	RAR	BPV	BPX	R$
12 SEA	14	11	0	217	141	3.85	4.37	1.18	714	705	717	26.9	2.3	5.8	2.6	60%	9%	40	19	40	26%	74%	13%	33	102	33%	36%			4.4	62	80	$13
13 LAA	9	8	0	150	109	4.02	4.30	1.39	758	789	747	26.8	2.8	6.5	2.4	61%	9%	40	21	38	32%	74%	9%	24	99	33%	42%			-2.9	61	80	$0
14 KC	11	10	0	187	128	3.71	4.13	1.27	713	661	731	26.3	2.0	6.2	3.1	63%	9%	38	23	39	31%	74%	8%	30	100	27%	30%			0.8	74	88	$5
15 KC	5	2	0	43	27	3.98	4.71	1.35	740	809	712	20.3	2.5	5.7	2.3	65%	8%	41	19	40	30%	74%	9%	9	76	0%	22%			-0.1	53	63	-$2
16 KC *	0	2	0	28	25	5.52	6.09	1.39	552	1333	430	16.8	1.3	7.9	5.9	64%	11%	36	15	48	34%	68%	6%	3	70	33%	0%			-4.6	98	117	-$5
1st Half																																	
2nd Half	0	2	0	28	25	5.52	6.09	1.39	552	1333	430	16.8	1.3	7.9	5.9	64%	11%	36	15	48	34%	68%	6%	3	70	33%	0%			-4.6	98	117	-$5
17 Proj	**7**	**7**	**0**	**131**	**96**	**4.35**	**4.56**	**1.37**	**782**	**798**	**776**	**21.4**	**2.4**	**6.6**	**2.8**	**62%**	**9%**	**40**	**21**	**39**	**32%**	**72%**	**11%**	**26**						**-2.6**	**74**	**88**	**-$1**

Velasquez,Vincent

Age: 25	Th: R	Role: RP	Health: B	LIMA Plan: A
Ht: 6' 3"	Wt: 203	Type: Pwr FB	PT/Exp: D	Rand Var: +3
			Consist: B	MM: 2503

Turned heads with 16-K gem on 4/14, but endured rough 2nd half and Sept shutdown. PRO: Top-shelf Dom came with full SwK support; RandVar points to improvement if H%, hr/f regress. CON: Ctl risk augmented by 2nd half FpK; low GB%; lasted 7+ IP in just 3 starts. Growth stock, but a few hurdles left.

Yr Tm	W	L	Sv	IP	K	ERA	xERA	WHIP	oOPS	vL	vR	BF/G	Ctl	Dom	Cmd	FpK	SwK	G	L	F	H%	S%	hr/f	GS	APC	DOM%	DIS%	Sv%	LI	RAR	BPV	BPX	R$
12																																	
13																																	
14																																	
15 HOU *	5	1	0	89	97	3.54	3.01	1.20	720	644	808	12.7	3.4	9.9	2.9	61%	11%	31	22	47	30%	72%	7%	7	51	14%	0%	0	0.64	4.6	108	129	$4
16 PHI	8	6	0	131	152	4.12	3.81	1.33	765	780	750	23.0	3.1	10.4	3.4	60%	12%	35	24	41	33%	75%	15%	24	92	17%	13%			1.1	117	140	$5
1st Half	7	2	0	73	87	3.34	3.61	1.24	690	700	681	21.4	3.0	10.8	3.6	63%	13%	37	22	42	33%	78%	12%	14	86	21%	14%			7.6	128	153	$12
2nd Half	1	4	0	58	65	5.09	4.05	1.44	857	870	841	25.1	3.2	10.0	3.1	56%	11%	32	27	41	34%	71%	19%	10	101	10%	10%			-6.5	104	123	-$5
17 Proj	**9**	**6**	**0**	**174**	**196**	**4.04**	**3.87**	**1.25**	**720**	**697**	**744**	**17.4**	**3.3**	**10.1**	**3.1**	**60%**	**11%**	**35**	**22**	**43**	**31%**	**72%**	**12%**	**30**						**3.2**	**108**	**128**	**$8**

Ventura,Yordano

Age: 26	Th: R	Role: SP	Health: B	LIMA Plan: C
Ht: 5' 11"	Wt: 140	Type: Pwr GB	PT/Exp: A	Rand Var: 0
			Consist: B	MM: 1205

Lighting up radar guns can only get him so far, as Ctl issues worsened with plunging FpK. Recovered SwK dip in 2nd half, so Dom should rebound, while GB% limits HR risk. Owns better skills, but xERA says this disaster was well-deserved. Waiting for that breakout? You'll be disappointed.

Yr Tm	W	L	Sv	IP	K	ERA	xERA	WHIP	oOPS	vL	vR	BF/G	Ctl	Dom	Cmd	FpK	SwK	G	L	F	H%	S%	hr/f	GS	APC	DOM%	DIS%	Sv%	LI	RAR	BPV	BPX	R$
12 aa	1	2	0	29	21	5.20	2.98	1.28				20.1	3.8	6.5	1.7						28%	56%								-4.3	74	97	-$4
13 KC *	8	7	0	150	140	3.71	3.76	1.37	693	687	700	21.7	3.5	8.4	2.4	53%	8%	49	15	36	33%	74%	18%	3	81	0%	33%			2.9	86	112	$3
14 KC	14	10	0	183	159	3.20	3.78	1.30	669	642	705	25.2	3.4	7.8	2.3	61%	11%	48	21	31	30%	77%	8%	30	96	30%	17%	0	0.77	12.3	75	89	$10
15 KC	13	8	0	163	156	4.08	3.56	1.30	698	734	658	24.8	3.2	8.6	2.7	60%	11%	52	21	27	31%	70%	11%	28	95	32%	36%			-2.3	98	117	$6
16 KC	11	12	0	186	144	4.45	4.60	1.44	754	756	753	25.5	3.8	7.0	1.8	56%	9%	50	19	31	31%	72%	13%	32	95	22%	34%			-6.0	52	61	$0
1st Half	6	6	0	87	64	5.26	4.99	1.45	752	777	727	24.3	4.0	6.6	1.6	57%	8%	47	18	35	29%	67%	13%	16	91	13%	50%			-11.5	36	42	-$4
2nd Half	5	6	0	99	80	3.74	4.26	1.43	757	735	774	26.8	3.6	7.3	2.1	55%	11%	53	20	27	32%	76%	12%	16	100	31%	19%			5.5	66	79	$3
17 Proj	**12**	**11**	**0**	**189**	**161**	**4.04**	**4.15**	**1.38**	**724**	**728**	**719**	**24.3**	**3.5**	**7.7**	**2.2**	**58%**	**10%**	**51**	**20**	**29**	**31%**	**73%**	**12%**	**33**						**3.4**	**71**	**85**	**$4**

RYAN BLOOMFIELD

Verlander,Justin

Age: 34	Th: R	Role: SP	Health: D	LIMA Plan: D+
Ht: 6' 5"	Wt: 200	Type: Pwr xFB	PT/Exp: A	Rand Var: -1
			Consist: A	MM: 2305

Took a while, but by season's end hung some of the best numbers of his career. Key components were working into 6th inning in 29 of 34 starts while perfecting slider and dialing up heater—leading to .100 reduction in RHB oBA since 2014. Full repeat would be tall order, but he's a tall man. Give him the ball.

Yr Tm	W	L	Sv	IP	K	ERA	xERA	WHIP	oOPS	vL	vR	BF/G	Ctl	Dom	Cmd	FpK	SwK	G	L	F	H%	S%	hr/f	GS	APC	DOM%	DIS%	Sv%	LI	RAR	BPV	BPX	R$
12 DET	17	8	0	238	239	2.64	3.35	1.06	601	608	593	29.0	2.3	9.0	4.0	61%	12%	42	22	36	29%	78%	8%	33	114	55%	15%			40.3	121	158	$36
13 DET	13	12	0	218	217	3.46	3.75	1.31	691	658	739	27.2	3.1	8.9	2.9	65%	11%	38	23	39	33%	76%	8%	34	109	38%	21%			10.9	94	122	$11
14 DET	15	12	0	206	159	4.54	4.27	1.40	756	686	849	27.9	2.8	6.9	2.4	62%	9%	40	20	41	33%	68%	7%	32	107	31%	31%			-20.4	66	79	-$3
15 DET	5	8	0	133	113	3.38	4.03	1.09	634	620	650	26.8	2.2	7.6	3.5	64%	10%	35	20	46	28%	72%	7%	20	108	40%	30%			9.7	92	110	$9
16 DET	16	9	0	228	254	3.04	3.63	1.00	630	603	657	26.6	2.3	10.0	4.5	64%	13%	34	19	48	27%	76%	11%	34	108	62%	9%			32.2	132	157	$33
1st Half	8	6	0	112	115	4.11	3.87	1.10	694	653	731	26.5	2.3	9.3	4.0	61%	12%	35	18	47	28%	67%	12%	17	106	65%	18%			1.1	117	140	$20
2nd Half	8	3	0	116	139	2.02	3.40	0.91	567	556	579	26.6	2.2	10.8	5.0	67%	14%	32	19	49	25%	87%	10%	17	110	59%	0%			31.1	145	174	$46
17 Proj	**15**	**11**	**0**	**218**	**216**	**3.26**	**3.85**	**1.09**	**647**	**621**	**677**	**26.1**	**2.4**	**8.9**	**3.8**	**64%**	**12%**	**35**	**20**	**45**	**28%**	**74%**	**9%**	**33**						**25.0**	**111**	**132**	**$24**

Villanueva,Carlos

Age: 33	Th: R	Role: RP	Health: A	LIMA Plan: C
Ht: 6' 3"	Wt: 220	Type:	PT/Exp: C	Rand Var: +5
			Consist: A	MM: 1201

Undistinguished swingman has morphed into anonymous reliever with equally bland results. Despite career-best Ctl and tightened Cmd, was still battered soundly. Calls for reinforcements were frequent, but judging by 2nd half S%, it appears bullpen mates turned a deaf ear. You should do the same.

Yr Tm	W	L	Sv	IP	K	ERA	xERA	WHIP	oOPS	vL	vR	BF/G	Ctl	Dom	Cmd	FpK	SwK	G	L	F	H%	S%	hr/f	GS	APC	DOM%	DIS%	Sv%	LI	RAR	BPV	BPX	R$
12 TOR	7	7	0	125	122	4.16	4.02	1.27	758	816	703	13.7	3.3	8.8	2.7	59%	11%	37	19	44	28%	74%	15%	16	53	25%	19%	0	0.79	-2.3	84	109	$3
13 CHC	7	8	0	129	103	4.06	3.91	1.22	726	731	721	11.1	2.8	7.2	2.6	58%	11%	40	21	39	28%	69%	10%	15	42	40%	33%	0	0.85	-3.0	72	94	$3
14 CHC	5	7	2	78	72	4.64	3.79	1.39	754	758	751	8.2	2.2	8.3	3.8	59%	12%	41	20	38	36%	67%	6%	5	31	0%	60%	100	0.96	-8.6	110	131	-$2
15 STL	4	3	2	61	55	2.95	3.94	1.16	677	661	689	7.1	3.1	8.1	2.6	62%	13%	42	19	39	27%	78%	9%	0	26			100	0.67	7.6	82	98	$4
16 SD	2	2	1	74	61	5.96	4.16	1.39	886	866	899	6.3	1.7	7.4	4.4	65%	11%	42	24	34	33%	63%	21%	0	23			50	0.81	-16.2	108	128	-$7
1st Half	1	0	1	48	41	4.53	3.83	1.30	824	733	887	6.2	1.5	7.7	5.1	65%	12%	45	24	31	32%	73%	21%	0	23			100	0.84	-2.0	121	145	-$2
2nd Half	1	2	0	26	20	8.54	4.77	1.56	990	1114	917	6.6	2.1	6.8	3.3	66%	9%	38	24	38	34%	47%	21%	0	25			0	0.75	-14.1	83	100	-$14
17 Proj	**3**	**4**	**0**	**73**	**62**	**4.69**	**4.20**	**1.35**	**824**	**836**	**816**	**6.9**	**2.3**	**7.7**	**3.3**	**63%**	**11%**	**41**	**22**	**37**	**32%**	**70%**	**15%**	**0**						**-4.5**	**94**	**112**	**-$3**

Vincent,Nick

Age: 30	Th: R	Role: RP	Health: D	LIMA Plan: A
Ht: 5' 11"	Wt: 185	Type: Pwr FB	PT/Exp: D	Rand Var: +1
			Consist: B	MM: 2400

Always questioned lack of save opps, no more so than in 2016 when Dom, Cmd, FpK and SwK held court. But he gave up a slew of 1st half bombs and lost a month to a strained back, which diluted his usage in the second. Not the imposing type, he's now in his 30s and throws in the 80s. Ah, there's the answer.

Yr Tm	W	L	Sv	IP	K	ERA	xERA	WHIP	oOPS	vL	vR	BF/G	Ctl	Dom	Cmd	FpK	SwK	G	L	F	H%	S%	hr/f	GS	APC	DOM%	DIS%	Sv%	LI	RAR	BPV	BPX	R$
12 SD *	4	1	2	58	56	3.17	3.09	1.20	551	475	598	3.9	2.7	8.8	3.2	56%	13%	37	24	39	31%	75%	8%	0	17			40	1.03	6.0	110	144	$3
13 SD *	10	6	1	72	69	2.61	2.88	1.17	525	781	313	4.1	2.8	8.6	3.1	56%	12%	43	23	34	30%	80%	3%	0	16			50	1.08	11.1	107	140	$8
14 SD	1	2	0	55	62	3.60	3.00	1.00	626	825	507	3.4	1.8	10.1	5.6	61%	12%	33	22	45	30%	66%	8%	0	14			0	1.07	1.0	145	173	$2
15 SD *	5	4	1	73	75	2.98	4.31	1.45	698	756	649	4.7	3.1	9.1	2.9	63%	10%	32	28	40	36%	81%	0%	0	16			20	0.55	8.9	97	115	$2
16 SEA	4	4	3	60	65	3.73	3.90	1.13	700	658	723	4.1	2.2	9.7	4.3	69%	14%	32	20	48	29%	75%	14%	0	16			33	1.26	3.4	124	147	$4
1st Half	2	3	1	36	42	3.47	3.59	1.05	684	779	625	4.2	2.2	10.4	4.7	69%	14%	36	17	47	27%	77%	16%	0	16			17	1.39	3.2	141	168	$6
2nd Half	2	1	2	24	23	4.13	4.36	1.25	722	469	861	4.0	2.3	8.6	3.8	70%	15%	26	25	49	31%	73%	12%	0	15			67	1.08	0.2	99	118	$1
17 Proj	**4**	**3**	**0**	**58**	**60**	**3.81**	**3.92**	**1.21**	**713**	**770**	**677**	**4.0**	**2.4**	**9.4**	**3.8**	**65%**	**13%**	**33**	**22**	**45**	**31%**	**73%**	**10%**	**0**						**2.7**	**114**	**136**	**$1**

Vizcaino,Arodys

Age: 26	Th: R	Role: RP	Health: F	LIMA Plan: C
Ht: 6' 0"	Wt: 230	Type: Pwr	PT/Exp: D	Rand Var: +3
			Consist: B	MM: 2420

Was handed the keys and hit full throttle (12.7 Dom in April/May), only to pump the brakes (8.8 Ctl in June) and screech to halt (2nd half oblique, shoulder injuries). Be prepared for Cmd, xERA detours and rest stops at the trainer's room, but if 1st half groundball tilt, SwK are for real, there's wide-open highway ahead.

Yr Tm	W	L	Sv	IP	K	ERA	xERA	WHIP	oOPS	vL	vR	BF/G	Ctl	Dom	Cmd	FpK	SwK	G	L	F	H%	S%	hr/f	GS	APC	DOM%	DIS%	Sv%	LI	RAR	BPV	BPX	R$
12																																	
13																																	
14 CHC *	1	1	1	37	31	4.91	4.85	1.58	837	200	1318	4.5	4.2	7.6	1.8	59%	7%	40	20	40	34%	69%	17%	0	19			50	0.02	-5.3	59	70	-$5
15 ATL	3	1	9	34	37	1.60	3.66	1.19	615	583	641	3.9	3.5	9.9	2.8	58%	12%	35	28	37	31%	87%	3%	0	15			90	1.12	9.8	97	116	$6
16 ATL	1	4	10	39	50	4.42	4.09	1.63	681	607	748	4.2	6.1	11.6	1.9	56%	14%	54	16	30	37%	73%	10%	0	17			71	1.15	-1.1	78	93	$0
1st Half	1	3	10	35	47	2.31	3.53	1.40	598	527	663	4.2	5.1	12.1	2.4	58%	16%	55	16	30	34%	85%	8%	0	17			83	1.23	8.1	111	133	$2
2nd Half	0	1	0	4	3	24.55	12.35	3.82	1244	1250	1236	4.3	14.7	7.4	0.5	46%	7%	50	19	31	49%	31%	20%	0	17			0	0.66	-9.2	-237	-283	-$21
17 Proj	**2**	**2**	**18**	**51**	**56**	**3.16**	**3.88**	**1.35**	**656**	**569**	**734**	**4.1**	**4.3**	**9.9**	**2.3**	**58%**	**14%**	**47**	**21**	**33**	**32%**	**79%**	**9%**	**0**						**6.5**	**86**	**102**	**$7**

Volquez,Edinson

Age: 33	Th: R	Role: SP	Health: A	LIMA Plan: D+
Ht: 6' 0"	Wt: 210	Type: Pwr	PT/Exp: A	Rand Var: +2
			Consist: A	MM: 1105

Skills have been wobbly for awhile; this year they locked arms and stepped off the ledge. Command led the plunge, fewer strikes yielded second most ER in MLB, overwhelmed xERA. That sound you heard in 2nd half was collective owners clicking their Drop buttons. Even with slight rebound, only marginally rosterable.

Yr Tm	W	L	Sv	IP	K	ERA	xERA	WHIP	oOPS	vL	vR	BF/G	Ctl	Dom	Cmd	FpK	SwK	G	L	F	H%	S%	hr/f	GS	APC	DOM%	DIS%	Sv%	LI	RAR	BPV	BPX	R$
12 SD	11	11	0	183	174	4.14	4.14	1.45	706	700	711	25.1	5.2	8.6	1.7	53%	11%	51	21	28	30%	72%	10%	32	101	25%	25%			-2.8	44	57	$1
13 2 NL	9	12	0	170	142	5.71	4.28	1.59	804	836	771	23.5	4.1	7.5	1.8	57%	9%	48	23	30	34%	65%	12%	32	91	9%	41%	0	0.77	-38.7	51	67	-$16
14 PIT	13	7	0	193	140	3.04	3.95	1.23	674	728	634	25.3	3.3	6.5	2.0	60%	9%	50	17	33	27%	78%	9%	31	93	29%	29%	0	0.76	16.7	56	67	$12
15 KC	13	9	0	200	155	3.55	4.22	1.31	692	692	691	25.0	3.2	7.0	2.2	58%	10%	46	21	33	30%	74%	8%	33	97	33%	27%	0	0.77	10.2	62	74	$10
16 KC	10	11	0	189	139	5.37	4.73	1.55	794	799	788	25.1	3.6	6.6	1.8	56%	9%	51	20	29	33%	67%	13%	34	95	12%	41%			-27.6	50	60	-$11
1st Half	7	7	0	99	77	4.80	4.45	1.43	721	657	785	25.6	3.4	7.0	2.1	55%	9%	53	16	30	32%	67%	10%	17	98	24%	29%			-7.5	66	79	-$2
2nd Half	3	4	0	90	62	6.00	5.04	1.68	871	936	791	24.5	3.9	6.2	1.6	58%	8%	49	24	27	34%	66%	15%	17	92	0%	53%			-20.1	33	40	-$21
17 Proj	**10**	**11**	**0**	**189**	**142**	**4.60**	**4.53**	**1.45**	**758**	**780**	**735**	**24.2**	**3.6**	**6.8**	**1.9**	**57%**	**9%**	**49**	**20**	**30**	**31%**	**70%**	**11%**	**33**						**-9.4**	**52**	**62**	**-$4**

Wacha,Michael

Age: 26	Th: R	Role: SP	Health: D	LIMA Plan: C
Ht: 6' 6"	Wt: 195	Type:	PT/Exp: A	Rand Var: +3
			Consist: A	MM: 1201

Recurrence of 2014 shoulder issue cost him much of 2nd half and puts 2017 role in limbo. Impact on Cmd, between-starts regimen reached zenith in Aug; returned as RP and was pummelled. 2015 showed us what can go right, but for now, uncertain health says he's not among young bulls around whom to build.

Yr Tm	W	L	Sv	IP	K	ERA	xERA	WHIP	oOPS	vL	vR	BF/G	Ctl	Dom	Cmd	FpK	SwK	G	L	F	H%	S%	hr/f	GS	APC	DOM%	DIS%	Sv%	LI	RAR	BPV	BPX	R$
12																																	
13 STL *	9	4	0	150	127	2.79	2.68	1.06	603	493	710	19.3	2.2	7.7	3.5	58%	12%	44	17	39	27%	77%	7%	9	69	22%	33%	0	0.66	19.9	105	137	$16
14 STL	5	6	0	107	94	3.20	3.70	1.20	636	581	687	23.5	2.8	7.9	2.8	64%	11%	42	22	36	30%	74%	5%	19	89	26%	21%			7.2	87	104	$5
15 STL	17	7	0	181	153	3.38	3.91	1.21	672	617	716	25.4	2.9	7.6	2.6	63%	10%	46	22	32	29%	76%	11%	30	98	23%	23%			13.1	83	99	$16
16 STL	7	7	0	138	114	5.09	4.33	1.48	800	733	849	22.4	2.9	7.4	2.5	59%	9%	47	24	30	34%	67%	12%	24	86	25%	33%	0	0.72	-15.3	80	95	-$6
1st Half	5	7	0	99	85	4.38	4.22	1.41	743	764	729	25.1	3.1	7.8	2.5	59%	9%	45	25	29	34%	69%	8%	17	96	29%	18%			-2.3	79	94	-$1
2nd Half	2	0	0	39	29	6.86	4.61	1.65	931	676	1179	18.0	2.5	6.6	2.6	59%	9%	49	21	30	36%	61%	20%	7	69	14%	71%	0	0.64	-13.0	79	94	-$16
17 Proj	**6**	**4**	**0**	**102**	**83**	**4.27**	**4.18**	**1.37**	**758**	**644**	**855**	**21.1**	**2.7**	**7.4**	**2.7**	**61%**	**10%**	**46**	**22**	**32**	**32%**	**71%**	**12%**	**20**						**-1.0**	**83**	**99**	**-$1**

Wainwright,Adam

Age: 35	Th: R	Role: SP	Health: F	LIMA Plan: B+
Ht: 6' 7"	Wt: 230	Type:	PT/Exp: A	Rand Var: +2
			Consist: A	MM: 2203

Successful comeback from Achilles injury? YES: Missed nary a turn; reached pre-injury Dom, FpK; middle months were vintage. NO: Fewest full-year IP; spotty Cmd throughout; battered vL in leading league in ER and hits allowed. VERDICT: Requires more TLC than in ace years, but this iteration still has utility.

Yr Tm	W	L	Sv	IP	K	ERA	xERA	WHIP	oOPS	vL	vR	BF/G	Ctl	Dom	Cmd	FpK	SwK	G	L	F	H%	S%	hr/f	GS	APC	DOM%	DIS%	Sv%	LI	RAR	BPV	BPX	R$
12 STL	14	13	0	199	184	3.94	3.36	1.25	701	724	681	26.0	2.4	8.3	3.5	64%	9%	51	23	26	32%	69%	10%	32	97	38%	22%			1.8	115	151	$11
13 STL	19	9	0	242	219	2.94	2.94	1.07	636	631	639	28.1	1.3	8.2	6.3	65%	10%	49	23	28	31%	74%	8%	34	104	59%	9%			27.5	139	181	$29
14 STL	20	9	0	227	179	2.38	3.31	1.03	580	625	542	28.1	2.0	7.1	3.6	61%	9%	46	24	30	27%	78%	5%	32	102	56%	22%			38.1	98	117	$30
15 STL	2	1	0	28	20	1.61	3.35	1.04	590	661	540	15.9	1.3	6.4	5.0	54%	8%	51	26	23	30%	83%	0%	4	55	25%	0%	0	0.51	8.1	110	131	$1
16 STL	13	9	0	199	161	4.62	4.23	1.40	785	841	739	25.7	2.7	7.3	2.7	61%	9%	44	25	31	33%	69%	12%	33	97	27%	33%			-10.6	81	96	$1
1st Half	7	5	0	103	77	4.70	4.25	1.35	743	721	760	25.7	2.4	6.7	2.8	63%	9%	44	26	30	33%	65%	8%	17	94	35%	35%			-6.5	77	92	$2
2nd Half	6	4	0	95	84	4.53	4.20	1.46	830	965	717	25.6	2.9	7.9	2.7	59%	8%	43	25	32	34%	73%	15%	16	100	19%	31%			-4.0	85	101	-$1
17 Proj	**12**	**7**	**0**	**174**	**146**	**3.73**	**3.85**	**1.25**	**711**	**759**	**670**	**26.1**	**2.3**	**7.6**	**3.3**	**62%**	**9%**	**46**	**25**	**30**	**31%**	**72%**	**10%**	**27**						**9.9**	**98**	**116**	**$9**

ROB CARROLL

Walker,Taijuan

Age: 24	Th: R	Role SP	Health D	LIMA Plan B	
Ht: 6' 4"	Wt: 210	Type Pwr	PT/Exp C	Rand Var +2	
			Consist A	MM 2203	

8-11, 4.22 ERA in 134 IP at SEA. Flat feet apparently caused foot, ankle issue that led to flat skills in 2nd half, but 1st half was strong continuation of 2015 growth. Yet to post full season ERA under 4.00, but xERA says it's there for the taking if hr/f ever falls in line. He's on the precipice of bigger, better things.

Yr Tm	W	L	Sv	IP	K	ERA	xERA	WHIP	oOPS	vL	vR	BF/G	Ctl	Dom	Cmd	FpK	SwK	G	L	F	H%	S%	hr/f	GS	APC	DOM%	DIS%	Sv%	LI	RAR	BPV	BPX	R$
12 aa	7	10	0	127	110	5.27	4.37	1.45				21.6	3.5	7.8	2.3						33%	63%								-19.7	71	93	-$7
13 SEA *	10	10	0	156	156	3.33	3.04	1.22	546	536	563	22.6	3.3	9.0	2.7	57%	10%	38	21	40	30%	74%	0%	3	78	0%	0%			10.3	101	132	$11
14 SEA *	9	7	0	116	109	3.85	3.70	1.25	642	729	501	20.5	3.2	8.4	2.7	61%	10%	47	27	26	29%	73%	7%	5	78	20%	0%	0	0.57	-1.5	82	97	$4
15 SEA	11	8	0	170	157	4.56	3.78	1.20	716	714	719	24.3	2.1	8.3	3.9	63%	11%	39	22	39	30%	66%	13%	29	91	34%	34%			-12.6	110	131	$5
16 SEA *	9	11	0	149	124	4.18	4.43	1.25	767	721	809	21.7	2.7	7.5	2.8	64%	10%	44	18	38	28%	74%	18%	25	92	28%	40%			0.2	58	68	$6
1st Half	4	6	0	82	75	3.29	3.86	1.12	702	638	764	22.7	1.9	8.2	4.4	61%	10%	44	19	38	28%	81%	16%	15	94	33%	33%			9.1	120	143	$13
2nd Half	4	5	0	52	44	5.68	4.66	1.41	867	861	871	23.3	3.4	7.6	2.2	67%	11%	44	17	38	29%	66%	19%	10	90	20%	50%			-9.6	66	78	-$3
17 Proj	**11**	**12**	**0**	**167**	**150**	**4.08**	**4.05**	**1.27**	**729**	**721**	**738**	**22.1**	**2.8**	**8.1**	**2.9**	**64%**	**10%**	**43**	**21**	**37**	**30%**	**72%**	**13%**	**31**						**2.2**	**92**	**110**	**$6**

Warren,Adam

Age: 29	Th: R	Role RP	Health A	LIMA Plan C	
Ht: 6' 2"	Wt: 215	Type Pwr	PT/Exp C	Rand Var 0	
			Consist B	MM 1200	

Looked great as reliever in 2014, then again in 2nd half of 2015 (3.06 xERA, 9.3 Dom, 132 BPV). Ctl, FB, hr/f spike were the major causes of this year's inflated ERA/xERA. However, Ctl woes might have been predicted from his flat, average FpK. hr/f regression should provide some bounce but needs to get walks back down.

Yr Tm	W	L	Sv	IP	K	ERA	xERA	WHIP	oOPS	vL	vR	BF/G	Ctl	Dom	Cmd	FpK	SwK	G	L	F	H%	S%	hr/f	GS	APC	DOM%	DIS%	Sv%	LI	RAR	BPV	BPX	R$
12 NYY *	7	8	0	155	87	5.19	6.13	1.71	1588	1500	1636	26.0	3.0	5.1	1.7	59%	5%	29	29	43	36%	71%	33%	1	77	0%	100%			-22.5	25	33	-$18
13 NYY	3	2	1	77	64	3.39	4.02	1.43	766	896	625	9.7	3.5	7.5	2.1	56%	11%	45	22	32	31%	81%	13%	2	38	0%	50%	100	0.58	4.5	63	82	-$1
14 NYY	3	6	3	79	76	2.97	3.31	1.11	615	525	690	4.7	2.7	8.7	3.2	58%	12%	45	24	31	29%	73%	6%	0	19			50	1.26	7.4	105	126	$6
15 NYY	7	7	1	131	104	3.29	3.84	1.16	648	603	680	12.4	2.7	7.1	2.7	60%	9%	45	23	32	28%	73%	8%	17	50	18%	12%	100	1.01	10.9	79	94	$9
16 2 TM	7	4	0	65	52	4.68	4.80	1.35	742	635	800	4.8	4.0	7.2	1.8	60%	10%	44	17	40	27%	70%	14%	1	20	0%	0%	0	1.05	-4.0	43	51	-$1
1st Half	3	1	0	26	18	4.56	5.34	1.40	727	812	686	4.4	4.9	6.3	1.3	56%	11%	46	15	38	25%	72%	13%	0	19			0	1.15	-1.2	5	6	-$1
2nd Half	4	3	0	40	34	4.76	4.47	1.31	752	531	879	5.0	3.4	7.7	2.3	62%	10%	42	18	40	28%	69%	15%	1	22	0%	0%	0	0.97	-2.8	67	80	-$1
17 Proj	**4**	**3**	**0**	**58**	**49**	**3.88**	**4.15**	**1.25**	**690**	**629**	**731**	**5.9**	**3.1**	**7.6**	**2.5**	**59%**	**10%**	**46**	**20**	**35**	**29%**	**72%**	**11%**	**0**						**2.2**	**77**	**91**	**$0**

Watson,Tony

Age: 32	Th: L	Role RP	Health A	LIMA Plan B	
Ht: 6' 4"	Wt: 210	Type	PT/Exp C	Rand Var -3	
			Consist B	MM 2221	

H%, S% helped get him shot at saves, but skills raise doubts about ability to stick. Dom still struggling to match SwK, and FpK should be generating better Ctl. Rising FB% and inflated hr/f were the big killers, though. The seeds are here, but 32-year-old southpaws often are better fits in setup roles.

Yr Tm	W	L	Sv	IP	K	ERA	xERA	WHIP	oOPS	vL	vR	BF/G	Ctl	Dom	Cmd	FpK	SwK	G	L	F	H%	S%	hr/f	GS	APC	DOM%	DIS%	Sv%	LI	RAR	BPV	BPX	R$
12 PIT	5	2	0	53	53	3.38	3.86	1.13	623	554	691	3.2	3.9	8.9	2.3	64%	12%	40	18	42	25%	73%	9%	0	13			0	1.21	4.2	74	97	$3
13 PIT	3	1	2	72	54	2.39	3.44	0.88	544	483	582	4.2	1.5	6.8	4.5	63%	12%	44	19	37	24%	76%	7%	0	16			50	1.14	13.1	103	135	$9
14 PIT	10	2	2	77	81	1.63	2.76	1.02	613	531	646	3.9	1.7	9.4	5.4	65%	14%	48	21	32	30%	88%	8%	0	15			22	1.34	20.1	149	177	$13
15 PIT	4	1	1	75	62	1.91	3.42	0.96	525	493	536	3.8	2.0	7.4	3.6	66%	12%	48	21	32	26%	81%	5%	0	14			33	1.38	19.1	104	124	$10
16 PIT	2	5	15	68	58	3.06	4.01	1.06	672	577	711	3.9	2.7	7.7	2.9	64%	13%	44	18	38	24%	79%	14%	0	15			75	1.07	9.4	89	106	$10
1st Half	1	2	0	35	32	3.09	3.83	1.03	633	606	647	4.0	3.1	8.2	2.7	69%	14%	46	20	35	23%	75%	13%	0	15			0	0.99	4.8	88	105	$5
2nd Half	1	3	15	33	26	3.03	4.20	1.10	713	533	771	3.8	2.2	7.2	3.3	59%	13%	42	16	42	25%	83%	15%	0	14			83	1.15	4.7	89	107	$16
17 Proj	**4**	**4**	**18**	**73**	**63**	**3.16**	**3.84**	**1.14**	**682**	**594**	**718**	**3.8**	**2.3**	**7.8**	**3.4**	**64%**	**13%**	**45**	**19**	**36**	**28%**	**76%**	**10%**	**0**						**9.2**	**102**	**121**	**$11**

Weaver,Jered

Age: 34	Th: R	Role SP	Health D	LIMA Plan D+	
Ht: 6' 7"	Wt: 215	Type Con xFB	PT/Exp A	Rand Var 0	
			Consist B	MM 0001	

Since 2010, as FB velocity slid from 90 to 83mph, xERA rose from 3.46 to the nightmare he posted last year. When you throw that slow with this many fly balls, giving up 37 HR in 178 IP seems inevitable. Tried throwing more FpK, but there's no fixing this without velocity and/or GB%. Does he even get another contract?

Yr Tm	W	L	Sv	IP	K	ERA	xERA	WHIP	oOPS	vL	vR	BF/G	Ctl	Dom	Cmd	FpK	SwK	G	L	F	H%	S%	hr/f	GS	APC	DOM%	DIS%	Sv%	LI	RAR	BPV	BPX	R$
12 LAA	20	5	0	189	142	2.81	4.01	1.02	605	541	690	24.6	2.1	6.8	3.2	61%	9%	36	21	43	25%	77%	9%	30	95	37%	17%			27.9	78	102	$29
13 LAA	11	8	0	154	117	3.27	4.17	1.14	671	638	725	26.4	2.2	6.8	3.2	60%	10%	31	22	47	28%	75%	8%	24	100	33%	29%			11.4	74	96	$12
14 LAA	18	9	0	213	169	3.59	4.25	1.21	684	723	620	26.1	2.7	7.1	2.6	56%	9%	33	19	48	28%	75%	9%	34	99	26%	29%			4.1	65	78	$13
15 LAA	7	12	0	159	90	4.64	4.83	1.23	767	777	757	25.7	1.9	5.1	2.7	61%	9%	34	19	47	28%	66%	10%	26	94	15%	50%			-13.3	53	63	-$1
16 LAA	12	12	0	178	103	5.06	5.54	1.46	862	857	866	24.7	2.6	5.2	2.0	64%	8%	29	23	48	30%	72%	13%	31	91	6%	61%			-19.0	31	37	-$5
1st Half	6	7	0	95	54	5.51	5.56	1.48	870	853	883	25.8	2.5	5.1	2.1	65%	8%	30	23	48	31%	68%	13%	16	93	6%	63%			-15.5	33	40	-$7
2nd Half	6	5	0	83	49	4.54	5.52	1.44	853	861	846	23.6	2.7	5.3	2.0	63%	8%	28	23	49	30%	76%	13%	15	90	7%	60%			-3.6	28	33	-$3
17 Proj	**5**	**6**	**0**	**87**	**51**	**4.88**	**5.28**	**1.39**	**824**	**816**	**831**	**25.0**	**2.4**	**5.3**	**2.2**	**62%**	**9%**	**31**	**21**	**47**	**30%**	**70%**	**11%**	**15**						**-7.4**	**40**	**48**	**-$4**

Weaver,Luke

Age: 23	Th: R	Role SP	Health A	LIMA Plan B	
Ht: 6' 2"	Wt: 160	Type Pwr FB	PT/Exp F	Rand Var +2	
			Consist F	MM 2401	

1-4, 5.70 ERA in 36 IP at STL. Ignore high MLB ERA that was bloated by 40% hit rate and unlucky LD%, and focus on underlying skills like 11.1 Dom, 3.8 Cmd, and 3.76 xERA. This is a quality prospect coming off a great AA season whose strong debut was obscured by noise. A buying opportunity awaits.

Yr Tm	W	L	Sv	IP	K	ERA	xERA	WHIP	oOPS	vL	vR	BF/G	Ctl	Dom	Cmd	FpK	SwK	G	L	F	H%	S%	hr/f	GS	APC	DOM%	DIS%	Sv%	LI	RAR	BPV	BPX	R$
12																																	
13																																	
14																																	
15																																	
16 STL *	8	7	0	119	127	2.78	3.55	1.19	870	1025	761	21.8	1.8	9.6	5.3	56%	10%	31	37	33	34%	80%	21%	8	76	13%	38%	0	0.71	20.8	146	174	$12
1st Half	4	1	0	37	37	1.17	3.41	1.25				25.3	1.5	9.0	6.0						37%	92%	0%	0						13.9	173	206	$10
2nd Half	4	6	0	82	89	3.54	3.69	1.18	870	1025	761	20.5	2.0	9.8	5.0	56%	10%	31	37	33	33%	74%	21%	8	76	13%	38%	0	0.71	6.6	134	160	$13
17 Proj	**9**	**7**	**0**	**123**	**129**	**3.47**	**3.76**	**1.14**	**553**	**656**	**480**	**24.0**	**2.6**	**9.4**	**3.6**	**56%**	**10%**	**38**	**23**	**39**	**30%**	**73%**	**9%**	**20**						**11.0**	**114**	**136**	**$10**

Wheeler,Zack

Age: 27	Th: R	Role SP	Health F	LIMA Plan B+	
Ht: 6' 3"	Wt: 185	Type Pwr	PT/Exp C	Rand Var 0	
			Consist F	MM 1201	

Return from TJS was pushed back multiple times by elbow pain, and he threw only 1 IP of rehab work. Was finally shut down, and won't resume work until pitchers and catchers report for spring training. Previous skills offer solid upside potential, but health risk means you should only acquire at a massive discount.

Yr Tm	W	L	Sv	IP	K	ERA	xERA	WHIP	oOPS	vL	vR	BF/G	Ctl	Dom	Cmd	FpK	SwK	G	L	F	H%	S%	hr/f	GS	APC	DOM%	DIS%	Sv%	LI	RAR	BPV	BPX	R$
12 a/a	12	8	0	149	132	3.44	2.58	1.19				23.9	3.3	8.0	2.4						29%	69%								10.5	101	132	$12
13 NYM *	11	7	0	169	148	3.38	3.58	1.29	696	766	639	23.1	3.7	7.9	2.2	52%	9%	43	23	33	29%	77%	10%	17	102	29%	35%			10.2	72	94	$9
14 NYM	11	11	0	185	187	3.54	3.37	1.33	678	745	615	24.8	3.8	9.1	2.4	54%	10%	54	19	27	31%	75%	10%	32	103	31%	22%			4.5	92	109	$6
15																																	
16																																	
1st Half																																	
2nd Half																																	
17 Proj	**7**	**5**	**0**	**102**	**89**	**3.90**	**4.19**	**1.35**	**674**	**739**	**617**	**24.3**	**3.9**	**7.9**	**2.0**	**53%**	**10%**	**50**	**21**	**30**	**31%**	**71%**	**7%**	**17**						**3.6**	**63**	**75**	**$2**

Whitley,Chase

Age: 28	Th: R	Role RP	Health F	LIMA Plan C	
Ht: 6' 4"	Wt: 220	Type	PT/Exp D	Rand Var -1	
			Consist B	MM 1100	

0-0, 2.51 ERA in 14 IP at TAM. Posted 9.4 Dom, 13% SwK in MLB cup of coffee, working primarily as reliever; had 8.6 Dom, 3.3 Cmd in 2nd half of 2014 in same role. Rest of skill history is barely average, including fastball that tops out at 91mph, so not much reason to buy in yet, but he merits further observation.

Yr Tm	W	L	Sv	IP	K	ERA	xERA	WHIP	oOPS	vL	vR	BF/G	Ctl	Dom	Cmd	FpK	SwK	G	L	F	H%	S%	hr/f	GS	APC	DOM%	DIS%	Sv%	LI	RAR	BPV	BPX	R$
12 a/a	9	5	2	84	61	3.90	3.41	1.20				7.9	3.0	6.5	2.2						27%	70%								1.2	64	84	$4
13 aaa	3	2	3	68	51	4.21	4.33	1.47				10.0	3.1	6.8	2.2						34%	71%								-2.9	69	89	-$3
14 NYY *	7	5	0	107	91	4.38	4.37	1.36	831	866	792	13.2	2.2	7.6	3.5	62%	11%	45	21	34	34%	69%	12%	12	53	17%	50%	0	0.83	-8.4	91	109	-$2
15 NYY *	3	2	0	36	27	3.63	3.93	1.34	763	1204	484	21.6	2.9	6.6	2.2	61%	11%	49	14	37	31%	74%	14%	4	81	25%	50%			1.5	66	79	-$2
16 TAM *	2	1	0	42	33	3.35	3.18	1.09	607	353	1000	14.9	2.5	7.0	2.8	67%	13%	42	19	40	25%	75%	12%	1	48	0%	100%	0	0.88	4.4	76	90	$0
1st Half																																	
2nd Half	2	1	0	42	33	3.35	3.18	1.09	607	353	1000	14.9	2.5	7.0	2.8	67%	13%	42	19	40	25%	75%	12%	1	48	0%	100%	0	0.88	4.4	76	90	$0
17 Proj	**3**	**3**	**0**	**58**	**45**	**3.90**	**4.29**	**1.28**	**634**	**662**	**603**	**13.1**	**2.7**	**7.0**	**2.6**	**62%**	**11%**	**45**	**21**	**34**	**30%**	**71%**	**8%**	**6**						**2.1**	**78**	**93**	**-$1**

BRANDON KRUSE

Wilson,Alex

Age: 30 Th: R Role RP | Health D | LIMA Plan B
Ht: 6' 1" Wt: 205 Type | PT/Exp D | Rand Var -3
Consist A | MM 0000

Claimed that minor mechanical tweaks turned season around, but 2H skills were actually worse (thank you, low H%, LD%). Has GB tilt, but not to degree that might make up for subpar Dom. Somewhat inexplicably keeping his head above water in high-leverage work, but that seems destined to end badly sooner or later.

Yr Tm	W	L	Sv	IP	K	ERA	xERA	WHIP	oOPS	vL	vR	BF/G	Ctl	Dom	Cmd	FpK	SwK	G	L	F	H%	S%	hr/f	GS	APC	DOM%	DIS%	Sv%	LI	RAR	BPV	BPX	R$
12 aaa	5	3	1	73	61	5.43	6.02	1.88				8.5	4.6	7.6	1.6						40%	70%								-12.7	55	72	-$12
13 BOS *	4	2	0	45	34	4.89	5.08	1.68	818	567	1108	5.0	3.9	6.9	1.8	56%	9%	31	30	39	37%	70%	0%	0	18			0	0.88	-5.7	58	76	-$6
14 BOS *	7	1	5	70	49	4.38	4.18	1.45	624	787	476	5.6	4.1	6.3	1.6	61%	8%	44	18	38	30%	70%	10%	0	23			50	0.54	-5.5	52	62	-$1
15 DET	3	3	2	70	38	2.19	3.98	1.03	609	566	645	4.6	1.4	4.9	3.5	62%	7%	50	15	35	26%	82%	7%	1	17	0%	0%	50	0.94	15.3	78	93	$7
16 DET	4	0	0	73	49	2.96	4.50	1.22	692	728	665	4.8	2.6	6.0	2.3	58%	9%	44	19	37	29%	77%	6%	0	18			0	1.10	11.1	61	72	$4
1st Half	0	0	0	34	27	3.93	4.10	1.40	765	773	758	4.9	2.6	7.1	2.7	60%	10%	48	26	26	34%	72%	7%	0	18			0	0.79	1.1	83	99	-$2
2nd Half	4	0	0	39	22	2.09	4.85	1.06	621	689	567	4.7	2.6	5.1	2.0	56%	9%	41	12	47	24%	84%	6%	0	19			0	1.39	10.0	42	50	$8
17 Proj	2	2	0	51	33	4.20	4.67	1.35	761	763	759	5.1	2.7	5.8	2.2	59%	8%	47	17	37	31%	70%	7%	0						-0.1	57	68	-$3

Wilson,Justin

Age: 29 Th: L Role RP | Health A | LIMA Plan A
Ht: 6' 2" Wt: 233 Type Pwr GB | PT/Exp C | Rand Var +4
Consist A | MM 3410

Trucking right along with elite 1H skills, then things took a turn. Did elbow woes, which surfaced in mid-June and required Aug cortisone shot, play role? If so, health could bring back closer-worthy skills. That's right, closer-worthy. See vR, Dom, GB%: Which box doesn't he check? Long shot, maybe, but... UP: 25 Sv

Yr Tm	W	L	Sv	IP	K	ERA	xERA	WHIP	oOPS	vL	vR	BF/G	Ctl	Dom	Cmd	FpK	SwK	G	L	F	H%	S%	hr/f	GS	APC	DOM%	DIS%	Sv%	LI	RAR	BPV	BPX	R$
12 PIT *	9	6	0	140	113	4.69	3.58	1.35	1111	1053	1161	15.8	4.5	7.3	1.6	58%	10%	20	53	27	28%	66%	0%	0	13			0	0.43	-11.7	63	82	-$1
13 PIT	6	1	0	74	59	2.08	3.59	1.06	543	501	563	5.1	3.4	7.2	2.1	59%	10%	53	17	30	24%	82%	7%	0	21			0	1.11	16.3	68	89	$8
14 PIT	3	4	0	60	61	4.20	3.68	1.32	643	681	622	3.7	4.5	9.2	2.0	61%	10%	51	14	34	29%	68%	7%	0	15			0	1.05	-3.4	72	86	-$2
15 NYY	5	0	0	61	66	3.10	3.17	1.13	602	629	588	3.3	3.0	9.7	3.3	60%	13%	44	27	29	30%	73%	7%	0	14			0	1.26	6.5	118	140	$4
16 DET	4	5	1	59	65	4.14	3.37	1.33	708	772	667	3.8	2.6	10.0	3.8	59%	13%	55	15	30	35%	71%	12%	0	15			17	1.25	0.3	142	169	$0
1st Half	2	1	0	31	39	3.19	2.32	1.03	590	619	569	3.5	1.5	11.3	7.8	63%	16%	57	23	20	35%	68%	7%	0	14			0	1.19	3.8	199	238	$5
2nd Half	2	4	1	28	26	5.20	4.67	1.66	825	939	758	4.1	3.9	8.5	2.2	55%	10%	53	8	39	36%	73%	15%	0	17			33	1.31	-3.5	78	93	-$5
17 Proj	5	4	2	65	70	3.53	3.43	1.21	633	686	603	3.7	3.0	9.6	3.2	59%	12%	51	18	31	32%	72%	9%	0						5.3	121	145	$3

Wisler,Matthew

Age: 24 Th: R Role SP | Health A | LIMA Plan C
Ht: 6' 3" Wt: 205 Type | PT/Exp C | Rand Var +1
Consist A | MM 0103

7-13, 5.00 ERA in 157 IP at ATL. Through 5/31, ERA sat at 3.16, but "progress" proved a mirage. Once hr/f luck evaporated, results took hard turn for the worse. Signs of true growth almost imperceptible—few more swings-and-misses, GBs in 2nd half, we suppose. For now, probably still too volatile to roster.

Yr Tm	W	L	Sv	IP	K	ERA	xERA	WHIP	oOPS	vL	vR	BF/G	Ctl	Dom	Cmd	FpK	SwK	G	L	F	H%	S%	hr/f	GS	APC	DOM%	DIS%	Sv%	LI	RAR	BPV	BPX	R$
12																																	
13 aa	8	5	0	105	94	3.31	2.87	1.12				20.7	2.2	8.1	3.7						30%	72%								7.2	115	150	$8
14 a/a	10	5	0	147	121	4.06	4.32	1.32				21.7	2.3	7.4	3.2						32%	72%								-5.7	82	97	$2
15 ATL *	11	12	0	174	116	5.00	4.95	1.46	819	986	664	23.3	2.8	6.0	2.1	59%	8%	34	23	43	32%	68%	10%	19	89	11%	53%	0	0.74	-22.2	45	53	-$8
16 ATL *	9	14	1	183	134	4.95	4.67	1.34	756	769	741	24.6	2.7	6.6	2.5	58%	9%	40	21	38	30%	67%	14%	26	90	12%	35%	100	0.83	-17.2	49	59	-$1
1st Half	3	8	1	102	76	4.16	4.70	1.26	711	775	639	25.4	2.6	6.7	2.6	62%	9%	38	20	42	29%	70%	10%	16	91	19%	25%	100	0.86	0.4	68	81	$5
2nd Half	6	6	0	82	58	5.93	5.49	1.44	836	756	891	24.8	2.8	6.4	2.3	51%	10%	44	24	32	31%	63%	23%	10	89	0%	50%			-17.6	31	37	-$9
17 Proj	9	10	0	152	113	4.81	4.60	1.36	767	820	718	23.4	2.6	6.7	2.6	57%	9%	38	23	39	31%	68%	11%	27						-11.7	66	79	-$2

Withrow,Chris

Age: 28 Th: R Role RP | Health F | LIMA Plan C
Ht: 6' 3" Wt: 220 Type Pwr FB | PT/Exp F | Rand Var -3
Consist B | MM 1300

In some ways, Cmd, xERA tell you all you need to know. High SwK offers some hope that Dom of yore will return; however, velocity also down 2.5 mph from 2013. FpK less optimistic that Ctl will improve. Might be onto something if 2nd half GB rate proves sustainable, but there's nothing projectable about 16 IP.

Yr Tm	W	L	Sv	IP	K	ERA	xERA	WHIP	oOPS	vL	vR	BF/G	Ctl	Dom	Cmd	FpK	SwK	G	L	F	H%	S%	hr/f	GS	APC	DOM%	DIS%	Sv%	LI	RAR	BPV	BPX	R$
12 aa	3	3	2	60	55	5.35	4.17	1.57				12.0	5.4	8.2	1.5						33%	64%								-9.9	71	92	-$7
13 LA *	7	0	1	61	71	2.20	2.73	1.16	536	533	538	4.8	3.6	10.4	2.9	55%	12%	36	21	44	29%	85%	15%	0	23			33	1.51	12.6	113	148	$7
14 LA	0	0	0	21	28	2.95	3.79	1.31	551	97	813	4.5	7.6	11.8	1.6	47%	14%	47	16	37	22%	78%	6%	0	19			0	1.08	2.1	33	39	-$2
15																																	
16 ATL	3	0	0	38	28	3.58	4.78	1.22	639	573	679	3.4	4.1	6.7	1.6	53%	12%	45	17	38	23%	76%	12%	0	14			0	1.02	2.8	34	40	-$1
1st Half	2	0	0	22	16	3.68	4.97	1.27	619	634	610	3.3	4.5	6.5	1.5	52%	12%	41	23	36	25%	73%	9%	0	14			0	0.92	1.4	15	18	$0
2nd Half	1	0	0	16	12	3.45	4.51	1.15	665	507	792	3.7	3.4	6.9	2.0	53%	12%	52	7	41	22%	80%	17%	0	15			0	1.19	1.4	61	73	-$1
17 Proj	1	2	0	36	33	4.35	4.48	1.35	693	645	724	4.4	4.0	8.3	2.1	54%	12%	43	16	41	29%	70%	10%	0						-0.7	61	73	-$3

Wittgren,Nick

Age: 26 Th: R Role RP | Health A | LIMA Plan A
Ht: 6' 2" Wt: 215 Type | PT/Exp D | Rand Var -2
Consist B | MM 1100

Purdue's all-time saves leader earned early-season call-up, was up for good by end of May. Body of work in minors featured 1.6 Ctl, 9.6 Dom. Ctl came with him, looked in 1st half like Dom did, too, but that proved unsustainable, as low SwK suggested. On his way to establishing himself as LIMA asset, albeit a boring one.

Yr Tm	W	L	Sv	IP	K	ERA	xERA	WHIP	oOPS	vL	vR	BF/G	Ctl	Dom	Cmd	FpK	SwK	G	L	F	H%	S%	hr/f	GS	APC	DOM%	DIS%	Sv%	LI	RAR	BPV	BPX	R$
12																																	
13																																	
14 aa	5	5	20	66	46	4.02	4.79	1.44				5.4	1.9	6.3	3.4						35%	73%								-2.2	82	98	$5
15 a/a	1	6	20	64	54	3.75	3.89	1.21				4.9	1.2	7.7	6.4						33%	71%								1.7	156	185	$7
16 MIA	4	3	0	52	42	3.14	4.16	1.16	671	618	717	4.4	1.7	7.3	4.2	62%	7%	39	21	40	30%	78%	10%	0	18			0	1.01	6.7	102	121	$2
1st Half	3	1	0	23	25	3.18	3.67	1.06	618	587	643	5.2	2.0	9.9	5.0	56%	8%	37	19	44	29%	76%	11%	0	21			0	1.00	2.8	140	167	$4
2nd Half	1	2	0	29	17	3.10	4.57	1.24	714	642	779	4.0	1.6	5.3	3.4	66%	6%	41	22	38	30%	79%	9%	0	16			0	1.01	3.9	72	86	$1
17 Proj	3	4	0	51	40	3.49	4.11	1.22	699	645	746	4.6	1.5	7.2	4.6	62%	7%	39	21	40	32%	75%	8%	0						4.4	105	125	$0

Wood,Alex

Age: 26 Th: L Role SP | Health F | LIMA Plan A
Ht: 6' 4" Wt: 215 Type Pwr | PT/Exp A | Rand Var +1
Consist B | MM 3303

Shook off sluggish beginning of year with 6 GS stretch that featured 2.80 ERA, 6.3 Cmd in 35 IP; then elbow woes, which eventually required surgery, set in. Health is huge question, but return of FB velocity, 4.2 Cmd vR are encouraging, and rising GB/Dom combo is extremely intriguing. May be worth risk at right price.

Yr Tm	W	L	Sv	IP	K	ERA	xERA	WHIP	oOPS	vL	vR	BF/G	Ctl	Dom	Cmd	FpK	SwK	G	L	F	H%	S%	hr/f	GS	APC	DOM%	DIS%	Sv%	LI	RAR	BPV	BPX	R$
12																																	
13 ATL *	8	5	0	140	132	2.43	2.83	1.22	670	622	690	13.4	2.8	8.5	3.0	62%	10%	49	24	27	32%	80%	5%	11	42	27%	36%	0	0.60	24.7	113	147	$13
14 ATL	11	11	0	172	170	2.78	3.20	1.14	651	667	645	19.8	2.4	8.9	3.8	62%	10%	46	19	35	30%	79%	10%	24	77	42%	13%	0	0.91	20.4	121	144	$16
15 2 NL	12	12	0	190	139	3.84	4.01	1.36	724	517	788	25.0	2.8	6.6	2.4	63%	8%	49	23	28	32%	73%	9%	32	91	28%	22%			2.8	70	84	$5
16 LA	1	4	0	60	66	3.73	3.32	1.26	660	774	620	18.2	3.0	9.8	3.3	64%	10%	53	20	27	33%	72%	12%	10	70	30%	20%	0	0.60	3.4	128	152	$0
1st Half	1	4	0	56	62	3.99	3.37	1.31	684	862	626	24.2	3.0	9.9	3.3	65%	10%	53	21	26	34%	71%	13%	10	93	30%	20%			1.4	127	152	$0
2nd Half	0	0	0	4	4	0.00	2.61	0.50	237	125	400	3.3	2.3	9.0	4.0	46%	7%	63	0	38	12%	100%	0%	0	15			0	0.21	2.1	142	169	-$4
17 Proj	7	7	0	145	140	3.31	3.62	1.25	671	681	667	23.1	2.7	8.7	3.2	63%	10%	49	21	30	32%	75%	10%	26						15.8	110	131	$9

Wood,Blake

Age: 31 Th: R Role RP | Health D | LIMA Plan B+
Ht: 6' 4" Wt: 225 Type Pwr GB | PT/Exp D | Rand Var +2
Consist D | MM 1300

CIN bullpen was butt of many jokes, so heights that 2nd half skills reached likely flew under radar, given way LHB teed off, and impact 30%+ hr/f did to stats from 8/1 on. GB% abated, but still decent; SwK validated Dom spike. Went 1-for-6 in Sv chances, so opps may never return. But may not be as bad as you think.

Yr Tm	W	L	Sv	IP	K	ERA	xERA	WHIP	oOPS	vL	vR	BF/G	Ctl	Dom	Cmd	FpK	SwK	G	L	F	H%	S%	hr/f	GS	APC	DOM%	DIS%	Sv%	LI	RAR	BPV	BPX	R$
12																																	
13 CLE *	2	0	0	24	23	3.31	4.41	1.82	700	500	833	4.1	7.1	8.8	1.2	50%	12%	50	25	25	36%	80%	0%	0	21			0	0.15	1.7	80	105	-$4
14 CLE *	0	2	0	39	36	7.04	6.97	2.26	673	625	729	5.5	8.9	8.3	0.9	67%	6%	40	20	40	38%	68%	0%	0	18			0	0.20	-16.0	39	47	-$13
15 aaa	2	5	29	59	49	5.19	5.05	1.71				4.7	4.5	7.6	1.7						37%	68%								-8.9	64	77	$3
16 CIN	6	5	1	77	81	3.99	3.86	1.43	752	722	775	4.7	4.5	9.5	2.1	56%	11%	53	19	28	32%	75%	16%	0	19			17	1.05	1.9	82	97	$1
1st Half	5	1	1	40	38	3.38	4.47	1.55	667	551	766	4.8	5.9	8.6	1.5	56%	10%	57	19	24	32%	77%	4%	0	20			25	0.95	4.0	31	37	$3
2nd Half	1	4	0	37	43	4.66	3.28	1.31	843	927	781	4.6	2.9	10.6	3.6	57%	13%	48	20	32	32%	73%	27%	0	17			0	1.17	-2.1	137	163	-$2
17 Proj	3	5	0	65	63	4.14	4.21	1.49	741	720	758	4.6	4.7	8.7	1.9	56%	11%	52	20	29	32%	73%	10%	0						0.4	61	73	-$3

KRISTOPHER OLSON

Wood,Travis

Age: 30	Th: L	Role RP	Health A	LIMA Plan B+	
Ht: 5' 11"	Wt: 166	Type Pwr FB	PT/Exp B	Rand Var -5	
			Consist C	MM 1200	

Unable to hold SwK, Dom gains he made when he moved to pen in 2015, though fortunate H%, S% hid the decline in 1st half. Upward trending FpK provides at least some hope for improved Ctl, but FB tendencies leaves him very susceptible to long ball vR. Bottom line: odds are stacked against a repeat.

Yr	Tm	W	L	Sv	IP	K	ERA	xERA	WHIP	oOPS	vL	vR	BF/G	Ctl	Dom	Cmd	FpK	SwK	G	L	F	H%	S%	hr/f	GS	APC	DOM%	DIS%	Sv%	LI	RAR	BPV	BPX	R$
12	CHC *	9	16	0	197	151	4.47	4.25	1.28	745	614	779	24.5	3.0	6.9	2.3	58%	7%	34	22	44	28%	70%	13%	26	96	27%	38%			-11.2	53	69	$2
13	CHC	9	12	0	200	144	3.11	4.34	1.15	643	599	656	25.7	3.0	6.5	2.2	61%	8%	33	22	44	26%	76%	7%	32	97	34%	22%			18.8	47	62	$15
14	CHC	8	13	0	174	146	5.03	4.59	1.53	782	619	837	25.2	3.9	7.6	1.9	57%	7%	34	23	42	33%	69%	9%	31	98	19%	42%			-27.5	42	50	-$11
15	CHC	5	4	4	101	118	3.84	3.67	1.24	663	597	698	7.8	3.5	10.5	3.0	62%	11%	35	23	43	31%	72%	10%	9	32	22%	22%	100	0.79	1.5	108	128	$5
16	CHC	4	0	0	61	47	2.95	4.75	1.13	664	447	865	3.3	3.5	6.9	2.0	66%	8%	37	22	41	23%	80%	11%	0	13			0	1.02	9.3	44	53	$4
1st Half		3	0	0	34	26	2.14	4.55	0.92	544	548	540	3.3	3.5	7.0	2.0	67%	7%	35	18	47	18%	82%	7%	0	13			0	1.21	8.5	44	53	$8
2nd Half		1	0	0	27	21	3.95	4.99	1.39	789	327	1164	3.3	3.6	6.9	1.9	64%	8%	40	26	34	28%	79%	16%	0	14			0	0.81	0.8	45	53	-$2
17	**Proj**	**3**	**2**	**0**	**65**	**57**	**3.71**	**4.46**	**1.26**	**706**	**488**	**840**	**5.0**	**3.5**	**7.9**	**2.2**	**63%**	**8%**	**36**	**23**	**41**	**28%**	**75%**	**11%**	**0**						**3.9**	**61**	**72**	**$1**

Worley,Vance

Age: 29	Th: R	Role RP	Health B	LIMA Plan B	
Ht: 6' 2"	Wt: 220	Type	PT/Exp C	Rand Var -2	
			Consist B	MM 0001	

Prior to June groin strain, was putting together decent year, though skills didn't support sub-3.00 ERA at the time. Upon return, was saved by extremely low H%, as Cmd, Fpk, and SwK were abysmal. Even if he wasn't 100% healthy, Dom history is lousy, and a reliever who doesn't miss bats isn't worth targeting.

Yr	Tm	W	L	Sv	IP	K	ERA	xERA	WHIP	oOPS	vL	vR	BF/G	Ctl	Dom	Cmd	FpK	SwK	G	L	F	H%	S%	hr/f	GS	APC	DOM%	DIS%	Sv%	LI	RAR	BPV	BPX	R$
12	PHI	6	9	0	133	107	4.20	4.16	1.51	806	847	764	25.7	3.2	7.2	2.3	61%	6%	46	24	30	35%	74%	10%	23	95	17%	39%			-3.0	68	89	-$5
13	MIN *	7	8	0	107	51	5.81	6.57	1.79	1004	1013	994	25.9	2.7	4.3	1.6	59%	4%	47	22	31	37%	68%	16%	10	92	10%	80%			-25.6	15	19	-$17
14	PIT *	11	6	0	157	111	3.44	3.75	1.23	679	666	691	25.4	1.5	6.4	4.3	63%	6%	49	20	30	32%	73%	9%	17	88	35%	18%	0	0.76	5.9	109	129	$7
15	PIT *	7	7	0	106	64	3.81	4.59	1.39	761	800	736	15.9	2.3	5.5	2.4	58%	6%	46	21	33	32%	75%	8%	8	50	0%	50%	0	0.80	1.9	54	64	-$1
16	BAL	2	2	1	87	56	3.53	4.81	1.37	746	763	731	10.4	3.6	5.8	1.6	55%	5%	48	18	34	28%	79%	12%	4	37	0%	25%	100	0.80	7.0	33	39	$0
1st Half		2	0	0	43	33	3.12	4.44	1.43	740	819	681	10.5	3.1	6.9	2.2	60%	7%	46	25	29	33%	81%	10%	2	37	0%	0%	0	1.02	5.7	64	76	$2
2nd Half		0	2	1	43	23	3.95	5.19	1.32	753	708	794	10.4	4.2	4.8	1.2	50%	3%	50	11	39	23%	76%	14%	2	37	0%	50%	100	0.57	1.3	2	2	-$1
17	**Proj**	**4**	**4**	**0**	**87**	**55**	**4.20**	**4.69**	**1.38**	**758**	**770**	**747**	**13.6**	**3.0**	**5.7**	**1.9**	**57%**	**5%**	**48**	**19**	**33**	**30%**	**72%**	**11%**	**10**						**-0.1**	**49**	**58**	**-$2**

Wright,Steven

Age: 32	Th: R	Role SP	Health F	LIMA Plan C	
Ht: 6' 2"	Wt: 220	Type	PT/Exp C	Rand Var -2	
			Consist A	MM 0103	

Remember - knuckleballers don't follow no stinkin' rules. Uptick in SwK and Dom—along with luck—fueled 1st half breakout. Stopped getting ahead of hitters in 2nd half, hurt his shoulder, and random fortune came back to bite him. ERA/xERA gap indicates he's due for some regression. DN: 5.00 ERA

Yr	Tm	W	L	Sv	IP	K	ERA	xERA	WHIP	oOPS	vL	vR	BF/G	Ctl	Dom	Cmd	FpK	SwK	G	L	F	H%	S%	hr/f	GS	APC	DOM%	DIS%	Sv%	LI	RAR	BPV	BPX	R$
12	a/a	10	7	0	142	90	4.05	4.84	1.63				25.2	5.2	5.7	1.1						31%	76%								-0.6	35	46	-$7
13	BOS *	10	7	0	149	83	4.86	5.62	1.79	659	760	350	24.5	5.0	5.0	1.0	46%	9%	38	26	36	34%	73%	0%	1	61	0%	100%	0	0.57	-18.2	23	30	-$15
14	BOS *	6	6	0	121	74	4.55	5.06	1.46	632	667	603	23.5	2.4	5.5	2.4	56%	10%	59	21	21	33%	71%	17%	1	58	0%	0%	0	0.26	-12.1	46	55	-$6
15	BOS *	7	9	0	125	83	4.95	5.17	1.54	722	671	770	22.6	3.3	6.0	1.8	55%	9%	43	14	43	33%	70%	12%	9	74	22%	56%	0	0.76	-15.3	38	46	-$9
16	BOS	13	6	0	157	127	3.33	4.42	1.24	653	608	686	27.3	3.3	7.3	2.2	55%	11%	44	19	37	29%	75%	7%	24	104	46%	25%			16.6	65	77	$13
1st Half		9	5	0	108	87	2.42	4.27	1.19	609	545	648	27.9	3.5	7.3	2.1	58%	11%	47	21	32	27%	81%	6%	16	108	56%	19%			23.6	61	72	$21
2nd Half		4	1	0	49	40	5.36	4.74	1.38	745	707	785	26.1	2.8	7.4	2.7	48%	11%	37	17	46	32%	62%	9%	8	97	25%	38%			-7.0	74	88	-$5
17	**Proj**	**11**	**7**	**0**	**160**	**118**	**4.13**	**4.80**	**1.44**	**770**	**722**	**813**	**24.7**	**3.2**	**6.6**	**2.1**	**53%**	**10%**	**44**	**16**	**39**	**32%**	**74%**	**9%**	**28**						**1.3**	**54**	**65**	**$0**

Young,Chris

Age: 38	Th: R	Role RP	Health C	LIMA Plan D+	
Ht: 6' 10"	Wt: 280	Type Pwr xFB	PT/Exp B	Rand Var +5	
			Consist A	MM 0201	

Luck finally ran out after years of outperforming skills. Fly balls left park at an alarming rate, including 26 HR in 56 IP as SP. Dramatic increase in sliders led to surge in SwK and Dom, particularly out of pen in 2nd half, but that's lone positive takeaway. As xERA history shows, "A" Consistency grade not always a good thing.

Yr	Tm	W	L	Sv	IP	K	ERA	xERA	WHIP	oOPS	vL	vR	BF/G	Ctl	Dom	Cmd	FpK	SwK	G	L	F	H%	S%	hr/f	GS	APC	DOM%	DIS%	Sv%	LI	RAR	BPV	BPX	R$
12	NYM	4	9	0	115	80	4.15	5.20	1.35	784	843	727	24.7	2.8	6.3	2.2	63%	9%	22	20	58	30%	73%	8%	20	92	15%	50%			-1.9	37	48	-$2
13	aaa	1	2	0	32	11	10.08	11.33	2.46				24.1	4.2	3.2	0.8						40%	63%								-24.5	-80	-104	-$18
14	SEA	12	9	0	165	108	3.65	5.06	1.23	733	810	632	22.9	3.3	5.9	1.8	59%	8%	22	19	59	25%	77%	9%	29	91	17%	41%	0	0.78	1.8	18	21	$7
15	KC	11	6	0	123	83	3.06	5.09	1.09	640	732	542	14.7	3.1	6.1	1.9	58%	10%	25	17	58	22%	78%	8%	18	58	17%	39%	0	0.69	13.6	27	33	$13
16	KC	3	9	1	89	94	6.19	5.01	1.66	942	1163	752	11.9	4.4	9.5	2.2	59%	12%	31	19	49	33%	72%	21%	13	49	0%	62%	100	0.56	-21.9	63	75	-$11
1st Half		2	7	0	58	60	6.24	5.20	1.58	961	1312	657	18.5	4.5	9.4	2.1	61%	11%	28	17	55	28%	74%	24%	12	77	0%	58%	0	0.72	-14.6	52	62	-$10
2nd Half		1	2	1	31	34	6.10	4.65	1.81	910	897	918	7.4	4.1	9.9	2.4	56%	13%	37	24	39	40%	70%	16%	1	30	0%	100%	100	0.44	-7.3	83	99	-$12
17	**Proj**	**6**	**8**	**0**	**116**	**99**	**5.11**	**5.21**	**1.50**	**851**	**951**	**753**	**12.1**	**3.8**	**7.7**	**2.1**	**59%**	**11%**	**29**	**19**	**52**	**31%**	**73%**	**13%**	**9**						**-13.1**	**44**	**52**	**-$7**

Ziegler,Brad

Age: 37	Th: R	Role RP	Health A	LIMA Plan C+	
Ht: 6' 4"	Wt: 195	Type Pwr xGB	PT/Exp B	Rand Var -5	
			Consist A	MM 4210	

Saves dried up following trade to BOS, but skills took off: more than doubled SwK on changeup (29%), while lifting Dom, SwK to career-best marks. Lack of velocity will make it tough to duplicate 2nd half performance. But elite GB% remains intact; recent success as closer could lead to more 9th inning opps.

Yr	Tm	W	L	Sv	IP	K	ERA	xERA	WHIP	oOPS	vL	vR	BF/G	Ctl	Dom	Cmd	FpK	SwK	G	L	F	H%	S%	hr/f	GS	APC	DOM%	DIS%	Sv%	LI	RAR	BPV	BPX	R$
12	ARI	6	1	0	69	42	2.49	2.92	1.09	578	749	501	3.4	2.8	5.5	2.0	65%	10%	76	17	8	26%	77%	13%	0	12			0	0.93	12.9	79	103	$7
13	ARI	8	1	13	73	44	2.22	3.16	1.14	594	647	550	3.8	2.7	5.4	2.0	63%	10%	70	19	11	26%	81%	13%	0	13			87	1.50	14.8	72	94	$13
14	ARI	5	3	1	67	54	3.49	3.23	1.25	681	596	734	4.1	3.2	7.3	2.3	59%	11%	64	17	19	29%	73%	14%	0	14			11	1.39	2.1	86	102	$2
15	ARI	0	3	30	68	36	1.85	3.24	0.96	524	621	430	4.0	2.3	4.8	2.1	59%	9%	73	14	14	22%	82%	11%	0	14			94	1.37	17.7	76	91	$18
16	2 TM	4	7	22	68	58	2.25	3.59	1.37	669	723	630	4.2	3.4	7.7	2.2	56%	12%	63	19	18	33%	84%	6%	0	15			79	1.48	16.3	86	102	$13
1st Half		2	3	17	37	25	2.65	3.99	1.42	691	746	634	4.5	3.6	6.0	1.7	60%	10%	65	18	17	32%	79%	0%	0	16			89	1.46	7.1	54	64	$16
2nd Half		2	4	5	31	33	1.76	3.15	1.30	643	678	626	3.8	3.2	9.7	3.0	52%	14%	61	20	19	34%	89%	13%	0	14			56	1.50	9.2	126	150	$9
17	**Proj**	**3**	**5**	**7**	**65**	**54**	**3.11**	**3.30**	**1.21**	**625**	**669**	**594**	**3.9**	**3.0**	**7.5**	**2.5**	**57%**	**11%**	**66**	**18**	**16**	**30%**	**74%**	**10%**	**0**						**8.7**	**98**	**116**	**$5**

Zimmermann,Jordan

Age: 31	Th: R	Role SP	Health D	LIMA Plan B+	
Ht: 6' 2"	Wt: 220	Type	PT/Exp A	Rand Var 0	
			Consist B	MM 1003	

9-7, 4.87 ERA in 105 IP at DET. Allowed only 2 ER in five April GS, but all downhill from there. Neck, back issues limited him to four ineffective starts in 2nd half, but Dom, SwK, and velocity were down well before that. Should bounce back some, but with questions regarding whiffs and health, he's now a risky investment.

Yr	Tm	W	L	Sv	IP	K	ERA	xERA	WHIP	oOPS	vL	vR	BF/G	Ctl	Dom	Cmd	FpK	SwK	G	L	F	H%	S%	hr/f	GS	APC	DOM%	DIS%	Sv%	LI	RAR	BPV	BPX	R$
12	WAS	12	8	0	196	153	2.94	3.78	1.17	686	650	723	25.2	2.0	7.0	3.6	69%	9%	43	23	33	30%	78%	9%	32	97	28%	28%			25.8	94	123	$20
13	WAS	19	9	0	213	161	3.25	3.50	1.09	654	702	601	27.0	1.7	6.8	4.0	67%	9%	48	21	31	28%	73%	10%	32	96	47%	16%			16.2	103	134	$22
14	WAS	14	5	0	200	182	2.66	3.22	1.07	631	655	606	25.0	1.3	8.2	6.3	71%	11%	40	24	36	31%	77%	6%	32	91	50%	13%			26.6	130	155	$22
15	WAS	13	10	0	202	164	3.66	3.82	1.20	699	776	617	25.2	1.7	7.3	4.2	67%	9%	42	22	36	31%	74%	11%	33	94	27%	18%			7.5	105	125	$13
16	DET *	9	8	0	126	74	4.42	4.91	1.40	804	738	862	22.1	2.2	5.3	2.4	65%	8%	43	18	39	31%	72%	10%	18	90	17%	39%	0	0.73	-3.5	42	50	-$1
1st Half		9	4	0	96	60	3.95	4.51	1.24	731	665	789	26.4	1.7	5.6	3.3	65%	8%	45	18	37	31%	69%	7%	15	101	20%	27%			2.8	79	94	$5
2nd Half		0	4	0	30	14	5.91	8.35	1.90	1419	1309	1521	15.7	3.9	4.1	1.0	67%	9%	30	19	51	33%	77%	32%	3	49	0%	100%	0	0.60	-6.4	-46	-55	-$18
17	**Proj**	**10**	**11**	**0**	**160**	**109**	**4.21**	**4.53**	**1.36**	**802**	**812**	**793**	**22.7**	**2.3**	**6.1**	**2.6**	**68%**	**9%**	**43**	**21**	**35**	**31%**	**73%**	**12%**	**32**						**-0.5**	**69**	**82**	**$1**

Zych,Tony

Age: 26	Th: R	Role RP	Health F	LIMA Plan C+	
Ht: 6' 3"	Wt: 190	Type Pwr	PT/Exp F	Rand Var 0	
			Consist D	MM 3400	

Prior to May shoulder issue that led to extended absence, Ctl had been trending in right direction, so drop can likely be attributed to small sample/injury. Status needs to be monitored after offseason surgery, but with ability to miss bats and keep ball down, could emerge as late-inning option in short order.

Yr	Tm	W	L	Sv	IP	K	ERA	xERA	WHIP	oOPS	vL	vR	BF/G	Ctl	Dom	Cmd	FpK	SwK	G	L	F	H%	S%	hr/f	GS	APC	DOM%	DIS%	Sv%	LI	RAR	BPV	BPX	R$
12	aa	2	1	0	25	24	5.17	4.94	1.68				5.6	4.5	8.9	2.0						39%	68%								-3.5	79	104	-$6
13	aa	5	5	3	56	34	3.69	3.90	1.44				5.1	3.5	5.4	1.6						31%	74%								1.2	55	72	-$1
14	aa	4	5	2	58	30	5.80	6.00	1.77				5.9	2.8	4.6	1.6						38%	66%								-14.8	34	40	-$9
15	SEA *	1	2	9	67	70	2.91	3.06	1.16	628	588	642	5.0	1.5	9.5	6.2	74%	15%	50	13	37	35%	75%	6%	1	21	0%	0%	82	1.22	8.7	179	214	$6
16	SEA	1	0	0	14	21	3.29	3.48	1.46	642	630	652	5.0	6.6	13.8	2.1	48%	11%	50	14	36	36%	75%	0%	0	21			0	0.44	1.5	99	118	-$3
1st Half		1	0	0	12	19	3.00	3.04	1.25	564	606	520	5.0	6.0	14.3	2.4	47%	12%	55	5	41	32%	73%	0%	0	21			0	0.49	1.8	127	152	-$2
2nd Half		0	0	0	2	2	5.40	7.42	3.00	1071	733	1750	5.0	10.8	10.8	1.0	50%	4%	33	50	17	53%	80%	0%	0	23			0	0.19	-0.2	-86	-102	-$8
17	**Proj**	**3**	**4**	**0**	**58**	**61**	**3.36**	**3.43**	**1.20**				**5.0**	**2.9**	**9.4**	**3.2**	**55%**	**11%**	**50**	**20**	**30**	**31%**	**75%**	**12%**	**0**						**5.9**	**119**	**141**	**$2**

BRIAN RUDD

The preceding section provided player boxes and analysis for 406 pitchers. As we know, far more than 406 pitchers will play in the major leagues in 2017. Many of those additional pitchers are covered in the minor league section, but that still leaves a gap: established major leaguers who don't play enough, or well enough, to merit a player box.

This section looks to fill that gap. Here, you will find "The Next Tier" of pitchers who are mostly past their growth years, but who are likely to see some playing time in 2017. We are including their 2015-16 MLB stats here for reference for you to do your own analysis. This way, if Ross Detwiler is rumored to be pushing for rotation spot at some point in 2017, a quick check here would confirm that his past skills do not indicate long-term success as a starter. Or if Josh Fields sneaks into a more promient bullpen role in 2017, this chart shows that if he could cut back on the fly balls, Cmd and BPV show some latent upside in shorter stints.

Pitcher	T	Yr	Age	W	Sv	IP	K	ERA	xERA	WHIP	vL	vR	CTL	DOM	CMD	SwK	FpK	G/L/F	H%	S%	BPV
Abad, Fernando	L	15	29	2	0	47	45	4.19	4.40	1.36	859	753	3.6	8.6	2.4	11.0	52	39/14/47	26	79	73
		16	30	1	1	46	41	3.70	4.61	1.34	459	789	4.3	8.0	1.9	8.3	61	43/19/38	28	26	49
Bastardo, Antonio	L	15	29	4	1	57	64	2.99	4.07	1.14	448	626	4.1	10.1	2.5	15.0	62	31/18/51	25	75	80
		16	30	3	0	67	74	4.55	4.58	1.37	816	705	4.3	9.9	2.3	14.7	60	30/22/48	28	28	70
Belisle, Matt	R	15	35	1	0	33	25	2.71	4.38	1.48	784	639	4.1	6.8	1.7	8.9	67	52/19/28	31	81	42
		16	36	0	0	46	32	1.76	3.93	1.09	443	736	1.4	6.3	4.6	9.5	68	47/22/31	29	15	101
Bolsinger, Mike	R	15	27	6	0	109	98	3.63	3.87	1.37	793	636	3.7	8.1	2.2	9.1	55	53/18/29	30	76	76
		16	28	1	0	27	25	6.95	4.49	1.54	961	876	3.0	8.3	2.8	9.8	61	34/28/39	34	40	79
Boyer, Blaine	R	16	34	2	1	66	26	3.95	5.09	1.47	778	758	2.3	3.5	1.5	6.5	64	49/22/29	33	27	28
		15	33	3	1	65	33	2.49	4.48	1.25	436	823	2.6	4.6	1.7	8.0	63	48/24/28	27	83	37
Coleman, Louis	R	15	29	1	0	3	1	0.00	5.70	1.00	400	500	6.0	3.0	0.5	11.9	67	38/25/38	13	100	-92
		16	30	2	0	48	45	4.69	4.81	1.44	980	696	4.5	8.4	1.9	12.8	63	35/24/41	31	31	43
Collmenter, Josh	R	15	29	4	1	121	63	3.79	4.73	1.26	737	834	1.8	4.7	2.6	7.3	59	34/26/40	28	76	48
		16	30	3	0	41	33	3.72	4.41	1.27	751	742	3.5	7.2	2.1	8.0	61	45/19/36	26	22	58
Dean, Pat	L	16	27	1	0	67	50	6.30	4.90	1.65	832	937	3.1	6.7	2.2	6.8	61	44/19/36	35	35	59
Detwiler, Ross	L	16	30	2	0	48	26	6.16	5.61	1.62	644	845	3.5	4.9	1.4	6.5	57	43/22/35	32	38	13
		15	29	1	0	58	41	7.28	5.72	2.03	660	1136	5.6	6.4	1.1	7.5	53	44/22/33	37	66	-14
Diaz, Jumbo	R	15	31	2	1	60	70	4.19	3.28	1.26	774	737	2.7	10.5	3.9	14.8	60	44/22/35	32	72	137
		16	32	1	0	43	37	3.14	4.51	1.28	693	727	4.0	7.7	1.9	11.0	57	47/16/38	25	15	57
Dunn, Mike	L	15	30	2	0	54	65	4.50	3.92	1.39	655	754	4.8	10.8	2.2	12.6	59	39/22/39	30	70	82
		16	31	6	0	42	38	3.42	4.26	1.28	702	766	2.4	8.1	3.5	12.6	59	28/30/43	32	22	88
Estevez, Carlos	R	16	23	3	11	55	59	5.24	4.42	1.42	539	855	4.6	9.7	2.1	11.8	57	44/16/40	30	36	72
Fields, Josh	R	15	29	4	0	50	67	3.59	3.37	1.16	705	530	3.4	12.0	3.5	13.5	60	34/18/48	31	68	135
		16	30	1	0	35	42	4.63	4.18	1.54	788	869	2.8	10.8	3.8	13.8	59	36/16/49	39	28	132
Fien, Casey	R	16	32	1	0	39	35	5.52	4.49	1.41	886	945	2.3	8.1	3.5	12.9	65	34/21/45	30	26	94
		15	31	4	0	63	41	3.57	4.29	1.09	717	597	1.1	5.8	5.1	9.3	68	37/20/43	27	70	89
Hatcher, Chris	R	15	30	3	4	39	45	3.69	3.47	1.23	688	682	3.0	10.4	3.5	13.0	60	43/18/39	31	73	127
		16	31	5	0	40	43	5.60	4.47	1.52	482	1028	4.7	9.6	2.0	10.4	60	44/17/38	30	32	68
Henderson, Jim	R	16	33	2	0	35	40	4.37	4.57	1.40	756	822	3.6	10.3	2.9	11.1	56	26/20/54	31	24	92
Howell, J.P.	L	15	32	6	1	44	39	1.43	3.50	1.39	518	823	2.9	8.0	2.8	10.4	59	60/15/24	33	93	104
		16	33	1	0	50	44	4.12	3.65	1.41	752	709	2.7	7.9	2.9	9.2	58	59/19/22	35	28	106
Hughes, Jared	R	15	30	3	0	67	36	2.28	3.86	1.33	684	741	2.6	4.8	1.9	10.0	61	64/18/19	31	84	60
		16	31	1	1	59	34	3.05	4.62	1.42	849	751	3.4	5.2	1.5	9.8	60	58/16/26	30	18	39
Hunter, Tommy	R	15	29	4	1	60	47	4.19	3.93	1.25	754	674	2.1	7.0	3.4	10.8	66	45/21/35	30	69	93
		16	30	2	0	34	23	3.18	3.98	1.26	715	656	2.1	6.1	2.9	9.9	65	50/25/26	33	26	80
Kontos, George	R	16	31	3	0	53	35	2.54	4.56	1.17	660	569	3.4	5.9	1.8	10.6	61	44/23/32	25	20	37
		15	30	4	0	73	44	2.34	3.98	0.94	684	544	1.5	5.4	3.7	10.4	58	43/22/35	22	83	78
Latos, Mat	R	16	28	7	0	70	42	4.89	5.46	1.49	767	828	3.9	5.4	1.4	7.3	57	43/19/38	29	29	14
		15	27	4	0	116	100	4.96	3.89	1.31	803	688	2.5	7.8	3.1	10.7	61	44/24/32	31	63	94
Layne, Tom	L	15	30	2	1	47	45	4.00	3.97	1.44	418	950	5.1	8.6	1.7	8.8	54	55/22/23	29	72	48
		16	31	2	1	44	38	3.67	4.27	1.31	571	750	4.3	7.7	1.8	9.5	56	51/18/32	29	27	53
LeBlanc, Wade	L	16	31	4	2	62	51	3.77	4.27	1.13	680	801	1.6	7.4	4.6	9.5	63	34/21/45	26	21	102
Logan, Boone	L	15	30	0	0	35	44	4.36	3.90	1.62	602	909	4.4	11.3	2.6	15.8	61	43/19/38	37	74	106
		16	31	2	1	46	57	3.71	3.25	1.02	477	759	3.9	11.1	2.9	16.7	65	50/17/33	23	35	122
Lopez, Javier	L	15	37	1	0	39	26	1.61	3.41	0.90	323	734	3.7	6.0	1.6	8.8	60	67/14/18	17	82	53
		16	38	1	1	26	15	4.12	5.04	1.49	634	948	5.2	5.2	1.0	6.8	61	62/15/23	26	25	-6
Lowe, Mark	R	15	32	1	1	55	61	1.96	2.97	1.05	724	523	2.0	10.0	5.1	14.4	67	40/27/32	31	85	145
		16	33	1	0	49	49	7.15	4.82	1.59	849	985	3.8	9.0	2.3	10.6	62	37/20/44	32	41	72

THE NEXT TIER

Pitchers

Pitcher	T	Yr	Age	W	Sv	IP	K	ERA	xERA	WHIP	vL	vR	CTL	DOM	CMD	SwK	FpK	G/L/F	H%	S%	BPV
Manship, Jeff	R	15	30	1	0	39	33	0.92	3.14	0.77	644	310	2.3	7.6	3.3	11.1	62	50/22/28	19	90	102
		16	31	2	0	43	36	3.13	4.80	1.44	795	725	4.6	7.5	1.6	12.0	60	51/13/36	27	15	40
Matusz, Brian	L	15	28	1	0	49	56	2.94	3.80	1.18	565	721	3.7	10.3	2.8	13.3	61	35/20/45	27	79	99
		16	29	0	0	9	3	14.00	10.14	2.89	1552	1298	9.0	3.0	0.3	8.3	47	38/23/38	33	40	-173
McGowan, Dustin	R	16	34	1	1	67	63	2.82	4.00	1.22	918	468	4.4	8.5	1.9	14.5	59	54/17/28	24	19	65
		15	33	1	0	23	21	7.01	6.23	2.12	1096	818	7.8	8.2	1.1	11.4	56	39/26/35	31	74	-45
Medlen, Kris	R	16	30	1	0	24	18	7.84	6.50	2.07	891	877	7.5	6.7	0.9	9.1	43	47/21/32	35	40	-55
		15	29	6	0	58	40	4.03	4.21	1.27	734	671	2.8	6.2	2.2	8.8	58	50/17/33	28	71	64
Miller, Justin	R	16	29	1	0	42	45	5.76	4.57	1.66	1125	740	4.3	9.6	2.3	10.6	60	35/27/38	37	33	70
		15	28	3	1	33	38	4.08	3.25	0.97	542	558	3.0	10.3	3.5	13.5	62	38/24/39	24	57	120
Milone, Tommy	L	15	28	9	1	128	91	3.93	4.34	1.28	603	772	2.5	6.4	2.5	8.2	64	42/23/35	28	73	67
		16	29	3	0	69	49	5.73	4.73	1.53	851	859	2.9	6.4	2.2	9.1	65	46/24/30	32	32	61
Morton, Charlie	R	15	31	9	0	129	96	4.81	3.79	1.38	894	633	2.9	6.7	2.3	8.5	62	57/21/21	31	66	78
		16	32	1	0	17	19	4.21	3.10	1.35	743	559	4.2	10.0	2.4	12.7	62	63/21/16	33	32	106
Moylan, Peter	R	16	37	2	0	44	34	3.46	3.91	1.31	973	542	3.3	6.9	2.1	9.9	57	61/17/21	29	24	75
		15	36	1	0	10	8	3.56	2.99	1.19	2250	475	0.0	7.1	-	8.9	57	69/8/22	31	73	172
Oberholtzer, Brett	L	16	27	3	1	70	54	5.91	5.12	1.63	829	952	3.7	6.9	1.9	8.5	62	42/21/36	31	29	44
		15	26	2	0	38	27	4.49	4.80	1.60	959	754	4.0	6.4	1.6	7.3	60	49/18/34	33	74	33
O'Flaherty, Eric	L	16	31	1	0	28	22	7.02	4.74	1.77	768	1000	3.5	7.0	2.0	8.9	62	54/18/28	37	40	63
		15	30	1	0	30	21	8.10	5.36	2.17	677	1162	5.4	6.3	1.2	10.4	65	58/23/19	39	60	4
Ohlendorf, Ross	R	16	33	5	2	65	68	4.69	4.67	1.40	651	905	4.4	9.4	2.1	11.0	56	32/22/46	27	26	59
		15	32	3	1	19	19	3.77	4.28	1.47	747	827	3.3	9.0	2.7	10.9	54	36/24/41	31	83	85
Osich, Josh	L	16	27	1	0	36	25	4.74	4.54	1.39	502	1089	4.7	6.2	1.3	10.9	53	65/12/24	23	28	27
		15	26	2	0	28	27	2.23	3.85	1.13	629	638	2.6	8.6	3.4	17.9	57	49/10/42	25	89	112
Otero, Dan	R	15	30	2	0	46	28	6.82	4.15	1.52	884	887	1.2	5.5	4.7	7.3	73	49/23/28	35	56	93
		16	31	5	1	70	57	1.54	2.95	0.91	522	529	1.3	7.3	5.7	8.0	67	62/18/20	26	16	136
Perez, Oliver	L	15	33	2	0	41	51	4.17	3.61	1.32	533	867	3.3	11.2	3.4	13.0	66	36/24/40	32	70	127
		16	34	2	0	40	46	4.95	4.19	1.45	720	790	4.5	10.4	2.3	9.7	54	39/23/38	34	33	82
Petit, Yusmeiro	R	16	31	3	1	62	49	4.50	4.51	1.32	925	698	2.2	7.1	3.3	9.0	64	42/17/41	30	27	89
		15	30	1	1	76	59	3.67	4.34	1.18	828	680	1.8	7.0	3.9	10.1	63	33/21/46	28	75	89
Putnam, Zach	R	16	29	1	0	27	30	2.32	3.64	1.33	546	694	3.7	10.0	2.7	18.0	57	40/33/26	33	15	98
		15	28	3	0	48	64	4.11	3.36	1.37	770	702	4.5	12.0	2.7	17.4	58	44/21/35	31	75	115
Qualls, Chad	R	15	36	3	4	49	46	4.40	3.00	1.12	614	714	1.6	8.4	5.1	12.1	65	60/15/25	29	63	145
		16	37	2	0	32	22	5.31	4.62	1.61	978	796	2.5	6.1	2.4	10.1	64	55/20/25	33	30	75
Ramos, Cesar	L	15	31	2	0	52	43	2.76	3.80	1.34	662	707	2.6	7.4	2.9	9.1	63	47/24/29	34	79	88
		16	32	3	1	47	27	6.10	5.54	1.69	851	1017	3.8	5.1	1.4	7.6	64	43/20/37	32	29	11
Rasmus, Cory	R	16	28	0	0	24	17	5.95	6.58	1.69	718	876	6.0	6.3	1.1	10.1	51	30/18/52	28	32	-38
		15	27	0	0	20	27	5.35	3.83	1.29	731	653	4.9	12.0	2.5	14.3	55	38/10/52	26	61	98
Rodriguez, Fernando	R	15	31	4	0	58	65	3.87	3.76	1.15	466	672	3.7	10.1	2.7	13.7	60	39/18/43	26	67	97
		16	32	2	0	40	37	4.25	4.33	1.17	963	450	3.8	8.3	2.2	13.0	59	36/22/42	26	36	60
Rzepczynski, Marc	L	16	30	1	0	47	46	2.67	3.99	1.59	674	716	5.5	8.8	1.6	11.7	50	67/12/20	34	18	53
		15	29	2	0	35	41	5.66	2.75	1.54	661	972	3.6	10.5	2.9	14.6	61	67/20/12	38	63	138
Shreve, Chasen	L	15	24	6	0	58	64	3.10	4.13	1.41	738	738	5.1	9.9	1.9	11.5	53	46/13/41	27	86	64
		16	25	2	1	33	33	5.18	4.14	1.27	1058	711	3.5	9.0	2.5	14.4	62	45/15/40	26	32	89
Simon, Alfredo	R	15	34	#	0	187	117	5.05	4.81	1.44	862	734	3.3	5.6	1.7	8.4	56	44/22/35	29	67	35
		16	35	2	0	58	39	9.43	5.84	2.06	1104	949	4.8	6.0	1.3	7.7	54	50/20/31	36	44	7
Sipp, Tony	L	16	32	1	1	43	40	5.00	4.96	1.62	894	1012	3.8	8.3	2.2	13.3	55	36/18/46	32	21	62
		15	31	3	0	54	62	2.00	3.32	1.04	593	619	2.5	10.3	4.1	14.7	65	39/17/44	27	86	135
Smith, Carson	R	15	25	2	#	70	92	2.31	2.20	1.01	593	502	2.8	11.8	4.2	12.9	59	65/17/18	29	77	180
		16	26	0	0	2	2	0.00	3.69	1.36	250	571	4.1	8.2	2.0	4.2	36	75/0/25	25	0	83
Smith, Josh	R	15	27	0	0	32	30	6.99	5.26	1.96	1120	758	5.9	8.4	1.4	9.1	57	38/28/34	37	66	9
		16	28	3	0	59	48	4.71	4.97	1.40	890	664	4.0	7.3	1.8	11.1	64	42/17/41	27	28	44
Solis, Sammy	L	16	27	2	0	41	47	2.41	3.84	1.27	556	639	4.6	10.3	2.2	12.8	65	42/26/32	30	20	81
		15	26	1	0	21	17	3.41	4.04	1.37	718	718	1.7	7.3	4.3	9.9	54	45/21/34	33	78	107
Vogelsong, Ryan	R	15	37	9	0	135	108	4.67	4.62	1.47	906	679	3.9	7.2	1.9	6.7	60	45/19/36	30	71	48
		16	38	3	0	82	61	4.82	5.22	1.47	917	727	4.4	6.7	1.5	6.6	58	40/21/38	29	30	20
Wilhelmsen, Tom	R	16	32	2	1	46	28	6.83	5.25	1.71	901	999	3.7	5.5	1.5	8.8	55	51/15/34	34	35	27
		15	31	2	#	62	60	3.19	4.19	1.37	874	564	4.2	8.7	2.1	11.2	53	42/20/37	31	77	63
Wright, Mike	R	15	25	3	0	44	26	6.11	5.48	1.58	919	855	3.7	5.3	1.4	7.6	54	38/19/43	29	66	12
		16	26	3	0	74	50	5.82	4.99	1.44	990	750	3.2	6.1	1.9	7.1	59	42/19/39	30	38	44
Yates, Kirby	R	15	28	1	0	20	21	8.06	4.61	1.49	1254	840	3.1	9.4	3.0	10.3	65	27/21/52	25	60	89
		16	29	2	0	41	50	5.26	3.80	1.46	584	829	4.2	10.9	2.6	12.3	64	44/23/34	34	35	106

5-Year Injury Log

The following chart details the disabled list stints for all players during the past five years. Use this as a supplement to our health grades in the player profile boxes as well as the "Risk Management" charts that start on page 249. It's also where to turn when in May you want to check whether, say, Desmond Jennings' left knee soreness should be concerning (answer: Yes, very).

For each injury, the number of days the player missed during the season is listed. A few DL stints are for fewer than 15 days; these are cases when a player was placed on the DL prior to Opening Day (only in-season time lost is listed).

Abbreviations:
Lt, L = left
Rt, R = right
fx = fractured
R/C = rotator cuff
str = strained
surg = surgery
TJS = Tommy John surgery (ulnar collateral ligament reconstruction)
x 2 = two occurrences of the same injury
x 3 = three occurrences of the same injury

Throughout the spring and all season long, BaseballHQ.com has comprehensive injury coverage.

FIVE-YEAR INJURY LOG — Batters

Batter	Yr	Days	Injury
Abreu,Jose	14	15	L ankle tendinitis
Ackley,Dustin	15	28	R lumbar strain
	16	126	Dislocated R should
Adams,Matt	13	15	R oblique strain
	14	14	Tightness in L calf
	15	105	Strained R quad
	16	22	L should inflammation
Adrianza,Ehire	14	82	Strained R hamstring x 2
	16	109	Fractured L foot
Ahmed,Nick	16	72	R hip impingement
Alonso,Yonder	13	41	R hand contusion
	14	55	Strained R forearm/R wrist tend
	15	46	Low back strain; bruised R shoulder
Altherr,Aaron	16	117	Repair torn tendon L wrist
Aoki,Norichika	14	20	Strained L groin
	15	40	Concussion; fx fibula
Arcia,Oswaldo	14	35	Strained R wrist
	15	30	R hip flexor strain
	16	21	Strained R elbow
Arenado,Nolan	14	40	Fractured L middle finger
Asche,Cody	14	26	Strained L hamstring
	16	61	Strained R oblique muscle
Avila,Alex	12	15	Strained R. hamstring
	13	31	L forearm bruise; Concussion
	14	5	Concussion
	15	55	Loose bodies in L knee
	16	66	Strained R hamstring x 2
Aybar,Erick	12	15	Fractured R. toe
	13	20	Bruised L heel
	16	15	Bruised R foot
Baez,Javier	16	12	Bruised L thumb
Barney,Darwin	13	15	L knee laceration
Bautista,Jose	12	77	Inflam R. wrist/Surgery on R. wrist
	13	40	L hip bone bruise
	16	53	Sprnd L knee; L big toe
Beckham,Gordon	13	54	Fractured hamate bone, L wrist
	14	25	Strained L oblique
	16	56	Strained L hamstring x2

FIVE-YEAR INJURY LOG — Batters

Batter	Yr	Days	Injury
Beckham,Tim	14	133	Rec. from surgery R Knee- torn ACL
	15	25	R hamstring strain
Belt,Brandon	14	81	Concussion x 2/Fx L thumb
Beltran,Carlos	14	29	Concussion; hyper ext. Rt elbow
	15	16	Strained L oblique
Beltre,Adrian	14	12	Strained L quadriceps
	15	21	Sprained L thumb
Benintendi,Andrew	16	20	Sprnd L knee
Bethancourt,Christian	16	33	Strnd L intercostal
Betts,Mookie	15	13	Concussion
Bird,Gregory	16	183	Rec fr surg.-torn labrum R should
Blackmon,Charlie	12	135	Turf toe
	16	15	Turf toe on L foot
Blanco,Andres	16	39	Fractured L index finger
Blanco,Gregor	15	9	Concussion
	16	24	R should impingement
Blanks,Kyle	12	173	Labrum tear L. shoulder
	13	80	L Achilles tendinitis
	14	109	Strnd L calf; L Achilles tendinitis
	15	129	Achilles tendinitis; cyst removal
Blash,Jabari	16	42	Sprnd L middle finger
Bogaerts,Xander	14	7	Concussion
Bonifacio,Emilio	12	112	Sprained L. thumb x2; spr. R. knee
	14	39	Strained R ribcage
	15	16	Strained L oblique
Bour,Justin	16	62	Sprnd R ankle
Bourgeois,Jason	15	84	Fractured L shoulder
Bourjos,Peter	12	15	Sore R. wrist
	13	100	Fx Rt wrist; Strained Lt hammy
	16	15	Sprnd R should
Bourn,Michael	13	25	R hand laceration
	14	56	Rec from surg: strained L hamstring
Brantley,Michael	16	164	R should fatigue; rec fr R should surg.
Brantly,Rob	15	45	Avulsion fracture, L thumb
Braun,Ryan	13	28	R thumb contusion
	14	10	strained R oblique muscle
Brett,Ryan	15	166	Subluxation of L shoulder
Brignac,Reid	14	31	Sprained L ankle

FIVE-YEAR INJURY LOG — Batters

Batter	Yr	Days	Injury
Brito,Socrates	16	42	Fractured toe R foot
Brown,Domonic	13	13	Concussion
	15	28	L Achilles tendinitis
Bruce,Jay	14	16	Rec from meniscus repair on L knee
Butler,Billy	16	7	Concussion
Buxton,Byron	15	45	Sprained L thumb
Byrd,Marlon	15	16	Fractured R wrist
Cabrera,Asdrubal	13	22	R quadriceps strain
	15	16	Strained R hamstring
	16	17	Strained patella tendon L knee
Cabrera,Everth	13	18	Strained L hamstring
	14	75	Strained L hamstring x 2
	15	15	L foot contusion
Cabrera,Melky	13	82	Strained L knee; Tendinitis
	14	21	Fractured R pinky finger
Cabrera,Miguel	15	41	L calf strain
Cain,Lorenzo	12	89	Strained L. groin
	13	26	Strained L oblique
	14	18	Strained L groin
	16	30	Strained L hamstring
Calhoun,Kole	14	35	Sprained R ankle
Canha,Mark	16	146	Strained back
Carpenter,Matt	12	30	R. oblique strain
	16	29	Strained R oblique muscle
Carrera,Ezequiel	16	15	Strained L Achilles tendon
Casali,Curtis	14	5	Concussion
	15	40	Strained L hamstring
Castellanos,Nick	16	51	Fractured L hand
Castillo,Welington	12	71	MCL sprain in R. knee
	13	5	Surgery - R knee
	14	19	L ribcage inflammation
Castro,Jason	12	36	R. knee swelling
	13	13	Cyst on R knee
	15	19	Strained R quad
Ceciliani,Darrell	15	27	Strained L hamstring
Cervelli,Francisco	13	156	Fractured R hand
	14	64	Hamstring injury
	16	38	Fractured L hand
Cespedes,Yoenis	12	25	Strained muscle in L. hand
	13	15	Strained muscle, L hand
	16	15	Strained R quadriceps
Chirinos,Robinson	12	182	Concussion
	15	37	L shoulder strain
	16	60	Fractured R forearm
Chisenhall,Lonnie	12	71	Fractured R. ulna
	16	17	R forearm injury
Choo,Shin-Soo	14	35	Bone spur in L elbow
	16	124	Strnd R calf/L ham/back; fract L frarm
Clevenger,Steve	12	33	Strained R. oblique
	13	169	L oblique strain
	16	95	Fractured R hand
Coghlan,Chris	13	84	R calf irritation
	14	41	Sore/strained R ribcage
Colon,Christian	14	12	fractured right middle finger
Corporan,Carlos	13	20	Concussion
	15	46	Sprained L thumb

FIVE-YEAR INJURY LOG — Batters

Batter	Yr	Days	Injury
Cowgill,Collin	12	24	Sprained L. ankle
	14	22	Fractured nose
	15	96	Sprained R wrist
Cozart,Zack	15	116	R knee surgery
	16	7	Sore R knee
Craig,Allen	12	43	Surg recovery; L. hamstring strain
	14	16	Sprained L foot
Crawford,Carl	12	148	Recovery from L. wrist surgery+ TJS
	13	33	Strained L hamstring
	14	43	Sprained L ankle
	15	84	Strained R oblique
	16	18	Sore lower back
Crisp,Coco	12	18	Infected ear/sinus
	13	15	Strained L hamstring
	15	104	Cervical strain; R elbow surg.
Cron,C.J.	16	42	Fractured L hand
Culberson,Charlie	15	67	Lumbar disc inflammation
d Arnaud,Travis	14	14	Concussion
	15	88	Hyperextended L elbow; fx R hand
	16	56	Strained R rotator cuff
d'Arnaud,Chase	13	61	L thumb surgery
Davidson,Matthew	16	94	Fractured R foot
Davis,Chris	14	14	Strained L oblique
Davis,Ike	13	21	Strained R oblique
	15	80	Strained L hip; quad
Davis,Khristopher	15	37	Torn meniscus, R knee
Davis,Rajai	13	24	Strained oblique
De Aza,Alejandro	12	15	Bruised L. ribs
Decker,Jaff	15	13	L calf strain
DeJesus,David	13	39	R shoulder sprain
	14	74	Fractured L hand
Denorfia,Chris	15	45	Strained L hamstring x2
Descalso,Daniel	16	40	Fractured L hand
DeShields Jr.,Delino	15	20	Strained L hamstring
Desmond,Ian	12	26	Torn L. oblique
Diaz,Aledmys	16	40	Fractured R thumb
Diaz,Elias	16	128	Disc R elbow, cellulitis L knee
Diaz,Jonathan	14	182	L hamstring injury
Dickerson,Corey	15	98	Non-displaced rib fx; fasciitis L ft x2
Dietrich,Derek	14	53	Strained R wrist
	16	11	Bruised R knee
Drew,Stephen	12	83	Recovering from R. ankle surgery
	13	31	R Hamstring tight; Concussion
	16	42	Vertigo
Duda,Lucas	13	46	Strained L intercostal
	15	16	Lower back strain
	16	117	Stress fracture lower back
Duffy,Matt	16	78	Recovering from surg. on L Achilles
Dyson,Jarrod	13	37	R ankle sprain
	16	16	Strained R oblique muscle
Eaton,Adam	13	100	L elbow strain
	14	31	Rt oblique muscle; Rt hamstring
Eibner,Brett	16	15	Sprnd L ankle
Ellis,A.J.	13	15	L oblique strain
	14	54	Sprained R ankle/L knee surgery
	15	15	R knee inflammation
Ellsbury,Jacoby	12	90	Subluxation of R. shoulder
	15	49	R knee sprain

FIVE-YEAR INJURY LOG — Batters

Batter	Yr	Days	Injury
Elmore,Jake	14	74	Strained L quadriceps
Encarnacion,Edwin	13	13	Surgery (cart) - L wrist
	14	39	Strained R quadriceps
Escobar,Alcides	14	16	Sore R shoulder
	15	7	Concussion & L cheek contusion
Escobar,Yunel	16	13	Concussion
Espinosa,Danny	13	15	Broken bone in R wrist
Ethier,Andre	12	15	Strained L. oblique
	16	160	Fractured tibia R leg
Featherston,Taylor	15	16	Uppen back strain
Federowicz,Tim	15	128	Torn meniscus, R knee
Fielder,Prince	14	129	Herniated disc in neck (surgery)
	16	75	Herniated discs neck
Flaherty,Ryan	15	30	Strained R groin x2
Flores,Wilmer	16	17	Strained L hamstring
Flowers,Tyler	13	28	R shoulder surgery
	16	33	Fractured L hand
Forsythe,Logan	12	60	L. foot fracture
	13	71	Plantar fasciitis, R foot
	16	27	Fractured L scapula
Fowler,Dexter	13	15	R wrist soreness
	14	43	Strained R intercostal
	16	32	Strained R hamstring
Franco,Maikel	15	48	Fractured L wrist
Franklin,Nick	15	42	Strained L oblique
	16	7	Concussion
Freeman,Freddie	13	15	Strained R oblique
	15	47	Strained R oblique; bruised R wrist
Freese,David	13	8	Strained lower back
	14	17	Fractured R middle finger
	15	40	Fractured R index finger
Fuld,Sam	12	110	Surgery - R. wrist
	14	36	Concussion
	16	183	Strained L should
Galvis,Freddy	12	119	Fracture of L4-5 veR.ebra
	14	15	Staph infection in L knee
Garcia,Avisail	13	30	Bruised R heel
	14	128	Surgery on L shoulder torn labrum
	16	14	Sprnd R knee
Gardner,Brett	12	164	Sore R. elbow
Gattis,Evan	13	26	Oblique strain
	14	21	Bulging thoracic disc in back
	16	11	Rec fr surg. to repair sports hernia
Gennett,Scooter	15	14	L hand laceration
	16	14	Strained R oblique muscle
Gentry,Craig	13	27	Fractured L hand
	14	39	Fx R hand; lower back strain
	16	90	Strained R lumbar spine
Giavotella,Johnny	15	41	Personal medical condition
Gillaspie,Conor	14	11	Sore/bruised L hand
Gillespie,Cole	14	25	Strained oblique muscle
Goldschmidt,Paul	14	58	Fractured L hand
Gomes,Yan	14	7	Concussion
	15	42	R knee sprain
	16	77	Separated R should
Gomez,Carlos	12	15	Strained L. hamstring
	15	15	R hamstring strain
	16	15	Bruised L rib cage

FIVE-YEAR INJURY LOG — Batters

Batter	Yr	Days	Injury
Gonzalez,Carlos	13	29	Sprained R middle finger
	14	51	L knee tendinitis/L finger inflam
Gonzalez,Marwin	12	38	Bruised R. heel
Gordon,Alex	15	54	Strained L groin
	16	33	Fractured R wrist
Gordon,Dee	12	68	Torn R. thumb ligament
	15	11	Dislocated L thumb
Gosewisch,Tuffy	15	129	Torn L ACL
Gosselin,Phil	15	105	Avulsion fracture, L thumb
Grandal,Yasmani	12	17	Strained R. oblique
	13	85	R knee sprain
	15	7	Concussion
	16	9	Sore R forearm
Granderson,Curtis	13	113	Fx finger Lt hand; Fx Lt finger
Green,Grant	14	39	Lumbar strain
Gregorius,Didi	13	23	Concussion; R elbow strain
Grichuk,Randal	15	47	R elbow strain
Guerrero,Alexander	16	58	Bruised L knee
Gutierrez,Franklin	12	128	Concussion + torn R. pec muscle
	13	123	Strained R hamstring x 2
Guyer,Brandon	12	144	Strained L. shoulder
	13	60	Fractured R middle finger
	14	24	Fractured L thumb
	16	23	Strained L hamstring
Gyorko,Jedd	13	32	Strained R groin
	14	52	Plantar fasciitis in L foot
Hamilton,Billy	16	25	Strained L oblique; concussion
Hamilton,Josh	14	55	Surgery on L thumb torn UCL
	15	38	Jammed & spriened R Shoulder;
	15	89	L knee infl; L hammy; rec R shldr surg
	16	142	Recovering from surg. on L knee
Hanigan,Ryan	13	50	Sprained L wrist; L oblique
	14	54	Strained L oblique; Rt hamstring
	15	61	Fractured knuckle, R hand
	16	58	L ankle tendinitis; neck strain
Hardy,J.J.	15	47	Groin strain; L shoulder strain
	16	46	Fractured L foot
Harper,Bryce	13	35	L knee bursitis
	14	64	Surgery on L thumb
Harrison,Josh	15	46	Torn L thumb ligaments
	16	7	Strained R groin
Headley,Chase	13	17	Broken L thumb
	14	15	Strained R calf
Heathcott,Zachary	15	62	Strained R quad
Hechavarria,Adeiny	13	15	Bruised L elbow
	14	11	Strained R triceps
Heisey,Chris	13	58	Strained R hamstring
Hernandez,Cesar	15	21	Dislocated L thumb
	15	35	L hamstring strain
Hernandez,Enrique	16	32	L ribcage inflammation
Hernandez,Gorkys	15	11	L shoulder discomfort
Hernandez,Oscar	15	91	Fractured L hand
Herrera,Dilson	15	26	Fractured R middle finger
Herrmann,Chris	16	51	Strained R hamstring; fx L wrist
Heyward,Jason	13	55	Fx R jaw; appendectomy

FIVE-YEAR INJURY LOG — Batters

Batter	Yr	Days	Injury
Hicks,Aaron	13	22	L hamstring strain
	14	22	Strained R shoulder;concussion
	15	34	Strained L ham; R forearm
	16	15	Strained R hamstring
Hill,Aaron	13	71	Broken L hand
Holliday,Matt	13	15	Strained R hamstring
	15	85	Strained R quad x 2
	16	52	Fractured L thumb
Holt,Brock	14	23	Concussion
	16	42	Concussion
Hosmer,Eric	14	31	Stress fracture in R hand
Howard,Ryan	12	93	Recov. Fr. L. Achilles tendon surg.
	13	86	L knee inflammation
Hundley,Nick	12	49	Torn meniscus in R. knee
	15	24	Cervical strain
	16	37	Strained L oblique; concussion
Iannetta,Chris	12	80	Fractured R. wrist
Iglesias,Jose	14	184	Stress fracture in both shins
	16	15	Strained L hamstring
Inciarte,Ender David	14	7	Concussion
	15	31	Strained R hamstring
	16	26	Strained L hamstring
Infante,Omar	13	39	Sprained L ankle
	14	15	Disc irritation in lower back
Ishikawa,Travis	15	65	Lower back strain x2
Jackson,Austin	12	15	Strained abdominal
	13	33	Strained R hamstring
	15	22	Sprained R ankle
	16	115	Torn meniscus L knee
Janish,Paul	13	40	Recovery from L shoulder surgery
Jaso,John	13	67	Concussion
	14	15	Concussion
	15	88	L wrist contusion; L knee bursitis
Jay,Jon	12	38	Sprained R. shoulder
	15	79	Bone bruise, L wrist + tendon
	16	70	Fractured R forearm
Jennings,Desmond	12	24	Sprained L. knee
	13	39	Fractured L middle finger
	14	30	Bruised L Knee
	15	142	L knee bursitis
	16	48	Bruised L knee; strained L hamstring
Johnson,Chris	15	40	Infection, L hand, Fx L hand
Johnson,Kelly	15	26	R oblique strain
Johnson,Reed	13	43	L knee tendinitis
	15	159	Strained L calf
Joseph,Caleb	16	30	Testicular injury
Joyce,Matt	12	27	Tightness in lower back
	15	35	Concussion
Judge,Aaron	16	19	Strained R oblique
Kang,Jung-Ho	15	14	Torn L meniscus, fx L tibia
	16	49	Sore L should; recov L knee surg.
Kelly,Don	15	175	Fractured R ring finger
Kemp,Matt	12	58	Strained L. hamstring
	13	97	Str R ham; Sore A/c joint, L ankle
	14	16	Recovering from surgery on L ankle
Kendrick,Howie	13	35	Sprained L knee
	15	56	Strained L hamstring
	16	9	Strained L calf

FIVE-YEAR INJURY LOG — Batters

Batter	Yr	Days	Injury
Kiermaier,Kevin	16	54	Fractured L hand
Kim,Hyun-soo	16	15	Strained R hamstring
Kinsler,Ian	13	28	R intercostal strain
Kipnis,Jason	14	26	Strained R oblique
	15	15	R shoulder inflammation
Kratz,Erik	13	35	L knee surgery
	15	36	Plantar fasciitis, L foot
La Stella,Tommy	15	119	Strained R oblique
	16	27	Strained R hamstring
Ladendorf,Tyler	15	91	Recovery from ankle surgery
Lagares,Juan	14	39	Strnd R intercostal/strnd R hamstring
	16	66	Torn lig L thumb; sprnd L thumb
Laird,Gerald	13	16	Kidney stone
	15	130	Lower back spasms
Lamb,Jacob	15	46	Stress reaction, L foot
Lambo,Andrew	15	152	Plantar fasciitis, L foot
	16	91	Testicular cancer
LaRoche,Adam	14	13	Strained R quadriceps
Lawrie,Brett	12	34	Strained R. oblique
	13	61	Sprained L ankle; L ribcage
	14	95	Strained L oblique; fx Rt finger
	16	68	Strained L hamstring
Lind,Adam	12	31	Strained mid-back
	14	52	Fx R foot; lower back tightness
Liriano,Rymer	16	183	Facial bone fractures
Lobaton,Jose	12	45	Sore R. shoulder
	16	22	L elbow tendinitis
Loney,James	15	55	Broken finger; R oblique
Longoria,Evan	12	98	Torn L. hamstring
Lough,David	15	8	Strained L hamstring
Lowrie,Jed	12	66	R. ankle + R. thumb sprains
	14	18	Fractured R index finger
	15	93	Torn ligament, R thumb
	16	74	Bunion on L foot; bruised R shin
Lucroy,Jonathan	12	58	R. hand fracture
	15	41	Broken L toe
Machado,Manny	13	5	Torn ligament - L knee
	14	79	Surgery L knee 10/13; R knee surgery
Mahtook,Mikie	16	46	Fractured L hand
Marisnick,Jake	15	16	Strained L hamstring
Markakis,Nick	12	40	Fractured R. hand
Marte,Ketel	16	32	Sprnd L thumb; mono
Marte,Starling	12	19	Strained R. oblique
	13	19	R hand contusion
	14	13	Concussion
Martin,Leonys	16	14	Strained L hamstring
Martin,Russell	14	26	Strained L hamstring
Martinez,J.D.	13	65	Sprnd R knee; Sprained L wrist
	16	48	Fractured R elbow
Martinez,Michael	12	65	R. foot fracture
Martinez,Victor	12	183	Recovery from surgery - L. knee
	15	31	L knee inflammation
Mastroianni,Darin	16	40	Strained L oblique
Mathis,Jeff	13	44	Broken R collarbone
	15	53	Fractured R ring finger
Mauer,Joe	13	41	Concussion
	14	40	Strained R oblique muscle

FIVE-YEAR INJURY LOG — Batters

Batter	Yr	Days	Injury
Maxwell,Justin	12	17	Loose bodies in L. ankle
	13	69	Fractured L hand; Concussion
Maybin,Cameron	13	163	Strained L knee; Sore R wrist
	14	29	Ruptured L biceps tendon
	16	60	Sprnd L thumb; fractured L wrist
McCann,Brian	13	36	Recovery from R shoulder surgery
	14	8	Concussion
McCann,James	16	21	Sprnd R ankle
McCutchen,Andrew	14	15	Fractured L rib
McKenry,Michael	13	64	L knee surgery
	15	47	Lateral meniscus tear, R knee
Mercer,Jordy	15	34	Lower leg contusion
Mesoraco,Devin	12	8	Concussion
	14	20	strnd L hamstring/strnd L oblique
	15	133	L hip strain
	16	154	Torn labrum L should
Middlebrooks,Will	12	54	Fractured R. wrist
	13	17	Low back strain
	14	94	Fx Rt index finger; strained Rt calf
	16	36	Strained R lower leg
Molina,Yadier	13	15	Sprained R knee
	14	50	Torn ligament in R thumb
Montero,Miguel	13	28	Lower back strain
	15	21	Sprained L thumb
Moreland,Mitch	12	40	Strained L. hamstring
	13	15	Strained R hamstring
	15	14	L elbow surgery
Morneau,Justin	12	15	Sore R. wrist
	14	8	Strained neck
	15	111	Concussion
	16	36	Recovering from surg. on L elbow
Morrison,Logan	12	67	R. knee Inflam
	13	70	Recovery from R knee surgery
	14	56	Strained R hamstring
	16	34	Strained R forearm,strained L wrist
Morse,Michael	12	58	Strained R. lat
	13	38	Strained R quad
	15	40	R ring finger strain
Moss,Brandon	16	28	Sprnd L ankle
Moustakas,Mike	16	146	Torn ACL R knee; fractured L thumb
Murphy,Daniel	14	11	Strained R calf
	15	25	Strained L quad
Myers,Wil	14	80	Sprained R wrist
	15	104	Bone spurs, L wrist + tend
Napoli,Mike	12	35	Strained L. quadriceps
	14	14	Sprained L ring finger
Nava,Daniel	12	40	Sprained L. wristx2
	15	54	Strained L thumb
	16	51	Strained L groin; tend. L kneecap
Navarro,Dioner	15	40	Strained L hamstring
Negron,Kristopher	12	34	R. knee injury
	15	21	Torn labrum Lt shdlr
Nieuwenhuis,Kirk	15	30	Pinched nerve in back
Nieves,Wil	12	31	Turf toe in R. foot
	14	27	Strained R quadriceps
Norris,Derek	13	15	Fractured big toe, L foot

FIVE-YEAR INJURY LOG — Batters

Batter	Yr	Days	Injury
Nunez,Eduardo	13	61	L ribcage strain
	14	16	Strained R hamstring
	15	12	L oblique strain
Ortiz,David	12	78	Strained R. achilles tendonx2
	13	20	R Achilles tendon soreness
Owings,Christopher	14	65	Strained L shoulder
	16	42	Plantar fasciitis L foot
Ozuna,Marcell	13	69	Torn L thumb ligament
Pacheco,Jordan	14	33	R shoulder tendinitis
	16	122	R should tendinitis
Pagan,Angel	13	125	Strained R hamstring
	14	43	Strained back
	15	21	R patella tendinitis
	16	21	Strained L hamstring
Panik,Joe	15	54	Lower back discomfort + inflam
	16	29	Concussion
Paredes,Jimmy	15	13	Lower back strain
	16	43	Strained L wrist
Parmelee,Chris	16	64	Strained R hamstring
Parra,Gerardo	16	53	Sprnd L ankle
Pearce,Steve	13	61	L wrist tendinitis x2
	15	33	L oblique strain
	16	43	Strnd R ham, strnd flexor R elbow
Pederson,Joc	16	18	Sprnd AC joint R should
Pedroia,Dustin	12	15	Sprained R. thumb
	14	29	L thumb/wrist surgery
	15	67	R hamstring strain x2
Pena,Brayan	16	147	L knee inflammation + surg.
Pena,Ramiro	13	105	R shoulder impingement
Pence,Hunter	15	112	L oblique; Fx L forearm; sore L wrist
	16	58	Strained R hamstring
Pennington,Cliff	12	18	Tendinitis in L. elbow
	14	64	Sprained ligament in L thumb
	16	77	Strained L hamstring x 2
Peralta,David	16	118	R wrist inflam; lower back strain
Peralta,Jhonny	16	80	Strained + torn ligament L thumb
Perez,Eury	14	70	Fractured L toe
Perez,Juan	15	12	Left oblique strain
Perez,Roberto	16	78	Fractured R thumb
Perez,Salvador	12	78	Surgery for torn L. meniscus
	13	7	Concussion
Petit,Gregorio	15	37	R hand contusion
Pham,Thomas	15	63	L quadriceps strain
	16	43	Strained L oblique
Phillips,Brandon	14	38	Surgery for torn ligament on L thumb
Pierzynski,A.J.	13	15	Strained R oblique
	16	37	Strained L hamstring x2
Pillar,Kevin	16	15	Sprnd L thumb
Pirela,Jose	15	32	Concussion
Plouffe,Trevor	12	23	Bruised R. thumb
	13	23	Concussion; Strained L calf
	14	15	Strained L oblique
	16	73	Fract L rib; strnd L oblique
Pollock,A.J.	14	93	Fractured R hand
	16	146	Fractured R elbow; strained L groin
Prado,Martin	14	14	Appendectomy
	15	29	R shoulder sprain

FIVE-YEAR INJURY LOG — Batters

Batter	Yr	Days	Injury
Presley,Alex	12	12	Concussion
	14	56	Strained R oblique muscle
Profar,Jurickson	14	183	Torn muscle in R shoulder
	15	183	Recovery from shoulder surgery
Puello,Cesar	15	182	Stress fracture in lower back
Puig,Yasiel	15	79	Strained R hamstring
	16	18	Strained L hamstring
Pujols,Albert	13	65	Plantar fasciitis
Raburn,Ryan	12	52	Sprain R. thumb; Strain R. quad
	13	15	Strained L Achilles
	14	14	Sore R wrist
Ramirez,Aramis	13	64	Sprained L knee x 2
	14	22	Strained L hamstring
Ramirez,Hanley	13	60	Str L hamMY; R thumb ligament
	14	14	Strained R oblique
	15	30	R shoulder inflammation
Ramos,Wilson	12	144	Torn R. knee ligament
	13	64	Strained L hamstring x 2
	14	50	Strained R hamstring/Fx L hand
Rasmus,Colby	13	41	L oblique str; contusion - L eye
	14	33	Tightness in R hamstring
	16	23	Ear infection
Reddick,Josh	13	39	Sprained R wrist x 2
	14	44	Strained R knee;hyper Rt knee
	15	8	Strained R oblique
	16	39	Fractured L thumb
Reimold,Nolan	12	156	Surgery for herniated disk
	13	129	Str Rt hammy; Nerve inflam neck
	14	108	Strnd L calf; cervical spine fusion
Rendon,Anthony	15	89	Strained L quad; Sprain L knee
Revere,Ben	13	78	Broken R foot
	16	30	Strained R oblique muscle
Reyes,Jose	13	74	Sprained L ankle
	14	19	Tightness in L hamstring
	15	27	Cracked L rib
	16	14	Strained L intercostal
Reynolds,Mark	12	17	Strained L. oblique
	16	19	Recovering from L wrist surg.
Rickard,Joey	16	73	R thumb ligament injury
Robinson,Shane	13	15	Strained R shoulder
	14	34	Surgery on L shoulder
	16	48	Strained R hip flexor; R ankle
Rodriguez,Alex	16	22	Strained R hamstring
Rodriguez,Sean	12	15	Fractured R. hand
Rodriguez,Yorman	12	40	Broken L. hand
	13	127	L hip surgery
	16	183	Strained L hamstring
Romine,Austin	12	182	Strained lower back
Rosales,Adam	13	25	Strained L intercostal
Rosario,Eddie	16	1	Fractured L thumb
Ross,David	14	18	Plantar fasciitis in R foot
	15	8	Concussion
	16	9	Concussion
Rua,Ryan	15	69	Sprained R ankle
Ruf,Darin	14	49	Strained L oblique
Ruggiano,Justin	14	65	Surgery L ankle/strnd L hamstring
	16	53	L should strain; L hamstring strain

FIVE-YEAR INJURY LOG — Batters

Batter	Yr	Days	Injury
Ruiz,Carlos	12	35	Plantar fasciitis in L. foot
	13	29	Strained R hamstring
	14	26	Concussion
Rutledge,Josh	14	11	Viral infection
	16	108	Patellar tendinitis L knee
Ryan,Brendan	14	36	Pinched nerve in neck
	15	90	Upper back strain; strain R calf
Saltalamacchia,Jarrod	14	17	Concussion
	15	10	Strained neck
Sanchez,Hector	12	15	L. knee sprain
	13	15	Strained R shoulder
	14	37	Concussion
	15	27	Strained L hamstring
Sandoval,Pablo	12	56	Strained L. hamstring+ Fx R. hand
	13	15	Strained L foot
	16	173	Strained L should
Sands,Jerry	14	98	Strained L wrist
Sano,Miguel	16	30	Strained L hamstring
Santana,Carlos	12	10	Concussion
	14	10	Concussion
	14	21	Bone bruise in L knee
Santana,Daniel	16	69	Sprnd AC joint L should; strain ham.
Santana,Domingo	16	85	Sore R elbow; sore R should
Saunders,Michael	13	18	Sprained R shoulder
	14	74	Strained Lt oblique; A/C joint inflam
	15	168	L knee inflam; rec L knee surg
Schafer,Jordan	12	25	Shoulder
	13	37	R ankle contusion
	15	33	R knee MCL sprain
Schafer,Logan	14	13	Strained R hamstring
Schoop,Jonathan	15	78	R knee sprain
Schumaker,Skip	12	36	R. hammy strain+torn R. oblique
Schwarber,Kyle	16	178	Torn ligaments L knee
Segura,Jean	15	15	Fractured R pinky finger
Shuck,J.B.	15	15	Strained L hamstring
Simmons,Andrelton	12	63	Non-displaced fract. R. hand
	16	36	Torn ligament L thumb
Sizemore,Grady	12	183	Recovery from back surgery
Skipworth,Kyle	16	67	Recovering from surg. on L ankle
Smith,Kevan	16	26	Back injury (sacroiliac joint dysfunct)
Smith,Mallex	16	87	Fractured L thumb
Smith,Seth	12	18	Strained L. hamstring
Smoak,Justin	13	19	R oblique strain
	14	23	Strained L quadriceps
Smolinski,Jacob	14	53	Bone bruise in L foot
Sogard,Eric	12	58	Strained back/sprained ankle
	16	183	Cervical strain
Solano,Donovan	13	34	Strained L intercostal muscle
Solarte,Yangervis	16	41	Strained R hamstring
Soler,Jorge	15	56	L oblique; Sprain L ankle
	16	59	Strained L hamstring
Soto,Geovany	12	30	Torn L. meniscus
	14	126	Strained R groin; surg. Rt knee
	16	121	L knee infl; R knee inf.; torn meniscus
Souza,Steven	14	22	Bruised L shoulder
	15	54	Fractured L hand; cut finger
	16	28	Brsd/strnd L hip, rec from surg. L hip

FIVE-YEAR INJURY LOG — Batters

Batter	Yr	Days	Injury
Span,Denard	12	15	Strained R. sternoclavicular joint
	14	7	Concussion
	15	98	Core muscle surg; back; torn labr.
Spangenberg,Cory	15	45	L knee contusion
	16	166	Strained L quadriceps
Springer,George	14	68	L quadriceps injury
	15	70	Fx R wrist; concussion
Stanton,Giancarlo	12	30	AR.hroscopic R. knee surgery
	13	41	Strained R hamstring
	15	100	L wrist hamate fracture
	16	23	Strained L groin
Stassi,Max	13	32	Concussion
	16	37	Surg. to repair fractured L wrist
Stewart,Chris	14	21	Surgery on R knee
	15	12	Strained R hamstring
	16	80	L knee injury
Story,Trevor	16	62	Torn ligament L thumb
Stubbs,Drew	12	19	Strained L. oblique
	16	79	Sprnd L little toe
Sucre,Jesus	13	72	L wrist sprain
	16	127	Fractured fibula leg
Susac,Andrew	15	58	Sprained R wrist
Swihart,Blake	15	17	Sprained L foot
	16	120	Sprnd L ankle
Swisher,Nick	14	66	Hyperextend L knee; R knee soreness
	15	84	L knee inflam; rec knee surg (both)
Szczur,Matthew	16	18	Strained R hamstring
Taylor,Chris	15	14	Fractured R wrist
Teixeira,Mark	13	167	Rt wrist surgery; Strained Rt wrist
	14	15	Strained R hamstring
	15	31	R shin bone bruise
	16	21	Torn cartilage R knee
Tejada,Ruben	12	48	Strained R. quadriceps
	13	37	R quad strain
	16	16	strnd L quadriceps
Terdoslavich,Joseph	15	61	Sprained L wrist
Thole,Josh	12	24	Concussion
Thompson,Trayce	16	79	Lower back injury
Tilson,Charlie	16	61	Torn L hamstring
Tolleson,Steve	15	31	Groin strain
Tomlinson,Kelby	16	31	Sprnd L thumb
Travis,Devon	15	101	L shoulder strain; inflam
	16	52	Recovering from surg. on L should
Trumbo,Mark	14	78	Stress fracture in L foot
Tucker,Preston	16	52	Strained R should
Tuiasosopo,Matt	13	15	Strained L intercostal
Tulowitzki,Troy	12	126	Strained L. groin muscle
	13	27	Fractured rib, R ribcage
	14	69	Strained L hip flexor
	16	21	Strained R quadriceps
Turner,Justin	12	18	Sprained R. ankle
	13	35	Intercostal strain
	14	19	Strained L hamstring
	15	13	R thigh skin infection
Upton,Melvin	12	15	Soreness in lower back
	13	21	R adductor strain
	15	66	Sesamoiditis, L foot

FIVE-YEAR INJURY LOG — Batters

Batter	Yr	Days	Injury
Uribe,Juan	12	28	L. wrist injury
	14	51	Strained R hamstring x 2
Utley,Chase	12	84	Worn caR.ilage behind L. kneecap
	13	31	Strained R oblique
	15	44	R ankle inflammation
Valbuena,Luis	13	29	R oblique strain
	16	66	Strained R hamstring
Valencia,Danny	14	21	Sprained L hand
	16	14	Strained L hamstring
Van Slyke,Scott	13	17	L shoulder bursitis
	15	15	L mid-back inflammation
	16	107	R wrist injury; lower back strain
Vazquez,Christian	15	189	R elbow sprain
	16	12	Recovering from TJS
Villanueva,Christian	16	183	Fractured fibula R leg
Votto,Joey	12	50	Torn medial meniscus in L. knee
	14	103	Strained L quadriceps x 2
Walker,Neil	13	32	Strained R oblique; R finger cut
	14	15	Appendectomy
	16	27	Herniated disk lower back
Walters,Zachary	15	19	Strained R oblique
Weeks,Jemile	16	148	Strained R hamstring
Weeks,Rickie	13	53	L hamstring surgery
Werth,Jayson	12	87	Broken L. wrist
	13	32	Strained R hamstring
	15	78	Rec. R shldr surg.; L wrist cont.
Wieters,Matt	14	94	Strained R Elbow; TJS
	15	61	Recovery from R elbow surgery
Williams,Mason	15	106	R shoulder inflammation
	16	106	Recovering from surg. on R should
Williamson,Mac	16	36	Strnd L should; strained R quadricep
Wilson,Bobby	12	13	Concussion
Wolters,Tony	16	12	Concussion
Wong,Kolten	14	15	Sore L shoulder
Wright,David	13	48	Strained R hamstring
	15	131	Strained R hamstring
	16	122	Herniated disc neck
Yelich,Christian	14	13	Strained lower back
	15	33	Rt knee contusion; lower back strain
Young,Chris	12	30	R. shoulder contusion
	14	15	Strained R quadriceps
	16	76	Strained R hamstring; R forearm
Zimmerman,Ryan	12	17	Sore R. shoulder
	13	15	Strained L hamstring
	14	110	Fx R thumb/strained R hamstring
	15	47	Plantar fasciitis, L foot
	16	33	Bruised L wrist; strained L ribcage
Zobrist,Ben	14	15	Dislocated L thumb
	15	30	Medial meniscus tear, L knee
Zunino,Mike	13	38	Fractured L hamate bone

FIVE-YEAR INJURY LOG — Pitchers

Pitchers	Yr	Days	Injury
Abad,Fernando	12	20	R. intercostal strain
Adleman,Timothy	16	74	Strnd L oblique
Albers,Matt	14	157	R shoulder tendinitis
	15	84	Broken finger,R hand
Alburquerque,Al	12	141	Recov. fr. surg. - R. elbow
Alvarez,Henderson	13	95	Mild R shoulder inflammation
	14	14	R shoulder inflammation
	15	169	R shoulder inflammation x2
	16	184	Rec fr surg. on R should
Alvarez,R.J.	16	71	Rec fr surg.R elbow remv bone chips
Amarista,Alexi	16	56	Strnd R hamstring x 2
Anderson,Brett	12	137	Recovery from TJS
	13	119	R foot stress fracture
	14	144	Strained lower back/fx L finger
	16	163	Rec fr back surg. - bulging disc
Anderson,Chase	15	19	R triceps inflammation
Anderson,Cody	15	18	L oblique strain
Anderson,Tyler	16	36	Strnd R oblique muscle
Araujo,Elvis	15	38	Strained L groin
Arrieta,Jake	14	34	Tightness in R shoulder
Atchison,Scott	12	60	Tightness In R. forearm
	13	60	R groin strain; R elbow
	15	16	Sprained L ankle
Baez,Pedro	15	43	R pectoral strain
Bailey,Andrew	12	132	R. thumb surgery
	13	100	Rt biceps soreness; Rt shoulder str
	16	14	Strnd L hamstring
Bailey,Homer	14	16	Strained flexor tendon in R elbow
	15	174	Torn UCL,R elbow; TJS surgery
	16	116	Rec fr TJS
Banuelos,Manny	15	35	L elbow inflammation
	16	51	Rec fr surg. L elbow spur
Barnes,Jacob	16	37	Sore R elbow
Barrett,Aaron	15	86	R elbow sprain; R biceps
	16	183	Rec fr TJS
Barrios,Yhonathan	16	184	Strnd R should
Bassitt,Chris	16	157	Torn ligament R elbow
Baumann,Buddy	16	89	Strnd lower back
Beachy,Brandon	12	109	TJS
	13	160	R elbow inflam; R elbow surgery
	14	184	Recovering from TJS
	15	103	Recovery from R elbow surgery
Bedrosian,Cam	16	55	Flexor tendinitis R finger
Beeler,Dallas	15	43	R shoulder inflammation
	16	183	R should inflammation
Beimel,Joe	15	14	L shoulder inflammation
Belisle,Matt	15	74	R elbow inflammation
	16	48	Strnd R calf
Beliveau,Jeff	15	171	L shoulder fatigue
Bellatti,Andrew	15	26	R shoulder tendinitis
Benoit,Joaquin	16	22	R should inflammation
Bergman,Christian	14	60	Fractured L hand/thumb
	15	32	R shoulder fatigue
	16	50	Strnd L oblique
Betances,Dellin	12	15	R. shoulder Inflam
Bettis,Chad	15	36	R elbow inflammation
Biddle,Jesse	16	183	Rec fr TJS

FIVE-YEAR INJURY LOG — Pitchers

Pitchers	Yr	Days	Injury
Billingsley,Chad	12	46	R. elbow pain
	13	177	R elbow surgery; finger bruise
	14	184	Recovering from TJS
	15	151	R flexor strain; R shlder; elbow surg
Black,Ray	16	30	Bone spur R elbow
Blair,Aaron	16	15	Strnd L knee
Blazek,Michael	15	52	Fractured R hand
	16	36	Strnd R forearm; R elbow imping
Blevins,Jerry	15	167	Fractured L forearm
Bolsinger,Michael	16	44	Strnd L oblique muscle
Boshers,Jeffrey	16	22	L elbow inflammation
Boxberger,Brad	16	116	Strnd L oblique; recov. core surg.
Boyer,Blaine	15	12	R elbow inflammation
Bradley,Archie	15	98	R shoulder tend; facial bruise
Breslow,Craig	13	36	L shoulder tendinitis
	14	13	Strained L shoulder
Britton,Zach	12	62	L. shoulder impingement
Brooks,Aaron	16	183	Bruised hip
Brown,Brooks	15	74	R shoulder inflammation x2
Broxton,Jonathan	13	108	R flexor strain x 2
	14	9	Rec from surgery R elbow/forearm
Buchholz,Clay	12	24	Gastro-intestinal problem
	13	93	Neck strain
	14	28	Hyperextended L knee
	15	86	R flexor strain
Bundy,Dylan	15	11	Strained right shoulder
Burgos,Enrique	15	27	Sore R shoulder
Butler,Eddie	14	40	R rotator cuff inflammation
Cahill,Trevor	13	47	R hip contusion
	16	32	Patellar tendinitis R knee
Cain,Matt	13	15	R forearm contusion
	14	93	R elbow inflam/R ham/cut R finger
	15	100	R elbow nerve irrit.; flexor strain
	16	67	Strnd R ham x 2; lower back strain
Caminero,Arquimedes	16	17	Strnd L quadriceps
Capps,Carter	14	97	Sprained R elbow
	15	63	R elbow strain
	16	183	Rec fr TJS
Capuano,Chris	13	39	L lat strain; Strained L calf
	15	43	Strained R quadriceps
	16	130	Sore L elbow
Carpenter,David	14	15	Strained R biceps
	15	80	R shoulder inflammation
Carrasco,Carlos	12	183	Recovery from TJS
	15	13	R shoulder inflammation
	16	38	Strnd L hamstring
Cashner,Andrew	12	59	Strained R. latissimus dorsi
	14	82	Sore R elbow/sore R shoulder
	16	37	Strnd R hamstring; str neck
Casilla,Santiago	13	53	Cyst on R knee
	14	24	Strained R hamstring
Castro,Miguel	16	26	R should inflammation
Cecil,Brett	13	13	L elbow soreness
	14	16	Strained L groin
	16	46	Strnd L triceps
Chacin,Jhoulys	12	111	R. shoulder Inflam
	13	15	L lower back strain
	14	128	R shoulder inflammation/strain

FIVE-YEAR INJURY LOG — Pitchers

Pitchers	Yr	Days	Injury
Chafin,Andrew	16	62	L should tendinitis
Chamberlain,Joba	12	117	Dislocated R. ankle
	13	30	Strained R oblique
	16	16	Strnd L intercostal
Chapman,Aroldis	14	41	Facial fractures,concussion
Chatwood,Tyler	13	31	R elbow inflammation
	14	168	Strnd R elbow/strnd L hamstring
	16	33	Tightness upper back x 2
Chavez,Jesse	15	19	Fractured rib
Chen,Wei-Yin	13	58	Strained R oblique
	16	57	Sprnd L elbow
Cingrani,Tony	13	15	Strained lower back
	14	17	L shoulder tendinitis
	15	37	Strained L shoulder
Cishek,Steve	16	15	Torn labrum L hip
Claudio,Alexander	16	148	R should stiffness
Cobb,Alex	13	60	Concussion
	14	38	Strained L oblique muscle
	15	183	R forearm tendinitis
	16	149	Rec fr TJS
Cole,Gerrit	14	63	Tightness R lat/R shoulder fatigue
	16	66	R elbow inflam; R triceps strain
Coleman,Louis	14	14	Bone bruised/sprained R middle finger
	16	29	R should fatigue
Collins,Tim	14	27	Strained flexor in L elbow
	15	183	L elbow surgery
	16	183	Rec fr TJS
Collmenter,Josh	12	22	Ulcers
	16	55	Tightness R should
Colome,Alex	13	94	Strained R elbow
	15	34	Pneumonia
	16	16	R biceps tendinitis
Colon,Bartolo	12	15	Strained R. oblique
	13	15	L groin strain
Colon,Joseph	16	24	R should inflammation
Conley,Adam	16	43	L middle finger tendinitis
Cook,Ryan	14	39	Strned R forearm; Rt shoulder inflam
	16	183	Strnd back muscle
Corbin,Patrick	14	184	Recovering from TJS
	15	91	Recovery from L elbow surgery
Cosart,Jarred	15	37	Vertigo
Cotham,Caleb	16	125	R should inflammation
Cravy,Tyler	15	17	R elbow impingement
Crow,Aaron	15	183	R elbow surgery
Cueto,Johnny	13	130	Strained R lat x 2; R shoulder
Cumpton,Brandon	15	106	R elbow surgery
Cunniff,Brandon	15	101	Strained R groin
Darnell,Logan	15	15	Pneumonia
Darvish,Yu	13	15	Upper back strain
	14	61	Rt elbow inflam; stiff neck
	15	183	R elbow surgery
	16	88	Rec fr TJS; R should strain
Davis,Erik	14	183	Sprained R elbow
	15	43	Recovery from R elbow surgery
Davis,Wade	16	48	Strnd flexor R forearm
De Fratus,Justin	12	152	R. elbow sprain

FIVE-YEAR INJURY LOG — Pitchers

Pitchers	Yr	Days	Injury
De La Rosa,Jorge	12	168	TJS
	15	15	Strained L groin
	16	27	Strnd L groin
De La Rosa,Rubby	16	105	R elbow inflammation
Deduno,Samuel	13	31	R shoulder soreness
	15	91	Lower back strain
deGrom,Jacob	14	12	Tendinitis in R rotator cuff
Delabar,Steve	13	29	R shoulder inflammation
Delgado,Randall	15	68	Sprained R ankle
DeSclafani,Anthony	16	68	Strnd oblique muscle
Detwiler,Ross	13	116	Back strain; x 2
	15	18	L shoulder inflammation
Diaz,Jairo	16	183	Rec fr TJS
Diekman,Jake	16	16	Lacerated L index finger
Doolittle,Sean	14	36	Strained R intercostal muscle
	15	136	L shoulder strain; torn rotator cuff
	16	64	Strnd L should
Doubront,Felix	12	15	Contusion in R. knee
	14	59	Strained L calf/strained L shoulder
	16	182	Sprnd L elbow
Drabek,Kyle	12	112	TJS
	13	95	Recovery from R elbow surgery
Duensing,Brian	15	15	R intercostal strain
	16	75	Surg. on L elbow
Duffy,Danny	12	143	TJS
	13	99	Recov Rt elbow surg; Rt flexor strain
	15	30	L biceps tendinitis
Dunn,Mike	16	58	Strnd L forearm
Edgin,Josh	16	37	Rec fr TJS
Edwards,Jonathan	16	183	Strnd flexor tendon R elbow
Eflin,Zach	16	55	Patellar tendinopathy both knees
Elias,Roenis	14	7	Strained flexor muscle in R elbow
Eovaldi,Nathan	13	79	Mild R shoulder inflammation
	16	52	R elbow tendon injury
Erlin,Robert	14	88	Sore L elbow
	16	165	Strnd L elbow
Escobar,Eduardo	16	16	Strnd L groin
Estrada,Marco	12	33	R. quadriceps strain
	13	64	Strained L hamstring
	16	24	Back strain
Familia,Jeurys	13	128	R elbow surgery
Feldman,Scott	14	18	R biceps tendinitis
	15	83	R shoulder sprain; R knee surg
Feliz,Neftali	12	136	TJS - R. elbow
	13	155	Recovery from R elbow surgery
	15	38	Axillary abscess on R side
Ferrell,Jeff	16	23	R should impingement
Fields,Josh	14	19	Sore R forearm
Fien,Casey	15	29	R shoulder strain
	16	27	R elbow tendinitis
Fister,Doug	12	47	Strained L. side
	14	41	Strained R lat
	15	34	R forearm tightness
Flores,Kendry	15	41	R shoulder tendinitis

FIVE-YEAR INJURY LOG — Pitchers

Pitchers	Yr	Days	Injury
Floyd,Gavin	12	31	Strain R. elbow flex+ tend R. Elbow
	13	155	R elbow surgery
	14	143	Recovery from TJS/fx R elbow
	15	149	R elbow surgery
	16	99	R should injury
Foltynewicz,Mike	15	13	Costochondritis
	16	26	Sore R elbow
Frasor,Jason	12	48	Tightness In R. forearm
	15	22	R shoulder strain
Frias,Carlos	15	61	R lower back tightness
	16	24	Strnd R oblique
Friedrich,Christian	12	67	Stress fract-R. side of lower spine
	13	53	Lower back inflammation
Furbush,Charlie	12	30	Strained L. triceps muscle
	15	88	L biceps tendinitis
	16	183	L biceps tendinitis
Gallardo,Yovani	13	17	Strained L hamstring
	16	56	R biceps tendinitis
Gant,John	16	54	Strnd L oblique
Garcia,Jaime	12	74	L. shoulder strain
	13	135	L shoulder strain
	14	69	L shoulder inflammation x 2
	15	75	L groin strain; recov L shldr surg
Garcia,Jason Emilio	15	85	R shoulder tendinitis
Garcia,Luis	14	13	Strained R forearm
Garcia,Yimi	16	163	Sore R biceps
Garza,Matt	12	68	R. elbow stress reaction
	13	51	Strained L lat
	14	27	Strained L oblique
	15	15	R shoulder tendinitis
	16	70	Strnd R lat
Gausman,Kevin	15	43	R shoulder tendinitis
	16	22	R should tendinitis
Gearrin,Cory	14	184	Sprained R elbow
	16	43	Strnd R should
Gee,Dillon	12	88	Damaged aR.ery in R. shoulder
	14	55	Tightness in R lat
	15	25	Groin strain
Germen,Gonzalez	14	29	Illness/Flu
Gibson,Kyle	16	45	Sore/strnd R should
Gimenez,Chris	16	30	Infection lower L leg
Glasnow,Tyler	16	35	Sore R should
Goeddel,Erik	15	81	Strained R elbow
Goins,Ryan	16	30	Tightness R forearm
Gomes,Brandon	13	146	Strained R lat
Gomez,Jeanmar	13	23	R forearm tightness
Gonzalez,Gio	14	30	L shoulder inflammation
Gonzalez,Miguel	13	17	R thumb blister
	14	11	Strained R oblique
	14	97	R arm fatigue
	15	45	R shoulder tend; R groin strain
	16	25	Strnd R groin
Gorzelanny,Tom	13	16	L shoulder tendinitis
	14	76	Rec from surgery on L shoulder
Graham,J.R.	15	16	R shoulder inflammation
Graveman,Kendall	15	100	Strained L oblique
Gray,Jonathan	16	20	Strnd abdominal muscle

FIVE-YEAR INJURY LOG — Pitchers

Pitchers	Yr	Days	Injury
Gray,Sonny	16	55	Strnd R forearm; R trap.
Green,Chad	16	26	Strnd tendon R forearm
Greene,Shane	16	37	Blister on R middle finger
Gregerson,Luke	16	17	Strnd L oblique
Greinke,Zack	13	33	Broken L collarbone
	16	37	Strnd L oblique
Griffin,A.J.	12	27	Strained R. shoulder
	14	184	Strained flexor muscle in R elbow
	15	172	R shoulder strain
	16	48	R should stiffness
Grilli,Jason	13	42	Strained R forearm
	14	28	Strained L oblique
	15	80	Torn L Achilles tendon
Grimm,Justin	15	26	R forearm inflammation
Grosser,Alec	16	58	Back strain
Guerra,Deolis	15	59	R knee inflammation
Guerra,Javy	12	63	Strained L. oblique+ R. knee Inflam
	15	16	R shoulder inflammation
Guerra,Junior	16	25	R elbow inflammation
Hagadone,Nick	15	89	Lower back strain
Hahn,Jesse	15	86	R forearm strain
	16	27	Strnd R should
Hale,David	15	61	Groin strain
Hamels,Cole	14	27	L biceps tendinitis
Hammel,Jason	12	54	Injured R. knee
	13	38	R forearm tenderness
Hand,Brad	14	40	Sprained R ankle
Happ,J.A.	12	30	Fractured R. foot
	13	89	Head contusion
	14	18	Strained back
Hardy,Blaine	16	16	L should impingement
Harrell,Lucas	16	47	Strnd R groin
Harris,Mitch	15	16	Groin strain
	16	183	Strnd R elbow
Harrison,Matt	13	177	Inflamed nerve in lower back
	14	55	Lower back inflam; back surg recovery
	15	156	Lower back inflam; back surg
	16	183	Lower back inflammation
Harvey,Matt	13	34	Torn R UCL
	14	183	Recovering from TJS
	16	90	Thoracic outlet synd, R should
Hatcher,Chris	15	58	L oblique strain
	16	75	Strnd L oblique
Heaney,Andrew	16	180	Strnd L flexor
Hellickson,Jeremy	12	15	Fatigued R. shoulder
	14	99	Recovering from surgery on R elbow
	15	22	Strained L hamstring
Hembree,Heath	15	37	R shoulder soreness
Henderson,Jim	13	15	Strained R hamstring
	14	150	R shoulder inflammation
	15	39	Recovery from R shoulder surgery
	16	60	R biceps tendinitis
Hendriks,Liam	16	40	Strnd R triceps
Hernandez,David	14	184	Surgery on R elbow torn ligament
	15	64	Recovery from R elbow surgery
Hernandez,Felix	16	49	Strnd R calf
Heston,Chris	16	96	Strnd oblique muscle

FIVE-YEAR INJURY LOG — Pitchers

Pitchers	Yr	Days	Injury
Hill,Rich	12	107	Rec fr TJS; +Soreness L forearm
	16	58	Blister L finger; L groin
Hinojosa,Dalier	16	64	Bruised R hand
Hochevar,Luke	14	184	TJS
	15	32	Recovery from R elbow surgery
	16	67	Thoracic outlet syndrome
Holaday,Bryan	16	26	Bruised L thumb
Holland,Derek	12	31	Fatigued L. shoulder
	14	164	Recovering from surgery on L knee
	15	130	Subscapular strain in R shoulder
	16	62	L should inflammation
Holland,Greg	12	21	Stress reaction in L. ribs
	15	18	R pectoral strain
Hollands,Mario	14	24	Strained flexor in L elbow
	15	183	Strained flexor tendon,L forearm
	16	61	Rec fr TJS
House,T.J.	15	20	L shoulder inflammation
Hudson,Daniel	12	137	R. shoulder impingement +TJS
	13	183	Recovery from R elbow surgery
	14	155	Recovering from TJS
Hughes,Jared	13	57	R shoulder inflammation
	16	27	Strnd L lat back
Hughes,Phil	13	6	R upper back thoracic injury
	15	32	Lower back inflammation
	16	115	L knee injury
Hunter,Tommy	14	17	Strained L groin
	16	39	Back strain; core muscle surg.
Hutchison,Drew	12	110	TJS - R. elbow
	13	131	Recovery from R elbow surgery
Iglesias,Raisel	15	36	Strained L oblique
	16	51	R should impingement
Iwakuma,Hisashi	14	35	Torn tendon in R middle finger
	15	73	R lat strain
Jackson,Edwin	14	29	Strained R lat
	16	31	Strnd R triceps
Jackson,Luke	16	10	Stress reaction lower back
Jansen,Kenley	15	40	L foot surgery
Janssen,Casey	14	42	Strained lower back
	15	47	R rotator cuff tendinitis
Jennings,Dan	14	24	Concussion
	15	24	Neck inflammation
Jepsen,Kevin	13	82	Rt tricep tightness; Appendectomy
Jimenez,Ubaldo	14	29	Sprained R ankle
Johnson,Erik	16	94	Sprnd R elbow
Johnson,Jim	16	24	Strnd R groin
Jones,Nate	14	184	Strained L hip;TJS
	15	131	Recovery from R elbow surgery
Jones,Zach	16	80	Sore R should
Jordan,Taylor	13	44	Lower back strain
	14	55	Sore R elbow
Kahnle,Thomas	14	17	R shoulder inflammation
Karns,Nathan	16	65	Strnd lower back
Kazmir,Scott	13	18	Strained R rib cage
	16	31	Inflammation cervical spine
Kela,Keone	16	85	R elbow impingement
Kelley,Shawn	14	29	Strained lumbar spine
	15	14	Strained L calf

FIVE-YEAR INJURY LOG — Pitchers

Pitchers	Yr	Days	Injury
Kelly,Casey	13	183	R elbow surgery
	14	184	Recovering from TJS
Kelly,Joe	14	85	Strained L hamstring
	15	8	R biceps tightness
	16	32	R should impingement
Kennedy,Ian	15	15	Strained L hamstring
Kershaw,Clayton	14	38	Back muscle inflam/strnd L shoulder
	16	47	Herniated disc lower back
Kimbrel,Craig	16	23	Torn meniscus L knee
Kintzler,Brandon	12	151	Sore R. forearm
	14	15	Strained R rotator cuff
	15	75	L knee tendinitis
Kluber,Corey	13	32	Sprained finger,R hand
Knebel,Corey	16	67	Strnd L oblique
Kontos,George	16	28	Strnd flexor R elbow
Krol,Ian	14	15	L shoulder inflammation
Lackey,John	12	182	TJS - R. elbow
	13	176	R biceps strain
	16	16	Strnd R should
Ladendorf,Tyler	16	47	Sprnd L wrist
Lamb,John	16	30	Rec fr back surg.
Latos,Mat	14	76	Recovering from surgery on L knee
	15	21	L knee inflammation
Law,Derek	16	17	Strnd R elbow
Lazo,Raudel	16	18	Strnd L should
League,Brandon	15	88	Sore R shoulder
Leake,Mike	15	15	Strained L hamstring
	16	9	Shingles
Lee,Chris	16	18	Strnd L should
Lewis,Colby	12	101	Surg. torn tendon R. elbow
	13	185	Recovery from R elbow surgery
	16	78	Strnd R lat muscle
Liberatore,Adam	16	16	L elbow inflammation
Lincecum,Tim	15	95	R forearm contusion
Lindgren,Jacob	15	28	L elbow surgery
Liriano,Francisco	13	41	Fractured R forearm
	14	32	Strained L oblique
Lobstein,Kyle	15	102	L shoulder soreness
Locke,Jeff	14	12	Strained R oblique
Logan,Boone	14	86	Diverticulitis/L elbow inflam x 3
	15	18	L elbow inflammation
	16	19	L should inflammation
Lorenzen,Michael	16	80	Sprnd UCL R elbow
Loup,Aaron	16	55	Sore L elbow
Lowe,Mark	12	45	Strained R. intercostal muscle
	13	16	Neck stiffness
Luebke,Cory	12	159	TJS
	13	183	Recovery from L elbow surgery
	14	184	Recovering from TJS
	15	183	Strained L elbow
	16	31	Tightness R hamstring
Lyles,Jordan	14	62	Fractured L hand
	15	126	Sprained L big toe
Lynn,Lance	15	13	Strained R forearm
	16	183	Rec fr TJS
Lyons,Tyler	14	36	Strained L shoulder
	16	62	Stress reaction R knee

FIVE-YEAR INJURY LOG — Pitchers

Pitchers	Yr	Days	Injury
Machi,Jean	15	18	Strained L groin
Madson,Ryan	12	183	TJS
	13	127	Recovery from R elbow surgery
Manaea,Sean	16	15	Strnd pronator L forearm
Maness,Seth	16	85	Strnd R elbow/inflammation
Manship,Jeff	14	37	Strained R quadriceps
	16	16	R wrist tendinitis
Mariot,Michael	14	32	Strained R hamstring
	16	46	Sprnd R ankle
Marksberry,Matt	16	64	L rotator cuff inflammation
Marshall,Evan	15	27	Fractured skull
Marshall,Sean	13	131	Sprained L shoulder; Tendinitis
	14	127	Strnd L shoulder/L shoulder inflam
	15	183	Recovery from L shoulder surgery
Martin,Chris	15	22	R elbow tendinitis
Martin,Ethan	14	51	Strained R shoulder
Martinez,Carlos	15	9	Right shoulder strain
Masterson,Justin	14	22	R knee inflammation
	15	40	R shoulder tendinitis
Mateo,Marcos	12	183	Sore R. elbow
	15	24	Strained neck
Mattheus,Ryan	12	27	Plantar fascia strain in L. foot
	13	67	Fractured R hand
Matusz,Brian	16	20	Strnd L intercostal
Matz,Steven	15	53	Partially torn L lat muscle
	16	42	Tightness L should
Matzek,Tyler	16	46	Anxiety disorder
Maurer,Brandon	15	55	R shoulder inflammation
May,Trevor	16	75	Strnd lower back x 2
Mazzoni,Cory	15	31	Strained R shoulder
McAllister,Zach	13	50	Sprained R middle finger
	14	27	Strained lower back
	16	22	R hip injury
McCarthy,Brandon	12	95	Strained R. shoulderx2; skull fract
	13	65	R shoulder inflammation
	15	161	Torn UCL,R elbow
	16	173	Rec fr TJS
McCullers,Lance	16	103	Sore R elbow; R should
McFarland,T.J.	16	57	L knee inflammation
McGee,Jake	15	86	Torn L knee menisc rec R elbow surg
	16	21	L knee inflammation
McGowan,Dustin	12	183	R. Plant. Fasciitis+R. should. surg.
	13	101	Strnd Rt oblique; Sore Rt shoulder
McHugh,Collin	14	15	R middle finger injury
McKirahan,Andrew	16	183	Rec fr TJS
Medlen,Kris	14	184	Recovering from TJS
	15	112	Recovery from R elbow surgery
	16	144	R rotator cuff inflammation
Mejia,Jenrry	13	160	R elbow inflamon; discomfort
	15	181	R elbow inflammation
Miley,Wade	16	12	Inflammation L should
Miller,Andrew	12	32	Strained L. hamstring
	13	85	L foot surgery
	15	27	L flexor forearm muscle strain
Miller,Justin	13	62	Recovery from R elbow surgery
	16	59	Strnd L oblique
Miller,Shelby	16	24	Sprnd R index finger

FIVE-YEAR INJURY LOG — Pitchers

Pitchers	Yr	Days	Injury
Milone,Tommy	14	23	Neck inflammation
	15	13	Strained L elbow
	16	28	L biceps tendinitis
Minor,Mike	14	37	L shoulder tendinitis
	15	185	L rotator cuff inflammation
	16	183	Rec fr surg. on L should
Mitchell,Bryan	15	10	Concussion,nasal fracture
	16	143	Surg. to repair fractured L big toe
Montas,Frankie	16	113	Rec fr rib re-section surg.
Montero,Miguel	16	16	Stiffness lower back
Montero,Rafael	15	158	R rotator cuff inflammation
Moore,Matt	13	36	L elbow soreness
	14	174	L elbow injury
	15	88	Recovery from L elbow surgery
Morales,Franklin	12	41	Fatigue in L. shoulder
	13	106	Strained lower back; L pectoral
	16	103	L should fatigue
Moran,Brian	14	184	L elbow inflammation
Moreland,Mitch	14	111	Surgery on L ankle impingement
Moreno,Diego	15	64	R elbow inflammation
Morin,Michael	14	15	Lacerated L foot
	15	38	L oblique strain
Morris,AJ	16	76	Strnd R should
Morris,Bryan	15	22	Lower back strain
	16	130	Herniated lumbar disc
Morrow,Brandon	12	74	Strained L. oblique
	13	121	R forearm strain
	14	122	Torn tendon sheath in R hand
	15	153	R shoulder inflammation
Morton,Charlie	12	137	Recovering from R. hip surgery+TJS
	13	74	Recovery from R elbow surgery
	14	35	R hip inflammation
	15	51	Hip injury
	16	162	Strnd L hamstring
Moscot,Jon	15	111	L shoulder surgery
	16	38	Strnd R intercostal; L should inflam
Motte,Jason	13	183	R elbow surgery
	14	77	Recovery TJS/strained lower back
	15	42	R shoulder strain
	16	96	Strnd R rotator cuff
Mujica,Edward	12	18	Fractured R. pinky toe
	15	28	Fractured R thumb
Mullee,Conor	16	93	Numbness R hand
Nathan,Joe	15	179	R elbow flexor strain
	16	68	Rec fr TJS
Nelson,Jimmy	15	13	Head contusion
Nesbitt,Angel	16	36	Sprnd R ankle
Nicasio,Juan	12	123	Strained L. knee
	15	11	L abdominal strain
Niese,Jon	13	51	Partially torn L rotator cuff
	14	30	Strained L shoulder/L elbow inflam
	16	41	Rec fr surg. on L knee
Nola,Aaron	16	61	Strnd R elbow
Nolasco,Ricky	14	38	Strained R elbow
	15	144	R ankle impinge.; R elbow inflam
Nolin,Sean	15	41	Recovery fr. bi-lateral core surgery
	16	183	Strnd L elbow

FIVE-YEAR INJURY LOG — Pitchers

Pitchers	Yr	Days	Injury
Norris,Bud	12	16	L. knee sprain
	14	11	Strained R groin
	15	20	Bronchitis
	16	15	Strnd mid-back
Norris,Daniel	15	27	R oblique strain
	16	52	Strnd R oblique muscle; lower back
Nova,Ivan	12	17	Inflam in R. rotator cuff
	13	27	R triceps inflammation
	14	162	Torn UCL R elbow
	15	81	Recovery from R elbow surgery
Nuno,Vidal	13	23	Strained L groin
O Day,Darren	16	87	Strnd R rotator cuff; R hamstring
O Flaherty,Eric	13	135	L elbow surgery
	14	95	Recovering from TJS
	15	31	L shoulder strain
	16	78	L elbow neuritis; strnd R knee
O Sullivan,Sean	15	20	L knee tendinitis
	16	32	L knee tendinitis
Oberg,Scott	16	42	Axillary artery thrombosis R arm
Oberholtzer,Brett	15	60	Blisters on pitching hand x2
Odorizzi,Jake	15	32	Strained L oblique
Ogando,Alexi	12	35	Strained R. groin
	13	87	R shoulder inflam x 2; R biceps
	14	117	R elbow inflammation
Ogando,Nefi	16	47	Fractured R rib
Ohlendorf,Ross	13	20	R shoulder inflammation
	14	184	Sprained R lumbar
	15	50	R groin strain
Olmos,Edgar	15	47	L shoulder impingement
Olson,Tyler	15	24	R knee contusion
Osich,Josh	16	35	Strnd L forearm
Ottavino,Adam	15	161	R triceps inflammation
	16	138	Rec fr TJS
Outman,Josh	12	37	Strained oblique
	15	120	L shoulder soreness
Papelbon,Jonathan	16	20	Strnd R intercostal
Parker,Jarrod	14	184	Recovering from TJS
	15	184	Recovery from R elbow surgery
	16	183	Fractured R elbow
Parnell,Bobby	13	61	Neck stiffness
	14	180	Torn MCL in R elbow
	15	81	R shoulder tend; rec R elbow surg
Paxton,James	14	115	Strained L lat in back
	15	107	Strained tendon in L middle finger
	16	16	Bruised L elbow
Peacock,Brad	15	184	L intercostal strain; rec R hip surg
Peavy,Jake	13	44	Fractured rib
	15	76	Back strain
	16	21	Strnd lower back
Pelfrey,Mike	12	165	TJS
	13	15	Back strain
	14	149	Strained L groin
	16	34	Strnd lower back
Peralta,Joel	14	16	Illness
	15	78	Neck sprain; R shoulder soreness
Peralta,Wily	15	63	Strained L oblique

FIVE-YEAR INJURY LOG — Pitchers

Pitchers	Yr	Days	Injury
Perez,Martin	13	43	Cracked ulna bone,L forearm
	14	141	L elbow inflammation
	15	109	Recovery from L elbow surgery
Perez,Rafael	12	161	Strained L. lat/ankle injury
Perez,Williams	15	34	L foot contusion
	16	86	Strnd R rotator cuff
Perkins,Glen	14	10	Strained L Forearm
	16	173	Strnd L should
Petricka,Jacob	15	15	Strained R forearm
	16	151	R hip impingement
Pettibone,Jonathan	13	63	Strained R shoulder
	15	183	Recovery from R shoulder surgery
Phegley,Joshua	16	109	Strnd R knee + inflammation
Phelps,David	13	71	R forearm strain
	14	56	R elbow inflammation/tendinitis
	15	49	Stress fracture,R forearm
	16	33	Strnd L oblique
Pimentel,Stolmy	14	56	Sprained R ankle/ R shoulder inflam
Pinder,Branden	16	164	Strnd R elbow
Pineda,Michael	12	182	Surgery torn labrum R. shoulder
	13	98	Recovery from R shoulder surgery
	14	99	Strained muscle in R shoulder
	15	27	Strained R forearm
Pomeranz,Drew	13	45	L bicep tendinitis
	14	26	Fractured R hand
	15	14	Sprained L AC joint
Porcello,Rick	15	24	Strained R triceps
Pressly,Ryan	15	91	R lat strain
Price,David	13	47	L triceps strain
Putnam,Zach	13	110	R elbow soreness
	14	15	R shoulder inflammation
	15	15	R groin strain
	16	104	Ulnar neuritis R elbow
Qualls,Chad	12	15	Irritation of L. toe
	15	14	Pinched nerve
	16	27	Illness
Ramirez,Erasmo	12	62	Strained R. elbow flexor
Ramirez,Neil	14	12	Sore R triceps
	15	113	L ab soreness; R shoulder inflam
Ramos,A.J.	14	17	R shoulder inflammation
	16	16	Fractured R middle finger
Rasmus,Cory	15	106	R forearm strain; core muscle surg
	16	135	Strnd R groin; strnd L groin
Ravin,Josh	15	34	L hernia
	16	140	Fractured L forearm; R triceps strain
Rea,Colin	16	63	R elbow injury
Reed,Cody	16	18	Back spasms
Richard,Clayton	13	122	L shoulder surgery; stomach virus
	16	24	Blister on L middle finger
Richards,Garrett	14	39	Torn patellar tendon in L knee
	15	15	Recovery from L knee surgery
	16	150	Torn UCL R elbow
Rienzo,Andre	15	20	L knee laceration
Rivero,Felipe	15	29	Gastrointestinal bleeding
Roberts,Kenneth	15	26	L elbow inflammation
Robertson,David	12	33	Strained L. oblique
	14	14	Strained L groin

FIVE-YEAR INJURY LOG — Pitchers

Pitchers	Yr	Days	Injury
Rodon,Carlos	16	22	Sprnd L wrist
Rodriguez,Eduardo	16	59	Dislocated R kneecap
Rodriguez,Fernando	13	183	R elbow surgery
	14	31	Recovering from TJS
	16	91	Strnd R should
Rodriguez,Paco	14	55	Strained L shoulder
	15	127	Strained L elbow
	16	183	Rec fr TJS
Roe,Chaz	15	22	R shoulder injury
Romero,Enny	16	15	Strnd back
Romo,Sergio	16	81	Strnd flexor tendon R elbow
Rondon,Bruce	14	184	Surgery on R elbow
	15	71	R biceps tendinitis
Rondon,Hector	16	18	Strnd R triceps
Rosenthal,Trevor	16	51	R rotator cuff inflammation
Ross,Joe	16	77	R should inflammation
Ross,Robbie	12	20	Sore L. forearm
Ross,Tyson	13	17	L shoulder subluxation
	16	178	R should inflammation
Rosscup,Zachary	14	31	Sore L shoulder
	15	58	L shoulder inflammation
	16	183	L should inflammation
Rumbelow,Nick	16	31	Rec fr TJS
Rusin,Chris	16	43	Strnd L should
Ryu,Hyun-Jin	14	35	Strained R hip/L shoulder inflam
	15	183	L shoulder inflammation
	16	171	L elbow tendinitis; L should surg.
Sabathia,C.C.	12	15	Sore L. elbow+ strain abductor
	13	5	Strained L hamstring
	14	141	Fluid in R knee
	15	16	R knee inflammation
	16	15	Strnd L groin
Sadler,Casey	15	34	R elbow discomfort
Salas,Fernando	13	36	R shoulder irritation
	14	21	R shoulder inflammation
Salazar,Danny	16	15	R elbow inflammation
Sale,Chris	14	30	Strained flexor muscle in R elbow
	15	7	Fractured R foot
Sampson,Adrian	16	101	Strnd R flexor mass
Sanchez,Aaron	15	40	R lat strain
Sanchez,Anibal	13	20	Strained R shoulder
	14	66	Strnd R pectoral muscle;cut Rt finger
	15	46	R rotator cuff inflammation
Santana,Ervin	16	16	Strnd lower back
Santos,Sergio	12	166	Surgery torn labrum in R. shoulder
	13	109	R triceps strain
	14	34	Strained R elbow/forearm
	15	108	R elbow surgery
Saupold,Warwick	16	46	Strnd R groin
Scahill,Rob	15	67	R forearm tightness
Scheppers,Tanner	14	158	R elbow inflammation x2
	15	29	L knee inflam; R ankle sprain
	16	159	Torn cartilage L knee
Schugel,Andrew	14	111	R hamstring injury
	16	10	R should injury
Schultz,Bo	16	48	Rec fr surg. on L hip
Schumaker,Skip	14	43	Concussion/dislocated L shoulder

FIVE-YEAR INJURY LOG — Pitchers

Pitchers	Yr	Days	Injury
Scribner,Evan	16	151	Strnd lat R should
Severino,Luis	16	16	Strnd R triceps
Shoemaker,Matthew	14	13	Strained Lt oblique
	16	28	Fractured skull,hematoma
Shreve,Chasen	16	24	Sprnd AC joint L should
Siegrist,Kevin	14	60	Strained L forearm
	16	14	Mononucleosis
Simmons,Shae	14	62	Strained R shoulder
	16	128	Rec fr TJS
Simon,Alfredo	16	68	Strnd R should
Skaggs,Tyler	14	81	Strained L forearm; Rt hammy
	15	184	Recovery from L elbow surgery
Smith,Burch	15	180	R elbow surgery
Smith,Carson	16	167	Tommy John surg.
Smith,Joe	16	39	Strnd L hamstring
Smith,Will	16	60	Torn LCL R knee
Smyly,Drew	12	37	Strain R. intercostal+ fing. blister
	15	118	L shoulder soreness x2
Solis,Sammy	15	20	L shoulder inflammation
	16	59	L should inflam; sore R knee
Soria,Joakim	12	182	Recovering from TJS
	13	99	Recovery from R elbow surgery
	14	50	Strained L oblique
Soriano,Rafael	15	27	R shoulder inflammation
Stammen,Craig	15	173	Torn R flexor tendon
Stauffer,Tim	12	182	R. elbow sprain
	15	21	R intercostal strain
Stites,Matthew	15	58	R elbow pain
Storen,Drew	12	106	Elbow injury
	16	16	R should inflammation
Strasburg,Stephen	13	15	Strained R latissimus dorsi
	15	58	L oblique; neck strain
	16	33	Sore R elbow; strnd upper back
Street,Huston	12	72	Strained L. calf+ L. lat str
	13	15	Strained L calf
	16	94	R knee inflammation; strnd L oblique
Stroman,Marcus	15	159	Torn ACL,L knee
Strop,Pedro	13	15	Lower back strain
	14	23	Strained L groin
	16	43	Torn meniscus L knee
Stults,Eric	12	48	Strained L. latissimus dorsi
Surkamp,Eric	12	182	TJS
	13	88	Recovery from L elbow surgery
	15	6	Strained upper back
Swarzak,Anthony	12	33	Strained R. rotator cuff
	13	7	Fractured ribs
	16	26	Strnd R rotator cuff
Taillon,Jameson	16	15	R should fatigue
Tanaka,Masahiro	14	74	R elbow inflammation
	15	35	Strained R forearm
Tazawa,Junichi	16	18	R should impingement
Teheran,Julio	16	17	Strnd R lat muscle
Thatcher,Joe	12	37	Mid-back strain
	14	57	Sprained L ankle
Thayer,Dale	15	14	Strained R shoulder
Thornburg,Tyler	14	114	Sore R elbow

FIVE-YEAR INJURY LOG — Pitchers

Pitchers	Yr	Days	Injury
Thornton,Matt	13	20	Strained R oblique
	16	50	Tendinitis L Achilles
Tillman,Chris	13	5	Strained L abdominal
	16	18	Bursitis R should
Tolleson,Shawn	13	170	Strained lower back
	16	41	Sprnd lower back
Tomlin,Josh	12	72	Inflam in R. elbow+R. wrist
	13	146	Recovery from R elbow surgery
	15	117	R shoulder surgery
Triggs,Andrew	16	14	Bruised L shin
Tropeano,Nicholas	16	96	Torn lig R elbow; strnd R should
Tsao,Chin-Hui	16	133	Strnd R triceps
Turner,Jacob	14	24	Strained R shoulder
	15	183	Strained flexor tendon,R elbow
Uehara,Koji	12	77	Strained R. lat
	15	66	Fx R wrist; Strain L ham
	16	47	Strnd R pectoral muscle
Urena,Jose	15	28	L knee contusion
Vargas,Cesar	16	127	Sore R elbow
Vargas,Jason	13	56	Blood clot,L arm
	14	23	Appendectomy
	15	131	Torn lig.,L elbow; L flexor strain x2
	16	166	Rec fr surg. on L elbow
Varvaro,Anthony	15	133	Torn flexor tendon in R elbow
Velasquez,Vincent	16	17	Strnd R biceps
Venditte,Patrick	15	51	Strained R shoulder
Ventura,Yordano	15	20	Ulnar neuritis
VerHagen,Drew	14	28	Stress reaction in spine
	16	108	Thoracic outlet syndrome R should
Verlander,Justin	15	66	Strained R triceps
Vincent,Nick	14	34	R shoulder fatigue
	16	39	Strnd mid-back
Vizcaino,Arodys	12	183	TJS
	13	183	Recovery from R elbow surgery
	16	67	R should inflam; strnd R oblique
Vogelsong,Ryan	12	10	Strained lower back
	13	80	Fractured R hand
	16	72	Facial bone fractures
Wacha,Michael	14	74	Stress reaction in R shoulder
	16	36	R should inflammation
Wainwright,Adam	15	162	Torn L Achilles
Walden,Jordan	12	41	Strained R. bicep
	13	17	R shoulder inflammation
	14	30	Strained L hamstring
	15	155	R biceps inflammation
	16	183	Strnd R should
Walker,Taijuan	14	73	R shoulder impingement
	16	31	R foot tendinitis
Wang,Chien-Ming	16	171	R biceps tendinitis
Weaver,Jered	12	22	Strained lower back
	13	51	Fractured L elbow
	15	49	L hip inflammation
Webb,Daniel	15	24	Mid R back strain
	16	157	Strnd flexor R elbow
Webb,Ryan	16	27	Strnd R pectoral muscle
Whalen,Rob	16	40	R should fatigue

FIVE-YEAR INJURY LOG — Pitchers

Pitchers	Yr	Days	Injury
Wheeler,Zack	15	183	Torn ligament,R elbow
	16	183	Rec fr TJS
Whitley,Chase	15	143	Sprained R elbow
	16	162	Rec fr TJS
Wilhelmsen,Tom	15	25	Hyperextended R elbow
	16	15	Lower back spasms
Wilson,Alex	13	83	Sprained R thumb
	16	14	Sore R should
Wilson,C.J.	14	23	Sprained R ankle
	15	66	L elbow inflammation
	16	183	L should tendinitis
Winkler,Daniel	15	158	Recovery from R elbow surgery
	16	175	Fractured R elbow
Withrow,Chris	12	32	R. shoulder strain
	14	127	TJS
	16	24	R elbow inflammation
Wood,Alex	16	112	Sore L tricep/elbow
Workman,Brandon	15	175	R elbow soreness
	16	183	Rec fr TJS
Worley,Vance	12	54	Loose bodies in R. elbow+ Inflam
	16	16	Strnd R groin
Wright,Mike	15	34	Strained L calf
Wright,Steven	14	70	Recovering from surgery sports hernia
	15	51	Concussion
	16	15	Bursitis R should
Wright,Wesley	15	95	L shoulder inflammation
Yates,Kirby	15	41	R pectoral strain
Young,Chris	13	18	Strained L quad
	16	18	R forearm strain
Zimmermann,Jordan	16	60	Strnd R lat; neck
Zych,Tony	16	112	R/C tendinitis R should

PROSPECTS

Top 75 Impact Prospects for 2017

by Rob Gordon and Jeremy Deloney

Looking for a rookie infusion in 2017? Here's the place to start. The following is a list of 75 prospects most likely to contribute and have an impact in the 2017 season. These capsules provide a primer on the strengths and weaknesses of rookie-eligible players, attempting to balance raw skill, readiness for the majors and likelihood of 2017 playing time. Prospects are presented in alphabetical order; the chart on page 221 ranks the prospects and includes projected 2017 Mayberry scores.

For additional information, including profiles of over 1000 minor-leaguers, statistics, and our overall HQ100 top prospect list, see our sister publication, the *2017 Minor League Baseball Analyst*—as well as the weekly scouting reports and minor league information on BaseballHQ.com. Happy prospecting!

Willy Adames (SS, TAM) continues to progress in all facets of the game as he set personal highs in doubles, HR, stolen bases, and walks. The well-rounded 21-year-old may not win the starting job in spring training, but he should begin the year in Triple-A and could force the Rays to summon him, especially if he proves himself with the glove.

Ozzie Albies (2B, ATL) gives the rebuilding Braves yet another elite infield prospect. The Braves moved Albies from SS to 2B mid-season with the emergence of Dansby Swanson. The switch-hitting Albies makes consistent contact and has a good understanding of the strike zone. He slashed .321/.391/.467 at Double-A. Albies could be in Atlanta by mid-season and his speed and ability to get on base make him an excellent fantasy target.

Jorge Alfaro (C, PHI) came over from the Rangers in the Cole Hamels deal and made his MLB debut in 2016. The 23-year-old Alfaro has plus raw power, but his aggressive approach results in low contact and limits his hit tool. He's made progress behind the plate, showing improved receiving skills and a plus arm (he nailed 44% of baserunners at Double-A). He will open in Triple-A, but Alfaro will soon have an opportunity with the rebuilding Phillies.

Anthony Banda (LHP, ARI) succeeds because of a solid three-pitch mix and his ability to throw strikes. The 23-year-old pitches off a good low-90s fastball and backs it up with a plus curve and an above-average change-up. He isn't going to light up the radar guns, but consistently induces weak contact and was 10-6 with a 2.88 ERA between Double- and Triple-A.

Franklin Barreto (2B/SS, OAK) has long been an outstanding hitter, which is even more incredible given he's always been among his league's youngest players. He performed admirably for a 20-year-old between Double-A and Triple-A in 2016, hitting .284/.342/.422 with 11 HR and 30 SB. He also makes easy contact with excellent plate coverage.

Jake Bauers (1B, TAM) came over from the Padres in the Wil Myers deal. His plus understanding of the strike zone (73 BB/89 K) allows his other average tools to play up. He uses a short, compact LH stroke to make consistent contact and shoots line-drives to all fields. Hit a career-high 14 HR with 10 SB and the cost-conscious Rays like his attitude and ability to play both the OF and 1B.

Tyler Beede (RHP, SF) has emerged as the Giants top pitching prospect. The 14th overall pick in '14, attacks hitters with a plus mid-90s fastball that hits 97 mph and has good late sink. He mixes in a good curve and a serviceable change-up and went 8-7 with a 2.81 ERA. Beede showed improved control and looks ready to make his big league debut in 2017.

Josh Bell (1B, PIT) is finally starting to tap into his power, hitting a career-high 17 home runs between Triple-A and the majors. The switch-hitter makes consistent contact with a good understanding of the strike zone and should be able to hit .300 with 15-20 HR potential. He is below-average on defense and is limited to 1B.

Cody Bellinger (1B/OF, LA) followed up his '15 breakout with a solid campaign hitting .271/.365/.507 with 26 HR between Double- and Triple-A. Bellinger has good athleticism and is a plus defender at 1B. He could handle the OF if needed, and with Adrian Gonzalez under contract Bellinger will have to bide his time until an injury or trade creates an opening.

Andrew Benintendi (OF, BOS) reached the majors in August and showcased his plethora of tools, which culminated in playoff appearances. He was a consistent producer in 2016 and hit over .300 with 11 HR and 17 SB at three levels. With a clean, textbook swing and a polished approach, the 22-year-old should secure significant playing time with the Red Sox in 2017.

Ty Blach (LHP, SF) is your prototypical command and control lefty. The 26-year-old has a fastball that sits at 88-92, topping out at 93 mph and his best offering is a plus change-up. He's a solid back-end starter but his low Dom limits him to NL-only formats.

Lewis Brinson (OF, MIL) was a highly-coveted player prior to his trade from Texas to Milwaukee at the trade deadline, and rightfully so. He has a wealth of tools, particularly his speed and power. At some point, he could become a 30 HR / 30 SB producer in the majors and he can also hit for a decent BA as his approach continues to evolve.

Zack Burdi (RHP, CHW) was very close to being promoted to the big leagues in 2016 despite being selected in the first round in June. The hard-throwing reliever touches triple digits on the gun and has a potent slider. He pitched 38 innings in the organization after signing, including 16 in Triple-A. Overall, he posted a 3.32 ERA, 12.1 Dom, and .174 oppBA.

Willie Calhoun (2B/OF, LA) has surprising pop for his size (5'8") and in 2016 he blasted 27 HR at Double-A. Calhoun has a good understanding of the strike zone, but can be overly aggressive as he sells out for power. He is below-average defensively, lacks speed, and so OF may be his eventual destination.

Gavin Cecchini (SS, NYM) isn't an elite shortstop but he does have a knack for making consistent contact. He uses a simple right-handed stroke to barrel the ball and had a breakout year hitting .325/.390/.448 with 8 HR at Triple-A. He's a solid defender with a strong, accurate arm, but his line-drive approach results in below-average power. He should see plenty of action in 2017 as a utility infielder, giving him some fantasy value.

Dylan Cozens (OF, PHI) is 6'6", 235, has some of the best raw power in the minors, and slugged 40 round-trippers to go along with 38 doubles and 125 RBI on his way to being named the Eastern League MVP. His swing can get long and he did strike out an alarming 186 times, but also drew 61 walks. Cozens runs well for his size and stole 21 bases and could be ready to contribute by mid-season.

Zack Collins (C, CHW) was the first of two first round selections of the White Sox and the pure hitter should breeze through the minors. He hit .258/.418/.467 in High-A upon signing and there will be opportunities given the dearth of catching in the organization. He owns a mature approach, plus power, and enough defensive skills to warrant big league consideration quickly.

Jharel Cotton (RHP, OAK) lacks ideal size for a frontline starter, but a plus fastball and outstanding change-up allow him to have success. He was obtained from the Dodgers at the trade deadline and made five effective starts for Oakland at the end of the season. His ability to hit his spots allows him to thrive even when his stuff isn't at its best.

J.P. Crawford (SS, PHI) remains an elite-level prospect, but one whose fantasy potential is mixed. At the plate, he has a quick bat and makes excellent contact, walking almost as often as he strikes out. The 21-year-old is an elite defender with plus range, soft hands, and a strong arm. He should develop average power once he matures and fills out his 6'2" frame, but isn't likely to develop into a fantasy stud.

Jose De Leon (RHP, LA) has had a hard time staying healthy, but has dominated when on the mound. The 24-year-old has a plus 92-94 mph fastball, a plus change-up, and a useable slider. He locates all three offerings well and keeps hitters off balance. He was roughed up in four starts with the Dodgers, but owns a career Dom rate of 12.1 and should have a chance to win a starting role in 2017.

Steven Duggar (OF, SF) has solid all-around tools and has moved quickly through the thin Giants system. The 23-year-old has plus speed, but swiped just 15 bases between High-A and Double-A. He has a good understanding of the strike zone and drew 71 walks while posting a slash line of .302/.388/.448 with 10 HR. The Giants have a good track record of utilizing toolsy, athletic players and Duggar could be in the majors by mid-season.

Adam Engel (OF, CHW) owns tools and elements that could aid fantasy teams as well as in real-life with the White Sox. He consistently steals 30+ bases, including 65 in 2015 and 45 in 2016. Regarded as one of the better defensive outfielders in the system, he won't produce much BA or power, but he sure can run.

Erick Fedde (RHP, WAS) was the 18th overall pick in '14 and is quickly developing into a solid mid-rotation starter. Fedde's best offering is a plus 92-94 mph fastball that has good late life. He backs it up with an average slider and a fringy change-up. The development of the change will determine his long-term upside, but his plus command gives him the chance to succeed once he reaches the majors.

Derek Fisher (OF, HOU) has a lot of competition for big league playing time in 2017, but he reached Triple-A in early August and showed he was capable of hitting upper-level pitching. He may not own an outstanding tool—though his speed is quite good—but he does everything well. At his peak, he could hit 20+ HR and steal 25+ bases, but he needs to make more contact.

Clint Frazier (OF, NYY) was acquired from Cleveland at the trade deadline in the Andrew Miller deal and struggled somewhat in Triple-A. Regardless, he's only 22 and has shown incremental improvement with his emerging power and plate approach. His bat speed is among the best in the minors and he can play all outfield positions.

Kyle Freeland (LHP, COL) is a hard-throwing lefty who hasn't yet lived up to the hype of being the 8th overall pick in 2014. He still has a good 92-95 mph fastball and a plus hard slider, but lacks an effective third offering. He doesn't miss as many bats as he could and has a career Dom rate of just 6.1. He remains worth a gamble in deep NL-only formats.

Carson Fulmer (RHP, CHW) may not know his long-term role, but he should be a success whether he'll be used as a starter or reliever. He was a highlight in the Double-A rotation before the White Sox used him out of the bullpen in July and August. Then, he returned to Triple-A as a starter. With a violent delivery and plus fastball and curveball, he has a high ceiling.

Amir Garrett (LHP, CIN) continues to make steady progress in making the transition from a thrower to a pitcher. The 24-year-old has a plus fastball that tops out at 96 mph with good location. His slider and change-up show potential, but remain inconsistent. Garrett posted a career-best 2.55 ERA between Double- and Triple-A and seems ready to join the Reds' young rotation.

Mitch Garver (C, MIN) was considered an average prospect prior to 2016, but he exceeded expectations and maintained his solid defensive skills. He owns a strong arm and is a sound receiver and blocker. Offensively, he can hit for moderate power and he gets on base consistently with a patient approach. He could compete for a back-up spot in spring training.

Lucas Giolito (RHP, WAS) can blow hitters away with a plus-plus mid-to-upper 90s fastball and a plus power curveball. The 22-year-old pitched at four different levels in '16, and made four starts with the Nationals. If his change-up continues to improve, Giolito has the size, stuff, and command to develop into a true #1 starter.

Tyler Glasnow (RHP, PIT) showed why he is considered one of best pitching prospects in baseball. The 23-year-old righty dominated at Triple-A, going 8-3 with a 1.87 ERA in 20 Triple-A starts, but a shoulder injury limited him to just four starts in the majors. Glasnow has a plus-plus upper-90s heater that he backs up with an above-average curve and developing change, though he still battles his control. He should be healthy for 2017.

Stephen Gonsalves (LHP, MIN) continued his rapid ascent up the ladder with another impressive campaign. He held hitters to a .179 oppBA between High-A and Double-A and has a career 2.13 ERA. He's added a few ticks to his fastball while his change-up is a potent offering that keeps hitters guessing. The rebuilding Twins could use him in the rotation.

Yulieski Gurriel (3B, HOU) didn't need much time in the minors (49 AB) after he signed out of Cuba in July. He hit .262/.292/.385 with 3 HR in 130 AB with the Astros and he could make a significant impact in 2017. He can play 3B, his natural position, but also 1B, LF, and DH. His bat is just too good to keep in the minors or on the bench.

Robert Gsellman (RHP, NYM) has come a long way since he was the 402nd player taken in the 2011 draft. He doesn't blow hitters away, choosing instead to pitch to contact off a low-90s sinker. He also has a good feel for a change and breaking ball with above-average command. Long-term he profiles as a solid back-end starter, but he should have fantasy value in 2017.

Josh Hader (RHP, MIL) is a former 19th-round pick who has a good low-to-mid-90s fastball with plus late movement. He mixes in a plus slider and a below-average changeup to keep hitters off balance. Hader breezed through Double-A, going 2-1 with a 0.95 ERA, but faltered when moved up to Triple-A (1-7, 5.22 ERA). Hader will have a chance to win a spot in the Brewers rotation.

Ian Happ (2B/OF, CHC) showed a mature approach at the plate, hitting .279/.365/.445 with 30 2B and 15 HR between High-A and Double-A. The switch hitter uses a quick, compact stroke to shoot balls to all fields. He has an advanced understanding of the strike zone and has the tools to hit for average and power. He remains a work-in-progress on defense and might end up in the OF.

Teoscar Hernandez (OF, HOU) has always been an aggressive hitter and that didn't change in 2016, but he made better contact and started to focus on using entire field. He has the power to eclipse 20 HR on an annual basis while also stealing 20+ bases. He earned time in the big leagues and showcased all of his impressive tools, including CF defense.

Jeff Hoffman (RHP, COL) has the best arm in the Rockies system and made his MLB debut, going 0-4 with a 4.88 ERA. Hoffman has a plus mid-90 fastball that tops out at 98 mph and he backs it up with a plus power curve and an inconsistent change-up. Hoffman led the PCL with 124 K, but didn't miss as many bats in the majors. Hoffman is a risky play in 2017, but has the stuff to be a top-end starter long-term.

Brent Honeywell (RHP, TAM) has been consistently solid at all levels of the minors, including 2016 when he succeeded at both High-A and Double-A. He toys with hitters with his exemplary four-pitch mix, including a screwball that is tough to square up.

The Rays could have an open rotation slot or two and he could be the answer due to his plus control and strikeout ability.

Rhys Hoskins (1B, PHI) has become a viable long-term option at 1B. The former 5th round pick has always had a good bat, and saw an uptick in power in '16, smashing 38 HR at Double-A. Hoskins has a good understanding of the strike zone (71 BB/116 K) and should be able to hit .260-.280 with at least average power.

Joe Jimenez (RHP, DET) did not allow an earned run until June and has one of the most electric arms in baseball. The 21-year-old appeared in the 2016 Futures Game, which highlighted his high-90s fastball and nasty slider. He accumulated 30 saves, a 1.51 ERA, and .144 oppBA in 2016. Many thought he deserved a call-up, but he's sure to make an impact in 2017.

JaCoby Jones (OF, DET) began the season in mid-May due to a drug suspension, but immediately hit upon his return. At this point, his best attribute may be his versatility, as he saw significant action in CF and 3B while also some time at LF and 1B. He only hit .214 in 28 AB with the Tigers and he struggled somewhat in Triple-A, but he has impressive strength and speed.

Aaron Judge (OF, NYY) smacked 23 HR between Triple-A and the majors and he has a lot more power packed into his gigantic frame. He can shorten his swing at times to make better contact, though strikeouts will always be a part of his game. The power is too good to ignore and he's proven his worth in RF with amazing arm strength and surprising agility and speed.

Reynaldo Lopez (RHP, WAS) was signed as an 18-year-old out of the D.R. for a paltry $17,000. Since then, he's seen his fastball velocity jump from the upper 80s to the mid-90s. He mixes in an average curve and a fringy change-up. Lopez impressed at Double- and Triple-A and then held his own in 44 innings with the Nationals. The Nationals rotation remains as deep as any in baseball, but Lopez will undoubtedly see significant action in '17.

Manny Margot (OF, SD) had a nice breakout, hitting .304 with 30 SB in the PCL in route to making his MLB debut. Once in the majors, the 22-year-old held his own in 10 late-season games. Margot has a contact-oriented approach at the plate with good strike zone awareness and plus speed. He should enter 2017 as the Padres starting CF, and his SB ability gives him plenty of fantasy value.

Francis Martes (RHP, HOU) struggled at the onset of the 2016 campaign, but started to dominate with his premium arm strength and dynamic fastball after May. Though he camped out at Double-A all year, he has a chance to make the Astros roster as a starter or reliever. He pumps mid-90s heat into the strike zone and has seen his curveball turn into a vicious, swing-and-miss offering.

Ryan McMahon (3B, COL) struggled in his Double-A debut, especially against RHP (.233/.305/.392). The Rockies hope that was an aberration and that he will return to form in 2017. When going well, McMahon has plus power and stroked 67 XBH in 2014-15. He split time between 3B and 1B and remains a below-average defender. Heading into 2017, the Rockies don't have any sure things at 1B, making McMahon a decent sleeper.

Austin Meadows (OF, PIT) had mixed results in 2016. He started the year on the DL after being hit in the eye, but came back red-hot at Double-A, hitting .311/.365/.611 with a 26-game hitting streak. A hamstring injury after being promoted to Triple-A hampered him and he hit just .214 with a 23% K rate. Nevertheless, Meadows has the tools to be an impact player and should hit for power and average once he reaches the majors.

Yohander Mendez (LHP, TEX) pitched on four levels, including the majors, in 2016. Given he played the entire 2015 season in Low-A, this was quite a revelation. Very projectable due to his 6'5" height and lean frame, he is a strike-thrower who can fool hitters with his plus fastball and advanced change-up. He could pitch out of the Rangers bullpen in 2017.

Ryan Merritt (LHP, CLE) is best known for his surprising success in the playoffs, but his ability to eat innings should be valued in 2017. He's not a flamethrower or strikeout artist and won't wow anybody with one particular pitch. However, he sequences his offerings and exhibits pinpoint command to all quadrants of the strike zone.

Yoan Moncada (2B/3B, BOS) struggled with strikeouts upon his September 2016 promotion, but his upside is higher than any prospect in baseball. Speed is the current ticket (49, 45 SB in his past two seasons), and he's just begininng to tap into his explosive bat (career .875 OPS). Originally a 2B, he switched to 3B to hasten his MLB arrival, which should take place for good in mid-season.

Frankie Montas (RHP, OAK) didn't see much action during the season (16 innings) due to a strained oblique, but was impressive in the Arizona Fall League. Now in his fourth organization after his acquisition from the Dodgers, he needs to throw more consistent strikes. Nevertheless, his arm strength and ability to dominate could be useful in the bullpen.

Tom Murphy (C, COL) has quietly developed into one of the better catching prospects in baseball. The 25-year-old has plus raw power and stroked 24 HR between Triple-A and the majors. He has some swing-and-miss to his game as he sells out for power, so the .327 BA at Triple-A isn't likely to be replicated in the majors. Still, Murphy has substantial fantasy value and should see plenty of action in Coors in 2017.

Sean Newcomb (LHP, ATL) has some of the best raw stuff of any LHP in the minors. His fastball sits at 92-95, topping out at 97 mph with a plus curve and improved change-up. As good as his stuff is, Newcomb stalled at Double-A, largely because of his below-average command and he has a career Ctl ratio of 4.7. Newcomb is tough to square up and could come quickly if he can develop more consistent mechanics.

Tyler O'Neill (OF, SEA) was phenomenal in 2015 while in High-A and matched the excitement with continued success while in Double-A in 2016. He profiles as a middle-of-the-order run producer as he smashed 24 HR while batting .295/.377/.512 in Double-A as a 21-year-old. There is a lot of swing-and-miss in his game, but he draws walks and has average speed.

David Paulino (RHP, HOU) was known for his injury history prior to 2016, but he vaulted to the majors on the consistency of his fastball. He pitched seven innings with the Astros and should have a shot at earning time in 2017. He stands 6'7", and his angle to the plate makes his pitches play up. Despite his lack of pro experience, he throws quality strikes consistently.

Brett Phillips (OF, MIL) has the potential to be a 5-tool player, but took a huge step backwards as he struggled to make contact all year. He whiffed an alarming 154 in 124 games, finishing with a .229/.332/.397 slash line. He did hit 16 HR and the rebuilding Brewers need him to prove that 2016 was a fluke. With a quick start, he could be in the majors by mid-season.

Roman Quinn (OF, PHI) has some of the best speed in the minors and swiped 36 bases in 77 games. The switch-hitter notched his second straight .300 season, dispelling doubts about his ability to hit for average. He uses a contact-oriented, line-drive approach to maximize his plus speed, but has shown gap power as well. Quinn has been injury-prone and again was limited to just 308 AB, but could make the team out of spring training.

Hunter Renfroe (OF, SD) had his best season as a pro, hitting .306 with 30 HR in the PCL and then blasting 4 HR in 11 games with the Padres. Renfroe has plus raw power but can be overly aggressive at the plate (22 BB/115 K) and will be hard-pressed to hit for average without an adjustment. Renfroe moves well in the OF with a plus arm and should open '17 as the Padres starting RF.

Alex Reyes (RHP, STL) has one of the most electric arms in baseball. He comes after hitters with a mid-90s fastball that tops out at 102 mph, and backs it up with a knee-buckling curveball. Reyes missed the first half of the season due to his second drug suspension, but was almost unhittable once he reached the majors. Like most young flamethrowers, control can still be an issue, but MLB hitters found him tough to square up, and hit just .201 against him in 46 innings of work.

Amed Rosario (SS, NYM) has quickly emerged as one of the top prospects in the NL, hitting .324/.374/.429 between High-A and Double-A. He uses a short, compact stroke to make consistent contact and shoots line drive to all fields. Rosario is a true shortstop with good range and a plus arm. At 20 years old, he's one of the youngest prospects on this list, but could reach the majors by mid-season.

Nick Senzel (3B, CIN) was considered the best college hitter in the 2016 draft class, and hit .329/.415/.567 with 23 2B and 7 HR in his pro debut at Low-A. Senzel has an advanced understanding of the strike zone and makes consistent, hard contact. He has only average speed, but is a good base runner (15 SB). Senzel is also a solid defender with good hands and a strong arm. If he continues to hit, he could force his way to Cincinnati by mid-season.

Matt Strahm (LHP, KC) is an ideal candidate to win a starting role with the Royals during spring training. He was in the Double-A rotation, though pitched out of the bullpen for the Royals. The 25-year-old was exceptional, posting a 1.23 ERA and 12.3 Dom in the majors. He can retire hitters with both his fastball and curveball and he rarely beats himself.

Dominic Smith (1B, NYM) had his best season yet, hitting .302/.367/.457. The 21-year-old has a smooth left-handed stroke that is geared more towards hard contact than over-the-fence power, though he did have a career-high 14 HR. At 6'0", 250 he's limited to 1B where he is a plus defender but with below-average speed. Smith should be in the majors by mid-season and could eventually hit .280 with 15 HR over a full season.

Robert Stephenson (RHP, CIN) has yet to tap into his full potential. The hard-throwing righthander has a plus mid-90s fastball that tops out at 97 mph with an average change and curveball, but struggles to repeat his mechanics with below-average command. Stephenson walked 4.6 batters per nine innings, both in the minors and in eight starts with the Reds. MLB hitters teed off when he fell behind; he will need to make adjustments in 2017.

Dansby Swanson (SS, ATL) enters 2017 as the top position prospect in the NL. The 22-year-old started the year at High-A where he hit .333 in 21 games, earning a quick promotion to Double-A. He made his MLB debut in August and quickly proved he was ready for the majors. He doesn't have off-the-charts raw tools but is a smart player who has a good understanding of how to hit and get on base and should develop at least average power.

Raimel Tapia (OF, COL) continues to exceed expectations. The 22-year-old had his best season yet, hitting .328 with 23 SB between Double and Triple-A and then .263 in 23 games for the Rockies. Tapia uses a slashing swing at the plate and is frequently off balance, but relies on quick hands, plus bat speed, and hand-eye-coordination to put the ball in play. He gets surprising pop from his rail-thin frame and should see plenty of action in Coors.

Andrew Toles (OF, LA) had one of the more unexpected turn-arounds of any prospect in baseball. Toles, who has a long history of off-field issues, was out of baseball and working in a grocery store when he was given another chance by the Dodgers. All he did was hit .331/.374/.511 with 23 SB at three minor league stops and .314/.365/.514 in 104 AB with the Dodgers. Toles has always had plus tools and seems to have worked his way into the Dodgers long-term plans.

Alex Verdugo (OF, LA) put together a solid season at Double-A, hitting .273/.336/.407 with 13 HR. Verdugo has a good approach at the plate with solid bat-on-ball skills, but can still be overly aggressive at the plate. Still just 20 years old, he should develop more power as he matures and a quick start could have him in LA if the Dodgers struggle with injuries again.

Dan Vogelbach (1B, SEA) has hit at every level of the minors, which was enticing enough for the Mariners to obtain him from the Cubs in late July. He hit a career-high 23 HR while continuing to get on base with an extremely patient approach. As a bat-only prospect, he still should see time with the Mariners in 2017, possibly as a DH.

Joey Wendle (2B, OAK) doesn't sit atop any top prospect list, but he reached the majors as a September call-up and hit .260/.398/.302 in 96 AB. The 26-year-old is a fundamentally-round hitter with a professional approach and moderate power. He'll have an excellent chance to make the Athletics roster in spring training.

Luke Weaver (RHP, STL) missed the first two months of the season with a broken wrist, but was lights-out when he returned. The 23-year-old was 7-3 with a 1.30 ERA in 13 starts in the minors and logged eight starts with the Cardinals. His 5.70 ERA in St. Louis isn't an accurate reflection of how well he pitched (3.76 xERA). Weaver makes an excellent sleeper pick for 2017, and his minor league Cmd rate is 5.5.

Nick Williams (OF, PHI) is a 23-year-old with plus bat speed and raw strength that should translate into power if he can learn to make more consistent contact. He can be overly aggressive at the plate (19 BB/136 K), which resulted in a .258 BA in 2016. He let those struggles impact his play and was twice disciplined for on-field issues. The plus athlete is likely to return to Triple-A, but a strong start there could land him in the majors by mid-season.

Jesse Winker (OF, CIN) put up solid numbers but was hampered by yet another wrist injury. The 23-year-old has a professional approach (61 BB/63 K in 2016). and now owns a career slash line of .296/.398/.455. Scouts remain divided on his long-term power upside, but the wrist injuries partially explain his lack of production. He should make his MLB debut this year.

Bradley Zimmer (OF, CLE) began the year in Double-A, where he showed a more patient approach and more consistent power, with impressive speed and base running acumen. His promotion to Triple-A wasn't as fruitful, as he continued to struggle with strikeouts (a stunning 56% ct% in AAA). An excellent defender with good secondary tools, Zimmer should see some time in Cleveland in 2017.

Top 75 Impact Prospects for 2017

The chart below lists projected Mayberry scores for the Top 75 Impact Prospects for 2017. Mayberry scores are explained in the Encyclopedia, and here reflect 2017 only, not a player's long-term impact. Batters are dark shaded; pitchers are lighter shaded.

RANK/BATTER/POS, TM	POWER	SPEED	BATAVG	PT '17	RANK/BATTER/POS, TM	POWER	SPEED	BATAVG	PT '17
RANK/PITCHER/POS, TM	ERA	DOM	SAVES	PT '17	RANK/PITCHER/POS, TM	ERA	DOM	SAVES	PT '17
1 Andrew Benintendi (OF, BOS)	2	1	4	5	39 Teoscar Hernandez (OF, HOU)	2	2	2	1
2 Dansby Swanson (SS, ATL)	1	2	3	5	40 Amir Garrett (LHP, CIN)	1	2	0	1
3 Alex Reyes (RHP, STL)	2	4	0	5	41 Sean Newcomb (LHP, ATL)	1	2	0	1
4 Yoan Moncada (2B/3B, BOS)	2	4	4	3	42 Ryan Merritt (LHP, CLE)	1	1	0	1
5 Lucas Giolito (RHP, WAS)	2	3	0	3	43 Derek Fisher (OF, HOU)	1	1	1	1
6 Josh Bell (1B, PIT)	2	1	3	3	44 David Paulino (RHP, HOU)	2	2	0	1
7 Manny Margot (OF, SD)	1	4	2	5	45 Zack Burdi (RHP, CHW)	2	3	1	0
8 J.P. Crawford (SS, PHI)	1	3	2	3	46 Josh Hader (RHP, MIL)	1	2	0	3
9 Hunter Renfroe (OF, SD)	3	1	2	3	47 Dan Vogelbach (1B, SEA)	2	0	3	1
10 Andrew Toles (OF, LA)	1	1	2	2	48 Yulieski Gurriel (3B, HOU)	2	0	4	5
11 Tyler Glasnow (RHP, PIT)	2	3	0	3	49 Ty Blach (LHP, SF)	2	1	1	1
12 Jose De Leon (RHP, LA)	2	2	0	3	50 Amed Rosario (SS, NYM)	1	2	2	1
13 Raimel Tapia (OF, COL)	1	3	2	3	51 Matt Strahm (LHP, KC)	3	2	0	1
14 Roman Quinn (OF, PHI)	1	4	2	3	52 Stephen Gonsalves (LHP, MIN)	2	2	0	1
15 Ozzie Albies (2B/SS, ATL)	1	3	3	1	53 Yohander Mendez (LHP, TEX)	1	1	0	0
16 Reynaldo Lopez (RHP, WAS)	1	2	1	3	54 Dominic Smith (1B, NYM)	2	1	2	3
17 Tom Murphy (C, COL)	2	0	1	3	55 Anthony Banda (LHP, ARI)	1	2	0	1
18 Aaron Judge (OF, NYY)	3	1	2	3	56 Tyler Beede (RHP, SF)	1	2	0	3
19 Franklin Barreto (2B/SS, OAK)	1	1	3	3	57 Cody Bellinger (1B, LA)	2	1	1	1
20 Austin Meadows (OF, PIT)	2	2	3	1	58 Gavin Cecchini (SS, NYM)	1	1	3	3
21 Jeff Hoffman (RHP, COL)	1	2	0	3	59 Nick Senzel (3B, CIN)	2	1	3	3
22 Clint Frazier (OF, NYY)	2	1	3	1	60 Willie Calhoun (2B, LA)	3	1	1	1
23 Tyler O'Neill (OF, SEA)	2	2	2	3	61 Ryan McMahon (3B, COL)	2	1	2	1
24 Lewis Brinson (OF, MIL)	1	2	3	1	62 Zack Collins (C, CHW)	2	0	1	1
25 Robert Stephenson (RHP, CIN)	1	2	0	3	63 JaCoby Jones (OF, DET)	1	2	1	1
26 Bradley Zimmer (OF, CLE)	2	2	1	1	64 Jesse Winker (OF, CIN)	2	2	2	3
27 Nick Williams (OF, PHI)	1	3	1	3	65 Mitch Garver (C, MIN)	1	0	1	1
28 Jorge Alfaro (C, PHI)	2	1	1	3	66 Dylan Cozens (OF, PHI)	3	1	1	1
29 Willy Adames (SS, TAM)	2	1	3	1	67 Rhys Hoskins (1B, PHI)	2	1	1	1
30 Luke Weaver (RHP, STL)	2	2	0	3	68 Erick Fedde (RHP, WAS)	2	2	0	1
31 Robert Gsellman (RHP, NYM)	2	1	0	3	69 Adam Engel (OF, CHW)	0	2	2	1
32 Carson Fulmer (RHP, CHW)	2	3	1	1	70 Ian Happ (2B/OF, CHC)	1	1	2	1
33 Brent Honeywell (RHP, TAM)	3	2	0	1	71 Joey Wendle (2B, OAK)	1	1	3	1
34 Jharel Cotton (RHP, OAK)	2	3	0	1	72 Kyle Freeland (LHP, COL)	1	1	1	3
35 Francis Martes (RHP, HOU)	1	3	1	1	73 Jake Bauers (OF, TAM)	1	1	2	1
36 Brett Phillips (OF, MIL)	2	2	1	1	73 Steven Duggar (OF, SF)	1	2	1	1
37 Frankie Montas (RHP, OAK)	1	3	1	0	75 Alex Verdugo (OF, LA)	2	1	2	1
38 Joe Jimenez (RHP, DET)	3	3	1	0					

Top International Players for 2017 and Beyond

Since the 2008 edition, the *Baseball Forecaster* has profiled a handful of Japanese prospects who may make the jump to Major League Baseball in the coming years. This provides owners in deep keeper leagues to get the jump on talent before they arrive in the states. For example, that first column in 2008 included names like Koji Uehara (who made his MLB debut in 2009), Norichika Aoki (2012), and even a "hugely talented young pitcher" named Yu Darvish (also 2012).

As more MLB teams now draw regularly from the international player pool, we've expanded our coverage to include both Korean players as well as top Carribean talent—both high-upside teenagers of the past international signing period and Cuban players that could draw the interest of mutliple MLB teams. With each, we list a "possible" MLB ETA—but for most of these, you'll need to be patient.

Japanese and Korean Players *(by Tom Muhall)*

Several players joined the major leagues in 2016, and as usual, the biggest impact came from pitchers. Seung-Hwan Oh proved to be as capable a closer for St. Louis as he was in Korea and Japan, and Kenta Maeda exceeded expectations to become a $20 starting pitcher. No such impact players loom on the immediate horizon, but this could be an excellent year to stock up your farm club, including possibly the best SP since Yu Darvish.

Shogo Akiyama (OF, Seibu Lions) became just the sixth player with a 200-hit season in NPB history in 2015 (a feat previously attained by only Ichiro Suzuki and Norichika Aoki), and the only player with 200 hits in a season since the "deader" ball was introduced in 2011. He followed up with a 171 hit/.296 BA season in 2016. Akiyama is a solid defender with decent five-category skills and could definitely play in the majors.
Possible ETA: 2018

Jae-Gyun Hwang (3B, Lotte Giants) has reached international free agency in Korea and wants to play in the U.S. Hwang can also play 1B and compares somewhat to Dae Ho Lee. He has no experience in the tougher Japanese League and isn't the best defender, but has some power (26 HR in both 2015 and 2016) and speed (six seasons with 17 SB or more) for a corner infielder. He likely profiles as a utility player in the majors.
Probable ETA: 2017

Yoshihiro Itoi (OF, Orix Buffaloes) is nearing the end of his solid career and is in his option year. Itoi is a good defender with plus speed and some power, and could prove to be a decent 4th outfielder for an MLB team. At age 35, he became the oldest player to lead his league in SB with 53.
Possible ETA: 2017

Takayuki Kajitani (OF, Yokohama DeNA Baystars) is somewhat similar to Aoki and could provide low double-digit HR and higher double-digit SB for an MLB team. Kajitani is getting close to domestic free agency and could be a productive utility player.
Possible ETA: 2018

Ryusuke Kikuchi (2B, Hiroshima Toyo Carp) is a plus defender with good batting skills. He's another player who does nothing great, but everything well. After knee surgery in 2015, he bounced back to hit .315 with a .358 OBP, 13 HR and 13 SB. Kikuchi could make an excellent utility man since he has shown he can handle 2B, SS and 3B.
Possible ETA: 2017

Yusei Kikuchi (LHP, Seibu Lions) drew interest from as many as 11 MLB teams when it looked like he might pass up the Japanese draft to sign stateside in 2009. Now 26 years old, Kikuchi is still a few years away from international free agency and would need to be posted by his Japanese team.
Possible ETA: 2018

Takayuki Kishi (RHP, Seibu Lions) may be one of the few players on this list to have any real impact in 2017. He has reached international free agency, which means no posting fee would be due to his Japanese team. His fastball hovers around 90 mph and he has the usual assortment of complementary pitches, including a solid change-up. Kishi is a notch below Iwakuma and Maeda but could prove to be a decent middle- or back-end starter. The drawback is his history of injuries, which makes him a gamble considering the more arduous MLB schedule. He is interested in playing in the U.S., but several Japanese teams will make a strong bid for his services.
Probable ETA: 2017

Yoshihiro Maru (OF, Hiroshima Toyo Carp) comes from a financially strapped team that sometimes has to post their players early for financial reasons, as they did with Kenta Maeda. Maru is a superior defender who could handle CF in the majors. At just age 28, he could has 15HR/15 SB potential.
Probable ETA: 2018

Sho Nakata (1B, Nippon-Ham Fighters) has some power potential but struggles with breaking pitches and does not do much else other than hit HR. He is limited defensively, so a full time MLB job does not seem probable.
Possible ETA: 2018

Shohei Otani (RHP, Nippon Ham Fighters) would be a top pitching prospect if he were not playing in Japan. Otani has an excellent fastball routinely touching 98-99 mph and tops out at 103 mph. He's had games where as many as 30 of his pitches hit 99 mph. In 2016, he struck out 174 batters in 140 IP on the way to a 1.86 ERA. And Otani has the usual complement of supporting pitches including a splitter and curve. He could be better than Darvish, which is about the highest praise you can give. The best thing about Otani is that he seems to have an understanding with his team that he can leave for the U.S anytime he desires. Otani could be worth more than every other player on this list combined.
Possible ETA: 2018

Shohei Otani (OF, Nippon Ham Fighters) would be a top ML hitting prospect if he were not playing in Japan. *That's right, it's the same guy.* He hits as well as pitches! Otani hit .322 with 22 HR and 67 RBIs in 323 ABs. He is adamant that he wants to bat as well as pitch. Would some AL team tempt him by promising the DH slot? Your fantasy league would probably treat him as two players—a pitcher and a hitter. He is a unique talent.
Possible ETA: 2018

Tetsuto Yamada (2B/SS, Tokyo Yakult Swallows) became only the ninth player in Japanese baseball history to hit for the "Triple 3" with a .329 BA, 38 HR and 34 SB in 2015, leading his league in both HR and SB and earning the MVP award. He followed that up with a .304, 38 HR, 30 SB campaign to prove 2015 was no fluke. Possibly the best all-around hitter in Japan, Yamada is just turning 25 and unfortunately is on a team that will probably not post him early. Keep him on your radar.
Possible ETA: 2018

Yuki Yanagita (OF, Softbank Hawks) is the other player to hit for the "Triple 3" in 2015 but did not follow up with such a successful 2016 after off-season elbow surgery. Yanagita is also on a financially solid team with little incentive to post him early. Only target him if your league allows a large and long-term farm team.
Possible ETA: 2018

Caveat about pitching stats in Japan: Japan instituted a new ball in 2011 which had lower-elasticity rubber surrounding the cork. The new design limited offense and inflated pitching stats. A more hitter-friendly ball was introduced in 2013 and HR increased to pre-2011 levels, but the slightly smaller and lighter ball still favors pitchers. Continue to be somewhat skeptical when analyzing pitching stats.

Caveat about hitting stats in Korea: Korean ball parks are notoriously hitter-friendly. Remember, Kang hit 40 HR in Korea the year before he joined the Pirates.

Carribean Players *(by Jeremy Deloney)*

Kevin Maitan (SS, ATL) was widely considered to be the best prospect part of the July international signing class, and the 16-year-old switch-hitter has a chance to be special. The Braves gave him a $4.25 million bonus and he has as much upside as any prospect in baseball. Maitan has no weakness in his game, though will need time to polish his arsenal. He has immense power potential while displaying a textbook swing from both sides of the plate. Many scouts consider him good enough to stick at shortstop, though he could slide over to 3B because of his projected body and arm strength.
Possible ETA: 2022

Norge Ruiz (RHP, Cuba) is not yet signed, but the durable 22-year-old could make an impact in the majors at some point in 2017 or 2018. Though he's not a flamethrower, his deep arsenal is enhanced by his ability to vary his arm slots and speeds. He establishes the plate with a low-90s sinker and he induces a high amount of groundballs. His other pitches include a slider, plus change-up, splitter, and cutter. Ruiz has been tough to make hard contact against and should become a mid-rotation starter very quickly.
Possible ETA: 2018

Adrian Morejon (LHP, SD) signed an $11 million bonus out of Cuba as a 17-year-old. Morejon has immense upside and could evolve into a #2-type starter for the Padres. He shows exemplary feel for pitching despite his age and simply knows how to hit his spots. His fastball currently sits between 90-94 mph and he complements it with a solid-average curveball and change-up. If his secondary pitches continue to develop and show consistency, he could prove to be a valuable member of the Padres rotation down the road.
Possible ETA: 2022

Vladimir Gutierrez (RHP, CIN) immediately became one of the Reds top prospects when the 21-year-old was signed to a $4.75 million bonus in September 2016. Gutierrez has the potential to reach the majors quickly, possibly as a reliever. His best pitch is a knockout curveball that shows break and tremendous consistency. He has a tall, strong frame with a solid-average fastball that sits in the 90-95 mph range. If he can develop a change-up, he could become a #2-3 starter in the big leagues.
Possible ETA: 2017

Lourdes Gurriel (INF/OF, TOR) defected with his brother Yulieski from Cuba, and the 22-year-old signed a seven-year, $22 million contract with the Blue Jays in November 2016. Much like other Cubans, his stint in the minors could be a short one. He is a bit of a free-swinger at present, though has the tools to be a middle-of-the-order run producer. He offers above average pop from the right side and has enough athleticism to be an asset on the bases as well as in the middle of the diamond.
Possible ETA: 2018

Luis Almanzar (SS, SD) is 16 years old, and is one of the better pure hitters among the July international signees. The right-handed hitter has a clean, quick stroke and likes to use the entire field in his professional and mature approach. Though he doesn't exhibit much over-the-wall pop now, he has natural strength and should develop at least average power. Signed to a $4 million bonus, Almanzar has the talent to stick at shortstop, though could slide over to either 2B or 3B given his nimble footwork and range.
Possible ETA: 2022

Luis Garcia (SS, WAS) is an example of the strength in the July international class at the shortstop position; the 16-year-old is one of the best. He is extremely athletic and has a great chance to stick at the position over the long-term. Garcia has quick, clean hands and above average range to both sides. As a hitter, he makes easy contact with a fast bat and should be able to hit for more power as he grows in his lean frame. His overall skill set is enhanced by his instincts and poise.
Possible ETA: 2022

MAJOR LEAGUE EQUIVALENTS

In his 1985 *Baseball Abstract*, Bill James introduced the concept of major league equivalencies. His assertion was that, with the proper adjustments, a minor leaguer's statistics could be converted to an equivalent major league level performance with a great deal of accuracy.

Because of wide variations in the level of play among different minor leagues, it is difficult to get a true reading on a player's potential. For instance, a .300 batting average achieved in the high-offense Pacific Coast League is not nearly as much of an accomplishment as a similar level in the Eastern League. MLEs normalize these types of variances, for all statistical categories.

The actual MLEs are not projections. They represent how a player's previous performance might look at the major league level. However, the MLE stat line can be used in forecasting future performance in just the same way as a major league stat line would.

The model we use contains a few variations to James' version and updates all of the minor league and ballpark factors. In addition, we designed a module to convert pitching statistics, which is something James did not originally do.

Players are listed if they spent at least part of 2015 or 2016 in Triple-A or Double-A and had at least 100 AB or 30 IP within those two levels (players who split a season at both levels are indicated as a/a). Major league and Single-A (and lower) stats are excluded. Each player is listed in the organization with which they finished the season. Some players over age 30 with major-league experience have been omitted for space.

These charts also provide the unique perspective of looking at two years' worth of data. These are only short-term trends, for sure. But even here we can find small indications of players improving their skills, or struggling, as they rise through more difficult levels of competition. Since players—especially those with any modicum of talent —are promoted rapidly through major league systems, a two-year scan is often all we get to spot any trends. Five-year trends do appear in the *Minor League Baseball Analyst*.

Used correctly, MLEs are excellent indicators of potential. But, just like we cannot take traditional major league statistics at face value, the same goes for MLEs. The underlying measures of base skill—contact rates, pitching command ratios, BPV, etc.—are far more accurate in evaluating future talent than raw home runs, batting averages or ERAs. This chart format focuses more on those underlying gauges.

Here are some things to look for as you scan these charts:

Target players who...
- had a full season's worth of playing time in AA and then another full year in AAA
- had consistent playing time from one year to the next
- improved their base skills as they were promoted

Raise the warning flag for players who...
- were stuck at the same level both years, or regressed
- displayed marked changes in playing time from one year to the next
- showed large drops in BPIs from one year to the next

BATTER	yr	b	age	pos	lvl	org	ab	hr	sb	ba	bb%	ct%	px	sx	bpv
Acevedo,Jhohan	16	R	23	DH	aa	STL	47	0	0	111	3	76	0	43	-76
Adames,Willy	16	R	21	SS	aa	TAM	486	9	11	247	11	72	92	114	21
Adams,Caleb	16	R	23	LF	aa	LAA	246	3	8	211	6	63	57	123	-53
Adams,David	15	R	28	2B	aa	MIA	371	4	2	237	11	83	45	61	9
	16	R	29	2B	aaa	TOR	206	2	2	203	10	72	80	49	-13
Adams,Lane	15	R	26	CF	a/a	KC	488	12	23	237	7	72	93	115	14
	16	R	27	RF	a/a	CHC	428	7	31	215	7	66	72	123	-28
Adams,Trever	15	R	27	1B	a/a	TEX	418	7	4	184	6	62	77	77	-55
	16	R	28	RF	aaa	TEX	38	1	0	147	2	59	119	115	-28
Adrianza,Ehire	15	B	26	SS	aaa	SF	171	2	4	254	7	74	51	74	-27
	16	B	27	3B	aaa	SF	35	1	1	204	4	86	61	101	33
Aguila,Osmel	16	R	27	CF	a/a	PHI	132	5	1	205	7	70	124	68	15
Aguilar,Jesus	15	R	25	1B	aaa	CLE	510	16	0	235	7	73	107	25	3
	16	R	26	1B	aaa	CLE	515	25	0	217	8	76	117	15	19
Aguilera,Eric	15	L	25	1B	aa	LAA	33	0	0	104	2	61	62	15	-93
	16	L	26	1B	aa	LAA	459	11	0	235	5	66	99	52	-30
Ahart,Devan	16	L	24	LF	aa	LA	79	1	1	194	4	76	60	66	-19
Alberto,Hanser	15	R	23	SS	aaa	TEX	310	3	4	279	2	88	68	91	41
	16	R	24	SS	aaa	TEX	265	5	2	238	2	88	62	58	25
Albies,Ozhaino	16	B	19	2B	a/a	ATL	552	6	29	287	9	81	77	142	48
Alcantara,Arismendy	15	B	24	2B	aaa	CHC	454	9	12	198	6	68	94	145	5
	16	B	25	2B	aaa	OAK	398	9	28	250	6	67	106	165	18
Alfaro,Jorge	15	R	22	C	aa	TEX	190	4	2	225	4	65	126	89	-2
	16	R	23	C	aa	PHI	404	14	2	253	4	70	106	75	-3
Allday,Forrestt	16	L	25	CF	a/a	LAA	133	0	4	221	8	82	41	63	-1
Allen,Greg	16	B	23	CF	aa	CLE	145	3	6	270	10	80	79	121	42
Allie,Stetson	15	R	24	RF	aa	PIT	409	11	5	172	8	64	96	55	-32
	16	R	25	RF	aa	PIT	365	12	1	209	8	67	108	60	-11
Almanzar,Michael	15	R	25	3B	aaa	BAL	502	4	1	208	5	79	56	38	-15
	16	R	26	3B	aaa	BAL	410	10	1	214	6	71	88	47	-19
Almonte,Abraham	15	B	26	CF	aaa	CLE	252	3	9	239	10	77	88	118	36
	16	B	27	CF	aaa	CLE	27	1	2	386	13	83	119	117	89
Almora,Albert	15	R	21	CF	aa	CHC	405	5	7	249	6	87	74	108	55
	16	R	22	CF	aaa	CHC	320	3	8	272	2	85	60	106	24
Alonso,Carlos	15	R	27	2B	aa	PHI	42	0	1	206	13	82	51	79	21
	16	R	28	3B	a/a	PHI	103	1	1	166	9	69	68	55	-32
Alvarez,Dariel	15	R	27	RF	aaa	BAL	512	16	6	245	3	86	82	76	39
	16	R	28	RF	aaa	BAL	524	4	6	244	4	82	59	59	3
Alvarez,Eddy	16	B	26	SS	a/a	CHW	430	5	8	217	9	76	53	84	-9
Amaral,Beau	16	L	25	CF	a/a	CIN	256	4	4	221	8	76	61	93	-3
Amaya,Gioskar	16	R	24	1B	aa	CHC	131	1	0	158	7	62	32	59	-91
Anderson,Brian	16	R	23	3B	aa	MIA	301	6	0	222	10	79	57	43	-4
Anderson,Lars	15	L	28	1B	a/a	LA	458	11	2	193	12	74	99	32	13
	16	L	29	1B	a/a	LA	286	6	2	211	10	75	84	58	4
Anderson,Tim	15	R	22	SS	aa	CHW	513	5	43	292	4	75	70	169	19
	16	R	23	SS	aaa	CHW	247	3	9	267	3	73	60	118	-19
Andreoli,John	15	R	25	CF	aaa	CHC	379	4	24	234	10	70	77	148	6
	16	R	26	CF	aaa	CHC	507	9	31	211	12	61	82	139	-22
Andujar,Miguel	16	R	21	3B	aa	NYY	282	2	2	262	7	84	59	67	19
Aplin,Andrew	15	L	24	CF	a/a	HOU	338	2	23	248	13	81	41	135	25
	16	L	25	CF	aaa	HOU	399	4	15	182	7	71	53	123	-23
Araiza,Armando	16	R	23	C	aa	TAM	27	0	0	259	11	70	61	21	-41
Arakawa,Tim	16	L	23	LF	a/a	LAA	149	0	6	151	8	76	30	95	-23
Arcia,Francisco	16	L	27	C	a/a	MIA	311	1	0	194	7	72	38	29	-57
Arcia,Orlando	15	R	21	SS	aa	MIL	512	9	23	297	5	85	94	132	66
	16	R	22	SS	aaa	MIL	404	6	11	236	5	79	66	113	15
Arnold,Jeff	16	R	28	C	aa	SF	164	2	1	183	6	61	83	73	-54
Arroyo,Carlos	16	L	23	LF	a/a	TEX	53	0	2	253	3	77	14	68	-50
Arroyo,Christian	16	R	21	SS	aa	SF	474	2	1	263	6	84	68	55	18
Arruebarrena,Erisbel	15	R	25	SS	aa	LA	136	1	1	251	3	70	57	55	-50
	16	R	26	SS	aa	LA	55	4	0	158	4	55	136	16	-55
Arteaga,Humberto	16	R	22	SS	aa	KC	207	0	1	193	2	78	33	84	-29
Asche,Cody	15	L	25	LF	aaa	PHI	61	1	0	250	7	82	59	21	-2
	16	L	26	LF	a/a	PHI	127	6	1	226	8	69	138	54	22
Asencio,Yeison	15	R	26	LF	aa	SD	482	10	5	245	2	90	59	53	29
	16	R	27	RF	a/a	SD	191	1	2	212	2	83	31	73	-13
Astudillo,Willians	16	R	25	C	aa	ATL	322	4	1	241	1	96	31	33	23
Asuaje,Carlos	16	L	25	2B	aaa	SD	535	6	7	257	6	81	67	100	21
Austin,Tyler	16	R	25	1B	a/a	NYY	378	18	5	270	13	68	161	72	51
Avelino,Abiatal	16	R	21	2B	aa	NYY	127	0	1	239	7	84	67	57	23
Avery,Xavier	15	L	25	LF	aaa	MIN	476	5	16	253	7	72	68	111	-7
	16	L	26	CF	aaa	BAL	303	6	16	220	9	54	97	109	-53
Bader,Harrison	16	R	22	CF	a/a	STL	465	15	10	235	6	68	98	98	-8
Ballou,Isaac	15	L	25	LF	a/a	WAS	178	4	8	268	8	79	95	124	47
	16	L	26	RF	a/a	WAS	400	5	6	225	9	76	61	103	3
Bandy,Jett	15	R	25	C	aaa	LAA	309	7	0	227	3	75	88	33	-11
	16	R	26	C	aaa	LAA	95	1	1	213	1	75	72	70	-16
Barnes,Austin	15	R	26	C	aaa	LA	292	7	9	257	8	85	80	87	47
	16	R	27	C	aaa	LA	336	5	14	239	8	81	74	123	37
Barnes,Barrett	15	R	24	LF	aa	PIT	126	2	3	210	9	78	65	66	5
	16	R	25	LF	aa	PIT	405	7	8	263	7	71	95	110	10
Barnum,Keon	16	L	23	1B	aa	CHW	283	3	1	167	7	63	60	38	-73
Baron,Steven	15	R	25	C	a/a	SEA	291	2	5	215	7	73	62	88	-17
	16	R	26	C	a/a	SEA	232	2	2	236	10	71	43	72	-36
Barreto,Franklin	16	R	20	SS	a/a	OAK	479	9	27	271	6	80	78	119	32
Basto,Nick	16	R	22	LF	aa	CHW	80	0	0	163	7	84	34	23	-12
Bauers,Jake	15	L	20	1B	aa	TAM	257	4	5	249	6	83	78	70	29
	16	L	21	RF	aa	TAM	493	12	8	246	11	80	78	69	27
Bautista,Claudio	16	R	23	2B	aa	CLE	63	1	1	117	0	67	40	41	-87
Bautista,Rafael	16	R	23	CF	aa	WAS	543	3	49	263	7	81	29	129	3
Bayardi,Brandon	16	R	26	RF	a/a	LAA	60	1	0	204	1	69	60	41	-57
Beck,Preston	15	L	25	RF	aa	TEX	343	4	6	189	8	80	51	96	7
	16	L	26	RF	a/a	TEX	357	6	5	232	7	79	83	109	29
Bednar,Brandon	16	R	24	2B	aa	SF	224	2	4	262	3	80	53	95	-2
Bell,Josh	15	B	23	1B	a/a	PIT	489	5	8	285	10	86	65	101	47
	16	B	24	1B	aaa	PIT	421	12	3	268	11	81	87	59	35
Bellinger,Cody	16	L	21	1B	a/a	LA	410	24	7	253	11	75	129	70	48
Belza,Thomas	15	L	26	3B	a/a	ARI	316	3	3	180	6	69	62	75	-39
	16	L	27	3B	aa	MIL	181	1	3	202	7	69	64	80	-33
Bemboom,Anthony	15	L	25	C	aa	LAA	257	4	2	220	7	73	53	63	-33
	16	L	26	C	a/a	LAA	239	1	4	181	7	76	45	92	-19
Benintendi,Andrew	16	L	22	CF	aa	BOS	237	6	7	285	8	86	112	117	88
Benjamin,Michael	16	R	24	2B	aa	COL	285	4	4	203	5	72	64	60	-33
Bennie,Joe	16	R	25	2B	aa	OAK	74	1	0	144	8	73	30	33	-56
Berberet,Parker	15	R	26	C	aa	MIL	164	2	2	203	7	75	55	57	-23
	16	R	27	C	a/a	MIL	35	1	0	92	6	56	100	10	-79
Beresford,James	15	L	26	2B	aaa	MIN	498	1	2	269	5	87	35	46	1
	16	L	27	3B	aaa	MIN	465	0	2	233	7	81	26	72	-18
Bernard,Wynton	16	R	26	LF	a/a	DET	376	5	18	242	7	80	57	135	21
Berset,Chris	15	B	27	C	a/a	CIN	182	0	0	162	5	74	44	31	-45
	16	B	28	C	aaa	CIN	289	2	1	209	7	75	28	45	-50
Berti,Jon	15	R	25	2B	a/a	TOR	405	3	19	225	8	82	48	119	18
	16	R	26	2B	a/a	TOR	292	3	26	218	10	76	63	158	23
Betancourt,Javier	16	R	21	2B	aa	MIL	343	5	3	219	8	81	55	64	3
Bethea,Danny	15	R	25	C	aa	BOS	44	0	0	290	0	64	129	44	-25
	16	R	26	C	a/a	BOS	104	2	0	160	3	73	96	55	-8
Betts,Jordan	16	R	25	3B	aa	BOS	46	1	0	138	3	63	98	33	-50
Bichette,Dante	15	R	23	1B	aa	NYY	254	2	0	210	4	79	56	44	-15
	16	R	24	1B	aa	NYY	367	10	4	229	12	75	85	63	14
Bierfeldt,Conor	16	R	25	RF	aa	BAL	43	2	0	179	5	58	123	11	-53
Black,Daniel	16	B	29	1B	aaa	MIA	84	1	1	171	6	64	39	29	-92
Blair,Carson	15	R	28	C	a/a	OAK	286	6	1	197	10	59	118	77	-25
	16	R	29	C	a/a	TEX	140	3	1	184	9	54	78	55	-85
Blair,Pat	16	R	25	2B	aa	TAM	123	1	5	147	8	66	44	81	-57
Blanco,Felipe	16	R	23	SS	a/a	SD	75	1	0	113	3	57	75	47	-88
Blandino,Alex	15	R	23	SS	aa	CIN	115	3	2	214	12	79	92	50	30
	16	R	24	2B	aa	CIN	401	9	13	219	12	67	80	79	-19
Blash,Jabari	15	R	26	RF	a/a	SEA	406	22	6	216	9	63	169	88	32
	16	R	27	LF	aaa	SD	177	7	1	198	13	52	159	30	-27
Bonifacio,Jorge	16	R	23	RF	aaa	KC	495	13	5	243	7	72	93	98	6
Borenstein,Zachary	15	L	25	LF	aa	ARI	332	7	4	244	7	76	92	92	21
	16	L	26	LF	aaa	ARI	357	6	10	222	6	61	105	135	-17
Bortnick,Tyler	15	R	28	2B	aa	SEA	222	1	9	218	7	78	50	74	-8
	16	R	29	2B	a/a	DET	167	4	3	214	8	76	74	104	13
Bostick,Christopher	16	R	23	2B	a/a	WAS	484	7	10	232	7	72	74	107	-3
Bote,David	16	R	23	3B	a/a	CHC	47	1	0	244	6	73	28	18	-64
Bousfield,Auston	15	R	22	CF	aa	SD	73	0	1	216	8	74	34	40	-47
	16	R	23	CF	aa	SD	367	3	8	153	8	66	55	89	-45
Boyd,B.J.	16	L	23	RF	aaa	OAK	30	0	0	248	6	89	0	15	-25
Boyd,Bobby	16	L	23	LF	aa	HOU	76	0	3	191	7	67	59	144	-25
Boyd,Jayce	15	R	25	LF	a/a	NYM	299	1	1	226	6	84	67	37	15
	16	R	26	LF	aa	NYM	270	2	2	212	8	77	49	37	-23
Brady,Patrick	15	R	27	2B	a/a	SEA	85	1	3	201	4	75	58	79	-21
	16	R	28	3B	aa	SEA	251	2	5	190	11	63	70	115	-35
Brantly,Rob	15	L	26	C	a/a	CHW	203	7	0	267	3	82	90	40	19
	16	L	27	C	aaa	SEA	303	10	0	192	2	78	79	41	-8
Bregman,Alex	16	R	22	SS	a/a	HOU	314	17	5	274	10	86	125	88	94
Brentz,Bryce	15	R	27	RF	aaa	BOS	220	6	0	209	8	62	108	27	-40
	16	R	28	LF	a/a	BOS	244	4	2	212	5	68	104	65	-15
Brinson,Lewis	15	R	21	CF	a/a	TEX	140	6	4	295	7	74	133	95	46
	16	R	22	CF	a/a	MIL	393	13	12	249	4	77	106	131	40
Brito,Socrates	15	L	23	RF	aa	ARI	490	8	17	283	5	81	81	138	42
	16	L	24	RF	aaa	ARI	303	4	5	253	3	77	68	114	6
Brockmeyer,Cael	15	R	24	C	a/a	CHC	29	1	0	177	5	76	101	-10	-5
	16	R	25	1B	a/a	CHC	133	2	0	216	4	65	96	42	-40
Brown,Aaron	16	L	24	CF	aa	PHI	228	3	2	193	7	68	85	115	-11
Brown,Domonic	15	L	28	RF	aaa	PHI	210	2	7	203	5	77	59	95	-4
	16	L	29	RF	aaa	TOR	464	6	4	199	6	73	64	41	-31
Broxton,Keon	15	R	25	CF	a/a	PIT	491	7	31	234	9	65	101	158	8
	16	R	26	CF	aaa	MIL	178	6	12	234	7	60	146	146	16
Brugman,Jaycob	16	L	24	CF	a/a	OAK	543	9	6	255	7	76	86	95	17
Bruno,Stephen	15	R	25	2B	aa	CHC	342	1	7	224	6	78	50	84	-10
	16	R	26	2B	a/a	CHC	73	1	1	204	4	62	67	101	-58
Bryan,Vaughn	16	B	23	LF	aa	STL	66	0	4	200	12	63	14	100	-80
Bueno,Ronald	16	B	24	2B	aa	CIN	33	0	0	227	13	57	0	64	-123
Burg,Alex	15	R	28	DH	a/a	TEX	197	5	1	204	8	68	98	37	-22
	16	R	29	DH	a/a	TEX	270	5	1	166	6	69	83	35	-32
Burns,Andrew	16	R	26	2B	aaa	TOR	418	7	11	205	6	77	79	83	9
Buxton,Byron	15	R	22	CF	a/a	MIN	292	5	18	289	8	77	101	161	56
	16	R	23	CF	aaa	MIN	190	10	6	288	6	68	155	156	57
Cabrera,Ramon	15	B	26	C	aaa	CIN	317	2	1	248	7	83	42	29	-11
	16	B	27	C	aaa	CIN	54	0	0	222	2	86	13	15	-36
Caldwell,Bruce	15	L	24	2B	aa	STL	294	6	3	225	10	67	106	64	-4
	16	L	25	2B	a/a	STL	375	8	1	202	8	60	90	58	-54
Calhoun,Willie	16	L	22	2B	aa	LA	503	26	0	241	7	86	110	36	59

BATTER	yr	b	age	pos	lvl	org	ab	hr	sb	ba	bb%	ct%	px	sx	bpv
Calixte,Orlando	16	R	24	RF	a/a	KC	471	8	15	243	6	77	79	122	21
Camargo,Johan	16	B	23	2B	aa	ATL	446	4	1	252	5	79	69	74	6
Campbell,Eric	15	R	28	3B	aaa	NYM	113	3	4	271	12	76	109	97	48
	16	R	29	1B	aaa	NYM	302	4	4	214	8	76	61	94	-4
Candelario,Jeimer	16	B	23	3B	a/a	CHC	474	11	0	250	10	76	104	51	26
Cantwell,Patrick	15	R	25	C	a/a	TEX	242	2	0	151	5	74	35	78	-39
	16	R	26	C	aaa	TEX	183	0	3	217	6	69	35	48	-68
Caratini,Victor	16	B	23	C	aa	CHC	412	5	2	259	10	78	68	56	4
Carhart,Ben	16	R	26	1B	a/a	CHC	210	5	1	208	3	79	76	49	1
Carrillo,Xorge	15	R	26	C	aa	NYM	325	8	1	198	6	80	73	47	7
	16	R	27	C	a/a	NYM	290	3	0	209	6	79	47	20	-27
Carrizales,Omar	16	L	21	CF	aa	COL	80	0	4	250	4	80	21	108	-21
Casali,Curtis	15	R	27	C	aaa	TAM	112	3	1	164	11	68	77	44	-29
	16	R	28	C	aaa	TAM	63	2	0	205	16	76	49	3	-23
Casteel,Ryan	15	R	24	C	a/a	COL	145	2	1	279	1	72	88	68	-16
	16	R	25	1B	a/a	SEA	337	5	2	202	6	65	74	80	-42
Castillo,Ali	15	R	26	SS	a/a	NYY	347	2	24	253	6	86	34	90	13
	16	R	27	2B	a/a	SF	380	0	8	264	4	86	35	99	11
Castillo,Ivan	16	B	21	SS	a/a	CLE	244	2	9	189	3	83	49	136	19
Castillo,Rusney	15	R	28	CF	aaa	BOS	156	2	8	244	7	79	64	79	5
	16	R	29	CF	aaa	BOS	395	2	8	234	5	79	57	119	10
Castro,Daniel	15	R	23	SS	a/a	ATL	400	0	4	270	5	88	26	47	1
	16	R	24	SS	aaa	ATL	214	2	0	224	3	86	47	49	5
Castro,Harold	15	L	22	2B	aa	DET	336	1	14	234	3	81	38	117	-3
	16	L	23	2B	aa	DET	392	3	5	220	2	83	43	67	-7
Cave,Jake	16	L	24	LF	a/a	NYY	426	8	6	249	7	72	99	111	17
Cecchini,Garin	15	L	24	LF	aaa	BOS	422	6	8	201	8	74	58	69	-19
	16	L	25	1B	aaa	MIL	424	4	9	225	5	82	51	92	10
Cecchini,Gavin	16	R	23	SS	aaa	NYM	446	6	3	264	7	85	59	61	23
Ceciliani,Darrell	15	L	25	CF	aaa	NYM	229	6	11	274	6	74	122	136	48
	16	L	26	LF	aaa	TOR	304	9	9	239	7	80	97	100	42
Centeno,Juan	15	L	26	C	aaa	MIL	176	0	1	237	2	87	32	62	-3
	16	L	27	C	aaa	MIN	49	1	1	211	6	91	34	48	19
Chapman,Matt	16	R	23	3B	a/a	OAK	514	28	6	212	10	64	160	102	37
Chen,Pin-Chieh	15	L	24	LF	aa	CHC	97	1	1	216	11	76	78	104	22
	16	L	25	RF	aa	LA	33	0	1	159	15	79	24	59	-16
Choi,Ji-Man	15	L	24	1B	aaa	SEA	57	1	0	240	10	70	80	35	-21
	16	L	25	1B	aaa	LAA	188	3	3	279	10	78	96	63	29
Choice,Michael	15	R	26	LF	aaa	CLE	460	11	2	206	6	65	113	66	-17
	16	R	27	DH	aaa	CLE	252	12	0	212	4	63	127	32	-26
Ciriaco,Juan	15	R	25	2B	aa	COL	297	0	14	246	1	85	28	127	4
	16	R	26	SS	a/a	COL	240	2	7	231	2	87	40	93	14
Coats,Jason	16	R	26	RF	aaa	CHW	297	8	1	273	6	71	106	53	0
Cole,Hunter	15	R	23	RF	aa	SF	192	2	1	276	7	74	120	97	35
	16	R	24	RF	aa	SF	469	10	2	247	6	72	88	71	-6
Coleman,Dusty	15	R	28	SS	a/a	KC	343	6	9	238	6	68	90	86	-18
	16	R	29	SS	aaa	KC	188	3	4	184	4	62	90	113	-35
Collier,Zach	16	L	26	RF	a/a	WAS	362	3	6	217	7	63	71	111	-41
Collins,Tyler	15	L	25	LF	aaa	DET	190	2	7	207	8	77	54	74	-9
	16	L	26	LF	aaa	DET	257	6	3	186	6	70	60	63	-37
Colon,Christian	15	R	26	SS	aaa	KC	192	1	6	239	8	89	38	65	25
	16	R	27	SS	aaa	KC	77	1	1	220	5	83	56	56	6
Conde,Vicente	15	R	22	SS	a/a	NYY	28	0	2	134	6	65	0	106	-94
	16	R	23	2B	aa	NYY	26	0	1	183	13	75	32	93	-20
Cone,Zach	15	R	26	RF	aa	TEX	144	2	0	210	3	62	102	10	-58
	16	R	27	LF	aa	TEX	125	4	2	171	5	61	117	106	-20
Conforto,Michael	15	L	22	LF	aa	NYM	173	5	1	282	10	77	113	75	44
	16	L	23	LF	aaa	NYM	128	6	1	353	7	83	122	85	70
Contreras,Willson	16	R	24	C	aaa	CHC	204	7	3	307	10	82	116	87	66
Cooper,Garrett	15	R	25	1B	aa	MIL	29	0	0	504	18	92	71	58	79
	16	R	26	1B	a/a	MIL	428	7	2	248	5	79	70	39	-3
Corcino,Edgar	16	B	24	RF	aa	MIN	183	2	1	254	5	79	64	100	11
Cordell,Ryan	16	R	24	CF	aa	TEX	405	16	10	234	6	74	114	123	37
Cordero,Franchy	16	L	22	CF	a/a	SD	258	5	9	262	6	68	81	121	-11
Coulter,Clint	16	R	23	RF	aa	MIL	95	2	1	321	4	82	61	60	3
Court,Ryan	16	R	28	3B	a/a	BOS	364	3	3	242	9	72	68	82	-12
Cousino,Austin	16	L	23	CF	aaa	LAA	29	0	2	142	2	57	25	167	-97
Cowart,Kaleb	15	B	23	3B	aaa	LAA	220	4	1	266	8	66	97	80	-18
	16	B	24	3B	aaa	LAA	414	6	13	228	6	71	94	114	8
Coyle,Sean	15	R	23	2B	aaa	BOS	126	4	4	150	12	63	97	90	-18
	16	R	24	2B	a/a	LAA	375	6	7	153	7	56	78	88	-70
Coyle,Tommy	15	L	25	2B	aa	TAM	354	4	15	188	11	63	79	116	-25
	16	L	26	2B	aa	TAM	181	1	8	145	7	67	61	144	-24
Cozens,Dylan	16	L	22	RF	aa	PHI	521	37	17	254	9	60	217	126	70
Crawford,J.P.	15	L	20	SS	aa	PHI	351	4	6	241	10	86	78	110	61
	16	L	21	SS	a/a	PHI	472	7	11	235	12	81	55	70	16
Cron,Kevin	16	R	23	1B	aa	ARI	465	23	3	209	6	69	130	68	13
Cruz,Luis	16	R	23	C	a/a	STL	175	2	1	217	5	64	59	77	-63
Cruzado,Victor	16	B	24	LF	aa	NYM	364	7	5	223	10	74	61	63	-16
Cuevas,Noel	15	R	24	LF	aa	COL	406	4	24	245	3	77	64	117	3
	16	R	25	CF	a/a	COL	331	3	6	274	3	83	66	111	26
Culberson,Charlie	15	R	26	SS	aaa	COL	20	1	0	164	0	66	113	48	-29
	16	R	27	SS	aaa	LA	265	3	5	210	5	72	74	85	-17
Culver,Cito	15	R	23	SS	a/a	NYY	387	3	7	189	5	72	56	108	-23
	16	R	24	SS	a/a	NYY	398	4	2	236	8	66	71	72	-39
Cunningham,Todd	15	B	26	RF	aaa	ATL	329	2	7	226	5	87	44	104	29
	16	B	27	RF	aaa	LAA	349	4	15	212	9	80	48	111	9
Curletta,Joey	16	R	22	RF	aa	LA	97	4	0	194	8	59	125	4	-45
Curley,Chris	15	R	28	3B	a/a	CHW	126	3	0	168	4	74	75	39	-21
	16	R	29	1B	aa	MIA	282	5	1	197	7	65	70	46	-54
Curtis,Jermaine	15	R	28	3B	aaa	CIN	227	2	4	223	7	86	42	68	13
	16	R	29	3B	aaa	CIN	285	8	5	241	11	80	75	56	21
Cuthbert,Cheslor	15	R	23	3B	aaa	KC	397	9	4	250	7	84	79	69	36
	16	R	24	3B	aaa	KC	93	5	0	287	8	83	113	57	58
Daal,Calten	16	R	23	SS	aa	CIN	116	1	5	299	7	74	44	102	-21
Dahl,David	16	L	22	CF	a/a	COL	350	16	14	307	9	73	152	122	73
Daniel,Andrew	16	R	23	3B	aa	LAA	448	4	8	247	7	74	58	84	-14
Davidson,Matthew	15	R	24	3B	aaa	CHW	528	20	1	179	9	59	128	33	-32
	16	R	25	3B	aaa	CHW	284	8	0	224	9	63	115	20	-29
Davis,Glynn	15	R	24	CF	aa	BAL	365	2	18	240	7	76	59	98	-3
	16	R	25	CF	aa	BAL	247	4	5	214	6	73	70	81	-16
Davis,Ike	15	L	28	1B	aaa	OAK	21	0	0	190	0	71	40	38	-69
	16	L	29	1B	aaa	NYY	234	8	0	208	10	63	114	24	-27
Davis,J.D.	16	R	23	3B	aa	HOU	485	20	1	236	7	66	135	34	-2
Davis,Johnny	16	B	26	LF	aa	MIL	218	1	14	234	5	67	38	158	-43
Davis,Taylor	15	R	26	C	a/a	CHC	331	7	0	259	6	82	93	38	28
	16	R	27	C	a/a	CHC	279	2	1	217	8	85	48	62	15
De La Cruz,Maikis	16	R	26	RF	aa	NYM	330	3	5	185	6	73	53	59	-36
de San Miguel,Allan	16	R	28	C	a/a	KC	91	1	0	150	4	79	42	44	-26
Dean,Austin	16	R	23	LF	aa	MIA	480	8	1	220	8	75	77	74	4
Dean,Matt	16	R	24	3B	aa	TOR	233	5	1	195	8	59	78	44	-72
Decker,Cody	15	R	28	1B	aaa	SD	373	12	1	178	6	62	118	43	-28
	16	R	29	1B	a/a	BOS	304	14	1	194	5	56	166	71	-10
Decker,Jaff	15	L	25	LF	aaa	PIT	218	2	15	232	12	81	55	116	27
	16	L	26	CF	aaa	TAM	349	10	15	215	12	73	88	102	18
Deglan,Kellin	15	L	23	C	aa	TEX	70	1	0	186	3	66	61	17	-76
	16	L	24	C	aa	TEX	268	7	1	170	5	56	92	53	-74
DeJong,Paul	16	R	23	3B	aa	STL	496	17	2	228	6	66	117	58	-10
Del Castillo,Miguel	16	R	25	C	a/a	SD	65	0	0	176	4	65	27	29	-100
Delfino,Mitch	15	R	24	3B	aa	SF	445	2	4	234	8	82	41	61	-4
	16	R	25	3B	aaa	SF	186	2	0	201	6	75	33	31	-49
Delmonico,Nick	16	L	24	1B	a/a	CHW	402	14	2	239	8	68	125	65	11
DeMichele,Joey	15	L	24	2B	aa	CHW	488	2	13	219	7	72	56	111	-18
	16	L	25	2B	aa	CHW	468	9	2	194	7	68	77	96	-20
DeMuth,Dustin	16	L	25	1B	aa	MIL	115	0	0	246	5	69	45	81	-53
Den Dekker,Matthew	15	L	28	CF	aaa	WAS	269	6	6	207	6	72	79	99	-3
	16	L	29	LF	aaa	WAS	372	6	16	172	8	64	65	94	-45
Dent,Ryan	15	R	26	SS	a/a	CHC	278	4	1	208	6	67	77	61	-39
	16	R	27	1B	aa	CHC	58	0	0	110	8	66	14	47	-91
DePew,Jake	15	R	23	C	aa	TAM	197	2	0	196	5	63	77	59	-58
	16	R	24	C	aa	TAM	284	7	2	182	7	70	72	55	-28
Deshields Jr.,Delino	15	R	23	DH	aaa	TEX	26	0	0	273	3	74	98	16	-11
	16	R	24	CF	aaa	TEX	207	2	17	225	12	68	60	101	-24
Diaz,Argenis	15	R	28	SS	aaa	MIN	302	0	3	216	6	79	34	79	-19
	16	R	29	2B	aaa	DET	323	2	1	197	5	79	38	36	-32
Diaz,Carlos	16	R	24	SS	a/a	KC	58	0	1	212	5	87	12	51	-16
Diaz,Chris	16	R	26	SS	aa	PIT	226	1	4	188	10	79	46	68	-7
Diaz,Elias	15	R	25	C	aaa	PIT	325	3	1	237	7	84	59	61	17
	16	R	26	C	a/a	PIT	101	0	1	229	3	80	21	26	-47
Diaz,Francisco	16	B	26	C	a/a	NYY	90	0	0	218	12	86	21	56	1
Diaz,Yandy	16	R	25	3B	a/a	CLE	444	8	9	285	12	79	72	90	24
Dickerson,Alex	15	L	25	LF	aaa	SD	459	8	3	237	6	74	98	105	20
	16	L	26	LF	aaa	SD	217	7	0	304	4	84	99	64	44
Dickson,OKoyea	15	R	25	1B	aaa	LA	386	10	1	217	4	81	94	48	21
	16	R	26	LF	aaa	LA	329	15	1	275	7	77	137	59	50
Difo,Wilmer	15	R	23	SS	aa	WAS	359	2	22	256	3	77	69	157	16
	16	R	24	SS	a/a	WAS	415	5	25	237	7	84	47	116	24
Dixon,Brandon	16	R	24	2B	aa	CIN	419	17	14	248	7	62	135	100	1
Dominguez,Matt	15	R	26	3B	aaa	MIL	442	8	0	215	3	82	75	29	4
	16	R	27	3B	aaa	TOR	475	16	1	235	5	82	78	27	10
Dosch,Drew	15	L	23	3B	aa	BAL	231	1	2	217	5	79	40	71	-19
	16	L	24	3B	aa	BAL	422	8	1	227	5	76	75	85	1
Dowdy,Jeremy	15	R	25	C	a/a	CHW	91	1	0	170	15	82	57	17	12
	16	R	26	C	aa	CHW	183	3	0	201	10	81	61	30	3
Dozier,Hunter	16	R	25	3B	a/a	KC	486	17	5	256	8	72	135	76	35
Drake,Blake	16	R	23	CF	aa	STL	193	4	2	223	8	68	75	77	-28
Drake,Yadir	15	R	25	RF	aa	LA	361	3	0	235	6	87	39	30	1
	16	R	26	RF	aa	LA	55	0	1	93	4	77	14	80	-48
Dubon,Mauricio	16	R	22	SS	aa	BOS	251	5	5	327	4	85	109	130	74
Duenez,Samir	16	L	20	DH	aa	KC	54	0	2	273	8	78	83	52	10
Duffy,Matthew	15	R	26	3B	aaa	HOU	490	14	3	231	6	77	93	76	20
	16	R	27	3B	aaa	TEX	401	10	1	185	5	63	86	63	-46
Dugan,Kelly	15	L	25	RF	a/a	PHI	299	2	2	228	5	70	56	59	-44
	16	L	26	LF	a/a	CHC	274	10	1	222	7	72	108	40	4
Duggar,Steven	16	L	23	CF	aa	SF	243	1	8	306	10	77	77	120	26
Duran,Juan	15	R	24	RF	aa	CIN	219	6	2	230	4	53	169	109	-10
	16	R	25	LF	aa	CIN	46	0	0	200	8	51	54	17	-132
Dykstra,Cutter	15	R	26	2B	a/a	WAS	407	4	6	197	10	68	49	56	-53
	16	R	27	LF	aa	WAS	74	0	1	255	10	65	44	55	-65
Eaves,Kody	16	L	23	3B	aa	DET	325	9	5	199	9	66	126	105	17
Eibner,Brett	16	R	28	CF	aaa	OAK	197	9	4	241	13	67	124	94	25
Elizalde,Sebastian	16	L	25	RF	aa	CIN	408	5	5	274	4	82	53	91	8
Elmore,Jake	15	R	28	3B	aaa	TAM	198	0	3	196	13	81	14	42	-25
	16	R	29	2B	aaa	MIL	150	1	8	245	10	84	24	77	0
Engel,Adam	16	R	25	CF	a/a	CHW	455	6	30	209	8	68	80	160	3
Ervin,Phillip	16	R	24	LF	aa	CIN	419	14	34	227	13	76	100	130	49

BATTER	yr	b	age	pos	lvl	org	ab	hr	sb	ba	bb%	ct%	px	sx	bpv
Escalera,Alfredo	16	R	21	CF	aa	KC	202	2	4	266	3	74	77	79	-12
Escobar,Elvis	16	L	22	CF	aa	PIT	112	2	2	220	7	76	48	124	-5
Espinal,Edwin	16	R	22	1B	aa	PIT	394	6	0	264	4	82	69	28	2
Evans,Phillip	16	R	24	SS	aa	NYM	361	7	1	289	4	80	88	39	14
Evans,Zane	15	R	24	C	aa	KC	238	4	1	219	3	71	87	34	-30
	16	R	25	C	a/a	KC	246	4	0	195	3	73	54	38	-46
Farmer,Kyle	15	R	25	C	aa	LA	283	2	0	238	4	77	89	38	1
	16	R	26	C	aa	LA	266	4	2	221	7	80	79	72	23
Featherston,Taylor	15	R	26	SS	aaa	LAA	29	0	0	131	4	67	50	106	-52
	16	R	27	3B	aaa	PHI	402	13	5	223	5	70	109	101	10
Feliz,Anderson	16	B	24	SS	aa	PIT	347	3	6	224	8	72	73	98	-5
Ferguson,Andrew	16	R	24	LF	aa	HOU	52	3	2	288	8	71	159	138	69
Ficociello,Dominic	15	B	23	1B	aa	DET	155	2	0	256	3	77	103	83	23
	16	B	24	1B	aa	DET	423	4	4	218	9	72	62	73	-20
Field,Johnny	15	R	23	RF	aa	TAM	432	10	14	218	6	71	116	133	32
	16	R	24	CF	a/a	TAM	450	10	13	237	5	72	103	116	19
Field,Tommy	15	R	28	2B	aaa	TEX	369	10	4	197	9	73	102	81	18
	16	R	29	2B	aaa	MIN	318	8	2	186	7	73	80	64	-7
Fields,Daniel	15	L	24	CF	aaa	DET	447	5	13	200	10	65	95	126	-3
	16	L	25	RF	a/a	LA	159	1	5	182	10	50	46	117	-108
Fields,Roemon	15	L	25	CF	a/a	TOR	225	1	21	227	7	80	22	128	-7
	16	L	26	CF	aa	TOR	497	4	36	197	7	76	38	133	-9
Figueroa,Cole	15	L	28	3B	aaa	NYY	449	3	3	241	7	92	36	42	28
	16	L	29	2B	aaa	MIA	229	1	4	214	7	86	46	102	25
Fiorito,Dan	15	R	25	1B	a/a	NYY	266	1	3	195	9	75	43	63	-29
	16	R	26	3B	a/a	NYY	119	1	0	165	6	64	46	25	-83
Fisher,Derek	16	L	23	CF	a/a	HOU	478	17	21	223	12	63	115	110	2
Fisher,Joel	16	R	23	C	aa	PHI	20	2	0	272	11	65	252	3	88
Fleming,Billy	15	R	23	1B	aa	NYY	36	0	0	226	7	75	140	84	54
	16	R	24	2B	aa	NYY	128	1	0	227	9	80	59	42	0
Fletcher,David	16	R	22	SS	aa	LAA	80	0	1	285	3	82	58	60	1
Flores,Jorge	15	R	24	SS	aa	TOR	395	2	8	250	9	81	53	66	8
	16	R	25	SS	aa	TOR	252	2	3	165	6	82	35	58	-10
Flores,Ramon	15	L	23	LF	aaa	SEA	328	6	2	254	9	82	70	60	24
	16	L	24	RF	aaa	MIL	28	1	0	211	5	71	71	17	-40
Flores,Rudy	15	L	25	1B	aa	ARI	440	12	1	212	5	64	109	36	-32
	16	L	26	LF	aa	ARI	160	4	1	270	6	62	127	98	-5
Fontana,Nolan	15	L	24	SS	aaa	HOU	361	2	4	196	12	68	75	87	-17
	16	L	25	SS	a/a	HOU	395	2	4	165	7	66	51	52	-64
Ford,Mike	16	L	24	1B	aa	NYY	143	5	0	264	18	80	108	18	52
Fowler,Dustin	16	L	22	CF	aa	NYY	541	13	25	275	4	83	96	145	61
Franco,Angel	15	B	25	2B	a/a	KC	269	3	1	235	6	88	70	61	39
	16	B	26	2B	aaa	KC	209	1	0	183	4	83	47	72	0
Franco,Carlos	16	L	25	3B	aa	ATL	424	4	3	231	11	62	54	58	-67
Franklin,Nick	15	B	24	2B	aaa	TAM	192	8	3	228	10	71	128	70	30
	16	B	25	2B	aaa	TAM	240	4	8	218	8	72	83	94	2
Frawley,Casey	16	R	29	SS	aa	DET	121	1	1	182	4	69	35	72	-63
Frazier,Adam	16	L	25	LF	aaa	PIT	261	0	15	300	9	89	51	110	48
Frazier,Clint	16	R	22	LF	a/a	NYY	463	18	13	258	9	71	122	117	39
Freeman,Michael	16	L	29	2B	aaa	SEA	446	3	8	238	7	72	54	110	-21
Freeman,Ronnie	15	R	24	C	aa	ARI	233	1	0	207	6	82	34	25	-22
	16	R	25	C	aa	ARI	219	2	0	216	5	74	61	29	-33
Freitas,David	15	R	26	C	a/a	BAL	261	7	1	213	5	84	83	41	26
	16	R	27	C	a/a	CHC	332	5	2	239	6	75	83	62	-2
Fuenmayor,Balbino	15	R	26	1B	a/a	KC	360	12	1	305	2	81	118	66	46
	16	R	27	1B	aaa	KC	358	4	0	234	3	75	66	11	-37
Fuentes,Reymond	15	L	24	CF	aaa	KC	396	7	23	275	6	80	56	139	21
	16	L	25	CF	aaa	KC	240	0	12	215	6	71	41	128	-30
Gallagher,Cameron	16	R	24	C	aa	KC	301	3	2	236	9	81	60	42	6
Gallo,Joey	15	L	22	3B	a/a	TEX	321	19	2	215	11	53	210	47	20
	16	L	23	3B	aaa	TEX	359	20	2	212	14	55	186	103	28
Galloway,Isaac	15	R	26	CF	a/a	MIA	468	5	12	210	3	73	59	125	-16
	16	R	27	CF	aaa	MIA	441	7	25	214	6	70	66	124	-15
Galvez,Cesar	16	B	25	2B	a/a	COL	29	0	2	283	3	89	23	58	0
Gamache,Dan	15	L	25	3B	a/a	PIT	346	3	3	269	5	81	59	55	-2
	16	L	26	DH	aaa	PIT	176	2	0	213	11	68	54	35	-49
Gamel,Benjamin	16	L	24	CF	aaa	NYY	483	6	17	286	8	78	68	115	18
Garcia,Alejandro	16	R	25	LF	a/a	HOU	253	2	7	249	3	84	42	76	1
Garcia,Anthony	16	R	24	RF	a/a	STL	340	8	2	200	7	76	76	46	-6
Garcia,Carlos	16	B	24	LF	aa	KC	279	2	8	233	7	80	53	110	13
Garcia,Edwin	15	B	24	3B	a/a	TEX	98	0	0	222	5	78	24	70	-36
	16	R	25	1B	a/a	TEX	215	0	4	182	4	83	25	59	-21
Garcia,Greg	15	L	26	SS	aaa	STL	330	0	11	240	9	80	48	96	9
	16	L	27	SS	aaa	STL	104	0	1	210	7	75	32	80	-34
Garcia,Leury	15	B	24	SS	aaa	CHW	349	3	25	263	5	78	63	137	16
	16	B	25	LF	aaa	CHW	310	5	14	265	6	75	55	111	-9
Garcia,Omar	16	R	23	LF	aa	MIL	27	0	5	176	24	60	0	125	-73
Garcia,Rene	16	R	26	C	a/a	MIL	182	0	1	209	3	87	25	38	-12
Garcia,Willy	15	R	23	RF	a/a	PIT	480	11	3	245	4	73	83	86	-8
	16	R	24	RF	aaa	PIT	462	5	5	222	6	70	82	79	-19
Garia,Chris	15	B	23	CF	a/a	TEX	92	1	4	144	2	78	31	118	-24
	16	B	24	LF	aa	TEX	38	0	1	115	2	68	0	66	-100
Garlick,Kyle	16	R	24	RF	aa	LA	292	7	1	258	5	68	141	72	17
Garver,Mitch	16	R	25	C	a/a	MIN	434	9	1	237	8	73	92	25	-9
Gaylor,Stephen	16	L	25	RF	a/a	ATL	111	1	3	221	5	70	20	88	-66
Gelalich,Jeff	16	L	25	CF	aa	CIN	237	2	9	230	6	53	100	150	-49
Gerber,Mike	16	L	24	CF	aa	DET	153	3	5	233	10	71	94	116	17

BATTER	yr	b	age	pos	lvl	org	ab	hr	sb	ba	bb%	ct%	px	sx	bpv
Giansanti,Anthony	16	R	28	1B	aa	CHC	35	1	1	181	4	64	62	82	-59
Gibson,Derrik	16	R	27	3B	aa	NYM	392	2	11	225	8	78	45	112	-1
Gillaspie,Casey	16	B	23	1B	a/a	TAM	472	15	4	253	13	72	114	70	25
Glaesmann,Todd	15	R	25	CF	a/a	ARI	343	11	3	224	3	74	131	100	40
	16	R	26	CF	a/a	ARI	357	10	4	232	4	75	99	104	19
Glenn,Alex	15	L	24	LF	aa	ARI	172	3	3	221	6	77	112	122	49
	16	L	25	RF	aa	MIA	214	6	0	242	6	75	85	54	0
Goebbert,Jake	15	L	28	LF	aaa	SD	354	6	2	211	9	74	72	59	-9
	16	L	29	LF	aaa	TAM	321	7	0	171	8	65	79	42	-48
Goetzman,Granden	16	R	24	LF	aa	TAM	313	4	19	208	4	74	63	155	2
Goins,Ryan	15	L	27	SS	aaa	TOR	20	0	0	309	0	69	50	8	-79
	16	L	28	SS	aaa	TOR	98	2	0	227	6	71	84	27	-27
Gomez,Raywilly	16	B	26	C	aa	NYM	33	0	0	147	7	82	41	17	-20
Gonzalez,Alfredo	16	R	24	C	a/a	CHW	284	0	2	187	7	73	32	59	-49
Gonzalez,Benji	15	B	25	SS	a/a	SD	241	1	2	204	6	83	48	76	8
	16	B	26	SS	aa	SEA	502	4	17	237	9	80	67	116	28
Gonzalez,Erik	16	R	25	SS	aaa	CLE	429	9	10	267	4	77	95	78	18
Gonzalez,Jay	16	L	25	CF	aa	BAL	61	0	2	210	10	72	0	51	-74
Gonzalez,Miguel	15	R	25	C	a/a	DET	219	2	2	203	4	79	74	58	2
	16	R	26	C	aaa	DET	214	2	0	212	7	76	55	17	-30
Goodrum,Niko	15	B	23	SS	aa	MIN	209	4	13	216	9	74	75	152	21
	16	B	24	3B	aa	MIN	182	5	6	243	9	68	100	108	5
Goodwin,Brian	15	L	25	CF	aa	WAS	429	6	12	197	6	76	62	111	2
	16	L	26	CF	aaa	WAS	436	11	13	248	9	72	92	79	6
Gore,Terrance	15	R	24	LF	aa	KC	222	0	30	249	8	75	19	154	-18
	16	R	25	CF	aa	KC	253	0	37	207	8	75	10	144	-33
Goris,Diego	15	R	25	2B	a/a	SD	404	4	1	203	2	83	52	44	-9
	16	R	26	3B	a/a	SD	342	7	1	204	3	78	58	46	-18
Gose,Anthony	16	L	26	CF	a/a	DET	340	5	13	174	7	58	74	118	-57
Gotta,Cade	16	R	25	RF	aa	TAM	291	4	17	218	6	81	75	135	38
Graeter,Steven	16	R	27	2B	aa	COL	250	5	4	247	7	77	72	64	1
Granite,Zach	16	L	24	CF	aa	MIN	525	3	44	263	6	91	39	149	55
Graterol,Juan	16	R	27	C	aaa	LAA	227	1	1	230	3	85	34	41	-14
Green,Austin	15	R	25	C	aa	DET	294	2	0	222	5	79	55	47	-13
	16	R	26	C	aa	DET	186	3	0	192	2	81	56	24	-16
Green,Dean	15	L	26	DH	a/a	DET	403	12	0	251	8	83	74	22	17
	16	L	27	DH	a/a	DET	476	18	2	247	6	79	96	34	19
Green,Grant	15	R	28	LF	aaa	LAA	385	3	1	227	3	76	70	83	-7
	16	R	29	3B	aaa	SF	348	4	1	249	2	78	62	83	-6
Gregor,Conrad	15	L	23	1B	aa	HOU	435	8	4	206	10	73	92	71	10
	16	L	24	1B	aa	HOU	370	7	0	181	9	80	70	46	9
Greiner,Grayson	16	R	24	C	a/a	DET	212	6	1	256	4	71	94	76	-7
Grossman,Robert	15	B	26	LF	aaa	HOU	347	3	9	197	10	70	57	80	-31
	16	B	27	CF	aaa	MIN	121	5	3	220	12	75	93	53	19
Guerrero,Alexander	16	R	30	3B	a/a	LA	40	0	0	38	2	65	0	75	-111
Guerrero,Emilio	15	R	23	3B	aa	TOR	183	2	1	213	4	68	81	70	-30
	16	R	24	3B	aa	TOR	149	5	3	259	5	73	109	103	23
Guerrero,Gabriel	16	R	23	RF	a/a	ARI	418	7	5	214	5	74	88	105	8
Guez,Ben	15	R	28	CF	aaa	MIL	115	5	5	222	11	64	128	86	10
	16	R	29	RF	aaa	MIL	41	1	2	126	10	29	186	63	-93
Gurriel,Yulieski	16	R	32	3B	a/a	HOU	35	1	0	127	4	63	60	21	-86
Guzman,Ronald	16	L	22	1B	a/a	TEX	463	13	2	251	7	76	91	79	16
Haase,Eric	16	R	24	C	aa	CLE	226	10	0	190	6	64	149	50	5
Hager,Jake	16	R	23	2B	a/a	TAM	451	3	6	205	6	76	62	85	-11
Hagerty,Jason	15	B	28	C	a/a	SD	286	4	2	188	7	70	75	64	-25
	16	B	29	1B	aaa	SD	129	3	0	197	5	71	90	49	-18
Haniger,Mitch	16	R	26	CF	a/a	ARI	458	19	9	273	10	74	133	97	55
Hankins,Todd	15	R	25	2B	aa	CLE	445	5	18	231	6	72	69	115	-7
	16	R	26	2B	a/a	CLE	484	8	17	198	5	68	70	137	-18
Hannemann,Jacob	15	L	24	CF	aa	CHC	434	5	13	202	5	70	77	150	0
	16	L	25	CF	aa	CHC	291	8	20	211	6	78	85	132	33
Hanson,Alen	15	B	23	2B	aaa	PIT	475	4	31	240	6	80	63	160	32
	16	B	24	2B	aaa	PIT	432	7	33	243	6	81	59	146	28
Happ,Ian	16	B	22	2B	aa	CHC	248	7	5	237	6	73	91	69	0
Harrell,Connor	15	R	24	CF	aa	DET	436	6	6	195	5	69	69	95	-27
	16	R	25	CF	aa	DET	366	8	5	231	5	68	75	73	-36
Harris,James	16	R	23	LF	aa	OAK	37	0	2	189	4	68	24	131	-59
Harrison,Travis	16	R	24	LF	aa	MIN	434	5	12	203	10	69	69	87	-23
Hassan,Alexander	15	R	27	LF	aaa	TOR	351	2	0	263	6	78	73	46	1
	16	R	28	1B	aaa	LA	254	1	1	182	9	71	27	46	-62
Hawkins,Courtney	15	R	22	LF	aa	CHW	300	9	1	227	6	63	130	68	-8
	16	R	23	LF	aa	CHW	418	10	0	175	5	63	100	18	-52
Hawkins,Joey	16	R	23	SS	aa	STL	20	0	0	43	11	49	0	0	-180
Hayes,Danny	15	L	25	1B	aa	CHW	431	6	0	217	17	70	75	37	-12
	16	L	26	1B	aaa	CHW	184	8	0	206	12	66	134	41	9
Hazelbaker,Jeremy	16	L	29	CF	aaa	STL	40	1	1	244	9	59	96	73	-44
Healy,Ryon	15	R	23	3B	aa	OAK	507	7	0	257	4	82	70	31	4
	16	R	24	1B	a/a	OAK	337	11	1	292	7	76	127	80	44
Heathcott,Zachary	15	L	25	CF	aaa	NYY	251	2	5	235	6	72	45	88	-38
	16	L	26	CF	aaa	CHW	180	2	2	200	11	58	62	103	-63
Hebert,Brock	16	R	25	3B	aa	SEA	170	1	3	194	18	59	78	116	-28
Hedges,Austin	15	R	23	C	aaa	SD	71	1	1	259	7	86	101	50	58
	16	R	24	C	aaa	SD	313	15	1	268	3	80	116	48	35
Heineman,Tyler	15	B	24	C	a/a	HOU	277	2	1	236	5	91	52	55	34
	16	B	25	C	aaa	HOU	239	2	1	213	7	78	47	58	-18
Henry,Jabari	15	R	25	LF	aa	SEA	288	8	5	142	10	59	118	105	-14
	16	R	26	DH	aa	LAA	352	12	2	184	8	63	96	48	-40
Heredia,Guillermo	16	R	25	CF	a/a	SEA	343	3	4	258	10	83	44	84	17

BATTER	yr	b	age	pos	lvl	org	ab	hr	sb	ba	bb%	ct%	px	sx	bpv
Hernandez,Gorkys	15	R	28	CF	aaa	PIT	340	4	13	236	8	73	66	118	-2
	16	R	29	CF	aaa	SF	437	5	14	234	8	77	57	101	2
Hernandez,Marco	16	L	24	SS	aaa	BOS	223	4	4	303	5	75	77	108	6
Hernandez,Oscar	15	R	22	C	aaa	ARI	25	0	0	202	3	78	97	20	2
	16	R	23	C	aa	ARI	144	6	3	183	3	80	99	56	23
Hernandez,Teoscar	16	R	24	RF	a/a	HOU	423	8	25	263	7	78	83	118	29
Herrera,Dilson	15	R	21	2B	aa	NYM	327	8	9	278	6	79	99	97	39
	16	R	22	2B	aaa	CIN	423	16	6	264	8	77	110	90	40
Herrera,Juan	16	R	23	SS	aa	STL	150	0	2	145	3	73	26	73	-58
Herrera,Rosell	16	B	24	LF	aa	COL	425	5	30	280	10	81	51	119	24
Hicks,D.J.	15	L	25	1B	aa	MIN	225	4	1	188	9	67	71	48	-40
	16	L	26	1B	aa	MIN	420	4	2	223	8	71	70	40	-31
Hicks,John	15	R	26	C	aaa	SEA	298	4	6	187	3	70	65	90	-31
	16	R	27	C	a/a	DET	323	8	3	260	5	74	94	72	6
Higashioka,Kyle	16	R	26	C	a/a	NYY	370	21	0	250	8	77	136	25	43
Hinojosa,C.J.	16	R	22	SS	aa	SF	226	2	1	238	8	79	51	83	1
Hinshaw,Chad	15	R	25	CF	aa	LAA	263	1	23	252	10	66	68	119	-22
	16	R	26	CF	aa	LAA	205	4	12	164	8	60	72	126	-48
Hobson,K.C.	15	L	25	1B	aa	TOR	499	12	1	213	5	75	78	33	-16
	16	L	26	DH	aa	TOR	141	3	0	143	8	72	66	43	-27
Hoenecke,Paul	15	L	25	1B	aa	LA	20	1	0	133	4	37	155	29	-112
	16	L	26	C	aa	LA	139	6	0	250	2	82	96	36	23
Hoes,LJ	15	R	25	RF	aaa	HOU	370	2	18	236	9	79	62	115	22
	16	R	26	CF	aaa	BAL	396	6	7	216	8	83	46	70	10
Hood,Destin	16	R	26	LF	aaa	MIA	476	11	9	230	6	73	92	93	7
Horan,Tyler	16	L	26	LF	aa	SF	287	9	4	233	9	67	107	110	8
Hoskins,Rhys	16	R	23	1B	aa	PHI	498	34	6	253	10	71	159	65	54
Hoying,Jared	16	L	27	CF	aaa	TEX	390	12	13	219	7	76	92	129	33
Hudson,Joe	16	R	25	C	aa	CIN	207	2	0	187	13	66	73	23	-44
Hunter,Cedric	15	L	27	LF	aaa	ATL	474	10	9	239	5	82	70	85	23
	16	L	28	RF	aaa	PHI	330	10	5	252	4	79	79	52	3
Hyams,Levi	15	L	26	2B	aa	ATL	223	2	2	235	12	69	71	88	-15
	16	L	27	1B	a/a	ATL	242	4	0	190	4	65	75	54	-53
Hyde,Mott	16	R	24	SS	aa	HOU	280	2	2	187	7	65	55	76	-59
Ibanez,Andy	16	R	23	2B	aa	TEX	307	5	4	235	7	83	69	83	29
Ijames,Stewart	15	L	27	RF	aa	ARI	73	2	1	236	5	76	160	88	68
	16	L	28	LF	aa	ARI	244	8	1	206	9	65	131	37	-5
Jackson,Joe	16	L	24	LF	aa	TEX	413	4	2	238	6	76	63	58	-13
Jackson,Ryan	15	R	27	SS	aaa	LAA	373	1	1	222	7	73	48	44	-40
	16	R	28	SS	aaa	LAA	290	0	3	185	9	68	28	38	-72
Jacobs,Chris	16	R	28	DH	aa	STL	113	3	0	166	4	55	69	39	-102
Jagielo,Eric	16	L	24	3B	aa	CIN	365	7	0	194	11	59	87	21	-65
Jamieson,Sean	15	R	26	3B	aa	ARI	294	5	8	235	9	69	77	82	-19
	16	R	27	2B	aaa	ARI	172	1	0	194	6	60	56	64	-81
Jenner,Jesse	16	R	23	C	a/a	STL	118	2	0	257	4	78	63	38	-17
Jensen,Chase	16	R	25	2B	aa	SD	78	3	2	123	4	56	96	92	-61
Jensen,Kyle	15	R	27	RF	aaa	LA	417	15	0	206	5	67	130	43	-3
	16	R	28	1B	aaa	ARI	498	19	1	224	5	57	148	50	-24
Jhang,Jin-De	16	L	23	C	a/a	PIT	208	1	1	263	5	93	49	43	35
Jimenez,A.J.	15	R	25	C	a/a	TOR	108	0	2	177	6	80	64	74	10
	16	R	26	C	aaa	TOR	228	4	1	217	5	83	84	59	27
Johnson,Kyle	15	R	26	CF	aaa	NYM	94	1	5	168	3	67	83	121	-21
	16	R	27	CF	a/a	NYM	249	2	3	161	6	66	59	59	-56
Johnson,Micah	15	L	25	2B	aaa	CHW	311	7	22	274	8	76	89	129	32
	16	L	26	2B	aaa	LA	464	4	20	215	6	73	57	114	-15
Johnson,Sherman	16	L	26	2B	a/a	LAA	459	9	14	201	11	74	70	109	8
Jones,Corey	15	L	28	2B	a/a	DET	343	1	2	225	6	80	48	54	-11
	16	L	29	2B	a/a	DET	420	6	6	220	7	83	60	73	19
Jones,Hunter	16	R	25	CF	aa	CHW	133	2	2	187	6	74	63	81	-16
Jones,JaCoby	16	R	24	CF	a/a	DET	369	6	11	234	7	66	97	124	-6
Jones,James	15	L	27	CF	aaa	SEA	265	1	16	203	8	79	47	148	17
	16	L	28	LF	aaa	TEX	276	2	9	184	6	62	57	115	-58
Jones,Matt	16	R	24	C	a/a	ARI	32	0	0	138	0	76	76	78	-11
Jones,Ryder	16	L	22	3B	aa	SF	474	12	1	231	5	82	80	35	14
Joseph,Corban	15	L	27	2B	aa	BAL	369	5	2	233	5	88	55	46	23
	16	L	28	2B	a/a	BAL	371	7	4	261	6	87	59	68	29
Joseph,Tommy	15	R	24	1B	aaa	PHI	166	3	0	165	1	77	70	11	-29
	16	R	25	1B	aaa	PHI	95	6	0	321	4	85	143	18	70
Judge,Aaron	15	R	23	RF	a/a	NYY	478	20	6	237	9	66	137	81	20
	16	R	24	RF	aaa	NYY	352	20	5	254	11	69	142	80	36
Juengel,Matt	15	R	25	LF	aa	MIA	437	11	2	208	5	83	84	83	36
	16	R	26	3B	aa	MIA	466	8	1	231	6	80	79	80	21
Kalish,Ryan	16	L	28	RF	aaa	CHC	57	0	2	295	11	80	68	132	37
Katz,Mason	16	R	26	2B	aa	STL	42	2	2	319	10	67	134	60	15
Kelly,Carson	16	R	22	C	a/a	STL	329	5	0	255	6	78	60	31	-18
Kelly,Tyler	15	B	27	LF	aaa	TOR	371	3	3	200	11	83	40	69	6
	16	B	28	LF	aaa	NYM	271	1	3	240	8	80	58	58	0
Kemmer,Jon	15	L	25	RF	aa	HOU	364	14	7	275	8	70	144	109	48
	16	L	26	RF	aaa	HOU	407	13	6	215	6	61	123	81	-18
Kemp,Anthony	15	L	24	2B	a/a	HOU	464	2	25	258	8	83	43	116	20
	16	L	25	2B	aaa	HOU	255	2	7	254	9	84	42	99	18
Kemp,Jeff	16	R	26	2B	aa	BAL	153	3	3	153	8	59	67	72	-71
Kennedy,A.J.	16	R	22	C	aa	SD	31	0	0	148	10	57	0	17	-145
Kennelly,Matt	16	R	27	C	aa	ATL	71	1	0	133	7	79	38	39	-25
Kepler,Max	15	L	22	1B	aa	MIN	407	7	14	294	11	84	112	135	88
	16	L	23	RF	aaa	MIN	110	1	1	271	11	87	75	99	61
Keyes,Kevin	15	R	26	1B	a/a	WAS	473	9	2	213	7	69	77	39	-35
	16	R	27	DH	a/a	WAS	324	9	1	175	10	61	105	32	-39

BATTER	yr	b	age	pos	lvl	org	ab	hr	sb	ba	bb%	ct%	px	sx	bpv
Kieboom,Spencer	16	R	25	C	aa	WAS	309	4	0	205	11	78	47	15	-21
Kiner-Falefa,Isiah	16	R	21	3B	aa	TEX	402	0	5	239	8	87	18	75	3
King,Jared	15	B	24	RF	aa	NYM	420	3	4	183	5	79	42	58	-21
	16	B	25	RF	aa	NYM	85	0	2	156	8	67	70	80	-34
Kingery,Scott	16	R	22	2B	aa	PHI	156	2	3	224	3	74	56	67	-32
Kirkland,Wade	15	R	26	SS	aa	OAK	229	3	3	204	2	62	66	94	-67
	16	R	27	2B	aa	OAK	256	1	1	173	3	62	48	83	-80
Kivlehan,Patrick	15	R	26	LF	aaa	SEA	472	14	9	196	5	70	97	73	-9
	16	R	27	3B	aaa	SD	370	8	3	192	4	63	85	68	-51
Knapp,Andrew	16	B	25	C	aaa	PHI	403	8	2	242	8	69	90	59	-18
Kozma,Pete	16	R	28	SS	aaa	NYY	445	2	9	177	6	75	38	82	-33
Krauss,Marc	15	L	28	1B	aaa	DET	244	3	1	222	13	69	81	87	-3
	16	L	29	1B	aaa	NYM	229	8	1	150	9	55	112	53	-56
Krizan,Jason	15	L	26	RF	a/a	DET	485	6	10	209	8	87	54	79	32
	16	L	27	LF	a/a	DET	456	8	2	249	9	90	74	65	58
Kubitza,Kyle	15	L	25	3B	aaa	LAA	457	4	5	212	8	67	105	88	-5
	16	L	26	LF	aaa	ATL	396	5	10	177	11	62	72	125	-34
Ladendorf,Tyler	15	R	27	SS	aaa	OAK	83	1	0	218	5	67	49	48	-66
	16	R	28	CF	aaa	OAK	128	1	0	195	4	76	39	45	-41
Lake,Junior	15	R	25	LF	aaa	BAL	247	7	11	290	13	69	104	68	7
	16	R	26	RF	aaa	TOR	281	6	8	206	9	67	81	97	-16
LaMarre,Ryan	15	R	27	CF	aaa	CIN	300	8	9	217	5	63	107	89	-24
	16	R	28	CF	aaa	BOS	317	8	15	271	7	70	88	83	-8
Lambo,Andrew	16	L	28	DH	aaa	OAK	216	3	1	215	7	77	67	89	3
Landoni,Emerson	15	R	26	SS	aa	ATL	411	1	3	255	5	87	49	75	21
	16	R	27	2B	a/a	ATL	147	0	1	211	3	80	24	47	-38
Landry,Leon	15	L	26	CF	a/a	SEA	220	6	11	217	6	78	65	101	9
	16	L	27	LF	aa	SEA	465	5	4	197	6	80	49	93	2
Lara,Jordy	15	R	24	3B	aa	SEA	443	6	0	207	6	78	78	58	4
	16	R	25	RF	aa	ATL	155	4	0	203	5	76	71	38	-15
Latimore,Quincy	15	R	26	RF	aa	BAL	442	18	5	237	7	72	140	101	47
	16	R	27	LF	aa	BAL	392	11	2	171	8	66	85	65	-28
Laureano,Ramon	16	R	22	CF	aa	HOU	124	4	8	294	11	70	136	129	52
Lavarnway,Ryan	15	R	28	C	aaa	ATL	41	2	0	221	13	78	99	12	24
	16	R	29	C	a/a	TOR	331	5	1	220	9	75	75	33	-11
Law,Adam	15	R	25	LF	aa	LA	229	0	8	205	6	82	34	103	-1
	16	R	26	3B	aa	SEA	238	3	12	270	9	78	57	98	8
Leblebijian,Jason	16	R	25	3B	aa	TOR	270	6	4	263	8	65	116	77	-7
Lee,Braxton	16	L	23	CF	aa	TAM	387	0	11	182	6	83	26	90	-7
Lee,Dae-ho	16	R	34	DH	aaa	SEA	27	1	0	403	5	90	154	-1	93
Lee,Hak-Ju	15	L	25	SS	aaa	TAM	313	2	16	185	8	61	66	111	-53
	16	L	26	SS	aaa	SF	162	2	3	219	8	63	67	86	-50
Lemon,Marcus	15	L	27	LF	aa	CHW	265	3	2	225	5	72	60	79	-27
	16	L	28	SS	a/a	CHW	278	1	1	171	7	70	34	69	-55
Leon,Sandy	15	B	26	C	aaa	BOS	99	1	0	238	8	74	54	23	-38
	16	B	27	C	aaa	BOS	115	2	0	223	8	76	53	55	-20
Leonard,Patrick	15	R	23	3B	aa	TAM	446	7	9	219	9	67	103	108	2
	16	R	24	3B	aa	TAM	407	7	7	223	6	61	103	88	-33
Leonards,Ryan	15	R	24	SS	aa	CHW	21	0	0	169	8	73	0	31	-81
	16	R	25	2B	a/a	CHW	69	0	0	130	3	74	32	44	-56
Leyba,Domingo	16	B	21	SS	aa	ARI	156	4	4	295	9	85	75	84	46
Lien,Connor	16	R	22	CF	aa	ATL	223	6	12	226	9	57	121	142	-10
Lin,Tzu-Wei	15	L	21	SS	aa	BOS	173	0	7	193	7	84	38	131	21
	16	L	22	SS	aa	BOS	372	2	8	213	7	84	38	100	14
Lindsey,Taylor	15	L	24	2B	a/a	SD	291	3	3	150	9	77	56	63	-7
	16	L	25	1B	a/a	SD	392	8	3	183	7	72	72	68	-18
Lino,Gabriel	15	R	22	C	a/a	PHI	304	3	0	206	5	70	77	23	-41
	16	R	23	C	aa	PHI	63	3	0	284	8	76	104	33	16
Lipka,Matthew	15	R	23	CF	aa	ATL	402	2	14	224	3	82	40	114	1
	16	R	24	CF	a/a	ATL	378	3	14	219	7	70	66	142	-9
Littlewood,Marcus	15	B	23	C	aa	SEA	195	6	1	203	8	76	91	34	6
	16	B	24	C	a/a	SEA	214	0	2	245	12	74	79	52	-1
Locastro,Tim	16	R	24	SS	aa	LA	191	1	8	249	3	90	38	112	35
Lockhart,Daniel	16	L	24	2B	aa	CHC	155	1	2	183	5	74	44	46	-43
Lollis,Ryan	15	L	29	CF	a/a	SF	296	2	5	266	6	84	71	84	32
	16	L	30	RF	aaa	SF	372	2	4	193	7	80	31	87	-11
Lombardozzi,Steve	15	B	27	2B	aaa	PIT	355	0	11	237	6	87	30	69	8
	16	B	28	2B	aaa	WAS	225	0	2	217	5	86	23	72	-4
Longley,Drew	15	R	27	C	aa	DET	104	3	0	174	4	54	141	55	-44
	16	R	28	C	a/a	DET	119	2	0	114	8	53	102	44	-78
Lopes,Christian	15	R	23	2B	aa	TOR	92	0	1	157	9	83	0	38	-38
	16	R	24	2B	aa	TOR	404	3	8	270	6	80	76	85	20
Lopes,Tim	16	R	22	2B	aa	SEA	510	1	25	271	9	81	45	126	17
Lopez,Jack	16	R	24	SS	aa	KC	267	5	8	169	4	76	53	96	-15
Lopez,Rafael	15	L	28	C	aaa	LAA	218	1	2	195	6	70	42	56	-54
	16	L	29	C	aaa	CIN	155	1	1	174	5	67	64	42	-57
Loveless,Derrick	16	L	23	RF	aa	TOR	169	7	3	195	11	63	138	96	16
Lucas,Jeremy	15	R	24	C	aa	CLE	238	2	0	217	8	80	51	32	-11
	16	R	25	C	a/a	CLE	357	10	1	227	9	76	98	41	14
Lugo,Dawel	16	R	22	3B	aa	ARI	173	4	1	299	2	91	77	92	58
Lutz,Donald	15	L	26	LF	aaa	CIN	42	0	0	160	9	71	61	19	-43
	16	L	27	1B	a/a	CIN	211	2	1	173	5	53	51	55	-120
Machado,Dixon	15	R	23	SS	aaa	DET	509	3	12	230	5	82	44	91	4
	16	R	24	SS	aaa	DET	492	3	15	244	10	84	55	92	28
Macias,Brandon	15	R	27	3B	a/a	MIL	158	2	2	202	6	83	59	92	21
	16	R	28	3B	a/a	MIL	170	3	0	160	5	78	58	35	-17
Mack,Chantz	16	L	25	RF	aa	SEA	20	0	0	224	12	88	28	106	32
Maffei,Justin	16	R	25	LF	a/a	PIT	71	0	1	147	7	74	11	82	-54

BATTER	yr	b	age	pos	lvl	org	ab	hr	sb	ba	bb%	ct%	px	sx	bpv
Maggi,Drew	15	R	26	SS	aa	LAA	422	0	24	206	8	77	35	95	-19
	16	R	27	SS	a/a	LA	336	3	13	238	6	76	57	99	-6
Mahtook,Mikie	15	R	26	RF	aaa	TAM	385	3	8	206	4	69	81	102	-17
	16	R	27	CF	aaa	TAM	105	1	4	255	8	72	69	129	-1
Maile,Luke	15	R	24	C	aaa	TAM	294	4	1	178	9	80	46	58	-4
	16	R	25	C	aaa	TAM	194	2	0	207	6	78	61	19	-19
Maloney,Joe	16	R	26	DH	aa	MIN	145	1	1	204	7	60	88	60	-55
Mancini,Trey	16	R	24	1B	a/a	BAL	546	19	2	255	8	72	100	63	4
Margot,Manuel	16	R	22	CF	aaa	SD	517	4	21	258	5	86	51	138	36
Marin,Adrian	16	R	22	SS	aa	BAL	406	4	9	210	5	79	39	86	-16
Marincov,Tyler	16	R	25	RF	aa	OAK	374	7	5	226	8	73	69	82	-13
Marjama,Mike	16	R	27	C	aa	TAM	278	4	2	230	5	79	84	65	15
Marlette,Tyler	15	R	22	C	aa	SEA	178	2	0	232	4	80	85	33	10
	16	R	23	C	aa	SEA	50	1	1	281	5	75	63	39	-26
Marmolejos,Jose	16	L	23	1B	aa	WAS	127	2	0	280	3	76	80	28	-17
Maron,Camden	15	L	24	C	aa	TEX	87	1	0	196	11	79	40	32	-16
	16	L	25	C	aa	MIA	162	1	1	268	11	84	43	33	5
Marrero,Deven	15	R	25	SS	aaa	BOS	375	5	10	236	7	74	59	88	-14
	16	R	26	SS	aaa	BOS	363	1	9	188	5	72	36	88	-45
Marte,Alfredo	15	R	26	RF	aaa	LAA	343	4	5	245	6	70	86	83	-11
	16	R	27	RF	aaa	PHI	36	0	0	120	2	73	0	12	-98
Marte,Jefry	15	R	24	3B	aaa	DET	357	12	6	238	6	81	112	90	54
	16	R	25	1B	aaa	LAA	162	2	2	211	8	74	76	66	-6
Marte,Ketel	15	B	22	SS	a/a	SEA	268	2	15	277	6	86	52	113	34
	16	B	23	SS	aaa	SEA	28	0	2	182	5	96	43	116	65
Marte,Luis	15	R	22	SS	aa	TEX	228	2	7	183	1	81	43	111	-5
	16	R	23	SS	aa	TEX	265	4	5	238	2	76	71	84	-8
Martin,Trey	16	R	24	CF	aa	CHC	215	2	11	161	5	71	27	116	-49
Martinez,Alberth	15	R	24	CF	aa	SD	479	9	5	234	7	79	63	71	4
	16	R	25	LF	aa	SD	32	0	0	135	3	78	47	51	-29
Martinez,Harold	15	R	25	3B	aa	PHI	260	3	1	242	5	78	58	67	-8
	16	R	26	3B	aa	PHI	255	8	0	229	5	71	95	32	-16
Martinez,Jose	16	R	28	1B	aaa	STL	442	7	7	212	6	78	67	73	1
Martinez,Osvaldo	15	R	27	SS	aa	BAL	433	2	7	211	6	82	31	70	-11
	16	R	28	SS	aaa	BAL	343	4	6	201	4	81	36	74	-14
Martini,Nick	15	L	25	LF	a/a	STL	369	4	6	236	10	82	63	78	24
	16	L	26	RF	a/a	STL	401	4	7	210	9	79	46	97	4
Martinson,Jason	15	R	27	3B	aaa	WAS	495	14	7	184	7	56	112	75	-47
	16	R	28	3B	aaa	WAS	455	9	9	183	6	53	104	109	-57
Marzilli,Evan	15	L	24	CF	a/a	ARI	152	1	5	221	8	74	59	121	-2
	16	L	25	CF	a/a	ARI	409	1	11	199	11	67	57	120	-26
Maxwell III,Bruce	15	L	25	C	aa	OAK	338	1	0	196	8	82	41	22	-16
	16	L	26	C	aaa	OAK	193	8	1	280	10	78	111	35	31
May,Jacob	16	B	24	CF	aaa	CHW	301	1	15	226	4	72	58	118	-22
Mayfield,Jack	15	R	25	2B	aa	HOU	173	5	2	216	8	75	80	74	3
	16	R	26	2B	a/a	HOU	250	8	3	175	5	74	88	59	-5
Mazzilli,L.J.	15	R	25	2B	aa	NYM	335	0	4	220	8	80	49	87	1
	16	R	26	2B	a/a	NYM	414	4	6	187	8	78	51	89	-1
McBroom,Ryan	16	R	24	1B	a/a	TOR	29	1	0	124	8	76	48	29	-29
McDonald,Chase	16	R	24	DH	aa	HOU	392	14	0	195	7	64	92	13	-50
McElroy,C.J.	16	B	23	LF	aa	STL	130	1	7	230	8	74	28	83	-39
McElroy,Casey	15	L	26	2B	a/a	SD	475	4	1	206	6	77	53	71	-13
	16	L	27	3B	aaa	SD	222	1	0	215	6	80	58	49	-7
McFarland,Chris	16	R	24	2B	aa	MIL	227	2	4	171	3	73	35	66	-52
McGee,Stephen	15	R	24	C	a/a	LAA	40	1	0	297	8	79	87	4	6
	16	R	25	C	a/a	MIA	124	2	1	147	9	65	69	38	-53
McGuire,Reese	16	L	21	C	aa	TOR	319	1	5	243	9	88	53	73	38
McKinney,Billy	15	L	21	RF	aa	CHC	274	2	0	262	8	81	97	30	28
	16	L	22	RF	aa	NYY	426	4	4	241	12	75	61	70	-3
McMahon,Ryan	16	L	22	3B	aa	COL	466	11	9	243	9	67	112	101	8
McVaney,Jeff	15	R	25	RF	a/a	DET	453	2	13	223	7	77	54	111	2
	16	R	26	RF	a/a	DET	368	5	10	253	11	85	83	127	68
Meadows,Austin	16	L	21	CF	a/a	PIT	293	10	15	252	9	77	143	155	88
Medina,Yhoxian	16	R	26	2B	a/a	CLE	255	3	4	220	3	84	62	95	21
Medrano,Kevin	15	L	25	2B	aa	ARI	71	0	2	261	4	85	44	85	13
	16	L	26	3B	a/a	ARI	269	0	4	224	5	86	39	89	12
Mejia,Alejandro	15	R	24	SS	a/a	STL	282	4	3	230	6	82	56	79	13
	16	R	25	SS	a/a	STL	269	1	1	196	5	83	43	59	-6
Mejias-Brean,Seth	15	R	24	3B	aa	CIN	405	6	7	221	12	72	75	91	1
	16	R	25	3B	aaa	CIN	435	6	4	204	6	75	56	62	-23
Mendez,Luis	15	B	22	3B	aa	TEX	335	2	7	214	6	77	41	95	-16
	16	B	23	3B	a/a	TEX	242	1	5	191	8	75	24	68	-40
Meneses,Heiker	15	R	24	2B	aa	MIN	340	0	11	222	5	77	29	99	-29
	16	R	25	SS	a/a	MIN	74	0	1	132	9	62	38	115	-68
Meneses,Joey	16	R	24	RF	aa	ATL	222	2	0	217	6	79	54	54	-10
Merrifield,Whit	16	R	27	2B	aaa	KC	274	5	14	214	5	76	81	110	15
Mesa,Melky	15	R	28	CF	a/a	TOR	420	7	2	214	3	58	123	83	-34
	16	R	29	CF	a/a	TOR	253	4	4	200	5	63	90	88	-40
Michael,Levi	15	B	24	2B	aa	MIN	221	4	13	232	9	74	93	160	37
	16	R	25	2B	aa	MIN	316	1	4	187	5	71	34	123	-39
Michalczewski,Trey	16	B	21	3B	aa	CHW	487	10	3	202	9	65	88	90	-23
Middlebrooks,Will	15	R	27	3B	aaa	SD	153	2	1	186	3	71	56	52	-49
	16	R	28	3B	a/a	MIL	252	7	1	231	3	71	121	76	9
Mier,Jio	15	R	25	SS	aa	HOU	376	5	7	214	9	75	66	84	0
	16	R	26	SS	aaa	TOR	224	3	2	195	7	77	64	57	-8
Miguel,Angel	16	R	26	SS	aa	CLE	29	0	0	120	5	69	31	22	-80
Miller,Derek	16	R	24	LF	aa	BOS	38	0	1	192	10	68	27	57	-69
Miller,Ian	16	L	24	CF	aa	SEA	430	0	46	232	9	85	23	169	30
Miller,Michael	16	R	27	2B	a/a	BOS	335	1	11	202	7	86	40	97	19
Miller,Ryan	16	R	24	C	aa	SD	198	6	3	208	5	65	126	103	2
Mitchell,Jared	15	L	27	CF	a/a	LAA	311	3	10	163	8	52	76	120	-80
	16	L	28	RF	aa	NYY	72	1	4	215	11	57	80	112	-49
Mitchell,Ronnie	16	L	25	RF	aa	MIA	184	4	1	233	8	78	87	49	15
Moncada,Yoan	16	B	21	2B	aa	BOS	177	9	8	264	12	61	149	137	31
Moncrief,Carlos	15	L	27	RF	a/a	CLE	365	9	9	191	13	71	79	90	2
	16	L	28	LF	aa	SF	176	4	5	216	12	73	81	79	7
Mondesi,Raul	16	B	21	SS	a/a	KC	172	5	18	263	7	70	109	176	37
Monsalve,Alex	16	R	24	C	a/a	CLE	68	1	0	269	6	86	48	66	14
Montero,Jesus	15	R	26	1B	aaa	SEA	394	12	2	278	5	77	90	79	15
	16	R	27	DH	aaa	TOR	489	10	1	276	4	80	70	32	-3
Moon,Chan	15	B	24	2B	a/a	HOU	254	2	12	212	9	77	45	106	-3
	16	B	25	2B	a/a	HOU	161	2	4	221	7	71	36	71	-51
Moon,Logan	16	R	24	RF	aa	KC	351	3	3	231	6	68	72	72	-34
Mooney,Peter	16	L	26	SS	a/a	MIA	406	3	2	224	8	87	39	53	13
Moore,Logan	15	L	25	C	a/a	PHI	229	3	0	211	6	75	61	40	-24
	16	L	26	C	a/a	PHI	177	5	0	190	7	63	89	31	-52
Moore,Tyler	16	R	29	1B	aaa	ATL	96	2	0	178	5	61	87	24	-65
Mora,Angelo	15	B	22	2B	aa	PHI	113	3	0	293	10	72	114	96	32
	16	B	23	SS	aa	PHI	367	4	2	221	6	75	65	80	-9
Morales,Tomas	16	R	25	C	a/a	PIT	56	2	1	218	3	86	70	122	45
Moran,Colin	15	L	23	3B	aa	HOU	366	7	1	266	8	75	95	53	10
	16	L	24	3B	aaa	HOU	459	8	2	216	7	68	63	46	-48
Moreno,Rando	15	B	23	SS	aa	SF	429	1	11	260	7	84	45	105	19
	16	B	24	SS	a/a	SF	324	1	4	226	4	82	41	96	-2
Morin,Parker	15	L	24	C	aa	KC	178	3	1	275	5	78	96	92	28
	16	L	25	C	aaa	KC	234	1	0	153	6	68	38	41	-70
Moroff,Max	16	B	23	2B	aaa	PIT	421	7	8	213	16	68	74	89	-8
Motter,Taylor	16	R	27	SS	aaa	TAM	350	10	16	187	7	77	78	95	15
Moya,Steven	15	L	24	RF	aaa	DET	500	16	4	205	4	65	116	44	-24
	16	L	25	RF	aaa	DET	409	17	3	254	3	75	117	93	28
Muncy,Max	15	L	25	3B	aaa	OAK	212	3	0	235	9	69	91	46	-17
	16	L	26	LF	aaa	OAK	223	6	4	219	12	73	79	101	10
Muno,Daniel	15	B	26	3B	aaa	NYM	274	2	4	211	8	77	51	69	-13
	16	B	27	3B	a/a	MIA	215	1	1	191	13	71	56	67	-25
Munoz,Yairo	16	R	21	SS	aa	OAK	387	7	5	217	5	79	64	80	4
Murphy,Jack	15	B	27	C	aa	TOR	286	3	0	187	9	75	63	53	-14
	16	B	28	C	aaa	LA	208	2	0	197	11	67	47	20	-66
Murphy,John	16	R	25	C	aaa	MIN	263	2	0	212	6	79	56	23	-18
Murphy,Taylor	16	L	24	RF	aa	CLE	81	2	2	215	12	64	114	70	-6
Murphy,Tom	15	R	24	C	a/a	COL	394	16	4	231	5	66	150	80	21
	16	R	25	C	aaa	COL	303	15	1	296	4	73	169	87	64
Myles,Bryson	15	R	26	LF	aa	CLE	365	8	21	233	9	72	103	126	30
	16	R	27	LF	a/a	CLE	208	6	8	198	8	71	92	104	8
Naquin,Tyler	16	L	25	CF	aaa	CLE	70	1	1	257	9	76	64	72	-3
Narvaez,Omar	16	B	24	C	a/a	CHW	188	2	0	203	6	84	41	24	-10
Nathans,Tucker	15	L	27	LF	aa	BAL	115	3	2	198	4	74	72	93	-7
	16	L	28	LF	aa	BAL	212	3	1	200	4	76	51	45	-30
Navarro,Reynaldo	15	B	26	2B	aaa	BAL	360	6	4	236	6	85	69	72	31
	16	B	27	SS	aaa	LAA	163	1	0	172	2	78	47	45	-30
Newman,Kevin	16	R	23	SS	aa	PIT	233	2	5	258	8	89	45	98	40
Ngoepe,Gift	15	R	25	SS	a/a	PIT	307	2	3	221	7	71	63	69	-30
	16	R	26	SS	aaa	PIT	332	6	4	187	7	56	105	83	-49
Nicholas,Brett	16	L	28	C	aaa	TEX	400	9	1	228	7	73	87	50	-7
Nieto,Adrian	15	B	26	C	aa	CHW	256	4	0	177	15	64	74	42	-39
	16	B	27	C	aaa	MIA	113	1	1	163	10	61	46	37	-87
Nimmo,Brandon	15	L	22	CF	a/a	NYM	360	4	4	237	9	76	59	71	-7
	16	L	23	CF	aaa	NYM	392	8	5	290	8	78	87	89	25
Nina,Angelys	16	R	28	3B	aaa	PHI	83	2	0	165	4	79	61	3	-25
Noel,Rico	15	R	26	CF	a/a	NYY	116	0	19	156	12	65	14	169	-52
	16	R	27	CF	aaa	LA	126	0	6	183	3	70	40	126	-42
Nogowski,John	16	R	23	1B	aa	OAK	23	1	0	111	9	86	73	-8	21
Nola,Austin	15	R	26	SS	a/a	MIA	463	1	0	205	8	78	48	40	-22
	16	R	27	2B	aaa	MIA	372	4	3	220	5	82	62	60	9
Noonan,Nick	15	L	26	SS	aaa	SF	308	2	1	209	5	67	50	44	-66
	16	L	27	SS	aaa	SD	342	3	0	229	4	73	73	33	-28
Norfork,Khayyan	16	R	27	2B	a/a	WAS	76	0	1	137	8	67	35	68	-67
Noriega,Gabriel	15	R	25	SS	a/a	KC	120	0	1	193	1	77	21	40	-59
	16	R	26	3B	aa	MIL	331	3	4	223	4	81	39	58	-17
Nottingham,Jacob	16	R	21	C	aa	MIL	415	11	9	228	6	65	79	77	-39
Nunez,Antonio	16	R	23	SS	aa	HOU	69	0	1	267	10	75	11	33	-59
Nunez,Gustavo	15	B	27	SS	aaa	PIT	340	1	15	232	5	82	30	101	-4
	16	B	28	SS	aa	DET	348	1	10	225	7	83	35	92	3
Nunez,Renato	16	R	22	3B	aaa	OAK	505	19	2	214	5	76	98	67	13
O Brien,Peter	15	R	25	LF	aaa	ARI	490	17	1	229	4	70	138	77	23
	16	R	26	LF	aaa	ARI	406	16	1	206	4	57	143	96	-20
O Conner,Justin	15	R	23	C	aa	TAM	429	7	8	197	2	66	94	115	-20
	16	R	24	C	aa	TAM	25	1	0	135	0	58	62	29	-106
O Malley,Shawn	15	B	28	2B	aaa	SEA	310	3	13	219	4	80	47	118	2
	16	B	29	2B	aaa	SEA	82	1	3	241	10	71	64	105	-14
O Neill,Tyler	16	R	21	RF	aa	SEA	492	23	12	282	11	66	141	103	33
Oberacker,Chad	15	L	26	CF	aa	OAK	395	3	13	236	7	78	74	124	24
	16	L	27	LF	aa	ARI	50	1	2	155	13	76	41	73	-12
Oberste,Matt	16	R	25	DH	aa	NYM	413	7	1	238	7	77	68	49	-7
O'Brien,Chris	15	B	26	C	aa	BAL	115	4	0	210	5	83	102	36	37
	16	B	27	C	a/a	BAL	249	6	0	152	12	74	59	19	-25

BATTER	yr	b	age	pos	lvl	org	ab	hr	sb	ba	bb%	ct%	px	sx	bpv
OConnell,Sean	16	L	25	C	a/a	CHW	81	0	0	173	1	61	55	17	-101
Odom,Joseph	16	R	24	C	aa	ATL	135	1	0	239	5	77	52	19	-34
O'Dowd,Chris	15	B	25	C	aa	ATL	79	2	2	267	16	71	104	96	29
	16	B	26	C	a/a	CHW	83	0	1	175	12	64	30	50	-77
Ogle,Tyler	16	R	26	C	a/a	LA	141	3	0	185	6	71	84	51	-17
Oh,Danny	15	L	26	LF	aa	NYY	242	1	8	255	5	84	58	111	27
	16	L	27	LF	aa	OAK	276	0	9	189	5	78	29	89	-25
OHearn,Ryan	16	L	23	1B	aa	KC	414	12	3	240	9	66	116	55	-5
Ohlman,Mike	15	R	25	C	aa	STL	365	8	0	225	8	76	75	28	-9
	16	R	26	C	a/a	STL	251	5	1	233	7	64	83	73	-40
Olivera,Hector	15	R	30	3B	a/a	ATL	92	1	0	243	4	83	62	60	8
	16	R	31	LF	aaa	ATL	35	0	0	86	2	81	18	15	-50
Olson,Matt	15	L	21	1B	aa	OAK	466	12	4	216	15	68	123	57	20
	16	L	22	RF	aaa	OAK	464	14	1	222	12	70	123	54	23
Olt,Mike	15	R	27	3B	a/a	CHC	220	6	0	221	7	58	143	51	-23
	16	R	28	1B	a/a	SD	166	4	1	196	11	55	98	39	-66
ONeill,Michael	16	R	24	RF	aa	NYY	176	1	4	218	6	69	60	114	-29
Opitz,Shane	15	L	23	2B	aa	TOR	358	3	3	223	5	84	57	94	23
	16	L	24	SS	a/a	TOR	240	2	6	199	7	80	53	84	2
Orf,Nate	15	R	25	3B	aa	MIL	424	2	4	245	12	81	63	84	24
	16	R	26	2B	a/a	MIL	454	2	7	226	8	84	43	82	11
Oropesa,Ricky	15	L	26	1B	aa	SF	453	13	1	219	7	67	106	36	-22
	16	L	27	1B	a/a	SF	252	6	0	173	8	64	71	16	-62
Ortega,Angel	16	R	23	SS	aa	MIL	247	3	4	222	1	82	47	49	-16
Ortega,Rafael	15	L	24	CF	aaa	STL	437	1	13	246	8	82	53	109	21
	16	L	25	LF	aaa	LAA	322	3	10	255	3	85	57	116	29
Ortiz,Danny	15	L	25	CF	aaa	MIN	484	14	3	221	5	76	108	85	29
	16	L	26	CF	aaa	PIT	436	13	5	204	5	77	87	71	9
Osborne,Zach	15	R	25	SS	a/a	COL	132	0	0	219	4	91	32	61	17
	16	R	26	SS	aa	COL	206	0	1	217	4	89	23	45	-1
Osuna,Jose	15	R	23	LF	aa	PIT	323	6	5	253	4	80	82	86	20
	16	R	24	1B	a/a	PIT	473	10	3	248	6	82	94	71	37
Othman,Sharif	15	B	26	C	aa	MIA	282	2	0	198	5	72	43	35	-54
	16	B	27	C	aa	MIA	102	0	0	154	6	64	56	82	-61
Palka,Daniel	16	L	25	RF	a/a	MIN	503	27	7	223	8	59	161	87	10
Paolini,Daniel	15	R	26	1B	a/a	SEA	359	3	4	203	9	72	49	61	-36
	16	R	27	DH	aa	SEA	99	0	0	173	9	68	17	32	-87
Papi,Mike	16	L	24	LF	aa	CLE	259	7	3	208	12	70	107	79	14
Paredes,Jimmy	16	B	28	DH	a/a	BAL	64	2	2	232	7	62	104	71	-30
Park,Byung Ho	16	R	30	DH	aaa	MIN	116	7	0	180	4	67	149	36	6
Parker,Jarrett	15	L	26	RF	aaa	SF	434	14	14	223	9	54	144	108	-16
	16	L	27	RF	aaa	SF	194	10	1	216	9	58	157	106	8
Parker,Kyle	15	R	26	1B	aaa	COL	357	7	4	234	4	67	91	90	-20
	16	R	27	1B	aa	CIN	141	4	1	171	16	68	92	50	-5
Parmelee,Chris	15	L	27	RF	aaa	BAL	239	6	3	279	10	75	88	51	6
	16	L	28	1B	aaa	NYY	214	10	0	214	10	76	109	19	19
Parmley,Ian	15	L	26	CF	aa	TOR	133	1	2	241	6	81	46	98	4
	16	L	27	RF	aa	TOR	282	2	10	250	7	67	47	137	-36
Patterson,Jordan	16	L	24	RF	aaa	COL	427	11	7	270	7	72	106	130	29
Paulino,Carlos	15	R	26	C	a/a	MIN	172	0	0	223	7	90	45	63	31
	16	R	27	C	a/a	MIN	109	0	0	194	8	74	36	25	-50
Paulsen,Benjamin	15	L	28	1B	aaa	COL	125	2	1	205	7	68	98	90	-8
	16	L	29	1B	aaa	COL	288	4	1	229	5	75	80	89	3
Payton,Mark	15	L	24	RF	aa	NYY	264	5	4	228	7	74	64	66	-15
	16	L	25	LF	a/a	NYY	345	7	8	252	8	83	71	120	44
Paz,Andy	16	R	23	C	aa	OAK	150	1	2	283	9	84	58	55	18
Peguero,Carlos	15	L	28	RF	aaa	BOS	103	5	0	225	7	61	172	44	10
	16	L	29	RF	aaa	STL	138	3	2	210	7	60	81	55	-64
Pena,Francisco	15	R	26	C	aaa	KC	342	10	3	212	5	82	90	67	30
	16	R	27	C	aaa	BAL	191	4	0	213	6	85	68	39	20
Pena,Roberto	15	R	23	C	aa	HOU	257	1	1	203	5	83	34	42	-15
	16	R	24	C	a/a	HOU	255	6	0	198	3	81	69	34	-4
Penalver,Carlos	16	R	22	SS	aa	CHC	407	0	2	187	5	80	41	52	-18
Peraza,Jose	15	R	21	2B	aaa	LA	481	3	26	260	3	90	37	136	36
	16	R	22	SS	aaa	CIN	288	2	9	269	7	83	58	104	25
Perez,Audry	15	R	27	C	aaa	BAL	267	2	0	215	4	86	38	17	-9
	16	R	28	C	aaa	BAL	306	6	0	248	5	79	51	21	-23
Perez,Carlos	15	R	25	C	aaa	LAA	72	1	1	287	6	88	98	43	57
	16	R	26	C	aaa	LAA	39	2	0	283	2	77	146	78	54
Perez,Eury	15	R	25	CF	aaa	ATL	236	2	24	262	7	80	45	137	14
	16	R	26	LF	aaa	TAM	223	2	16	217	4	77	46	170	4
Perez,Juan	15	L	24	SS	a/a	CIN	387	3	17	203	7	77	64	133	13
	16	L	25	2B	aaa	CIN	367	6	10	223	7	71	65	102	-17
Perez,Michael	16	L	24	C	aa	ARI	122	3	0	191	5	74	72	52	-20
Perez,Stephen	15	B	25	SS	aa	WAS	54	0	1	113	14	80	29	63	-10
	16	B	26	2B	aa	WAS	301	4	10	217	12	78	45	89	-2
Perez,Yefri	16	B	25	CF	aa	MIA	328	1	33	231	9	78	28	143	-4
Perkins,Cameron	15	R	25	LF	aa	PHI	377	9	5	209	5	83	86	78	36
	16	R	26	CF	aaa	PHI	408	8	10	261	4	83	70	100	27
Peter,Jake	16	L	23	2B	a/a	CHW	481	5	7	246	8	77	58	60	-11
Peterson,D.J.	15	R	24	1B	a/a	SEA	372	5	4	187	6	71	74	75	-20
	16	R	25	1B	a/a	SEA	455	15	1	226	6	69	110	38	-12
Peterson,Dustin	16	R	22	LF	aa	ATL	524	11	4	271	8	79	95	73	30
Peterson,Jace	16	L	26	2B	aaa	ATL	97	0	2	155	8	81	34	96	-1
Peterson,Shane	15	L	27	RF	aaa	MIL	172	5	0	254	6	70	111	57	1
	16	L	28	RF	aaa	MIL	49	2	3	272	8	59	207	138	59
Petty,Kyle	16	R	25	1B	aa	SEA	129	0	0	172	8	68	60	58	-45
Pham,Thomas	16	R	28	CF	a/a	STL	124	3	6	193	11	66	75	100	-21
Phillips,Anthony	16	R	26	SS	aa	LAA	347	1	8	227	8	73	35	87	-36
Phillips,Brett	15	L	21	CF	aa	MIL	214	1	8	285	9	72	105	143	33
	16	L	22	CF	aa	MIL	441	15	11	222	13	63	109	111	-1
Pina,Eudy	15	R	24	RF	aa	MIA	336	2	10	274	4	75	62	125	-4
	16	R	25	DH	aa	CHW	382	3	5	207	5	72	37	73	-50
Pinder,Chad	15	R	23	SS	aa	OAK	477	10	5	270	4	76	96	71	12
	16	R	24	SS	aaa	OAK	426	11	4	236	5	73	97	110	13
Pineda,Jeremias	16	B	26	CF	aa	MIA	203	0	14	158	8	57	27	130	-93
Pinto,Eduard	16	L	22	RF	aa	TEX	110	0	3	294	7	92	30	59	26
Pinto,Josmil	15	R	26	C	aaa	MIN	237	5	0	197	7	74	72	37	-18
	16	R	27	C	aaa	MIL	286	8	0	245	6	71	105	53	-1
Pirela,Jose	15	R	26	3B	a/a	NYY	241	3	4	274	8	88	63	81	43
	16	R	27	LF	aaa	SD	137	1	1	193	4	80	57	88	3
Pizzano,Dario	15	L	24	DH	aa	SEA	221	3	2	267	6	89	72	83	55
	16	L	25	LF	a/a	SEA	320	2	0	203	6	81	49	59	-5
Plaia,Colton	16	R	26	C	aa	NYM	216	1	0	192	6	69	40	25	-70
Plawecki,Kevin	15	R	24	C	aaa	NYM	85	1	0	175	2	83	58	48	0
	16	R	25	C	aaa	NYM	190	5	0	233	4	88	72	30	28
Pleffner,Shawn	15	L	26	1B	aa	WAS	394	2	2	232	7	81	53	43	-4
	16	L	27	1B	aa	WAS	300	2	1	225	8	77	50	58	-15
Polanco,Jorge	15	B	22	SS	a/a	MIN	482	5	16	266	6	84	59	96	27
	16	B	23	2B	aaa	MIN	293	8	4	262	7	82	91	99	47
Pompey,Dalton	15	B	23	CF	a/a	TOR	386	7	20	291	10	81	62	139	37
	16	B	24	CF	aaa	TOR	337	4	16	250	10	76	57	97	-2
Powell,Boog	16	L	23	CF	aaa	SEA	248	2	8	232	6	80	44	103	2
Prime,Correlle	16	R	22	1B	aa	COL	324	2	3	233	6	69	69	45	-41
Profar,Jurickson	16	B	23	SS	aaa	TEX	169	4	3	251	7	83	71	67	26
Puello,Cesar	16	R	25	RF	aaa	NYY	230	5	16	257	12	72	83	96	9
Puig,Yasiel	16	R	26	RF	aaa	LA	69	3	0	291	6	86	100	65	57
Pullin,Andrew	16	L	23	LF	aa	PHI	188	9	0	311	5	78	114	26	22
Querecuto,Juniel	16	B	24	3B	a/a	TAM	340	2	2	209	6	75	60	80	-15
Quinn,Roman	15	B	22	CF	aa	PHI	232	4	23	272	6	79	63	171	32
	16	B	23	CF	aa	PHI	286	5	25	255	8	72	85	168	26
Quintana,Gabriel	15	R	23	3B	aa	SD	39	3	0	265	0	61	272	96	93
	16	R	24	3B	aa	SD	456	18	4	216	4	65	131	71	-6
Radack,Collin	16	R	24	LF	aa	STL	134	0	3	232	8	72	12	57	-68
Rademacher,Bijan	15	L	24	RF	aa	CHC	357	3	5	227	13	81	64	84	26
	16	L	25	LF	a/a	CHC	326	8	0	260	9	77	87	27	5
Ramirez,Harold	16	R	22	CF	aa	TOR	383	2	6	295	5	81	58	110	15
Ramirez,Nick	15	L	26	1B	aa	MIL	432	14	2	215	11	69	104	47	-4
	16	L	27	1B	aa	MIL	282	12	0	178	12	65	116	32	-10
Ramos,Henry	16	B	24	RF	a/a	BOS	361	6	6	249	5	79	74	102	18
Ramos,Mauricio	16	R	24	3B	aa	KC	483	7	4	262	3	79	71	53	-2
Ramsay,James	16	L	24	LF	aa	HOU	338	3	3	167	8	77	57	79	-4
Ramsey,Caleb	15	L	27	RF	a/a	WAS	429	1	10	244	7	79	24	103	-16
	16	L	28	RF	aaa	WAS	427	3	4	227	7	76	59	72	-10
Ramsey,James	15	L	26	LF	aaa	CLE	440	10	3	209	9	65	94	50	-29
	16	L	27	RF	aaa	SEA	351	6	4	209	7	59	89	79	-53
Ravelo,Rangel	15	R	23	1B	a/a	OAK	189	2	0	260	6	77	76	60	3
	16	R	24	1B	aaa	OAK	367	6	1	239	8	81	77	65	24
Reed,A.J.	15	L	22	1B	aa	HOU	205	9	0	296	10	73	142	48	40
	16	L	23	1B	aaa	HOU	261	12	0	251	8	70	148	37	29
Reed,Michael	15	R	23	RF	a/a	MIL	439	5	20	239	12	71	97	126	27
	16	R	24	CF	aaa	MIL	411	6	14	209	12	66	70	93	-29
Refsnyder,Rob	15	R	24	2B	aaa	NYY	450	9	10	244	10	81	81	91	39
	16	R	25	3B	aaa	NYY	209	2	5	287	7	83	51	87	16
Reginatto,Leonardo	15	R	25	SS	a/a	TAM	360	2	0	226	5	84	53	60	10
	16	R	26	SS	a/a	MIN	483	2	7	229	5	80	38	75	-14
Regis,Cody	16	L	25	3B	aa	ARI	72	0	0	175	10	67	26	40	-76
Reinheimer,Jack	15	R	23	SS	aa	ARI	485	4	17	249	8	79	64	111	18
	16	R	24	SS	aaa	ARI	500	1	14	246	6	79	57	107	7
Renda,Tony	16	R	25	LF	a/a	CIN	366	3	15	284	6	88	71	117	58
Renfroe,Hunter	15	R	23	RF	a/a	SD	511	14	4	226	5	70	102	85	-1
	16	R	24	RF	aaa	SD	533	21	3	248	3	74	116	84	21
Reynolds,Matt	15	R	25	SS	aaa	NYM	445	4	9	208	5	75	76	111	4
	16	R	26	3B	aaa	NYM	269	1	6	199	6	70	53	101	-32
Richmond,Josh	16	R	27	RF	aa	CHW	78	2	0	206	7	64	77	63	-47
Rickles,Nick	16	R	26	C	a/a	WAS	92	3	0	200	3	73	82	22	-29
Riddle,J.T.	15	L	24	SS	a/a	MIA	176	3	0	260	4	85	61	61	17
	16	L	25	SS	a/a	MIA	445	3	5	249	6	80	52	95	3
Rijo,Wendell	16	R	21	2B	aa	MIL	177	1	2	181	7	73	64	62	-24
Rios,Edwin	16	L	22	3B	aa	LA	122	5	0	240	5	72	116	23	2
Rivera,T.J.	16	R	28	3B	aaa	NYM	405	7	2	260	3	82	73	48	11
Rivera,Yadiel	15	R	23	SS	a/a	MIL	473	2	9	223	4	80	45	103	-2
	16	R	24	SS	aaa	MIL	304	1	3	192	2	71	43	118	-40
Rivero,Carlos	15	R	27	3B	aaa	BOS	453	7	2	224	5	75	64	54	-22
	16	R	28	3B	aaa	ARI	415	12	1	214	4	75	95	44	-3
Roache,Victor	15	R	24	LF	aa	MIL	223	8	2	229	8	68	127	78	14
	16	R	25	LF	aa	MIL	148	4	2	221	11	69	112	78	12
Roberson,Tim	15	R	26	DH	aa	BOS	217	3	1	262	4	75	77	55	-9
	16	R	27	DH	aa	BOS	223	3	0	213	5	68	85	21	-42
Roberts,James	16	R	25	2B	aa	MIA	181	0	1	185	9	78	22	43	-37
Robertson,Daniel	15	R	21	SS	aa	TAM	299	3	2	245	8	78	84	100	30
	16	R	22	SS	aaa	TAM	436	4	2	237	11	74	60	66	-11
Robinson,Drew	15	L	23	2B	a/a	TEX	455	17	12	208	13	66	132	110	29
	16	L	24	RF	aaa	TEX	467	16	13	224	10	65	124	130	20

BATTER	yr	b	age	pos	lvl	org	ab	hr	sb	ba	bb%	ct%	px	sx	bpv
Rodriguez,Jairo	16	R	28	C	aa	MIN	44	0	0	109	0	74	17	28	-82
Rodriguez,Jonathan	15	R	26	1B	aa	STL	454	9	6	221	8	74	76	58	-8
	16	R	27	1B	a/a	STL	437	10	3	202	8	61	86	53	-52
Rodriguez,Luigi	16	B	24	LF	aa	CLE	158	3	5	201	4	62	73	116	-47
Rodriguez,Nellie	15	R	21	1B	aa	CLE	93	4	0	112	8	57	115	14	-56
	16	R	22	1B	aa	CLE	492	23	1	238	12	61	158	46	9
Rodriguez,Ronny	16	R	24	2B	aaa	CLE	450	9	3	237	4	79	80	82	14
Rodriguez,Steve	15	L	25	C	aa	ATL	166	0	0	178	9	72	32	32	-57
	16	L	26	C	aa	ATL	43	0	0	185	6	66	0	12	-118
Rogers,Jason	15	R	27	1B	aaa	MIL	122	6	0	276	12	76	132	20	42
	16	R	28	3B	aaa	PIT	372	5	1	220	9	75	58	49	-18
Rohlfing,Danny	15	R	26	C	aaa	NYM	161	2	0	173	4	63	95	37	-52
	16	R	27	C	a/a	ARI	154	4	0	225	4	66	100	33	-37
Rojas Jr.,Mel	15	B	25	CF	aaa	PIT	370	1	7	223	7	74	53	86	-21
	16	B	26	RF	a/a	ATL	379	10	10	218	8	71	97	110	14
Roller,Kyle	15	L	27	1B	aaa	NYY	426	13	0	197	10	61	109	38	-34
	16	L	28	DH	aaa	TAM	162	4	0	173	9	54	111	36	-65
Romanski,Jake	15	R	25	C	aa	BOS	56	1	0	235	4	88	34	11	-8
	16	R	26	C	aa	BOS	334	3	0	272	3	84	64	21	1
Romero,Avery	16	R	23	2B	aa	MIA	100	1	2	179	12	82	51	116	29
Romero,Stefen	15	R	27	RF	aaa	SEA	476	11	6	220	4	77	96	94	22
	16	R	28	RF	aaa	SEA	418	15	1	235	6	79	96	71	27
Rondon,Jose	16	R	22	SS	a/a	SD	456	5	10	250	3	80	59	88	3
Rosa,Angel	15	R	23	SS	aaa	LAA	45	0	0	277	6	76	49	73	-20
	16	R	24	3B	a/a	LAA	308	4	6	162	5	64	59	114	-50
Rosa,Garabez	15	R	26	2B	a/a	BAL	378	5	3	219	4	78	56	66	-14
	16	R	27	2B	a/a	BAL	529	8	2	248	2	72	58	36	-49
Rosa,Viosergy	15	L	25	1B	aa	MIA	387	7	0	183	13	73	68	26	-17
	16	L	26	1B	aa	OAK	459	6	1	210	11	65	86	23	-41
Rosario,Alberto	16	R	29	C	aaa	STL	114	0	0	209	3	76	29	14	-59
Rosario,Amed	16	R	21	SS	aa	NYM	214	2	5	311	7	73	86	127	17
Rosario,Eddie	15	L	24	CF	aaa	MIN	95	2	1	221	4	81	68	89	14
	16	L	25	CF	aaa	MIN	160	6	4	287	4	83	117	78	58
Rosario,Jose	15	R	24	2B	a/a	NYY	351	2	10	223	2	78	51	115	-5
	16	R	25	2B	a/a	NYY	258	4	4	252	2	77	63	91	-10
Rosario,Rainel	16	R	27	LF	a/a	BOS	330	2	2	222	6	84	47	70	7
Ruf,Darin	15	R	29	1B	aaa	PHI	26	0	0	238	0	90	25	35	-8
	16	R	30	1B	aaa	PHI	350	19	0	246	6	71	132	49	20
Ruiz,Rio	16	L	22	3B	aaa	ATL	465	8	1	246	10	71	78	43	-16
Sabol,Stefan	16	R	24	RF	aa	NYM	218	4	2	195	9	54	103	61	-61
Saez,Jorge	16	R	26	C	aa	TOR	125	5	0	205	6	63	135	31	-17
Salgado,Ismael	16	R	23	LF	aa	DET	20	0	0	88	0	69	0	47	-108
Salters,Daniel	16	L	23	C	aa	CLE	136	1	0	220	6	70	74	31	-39
Sanchez,Adrian	15	R	25	3B	aa	WAS	179	1	2	216	5	86	55	80	25
	16	R	26	3B	a/a	WAS	350	0	6	220	4	84	41	82	3
Sanchez,Carlos	15	B	23	2B	aaa	CHW	131	2	4	311	3	76	89	71	3
	16	B	24	2B	aaa	CHW	235	7	8	219	6	72	88	104	5
Sanchez,Gary	15	R	23	C	a/a	NYY	365	18	6	256	7	76	135	65	47
	16	R	24	C	aaa	NYY	284	10	6	263	6	82	109	86	56
Sanchez,Hector	15	B	26	C	aaa	SF	139	2	0	216	5	78	60	29	-20
	16	B	27	1B	aaa	SD	204	10	0	229	6	71	142	8	14
Sands,Jerry	15	R	28	DH	aaa	CLE	223	11	1	237	14	78	127	47	55
	16	R	29	1B	aaa	CHW	270	6	0	193	7	70	72	37	-37
Santos,Trae	16	L	24	1B	aa	SD	71	2	0	125	0	58	94	34	-82
Sardinas,Luis	15	B	22	SS	aaa	MIL	390	1	12	245	4	84	43	115	16
	16	B	23	SS	aaa	SD	182	0	6	207	4	85	22	75	-9
Scavuzzo,Jacob	16	R	22	LF	aa	LA	421	10	4	248	5	74	84	81	1
Schebler,Scott	15	L	25	RF	aaa	LA	432	10	11	198	6	74	81	122	13
	16	L	26	CF	aaa	CIN	289	12	2	277	5	75	135	97	49
Schimpf,Ryan	16	L	28	3B	aaa	SD	166	10	0	270	7	73	166	31	52
Schlehuber,Braeden	16	R	28	C	aaa	ATL	110	0	0	188	1	68	50	43	-69
Schoop,Sharlon	15	R	28	2B	a/a	BAL	251	1	1	184	7	76	31	36	-46
	16	R	29	2B	a/a	BAL	305	4	0	182	7	72	57	51	-38
Schrader,Jake	16	R	25	1B	aa	ATL	341	11	2	208	7	61	114	50	-35
Schrock,Max	16	L	22	2B	aa	OAK	23	0	0	357	0	100	28	51	40
Schulz,Nick	16	R	25	RF	aa	SD	393	9	4	247	8	69	90	50	-17
Schwind,Jonathan	15	R	25	RF	aa	PIT	46	0	2	91	3	64	57	167	-38
	16	R	26	RF	a/a	PIT	168	2	2	198	9	73	58	74	-21
Schwindel,Frank	15	R	23	1B	aa	KC	170	3	0	187	1	77	64	34	-27
	16	R	24	1B	aa	KC	455	16	1	244	3	79	87	39	7
Scruggs,Xavier	15	R	28	1B	aaa	STL	383	9	3	183	9	67	96	57	-18
	16	R	29	1B	aaa	MIA	317	14	3	231	13	65	146	63	22
Segedin,Robert	16	R	28	3B	aaa	LA	373	16	2	254	7	73	130	95	39
Seitzer,Cameron	15	L	25	1B	a/a	TAM	413	9	0	262	8	74	95	34	0
	16	L	26	1B	aaa	TAM	135	0	0	148	5	67	18	17	-100
Selsky,Steve	16	R	27	1B	aaa	CIN	296	8	2	243	8	69	120	56	4
Serna,KC	15	R	26	SS	a/a	PHI	381	1	7	200	5	83	29	93	-3
	16	R	27	SS	aa	PHI	336	3	4	239	8	78	53	60	-9
Sever,Joe	15	R	25	1B	aa	CLE	105	2	0	194	5	72	55	18	-49
	16	R	26	3B	aa	CLE	419	3	2	219	4	70	57	48	-49
Severino,Pedro	15	R	22	C	aa	WAS	329	4	1	230	5	84	50	36	-3
	16	R	23	C	aaa	WAS	291	2	3	260	6	84	43	39	-5
Shaffer,Richie	15	R	24	3B	a/a	TAM	393	19	3	226	10	63	166	65	28
	16	R	25	3B	aaa	TAM	428	9	3	193	11	63	96	49	-33
Shank,Zach	15	R	24	2B	a/a	SEA	308	1	4	206	6	77	49	115	-7
	16	R	25	3B	a/a	SEA	414	2	1	249	6	74	51	65	-30
Shaw,Chris	16	L	23	1B	aa	SF	232	4	0	233	8	74	105	78	20

BATTER	yr	b	age	pos	lvl	org	ab	hr	sb	ba	bb%	ct%	px	sx	bpv
Shaw,Nick	16	L	28	SS	aa	MIL	116	0	2	213	7	71	34	71	-51
Shoemaker,Brady	15	R	28	LF	aaa	MIA	324	6	0	231	8	82	63	25	3
	16	R	29	1B	a/a	CHW	329	7	0	169	9	69	70	27	-40
Shuck,J.B.	16	L	29	LF	aaa	CHW	154	2	3	230	5	89	52	87	35
Sierra,Moises	15	R	27	RF	aaa	KC	235	2	10	240	6	75	43	70	-31
	16	R	28	RF	aa	MIA	268	6	5	280	8	80	86	97	36
Silva,Juan	15	L	24	RF	a/a	CIN	260	2	6	188	12	76	61	104	8
	16	L	25	DH	aa	NYY	118	1	2	202	12	71	58	47	-30
Silverio,Louis	16	R	23	RF	aaa	CHW	21	0	0	204	0	83	65	-10	-15
Singleton,Jonathan	15	L	24	1B	aaa	HOU	378	16	1	207	10	69	137	67	28
	16	L	25	1B	aaa	HOU	410	15	0	165	12	64	102	22	-29
Sisco,Chance	16	L	21	C	a/a	BAL	426	6	2	300	11	78	74	40	9
Skipworth,Kyle	15	L	25	C	a/a	CIN	241	11	0	178	8	43	222	52	-19
	16	L	26	C	a/a	CIN	106	4	0	137	10	53	114	32	-66
Skole,Matt	15	L	26	3B	a/a	WAS	465	15	2	200	11	69	104	41	-5
	16	L	27	1B	aaa	WAS	499	19	2	212	10	72	99	49	6
Slater,Austin	15	R	23	2B	a/a	SF	199	0	1	278	6	73	57	62	-28
	16	R	24	LF	a/a	SF	390	13	7	265	11	74	98	65	17
Smalling,Tim	15	R	28	3B	aaa	COL	367	4	4	203	4	80	43	66	-15
	16	R	29	3B	aaa	COL	232	2	0	190	4	82	28	49	-23
Smith,Bryson	15	R	27	CF	a/a	CIN	168	3	2	230	5	74	77	81	-7
	16	R	28	CF	a/a	CIN	166	0	1	153	6	71	19	76	-62
Smith,Dominic	16	L	21	1B	aa	NYM	484	12	2	273	8	83	83	54	33
Smith,Dwight	15	L	23	LF	aa	TOR	460	6	3	246	8	84	73	76	35
	16	L	24	LF	aa	TOR	471	14	10	243	7	78	95	90	31
Smith,Jordan	15	L	25	RF	aa	CLE	475	4	16	227	8	77	65	108	11
	16	L	26	RF	a/a	CLE	403	7	14	229	8	75	90	107	23
Smith,Kevan	15	R	27	C	aaa	CHW	319	5	0	215	7	75	63	52	-20
	16	R	28	C	aaa	CHW	183	6	0	171	6	75	86	13	-14
Smith,Mallex	16	L	23	CF	a/a	ATL	31	0	4	393	11	70	110	166	41
Smith,Mason	16	R	21	DH	aa	SD	24	0	0	77	10	54	48	15	-117
Smith,Tyler	16	R	25	SS	aaa	SEA	392	4	5	220	4	79	50	59	-18
Smolinski,Jacob	15	R	26	LF	aaa	OAK	131	7	2	316	7	86	154	53	98
	16	R	27	CF	aaa	OAK	145	2	5	213	6	82	93	92	43
Snider,Travis	15	L	27	LF	aaa	PIT	35	1	0	263	8	90	48	27	25
	16	L	28	LF	aaa	KC	277	2	0	194	9	73	60	51	-27
Snyder,Brandon	15	R	29	DH	aaa	BAL	334	9	1	227	8	61	134	72	-10
	16	R	30	RF	aaa	ATL	147	2	4	254	4	68	67	76	-43
Sohn,Andrew	16	R	23	SS	aa	STL	28	0	0	252	8	66	63	23	-58
Solano,Donovan	15	R	28	SS	aaa	MIA	140	0	0	222	2	79	17	27	-55
	16	R	29	3B	aaa	NYY	511	7	2	265	4	80	66	60	2
Sole,Alec	16	L	23	SS	a/a	TAM	26	1	0	101	9	53	70	64	-95
Solis,Ali	15	R	28	C	a/a	LA	234	1	0	114	3	65	40	16	-96
	16	R	29	C	a/a	BOS	99	1	0	161	5	80	37	13	-34
Soriano,Wilson	16	R	25	3B	aa	COL	60	0	2	300	4	86	38	89	13
Soto,Elliot	15	R	26	SS	aa	MIA	414	0	5	215	11	77	26	76	-23
	16	R	27	2B	aaa	MIA	158	1	2	204	13	73	33	86	-27
Soto,Neftali	15	R	26	1B	aaa	CHW	199	2	0	208	11	76	38	26	-34
	16	R	27	1B	a/a	WAS	456	8	2	237	5	76	74	54	-8
Sparks,Taylor	16	R	23	3B	aa	CIN	224	9	2	174	7	57	103	74	-50
Sportman,J.P.	16	R	24	LF	aa	OAK	483	4	14	232	4	81	62	117	20
Stallings,Jacob	16	R	27	C	aaa	PIT	257	5	0	181	3	71	83	34	-32
Stamets,Eric	15	R	24	SS	aa	CLE	331	4	6	207	6	87	52	81	27
	16	R	25	SS	a/a	CLE	317	6	7	212	6	67	90	128	-8
Starling,Bubba	16	R	24	CF	a/a	KC	399	5	9	161	4	61	86	110	-46
Stassi,Brock	15	L	26	1B	aa	PHI	466	12	2	245	11	83	90	46	41
	16	L	27	1B	aaa	PHI	375	12	1	234	12	75	105	39	23
Stassi,Max	15	R	24	C	aaa	HOU	294	9	1	171	6	63	94	63	-41
	16	R	25	C	aaa	HOU	243	5	1	188	5	68	80	42	-39
Staton,Allen	16	R	24	2B	aa	STL	180	2	2	240	7	77	60	83	-4
Stevens,River	16	L	24	3B	aa	SD	276	4	4	206	6	78	41	85	-18
Stevenson,Andrew	16	L	22	CF	aa	WAS	256	2	11	233	7	79	49	112	4
Stewart,Christin	16	L	23	LF	aa	DET	87	5	0	192	10	69	112	42	-1
Strausborger,Ryan	15	R	27	RF	aaa	TEX	345	7	20	228	5	77	85	129	27
	16	R	28	RF	aaa	SEA	274	4	11	179	5	65	56	93	-55
Stuart,Champ	16	R	24	CF	aa	NYM	184	2	12	170	6	54	42	133	-96
Stubbs,Drew	15	R	31	CF	aaa	TEX	164	1	7	200	10	65	57	132	-34
	16	R	32	CF	aaa	TEX	39	1	1	174	16	74	125	87	56
Stubbs,Garrett	16	L	23	C	aa	HOU	120	3	4	289	8	89	93	105	82
Sturgeon,Cole	15	L	24	RF	aa	BOS	133	0	3	187	3	75	64	101	-10
	16	L	25	CF	a/a	BOS	436	5	5	249	4	84	60	66	14
Sucre,Jesus	15	R	27	C	aaa	SEA	23	0	0	196	7	56	0	42	-148
	16	R	28	C	aaa	SEA	99	0	0	210	2	80	31	50	-33
Susac,Andrew	15	R	25	C	aaa	SF	28	1	0	261	7	57	162	45	-12
	16	R	26	C	aaa	MIL	249	6	0	201	7	71	79	31	-29
Swanner,Will	15	R	24	1B	aa	COL	358	15	5	242	9	63	142	38	-5
	16	R	25	1B	aaa	COL	31	1	0	171	8	57	86	39	-74
Swanson,Dansby	16	R	22	SS	aa	ATL	333	8	7	252	10	76	80	125	27
Sweeney,Darnell	15	B	24	2B	aaa	LA	472	7	24	229	6	71	87	117	4
	16	B	25	2B	aaa	PHI	400	6	11	212	8	71	72	107	-10
Swihart,Blake	15	B	23	C	a/a	BOS	81	0	1	305	6	79	49	40	-20
	16	B	24	C	aaa	BOS	103	1	2	238	14	82	47	54	11
Tabata,Jose	15	R	27	RF	aaa	LA	237	2	2	210	6	85	40	56	3
	16	R	28	RF	aaa	LA	90	1	2	193	8	78	52	58	-12
Taijeron,Travis	16	R	27	RF	aaa	NYM	459	12	1	204	8	54	150	68	-25
Tanielu,Nick	16	R	24	2B	aa	HOU	371	6	1	217	4	81	53	40	-11
Tapia,Raimel	16	L	22	CF	a/a	COL	528	7	19	322	4	89	68	130	59
Tarsovich,Jordan	16	R	25	3B	aa	LA	169	4	5	194	11	78	74	77	19

BATTER	yr	b	age	pos	lvl	org	ab	hr	sb	ba	bb%	ct%	px	sx	bpv
Tauchman,Mike	15	L	25	LF	aa	COL	507	3	19	270	7	85	53	108	31
	16	L	26	CF	aaa	COL	475	1	16	252	6	83	49	121	20
Tavarez,Aneury	15	L	23	RF	a/a	BOS	252	5	5	226	4	71	101	89	1
	16	L	24	RF	a/a	BOS	400	6	17	317	6	82	85	130	48
Taylor,Beau	15	L	25	C	aa	OAK	58	1	0	209	8	78	63	43	-6
	16	L	26	C	aa	OAK	339	3	1	232	11	71	77	37	-21
Taylor,Chris	15	R	25	SS	aaa	SEA	343	3	11	237	9	78	64	104	14
	16	R	26	SS	aaa	LA	304	2	13	268	8	74	88	123	21
Taylor,Chuck	16	B	23	LF	aa	ARI	84	1	1	225	6	81	74	61	14
Taylor,Michael	15	R	24	CF	aa	WAS	26	1	2	353	11	58	110	62	-37
	16	R	25	CF	aaa	WAS	117	1	6	186	8	69	56	127	-23
Taylor,Tyrone	15	R	21	CF	aa	MIL	454	3	9	250	6	87	50	86	28
	16	R	22	RF	aa	MIL	465	9	8	225	7	83	52	75	14
Tejada,Luis	16	R	24	LF	aa	SD	195	4	3	229	9	75	92	103	26
Telis,Tomas	15	B	24	C	aaa	MIA	330	4	3	265	5	88	53	67	24
	16	B	25	C	aaa	MIA	336	4	3	276	6	86	59	86	32
Tellez,Rowdy	16	L	21	1B	aa	TOR	438	22	4	288	11	77	141	59	63
Terdoslavich,Joseph	15	B	27	1B	a/a	ATL	149	3	1	237	14	70	113	61	20
	16	B	28	1B	a/a	BAL	451	12	1	192	11	78	77	39	8
Thomas,Dillon	16	L	24	RF	aa	COL	374	4	11	274	6	74	103	79	16
Thomas,Mark	15	R	27	C	aa	ARI	195	4	2	148	7	62	115	73	-21
	16	R	28	C	aaa	ARI	79	1	0	145	9	45	110	11	-107
Thompson,Nick	16	R	24	LF	aa	STL	25	1	0	170	6	76	77	71	2
Tilson,Charlie	16	L	24	CF	aaa	STL	351	3	11	236	7	82	55	133	29
Toles,Andrew	16	L	24	CF	a/a	LA	231	6	12	280	5	81	109	113	57
Tomlinson,Kelby	15	R	25	2B	a/a	SF	389	2	17	277	6	82	54	121	23
	16	R	26	SS	aaa	SF	185	0	9	238	8	83	33	109	10
Torres,Nick	16	R	23	LF	a/a	SD	503	10	8	250	3	70	96	71	-15
Torres,Ramon	15	B	22	SS	aa	KC	189	3	3	251	7	87	69	67	40
	16	B	23	SS	a/a	KC	461	2	17	237	5	82	39	100	0
Toscano,Dian	16	L	27	RF	aa	LA	177	0	2	188	9	64	21	90	-81
Toups,Corey	16	R	23	2B	aa	KC	338	8	14	256	8	70	115	128	28
Tovar,Wilfredo	15	R	24	SS	aaa	NYM	357	2	21	225	4	86	38	101	17
	16	R	25	SS	aaa	MIN	450	1	25	226	6	86	47	123	31
Towey,Cal	15	L	25	RF	aa	LAA	316	2	9	187	12	59	73	109	-45
	16	L	26	RF	a/a	LAA	450	9	11	217	11	61	95	109	-25
Travis,Sam	16	R	23	1B	aaa	BOS	173	5	1	272	8	75	106	53	20
Trinkwon,Brandon	15	L	23	2B	aa	LA	190	2	4	210	11	85	33	100	18
	16	L	24	3B	aa	LA	270	3	4	202	9	83	44	80	10
Triunfel,Alberto	16	R	22	SS	aa	TEX	293	1	3	168	4	77	36	62	-36
Triunfel,Carlos	15	R	25	SS	aaa	SF	314	3	2	217	2	78	69	90	-1
	16	R	26	2B	aaa	CIN	378	4	1	244	1	77	76	50	-12
Tucker,Preston	15	L	25	LF	aaa	HOU	129	8	1	238	6	76	123	30	27
	16	L	26	LF	a/a	HOU	230	6	1	233	5	69	104	86	-3
Turgeon,Casey	16	L	24	3B	aa	STL	28	0	0	152	15	83	24	23	-10
Turner,Stuart	15	R	24	C	aa	MIN	327	3	4	190	9	77	49	66	-14
	16	R	25	C	aa	MIN	322	4	4	206	8	75	75	57	-5
Turner,Trea	15	R	22	SS	a/a	WAS	454	6	25	304	7	78	80	134	30
	16	R	23	SS	aaa	WAS	331	5	23	285	10	77	94	164	52
Urena,Richard	16	B	20	SS	aa	TOR	124	0	0	262	3	84	69	96	26
Urrutia,Henry	15	L	28	DH	aaa	BAL	460	10	1	253	7	79	72	37	1
	16	L	29	RF	a/a	BAL	396	4	1	240	6	80	51	38	-12
Urshela,Giovanny	15	R	24	3B	aaa	CLE	81	3	0	244	3	83	106	67	45
	16	R	25	3B	aaa	CLE	468	7	0	246	3	86	59	36	10
Valaika,Pat	16	R	24	SS	a/a	COL	541	12	8	240	4	77	101	93	27
Valdespin,Jordany	15	L	28	LF	aaa	MIA	256	1	5	242	5	85	50	107	26
	16	L	29	2B	aaa	DET	293	2	8	196	5	76	45	100	-17
Valdez,Ordomar	16	B	22	2B	a/a	CLE	21	0	2	179	4	75	0	149	-44
Valentin,Jesmuel	16	B	22	2B	a/a	PHI	446	9	4	252	9	80	71	90	24
Valenzuela,Ricardo	16	R	26	C	a/a	SD	46	0	0	156	7	73	0	7	-88
Valera,Breyvic	15	B	23	2B	aa	STL	360	2	1	201	6	92	29	51	20
	16	B	24	2B	a/a	STL	395	0	9	259	7	88	34	78	19
Valle,Sebastian	15	R	25	C	aa	PIT	247	3	1	236	6	75	90	35	-5
	16	R	26	C	aa	NYY	228	4	0	182	5	63	79	38	-62
Van Hoosier,Evan	16	R	23	2B	aa	TEX	80	0	1	241	4	81	28	101	-12
VanMeter,Josh	16	L	21	3B	aa	SD	106	2	2	185	6	81	40	59	-12
Vargas,Ildemaro	16	B	25	SS	a/a	ARI	521	5	16	264	6	92	50	108	53
Vargas,Kennys	15	B	25	1B	a/a	MIN	244	10	0	244	14	67	117	52	9
	16	B	26	1B	aaa	MIN	330	12	1	205	14	70	106	44	8
Varona,Dayron	15	R	27	CF	aa	TAM	277	7	3	211	4	77	85	108	17
	16	R	28	RF	aaa	TAM	435	11	8	185	3	71	96	94	-1
Vasquez,Danry	15	L	21	LF	aa	HOU	277	0	2	217	4	83	39	61	-7
	16	L	22	LF	aa	HOU	211	3	6	238	6	87	59	76	33
Vazquez,Christian	16	R	26	C	aaa	BOS	152	2	2	255	8	77	71	56	0
Vazquez,Jan	15	B	24	C	aa	COL	211	3	2	209	9	69	70	80	-23
	16	B	25	C	a/a	COL	205	1	5	207	8	78	55	81	0
Verdugo,Alex	16	L	20	CF	aa	LA	477	13	2	264	8	85	77	39	31
Vertigan,Brett	16	L	26	CF	aa	OAK	415	1	10	203	7	75	44	98	-20
Vielma,Engelb	16	B	22	SS	aa	MIN	314	0	8	251	8	79	27	107	-10
Villalona,Angel	15	R	25	1B	aa	SF	56	0	0	127	5	65	36	25	-91
	16	R	26	DH	aa	SF	56	1	0	122	9	58	63	21	-93
Villegas,Luis	16	R	24	C	a/a	KC	27	0	0	130	8	80	29	24	-32
Vincej,Zach	15	R	24	SS	aa	CIN	286	5	6	215	12	80	55	57	7
	16	R	25	SS	aa	CIN	399	3	7	259	6	75	68	86	-8
Vinicio,Jose	16	B	23	2B	a/a	BOS	228	2	6	249	3	80	37	106	-12
Vogelbach,Daniel	16	L	24	1B	aaa	SEA	459	17	0	246	14	74	104	38	19
Voit,Luke	16	R	25	1B	aa	STL	482	14	1	252	8	79	81	56	15
Vosler,Jason	16	L	23	3B	aa	CHC	92	1	0	220	7	68	82	27	-38
Wade,Tyler	15	L	21	SS	aa	NYY	113	1	2	194	2	77	46	50	-35
	16	L	22	SS	aa	NYY	505	6	27	254	12	78	52	143	21
Walding,Mitch	16	L	24	3B	aa	PHI	70	3	1	186	11	62	99	67	-30
Waldrop,Kyle	15	L	24	RF	a/a	CIN	447	7	2	210	3	70	73	51	-38
	16	L	25	RF	aaa	CIN	325	5	3	227	5	79	72	59	2
Walker,Adam	15	R	24	LF	aa	MIN	502	22	9	203	7	57	171	99	11
	16	R	25	LF	aaa	MIN	478	22	6	218	7	54	165	96	-7
Walker,Christian	15	R	24	1B	aaa	BAL	534	19	1	243	8	72	120	38	14
	16	R	25	LF	aaa	BAL	504	18	1	240	6	70	110	46	-5
Walker,Keenyn	15	B	25	CF	aa	CHW	203	2	10	163	8	69	25	85	-62
	16	B	26	RF	aa	CHW	329	2	16	195	10	60	66	131	-46
Walker,Ryan	16	L	24	2B	aa	MIN	297	2	10	242	8	77	44	122	-4
Wallach,Chad	16	R	25	C	aa	CIN	200	8	0	224	15	73	110	23	17
Walsh,Colin	16	B	27	LF	aaa	OAK	201	3	0	222	14	64	89	49	-28
Walters,Zachary	15	B	26	LF	aaa	CLE	341	8	3	214	7	72	103	75	10
	16	B	27	1B	aaa	LA	333	8	2	224	5	77	82	79	8
Ward,Drew	16	L	22	3B	aa	WAS	178	2	0	208	10	70	60	29	-41
Ward,Nelson	16	L	24	2B	aa	SD	453	5	26	196	10	68	53	111	-33
Washington,David	15	L	25	RF	aa	STL	340	11	3	224	6	59	123	45	-37
	16	L	26	RF	a/a	STL	421	21	3	209	11	50	178	56	-19
Wass,Wade	16	R	25	C	aa	LAA	127	1	4	168	12	55	38	95	-96
Watkins,Logan	16	L	27	2B	aaa	CHC	337	1	10	210	5	75	46	126	-11
Way,Bo	16	L	25	CF	aa	LAA	425	2	19	233	6	76	33	100	-26
Webb,Brenden	16	L	26	LF	aa	WAS	51	1	2	153	15	67	61	51	-37
Weber,Garrett	15	R	26	2B	a/a	ARI	404	7	1	249	7	76	89	72	12
	16	R	27	2B	a/a	MIA	251	2	0	200	7	72	37	61	-47
Weems,Jordan	15	L	23	C	aa	BOS	67	1	1	211	5	74	106	96	22
	16	L	24	1B	aa	BOS	67	0	0	108	12	60	17	15	-115
Weiss,Erich	15	L	24	2B	aa	PIT	112	0	3	216	5	79	35	102	-15
	16	L	25	2B	aa	PIT	456	4	5	237	8	78	65	95	11
Welz,Zach	16	R	24	RF	aa	LAA	68	1	1	186	11	53	93	125	-54
Wendle,Joe	15	L	25	2B	aaa	OAK	577	7	10	250	3	78	92	127	30
	16	L	26	2B	aaa	OAK	491	9	12	247	4	74	98	148	31
Westbrook,Jamie	16	R	21	2B	aa	ARI	435	5	9	256	5	85	56	81	23
White,T.J.	16	R	24	3B	aa	MIN	197	0	7	194	6	74	39	152	-14
White,Tyler	15	R	25	3B	a/a	HOU	403	10	1	267	13	78	91	40	24
	16	R	26	1B	aaa	HOU	174	10	1	196	6	79	102	61	29
Wickens,Stephen	15	R	26	3B	aa	MIN	264	1	11	209	9	80	50	124	18
	16	R	27	3B	aaa	MIN	80	2	2	171	9	67	73	75	-30
Wilkerson,Shannon	15	R	27	CF	aa	MIN	185	1	8	238	6	84	40	140	24
	16	R	28	CF	aa	MIN	199	1	1	195	5	83	46	66	2
Wilkins,Andrew	15	L	27	1B	aaa	LA	434	14	0	199	7	73	108	33	4
	16	L	28	RF	aaa	MIL	327	8	2	181	8	65	95	70	-24
Williams,Justin	16	L	21	RF	aa	TAM	148	5	0	219	3	77	91	82	15
Williams,Mason	15	L	24	CF	a/a	NYY	201	0	11	288	11	87	54	87	40
	16	L	25	CF	aaa	NYY	125	0	1	267	4	80	52	87	-1
Williams,Matt	15	R	26	SS	a/a	STL	206	2	5	187	11	79	41	77	-6
	16	R	27	SS	aaa	STL	338	1	8	205	9	74	47	82	-19
Williams,Nick	15	L	22	CF	aa	PHI	475	15	10	270	6	77	107	101	35
	16	L	23	LF	aaa	PHI	497	14	6	246	4	69	119	124	18
Williamson,Mac	15	R	25	RF	a/a	SF	448	9	3	232	9	72	93	87	7
	16	R	26	LF	aaa	SF	208	7	2	217	4	69	112	67	-4
Wilson,Jacob	15	R	25	3B	a/a	STL	427	12	1	188	6	75	88	48	0
	16	R	26	3B	a/a	STL	310	10	2	178	7	68	98	53	-18
Wilson,Kenneth	15	R	25	CF	aa	MIA	497	5	29	233	8	75	72	145	22
	16	R	26	CF	a/a	MIA	428	2	25	222	10	73	53	119	-9
Winker,Jesse	15	L	22	LF	aa	CIN	443	14	7	264	13	79	99	73	43
	16	L	23	RF	aaa	CIN	380	3	0	284	13	82	56	16	5
Winn,Matt	16	R	24	C	aa	SF	56	2	0	224	5	76	87	27	-9
Wisdom,Patrick	15	R	24	3B	aa	STL	414	10	8	198	6	71	91	97	0
	16	R	25	3B	aaa	STL	262	3	4	187	7	66	89	76	-27
Witt,Tanner	16	R	25	DH	aa	MIN	31	0	2	166	2	79	24	107	-27
Witte,Jantzen	15	R	25	1B	aa	BOS	314	3	2	255	8	83	88	55	38
	16	R	26	3B	a/a	BOS	396	3	4	246	8	82	76	63	25
Wong,Joey	15	L	27	3B	a/a	COL	225	0	3	221	5	80	54	84	0
	16	L	28	SS	aaa	COL	257	1	1	195	10	77	41	54	-20
Wong,Kean	16	L	21	2B	aa	TAM	446	4	8	249	6	82	50	74	3
Wong,Kolten	16	L	26	2B	aaa	STL	28	3	1	352	10	72	184	124	94
Wood,Eric	15	R	23	3B	aa	PIT	334	1	2	208	7	72	43	72	-41
	16	R	24	3B	aa	PIT	402	12	4	216	9	76	92	88	26
Woodward,Trent	16	B	24	C	aa	HOU	48	1	0	213	7	71	96	12	-20
Wren,Kyle	15	L	24	CF	a/a	MIL	518	1	28	235	6	83	31	103	4
	16	L	25	LF	a/a	MIL	398	2	23	281	11	79	44	134	16
Wynns,Austin	16	R	26	C	a/a	BAL	91	1	1	216	6	82	74	66	22
Yarbrough,Alex	15	B	24	2B	aaa	LAA	500	2	1	187	3	68	60	57	-55
	16	B	25	2B	aaa	LAA	524	3	9	223	4	71	64	76	-33
Yastrzemski,Mike	15	L	25	LF	aa	BAL	476	5	7	215	7	76	79	95	12
	16	L	26	RF	a/a	BAL	466	12	11	201	9	71	90	107	9
Ynoa,Rafael	15	B	28	2B	aaa	COL	224	1	3	229	4	81	56	100	9
	16	B	29	2B	aaa	COL	482	2	5	213	6	80	54	76	-2
Young,Chesny	16	R	24	2B	aa	CHC	491	3	12	265	8	85	48	65	16
Zagunis,Mark	16	R	23	LF	a/a	CHC	358	8	4	255	10	75	100	93	31
Zarraga,Shawn	15	B	26	C	a/a	LA	185	1	0	238	7	80	52	18	-16
	16	B	27	C	a/a	LA	133	0	0	211	8	79	50	33	-16
Zimmer,Bradley	15	L	23	CF	aa	CLE	187	5	11	202	8	68	107	119	10
	16	L	24	CF	a/a	CLE	468	13	32	229	12	61	121	133	5
Zunino,Mike	15	R	24	DH	aaa	SEA	41	2	0	257	0	76	119	32	12

PITCHER	yr	t	age	lvl	org	ip	era	whip	bf/g	ctl	dom	cmd	hr/9	h%	s%	bpv
Achter,A.J.	15	R	27	aaa	MIN	48	3.87	1.09	4.4	2.8	6.6	2.4	1.2	24	69	65
	16	R	28	aaa	LAA	46	3.89	1.09	6.2	2.8	5.0	1.8	1.7	21	73	30
Adams,Austin	15	R	24	a/a	LAA	40	3.90	1.54	6.1	8.2	9.4	1.1	0.0	26	72	99
	16	R	25	aa	LAA	41	4.26	1.53	5.6	5.7	11.1	1.9	0.5	34	72	99
Adams,Austin	16	R	30	aaa	CLE	38	6.99	1.92	5.3	2.6	7.0	2.7	0.3	44	61	70
Adams,Chance	16	R	22	aa	NYY	70	3.01	1.01	20.5	3.4	8.1	2.4	1.0	21	75	87
Adams,Spencer	16	R	20	aa	CHW	55	4.39	1.34	25.6	1.7	3.9	2.4	0.4	32	66	59
Additon,Nick	15	L	28	a/a	BAL	111	7.16	1.82	19.0	3.5	4.7	1.3	0.8	37	59	21
	16	L	29	aaa	BAL	80	6.30	1.90	23.7	3.2	4.1	1.3	1.3	37	68	-4
Adkins,Hunter	16	R	26	a/a	MIA	84	7.55	1.77	14.3	4.5	5.8	1.3	1.6	33	59	6
Adleman,Timothy	16	R	29	aaa	CIN	57	3.76	1.51	24.6	2.0	4.8	2.4	1.0	34	78	39
Alaniz,Ruben	15	R	24	aa	HOU	57	5.30	1.78	18.8	3.7	3.4	0.9	0.3	35	68	18
	16	R	25	a/a	DET	74	3.59	1.65	6.3	4.0	7.0	1.8	0.1	37	77	69
Alcantara,Raul	16	R	24	a/a	OAK	136	4.52	1.44	23.1	2.1	5.6	2.7	0.8	34	70	60
Alcantara,Victor	16	R	23	a/a	LAA	111	5.76	1.70	17.3	4.9	5.6	1.1	0.8	33	66	29
Alexander,Scott	15	L	26	aaa	KC	63	3.39	1.23	6.3	2.6	5.4	2.1	0.8	28	75	56
	16	L	27	aaa	KC	30	3.73	1.65	6.1	3.1	5.4	1.7	0.6	36	78	42
Alexander,Tyler	16	L	22	aa	DET	34	3.73	1.30	23.6	1.1	4.9	4.6	1.1	32	75	89
Alger,Brandon	15	L	24	aa	SD	60	4.28	1.60	5.5	5.9	7.0	1.2	0.8	30	74	50
	16	L	25	aa	SD	21	11.47	2.16	7.4	6.6	7.7	1.2	2.7	36	48	-24
Almonte,Miguel	15	R	22	a/a	KC	104	5.42	1.48	15.9	3.6	6.9	1.9	0.6	33	62	62
	16	R	23	a/a	KC	76	7.14	1.94	11.3	5.4	7.0	1.3	1.1	37	63	27
Almonte,Yency	16	R	22	aa	COL	30	4.58	1.53	26.1	5.3	5.2	1.0	1.8	25	77	2
Altavilla,Dan	16	R	24	aa	SEA	57	2.53	1.26	5.4	3.6	8.9	2.5	0.6	30	82	96
Alvarado,Carlos	16	R	27	aa	SF	19	4.05	0.89	4.5	0.0	8.9	0.0	1.0	30	57	0
Alvarez,Dario	15	L	26	a/a	NYM	42	3.38	1.24	3.6	4.5	10.9	2.4	0.5	30	73	115
	16	L	27	aaa	TEX	31	7.70	2.00	4.9	5.6	11.2	2.0	1.4	44	62	56
Alvarez,R.J.	15	R	24	aaa	OAK	35	5.04	1.72	5.1	4.6	8.6	1.9	0.5	38	70	70
	16	R	25	a/a	CHC	25	8.69	2.10	5.9	4.5	9.8	2.2	0.8	47	57	62
Ames,Jeff	15	R	24	aa	TAM	25	0.84	1.45	7.5	5.1	8.0	1.6	0.0	31	94	89
	16	R	25	aa	TAM	63	3.36	1.51	5.7	6.0	7.3	1.2	1.1	27	82	45
Anderson,Chris	15	R	23	a/a	LA	133	5.46	1.64	22.8	4.3	5.8	1.4	1.1	32	68	28
	16	R	24	aa	LA	40	7.86	2.01	10.6	7.8	4.7	0.6	0.9	31	59	13
Anderson,Cody	15	R	25	a/a	CLE	71	2.59	1.28	22.5	1.9	5.6	3.0	0.3	32	80	87
	16	R	26	aaa	CLE	32	5.15	1.62	11.0	3.1	8.6	2.8	1.5	37	72	58
Anderson,Isaac	16	R	23	aa	LA	22	8.67	1.76	19.8	2.4	5.7	2.4	1.5	38	50	23
Anderson,John	15	L	27	a/a	TOR	124	7.06	1.95	19.7	3.6	4.4	1.2	1.0	38	63	7
	16	L	28	a/a	TOR	115	8.17	2.28	19.5	4.0	5.8	1.4	1.5	43	65	-4
Anderson,Matt	15	R	24	a/a	SEA	71	4.65	1.38	6.3	3.0	7.3	2.4	0.7	33	67	73
	16	R	25	aa	SEA	62	4.94	1.55	6.6	2.5	6.9	2.8	0.4	38	66	82
Anderson,Tyler	16	L	27	a/a	COL	27	3.17	1.43	22.9	3.2	5.7	1.8	0.5	32	79	55
Andriese,Matt	15	R	26	aaa	TAM	65	3.02	1.39	21.1	1.5	7.7	5.2	0.3	38	78	140
	16	R	27	aaa	TAM	34	4.74	1.43	24.3	2.1	9.2	4.5	0.6	39	67	125
Antolin,Dustin	16	R	27	aaa	TOR	53	3.04	1.65	5.2	5.6	8.3	1.5	0.8	33	84	60
Appel,Mark	15	R	24	a/a	HOU	132	4.84	1.52	22.9	3.4	6.4	1.9	0.9	33	69	47
	16	R	25	aaa	PHI	38	6.85	2.00	23.1	5.5	6.7	1.2	1.1	38	66	22
Aquino,Jayson	16	L	24	a/a	BAL	128	5.07	1.67	23.1	2.7	5.1	1.9	0.7	36	69	39
Arano,Victor	16	R	21	aa	PHI	17	2.54	0.98	5.8	2.1	11.8	5.5	1.3	28	83	160
Araujo,Victor	16	R	24	aa	MIA	16	4.59	2.14	8.8	6.8	5.5	0.8	0.6	37	79	21
Archer,Tristan	16	R	26	aa	MIL	82	5.26	1.50	7.2	1.2	7.2	6.0	0.6	39	64	141
Armenteros,Roge	16	R	22	aa	HOU	18	2.23	1.24	24.8	1.9	5.7	3.0	0.6	31	84	82
Armstrong,Shawn	15	R	25	aaa	CLE	50	3.18	1.48	4.6	5.0	12.0	2.4	0.0	38	76	128
	16	R	26	aaa	CLE	49	2.61	1.37	4.4	5.9	10.2	1.7	0.0	30	79	112
Aro,Jonathan	15	R	25	a/a	BOS	74	4.21	1.26	8.9	2.4	7.0	2.9	0.3	32	65	97
	16	R	26	aaa	SEA	36	2.74	1.18	6.0	2.4	5.1	2.1	0.5	28	78	67
Ascher,Steve	16	L	23	aa	TAM	46	5.11	1.48	7.6	3.5	6.1	1.7	1.0	31	67	42
Ash,Brett	16	R	25	aa	SEA	135	6.04	1.87	25.4	2.2	3.3	1.5	0.7	39	67	12
Asher,Alec	15	R	24	a/a	PHI	134	4.72	1.49	24.0	2.8	6.3	2.3	1.8	32	75	28
	16	R	25	a/a	PHI	59	3.40	1.10	25.5	1.4	5.2	3.8	1.1	27	74	83
Astin,Barrett	15	R	24	aa	CIN	77	7.38	1.90	25.8	5.0	6.2	1.3	1.5	36	62	8
	16	R	25	aa	CIN	103	3.52	1.25	11.4	2.6	7.2	2.7	1.1	29	76	72
Avila,Andres	15	R	25	aa	OAK	48	4.47	1.54	6.6	2.6	6.2	2.4	0.9	35	72	55
	16	R	26	aa	OAK	73	4.39	1.42	7.7	2.7	7.4	2.7	1.1	33	72	65
Avilan,Luis	16	L	27	aaa	LA	34	5.34	1.73	4.7	4.2	7.7	1.8	1.0	37	70	49
Aviles,Robbie	16	R	25	aa	CLE	55	6.02	1.89	8.1	3.3	4.4	1.3	1.0	38	69	8
Bacus,Dakota	15	R	24	a/a	WAS	95	4.77	1.53	17.1	3.2	4.2	1.3	0.8	31	70	24
	16	R	25	a/a	WAS	15	10.81	2.40	8.7	9.5	6.2	0.7	0.7	37	52	21
Baker,Corey	15	R	26	aa	STL	97	4.40	1.44	10.9	3.6	6.4	1.8	0.5	32	69	60
	16	R	27	a/a	STL	130	7.12	1.89	21.1	3.9	6.2	1.6	2.0	37	66	-1
Baldonado,Albert(	16	L	23	aa	NYM	40	5.86	1.90	5.6	5.1	9.1	1.8	1.2	40	71	47
Ballew,Travis	15	R	24	a/a	HOU	67	4.43	1.58	5.9	3.2	6.5	2.1	0.3	36	70	68
	16	R	25	aa	MIA	15	7.33	1.48	6.0	5.9	3.7	0.6	0.6	24	47	27
Balog,Alex	16	R	24	aa	COL	55	7.58	2.11	24.5	4.0	3.9	1.0	2.3	37	68	-46
Banda,Anthony	16	L	23	a/a	ARI	150	3.49	1.47	24.7	3.3	7.7	2.3	0.7	34	77	74
Banuelos,Manuel	15	L	24	aaa	ATL	85	2.97	1.43	22.5	4.6	6.4	1.4	0.3	30	78	66
	16	L	25	a/a	ATL	49	6.90	2.09	18.4	6.2	6.3	1.0	1.3	37	68	8
Barbato,John	16	R	24	aaa	NYY	48	3.81	1.55	6.81	4.9	7.7	1.6	0.8	32	77	57
Barker,Brandon	16	R	24	aa	BAL	145	4.93	1.50	23.3	2.9	5.4	1.9	1.3	32	71	28
Barlow,Scott	16	R	24	aa	LA	124	5.30	1.64	23.1	3.7	6.2	1.7	0.8	35	68	42
Barnes,Daniel	16	R	27	a/a	TOR	61	1.07	0.61	5.13	1.0	9.0	8.9	0.6	19	91	247
Barnes,Jacob	16	R	26	a/a	MIL	25	1.45	1.12	4.92	2.8	7.7	2.7	0.4	28	90	101
Barnette,Tyler	15	R	23	aa	CHW	76	3.22	1.54	11.4	3.4	5.2	1.5	0.5	33	80	46
	16	R	24	a/a	CHW	84	7.26	1.87	10.6	4.3	5.5	1.3	0.9	37	60	22
Bartsch,Kyle	16	L	25	aa	KC	46	5.17	1.80	8.51	3.4	5.1	1.5	1.1	37	73	15
Baumann,Buddy	16	L	29	aaa	SD	29	3.47	1.34	4.97	3.9	7.5	1.9	1.0	29	78	62
Bawcom,Logan	15	R	27	aaa	SEA	76	4.86	1.65	7.51	3.5	5.9	1.7	0.7	35	70	44
	16	R	28	a/a	LA	98	2.64	1.34	11.3	3.2	5.6	1.8	0.7	29	83	53
Baxendale,D.J.	16	R	26	a/a	MIN	116	3.87	1.43	13.3	2.0	5.9	2.9	0.5	35	73	77
Beal,Evan	16	R	23	a/a	KC	58	4.74	1.46	8.0	3.2	6.0	1.8	1.6	30	73	26
Beck,Chris	15	R	25	aaa	CHW	54	4.28	1.45	23.2	2.7	5.5	2.0	0.7	33	71	52
	16	R	26	aaa	CHW	66	5.33	1.84	14.1	3.9	5.6	1.4	0.8	38	71	27
Beede,Tyler	16	R	23	aa	SF	147	3.82	1.51	26.6	3.5	7.1	2.0	0.6	34	75	67
Beeks,Jalen	16	L	23	aa	BOS	65	6.06	1.76	23.0	4.0	6.5	1.6	0.9	37	66	38
Bell,Chadwick	15	L	26	aa	TEX	141	5.75	1.64	23.3	2.9	5.9	2.1	0.8	36	65	46
	16	L	27	aaa	DET	98	4.87	1.76	13.6	4.7	5.9	1.3	0.5	35	71	42
Bencomo,Omar	16	R	27	a/a	MIN	84	5.29	1.71	15.9	2.7	5.1	1.9	0.9	37	70	31
Benincasa,Robert	16	R	26	aa	WAS	30	6.37	1.87	6.7	4.8	8.2	1.7	1.8	37	69	22
Benjamin,Ramon	15	L	28	aa	LA	26	6.25	1.77	5.0	6.0	5.9	1.0	1.9	29	69	-1
	16	L	29	aa	SD	22	9.57	2.15	7.2	5.4	6.1	1.1	4.0	34	64	-76
Berg,Dave	16	R	23	aa	CHC	43	7.41	2.04	6.1	2.3	5.4	2.3	0.0	44	60	59
Bergman,Christiai	16	R	28	aaa	COL	52	5.57	1.65	23.1	2.5	4.0	1.6	2.1	32	73	-16
Berrios,Jose	15	R	21	a/a	MIN	166	3.44	1.15	24.5	2.0	8.0	4.0	0.7	31	71	117
	16	R	22	aaa	MIN	111	3.39	1.13	25.9	3.0	8.4	2.8	0.8	28	72	97
Berry,Timothy	15	L	24	aa	BAL	82	9.87	2.05	17.4	4.0	5.1	1.3	1.2	39	50	4
	16	L	25	aa	SD	69	9.96	2.53	19.4	6.1	5.4	0.9	1.5	43	60	-18
Bibens-Dirkx,Aust	15	R	30	a/a	TOR	114	6.59	1.83	21.3	3.1	6.3	2.0	1.5	38	66	22
	16	R	31	aaa	TEX	85	6.16	1.70	22.6	3.2	4.7	1.5	1.5	34	66	5
Binford,Christian	15	R	23	a/a	KC	119	6.39	1.78	24.9	2.9	4.2	1.5	0.8	37	63	19
	16	R	24	a/a	KC	141	6.49	1.61	25.0	3.0	5.2	1.8	1.3	34	61	20
Bird,Kyle	16	L	23	aa	TAM	49	3.49	1.40	6.5	3.1	6.1	1.9	0.8	31	77	55
Blach,Ty	16	L	26	aaa	SF	163	4.13	1.32	25.9	2.2	5.1	2.3	0.5	31	68	64
Black,Corey	15	R	24	aa	CHC	86	5.94	1.58	10.2	5.2	8.9	1.7	0.8	33	62	68
	16	R	25	a/a	CHC	53	5.12	1.78	5.1	6.4	8.7	1.4	0.2	36	69	75
Black,Ray	16	R	26	aa	SF	31	6.92	1.87	4.2	10.6	12.3	1.2	0.3	31	60	104
Blackburn,Claytor	15	R	22	aaa	SF	123	2.69	1.30	22.1	2.2	6.3	2.9	0.3	33	79	88
	16	R	23	aaa	SF	136	4.92	1.42	23.1	2.3	5.8	2.5	1.0	32	67	53
Blackburn,Paul	16	R	23	aa	SEA	143	4.25	1.40	23.2	2.2	5.5	2.5	0.6	33	70	64
Blackford,Alex	16	R	26	aa	LAA	111	4.38	1.36	21.2	4.4	6.9	1.6	1.3	26	72	44
Blackmar,Mark	15	R	23	aa	CHW	151	4.91	1.55	25.5	3.7	3.3	0.9	0.6	31	68	19
	16	R	24	aa	WAS	57	7.29	1.60	28.0	3.7	3.2	0.9	1.3	30	54	-4
Blair,Aaron	15	R	23	a/a	ARI	160	3.29	1.25	25.1	2.7	5.7	2.1	0.8	28	76	59
	16	R	24	aaa	ATL	72	5.84	1.75	25.2	4.3	7.8	1.8	0.5	38	65	61
Bleich,Jeremy	15	L	28	a/a	PIT	53	3.98	1.51	6.1	2.5	4.8	1.9	0.3	34	73	53
Bleier,Richard	16	L	29	aaa	NYY	58	6.08	1.87	22.7	2.2	2.9	1.4	0.5	39	66	12
Bonilla,Lisalverto	16	R	26	a/a	LA	111	5.19	1.58	15.7	3.2	7.7	2.4	0.6	37	66	73
Borden,Buddy	16	R	24	aa	PIT	29	6.47	1.85	9.8	6.5	5.9	0.9	0.6	33	64	33
Boscan,Wilfredo	15	R	26	aaa	PIT	126	4.04	1.65	22.5	3.3	4.7	1.4	0.2	35	74	44
	16	R	27	aaa	ATL	93	5.58	1.82	21.6	2.3	4.6	2.0	0.7	39	69	33
Boshers,Jeffrey	16	L	28	aaa	MIN	26	1.60	1.44	5.0	4.4	7.3	1.6	0.5	31	91	69
Boyd,Matt	15	L	24	a/a	DET	115	2.05	0.98	22.9	2.2	6.7	3.0	0.7	24	84	95
	16	L	25	aaa	DET	64	3.19	1.38	24.4	2.9	6.2	2.1	0.9	31	80	56
Bracewell,Ben	16	R	26	aa	OAK	88	2.62	1.25	12.4	2.7	4.6	1.7	0.4	28	80	56
Bracho,Silvino	15	R	23	aa	ARI	45	2.38	1.12	4.8	1.9	10.1	5.4	0.8	33	83	156
	16	R	24	aaa	ARI	34	5.27	1.35	3.9	2.1	9.5	4.6	0.5	38	59	136
Bradford,Chase	15	R	26	aaa	NYM	64	4.18	1.69	5.4	1.9	5.3	2.8	0.4	39	74	65
	16	R	27	aaa	NYM	66	4.93	1.61	5.2	1.7	5.9	3.4	0.6	38	69	76
Bradley,Archie	15	R	23	aaa	ARI	21	2.91	1.48	22.9	1.9	7.1	3.8	1.2	36	86	79
	16	R	24	aaa	ARI	41	2.18	1.14	23.0	3.8	8.6	2.3	0.0	28	79	114
Bradley,Jed	16	L	26	a/a	ATL	108	4.37	1.69	13.9	3.8	7.5	1.9	0.2	38	72	72
Brady,Michael	16	R	29	a/a	WAS	81	4.51	1.44	19.2	1.8	5.8	3.2	1.0	34	71	66
Bragg,Sam	16	R	23	aa	OAK	65	4.93	1.32	7.5	2.6	7.7	3.0	1.2	32	65	75
Brantley,Justin	16	R	25	aa	CLE	16	10.23	2.64	7.1	8.7	6.3	0.7	2.2	40	63	-32
Brasoban,Jimmy	16	R	22	aa	SD	36	3.75	1.33	5.1	4.1	7.9	1.9	0.3	30	71	87
Brault,Steven	16	L	24	aaa	PIT	71	5.40	1.68	20.0	4.7	8.1	1.7	0.9	36	68	56
Brebbia,John	16	R	26	a/a	STL	68	6.17	1.75	7.2	2.7	7.5	2.8	1.3	40	66	53
Bremer,Tyler	15	R	26	a/a	MIA	20	2.96	1.36	9.4	3.9	5.9	1.5	2.3	24	93	4
	16	R	27	a/a	MIA	73	4.97	1.64	8.0	4.4	5.5	1.2	0.8	32	70	32
Brennan,Brandon	16	R	25	aa	CHW	66	9.97	2.12	13.5	4.4	6.2	1.4	0.8	42	50	24
Brice,Austin	16	R	24	a/a	MIA	102	3.71	1.31	13.2	2.9	6.4	2.2	0.6	31	72	71
Bridwell,Parker	16	R	25	a/a	BAL	66	5.73	1.64	13.3	4.4	5.7	1.3	1.5	31	68	12
Britton,Drake	15	L	26	aaa	CHC	83	6.18	1.57	13.1	3.8	3.9	1.0	0.8	31	60	17
	16	L	27	aaa	DET	41	6.76	1.99	5.4	5.5	2.7	0.5	0.9	34	65	-10
Brooks,Aaron	16	R	24	aa	SEA	23	6.65	2.03	7.1	3.2	8.0	2.5	0.0	46	64	81
	15	R	25	aaa	OAK	119	4.46	1.47	25.5	1.7	6.2	3.6	0.8	36	71	82
Brooks,Aaron	16	R	26	aaa	CHC	16	9.33	1.94	15.5	2.3	5.4	2.3	3.2	37	57	-35
Broussard,Geoff	16	R	26	a/a	LAA	62	7.92	1.78	6.5	3.7	7.6	2.0	2.0	37	58	19
Broussard,Joe	16	R	25	a/a	LA	44	2.62	1.23	5.1	2.4	9.1	3.8	0.5	33	80	123
Brown,Dennis	15	R	25	aa	CLE	30	4.53	1.51	26.3	1.3	5.4	4.3	1.5	35	75	66
	16	R	26	a/a	CLE	137	6.88	1.75	22.3	3.3	6.1	1.9	1.4	36	62	23
Browning,Wil	15	R	27	aa	TOR	19	5.46	1.47	6.16	3.8	6.2	1.6	0.0	33	59	73
	16	R	28	a/a	TOR	52	3.07	1.40	4.7	3.0	8.6	2.8	0.8	34	80	89
Broyles,Shane	15	R	24	a/a	COL	47	5.30	1.59	6.43	5.2	7.4	1.4	1.1	31	68	43
	16	R	25	aa	COL	51	9.16	1.97	6.78	6.9	9.0	1.3	1.1	37	52	42
Buchanan,David	15	R	26	aaa	PHI	55	3.58	1.70	24.7	3.6	4.1	1.1	0.4	35	79	27
	16	R	27	aaa	PHI	167	6.39	1.64	27.7	2.6	4.1	1.6	1.3	34	62	8
Buchanan,Jake	15	R	26	aaa	HOU	81	5.23	1.68	12.2	2.4	4.2	1.7	0.6	36	68	32
	16	R	27	aaa	CHC	141	5.37	1.62	26.1	2.6	5.3	2.0	0.5	36	65	51
Bundy,Bobby	15	R	25	aa	BAL	15	5.78	2.00	9.03	6.7	6.8	1.0	0.0	38	68	55
	16	R	26	a/a	BAL	50	4.87	1.64	6.03	3.8	6.4	1.7	1.0	34	72	38
Burdi,Zack	16	R	21	a/a	CHW	64	3.56	1.20	6.13	5.8	11.7	2.0	0.6	24	71	116
Burgos,Enrique	15	R	25	a/a	ARI	24	4.34	1.92	4.61	7.4	11.4	1.5	1.3	38	81	62
	16	R	26	aaa	ARI	28	2.23	1.58	5.07	5.5	7.5	1.4	0.3	32	86	67
Burgos,Hiram	15	R	28	a/a	MIL	110	4.68	1.47	23.6	3.9	6.4	1.7	0.7	31	68	53
	16	R	29	aaa	MIL	143	5.63	1.82	24.6	3.9	5.4	1.4	0.9	37	69	23

PITCHER	yr	t	age	lvl	org	ip	era	whip	bf/g	ctl	dom	cmd	hr/9	h%	s%	bpv
Burke,Devin	16	R	25	a/a	COL	16	3.34	1.66	12.2	1.9	5.3	2.8	1.7	36	87	28
Busenitz,Alan	15	R	25	aa	LAA	53	8.78	2.14	16.5	2.7	5.3	1.9	1.3	43	58	10
	16	R	26	a/a	MIN	61	4.91	1.54	5.91	2.4	6.2	2.6	0.5	36	67	68
Butler,Eddie	15	R	24	aaa	COL	63	6.76	1.73	26.2	3.7	4.2	1.1	1.1	34	61	7
	16	R	25	aaa	COL	89	6.34	1.66	26.6	2.9	2.6	0.9	1.3	32	63	-13
Buttrey,Ty	16	R	23	aa	BOS	79	5.75	1.82	11.1	5.5	5.0	0.9	0.7	33	68	22
Cabrera,Mauricio	16	R	23	aa	ATL	34	4.60	1.48	5.79	6.6	8.3	1.3	0.0	28	65	90
Camarena,Daniel	16	L	24	a/a	NYY	136	5.63	1.48	21.6	1.7	6.2	3.5	1.3	35	64	64
Campos,Leonel	15	R	28	aaa	SD	50	2.92	1.09	5.11	3.8	9.6	2.6	0.3	27	73	119
	16	R	29	aaa	SD	50	4.78	1.73	6.15	5.6	8.6	1.5	0.4	36	71	71
Campos,Vicente	16	R	24	a/a	ARI	83	3.74	1.31	22.9	2.2	5.7	2.6	0.1	32	69	86
Caramo,Yender	16	R	25	a/a	KC	118	3.14	1.29	13.8	1.8	4.2	2.3	0.5	30	76	57
Carasiti,Matt	16	R	25	a/a	COL	46	2.97	1.08	4.08	2.0	6.9	3.4	1.5	25	82	78
Carle,Shane	15	R	24	a/a	COL	166	5.06	1.52	26.7	1.9	4.4	2.4	1.0	34	68	38
	16	R	25	aaa	COL	111	7.72	2.01	19.9	2.9	5.3	1.8	1.0	41	61	19
Carpenter,Ryan	15	L	25	aa	COL	167	6.29	1.58	26.2	2.3	5.5	2.4	1.7	34	63	25
	16	L	26	aaa	COL	69	10.87	2.35	13.7	3.7	6.4	1.7	3.0	43	57	-43
Carpenter,Tyler	16	R	24	aa	LAA	71	7.63	1.88	22.3	2.3	5.4	2.3	0.9	41	58	37
Carter,Anthony	16	R	30	aaa	TEX	21	8.65	1.92	4.66	2.7	5.3	2.0	2.2	38	57	-11
Carter,Will	16	R	23	aa	NYY	43	6.53	1.75	24.6	4.3	5.1	1.2	0.3	36	60	38
Cash,Ralston	15	R	24	a/a	LA	58	4.01	1.33	4.82	4.2	7.6	1.8	1.2	27	74	55
	16	R	25	a/a	LA	69	3.67	1.36	6.27	4.2	9.0	2.1	0.3	32	72	96
Casilla,Jose	15	R	26	aa	SF	56	1.99	1.59	5.29	3.3	4.1	1.2	0.0	34	86	45
	16	R	27	a/a	SF	53	4.77	1.80	6.95	3.5	4.7	1.4	0.9	36	75	19
Castillo,Fabio	16	R	27	a/a	SD	78	5.40	1.70	25.1	4.0	6.2	1.5	1.2	34	70	27
Castillo,Lendy	15	R	26	aa	TOR	32	6.55	2.12	8.41	7.1	5.3	0.7	1.5	34	71	-8
	16	R	27	aa	CLE	51	8.13	1.92	5.71	5.4	7.0	1.3	0.9	37	56	32
Castro,Miguel	15	R	21	aaa	COL	33	3.85	1.64	6.19	5.0	7.0	1.4	1.3	31	81	31
	16	R	22	aaa	COL	16	13.85	2.08	4.79	4.2	6.8	1.6	3.8	36	33	-58
Castro,Simon	15	R	27	aaa	COL	57	5.06	1.56	6.94	3.5	8.7	2.5	1.3	36	71	62
	16	R	28	aaa	COL	53	5.14	1.60	4.71	2.4	6.8	2.8	1.3	37	71	52
Cessa,Luis	16	R	24	aaa	NYY	77	4.43	1.43	21.9	3.0	6.8	2.2	1.4	31	74	45
Chacin,Alejandro	16	R	23	aa	CIN	61	2.65	1.57	5.12	4.5	10.0	2.2	0.5	37	84	93
Chaffee,Ryan	16	R	28	a/a	MIA	47	5.99	2.00	7.26	5.3	6.0	1.1	0.4	39	68	35
Chapman,Jaye	15	R	28	a/a	MIL	65	3.22	1.44	4.67	3.6	7.2	2.0	0.8	32	80	62
	16	R	29	a/a	TAM	54	5.64	1.36	4.23	2.9	8.2	2.8	1.0	33	59	78
Chapman,Kevin	15	L	27	aaa	HOU	53	5.34	1.82	5.01	4.5	8.3	1.8	0.5	40	70	63
	16	L	28	aaa	HOU	61	5.85	1.82	5.55	4.2	8.8	2.1	0.9	40	68	60
Chargois,J.T.	16	R	26	a/a	MIN	47	1.87	1.26	4.88	2.7	8.1	3.0	0.5	32	87	101
Chirinos,Yonny	16	R	23	aa	TAM	67	5.28	1.45	20.3	1.6	5.1	3.1	0.7	34	63	68
Church,John	15	R	29	aaa	NYM	71	4.29	1.37	4.87	2.1	4.3	2.1	0.8	31	70	42
	16	R	30	aaa	STL	30	4.22	1.56	5.2	4.5	5.8	1.3	0.0	33	70	63
Cimber,Adam	15	R	25	a/a	SD	59	3.18	1.38	5.38	2.2	5.9	2.6	0.7	33	79	67
	16	R	26	a/a	SD	57	4.41	1.41	5.28	2.4	4.0	1.6	0.7	31	69	35
Claiborne,Prestor	16	R	28	aa	SF	45	3.53	1.24	5.41	3.1	7.5	2.4	0.9	29	74	76
Clark,Brian	16	L	23	a/a	CHW	57	3.20	1.46	6.55	2.0	6.7	3.3	0.2	37	77	98
Clarke,Taylor	16	R	23	aa	ARI	98	5.00	1.49	24.7	2.1	5.6	2.7	1.1	34	68	52
Claudio,Alexande	15	L	23	aaa	TEX	40	3.61	1.43	5.87	1.6	6.6	4.1	0.5	36	75	103
	16	L	24	aaa	TEX	16	0.69	0.77	9.78	2.4	3.6	1.5	0.0	17	90	77
Clemens,Paul	15	R	27	a/a	KC	47	7.97	2.01	14.1	5.9	5.0	0.9	1.3	35	60	-2
	16	R	28	aaa	MIA	75	6.35	1.57	23.6	3.6	5.9	1.7	0.8	33	59	41
Cleto,Maikel	15	R	26	aaa	CHW	51	4.17	1.34	6.84	5.1	8.7	1.7	1.5	25	74	56
	16	R	27	aaa	ATL	21	2.87	1.91	4.96	6.3	10.8	1.7	1.5	39	91	51
Clevinger,Michael	16	R	26	aaa	CLE	93	4.27	1.50	23.6	3.8	7.2	1.9	1.0	32	74	53
Cochran-Gill,Trey	15	R	23	a/a	SEA	56	5.46	1.76	7.28	5.0	4.7	0.9	0.0	34	66	43
	16	R	24	aa	OAK	73	3.59	1.45	7.46	3.1	5.7	1.9	0.7	32	77	50
Cole,A.J.	15	R	23	aaa	WAS	106	4.16	1.37	21.1	3.0	5.3	1.8	0.8	30	71	45
	16	R	24	aaa	WAS	125	6.15	1.66	25.4	2.9	6.4	2.2	1.4	36	65	34
Cole,Taylor	15	R	26	aa	TOR	164	5.62	1.72	26.6	3.3	5.8	1.7	1.4	36	70	21
	16	R	27	aa	TOR	62	5.39	1.80	23.7	2.8	6.3	2.2	1.2	39	72	34
Coleman,Casey	15	R	28	aaa	KC	82	6.81	2.18	12.5	5.1	4.3	0.9	0.8	39	68	2
	16	R	29	aaa	TAM	53	3.71	1.40	5.88	3.4	7.0	2.1	0.7	32	74	67
Collier,Tommy	15	R	26	aa	DET	108	5.82	1.56	26.4	2.6	4.8	1.8	0.6	35	61	42
	16	R	27	aa	DET	131	5.54	1.70	23.6	2.7	4.4	1.6	1.2	35	69	13
Colon,Joseph	16	R	26	aaa	CLE	22	1.16	1.07	4.28	5.4	6.6	1.2	0.0	18	88	92
Concepcion,Gera	16	L	24	a/a	CHC	60	6.06	1.68	6.39	4.3	6.6	1.5	1.0	34	64	36
Conway,Josh	16	R	25	aa	CHC	23	6.64	2.19	5.31	11.5	5.7	0.5	0.5	28	68	37
Coonrod,Sam	16	R	24	aa	SF	77	4.11	1.48	25.6	4.9	5.1	1.0	0.8	27	74	32
Cooper,Matt	16	R	25	a/a	CHW	41	3.79	1.20	8.67	2.9	8.7	3.0	0.8	30	70	99
Copeland,Scott	15	R	28	aaa	TOR	125	4.76	1.70	26.9	3.2	3.8	1.2	0.9	34	73	10
	16	R	29	aaa	TOR	50	4.74	1.66	25.1	3.7	4.5	1.2	0.8	33	72	21
Corcino,Daniel	16	R	26	aa	LA	36	4.91	1.29	5.43	2.6	6.3	2.4	1.3	29	65	51
Cordero,Estarlin	16	L	23	aa	KC	17	14.83	2.41	8.09	4.4	7.0	1.6	3.0	44	37	-40
Coshow,Cale	15	R	23	aa	NYY	33	4.73	1.48	23.9	3.8	4.9	1.3	0.4	31	66	46
	16	R	24	aa	NYY	89	6.11	1.87	11.6	5.8	6.0	1.0	0.9	34	68	23
Cotton,Chris	15	L	25	a/a	HOU	44	3.72	1.32	5.16	2.5	6.0	2.4	0.9	31	74	61
	16	L	26	a/a	HOU	61	4.74	1.67	8.55	2.4	3.7	1.5	0.9	35	73	17
Cotton,Jharel	15	R	23	a/a	LA	70	2.96	1.24	17.8	2.8	8.9	3.2	0.6	32	77	109
	16	R	24	aaa	OAK	136	5.90	1.30	20	2.8	8.3	2.9	1.5	30	57	69
Couch,Keith	15	R	26	aaa	BOS	125	9.18	2.08	23.5	4.2	3.5	0.8	1.0	38	54	-10
	16	R	27	a/a	BOS	127	6.11	1.80	26.7	3.1	4.0	1.3	0.9	36	66	11
Coulombe,Daniel	15	L	26	aaa	LA	41	3.72	1.54	4.74	5.0	7.2	1.4	0.2	32	74	70
	16	L	27	aaa	OAK	25	1.58	1.23	5.06	2.5	9.5	3.8	0.0	35	86	141
Covey,Dylan	16	R	25	aa	OAK	29	2.20	1.43	20.8	5.3	6.3	1.2	0.6	27	87	53
Cravy,Tyler	15	R	26	aaa	MIL	95	4.59	1.47	24.1	3.1	5.7	1.8	0.7	32	69	50
	16	R	27	aaa	MIL	56	7.23	1.74	12.2	4.8	8.1	1.7	0.9	36	57	52
Creasy,Jason	15	R	23	aa	PIT	147	4.95	1.56	23.8	2.9	3.5	1.2	0.6	32	68	21
	16	R	24	a/a	PIT	34	6.98	1.66	15.1	3.9	3.6	0.9	0.6	32	55	18

PITCHER	yr	t	age	lvl	org	ip	era	whip	bf/g	ctl	dom	cmd	hr/9	h%	s%	bpv
Crichton,Stefan	16	R	24	aa	BAL	72	4.71	1.57	6.62	3.3	6.2	1.8	0.6	35	70	52
Crick,Kyle	15	R	23	aa	SF	63	4.28	2.02	8.48	10.2	8.9	0.9	0.3	32	78	70
	16	R	24	aa	SF	109	6.84	1.92	22.5	6.1	6.0	1.0	0.7	35	63	30
Crockett,Kyle	15	L	24	aaa	CLE	29	7.89	2.18	4.95	3.6	7.2	2.0	1.1	45	64	28
	16	L	25	aaa	CLE	30	5.43	1.62	4.59	3.6	6.1	1.7	0.8	35	66	44
Crouse,Matt	15	L	25	aa	DET	25	3.31	1.72	8	4.4	3.7	0.8	0.9	32	83	7
	16	L	26	a/a	DET	126	5.06	1.61	18	3.7	4.2	1.1	0.7	32	68	23
Cuevas,William	16	R	26	aaa	BOS	131	7.00	1.85	24.5	3.8	4.6	1.2	1.7	35	65	-11
Culver,Malcom	15	R	25	aa	KC	58	5.27	1.74	6.15	4.8	7.1	1.5	0.3	36	68	59
	16	R	26	aaa	KC	68	4.69	1.66	6.89	3.7	6.2	1.7	0.5	36	71	49
Cunniff,Brandon	16	R	28	a/a	ATL	55	4.80	1.52	5.58	4.7	6.4	1.4	0.6	30	68	51
Curtis,Zac	16	L	24	aa	ARI	20	4.55	1.43	4.4	3.0	11.4	3.8	1.8	36	75	93
Dahlstrand,Jacob	16	R	24	aa	BOS	19	7.99	1.89	22.8	4.0	3.1	0.8	1.6	34	58	-25
Danish,Tyler	16	R	22	a/a	CHW	105	5.59	1.44	23.5	2.3	5.3	2.2	0.3	34	58	66
Darnell,Logan	15	L	26	aaa	MIN	78	4.01	1.65	9.92	3.3	5.9	1.8	0.4	36	75	52
	16	L	27	aaa	MIN	110	5.31	1.66	27.3	3.4	3.2	1.0	0.8	33	68	9
Davis,Erik	15	R	29	a/a	WAS	46	6.10	2.21	6.57	6.3	6.4	1.0	0.5	41	71	30
	16	R	30	aaa	WAS	52	6.73	1.91	5.51	4.9	7.9	1.6	0.7	40	64	50
Davis,Rookie	16	R	23	a/a	CIN	125	5.48	1.60	23	3.0	5.0	1.6	1.4	33	69	16
Dawson,Shane	16	L	23	aa	TOR	134	5.50	1.76	23.6	5.1	5.5	1.1	0.9	33	69	26
Dayton,Grant	16	L	29	a/a	LA	52	3.39	0.99	5.21	2.0	11.8	5.8	0.5	32	65	192
De Fratus,Justin	16	R	29	a/a	WAS	58	5.82	1.80	5.95	4.7	4.9	1.0	0.8	34	67	19
De Jong,Chase	16	R	23	a/a	LA	147	3.46	1.14	22.4	2.3	7.0	3.0	1.1	27	74	81
De La Cruz,Joel	15	R	26	a/a	NYY	84	4.69	1.57	16.1	2.7	3.6	1.3	0.9	33	71	15
	16	R	27	aaa	ATL	58	6.28	1.83	12.8	4.2	5.6	1.3	0.9	36	66	24
De Leon,Jose	15	R	23	aa	LA	77	4.54	1.30	19.7	3.3	10.6	3.2	1.6	32	71	90
	16	R	24	aaa	LA	86	3.45	1.04	20.8	1.9	9.7	5.0	1.1	29	71	141
De Los Santos,Ab	15	R	23	aa	WAS	58	4.35	1.30	6.09	1.9	7.0	3.7	1.0	32	69	89
	16	R	24	a/a	CIN	58	4.12	1.60	5.55	5.4	8.8	1.6	0.7	33	75	68
De Paula,Rafael	16	R	25	a/a	SD	64	3.04	1.36	5.98	3.1	10.3	3.3	0.3	37	77	124
Dean,Pat	15	L	26	aaa	MIN	179	4.06	1.46	28.4	2.0	3.8	1.9	0.6	33	73	37
	16	L	27	aaa	MIN	87	8.37	1.99	26.2	2.2	3.8	1.7	1.4	40	58	-4
Delgado,Casey	16	R	26	aa	NYM	58	5.88	1.84	26.8	3.3	5.8	1.8	0.9	39	68	32
DeLoach,Tyler	15	L	24	a/a	LAA	139	5.43	1.53	24.2	3.4	7.3	2.1	0.8	35	64	61
	16	L	25	a/a	LAA	63	3.43	1.42	5.2	3.5	8.3	2.4	0.3	34	75	92
Dermody,Matt	16	L	26	a/a	TOR	36	2.49	1.44	4.95	2.0	5.5	2.8	0.4	35	83	76
Diamond,Scott	15	L	29	aaa	TAM	150	5.10	1.77	24.7	1.8	4.1	2.3	0.9	38	72	28
	16	L	30	aaa	TOR	166	7.11	1.87	27.8	2.1	4.1	1.9	0.9	39	61	18
Diaz,Dayan	16	R	27	aaa	CIN	56	4.61	1.59	6.18	3.1	6.1	2.0	0.5	36	70	56
Diaz,Edwin	16	R	22	aa	SEA	41	2.82	1.09	9.95	1.5	10.7	7.0	0.7	34	77	194
Diaz,Luis	15	R	23	aa	BOS	137	6.87	1.79	23.3	4.0	4.7	1.2	0.8	35	60	20
	16	R	24	aa	SD	56	7.46	1.80	25.9	3.1	6.5	2.1	1.6	38	60	23
Diaz,Miller	16	R	24	aa	ARI	22	4.01	1.69	5.92	4.0	8.0	2.0	1.1	37	79	53
Dickson,Cody	16	L	24	aa	PIT	140	4.46	1.74	22.8	6.1	5.4	0.9	0.5	31	74	35
Dimock,Michael	15	R	26	a/a	SD	60	2.23	1.03	4.71	0.9	8.6	9.6	0.8	31	84	233
	16	R	27	a/a	SD	46	6.04	1.35	6.23	3.3	9.0	2.7	1.6	31	58	68
Dirks,Caleb	16	R	23	aa	ATL	61	1.69	1.22	5.02	3.0	8.8	2.9	0.6	31	89	105
Dominguez,Jose	15	R	25	aaa	TAM	28	7.77	2.33	4.75	6.9	6.7	1.0	1.7	40	69	-7
	16	R	26	aaa	SD	36	3.91	1.55	5.77	6.1	7.5	1.2	0.2	30	73	71
Donatello,Sean	15	R	25	aa	MIA	33	5.18	1.51	5.16	3.1	5.6	1.8	0.5	33	64	51
	16	R	26	aa	MIA	50	4.82	1.50	4.73	2.4	3.6	1.5	0.2	33	65	41
Donofrio,Joey	15	R	26	a/a	STL	73	4.93	1.58	7.65	4.5	4.7	1.0	0.7	30	69	28
	16	R	27	aa	STL	23	5.24	1.75	6.91	5.8	6.2	1.1	0.9	32	71	30
Doolittle,Ryan	15	R	27	aa	OAK	57	3.78	1.57	6.25	2.7	5.5	2.1	0.8	35	77	47
	16	R	28	a/a	OAK	44	3.94	1.54	6.4	3.3	4.4	1.3	0.9	32	77	22
Doyle,John	15	R	30	a/a	BAL	159	3.51	1.42	25.9	1.6	4.5	2.9	0.9	33	78	53
	16	R	31	a/a	ARI	35	7.26	1.92	27.4	2.4	4.0	1.7	0.0	41	58	40
Dragmire,Brady	16	R	23	aa	TOR	72	5.70	1.71	7.24	3.7	4.5	1.2	1.6	32	70	-4
Drake,Oliver	15	R	28	aaa	BAL	44	1.38	1.22	4.23	4.2	10.2	2.4	0.3	30	90	115
	16	R	29	aaa	BAL	56	4.49	1.68	5.39	5.0	9.2	1.8	1.3	35	77	52
Drehoff,Jake	16	L	24	aa	BOS	36	7.33	2.13	8.4	5.9	6.7	1.1	1.7	38	68	0
Drummond,Calvin	16	R	27	aa	DET	25	6.55	2.09	9.58	7.2	6.8	0.9	0.8	37	68	28
Duffey,Tyler	15	R	25	a/a	MIN	138	3.28	1.28	25.7	2.1	6.3	3.0	0.1	33	72	100
	16	R	26	aaa	MIN	31	4.32	1.46	26.3	3.9	5.6	1.4	1.5	28	76	20
Duncan,Frank	16	R	24	a/a	PIT	139	3.05	1.40	21.7	2.4	6.0	2.5	0.3	34	77	77
Dunning,Jake	15	R	27	aaa	SF	46	7.56	2.15	17.6	4.3	5.4	1.3	1.5	40	66	-5
	16	R	28	aaa	SF	59	6.10	1.82	5.62	4.9	5.1	1.0	0.6	35	65	27
DuRapau,Montan	16	R	24	aa	PIT	49	4.52	1.42	4.18	3.5	7.4	2.1	1.1	31	71	56
Dykstra,James	16	R	26	aa	CHW	102	6.20	1.97	17.5	3.9	4.8	1.2	0.4	39	67	26
Dziedzic,Jonathar	15	L	24	a/a	KC	142	4.45	1.51	22.7	2.4	4.9	2.0	0.8	33	72	41
	16	L	25	aaa	KC	140	4.82	1.57	23.6	4.1	5.4	1.3	0.8	32	70	36
Eades,Ryan	16	R	25	aa	MIN	113	5.91	1.60	19.3	3.6	5.6	1.6	0.4	35	60	51
Echemendia,Pedr	16	R	25	a/a	STL	49	4.00	1.42	6.89	3.5	5.5	1.6	1.3	29	77	27
Edwards,Andrew	16	R	25	a/a	KC	61	5.08	1.71	6.61	5.0	8.6	1.7	1.1	35	72	51
Edwards,Carl	15	R	24	a/a	CHC	55	3.28	1.31	6.35	6.9	10.3	1.5	0.2	24	73	111
	16	R	25	aaa	CHC	25	5.05	1.48	4.54	6.3	10.3	1.6	0.4	31	64	96
Eflin,Zach	16	R	22	aaa	PHI	68	4.18	1.07	24.2	1.6	6.5	4.1	0.4	29	59	120
Ege,Cody	15	L	24	a/a	MIA	52	1.11	1.30	5.49	4.2	8.6	2.1	0.5	29	95	89
	16	L	25	aaa	LAA	51	4.75	1.56	5.35	4.8	6.7	1.4	0.3	32	68	62
Ehret,Jake	16	R	23	aa	CIN	30	8.05	2.05	6.64	7.3	8.3	1.1	0.9	38	59	41
Eitel,Derek	15	R	28	a/a	MIL	25	7.36	2.15	5.92	6.8	7.0	1.0	1.1	38	66	21
	16	R	29	aaa	SD	69	4.06	1.55	5.56	5.5	7.2	1.3	0.7	30	75	55
Elias,Roenis	15	L	27	aaa	SEA	61	7.68	1.74	23.3	2.5	5.5	2.2	1.2	37	55	29
	16	L	28	aaa	BOS	125	6.28	1.93	28.3	5.3	6.2	1.2	1.1	37	68	21
Ellington,Brian	15	R	25	a/a	MIA	44	3.19	1.09	6.67	2.8	7.8	2.7	0.0	28	67	116
	16	R	26	aaa	MIA	35	4.40	1.48	4.66	7.7	10.9	1.4	0.6	26	70	97
Ellis,Chris	15	R	23	aa	LAA	78	4.89	1.69	23.5	4.8	6.2	1.3	1.1	33	73	28
	16	R	24	a/a	ATL	146	6.07	1.68	23.5	5.9	6.7	1.1	0.4	32	62	53

PITCHER	yr	t	age	lvl	org	ip	era	whip	bf/g	ctl	dom	cmd	hr/9	h%	s%	bpv
Emanuel,Kent	16	L	24	aa	HOU	83	6.19	1.60	21.5	2.2	5.4	2.5	1.0	36	61	43
Enns,Dietrich	16	L	25	a/a	NYY	135	2.64	1.48	22.3	4.4	6.8	1.6	0.6	31	84	58
Eppler,Tyler	16	R	23	aa	PIT	162	4.85	1.46	25.7	1.8	4.8	2.6	0.8	34	67	54
Esch,Jacob	16	R	26	a/a	MIA	142	6.10	1.67	24.5	3.3	4.7	1.4	0.7	35	62	29
Escobar,Edwin	15	L	23	aaa	BOS	50	7.13	1.86	12.2	5.0	3.6	0.7	1.7	31	64	-23
	16	L	24	aaa	ARI	98	4.33	1.55	22.6	3.3	4.9	1.5	0.7	33	73	35
Eshelman,Tom	16	R	22	aa	PHI	61	6.10	1.73	21.5	2.5	7.2	2.9	0.7	41	64	70
Espino,Paolo	15	R	28	a/a	WAS	156	4.99	1.51	24.1	2.0	5.1	2.6	1.1	34	69	43
	16	R	29	aaa	WAS	153	5.32	1.60	26	2.2	5.7	2.6	1.0	36	68	48
Faria,Jake	16	R	23	a/a	TAM	151	4.91	1.31	23.1	4.1	8.2	2.0	0.8	28	62	76
Farmer,Buck	15	R	24	aaa	DET	87	5.07	1.45	23.1	2.7	6.2	2.3	0.7	33	65	61
	16	R	25	aaa	DET	100	5.48	1.66	22.4	2.9	6.5	2.2	1.2	36	69	39
Farrell,Luke	15	R	24	aa	KC	93	3.80	1.44	20.9	2.9	5.0	1.7	0.7	31	75	43
	16	R	25	aaa	KC	91	4.47	1.53	20.8	4.0	6.1	1.5	1.2	31	74	32
Farris,James	16	R	24	aa	CHC	36	3.31	1.16	5.51	2.6	8.0	3.1	0.6	30	72	104
Fasola,John	16	R	25	a/a	TEX	40	4.42	1.47	5.96	2.5	8.2	3.3	0.5	37	69	97
Faulkner,Andrew	15	L	23	a/a	TEX	100	4.65	1.47	12.7	4.4	7.7	1.8	0.9	31	70	60
	16	L	24	aaa	TEX	45	4.99	1.50	4.78	4.3	6.3	1.5	0.7	31	66	50
Fedde,Erick	16	R	23	aa	WAS	29	5.30	1.73	26.7	3.3	7.1	2.2	0.3	39	67	68
Fernandez,Anthoı	16	L	26	aa	DET	24	6.67	1.63	21.7	2.9	4.5	1.6	1.3	34	60	13
Fernandez,Pedro	16	R	22	aa	KC	29	5.27	1.54	15.8	3.2	4.9	1.6	0.7	33	65	38
Fernandez,Raul	15	R	25	aa	CHW	61	6.01	1.61	7.55	3.8	5.5	1.4	0.8	33	62	34
	16	R	26	aa	MIN	38	4.66	1.56	6.4	3.7	5.2	1.4	0.5	33	69	42
Feyereisen,J.P.	16	R	23	aa	NYY	58	2.52	1.34	5.77	4.5	10.4	2.3	0.7	31	84	98
Fife,Stephen	16	R	30	aaa	CHC	27	6.04	1.74	17.8	3.8	6.2	1.6	0.4	37	63	50
Fillmyer,Heath	16	R	22	aa	OAK	39	2.85	1.07	19	1.8	5.6	3.1	0.6	27	76	88
Filomeno,Joe	16	L	23	aa	TEX	41	2.87	1.47	5.87	7.2	8.9	1.2	0.8	24	83	73
Finnegan,Kyle	16	R	25	aa	OAK	42	2.56	1.35	5.84	4.4	6.9	1.6	0.6	28	83	63
Fleck,Kaleb	15	R	26	aaa	ARI	52	3.64	1.44	5.28	4.0	9.1	2.3	0.4	35	74	95
	16	R	27	aaa	ARI	31	6.79	1.97	5.12	5.4	8.3	1.6	0.9	40	65	44
Fleet,Austin	15	R	28	aaa	SF	32	7.62	1.84	21.3	3.3	4.3	1.3	1.0	37	57	11
	16	R	29	aaa	SF	37	4.42	1.67	7.16	4.5	3.9	0.9	0.7	32	74	16
Flemer,Matt	15	R	25	aa	COL	170	6.03	1.68	27.2	2.4	3.4	1.4	1.0	35	64	8
	16	R	26	a/a	COL	102	5.59	1.62	18.2	2.6	4.0	1.6	1.8	32	70	-5
Flores,Kendry	15	R	24	a/a	MIA	115	3.00	1.12	23.9	2.4	5.3	2.2	0.5	26	74	74
	16	R	25	a/a	MIA	97	6.04	1.88	24	4.0	5.8	1.4	0.8	38	67	28
Floro,Dylan	16	R	26	aaa	TAM	50	3.92	1.54	6.81	1.8	5.9	3.3	1.3	36	79	56
Flynn,Brian	16	L	26	aaa	KC	24	3.70	1.63	11.7	4.7	8.2	1.8	0.4	36	77	73
Foltynewicz,Mike	15	R	24	aaa	ATL	57	4.65	1.61	25.1	4.4	8.7	2.0	1.3	34	75	52
	16	R	25	aaa	ATL	27	2.14	1.15	21.4	5.1	7.1	1.4	0.0	22	79	93
Font,Wilmer	16	R	26	a/a	TOR	66	5.24	1.40	23.2	1.9	6.1	3.3	1.5	32	67	56
Frankoff,Seth	15	R	27	a/a	OAK	61	4.51	1.49	5.56	3.7	6.4	1.7	1.1	31	72	43
	16	R	28	a/a	LA	68	5.61	1.75	12.4	2.3	6.3	2.7	0.5	40	66	65
Freeland,Kyle	16	L	23	a/a	COL	162	5.66	1.59	27.5	2.7	4.6	1.7	1.3	33	66	18
Freeman,Michael	16	L	25	aa	HOU	56	8.70	2.31	7.81	5.9	3.9	0.7	1.0	39	61	-11
Freeman,Sam	16	L	29	aaa	MIL	55	6.66	2.02	8.92	5.2	5.6	1.1	0.8	38	66	20
Frias,Carlos	15	R	26	aaa	LA	21	3.37	1.53	11.6	2.0	6.5	3.2	0.9	36	81	70
	16	R	27	a/a	LA	43	5.27	1.43	18.4	2.3	5.2	2.2	0.5	33	61	59
Frias,Edison	15	R	25	aa	HOU	34	6.36	1.83	19.6	2.8	9.4	3.4	0.9	45	65	85
	16	R	26	a/a	HOU	93	4.74	1.56	21.3	3.9	5.6	1.4	0.8	32	70	37
Fry,Paul	16	L	24	aaa	SEA	55	2.95	1.48	4.92	4.7	9.2	2.0	0.2	34	79	96
Fulmer,Carson	16	R	23	a/a	CHW	103	5.49	1.65	21.9	5.2	8.0	1.5	0.8	34	67	56
Fulmer,Michael	15	R	22	aa	DET	118	2.61	1.23	22.7	2.3	7.3	3.1	0.6	31	81	94
	16	R	23	aaa	DET	15	5.58	1.64	22.8	3.2	9.4	2.9	2.1	37	73	47
Gabryszwski,Jere	16	R	23	aa	TOR	146	6.82	1.72	22.9	3.2	5.1	1.6	1.3	35	61	17
Gage,Matt	15	L	22	aa	SF	39	5.94	1.46	18.4	2.5	6.1	2.5	0.5	35	57	71
	16	L	23	aa	SF	136	4.49	1.43	25.1	2.4	6.1	2.5	0.1	35	66	81
Gagnon,Drew	15	R	25	a/a	MIL	111	8.51	2.03	20.6	5.6	4.6	0.8	1.6	35	58	-13
	16	R	26	a/a	MIL	68	6.03	1.59	8.37	3.7	6.6	1.8	0.7	35	61	53
Gallegos,Giovann	16	R	25	a/a	NYY	78	2.11	1.07	7.22	2.3	10.1	4.4	0.9	30	86	137
Gant,John	16	R	24	aaa	ATL	56	5.25	1.65	20.8	3.8	8.0	2.1	0.9	37	69	60
Garces,Frank	15	L	25	aaa	SD	22	2.74	1.46	4.88	5.8	5.9	1.0	0.7	25	84	46
	16	L	26	aaa	SD	114	4.56	1.57	13.6	3.0	6.4	2.1	1.2	34	74	40
Garcia,Edgar	15	R	28	a/a	ARI	104	5.63	1.61	18.5	3.8	4.1	1.1	1.5	30	68	-1
	16	R	29	a/a	ARI	123	7.16	1.84	22.1	4.1	5.0	1.2	1.1	36	61	12
Garcia,Jarlin	16	L	23	aa	MIA	40	6.04	1.46	18.8	2.7	5.1	1.9	0.9	32	58	39
Garcia,Jason	15	R	23	aa	BAL	15	5.54	1.60	7.37	5.8	7.0	1.2	1.6	28	69	24
	16	R	24	aa	BAL	124	5.97	1.77	23.7	4.1	4.2	1.0	0.5	35	64	24
Garcia,Luis	16	R	29	aaa	PHI	55	3.59	1.57	5	5.1	6.7	1.3	0.8	31	79	45
Garner,David	16	R	24	aa	CHC	54	5.05	1.85	5.83	6.1	7.9	1.3	0.4	37	71	60
Garner,Perci	16	R	28	a/a	CLE	79	2.70	1.21	7.74	2.9	5.9	2.0	0.3	28	77	76
Garrett,Amir	16	L	24	a/a	CIN	145	3.74	1.35	24.1	4.2	7.2	1.7	0.6	29	73	70
Garrett,Reed	16	R	23	a/a	TEX	99	7.38	1.78	16.9	4.4	6.0	1.4	1.0	35	58	26
Garrido,Santiago	16	R	27	aa	DET	43	9.85	2.35	9.75	4.5	6.1	1.4	1.7	44	58	-10
Garton,Ryan	16	R	27	aaa	TAM	32	4.30	1.60	6.43	3.2	8.8	2.8	0.3	40	72	94
Gaviglio,Sam	15	R	25	aaa	SEA	102	5.15	1.40	20.4	2.9	5.8	2.0	1.3	30	66	39
	16	R	26	a/a	SEA	165	4.90	1.41	24.9	2.0	5.5	2.8	0.8	33	66	62
Geltz,Steve	16	R	29	aaa	TAM	36	4.41	1.70	5.2	5.1	7.7	1.5	1.0	34	76	46
Gibson,Daniel	15	L	24	aa	ARI	24	2.01	1.53	4.02	5.5	6.2	1.1	0.0	30	85	67
	16	L	25	a/a	ARI	44	4.43	1.82	4.5	4.7	5.7	1.2	1.0	35	78	23
Gilmartin,Sean	16	L	26	aaa	NYM	107	4.76	1.49	24.4	2.5	6.4	2.6	0.9	35	69	60
Giolito,Lucas	15	R	21	aa	WAS	47	4.68	1.52	25.7	3.2	7.2	2.3	0.4	36	68	76
	16	R	22	a/a	WAS	108	3.79	1.53	22.4	3.9	7.9	2.0	0.5	35	75	75
Girodo,Chad	16	L	25	aaa	TOR	36	5.40	2.02	5.96	3.7	5.1	1.4	1.8	39	78	-12
Glasnow,Tyler	15	R	22	a/a	PIT	104	2.69	1.16	20.7	3.3	9.3	2.8	0.2	30	76	120
	16	R	23	a/a	PIT	117	2.47	1.30	21.8	5.3	9.0	1.7	0.4	27	82	92
Glover,Koda	16	R	23	a/a	WAS	46	3.73	1.19	5.63	2.1	8.2	3.9	0.7	32	70	115
Godley,Zachary	16	R	26	a/a	ARI	82	4.68	1.61	24.2	3.0	6.0	2.0	0.9	35	72	43
Goeddel,Erik	16	R	28	aaa	NYM	29	4.17	1.61	5.29	4.7	8.3	1.8	0.6	35	74	68
Goforth,David	15	R	27	aaa	MIL	47	3.18	1.54	5.39	5.6	5.2	0.9	0.5	28	80	42
	16	R	28	aaa	MIL	51	6.14	2.10	6.02	6.8	5.1	0.7	0.6	36	70	18
Goldberg,Brad	16	R	26	a/a	CHW	57	3.41	1.51	5.22	4.7	6.7	1.4	0.6	31	78	56
Gomber,Austin	16	L	23	aa	STL	19	1.69	1.14	19.1	4.3	6.2	1.4	0.0	24	83	85
Gonsalves,Stephe	16	L	22	aa	MIN	74	2.19	1.14	22.7	4.3	8.9	2.1	0.1	26	80	110
Gonzalez,Alex	15	R	23	aaa	TEX	88	4.40	1.61	24.5	3.3	4.8	1.5	0.3	35	71	43
	16	R	24	aaa	TEX	138	5.90	1.67	24.8	3.1	4.8	1.6	0.6	36	63	35
Gonzalez,Carlos	15	R	25	aa	CIN	27	5.87	1.93	6.03	4.9	3.2	0.7	0.5	35	68	7
	16	R	26	aa	CIN	62	5.99	1.54	5.51	3.9	7.0	1.8	0.9	33	61	50
Gonzalez,Felipe	16	R	25	aa	LA	16	12.74	2.58	17.6	6.7	4.5	0.7	2.1	41	50	-47
Gonzalez,Juan	15	R	25	a/a	LA	50	1.95	1.11	4.47	2.8	7.6	2.7	0.2	28	82	107
	16	R	26	aaa	STL	43	6.40	1.91	5.18	6.6	6.9	1.0	0.6	35	65	40
Gonzalez,Nelson	15	R	25	a/a	COL	69	4.21	1.42	6.97	2.9	6.3	2.2	1.0	32	72	54
	16	R	26	aaa	COL	35	7.42	1.92	5.98	4.3	5.9	1.4	2.6	35	67	-26
Gonzalez,Rayan	16	R	26	aa	COL	52	5.16	1.71	5.13	4.8	6.1	1.3	0.6	34	69	42
Gonzalez,Severin	15	R	23	aaa	PHI	88	6.13	1.59	24.3	1.9	4.1	2.1	1.0	35	62	29
	16	R	24	a/a	PHI	46	3.98	1.42	9.3	1.7	5.9	3.5	0.8	35	74	78
Goody,Nicholas	15	R	24	a/a	NYY	62	2.16	1.22	5.86	3.3	10.3	3.1	0.4	32	83	123
	16	R	25	aaa	NYY	23	2.88	0.87	4.79	1.8	11.2	6.3	2.4	21	91	143
Gorski,Darin	15	L	28	aaa	NYM	137	5.89	1.82	22.7	4.5	5.6	1.2	1.3	35	70	12
	16	L	29	aaa	NYM	69	6.17	1.66	20.5	3.8	5.3	1.4	1.0	33	63	24
Gossett,Daniel	16	R	24	a/a	OAK	108	3.06	1.22	24.2	2.4	6.6	2.7	0.4	30	75	90
Gott,Trevor	15	R	23	a/a	LAA	28	2.41	1.39	4.72	3.5	8.3	2.4	0.0	35	81	103
	16	R	24	aaa	WAS	39	6.28	1.80	5.51	3.4	5.8	1.7	0.6	38	63	42
Goudeau,Ashton	16	R	24	aa	KC	93	7.27	1.73	21.1	2.4	5.3	2.2	1.4	37	59	22
Grace,Matt	15	L	27	aaa	WAS	49	3.45	1.53	5.57	3.4	4.3	1.3	0.2	33	76	43
	16	L	28	aaa	WAS	47	4.49	1.82	6.28	2.1	4.5	2.1	0.3	40	74	48
Graham,J.R.	16	R	26	a/a	NYY	41	5.46	1.78	6.99	4.2	7.8	1.9	0.7	39	69	56
Green,Chad	16	R	25	aaa	NYY	95	2.27	1.20	23.8	2.3	7.9	3.4	0.4	31	82	111
Greene,Conner	15	R	20	aa	TOR	25	5.78	1.61	22.2	4.3	5.0	1.2	0.4	32	62	39
	16	R	21	aa	TOR	69	5.31	1.45	24.5	4.4	5.7	1.3	0.8	28	63	40
Greenwood,Nick	15	L	28	aaa	STL	129	7.00	1.77	18.5	1.8	3.1	1.7	1.2	37	60	3
	16	L	29	a/a	MIN	112	4.75	1.51	23.1	1.2	3.3	2.7	0.9	34	70	38
Gregorio,Joan	15	R	23	aa	SF	79	4.02	1.41	9	4.0	7.0	1.8	0.7	31	72	63
	16	R	24	a/a	SF	134	5.85	1.50	22.3	3.5	8.6	2.5	0.9	35	61	75
Grendell,Kevin	16	L	23	a/a	LAA	20	1.84	1.07	6.96	5.8	9.2	1.6	0.5	17	86	101
Griggs,Scott	16	R	25	aa	LA	34	6.18	1.82	5.04	5.4	4.6	0.9	1.0	32	67	9
Grills,Evan	16	L	24	a/a	HOU	112	4.30	1.31	24.4	1.4	5.4	4.0	1.4	31	72	70
Grimes,Matthew	16	R	25	aa	BAL	58	6.04	1.69	23.6	3.8	4.6	1.2	1.0	33	65	15
Grover,Taylor	16	R	25	aa	BOS	45	6.74	1.85	10	3.5	6.8	2.0	1.1	39	64	35
Grullon,Juan	15	L	25	aa	TEX	40	6.68	1.68	7.13	4.0	6.0	1.5	2.3	31	66	-8
	16	L	26	a/a	TEX	61	5.55	1.67	8.61	4.5	7.1	1.6	1.2	34	69	34
Gsellman,Robert	16	R	23	a/a	NYM	115	4.06	1.29	23.6	2.3	5.9	2.6	0.7	31	69	70
Guduan,Reymin	15	L	23	aa	HOU	16	13.20	2.52	5.46	10.4	9.1	0.9	1.8	39	45	9
	16	L	24	a/a	HOU	56	4.77	1.67	5.84	5.9	8.6	1.5	0.5	34	71	69
Guerrero,Jordan	16	L	22	aa	CHW	136	5.60	1.66	24.3	5.1	6.4	1.3	1.0	32	67	35
Guerrero,Tayron	16	R	25	aa	MIA	50	6.02	1.59	4.97	4.4	7.4	1.7	0.8	33	61	55
Guerrieri,Taylor	16	R	24	aa	TAM	146	4.55	1.36	21.8	2.9	4.7	1.6	0.7	29	67	42
Guilmet,Preston	15	R	28	aaa	MIL	50	2.60	1.20	5.19	2.8	6.4	2.3	0.2	29	78	86
	16	R	29	aaa	DET	68	4.28	1.67	4.72	2.0	7.6	3.8	0.7	41	75	92
Gunkel,Joe	15	R	24	aa	BAL	123	3.76	1.32	24.2	1.8	5.5	3.0	0.8	32	73	70
	16	R	25	a/a	BAL	161	5.60	1.57	25.3	1.3	4.8	3.8	1.3	36	66	58
Gurka,Jason	15	L	27	a/a	COL	63	4.19	1.57	7.9	3.0	5.6	1.9	0.7	35	74	48
	16	L	28	aaa	COL	21	2.57	1.93	5.63	3.0	9.0	3.0	1.9	43	96	43
Gustave,Jandel	16	R	24	aaa	HOU	57	4.17	1.29	4.99	3.5	7.4	2.1	0.2	31	65	90
Hader,Joshua	16	L	22	a/a	MIL	126	4.07	1.38	21.2	4.1	9.9	2.4	0.5	34	70	102
Haley,Justin	15	R	24	aa	BOS	124	6.61	1.80	21.2	3.9	5.7	1.5	0.6	37	61	38
	16	R	25	a/a	BOS	147	4.44	1.41	23	3.1	6.3	2.0	0.7	32	69	59
Haley,Trey	16	R	26	a/a	PIT	56	7.49	2.06	5.78	7.5	5.3	0.7	0.7	34	62	19
Hall,Brooks	15	R	25	aa	MIL	106	6.43	1.60	18.8	2.8	5.6	2.0	1.3	34	61	27
	16	R	26	a/a	MIL	98	5.79	1.51	12.9	2.6	5.1	2.0	1.3	33	63	29
Hall,Cody	15	R	27	aaa	SF	68	3.82	1.54	6.86	3.6	5.7	1.6	0.3	34	74	56
	16	R	28	aaa	MIA	18	9.60	2.33	5.8	4.2	5.2	1.3	1.1	44	57	-2
Hall,Kris	15	R	24	a/a	OAK	74	3.05	1.72	8.61	7.1	7.6	1.1	0.6	31	83	56
	16	R	25	aa	OAK	34	8.23	2.17	6.29	8.7	5.4	0.6	1.6	32	63	-7
Hansen,Kyle	15	R	24	aa	CHW	67	5.18	1.67	7.03	4.7	5.3	1.1	0.6	33	68	36
	16	R	25	aa	CHW	21	8.59	1.80	6.83	4.9	9.2	1.9	0.5	40	49	72
Hardy,Blaine	16	L	29	aaa	DET	31	2.67	1.09	3.83	1.8	3.9	2.1	0.4	26	76	63
Harper,Bryan	15	L	26	a/a	WAS	46	4.07	1.46	5.14	4.1	5.2	1.3	1.1	28	76	26
	16	L	27	a/a	WAS	45	3.26	1.30	4.67	4.3	6.2	1.5	1.2	24	81	40
Harper,Ryne	15	R	26	a/a	ATL	34	2.54	1.19	5.86	3.2	8.9	2.7	0.3	30	79	111
	16	R	27	aa	SEA	68	3.56	1.40	6.84	3.7	10.2	2.8	0.3	36	74	112
Harrell,Lucas	16	R	31	a/a	DET	62	4.52	2.12	20.3	6.3	4.8	0.8	0.4	38	78	21
Harrison,Jordan	16	L	24	aa	TAM	24	3.13	1.42	4.13	7.2	5.4	0.7	0.0	22	75	67
Hart,Donnie	16	L	26	aa	BAL	46	3.58	1.26	4.73	1.5	7.6	5.2	0.3	35	70	145
Hathaway,Steve	16	L	26	a/a	ARI	45	3.36	1.48	4.72	4.7	6.2	1.3	0.5	30	78	55
Hauschild,Mike	15	R	25	a/a	HOU	138	3.82	1.40	23.3	2.3	6.3	2.8	0.6	34	73	76
	16	R	26	aaa	HOU	140	3.70	1.44	24.8	2.6	6.3	2.4	0.5	34	74	70
Haviland,Shawn	15	R	30	aaa	BOS	114	6.78	1.87	21.4	2.8	4.7	1.7	1.2	38	64	11
	16	R	31	aaa	CLE	42	5.24	1.64	27	2.6	4.5	1.8	1.2	34	70	18
Hawkins,Chandle	16	L	23	aa	STL	24	5.00	1.44	7.3	3.9	5.7	1.5	1.2	29	68	31
Hayes,Drew	16	R	29	aaa	CIN	59	6.50	2.04	7.54	5.2	4.9	0.9	0.7	38	67	14
Haynes,Kyle	15	R	24	a/a	NYY	116	4.94	1.70	15.5	4.1	5.7	1.4	0.8	35	71	35
	16	R	25	a/a	NYY	124	8.08	1.97	25.7	4.3	6.0	1.4	1.6	38	60	3
Head,Louis	15	R	25	aa	CLE	60	5.59	1.71	5.82	5.3	7.3	1.4	0.4	35	65	59
	16	R	26	aa	CLE	68	3.72	1.35	6.27	2.6	6.3	2.4	0.5	32	73	72

PITCHER	yr	t	age	lvl	org	ip	era	whip	bf/g	ctl	dom	cmd	hr/9	h%	s%	bpv
Healy,Tucker	15	R	25	aa	OAK	55	2.13	1.12	4.85	4.1	6.9	1.7	0.0	24	79	93
	16	R	26	aaa	OAK	52	5.16	1.50	5.14	5.1	10.1	2.0	0.6	34	65	89
Hedges,Zach	16	R	24	aa	CHC	47	2.98	1.30	24.4	1.8	5.1	2.9	0.4	32	78	77
Hefner,Jeremy	16	R	30	aaa	STL	98	6.64	1.79	25	4.1	5.8	1.4	1.2	36	64	19
Heller,Ben	16	R	25	a/a	NYY	48	2.57	1.06	3.8	3.1	8.5	2.8	0.6	26	78	107
Hellweg,John	15	R	27	aa	MIL	15	14.61	3.60	19.3	16.2	5.2	0.3	3.9	38	63	-99
	16	R	28	a/a	SD	25	13.38	2.72	13.7	7.5	4.9	0.7	0.9	44	47	-8
Hemmer,Gabe	16	R	26	aa	DET	19	6.72	1.86	6.84	6.8	6.4	0.9	0.0	34	60	57
Hepple,Mike	16	R	26	aa	NYM	20	7.66	2.13	6.19	9.5	6.2	0.7	1.5	30	65	5
Herb,Tyler	16	R	24	aa	SEA	55	6.69	1.76	23.1	4.6	5.8	1.3	0.8	35	61	31
Herget,Kevin	16	R	25	a/a	STL	39	3.84	1.63	4.73	2.9	7.8	2.7	0.2	40	75	88
Hernandez,Carlos	15	L	28	a/a	COL	41	7.30	1.97	24.3	1.8	3.9	2.1	2.8	38	70	-37
	16	L	29	a/a	COL	130	7.79	2.23	23.5	1.6	4.4	2.7	1.1	45	65	19
Hernandez,Jefri	16	R	25	a/a	TEX	32	4.05	1.76	6.17	6.2	7.1	1.1	0.3	34	76	57
Herrera,Ronald	15	R	20	aa	SD	44	4.82	1.46	23.4	2.7	6.6	2.4	0.8	34	67	64
	16	R	21	a/a	NYY	137	5.58	1.54	24.9	2.7	7.7	2.8	1.0	36	64	70
Herron,Tyler	16	R	30	a/a	NYM	64	6.96	2.04	25.8	3.0	5.5	1.8	1.4	41	67	9
Hess,David	16	R	23	aa	BAL	127	6.65	1.79	23.5	2.8	5.0	1.8	1.7	36	66	3
Hessler,Keith	15	L	26	a/a	ARI	44	3.41	1.13	4.27	2.7	7.3	2.7	0.9	26	73	81
	16	L	27	a/a	SD	42	3.84	1.49	5.17	3.4	8.1	2.4	0.2	36	73	90
Heyer,Kurt	15	R	24	a/a	STL	84	4.48	1.55	8.91	2.4	5.0	2.1	0.6	35	71	48
	16	R	25	a/a	STL	94	6.41	1.68	12.5	2.6	5.4	2.1	0.8	37	61	42
Higgins,Tyler	15	R	24	aa	MIA	24	5.24	1.45	5.62	3.2	6.2	2.0	0.7	32	64	55
	16	R	25	aa	MIA	73	4.79	1.41	7.02	2.6	4.4	1.7	0.8	31	67	36
Hildenberger,Trev	16	R	26	aa	MIN	39	0.92	0.84	4.42	1.5	8.0	5.4	0.5	24	95	162
Hill,Cameron	16	R	22	a/a	CLE	17	2.75	1.02	5.94	1.1	5.3	5.0	1.3	25	81	104
Hill,Taylor	15	R	26	aaa	WAS	119	7.35	2.03	26.2	2.4	4.1	1.7	0.8	41	63	14
	16	R	27	aaa	WAS	155	7.08	1.77	26.3	2.7	4.3	1.6	1.4	36	61	3
Hill,Tim	16	L	26	aa	KC	45	4.29	1.61	6.38	3.8	7.5	2.0	1.4	34	78	39
Hinojosa,Dalier	15	R	29	aaa	PHI	55	5.14	1.73	8.63	4.2	6.6	1.6	0.7	36	70	45
	16	R	30	aaa	PHI	24	5.03	2.26	5.61	6.7	6.5	1.0	1.3	39	80	6
Hissong,Travis	16	R	25	aa	NYY	33	4.18	1.29	9.13	2.2	7.2	3.2	1.3	31	72	72
Hoffman,Jeff	16	R	23	aaa	COL	119	5.49	1.60	23.9	3.5	7.2	2.0	1.1	35	67	47
Holder,Jonathan	16	R	23	a/a	NYY	61	2.57	0.83	5.6	1.2	11.9	10.3	0.7	30	72	284
Hollands,Mario	16	L	28	a/a	PHI	37	6.54	2.16	7.03	5.3	5.6	1.1	1.5	39	72	-5
Holmberg,David	15	L	24	aaa	CIN	120	5.75	1.81	26.5	3.3	4.6	1.4	1.5	36	71	-2
	16	L	25	a/a	CHW	169	4.75	1.43	25.6	2.5	4.8	1.9	0.8	32	67	42
Holmes,Brian	15	L	24	aa	HOU	71	5.91	1.76	20.3	4.0	7.6	1.9	1.6	37	70	30
	16	L	25	a/a	HOU	52	4.87	1.51	18.6	2.5	7.7	3.1	1.2	36	70	70
Holmes,Clay	16	R	23	aa	PIT	136	5.13	1.64	23.4	4.2	5.4	1.3	0.7	33	68	36
Honeywell,Brent	16	R	21	aa	TAM	59	2.62	1.18	23.7	2.1	7.2	3.5	0.6	30	80	103
Hoover,J.J.	16	R	29	aaa	CIN	38	5.56	1.80	5.53	3.3	9.2	2.8	0.8	43	69	80
Horstman,Ryan	16	L	24	aa	SEA	24	7.57	2.52	5.5	10.6	8.5	0.8	0.4	41	68	45
House,Austin	15	R	24	aa	COL	52	6.29	2.22	5.07	3.5	5.3	1.5	0.3	45	69	32
	16	R	25	a/a	COL	61	7.43	1.94	6.42	3.6	6.5	1.8	0.9	41	61	34
House,T.J.	15	L	26	aaa	CLE	21	5.32	1.94	25	6.0	4.5	0.8	1.6	32	77	-13
	16	L	27	aaa	CLE	72	5.79	2.30	11.2	6.1	4.7	0.8	1.0	40	76	-4
Houser,Adrian	15	R	22	aa	MIL	70	6.14	1.57	22.1	3.0	6.2	2.1	1.9	33	65	18
	16	R	23	aa	MIL	70	7.59	1.72	24.5	3.2	6.1	1.9	0.9	37	54	41
Howard,Sam	16	L	23	aa	COL	90	6.20	1.99	27.1	3.2	5.1	1.6	1.7	39	72	-4
Hoyt,James	16	R	30	aaa	HOU	55	2.04	1.04	4.34	3.4	11.5	3.4	0.4	29	82	145
Hu,Chih-Wei	16	R	23	a/a	TAM	147	3.46	1.33	24.5	2.4	6.1	2.6	0.5	32	74	74
Huchingson,Chas	15	L	26	a/a	NYM	56	4.68	1.77	5.07	6.4	6.7	1.0	0.3	33	72	52
	16	L	27	aaa	NYM	27	5.92	1.98	5.97	6.7	6.8	1.0	0.6	36	69	38
Hunter,Kyle	15	L	26	aa	SEA	44	3.55	1.42	7.84	4.0	4.7	1.2	0.5	29	75	42
	16	L	27	a/a	SEA	76	5.63	1.72	12	3.9	4.4	1.1	0.8	34	67	18
Hurlbut,David	15	L	26	a/a	MIN	107	4.65	1.69	26.8	3.2	4.0	1.2	0.4	35	71	29
	16	L	27	a/a	MIN	162	5.20	1.79	26.7	1.8	4.3	2.4	0.8	39	71	37
Hursh,Jason	15	R	24	a/a	ATL	97	6.82	1.99	13.8	3.6	5.2	1.4	0.5	41	64	28
	16	R	25	a/a	ATL	73	2.72	1.46	7.27	4.3	5.3	1.2	0.0	31	79	61
Hutchison,Drew	16	R	26	aaa	PIT	138	5.17	1.49	23.8	3.6	6.9	1.9	1.2	31	68	43
Infante,Gregory	15	R	28	a/a	TOR	57	4.85	2.14	5.51	7.3	6.3	0.9	0.7	37	78	25
	16	R	29	a/a	PHI	62	7.74	2.17	7.89	6.2	7.3	1.2	1.6	39	66	8
Irvine,Lucas	16	R	28	a/a	ARI	32	7.52	1.86	21.6	5.0	5.5	1.1	1.4	34	60	6
Jackson,Luke	15	R	24	aaa	TEX	66	5.47	1.67	7.63	5.0	8.8	1.8	0.5	37	66	74
	16	R	25	a/a	TEX	46	4.88	1.84	5.99	7.0	9.1	1.3	1.4	33	77	41
Janas,Stephen	15	R	23	aa	ATL	68	6.22	1.74	24	2.7	3.9	1.4	0.2	37	61	36
	16	R	24	a/a	ATL	85	3.72	1.25	7.87	1.9	5.2	2.8	0.6	30	71	71
Jankowski,Jordan	15	R	26	aaa	HOU	62	3.49	1.55	4.95	4.9	9.1	1.8	0.0	36	75	96
	16	R	27	aaa	HOU	72	4.42	1.34	5.85	4.0	10.4	2.6	0.9	32	68	97
Jannis,Mickey	16	R	29	aa	NYM	121	7.25	1.88	24.7	5.5	4.0	0.7	0.8	33	60	8
Jaye,Myles	15	R	24	aa	CHW	148	4.55	1.51	24.6	3.3	5.4	1.6	0.7	32	70	43
	16	R	25	a/a	DET	162	5.27	1.48	24.9	2.5	5.8	2.3	0.9	34	65	52
Jemiola,Zach	16	R	22	aa	COL	162	6.69	1.79	27.6	2.8	4.0	1.4	1.3	36	63	2
Jenkins,Chad	15	R	28	aaa	TOR	94	4.81	1.81	10.6	3.0	4.6	1.5	0.8	37	74	22
	16	R	29	aaa	TOR	30	8.05	2.64	8.09	6.3	4.9	0.8	0.5	45	67	5
Jenkins,Tyrell	15	R	23	a/a	ATL	138	4.11	1.55	24.2	4.1	5.1	1.2	0.5	31	73	40
	16	R	24	aaa	ATL	84	3.11	1.67	22.1	4.0	5.2	1.3	0.4	34	81	42
Jensen,Chris	15	R	25	aa	OAK	166	5.31	1.61	26.3	3.4	3.9	1.1	0.9	32	68	15
	16	R	26	a/a	OAK	147	6.03	1.52	23.7	3.0	4.8	1.6	1.3	31	62	21
Jensen,Michael	15	R	25	aa	CHC	32	2.75	1.60	6.49	4.8	6.7	1.4	0.0	34	81	70
	16	R	26	aa	CHC	21	10.40	2.26	8.74	7.1	5.3	0.7	1.6	37	53	-13
Jerez,Williams	16	L	24	aa	BOS	65	6.21	1.80	7.51	4.4	7.5	1.7	0.9	38	65	44
Jester,Jason	16	R	25	a/a	SD	56	3.66	1.45	5.12	2.1	9.0	4.3	0.7	39	76	118
Jimenez,Joe	16	R	21	a/a	DET	36	2.77	1.01	3.66	3.1	10.3	3.3	0.3	27	72	140
Jiminian,Johendi	16	R	24	aa	COL	59	3.66	1.71	6.99	4.1	5.8	1.4	1.0	34	81	29
Johnson,Brian	15	L	25	aaa	BOS	96	3.71	1.38	22.4	3.4	6.8	2.0	0.7	31	74	64
	16	L	26	aaa	BOS	77	6.83	1.92	24.3	5.2	5.0	1.0	1.5	34	66	-3

PITCHER	yr	t	age	lvl	org	ip	era	whip	bf/g	ctl	dom	cmd	hr/9	h%	s%	bpv
Johnson,Chase	16	R	24	aa	SF	52	4.44	1.49	9.4	3.4	5.4	1.6	0.4	32	69	53
Johnson,Cole	15	R	27	a/a	MIN	52	4.43	1.72	6.74	3.8	6.3	1.6	0.6	37	74	46
	16	R	28	a/a	ARI	52	5.80	1.54	19	1.7	5.1	3.0	0.9	36	62	57
Johnson,D.J.	15	R	26	aa	MIN	50	5.89	1.82	6.11	4.8	5.7	1.2	0.4	36	66	40
	16	R	27	aa	LAA	69	5.87	2.02	7.13	4.8	7.0	1.5	0.2	42	68	54
Johnson,Erik	15	R	26	aaa	CHW	133	3.30	1.41	24.4	3.3	7.5	2.2	0.5	33	77	79
	16	R	27	aaa	CHW	49	3.80	1.52	26.6	3.6	5.2	1.4	1.6	30	82	11
Johnson,Hobbs	15	L	24	aa	MIL	117	5.47	1.73	21.3	6.8	6.1	0.9	0.6	30	67	41
	16	L	25	aa	MIL	25	9.10	2.48	8.4	8.3	5.5	0.7	1.0	40	62	1
Johnson,Jeff	16	R	26	aaa	CLE	53	4.08	1.59	4.9	4.5	7.4	1.7	0.7	34	75	58
Johnson,Michael	16	L	25	aa	LA	57	5.19	1.86	5.76	3.8	7.4	1.9	1.4	39	75	30
Johnson,Patrick	16	R	28	aa	MIA	128	4.99	1.57	18.2	2.8	5.9	2.1	1.2	34	71	37
Johnson,Pierce	16	R	25	aaa	CHC	63	7.27	1.82	13.3	6.4	8.9	1.4	1.3	34	60	42
Johnson,Stephen	16	R	25	aaa	CIN	75	6.96	1.79	9.84	5.6	6.5	1.2	1.6	32	63	12
Johnson,Steve	15	R	28	aaa	BAL	55	3.90	1.50	7.39	3.4	8.3	2.5	0.6	36	74	83
	16	R	29	aaa	SEA	22	2.42	1.06	7.76	2.5	8.2	3.2	0.4	28	78	116
Jokisch,Eric	15	L	26	aaa	CHC	70	5.32	1.74	22.8	3.2	4.1	1.3	0.8	35	70	15
	16	L	27	a/a	TEX	63	5.52	1.92	11.1	4.0	4.6	1.1	0.9	37	72	11
Jones,Chris	15	L	27	aaa	BAL	150	4.86	1.71	22.7	2.2	4.8	2.2	1.5	36	76	18
	16	L	28	aaa	LAA	118	7.19	1.86	24.1	3.0	4.8	1.6	0.7	39	60	25
Jones,Christian	16	L	25	aa	SF	63	5.52	1.57	5.8	4.5	5.5	1.2	0.3	32	62	50
Jones,Tyler	15	R	26	aa	ATL	44	4.17	1.69	5.08	4.1	8.4	2.1	0.0	39	73	87
	16	R	27	aa	NYY	46	3.51	1.67	6.21	2.7	10.5	3.9	0.3	45	78	125
Jones,Zach	16	R	26	a/a	MIN	33	4.16	1.52	6.22	5.3	9.6	1.8	0.3	34	71	91
Jordan,Taylor	15	R	26	aaa	WAS	104	4.15	1.43	23.2	2.6	4.1	1.6	0.4	32	70	43
	16	R	27	aaa	WAS	16	2.65	1.77	24	3.5	5.3	1.5	0.0	38	83	52
Jorge,Felix	16	R	22	aa	MIN	74	4.96	1.43	28.7	1.4	3.2	2.3	0.9	32	66	33
Jose,Jose	16	L	26	aa	MIA	16	13.28	1.93	5.96	3.1	9.4	3.0	3.0	41	28	12
Jungmann,Taylor	15	R	26	aaa	MIL	59	7.38	1.72	24.5	4.7	6.6	1.4	0.4	36	54	54
	16	R	27	a/a	MIL	106	6.41	1.87	23.7	6.8	6.9	1.0	0.9	33	65	35
Junis,Jakob	16	R	24	a/a	KC	149	5.08	1.42	23.4	2.1	6.9	3.3	1.1	34	66	73
Jurado,Ariel	16	R	20	aa	TEX	44	4.10	1.39	23	2.1	6.3	2.9	0.7	34	71	76
Kaminsky,Rob	16	L	22	aa	CLE	137	4.23	1.40	23.1	3.2	5.1	1.6	0.6	30	70	48
Keel,Jerry	16	L	23	aa	SD	17	8.69	2.16	28.2	4.4	5.1	1.2	1.3	40	59	-2
Kehrt,Jeremy	15	R	30	aa	LA	120	4.87	1.60	24	2.3	5.3	2.3	0.7	36	70	49
	16	R	31	a/a	LA	122	7.93	1.94	23.2	3.0	4.4	1.4	1.0	39	58	9
Keller,Jon	16	R	24	aa	BAL	36	8.45	2.16	7.53	8.2	6.2	0.8	1.3	34	60	9
Kelly,Casey	15	R	26	a/a	SD	96	5.61	1.71	14.5	3.7	5.5	1.5	0.6	36	66	38
	16	R	27	aaa	ATL	74	4.73	1.52	21.4	3.9	4.7	1.2	0.8	30	70	27
Kelly,Joe	15	R	27	aaa	BOS	19	4.35	1.38	19.9	3.4	6.6	1.9	0.6	31	68	64
	16	R	28	aaa	BOS	35	2.69	1.43	8.75	2.0	9.0	4.6	0.4	39	81	133
Kelly,Michael	16	R	24	a/a	SD	99	4.37	1.44	22.3	3.6	7.0	2.0	0.7	32	70	64
Kent,Steve	16	L	27	a/a	ATL	57	5.66	1.92	6.47	3.9	7.8	2.0	1.0	41	71	46
Kiekhefer,Dean	16	L	27	aaa	STL	35	2.48	1.35	4.99	2.2	4.2	1.9	0.5	31	83	48
Kinley,Tyler	16	R	25	a/a	MIA	60	6.27	1.75	6.19	4.9	7.6	1.6	0.6	36	63	54
Kipper,Jordan	16	R	24	aa	LAA	153	4.58	1.48	26.3	2.6	4.3	1.7	0.7	32	69	36
Kirsch,Chris	15	L	24	aa	TAM	55	6.56	1.73	22.9	3.9	6.2	1.6	0.5	37	60	48
	16	L	25	aa	TAM	145	3.98	1.55	25.4	3.7	5.9	1.6	0.5	33	74	50
Kittredge,Andrew	15	R	25	a/a	SEA	75	4.76	1.49	8.99	3.3	6.0	1.8	0.7	33	68	51
	16	R	26	a/a	SEA	72	4.31	1.54	8.48	2.4	8.7	3.6	0.7	39	72	100
Klein,Phil	15	R	26	aaa	TEX	64	3.90	1.42	15	4.2	6.4	1.5	0.3	30	71	65
	16	R	27	aaa	PHI	78	3.15	1.31	14.7	2.5	8.2	3.2	1.1	32	81	84
Kleven,Colin	15	R	24	aa	PHI	26	9.98	1.79	24	3.5	4.5	1.3	0.4	37	39	30
	16	R	25	aa	CHW	17	6.52	1.53	5.68	1.8	8.5	4.8	0.6	40	55	124
Klonowski,Alex	16	R	24	aa	LAA	20	7.26	2.01	19.6	3.8	5.3	1.4	0.0	42	60	44
Knapp,Ricky	16	R	24	a/a	NYM	58	3.85	1.26	26.4	2.5	6.7	2.7	0.3	31	68	90
Knudson,Guido	15	R	26	a/a	DET	60	3.33	1.44	6.36	4.8	6.8	1.4	0.5	29	78	61
	16	R	27	a/a	SEA	47	4.85	1.39	6.34	4.0	6.2	1.6	1.1	28	67	42
Koch,Matt	16	R	26	a/a	ARI	121	5.27	1.61	25.6	1.5	4.4	2.9	0.9	36	68	48
Kohlscheen,Steph	16	R	28	aa	MIL	50	4.09	1.59	4.38	3.9	9.2	2.4	0.8	37	76	78
Kolarek,Adam	15	L	26	aa	NYM	67	5.56	1.51	5.69	4.0	6.7	1.7	0.6	32	62	56
	16	L	27	a/a	TAM	60	4.20	1.53	5.58	5.8	7.5	1.3	0.2	30	70	74
Krehbiel,Joey	16	R	24	aa	ARI	56	3.91	1.41	4.52	4.1	8.8	2.2	0.8	32	74	78
Kubitza,Austin	15	R	24	aa	DET	134	7.34	2.09	24.3	3.4	5.1	1.5	0.5	42	63	27
	16	R	25	aa	DET	20	6.81	2.19	14.3	7.8	3.8	0.5	0.5	35	67	9
Kuchno,John	15	R	24	aa	PIT	68	3.96	1.39	7.13	2.9	3.4	1.2	0.9	28	74	16
	16	R	25	a/a	PIT	84	6.12	1.64	9.9	3.4	3.6	1.1	1.2	32	64	1
Kuhl,Chad	16	R	24	aaa	PIT	84	3.27	1.41	22.1	1.8	5.7	3.1	1.1	33	81	60
Kurcz,Aaron	15	R	25	aaa	OAK	59	4.58	1.84	5.61	5.9	8.4	1.4	0.6	37	75	57
	16	R	26	a/a	OAK	68	3.99	1.22	6	2.4	5.6	2.3	0.6	29	67	69
Lail,Brady	15	R	22	a/a	NYY	143	3.93	1.45	22.7	2.9	4.2	1.5	0.5	31	73	39
	16	R	23	a/a	NYY	124	6.88	1.71	24.4	3.4	4.7	1.4	1.4	34	61	5
Lakind,Jared	16	L	24	aa	PIT	66	3.21	1.32	5.82	3.9	6.7	1.7	0.4	29	76	71
Lamb,John	15	L	25	aaa	CIN	111	3.61	1.41	23.6	3.2	8.1	2.5	0.8	33	77	76
	16	L	26	aaa	CIN	29	7.70	1.93	23.2	3.3	6.7	2.1	0.5	42	57	53
Lamb,Will	15	L	25	a/a	TEX	57	5.55	1.73	5.51	4.4	6.5	1.5	0.5	36	67	47
	16	L	26	aaa	CHW	54	6.92	1.80	6.44	5.1	5.7	1.1	1.8	32	65	-2
Lambson,Mitch	15	L	25	a/a	ATL	57	3.17	1.38	6.01	3.4	7.0	2.0	0.4	32	77	76
	16	L	26	a/a	MIL	15	5.66	1.53	4.35	4.7	7.6	1.6	1.5	30	66	37
Lamet,Dinelson	16	R	24	a/a	SD	85	3.92	1.33	22.1	3.7	9.5	2.6	0.5	33	70	103
Lara,Braulio	15	L	27	a/a	SF	50	7.33	1.99	7.56	3.9	6.5	1.6	0.7	41	61	37
	16	L	28	aaa	SF	28	4.91	1.73	5.04	4.7	6.3	1.3	0.9	34	73	33
Lara,Confesor	15	R	25	aa	DET	42	6.05	1.75	7.44	2.5	3.8	1.5	0.8	37	65	17
	16	R	26	aa	MIN	17	11.10	2.18	7.09	3.9	6.1	1.6	1.2	43	46	11
Lara,Rainy	15	R	24	a/a	NYM	134	4.42	1.44	23.8	2.5	5.5	2.2	1.0	32	71	47
	16	R	25	a/a	NYM	113	5.48	1.56	19.9	3.3	4.7	1.4	1.0	32	66	23
Lawrence,Casey	15	R	28	a/a	TOR	168	6.96	2.00	29.9	2.0	4.1	2.0	0.8	42	64	21
	16	R	29	a/a	TOR	162	6.34	1.80	26.7	2.5	4.6	1.8	1.1	38	65	18

PITCHER	yr	t	age	lvl	org	ip	era	whip	bf/g	ctl	dom	cmd	hr/9	h%	s%	bpv
Lazo,Raudel	15	L	26	aa	MIA	29	2.81	1.48	7.01	2.3	7.6	3.3	0.6	37	83	91
	16	L	27	a/a	MIA	42	3.10	1.50	5.33	2.7	5.7	2.1	0.2	35	78	66
Leathersich,Jack	16	L	26	a/a	CHC	15	2.89	1.56	4.2	6.3	8.6	1.4	0.0	32	79	88
Leclerc,Jose	16	R	23	a/a	TEX	66	3.80	1.34	7.03	5.6	8.8	1.6	0.6	26	72	82
Ledbetter,Ryan	16	R	24	aa	TEX	28	7.72	2.00	7.1	5.4	6.8	1.3	1.9	36	64	-2
Lee,Brett	15	L	25	aa	MIN	96	3.68	1.34	24.9	2.8	3.3	1.2	0.4	29	72	35
	16	L	26	aa	MIL	27	11.66	2.77	6.36	6.3	3.9	0.6	1.4	44	56	-35
Lee,Chris	16	L	24	aa	BAL	51	3.76	1.21	25.9	2.4	2.7	1.2	0.9	25	71	18
Lee,Nick	16	L	25	aa	WAS	50	5.99	2.03	5.39	8.5	7.9	0.9	1.0	33	71	35
Lee,Thomas	15	R	26	a/a	STL	142	3.92	1.35	21.1	2.0	4.2	2.1	0.9	31	73	40
	16	R	27	aaa	STL	56	7.29	2.05	14.4	3.1	4.5	1.4	0.5	42	62	22
Lee,Zach	15	R	24	aaa	LA	113	2.95	1.20	24	1.4	5.4	3.9	0.4	31	76	103
	16	R	25	aaa	SEA	148	6.65	1.70	24.8	2.2	5.5	2.4	1.3	37	62	33
Leiter,Mark	15	R	24	aa	PHI	47	5.52	1.59	25.9	2.1	6.3	2.9	0.7	38	65	69
	16	R	25	aa	PHI	104	4.28	1.36	18.9	2.8	6.9	2.5	1.0	31	71	64
Leone,Dominic	15	R	24	a/a	ARI	37	5.60	1.43	5.83	4.0	7.3	1.8	0.5	31	59	68
	16	R	25	aaa	ARI	35	3.74	1.12	4.18	2.8	7.5	2.7	1.1	26	70	81
Lewicki,Artie	16	R	24	aa	DET	67	4.29	1.38	23.6	1.8	6.0	3.3	0.6	34	69	83
Leyer,Robinson	15	R	22	aa	CHW	38	6.55	1.81	14.8	4.5	6.2	1.4	0.9	36	63	30
	16	R	23	aa	CHW	33	6.84	2.05	6.63	5.9	8.0	1.4	0.3	41	64	56
Light,Pat	16	R	25	aaa	MIN	38	3.41	1.43	5.2	4.9	7.8	1.6	0.3	30	75	78
Liranzo,Jesus	16	R	21	aa	BAL	19	4.05	1.12	6.68	5.7	8.2	1.5	1.8	13	72	53
Littrell,Corey	16	L	24	a/a	STL	67	4.58	1.47	5.42	4.1	7.4	1.8	1.0	31	71	55
Lively,Ben	15	R	23	aa	PHI	144	4.67	1.55	25.1	2.8	6.1	2.2	1.0	35	72	46
	16	R	24	a/a	PHI	171	3.65	1.12	24	2.4	6.3	2.6	0.8	27	69	77
Lloyd,Kyle	16	R	26	aa	SD	130	4.46	1.52	18.8	2.9	5.6	1.9	0.8	34	72	46
Lobstein,Kyle	15	L	26	aaa	DET	18	8.43	2.35	22.8	5.0	5.0	1.0	1.2	42	64	-8
	16	L	27	aaa	BAL	51	6.37	1.89	12.1	3.8	5.6	1.5	0.8	39	66	26
Lockett,Walker	16	R	22	a/a	SD	53	3.13	1.09	22.9	0.7	5.8	9.0	0.7	30	74	204
Lollis,Matt	15	R	25	aa	TAM	64	4.16	1.36	5.66	4.5	7.3	1.6	0.8	28	71	61
	16	R	26	a/a	CHW	56	4.64	1.49	6.56	6.0	7.3	1.2	1.2	26	72	44
Long,Jaron	15	R	24	a/a	NYY	155	5.77	1.80	24.6	1.9	5.1	2.6	0.8	40	68	45
	16	R	25	a/a	WAS	107	4.57	1.59	24.8	2.1	4.8	2.3	1.0	35	73	37
Lopez,Frank	15	L	21	aa	TEX	75	5.62	1.72	21.3	4.0	6.0	1.5	1.1	35	69	26
	16	L	22	aa	TEX	92	6.76	1.80	18.5	3.6	6.4	1.8	1.0	38	62	34
Lopez,Jorge	15	R	22	aa	MIL	143	3.10	1.29	24.6	3.6	7.6	2.1	0.8	29	79	71
	16	R	23	a/a	MIL	125	7.30	1.98	23.9	5.4	6.9	1.3	1.4	37	64	15
Lopez,Reynaldo	16	R	22	a/a	WAS	109	4.31	1.33	23.9	3.1	8.8	2.8	1.2	32	71	79
Lopez,Yoan	16	R	23	aa	ARI	62	7.68	1.89	20.9	5.0	4.4	0.9	1.9	33	62	-20
Lowry,Thaddius	16	R	22	aa	CHW	24	4.78	1.25	24.4	1.6	3.7	2.4	0.0	31	57	72
Lucas,Josh	16	R	26	a/a	STL	60	4.94	1.40	5.65	2.6	8.2	3.2	0.8	35	65	91
Luetge,Lucas	15	L	28	aaa	SEA	49	5.70	1.79	7.79	4.1	5.3	1.3	1.4	35	71	8
	16	L	29	aaa	LAA	56	5.52	1.73	5.28	4.4	7.2	1.6	0.6	37	67	53
Lugo,Seth	16	R	27	aaa	NYM	73	6.50	1.80	16.1	2.4	6.0	2.5	1.1	40	64	40
Lujan,Matt	15	L	27	aa	SF	108	4.50	1.81	24.9	4.1	5.8	1.4	0.5	37	75	38
	16	L	28	aaa	SF	49	5.08	1.84	19	4.7	6.4	1.4	1.4	36	76	16
Lyman,Scott	15	R	25	aa	MIA	79	7.87	2.05	25.7	4.8	4.7	1.0	0.6	39	59	17
	16	R	26	aa	MIA	18	7.22	1.96	7.67	5.8	4.4	0.8	0.0	36	59	33
Maddox,Austin	16	R	25	a/a	BOS	43	5.52	1.44	7.1	4.0	6.7	1.7	1.0	30	62	48
Mader,Michael	16	L	22	aa	ATL	30	3.37	1.33	24.9	2.0	7.1	3.6	0.0	35	72	116
Magill,Matthew	16	R	27	a/a	CIN	52	7.58	2.01	6.61	5.8	8.4	1.5	1.7	39	64	21
Magnifico,Damien	16	R	25	aaa	MIL	62	4.76	1.62	5.29	5.0	7.2	1.4	0.3	34	69	64
Mahle,Greg	16	L	23	aaa	LAA	33	7.71	1.87	5.11	3.0	5.8	1.9	1.6	38	60	10
Mahle,Tyler	16	R	22	aa	CIN	71	7.00	1.69	23	2.9	7.5	2.6	2.3	36	63	22
Malm,Jeff	16	L	26	aa	LA	19	3.88	1.57	5	2.9	6.4	2.2	1.2	35	79	41
Manaea,Sean	15	L	23	aa	OAK	50	2.46	1.34	22.9	3.7	9.3	2.5	0.6	32	84	95
	16	L	24	aaa	OAK	18	2.05	1.34	25	2.2	8.4	3.9	0.6	36	87	114
Mantiply,Joe	16	L	25	a/a	DET	59	3.64	1.29	4.35	2.0	8.1	4.0	0.4	35	71	121
Mapes,Tyler	16	R	25	aa	WAS	155	4.43	1.54	27	2.5	3.6	1.4	0.7	33	72	23
Marin,Terance	15	R	26	aaa	CHW	77	4.08	1.48	17.4	2.4	4.1	1.7	0.7	33	73	36
	16	R	27	aaa	CHW	110	6.04	1.70	19.1	3.2	3.9	1.2	1.3	33	66	0
Mariot,Michael	15	R	27	aaa	KC	62	3.15	1.35	6.16	2.6	7.8	3.0	0.5	34	77	95
	16	R	28	a/a	PHI	36	3.67	1.27	5.13	4.1	5.5	1.3	1.5	23	78	26
Markel,Parker	15	R	25	a/a	TAM	60	4.17	1.71	5.82	4.8	5.7	1.2	0.8	33	77	32
	16	R	26	a/a	TAM	71	3.64	1.63	7.38	3.6	6.0	1.7	0.1	36	76	61
Markey,Brad	16	R	24	aa	CHC	131	3.82	1.51	21.7	3.2	3.8	1.2	1.0	30	78	13
Marks,Justin	15	L	27	aaa	ARI	109	6.05	1.71	17.6	4.0	5.4	1.3	1.0	34	65	23
	16	L	28	aaa	TAM	140	5.49	1.62	24.8	3.9	6.4	1.6	1.1	33	68	34
Marksberry,Matt	16	L	26	a/a	ATL	43	3.27	1.57	5.51	4.1	6.9	1.7	0.5	34	80	59
Maronde,Nick	15	L	26	a/a	CLE	92	6.57	1.95	12.5	3.5	7.4	2.1	1.2	42	67	35
	16	L	27	a/a	CLE	48	4.60	1.67	5.67	3.0	5.5	1.9	0.8	36	73	40
Marquez,German	16	R	21	a/a	COL	167	4.42	1.38	26.9	2.2	6.6	3.0	1.1	33	71	68
Marshall,Brett	15	R	25	aa	COL	42	8.41	1.77	27.3	3.5	5.2	1.5	1.1	36	51	20
	16	R	26	aa	TAM	20	10.41	2.65	7.18	8.3	4.9	0.6	0.5	42	58	5
Marshall,Evan	15	R	25	aaa	ARI	32	6.58	1.95	4.98	3.4	5.6	1.7	0.3	41	64	44
	16	R	26	aaa	ARI	33	5.25	1.73	4.6	4.3	6.0	1.4	0.3	36	68	50
Marte,Kelvin	16	L	29	aaa	PIT	74	5.65	1.57	9.5	3.1	5.0	1.6	0.6	34	63	39
Martes,Francis	16	R	21	aa	HOU	125	3.72	1.27	20.5	3.2	8.5	2.6	0.3	32	69	102
Martin,Cody	15	R	26	aaa	OAK	94	5.12	1.54	22.9	4.2	6.8	1.6	0.8	32	67	49
	16	R	27	aaa	SEA	114	4.10	1.36	19.1	2.6	7.3	2.8	0.5	34	69	88
Martin,Josh	16	R	27	aaa	CLE	66	4.96	1.54	6.12	3.6	6.2	1.7	0.7	33	68	49
Martin,Kyle	15	R	24	aa	BOS	42	5.77	1.63	6.93	3.6	8.4	2.3	0.7	38	64	73
	16	R	25	aaa	BOS	67	5.51	1.57	8.13	3.4	8.5	2.5	0.9	37	65	72
Martinez,David	15	R	28	a/a	TEX	67	4.30	1.66	6.15	3.9	4.9	1.3	0.8	33	75	26
	16	R	29	a/a	DET	94	8.69	2.18	15.1	2.7	5.1	1.9	1.7	43	61	-7
Martinez,Nicholas	15	R	25	aaa	TEX	31	3.73	1.50	22.3	2.2	4.2	1.9	0.3	34	74	49
	16	R	26	a/a	TEX	105	5.21	1.55	24.2	1.8	4.9	2.8	0.8	36	67	53
Martinez,Rodolfo	16	R	22	aa	SF	23	8.67	2.19	4.61	6.2	5.9	0.9	0.4	40	57	29

PITCHER	yr	t	age	lvl	org	ip	era	whip	bf/g	ctl	dom	cmd	hr/9	h%	s%	bpv
Mateo,Luis	16	R	26	a/a	NYM	67	2.91	1.44	5.6	2.7	5.7	2.1	0.4	33	80	64
Mateo,Victor	15	R	26	a/a	ATL	148	4.69	1.63	24.3	3.7	4.0	1.1	0.6	33	71	23
	16	R	27	a/a	ATL	51	9.67	2.58	12.5	5.8	4.5	0.8	1.5	43	62	-30
Mayers,Mike	16	R	25	a/a	STL	144	3.83	1.44	24.5	3.1	6.8	2.2	0.8	33	75	62
Mayza,Tim	16	L	24	aa	TOR	15	5.47	2.32	5.63	9.4	6.5	0.7	0.0	38	74	46
Mazza,Chris	16	R	27	aa	MIA	80	6.03	1.69	19	3.7	4.4	1.2	1.0	33	65	13
McAvoy,Kevin	16	R	23	aa	BOS	116	7.50	1.75	24.2	4.2	5.2	1.2	0.8	35	55	24
McCarthy,Kevin	16	R	24	a/a	KC	68	3.65	1.30	5.96	3.2	6.3	1.9	1.0	28	75	54
McCarthy,Mike	15	R	28	a/a	BOS	122	7.10	1.83	18.9	3.9	3.4	0.9	1.1	34	61	-6
	16	R	29	a/a	BOS	40	8.65	2.33	16	4.4	2.0	0.4	1.5	39	63	-48
McCormick,Phil	15	L	27	aa	SF	57	2.89	1.75	4.52	3.9	4.7	1.2	0.0	36	82	45
	16	L	28	a/a	SF	31	4.69	1.93	5.72	4.0	4.0	1.0	0.6	37	76	13
McCoy,Patrick	15	L	27	a/a	BAL	69	6.19	1.98	8.12	3.6	5.1	1.4	1.0	40	69	13
	16	L	28	aaa	COL	44	8.40	2.37	5.85	6.8	5.1	0.8	0.9	40	63	1
McCurry,Brendan	15	R	23	aa	OAK	17	1.69	0.93	4.46	3.1	11.6	3.7	0.5	26	85	155
	16	R	24	a/a	HOU	82	3.51	1.29	6.02	2.3	8.8	3.9	0.7	34	75	113
McFarland,T.J.	15	L	26	aaa	BAL	53	4.70	1.42	14	2.9	4.2	1.4	0.0	32	63	54
	16	L	27	a/a	BAL	29	6.25	1.94	14	2.5	3.3	1.3	1.8	37	72	-26
McGough,Scott	15	R	26	a/a	MIA	30	3.18	1.49	5.69	4.9	3.7	0.8	0.6	27	80	24
	16	R	27	a/a	BAL	76	7.78	2.02	8.51	3.5	5.3	1.5	1.4	40	62	3
McGowan,Kevin	16	R	25	a/a	NYM	51	3.53	1.42	8.05	3.1	7.3	2.4	0.5	34	75	77
McGowin,Kyle	15	R	24	aa	LAA	154	5.58	1.46	24.4	2.9	6.2	2.1	1.0	33	62	49
	16	R	25	a/a	LAA	142	6.96	1.76	24.1	3.5	6.9	1.9	1.3	37	61	33
McGrath,Kyle	16	L	24	a/a	SD	50	1.40	0.91	5.53	1.6	8.0	5.0	0.8	25	91	144
McGuire,Deck	15	R	26	a/a	LA	137	4.53	1.39	19.2	2.4	6.4	2.7	0.9	33	68	67
	16	R	27	a/a	STL	141	6.08	1.59	23	3.7	6.2	1.7	1.5	32	64	22
McKinney,Brett	15	R	25	aa	PIT	30	8.78	2.07	6.12	4.0	7.2	1.8	1.4	42	57	22
	16	R	26	aa	PIT	67	5.04	1.66	6.82	3.8	6.7	1.7	0.4	36	68	58
McMyne,Kyle	15	R	26	aa	CIN	62	3.79	1.79	5.47	5.4	3.7	0.7	0.4	32	79	18
	16	R	27	aa	CIN	57	8.51	2.14	6.12	3.8	4.8	1.3	0.8	42	58	11
McRae,Alex	16	R	23	aa	PIT	88	5.82	1.77	25.4	2.5	5.5	2.2	0.7	39	67	44
Means,John	16	L	23	aa	BAL	96	5.80	1.64	23.8	2.4	4.0	1.7	0.8	35	64	24
Medina,Jhondani(	15	R	22	aa	PIT	62	3.04	1.28	5.65	4.9	5.3	1.1	0.2	24	75	61
	16	R	23	a/a	PIT	70	4.46	1.48	6.5	5.0	7.3	1.5	0.8	29	71	56
Mejia,Adalberto	16	L	23	a/a	MIN	132	3.90	1.30	24.7	2.1	7.0	3.4	0.9	32	72	84
Mejia,Miguel	16	R	28	a/a	CHC	61	6.50	1.76	7.32	3.0	6.9	2.3	0.7	40	62	55
Melotakis,Mason	16	L	25	aa	MIN	33	3.81	1.68	4.17	3.3	8.8	2.6	0.9	40	80	73
Mendez,Gilberto	15	R	23	aa	WAS	61	4.86	1.58	6.1	2.6	6.3	2.5	0.8	36	70	58
	16	R	24	aa	WAS	27	9.62	2.15	10.2	5.6	6.6	1.2	2.3	38	57	-20
Mendez,Roman	15	R	25	aaa	TEX	36	3.57	1.36	4.97	2.4	6.7	2.7	1.5	31	81	52
	16	R	26	aaa	BOS	64	5.63	1.59	8.82	4.6	6.6	1.4	1.2	31	66	34
Mendez,Yohande	16	L	21	a/a	TEX	78	2.55	1.15	18.2	3.6	6.7	1.9	0.3	26	77	85
Mendoza,Francis(	15	R	28	a/a	TEX	67	2.90	1.70	6.85	4.7	5.5	1.2	0.0	35	81	53
	16	R	29	aaa	TEX	54	8.70	1.89	6.02	3.6	5.7	1.6	0.8	39	51	28
Mengden,Daniel	16	R	23	a/a	OAK	98	1.81	1.12	22.8	2.7	7.1	2.6	0.4	28	85	97
Mercedes,Simon	15	R	23	aa	BOS	79	6.13	1.76	9.82	4.5	6.0	1.3	1.0	35	65	28
	16	R	24	aa	BOS	23	10.85	2.57	8.26	8.3	6.5	0.8	1.7	41	57	-15
Merritt,Ryan	16	L	24	aaa	CLE	143	5.05	1.52	25.9	1.5	4.6	3.0	1.2	35	69	46
Merryweather,Juli	16	R	25	aa	CLE	74	5.33	1.52	24.7	2.2	5.8	2.6	0.9	35	65	55
Meyer,Alex	15	R	25	aaa	MIN	92	6.76	1.97	11.6	5.2	7.7	1.5	0.5	41	64	52
	16	R	26	aaa	LAA	21	0.90	0.86	19.6	1.6	8.6	5.3	0.0	27	88	179
Middleton,Keynar	16	R	23	a/a	LAA	30	3.47	1.21	5.69	2.4	8.5	3.6	0.6	32	72	113
Miller,Adam	15	R	26	aa	ARI	56	4.02	1.91	5.33	4.9	8.0	1.6	0.0	41	77	72
	16	R	27	aa	ARI	24	6.73	2.22	5.83	6.5	6.9	1.1	0.5	41	68	34
Miller,Jared	16	L	23	a/a	ARI	33	5.01	1.27	5.57	4.1	9.1	2.2	0.9	28	61	83
Mills,Alec	16	R	25	a/a	KC	126	4.13	1.41	22.1	2.3	6.9	3.0	0.8	34	72	78
Milner,Hoby	15	L	24	aa	PHI	61	4.25	1.42	8.92	2.5	5.1	2.0	1.0	31	73	39
	16	L	25	a/a	PHI	65	3.45	1.36	5.55	2.3	8.9	3.8	1.0	35	78	103
Minaya,Juan	16	R	26	aaa	CHW	52	4.60	1.56	6.7	4.0	6.7	1.7	0.6	34	70	55
Minnis,Albert	16	L	25	a/a	HOU	37	4.86	1.57	7.67	4.2	4.5	1.1	1.1	30	71	14
Minter,A.J.	16	L	23	aa	ATL	19	3.46	1.24	4.21	3.2	13.3	4.1	0.0	39	69	173
Miranda,Ariel	16	L	27	aaa	BAL	101	6.22	1.67	23.8	3.3	5.9	1.8	1.6	34	65	18
Mitchell,Bryan	15	R	24	aaa	NYY	75	4.18	1.57	22	4.9	6.2	1.3	0.2	32	71	60
	16	R	25	a/a	NYY	16	4.37	1.55	17.1	3.4	9.5	2.8	0.9	38	74	85
Mitchell,Evan	16	R	24	aa	CIN	47	4.11	1.44	6.03	3.4	5.4	1.6	0.6	31	72	48
Mizenko,Tyler	15	R	25	aa	SF	50	2.69	1.57	5.93	2.6	4.1	1.6	0.4	34	83	39
	16	R	26	aa	SF	54	6.10	1.98	5.11	4.8	5.5	1.2	1.3	37	71	7
Molina,Jose	16	L	25	aa	LAA	62	7.75	2.01	11.9	3.7	5.9	1.6	0.9	41	60	25
Molina,Nestor	16	R	27	aa	SF	18	4.27	1.34	19.1	1.7	5.1	2.9	1.1	31	71	56
Moll,Sam	16	L	24	aaa	COL	47	6.90	1.89	5.31	3.9	5.6	1.4	1.3	37	64	11
Molleken,Dustin	16	R	32	aaa	DET	60	5.61	1.78	6.6	5.7	5.8	1.0	0.8	33	69	29
Monegro,Jose	15	R	26	a/a	TEX	18	8.34	1.66	6.2	3.3	5.5	1.7	1.2	35	48	25
	16	R	27	a/a	TEX	33	10.81	2.29	13.1	5.7	5.1	0.9	2.3	38	54	-40
Montas,Frankie	15	R	22	aa	CHW	112	3.95	1.43	20.7	4.3	7.6	1.8	0.3	32	71	78
	16	R	23	a/a	LA	16	2.76	1.19	9.17	1.6	10.6	6.7	0.7	36	79	186
Montero,Rafael	16	R	26	a/a	NYM	129	5.75	1.73	23.5	4.1	6.1	1.5	1.1	35	68	27
Montgomery,Jord:	16	L	24	a/a	NYY	139	3.17	1.50	24.1	3.3	7.3	2.2	0.5	35	79	73
Montgomery,Mark	15	R	25	a/a	NYY	51	3.70	1.20	4.43	3.4	7.8	2.3	0.5	28	69	90
	16	R	26	a/a	NYY	46	3.98	1.49	5.97	5.2	10.1	1.9	0.6	33	74	88
Moore,Andrew	16	R	22	aa	SEA	108	4.02	1.38	23.9	1.5	6.4	4.3	0.8	35	72	99
Morales,Andrew	15	R	22	aa	STL	130	5.19	1.70	22.6	2.9	5.0	1.7	1.1	36	71	23
	16	R	23	aa	STL	78	4.06	1.29	22.9	2.1	6.8	3.2	1.2	31	73	71
Morgan,Adam	15	L	25	aaa	PHI	68	5.93	1.84	24.5	3.8	3.7	1.0	1.2	35	69	-5
	16	L	26	aaa	PHI	50	4.77	1.40	26.5	2.1	7.5	3.5	1.1	34	68	81
Morimando,Shawı	16	L	24	a/a	CLE	152	4.40	1.54	24.6	3.6	5.7	1.6	0.7	33	72	42
Morris,AJ	16	R	30	aaa	CIN	39	6.32	2.06	10.5	3.3	5.8	1.8	1.9	41	73	-5
Morris,Akeel	15	R	23	aa	NYM	29	2.89	1.17	5.09	4.6	9.4	2.0	0.3	26	75	106
	16	R	24	aa	ATL	61	4.75	1.66	5.82	6.3	11.0	1.8	0.7	36	72	85

PITCHER	yr	t	age	lvl	org	ip	era	whip	bf/g	ctl	dom	cmd	hr/9	h%	s%	bpv
Morrow,Bryce	15	R	27	a/a	SD	75	5.07	1.61	17.6	2.9	4.9	1.7	0.7	35	68	36
	16	R	28	aa	SD	50	8.36	2.14	27.5	4.6	4.0	0.9	1.5	38	61	-20
Mortensen,Jared	15	R	27	a/a	TAM	127	4.67	1.47	21	2.9	6.1	2.1	1.1	32	70	45
	16	R	28	aa	TAM	72	6.90	1.81	9.85	7.9	8.4	1.1	1.0	30	61	47
Moscot,Jon	15	R	24	aaa	CIN	54	4.17	1.50	26.1	3.4	4.9	1.4	1.2	30	76	21
	16	R	25	aaa	CIN	50	7.59	1.88	25.9	3.4	4.8	1.4	2.4	35	64	-28
Moskos,Daniel	16	L	30	aaa	SD	61	3.80	1.77	5.28	3.4	5.3	1.5	0.3	38	78	44
Muhammad,ElHaj	16	R	25	a/a	CIN	51	6.08	1.87	7.03	4.8	5.6	1.2	1.1	36	68	17
Mullee,Conor	16	R	28	a/a	NYY	38	1.94	1.23	5.86	3.3	8.7	2.7	0.8	29	89	92
Munson,Kevin	15	R	26	a/a	ARI	35	4.89	1.56	4.84	6.5	6.9	1.1	1.2	26	71	37
	16	R	27	aaa	SEA	26	5.03	1.79	6.39	5.7	7.7	1.3	0.3	36	70	61
Murata,Toru	15	R	30	aaa	CLE	164	4.33	1.56	26.7	2.9	4.1	1.4	1.2	32	76	13
	16	R	31	aaa	CLE	102	5.83	1.67	13.9	2.5	3.9	1.5	0.9	35	65	18
Murray,Colton	15	R	25	a/a	PHI	78	3.23	1.26	6.09	3.8	7.5	2.0	0.4	28	74	83
	16	R	26	aaa	PHI	37	4.62	1.64	6.05	4.4	7.3	1.7	0.8	35	73	52
Musgrave,Harriso	15	L	23	aa	COL	57	4.75	1.50	22.3	2.3	6.8	3.0	1.7	34	74	46
	16	L	24	a/a	COL	153	5.32	1.51	26.6	3.2	4.8	1.5	1.6	30	69	11
Musgrove,Joe	16	R	24	a/a	HOU	85	3.13	1.16	21.3	1.0	7.8	7.5	1.1	32	78	173
Naile,James	16	R	23	a/a	OAK	28	6.36	1.58	24.7	2.6	4.0	1.5	0.7	34	58	28
Nappo,Gregory	15	L	27	a/a	MIA	65	3.41	1.28	6.19	2.8	7.2	2.6	0.7	30	75	79
	16	L	28	aaa	MIA	68	6.84	1.94	12.5	5.2	5.9	1.1	1.5	36	67	4
Neal,Zachary	15	R	27	a/a	OAK	168	5.68	1.62	26.6	2.0	4.1	2.0	0.9	35	65	27
	16	R	28	aaa	OAK	62	4.79	1.51	24.3	1.4	3.4	2.5	0.9	34	69	36
Nesbitt,Angel	15	R	25	aaa	DET	40	7.78	2.16	7.43	5.0	5.2	1.0	0.8	40	62	12
	16	R	26	a/a	DET	44	6.97	2.17	5.63	3.7	5.7	1.5	0.7	43	67	22
Neverauskas,Dov	16	R	23	a/a	PIT	58	3.97	1.37	5.17	3.5	7.1	2.0	0.2	32	69	83
Newcomb,Sean	15	L	22	aa	LAA	36	3.36	1.34	21.4	5.7	8.6	1.5	0.5	26	75	83
	16	L	23	aa	ATL	140	5.53	1.58	22.8	5.1	8.7	1.7	0.3	35	63	80
Nicolino,Justin	15	L	24	aaa	MIA	115	4.64	1.69	25.9	2.4	4.0	1.7	0.9	36	74	21
	16	L	25	aaa	MIA	85	5.71	1.46	26	1.5	4.1	2.7	1.1	33	62	39
Nielsen,Trey	16	R	25	a/a	STL	127	4.50	1.57	23.3	3.1	5.1	1.6	1.0	33	74	29
Nina,Aroni	15	R	25	aa	KC	51	6.48	2.06	5.75	8.5	6.9	0.8	0.4	34	66	45
	16	R	26	a/a	KC	36	3.60	1.65	6.19	5.8	7.5	1.3	0.0	33	76	75
Norris,Daniel	15	L	22	aaa	TOR	91	6.06	1.80	26.2	4.4	7.0	1.6	0.7	38	65	46
	16	L	23	a/a	DET	80	5.76	1.65	23.8	3.7	7.6	2.0	0.5	37	63	67
Northcraft,Aaron	15	R	25	a/a	SD	83	4.39	1.54	9.33	4.2	5.3	1.3	0.6	31	71	40
	16	R	26	a/a	SD	91	4.76	1.56	14.2	3.1	6.0	1.9	1.0	34	71	42
Nuding,Zach	15	R	25	aa	CLE	41	4.60	1.44	7.22	4.0	4.8	1.2	0.8	28	69	31
	16	R	26	a/a	LAA	106	6.33	1.80	18.1	3.6	4.8	1.3	1.2	36	66	8
Nunez,Miguel	16	R	24	aa	PHI	46	3.84	1.65	4.6	5.7	8.4	1.5	0.5	34	77	69
O Grady,Chris	16	L	26	a/a	LAA	96	4.01	1.55	11.3	2.1	5.7	2.7	0.6	36	74	64
O Rourke,Ryan	15	L	27	a/a	MIN	15	7.27	1.78	3.14	4.6	11.3	2.4	0.7	43	57	91
	16	L	28	aaa	MIN	28	2.97	1.52	3.69	2.2	6.8	3.0	0.4	37	81	84
Oaks,Trevor	16	R	23	a/a	LA	126	3.16	1.24	25.6	1.2	5.3	4.4	0.7	32	76	102
Oberg,Scott	16	R	26	aaa	COL	30	3.53	1.12	4.33	3.8	7.9	2.1	0.4	25	68	93
Ogando,Nefi	15	R	26	a/a	PHI	63	3.54	1.52	6.08	4.8	6.5	1.4	0.5	31	77	54
	16	R	27	aaa	MIA	24	4.81	1.50	4.78	4.7	5.4	1.1	0.8	28	69	35
Okert,Steven	16	L	25	aaa	SF	47	4.48	1.52	5.01	2.2	9.4	4.4	0.3	41	69	131
Oliver,Andrew	15	L	28	aaa	BAL	57	6.41	1.98	6.67	8.0	7.8	1.0	1.1	33	68	35
	16	L	29	aaa	BAL	87	5.67	1.93	14.7	4.7	6.3	1.4	1.0	38	72	24
Olmos,Edgar	15	L	25	aaa	SEA	33	3.55	1.40	6.96	3.2	7.8	2.4	0.0	35	72	98
	16	L	26	aaa	BAL	69	4.46	1.71	7.41	4.3	7.8	1.8	0.8	37	75	54
Olson,Tyler	15	L	26	aaa	SEA	54	4.58	1.52	9.43	2.6	7.2	2.7	1.1	35	72	63
	16	L	27	aaa	CLE	44	7.39	1.99	8.53	3.7	5.1	1.4	1.1	39	63	9
Omahen,John	15	R	26	aa	ARI	78	3.89	1.64	26.6	3.4	4.3	1.3	0.0	35	74	46
	16	R	27	a/a	ARI	127	7.48	1.95	23.3	3.5	4.2	1.2	1.2	38	62	-2
Ortega,Jorge	16	R	23	a/a	MIL	97	7.22	1.63	24	1.6	4.2	2.7	1.2	36	55	32
Ortiz,Luis	16	R	21	aa	MIL	63	4.61	1.71	19	2.7	6.2	2.3	0.9	38	75	47
Overton,Dillon	16	L	25	aaa	OAK	126	4.60	1.60	26.5	2.5	5.9	2.4	0.5	37	71	62
Owens,Henry	15	L	23	aaa	BOS	122	4.44	1.36	24.3	4.5	6.3	1.4	0.6	27	67	58
	16	L	24	aaa	BOS	138	5.65	1.73	26.1	6.2	7.3	1.2	1.1	31	69	35
Paez,Paul	16	L	24	aa	NYM	20	10.66	2.05	6.84	3.2	10.4	3.2	2.0	47	47	52
Pagan,Emilio	16	R	25	a/a	SEA	65	3.00	1.30	6.52	4.0	9.8	2.5	1.0	30	81	88
Paniagua,Juan	15	R	25	aa	CHC	20	9.04	2.21	8.99	7.4	5.3	0.7	1.5	35	59	-10
	16	R	26	aa	CHC	65	5.07	1.57	6.93	5.9	7.0	1.2	0.8	29	68	48
Paredes,Eduardo	16	R	21	aa	LAA	48	4.36	1.42	5.85	2.7	7.2	2.7	1.2	33	73	61
Paredes,Edward	16	L	30	aa	LAA	44	3.50	1.38	3.99	5.3	8.3	1.6	0.5	28	75	77
Parker,Blake	16	R	31	aaa	SEA	40	3.26	1.04	4.03	2.6	9.7	3.7	1.0	27	73	120
Parks,Adam	16	R	24	aa	TEX	19	2.48	0.74	4.05	1.6	11.3	7.3	1.7	20	84	192
Partch,Curtis	15	R	28	aaa	SF	64	4.15	1.54	5.79	3.9	8.8	2.3	0.4	37	72	88
	16	R	29	aaa	PIT	60	3.45	1.54	6.26	5.3	6.4	1.2	0.2	30	76	62
Pasquale,Nick	16	R	26	a/a	CLE	77	5.44	1.75	25.2	4.5	5.0	1.1	0.6	34	68	28
Patton,Spencer	15	R	27	aaa	TEX	27	2.24	1.36	4.34	3.4	9.2	2.7	0.4	34	85	104
	16	R	28	aaa	CHC	36	0.95	1.19	4.12	4.2	11.4	2.7	0.0	32	91	140
Paulino,David	16	R	22	a/a	HOU	78	2.40	1.09	17.9	1.9	9.4	5.1	0.5	32	79	155
Payano,Victor	15	L	23	aa	TEX	93	5.95	1.81	14.8	6.3	6.3	1.0	1.4	31	69	16
	16	L	24	a/a	TEX	128	5.66	1.68	23	4.6	6.6	1.4	1.3	33	68	27
Pazos,James	15	L	24	a/a	NYY	43	1.72	1.23	6.4	3.5	8.7	2.5	0.3	30	87	105
	16	L	25	aaa	NYY	27	3.94	1.71	5.39	7.2	11.2	1.5	0.5	35	77	90
Pearce,Matt	16	R	22	a/a	STL	27	7.52	1.75	24.7	3.6	6.7	1.8	1.6	36	58	20
Pena,Ariel	15	R	26	aaa	MIL	83	4.79	1.50	8.3	3.7	7.3	2.0	1.0	33	69	56
	16	R	27	aaa	MIL	38	10.23	2.56	12.7	8.3	6.5	0.8	1.9	41	61	-20
Pena,Felix	16	R	26	aaa	CHC	63	4.13	1.25	7.16	3.5	9.3	2.7	0.7	31	67	101
Pena,Richelson	16	R	23	a/a	TEX	61	6.36	1.76	12.7	4.1	6.7	1.6	1.7	35	67	16
Peoples,Michael	16	R	25	a/a	CLE	165	5.05	1.66	26.4	3.2	3.7	1.2	0.5	34	68	24
Perakslis,Stepher	15	R	24	aa	CHC	21	5.10	1.38	6.4	3.5	5.7	1.6	0.9	29	64	44
	16	R	25	a/a	CHC	75	4.34	1.41	9.92	2.4	5.8	2.4	1.1	32	72	49

PITCHER	yr	t	age	lvl	org	ip	era	whip	bf/g	ctl	dom	cmd	hr/9	h%	s%	bpv
Peralta,Starling	16	R	26	a/a	CHC	71	5.03	1.58	8.41	3.8	3.7	1.0	0.6	31	68	21
Peralta,Wandy	16	L	25	a/a	CIN	76	3.74	1.46	6.48	3.7	5.9	1.6	0.5	32	75	54
Perez,David	16	R	24	aa	TEX	54	6.45	1.86	9.03	5.8	6.9	1.2	1.0	35	65	31
Perez,Williams	15	R	24	aaa	ATL	39	1.55	1.29	19.9	2.5	7.3	2.9	0.3	33	89	99
	16	R	25	aaa	ATL	24	3.32	1.06	23.6	2.8	7.6	2.7	0.8	25	71	90
Perry,Chris	15	R	25	aa	STL	28	6.75	1.71	7.04	5.6	6.1	1.1	0.3	33	57	50
	16	R	26	aa	STL	53	4.36	1.61	6.38	7.4	8.4	1.1	0.4	28	72	75
Peters,Dillon	16	L	24	aa	MIA	23	2.70	1.12	22.3	1.7	5.2	3.0	0.8	27	80	74
Peterson,Brandor	15	R	24	aa	MIN	29	3.92	1.61	6.49	3.9	8.1	2.1	0.3	37	74	79
	16	R	25	aa	MIN	26	5.33	1.53	7.06	5.3	8.4	1.6	0.4	32	63	77
Peterson,David	15	R	25	a/a	ATL	29	2.50	1.41	5.34	2.7	4.5	1.7	0.7	31	85	38
	16	R	26	a/a	ATL	52	8.06	2.16	6.17	4.8	6.2	1.3	0.6	42	61	27
Peterson,Eric	16	R	23	aa	HOU	54	4.28	1.26	8.11	1.5	8.0	5.4	0.8	34	67	137
Peterson,Mark	15	R	25	aa	KC	73	3.55	1.56	8.24	3.4	4.2	1.2	0.9	31	80	19
	16	R	26	a/a	KC	60	4.94	1.61	6.3	3.8	6.3	1.6	1.3	33	73	28
Peterson,Stephen	16	L	29	a/a	MIL	62	4.60	1.75	4.89	5.1	5.7	1.1	0.0	35	71	54
Peterson,Tim	16	R	25	aa	NYM	44	4.87	1.58	5.37	3.0	9.0	3.0	0.9	39	70	84
Phillips,Evan	16	R	22	aa	ATL	34	6.26	1.70	7.05	4.6	10.2	2.2	0.6	40	62	85
Pierpont,Matt	16	R	25	aa	COL	67	4.77	1.60	7.63	3.6	7.1	2.0	1.1	35	72	47
Pill,Tyler	15	R	25	a/a	NYM	118	6.47	1.69	22.2	3.5	4.7	1.3	1.2	34	62	12
	16	R	26	a/a	NYM	166	4.64	1.46	26.3	2.2	5.8	2.7	0.7	34	68	65
Pimentel,Carlos	15	R	26	aaa	CHC	143	3.59	1.52	23	4.6	6.0	1.3	0.8	30	78	41
	16	R	27	aaa	SD	145	5.97	1.77	23.8	3.8	6.1	1.6	1.1	36	67	29
Pimentel,Stolmy	15	R	25	aaa	TEX	72	6.94	1.95	20.1	4.5	6.1	1.4	1.3	38	65	12
	16	R	26	aaa	NYM	31	10.22	2.38	11.5	4.9	6.8	1.4	0.8	46	54	23
Pineyro,Ivan	15	R	24	a/a	MIA	146	4.59	1.43	23.9	2.7	5.9	2.2	0.5	33	67	65
	16	R	25	a/a	MIA	25	10.33	2.11	15.6	5.5	4.0	0.7	0.8	37	47	2
Pinto,Ricardo	16	R	22	aa	PHI	156	4.86	1.42	24.5	2.9	5.2	1.8	1.4	29	69	26
Pivetta,Nick	16	R	23	a/a	PHI	149	4.35	1.41	23.3	3.3	7.4	2.2	1.0	32	71	62
Plutko,Adam	16	R	25	a/a	CLE	162	5.15	1.48	24.8	2.8	5.7	2.1	0.9	33	66	46
Polanco,Andersor	16	L	24	aa	CLE	22	10.81	2.25	18.9	5.9	6.8	1.1	1.0	42	49	17
Poncedeleon,Dan	16	R	24	aa	STL	151	4.35	1.39	23.5	3.5	6.3	1.8	0.6	30	69	59
Pounders,Brooks	16	R	26	aaa	KC	80	3.81	1.47	11.1	4.2	7.8	1.8	0.6	32	74	71
Povse,Max	16	R	23	a/a	ATL	71	4.20	1.27	26.3	1.7	5.4	3.2	0.6	31	67	80
Pries,Jordan	15	R	25	aaa	SEA	88	5.21	1.44	23.5	2.5	5.1	2.0	0.9	32	64	43
	16	R	26	a/a	CHC	131	6.20	1.71	20.4	3.3	6.6	2.0	1.2	37	65	36
Pruitt,Austin	15	R	26	aa	TAM	160	3.72	1.44	26.2	2.2	5.6	2.5	0.2	35	72	76
	16	R	27	aaa	TAM	163	5.23	1.50	25.1	1.7	6.6	3.9	1.4	36	69	70
Pruneda,Benino	15	R	27	aa	KC	38	4.94	1.72	5.61	4.9	6.0	1.2	0.3	35	69	50
	16	R	28	a/a	KC	58	4.92	1.51	7.56	5.9	8.6	1.5	0.7	29	67	69
Purke,Matt	15	L	25	aa	WAS	24	8.31	1.98	11.7	2.8	5.5	2.0	0.8	42	56	31
	16	L	26	aaa	CHW	38	4.46	1.64	6.57	6.2	7.4	1.2	1.1	29	76	39
Ramirez,Jose	15	R	25	aaa	SEA	63	4.17	1.39	6.44	3.9	7.9	2.0	0.8	31	71	71
	16	R	26	aaa	ATL	41	2.86	1.50	4.96	4.3	8.2	1.9	0.7	33	83	68
Ramirez,Luis	16	R	24	aa	ARI	26	7.38	1.76	5.18	4.9	8.6	1.7	1.4	36	58	42
Ramirez,Noe	15	R	26	aaa	BOS	43	3.47	1.52	6.17	4.4	6.3	1.4	0.3	32	76	61
	16	R	27	aaa	BOS	44	3.17	1.59	6.42	2.8	8.7	3.0	0.9	39	83	82
Ramos,Cesar	16	L	32	aaa	DET	32	7.85	1.93	14	2.8	5.6	2.0	1.2	40	59	23
Ramos,Edubray	16	R	24	a/a	PHI	39	1.58	0.88	5.5	1.0	8.2	8.1	0.3	28	83	222
Ranaudo,Anthony	15	R	26	aaa	TEX	118	6.01	1.72	25.5	3.8	5.4	1.4	1.3	34	67	15
	16	R	27	aaa	CHW	110	4.13	1.27	23.7	1.4	5.5	3.8	1.5	30	74	66
Ravenelle,Adam	16	R	24	aa	DET	30	6.00	1.76	5.04	5.2	5.5	1.1	1.3	32	68	11
Redman,Reid	15	R	27	aa	KC	17	4.78	1.29	7.92	0.6	5.4	9.6	2.4	30	74	157
	16	R	28	aa	KC	26	4.11	1.55	7.1	3.2	5.4	1.7	1.7	31	80	11
Reed,Chris	15	L	25	a/a	MIA	55	6.82	1.81	6.74	6.1	5.7	0.9	0.8	32	61	27
	16	L	26	a/a	MIA	81	5.17	1.49	14.6	4.0	5.6	1.4	1.1	30	67	31
Reed,Cody	15	L	22	aa	CIN	78	3.32	1.28	24.7	2.9	8.2	2.9	0.6	32	75	95
	16	L	23	aaa	CIN	73	4.27	1.51	24.3	2.7	7.2	2.6	1.0	35	74	62
Reed,Jake	16	R	24	a/a	MIN	71	4.74	1.37	5.93	3.2	7.2	2.3	0.3	33	63	84
Regnault,Kyle	16	L	28	aa	NYM	21	5.53	1.85	6.44	1.4	6.1	4.2	0.5	43	69	90
Reyes,Alex	16	R	22	aaa	STL	65	5.33	1.51	20.2	4.2	11.6	2.7	0.8	38	64	105
Reyes,Arturo	15	R	23	a/a	STL	124	3.96	1.50	24.4	3.0	5.8	2.0	0.3	34	72	64
	16	R	24	aaa	STL	101	4.67	1.43	22.7	3.2	6.0	1.9	1.0	31	69	44
Reyes,Genison	16	R	25	aa	BAL	28	8.19	2.05	6	5.7	6.6	1.2	1.2	38	60	14
Reyes,James	15	L	26	aaa	TEX	62	3.03	1.57	6.68	2.7	4.5	1.7	0.2	35	80	50
	16	L	27	aaa	TEX	72	5.56	1.69	7.51	2.8	4.9	1.8	0.8	36	67	33
Reynolds,Danny	15	R	24	a/a	LAA	43	5.82	1.58	4.44	5.8	8.8	1.5	0.2	33	60	83
	16	R	25	a/a	LAA	34	7.84	1.80	7.07	7.0	6.9	1.0	0.6	32	54	45
Reynolds,Greg	16	R	31	aaa	SD	25	8.17	2.08	24.2	3.1	1.4	0.5	1.9	36	63	-62
Rhame,Jacob	15	R	22	aa	LA	50	3.74	1.14	5.08	3.3	9.0	2.8	1.1	27	71	92
	16	R	23	aaa	LA	63	3.81	1.35	4.87	3.6	8.5	2.4	0.8	32	74	82
Richman,Jason	16	L	23	a/a	TEX	21	2.72	1.14	5.94	3.7	3.9	1.1	0.5	22	77	45
Richy,John	16	R	24	aa	PHI	69	6.32	1.70	23.8	3.8	5.1	1.3	1.2	34	63	17
Riefenhauser,Cha	15	L	25	aaa	TAM	35	3.59	1.08	4.66	1.9	7.3	3.8	0.3	29	65	123
	16	L	26	aaa	CHC	28	5.51	1.42	4.19	6.2	6.9	1.1	0.8	24	61	55
Rienzo,Andre	15	R	27	aaa	MIA	78	4.23	1.57	22.7	4.2	4.9	1.2	0.6	31	73	34
	16	R	28	a/a	MIA	33	4.79	1.77	5.47	5.8	7.0	1.2	0.6	34	73	47
Rincon,Junior	16	R	25	aa	MIL	24	5.73	1.54	4.91	5.4	9.0	1.7	0.0	34	59	94
Riordan,Cory	16	R	30	a/a	DET	154	7.17	1.89	26.8	2.2	4.6	2.1	1.4	39	63	12
Rios,Yacksel	16	R	23	aa	PHI	18	5.55	2.12	6.71	7.3	9.4	1.3	0.0	42	71	75
Rivero,Alexis	16	R	22	aa	PHI	33	4.81	1.71	6.57	3.8	7.8	2.1	1.3	37	75	43
Rivero,Armando	16	R	28	aaa	CHC	68	2.69	1.33	6.53	5.2	10.8	2.1	0.5	30	81	107
Roach,Donn	15	R	26	aaa	TOR	143	5.15	1.62	25.4	1.9	2.8	1.4	0.8	35	68	12
	16	R	27	aaa	DET	138	5.70	1.61	22.6	1.9	4.0	2.1	0.7	36	64	37
Roberts,Will	15	R	25	a/a	CLE	157	4.72	1.36	25.2	1.4	4.0	2.8	1.3	31	69	40
	16	R	26	a/a	CLE	89	6.59	1.82	24.2	4.3	3.3	0.8	1.6	32	66	-22
Robinson,Andrew	15	R	27	aa	BAL	62	4.57	1.31	5.36	2.7	5.9	2.2	1.3	29	69	46
	16	R	28	aa	WAS	58	2.97	1.32	6.9	3.2	7.5	2.4	1.0	30	82	70

PITCHER	yr	t	age	lvl	org	ip	era	whip	bf/g	ctl	dom	cmd	hr/9	h%	s%	bpv
Rodgers,Brady	16	R	26	aaa	HOU	132	3.29	1.31	24.8	1.6	6.5	4.1	0.5	34	76	106
Rodriguez,Bryan	15	R	24	a/a	SD	146	4.98	1.66	24.2	2.4	4.6	1.9	0.4	37	69	43
	16	R	25	a/a	SD	145	5.10	1.68	25.2	2.7	4.3	1.6	1.0	35	71	19
Rodriguez,Eduarc	15	L	22	aaa	BOS	48	4.10	1.32	25	1.4	7.0	5.0	0.4	35	68	130
	16	L	23	aaa	BOS	38	4.83	1.35	22.6	1.9	4.8	2.5	1.9	29	71	23
Rodriguez,Joely	15	L	24	a/a	PHI	129	7.27	1.90	19.1	4.1	4.4	1.1	0.9	37	61	9
	16	L	25	a/a	PHI	68	3.65	1.50	6.42	3.2	6.6	2.0	0.6	34	76	62
Rodriguez,Richar	15	R	25	a/a	BAL	84	3.64	1.27	7.43	2.7	6.4	2.4	1.3	28	77	54
	16	R	26	aaa	BAL	82	3.92	1.43	7.23	3.2	7.0	2.2	0.9	32	75	61
Roe,Chaz	15	R	29	a/a	BAL	26	3.90	1.42	6.12	3.9	5.6	1.4	0.0	31	69	67
	16	R	30	aaa	BAL	38	4.00	1.38	4.79	3.0	7.7	2.6	0.4	34	70	89
Rogers,Chad	16	R	27	aaa	ATL	62	6.39	1.63	8.16	4.1	6.5	1.6	1.5	33	63	23
Rogers,Rob	16	R	26	a/a	LA	28	5.53	1.65	6.51	3.6	5.5	1.5	0.0	36	63	59
Rogers,Taylor	16	L	26	aaa	MIN	18	6.62	2.12	12.7	3.3	5.7	1.7	0.6	43	68	29
Rogers,Tyler	16	R	26	a/a	SF	66	4.26	1.58	4.92	3.6	5.1	1.4	0.1	34	71	52
Roibal,Reinier	15	R	26	aa	PHI	49	2.00	1.10	7.62	2.0	7.2	3.7	0.7	28	86	107
	16	R	27	a/a	PHI	35	10.05	2.17	9.2	3.3	6.9	2.1	1.9	44	54	5
Rollins,David	16	L	27	aaa	SEA	45	4.27	1.13	4.84	1.2	5.1	4.4	0.8	29	63	101
Romano,Sal	16	R	23	aa	CIN	156	5.25	1.54	25.2	2.3	7.5	3.3	0.9	37	66	80
Romero,Antonio	16	R	26	aa	CLE	21	10.63	2.18	8.89	5.6	5.5	1.0	1.1	39	49	5
Rondon,Bruce	16	R	26	aaa	DET	22	5.41	2.25	4.99	7.8	9.4	1.2	0.5	43	75	55
Rondon,Jorge	15	R	27	aaa	BAL	61	3.68	1.32	7.17	3.5	5.7	1.6	0.0	30	69	74
	16	R	28	aaa	PIT	57	4.02	1.55	5.83	4.4	4.2	1.0	0.4	30	73	34
Roney,Bradley	16	R	24	a/a	ATL	68	4.50	1.82	7.14	8.1	10.2	1.3	0.6	34	75	74
Rosario,Jose	16	R	25	a/a	CHC	38	3.46	1.41	4.82	2.3	6.5	2.9	0.3	35	74	88
Rosario,Miguel	16	R	23	aa	PIT	34	2.27	1.04	5.64	3.4	6.3	1.8	0.3	23	78	85
Roseboom,David	16	L	24	aa	NYM	58	2.18	0.99	4.23	2.8	7.1	2.5	0.8	22	83	87
Ross,Austin	15	R	27	a/a	MIL	70	6.14	1.87	6.73	3.4	7.9	2.3	0.7	42	66	60
	16	R	28	aaa	MIL	72	4.87	1.48	6.55	3.2	7.5	2.4	1.2	33	69	58
Ross,Greg	15	R	26	aa	ATL	138	5.42	1.72	25	3.4	4.4	1.3	0.5	36	67	29
	16	R	27	aa	WAS	54	1.21	1.22	21.8	2.2	4.1	1.9	0.2	29	91	61
Roth,Michael	15	L	25	aaa	CLE	124	6.55	1.79	18.5	3.3	4.5	1.4	1.8	35	67	-10
	16	L	26	aaa	TEX	145	3.90	1.49	22.4	2.9	4.5	1.5	0.7	32	75	37
Routt,Nick	16	L	25	a/a	CIN	68	2.96	1.41	5.78	3.9	6.6	1.7	0.4	31	79	66
Rowen,Benjamin	15	R	27	a/a	TOR	65	2.91	1.20	5.41	1.5	4.7	3.3	0.2	31	74	92
	16	R	28	aaa	MIL	58	2.91	1.48	5.55	2.4	5.3	2.2	0.2	35	79	68
Rucinski,Drew	15	R	27	aaa	LAA	112	5.67	1.71	23.1	3.2	5.6	1.8	1.4	35	69	20
	16	R	28	aaa	CHC	155	7.49	1.81	25.6	2.8	5.2	1.9	1.1	38	58	23
Runion,Sam	15	R	27	a/a	WAS	65	4.09	1.66	6.07	3.4	6.3	1.8	0.5	37	75	54
	16	R	28	a/a	WAS	49	9.47	1.84	6.96	3.6	4.3	1.2	0.2	38	43	32
Ruth,Eric	15	R	25	a/a	NYY	124	4.72	1.56	24.8	3.3	4.8	1.5	0.8	33	71	30
	16	R	26	a/a	NYY	47	4.17	1.44	13.3	3.7	6.8	1.9	0.3	33	70	72
Sadzeck,Connor	16	R	25	aa	TEX	141	5.67	1.55	24.6	3.8	6.8	1.8	1.4	32	66	34
Salas,Javier	16	R	24	aa	MIL	47	7.58	1.85	17	8.3	5.5	0.7	0.3	29	55	45
Sampson,Adrian	16	R	25	aaa	SEA	80	3.52	1.27	25.2	1.3	5.8	4.5	0.5	33	73	112
Sampson,Keyvius	15	R	24	a/a	CIN	83	4.45	1.71	23.4	5.4	7.0	1.3	0.5	34	73	54
	16	R	25	aaa	CIN	62	2.71	1.18	13.8	3.5	7.7	2.2	0.6	27	79	84
Sanabia,Alex	15	R	27	aaa	LAA	87	6.92	1.94	16	3.0	4.5	1.5	0.8	40	63	17
	16	R	28	aaa	CHC	25	12.13	2.16	21	3.9	4.1	1.0	2.2	39	42	-39
Sanburn,Nolan	15	R	24	aa	CHW	30	9.13	1.98	6.54	8.1	7.6	0.9	0.4	34	50	53
	16	R	25	aa	CHW	74	4.80	1.50	9.41	3.3	6.0	1.8	0.6	33	67	54
Sanchez,Jake	15	R	26	a/a	OAK	151	5.60	1.76	25.6	2.9	4.9	1.7	0.7	38	68	31
	16	R	27	aa	OAK	67	3.88	1.37	6.35	2.6	7.3	2.8	0.3	34	70	94
Santana,Edgar	16	R	25	a/a	PIT	57	4.61	1.48	7.25	2.8	6.2	2.2	0.9	33	70	54
Santos,Eduard	15	R	26	aa	LAA	58	3.08	1.28	6.13	5.1	9.8	1.9	0.5	27	77	98
	16	R	27	aaa	OAK	63	5.00	1.60	6.19	6.4	7.2	1.1	0.5	29	68	59
Santos,Luis	16	R	25	aa	TOR	82	5.82	1.62	21.4	2.6	6.9	2.6	1.2	37	65	52
Sappington,Mark	15	R	25	aa	TAM	68	4.49	1.75	6.5	6.1	7.7	1.3	0.4	34	73	61
	16	R	26	a/a	TAM	52	7.48	2.11	6.1	8.3	6.8	0.8	0.4	36	62	42
Sarianides,Nick	16	R	27	aa	CHC	37	4.65	1.79	5.74	5.3	6.3	1.2	0.9	34	75	31
Satterwhite,Cody	15	R	28	aaa	NYM	72	4.67	1.58	5.56	3.6	6.9	1.9	0.8	35	71	55
	16	R	29	aaa	LAA	25	2.05	1.24	5.64	3.0	6.1	2.0	0.7	28	87	64
Saupold,Warwick	15	R	25	a/a	DET	124	5.17	1.50	18.4	3.3	5.3	1.6	0.5	32	64	48
	16	R	26	aaa	DET	74	3.33	1.47	17.7	3.1	4.6	1.5	0.5	32	78	42
Sborz,Josh	16	R	23	aa	LA	17	4.93	1.57	7.32	3.1	7.8	2.5	1.3	36	72	54
Schafer,Jordan	16	L	30	a/a	LA	46	5.50	1.99	6.02	3.6	7.6	2.1	1.3	42	75	34
Schepel,Kyle	16	R	26	aa	SEA	38	2.95	1.35	6.88	4.9	7.8	1.6	0.9	27	81	65
Schlitter,Brian	15	R	30	aaa	CHC	45	2.12	1.87	4.65	6.1	5.3	0.9	0.2	34	89	38
	16	R	31	aaa	COL	42	5.74	2.03	5.65	5.5	6.2	1.1	0.7	39	71	28
Schlosser,Gus	15	R	27	aa	COL	47	7.84	2.13	8.25	4.9	4.5	0.9	1.3	38	63	-10
	16	R	28	a/a	LA	43	7.50	1.85	7.67	2.2	6.8	3.1	1.4	41	60	47
Schreiber,Brad	15	R	24	aa	TAM	28	4.07	1.32	4.83	4.2	7.6	1.8	0.6	28	69	74
	16	R	25	aa	TAM	37	7.49	1.98	5.92	3.4	6.1	1.8	1.4	40	63	16
Schugel,Andrew	15	R	26	a/a	ARI	115	5.81	1.71	24.9	2.5	4.9	1.9	0.8	37	66	33
	16	R	27	aaa	PIT	18	5.89	1.15	5.5	1.7	6.7	3.9	0.0	32	43	127
Schultz,Bo	15	R	30	aaa	TOR	21	2.82	1.44	5.68	3.7	5.8	1.6	0.7	30	83	48
	16	R	31	a/a	TOR	35	6.28	1.58	5.55	2.8	4.6	1.6	1.2	33	61	20
Schultz,Jaime	15	R	24	aa	TAM	135	4.22	1.56	21.9	6.0	9.5	1.6	0.7	31	74	76
	16	R	25	aaa	TAM	131	4.77	1.63	21.5	5.1	9.4	1.9	1.0	35	72	66
Schuster,Patrick	15	L	25	aa	CIN	54	4.46	1.68	4.67	4.8	6.4	1.3	0.2	35	72	56
	16	L	26	aaa	PHI	45	1.90	1.42	4.99	4.3	7.7	1.8	0.0	32	85	88
Scott,Robby	16	L	27	aaa	BOS	78	4.33	1.27	9.97	2.0	6.5	3.2	1.5	30	71	63
Scott,Tanner	16	L	22	aa	BAL	16	6.82	2.22	5.75	8.4	8.6	1.0	0.0	41	66	65
Scott,Tayler	15	R	23	aa	CHC	31	6.19	1.84	9.64	6.0	5.3	0.9	0.9	32	66	18
	16	R	24	aa	MIL	27	6.48	1.62	4.93	5.4	5.9	1.1	1.4	28	61	19
Scribner,Troy	16	R	25	a/a	LAA	132	4.07	1.30	22.7	3.9	6.7	1.7	0.8	27	70	59
Secrest,Kelly	16	L	25	aa	NYM	16	6.55	1.63	6.06	5.7	9.1	1.6	0.6	34	58	73
Seddon,Joel	16	R	24	aa	OAK	143	5.15	1.53	23.1	3.0	3.8	1.3	0.8	32	66	21
Self,Derek	16	R	26	a/a	WAS	56	6.06	1.86	8.24	3.4	5.5	1.6	1.0	38	68	24
Senzatela,Antonic	16	R	21	aa	COL	35	2.74	1.27	20.3	2.6	5.6	2.2	0.4	30	79	70
Severino,Luis	15	R	21	a/a	NYY	99	3.16	1.14	20.7	2.6	7.9	3.1	0.2	30	71	114
	16	R	22	aaa	NYY	77	4.90	1.45	25.4	2.3	8.0	3.5	0.7	37	66	97
Sewald,Paul	15	R	25	aa	NYM	51	2.15	0.99	4.44	1.8	8.2	4.5	0.6	27	81	137
	16	R	26	aaa	NYM	66	3.22	1.25	4.77	2.7	8.9	3.3	1.1	31	79	93
Shaban,Ronnie	15	R	25	aa	STL	49	3.05	1.24	4.62	2.7	6.7	2.5	0.5	30	76	82
	16	R	26	a/a	STL	58	3.59	1.44	5.53	2.6	5.4	2.0	1.1	32	79	38
Shackelford,Kevir	15	R	26	aa	CIN	39	5.09	1.97	5.29	4.5	4.9	1.1	0.4	39	73	28
	16	R	27	a/a	CIN	44	3.17	1.58	5.58	4.3	5.2	1.2	0.6	32	81	36
Shepherd,Chandl	16	R	24	a/a	BOS	64	4.07	1.15	6.35	2.8	7.2	2.6	1.0	26	67	76
Sherfy,Jimmie	15	R	24	aa	ARI	50	8.75	1.83	5.25	5.3	7.5	1.4	0.7	37	49	47
	16	R	25	a/a	ARI	43	4.50	1.16	4.28	3.9	9.9	2.5	1.5	25	66	82
Sherriff,Ryan	15	L	25	a/a	STL	40	3.30	1.48	5.69	3.3	6.0	1.8	1.1	31	82	39
	16	L	26	aaa	STL	67	3.31	1.52	5.9	3.2	6.2	1.9	0.5	34	79	58
Shibuya,Tim	15	R	26	a/a	MIN	49	5.76	1.65	8.17	2.0	3.4	1.7	0.6	36	64	25
	16	R	27	a/a	LA	79	5.35	1.49	17.8	1.4	3.9	2.8	1.2	34	66	37
Shipley,Braden	15	R	23	aa	ARI	157	4.60	1.49	24.1	3.3	5.7	1.7	0.5	33	68	53
	16	R	24	aaa	ARI	119	4.05	1.40	26.5	1.6	4.8	3.0	0.5	34	71	71
Shirley,Tommy	15	L	27	aaa	HOU	41	3.45	1.18	14.9	2.5	6.5	2.6	0.7	28	72	79
	16	L	28	a/a	DET	106	8.11	2.27	20	4.1	4.4	1.1	1.6	41	65	-23
Shreve,Chasen	16	L	26	aaa	NYY	17	2.47	0.82	4.66	4.5	8.8	2.0	0.9	11	75	103
Sides,Grant	15	R	26	aa	CLE	25	5.54	1.93	8.03	7.8	5.2	0.7	0.5	31	70	31
	16	R	27	aa	CLE	62	4.80	1.36	6.14	4.4	7.6	1.7	0.8	28	65	66
Simmons,Seth	15	R	27	a/a	ARI	75	3.66	1.32	5.88	3.6	8.1	2.2	0.6	31	73	84
	16	R	28	a/a	SD	121	3.64	1.33	14.8	3.0	6.3	2.1	1.0	30	76	54
Simms,John	15	R	23	aa	WAS	45	5.58	1.63	25	3.1	5.6	1.8	0.6	36	65	45
	16	R	24	aa	WAS	93	4.48	1.29	13.1	3.0	6.2	2.1	0.9	29	67	59
Sims,Lucas	15	R	21	aa	ATL	48	3.97	1.31	21.9	5.5	9.7	1.8	0.2	28	68	104
	16	R	22	a/a	ATL	141	5.72	1.70	22.7	6.2	9.2	1.5	1.1	33	67	56
Sitton,Kraig	15	L	27	aa	COL	58	4.82	1.84	5.85	2.6	4.3	1.6	0.0	40	71	44
	16	L	28	a/a	SEA	52	3.10	1.27	5.09	1.5	5.2	3.5	0.4	32	75	92
Skaggs,Tyler	16	L	25	aaa	LAA	32	1.74	0.88	17.1	2.1	10.5	5.0	0.5	26	83	170
Skoglund,Eric	16	L	24	aa	KC	156	4.70	1.33	24	2.3	6.2	2.7	1.3	30	68	56
Skulina,Tyler	16	R	25	aa	CHC	129	6.35	1.84	22.2	5.3	5.3	1.0	1.3	33	67	7
Slack,Ryne	15	L	23	aa	TEX	17	1.25	0.82	5.63	3.2	7.1	2.2	1.2	14	98	81
	16	L	24	aa	TEX	49	5.18	1.67	5.61	5.8	6.2	1.1	1.1	30	71	28
Slania,Dan	16	R	24	a/a	SF	96	2.93	1.23	13.4	2.6	7.4	2.9	0.5	31	77	93
Slegers,Aaron	16	R	24	aa	MIN	145	4.28	1.44	24.8	2.9	5.1	1.8	0.8	32	71	44
Smith,Alex	15	R	26	aa	NYY	39	3.61	1.54	6.86	3.2	5.7	1.8	0.0	35	74	68
	16	R	27	aa	TAM	32	4.40	1.64	6.42	5.6	6.6	1.2	0.3	32	72	56
Smith,Blake	16	R	29	aaa	CHW	71	4.79	1.58	8.05	3.7	7.3	2.0	1.0	35	71	52
Smith,Caleb	15	L	24	a/a	NYY	135	4.71	1.58	22.9	4.1	5.4	1.3	0.7	32	71	36
	16	L	25	aa	NYY	64	6.13	1.75	10.8	3.3	8.2	2.5	0.9	40	65	63
Smith,Chris	16	R	28	a/a	TOR	61	2.87	1.45	5.51	3.9	9.4	2.4	0.7	35	82	90
Smith,Gage	16	R	25	aa	MIL	16	4.33	1.58	6.26	1.3	2.3	1.7	0.8	34	74	14
Smith,Jake	16	R	26	aa	SD	26	7.92	2.03	4.51	9.6	8.6	0.9	0.4	33	58	61
Smith,Josh	16	L	27	a/a	PIT	65	9.11	2.06	6.44	5.2	7.1	1.3	1.5	39	55	13
	15	R	28	a/a	CIN	142	5.00	1.53	25.8	2.5	6.2	2.5	0.7	36	67	61
Smith,Josh	16	R	29	aaa	CIN	45	6.00	1.74	22.8	3.3	6.0	1.8	1.6	36	69	15
Smith,Joshua	15	L	26	aa	PIT	48	6.32	1.75	6.4	6.3	4.5	0.7	0.5	30	62	27
Smith,Kyle	16	R	24	aa	HOU	82	5.96	1.73	13.9	3.2	6.3	2.0	1.8	36	70	14
Smith,Murphy	16	R	29	a/a	TOR	73	2.25	1.40	7.16	3.9	6.5	1.7	0.9	29	89	50
Smith,Myles	16	R	24	a/a	ARI	33	8.02	2.12	8.67	6.3	6.5	1.0	1.5	37	63	3
Smith,Nate	16	L	25	aaa	LAA	150	4.80	1.48	24.9	2.5	6.1	2.4	1.0	34	69	54
Smoker,Josh	16	L	28	aaa	NYM	57	4.20	1.61	4.85	2.8	9.9	3.5	0.7	41	75	103
Sneed,Cy	16	R	24	aa	HOU	118	4.79	1.45	20.1	2.5	7.3	2.9	1.1	34	69	69
Snell,Blake	15	L	23	a/a	TAM	113	1.95	1.11	21.2	3.4	9.4	2.8	0.5	28	85	112
	16	L	24	aaa	TAM	63	3.91	1.55	22.9	4.2	11.0	2.6	0.7	39	76	100
Snodgrass,Jack	15	L	28	a/a	SF	72	5.53	1.70	19.3	4.5	4.5	1.0	0.7	33	67	21
	16	L	29	a/a	TEX	45	6.88	1.97	21.7	4.6	5.6	1.2	1.5	37	67	0
Snow,Forrest	15	R	27	aaa	SEA	121	4.26	1.38	17.5	2.8	5.8	2.1	1.5	29	75	33
	16	R	28	a/a	SEA	54	3.64	1.30	7.94	2.7	8.0	3.0	0.6	33	72	97
Somsen,Layne	16	R	27	aaa	LA	31	4.81	1.76	7.02	6.1	7.6	1.2	1.1	33	75	40
Sopko,Andrew	16	R	22	aa	LA	31	6.31	1.66	23.2	3.0	6.3	2.1	1.4	36	64	31
Soto,Giovanni	15	L	24	aaa	CLE	54	3.55	1.35	4.87	5.0	7.2	1.4	0.2	28	72	79
	16	L	25	aaa	CHC	49	6.09	1.87	6.97	5.9	8.4	1.4	0.6	38	66	56
Sparkman,Glenn	15	R	23	aa	KC	20	4.34	1.43	21.2	4.0	7.7	1.9	0.5	32	69	75
	16	R	24	aa	KC	18	6.24	1.77	20.3	2.7	8.2	3.0	1.2	41	66	64
Spomer,Kurt	15	R	26	a/a	LAA	64	4.46	1.55	6.11	3.1	4.1	1.3	1.3	31	75	8
	16	R	27	a/a	DET	56	4.01	1.67	6.16	2.6	5.8	2.2	0.6	38	76	53
Spurlin,Tyler	16	R	25	aa	MIL	41	5.25	1.86	4.69	6.1	6.4	1.0	0.0	35	68	57
Stanek,Ryne	15	R	24	aa	TAM	62	4.71	1.46	16.5	4.5	5.1	1.1	1.0	27	70	28
	16	R	25	aa	TAM	103	5.51	1.51	13.1	4.5	8.3	1.9	0.9	33	64	64
Stankiewicz,Tedd	16	R	23	aa	BOS	136	6.09	1.55	23.7	2.7	5.5	2.0	1.2	34	61	35
Staumont,Josh	16	R	23	aa	KC	50	4.05	1.77	21	6.9	10.7	1.6	0.4	37	77	87
Steckenrider,Drev	16	R	25	a/a	MIA	42	3.56	1.14	4.89	4.1	9.2	2.3	0.2	27	67	112
Stephens,Jacksor	16	R	22	aa	CIN	151	4.87	1.53	24.4	2.8	7.1	2.6	0.6	36	68	73
Stephenson,Robe	15	R	22	a/a	CIN	134	4.84	1.45	22.9	4.9	8.5	1.7	0.9	30	68	66
	16	R	23	aaa	CIN	137	6.11	1.62	25.3	5.2	7.1	1.4	1.6	30	65	25
Stewart,Brock	16	R	25	a/a	LA	110	2.41	1.05	22.4	1.4	8.0	5.9	0.4	31	78	166
Stewart,Kohl	16	R	22	aa	MIN	92	3.66	1.59	25.4	4.2	3.8	0.9	0.4	31	77	28
Stilson,John	16	R	26	a/a	TOR	50	5.41	1.64	6.33	4.7	6.2	1.3	0.5	33	66	48
Stites,Matthew	15	R	25	aaa	ARI	26	3.97	1.82	5.18	4.6	4.0	0.9	0.7	34	79	13
	16	R	26	a/a	ARI	52	3.55	1.45	4.76	4.4	6.3	1.4	0.2	31	74	66
Stoffel,Jason	15	R	27	a/a	BAL	57	6.35	1.47	5.29	4.2	7.3	1.7	1.0	31	56	54
	16	R	28	a/a	BAL	59	3.63	1.47	4.6	3.6	8.9	2.5	1.4	33	81	64
Stout,Eric	16	L	23	aa	KC	72	5.14	1.50	7.44	3.2	7.0	2.2	0.4	35	64	73

PITCHER	yr	t	age	lvl	org	ip	era	whip	bf/g	ctl	dom	cmd	hr/9	h%	s%	bpv
Strahm,Matt	16	L	25	aa	KC	102	4.77	1.50	20.1	2.2	7.4	3.4	1.4	36	72	66
Straka,John	16	R	26	aa	TOR	25	6.50	1.58	22	3.2	6.5	2.0	1.0	35	58	46
Stratton,Chris	15	R	25	a/a	SF	148	4.70	1.45	24.3	4.0	5.5	1.4	0.5	30	67	50
	16	R	26	aaa	SF	126	4.65	1.46	25.6	3.0	6.0	2.0	0.4	34	67	64
Strong,Michael	16	L	28	aa	MIN	18	11.87	2.42	5.79	7.3	3.7	0.5	0.6	39	47	-3
Stumpf,Daniel	16	L	25	a/a	KC	27	4.33	1.15	5.57	1.8	8.0	4.5	0.0	33	58	148
Suarez,Albert	15	R	26	aa	LAA	163	3.96	1.34	25.1	2.3	5.4	2.4	0.9	31	72	56
	16	R	27	aaa	SF	46	5.33	1.55	22.2	3.0	6.1	2.0	0.6	35	64	57
Suarez,Andrew	16	L	24	aa	SF	114	5.36	1.63	26.7	2.1	6.0	2.9	0.9	38	68	58
Suero,Wander	15	R	24	aa	WAS	34	8.22	1.92	9.48	3.9	6.2	1.6	1.1	39	56	22
	16	R	25	aa	WAS	55	3.38	1.64	6.32	3.8	6.2	1.6	0.6	35	80	49
Sulbaran,Juan	15	R	26	a/a	KC	132	6.83	1.79	21.8	3.6	5.1	1.4	2.0	34	66	-11
	16	R	27	a/a	STL	146	6.57	1.66	23.4	3.7	5.8	1.6	1.2	34	61	25
Sulser,Cole	16	R	26	a/a	CLE	45	6.26	1.67	6.69	2.9	7.0	2.4	0.3	39	60	75
Suter,Brent	16	L	27	aaa	MIL	111	4.28	1.55	18.6	1.2	4.7	3.9	0.5	37	72	84
Tago,Peter	15	R	23	aa	CHW	19	2.57	0.93	5.93	4.9	6.5	1.3	0.0	16	69	98
	16	R	24	aa	CHW	60	5.10	1.52	6.82	5.4	10.1	1.9	0.5	34	65	90
Taillon,Jameson	16	R	25	aaa	PIT	62	2.88	1.01	23.6	1.0	6.9	7.3	0.3	30	71	190
Taylor,Ben	16	R	25	aa	BOS	34	4.64	1.41	6.85	3.5	9.0	2.6	1.2	33	70	75
Taylor,Josh	16	L	23	aa	ARI	55	6.87	1.78	22.9	3.2	6.4	2.0	0.8	39	60	43
Taylor,Logan	16	R	25	aa	NYM	86	4.75	1.63	8.66	4.2	8.6	2.0	0.6	37	70	74
Tepera,Ryan	15	R	28	aaa	TOR	34	1.71	1.13	6.39	4.2	7.7	1.8	0.4	24	87	90
	16	R	29	aaa	TOR	45	4.03	1.45	5.23	3.9	7.3	1.9	0.9	31	74	57
Therrien,Jesen	16	R	23	aa	PHI	17	4.49	1.66	6.92	2.7	10.3	3.8	1.3	42	77	92
Thomas,Chris	15	R	27	a/a	STL	74	3.68	1.27	6.08	2.1	6.0	2.9	0.7	31	72	75
	16	R	28	aa	STL	17	9.11	2.10	6.1	3.6	6.6	1.9	1.8	42	57	3
Thompson,Jake	15	R	21	aa	PHI	133	4.09	1.34	23	2.8	6.9	2.5	0.8	32	71	73
	16	R	22	aaa	PHI	130	3.61	1.33	25.6	2.8	5.4	1.9	1.0	29	76	44
Thompson,Ryan	16	R	24	aa	HOU	40	2.13	1.18	6.95	2.3	4.4	1.9	0.0	28	80	73
Thornton,Trent	16	R	23	aa	HOU	46	2.72	1.14	26	1.0	6.0	6.2	1.1	30	82	133
Thornton,Zack	15	R	27	aaa	NYM	62	4.11	1.45	4.18	3.4	6.4	1.9	0.3	33	70	69
	16	R	28	aaa	NYM	40	7.19	1.90	5.35	3.4	4.4	1.3	0.9	38	61	13
Thurman,Andrew	15	R	24	aa	ATL	24	6.75	2.14	24.1	6.3	4.5	0.7	0.0	38	65	29
	16	R	25	aa	ATL	63	10.30	2.24	16.7	7.9	6.4	0.8	1.7	36	53	-5
Tillman,Daniel	16	R	27	aa	MIL	20	0.72	1.56	6.16	3.4	8.9	2.6	0.7	38	100	85
Tolliver,Ashur	16	L	28	a/a	LAA	40	3.13	1.52	5.83	3.6	7.3	2.0	1.0	33	83	56
Tomshaw,Matt	15	L	27	a/a	MIA	124	6.97	1.80	18.4	2.4	5.2	2.2	0.8	39	60	37
	16	L	28	a/a	MIA	89	4.94	1.45	16.5	2.2	7.6	3.5	0.9	36	67	86
Torres,Alexander	16	L	29	aaa	SF	38	5.48	2.09	4.67	8.6	6.8	0.8	0.2	35	72	48
Torres,Jose	16	L	23	a/a	SD	39	1.52	1.00	5.32	2.9	7.7	2.6	0.2	25	85	111
Tracy,Matthew	15	L	27	a/a	NYY	90	5.48	1.77	14.3	4.1	5.2	1.3	0.7	35	69	27
	16	L	28	aa	MIA	79	7.06	1.99	15.2	3.6	5.2	1.4	0.9	40	64	16
Travieso,Nick	16	R	22	aa	CIN	117	5.60	1.68	22.9	4.6	6.4	1.4	1.3	33	69	26
Triggs,Andrew	16	R	27	aaa	OAK	18	4.30	1.47	4.92	2.8	7.8	2.7	0.0	37	68	101
Trivino,Lou	16	R	23	aa	OAK	18	2.82	1.23	6.19	3.4	4.8	1.4	0.5	26	78	53
Tseng,Jen-Ho	16	R	22	aa	CHC	113	4.96	1.64	23	2.5	4.8	1.9	1.1	35	72	27
Tuivailala,Sam	15	R	23	aaa	STL	45	1.74	1.22	4.23	4.9	7.1	1.5	0.4	24	87	78
	16	R	24	aaa	STL	47	5.83	1.60	4.91	4.2	12.1	2.8	0.6	42	62	113
Turley,Josh	15	L	25	aa	DET	153	4.26	1.45	26.1	2.2	4.7	2.1	1.1	32	73	35
	16	L	26	a/a	DET	153	6.01	1.74	26.8	2.5	5.6	2.2	1.2	37	67	30
Turley,Nik	15	L	26	aaa	SF	103	4.92	1.49	23.3	4.3	6.0	1.4	1.1	29	69	35
	16	L	27	aa	BOS	36	6.04	1.84	8.31	8.0	9.4	1.2	0.9	32	67	59
Turner,Jacob	16	R	25	aaa	CHW	107	5.84	1.70	26.8	2.7	6.0	2.2	1.0	37	66	41
Underwood Jr.,Du	16	R	22	aa	CHC	59	5.68	1.78	20.8	4.7	6.2	1.3	1.2	35	70	22
Unsworth,Dylan	15	R	23	aa	SEA	66	5.09	1.52	22.2	1.7	6.0	3.5	0.9	37	67	76
	16	R	24	aa	SEA	47	1.54	1.25	21.1	1.4	5.8	4.2	0.5	33	90	108
Urena,Jose	15	R	24	aaa	MIA	68	3.50	1.47	26.4	2.7	4.4	1.6	0.5	32	77	41
	16	R	25	aaa	MIA	48	4.38	1.55	17.6	4.4	6.1	1.4	0.8	31	73	42
Urias,Julio	15	L	19	a/a	LA	73	3.99	1.19	19.4	2.3	9.1	4.0	0.5	33	66	127
	16	L	20	aaa	LA	45	1.54	0.89	15.2	1.4	8.8	6.4	0.4	27	85	187
Valdespina,Jose	16	R	24	a/a	TEX	64	4.73	1.69	7.22	3.6	4.7	1.3	0.8	34	73	23
Valdez,Cesar	16	R	31	aaa	HOU	138	3.88	1.40	19.5	0.9	5.6	6.0	0.6	36	73	133
Valdez,Jose	15	R	25	aaa	DET	57	4.13	1.74	6.04	6.4	5.2	0.8	0.5	30	76	34
	16	R	26	a/a	LAA	46	2.88	1.39	5.05	4.7	7.1	1.5	0.8	28	82	58
Valdez,Phillips	16	R	25	aa	WAS	88	6.40	1.90	25.9	4.2	4.7	1.1	0.8	37	66	14
Vasquez,Anthony	15	L	29	a/a	PHI	134	5.43	1.64	21.3	3.9	3.9	1.0	0.6	32	66	21
	16	L	30	a/a	PHI	172	4.72	1.67	27.6	2.8	4.7	1.7	1.2	35	75	18
Vasto,Jerry	16	L	24	aa	COL	30	4.82	1.85	4.47	5.3	7.8	1.5	1.0	37	75	42
Venditte,Patrick	15	L	30	aaa	OAK	41	2.14	1.32	7.32	4.0	6.4	1.6	0.5	28	86	64
	16	L	31	aaa	SEA	43	4.48	1.70	6.52	3.5	10.0	2.9	0.7	42	74	92
Ventura,Angel	16	R	23	aa	MIL	55	5.92	1.66	22.4	4.6	7.2	1.6	2.0	31	70	14
Viza,Tyler	16	R	22	aa	PHI	94	5.57	1.45	25.1	2.2	5.0	2.3	1.4	32	64	31
Voelker,Paul	15	R	23	aa	DET	17	3.22	1.55	4.73	5.4	7.1	1.3	0.6	30	80	57
	16	R	24	aa	DET	54	5.15	1.65	4.64	4.2	10.4	2.4	1.3	38	72	71
Voth,Austin	16	R	24	aaa	WAS	157	4.55	1.53	25.3	3.7	6.2	1.7	0.8	33	71	48
Waddell,Brandon	16	L	22	aa	PIT	118	4.90	1.67	24.1	4.5	5.9	1.3	0.7	34	71	39
Wade,Konner	16	R	25	aa	COL	77	8.38	1.98	9.96	3.6	4.2	1.2	1.7	37	59	-18
Wagman,Joey	16	R	25	aa	OAK	18	7.64	2.01	22.2	2.0	3.5	1.7	0.5	42	59	20
Wagner,Michael	15	R	24	a/a	CHC	25	5.98	1.55	8.4	5.6	5.8	1.0	0.4	29	59	50
	16	R	25	a/a	CHC	84	5.28	1.67	19.9	4.7	6.4	1.4	0.7	33	68	42
Wagner,Tyler	15	R	24	aa	MIL	152	3.20	1.42	25.8	3.1	6.0	2.0	0.6	32	79	58
	16	R	25	aaa	ARI	27	3.40	1.64	23.8	3.6	4.1	1.1	0.3	34	79	32
Wahl,Bobby	15	R	23	aa	OAK	32	4.37	1.61	5.97	3.8	8.3	2.2	0.5	38	72	77
	16	R	24	a/a	OAK	50	2.93	1.26	4.89	4.3	8.9	2.1	0.6	28	78	92
Walden,Marcus	16	R	28	a/a	MIN	56	3.47	1.36	5.61	2.9	4.7	1.6	0.2	31	73	57
Walter,Corey	16	R	24	aa	OAK	100	2.52	1.19	13.9	1.4	3.9	2.9	0.2	30	78	80
Walter,Johnny	16	R	25	aa	STL	49	7.89	1.72	24.7	4.0	5.5	1.4	0.6	35	51	36
Walters,Blair	16	L	27	aa	CHW	101	5.85	1.89	22.6	5.6	6.1	1.1	0.7	36	68	33
Walters,Jeffrey	16	R	29	aaa	NYM	66	6.16	1.65	5.24	3.9	5.0	1.3	1.3	32	64	12
Wang,Wei-Chung	16	L	24	a/a	MIL	133	4.88	1.49	24	2.5	6.4	2.5	0.7	35	67	64
Weathers,Casey	15	R	30	aa	CLE	22	5.56	1.96	4.85	5.3	6.6	1.3	0.6	39	71	39
	16	R	31	aa	CLE	28	5.36	2.02	5.89	6.1	6.9	1.1	0.9	38	74	28
Weaver,Luke	16	R	23	a/a	STL	83	1.50	1.01	24.5	1.3	8.9	6.8	0.4	31	88	190
Webb,Tyler	15	L	25	aaa	NYY	38	3.89	1.64	6.78	2.9	8.0	2.8	1.3	38	81	58
	16	L	26	aaa	NYY	73	5.48	1.61	8.94	3.4	8.2	2.4	1.0	37	67	65
Weber,Ryan	15	R	25	a/a	ATL	100	3.16	1.14	10.4	1.0	4.5	4.6	0.9	29	76	100
	16	R	26	aaa	ATL	62	3.62	1.55	10.4	2.3	5.0	2.2	0.2	36	75	63
Weber,Thad	15	R	31	aaa	DET	161	5.77	1.68	26.8	2.7	4.1	1.5	1.4	34	68	5
	16	R	32	a/a	DET	147	7.41	1.99	27.2	3.1	3.3	1.1	1.1	38	63	-10
Weigel,Patrick	16	R	22	aa	ATL	21	3.06	0.96	26.1	3.8	6.7	1.8	1.1	17	74	68
Weir,T.J.	16	R	25	aa	SD	49	7.93	1.76	14.1	3.8	6.9	1.8	1.4	37	55	29
Welker,Duke	16	R	30	aaa	SF	35	5.02	2.32	5.81	4.7	5.8	1.2	0.8	44	79	14
Weller,Blayne	15	R	25	a/a	ARI	62	6.48	1.55	20.8	3.3	4.8	1.5	0.8	32	57	31
	16	R	26	a/a	LAA	72	8.23	1.78	20.7	3.9	7.3	1.9	2.3	35	57	3
Wendelken,Jeffre	16	R	23	aaa	OAK	46	5.51	1.87	5.53	5.4	10.4	1.9	1.1	41	72	63
West,Aaron	15	R	25	aa	HOU	84	3.30	1.30	11.6	1.2	6.1	5.0	0.6	34	76	120
	16	R	26	a/a	HOU	82	4.30	1.54	7.32	1.8	6.2	3.4	0.5	37	72	84
West,Matthew	15	R	27	a/a	LA	51	4.62	1.48	6.7	3.0	7.1	2.3	0.6	35	69	69
	16	R	28	aaa	LA	46	3.01	1.12	4.69	1.6	5.7	3.6	0.2	30	72	107
Westphal,Luke	16	L	27	aa	MIN	30	7.24	2.30	8.54	7.4	8.3	1.1	1.1	42	69	28
Whalen,Rob	16	R	22	a/a	ATL	120	3.12	1.36	23.9	3.5	7.6	2.2	0.3	32	77	85
Wheeler,Andre	16	L	25	aa	CHW	26	8.64	2.42	7.08	4.7	7.4	1.6	2.1	46	67	-10
Wheeler,Beck	15	R	27	aa	NYM	59	4.33	1.45	5.83	4.3	6.9	1.6	0.4	31	69	67
	16	R	28	a/a	NYM	56	6.78	1.82	5.5	5.7	9.4	1.6	1.2	37	63	51
Wheeler,Jason	15	L	25	a/a	MIN	138	6.99	1.74	25.1	2.8	4.6	1.7	1.3	36	60	11
	16	L	26	a/a	MIN	169	4.57	1.44	25.7	2.3	5.5	2.4	0.8	33	69	53
Whitehead,David	16	R	24	aa	PIT	46	9.70	2.37	21.7	9.3	3.7	0.4	1.0	34	57	-9
Whiting,Boone	16	R	27	aa	WAS	25	8.45	2.32	25.4	6.0	3.9	0.6	1.3	39	64	-22
Whitley,Chase	15	R	26	aaa	NYY	17	2.96	1.38	23.8	3.6	5.6	1.5	0.0	31	76	69
	16	R	27	aa	TAM	28	3.78	1.08	18	2.8	5.7	2.0	1.1	23	69	55
Wick,Rowan	16	R	24	aa	STL	20	5.10	1.59	4.13	6.7	8.0	1.2	0.5	29	67	67
Wieck,Brad	16	L	25	aa	SD	20	0.58	1.03	5.22	3.8	11.6	3.0	0.0	28	94	152
Wieland,Joe	15	R	25	aaa	LA	114	5.13	1.55	22.6	1.9	6.0	3.2	0.6	37	66	77
	16	R	26	aaa	SEA	124	6.01	1.71	21.7	2.7	7.1	2.6	1.1	39	66	53
Wilk,Adam	15	L	28	aaa	LAA	145	5.82	1.73	24.4	2.3	5.1	2.2	0.9	38	66	36
	16	L	29	aaa	TAM	87	5.25	1.49	25.1	1.6	5.9	3.7	1.2	35	67	69
Wilkerson,Aaron	16	R	27	a/a	MIL	147	5.14	1.51	22.7	2.9	7.6	2.6	0.9	35	66	68
Williams,Austen	16	R	24	aa	WAS	51	7.71	2.09	24.9	4.3	4.3	1.0	1.0	39	62	-1
Williams,Corey	16	L	26	aa	MIN	37	5.42	1.74	7.68	6.7	5.0	0.8	1.7	27	73	-2
Williams,Ryan	15	R	24	aa	CHC	88	3.34	1.16	20.6	1.7	5.3	3.1	0.2	30	69	93
	16	R	25	aaa	CHC	44	3.88	1.42	20.7	2.6	5.1	2.0	0.9	31	75	42
Williams,Trevor	16	R	24	aaa	PIT	110	3.49	1.45	23.6	2.6	4.8	1.8	0.5	33	76	50
Wilson,Tyler	15	R	26	aaa	BAL	94	5.25	1.60	24.6	2.1	4.7	2.3	1.2	35	70	28
	16	R	27	aaa	BAL	24	7.21	1.66	17.7	1.4	5.8	4.3	0.6	40	54	91
Wimmers,Alex	16	R	28	a/a	MIN	57	5.76	1.72	5.72	4.5	6.5	1.4	0.4	36	65	52
Windle,Tom	15	L	23	aa	PHI	97	4.91	1.64	12.8	4.7	5.2	1.1	0.6	32	70	34
	16	L	24	aa	PHI	32	7.03	1.91	5.99	4.1	8.1	2.0	1.8	39	66	23
Winkler,Kyle	15	R	25	a/a	LAA	42	4.50	1.32	5.66	3.0	6.5	2.2	0.4	31	64	76
	16	R	26	a/a	TAM	33	3.61	1.30	4.49	3.9	8.1	2.1	1.0	29	75	71
Wisler,Matthew	15	R	23	aaa	ATL	65	5.60	1.46	23.2	1.9	6.0	3.2	0.8	35	61	72
	16	R	24	aaa	ATL	27	4.67	1.40	28.1	1.8	6.5	3.6	1.1	34	69	77
Wojciechowski,A	15	R	27	aaa	HOU	115	5.52	1.66	25.8	3.3	5.4	1.7	1.1	35	68	27
	16	R	28	aa	MIA	86	7.31	2.08	21	4.8	4.9	1.0	1.3	38	66	-5
Wolff,Sam	16	R	25	aa	TEX	50	6.58	1.92	23.8	6.3	5.5	0.9	1.5	32	68	0
Wood,Austin	15	R	25	aa	LAA	80	5.14	1.64	11.5	4.7	4.8	1.0	0.6	31	68	30
	16	R	26	aa	LAA	17	6.80	2.22	4.51	8.3	5.2	0.6	0.6	35	68	17
Wood,Hunter	16	R	23	aa	TAM	49	3.89	1.24	20	3.6	7.8	2.1	1.0	27	71	72
Woodruff,Brandon	16	R	23	aa	MIL	114	4.35	1.27	23.3	2.7	8.3	3.1	0.4	33	64	106
Wooten,Robert	15	R	30	aaa	MIL	52	5.86	1.67	5.3	2.8	6.5	2.3	2.1	35	71	15
	16	R	31	aaa	ATL	73	5.08	1.56	9.13	1.6	5.7	3.5	1.4	36	71	56
Wort,Rob	16	R	27	aa	BOS	28	9.50	2.22	8.3	6.2	6.7	1.1	1.1	40	56	14
Wotherspoon,Mat	16	R	25	a/a	NYY	90	3.80	1.41	10.6	4.0	7.3	1.8	0.6	31	74	67
Wright,Austin	16	L	27	aa	ARI	44	6.56	1.79	7.45	5.5	6.2	1.1	1.4	32	65	14
Wright,Daniel	16	R	25	a/a	CIN	104	7.54	1.84	19.3	3.0	6.5	2.2	1.3	39	59	30
Wright,Justin	15	L	26	a/a	STL	57	3.45	1.36	4.94	2.7	6.9	2.6	0.0	34	72	96
	16	L	27	a/a	STL	52	6.29	1.90	5.22	6.1	5.8	1.0	0.6	35	65	32
Wright,Mike	15	R	25	aaa	BAL	81	3.52	1.35	22.5	3.3	5.6	1.7	0.7	29	75	52
	16	R	26	aaa	BAL	76	4.74	1.48	25.3	1.9	4.4	2.3	1.5	32	73	23
Wyatt,Heath	15	R	27	a/a	STL	74	2.71	1.18	6.14	3.0	4.7	1.6	0.5	26	78	54
	16	R	28	a/a	STL	39	7.33	2.21	6.82	3.8	4.7	1.2	1.0	42	67	1
Yacabonis,Jimmy	16	R	24	aa	BAL	44	2.56	1.24	5.29	2.9	7.6	2.6	0.5	30	81	90
Yarbrough,Ryan	16	L	25	aa	SEA	128	3.99	1.33	21.3	2.3	5.9	2.5	0.6	32	70	71
Yardley,Eric	16	R	26	a/a	SD	71	3.43	1.49	6.22	2.1	4.9	2.3	0.7	34	79	51
Yates,Kirby	15	R	28	aaa	TAM	25	7.16	1.91	5.2	4.8	9.4	1.9	2.0	39	66	26
	16	R	29	aaa	NYY	17	2.65	1.49	5.13	4.1	7.8	1.9	0.0	34	80	88
Ynoa,Gabriel	16	R	23	aaa	NYM	154	3.64	1.34	25.7	2.1	3.9	1.9	0.7	30	74	40
Ynoa,Michael	16	R	25	a/a	CHW	28	4.82	1.56	5.77	4.4	6.6	1.5	0.8	32	69	48
Younginer IV,Mad	16	R	26	a/a	ATL	56	5.67	1.64	5.43	4.2	8.0	1.9	0.4	37	63	73
Ysla,Luis	16	L	24	a/a	BOS	56	5.78	1.78	6.48	4.8	8.2	1.7	0.8	38	67	56
Yuhl,Keegan	16	R	24	a/a	HOU	124	4.72	1.47	22.1	1.9	6.4	3.3	0.9	35	69	74
Zastryzny,Rob	16	L	24	a/a	CHC	136	5.10	1.38	23.7	3.5	6.7	1.9	1.0	30	64	54
Zeid,Joshua	15	R	28	aaa	DET	71	5.93	1.86	7.87	5.7	5.4	1.0	0.6	34	67	28
	16	R	29	a/a	NYM	92	5.35	1.66	25.6	4.6	5.4	1.2	1.3	31	70	17

This section provides rankings of projected skills indicators for 2017. Rather than take shots in the dark predicting league leaders in the exact number of home runs, or stolen bases, or strikeouts, the Forecaster's Leaderboards focus on the component elements of each skill.

For batters, we've ranked the top players in terms of pure power, speed, and batting average skill, breaking each down in a number of different ways. For pitchers, we rank some of the key base skills, differentiating between starters and relievers, and provide a few interesting cuts that might uncover some late round sleepers. Plus, some potential gainers/faders lists in several categories.

These are clearly not exhaustive lists of sorts and filters—drop us a note if you see something we should consider for next year's book. Also, the database at BaseballHQ.com allows you to construct your own custom sorts and filters. Finally, remember that these are just tools. Some players will appear on multiple lists—even mutually exclusive lists—so you have to assess what makes most sense and make decisions for your specific application.

Power

Top PX, 400+ AB: Top power skills among projected full-time players.

Top PX, –300 AB: Top power skills among projected part-time players. Possible end-game options are here.

Position Scarcity: A quick scan to see which positions have deeper power options than others.

Top PX, ct% over 80%: Top power skills among the top contact hitters. Best pure power options here.

Top PX, ct% under 70%: Top power skills among the worst contact hitters. These are free-swingers who might be prone to streakiness or lower batting averages.

Top PX, FB% over 40%: Top power skills among the most extreme fly ball hitters. Most likely to convert their power into home runs.

Top PX, FB% under 35%: Top power skills among those with lesser fly ball tendencies. There may be more downside to their home run potential.

Speed

Top Spd, 400+ AB: Top speed skills among projected full-time players.

Top Spd, -300 AB: Top speed skills among projected part-time players. Possible end-game options here.

Position Scarcity: A quick scan to see which positions have deeper speed options than others.

Top Spd, OB% .330 and above: Top speed skills among those who get on base most often. Best opportunities for stolen bases here.

Top Spd, OB% under .300: Top speed skills among those who have trouble getting on base. These names may bear watching if they can improve their on base ability.

Top Spd, SBO% over 20%: Top speed skills among those who get the green light most often. Most likely to convert their speed into stolen bases.

Top Spd, SBO% under 15%: Top speed skills among those who are currently not getting the green light. There may be sleeper SBs here if given more opportunities to run.

Batting Average

Top ct%, 400+ AB: Top contact skills among projected full-time players. Contact does not always convert to higher BAs, but is still strongly correlated.

Top ct%, -300 AB: Top contact skills among projected part-time players. Possible end-gamers here.

Low ct%, 400+ AB: The poorest contact skills among projected full-time players. Potential BA killers.

Top ct%, bb% over 9%: Top contact skills among the most patient hitters. Best batting average upside here.

Top ct%, bb% under 6%: Top contact skills among the least patient hitters. These are free-swingers who might be prone to streakiness or lower batting averages.

Top ct%, GB% over 50%: Top contact skills among the most extreme ground ball hitters. A ground ball has a higher chance of becoming a hit than a non-HR fly ball so there may be some batting average upside here.

Top ct%, GB% under 40%: Top contact skills from those with lesser ground ball tendencies. These players make contact but hit more fly balls, which tend to convert to hits at a lower rate than GB.

Pitching Skills

Top Command: Leaders in projected K/BB rates.

Top Control: Leaders in fewest projected walks allowed.

Top Dominance: Leaders in projected strikeout rate.

Top Ground Ball Rate: GB pitchers tend to have lower ERAs (and higher WHIP) than fly ball pitchers.

Top Fly Ball Rate: FB pitchers tend to have higher ERAs (and lower WHIP) than ground ball pitchers.

High GB, Low Dom: GB pitchers tend to have lower K rates, but these are the most extreme examples.

High GB, High Dom: The best at dominating hitters and keeping the ball down. These are the pitchers who keep runners off the bases and batted balls in the park, a skills combination that is the most valuable a pitcher can own.

Lowest xERA: Leaders in projected skills-based ERA.

Top BPV: Two lists of top skilled pitchers. For starters, those projected to be rotation regulars (180+ IP) and fringe starters with skill (<150 IP). For relievers, those projected to be frontline closers (10+ saves) and high-skilled bullpen fillers (<9 saves).

Potential Gainers and Faders

These charts look to identify upcoming changes in performance by highlighting 2016 results that were in conflict with their corresponding skill indicators.

PX Gainers/Faders: Compares PX to xPX.

BA Gainers/Faders: Compares batter hit rate (h%) to HctX.

Dom Gainers/Faders: Compares K/9 to SwK%.

Ctl Gainers/Faders: Compares BB/9 to FpK%.

Additional details are provided on the page in which the charts appear.

Risk Management

These lists include players who've accumulated the most days on the disabled list over the past five years (Grade "F" in Health) and whose performance was the most consistent over the past three years. Also listed are the most reliable batters and pitchers overall, with a focus on positional and skills reliability. As a reminder, reliability in this context is not tied to skill level; it is a gauge of which players manage to accumulate playing time and post consistent output from year to year, whether that output is good or bad.

Mayberry Portfolio3 Plan

Players are sorted and ranked based on how they fit into the three draft tiers of the Portfolio3 Plan used in conjunction with the Mayberry Method, as detailed on page 54.

Daily Fantasy Indicators

Players splits, teams and park factors designed to give you an edge in DFS.

BATTER SKILLS RANKING - Power

TOP PX, 400+ AB

NAME	POS	PX
Sano,Miguel	0 5 9	186
Stanton,Giancarlo	9	183
Carter,Chris	3	181
Story,Trevor	6	177
Davis,Chris	3	174
Bird,Gregory	0	169
Davis,Khristopher	0 7	167
Bryant,Kris	5 7	162
Pederson,Joc	8	161
Grichuk,Randal	8	158
Trout,Mike	8	154
Duvall,Adam	7	154
Alvarez,Pedro	0	151
Cruz,Nelson	0 9	151
Freeman,Freddie	3	151
Moss,Brandon	3 7 9	150
Santana,Domingo	9	150
Schwarber,Kyle	7	150
Encarnacion,Edwin	0 3	148
Lamb,Jacob	5	147
Carpenter,Matt	3 4 5	147
Arenado,Nolan	5	147
Martinez,J.D.	9	146
Gattis,Evan	0 2	144
Dozier,Brian	4	142
Cespedes,Yoenis	7 8	142
Harper,Bryce	9	141
Trumbo,Mark	0 9	141
Gonzalez,Carlos	9	141
Rizzo,Anthony	3	140
Upton,Justin	7	139
Donaldson,Josh	5	139
Sanchez,Gary	2	139
Kang,Jung-ho	5	138
Napoli,Mike	0 3	138
Votto,Joey	3	138
Bautista,Jose	0 9	137
Belt,Brandon	3	137
Dickerson,Corey	0 7	137
Tomas,Yasmany	7 9	136

TOP PX, 300 or fewer AB

NAME	POS	PX
O Brien,Peter	7	193
Gallo,Joey	5	189
Howard,Ryan	3	156
Chirinos,Robinson	2	148
Hazelbaker,Jeremy	7 8	132
Nieuwenhuis,Kirk	8 9	132
Shaffer,Richie	3	132
Austin,Tyler	3	132
Young,Chris	7	132
Beckham,Tim	6	131
Gutierrez,Franklin	9	129
Casali,Curtis	2	126
Smoak,Justin	3	125
Meadows,Austin		125
Saltalamacchia,Jarrod	2	124
Marte,Jefry	3 5 7	124
Moya,Steven	9	123
Rodriguez,Sean	3 4 6	123
Haniger,Mitch	8	118
Hamilton,Josh	0	117
Arcia,Oswaldo	9	117
Olson,Matt	9	117
Toles,Andrew	7	115

POSITIONAL SCARCITY

NAME	POS	PX
Sano,Miguel	DH	186
Bird,Gregory	2	169
Davis,Khristopher	3	167
Alvarez,Pedro	4	151
Cruz,Nelson	5	151
Encarnacion,Edwin	6	148
Murphy,Tom	CA	153
Chirinos,Robinson	2	148
Gattis,Evan	3	144
Sanchez,Gary	4	139
Grandal,Yasmani	5	135
Contreras,Willson	6	129
Zunino,Mike	7	129
Casali,Curtis	8	126
Carter,Chris	1B	181
Davis,Chris	2	174
Howard,Ryan	3	156
Freeman,Freddie	4	151
Moss,Brandon	5	150
Encarnacion,Edwin	6	148
Carpenter,Matt	7	147
Rizzo,Anthony	8	140
Napoli,Mike	9	138
Votto,Joey	10	138
Schimpf,Ryan	2B	174
Carpenter,Matt	2	147
Dozier,Brian	3	142
Rodriguez,Sean	4	123
Odor,Rougned	5	121
Coghlan,Chris	6	114
Murphy,Daniel	7	114
Turner,Trea	8	112
Gallo,Joey	3B	189
Sano,Miguel	2	186
Bryant,Kris	3	162
Lamb,Jacob	4	147
Carpenter,Matt	5	147
Arenado,Nolan	6	147
Donaldson,Josh	7	139
Kang,Jung-ho	8	138
Castellanos,Nick	9	130
Frazier,Todd	10	130
Story,Trevor	SS	177
Beckham,Tim	2	131
Machado,Manny	3	125
Rodriguez,Sean	4	123
Correa,Carlos	5	120
Russell,Addison	6	120
Seager,Corey	7	119
Miller,Bradley	8	118
O Brien,Peter	OF	193
Sano,Miguel	2	186
Stanton,Giancarlo	3	183
Davis,Khristopher	4	167
Bryant,Kris	5	162
Pederson,Joc	6	161
Grichuk,Randal	7	158
Trout,Mike	8	154
Duvall,Adam	9	154
Cruz,Nelson	10	151
Moss,Brandon	11	150
Santana,Domingo	12	150
Schwarber,Kyle	13	150
Martinez,J.D.	14	146
Cespedes,Yoenis	15	142
Harper,Bryce	16	141

TOP PX, Ct% over 80%

NAME	Ct%	PX
Arenado,Nolan	84	147
Rizzo,Anthony	81	140
Cabrera,Miguel	81	132
Benintendi,Andrew	83	125
Machado,Manny	81	125
Kepler,Max	80	121
Bregman,Alex	81	119
Seager,Kyle	82	118
Santana,Carlos	80	118
Turner,Justin	81	115
Blackmon,Charlie	82	114
Murphy,Daniel	89	114
Bour,Justin	80	113
Holliday,Matt	81	113
Moustakas,Mike	84	111
Drury,Brandon	81	110
Betts,Mookie	87	109
Diaz,Aledmys	82	108
Cano,Robinson	85	108
Beltran,Carlos	82	106
Gonzalez,Adrian	81	106
Beltre,Adrian	88	105
Pollock,A.J.	84	105
Perez,Salvador	81	105
Cabrera,Asdrubal	80	103
Lucroy,Jonathan	82	103
Jones,Adam	81	102
Walker,Neil	81	101
Gurriel,Yulieski	85	101
Flores,Wilmer	85	101
Franco,Maikel	83	101
Pujols,Albert	88	97.6
Kiermaier,Kevin	80	96.5
Zobrist,Ben	85	95.8
Chisenhall,Lonnie	80	95.8
Vogt,Stephen	82	95
Altuve,Jose	90	94.4
Peralta,Jhonny	80	93
Almora,Albert	85	92.9
Hosmer,Eric	80	92.8

TOP PX, Ct% under 70%

NAME	Ct%	PX
O Brien,Peter	62	193
Gallo,Joey	52	189
Sano,Miguel	61	186
Stanton,Giancarlo	68	183
Carter,Chris	62	181
Story,Trevor	68	177
Davis,Chris	62	174
Schimpf,Ryan	68	174
Pederson,Joc	66	161
Howard,Ryan	67	156
Moss,Brandon	67	150
Santana,Domingo	63	150
Judge,Aaron	64	139
Napoli,Mike	67	138
Hazelbaker,Jeremy	67	132
Nieuwenhuis,Kirk	63	132
Shaffer,Richie	63	132
Austin,Tyler	68	132
Beckham,Tim	69	131
Gutierrez,Franklin	67	129
Zunino,Mike	68	129
Saunders,Michael	70	128
Vargas,Kennys	68	128

Top PX, FB% over 40%

NAME	FB%	PX
O Brien,Peter	53	193
Sano,Miguel	44	186
Stanton,Giancarlo	43	183
Carter,Chris	50	181
Story,Trevor	47	177
Davis,Chris	42	174
Schimpf,Ryan	63	174
Bird,Gregory	48	169
Davis,Khristopher	40	167
Bryant,Kris	46	162
Pederson,Joc	40	161
Grichuk,Randal	43	158
Duvall,Adam	46	154
Moss,Brandon	51	150
Schwarber,Kyle	42	150
Chirinos,Robinson	44	148
Encarnacion,Edwin	42	148
Carpenter,Matt	43	147
Arenado,Nolan	44	147
Gattis,Evan	41	144
Dozier,Brian	45	142
Cespedes,Yoenis	42	142
Harper,Bryce	40	141
Trumbo,Mark	42	141
Rizzo,Anthony	41	140
Upton,Justin	42	139
Judge,Aaron	47	139
Napoli,Mike	43	138
Bautista,Jose	44	137
Belt,Brandon	44	137
Bruce,Jay	41	134
Renfroe,Hunter	43	133
Shaffer,Richie	45	132
Austin,Tyler	40	132
Young,Chris	48	132
Conforto,Michael	43	131
Joseph,Tommy	43	131
Castellanos,Nick	43	130
Frazier,Todd	46	130
Duda,Lucas	46	129

Top PX, FB% under 35%

NAME	FB%	PX
Alvarez,Pedro	34	151
Santana,Domingo	28	150
Kang,Jung-ho	35	138
Votto,Joey	31	138
Tomas,Yasmany	31	136
Goldschmidt,Paul	31	136
Hazelbaker,Jeremy	35	132
Nieuwenhuis,Kirk	33	132
Beckham,Tim	34	131
Contreras,Willson	28	129
Bradley,Jackie	34	127
Broxton,Keon	29	126
Naquin,Tyler	29	124
Moya,Steven	33	123
Springer,George	32	123
Correa,Carlos	28	120
Seager,Corey	28	119
Martin,Russell	34	118
Peralta,David	28	117
Dahl,David	33	117
Williamson,Mac	27	117
Souza,Steven	35	117
Braun,Ryan	29	115

BATTER SKILLS RANKING - Speed

TOP Spd, 400+ AB

NAME	POS	Spd
Gordon,Dee	4	196
Turner,Trea	4 8	187
Buxton,Byron	8	187
Anderson,Tim	6	179
Hamilton,Billy	8	178
Peraza,Jose	6	169
Segura,Jean	4 6	165
Hernandez,Cesar	4	161
LeMahieu,DJ	4	158
Fowler,Dexter	8	157
Revere,Ben	7 8	156
Marte,Starling	7	155
Inciarte,Ender	8	153
Swanson,Dansby	6	153
Nunez,Eduardo	5 6	150
Owings,Christopher	6 8	149
Pollock,A.J.	8	148
Dahl,David	7	144
Arcia,Orlando	6	143
Hechavarria,Adeiny	6	143
Escobar,Alcides	6	142
Broxton,Keon	8	142
Betts,Mookie	9	141
Rosario,Eddie	7 8	140
Upton,Melvin	7 8	137
Maybin,Cameron	8	137
Eaton,Adam	8 9	136
Herrera,Odubel	8	136
Perez,Hernan	5 9	136
Diaz,Aledmys	6	135
Harrison,Josh	4	133
Duffy,Matt	5	133
Reyes,Jose	5	131
Jackson,Austin	8	131
Bogaerts,Xander	6	131
Andrus,Elvis	6	130
Cain,Lorenzo	8 9	130
Kiermaier,Kevin	8	129
Springer,George	9	128
Naquin,Tyler	8	128

TOP Spd, 300 or fewer AB

NAME	POS	Spd
Bourjos,Peter	9	169
Tapia,Raimel	8	168
Mondesi,Raul	4	164
Rickard,Joey	7 9	163
Dyson,Jarrod	8 9	159
Torreyes,Ronald	5	157
Goeddel,Tyler	7	153
Heredia,Guillermo	7	147
Orlando,Paulo	8 9	144
Holt,Tyler	8 9	140
Beckham,Tim	6	140
Burns,Billy	8	139
Hernandez,Teoscar	7	138
Moncada,Yoan	5	137
Albies,Ozhaino	4 6	136
Santana,Danny	8	134
Deshields Jr.,Delino	7 8	134
Frazier,Adam	7	133
Tomlinson,Kelby	4	133
Jennings,Desmond	7 8	133
Pompey,Dalton	7	132
Wendle,Joe	4	132
O Malley,Shawn	6	132

POSITIONAL SCARCITY

NAME	POS	Spd
Zimmer,Bradley	DH	115
Dickerson,Corey	2	100
Bird,Gregory	3	98
Gattis,Evan	4	97
Garcia,Avisail	5	95
Sano,Miguel	6	94
Herrmann,Chris	CA	114
Murphy,Tom	2	114
Realmuto,Jacob	3	112
Lobaton,Jose	4	111
Brown,Trevor	5	106
Murphy,John	6	104
Joseph,Caleb	7	103
Contreras,Willson	8	103
Refsnyder,Rob	1B	124
Rua,Ryan	2	123
Myers,Wil	3	122
Miller,Bradley	4	115
Belt,Brandon	5	115
Paulsen,Benjamin	6	110
Ackley,Dustin	7	106
Rojas,Miguel	8	102
Flores,Wilmer	9	100
Ramirez,Hanley	10	98
Gordon,Dee	2B	196
Turner,Trea	2	187
Segura,Jean	3	165
Mondesi,Raul	4	164
Hernandez,Cesar	5	161
LeMahieu,DJ	6	158
Spangenberg,Cory	7	138
Albies,Ozhaino	8	136
Torreyes,Ronald	3B	157
Nunez,Eduardo	2	150
Moncada,Yoan	3	137
Perez,Hernan	4	136
Duffy,Matt	5	133
Reyes,Jose	6	131
Jones,JaCoby	7	131
Bregman,Alex	8	122
Villar,Jonathan	9	118
Bryant,Kris	10	117
Anderson,Tim	SS	179
Peraza,Jose	2	169
Segura,Jean	3	165
Swanson,Dansby	4	153
Nunez,Eduardo	5	150
Owings,Christopher	6	149
Arcia,Orlando	7	143
Hechavarria,Adeiny	8	143
Turner,Trea	OF	187
Buxton,Byron	2	187
Quinn,Roman	3	179
Hamilton,Billy	4	178
Bourjos,Peter	5	169
Tapia,Raimel	6	168
Rickard,Joey	7	163
Dyson,Jarrod	8	159
Fowler,Dexter	9	157
Revere,Ben	10	156
Marte,Starling	11	155
Inciarte,Ender	12	153
Goeddel,Tyler	13	153
Owings,Christopher	14	149
Margot,Manuel	15	149
Pollock,A.J.	16	148

TOP Spd, .330+ OBP

NAME	OBP	Spd
Turner,Trea	346	187
Quinn,Roman	338	179
Segura,Jean	333	165
Hernandez,Cesar	360	161
LeMahieu,DJ	373	158
Fowler,Dexter	377	157
Marte,Starling	350	155
Inciarte,Ender	338	153
Heredia,Guillermo	339	147
Dahl,David	331	144
Betts,Mookie	368	141
Holt,Tyler	336	140
Maybin,Cameron	330	137
Eaton,Adam	360	136
Herrera,Odubel	342	136
Albies,Ozhaino	340	136
Diaz,Aledmys	348	135
Frazier,Adam	343	133
Pompey,Dalton	342	132
Bogaerts,Xander	343	131
Andrus,Elvis	343	130
Cain,Lorenzo	335	130
Springer,George	357	128
Naquin,Tyler	339	128
Lindor,Francisco	344	128
Blanco,Gregor	337	128
Aoki,Norichika	347	128
Story,Trevor	331	126
Trout,Mike	421	126
Gardner,Brett	344	123
Myers,Wil	331	122
McCutchen,Andrew	374	122
Blackmon,Charlie	361	121
Altuve,Jose	373	121
Kepler,Max	337	120
Kinsler,Ian	339	119
Villar,Jonathan	340	118
Bryant,Kris	381	117
Forsythe,Logan	334	117
Barreto,Franklin	334	117

TOP Spd, OBP under .300

NAME	OBP	Spd
Anderson,Tim	292	179
Bourjos,Peter	288	169
Mondesi,Raul	279	164
Goeddel,Tyler	299	153
Owings,Christopher	295	149
Margot,Manuel	298	149
Orlando,Paulo	298	144
Arcia,Orlando	295	143
Hechavarria,Adeiny	294	143
Escobar,Alcides	299	142
Rosario,Eddie	292	140
Burns,Billy	291	139
Hernandez,Teoscar	280	138
Upton,Melvin	290	137
Perez,Hernan	288	136
Santana,Danny	285	134
Wendle,Joe	274	132
O Malley,Shawn	296	132
Brito,Socrates	279	131
Jones,JaCoby	295	131
Martin,Leonys	298	126
Brinson,Lewis	293	125
Ortega,Rafael	288	124

Top Spd, SBO% over 20%

NAME	SBO%	Spd
Gordon,Dee	42%	196
Turner,Trea	34%	187
Buxton,Byron	23%	187
Anderson,Tim	30%	179
Quinn,Roman	45%	179
Hamilton,Billy	56%	178
Peraza,Jose	36%	169
Tapia,Raimel	33%	168
Segura,Jean	26%	165
Mondesi,Raul	41%	164
Dyson,Jarrod	50%	159
Revere,Ben	24%	156
Marte,Starling	38%	155
Nunez,Eduardo	29%	150
Margot,Manuel	34%	149
Pollock,A.J.	21%	148
Smith,Mallex	44%	148
Lagares,Juan	20%	148
Jankowski,Travis	37%	147
Dahl,David	20%	144
Arcia,Orlando	21%	143
Broxton,Keon	42%	142
Burns,Billy	34%	139
Spangenberg,Cory	26%	138
Hernandez,Teoscar	35%	138
Upton,Melvin	25%	137
Moncada,Yoan	23%	137
Perez,Hernan	29%	136
Albies,Ozhaino	27%	136
Santana,Danny	31%	134
Deshields Jr.,Delino	33%	134
Frazier,Adam	21%	133
Davis,Rajai	45%	133
Tomlinson,Kelby	24%	133
Pompey,Dalton	27%	132
Reyes,Jose	21%	131
Jones,JaCoby	24%	131
Andrus,Elvis	21%	130
Cain,Lorenzo	22%	130
Kiermaier,Kevin	23%	129

Top Spd, SBO% under 15%

NAME	SBO%	Spd
LeMahieu,DJ	13%	158
Torreyes,Ronald	13%	157
Fowler,Dexter	12%	157
Swanson,Dansby	9%	153
Goeddel,Tyler	15%	153
Heredia,Guillermo	12%	147
Hechavarria,Adeiny	5%	143
Beckham,Tim	11%	140
Rosario,Eddie	14%	140
Eaton,Adam	13%	136
Diaz,Aledmys	11%	135
Jennings,Desmond	15%	133
Duffy,Matt	11%	133
Wendle,Joe	13%	132
Jackson,Austin	13%	131
Suzuki,Ichiro	14%	131
Bogaerts,Xander	8%	131
Nimmo,Brandon	9%	130
Springer,George	10%	128
Naquin,Tyler	13%	128
Gregorius,Didi	6%	128
Story,Trevor	15%	126
Gosselin,Phil	8%	126

BATTER SKILLS RANKING - Batting Average

TOP ct%, 400+ AB

NAME	ct%	BA
Simmons,Andrelton	91	284
Revere,Ben	90	271
Altuve,Jose	90	325
Murphy,Daniel	89	315
Panik,Joe	89	282
Brantley,Michael	89	280
Ramirez,Jose	89	280
Iglesias,Jose	89	266
Beltre,Adrian	88	295
Molina,Yadier	88	285
Pedroia,Dustin	88	305
Posey,Buster	88	301
Span,Denard	88	283
Prado,Martin	88	294
Pujols,Albert	88	265
Ramirez,Alexei	88	251
Cabrera,Melky	88	293
Peraza,Jose	87	279
Betts,Mookie	87	316
Inciarte,Ender	87	288
Phillips,Brandon	87	288
Escobar,Yunel	87	288
Martinez,Victor	87	273
Solarte,Yangervis	86	274
Aybar,Erick	86	259
Kim,Hyun-Soo	86	291
Andrus,Elvis	86	286
Escobar,Alcides	86	263
Zobrist,Ben	85	269
Pagan,Angel	85	271
Markakis,Nick	85	275
Sandoval,Pablo	85	269
Cano,Robinson	85	298
Gurriel,Yulieski	85	264
Kinsler,Ian	85	285
Reddick,Josh	85	265
Moustakas,Mike	84	269
Pillar,Kevin	84	269
Gregorius,Didi	84	264
Segura,Jean	84	290
Hechavarria,Adeiny	84	253
Harrison,Josh	84	278
Reyes,Jose	84	261
Arenado,Nolan	84	291
Nunez,Eduardo	84	273
Pollock,A.J.	84	281
Ellsbury,Jacoby	84	260
LeMahieu,DJ	84	307
Lindor,Francisco	84	292
Benintendi,Andrew	83	288
Gordon,Dee	83	282
Heyward,Jason	83	262
Wong,Kolten	83	253
Duffy,Matt	83	274
Mercer,Jordy	83	250
Franco,Maikel	83	264
Lucroy,Jonathan	82	286
Marte,Ketel	82	261
Blackmon,Charlie	82	304
Polanco,Jorge	82	269
Cozart,Zack	82	246
Barnhart,Tucker	82	255
Hardy,J.J.	82	253
Diaz,Aledmys	82	274
Seager,Kyle	82	273
Vogt,Stephen	82	257

LOW ct%, 400+ AB

NAME	ct%	BA
Sano,Miguel	61	238
Broxton,Keon	62	237
Carter,Chris	62	220
Davis,Chris	62	230
Santana,Domingo	63	252
Souza,Steven	65	242
Rasmus,Colby	66	220
Pederson,Joc	66	240
Buxton,Byron	67	247
Napoli,Mike	67	240
Moss,Brandon	67	226
Upton,Melvin	67	227
Story,Trevor	68	260
Stanton,Giancarlo	68	262
Soler,Jorge	68	248
Zunino,Mike	68	230
Rupp,Cameron	69	225
Springer,George	69	260
Saunders,Michael	70	247
Bird,Gregory	70	248
Duvall,Adam	70	232
Altherr,Aaron	70	235
Grichuk,Randal	70	255
Upton,Justin	70	255
Villar,Jonathan	70	270
Davis,Khristopher	71	249
Alvarez,Pedro	71	244
Naquin,Tyler	71	264
Lamb,Jacob	71	267
Schwarber,Kyle	71	243
Belt,Brandon	71	271
Martinez,J.D.	71	292
Bryant,Kris	72	288
Gomez,Carlos	72	250
Grandal,Yasmani	72	241
Castillo,Welington	72	250

TOP ct%, 300 or fewer AB

NAME	ct%	BA
Shuck,J.B.	90	226
Torreyes,Ronald	89	262
Loney,James	89	269
Giavotella,Johnny	88	264
Renda,Tony	87	250
Heredia,Guillermo	87	251
Rojas,Miguel	86	240
Suzuki,Ichiro	86	268
Frazier,Adam	86	288
La Stella,Tommy	85	271
Almora,Albert	85	249
Hill,Aaron	84	250
Ortega,Rafael	84	240
Rivera,T.J.	84	271
Dyson,Jarrod	84	267
Barney,Darwin	84	239
Gillaspie,Conor	83	261
Kemp,Anthony	83	249
Butler,Billy	83	270
Barnes,Austin	83	243
Ackley,Dustin	83	214
Tapia,Raimel	82	293
Centeno,Juan	82	246
Amarista,Alexi	82	239
Ramos,Wilson	82	274
Ahmed,Nick	82	234
Guyer,Brandon	81	264

TOP ct%, bb% over 9%

NAME	bb%	ct%
Posey,Buster	10	88
Heredia,Guillermo	10	87
Kim,Hyun-Soo	11	86
Zobrist,Ben	14	85
La Stella,Tommy	9	85
Markakis,Nick	10	85
Bell,Josh	10	84
LeMahieu,DJ	10	84
Crawford,J.P.	11	83
Heyward,Jason	9	83
Crisp,Coco	10	82
Diaz,Aledmys	9	82
Seager,Kyle	9	82
Mauer,Joe	12	81
Cabrera,Miguel	12	81
Holliday,Matt	10	81
Rizzo,Anthony	11	81
Winker,Jesse	13	81
Kepler,Max	10	80
Santana,Carlos	16	80
Bour,Justin	10	80
Encarnacion,Edwin	13	80
Rendon,Anthony	10	80
Ethier,Andre	10	80
Choi,Ji-Man	11	80
Contreras,Willson	9	80
Profar,Jurickson	10	79
McCann,Brian	10	79
Jaso,John	12	79
Donaldson,Josh	13	79
Blanco,Gregor	11	79
Peterson,Jace	11	79
Hernandez,Cesar	11	79
Gardner,Brett	11	78
Coghlan,Chris	12	78
Rickard,Joey	9	78
Votto,Joey	18	78
Kipnis,Jason	9	78
Bautista,Jose	17	78
Hicks,Aaron	9	78

TOP ct%, bb% under 6%

NAME	bb%	ct%
Revere,Ben	4	90
Torreyes,Ronald	5	89
Loney,James	5	89
Iglesias,Jose	5	89
Giavotella,Johnny	5	88
Ramirez,Alexei	5	88
Peraza,Jose	4	87
Phillips,Brandon	4	87
Suzuki,Kurt	6	87
Aybar,Erick	6	86
Rojas,Miguel	5	86
Escobar,Alcides	4	86
Almora,Albert	4	85
Flores,Wilmer	5	85
Margot,Manuel	5	85
Pillar,Kevin	5	84
Gregorius,Didi	5	84
Segura,Jean	5	84
Hechavarria,Adeiny	5	84
Harrison,Josh	4	84
Nunez,Eduardo	5	84
Rivera,T.J.	3	84
Gillaspie,Conor	6	83

Top ct%, GB% over 50%

NAME	GB%	ct%
Simmons,Andrelton	54	91
Revere,Ben	58	90
Aoki,Norichika	59	90
Shuck,J.B.	55	90
Torreyes,Ronald	55	89
Iglesias,Jose	54	89
Span,Denard	51	88
Ramirez,Alexei	50	88
Inciarte,Ender	51	87
Escobar,Yunel	56	87
Renda,Tony	56	87
Aybar,Erick	54	86
Rojas,Miguel	56	86
Suzuki,Ichiro	52	86
Kim,Hyun-Soo	52	86
Andrus,Elvis	50	86
Segura,Jean	56	84
Nunez,Eduardo	52	84
Ortega,Rafael	56	84
Dyson,Jarrod	56	84
Gordon,Dee	58	83
Duffy,Matt	51	83
Centeno,Juan	51	82
Marte,Ketel	53	82
Ramos,Wilson	56	82
Adames,Cristhian	61	81
Sardinas,Luis	59	81
Mauer,Joe	53	81
Garcia,Adonis	51	81
Eaton,Adam	54	81
Gosselin,Phil	54	81
Refsnyder,Rob	53	81
Arcia,Orlando	53	81
Drury,Brandon	51	81
Kendrick,Howie	59	80
Jay,Jon	56	80
Burns,Billy	52	80
Tomlinson,Kelby	50	80
Hosmer,Eric	55	80
Holt,Brock	54	80

Top ct%, GB% under 40%

NAME	GB%	ct%
Betts,Mookie	40	87
Martinez,Victor	39	87
La Stella,Tommy	38	85
Flores,Wilmer	37	85
Kinsler,Ian	34	85
Reddick,Josh	37	85
Moustakas,Mike	39	84
Gregorius,Didi	40	84
Hill,Aaron	38	84
Arenado,Nolan	36	84
Benintendi,Andrew	36	83
Gillaspie,Conor	40	83
Tapia,Raimel	37	82
Lucroy,Jonathan	40	82
Blackmon,Charlie	37	82
Polanco,Jorge	36	82
Seager,Kyle	36	82
Vogt,Stephen	32	82
Machado,Manny	40	81
Walker,Neil	39	81
Turner,Justin	39	81
Bregman,Alex	33	81
Rizzo,Anthony	38	81

POTENTIAL SKILLS GAINERS AND FADERS - Batters

Power Gainers

Batters whose 2016 Power Index (PX) fell significantly short of their underlying power skill (xPX). If they show the same xPX skill in 2017, they are good candidates for more power output.

Power Faders

Batters whose 2016 Power Index (PX) noticeably outpaced their underlying power skill (xPX). If they show the same xPX skill in 2017, they are good candidates for less power output.

BA Gainers

Batters who had strong Hard Contact Index levels in 2016, but lower hit rates (h%). Since base hits come most often on hard contact, if these batters can make hard contact at the same strong rate again in 2017, they may get better results in terms of hit rate, resulting in a batting average improvement.

BA Faders

Batters who had weak Hard Contact Index levels in 2016, but higher hit rates (h%). Since base hits come most often on hard contact, if these batters only make hard contact at the same weak rate again in 2017, they may get worse results in terms of hit rate, resulting in a batting average decline.

PX GAINERS

NAME	PX	xPX
De Aza,Alejandro	78	157
Choo,Shin-Soo	97	127
Beckham,Gordon	89	123
McCann,Brian	97	120
Montero,Miguel	84	115
Crawford,Brandon	92	114
McCann,James	88	112
Jones,Adam	92	110
Hardy,J.J.	89	110
Bethancourt,Christian	95	109
Headley,Chase	83	108
Markakis,Nick	82	105
Hicks,Aaron	72	104
Centeno,Juan	88	104
Hill,Aaron	66	102
Gillaspie,Conor	92	102
Bandy,Jett	90	101
Harrison,Josh	63	99
Gonzalez,Marwin	94	99
Dietrich,Derek	93	99
Descalso,Daniel	96	99
Jennings,Desmond	95	99
Marte,Starling	95	98
Jackson,Austin	66	97
LeMahieu,DJ	84	95
Butler,Billy	86	95
Gonzalez,Adrian	93	94
Alonso,Yonder	76	94
Iannetta,Chris	83	94
Coghlan,Chris	87	94
Mahtook,Mikie	81	94
Barnhart,Tucker	79	93
Fielder,Prince	76	92
Ahmed,Nick	50	92
Johnson,Chris	80	92
Ellis,A.J.	55	92
Franco,Maikel	95	91

PX FADERS

NAME	PX	xPX
Blanco,Andres	103	68
Marisnick,Jake	91	68
Crisp,Coco	98	69
Lee,Dae-ho	103	72
Eibner,Brett	105	72
Bogaerts,Xander	91	73
Chisenhall,Lonnie	93	77
Gregorius,Didi	96	78
Kiermaier,Kevin	98	78
Desmond,Ian	101	81
Leon,Sandy	112	82
Buxton,Byron	158	85
Almonte,Abraham	109	85
Gomez,Carlos	111	87
Morneau,Justin	113	88
Lawrie,Brett	119	92
Cano,Robinson	124	96
Hazelbaker,Jeremy	152	96
Braun,Ryan	127	97
Beckham,Tim	131	97
Castro,Jason	124	102
Healy,Ryon	137	102
Beltran,Carlos	124	103
Marte,Jefry	135	109
Frazier,Todd	142	111
Miller,Bradley	147	116
Gattis,Evan	157	119
Alvarez,Pedro	163	120
Cruz,Nelson	160	134
Davis,Khristopher	171	145

BA GAINERS

NAME	h%	HctX
Holliday,Matt	25	127
De Aza,Alejandro	26	127
Bautista,Jose	26	126
Howard,Ryan	21	122
Kang,Jung-ho	28	120
Bruce,Jay	27	119
Encarnacion,Edwin	28	118
Conforto,Michael	27	115
Dickerson,Alex	28	114
Bour,Justin	28	114
Granderson,Curtis	26	114
Lind,Adam	26	114
Marte,Jefry	27	113
Joseph,Tommy	27	113
Alvarez,Pedro	28	112
Hechavarria,Adeiny	27	112
Davis,Khristopher	27	111
McCann,Brian	27	111
Duvall,Adam	28	111
Grandal,Yasmani	25	111
Gillaspie,Conor	28	110
Moreland,Mitch	27	110
Dozier,Brian	28	109
Jones,Adam	28	108
Gyorko,Jedd	24	107
Loney,James	28	107
Harper,Bryce	27	106
Miller,Bradley	28	104
Cozart,Zack	28	104
Joyce,Matt	28	104
Kepler,Max	27	103
Carter,Chris	27	103
Kiermaier,Kevin	28	102
Franco,Maikel	27	102
Duda,Lucas	25	102
Ellis,A.J.	25	102
Iannetta,Chris	27	102

BA FADERS

NAME	h%	HctX
Buxton,Byron	34	67
Jankowski,Travis	34	68
Avila,Alex	35	71
Garcia,Greg	35	74
Bourn,Michael	34	78
Maybin,Cameron	38	81
Hernandez,Cesar	36	83
Francoeur,Jeff	34	84
Herrera,Odubel	35	85
Dietrich,Derek	35	86
Cervelli,Francisco	34	86
Gosselin,Phil	34	87
Baez,Javier	34	88
Fowler,Dexter	35	90
Grossman,Robert	36	91
Desmond,Ian	35	92
Jay,Jon	37	93
Leon,Sandy	40	94
Anderson,Tim	38	94
Healy,Ryon	35	95
Andrus,Elvis	34	95
Cain,Lorenzo	35	96
Almonte,Abraham	34	96
Contreras,Willson	34	96
Escobar,Yunel	34	96
Beckham,Tim	35	97
Freese,David	37	97
Dahl,David	40	97

PITCHER SKILLS RANKINGS - Starting Pitchers

Top Command (k/bb)

NAME	Cmd
Kershaw,Clayton	7.1
Scherzer,Max	5.2
Tomlin,Josh	5.2
Tanaka,Masahiro	5.1
Sale,Chris	5.1
Musgrove,Joe	4.9
Bumgarner,Madison	4.9
Strasburg,Stephen	4.9
Price,David	4.9
Syndergaard,Noah	4.6
Porcello,Rick	4.5
Carrasco,Carlos	4.3
Shoemaker,Matthew	4.3
Kluber,Corey	4.3
Chen,Wei-Yin	4.3
Pineda,Michael	4.3
Colon,Bartolo	4.2
Hughes,Phil	4.2
Lester,Jon	4.0
Nola,Aaron	4.0
Iwakuma,Hisashi	4.0
Cueto,Johnny	4.0
Andriese,Matt	3.9
Harvey,Matt	3.9
deGrom,Jacob	3.9
Verlander,Justin	3.8
De Leon,Jose	3.8
Stewart,Brock	3.8
Hendricks,Kyle	3.7
Stroman,Marcus	3.7
Taillon,Jameson	3.7

Top Control (bb/9)

NAME	Ctl
Tomlin,Josh	1.2
Neal,Zachary	1.4
Musgrove,Joe	1.4
Kershaw,Clayton	1.5
Colon,Bartolo	1.5
Hughes,Phil	1.6
Tanaka,Masahiro	1.6
Porcello,Rick	1.6
Chen,Wei-Yin	1.7
Shoemaker,Matthew	1.8
Alcantara,Raul	1.8
Iwakuma,Hisashi	1.8
Price,David	1.8
Leake,Mike	1.9
Sale,Chris	1.9
Nicolino,Justin	1.9
Eflin,Zach	2.0
Taillon,Jameson	2.0
Bumgarner,Madison	2.0
Stewart,Brock	2.0
Cueto,Johnny	2.0
Hendricks,Kyle	2.0
Andriese,Matt	2.0
Scherzer,Max	2.1
Stroman,Marcus	2.2
Carrasco,Carlos	2.2
Quintana,Jose	2.2
Pineda,Michael	2.2
DeSclafani,Anthony	2.2
Syndergaard,Noah	2.2
Lester,Jon	2.2

Top Dominance (k/9)

NAME	Dom
McCullers,Lance	11.2
Reyes,Alex	11.0
Darvish,Yu	10.9
Strasburg,Stephen	10.9
Scherzer,Max	10.9
Kershaw,Clayton	10.3
Velasquez,Vincent	10.1
De Leon,Jose	10.1
Snell,Blake	10.1
Syndergaard,Noah	10.1
Salazar,Danny	10.0
Archer,Chris	9.8
Ray,Robbie	9.8
Kluber,Corey	9.6
Bumgarner,Madison	9.6
Liriano,Francisco	9.6
Sale,Chris	9.5
Strahm,Matt	9.4
Weaver,Luke	9.4
Glasnow,Tyler	9.4
Carrasco,Carlos	9.4
Karns,Nathan	9.3
Pineda,Michael	9.3
Hader,Joshua	9.2
Nola,Aaron	9.1
Urias,Julio	9.1
Rodon,Carlos	9.1
Maeda,Kenta	9.1
Smyly,Drew	9.0
Price,David	9.0
Hamels,Cole	9.0

Top Ground Ball Rate

NAME	GB
Anderson,Brett	63
Perdomo,Luis	59
Keuchel,Dallas	59
Stroman,Marcus	58
Garcia,Jaime	58
Chatwood,Tyler	57
Richard,Clayton	57
Ross,Tyson	57
Cosart,Jarred	56
Cobb,Alex	55
Perez,Williams	55
Martinez,Carlos	55
Perez,Martin	54
Gsellman,Robert	54
Gray,Sonny	53
Anderson,Tyler	53
Neal,Zachary	53
Leake,Mike	53
McCullers,Lance	53
Hernandez,Felix	53
Nola,Aaron	52
Taillon,Jameson	52
Hahn,Jesse	52
Liriano,Francisco	52
Arrieta,Jake	52
Nova,Ivan	51
Peralta,Wily	51
Graveman,Kendall	51
Gibson,Kyle	51
Stripling,Ross	51
Ventura,Yordano	51

Top Fly Ball Rate

NAME	FB
Cole,A.J.	55
Miranda,Ariel	52
Santiago,Hector	50
Estrada,Marco	49
Owens,Henry	49
Straily,Dan	49
Stewart,Brock	49
Cotton,Jharel	48
Weaver,Jered	47
Boyd,Matt	47
Griffin,A.J.	47
Lewis,Colby	46
Smyly,Drew	46
Scherzer,Max	46
Peacock,Brad	46
Verlander,Justin	45
Peavy,Jake	44
Adleman,Timothy	44
Odorizzi,Jake	44
Velasquez,Vincent	43
Alcantara,Raul	43
Kennedy,Ian	43
Hughes,Phil	42
De Leon,Jose	42
Morgan,Adam	42
Conley,Adam	41
Reyes,Alex	41
Moore,Matt	41
Stephenson,Robert	41
Clevinger,Michael	41
Duffy,Danny	41

High GB, Low Dom

NAME	GB	Dom
Perdomo,Luis	59	6.4
Chatwood,Tyler	57	6.4
Richard,Clayton	57	4.6
Cosart,Jarred	56	5.6
Perez,Williams	55	5.5
Perez,Martin	54	5.3
Gsellman,Robert	54	6.1
Anderson,Tyler	53	7.0
Neal,Zachary	53	3.9
Leake,Mike	53	6.3
Hahn,Jesse	52	5.6
Nova,Ivan	51	7.0
Peralta,Wily	51	6.3
Graveman,Kendall	51	5.3
Gibson,Kyle	51	6.5
Stripling,Ross	51	6.4
Pelfrey,Mike	50	4.6
Hoffman,Jeff	50	6.8
Farmer,Buck	50	6.5
Bettis,Chad	50	6.7
Volquez,Edinson	49	6.8
Locke,Jeff	49	6.2
Garza,Matt	49	6.5
Duffey,Tyler	49	6.9
Niese,Jon	48	6.6
Jenkins,Tyrell	48	4.9
Mitchell,Bryan	48	6.7
Urena,Jose	48	5.4
Nicolino,Justin	48	4.0
Roark,Tanner	47	6.6
Butler,Eddie	47	4.2

High GB, High Dom

NAME	GB	Dom
Ross,Tyson	57	8.6
McCullers,Lance	53	11.2
Nola,Aaron	52	9.1
Liriano,Francisco	52	9.6
Arrieta,Jake	52	8.7
Carrasco,Carlos	50	9.4
Kershaw,Clayton	49	10.3
Wood,Alex	49	8.7
Syndergaard,Noah	49	10.1
Gonzalez,Gio	49	8.7
Hamels,Cole	48	9.0
Glasnow,Tyler	48	9.4
Archer,Chris	47	9.8
Lester,Jon	47	8.9
Strahm,Matt	47	9.4
Pineda,Michael	46	9.3
Rodon,Carlos	45	9.1
Pomeranz,Drew	45	9.0
deGrom,Jacob	45	8.6
Ray,Robbie	45	9.8
Kluber,Corey	44	9.6
Lynn,Lance	44	8.6
Maeda,Kenta	44	9.1
Urias,Julio	44	9.1
Salazar,Danny	44	10.0
Harvey,Matt	44	8.7
Reyes,Alex	43	11.0
Price,David	43	9.0
Sale,Chris	42	9.5
Paulino,David	42	8.7
Bumgarner,Madison	42	9.6

Lowest xERA

NAME	xERA
Kershaw,Clayton	2.67
Syndergaard,Noah	3.09
Strasburg,Stephen	3.18
McCullers,Lance	3.20
Carrasco,Carlos	3.24
Scherzer,Max	3.27
Sale,Chris	3.33
Bumgarner,Madison	3.35
Stroman,Marcus	3.35
Kluber,Corey	3.36
Nola,Aaron	3.37
Lester,Jon	3.39
Darvish,Yu	3.41
Archer,Chris	3.42
Keuchel,Dallas	3.45
Tanaka,Masahiro	3.47
Urias,Julio	3.48
Price,David	3.48
Pineda,Michael	3.48
Arrieta,Jake	3.50
Cueto,Johnny	3.55
Matz,Steven	3.55
Hendricks,Kyle	3.60
Ross,Tyson	3.60
Harvey,Matt	3.61
Wood,Alex	3.62
deGrom,Jacob	3.62
Taillon,Jameson	3.64
Anderson,Brett	3.66
Martinez,Carlos	3.66
Cobb,Alex	3.69

Top BPV, 180+ IP

NAME	BPV
Kershaw,Clayton	174
Scherzer,Max	152
Syndergaard,Noah	149
Sale,Chris	141
Bumgarner,Madison	140
Carrasco,Carlos	138
Kluber,Corey	135
Price,David	133
Darvish,Yu	128
Tanaka,Masahiro	127
Lester,Jon	125
Archer,Chris	124
Stroman,Marcus	122
Cueto,Johnny	115
Verlander,Justin	111
Porcello,Rick	110
Maeda,Kenta	110
Hendricks,Kyle	109
Keuchel,Dallas	109
Taillon,Jameson	107
Gausman,Kevin	107
Duffy,Danny	105
Iwakuma,Hisashi	104
McHugh,Collin	103
Greinke,Zack	103
Hamels,Cole	101
Quintana,Jose	101
Arrieta,Jake	100
Samardzija,Jeff	97
Gonzalez,Gio	97
Fulmer,Michael	96

Top BPV, <150 IP

NAME	BPV
De Leon,Jose	128
McCullers,Lance	120
Urias,Julio	115
Weaver,Luke	114
Matz,Steven	114
Wood,Alex	110
Paulino,David	109
Ryu,Hyun-Jin	106
Stewart,Brock	101
Cobb,Alex	98
Severino,Luis	97
Strahm,Matt	96
Cotton,Jharel	96
Green,Chad	94
Ross,Tyson	94
Bailey,Homer	94
Garcia,Jaime	94
Skaggs,Tyler	91
Sanchez,Anibal	89
Anderson,Brett	88
Hughes,Phil	88
Kazmir,Scott	87
Lynn,Lance	87
Duffey,Tyler	87
Lopez,Reynaldo	86
Peavy,Jake	85
Miley,Wade	84
Wacha,Michael	83
Norris,Daniel	82
Richards,Garrett	82
Stripling,Ross	81

PITCHER SKILLS RANKINGS - Relief Pitchers

Top Command (k/bb)

NAME	Cmd
Jansen,Kenley	7.8
Miller,Andrew	6.9
Uehara,Koji	6.9
Romo,Sergio	5.5
Hendriks,Liam	5.5
Melancon,Mark	5.5
Doolittle,Sean	5.5
Cecil,Brett	5.4
Osuna,Roberto	5.3
Oh,Seung-Hwan	5.2
Dayton,Grant	5.2
Law,Derek	5.2
Kelley,Shawn	4.9
Rondon,Hector	4.9
Perkins,Glen	4.8
Reed,Addison	4.8
Wittgren,Nick	4.6
Chapman,Aroldis	4.4
Ramos,Edubray	4.3
Diaz,Edwin	4.3
Bush,Matt	4.2
Devenski,Christopher	4.2
Baez,Pedro	4.2
Neshek,Pat	4.1
Britton,Zach	4.1
Salas,Fernando	4.1
Colome,Alexander	4.1
Herrera,Kelvin	4.0
Lyons,Tyler	4.0
Hochevar,Luke	4.0
Jones,Nate	4.0

Top Control (bb/9)

NAME	Ctl
Melancon,Mark	1.5
Law,Derek	1.5
Wittgren,Nick	1.5
Uehara,Koji	1.6
Jansen,Kenley	1.7
Hendriks,Liam	1.7
Romo,Sergio	1.8
Osuna,Roberto	1.8
Doolittle,Sean	1.8
Nuno,Vidal	1.8
Perkins,Glen	1.9
Claudio,Alexander	2.0
Ramos,Edubray	2.0
Rondon,Hector	2.0
Triggs,Andrew	2.0
Neshek,Pat	2.0
Bush,Matt	2.0
Kintzler,Brandon	2.0
Devenski,Christopher	2.1
Dayton,Grant	2.1
Reed,Addison	2.1
Miller,Andrew	2.1
Cecil,Brett	2.1
Oh,Seung-Hwan	2.1
Lyons,Tyler	2.1
Salas,Fernando	2.2
Storen,Drew	2.2
Feldman,Scott	2.2
Britton,Zach	2.3
Watson,Tony	2.3
Baez,Pedro	2.3

Top Dominance (k/9)

NAME	Dom
Chapman,Aroldis	15.1
Miller,Andrew	14.5
Kimbrel,Craig	14.1
Betances,Dellin	14.0
Jansen,Kenley	13.5
Giles,Kenneth	13.0
Barraclough,Kyle	12.4
Grilli,Jason	11.8
Allen,Cody	11.8
Robertson,David	11.7
Kelley,Shawn	11.6
Rosenthal,Trevor	11.6
Cecil,Brett	11.5
Edwards,Carl	11.5
Diaz,Edwin	11.5
Smith,Will	11.3
Holland,Greg	11.3
Hoyt,James	11.3
Uehara,Koji	11.1
Givens,Mychal	11.1
Boxberger,Brad	11.0
Oh,Seung-Hwan	11.0
Alvarez,Dario	11.0
Feliz,Michael	10.9
Dayton,Grant	10.8
May,Trevor	10.8
Grimm,Justin	10.8
Hand,Brad	10.7
Colome,Alexander	10.7
Kela,Keone	10.7
Jones,Nate	10.5

Top Ground Ball Rate

NAME	GB
Britton,Zach	77
Dyson,Sam	67
Ziegler,Brad	66
Treinen,Blake	64
Coulombe,Daniel	62
Claudio,Alexander	62
Bowman,Matthew	61
Familia,Jeurys	61
Jeffress,Jeremy	61
Kintzler,Brandon	59
Gregerson,Luke	58
Cahill,Trevor	58
Duke,Zach	58
Sanchez,Aaron	58
Johnson,Jim	58
Ottavino,Adam	57
Lorenzen,Michael	56
Melancon,Mark	56
Chargois,J.T.	56
Strop,Pedro	56
Gearrin,Cory	56
Montgomery,Michael	55
Jennings,Dan	55
Flynn,Brian	55
Ramirez,J.C.	55
Rusin,Chris	54
Axford,John	54
Simmons,Shae	54
Hoyt,James	54
Socolovich,Miguel	53
Harris,Will	53

Top Fly Ball Rate

NAME	FB
Buchter,Ryan	59
Clippard,Tyler	54
Uehara,Koji	53
Young,Chris	52
Doolittle,Sean	52
Jansen,Kenley	51
Dull,Ryan	50
Grilli,Jason	48
Osuna,Roberto	47
Neshek,Pat	47
Dayton,Grant	46
Hochevar,Luke	46
Kelley,Shawn	46
Bracho,Silvino	46
Siegrist,Kevin	46
Meyer,Alex	46
Vincent,Nick	45
Clemens,Paul	44
Robles,Hansel	44
Thornburg,Tyler	43
Goeddel,Erik	43
Salas,Fernando	43
Bundy,Dylan	42
Street,Huston	42
Devenski,Christopher	42
May,Trevor	41
Hembree,Heath	41
Rondon,Bruce	41
Papelbon,Jonathan	41
Bailey,Andrew	41
Wood,Travis	41

High GB, Low Dom

NAME	GB	Dom
Dyson,Sam	67	7.0
Ziegler,Brad	66	7.5
Claudio,Alexander	62	6.1
Bowman,Matthew	61	6.0
Jeffress,Jeremy	61	7.4
Kintzler,Brandon	59	5.5
Sanchez,Aaron	58	7.3
Gearrin,Cory	56	7.4
Montgomery,Michael	55	7.2
Flynn,Brian	55	6.7
Ramirez,J.C.	55	6.1
Ryan,Kyle	53	5.0
Biagini,Joe	52	6.9
Lyles,Jordan	51	5.2
Godley,Zachary	51	6.7
Gomez,Jeanmar	50	6.1
Madson,Ryan	50	7.3
Feldman,Scott	50	6.1
Rogers,Taylor	49	7.0
Worley,Vance	48	5.7
Ramirez,Erasmo	48	6.5
Suarez,Albert	47	5.6
Wilson,Alex	47	5.8
Whitley,Chase	45	7.0
Alvarez,Jose	45	7.0
De La Cruz,Joel	44	4.7
Scheppers,Tanner	44	7.3
Jackson,Edwin	43	7.1
Anderson,Cody	42	6.8
Guerra,Deolis	42	6.8
Blazek,Michael	41	7.3

High GB, High Dom

NAME	GB	Dom
Britton,Zach	77	9.4
Coulombe,Daniel	62	9.0
Familia,Jeurys	61	9.5
Gregerson,Luke	58	9.3
Cahill,Trevor	58	9.0
Duke,Zach	58	9.7
Ottavino,Adam	57	9.9
Strop,Pedro	56	10.5
Axford,John	54	9.3
Simmons,Shae	54	10.1
Hoyt,James	54	11.3
Harris,Will	53	9.3
Rodney,Fernando	53	9.7
Roe,Chaz	53	8.7
Edwards,Carl	53	11.5
Barraclough,Kyle	52	12.4
Wood,Blake	52	8.7
Wilson,Justin	51	9.6
Miller,Andrew	51	14.5
Betances,Dellin	51	14.0
Cabrera,Mauricio	51	8.5
Zych,Tony	50	9.4
Cedeno,Xavier	50	8.9
Diekman,Jake	50	10.2
Krol,Ian	49	9.2
Bedrosian,Cam	49	10.3
Broxton,Jonathan	49	8.7
Jones,Nate	49	10.5
Casilla,Santiago	48	8.9
Cecil,Brett	48	11.5
Kelly,Joe	48	9.6

Lowest xERA

NAME	xERA
Miller,Andrew	1.89
Britton,Zach	2.21
Chapman,Aroldis	2.21
Betances,Dellin	2.52
Jansen,Kenley	2.62
Kimbrel,Craig	2.63
Cecil,Brett	2.67
Giles,Kenneth	2.90
Melancon,Mark	2.90
Strop,Pedro	2.93
Edwards,Carl	2.94
Diaz,Edwin	2.97
Barraclough,Kyle	3.01
Jones,Nate	3.02
Gregerson,Luke	3.05
Ottavino,Adam	3.10
Hoyt,James	3.10
Oh,Seung-Hwan	3.10
Colome,Alexander	3.13
Rondon,Hector	3.14
Familia,Jeurys	3.15
Kelley,Shawn	3.16
Holland,Greg	3.20
Harris,Will	3.21
Allen,Cody	3.22
Robertson,David	3.23
Law,Derek	3.24
Simmons,Shae	3.25
Kelly,Joe	3.25
Herrera,Kelvin	3.25
Romo,Sergio	3.26

Top BPV, 10+ Saves

NAME	BPV
Miller,Andrew	233
Jansen,Kenley	207
Chapman,Aroldis	200
Betances,Dellin	172
Kimbrel,Craig	169
Giles,Kenneth	165
Britton,Zach	163
Diaz,Edwin	159
Oh,Seung-Hwan	158
Romo,Sergio	150
Rondon,Hector	146
Colome,Alexander	143
Melancon,Mark	141
Allen,Cody	139
Robertson,David	138
Osuna,Roberto	138
Ottavino,Adam	134
Law,Derek	131
Holland,Greg	127
Davis,Wade	120
Familia,Jeurys	117
Bedrosian,Cam	116
Lorenzen,Michael	109
Watson,Tony	102
Iglesias,Raisel	102
Rodriguez,Francisco	94
Maurer,Brandon	94
Hudson,Daniel	94
Dyson,Sam	88
Thornburg,Tyler	87
Johnson,Jim	86

Top BPV, <10 Saves

NAME	BPV
Cecil,Brett	176
Uehara,Koji	162
Kelley,Shawn	161
Dayton,Grant	149
Hoyt,James	148
Hendriks,Liam	145
Jones,Nate	145
Doolittle,Sean	140
Reed,Addison	139
Feliz,Michael	136
Gregerson,Luke	136
Hand,Brad	133
Kelly,Joe	131
Herrera,Kelvin	131
Baez,Pedro	130
Edwards,Carl	126
Smith,Will	126
O Day,Darren	126
Harris,Will	126
Perkins,Glen	125
Storen,Drew	123
Wilson,Justin	121
Hochevar,Luke	121
Givens,Mychal	119
Blevins,Jerry	119
Lyons,Tyler	119
McGee,Jake	119
Zych,Tony	119
Krol,Ian	119
Bush,Matt	118
Tazawa,Junichi	117

POTENTIAL SKILLS GAINERS AND FADERS - Pitchers

Dom Gainers

From a pitcher's swinging-strike rate (SwK%), we can establish a typical range in which we would expect to find their Dom (k/9). The pitchers on this list posted a 2016 Dom that was in the bottom of that expected range based on their SwK%. The names above the break line are in the bottom 10% of that range, and are the strongest candidates for Dom gains. The names below the break line are in the bottom 25%, and are also good candidates for strikeout gains.

Dom Faders

From a pitcher's swinging-strike rate (SwK%), we can establish a typical range in which we would expect to find their Dom (k/9). The pitchers on this list posted a 2016 Dom that was in the top of that expected range based on their SwK%. The names above the break line are in the top 10% of that range, and are the strongest candidates for a Dom fade. The names below the break line are in the top 25%, and are also good candidates for a Dom fade.

Ctl Gainers

From a pitcher's first-pitch strike rate (FpK%), we can establish a typical range in which we would expect to find their Ctl (bb/9). These pitchers posted a 2016 Ctl that was in the bottom of that expected range based on their FpK%. The names above the break line are in the bottom 10% of that range, and are the strongest candidates for Ctl gains. The names below the break line are in the bottom 25%, and are also good candidates for Ctl gains.

Ctl Faders

From a pitcher's first-pitch strike rate (FpK%), we can establish a typical range in which we would expect to find their Ctl (bb/9). These pitchers posted a 2016 Ctl that was in the top 10% of that expected range based on their FpK%, making them the strongest candidates for a Ctl fade.

DOM GAINERS

NAME	SwK	K/9
Manaea,Sean	12	7.7
Guerra,Junior	11	7.4
Hellickson,Jeremy	11	7.3
Dickey,R.A.	11	6.7
Wright,Steven	11	7.3
de la Rosa,Jorge	11	7.3
Fulmer,Michael	11	7.5
Harvey,Matt	11	7.4
Gibson,Kyle	10	6.4
Buchholz,Clay	10	6.0
Ramirez,Erasmo	9	6.3
Devenski,Christopher	14	8.7
Shoemaker,Matt	13	8.0
Paxton,James	12	8.7
Torres,Carlos	12	8.6
Lackey,John	12	8.6
Ross,Joe	11	8.0
Tanaka,Masahiro	11	7.5
Morgan,Adam	11	7.6
Peavy,Jake	11	7.8
Andriese,Matt	11	7.7
Greinke,Zack	11	7.6
Hammel,Jason	11	7.8
Straily,Dan	11	7.6
Jackson,Edwin	10	6.5
Nolasco,Ricky	9	6.6
Wisler,Matt	9	6.6
Shields,James	9	6.7
Bettis,Chad	9	6.7

DOM FADERS

NAME	SwK	K/9
Vogelsong,Ryan	7	6.7
Gallardo,Yovani	7	6.5
Rea,Colin	7	7.0
Cashner,Andrew	8	7.6
Bradley,Archie	9	9.1
Nola,Aaron	10	9.8
Phelps,David	10	11.9
Nicasio,Juan	11	10.5
Hill,Rich	11	10.5
Salazar,Danny	12	10.6
Strasburg,Stephen	12	11.2
Ray,Robbie	12	11.3
Hand,Brad	13	11.2
Colon,Bartolo	6	6.0
Quintana,Jose	8	7.8
Jimenez,Ubaldo	9	7.9
Kazmir,Scott	10	8.9
Rodon,Carlos	11	9.2
Karns,Nathan	11	9.7
Snell,Blake	12	9.9
Young,Chris	12	9.6
Pomeranz,Drew	12	9.8
Velasquez,Vince	12	10.4
Archer,Chris	13	10.4

CTL GAINERS

NAME	FpK	BB/9
Lackey,John	68	2.5
Pineda,Michael	67	2.7
Sanchez,Anibal	67	3.1
Perez,Martin	64	3.5
Conley,Adam	64	4.2
Nicasio,Juan	63	3.4
Verrett,Logan	63	4.2
Niese,Jon	63	3.5
Buchholz,Clay	62	3.6
Norris,Bud	62	3.9
Dickey,R.A.	62	3.4
Koehler,Tom	59	4.2
Miller,Shelby	59	3.7
Young,Chris	59	4.4
Hernandez,Felix	59	3.8
Jimenez,Ubaldo	58	4.6
Snell,Blake	57	5.2
McCullers,Lance	57	5.0
McHugh,Collin	67	2.6
Harvey,Matt	66	2.4
Strasburg,Stephen	65	2.7
Eovaldi,Nathan	64	2.9
Peavy,Jake	64	2.7
Cain,Matt	63	3.2
Gray,Jon	62	3.2
Martinez,Carlos	62	3.2
Moore,Matt	62	3.3
Chacin,Jhoulys	61	3.4
Gray,Sonny	61	3.2
Bundy,Dylan	61	3.5
Straily,Dan	61	3.4
Friedrich,Christian	60	3.6
Rea,Colin	60	3.9
Kazmir,Scott	60	3.4
Hand,Brad	59	3.6
Vogelsong,Ryan	58	4.4
Nelson,Jimmy	58	4.3
Karns,Nathan	57	4.3
Bradley,Archie	57	4.3
Liriano,Francisco	56	4.7

CTL FADERS

NAME	FpK	BB/9
Rodon,Carlos	54	2.9
DeSclafani,Anthony	58	2.2
Nolasco,Ricky	61	2.0
Eickhoff,Jerad	61	1.9
Taillon,Jameson	62	1.5
Teheran,Julio	62	2.0
Nova,Ivan	62	1.6
Leake,Mike	62	1.5
Sale,Chris	62	1.8
Paxton,James	62	1.8
Wright,Steven	55	3.3
Peralta,Wily	56	3.0
Ross,Joe	56	2.5
Gausman,Kevin	57	2.4
Wilson,Tyler	57	2.3
Rusin,Chris	58	2.5
Odorizzi,Jake	58	2.6
Smyly,Drew	58	2.5
Santana,Ervin	59	2.6
Morgan,Adam	60	2.3
Nola,Aaron	61	2.4
Gonzalez,Miguel	61	2.3
Stroman,Marcus	61	2.4
Hellickson,Jeremy	61	2.1
Fulmer,Michael	61	2.4
Davies,Zach	62	2.1
Carrasco,Carlos	62	2.1

RISK MANAGEMENT

GRADE "F" in HEALTH

Pitchers	Pitchers
Anderson,Brett	Street,Huston
Bailey,Homer	Stroman,Marcus
Blevins,Jerry	Tolleson,Shawn
Boxberger,Brad	Tomlin,Josh
Buchholz,Clay	Uehara,Koji
Cain,Matt	Vargas,Jason
Cashner,Andrew	Vizcaino,Arodys
Chacin,Jhoulys	Wainwright,Adam
Chatwood,Tyler	Wheeler,Zack
Claudio,Alexander	Whitley,Chase
Cobb,Alex	Withrow,Chris
Cole,Gerrit	Wood,Alex
Corbin,Patrick	Wright,Steven
Darvish,Yu	Zych,Tony
De La Rosa,Rubby	
Doolittle,Sean	**Batters**
Feliz,Neftali	Ackley,Dustin
Flynn,Brian	Adams,Matt
Garcia,Jaime	Avila,Alex
Garza,Matt	Bird,Gregory
Griffin,A.J.	Brantley,Michael
Grilli,Jason	Canha,Mark
Harvey,Matt	Cervelli,Francisco
Hernandez,David	Chirinos,Robinson
Hill,Rich	D Arnaud,Travis
Hochevar,Luke	Duda,Lucas
Holland,Derek	Ethier,Andre
Hughes,Phil	Hamilton,Josh
Iwakuma,Hisashi	Holliday,Matt
Jones,Nate	Iglesias,Jose
Kintzler,Brandon	Jackson,Austin
Lewis,Colby	Jay,Jon
Lyles,Jordan	Jennings,Desmond
Lynn,Lance	La Stella,Tommy
Madson,Ryan	Lawrie,Brett
McCarthy,Brandon	Lowrie,Jed
McCullers,Lance	Maybin,Cameron
Mitchell,Bryan	Mesoraco,Devin
Montas,Frankie	Moustakas,Mike
Moore,Matt	Myers,Wil
Nolasco,Ricky	Pagan,Angel
Nova,Ivan	Pence,Hunter
O Day,Darren	Pollock,A.J.
Ottavino,Adam	Profar,Jurickson
Paxton,James	Sandoval,Pablo
Peacock,Brad	Saunders,Michael
Peavy,Jake	Schwarber,Kyle
Pelfrey,Mike	Spangenberg,Cory
Perez,Martin	Stanton,Giancarlo
Perez,Williams	Swihart,Blake
Perkins,Glen	Travis,Devon
Phelps,David	Van Slyke,Scott
Pineda,Michael	Vazquez,Christian
Richards,Garrett	Wright,David
Romo,Sergio	Zimmerman,Ryan
Rondon,Bruce	
Ross,Tyson	
Ryu,Hyun-Jin	
Sabathia,CC	
Sanchez,Anibal	
Scheppers,Tanner	
Simmons,Shae	
Skaggs,Tyler	
Smyly,Drew	
Soria,Joakim	

Highest Reliability Grades - Health / Experience / Consistency (Min. Grade = BBB)

CA	POS	Rel
Perez,Salvador	2	AAA
Posey,Buster	2	AAB
McCann,Brian	20	ABA
Martin,Russell	2	ABB
Gattis,Evan	20	BBB

1B/DH	POS	Rel
Gonzalez,Adrian	3	AAA
Rizzo,Anthony	3	AAA
Butler,Billy	03	ABA
Lee,Dae-ho	3	ABA
Shaw,Travis	35	ABA
Miller,Bradley	36	ABB
Napoli,Mike	03	ABB
Mauer,Joe	03	BAA
Pujols,Albert	03	BAA
Carpenter,Matt	345	BAB
Encarnacion,Edwin	03	BAB
Loney,James	3	BBA
Belt,Brandon	3	BBB
Moss,Brandon	379	BBB

2B	POS	Rel
Kinsler,Ian	4	AAB
Wendle,Joe	4	ABA
Odor,Rougned	4	ABB
Carpenter,Matt	345	BAB
Phillips,Brandon	4	BAB
Zobrist,Ben	479	BAB
Walker,Neil	4	BBB

SS	POS	Rel
Semien,Marcus	6	AAA
Crawford,Brandon	6	AAB
Escobar,Alcides	6	AAB
Ramirez,Alexei	6	AAB
Miller,Bradley	36	ABB
Gregorius,Didi	6	ABB
Hechavarria,Adeiny	6	ABB
Cabrera,Asdrubal	6	BAB
Machado,Manny	56	BAB
Galvis,Freddy	6	BBA
Aybar,Erick	6	BBB
Simmons,Andrelton	6	BBB

3B	POS	Rel
Frazier,Todd	5	AAA
Headley,Chase	5	AAA
Arenado,Nolan	5	AAB
Longoria,Evan	5	AAB
Seager,Kyle	5	AAB
Shaw,Travis	35	ABA
Suarez,Eugenio	5	ABA
Prado,Martin	5	BAA
Machado,Manny	56	BAB
Carpenter,Matt	345	BAB
Reyes,Jose	5	BBA
Castellanos,Nick	5	BBB
Solarte,Yangervis	5	BBB

OF	POS	Rel
Jones,Adam	8	AAA
Markakis,Nick	9	AAA
Bruce,Jay	9	AAB
Calhoun,Kole	9	AAB
Cruz,Nelson	09	AAB
Ozuna,Marcell	8	AAB
Polanco,Gregory	79	AAB
Trout,Mike	8	AAB
Upton,Justin	7	AAB
Pillar,Kevin	8	ABA
Smith,Seth	79	ABA
Davis,Khristopher	07	ABB
Duvall,Adam	7	ABB
Herrera,Odubel	8	ABB
Kim,Hyun-Soo	7	ABB
Marte,Starling	7	ABB
Pederson,Joc	8	ABB
Eaton,Adam	89	BAA
Gardner,Brett	7	BAA
Zobrist,Ben	479	BAB
Cespedes,Yoenis	78	BAB
Granderson,Curtis	89	BAB
Yelich,Christian	78	BAB
Moss,Brandon	379	BBB
Hamilton,Billy	8	BBB
Inciarte,Ender	8	BBB
Trumbo,Mark	09	BBB

RP		Rel
Allen,Cody		AAA
Britton,Zach		AAA
Melancon,Mark		AAA
Rodriguez,Francisco		AAB
Ramirez,Erasmo		ABB
Kimbrel,Craig		BAA
Chapman,Aroldis		BAB
Robertson,David		BAB
Chavez,Jesse		BBA
Gregerson,Luke		BBA
Rondon,Hector		BBA
Ramos,A.J.		BBB
Rodney,Fernando		BBB

SP	Rel
Archer,Chris	AAA
Bauer,Trevor	AAA
Bumgarner,Madison	AAA
Hendricks,Kyle	AAA
Koehler,Tom	AAA
Lester,Jon	AAA
Martinez,Carlos	AAA
Miley,Wade	AAA
Quintana,Jose	AAA
Roark,Tanner	AAA
Santiago,Hector	AAA
Scherzer,Max	AAA
Volquez,Edinson	AAA
McHugh,Collin	AAB
Nelson,Jimmy	AAB
Samardzija,Jeff	AAB
Shields,James	AAB
Eickhoff,Jerad	ABA
Fiers,Mike	ABB
Locke,Jeff	ABB
Maeda,Kenta	ABB
Straily,Dan	ABB
Colon,Bartolo	BAA
Dickey,R.A.	BAA
Gonzalez,Gio	BAA
Hamels,Cole	BAA
Kennedy,Ian	BAA
Kluber,Corey	BAA
Leake,Mike	BAA
Odorizzi,Jake	BAA
Porcello,Rick	BAA
Price,David	BAA
Sale,Chris	BAA
Santana,Ervin	BAA
Teheran,Julio	BAA
Tillman,Chris	BAA
Arrieta,Jake	BAB
Jimenez,Ubaldo	BAB
Keuchel,Dallas	BAB
Miller,Shelby	BAB
Ventura,Yordano	BAB
Anderson,Chase	BBA
deGrom,Jacob	BBA
Rodon,Carlos	BBA
Salazar,Danny	BBB

RISK MANAGEMENT

GRADE "A" in CONSISTENCY (in order by Rel)

Pitchers (min 120 IP)	Pitchers (min 120 IP)
Archer,Chris	Garcia,Jaime
Bauer,Trevor	Garza,Matt
Bumgarner,Madison	Nolasco,Ricky
Hendricks,Kyle	Pineda,Michael
Koehler,Tom	Richards,Garrett
Lester,Jon	Ross,Tyson
Martinez,Carlos	Sabathia,CC
Miley,Wade	Corbin,Patrick
Quintana,Jose	Darvish,Yu
Roark,Tanner	Nova,Ivan
Santiago,Hector	Stroman,Marcus
Scherzer,Max	Tomlin,Josh
Volquez,Edinson	Wright,Steven
Eickhoff,Jerad	Skaggs,Tyler
Colon,Bartolo	
Dickey,R.A.	**Batters (min 400 AB)**
Gonzalez,Gio	Frazier,Todd
Hamels,Cole	Gonzalez,Adrian
Kennedy,Ian	Headley,Chase
Kluber,Corey	Jones,Adam
Leake,Mike	Markakis,Nick
Odorizzi,Jake	Perez,Salvador
Porcello,Rick	Rizzo,Anthony
Price,David	Semien,Marcus
Sale,Chris	McCann,Brian
Santana,Ervin	Pillar,Kevin
Teheran,Julio	Shaw,Travis
Tillman,Chris	Suarez,Eugenio
Anderson,Chase	Eaton,Adam
deGrom,Jacob	Gardner,Brett
Rodon,Carlos	Mauer,Joe
Davies,Zachary	Prado,Martin
Wisler,Matthew	Pujols,Albert
Andriese,Matt	Galvis,Freddy
Giolito,Lucas	Reyes,Jose
Morgan,Adam	Anderson,Tim
Musgrove,Joe	Castillo,Welington
Thompson,Jake	Wong,Kolten
Urias,Julio	Grandal,Yasmani
Bettis,Chad	Kiermaier,Kevin
Fulmer,Michael	Buxton,Byron
Manaea,Sean	Kendrick,Howie
Hammel,Jason	Plouffe,Trevor
Lackey,John	Garcia,Avisail
Pomeranz,Drew	Jackson,Austin
Sanchez,Aaron	Lawrie,Brett
Shoemaker,Matthew	Pence,Hunter
Anderson,Tyler	Bird,Gregory
Glasnow,Tyler	
Carrasco,Carlos	
Chen,Wei-Yin	
Estrada,Marco	
Gibson,Kyle	
Gray,Sonny	
Happ,J.A.	
Kazmir,Scott	
Kershaw,Clayton	
Strasburg,Stephen	
Tanaka,Masahiro	
Verlander,Justin	
Gonzalez,Miguel	
DeSclafani,Anthony	
Matz,Steven	
Walker,Taijuan	
Norris,Daniel	
Rodriguez,Eduardo	
Lewis,Colby	
Wainwright,Adam	

TOP COMBINATION OF SKILLS AND RELIABILITY — Maximum of one "C" in Reliability Grade

BATTING POWER (Min. 400 AB)

PX 105+	PX	Rel
Carter,Chris	181	ABC
Davis,Khristopher	167	ABB
Bryant,Kris	162	AAC
Pederson,Joc	161	ABB
Trout,Mike	154	AAB
Duvall,Adam	154	ABB
Alvarez,Pedro	151	ACB
Cruz,Nelson	151	AAB
Freeman,Freddie	151	BAC
Moss,Brandon	150	BBB
Encarnacion,Edwin	148	BAB
Lamb,Jacob	147	BBC
Carpenter,Matt	147	BAB
Arenado,Nolan	147	AAB
Martinez,J.D.	146	CBB
Gattis,Evan	144	BBB
Dozier,Brian	142	AAC
Cespedes,Yoenis	142	BAB
Trumbo,Mark	141	BBB
Gonzalez,Carlos	141	BBC
Rizzo,Anthony	140	AAA
Upton,Justin	139	AAB
Donaldson,Josh	139	AAC
Napoli,Mike	138	ABB
Belt,Brandon	137	BBB
Tomas,Yasmany	136	ACB
Grandal,Yasmani	135	BCA
Bruce,Jay	134	AAB
Kemp,Matt	133	CAB
Cabrera,Miguel	132	BAC
Castellanos,Nick	130	BBB
Frazier,Todd	130	AAA
Granderson,Curtis	126	BAB
Broxton,Keon	126	ACB
Machado,Manny	125	BAB
Longoria,Evan	125	AAB
Odor,Rougned	121	ABB
Correa,Carlos	120	ACB
Russell,Addison	120	ACB
Seager,Corey	119	ACB
Castillo,Welington	119	ACA
Seager,Kyle	118	AAB
Martin,Russell	118	ABB
Santana,Carlos	118	AAC
Miller,Bradley	118	ABB
Gomez,Carlos	116	BBC
Braun,Ryan	115	AAC
Turner,Justin	115	BCB
Cron,C.J.	114	BCB
Blackmon,Charlie	114	BAC
Shaw,Travis	114	ABA
Abreu,Jose	114	AAC
Polanco,Gregory	112	AAB
Yelich,Christian	111	BAB
Ozuna,Marcell	110	AAB
Betts,Mookie	109	AAC
Kipnis,Jason	108	AAC
Cano,Robinson	108	AAC
Piscotty,Stephen	107	ABC
Calhoun,Kole	107	AAB
Beltran,Carlos	106	BBC
Gonzalez,Adrian	106	AAA
Beltre,Adrian	105	BAC
Rosario,Eddie	105	ACB
Perez,Salvador	105	AAA

RUNNER SPEED (Min. 400 AB)

Spd 100+	SX	Rel
Anderson,Tim	179	ACA
Hamilton,Billy	178	BBB
Hernandez,Cesar	161	ABC
Fowler,Dexter	157	CAB
Marte,Starling	155	ABB
Inciarte,Ender	153	BBB
Hechavarria,Adeiny	143	ABB
Escobar,Alcides	142	AAB
Broxton,Keon	142	ACB
Betts,Mookie	141	AAC
Rosario,Eddie	140	ACB
Eaton,Adam	136	BAA
Herrera,Odubel	136	ABB
Harrison,Josh	133	BBC
Reyes,Jose	131	BBA
Bogaerts,Xander	131	AAC
Andrus,Elvis	130	AAC
Kiermaier,Kevin	129	BCA
Lindor,Francisco	128	AAC
Gregorius,Didi	128	ABB
Martin,Leonys	126	ABC
Trout,Mike	126	AAB
Simmons,Andrelton	124	BBB
Merrifield,Whit	123	ABC
Gardner,Brett	123	BAA
Wong,Kolten	123	ACA
Castro,Starlin	122	AAC
Semien,Marcus	122	AAA
Blackmon,Charlie	121	BAC
Kinsler,Ian	119	AAB
Dozier,Brian	119	AAC
Bryant,Kris	117	AAC
Piscotty,Stephen	116	ABC
Miller,Bradley	115	ABB
Belt,Brandon	115	BBB
Crawford,Brandon	115	AAB
Desmond,Ian	114	AAC
Ramirez,Jose	113	ABC
Ozuna,Marcell	113	AAB
Realmuto,Jacob	112	ACB
Yelich,Christian	112	BAB
Prado,Martin	111	BAA
Castellanos,Nick	111	BBB
Ramirez,Alexei	111	AAB
Longoria,Evan	110	AAB
Braun,Ryan	109	AAC
Galvis,Freddy	109	BBA
Kim,Hyun-Soo	109	ABB
Machado,Manny	108	BAB
Mazara,Nomar	108	ACB
Gomez,Carlos	108	BBC
Upton,Justin	106	AAB
Mercer,Jordy	106	ABC
Escobar,Yunel	105	BAC
Odor,Rougned	104	ABB
Cabrera,Asdrubal	104	BAB
Arenado,Nolan	103	AAB
Zobrist,Ben	103	BAB
Seager,Corey	102	ACB
Pedroia,Dustin	102	CAB
Russell,Addison	101	ACB
Martinez,J.D.	101	CBB
Lamb,Jacob	101	BBC
Kipnis,Jason	101	AAC

OVERALL PITCHING SKILL

BPV over 85	BPV	Rel
Jansen,Kenley	207	CAA
Chapman,Aroldis	200	BAB
Betances,Dellin	172	ACA
Kimbrel,Craig	169	BAA
Britton,Zach	163	AAA
Scherzer,Max	152	AAA
Syndergaard,Noah	149	ACB
Rondon,Hector	146	BBA
Sale,Chris	141	BAA
Melancon,Mark	141	AAA
Bumgarner,Madison	140	AAA
Allen,Cody	139	AAA
Reed,Addison	139	ACB
Robertson,David	138	BAB
Osuna,Roberto	138	ACA
Gregerson,Luke	136	BBA
Kluber,Corey	135	BAA
Hand,Brad	133	BCB
Price,David	133	BAA
Herrera,Kelvin	131	BCB
Harris,Will	126	ACA
Lester,Jon	125	AAA
Archer,Chris	124	AAA
Wilson,Justin	121	ACA
deGrom,Jacob	118	BBA
Cishek,Steve	112	BBC
Porcello,Rick	110	BAA
Shoemaker,Matthew	110	CBA
Salazar,Danny	110	BBB
Maeda,Kenta	110	ABB
Hendricks,Kyle	109	AAA
Keuchel,Dallas	109	BAB
Brach,Brad	108	ACA
Neshek,Pat	107	ACA
Duffy,Danny	105	CAB
McHugh,Collin	103	AAB
Duke,Zach	103	ACB
Watson,Tony	102	ACB
Lackey,John	101	CAA
Hamels,Cole	101	BAA
Quintana,Jose	101	AAA
Arrieta,Jake	100	BAB
Samardzija,Jeff	97	AAB
Chavez,Jesse	97	BBA
Gonzalez,Gio	97	BAA
Nuno,Vidal	97	ACA
Hammel,Jason	96	CAA
Martinez,Carlos	95	AAA
Villanueva,Carlos	94	ACA
Rodriguez,Francisco	94	AAB
Rodon,Carlos	94	BBA
Leake,Mike	94	BAA
Fiers,Mike	93	ABB
Pomeranz,Drew	92	CBA
Odorizzi,Jake	91	BAA
Liriano,Francisco	91	CAB
Colon,Bartolo	90	BAA
Kennedy,Ian	90	BAA
Teheran,Julio	90	BAA
Shaw,Bryan	90	ACA
Treinen,Blake	89	ACA
Eickhoff,Jerad	89	ABA
Dyson,Sam	88	ACB
Diekman,Jake	87	BCA
Davies,Zachary	87	ACA
Torres,Carlos	86	ACA

PORTFOLIO 3 PLAN — Hitters

TIER 1 Hitters
Rel BBB+; xBA score 3+; Power OR Speed score 3+

BATTERS	Age	Bats	Pos	MM	REL	MAY	R$
Trout,Mike	25	R	9	4445	AAB	108	$40
Marte,Starling	28	R	7	2545	ABB	97	$36
Arenado,Nolan	26	R	5	4155	AAB	95	$33
Machado,Manny	24	R	56	4345	BAB	97	$32
Rizzo,Anthony	27	L	3	4155	AAA	100	$30
Cespedes,Yoenis	31	R	79	4245	BAB	91	$29
Cruz,Nelson	37	R	08	4245	AAB	95	$29
Yelich,Christian	25	L	79	3345	BAB	91	$29
Odor,Rougned	23	L	4	4235	ABB	85	$29
Eaton,Adam	28	L	89	2445	BAA	95	$27
Kinsler,Ian	35	R	4	2335	AAB	83	$26
Polanco,Gregory	25	L	87	3345	AAB	95	$26
Seager,Kyle	29	L	5	3145	AAB	83	$25
Encarnacion,Edwin	34	R	03	4155	BAB	91	$24
Carpenter,Matt	31	L	534	4055	BAB	85	$24
Inciarte,Ender	26	L	9	1545	BBB	87	$24
Longoria,Evan	31	R	5	4135	AAB	83	$22
Calhoun,Kole	29	L	8	3135	AAB	76	$21
Davis,Khristopher	29	R	70	5135	ABB	85	$21
Bruce,Jay	30	L	8	4235	AAB	89	$20
Jones,Adam	31	R	9	3235	AAA	87	$20
Gonzalez,Adrian	35	L	3	3045	AAA	80	$20
Walker,Neil	31	B	4	3235	BBB	75	$20
Pillar,Kevin	28	R	9	1335	ABA	76	$19
Simmons,Andrelton	27	R	6	1445	BBB	81	$19
Gattis,Evan	30	R	02	4135	BBB	75	$19
Ozuna,Marcell	26	R	9	3135	AAB	76	$19
Escobar,Alcides	30	R	6	1535	AAB	89	$18
Cabrera,Asdrubal	31	B	6	3335	BAB	85	$18
Gregorius,Didi	27	L	6	2435	ABB	85	$17
Miller,Bradley	27	L	63	3335	ABB	85	$16
Granderson,Curtis	36	L	89	4235	BAB	85	$16
Perez,Salvador	27	R	2	3335	AAA	93	$14
Ramirez,Alexei	35	R	6	1343	AAB	42	$10
Lee,Dae-ho	35	R	3	3033	ABA	34	$7
Smith,Seth	34	L	87	3133	ABA	38	$7
Wendle,Joe	27	L	4	1431	ABA	11	$5

TIER 2 Hitters
Rel BCC+; 5 PT; xBA, Power, or Speed score 3+ — <$20

BATTERS	Age	Bats	Pos	MM	REL	MAY	R$
Hamilton,Billy*	26	B	9	0515	BBB	64	$38
Herrera,Odubel*	25	L	9	1525	ABB	79	$25
Posey,Buster*	30	R	2	2255	AAB	89	$24
Upton,Justin*	29	R	7	4325	AAB	89	$24
Frazier,Todd*	31	R	5	4225	AAA	87	$23
Pujols,Albert*	37	R	03	2145	BAA	76	$22
Phillips,Brandon*	36	R	4	1245	BAB	73	$22
Belt,Brandon*	29	L	3	4225	BBB	75	$21
Gardner,Brett	33	L	7	1425	BAA	76	$20
Harrison,Josh	29	R	4	1535	BBC	77	$19
Prado,Martin	33	R	5	1255	BAA	83	$19
Cabrera,Melky	32	B	7	2255	BAC	81	$19
Castro,Starlin	27	R	4	2335	AAC	79	$19
Zobrist,Ben	36	B	478	2255	BAB	85	$19
Reyes,Jose	34	B	5	1525	BBA	79	$18
Piscotty,Stephen	26	R	8	3235	ABC	75	$18
Santana,Carlos	31	B	03	3235	AAC	79	$18
Realmuto,Jacob	26	R	2	2335	ACB	75	$18
Beltran,Carlos	40	B	08	3135	BBC	66	$18
Trumbo,Mark	31	R	80	4125	BBB	69	$18
Cron,C.J.	27	R	3	3135	BCB	66	$17
Suarez,Eugenio	25	R	5	3215	ABA	70	$17
Castellanos,Nick	25	R	5	4125	BBB	69	$17
Russell,Addison	23	R	6	3225	ACB	69	$17
Duvall,Adam	28	R	7	4225	ABB	79	$17
Crawford,Brandon	30	L	6	2325	AAB	76	$17

TIER 2 Hitters (Cont.)
Rel BCC+; 5 PT; xBA, Power, or Speed score 3+ — <$20

BATTERS	Age	Bats	Pos	MM	REL	MAY	R$
Solarte,Yangervis	29	B	5	2145	BBB	69	$17
Martin,Leonys	29	L	9	1505	ABC	64	$16
Sanchez,Gary	24	R	2	4145	ACC	77	$16
Semien,Marcus	26	R	6	3425	AAA	93	$16
Pederson,Joc	25	L	9	5125	ABB	79	$16
Markakis,Nick	33	L	8	1035	AAA	60	$16
Marte,Ketel	23	B	6	1425	BCC	63	$15
Carter,Chris	30	R	3	5115	ABC	69	$15
Escobar,Yunel	34	R	5	1035	BAC	52	$15
Rosario,Eddie	25	L	79	3425	ACB	81	$15
Mauer,Joe	34	L	30	1255	BAA	83	$15
Kim,Hyun-Soo	29	L	7	1145	ABB	67	$15
Molina,Yadier	34	R	2	1145	BBC	61	$14
Alvarez,Pedro	30	L	0	4135	ACB	75	$14
Napoli,Mike	35	R	30	4115	ABB	67	$13
Martin,Russell	34	R	2	3125	ABB	67	$13
Chisenhall,Lonnie	28	L	8	2325	BCC	63	$13
Wong,Kolten	26	L	4	1425	ACA	73	$13
Gyorko,Jedd	28	R	456	3025	BCC	53	$13
Grandal,Yasmani	28	B	2	4025	BCA	64	$13
Merrifield,Whit	28	R	4	1425	ABC	69	$12
Castillo,Welington	30	R	2	3225	ACA	73	$12
Vogt,Stephen	32	L	20	2035	ACB	58	$12
Moss,Brandon	33	L	378	4215	BBB	69	$11
Garcia,Adonis	32	R	5	2135	ACB	64	$11
Aybar,Erick	33	B	6	1245	BBB	69	$11
Gennett,Scooter	27	L	4	2235	ACC	66	$9
Hechavarria,Adeiny	28	R	6	1425	ABB	73	$9
Shaw,Travis	27	L	53	3115	ABA	64	$9
Zunino,Mike	26	R	2	4005	ACC	50	$8

TIER 3 Hitters
Health>"F"; xBA score 3+; Power or Speed score 3+ — <$15

BATTERS	Age	Bats	Pos	MM	REL	MAY	R$
Joseph,Tommy	25	R	3	4035	AFF	53	$15
Drury,Brandon	24	R	785	3045	ACD	63	$15
Reddick,Josh	30	L	8	2335	CCB	68	$15
Margot,Manuel	22	R	9	1533	AFB	37	$14
Healy,Ryon	25	R	5	3035	ADF	52	$14
Polanco,Jorge	23	B	6	1335	ADB	66	$14
Kendrick,Howie	33	R	74	1345	CAA	79	$14
Aoki,Norichika	35	L	7	1453	BCA	45	$13
Albies,Ozhaino	20	B	46	2533	AFF	35	$13
Bour,Justin	29	L	3	3045	CCC	60	$13
Flores,Wilmer	25	R	53	3043	ACB	35	$13
Peralta,David	29	L	8	3355	DCF	65	$13
Lind,Adam	33	L	3	3033	BCC	28	$12
Murphy,Tom	26	R	2	4233	AFD	34	$12
Dickerson,Alex	27	L	7	4245	ADC	78	$12
Pearce,Steve	34	R	3	4033	DDF	23	$11
Morrison,Logan	29	L	3	3135	DCB	57	$10
Tapia,Raimel	23	L	9	1541	AFF	10	$10
Toles,Andrew	25	L	7	3351	AFF	11	$10
Holt,Brock	29	L	7	1343	BCA	38	$9
Jaso,John	33	L	3	3043	DDC	26	$8
Barreto,Franklin	21	R	6	2331	AFF	8	$8
Frazier,Adam	25	L	7	1441	AFB	10	$8
Suzuki,Ichiro	43	L	8	0543	ACD	38	$8
Guyer,Brandon	31	R	7	2331	DDA	8	$8
Heredia,Guillermo	26	R	7	1333	AFF	27	$7
Gosselin,Phil	28	R	4	1431	CFF	7	$7
Almora,Albert	23	R	9	2353	ADB	43	$7
Coghlan,Chris	32	L	74	3243	CCC	36	$7
Marte,Jefry	26	R	375	4231	ACA	12	$7
Tomlinson,Kelby	27	R	4	0531	BCC	9	$6
Saladino,Tyler	27	R	46	1431	ADC	9	$6
Brito,Socrates	24	L	9	3431	BFD	10	$6
Refsnyder,Rob	26	R	38	1441	ACA	12	$5
Renda,Tony	26	R	4	0341	ADB	9	$5
Torreyes,Ronald	24	R	5	1541	ADB	12	$4
Choi,Ji-Man	26	L	37	3131	AFA	9	$4

* Tier 2 players should generally be less than $20. If you pay more than $20, you should be aware of the extra risk.

PORTFOLIO 3 PLAN — Pitchers

TIER 1 Pitchers

Rel BBB+; xERA score 3+ and K/9 score 3+

PITCHERS	Age	Th	MM	REL	MAY	R$
Scherzer,Max	32	R	4505	AAA	120	$30
Bumgarner,Madison	27	L	4405	AAA	113	$28
Chapman,Aroldis	29	L	5530	BAB	65	$28
Britton,Zach	29	L	5430	AAA	68	$26
Lester,Jon	33	L	3305	AAA	93	$26
Kluber,Corey	31	R	3405	BAA	95	$25
Sale,Chris	28	L	4405	BAA	108	$24
Kimbrel,Craig	29	R	5530	BAA	69	$21
Archer,Chris	28	R	3405	AAA	100	$21
Price,David	31	L	3305	AAA	89	$21
Arrieta,Jake	31	R	3305	BAB	85	$21
Robertson,David	32	R	4531	BAB	82	$20
Rodriguez,Francisco	35	R	3330	AAB	46	$19
Allen,Cody	28	R	4530	AAA	64	$18
Martinez,Carlos	25	R	3305	AAA	93	$16
deGrom,Jacob	29	R	3303	BBA	44	$14
Rondon,Hector	29	R	4420	BBA	34	$14
Gregerson,Luke	33	R	5410	BBA	18	$5

TIER 2 Pitchers

Rel BCC+; PT score 3+; xERA or K/9 score 3+   <$20

PITCHERS	Age	Th	MM	REL	MAY	R$
Syndergaard,Noah*	24	R	4405	ACB	98	$23
Hendricks,Kyle*	27	R	3205	AAA	87	$20
Maeda,Kenta	29	R	2305	ABB	73	$16
Keuchel,Dallas	29	L	3205	BAB	79	$13
Hamels,Cole	33	L	2305	BAA	76	$12
Salazar,Danny	27	R	2403	BBB	38	$9
Kennedy,Ian	32	R	1305	BAA	64	$9
Gonzalez,Gio	31	L	2305	BAA	76	$7
Rodon,Carlos	24	L	2305	BBA	73	$7
Finnegan,Brandon	24	L	1305	ACC	55	$3

* Tier 2 players should generally be less than $20. If you pay more than $20, you should be aware of the extra risk.

TIER 3 Pitchers

Health > "F"; xERA score 3+   <$15

PITCHERS	Age	Th	MM	REL	MAY	R$
Matz,Steven	26	L	3303	DCA	36	$13
Bedrosian,Cam	25	R	3530	DDD	34	$13
Urias,Julio	20	L	3303	ADA	41	$12
Bush,Matt	31	R	4311	AFF	23	$12
Kelley,Shawn	33	R	4511	CCA	33	$10
Herrera,Kelvin	27	R	4411	BCB	31	$9
Nola,Aaron	24	R	3303	DCB	34	$9
Barraclough,Kyle	27	R	5511	ADA	39	$8
Neris,Hector	28	R	3511	ADC	27	$7
Holland,Greg	31	R	4520	BCD	30	$7
Baez,Pedro	29	R	3411	CDA	25	$7
Hand,Brad	27	L	4511	BCB	33	$7
Brach,Brad	31	R	3401	ACA	13	$6
Reed,Addison	28	R	3411	ACB	28	$6
Casilla,Santiago	36	R	3310	DBA	10	$6
Givens,Mychal	27	R	3501	ADD	12	$6
Strickland,Hunter	28	R	3310	ADC	10	$6
Harris,Will	32	R	4410	ACA	16	$6
Altavilla,Dan	24	R	3310	AFF	9	$5
Feliz,Michael	24	R	4511	ADA	34	$5
Dayton,Grant	29	L	3510	ADD	12	$5
Rivero,Felipe	25	L	3411	BDB	25	$5
Strop,Pedro	32	R	5500	DCA	0	$4
Cecil,Brett	30	L	5500	DDA	0	$4
Smith,Will	27	L	3510	DDB	11	$4
Rosenthal,Trevor	27	R	3510	DAB	12	$4
Kelly,Joe	29	R	4401	DCA	13	$4
Cishek,Steve	31	R	3410	BBC	12	$4
Kela,Keone	24	R	3510	DDB	11	$4
Storen,Drew	29	R	3310	CCA	11	$3
Wilson,Justin	29	L	3410	ACA	13	$3
Edwards,Carl	25	R	5500	ADA	0	$3
Barnette,Tony	33	R	3300	ACF	0	$3
Cedeno,Xavier	30	L	3310	ADA	11	$3
Knebel,Corey	25	R	3410	DDB	10	$2
Nicasio,Juan	30	R	3401	CCC	11	$2
Duke,Zach	34	L	3400	ACB	0	$2
Hendriks,Liam	28	R	3400	CCA	0	$2
Krol,Ian	26	L	3400	ADB	0	$1

DAILY FANTASY INDICATORS

Top OPS v LHP, 2015-2016

Hitter	OPS
Goldschmidt,Paul	1075
Cruz,Nelson	1061
Stanton,Giancarlo	1036
Flores,Wilmer	1024
Trout,Mike	1011
Braun,Ryan	984
Cain,Lorenzo	978
Donaldson,Josh	975
Prado,Martin	969
Tomas,Yasmany	968
Beltre,Adrian	966
Cabrera,Miguel	959
Rupp,Cameron	954
Bryant,Kris	945
Springer,George	941
Votto,Joey	940
Piscotty,Stephen	934
Werth,Jayson	933
Altuve,Jose	932
Ramirez,Hanley	918
Guyer,Brandon	912
Ozuna,Marcell	908
Forsythe,Logan	895
Zobrist,Ben	891
Kemp,Matt	891
Martinez,J.D.	889
Villar,Jonathan	886
Bogaerts,Xander	883
Napoli,Mike	883
Harper,Bryce	880
Posey,Buster	879
Valencia,Danny	878
McCann,James	878
Cespedes,Yoenis	875
Encarnacion,Edwin	873
Zimmerman,Ryan	872
Fowler,Dexter	870
Cervelli,Francisco	867
Beltran,Carlos	864
Frazier,Todd	861
Longoria,Evan	861

600+ PA, 2015-2016

Consistent High-PQS SP

Pitcher	QC*
Kershaw,Clayton	132
Verlander,Justin	88
Fernandez,Jose	84
Scherzer,Max	82
Sale,Chris	80
Bumgarner,Madison	76
Porcello,Rick	74
Strasburg,Stephen	64
Syndergaard,Noah	60
Kluber,Corey	54
Darvish,Yu	46
Cueto,Johnny	42
Hill,Rich	40
Hendricks,Kyle	38
Lester,Jon	36
deGrom,Jacob	24
Quintana,Jose	18
Sanchez,Aaron	18
Duffy,Danny	16

10+ Games Started, 2016

Consistent Low-PQS SP

Pitcher	QC*	Pitcher	QC*
Pelfrey,Mike	(292)	Adleman,Timothy	(246)
Nicolino,Justin	(276)	Clevinger,Michael	(240)
Blair,Aaron	(268)	Perez,Williams	(238)
Milone,Tommy	(268)	Severino,Luis	(238)
Wilson,Tyler	(260)	Simon,Alfredo	(238)
Hughes,Phil	(256)	Weaver,Jered	(232)
Young,Chris	(248)	Eflin,Zach	(220)

*Quality-Consistency score

Top OPS v RHP, 2015-2016

Hitter	OPS
Votto,Joey	1015
Harper,Bryce	998
Trout,Mike	985
Cabrera,Miguel	965
Freeman,Freddie	963
Seager,Corey	958
Arenado,Nolan	941
Gonzalez,Carlos	939
Donaldson,Josh	939
Rizzo,Anthony	936
Carpenter,Matt	923
Goldschmidt,Paul	918
Murphy,Daniel	914
Encarnacion,Edwin	914
Turner,Justin	913
Davis,Chris	906
Blackmon,Charlie	896
Martinez,J.D.	893
Bautista,Jose	889
Peralta,David	886
Bryant,Kris	886
Cano,Robinson	885
Machado,Manny	878
Cespedes,Yoenis	877
Brantley,Michael	872
Bradley,Jackie	872
Betts,Mookie	870
Yelich,Christian	866
Cruz,Nelson	865
Kang,Jung-ho	865
Kipnis,Jason	862
Granderson,Curtis	861
Abreu,Jose	860
Dietrich,Derek	857
Pollock,A.J.	855
Gonzalez,Adrian	854
Belt,Brandon	853
Bour,Justin	850
Altuve,Jose	848
Choo,Shin-Soo	848
Hosmer,Eric	847

Most DOMinant SP

Pitcher	DOM
Kershaw,Clayton	76%
Sale,Chris	66%
Scherzer,Max	65%
Verlander,Justin	62%
Kluber,Corey	59%
Strasburg,Stephen	58%
Bumgarner,Madison	56%
Porcello,Rick	55%
Cueto,Johnny	53%
Lester,Jon	50%
Syndergaard,Noah	50%
Fernandez,Jose	48%
Quintana,Jose	47%
Darvish,Yu	47%
Wright,Steven	46%
Teheran,Julio	43%
Sanchez,Aaron	43%
Arrieta,Jake	42%
Gray,Jonathan	41%

Top L-R Splits, 2015-2016

Hitter	OPS vL-vR
Flores,Wilmer	385
McCann,James	311
Rupp,Cameron	295
Rollins,Jimmy	276
Prado,Martin	274
Werth,Jayson	269
Tomas,Yasmany	266
Guyer,Brandon	262
Cain,Lorenzo	250
Zimmerman,Ryan	223
Ozuna,Marcell	215
Stanton,Giancarlo	210
Cruz,Nelson	196
Beltre,Adrian	183
Iannetta,Chris	183
Upton,Melvin	182
Suzuki,Ichiro	180
Springer,George	173
Ahmed,Nick	171

Top R-L Splits, 2015-2016

Hitter	OPS vR-vL
Coghlan,Chris	377
Howard,Ryan	376
Dietrich,Derek	316
Reddick,Josh	310
Bour,Justin	289
Gonzalez,Carlos	276
Jaso,John	267
Smith,Seth	257
Span,Denard	253
Pederson,Joc	239
Castro,Jason	237
Lamb,Jacob	231
Dickerson,Corey	231
Turner,Justin	229
Barnhart,Tucker	222
Lind,Adam	218
Gose,Anthony	218
Granderson,Curtis	216
Miller,Bradley	210

Most DISastrous SP

Pitcher	DIS
Pelfrey,Mike	73%
Adleman,Timothy	69%
Wilson,Tyler	69%
Nicolino,Justin	69%
Blair,Aaron	67%
Milone,Tommy	67%
Eflin,Zach	64%
Perez,Williams	64%
Severino,Luis	64%
Simon,Alfredo	64%
Hughes,Phil	64%
Locke,Jeff	63%
Young,Chris	62%
Weaver,Jered	61%
Thompson,Jake	60%
Clevinger,Michael	60%
Chacin,Jhoulys	59%
Wright,Mike	58%
Peralta,Wily	57%

Best Parks - BB

Ballpark	Factor
NYM	19%

Worst Parks - BB

Ballpark	Factor
LA	-14%

Best Parks - LH HR

Ballpark	Factor
MIL	49%
NYY	46%
CIN	29%
LA	17%
COL	16%
BAL	16%
CHW	13%
SEA	10%
CLE	10%

Best Parks - RH HR

Ballpark	Factor
NYY	25%
COL	25%
PHI	23%
NYM	19%
CHC	16%
MIL	11%
CIN	11%
TOR	9%
BAL	8%

Worst Parks - LH HR

Ballpark	Factor
SF	-41%
SD	-26%
BOS	-25%
ATL	-21%
OAK	-20%
KC	-20%
CHC	-19%
WAS	-17%
LAA	-13%
MIN	-10%

Worst Parks - RH HR

Ballpark	Factor
SF	-26%
PIT	-24%
MIA	-23%
OAK	-19%
KC	-19%
STL	-15%
TB	-15%
ATL	-10%

Best Parks - Runs

Ballpark	Factor
COL	43%
BOS	16%
ARI	15%
CLE	13%
TEX	12%

Worst Parks - Runs

Ballpark	Factor
MIA	-17%
LA	-12%
SEA	-12%
LAA	-10%
HOU	-9%

Note: for Runs, best parks for hitters = worst for pitchers

Best Parks - Ks

Ballpark	Factor
NYM	12%
HOU	9%
ATL	9%

Worst Parks - Ks

Ballpark	Factor
COL	-16%
MIN	-10%

Universal Draft Grid

Most publications and websites provide cheat sheets with ranked player lists for different fantasy draft formats. The biggest problem with these tools is that they perpetuate the myth that players can be ranked in a linear fashion.

Since rankings are based on highly variable projections, it is foolhardy to draw conclusions that a $24 player is better than a $23 player is better than a $22 player. Yes, a first round pick is better than a 10th round pick, but within most rounds, all players are pretty much interchangeable commodities.

But typical cheat sheets don't reflect that reality. Auction sheets rank players by dollar value. Snake draft sheets rank players within round, accounting for position and categorical scarcity. But just as ADPs have a ridiculously low success rate, these cheat sheets are similarly flawed.

We have a tool at BaseballHQ.com called the Rotisserie Grid. It is a chart—that can be customized to your league parameters—which organizes players into pockets of skill, by position. It is one of the most popular tools on the site. One of the best features of this grid is that its design provides immediate insight into position scarcity.

So in the *Forecaster*, we have transitioned to this format as a sort of Universal Draft Grid.

How to use the chart

Across the top of the grid, players are sorted by position. First and third base, and second and shortstop are presented side-by-side for easy reference when considering corner and middle infielders, respectively.

The vertical axis separates each group of players into tiers based on potential fantasy impact. At the top are the Elite players; at the bottom are the Fringe players.

Auction leagues: The tiers in the grid represent rough breakpoints for dollar values. Elite players could be considered those that are purchased for $30 and up. Each subsequent tier is a step down of approximately $5.

Snake drafters: Tiers can be used to rank players similarly, though most tiers will encompass more than one round. Any focus on position scarcity will bump some players up a bit. For instance, with the dearth of Elite catchers and the wealth of Elite outfielders, one might opt to draft Buster Posey (from the Stars tier) before the Elite level Starling Marte. The reason we target scarce positions early is that there will be plenty of solid outfielders and starting pitchers later on.

To build the best foundation, you should come out of the first 10 rounds with all your middle infielders, all your corner infielders, one outfielder, at least one catcher and two pitchers (at least one closer).

The players are listed at the position where they both qualify and provide the most fantasy value. Additional position eligibility (20 games) is listed in parentheses. Listings in bold are players with high reliability grades (minimum "B" across the board).

Each player is presented with his 7-character Mayberry score. The first four digits (all on a 0-5 scale) represent skill: power, speed, batting average and playing time for batters; ERA, dominance, saves potential and playing time for pitchers. The last three alpha characters are the reliability grade (A-F): health, experience and consistency.

Within each tier, players are sorted by the first character of their Mayberry score. This means that batters are sorted by power; pitchers by ERA potential. If you need to prospect for the best skill sets among players in a given tier, target those with 4s and 5s in whatever skill you need.

CAVEATS and DISCLAIMERS

The placement of players in tiers does not represent average draft positions (ADP) or average auction values (AAV). It represents where each player's true value may lie. It is the variance between this true value and the ADP/AAV market values—or better, the value that your league-mates place on each player—where you will find your potential for profit or loss.

That means *you cannot take this chart right into your draft with you*. You have to compare these rankings with your ADPs and AAVs, and build your draft list from there. In other words, if we project Trea Turner as a "Elite" level pick but you know the other owners (or your ADPs) see him as a third-rounder, you can probably wait to pick him up in round two. If you are in an auction league with owners who overvalue Red Sox, and Dustin Pedroia (projected at $26) gets bid past $30, you will likely take a loss should you decide to chase the bidding, especially given the depth of second basemen in 2017.

Finally, this chart is intended as a preliminary look based on current factors. For Draft Day, you will need to make your own adjustments based upon many different criteria that will impact the world between now and then. Daily updates appear online at BaseballHQ.com. A free projections update is available in March at **http://www.baseballhq.com/bf2017**

Simulation League Cheat Sheet

Using Runs Above Replacement creates a more real-world ranking of player value, which serves simulation gamers well. Batters and pitchers are integrated, and value break-points are delineated.

Universal Draft Grid

Elite

FIRST BASE		THIRD BASE		SECOND BASE		SHORTSTOP	
Goldschmidt,Paul	(4345 BAD)	Bryant,Kris (O)	(5335 AAC)	Turner,Trea (O)	(3545 ADD)	**Machado,Manny (3)**	**(4345 BAB)**
Votto,Joey	(4155 CBD)	**Arenado,Nolan**	**(4155 AAB)**	Altuve,Jose	(2455 AAD)	Villar,Jonathan (3)	(2525 ABD)
Cabrera,Miguel	(4055 BAC)	Donaldson,Josh	(4345 AAC)	Gordon,Dee	(0535 ABD)		
Rizzo,Anthony	**(4155 AAA)**						

Gold

FIRST BASE		THIRD BASE		SECOND BASE		SHORTSTOP	
Freeman,Freddie	(4245 BAC)	Beltre,Adrian	(3155 BAC)	**Odor,Rougned**	**(4235 ABB)**	Story,Trevor	(5325 CCD)
		Ramirez,Jose (O)	(2445 ABC)	Dozier,Brian	(4435 AAC)	Correa,Carlos	(4355 ACB)
				Murphy,Daniel (1)	(3255 BAF)	Seager,Corey	(3255 ACB)
				Cano,Robinson	(3055 AAC)	Bogaerts,Xander	(2435 ACA)
				Kinsler,Ian	**(2335 AAB)**	Anderson,Tim	(2525 ACA)
				LeMahieu,DJ	(1555 AAF)	Segura,Jean (2)	(1545 AAD)
				Pedroia,Dustin	(1255 CAB)	Lindor,Francisco	(1445 AAC)
						Nunez,Eduardo (3)	(1535 BDB)
						Andrus,Elvis	(1545 AAC)
						Peraza,Jose	(0545 ADC)

Stars

FIRST BASE		THIRD BASE		SECOND BASE		SHORTSTOP	
Encarnacion,Edwin	**(4155 BAB)**	Frazier,Todd	(4225 AAA)	**Carpenter,Matt (31)**	**(4055 BAB)**	Baez,Javier (23)	(2415 ACC)
Belt,Brandon	**(4225 BBB)**	Longoria,Evan	(4135 AAB)	Kipnis,Jason	(3345 AAC)		
Abreu,Jose	(3045 AAC)	Lamb,Jacob	(4335 BBC)	**Phillips,Brandon**	**(1245 BAB)**		
Ramirez,Hanley	(3245 CBD)	**Seager,Kyle**	**(3145 AAB)**	Hernandez,Cesar	(1535 ABC)		
Myers,Wil	(3425 FCC)	Turner,Justin	(3255 BCB)				
Hosmer,Eric	(2145 AAC)	Bregman,Alex	(3335 AFF)				
Pujols,Albert	**(2145 BAA)**	Perez,Hernan (O)	(2525 ACC)				

Regulars

FIRST BASE		THIRD BASE		SECOND BASE		SHORTSTOP	
Davis,Chris	(5115 AAF)	Sano,Miguel (O)	(5215 BDC)	**Walker,Neil**	**(3235 BBB)**	Diaz,Aledmys	(3335 BDF)
Gonzalez,Adrian	**(3045 AAA)**	Kang,Jung-ho	(4145 CCF)	Forsythe,Logan	(3325 CBC)	Tulowitzki,Troy	(3235 DBF)
Santana,Carlos	(3235 AAC)	**Castellanos,Nick**	**(4125 BBB)**	Schoop,Jonathan	(3125 CBD)	**Cabrera,Asdrubal**	**(3335 BAB)**
Cron,C.J.	(3135 BCB)	Franco,Maikel	(3235 BBF)	Travis,Devon	(2335 FDB)	Russell,Addison	(3225 ACB)
		Moustakas,Mike	(3045 FCD)	Castro,Starlin	(2335 AAC)	**Semien,Marcus**	**(3425 AAA)**
		Suarez,Eugenio	**(3215 ABA)**	**Zobrist,Ben (O)**	**(2255 BAB)**	**Miller,Bradley (1)**	**(3335 BAB)**
		Gurriel,Yulieski	(3245 ADF)	Harrison,Josh	(1535 BBC)	Swanson,Dansby	(2525 AFF)
		Valencia,Danny (O)	(3135 BCD)	Panik,Joe	(1345 CBF)	**Crawford,Brandon**	**(2325 AAB)**
		Rendon,Anthony	(2335 CBD)			Owings,Christopher (O)	(2535 CCC)
		Solarte,Yangervis	**(2145 BBB)**			**Gregorius,Didi**	**(2435 ABB)**
		Prado,Martin	**(1255 BAA)**			**Simmons,Andrelton**	**(1445 BBB)**
		Reyes,Jose	**(1525 BBA)**			Arcia,Orlando	(1535 ADF)
		Duffy,Matt				**Escobar,Alcides**	**(1535 BAB)**
						Marte,Ketel	(1425 BCC)

Mid-Level

FIRST BASE		THIRD BASE		SECOND BASE		SHORTSTOP	
Carter,Chris	(5115 ABC)	Drury,Brandon (O)	(3045 ACD)	Lawrie,Brett	(3215 FCA)	Gyorko,Jedd (23)	(3025 BCC)
Joseph,Tommy	(4035 AFF)	Healy,Ryon	(3035 ADF)	Kendrick,Howie (O)	(1345 CAA)	Albies,Ozhaino (2)	(2533 AFF)
Napoli,Mike	**(4115 ABB)**	Flores,Wilmer (1)	(3043 ACA)	Wong,Kolten	(1425 ACA)	Cozart,Zack	(2325 DCC)
Moss,Brandon (O)	**(4215 BBB)**	Valbuena,Luis	(3123 CBB)	Mondesi,Raul	(1503 AFB)	Gonzalez,Marwin (3)	(2233 ADB)
Pearce,Steve	(4033 DDF)	**Headley,Chase**	**(2225 AAA)**	Merrifield,Whit	(1425 ABC)	Polanco,Jorge	(1335 ADB)
Bour,Justin	(3045 CCC)	Garcia,Adonis	(2135 ACB)	Spangenberg,Cory	(1523 FFA)	**Aybar,Erick**	**(1245 BBB)**
Park,Byung Ho	(3103 ABF)	Plouffe,Trevor	(2225 DBA)			**Ramirez,Alexei**	**(1343 AAB)**
Lind,Adam	(3033 BCC)	Peralta,Jhonny	(2033 DBA)				
Moreland,Mitch	(3125 DCD)	Escobar,Yunel	(1035 BAC)				
Zimmerman,Ryan	(3225 FCC)	Sandoval,Pablo	(1035 FCF)				
Morrison,Logan	(3135 DCB)						
Mauer,Joe	**(1255 BAA)**						

Bench

FIRST BASE		THIRD BASE		SECOND BASE		SHORTSTOP	
Adams,Matt	(4023 FCC)	Gallo,Joey	(5303 ADA)	Schimpf,Ryan	(5013 ACC)	Rodriguez,Sean (21)	(4213 ADD)
Duda,Lucas	(4025 FCB)	Marte,Jefry (1O)	(4231 ACA)	Dietrich,Derek	(3213 BDB)	Beckham,Tim	(4421 DFC)
Austin,Tyler	(4213 ACD)	**Shaw,Travis (1)**	**(3115 ABA)**	Coghlan,Chris (O)	(3243 CCC)	Espinosa,Danny	(3303 ACB)
Vargas,Kennys	(4013 ACA)	Wright,David	(3223 FDC)	Gennett,Scooter	(2235 ACC)	Barreto,Franklin	(2331 AFF)
Howard,Ryan	(4021 CBA)	Jones,JaCoby	(3501 AFB)	Gosselin,Phil	(1431 CFF)	**Galvis,Freddy**	**(2313 BBA)**
Smoak,Justin	(4013 ADB)	Moncada,Yoan	(3411 AFF)	**Wendle,Joe**	**(1431 ABA)**	Mercer,Jordy	(1125 ABC)
Canha,Mark	(3223 FDF)	Profar,Jurickson	(2235 FFF)	Tomlinson,Kelby	(0531 BCC)	**Hechavarria,Adeiny**	**(1425 ABB)**
Jaso,John	(3043 DDC)	Freese,David (1)	(2013 BCA)			Hardy,J.J.	(1215 DBD)
Reynolds,Mark	**(3113 BCB)**	Gillaspie,Conor	(2033 ADC)			Crawford,J.P.	(1313 ADA)
Lee,Dae-ho	**(3033 ABA)**					Saladino,Tyler (2)	(1431 ADC)
Reed,A.J.	(3003 AFF)					Escobar,Eduardo (3)	(1123 ACB)
Butler,Billy	**(2043 ABA)**					Iglesias,Jose	(0335 FDC)
Bell,Josh	(1143 ACC)					Sardinas,Luis	(0423 ADA)
Alonso,Yonder	(1133 CCB)						
Loney,James	**(1043 BBA)**						
Refsnyder,Rob (O)	(1441 ACA)						

Fringe

FIRST BASE		THIRD BASE		SECOND BASE		SHORTSTOP	
Shaffer,Richie	(4201 ACC)	Cuthbert,Cheslor	(2321 ACB)	Utley,Chase	(2133 CBC)	Descalso,Daniel	(1221 BFC)
Vogelbach,Daniel	(3011 AFA)	Nunez,Renato	(2311 ADB)	Johnson,Kelly (3)	(2221 BDB)	O Malley,Shawn	(1411 ADB)
Choi,Ji-Man (O)	(3131 AFA)	Wallace,Brett (1)	(2001 ADB)	Pinder,Chad	(2201 ADB)	Ahmed,Nick	(1311 CCA)
Aguilar,Jesus	(3011 ACA)	Flaherty,Ryan	(2401 ADA)	Beckham,Gordon	(2211 DDA)	Barney,Darwin (23)	(1221 ADC)
Paulsen,Benjamin	(3111 ACB)	La Stella,Tommy	(1141 FFA)	Giavotella,Johnny	(1241 BCB)	Garcia,Greg (23)	(1221 ADB)
Rua,Ryan (O)	(2501 BDF)	Torreyes,Ronald	(1541 ADB)	Peterson,Jace	(1223 ACA)	Rojas,Miguel (21)	(1131 ADC)
White,Tyler	(2111 ADD)			Hill,Aaron (3)	(1121 BCA)	Petit,Gregorio (2)	(1111 BFC)
Johnson,Chris	(1211 BCA)			Rivera,T.J.	(1131 ACA)	Adames,Cristhian	(0221 ADB)
Ackley,Dustin	(1211 FDC)			Asuaje,Carlos	(1211 ADB)		
				Sanchez,Carlos	(1211 ACA)		
				Lowrie,Jed	(1313 FCA)		
				Muncy,Max	(1301 ACA)		
				Renda,Tony	(0341 ADB)		
				Amarista,Alexi	(0411 BDB)		

Universal Draft Grid

TIER	CATCHER		DH		OUTFIELD			
Elite					Trout,Mike	**(4445 AAB)**	Hamilton,Billy	(0515 BBB)
					Betts,Mookie	(3555 AAC)		
					Blackmon,Charlie	(3455 BAC)		
					Marte,Starling	**(2545 ABB)**		
Gold					**Cespedes,Yoenis**	**(4245 BAB)**	Desmond,Ian	(2425 AAC)
					Cruz,Nelson	**(4245 AAB)**		
					Harper,Bryce	(4235 BBF)		
					Yelich,Christian	**(3345 BAB)**		
					Braun,Ryan	(3345 AAC)		
					Dahl,David	(3535 ADF)		
					Pollock,A.J.	(3545 FDF)		
					Polanco,Gregory	**(3345 AAB)**		
					Eaton,Adam	**(2445 BAA)**		
					Cain,Lorenzo	(2535 CBC)		
Stars	Lucroy,Jonathan	(3345 BBD)			Stanton,Giancarlo	(5235 FBC)	Broxton,Keon	(4505 ACB)
	Posey,Buster	**(2255 AAB)**			**Davis,Khristopher**	**(5135 ABB)**	McCutchen,Andrew	(3335 BAD)
					Gonzalez,Carlos	(4245 BBC)	Buxton,Byron	(3505 BFA)
					Upton,Justin	**(4325 AAB)**	Gomez,Carlos	(3425 BBC)
					Kemp,Matt	(4135 CAB)	**Calhoun,Kole**	**(3135 AAB)**
					Martinez,J.D.	(4235 CBB)	Fowler,Dexter	(3525 CAB)
					Tomas,Yasmany	(4145 ACB)	**Jones,Adam**	**(3235 AAA)**
					Benintendi,Andrew	(4355 AFF)	Kiermaier,Kevin	(2535 BCA)
					Springer,George	(4325 DBB)	Davis,Rajai	(2523 ACA)
					Bruce,Jay	**(4235 AAB)**	**Herrera,Odubel**	**(1525 ABB)**
					Kepler,Max	(4345 ADC)	**Inciarte,Ender**	**(1545 BBB)**
Regulars	Contreras,Willson (O)	(4155 ADB)	Morales,Kendrys	(3035 ABF)	**Pederson,Joc**	**(5125 ABB)**	Puig,Yasiel	(3235 CCB)
	Gattis,Evan	**(4135 BBB)**	Martinez,Victor	(2045 CAF)	Bautista,Jose	(4135 DAC)	Cabrera,Melky	(2255 BAC)
	Sanchez,Gary	(4145 ACC)			Grichuk,Randal	(4325 BCF)	Heyward,Jason	(2335 AAD)
	Realmuto,Jacob	(2335 ACB)			**Trumbo,Mark**	**(4125 BBB)**	Brantley,Michael	(2355 FCF)
					Conforto,Michael	(4035 AFB)	**Gardner,Brett**	**(1425 BAA)**
					Bradley,Jackie	(4235 ABD)	Span,Denard	(1355 DBC)
					Duvall,Adam	**(4225 ABB)**	Smith,Mallex	(1523 CFA)
					Naquin,Tyler	(4435 ADB)	Quinn,Roman	(1503 AFA)
					Santana,Domingo	(4125 CCB)	**Pillar,Kevin**	**(1335 ABA)**
					Schwarber,Kyle	(4125 FFF)	Ellsbury,Jacoby	(1435 CAC)
					Dickerson,Corey	(4145 CCC)	Dyson,Jarrod	(1543 BDA)
					Granderson,Curtis	**(4235 BAB)**	Maybin,Cameron	(1535 FCC)
					Ozuna,Marcell	**(3135 AAB)**	Pagan,Angel	(1445 FBC)
					Pence,Hunter	(3235 FCA)	Martin,Leonys	(1505 ABC)
					Piscotty,Stephen	(3235 ABC)	**Markakis,Nick**	**(1035 AAA)**
					Beltran,Carlos	(3135 BBC)	Revere,Ben	(0555 CBC)
Mid-Level	Grandal,Yasmani	(4025 BCA)	Bird,Gregory	(5135 FFA)	Dickerson,Alex	(4245 ADC)	Jackson,Austin	(2435 FCA)
	Murphy,Tom	(4233 AFD)	Alvarez,Pedro	(4135 ACB)	Saunders,Michael	(4225 FDF)	Chisenhall,Lonnie	(2325 BCC)
	Perez,Salvador	**(3335 AAA)**			Gordon,Alex	(3225 CCB)	Mazara,Nomar	(2125 ACB)
	Martin,Russell	**(3125 ABB)**			Souza,Steven	(3205 CCB)	Garcia,Avisail	(2225 DCA)
	Castillo,Welington	(3225 ACA)			Rosario,Eddie	(3425 ACB)	Parra,Gerardo	(2243 BBD)
	Wieters,Matt	(2035 DDC)			Upton,Melvin	(3505 CCB)	Altherr,Aaron	(2425 DDF)
	Vogt,Stephen	(2035 ACB)			Werth,Jayson	(3215 DBD)	Schebler,Scott	(2223 ACD)
	McCann,Brian	**(2225 ABA)**			Peralta,David	(3355 DCF)	**Kim,Hyun-Soo**	**(1145 ABB)**
	Molina,Yadier	(1145 BBC)			Ethier,Andre	(3143 FDF)	Margot,Manuel	(1533 AFB)
	Cervelli,Francisco	(1215 FDB)			Brinson,Lewis	(3423 AFF)	Jankowski,Travis	(1523 ADB)
					Soler,Jorge	(3215 DDD)	Aoki,Norichika	(1453 BCA)
					Choo,Shin-Soo	(2125 CCD)	Deshields Jr.,Delino	(1513 ACD)
					Reddick,Josh	(2335 CCB)	Tapia,Raimel	(1541 AFF)
Bench	Zunino,Mike	(4005 ACC)	Zimmer,Bradley	(2503 AFB)	Judge,Aaron	(4203 ADB)	Grossman,Robert	(2113 ACF)
	Gomes,Yan	(3213 DCD)			Renfroe,Hunter	(4213 ACB)	Almora,Albert	(2353 ADB)
	Norris,Derek	(3203 ABC)			Young,Chris	(4221 DDB)	Jennings,Desmond	(2413 FDA)
	Flowers,Tyler	(3003 BCC)			Moya,Steven	(4223 ACD)	Smolinski,Jacob	(2233 BDC)
	Hundley,Nick	(3123 CDC)			Gutierrez,Franklin	(4111 CFA)	Pompey,Dalton	(1501 ADB)
	Mesoraco,Devin	(2023 FFF)			Meadows,Austin	(4421 AFF)	Lagares,Juan	(1523 CDA)
	McCann,James	(2113 ADB)			Toles,Andrew	(3351 AFF)	Blanco,Gregor	(1513 BCD)
	Montero,Miguel	(2113 BCB)			Holliday,Matt	(3033 FCA)	Holt,Brock	(1343 BCA)
	Ramos,Wilson	(2031 CBF)			Taylor,Michael	(3503 ACB)	Santana,Danny	(1523 CDC)
	Barnhart,Tucker	(1025 ADC)			Pham,Thomas	(3313 DDC)	Frazier,Adam	(1441 AFB)
	D Arnaud,Travis	(1213 FDC)			Rasmus,Colby	(3203 BCC)	Hicks,Aaron	(1213 CCD)
					Hernandez,Teoscar	(3511 ADC)	Heredia,Guillermo	(1333 AFF)
					Thompson,Trayce	(3223 CCB)	Bourn,Michael	(1413 BCB)
					Smith,Seth	**(3133 ABA)**	Orlando,Paulo	(1521 ACC)
					Franklin,Nick	(3413 BDA)	O Neill,Tyler	(1301 AFF)
					Haniger,Mitch	(3221 ADC)	Crisp,Coco	(1323 DCF)
					Williamson,Mac	(3113 BFA)	Swihart,Blake	(1323 FDB)
					Brito,Socrates	(3431 BFD)	Rickard,Joey	(1501 CDF)
					Winker,Jesse	(2123 ADC)	Burns,Billy	(0511 ACF)
					Almonte,Abraham	(2223 ADC)	Suzuki,Ichiro	(0543 ACD)
					Guyer,Brandon	(2331 DDA)	Jay,Jon	(0233 FDF)
					Gamel,Benjamin	(2321 ADC)	Kemp,Anthony	(0321 ACA)
Fringe	Chirinos,Robinson	(4021 FFB)	Hamilton,Josh	(3221 FFA)	O Brien,Peter	(5101 ACB)	Williams,Nick	(2201 ACD)
	Saltalamacchia,Jarrod	(4001 ADA)	Tucker,Preston	(3011 BCB)	Nieuwenhuis,Kirk	(4101 ADA)	Hernandez,Enrique	(2311 CDB)
	Casali,Curtis	(4201 BFB)	Rodriguez,Alex	(2201 DDF)	Hazelbaker,Jeremy	(4411 ADC)	Collins,Tyler	(2211 ADA)
	Rupp,Cameron	(3003 ADD)			Arcia,Oswaldo	(3001 CDC)	Asche,Cody	(2211 CCA)
	Susac,Andrew	(3303 BFB)			Mahtook,Mikie	(3301 BCB)	Szczur,Matthew	(1311 ADB)
	Castro,Jason	(3103 ACA)			Joyce,Matt	(3011 BDF)	Carrera,Ezequiel	(1411 ADA)
	Perez,Roberto	(3101 CFC)			Olson,Matt	(3211 ADA)	Nimmo,Brandon	(1221 ADB)
	Sanchez,Hector	(3011 BFC)			Dozier,Hunter	(3211 ACC)	Goeddel,Tyler	(1501 AFC)
	Bandy,Jett	(2113 ADA)			Parker,Jarrett	(3201 ACA)	Perez,Eury	(0431 BDA)
	Wolters,Tony	(2221 ADC)			Bourjos,Peter	(2511 BDC)	Holt,Tyler	(0501 ACA)
	Herrmann,Chris	(2401 BFF)			Van Slyke,Scott	(2211 FFF)	Shuck,J.B.	(0231 ADD)
	Maldonado,Martin	(2003 AFC)			Marisnick,Jake	(2401 ADB)	Ortega,Rafael	(0421 ACA)
	Rivera,Rene	(2001 ADF)			Eibner,Brett	(2201 ADC)		
	Avila,Alex	(2001 FDC)			Francoeur,Jeff	(2101 ADC)		

Universal Draft Grid

TIER	STARTING PITCHERS				RELIEF PITCHERS			
Elite	Kershaw,Clayton	(5505 DAA)						
Gold	**Bumgarner,Madison**	**(4405 AAA)**			Britton,Zach	(5430 AAA)	Melancon,Mark	(5231 AAA)
	Scherzer,Max	**(4505 AAA)**			Chapman,Aroldis	(5530 BAB)	Osuna,Roberto	(3431 ACA)
	Lester,Jon	(3305 AAA)			Jansen,Kenley	(5530 CAA)		
Stars	Sale,Chris	**(4405 BAA)**	Hendricks,Kyle	(3205 AAA)	Betances,Dellin	(5531 ACA)	Colome,Alexander	(4530 DCB)
	Syndergaard,Noah	(4405 ACB)	Kluber,Corey	**(3405 BAA)**	Diaz,Edwin	(5530 ADB)	Familia,Jeurys	(4431 DAB)
	Archer,Chris	(3405 AAA)	Price,David	(3305 BAA)	Giles,Kenneth	(5530 ACC)	Oh,Seung-Hwan	(4531 AAD)
	Arrieta,Jake	(3305 BAB)	Verlander,Justin	(2305 DAA)	Kimbrel,Craig	(5530 BAA)	Robertson,David	(4531 BAB)
	Cueto,Johnny	(3205 DAB)						
Regulars	Carrasco,Carlos	(4405 DAA)	Greinke,Zack	(2205 DAB)	Miller,Andrew	(5521 DBA)		
	Strasburg,Stephen	(4503 DAA)	**Maeda,Kenta**	**(2305 ABB)**	**Allen,Cody**	**(4530 AAA)**		
	Darvish,Yu	(3505 FCA)	**Porcello,Rick**	**(2205 BAA)**	Davis,Wade	(4530 DCB)		
	Martinez,Carlos	**(3305 AAA)**	**Quintana,Jose**	**(2205 AAA)**	Rodriguez,Francisco	(3330 AAB)		
	Tanaka,Masahiro	(3205 DAA)	Sanchez,Aaron	(2205 CBA)	Ramos,A.J.	(2530 BBB)		
	Duffy,Danny	(2305 CAB)						
Mid-Level	Stroman,Marcus	(4205 FCA)	Hammel,Jason	(2303 CAA)	Bush,Matt	(4311 AFF)		
	deGrom,Jacob	**(3303 BBA)**	Hernandez,Felix	(2205 DAB)	Ottavino,Adam	(4430 FDB)		
	Harvey,Matt	(3303 FCC)	Iwakuma,Hisashi	(2105 FAB)	**Rondon,Hector**	**(4420 BBA)**		
	Keuchel,Dallas	**(3205 BAB)**	Lackey,John	(2203 CAA)	Bedrosian,Cam	(3530 DDD)		
	Matz,Steven	(3303 DCA)	Manaea,Sean	(2303 BDA)	Dyson,Sam	(3130 ACB)		
	Taillon,Jameson	(3205 BDF)	Pomeranz,Drew	(2303 CBA)	Lorenzen,Michael	(3221 DDD)		
	Urias,Julio	(3303 ADA)	Reyes,Alex	(2503 AFD)	Iglesias,Raisel	(2321 DDA)		
	Cole,Gerrit	(2203 FBB)	Ross,Joe	(2203 DDC)	Kintzler,Brandon	(2030 FDF)		
	Fulmer,Michael	(2205 BDA)	Weaver,Luke	(2401 AFF)	Madson,Ryan	(2230 FCC)		
	Gausman,Kevin	(2305 DCB)	Happ,J.A.	(1203 DAA)	Watson,Tony	(2221 ACB)		
	Gray,Sonny	(2205 DAA)	**Odorizzi,Jake**	**(1205 BAA)**	Thornburg,Tyler	(1430 DDF)		
	Hamels,Cole	**(2305 BAA)**	Teheran,Julio	(1205 BAA)				
Bench	McCullers,Lance	(4501 FDB)	Shoemaker,Matthew	(2203 CBA)	Barraclough,Kyle	(5511 ADA)	Triggs,Andrew	(3201 ADC)
	Nola,Aaron	(3303 DCB)	Skaggs,Tyler	(2303 FDA)	**Gregerson,Luke**	**(5410 BBA)**	Devenski,Christopher	(2301 ADB)
	Pineda,Michael	(3403 FBA)	Smyly,Drew	(2303 FBB)	Jones,Nate	(5511 FDC)	Hill,Rich	(2401 FDA)
	Ross,Tyson	(3303 FBA)	Snell,Blake	(2503 ADF)	Feliz,Michael	(4511 ADA)	Hudson,Daniel	(2320 BDA)
	Wood,Alex	(3303 FAB)	Velasquez,Vincent	(2503 BDB)	Hand,Brad	(4511 BCB)	Johnson,Jim	(2220 CCA)
	Anderson,Tyler	(2103 CDA)	Wainwright,Adam	(2203 FAA)	Harris,Will	(4410 ACA)	Maurer,Brandon	(2220 CCA)
	Andriese,Matt	(2203 ADA)	Walker,Taijuan	(2203 DCA)	Herrera,Kelvin	(4411 BCB)	Phelps,David	(2411 FBB)
	Chen,Wei-Yin	(2103 DAA)	Colon,Bartolo	(1003 DAA)	Holland,Greg	(4520 BCD)	Vizcaino,Arodys	(2420 FDB)
	Davies,Zachary	(2103 ACA)	Cotton,Jharel	(1303 ADB)	Kelley,Shawn	(4511 CCA)	Dull,Ryan	(1301 ADD)
	De Leon,Jose	(2503 ADB)	DeSclafani,Anthony	(1205 DCA)	Law,Derek	(4220 BDF)		
	Gonzalez,Gio	**(2305 BAA)**	**Eickhoff,Jerad**	**(1205 ABA)**	Romo,Sergio	(4420 FCB)		
	Leake,Mike	**(2105 BAA)**	Estrada,Marco	(1203 DAA)	**Ziegler,Brad**	**(4210 ABA)**		
	Liriano,Francisco	(2403 CAB)	**Fiers,Mike**	**(1203 ABB)**	Altavilla,Dan	(3310 AFF)		
	Lynn,Lance	(2301 FBA)	Guerra,Junior	(1203 CDD)	Baez,Pedro	(3411 CDA)		
	McHugh,Collin	**(2205 AAB)**	**Kennedy,Ian**	**(1305 BAA)**	Brach,Brad	(3401 ACA)		
	Musgrove,Joe	(2103 ADA)	Moore,Matt	(1303 FCB)	Casilla,Santiago	(3310 DBA)		
	Nova,Ivan	(2105 FCA)	**Roark,Tanner**	**(1103 AAA)**	Givens,Mychal	(3501 ADD)		
	Paxton,James	(2205 FCB)	Rodriguez,Eduardo	(1203 DDA)	Jeffress,Jeremy	(3210 BCB)		
	Richards,Garrett	(2203 FBA)	**Santana,Ervin**	**(1203 BAA)**	Neris,Hector	(3511 ADC)		
	Rodon,Carlos	**(2305 BBA)**	Stewart,Brock	(1203 AFF)	O Day,Darren	(3510 FCA)		
	Salazar,Danny	**(2403 BBB)**	**Tillman,Chris**	**(1103 BAA)**	Reed,Addison	(3411 ACB)		
	Samardzija,Jeff	**(2205 AAB)**	Tomlin,Josh	(1103 FCA)	Strickland,Hunter	(3310 ADC)		
Fringe	Anderson,Brett	(3101 FCC)	**Dickey,R.A.**	**(1103 BAA)**	Cecil,Brett	(5500 DDA)	Diekman,Jake	(2510 BCA)
	Bailey,Homer	(2203 FDF)	Duffey,Tyler	(1103 ADD)	Edwards,Carl	(5500 ADA)	Gearrin,Cory	(2210 BDA)
	Cobb,Alex	(2203 FCF)	Finnegan,Brandon	(1305 ACC)	Strop,Pedro	(5500 DCA)	Glover,Koda	(2300 BFF)
	Garcia,Jaime	(2203 FBA)	Foltynewicz,Mike	(1203 CDD)	Kelly,Joe	(4401 DCA)	Greene,Shane	(2301 CDC)
	Glasnow,Tyler	(2403 CDA)	Gonzalez,Miguel	(1103 DBA)	Simmons,Shae	(4410 FFB)	Grilli,Jason	(2510 FCB)
	Gray,Jonathan	(2305 BCD)	Graveman,Kendall	(1005 DCB)	Uehara,Koji	(4510 FCB)	May,Trevor	(2500 DCA)
	Gsellman,Robert	(2001 ADA)	Green,Chad	(1301 BDD)	Barnette,Tony	(3300 ACF)	McGee,Jake	(2410 DCC)
	Kazmir,Scott	(2303 DAA)	Hellickson,Jeremy	(1205 DBC)	Blevins,Jerry	(3510 FDD)	Montgomery,Michael	(2101 ACB)
	Paulino,David	(2300 AFF)	Kuhl,Chad	(1003 BDC)	Cedeno,Xavier	(3310 ADA)	Morin,Michael	(2310 CDB)
	Ray,Robbie	(2403 ACC)	Lopez,Reynaldo	(1301 ADF)	Cishek,Steve	(3410 BBC)	Neshek,Pat	(2300 ACA)
	Ryu,Hyun-Jin	(2201 FDF)	Norris,Daniel	(1303 DDA)	Claudio,Alexander	(3000 FDD)	Ramos,Edubray	(2311 AFB)
	Severino,Luis	(2301 BDC)	**Ventura,Yordano**	**(1205 BAB)**	Dayton,Grant	(3510 ADD)	**Rodney,Fernando**	**(2420 BBB)**
	Strahm,Matt	(2401 AFF)	Wheeler,Zack	(1201 FCF)	Doolittle,Sean	(3410 FCB)	Salas,Fernando	(2310 CCA)
	Anderson,Chase	**(1103 BBA)**	Zimmermann,Jordan	(1003 DAB)	Duke,Zach	(3400 ACB)	Shaw,Bryan	(2300 ACA)
	Bauer,Trevor	**(1205 AAA)**	**Santiago,Hector**	**(0203 AFD)**	Hendriks,Liam	(3400 CCA)	Smith,Joe	(2200 DCA)
	Berrios,Jose	(1201 ADB)	**Straily,Dan**	**(0203 ABB)**	Hochevar,Luke	(3400 FDA)	Torres,Carlos	(2201 ACA)
	Boyd,Matt	(1203 ADD)	Wright,Steven	(0103 FCA)	Kela,Keone	(3510 DDB)	Vincent,Nick	(2400 DDB)
	Buchholz,Clay	(1103 FAC)			Knebel,Corey	(3410 DDB)	Bundy,Dylan	(1303 ADB)
					Krol,Ian	(3400 ADB)	Cabrera,Mauricio	(1311 AFD)
					Lyons,Tyler	(3300 DDB)	Clippard,Tyler	(1410 ACC)
					Nicasio,Juan	(3401 CCC)	Feliz,Neftali	(1310 FDC)
					Rivero,Felipe	(3411 BDB)	Gomez,Jeanmar	(1021 ACA)
					Rosenthal,Trevor	(3510 DAB)	Papelbon,Jonathan	(1310 CBB)
					Smith,Will	(3510 DDB)	Pressly,Ryan	(1211 DDA)
					Soria,Joakim	(3401 FCB)	Quackenbush,Kevin	(1200 ACB)
					Storen,Drew	(3310 CCA)	**Ramirez,Erasmo**	**(1101 ABB)**
					Treinen,Blake	(3300 ACA)	Robles,Hansel	(1401 ADB)
					Wilson,Justin	(3410 ACA)	Siegrist,Kevin	(1410 DCA)
					Zych,Tony	(3400 FFD)	Warren,Adam	(1200 ACB)
					Benoit,Joaquin	(2400 CCB)	Wittgren,Nick	(1100 ADB)
					Biagini,Joe	(2110 ADA)	Wood,Travis	(1200 ABC)
					Blanton,Joe	(2301 ADA)	Buchter,Ryan	(0410 ADC)
					Boxberger,Brad	(2510 FCD)	Street,Huston	(0220 FBC)
					Broxton,Jonathan	(2301 DCA)		

Universal Draft Grid

TIER	STARTING PITCHERS				RELIEF PITCHERS			
Below Fringe	Corbin,Patrick	(2203 FCA)	Alcantara,Raul	(0001 ADF)	Hoyt,James	(4500 ADC)	Rondon,Bruce	(1500 FDA)
	Perdomo,Luis	(2103 ADF)	Blair,Aaron	(0101 BDD)	Coulombe,Daniel	(3300 ADA)	Ryan,Kyle	(1000 ACB)
	Bettis,Chad	(1103 BCA)	Butler,Eddie	(0001 BDB)	Grimm,Justin	(3500 BDA)	Scheppers,Tanner	(1200 FFA)
	Bolsinger,Michael	(1200 CDF)	Cessa,Luis	(0101 ADB)	Alvarez,Dario	(2500 AFF)	Socolovich,Miguel	(1200 ADC)
	Bradley,Archie	(1203 DDB)	Clevinger,Michael	(0203 ADB)	Axford,John	(2400 ACA)	Villanueva,Carlos	(1201 ACA)
	Brault,Steven	(1201 ADF)	Cole,A.J.	(0101 ADB)	Barnes,Jacob	(2200 CDD)	Whitley,Chase	(1100 FDB)
	Cashner,Andrew	(1203 FAB)	Conley,Adam	(0203 CCB)	Bowman,Matthew	(2000 ADF)	Withrow,Chris	(1300 FFB)
	Chacin,Jhoulys	(1103 FCB)	Cosart,Jarred	(0001 BCB)	Cahill,Trevor	(2301 DDA)	Wood,Blake	(1300 DDD)
	Chatwood,Tyler	(1103 FCB)	Eflin,Zach	(0001 DDB)	Chargois,J.T.	(2210 AFA)	Bailey,Andrew	(0200 DFA)
	de la Rosa,Jorge	(1203 DAB)	Farmer,Buck	(0101 ADB)	Farquhar,Daniel	(2300 ADB)	Barrett,Jake	(0210 ADC)
	De La Rosa,Rubby	(1201 FBA)	Fister,Doug	(0003 DAB)	Jennings,Dan	(2200 CDA)	Blazek,Michael	(0200 DDF)
	Garza,Matt	(1103 FBA)	Friedrich,Christian	(0101 CCC)	Liberatore,Adam	(2400 BDB)	Cain,Matt	(0201 FCC)
	Gibson,Kyle	(1103 DAA)	Fulmer,Carson	(0301 AFF)	Montas,Frankie	(2400 FFA)	Cervenka,Hunter	(0300 ADF)
	Giolito,Lucas	(1203 ADA)	Gallardo,Yovani	(0103 DAB)	Perkins,Glen	(2300 FCC)	Cingrani,Tony	(0310 DCA)
	Godley,Zachary	(1100 ADD)	Gant,John	(0201 DDB)	Roe,Chaz	(2300 BDB)	Clemens,Paul	(0001 ADF)
	Hader,Joshua	(1401 ADA)	Garrett,Amir	(0101 AFF)	Ross,Robbie	(2200 ACB)	De La Cruz,Joel	(0000 ADA)
	Hoffman,Jeff	(2203 AFF)	Gee,Dillon	(1200 FFF)	Rusin,Chris	(2201 CCD)	Gustave,Jandel	(0200 AFB)
	Hughes,Phil	(2201 DDB)	Griffin,A.J.	(1101 ADB)	Tazawa,Junichi	(2400 BDA)	Jackson,Edwin	(0101 DCB)
	Jimenez,Ubaldo	**(2203 AFF)**	Hahn,Jesse	(1200 FFF)	Tolleson,Shawn	(2300 FCB)	Jepsen,Kevin	(0200 CCC)
	Karns,Nathan	(2201 DDB)	Heaney,Andrew	(1101 ADB)	Tonkin,Michael	(2301 ADC)	Light,Pat	(0200 AFA)
	McCarthy,Brandon	(1101 FCB)	Holland,Derek	(0103 FCB)	Alvarez,Jose	(1100 ADC)	Lyles,Jordan	(0001 FCC)
	Mengden,Daniel	(1200 ADF)	Hutchison,Drew	(0201 DBB)	Anderson,Cody	(1101 ADF)	Sampson,Keyvius	(0301 ADB)
	Miley,Wade	**(1203 AAA)**	Jenkins,Tyrell	(0000 ADB)	Barnes,Matt	(1301 ADF)	Schugel,Andrew	(0101 DDF)
	Miller,Shelby	**(1103 BAB)**	Koehler,Tom	**(0103 AAA)**	Bracho,Silvino	(1300 AFF)	Suarez,Albert	(0000 ADB)
	Nelson,Jimmy	**(1203 AAB)**	Lewis,Colby	(0103 FAA)	Burgos,Enrique	(1510 BFB)	Wilson,Alex	(0000 DDA)
	Niese,Jon	(1101 DAB)	Locke,Jeff	**(0003 ABB)**	Caminero,Arquimedes	(1200 BDD)	Worley,Vance	(0001 BCB)
	Nolasco,Ricky	(1105 FBA)	Lugo,Seth	(0101 ADB)	**Chavez,Jesse**	**(1201 BBA)**	Young,Chris	(0201 CBA)
	Peavy,Jake	(1201 FBA)	Mejia,Adalberto	(0101 ADC)	Delgado,Randall	(1300 DCA)		
	Peralta,Wily	(1103 DBC)	Meyer,Alex	(0301 CDF)	Feldman,Scott	(1001 DBA)		
	Perez,Martin	(1003 FCB)	Miranda,Ariel	(0103 ADB)	Flynn,Brian	(1100 FDF)		
	Perez,Williams	(1001 FCB)	Mitchell,Bryan	(0101 FDA)	Goeddel,Erik	(1300 DDC)		
	Reed,Cody	(1203 BDF)	Morgan,Adam	(0103 ADA)	Guerra,Deolis	(1100 DDB)		
	Sabathia,CC	(1203 FBA)	Neal,Zachary	(0000 ADC)	Hembree,Heath	(1200 BDB)		
	Sanchez,Anibal	(1203 FAB)	Nicolino,Justin	(0001 ACB)	Hernandez,David	(1401 FDA)		
	Shields,James	**(1203 AAB)**	Owens,Henry	(0200 ACC)	Marinez,Jhan	(1200 ADC)		
	Stripling,Ross	(1101 ADB)	Peacock,Brad	(0200 FCA)	McAllister,Zach	(1300 DCB)		
	Vargas,Jason	(1103 FCB)	Pelfrey,Mike	(0001 FBD)	Norris,Bud	(1201 DBA)		
	Volquez,Edinson	(1105 AAA)	Richard,Clayton	(0001 DDF)	Nuno,Vidal	(1200 ACA)		
	Wacha,Michael	(1201 DAA)	Shipley,Braden	(0001 ADA)	Ramirez,J.C.	(1000 ADA)		
	Adleman,Timothy	(0101 DDA)	Stephenson,Robert	(0203 ADC)	Rogers,Taylor	(1100 ADB)		

SIMULATION LEAGUE DRAFT   TOP 500+

NAME	POS	RAR	NAME	POS	RAR	NAME	POS	RAR	NAME	POS	RAR
Trout,Mike	8	62.1	Benintendi,Andrew	7	17.7	Harris,Will	P	11.8	Kim,Hyun-Soo	7	8.3
Votto,Joey	3	57.8	Carrasco,Carlos	P	17.4	Davis,Chris	3	11.7	Simmons,Shae	P	8.3
Kershaw,Clayton	P	51.0	Manaea,Sean	P	17.4	Kepler,Max	9	11.7	Salazar,Danny	P	8.1
Goldschmidt,Paul	3	42.5	Fulmer,Michael	P	16.9	Bogaerts,Xander	6	11.6	Martin,Russell	2	8.1
Cabrera,Miguel	3	42.1	McCullers,Lance	P	16.8	Jones,Nate	P	11.4	Skaggs,Tyler	P	8.1
Betts,Mookie	9	42.0	Fowler,Dexter	8	16.7	Tomas,Yasmany	79	11.4	Law,Derek	P	8.0
Bryant,Kris	57	37.6	Conforto,Michael	7	16.7	Porcello,Rick	P	11.4	Ozuna,Marcell	8	8.0
Freeman,Freddie	3	36.1	Tulowitzki,Troy	6	16.5	Pederson,Joc	8	11.4	Holland,Greg	P	7.9
Donaldson,Josh	5	34.6	Encarnacion,Edwin	3	16.4	Barraclough,Kyle	P	11.3	Casilla,Santiago	P	7.9
Altuve,Jose	4	34.1	Oh,Seung-Hwan	P	16.2	Brantley,Michael	7	11.2	Robertson,David	P	7.8
Arenado,Nolan	5	33.7	Hamels,Cole	P	16.0	Givens,Mychal	P	11.1	Molina,Yadier	2	7.8
Bumgarner,Madison	P	33.1	Hernandez,Felix	P	15.9	Dyson,Sam	P	11.0	Hand,Brad	P	7.8
Harper,Bryce	9	32.6	Wood,Alex	P	15.8	Weaver,Luke	P	11.0	Bregman,Alex	5	7.7
Cueto,Johnny	P	32.1	Urias,Julio	P	15.5	Colome,Alexander	P	11.0	Kuhl,Chad	P	7.5
Cespedes,Yoenis	78	31.1	Pedroia,Dustin	4	15.3	Giles,Kenneth	P	10.8	Gonzalez,Adrian	3	7.5
Murphy,Daniel	34	30.9	Cabrera,Melky	7	15.3	Zobrist,Ben	479	10.8	Naquin,Tyler	8	7.5
Syndergaard,Noah	P	30.4	Sanchez,Gary	2	15.2	Iwakuma,Hisashi	P	10.7	Ramirez,Hanley	3	7.4
Seager,Corey	6	30.3	Belt,Brandon	3	15.1	Odorizzi,Jake	P	10.6	Kennedy,Ian	P	7.4
Blackmon,Charlie	8	30.1	Lamb,Jacob	5	15.0	Kipnis,Jason	4	10.6	O Day,Darren	P	7.4
Posey,Buster	2	29.9	Hill,Rich	P	14.9	Brach,Brad	P	10.5	Krol,Ian	P	7.3
Scherzer,Max	P	28.9	Dahl,David	7	14.9	Stroman,Marcus	P	10.5	Pineda,Michael	P	7.3
Rizzo,Anthony	3	28.8	Betances,Dellin	P	14.6	Pence,Hunter	9	10.5	Hendriks,Liam	P	7.2
Lester,Jon	P	28.7	Davis,Khristopher	7	14.5	Andriese,Matt	P	10.5	Longoria,Evan	5	7.2
Yelich,Christian	78	28.4	Grandal,Yasmani	2	14.3	Lynn,Lance	P	10.4	Sano,Miguel	59	7.1
Turner,Trea	48	27.7	Maeda,Kenta	P	14.2	Kelley,Shawn	P	10.3	Strickland,Hunter	P	7.1
Carpenter,Matt	345	27.4	Ross,Tyson	P	14.1	Teheran,Julio	P	10.2	Claudio,Alexander	P	7.1
Martinez,J.D.	9	26.3	Pollock,A.J.	8	14.0	Allen,Cody	P	10.1	Bruce,Jay	9	7.1
Correa,Carlos	6	25.7	Strasburg,Stephen	P	14.0	Dull,Ryan	P	10.0	Realmuto,Jacob	2	7.0
Braun,Ryan	7	25.5	Lindor,Francisco	6	13.9	Rodon,Carlos	P	10.0	Gregerson,Luke	P	7.0
Hendricks,Kyle	P	25.4	Seager,Kyle	5	13.9	Duke,Zach	P	9.9	Clippard,Tyler	P	7.0
McCutchen,Andrew	8	25.2	Jansen,Kenley	P	13.9	Wainwright,Adam	P	9.9	Ramos,Edubray	P	6.9
Verlander,Justin	P	25.0	Paxton,James	P	13.9	Triggs,Andrew	P	9.6	Biagini,Joe	P	6.9
Kluber,Corey	P	24.9	Ross,Joe	P	13.8	Baez,Pedro	P	9.5	Smith,Will	P	6.9
Archer,Chris	P	24.6	Jeffress,Jeremy	P	13.7	Iglesias,Raisel	P	9.5	Rivero,Felipe	P	6.9
Martinez,Carlos	P	24.6	Richards,Garrett	P	13.7	Lorenzen,Michael	P	9.5	Barnette,Tony	P	6.9
Stanton,Giancarlo	9	24.4	Gray,Sonny	P	13.7	Ramos,A.J.	P	9.4	Andrus,Elvis	6	6.7
Lucroy,Jonathan	2	24.1	Osuna,Roberto	P	13.6	Bradley,Jackie	8	9.3	Soria,Joakim	P	6.7
Darvish,Yu	P	23.9	Taillon,Jameson	P	13.6	Davies,Zachary	P	9.3	Estrada,Marco	P	6.7
Cano,Robinson	4	23.8	Marte,Starling	7	13.5	Watson,Tony	P	9.2	Dayton,Grant	P	6.7
Contreras,Willson	27	23.7	Lackey,John	P	13.5	Stewart,Brock	P	9.2	Treinen,Blake	P	6.7
Sale,Chris	P	23.3	Eaton,Adam	89	13.3	Diaz,Edwin	P	9.2	Cishek,Steve	P	6.7
Machado,Manny	56	22.6	Abreu,Jose	3	13.3	Nola,Aaron	P	9.1	Peralta,David	9	6.6
Quintana,Jose	P	21.8	Kang,Jung-ho	5	13.1	Granderson,Curtis	89	9.1	Cedeno,Xavier	P	6.5
deGrom,Jacob	P	21.7	Herrera,Kelvin	P	12.9	Roark,Tanner	P	9.1	Vizcaino,Arodys	P	6.5
Arrieta,Jake	P	21.7	Happ,J.A.	P	12.9	Kimbrel,Craig	P	9.1	Cain,Lorenzo	89	6.3
Sanchez,Aaron	P	21.4	Bush,Matt	P	12.9	Bedrosian,Cam	P	9.1	Puig,Yasiel	9	6.3
Gonzalez,Carlos	9	20.9	Gausman,Kevin	P	12.9	DeSclafani,Anthony	P	9.0	Dickerson,Corey	7	6.3
Bautista,Jose	9	20.5	Turner,Justin	5	12.8	Murphy,Tom	2	8.9	Guerra,Junior	P	6.3
Beltre,Adrian	5	20.5	Schwarber,Kyle	7	12.6	Neris,Hector	P	8.9	Strahm,Matt	P	6.3
Duffy,Danny	P	20.2	Upton,Justin	7	12.5	Liriano,Francisco	P	8.8	Herrera,Odubel	8	6.3
Cruz,Nelson	9	19.6	Diaz,Aledmys	6	12.4	Cecil,Brett	P	8.7	Rodriguez,Francisco	P	6.2
Chapman,Aroldis	P	19.6	Keuchel,Dallas	P	12.4	Strop,Pedro	P	8.7	Ottavino,Adam	P	6.2
Price,David	P	19.4	Familia,Jeurys	P	12.4	Walker,Neil	4	8.7	Cabrera,Mauricio	P	6.1
Story,Trevor	6	19.4	Harvey,Matt	P	12.3	Ziegler,Brad	P	8.7	Cabrera,Asdrubal	6	6.1
Tanaka,Masahiro	P	19.2	Davis,Wade	P	12.2	Calhoun,Kole	9	8.6	Musgrove,Joe	P	6.1
Greinke,Zack	P	19.0	Kemp,Matt	79	12.1	Rondon,Hector	P	8.6	Blanton,Joe	P	6.1
Miller,Andrew	P	18.8	Phelps,David	P	12.1	Springer,George	9	8.6	Hammel,Jason	P	6.0
Matz,Steven	P	18.7	Dozier,Brian	4	12.0	Shaw,Bryan	P	8.5	Odor,Rougned	4	6.0
Melancon,Mark	P	18.6	Reyes,Alex	P	12.0	Ethier,Andre	7	8.5	Coghlan,Chris	47	6.0
Anderson,Tyler	P	18.3	Pomeranz,Drew	P	11.9	Holliday,Matt	7	8.4	Dickerson,Alex	7	5.9
Cole,Gerrit	P	18.3	Devenski,Christopher	P	11.9	Ryu,Hyun-Jin	P	8.4	Zych,Tony	P	5.9
Britton,Zach	P	18.3	Reed,Addison	P	11.9	Kelly,Joe	P	8.4	Kinsler,Ian	4	5.8
LeMahieu,DJ	4	18.2	Altavilla,Dan	P	11.9	Romo,Sergio	P	8.3	Jennings,Dan	P	5.8

SIMULATION LEAGUE DRAFT TOP 500+

NAME	POS	RAR	NAME	POS	RAR	NAME	POS	RAR	NAME	POS	RAR
Villar,Jonathan	56	5.7	Nova,Ivan	P	3.7	Tolleson,Shawn	P	2.1	Wilson,Alex	P	-0.1
McAllister,Zach	P	5.7	Street,Huston	P	3.7	Whitley,Chase	P	2.1	Werth,Jayson	7	-0.1
Rosenthal,Trevor	P	5.7	Lyons,Tyler	P	3.7	Young,Chris	7	2.1	Worley,Vance	P	-0.1
Neshek,Pat	P	5.7	Santana,Domingo	9	3.6	Kazmir,Scott	P	2.0	Solarte,Yangervis	5	-0.1
Grichuk,Randal	8	5.6	Barnes,Jacob	P	3.6	Miller,Bradley	36	2.0	Vogelbach,Daniel	3	-0.1
Benoit,Joaquin	P	5.6	Pearce,Steve	3	3.6	Johnson,Jim	P	2.0	Desmond,Ian	78	-0.1
Snell,Blake	P	5.4	Wheeler,Zack	P	3.6	Buchholz,Clay	P	2.0	Scheppers,Tanner	P	-0.2
Santana,Ervin	P	5.4	Bowman,Matthew	P	3.5	Kiermaier,Kevin	8	1.9	Barrett,Jake	P	-0.2
Doolittle,Sean	P	5.4	Bour,Justin	3	3.5	Fiers,Mike	P	1.9	Piscotty,Stephen	9	-0.2
Crawford,Brandon	6	5.4	Gsellman,Robert	P	3.5	Papelbon,Jonathan	P	1.9	Napoli,Mike	3	-0.3
Gonzalez,Gio	P	5.3	Tillman,Chris	P	3.4	Bird,Gregory	0	1.8	Stripling,Ross	P	-0.3
Wilson,Justin	P	5.3	Ventura,Yordano	P	3.4	Jones,Adam	8	1.8	Smith,Seth	79	-0.3
Madson,Ryan	P	5.3	Ross,Robbie	P	3.4	Perez,Salvador	2	1.8	Dyson,Jarrod	89	-0.3
Toles,Andrew	7	5.3	Farquhar,Daniel	P	3.4	Guerra,Deolis	P	1.8	Montas,Frankie	P	-0.3
Trumbo,Mark	9	5.2	Anderson,Brett	P	3.4	Ryan,Kyle	P	1.7	Beckham,Tim	6	-0.4
Graveman,Kendall	P	5.2	Grimm,Justin	P	3.3	Zunino,Mike	2	1.7	Zimmermann,Jordan	P	-0.5
Shoemaker,Matthew	P	5.2	Salas,Fernando	P	3.3	Caminero,Arquimedes	P	1.7	Morin,Michael	P	-0.5
Smith,Joe	P	5.1	Valbuena,Luis	5	3.3	Liberatore,Adam	P	1.7	Thompson,Trayce	789	-0.6
Green,Chad	P	5.1	Paulino,David	P	3.3	Swanson,Dansby	6	1.6	Tapia,Raimel	8	-0.6
Thornburg,Tyler	P	5.1	Velasquez,Vincent	P	3.2	Choo,Shin-Soo	9	1.6	Severino,Luis	P	-0.6
Polanco,Gregory	79	5.1	Feliz,Neftali	P	3.2	Hernandez,David	P	1.6	Cervenka,Hunter	P	-0.6
Gearrin,Cory	P	5.1	Rodney,Fernando	P	3.2	Coulombe,Daniel	P	1.6	Descalso,Daniel	6	-0.7
Vogt,Stephen	2	5.1	Robles,Hansel	P	3.2	Healy,Ryon	5	1.5	Forsythe,Logan	4	-0.7
Samardzija,Jeff	P	5.0	Rendon,Anthony	5	3.2	Giolito,Lucas	P	1.5	Withrow,Chris	P	-0.7
Garcia,Jaime	P	5.0	McCann,Brian	2	3.2	Chirinos,Robinson	2	1.4	Grilli,Jason	P	-0.8
Montgomery,Michael	P	5.0	Cervelli,Francisco	2	3.1	Jaso,John	3	1.3	Cingrani,Tony	P	-0.8
Torres,Carlos	P	5.0	Socolovich,Miguel	P	3.1	Goeddel,Erik	P	1.3	Lind,Adam	3	-0.8
Kintzler,Brandon	P	5.0	Quackenbush,Kevin	P	3.1	Wright,Steven	P	1.3	Conley,Adam	P	-0.8
Wieters,Matt	2	5.0	Gordon,Alex	7	3.1	Colon,Bartolo	P	1.2	Rondon,Bruce	P	-0.9
McHugh,Collin	P	4.9	Moore,Matt	P	3.0	Buchter,Ryan	P	1.1	Guyer,Brandon	7	-1.0
Leake,Mike	P	4.9	Chatwood,Tyler	P	3.0	Ramirez,J.C.	P	1.1	Wacha,Michael	P	-1.0
Siegrist,Kevin	P	4.9	Adleman,Timothy	P	3.0	Gardner,Brett	7	1.1	Jenkins,Tyrell	P	-1.0
Cahill,Trevor	P	4.8	Prado,Martin	5	3.0	Rusin,Chris	P	1.1	Rogers,Taylor	P	-1.1
Saunders,Michael	79	4.8	Boxberger,Brad	P	2.9	Frazier,Adam	7	1.0	Heyward,Jason	89	-1.1
Nicasio,Juan	P	4.7	Eickhoff,Jerad	P	2.8	Segura,Jean	46	1.0	Chavez,Jesse	P	-1.1
Smyly,Drew	P	4.7	Roe,Chaz	P	2.8	Travis,Devon	4	0.9	Gurriel,Yulieski	5	-1.2
Ramirez,Erasmo	P	4.7	Castellanos,Nick	5	2.8	Barreto,Franklin	6	0.9	Casali,Curtis	2	-1.2
Rodriguez,Eduardo	P	4.6	Diekman,Jake	P	2.8	Wright,David	5	0.9	Pompey,Dalton	7	-1.2
Feliz,Michael	P	4.6	Soler,Jorge	7	2.8	Lopez,Reynaldo	P	0.9	Joyce,Matt	79	-1.2
Hoyt,James	P	4.5	Vincent,Nick	P	2.7	Axford,John	P	0.8	Simmons,Andrelton	6	-1.3
Castillo,Welington	2	4.5	Santana,Carlos	3	2.6	Inciarte,Ender	8	0.8	Duvall,Adam	7	-1.4
Span,Denard	8	4.5	Ray,Robbie	P	2.6	Haniger,Mitch	8	0.8	Mauer,Joe	3	-1.4
De Leon,Jose	P	4.5	Barnes,Matt	P	2.6	Mejia,Adalberto	P	0.8	Holt,Brock	7	-1.4
Edwards,Carl	P	4.5	Bailey,Homer	P	2.6	Chen,Wei-Yin	P	0.7	Delgado,Randall	P	-1.5
Bundy,Dylan	P	4.5	Glover,Koda	P	2.5	Broxton,Jonathan	P	0.7	Pagan,Angel	7	-1.5
Hochevar,Luke	P	4.5	Panik,Joe	4	2.5	Cashner,Andrew	P	0.7	Suarez,Albert	P	-1.6
Knebel,Corey	P	4.4	Storen,Drew	P	2.5	Heaney,Andrew	P	0.6	Feldman,Scott	P	-1.6
Wittgren,Nick	P	4.4	Nuno,Vidal	P	2.5	Aoki,Norichika	7	0.6	Beltran,Carlos	9	-1.6
Kela,Keone	P	4.4	Foltynewicz,Mike	P	2.4	Russell,Addison	6	0.5	Perez,Williams	P	-1.6
Uehara,Koji	P	4.4	Hembree,Heath	P	2.4	Wood,Blake	P	0.4	Gosselin,Phil	4	-1.6
Glasnow,Tyler	P	4.4	Boyd,Matt	P	2.4	Tonkin,Michael	P	0.4	Sampson,Keyvius	P	-1.7
Cobb,Alex	P	4.3	Greene,Shane	P	2.4	May,Trevor	P	0.4	Chisenhall,Lonnie	9	-1.7
Moustakas,Mike	5	4.3	Perkins,Glen	P	2.3	Jepsen,Kevin	P	0.4	Lugo,Seth	P	-1.7
McGee,Jake	P	4.3	Maurer,Brandon	P	2.3	Mengden,Daniel	P	0.3	Gibson,Kyle	P	-1.8
Blevins,Jerry	P	4.2	Hundley,Nick	2	2.3	Anderson,Cody	P	0.3	Finnegan,Brandon	P	-1.8
Alvarez,Jose	P	4.2	Walker,Taijuan	P	2.2	Montero,Miguel	2	0.3	Duffey,Tyler	P	-1.9
Drury,Brandon	579	4.1	Tazawa,Junichi	P	2.2	Jackson,Austin	8	0.3	Susac,Andrew	2	-1.9
Chargois,J.T.	P	4.1	Warren,Adam	P	2.2	Gamel,Benjamin	9	0.3	Burgos,Enrique	P	-1.9
Ramos,Wilson	2	3.9	Reddick,Josh	9	2.2	Schimpf,Ryan	4	0.2	Austin,Tyler	3	-2.0
Wood,Travis	P	3.9	Hudson,Daniel	P	2.2	Gustave,Jandel	P	0.1	Mesoraco,Devin	2	-2.1
Cotton,Jharel	P	3.9	Flynn,Brian	P	2.2	Hellickson,Jeremy	P	0.0	Norris,Derek	2	-2.2
Marinez,Jhan	P	3.8	Pressly,Ryan	P	2.1	Markakis,Nick	9	0.0	Garrett,Amir	P	-2.2
Norris,Daniel	P	3.8	Valencia,Danny	59	2.1	Ramirez,Jose	57	0.0	Clevinger,Michael	P	-2.2

In-person answers to all your fantasy baseball questions.

Just in time for Draft Day.

Get ready for an unforgettable experience—BaseballHQ.com's **First Pitch Forums**. These 3+ hour events—with a new format in 2017—will be packed full of fantasy baseball talk, interactive activities and fun! The forums will come to seven cities in 2017 and help you prepare for your championship season. Top national baseball analysts disclose competitive secrets unique to 2017: Players to watch, trends to monitor, new strategies to employ and more! Plus, they answer YOUR questions as you look for the edge that will lead to a 2017 championship.

BaseballHQ.com founder Ron Shandler, along with current co-GMs Brent Hershey and Ray Murphy chair the sessions and bring a dynamic energy to every event. They are joined by experts from BaseballHQ. com as well as other sports media sources, such as ESPN.com, MLB. com, RotoWire, FanGraphs, Baseball Prospectus, Mastersball, Sirius/XM Radio and more.

PRELIMINARY* 2017
FIRST PITCH FORUMS DATES & SITES

Sat, February 25	CHICAGO
Sun, February 26	ST. LOUIS
Fri, March 3	WASHINGTON DC
Sat, March 4	NEW YORK
Sun, March 5	BOSTON
Sat, March 11	LOS ANGELES
Sun, March 12	SAN FRANCISCO

*Dates are subject to change, but will be confirmed soon. PLUS—check out the link below during March for more info about our NEW online version of the program. Find complete description and details at:

www.firstpitchforums.com

Registration:
$39 per person in advance // $49 per person at the door

Plus, don't forget First Pitch Arizona: November 3-5, 2017 in Phoenix, AZ, at the Arizona Fall League!!

2017 CHEATER'S BOOKMARK

BATTING STATISTICS

Abbrv	Term	Formula / Desc.	BAD UNDER	'16 LG AVG AL	'16 LG AVG NL	BEST OVER
Avg	Batting Average	h/ab	235	257	260	280
xBA	Expected Batting Average	See glossary		262	265	
OB	On Base Average	(h+bb)/(ab+bb)	290	318	326	340
Slg	Slugging Average	total bases/ab	350	424	425	450
OPS	On Base plus Slugging	OB+Slg	650	742	751	780
bb%	Walk Rate	bb/(ab+bb)	6%	8%	9%	10%
ct%	Contact Rate	(ab-k) / ab	73%	77%	77%	83%
Eye	Batting Eye	bb/k	0.30	0.39	0.42	0.50
PX	Power Index	Normalized power skills	80	100	100	120
Spd	Speed Score	Normalized speed skills	80	100	100	120
SBO	Stolen Base Opportunity %	(sb+cs)/(singles+bb)		8%	9%	
G/F	Groundball/Flyball Ratio	gb / fb		1.2	1.3	
G	Ground Ball Per Cent	gb / balls in play		44%	45%	
L	Line Drive Per Cent	ld / balls in play		20%	21%	
F	Fly Ball Per Cent	fb / balls in play		36%	34%	
BPV	Base Performance Value	See glossary	20	37	38	55
RC/G	Runs Created per Game	See glossary	3.00	4.61	4.74	5.00
RAR	Runs Above Replacement	See glossary	0.0			10.0

Batting statistics do not include pitchers' batting statistics

PITCHING STATISTICS

Abbrv	Term	Formula / Desc.	BAD OVER	'16 LG AVG AL	'16 LG AVG NL	BEST UNDER
ERA	Earned Run Average	er*9/ip	4.75	4.21	4.17	3.00
xERA	Expected ERA	See glossary		3.75	3.70	
WHIP	Baserunners per Inning	(h+bb)/ip	1.50	1.32	1.33	1.15
BF/G	Batters Faced per Game	((ip*2.82)+h+bb)/g	28.0			
PC	Pitch Counts per Start		120	94	92	
OBA	Opposition Batting Avg	Opp. h/ab	280	257	254	235
OOB	Opposition On Base Avg	Opp. (h+bb)/(ab+bb)	350	317	318	290
BABIP	BatAvg on balls in play	(h-hr)/(ip*2.82)+h-k-hr)		298	298	
Ctl	Control Rate	bb*9/ip		3.0	3.2	2.5
hr/9	Homerun Rate	hr*9/ip		1.2	1.1	1.0
hr/f	Homerun per Fly ball	hr/fb		13%	13%	
S%	Strand Rate	(h+bb-er)/(h+bb-hr)		72%	72%	
DIS%	PQS Disaster Rate	% GS that are PQS 0/1		36%	34%	15%

Abbrv	Term	Formula / Desc.	BAD UNDER	'16 LG AVG AL	'16 LG AVG NL	BEST OVER
RAR	Runs Above Replacement	See glossary	-0.0			+10
Dom	Dominance Rate	k*9/ip		8.0	8.2	9.0
Cmd	Command Ratio	k/bb		2.6	2.5	3.3
G/F	Groundball/Flyball Ratio	gb / fb		1.25	1.34	
SwK	Swinging Strike Percentage	swinging strikes/pitches		10.6%	10.5%	11.5%
FpK	First Pitch Strike Percentage	first pitch strikes/batters		60%	60%	63%
BPV	Base Performance Value	See glossary	50	85	83	100
DOM%	PQS Dominance Rate	% GS that are PQS 4/5		24%	24%	50%
Sv%	Saves Conversion Rate	(saves / save opps)		69%	67%	80%
REff%	Relief Effectiveness Rate	See glossary		67%	67%	80%

NOTES

Home page for year-round fanalytic coverage:
www.BaseballHQ.com

For March projections update and any other information related to this book:
www.baseballhq.com/bf2017

For the schedule of dates and cities on our Spring 2017 First Pitch tour, including registration information:
www.FirstPitchForums.com

Facebook: **www.facebook.com/baseballhq**
Twitter: **www.twitter.com/baseballhq**
HQ staffers on Twitter:
www.twitter.com/BaseballHQ/lists/hq-staff